Understanding Human Sexuality

Fifth Edition

Understanding Human Sexuality

Janet Shibley Hyde

University of Wisconsin—Madison

McGraw-Hill, Inc.
New York   St. Louis   San Francisco   Auckland   Bogotá   Caracas
Lisbon   London   Madrid   Mexico City   Milan   Montreal
New Delhi   San Juan   Singapore   Sydney   Tokyo   Toronto

Understanding Human Sexuality

Acknowledgments appear on pages 733–738, and on this page by reference.

This book is printed on acid-free paper.

3 4 5 6 7 8 9 0 DOW DOW 9 0 9 8 7 6 5

ISBN 0-07-031615-5

This book was set in Sabon by Ruttle, Shaw, & Wetherill, Inc.
The editors were Jane Vaicunas and Scott Amerman;
the designer was Robin Hoffmann;
the production supervisor was Paula Keller.
The photo editor was Suzanne Skloot.
R. R. Donnelley & Sons Company was printer and binder.

Library of Congress Cataloging-in-Publication Data

Hyde, Janet Shibley.
    Understanding human sexuality / Janet Shibley Hyde. — 5th ed.
        p.   cm.
    Includes bibliographical references and index.
    ISBN 0-07-031615-5 (alk. paper)
    1. Sex.   2. Sex customs.   3. Hygiene, Sexual.   4. Sex (Psychology).
    I. Title.
    HQ12.H82   1994
    306.7—dc20   93-24355

About the Author

Janet Shibley Hyde is Professor of Psychology and Women's Studies at the University of Wisconsin—Madison, having received her education at Oberlin College and the University of California—Berkeley. She has taught a course in human sexuality since 1974, first at Bowling Green State University, then at Denison University, and now at the University of Wisconsin. Her research interests are in gender differences and gender-role development in children. Author of the textbook *Half the Human Experience: The Psychology of Women,* she is a member of the Board of Directors of the Society for the Scientific Study of Sex, and a Fellow of the American Psychological Association. She has received many other honors, including an award for excellence in teaching at Bowling Green State University, an award for excellence in teaching from the Wisconsin Students Association at the University of Wisconsin, and the Kinsey Award from the Society for the Scientific Study of Sex for career contributions to sex research.

To my family—
my mother, Dorothy Shibley,
my children, Margaret and Luke,
and my new family, the DeLamaters—
who have been constant sources
of support in all my work.

Contents in Brief

Contents

xi

Chapter 3

Sex Research   49

Chapter 4

Sexual Anatomy   80

Chapter 5 Sex Hormones and Sexual Differentiation 108

Chapter 6 Menstruation and Menopause 129

Chapter 9   *The Physiology of Sexual Response   241*

Chapter 10   *Techniques of Arousal and Communication   270*

Chapter 11

Sexuality and the Life Cycle: Childhood and Adolescence   308

Chapter 14   *Gender Roles, Female Sexuality, and Male Sexuality 386*

Chapter 15   *Sexual Orientation: Gay, Straight, or Bi? 420*

Chapter 16

Variations in Sexual Behavior   459

Chapter 20   *Sexually Transmitted Diseases* 567

Chapter 21   Ethics, Religion, and Sexuality   597

Chapter 22   Sex and the Law   630

Preface

I suspect that my motivation for writing this text was quite similar to that of many people who write textbooks. When I began teaching an undergraduate course in human sexuality, in the fall of 1974, I was unable to find a text that suited my needs or tastes. One text treated the biological aspects of sexuality with so many forbidding Latin terms that students seemed too intimidated to study it effectively. Another had a preaching tone and a bias in favor of very traditional gender roles, neither of which seemed to be in touch with today's students. Others were far too brief and omitted important topics. As a result, I set out to write a text that would meet the needs that the other texts neglected.

Today, approximately 20 years later, there are many sexuality texts available, and many of them are quite good. Nonetheless, I feel that this text has a unique combination of three features that are of utmost importance in a textbook: a writing style that is readable and appealing to the student; coverage that is interdisciplinary and comprehensive; and excellent scholarship. Of the other texts available, some are quite readable, but they tend to be weak in scholarship. Some are very scholarly, but they are not readable. Others lack comprehensiveness, omitting such important topics as the legal aspects of sexuality, or focusing on biology to the exclusion of psychology. My goal in this text is to provide the best in all three of these features—readability, scholarship, and comprehensiveness. This approach has beeen well-received in the previous editions, and I have worked to maintain and improve these features in the fifth edition.

PLAN OF THE BOOK

First and foremost, I tried to keep in mind at all times that students *want* to learn about sexuality and that my job as writer was to help them learn. I covered topics completely, in as clear a presentation as possible, and made a special effort to use language that would enlighten rather than intimidate; because students so often know only slang terminology regarding sex, I have included slang terms in parentheses following definitions of scientific sexual terms, to connect the two terminologies. Similarly, in the selection and preparation of illustrations for the book, the goal was always to convey as much information as possible, simply and clearly.

The book assumes no prior college courses in biology, psychology, or sociology. It is designed as an introduction following the three major objectives of my own courses in human sexuality:

1. To provide practical information needed for everyday living (information about sexual anatomy, contraception, and sexually transmitted diseases, for example) and to deal with problems in a more psychological area (such as erection problems or inability to have an orgasm).

2. To help students feel more comfortable with thinking and talking about sex, both to minimize their own personal anguish about a tension-causing topic and to help them become rational decision makers in an important aspect of their lives.

3. To familiarize students with methods used in research on sexual behavior, and particularly with problems inherent in some of these methods, so that they can read research reports critically and intelligently.

My own course is a survey course, designed to provide students with a broad range of information about sexuality. Reflecting that approach, this book is intended to be complete and balanced in its coverage, so that students will want to save it after the course for use as a reference in future years. My own training was quite compatible with this interdisciplinary, survey approach. My original graduate training was in psychology, with specialties in behavior genetics and statistics; later my interests expanded to include psychology of women and gender roles. As a result, I feel comfortable in discussing sexuality from biological, psychological, and sociological viewpoints. I did not want to write a book just about the biology of sex, nor just about the psychology of sex, nor just about the sociology of sex. I wanted to cover all those areas with integrity.

Nonetheless, for instructors who feel they lack the time to deal with all the material or who are not prepared to cover certain topics, the chapters have been written to be fairly independent. For example, any of the following chapters could be omitted without loss of continuity: Chapter 13, "Attraction, Love and Intimacy"; Chapter 17, "Sexual Coercion"; Chapter 21, "Ethics, Religion, and Sexuality"; Chapter 22, "Sex and the Law."

It is my belief that, in modern American culture, we are in danger of taking sex far too seriously. We may not be serious about it in the same way as were our Victorian ancestors, but we are serious nonetheless—serious about whether we are using the best and most up-to-date sexual techniques, serious about whether our partners are having as many orgasms as possible, and so on. To counteract this tendency, I have tried to use a light touch, with occasional bits of humor, in this book. I am not advocating that we treat sex in a flippant or frivolous manner, but rather that we keep it in perspective and remember that there are some very funny things about it.

THE FIFTH EDITION

The fifth edition represents a major revision. What is new about the fifth edition? Most importantly, I have expanded the coverage of the multicultural perspective. Several chapters have received major rewrites, and the number of chapters has been reduced by one.

Two chapters have received major revisions: Chapter 8, "Contraception and Abortion"; and Chapter 10, "Sexually Transmitted Diseases." These rewrites reflect an explosion of new research on topics such as HIV/AIDS, genital warts, and newly introduced methods of contraception such as Norplant.

Faculty had requested that I reduce the number of chapters to make it more feasible to get through the book in a semester, or perhaps even a quarter. I was able to reduce the number of chapters by one by combining two chapters from the previous edition, one on gender roles and the other on female sexuality and male sexuality, into a single chapter, Chapter 14, "Gender Roles, Female Sexuality, and Male Sexuality."

Faculty had also requested that the chapter on methodology in sex research be moved to the front of the book because they like covering this material early in the course. I have responded to this request, too, by making "Sex Research" Chapter 3 in the text. As in previous editions, though, I have tried to keep the chapters fairly independent of each other so that instructors can use them in a different order from the one I have set. Many colleagues have told me that they do use the chapters in a different order (although no two of them seem to share the same re-ordering), and that this is done with ease.

All other chapters have been updated throughout, and special care has been taken to present the most recent available statistics at every point.

To give you some idea of the extent of the revision, there were well over 1000 references in the fourth edition of the book. To these, 265 new references have been added for the fifth edition, after considerable winnowing to pick the best studies and not to expand the book to 1000 pages in length!

Multicultural/Multiethnic Perspective

Beginning with the very first edition of this book, published in 1978, I have included cross-cultural perspectives. The multicultural/multiethnic perspective has really come into full flower in this edition, in which I have been able to integrate into nearly every chapter studies on sexuality in various cultures around the world, as well as on various ethnic groups in the United States. I will give just a few examples here. In Chapter 1 a Focus box has been added, "Sex in China," covering the history of sexual norms in China as well as the current sexual scene in mainland China. In Chapter 3 on methodology, I have added a new exemplar study on African American and Hispanic youth, with discussion of methodological issues that must be addressed in doing multiethnic research. Chapter 15 includes a new discussion of issues surrounding ethnicity and sexual orientation, and Chapter 14 includes a discussion of ethnicity and gender roles. And the important multicultural studies already in the fourth edition—such as the Goldmans' research on the sexual knowledge of children in four cultures—has of course been retained in this edition.

LEARNING RESOURCES

This book also emphasizes learning resources for the student. There is a running glossary of terms, with pronunciations. A chapter outline appears at the opening of each chapter. Since research in cognitive psychology indicates that learning and memory are improved considerably if the learner knows the organization of the material in advance, the chapter outlines are designed to facilitate this learning. There are Review Questions and Questions for Thought, Discussion, and Debate at the end of each chapter. These questions are designed to help students review for exams as well as stimulate them to think beyond the material presented in the text.

SPECIAL FEATURES

Finally, there is an Appendix—"A Directory of Resources in Human Sexuality." It lists the names, addresses, and functions of many major organizations in the field of human sexuality, on topics ranging from birth control to toll-free hotlines on sexually transmitted diseases, to scholarly journals. I hope that this listing will serve as a useful reference for both instructors and students. I personally have used the one in the previous edition a greal deal.

SUPPLEMENTARY MATERIALS

A full teaching resource package accompanies this text. The package includes an instructor's manual which contains both a set of test questions for every chapter, and a resource section which offers a wide variety of teaching aids for new and experienced instructors. The test questions are available in computerized format for IBM and Macintosh computers. The teaching package also includes a set of 65 full-color overhead transparencies, revised and expanded for this edition.

ACKNOWLEDGMENTS

Over the course of the first four editions, numerous reviewers contributed to the development of *Understanding Human Sexuality*. I don't have the space to cite them all, but their contributions remain and I am grateful to them.

In addition, I am enormously grateful to the following reviewers who helped shape this revision: Michael H. Birnbaum, California State University, Fullerton; Robert Brush, Purdue University; Clive Davis, Syracuse University; John D. DeLamater, University of Wisconsin; Beverly Drinnin, Des Moines Area Community College; Randy D. Fisher, University of Central Florida; Gere B. Fulton, University of Toledo; Susan D. Lonborg, Central Washington University; John T. Long, Mount San Antonio College; and David P. J. Przybyla, Denison University. Wendy Theobald, my student library assistant, deserves special thanks for tracking down hundreds of articles and books at the numerous libraries spread around the University of Wisconsin. She was creative and thorough and often found studies that even I was not aware of. This book is noticeably better because of her work.

Finally, I owe many thanks to the editors and staff at McGraw-Hill: Jane Vaicunas, who has offered consistent support and encouragement and many excellent ideas for the book; and Scott Amerman, editing supervisor, who did an excellent job carrying the book through to completion.

I love teaching the human sexuality course and I've loved writing and rewriting this text for it. I hope that you will enjoy reading it, learning from it, and teaching with it.

Janet Shibley Hyde

*Understanding
Human
Sexuality*

Sexuality in Perspective

1

Her voice was the merest whisper as he slowly undressed her, until at last she stood before him, tiny, perfectly formed, her flesh shining in the moonlight, her blond hair almost silver. He picked her up then and slid her into the bed, and carefully took off his own clothes, dropped them to the floor, and slid in beside her. The feel of her satin skin was almost more than he could bear, and he had a hunger for her that was impossible to control as he lay beside her. But it was she who took his face in her hands, who held him close as she arched her body toward him, as slowly, like a forgotten memory come to life with a delicious vengeance, she felt him slip inside her, and she soared to heights that, even with Jeffrey, she had never known. *

The biologist considers sexual behavior to be of fundamental significance because it leads to perpetuation of the species and thus to the continuity of life itself. The psychologist finds in the sexual impulse wellsprings of human conduct, deep reservoirs of motivation that impel men and women to action and furnish the driving force for many of their day-do-day activities. Sociologists recognize the integrating, cohesive functioning of sex as contributing to the stability of the family unit and thus to the entire structure of the social group. For the moralist, man's perpetual attempt to reconcile his basic sexual tendencies with the ethical standards and ideal demands of his social group presents a primary problem. [†]

---

* *Source:* Danielle Steel. (1982). *Once in a lifetime.* New York: Dell Publishing, p. 130.

[†] *Source:* Clellan S. Ford and Frank A. Beach. (1951). *Patterns of sexual behavior.* New York: Harper & Row, p. 1.

Odd though it may seem, both of the quotations on page 1 are talking about the same thing—sex. The first quotation is from a romance novel. It stimulates the reader's fantasies and arousal response. The second is from a scholarly book about sex. It stimulates the brain but not the genitals. From these two brief excerpts we can quickly see that the topic of sexuality is diverse, complex, and fascinating.

Introductory textbooks on most subjects generally begin with a section designed to motivate students to study whatever topic the text is about. No such section appears in this book; the reason people want to study sex is obvious, and your motivation for studying it is probably already quite high. Sex is an important force in many people's lives, so there are practical reasons for wanting to learn about it. Most people are curious about sex, particularly because exchanging sexual information is somewhat taboo in our culture, so curiosity also motivates us to study sex. Finally, most of us at various times experience problems with our sexual functioning or wish that we could function better, and we hope that learning more about sex will help us. This book is designed to meet all those needs. And so, without further comment, let us consider various perspectives on sexuality. This will give you a glimpse of the forest before you study the trees: sexual anatomy and physiology (the "plumbing" part), and sexual behavior (the "people" part), which is discussed in the later chapters.

SEX AND GENDER

We sometimes use the word "sex" ambiguously. Sometimes it refers to being male or female, and sometimes it refers to sexual behavior or reproduction. In most cases, of course, the meaning is clear from the context. If you are filling out a job application form and one item says, "Sex: _____," you do not write, "I like it" or "As often as possible." It is clear that your prospective employer wants to know whether you are a male or female. In other cases, though, the meaning is ambiguous. For example, when a book has the title *Sex and Temperament in Three Primitive Societies,* what is it about? Is it about the sexual practices of primitive people and whether having sex frequently gives them pleasant temperaments? Or is it about the kinds of personalities that males and females are expected to have in those societies? Not only does this use of "sex" create ambiguities, but it also clouds our thinking about some important issues.

To remove—or at least reduce—this ambiguity, the term "sex" will be used in this book to refer specifically to sexual anatomy and sexual behavior, and the term **gender** will be used to refer to the state of being male or female. This convention will be maintained throughout the book in the hope that it will help clarify some issues as we proceed.

This is a book about sex, not gender; it is about sexual behavior and the biological, psychological, and social forces that influence it. Of course, although I am arguing that sex and gender are conceptually different, I would not try to argue that they are totally independent of each other. Certainly gender roles—the ways in which males and females are expected to behave—exert a powerful influence on the way people behave sexually, and so one chapter will be devoted to gender roles and their effects on sexuality.

How should we define "sex," aside from saying that it is different from "gender"? A biologist might define sexual behavior as "any behavior that increases the likelihood of gametic union [union of sperm and egg]" (Bermant and Davidson, 1974). This definition emphasizes the reproductive function of sex. However, particularly in the last few decades, technologies have been developed that allow us to

Gender: The state of being male or female.

separate reproduction from sex. Most Americans now use sex not only for procreation but also for recreation.[1]

Kinsey defined "sex" as behavior that leads to orgasm. Although this definition has some merits (it does not imply that sex must be associated with reproduction), it also presents some problems. If a wife has intercourse with her husband but does not have an orgasm, was that not sexual behavior for her?

Sexual behavior: Behavior that produces arousal and increases the chance of orgasm.

To try to avoid some of these problems, sexual behavior will be defined in this book as *behavior that produces arousal and increases the chance of orgasm.*[2] The term "sexual anatomy," then, refers to the parts of our bodies that are involved in sexual behavior (particularly intercourse) and reproduction.

UNDERSTANDING SEXUALITY

Religion

Throughout most of recorded history, at least until about 100 years ago, religion (and rumor) provided most of the information that people had about sexuality. Thus the ancient Greeks openly acknowledged both heterosexuality and homosexuality in their society and explained the existence of the two in a myth in which the original humans were double creatures with twice the normal number of limbs and organs; some were double males, some were double females, and some were half male and half female. The gods, fearing the power of these creatures, split them in half, and forever after each one continued to search for its missing half. Thus heterosexuals were thought to have resulted from the splitting of the half male, half female; male homosexuals, from the splitting of the double male; and female homosexuals, from the splitting of the double female. It was through this mythology that the ancient Greek understood sexuality.

The fifteenth-century Christian believed that "wet dreams" (nocturnal emissions) resulted from intercourse with tiny spiritual creatures called *incubi* and *succubi*, a notion put forth in a papal bull of 1484 and a companion book, the *Malleus Maleficarum* ("witch's hammer"); the person who had wet dreams was guilty of sodomy (see Chapter 21) as well as witchcraft.

The Muslim believed that sexual intercourse was one of the finest pleasures of life, reflecting the teachings of the great prophet Muhammad.

Different religions hold different understandings of human sexuality, and these religious views often have a profound impact on people growing up with them. A detailed discussion of religion and sexuality is provided in Chapter 21.

Science

It was against this background of religious understandings of sexuality that the scientific study of sex began in the late nineteenth century, although, of course,

---

[1] Actually, even in former times sex was not always associated with reproduction. For example, a man in 1850 might have fathered 10 children; using a very conservative estimate that he engaged in sexual intercourse 1500 times during his adult life (once a week for the 30 years from age 20 to age 50), one concludes that only 10 in 1500 of those acts, or less than 1 percent, resulted in reproduction.

[2] This definition, though an improvement over some, still has its problems. For example, consider a woman who feels no arousal at all during intercourse. According to the definition, intercourse would not be sexual behavior for her. However, intercourse would generally be something we would want to classify as sexual behavior. It should be clear that defining "sexual behavior" is very difficult. The definition given is good, though not perfect.

religious notions continue to influence our ideas about sexuality to the present day. In addition, the groundwork for an understanding of the biological aspects of sexuality had already been laid by the research of physicians and biologists. The Dutch microscopist Anton van Leeuwenhoek (1632–1723) and his student John Ham had discovered sperm swimming in human semen. In 1875 Oscar Hertwig first observed the actual fertilization of the egg by the sperm in sea urchins, although the ovum in humans was not directly observed until the twentieth century.

A major advance in the scientific understanding of the psychological aspects of human sexuality came with the work of the Viennese physician Sigmund Freud (1856–1939), founder of psychiatry and psychoanalysis. His ideas will be discussed in detail in Chapter 2.

It is important to recognize the cultural context in which Freud and the other early sex researchers began their research and writing. They began their work in the Victorian era, the late 1800s, both in the United States and Europe. Norms about sexuality were extraordinarily rigid and oppressive. Historian Peter Gay characterized this repressive aspect of Victorian cultural norms as

> . . . a devious and insincere world in which middle-class husbands slaked their lust by keeping mistresses, frequenting prostitutes, or molesting children, while their wives, timid, dutiful, obedient, were sexually anesthetic and poured all their capacity for love into their housekeeping and their child-rearing. (Gay, 1984, p. 6)

Certainly traces of these Victorian attitudes remain with us today. Yet at the same time the actual sexual behavior of Victorians was sometimes active and in violation of societal norms (see Focus 1.1: A Victorian Sex Survey). In his history of sexuality in the Victorian era, Peter Gay documents the story of Mabel Loomis Todd who, though married, carried on a sensual and lengthy affair with Austin Dickinson, a

FIGURE 1.1
Two important early sex researchers. (a) Sigmund Freud. (b) Henry Havelock Ellis.

(a)

(b)

A Victorian Sex Survey

In the late 1800s Queen Victoria reigned in England, and both there and in the United States the ideal seemed to be to repress sexuality as much as possible. Women, particularly, were to have no sexual desires. And standards of modesty were so great that pianos had "limbs" rather than vulgar "legs."

Out of the Victorian environment emerged a remarkable woman, Dr. Clelia Mosher. Born in Albany, New York, in 1863, she began college at Wellesley and finished at Stanford. For her Masters degree from Stanford, she collected data to debunk a popular myth of the time: that women could breathe only high in the chest, whereas men breathed deeply, using the diaphragm. Mosher concluded, quite reasonably, that any differences resulted purely from women being laced into tight-fitting corsets. Mosher began medical school at Johns Hopkins when she was 32 and earned her M.D. degree four years later. Interestingly, Gertrude Stein, the famous author, entered the same medical school one year after Mosher, but never finished her degree.

Over a period of 30 years, beginning when she was an undergraduate, Mosher conducted a sex survey of Victorian women, most of whom were born around the time of the Civil War. In all, she administered her nine-page questionnaire to 47 women. The sample is, admittedly, small and nonrandom. Many of the women were faculty wives at universities, or women from Mosher's medical practice, and surely they were a select sample to agree to answer the questions; 81 percent had attended college, a high level of education for women in those days. Nonetheless, the survey is remarkable because—despite well-known ideas about Victorian women—this is the only actual survey of those women known to exist. Here are some interesting findings from the study:

- Despite the stereotype that Victorian women felt no sexual desire, 35 of the 44 women (80 percent) answering the question said that they felt a desire for sexual intercourse.

- Thirty-four of the women (72 percent) indicated that they experienced orgasm. Interestingly, Mosher worded the question "Do you always have a venereal orgasm?" thus assuming that orgasm was to be expected.

- Mosher suspected that women's longer time to reach orgasm might be a cause of marital conflicts. Many of her respondents supported this idea. One said that sex had been unpleasant to her for years because of her "slow reaction," but "orgasm [occurs] if time is taken." Another complained that "Men have not been properly trained." And for some, not reaching orgasm was psychologically devastating (one can't help thinking that things haven't changed so much from the 1890s to the 1990s).

- At least 30 of the women (64 percent) used some form of birth control. Douching was the most popular method, followed by withdrawal and "timing." Several women's husbands used a "male sheath," and two women used a "rubber cap over the uterus." One women used cocoa butter. She did not explain how or why.

Clelia Mosher's survey is fascinating because it demonstrates that despite the Victorian era's repressive teachings, some women still managed to enjoy sex. True, some were affected by Victorian mores; three of the women said their ideal would be to abstain from intercourse entirely. But the majority of the women still expressed sexual desires and experienced orgasms and seemed to enjoy sex with their husbands.

Source: Kathryn A. Jacob. (1981). The Mosher report. *American Heritage*, pp. 57–64.

community leader in Amherst, Massachusetts. Many people actually knew about the "secret" affair, yet Mrs. Loomis did not become an outcast (Gay, 1984). Doubtless, this wide discrepancy between Victorian sexual norms and actual behavior created a great deal of personal tension. That tension probably propelled a good many people into Dr. Freud's office, providing data for his theory that emphasizes sexual tensions and conflict.

An equally great—though not so well known—early contributor to the scientific study of sex was Henry Havelock Ellis (1859–1939). A physician in Victorian England, he compiled a vast collection of information on sexuality—including medical and anthropological findings, as well as case histories—which was published in a series of volumes entitled *Studies in the Psychology of Sex* beginning in 1896. Havelock Ellis was a remarkably objective and tolerant scholar, particularly for his era. A sexual reformer, he believed that sexual deviations from the norm were often harmless, and he urged society to accept them. In his desire to collect information about human sexuality rather than to make judgments about it, he can be considered

FIGURE 1.2
The Victorian era, from which Freud and Ellis emerged, was characterized by extreme sexual repression. Here are some apparatuses that were sold to prevent onanism (masturbation).

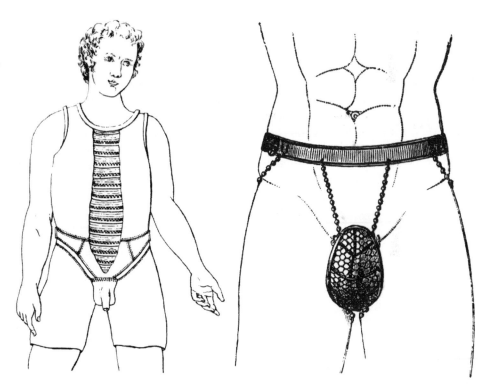

Fig. 350. Korsett von Lajade-Lafond zur Verhinderung der Onanie. Nach Fleck: Die Verirrungen des Geschlechtstriebes. Stuttgart 1830.

Fig. 351.
Onaniebandage
für weibliche Patienten.

Onaniebandage
für männliche Patienten.

the forerunner of modern sex research (for an autobiography, see Ellis, 1939; numerous biographies also exist).

Another important figure in nineteenth-century sex research was Richard von Krafft-Ebing (1840–1902). His special interest was "pathological" sexuality, and he managed to collect over 200 cases histories of pathological individuals, which appeared in his book entitled *Psychopathia Sexualis*. His work tended to be neither objective nor tolerant. One of his case histories is presented in Chapter 16.

One other early contributor to the scientific understanding of sexuality deserves mention, the German Magnus Hirschfeld (1868–1935). He founded the first sex research institute and administered the first large-scale sex survey, obtaining data from 10,000 people on a 130-item questionnaire. Unfortunately, most of the information he amassed was destroyed by Nazi hoodlums. Hirschfeld also established the first journal devoted to the study of sex, established a marriage counseling service, worked for legal reforms, and gave advice on contraception and sex problems. His special interest, however, was homosexuality. Doubtless some of his avant-garde approaches resulted from the fact that he was himself both a homosexual and a transvestite, but his contributions as a pioneer sex researcher cannot be denied (Bullough, 1976).

In the twentieth century, major breakthroughs in the scientific understanding of sex came with the massive surveys of human sexual behavior in the United States conducted by Alfred Kinsey and his colleagues in the 1940s and with Masters and Johnson's investigations of sexual dysfunctions and the physiology of sexual response. At about the same time that the Kinsey research was being conducted, some anthropologists—most notably Margaret Mead and Bronislaw Malinowski—were beginning to collect data on sexual behavior in other cultures. Other, smaller investigations also provided important information.

The scientific study of sex has not emerged as a separate, unified academic discipline like biology or psychology or sociology. Rather, it tends to be interdisciplinary—a joint effort by biologists, psychologists, sociologists, anthropologists, and physicians. In a sense, this is a major virtue in our current approach to understanding sexuality, since it gives us a better view of humans in all their sexual complexity.

Let us now consider the perspectives on sexuality provided by cross-cultural observations of humans in a wide variety of societies.

CROSS-CULTURAL PERSPECTIVES

We tend to be ethnocentric in our understanding of human sexual behavior. That is, most of us have had experience with sexuality in only one culture—the United

Homosexual: A person who is sexually attracted to, or engages in sexual activity primarily with, members of his or her own gender.

Transvestite: A person (usually a man) who dresses in the clothing of another gender.

FIGURE 1.3
The history of scientific research on sex.

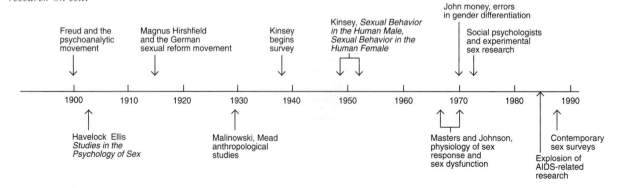

States, for example—and we tend to view it as the only pattern of sexual behavior in existence, and certainly as the only "natural" pattern. But anthropologists have discovered that there are wide variations in sexual behavior and attitudes from one culture to the next. Considering these variations should help us to put our own sexual behavior in perspective.

The data on the enormous cross-cultural variations in sexual behavior will be reviewed below. First, however, some generalizations that emerge in cross-cultural studies will be considered. One source of data for the conclusions that will be drawn is the classic study of anthropologist Clellan Ford and psychologist Frank Beach (1951), who surveyed sexual behavior in 190 societies around the world and also sexual behavior across various animal species. Other major sources are massive cross-cultural surveys of sexual practices done by anthropologists Edgar Gregersen (1983) and Suzanne Frayser (1985).

Before proceeding it is worth noting that Ford and Beach concluded, in 1951, that the United States culture was a relatively sexually restrictive one; the majority of the others studied were far more permissive. This may help us put our own standards in better perspective. On the other hand, most people would agree—and scientific research supports the notion (see Chapters 11 to 12)—that sexual behavior and attitudes among Americans have undergone substantial changes in the more than 40 years since Ford and Beach wrote their book. Modern America has been described as an "eroticized" culture (Gregor, 1985).

Generalizations

The major generalization that emerges from cross-cultural studies is that all societies regulate sexual behavior in some way, though the exact regulations vary greatly from one culture to the next (Gebhard, 1971; Jensen, 1976b). Apparently no society has seen fit to leave sexuality totally unregulated, perhaps because social disruption would result. As an example, incest taboos are nearly universal: Sex is regulated in that intercourse between relatives is prohibited. Most societies also condemn forced sexual relations, such as rape.

Beyond this generalization, though, regulations vary greatly from one society to the next, and sexual behavior and attitudes vary correspondingly (see Focus 1.2). The ways in which various societies treat some key areas of human sexual behavior will be considered below.

Sexual Techniques

Kissing is one of the most common sexual techniques in our culture. It is also very common in most other societies (Gregersen, 1983). There are a few societies, though, in which kissing is unknown. For example, when the Thonga of Africa first saw Europeans kissing, they laughed and said, "Look at them; they eat each other's saliva and dirt." There is also some variation in techniques of kissing. For example, among the Kwakiutl of Canada and the Trobriand Islanders, kissing consists of sucking the lips and tongue of the partner, permitting saliva to flow from one mouth to the other. Many Americans might find such a practice somewhat repulsive, but other peoples find it sexually arousing.

Grooming and delousing are widespread forms of behavior that act as a prelude to sexual relations. Describing the Siriono of South America, one observer wrote:

> Lovers also spend hours in grooming one another—extracting lice from their hair or wood ticks from their bodies, and eating them; removing worms and spines from their skin; gluing feathers into their hair; and covering their faces with utuku

Incest taboo: A regulation prohibiting sexual interaction between blood relatives, such as brother and sister or father and daughter.

Sexuality in Three Societies

Inis Beag

Inis Beag is a small island off the coast of Ireland. It is probably one of the most naive and sexually repressive societies in the world.

The people of Inis Beag seem to have no knowledge of a number of sexual activities such as French kissing, mouth stimulation of the breast, or hand stimulation of the partner's penis, much less cunnilingus, fellatio, or homosexuality. Sex education is virtually nonexistent; parents do not seem to be able to bring themselves to discuss such embarrassing matters with their children, and they simply trust that, after marriage, nature will take its course.

Menstruation and menopause are sources of fear for the island women because they have no idea of their physiological significance. It is commonly believed that menopause can produce insanity; in order to ward off this condition, some women have retired from life in their mid-forties, and a few have confined themselves to bed until death years later.

The men believe that intercourse is hard on one's health. They will desist from sex the night before they are to do a job that takes great energy. They do not approach women sexually during menstruation or for months after childbirth; a woman is considered dangerous to the male at these times.

The islanders abhor nudity. Only babies are allowed to bathe while nude. Adults wash only the parts of their bodies that extend beyond their clothing—face, neck, lower arms, hands, lower legs, and feet. The fear of nudity has even cost lives. Sailors who never learned to swim because it involved wearing scanty clothing have drowned when their ships have sunk.

Premarital sex is essentially unknown. In marital sex, foreplay is generally limited to kissing and rough fondling of the buttocks. The husband invariably initiates the activity. The male-on-top is the only position used, and both partners keep their underwear on during the activity. The man has orgasm quickly and falls asleep immediately. Female orgasm is unknown, or at least it is doubted to exist or is considered deviant.

Mangaia

In distinct contrast to Inis Beag is Mangaia, an island in the South Pacific. For the Mangaians, sex—for pleasure and for procreation—is a principal interest.

The Mangaian boy hears of masturbation when he is about 7, and he may begin to masturbate at age 8 or 9. At around age 13 he undergoes the superincision ritual (in which a slit is made on the top of the penis, along its entire length). This ritual initiates him into manhood; more important, however, the expert who performs the superincision gives him sexual instruction. He shows the boy how to perform cunnilingus, how to kiss and suck

. . . paint. This behavior often leads up to a sexual bout, especially when conditions for intercourse are favorable. (Holmberg, 1946, p. 182)

Cunnilingus (mouth stimulation of the female genitals) is fairly common in our society, and it occurs in a few other societies as well, especially in the South Pacific. A particularly exotic variation is reported on the island of Ponape; the man places a fish in the woman's vulva and then gradually licks it out prior to coitus.

Inflicting pain on the partner is also a part of the sexual technique in some

breasts, and how to bring his partner to orgasm several times before he has his own orgasm. About two weeks after the operation, the boy has intercourse with an experienced woman, which removes the scab. She provides him with practice in various acts and positions and trains him to hold back until he can have simultaneous orgasms with his partner.

After this, the Mangaian boy aggressively seeks out girls, or they seek him out; soon he has coitus every night. The girl, who has received sexual instruction from an older woman, expects demonstration of his virility as proof of his desire for her. What is valued is the ability of the male to continue vigorously the in-and-out action of coitus over long periods of time while the female moves her hips "like a washing machine." Nothing is despised more than a "dead" partner who does not move. A good man is expected to continue his actions for 15 to 30 minutes or more.

The average "nice" girl will have three or four successive boyfriends between the ages of 13 and 20; the average boy may have 10 or more girlfriends. Mangaian parents encourage their daughters to have sexual experiences with several men. They want her to find a marriage partner who is congenial.

At around age 18, the Mangaians typically have sex most nights of the week, with about three orgasms per night. By about age 48, they have sex two or three times per week, with one orgasm each time.

All women in Mangaia apparently learn to have orgasms. Bringing his partner to orgasm is one of the man's chief sources of sexual pleasure.

Mehinaku

In contrast to Inis Beag where there is little sex and plenty of anxiety, and Mangaia where there

is plenty of sex and little anxiety, lies Mehinaku, where there is plenty of sex and plenty of anxiety.

In the central Brazilian village of Mehinaku, sex is believed to be very fascinating and the culture is highly eroticized. There is an openness with children about sex, and children can easily list the names of their parents' extramarital lovers, who are typically many. The men have a very high libido, leading them to compete with each other for women's sexual favors by bringing small gifts such as fish.

On the other hand, the culture is very gender-segregated. There is a men's house and if a woman enters it and sees what she is forbidden to see, she is taken to the woods and gang raped, in a culture that is otherwise very nonviolent. Women are believed to have much less of a sex drive than men, and there seems to be no recognition of female orgasm. Women's menstruation is believed to be dangerous.

The dreams and mythic stories told by the people testify to their sexual anxieties—for example, those in myths who engage in extramarital sex typically die in fantastic ways. In reality the people continue with a great deal of sexual activity while feeling intense ambivalence and anxiety about it.

Sources: John C. Messenger. Sex and repression in an Irish folk community. Donald S. Marshall. Sexual behavior on Mangaia. Both in D. S. Marshall and R. C. Suggs (Eds.). (1971). *Human sexual behavior.* New York: Basic Books. Thomas Gregor. (1985). *Anxious pleasures: The sexual lives of an Amazonian people.* Chicago: University of Chicago Press.

societies. The Apinaye woman of South America may bite off bits of her partner's eyebrows, noisily spitting them aside. Ponapean men usually tug at the woman's eyebrows, occasionally yanking out tufts of hair. The Trukese women of the South Pacific poke a finger into the man's ear when they are highly aroused. People of various societies bite their partners to the point of drawing blood and leaving scars; most commonly it is the woman who inflicts the pain on the man (Ford & Beach, 1951).

The frequency of intercourse for married couples varies considerably from one culture to the next. The lowest frequency seems to be among the Keraki of the South Pacific, who copulate only about once a week. The Irish natives of Inis Beag, discussed in Focus 1.2, may hold a record by having an even lower frequency than this, perhaps only once or twice a month; however, the anthropologists who studied them were unable to determine how often couples did have sex because so much secrecy surrounds the act. At the opposite extreme, the Aranda of Australia have intercourse as often as three to five times a night, sleeping between episodes; the Mangaians, described in Focus 1.2, seem to have an equally high frequency, at least among the young. The Santals of southern Asia copulate as often as five times per day every day early in marriage (Gregersen, 1983). Our own culture, then, at the time of the Kinsey report, had a low frequency of intercourse compared with other societies. Surveys of United States sexuality in the 1980s indicated our frequency of intercourse had shifted to being about average compared with other societies (e.g., Blumstein & Schwartz, 1983).

Very few societies actually encourage people to engage in sexual intercourse at particular times (Frayser, 1985). Instead, most groups have restrictions that forbid intercourse at certain times or in certain situations. For example, almost every society has a postpartum sex taboo, that is, a prohibition on sexual intercourse for a period of time after a woman has given birth to a baby, although the taboo typically lasts less than six months (Frayser, 1985).

Masturbation

Masturbation: Self-stimulation of the genitals to produce sexual arousal.

Attitudes toward masturbation vary widely across cultures. Some societies tolerate or even encourage masturbation during childhood and adolescence, while others condemn the practice at any age. Almost all human societies express some disapproval of adult masturbation, ranging from mild ridicule to severe punishment (Gregersen, 1983). On the other hand, at least some adults in all societies appear to practice it.

Female masturbation certainly occurs in other societies. The African Azande woman does it with a phallus made of a wooden root; however, if her husband catches her masturbating, he may beat her severely. The following is a description of the Lesu of the South Pacific, who are one of the few societies that express no disapproval of adult female masturbation:

> A woman will masturbate if she is sexually excited and there is no man to satisfy her. A couple may be having intercourse in the same house, or near enough for her to see them, and she may thus become aroused. She then sits down and bends her right leg so that her heel presses against her genitalia. Even young girls of about six years may do this quite casually as they sit on the ground. The women and men talk about it freely, and there is no shame attached to it. It is a customary position for women to take, and they learn it in childhood. They never use their hands for manipulation. (Powdermaker, 1933, pp. 276–277)

Premarital and Extramarital Sex

Societies differ considerably in their rules regarding premarital sex (Frayser, 1985). At one extreme are the Marquesans of Eastern Polynesia. Both boys and girls in that culture have participated in a wide range of sexual experiences before puberty. Their first experience with intercourse occurs with a heterosexual partner who is 30 to 40 years old. Mothers are proud if their daughters have many lovers. Only later does marriage occur. In contrast are the Egyptians of Silwa. In this culture a girl's clitoris is removed at age 7 or 8 in order to decrease her potential for sexual excitement and intercourse. Premarital intercourse is believed to bring shame on the family. Marriage usually occurs around the age of 12 or 13, shortening the premarital period and any temptations it might contain.

These two cultures are fairly typical of their regions. According to one study, 90 percent of Pacific Island societies permit premarital sex, as do 88 percent of African and 82 percent of Eurasian societies; however, 73 percent of Mediterranean societies prohibit premarital sex (Frayser, 1985).

Extramarital sex is more complex and conflicted for most cultures. Extramarital sex ranks second only to incest as the most strictly prohibited type of sexual contact. One cross-cultural study found that it was forbidden for one or both partners in 74 percent of the cultures surveyed (Frayser, 1985). Even when extramarital sex is permitted, it is subjected to regulations; the most common pattern of restriction is to allow extramarital sex for husbands but not wives.

Homosexuality

There is a wide range of attitudes toward homosexuality in various cultures. At one extreme are societies that strongly disapprove of homosexual behavior for people of any age. In contrast, some societies tolerate homosexual behavior for children but disapprove of it in adults. Yet other societies actively force all their male members to engage in some homosexual behavior, usually in conjunction with puberty rites. In Africa, prominent Siwan men lend their sons to one another, and they discuss their homosexual love affairs as openly as they discuss the love of women. A few societies have a formalized role for the adult male homosexual that gives him status and dignity.

While there is wide variation in attitudes toward homosexuality and in homosexual behavior, four general rules do seem to emerge (Ford & Beach, 1951; Whitam, 1983): (1) No matter how a particular society treats homosexuality, the behavior always occurs in at least some individuals—that is, homosexuality is found universally in all societies; (2) males are more likely to engage in homosexual behavior than females; (3) homosexual behavior is never the predominant form of sexual behavior for adults in any of the societies studied; and (4) the incidence of homosexuality is stable across cultures and across time and does not exceed 5 percent of the total population.

Standards of Attractiveness

In all human societies physical characteristics are important in determining whom one chooses as a sex partner. What is considered attractive varies considerably, though. In the United States, the ideal is a slim woman with large eyes and a lovely complexion and long, shapely legs. For us, physical characteristics are probably less important in determining a man's attractiveness. More important is what he *does*; he is attractive if he is a star athlete or a wealthy businessman. But his physical characteristics are also considered important; the ideal is a tall, trim man with broad shoulders, narrow hips, and a firm jaw.

The region of the body that is judged for attractiveness varies considerably from one culture to the next. For some peoples, the shape and color of the eyes are especially significant. For others, the shape of the ears is most important. Some societies go directly to the heart of the matter and judge attractiveness by the appearance of the external genitals. In a few societies, elongated labia majora (the pads of fat on either side of the vaginal opening in women) are considered sexually attractive, and it is common practice for a woman to pull on hers in order to make

Sex in China

For the first 4000 years of Chinese history, there was a yin-yang philosophy and open, positive attitudes about human sexuality, including a rich erotic literature. Indeed, the oldest sex manuals in the world came from China, dating from approximately 200 B.C. The most recent 1000 years, however, have been just the opposite, characterized by repression of sexuality and censorship. Dr. Fang Fu Ruan, a physician and leading sex expert in China, came to the United States and has given us an insider's view of sexuality in Chinese culture in his book *Sex in China*.

A major philosophical concept in Chinese culture is yin and yang, originating around 300 B.C. and found in important writings on Confucianism and Taoism. According to yin-yang philosophy, all objects and events are the products of two elements: yin, which is negative, passive, weak, and destructive; and yang, which is positive, active, strong, and constructive. Yin is associated with the female, and yang with the male. For several thousand years, the Chinese have used yin and yang in words dealing with sexuality. For example, *yin fu* (the door of yin) means "vulva," and *yang ju* (the organ of yang) means "penis." *Huo yin yang* (the union of yin and yang) is the term used for sexual intercourse. This philosophy holds that the harmonious interaction between the male and female principles is vital, creating positive cultural attitudes toward sexuality.

Of the three major religions of China—Confucianism, Taoism, and Buddhism—Taoism is the only truly indigenous one, dating from the writings of Chang Ling around A.D. 143. Taoism is one of the few religions to advocate the cultivation of sexual techniques for the benefit of the individual. To quote from a classic Taoist work, *The Canon of the Immaculate Girl,*

Said P'eng, "One achieves longevity by loving the essence, cultivating the spiritual, and partaking of many kinds of medicines. If you don't know the ways of intercourse, taking herbs is of no benefit. The producing of man and woman is like the begetting of Heaven and Earth. Heaven and Earth have attained the method of intercourse and, therefore, they lack the limitation of finality. Man loses the method of intercourse and therefore suffers the mortification of early death. If you can avoid

them longer. Elongated labia majora among the Nawa women of Africa are considered a mark of beauty and are quite prominent.

Our society's standards are in the minority in one way: in most cultures, a plump woman is considered more attractive than a thin one.

One standard does seem to be a general rule: A poor complexion is considered unattractive in the majority of human societies.

Gender Roles

Margaret Mead did some of the most important studies on gender roles in cultures other than our own, and her books, among them *Sex and Temperament in Three*

mortification and injury and attain the arts of sex, you will have found the way of nondeath. (Ruan, p. 56)

The tradition of erotic literature and openness about sexuality began to change about 1000 years ago, led by several famous neo-Confucianists, so that negative and repressive attitudes become dominant. In 1422 there was a ban on erotic literature, and a second major ban occurred in 1664. A commoner involved in printing a banned book could be beaten and exiled.

When the communist government founded the People's Republic of China in 1949, it imposed a strict ban on all sexually explicit materials. The policy was quite effective in the 1950s and 1960s. By the late 1960s, however, erotica were produced much more in Western nations and in China there was increased openness to the West. By the late 1970s, X-rated videotapes were being smuggled into China from Hong Kong and other countries, and they quickly became a fad. Small parties were organized around the viewing of these tapes. The government reacted harshly, promulgating a new anti-pornography law in 1985. According to the law, "Pornography is very harmful, poisoning people's minds, inducing crimes . . . and must be banned. . . . The person who smuggled, produced, sold, or organized the showing of pornography, whether for sale or not, shall be punished according to the conditions, by imprisonment or administrative punishment" (Ruan, p. 100). Publishing houses were given stiff fines, and by 1986, 217 illegal publishers had been arrested and 42 publishing houses had been forced to close. In one incident, a Shanghai railway station employee was sentenced to death for having organized sex parties on nine different occasions, during which pornographic videotapes were viewed and he engaged in sexual activity with women at the party.

Male homosexuality is recognized in historical writings in China as early as 2000 years ago. Homosexuality was so widespread among the upper classes in ancient China that it is known as the Golden Age of Homosexuality in China. One historical book on the Han dynasty contained a special section describing the emperors' male sexual partners. There were tolerant attitudes toward lesbianism. But with the founding of the People's Republic in 1949, homosexuality, like all other sexuality, was severely repressed. Most Chinese today claim that they have never known a homosexual and that there must be very few in Chinese society.

China today is characterized by a puritanism that probably far exceeds that observed by the original Puritans. It is considered scandalous for a married couple to hold hands in public. Prostitution, premarital sex, homosexuality, and variant sexual behaviors are all illegal, and the laws are enforced. Even sexuality in marriage is given little encouragement. As part of recent reforms, sex education was introduced in the 1980s, in part because of concerns about pregnancy rates and the population problem. Yet political repression and sexual repression go hand in hand. Sexual freedom is unlikely to occur until there is a general openness in government.

Source: Ruan, Fang Fu (1991). *Sex in China.* New York: Plenum Press.

Primitive Societies, are classics. Those studies will not be discussed in detail here because they are well known; the interested reader may consult them directly.

The point that emerges from the cross-cultural studies is that gender roles vary tremendously from one society to the next. In particular, the roles that males and females play in sexual relations may be quite different from the ones that are played in our own society. There are a few societies in which the girl generally begins all love affairs (for example, the Maori and the Kwoma of the South Pacific and the Mataco of South America). Although the gender roles in our society lead us to believe that rape is always committed by men against women, Malinowski described a regular process of women raping men among the Trobriand Islands of the South Pacific:

(a)

(b)

FIGURE 1.4
*Cross-cultural differences,
cross-cultural similarities.
(a) Native women of Labe
Guinea, West Africa. (b)
Three beauty queens,
Cinco de Mayo parade,
San Jose, California. The
custom of female
adornment is found in
most cultures, although the
exact definition of beauty
varies from culture to
culture.*

If they perceive a stranger, a man from any village but their own, passing within sight, they have a customary right to attack him, a right which by all accounts they exercise with zeal and energy.

The man is the fair game of the women for all that sexual violence, obscene cruelty, filthy pollution, and rough handling can do to him. Thus first they pull off and tear up his pubic leaf, the protection of his modesty and, to a native, the symbol of his manly dignity. Then by masturbatory practices and exhibitionism, they try to produce an erection in their victim and, when their manoeuvres have brought about the desired result, one of them squats over him and inserts his penis into her vagina. After the first ejaculation he may be treated in the same manner by another woman. Worse things are to follow. Some of the women will defecate and micturate all over his body. . . . Local informants from the south confirmed this account in all essentials. They were by no means ashamed of their custom, regarding it rather as a sign of the general virility of the district, and passing on any possible opprobrium to the stranger-victims. (1929)

Suffice it to say that some cultures have gender roles very different from our own.

Social-Class and Ethnic-Group Variations in the United States

The discussion so far may have seemed to imply that there is one uniform standard of sexual behavior in the United States and that all Americans behave alike sexually. In fact, though, there are large variations in sexual behavior within our culture. Some of these subcultural variations can be classified as social-class differences and some as ethnic differences.

Social Class and Sex

Cunnilingus (kun-nih-LING-us): Mouth stimulation of the female genitals.

In the years between the Kinsey report of the 1940s and the sexual revolution of the 1970s, social-class differences in sexuality diminished. For example, Kinsey found that almost none of the males who had not gone beyond grade school ever performed **cunnilingus** on their wives, whereas about half the college-educated men did (Kinsey et al., 1948). Hunt (1974), in contrast, found that few social-class differences re-

FIGURE 1.5
Father and son in Mehinaku. Although there are many variations in sexual behaviors and gender roles across cultures, some things are also remarkably similar. The anthropologist who observed the Mehinaku commented: "Most men do not relish the job of babysitting. 'It is a nuisance to take care of children,' they complain" (Gregor, 1985).

Fellatio (fuh-LAY-sho): Mouth stimulation of the penis.

mained. Particularly for techniques such as mouth-genital sex (fellatio and cunnilingus), the mass media have given everyone, at all educational levels, glowing and detailed descriptions of how to do it, and social-class differences have thus declined.

On the other hand, 1980s data indicate that large social-class differences remain in areas such as contraceptive use and unwanted pregnancy. As Table 1.1 shows, among never-married women in their twenties, only 66 percent of those who did not graduate from high school use contraceptives, compared with 98 percent of those who graduated from college. Among the college graduates, only 19 percent had had an unwed pregnancy, compared with 82 percent for those who didn't finish high school.

In summary, there are not large social-class differences in sexual techniques; however, there are substantial social-class variations in contraceptive use and unwed pregnancy.

Ethnicity and Sexuality

The American population is composed of many ethnic groups, and there are some variations among these groups in sexual behavior. The most data are available on whites and African Americans, with some data on Hispanics, fewer on Asian Americans, and none that I could find on Native Americans.

The sexuality of African Americans, of course, is influenced by many of the same factors influencing the sexuality of white Americans, such as the legacies of the Victorian era and the influence of the Judeo-Christian religious tradition. In addition, at least three other factors may act to make the sexuality of blacks somewhat different from that of whites: (1) the African heritage, (2) the forces that acted upon blacks

Table 1.1

Social-Class Variations in the Sexual Behavior of Single (Never-Married) American Women in Their Twenties. (Education is used as an indicator of social class.)

	<12 years of Education, %	12 years of Education, %	13–15 years of Education, %	>15 years of Education, %
Ever had intercourse	90	86	77	81
Currently sexually active	66	56	50	47
Of those who are sexually active, use contraceptives	66	84	89	98
Of those who are sexually active, have been pregnant	82	35	25	19

Source: Koray Tanfer & Marjorie C. Horn. (1985, January/February). Contraceptive use, pregnancy and fertility patterns among single American women in their 20s. *Family Planning Perspectives, 17,* 10–19.

during slavery, and (3) current economic and social conditions, particularly high unemployment among African American men.

Given these forces, how do blacks and whites compare in their sexual behaviors and attitudes? Table 1.2 provides a summary of some statistics from several different studies. Notice that there are some similarities but also some differences between blacks and whites. For example, black males and white males, on the average, begin to masturbate at about the same age, although black females begin masturbating earlier than white females do. African American teenage girls and white teenage girls are about equally negligent in their use of contraception: 24 percent of whites and 25 percent of African Americans never use any method. On the other hand, black teenage girls are more likely to engage in premarital intercourse and to do so at a somewhat younger age. And blacks are less likely to engage in mouth-genital sex. Black teenage girls are somewhat less knowledgeable about important reproductive facts such as the time of the menstrual cycle during which the female is most fertile.

Notice in Table 1.2 that by their thirties, blacks are considerably less likely to have married. Many factors play into this pattern. One is the high rate of unemployment of black men, who may feel that they should not get married if they cannot support a family. The rules of the welfare system discourage marriage. Notice also that the sex ratio for blacks is at more of an imbalance than it is for whites. For whites there are nearly 100 males (101 to be precise) for every 100 females in the 30–34 age category. But for blacks, there are only 85.3 males for every 100 females; again, this means that the numbers do not work out quite right for everyone to be married, at least on the assumption (an accurate one) that most marriages are between two people of the same race.

There are also variations within black culture. Differences exist between the sexual behavior of black men and women that are similar to the differences between the sexual behavior of white men and women. For example, black men are more accepting of premarital sex than black women are. In addition, there are social-class variations; the sexual behavior of middle-class blacks is more similar to that of middle-class whites than it is to that of lower-class blacks (Staples, 1972).

Generally, the differences between blacks and whites in sexual behavior are not large, and they may be related more to social class than to anything else.

Hispanics have a cultural heritage distinct from that of both African Americans

Table 1.2
Comparison of the Sexuality of African Americans, Hispanics, and Whites

	Whites	African Americans	Hispanics
Percentage of unmarried women aged 15–19 who have ever had intercourse*	31	63	
Percentage of unmarried men aged 15–19 who have ever had intercourse†	57	81	60
Percentage of 19-year-olds who know the time of fertility during the menstrual cycle*	57	29	
Median age at first intercourse for women*	16.3 years	15.6 years	
Percentage of sexually active teenage girls who never use contraceptives*	24	25	
Percentage of males who used a condom at first intercourse†	64	37	66
Percentage of 30–34-year-old females who have never been married‡	14	35	17
Percentage of 30–34-year-old males who have never been married‡	25	45	25
Sex ratio (number of males per 100 females), 30–34-year-olds‡	101	85.3	98.0
Mean age of first masturbation, males§	13.1 years	13.3 years	
Mean age of first masturbation, females§	14.3 years	12.6 years	
Percentage of females who have performed fellatio§	81	47	
Percentage of males who have performed cunnilingus§	72	50	

* *Source:* Zelnik, M., & Kantner, J. F. (1977). Sexual and contraceptive experience of young unmarried women in the United States, 1976 and 1971. *Family Planning Perspectives, 9*(2), 55–71.

† *Source:* Sonenstein, F., et al. (1989). Sexual activity, condom use, and AIDS awareness among adolescent males. *Family Planning Perspectives 21*(4), 152–158.

‡ *Source:* U.S. Bureau of the Census (1990).

§ *Source:* Belcastro, P. A. (1985). Sexual behavior differences between black and white students. *Journal of Sex Research, 21,* 56–67.

and Anglos, although forces such as the Judeo-Christian religious tradition affect all three groups. In traditional Latin American cultures, gender roles are rigidly defined (Comas-Diaz, 1987). Such roles are emphasized early in the socialization process for children. Boys are given greater freedom and are encouraged in sexual exploits. Girls are expected to be passive, obedient, and weak. Latinos in the United States today have a cultural heritage that blends these traditional cultural values with the contemporary values of the dominant Anglo culture. Nonetheless, traditional Hispanic cultural values continue to have an influence.

The rigid gender roles are epitomized in the concepts of machismo and marianismo (Comas-Diaz, 1987). The term *machismo,* or *macho,* has come to be used loosely in American culture today. Literally, machismo means "maleness" or "virility." The cultural code of machismo among Latin Americans mandates that the man must be the one responsible for the well-being and honor of his family, but in extreme forms it also means that men's sexual infidelities should be tolerated. *Marianismo,* the female counterpart of machismo, derives from Catholic worship of Mary, the virgin mother. Thus motherhood is highly valued, but virginity until marriage is closely guarded. In Mexico, for example, 62 percent of males have had premarital intercourse by age 19, compared with only 14 percent of females (Liskin, 1985).

As discussed in Focus 1.3, traditional Asian cultures, particularly the Chinese culture, have been represssive about sexuality. Asian Americans today tend to be sexually conservative compared with other ethnic groups. For example, in one sample of Asian American college students ranging in age from 18 to 25, only 44 percent of the men and 50 percent of the women had engaged in premarital intercourse (Cochran et al., 1991).

The United States is truly a multicultural society today. The data on ethnic group variations in sexual patterns help us see the extent to which cultural traditions influence our sexuality.

The Significance of the Cross-Cultural Studies

What relevance do the cross-cultural data have to an understanding of human sexuality? They are important for two basic reasons. First, they give us a notion of the enormous variation that exists in human sexual behavior, and they help us put our own society's standards and our own behavior in perspective. Second, these studies provide us with impressive evidence concerning the importance of culture and learning in the shaping of our sexual behavior; they show us that human sexual behavior is not completely determined by biology or drives or instincts. For example, the woman of Inis Beag and the woman of Mangaia presumably have vaginas that are similarly constructed and clitorises that are approximately the same size and have the same nerve supply. But the woman of Inis Beag never has an orgasm, and all Mangaian women orgasm.[3] Why? Their cultures are different, and they and their partners learned different things about sex as they were growing up. Learning is the biggest determinant of human sexual behavior, and instincts or drives play only a minor role.

CROSS-SPECIES PERSPECTIVES

Humans are one of many animal species, and all of them display sexual behavior. To put our own sexual behavior in evolutionary perspective, it is helpful to explore the similarities and differences between our own sexuality and that of other species. There is one other motive behind this particular discussion. Some people classify sexual behaviors as "natural" or "unnatural" depending on whether other species do or do not exhibit those behaviors. Sometimes, though, the data are twisted to suit the purposes of the person making the argument, and so there is a need for a less biased view. Let us see exactly what some other species do!

Masturbation

Humans are definitely not the only species that masturbates. Masturbation is found among many species of mammals, and it is particularly common among the primates

---

[3] I like to use the word "orgasm" not only as a noun but also as a verb. The reason is that alternative expressions, such as "to *achieve* orgasm" and "to *reach* orgasm," reflect our tendency to make sex an achievement situation (an idea to be discussed further in Chapter 10). To avoid this, I use "to have an orgasm" or "to orgasm."

FIGURE 1.6
The sexual behavior of gorillas. (a) *The female "presents" to the male, soliciting copulation.* (b) *Copulation in the rear-mount position.* (c) *Copulation in the face-to-face position, which is rare among nonhumans.*

(a)

(b)

(c)

(monkeys and apes). Male monkeys and apes in zoos can be observed masturbating, often to the horror of the proper folk who have come to see them. At one time it was thought that this behavior might be the result of the unnatural living conditions of zoos. However, observations of free-living primates indicate that they, too, masturbate (e.g., Carpenter, 1942). Techniques include hand stimulation of the genitals or rubbing the genitals against an object. In terms of technique, monkeys and non-human apes have one advantage over humans: their bodies are so flexible that they can perform mouth-genital sex on themselves. A unique form of male masturbation is found among red deer; during the rutting season they move the tips of their antlers through low-growing vegetation, producing erection and ejaculation (Beach, 1976).

Female masturbation is also found among many species besides our own. The prize for the most inventive technique probably should go to the female porcupine. She holds one end of a stick in her paws and walks around while straddling the stick; as the stick bumps against the ground, it vibrates against her genitals (Ford & Beach, 1951). Human females are apparently not the first to enjoy vibrators.

Mouth-Genital Stimulation

Mouth-genital stimulation is also quite natural, judging from the behavior of other species. It is quite common for the male to apply his mouth to the female's genitals, in part because the sex scents, or *pheromones,* she produces stimulate sexual behavior (see Chapter 9). The following quotation describes this practice among chimpanzees (our nearest evolutionary relatives) and points out the pleasure the female apparently receives from it:

> Wendy was turning so that her face was away from Billy and her posterior parts were turned conspicuously towards him. . . . Billy showed interest in the protruding genitalia (and) . . . gradually the manipulations of his free hand became directed more and more (toward them). . . . He picked at them with his fingers and several times took them in his lips. Shortly after this manipulation began it became apparent that Wendy was sexually stimulated. The clitoris became noticeably erect, and I could detect occasional surges as though she were voluntarily increasing the erection (Bingham, 1928, pp. 98–99)

Observations indicate that it is less common for the female to stimulate the male's genitals with her mouth, although this does occur (Ford & Beach, 1951).

Homosexual Behavior

Homosexual behavior is found in many species besides our own (Beach, 1976). Indeed, observations of other species indicate that our basic mammalian heritage is bisexual; it is composed of both heterosexual and homosexual elements (Ford & Beach, 1951).

Males of many species will mount other males. Anal intercourse has even been observed in some male primates (Erwin & Maple, 1976; Hamilton, 1914; Kempf, 1917). Male porpoises have also been observed repeatedly attempting to insert their penis into the anus of an intended partner, even though females were available (McBride & Hebb, 1948). Such attempts at anal intercourse, however, have been observed only among captive animals and may not occur among animals in the wild. Females also mount other females. I have two female dogs, and they delight in mounting each other, particularly when company is present.

In species that form long-term bonds or relationships, long homosexual bonds have been observed. For example, Konrad Lorenz (1966) reported a long-term relationship between two male ducks.

Human Uniqueness

The general trend, as we move from lower species such as fish or rodents to higher species such as primates, is for sexual behavior to be more hormonally (instinctively) controlled among lower species and to be controlled more by the brain (and therefore by learning) in the higher species (Beach, 1947). Thus environmental influences are much more important in shaping primate—especially human—sexual behavior than they are in shaping the sexual behavior of other species.

An illustration of this is provided by studies of the adult sexual behavior of animals that have been raised in deprived environments. If mice are reared in isolation, their adult sexual behavior will nonetheless be normal (King, 1956, cited by Scott, 1964). But the research of the Harlows shows that if rhesus monkeys are reared in isolation, their adult sexual behavior is severely disturbed, to the point where they may be incapable of reproducing (Harlow et al., 1963). Thus environmental experiences are crucial in shaping the sexual behavior of the higher species, particularly humans; for us, sexual behavior is a lot more than just "doin' what comes naturally."

Female sexuality provides a particularly good illustration of the shift in hormonal control from lower to higher species. Throughout most of the animal kingdom, female sexual behavior is strongly controlled by hormones. In virtually all species, females do not engage in sexual behavior at all except when they are in "heat" (estrus), which is a particular hormonal and physiological state. In contrast, human females are capable of engaging in sexual behavior—and actually do engage in it—during any phase of their hormonal (menstrual) cycle. Thus the sexual behavior of the human female is not nearly so much under hormonal control as that of females of other species.

Traditionally it was thought that female orgasm is unique to humans and does not exist in other species. Then some studies found evidence of orgasm in rhesus macaques (monkeys), although under very artificial laboratory conditions involving

FIGURE 1.7
Sexual behavior may be used for a variety of nonsexual purposes, such as to express aggression. This primitive figure is defying his opponent by sticking out his tongue and his erect penis.

stimulation of the female by a mechanical penis (Burton, 1970; Zumpe & Michael, 1968). Now another study has shown the same physiological responses indicative of orgasm in human females—specifically, increased heart rate and uterine contractions—in stump-tailed macaques as a result of female homosexual activity, and perhaps for heterosexual activity as well (Goldfoot et al., 1980). Thus it seems that humans can no longer claim that they have a corner on the female orgasm market. This has interesting implications for understanding the evolution of sexuality. Perhaps the higher species, in which the females are not driven to sexual activity by their hormones, have the pleasure of orgasm as an alternative incentive.

The Nonsexual Uses of Sexual Behavior

Two male baboons are locked in combat. One begins to emerge as the victor. The other "presents" (the "female" sexual posture, in which the rump is directed toward the other and is elevated somewhat).

Two male monkeys are members of the same troop. Long ago they established which one is dominant and which one is subordinate. The dominant one mounts (the "male" sexual behavior) the subordinate one.

These are examples of the fact that animals sometimes use sexual behavior for nonsexual purposes (Ford & Beach, 1951; Jensen, 1976b). Commonly this is done to signal the end of a fight, as in the first example above. The loser indicates surrender by presenting, and the winner signals victory by mounting. Sexual behaviors can also symbolize an animal's rank in a dominance hierarchy. Dominant animals mount subordinate ones. As another example, male squirrel monkeys sometimes use an exhibitionist display of their erect penis as part of an aggressive display against another male, something that is called *phallic aggression* (Wickler, 1973).

All this is perfectly obvious when we observe it in monkeys. But do humans ever use sexual behavior for nonsexual purposes? Consider the rapist, who uses sex as an expression of aggression against and power over a woman (Holmstrom & Burgess, 1980), or power over another man, in the case of homosexual rape in prisons. Another example is the exhibitionist, who uses the display of his erect penis to shock and frighten women, much as the male squirrel monkey uses this display to shock and frighten his opponent. Humans also use sex for economic purposes; the best examples are prostitutes and **gigolos**.

There are also less extreme examples. Consider the couple who have a fight and then make love to signal an end to the hostilities.[4] Or consider the woman who goes to bed with an influential—though unattractive—politician because this gives her a vicarious sense of power.

You can probably think of other examples of the nonsexual use of sexual behavior. Humans, just like members of other species, can use sex for a variety of nonsexual purposes (Marmor, 1969).

Gigolo (JIH-guh-lo): A man who sells his sexual services to women.

Summary

"Sexual behavior" was defined as behavior that produces arousal and increases the chance of orgasm. A distinction was made between "sex" (sexual behavior and anatomy) and "gender" (being male or female).

---

[4] It has been my observation that this practice does not always mean the same thing to the man and to the woman. To the man it can mean that everything is fine again, but the woman can be left feeling dissatisfied and not at all convinced that the issues are resolved. Thus this situation can be a source of miscommunication between the two.

Throughout most of human history, religion was the main source of information concerning sexuality. In the late 1800s and early 1900s, important contributions to the scientific understanding of sex were made by Sigmund Freud, Havelock Ellis, Richard von Krafft-Ebing, and Magnus Hirschfeld. These early researchers emerged from the Victorian era, in which sexual norms were highly rigid; many people's actual behavior, though, violated these norms.

Studies in various human cultures around the world provide evidence of the enormous variations in human sexual behavior. For example, in a few societies kissing is unknown. Frequency of intercourse may vary from once a week in some cultures to three or four times a night in others. One generalization that does emerge is that all societies regulate sexual behavior in some way. Attitudes regarding premarital and extramarital sex, masturbation, homosexual behavior, and gender roles vary considerably from one culture to the next. The great variations provide evidence of the importance of learning in shaping our sexual behavior.

Even within the United States, sexual behavior varies with social class and ethnic group. Black women are more likely to engage in premarital intercourse as teenagers than white women are. In other areas, though, blacks and whites are quite similar. Traditional Hispanic cultures are characterized by rigid gender roles and restrictions on female sexuality, but not on male sexuality. Asian cultures tend to be conservative about sexuality for both males and females.

Studies of sexual behavior in various animal species show that masturbation, mouth-genital stimulation, and homosexual behavior are by no means limited to humans. They also illustrate how sexual behavior may be used for a variety of nonsexual purposes, such as expressing dominance.

Review Questions

1. H. Havelock Ellis was an important nineteenth-century sex researcher. True or false?

2. A sex survey of Victorian women found that none of them reported having orgasms during marital intercourse. True or false?

3. On Inis Beag, an island off the coast of Ireland, premarital intercourse is common and many babies are born out of wedlock. True or false?

4. Black teenage girls and white teenage girls are about equally irresponsible regarding contraception. True or false?

5. The wide variations in sexual behavior found cross-culturally provide evidence of the importance of learning and culture in shaping human sexual behavior. True or false?

6. Homosexual behavior is unknown among animals. True or false?

7. In traditional Hispanic cultures, males are far more likely to engage in premarital sex than females are. True or false?

8. This textbook uses the term "sex" to refer to sexual anatomy and sexual behavior, and the term _____ to refer to the state of being male or female.

9. The early sex researcher Richard von Krafft-Ebing focused on "pathological" sexual behavior. True or false?

10. All societies regulate sexuality in some way, although the exact regulations vary from culture to culture. True or false?

(The answers to all review questions are at the end of the book, beginning on page 731.)

1. In the wide spectrum of sexual practices in different cultures, from the conservatism of Inis Beag to the permissiveness of Mangaia, where would you place the United States today? Are we premissive, restrictive, or somewhere in between? Why?

2. Research indicates that masturbation, mouth-genital stimulation, and homosexual behaviors are present in other species besides humans. What is the significance of that finding?

Suggestions for Further Reading

Gay, Peter. (1984). *The bourgeois experience: Victoria to Freud.* Vol. I. *Education of the senses.* New York: Oxford University Press. This well-known historian analyzes sexuality in the Victorian era.

Gregersen, Edgar. (1983). *Sexual practices. The story of human sexuality.* New York: Franklin Watts. Gregersen, an anthropologist, has compiled a vast amount of information about sexuality in cultures around the world. The book also includes a treasure trove of fascinating illustrations.

Hopson, Janet L. (1987, August). Boys will be boys, girls will . . . sex and the spotted hyena. *Psychology Today,* 60–66. The fascinating story of the female spotted hyena, who dominates the male and whose clitoris is the size of a penis.

Mead, Margaret. (1935). *Sex and temperament in three primitive societies.* New York: Morrow. A fascinating description of Mead's investigations of sex and gender in other cultures.

Theoretical Perspectives on Sexuality

2

C h a p t e r   H i g h l i g h t s

I. Sociobiology

II. Psychological Theories
   Psychoanalytic Theory
   Learning Theory
   Cognitive Theories

III. The Sociological Perspective
   Sexual Scripts
   The Sociological Approach:
   Levels of Analysis
   Social Institutions
   Reiss's Sociological Theory of Sexuality

One of the discoveries of psychoanalysis consists in the assertion that impulses, which can only be described as sexual in both the narrower and the wider sense, play a peculiarly large part, never before sufficiently appreciated, in the causation of nervous and mental disorders. Nay, more, that these sexual impulses have contributed invaluably to the highest cultural, artistic, and social achievements of the human mind. [*]

On the face of it, sex is at best a peculiar way to reproduce; at worst, it seems profoundly self-defeating. [†]

Imagine, for a moment, a heterosexual couple making love. Imagine, too, that sitting with you in the room, thinking your same thoughts, are Freud, E. O. Wilson (a leading sociobiologist), Albert Bandura (a leading social learning theorist), and John Gagnon and William Simon (proponents of script theory in sociology). The scene you are imagining may evoke arousal and nothing more in you, but your imaginary companions have a rich set of additional thoughts as they view the scene through the special-colored lenses of their own theoretical perspectives. Freud might be marveling at how the biological sex drive, the *libido*, expresses itself so strongly and directly in these people. Wilson, the sociobiologist, is thinking how mating behavior in humans is similar to mating behavior in other species of animals, and how it is clearly the product of evolutionary selection for behaviors that lead to successful reproduction. Bandura might be thinking how sexual arousal and orgasm act as powerful positive reinforcers that will lead the couple to repeat the act frequently, and how they are imitating a technique of neck nibbling that they saw in an X-rated film last week. Finally, Gagnon and Simon's thoughts may be about the social

[*] *Source:* Sigmund Freud. (1924). *A general introduction to psychoanalysis.* New York: Permabooks, 1953 (Boni & Liveright edition, 1924), pp. 26–27.

[†] *Source:* D. P. Barash, (1982). *Sociobiology and behavior.* New York: Elsevier, p. 216.

scripting of sexuality; this couple begins with kissing, moves on to petting, and finishes up with intercourse, following a script written by society.

Some of the major theories in the social sciences have had many—and different—things to say about sexuality, and it is these theories that we consider in this chapter.

SOCIOBIOLOGY

Sociobiology: The application of evolutionary biology to understanding the social behavior of animals, including humans.

Sociobiology is a highly controversial theory. It was heralded by Harvard biologist E. O. Wilson's book *Sociobiology: The New Synthesis* (1975). Sociobiology is defined as the application of evolutionary biology to understanding the social behavior of animals, including humans (Barash, 1977). Sexual behavior, of course, is a form of social behavior, and so the sociobiologists, often through observations of other species, try to understand why certain patterns of sexual behavior have evolved in humans. Donald Symons has applied sociobiological thinking to human sexuality in his book *The Evolution of Human Sexuality* (1979; Symons, 1987).

Evolution: A theory that all living things have acquired their present forms through gradual changes in their genetic endowment over successive generations.

Before we proceed, we should note that in terms of **evolution** and **natural selection**, the thing that counts is producing lots of healthy, viable offspring who will carry on one's genes. It does not matter particularly how clever or talented one is. Advantage is measured in terms of how many of one's genes are passed on to the next generation, and that in turn depends heavily on how many offspring one produces.

Natural selection: A process in nature resulting in the survival of only those plants and animals that are adapted to their environment.

How do humans select mates? One major criterion is the physical attractiveness of the person (see Chapter 13). The sociobiologist would argue that many of the characteristics we evaluate in judging attractiveness—for example, physique and complexion—are indicative of the health and vigor of the individual. These in turn are probably related to the person's reproductive potential; the unhealthy are less likely to produce many vigorous offspring. Natural selection would favor those individuals preferring mates who would have maximum reproductive success. Thus, perhaps our concern with physical attractiveness is a product of evolution and natural selection. (See Barash, 1977, for an extended discussion of this point and the ones that follow.) We choose an attractive, healthy mate who will help us produce many offspring. Can you guess why the sociobiologist thinks men are attracted to women with large breasts?

From this viewpoint, dating, going steady, getting engaged, and similar customs are much like the courtship rituals of other species. For example, many falcons and eagles have a flying courtship in which objects are exchanged between the pair in midair. The sociobiologist views this courtship as an opportunity for each member of the prospective couple to assess the other's fitness. For example, any lack of speed or coordination would be apparent during the eagle acrobatics. Evolution would favor courtship patterns that permitted individuals to decide on mates who would increase their reproductive success. Perhaps that is exactly what we are doing in our human courtship rituals. The expenditure of money by men on dates indicates their ability to support a family. Dancing permits the assessment of physical prowess, and so on.

The sociobiologists even have an explanation for the double standard—specifically, our relatively permissive attitudes toward male promiscuity and our intolerance for female promiscuity. Sperm are cheap. A man can literally produce millions of them in a day, and he can always produce more. Eggs, in contrast, are far more precious to their owner. Only one can be produced per month, and if certain things happen to it, the result can be a 9-month (or perhaps more accurately, an 18-year) commitment of time and energy. It is therefore no wonder that the female is choosy about whom she has sex with and limits her number of partners compared with the male's number of partners.

Sociobiologists note that sex is fun. And they have an explanation for why it is fun. Natural selection simply favored individuals who found it to be fun and therefore did it more, and therefore reproduced more.

In addition to natural selection, Darwin also proposed a mechanism that is not so much a household word, sexual selection (Buss, 1988; Trivers, 1972). Sexual selection is the mechanism that is used by sociobiologists to explain the evolution of gender differences. Sexual selection consists of two processes: (1) competition among members of one gender (usually males) for mating access to members of the other gender; and (2) preferential choice by members of one gender (usually females) for certain members of the other gender. In other words, in many, though not all, species, males compete among themselves for the right to mate with females; and females, for their part, prefer certain males and mate with them while refusing to mate with other males. Researchers are currently testing with humans some of the predictions that come from the theory of sexual selection. For example, the theory predicts that men should compete with each other in ways that involve displaying material resources that should be attractive to women, and men should engage in these displays more than women (Buss, 1988). Examples might be giving impressive gifts to potential mates, flashy showing of possessions (e.g., cars, stereos), or displaying personality characteristics that are likely to lead to the acquisition of resources (e.g., ambition). Research shows that men engage in these behaviors significantly more than women do, and that both men and women believe these tactics are effective (Buss, 1988).

One of the most controversial ideas is the argument by some sociobiologists that rape is the product of evolutionary selection because it is adaptive for the male (Barash, 1977b; Shields & Shields, 1983; Symons, 1979; see Palmer, 1991, for a critical review). They have even suggested that human males are larger than human females as a result of evolutionary selection that made large males successful at rape.

Sexual selection: An evolutionary theory proposed to explain gender differences.

FIGURE 2.1
Courtship rituals in the Laysan albatross. According to sociobiologists, human customs of dating and becoming engaged are biologically produced and serve the same functions as courtship rituals in other species.

(a)

(b)

They have found evidence of the existence of male rape of females in a number of other species. The argument is that human males could reproduce either by courtship, bonding with a female and then reproducing, or else by rape. Rape would be predicted only for those males that lacked the resources to carry on a successful courtship and win a consenting female. One problem with this argument is that if rape is punished, it may lead to less reproduction, not more. For example, if there is capital punishment for rape, it becomes a poor reproductive strategy; the single act of rape produces a certain probability (but certainly not 100 percent) of impregnating the female, but if it leads to the man's death he cannot reproduce any more—scarcely a good strategy for passing on one's genes to the next generation. There are also problems internally with the sociobiological arguments about rape (Palmer, 1991) which are too complicated to discuss here. This example, though, will give you a flavor of some theorizing by sociobiologists.

Many criticisms of sociobiology have been made. Some protest that it ignores the importance of culture and learning in human behavior. However, most sociobiologists would argue that evolution should be recognized as one of several influences on behavior and would not exclude the influence of learning and culture. Other critics resent the biological determinism that it introduces. Sociobiology has been criticized for resting on an outmoded version of evolutionary theory that modern biologists consider naive (Gould, 1987). For example, sociobiology has focused mainly on individuals' struggle for survival, whereas modern biologists focus on more complex issues such as the survival of the species and the evolution of a successful adaptation between the species and its environment. Further, sociobiologists assume that the central function of sex is reproduction; this may have been true historically, but it probably is not at present. We really do not have sufficient research at this point to do a conclusive evaluation. Until we do have that evidence, sociobiology will remain a provocative source of ideas about human sexuality.

PSYCHOLOGICAL THEORIES

Four of the major theories in psychology are relevant to sexuality: psychoanalytic theory, learning theory, cognitive theory, and humanistic psychology.

Psychoanalytic Theory

Psychoanalytic theory: A psychological theory originated by Freud; it contains a basic assumption that part of human personality is unconscious.

Freud's psychoanalytic theory has been one of the most influential of all psychological theories. Because Freud saw sex as one of the key forces in human life, his theory gives full treatment to human sexuality.

Freud termed the sex drive or sex energy **libido**, and he saw it as one of the two major forces motivating human behavior (the other being *thanatos*, or the death instinct).

Libido (lih-BEE-doh): In psychoanalytic theory, the term for the sex energy or sex drive.

Id, Ego, and Superego

Freud described the human personality as being divided into three major parts: the id, the ego, and the superego. The **id** is the basic part of personality and is present at birth. It is the reservoir of psychic energy (including libido) and contains the instincts. Basically it operates on the *pleasure principle;* it cannot tolerate any increase in psychic tensions, and so it seeks to discharge these tensions.

While the id operates only on the pleasure principle and can thus be pretty

Id: According to Freud, the part of the personality containing the libido.

irrational, the ego operates on the *reality principle* and tries to keep the id in line. The ego functions to make the person have realistic, rational interactions with others.

Finally, the superego is the conscience. It contains the values and ideals of society that we learn, and it operates on *idealism.* Thus its aim is to inhibit the impulses of the id and to persuade the ego to strive for moral goals rather than realistic ones.

To illustrate the operation of these three components of the personality in a sexual situation, consider the case of the president of the corporation who is at a meeting of the board of directors; the meeting is also attended by her gorgeous, muscular colleague, Mr. Hunk. She looks at Mr. Hunk, and her id says, "I want to throw him on the table and make love to him immediately. Let's do it!" The ego intervenes and says "We can't do it now because the other members of the board are also here. Let's wait until 5 P.M., when they're all gone, and then do it." The superego says, "I shouldn't make love to Mr. Hunk at all because I'm a married woman." What actually happens? It depends on the relative strengths of this woman's id, ego, and superego.

The id, ego, and superego develop sequentially. The id contains the set of instincts present at birth. The ego develops later, as the child learns how to interact realistically with his or her environment and the people in it. The superego develops last, as the child learns moral values.

Erogenous Zones

Freud saw the libido as being focused in various regions of the body known as erogenous zones (a term that is used rather loosely by the general public). An erogenous zone is a part of the skin or mucous membrane which is extremely sensitive to stimulation; touching it in certain ways produces feelings of pleasure. The lips and mouth are one such erogenous zone, the genitals are a second, and the rectum and anus are a third. Thus sucking produces oral pleasure, defecating produces anal pleasure, and rubbing the genital area produces genital pleasure.

Stages of Psychosexual Development

Freud believed that the child passes through a series of stages of development. In each of these stages, a different erogenous zone is the focus of the child's striving.

The first stage, lasting from birth to about 1 year of age, is the *oral stage*. The child's chief pleasure is derived from sucking and otherwise stimulating the lips and mouth. Anyone who has observed children of this age knows how they delight in putting anything they can into their mouths. The second stage, which occurs during approximately the second year of life, is the *anal stage.* During this stage, the child's interest is focused on elimination.

The third stage of development, lasting from age 3 to perhaps age 5 or 6, is the *phallic stage.* The boy's interest is focused on his phallus (penis), and he derives great pleasure from masturbating.[1] Perhaps the most important occurrence in this stage is the development of the Oedipus complex, which derives its name from the Greek story of Oedipus, who killed his father and married his mother. In the Oedipus complex, the boy loves his mother and desires her sexually. He hates his father, whom he sees as a rival for the mother's affection. The boy's hostility toward his father grows, but eventually he comes to fear that his father will retaliate by cutting

---

[1]   Masturbation to orgasm is physiologically possible at this age, although males are not capable of ejaculation until they reach puberty.

off his prized penis (castration). Thus the boy feels *castration anxiety.* Eventually the castration anxiety becomes so great that he stops desiring his mother and shifts to identifying with his father, taking on the father's gender role and acquiring the characteristics expected of males by society. Freud considered the Oedipus complex and its resolution to be one of the key factors in human personality development.

As might be expected from the name of this stage, the girl will have a considerably different, and much more difficult, time passing through it, since she has none of what the stage is all about. For the girl, the stage begins with her traumatic realization that she has no penis, perhaps after observing that of her father or her brother. She feels envious and cheated, and she suffers from *penis envy,* wishing that she too had a wonderful wand. (Presumably she thinks her own clitoris is totally inadequate, or she is not even aware that she has it.) She believes that at one time she had a penis but that it was cut off, and she holds her mother responsible. Thus she begins to hate her mother and shifts to loving her father, forming her version of the Oedipus complex, sometimes called the Electra complex. In part, her incestuous desires for her father result from a desire to be impregnated by him, to substitute for the unobtainable penis. Unlike the boy, the girl does not have a strong motive of castration anxiety for resolving the Oedipus complex; she has already lost her penis. Thus the girl's resolution of the Electra complex is not so complete as the boy's resolution of the Oedipus complex, and for the rest of her life she remains somewhat immature compared with men.

Freud said that following the resolution of the Oedipus or Electra complex, children pass into a prolonged stage known as *latency,* which lasts until adolescence. During this stage, the sexual impulses are repressed or are in a quiescent state, and so nothing much happens sexually. The postulation of this stage is one of the weaker parts of Freudian theory, because it is clear from the data of modern sex researchers that children do continue to engage in sexual behavior during this period.

With adolescence, sexual urges reawaken, and the child passes into the *genital stage.* During this stage, sexual urges become more specifically genital, and the oral, anal, and genital urges all fuse together to promote the biological function of reproduction. Sexuality becomes less narcissistic (self-directed) than it was in childhood and is directed toward other people as appropriate sexual objects.

Of course, according to Freud, people do not always mature from one stage to the next as they should. A person might remain permanently fixated, for example, at the oral stage; symptoms of such a situation would include incessant cigarette smoking and fingernail biting, which gratify oral urges. Most adults have at least traces of earlier stages remaining in their personalities.

Freud on Women

In recent years a storm of criticism of Freudian theory has arisen from feminists. Let us first review what Freud had to say about women and then discuss what feminists object to in his theory (Lerman, 1986; Millett, 1969).

Essentially, Freud assumed that the female is biologically inferior to the male because she lacks a penis. He saw this absence as a key factor in her personality development. The penis envy she feels as a result of her biological deficiency causes her to develop the Electra complex. Yet she never adequately resolves this complex, and she is left, throughout her life, with feelings of jealousy and inferiority, all because of her lack of a penis. As Freud said, "Anatomy is destiny."

Freud believed that female sexuality is inherently passive (as opposed to the active aggressiveness of the male). He also felt that female sexuality is masochistic; in seeking intercourse, the female is trying to bring pain on herself, since childbirth, which may result, is painful and since intercourse itself may sometimes be painful.

Electra complex (eh-LEK-tra): According to Freud, the sexual attraction of a little girl for her father.

The following quotation from Marie Bonaparte, a follower of Freud, will illustrate the psychoanalytic position:

> Throughout the whole range of living creatures, animal or vegetable, passivity is characteristic of the female cell, the ovum whose mission is to *await* the male cell, the active mobile spermatozoan to come and *penetrate* it. Such penetration, however, implies infraction of its tissue, but infraction of a living creature's tissue may entail destruction: death as much as life. Thus the fecundation of the female cell is initiated by a kind of wound; in its way, the female cell is primordially "masochistic." (1953, p. 79)

Freud also originated the distinction between *vaginal orgasm* and *clitoral orgasm* in women. During childhood little girls rub their clitorises to produce orgasm (clitorial orgasm). Freud believed, though, that as they grow to adulthood they need to shift their focus to having orgasm during heterosexual intercourse, with the penis stimulating the vagina (vaginal orgasm). Thus, not only did he postulate two kinds of orgasm for women, but he also maintained that one kind was better (more mature) than the other. The evidence that Masters and Johnson have collected on this issue will be reviewed in Chapter 9; suffice it to say for now that there seems to be little or no physiological difference between the two kinds of orgasm. The assertion that the vaginal orgasm is more mature is not supported by Masters and Johnson's and others' findings that most adult women orgasm as a result of clitoral stimulation.

Feminists understandably object to several aspects of Freud's theory. A chief objection is to the whole notion that women are anatomically inferior to men because they lack a penis. What is so intrinsically valuable about a penis that makes it better than a clitoris, a vagina, or a pair of ovaries? In a creative approach, psychoanalyst Karen Horney (1926/1973) coined the concept of "womb envy," arguing that males have a powerful envy of females' reproductive capacity, more than females envy the penis. Similarly, feminists find the assertion that women are inherently passive, masochistic, and narcissistic to be offensive. Is it not likelier that men simply have higher status in our culture than women do and that women's feelings of jealousy or inferiority result from these cultural status differences? Feminists argue that psychoanalytic theory is essentially a male-centered theory which may have bad effects on women, particularly when it is used on a woman who seeks psychotherapy from a therapist who uses a psychoanalytic approach.

Evaluation of Psychoanalytic Theory

From a scientific point of view, one of the major problems with psychoanalytic theory is that most of its concepts cannot be evaluated scientifically to see whether they are accurate. Freud postulated that many of the most important forces in personality are unconscious, and thus they cannot be studied by any of the usual scientific techniques.

Another criticism is that Freud derived his data almost exclusively from his work with patients who sought therapy from him. Thus, his theory may provide a view not so much of the human personality as of *disturbances* in the human personality.

Finally, many modern psychologists feel that Freud overemphasized biological determinants of behavior and instincts and that he gave insufficient recognition to the importance of the environment and learning.

Nonetheless, Freud did make some important contributions to our understanding of human behavior. He managed to rise above the Victorian era of which he was a part and teach that sex is an important part of personality (although he may have overestimated its importance). His recognition that humans pass through stages in their psychological development was a great contribution. Perhaps most important from the perspective of this text, Freud took sex out of the closet; he brought it to the attention of the general public and suggested that we could talk about it and that it was an appropriate topic for scientific research.

Learning Theory

While psychoanalytic and sociobiological theories are based on the notion that much of human sexual behavior is biologically controlled, it is also quite apparent that much of it is learned. Some of the best evidence for this point comes from studies of sexual behavior across different human societies, which were considered in Chapter 1. Here the various principles of modern learning theory will be reviewed, because they can help us understand our own sexuality (for a more detailed discussion, see McConaghy, 1987).

Classical Conditioning

Classical conditioning: The learning process in which a previously neutral stimulus (conditioned stimulus) is repeatedly paired with an unconditioned stimulus that reflexively elicits an unconditioned response. Eventually the conditioned stimulus itself will evoke the response.

Classical conditioning is a concept usually associated with the work of Pavlov. Think of the following situations: You salivate in response to the sight or smell of food, you blink in response to someone poking a finger in your eye, or you experience sexual arousal in response to stroking the inner part of your thigh. In all these cases, an unconditioned stimulus (US, for example, appealing food) automatically, reflexively elicits an unconditioned response (UR, for example, salivation). The process of learning that occurs in classical conditioning takes place when a new stimulus, the conditioned stimulus (CS, for example, the sound of a bell) repeatedly occurs paired with the original unconditioned stimulus (food). After this happens many times, the conditioned stimulus (ringing bell) can eventually be presented without the unconditioned stimulus (food) and will evoke the original response, now called the conditioned response (CR, salivation).

As an example, suppose that Nadia's first serious boyfriend in high school always wears Eau de Male aftershave when they go out. As they advance in their sexual intimacy, they have many pleasant times in the back seat of the car, where he strokes her thighs and other sexy parts of her body and she feels highly aroused, always with the aroma of Eau de Male in her nostrils. One day she enters an elevator full of strangers in a department store. Someone is wearing Eau de Male and Nadia instantly feels sexually aroused, although nothing sexy is happening to her. From the point of view of classical conditioning, this makes perfect sense, although Nadia may wonder why she is feeling so aroused in the elevator. The thigh-stroking and sexy touching were the US. Her arousal was the UR. The aroma of Eau de Male, the CS, was repeatedly paired with the US. Eventually, the Eau de Male aroma occurred by itself, evoking arousal, the CR.

Classical conditioning is useful in explaining a number of phenomena in sexuality. One example is fetishes, as explained in Chapter 16.

Operant Conditioning

Operant conditioning (OP-ur-unt): The process of changing the frequency of a behavior (the operant) by following it with reinforcement (which will make the behavior more frequent in the future) or punishment (which should make the behavior less frequent in the future).

Operant conditioning, a concept that is often associated with the psychologist B. F. Skinner, refers to the following process: A person performs a particular behavior (the operant). That behavior may be followed by either a reward (positive reinforcement) or a punishment. If a reward follows, the person will be likely to repeat the behavior again in the future; if a punishment follows, the person will be less likely to repeat the behavior. Thus if a behavior is repeatedly rewarded, it may become very frequent, and if it is repeatedly punished, it may become very infrequent or even be eliminated.

Some rewards are considered to be primary reinforcers; that is, there is something intrinsically rewarding about them. Food is one such primary reinforcer, and sex is another. Rats, for example, can be trained to learn a maze if they find a willing sex partner at the end of it. Thus sexual behavior plays dual roles in learning theory: It can itself be a positive reinforcer, but it can also be the behavior that is rewarded or punished.

Simple principles of operant conditioning can help explain some aspects of sex (McGuire et al., 1965). For example, if a woman repeatedly experiences pain when she has intercourse (perhaps because she has a vaginal infection), she will probably want to have sex infrequently or not at all. In operant conditioning terms, sexual intercourse has repeatedly been associated with a punishment (pain), and so the behavior becomes less frequent.

What other principles of operant conditioning are useful in understanding sexual behavior? One principle is that positive reinforcements are most effective in shaping behavior when they occur immediately after a behavior and that the longer they are delayed after the behavior has occurred, the less effective they become. As an example of that principle, consider the male homosexual who continues to engage in homosexual behavior with his lover even though, because of this, his colleagues at work have rejected him and he is even in danger of being fired. Since he is being punished for the behavior, why does he persist in it? The delay-of-reinforcement principle might explain the situation as follows: Every time he engages in homosexual behavior, he enjoys it and finds it rewarding; this occurs immediately. These immediate rewards are effective in encouraging him to continue the behavior, and the punishments, which may not occur until a week after the behavior, are not effective in eliminating it.

Another principle that has emerged in operant conditioning studies is that, compared with rewards, punishments are not very effective in shaping behavior. Often, as in the case of the child who is punished for taking an illicit cookie, punishments do not eliminate a behavior but rather teach the person to be sneaky and engage in it without being caught. As an example, parents, particularly in earlier times in our culture, punished children for masturbating, and yet most of those children continued to masturbate. Punishment is simply not very effective in eliminating behavior. Still using masturbation as an example, children may instead learn to do it under circumstances (such as in a bathroom with the door locked) in which they are not likely to be caught.

One important difference between psychoanalytic theory and learning theory should be noticed. Psychoanalytic theorists believe that the determinants of human sexual behavior occur in early childhood, particularly during the Oedipal complex period. Learning theorists, in contrast, believe that sexual behavior can be learned and changed at any time in the lifespan—in childhood, in adolescence, in young adulthood, or later. When we try to understand the causes of certain sexual behaviors and how to treat people with sex problems, this distinction between the theories will have important implications.

Behavior Modification

Behavior modification: A set of operant conditioning techniques used to modify human behavior.

Behavior modification involves a set of techniques, based on principles of operant conditioning, that are used to change or modify human behavior. These techniques have been used to modify everything from problem behaviors of children in the classroom to the behavior of schizophrenics. In particular, these methods can be used to modify problematic sexual behaviors—sexual dysfunctions such as orgasm problems (see Chapter 19) or deviant sexual behavior such as child molesting. Behavior modification methods differ from more traditional methods of psychotherapy such as psychoanalysis in that the behavioral therapist considers only the problem behavior and how to modify it using learning-theory principles; the therapist does not worry about a depth analysis of the person's personality to see, for example, what unconscious forces might be motivating the behavior.

One example of a behavior modification technique that has been used in modifying sexual behavior is aversion therapy (Barlow, 1973). In *aversion therapy*, the problematic sexual behavior is punished using an aversive method. For example, a child molester might be shown pictures of children; if he responds with sexual arousal, he receives an electric shock. Trials are repeated until he no longer feels aroused when he sees a child's picture.

Social Learning

Social learning theory (Bandura, 1969; Bandura & Walters, 1963) is a somewhat more complex form of learning theory. It is based on principles of operant conditioning, but it also recognizes two processes at work besides conditioning: *imitation* and *identification*. Identification (the concept here is similar to the one in psychoanalytic theory) and imitation are useful in explaining the development of gender identity, or one's sense of maleness or femaleness. For example, it seems that a little girl acquires many characteristics of the female role by identifying with her mother and imitating her, as when she plays at dressing up after observing her mother getting ready to go to a party. Because most sexual behaviors in our society are kept rather private and hidden, imitation and identification have less of a chance to play a part. However, some of the more open forms of sexuality may be learned through imitation. In high school, for example, the sexiest girl in the senior class may find that other girls are imitating her behaviors and the way she dresses. Or a boy might see

FIGURE 2.2
Jesse and Rebecca from Full House? *According to social learning theory, children may acquire behaviors by imitating models they see on TV or in the movies.*

Learning Theory and Sexual Orientations in a Non-Western Society

The Sambia are a tribe living in Papua New Guinea in the South Pacific, which has been extensively studied by anthropologists (see Focus 15.3 in Chapter 15). The Sambia are interesting for a number of reasons, the chief one being that young males are expected to spend 10 or more years of their lives in exclusively homosexual relations. During this time they are taught to fear women and believe that women have polluting effects on them. After that stage of their lives, they are expected to marry women. They do, and their sexual behavior becomes exclusively heterosexual. These observations defy our Western notions that sexual orientation is a permanent characteristic throughout one's life. Indeed, the very concepts of having a "heterosexual identity" or "homosexual identity" are not present in Sambia culture.

Can social learning theory explain these patterns of sexual behavior? It can, according to the analysis of John and Janice Baldwin. The thing that is puzzling is how the Sambia male, who has had years of erotic conditioning to homosexual behavior just at puberty when he is most easily aroused and sensitive to conditioning, would then switch to heterosexual behavior and do so happily.

According to the Baldwins' analysis, several factors in social learning theory explain this switch. First, positive conditioning in the direction of heterosexuality occurs early in life. The boy spends the first 7 to 10 years of his life with his family. He has a close, warm relationship with his mother. In essence, he has been conditioned to positive feelings about women. Second, observational learning occurs. In those same first 7 to 10 years, he observes closely the heterosexual relationship between two adults, his mother and father. This observational learning then can be used a decade later when it is

time for him to marry and form a heterosexual relationship. Third, the boy is provided with much cognitive structuring, a notion present in the later revisions of social learning theory as well as cognitive psychology. He is instructed that there are a series of stages a boy must pass through to become a strong, masculine man. This includes first becoming the receptive partner to fellatio, then being the inserting partner to fellatio, marrying, defending himself from his wife's menarche (girls are usually married before puberty and undergo no homosexual stage of development), and then fathering a child by her. Essentially he is given all the cognitive structures necessary to convince him that it is perfectly natural, indeed desirable, to engage in sex with men for 10 years and then switch to women. Finally, there is some aversive conditioning to the homosexual behavior that leads it to be not particularly erotic. The boy performs fellatio for the first time after several days of initiation, when he is exhausted. The activities are staged so that the boy feels fearful about it. He must do it in darkness with an older boy who may be an enemy, and he is required to do it with many males in succession. In essence, unpleasantness or punishment is associated with homosexual behavior.

In summary, then, social learning theory provides a sensible explanation of the seemingly puzzling shift that Sambia males make from exclusive homosexual expression to exclusive heterosexual expression.

Source: Baldwin, John D., & Baldwin, Janice I. (1989). The socialization of homosexuality and heterosexuality in a non-Western society. *Archives of Sexual Behavior, 18,* 13–31. Herdt, Gilbert H. (Ed.) (1984). *Ritualized homosexuality in Melanesia,* Berkeley: University of California Press.

a movie in which the hero's technique seems to "turn women on"; then he tries to use this technique with his own dates.

Yet another process in social learning theory is *observational learning*. It is much like imitation except that the behavior is delayed. That is, the person may see someone perform an apparently enjoyable sexual behavior, and then carry it out themselves one year or ten years later.

In a later, revised version of his theory, Bandura (1977) added cognitive processes to conditioning and imitation as means by which social learning occurs. This brings us to our next topic, theories in cognitive psychology.

Cognitive Theories

Over the last two decades, a "cognitive revolution" has swept through psychology. In contrast to the older behaviorist tradition (which insisted that psychologists should study only behaviors that could be directly observed), cognitive psychologists believe that it is very important to study people's thoughts—that is, the way people think and perceive.

Cognitive psychology is increasingly being applied in understanding human sexuality (Walen & Roth, 1987). A basic assumption is that what we think influences what we feel. If we think happy, positive thoughts, we will tend to feel better than if we think negative ones. Therapists using a cognitive approach believe that psychological distress is often a result of unpleasant thoughts that are usually not tuned to reality and include misconceptions, distortion, exaggerations of problems, and unreasonably negative evaluations of events.

To the cognitive psychologist, how we perceive and evaluate a sexual event makes all the difference in the world (Walen & Roth, 1987). For example, suppose that a man engaged in lovemaking with his wife does not get an erection. Starting from that basic event, his thoughts might take one of two directions. In the first, he thinks that it is quite common for men in his age group (fifties) not to get an erection every time they have sex; this has happened to him a few times before, once every two or three months, and it's nothing to worry about. At any rate, the fellatio was fun, and so was the cunnilingus, and his wife had an orgasm from that, so all in all it was a nice enough encounter. In the second possibility, he began the lovemaking thinking that he had to have an erection, had to have coitus, and had to have an orgasm. When he didn't get an erection, he mentally labeled it *impotence* and imagined that he would never again have an erection. He thought of the whole episode as a frustrating disaster because he never had an orgasm.

As cognitive psychologists point out, perception, labeling, and evaluating events are crucial. In one case, the man perceived a slight problem, labeled it a temporary erection problem, and evaluated his sexual experience as pretty good. In the other case, the man perceived a serious problem, labeled it impotence, and evaluated the experience as horrible.

We shall see cognitive psychology several times again in this book, as theorists use it to understand the cycle of sexual arousal (see Chapter 9), the causes of some sexual variations such as fetishes (see Chapter 16), and the causes and treatment of sexual dysfunctions (see Chapter 19). Before we leave cognitive psychology, however, we will look at one cognitive theory, schema theory, that has been used especially to understand issues of sex and gender.

Gender Schema Theory

Psychologist Sandra Bem (1981) has proposed a schema theory to explain gender-role development and the impact of gender on people's daily lives and thinking.

"Schema" is a term taken from cognitive psychology. A **schema** is a general knowledge framework that a person has about a particular topic. A schema organizes and guides perception; it helps us remember, but it sometimes also distorts our memory, especially if the information is inconsistent with our schema. Thus, for example, you might have a "football game schema," the set of ideas you have about what elements should be present at the game (two teams, spectators, bleachers, etc.) and what kinds of activities should occur (opening kickoff, occasional touchdown, band playing at half-time, and so on).

It is Bem's contention that all of us possess a *gender schema*—the set of things (behaviors, personality, appearance) that we associate with males and females. Our gender schema, according to Bem, predisposes us to process information on the basis of gender. That is, we tend to want to think of things as gender-related and to want to dichotomize them on the basis of gender. A good example is the case of the infant whose gender isn't clear when we meet him or her. We eagerly seek out the information or feel awkward if we don't, because we seem to need to know the baby's gender in order to continue to process information about it.

Bem (1981) has done a number of experiments that provide evidence for her theory, and there are confirming experiments by other researchers as well, although the evidence is not always completely consistent (Ruble & Stagnor, 1986). In one of the most interesting of these experiments, 5- and 6-year-old children were shown pictures of males or females performing either stereotype-consistent activities (such as a girl baking cookies) or stereotype-inconsistent activities (such as girls boxing) (Martin & Halverson, 1983). One week later the children were tested for their recall of the pictures. The results indicated that the children distorted information by changing the gender of people in the stereotype-inconsistent pictures, while not making such changes for the stereotype-consistent pictures. That is, children tended to remember the pictures of the girls boxing as having been a picture of boys boxing. These results are just what would be predicted by gender schema theory. The schema helps us remember schema-consistent (stereotype-consistent) information well, but it distorts our memory of information that is inconsistent with the schema (stereotype-inconsistent).

One of the interesting implications of gender schema theory is that stereo-

FIGURE 2.3
Pictures like these were used in the Martin and Halverson research on gender schemas and children's memory. (a) A girl engaged in a stereotype-consistent activity. (b) Girls engaged in a stereotype-inconsistent activity. In a test of recall a week later, children tended to distort the stereotype-inconsistent pictures to make them stereotype-consistent; for example, they remembered that they had seen boys boxing.

(a)

(b)

types—whether they are about males and females, or heterosexuals and homosexuals, or other groups—may be very slow to change. The reason is that our schema tends to filter out stereotype-inconsistent (that is, schema-inconsistent) information so that we don't even remember it.

THE SOCIOLOGICAL PERSPECTIVE

Sociologists were most interested in the ways in which society or culture shapes human sexuality (for a detailed articulation of the sociological perspective, see DeLamater, 1987; the arguments that follow are taken from that source).

Sociologists approach the study of sexuality with three basic assumptions: (1) Every society regulates the sexuality of its members in some ways. (2) Basic institutions of society (such as religion and the family) affect the rules governing sexuality in that society. (3) The appropriateness or inappropriateness of a particular sexual behavior depends on the culture in which it occurs.

Sexual Scripts

The outcome of all these social influences is that each of us learns a set of sexual scenarios (DeLamater, 1987) or *sexual scripts* (Gagnon & Simon, 1973; Gagnon, 1977, 1990; Berne, 1970). The idea is that sexual behavior (and virtually all human behavior, for that matter) is scripted much as a play in a theater is. That is, sexual behavior is a result of elaborate prior learning that teaches us an etiquette of sexual behavior. According to this concept, little in human sexual behavior is spontaneous. Instead, we have learned an elaborate script that tells us who, what, when, where, and why we do what we do sexually. For example, the "who" part of the script tells us that sex should occur with someone of the other gender, of approximately our own age, of our own race, and so on. Even the sequence of sexual activity is scripted. Scripts also tell us the meaning we should attach to a particular sexual event (Gagnon, 1990). *Scripts,* then, are plans that people carry around in their heads for what they are doing and what they are going to do; they are also devices for helping people remember what they have done in the past (Gagnon, 1977, p. 6). Scripts, of course, vary from one culture to another, as we saw in Chapter 1.

One study attempted to identify the sequence of sexual behaviors that is scripted for males and females in a heterosexual relationship in our culture (Jemail & Geer, 1977). Subjects were given 25 sentences, each describing an event in a heterosexual interaction. They were asked to rearrange the sentences in a sequence that was "most sexually arousing" and then to do it again to indicate what was "the most likely to occur." There was a high degree of agreement among subjects about what the sequence should be. There was also high agreement between males and females. The standard sequence was kissing, hand stimulation of the breasts, hand stimulation of the genitals, mouth-genital stimulation, intercourse, and orgasm. Does it sound familiar? Interestingly, not only is this the sequence in a sexual encounter, it is also the sequence that occurs as a couple progresses in a relationship. These results suggest that there are culturally defined sequences of behaviors that we all have learned, much as the notion of "script" suggests.

Can you imagine a young man, on the first date, attempting mouth stimulation of the young lady's genitals before he has kissed her? The idea seems amazing, perhaps humorous or shocking. Why? Because the young man has performed Act IV before Act I.

The Sociological Approach:
Levels of Analysis

The sociological approach to understanding influences on sexuality is shown in Figure 2.4. As you look down the left side of the diagram, you will notice that sociologists view societal influences on human sexuality as occurring on four levels: the macro-level or society as a whole; the subcultural level, at which one's social class or ethnic group may have an impact on one's sexuality; the interpersonal level, in which interactions with parents, peers, or lovers influence us; and finally the individual level, at which each of us has her or his own level of sexual desire, a sexual orientation, and a set of sexual scripts stored in memory.

Social Institutions

FIGURE 2.4
A sociological approach to understanding human sexuality. Sociologists focus on four levels of analysis: the macro level, the subcultural level, the interpersonal level, and the level of the individual (DeLamater, 1987).

According to the sociological perspective, at the macro-level our sexuality is influenced by powerful social institutions, including religion, the family, the economy, medicine, and the law.

Religion

In our culture, the Judeo-Christian religious tradition has been a powerful shaper of sexual norms. A detailed discussion of that religious tradition and its teachings on

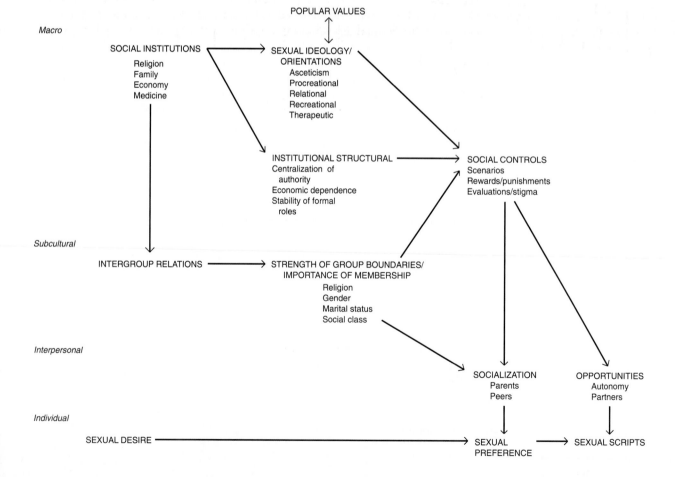

sexuality is provided in Chapter 21. Suffice it to say here that the Christian religion has contained within it a tradition of asceticism, in which abstinence from sexual pleasures—especially by certain persons such as monks and priests—is seen as virtuous. The tradition, at least until recently, has also been oriented toward procreation—that is, a belief that sexuality is legitimate only within traditional heterosexual marriage and only with the goal of having children. This view has created within our culture a set of norms that say, for example, that premarital sex, extramarital sex, and homosexual sex are wrong.

The Economy

The nature and structure of the economy is another macro-factor influencing sexuality. Before the industrial revolution, most work was done in the family unit in the home or farm. This kind of togetherness permitted rather strict surveillance of family members' sexuality and thus strict norms could be enforced. However, with the industrial revolution, people—most frequently men—spent many hours per day at work away from the home. Thus they were under less surveillance, and scenarios such as extramarital affairs and homosexual sex could be acted out more often.

Today we see much evidence of the extent to which economic conditions, and especially the unemployment rate, can affect the structure of the family and thus sexuality. For example, when a group of men—such as lower-class black men—have less access to jobs and have a high unemployment rate, they are understandably reluctant to marry, knowing that they cannot support a family. The result is many female-headed households, with sexuality occurring outside marriage and children born without a legal father, although the father may be present in the household, providing care for the children. The point is that a culture's economy may have a profound effect on patterns of sexuality, marriage, and childbearing.

The Family

The family is a third macro-level factor influencing sexuality. As we noted earlier, before the industrial revolution the family was an important economic unit, producing the goods necessary for survival. As that function waned after the industrial revolution, there was increased emphasis on the quality of interpersonal relationships in the family. At the same time, love was increasingly seen as an important reason for marriage. By 1850, popular American magazines sang the praises of marriage based on romantic love (Lantz et al., 1975). Thus a triple linkage between love, marriage, and sex was formed. Ironically, the linkage eventually became a direct one between love and sex (removing marriage as the middleman) so that, by the 1970s, people were arguing that premarital sex, if in the context of a loving relationship, was permissible, as was homosexual sex, again if the relationship was a loving one.

The family exerts a particularly important force on sexuality through *socialization* of children. That is, parents socialize their children—teach them appropriate norms for behavior—in many areas, including sexuality. Others, of course, such as the peer group, also have important socializing influences. Sociologists see these socializing influences occurring not at the macro-level, but at the interpersonal level (see Figure 2.4).

Medicine

The institution of medicine is another macro-level factor that, particularly in the last 100 years, has influenced our sexuality. Physicians tell us what is healthy and what is unhealthy. In the late 1800s, physicians warned that masturbation could cause

FIGURE 2.5
*According to the
sociological perspective, the
family is one of the macro-
level institutions
influencing sexuality.*

various pathologies. Today sex therapists tell us that sexual expression is natural and healthy and sometimes even "prescribe" masturbation as a cure. Because we tend to have great confidence in medical advice, these pronouncements have an enormous impact on sexuality.

The Law

The legal system is another institution influencing sexuality at the macro-level. A detailed discussion of laws relating to sexuality is provided in Chapter 22. The point to be made here is that from a sociological perspective, the law influences people's sexual behaviors in a number of ways. First, laws determine norms. Generally we think that what is legal is right and what is illegal is wrong. Thus, a society in which prostitution is illegal will have much different views of it than a society in which it is legal. Second, laws are mechanisms of social control. They can lead to punishments for certain acts and thus discourage people from engaging in them. An example is public sexual acts such as exhibitionism, or even nudity on beaches. One wonders how many people would prefer to be nude at the beach if they did not fear arrest because the behavior is generally illegal and if they did not fear possible embarrassing publicity such as having their names in the paper as a result of an arrest.

Third, the law reflects the interests of the powerful, dominant groups within a society. In part, the law functions to confirm the superiority of the ideologies of these dominant groups. Consider Mormons in the United States. Their religion was approving of polygamy (a man having several wives). Mormons did not become the dominant group in American society—although they might have, with the kind of reproduction one could achieve with polygamy. Rather, the Judeo-Christian tradition was the ideology of the dominant group, and the Judeo-Christian tradition takes a very dim view of polygamy. Accordingly, polygamy is illegal in the United States and Mormons were sometimes arrested for their practice. Also, one wonders what kinds of laws we would have on prostitution or sexual harassment if the composition of the United States Congress were 90 percent women rather than 90 percent men. Would prostitution, for example, be legal? Or would it still be illegal, but would the male customer be held as guilty as or guiltier than the female prostitute?

In summary, then, the sociological perspective focuses on how society or culture shapes and controls our sexual expression, at levels from insitutions such as religion and the law to the interpersonal level of socialization by family and peers.

Reiss's Sociological Theory of Sexuality

Ira Reiss (1986) has proposed a sociological theory of human sexuality. Borrowing from script theory discussed earlier in this section, he defines sexuality as "erotic and genital responses produced by the cultural scripts of a society" (p. 37). As he points out, a sociological theory, because it focuses on societal influences on sexuality, must be able to account for both cross-cultural variations in sexuality, as well as cross-cultural universals in sexuality.

One cross-cultural universal is that all societies believe that sexuality is important. Even in those cultures that are sexually repressive, sexuality is still accorded great importance as something that is dangeorus and must be controlled. Why is sexuality so important? Many previous theorists have claimed that it is the link of sexuality to making babies, which is undeniably important for any society. Reiss argues against this notion, however, citing instances of societies that do not understand the link between sex and reproduction, yet still find sex important. Indeed, in North America today effective methods of contraception have allowed us to separate much of sexuality from reproduction, yet we still think sex is important, even non-reproductive sex.

Reiss's explanation for the importance of sexuality has two components: (1) sexuality is associated with great physical pleasure, and (2) sexual interactions are associated with great personal self-disclosure, involving not only disclosure of one's body, but in an intimate interaction, of one's thoughts and feelings as well. Humans seem to find intrinsic value in the physical pleasures of sex and in the psychic satisfaction of the self-disclosures associated with sex—therefore its importance.

According to Reiss, sexuality is linked to the structures of any society in three areas: the kinship system, the power structure, and the ideology of the society.

First, because sexuality is the source of reproduction, it is always linked to

FIGURE 2.6
According to the sociological perspective, the law is an institution that influences sexuality by defining norms and exerting social control on sexual behaviors. Here gay activists are arrested for protesting at the Supreme Court over the Georgia sodomy case (see Chapter 22); the law (both the Supreme Court and the police) defined homosexual behaviors as violating norms.

kinship, and all societies seek to maintain social order through stable kinship systems. This linkage then becomes the explanation for sexual jealousy, which is universal cross-culturally although it exists in varied forms. Jealousy is a way of setting boundaries on a relationship that is considered very important, important enough so that it should not be breached. Marriage is typically such a relationship, and jealousy in marriage about extramarital affairs exists in all human societies. Kin define what relationships are and are not acceptable and enforce the resulting rules. Furthermore, all societies have structured ways of dealing with such jealousy. Even in societies that practice polygamy (one man with several wives), rituals develop to minimize jealousy among the wives—for example, the husband must sleep one night with one wife, the next with another, and so on, and has violated norms if he spends two nights with the same wife! Reiss argues, therefore, that no society will be able to eliminate sexual jealousy because jealousy is a statement of the value or importance kinship groups and individuals attach to a particular relationship such as marriage.

Second, sexuality is always linked to the *power structure* of a society. Reiss defines power as the ability to influence others and achieve one's objectives even if there is opposition from the other person. Powerful groups in any society generally seek to control the sexuality of the less powerful. Males are more powerful than females in most societies, so sexuality becomes linked to gender roles and males exercise control over female sexuality. Cross-cultural research shows, interestingly, that the closer females are in power to males in a society, the greater the sexual freedom for women; in societies in which women have little power, their sexuality is greatly restricted.

Third, sexuality is closely linked to the *ideologies* of a culture. Reiss defines "ideology" as fundamental assumptions about human nature. Societies define carefully what sexual practices are normal and abnormal, and which are right and wrong. Some cultures define homosexuality as abnormal, whereas others define it as normal—but the point is that all cultures define it one way or the other. Similarly, some cultures take a permissive attitude toward premarital sex both for males and females, some are permissive for males but not for females, and some are permissive for neither. A culture's ideologies define what is right and wrong sexually.

In summary, Reiss's sociological theory of sexuality argues that societies regard sexuality as important because it is associated with physical pleasure and with self-disclosure. Sexuality is powerfully connected to the fabric of any society because of its links to the kinship system, to power structures, and to the ideologies of the society.

Summary

Various theoretical perspectives on sexuality were reviewed. Sociobiologists view human sexual behaviors as the product of natural selection in evolution, and thus view these behavioral patterns as being genetically controlled.

Among the psychological theories, Freud's psychoanalytic theory views the sex energy, or libido, as a major influence on personality and behavior. Freud introduced the concepts of erogenous zones and psychosexual stages of development. Learning theory emphasizes how sexual behavior is learned and modified through reinforcements and punishments according to principles of operant conditioning. Behavior modification techniques—therapies based on learning theory—are used in treating sexual variations and sexual dysfunctions. Social learning theory adds imitation, identification, and observational learning to learning theory. Cognitive psychologists focus on people's thoughts and perceptions—whether positive or negative—and how these influence sexuality.

Sociologists study the ways in which society defines our sexual scripts. At the macro-level of analysis, sociologists investigate the ways in which institutions such as religion, the economy, the family, medicine, and the law influence sexuality. At the subcultural level, our social class or ethnic group may shape our sexuality. At an interpersonal level we are socialized by others—such as parents and peers—as to the appropriate norms for sexual expression. Reiss's sociological theory argues that all societies regard sexuality as important because it is associated with great physical pleasure and self-disclosure.

Review Questions

1. _____ is the term for the theory that applies evolutionary theory to social behaviors such as sexual behavior.
2. Freud termed the sex energy or sex drive _____.
3. According to Freud, the three major parts of the personality are the id, the ego, and the libido. True or false?
4. Freud believed that women could have either of two kinds of orgasms, vaginal orgasm or clitoral orgasm. True or false?
5. According to learning theory, teenagers are in the genital stage of development. True or false?
6. According to social learning theory, imitation is a powerful force shaping our sexual behaviors. True or false?
7. According to cognitive psychologists, how we perceive and evaluate a sexual event is at least as important as what occurred. True or false?
8. Sociologists study social influence at four levels of analysis: _____, _____, _____, and _____.
9. According to the notion of scripts, we have been socialized to believe that the appropriate sequence of social behaviors is kissing before engaging in intercourse. True or false?
10. According to Reiss's sociological theory, sex is important in any society because it involves physical pleasure and _____.

(The answers to all review questions are at the end of the book, beginning on page 731.)

Questions for Thought, Discussion, and Debate

1. Compare and contrast how a sociobiologist, a psychoanalyst, and a sociologist would explain why people engage in premarital intercourse.
2. Of the theories described in this chapter, which do you think provides the most insight into human sexuality? Why?
3. Compare how a sociobiologist and a social learning theorist would explain why most child care is done by women.
4. From a sociologist's point of view, how have social institutions controlled female sexuality?
5. Could script theory explain the pattern of homosexual and heterosexual behavior of Sambia males described in Focus 2.1?

Freud, S. *A general introduction to psychoanalysis.* (1943). Garden City, NY: Garden City Publishing. (Original in German, 1917). Good for the reader who wants a basic introduction to Freud. For a good one-chapter summary, see Hall, C. S., and Lindzey, G. (1970). *Theories of personality* (2nd ed.). New York: Wiley.

Gagnon, John H., & Simon, William (1987). The sexual scripting of oral-genital contacts. *Archives of Sexual Behavior, 16,* 1–26. An interesting discussion and application of script theory.

Symons, Donald. (1979). *The evolution of human sexuality.* New York: Oxford University Press. A sociobiological analysis of sexuality.

3

Sex Research

Chapter Highlights

According to the Kinsey Report
Every average man you know,
Much prefers to play his favorite sport,
When the temperature is low,
But when the thermometer goes way up,
And the weather is sizzling hot,
  Mr. Adam
  For his madam
  Is not.
    'Cause it's too darn hot. *

In the last few decades, sex research has made increasing advances, and the names of Kinsey and of Masters and Johnson have become household words. How do sex researchers do it? How valid are their conclusions?

There are many different types of sex research, but basically the techniques vary in terms of the following: (1) whether they rely on people's self-reports of their sexual behavior or whether the scientist observes the sexual behavior directly; (2) whether large numbers of people are studied (surveys) or whether a small number or just a single individual is studied (in laboratory studies or case studies); (3) whether the studies are conducted in the laboratory or in the field; and (4) whether sexual behavior is studied simply as it occurs naturally or whether some attempt is made to manipulate it experimentally.

Examples of studies using all these techniques will be considered and evaluated later in the chapter. First some issues in sex research—objections frequently made to studies that have been done—will be discussed.

It is important to have some knowledge of the techniques of sex research and their strengths as well as their limitations. This knowledge will help you evaluate the studies that are cited as evidence for various conclusions in later chapters and will

*   *Source: Kiss Me Kate,* a musical comedy. (1953). Music and lyrics by Cole Porter; book by Sam and Bella Spewack. New York: Knopf.

also help you decide how willing you are to accept these conclusions. Perhaps more important, this knowledge will help you evaluate future sex research. The knowledge we have of sexuality at present is based on relatively few studies. Many more will be done in the future. The information in this chapter should help you understand and evaluate sex research that appears 10 or 20 years from now.

ISSUES IN SEX RESEARCH

Sampling

Population: A group of people a researcher wants to study and make inferences about.

Sample: A part of a population.

Random sampling: An excellent method of sampling in research, in which each member of the population has an equal chance of being included in the sample.

Probability sampling: An excellent method of sampling in research, in which each member of the population has a known probability of being included in the sample.

Problem of refusal or nonresponse: The problem that some people will refuse to participate in a sex survey, thus making it difficult to have a random sample.

Volunteer bias: A problem in sex surveys caused by some people refusing to participate, so that those who are in the sample are volunteers who may in some ways differ from those who refuse to participate.

One of the first steps in conducting sex research is to identify the appropriate **population** of people to be studied. Does the population in question consist of all adult human beings, all adults in the United States, all adolescents in the United States, all people guilty of sex crimes, or all married couples who engage in swinging? Generally, of course, the scientist is unable to get data for all the people in the population, and so a **sample** is taken.

At this point, things begin to get sticky. If the sample is a **random sample** or representative sample of the population in question and if it is a reasonably large sample, then results obtained from it can safely be generalized to the population that was originally identified. That is, if a researcher has really randomly selected 1 out of every 50 adolescents in the United States, then the results obtained from that sample are probably true of all adolescents in the United States. One technique that is sometimes used to get such a sample is **probability sampling.**[1] But if the sample consists only of adolescents with certain characteristics—for example, only those whose parents would agree to let them participate in sex research—then the results obtained from that sample may not be true of all adolescents. Sampling has been a serious problem in sex research.

Typically, sampling proceeds in three phases: the population is identified, a method for obtaining a sample is adopted, and the people in the sample are contacted and asked to participate. The scientific techniques of the second phase—obtaining a sample—are by now fairly well developed and should not be a problem in future research, provided investigators use them. What is perhaps the thorniest problem, though, occurs in the last phase: getting the people identified for the sample to participate. If any of the people refuse to participate, then the nice probability sample is ruined. And generally in sex research, rather large numbers of people will refuse to participate; this is called the **problem of refusal** (or **nonresponse**). As a result, the researcher is essentially studying volunteers, that is, people who volunteer to be in the research. Therefore, this problem is also called **volunteer bias.** In casually conducted research such as the Hite report (see Chapter 14), the response rate was only 3 percent, making it impossible to reach any conclusions about the population based on the sample. The problem of refusal in sex research is very difficult, since there is no ethical way of forcing people to participate when they do not want to.

The problem of volunteer bias would not be so great if those who refused to participate were identical in their sexual behavior to those who participated. But it seems likely that those who refuse to participate differ in some ways from those who agree to, and that leads to a biased sample. Evidence suggests that volunteers who participate in sex research, compared with those who do not participate, hold more

---

[1] A detailed discussion of probability sampling is beyond the scope of this book. For a good description of this method as applied to sex research, see Cochran et al. (1953). A random sample is one example of a probability sample.

permissive attitudes about sexuality and are more sexually experienced—for example, they masturbate more frequently and have had more sexual partners (Saunders et al., 1985; Morokoff, 1986; Wolchik et al., 1985). In addition, women are less likely to volunteer for sex research than men are (e.g., Wolchik et al., 1985), so that female samples are even more highly selected than male samples. In sum, volunteer bias is potentially a serious problem when we try to reach conclusions based on sex research.

Reliability of Self-Reports of Sexual Behavior

Most sex researchers have not directly observed the sexual behavior of their subjects. Instead, most have relied on respondents' self-reports of their sexual practices. The question is: How accurately do people report their own sexual behavior? There are several ways in which inaccuracies may occur, and these inaccuracies are problems for sex surveys. These problems are discussed below.

Purposeful Distortion

Purposeful distortion: Purposely giving false information in a survey.

If you were an interviewer in a sex research project and a 90-year-old man said that he and his wife made love twice a day, would you believe him, or would you suspect that he might be exaggerating slightly? If a 35-year-old woman told you that she had never masturbated, would you believe her, or would you suspect that she had masturbated but was unwilling to admit it?

Respondents in sex research may, for one reason or another, give self-reports that are distortions of reality. These distortions may be in either of two directions. People may exaggerate their sexual activity (a tendency toward "enlargement"), or they may minimize their sexual activity or hide the fact that they have done certain things ("concealment"). Unfortunately, we do not know whether most people tend toward enlargement or concealment.

Distortion is a basic problem when using self-reports. To minimize distortion, subjects must be impressed with the fact that because the study will be used for scientific purposes, their reports must be as accurate as possible. They must also be assured that their responses will be completely anonymous; this is necessary, for example, so that a politician would not be tempted to hide a homosexual history or an extramarital affair for fear that the information could be used to blackmail him.

But even if all respondents were very truthful and tried to give as accurate information as possible, two factors might still cause their self-reports to be inaccurate: memory and ability to estimate.

Memory

Some of the questions asked in sex surveys require respondents to recall what their sexual behavior was like many years before. For example, some of the data we have on sexual behavior in childhood come from the Kinsey study, in which adults were asked about their childhood sex behavior. This might involve asking a 50-year-old man to remember at what age he began masturbating and how frequently he masturbated when he was 16 years old. It may be difficult to remember such facts accurately. The alternative is to ask people about their current sexual behavior, although getting data like this from children raises serious ethical and practical problems.

Ability to Estimate

One of the questions Kinsey asked was: How long, on the average, do you spend in precoital foreplay? If you were asked this question, how accurate a response do you think you could give? It is rather difficult to estimate time to begin with, and it is even more difficult to do so when engaged in an absorbing activity. The point is that in some sex surveys people are asked to give estimates of things that they probably cannot estimate very accurately. This may be another source of inaccuracy in self-report data (Leavitt, 1983).

Test-Retest Reliability

Test-retest reliability: A method for testing whether self-reports are reliable or accurate; subjects are interviewed (or given a questionnaire) and then interviewed a second time sometime later to determine whether their answers are the same both times.

One way of assessing how reliable or accurate people's reports are is the method of **test-retest reliability,** in which the respondent is asked a series of questions and then is asked the same set of questions after a period of time has passed, for example, a day or a week. The correlation[2] between answers at the two times (test and retest) measures the reliability of responses. If people answer identically both times, the correlation would be 1.0, meaning perfect reliability. If there was absolutely no relationship between what they said the first time and what they said the second time (a situation that never actually occurs), the correlation would be 0, indicating that the responses are not at all reliable.

In one study, heterosexual college students were asked to estimate their frequency of vaginal intercourse for a one-month period; the test-retest reliability was .89, which is excellent (Catania et al., 1990a). However, when they were asked their frequency of intercourse in a six-month period of time, the test-retest reliability fell to .65, and when they were asked about its frequency during a one-year period, reliability was only .36. Respondents can give their best estimates about short, recent time intervals.

Self-reports of sexuality are reasonably reliable, then, at least for those who volunteer to participate, and if the questions are asked in the best possible manner.

Interviews Versus Questionnaires

In the large-scale sex surveys, two methods of collecting data have been used. Either interviewers question people directly about their sexual behavior or people are given a questionnaire which they complete themselves. Each of these methods has some advantages when compared with the other.

The advantage of the personal interview is that the interviewer can establish rapport with the respondent and, it is hoped, convince that person of the research's worth and of the necessity for being honest. An interviewer can also vary the sequence of questions depending on the person's response. For example, in the Kinsey interviewing procedure, if a person mentioned having had a homosexual experience, this would be followed by a series of questions about the experience; however, those questions would be omitted if the person reported having had no homosexual experiences. It is hard to get this kind of flexibility in a printed questionnaire. Finally, interviews can be administered to persons who cannot read or write.

Questionnaires are much less costly, since they do not require hiring interviewers to spend the many hours necessary to interview subjects individually. Although it might seem that respondents would be more honest in answering a questionnaire because they are more anonymous, the evidence indicates that questionnaires and

---

[2]   The statistical concept of correlation is discussed in the last section of this chapter.

FIGURE 3.1
*Sex researchers have tried
to devise some ingenious
methods for overcoming
the problems of self-
reports.*

"Another one of those damned sex surveys, I suppose."

interviews yield equally valid self-reports (DeLamater, 1982). Questionnaires are less subject to the problem of responses being influenced by extraneous factors, such as the personality of the interviewer or a grimace from the interviewer when a particular behavior is reported.

Self-Reports Versus Direct Observations

As I noted earlier, one of the major ways of classifying techniques of sex research is according to whether the scientist relied on people's self-reports of their behavior or observed the sexual behavior directly.

The problems of self-reports have been discussed above. In a word, self-reports may be inaccurate. Direct observations—such as those done by Masters and Johnson in their work on the physiology of sexual response—have a major advantage over self-reports in that they are accurate. No purposeful distortion or poor memory can intervene. On the other hand, direct observations have their own set of problems. They are expensive and time-consuming, with the result that generally a rather small sample of subjects is studied. Further, obtaining a random or representative sample of the population is even more difficult than in survey research. While many people are reticent about completing a questionnaire concerning their sexual behavior, even more would be unwilling to come to a laboratory where their sexual behavior would be observed by a scientist or where they would be hooked up to recording instruments while they engaged in sex. Thus results obtained from the unusual group of volunteers who would be willing to do this might not be generalizable to the rest of the population. One study showed that volunteers for a laboratory study of male sexual arousal were less guilty, less sexually fearful, and more sexually experienced than nonvolunteers (Farkas et al., 1978; for similar results with females, see Wolchik et al., 1983).

Direct observations of sexual behavior in the laboratory, such as those made by Masters and Johnson, also involve one other problem: Is sexual behavior in the laboratory the same as sexual behavior in the privacy of one's own bedroom? For example, might sexual response in the laboratory be somewhat inhibited?

Extraneous Factors

Various extraneous factors may also influence the outcomes of sex research. For example, people report more sexual feelings to an interviewer of their own gender than to an interviewer of the opposite gender (Walters et al., 1962). Generally, respondents are most open with interviewers who are of their own gender (Benney et al., 1956; J. Ehrlich & Riesman, 1961). Thus such extraneous factors as the gender or age of the interviewer may influence the outcome of sex research. Questionnaires do not get around these problems, since such simple factors as the wording of a question may influence the results. For example, if a question reads "On the average, how many times do you have intercourse per month?" the estimates of frequency of intercourse that are obtained will not be the same as if the question had read "On the average, how many times do you have intercourse per day?" Thus sex researchers must be careful to control these extraneous factors so that they influence the results as little as possible.

Ethical Issues

In recent years, scientists as well as lay people have become more aware of the ethical problems involved in doing research. Such ethical problems are particularly difficult in sex research, because people are more likely to feel that their privacy has been invaded when you ask them about sex than when you ask them to name their favorite presidential candidate or memorize a list of words. The ethical standards of most scientific organizations—such as the American Psychological Association and the American Sociological Association—involve two basic principles: informed consent and protection from harm (see, for example, American Psychological Association, 1973).

Informed Consent

Informed consent: An ethical principle in research, in which subjects have a right to be informed, before participating, of what they will be asked to do in the research.

According to the principle of informed consent, participants have a right to be told, before they participate, what the purpose of the research is and what they will be asked to do. They may not be forced to participate or be forced to continue. An investigator may not coerce people to be in a study, and it is the scientist's responsibility to see to it that all subjects understand exactly what they are agreeing to do. In the case of children who may be too young to give truly informed consent, it is usually given by the parents.

The principle of informed consent was adopted by scientific organizations in the 1970s, and thus it was violated in some of the older sex studies, as will be discussed later in this chapter.

Protection from Harm

Investigators should minimize the amount of physical and psychological stress to those participating in their research. Thus, for example, if an investigator must shock subjects during a study, there should be a good reason for doing this. Questioning people about their sexual behavior may be psychologically stressful to them and might conceivably harm them in some way, and thus sex researchers must be careful to minimize the stress involved in their procedures. The principle of *anonymity* of response is important to ensure that subjects will not suffer afterward for their participation in research.

A Cost-Benefit Approach

Cost-benefit approach: An approach to analyzing the ethics of a research study, based on weighing the costs of the research (the subjects' time, stress to subjects, and so on) against the benefits of the research (gaining knowledge about human sexuality).

Considering the possible dangers involved in sex research, is it ever ethical to do such research? Officials in universities and government agencies sponsoring sex research must answer this question for every proposed sex research study. Typically they use a cost-benefit approach. That is, stress to subjects should be minimized as much as possible, but some stresses will remain; they are the cost. The question then becomes: Will the benefits that result from the research be greater than the cost? That is, will the subjects benefit in some way from participating, and will science and society in general benefit from the knowledge resulting from the study? Do these benefits outweigh the costs? If they do, the research is justifiable; otherwise, it is not.

As an example, Masters and Johnson considered these issues carefully and they feel that their subjects benefited from being in their research; they have collected data from former subjects that confirm this belief. Thus a cost-benefit analysis would suggest that their research is ethical, even though their subjects may be temporarily stressed by it. Even in such an ethically questionable study as Laud Humphreys's study of the tearoom trade (discussed in Focus 15.2 in Chapter 15), the potential cost to the subjects must be weighed against the benefits that accrue to society from being informed about this aspect of sexual behavior.

What Do Subjects Say About Ethics?

Psychologist Paul Abramson (1977) attempted to collect empirical data relevant to the problems of ethics in sex research. He administered standard sex research procedures to undergraduate volunteers; they filled out a questionnaire about their past sexual behavior, they completed a personality inventory on sexual attitudes, they read an erotic story and rated their arousal, they were observed in a waiting room with sexually explicit magazines, they responded to double entendres (words with double meanings, one of which is sexual), and they were tested for retention of information on reproductive biology. Afterward, subjects reported that they felt that their participation had been constructive and devoid of negative aftereffects. Thus this study suggests that volunteer subjects do not view their participation as having harmed them; instead, they feel good about having contributed something to knowledge in this area.

Having considered some of the problems with sex research—though these problems are by no means limited to sex research and are common in most research on human behavior—let us proceed to examine some of the studies that have been done.

THE MAJOR SEX SURVEYS

In the major sex surveys, the data were collected from a large sample of people by means of questionnaires or interviews. The best known of these studies is the one done by Kinsey. The data were collected in the 1940s and thus the results are now largely of historical interest. However, Kinsey documented his methods with extraordinary care and so his research is a good example to study for both the good and the bad points of surveys.

The Kinsey Report

Sampling

Kinsey and his colleagues interviewed a total of 5300 males, and their responses were reported in *Sexual Behavior in the Human Male* (1948); 5940 females contributed to *Sexual Behavior in the Human Female* (1953). Though some blacks were interviewed, only interviews with whites were included in the publications. The interviews were conducted between 1938 and 1949.

Initially, Kinsey was not much concerned with sampling issues. His goal was simply to collect sex histories from as wide a variety of people as possible. He began collecting interviews on his university campus and then moved to collecting others in large cities, such as Chicago.

Later he became more concerned with sampling issues and developed a technique called *100 percent sampling*. In this method he contacted a group, obtained its cooperation, and then got every one of its members to give a history. Once the cooperation of a group had been secured, peer pressure assured that all members would participate. Unfortunately, although he was successful in getting a complete sample from such groups, the groups themselves were by no means chosen randomly. Thus among the groups from which 100 percent samples were obtained were 2 sororities, 9 fraternities, and 13 professional groups.

In the 1953 volume, Kinsey said that he and his colleagues had deliberately chosen not to use probability sampling methods because of the problems of nonresponse. This is a legitimate point. But as a result, we have almost no information on how adequate the sample was.

As one scholar observed, the sampling was haphazard but not random (Kirby, 1977). For example, there were more subjects from Indiana than from any other state. Generally, the following kinds of subjects were overrepresented in the sample: college students, young people, well-educated people, Protestants, people living in cities, and people living in Indiana and the northeast. Underrepresented groups included manual laborers, less well-educated people, older people, Roman Catholics, Jews, members of racial minorities, and people living in rural areas.

Interviewing

Although scientists generally regard Kinsey's sampling methods with some dismay, his interviewing techniques are highly regarded. The interviewers made every attempt to establish rapport with the people they spoke to, and they treated all reports matter-of-factly. They were also skillful at phrasing questions in language that was easily understood. Questions were worded so as to encourage subjects to report anything they had done. For example, rather than asking "Have you ever masturbated?" the interviewers asked "At what age did you begin masturbating?" They also developed a number of methods for cross-checking a subject's report so that false information would be detected. Wardell Pomeroy recounted an example:

> Kinsey illustrated this point with the case of an older Negro male who at first was wary and evasive in his answers. From the fact that he listed a number of minor jobs when asked about his occupation and seemed reluctant to go into any of them [Kinsey] deduced that he might have been active in the underworld, so he began to follow up by asking the man whether he had ever been married. He denied it, at which Kinsey resorted to the vernacular and inquired if he had ever "lived common law." The man admitted he had, and that it had first happened when he was 14.

Alfred C. Kinsey

Alfred C. Kinsey was born in 1894 in New Jersey, the first child of uneducated parents. In high school he did not date, and a classmate recalled that he was "the shyest guy around girls you could think of."

His father was determined that Kinsey become a mechanical engineer. From 1912 to 1914 he tried studying mechanical engineering at Stevens Institute, but he showed little talent for it. At one point he was close to failing physics, but a compromise was reached with the professor, who agreed to pass him if he would not attempt any advanced work in the field! In 1914 Kinsey made the break and enrolled at Bowdoin College to pursue his real love: biology. Because this went against his father's wishes, Kinsey was put on his own financially; the only economic help he received from his parents after that was a single suit costing $25.

In 1916 he began graduate work at Harvard. There he developed an interest in insects, specializing in gall wasps. Even while a graduate student he wrote a definitive book on the edible plants of eastern North America.

In 1920 he went to Bloomington, Indiana, to take a job as assistant professor of zoology at Indiana University. That fall he met Clara McMillen, whom he married six months later. They soon had four children.

With his intense curiosity and driving ambition, Kinsey quickly gained academic success. He published a high school biology text in 1926, and it received enthusiastic reviews. By 1936 he had published two major books on gall wasps; they established his reputation as a leading authority in the field and contributed not only to knowledge of gall wasps but also to genetic theory.

Kinsey came to the study of human sexual behavior as a biologist, not as a social reformer. His shift to the study of sex began in 1938, when Indiana University began a "marriage" course; Kinsey chaired the faculty committee teaching it. Part of the course included individual conferences between students and faculty, and these were Kinsey's first sex interviews. When confronted with teaching the course, he also became aware of the incredible lack of information on human sexual behavior. Thus his research resulted in part from his realization of the need of people, especially young people, for sex information. In 1939 he made his first field trip to collect sex histories in Chicago. His lifetime goal was to collect 100,000 sex histories.

His work culminated with the publication of the Kinsey reports in 1948 *(Sexual Behavior in the Human Male)* and 1953 *(Sexual Behavior in the Human Female)*. While the scientific community generally received them as a landmark contribution, they also provoked hate mail.

In 1947 he founded the Institute for Sex Research (known popularly as the Kinsey Institute) at Indiana University. It was financed by a grant from

"How old was the woman?" [Kinsey] asked.

"Thirty-five," he admitted, smiling.

Kinsey showed no surprise. "She was a hustler, wasn't she?" he said flatly.

At this the subject's eyes opened wide. Then he smiled in a friendly way for the first time, and said, "Well, sir, since you appear to know something about these things, I'll tell you straight."

FIGURE 3.2
Alfred C. Kinsey (second from right, holding the folder), with colleagues Martin, Gebhard, and Pomeroy.

the Rockefeller Foundation and, later, by book royalties. But in the 1950s Senator Joseph McCarthy, the communist baiter, was in power. He made a particularly vicious attack on the Institute and its research, claiming that its effect was to weaken American morality and thus make the nation more susceptible to a communist takeover. Under his pressuring, support from the Rockefeller Foundation was terminated.

Kinsey's health began to fail, partly as a result of the incredible work load he set for himself, partly because he was so involved with the research that he took attacks personally, and partly because he saw financial support for the research collapsing. He died in 1956 at the age of 62 of heart failure, while

honoring a lecture engagement when his doctor had ordered him to convalesce.

Fortunately, by 1957 McCarthy had been discredited, and the grant funds returned. The Institute was headed by Paul Gebhard, an anthropologist who had been a member of the staff for many years. The Institute continues to do research today; it also houses a large library on sex and an archival collection including countless works of sexual art.

Sources: P. Gebhard. The Institute. In M. S. Weinberg (Ed.). (1976). *Sex research: Studies from the Kinsey Institute.* New York: Oxford University Press, pp. 10–22. C. V. Christensen. (1971), *Kinsey: A biography.* Bloomington: Indiana University Press.

After that, [Kinsey] got an extraordinary record of this man's history as a pimp. . . . (1972, pp. 115–116)

Strict precautions were taken to ensure that responses were anonymous and that they would remain anonymous. The data were stored on IBM cards, but using a code that had been memorized by only a few people directly in the project, and the code was never written down. They had even made contingency plans for destroying the data in the event that the police tried to demand access to the records for the purposes of prosecuting people.

Over 50 percent of the interviews were done by Kinsey himself, and the rest by his associates, whom he trained carefully.

Put simply, the interviewing techniques were probably very successful in minimizing purposeful distortion. However, other problems of self-report remained: the problems of memory and of inability to estimate some of the numbers requested.

Checking for Accuracy

Kinsey and his colleagues developed a number of methods for checking on the accuracy of subjects' self-reports.

They did retakes of the histories of 162 men and women, with a minimum of 18 months between the two interviews (recall that the correlation between the two reports estimates the test-retest reliability). Any discrepancies between the two histories would be accounted for by memory problems, purposeful distortion, and various chance factors. The results indicated a high degree of agreement between the first and second interviews for all measures. Correlations greater than .95 between the first and second interviews were obtained for reports of incidence of masturbation, extramarital coitus, and homosexual activity. Thus these data indicate that the self-reports were highly reliable.

Another method for checking accuracy is to interview a husband and a wife independently; their reports on many items should be identical and can thus be used as a check for accuracy. Kinsey did exactly this for 706 couples. The results indicated that reports of objective facts—such as the number of years they had been married, how long they were engaged, and how much time elapsed between their marriage and the birth of their first child—showed perfect or near-perfect agreement between spouses. However, as was noted earlier in this chapter, some other questions required much more subjective responses or estimates of things that might be difficult to estimate. On such items, there was less agreement between spouses. For example, the correlation between husband's and wife's estimate of the average frequency of intercourse early in marriage was only about .50 (this was the lowest correlation obtained). Even with these subjective reports, though, husbands and wives showed a fairly high degree of agreement.

Thus from the available data it appears that the self-reports varied from being fairly accurate (on the subjective items, such as reports of frequencies) to highly accurate (on items such as vital statistics and incidences of activities).

How Accurate Are the Kinsey Statistics?

When all is said and done, how accurate are the statistics presented by Kinsey?

The American Statistical Association appointed a blue-ribbon panel to evaluate the Kinsey reports (Cochran et al., 1953; for other evaluations, see Terman, 1948; Wallin, 1949). While they generally felt that the interview techniques had been excellent, they were dismayed by Kinsey's failure to use probability sampling, and they concluded, somewhat pessimistically:

> In the absence of a probability-sample benchmark, the present results must be regarded as subject to systematic errors of unknown magnitude due to selective sampling (via volunteering and the like). (Cochran et al., p. 711)

However, they also felt that this was a nearly insoluble problem for sex research; even if a probability sample were used, refusals would create serious problems:

> In our opinion, no sex study of a broad human population can expect to present incidence data for reported behavior that are *known* to be correct to within a few percentage points. . . . If the percentage of refusals is 10 percent or more, then however large the sample, there are no statistical principles which guarantee that the results are correct to within 2 or 3 percent. (Cochran et al., 1953, p. 675)

It is possible, then, that the Kinsey statistics are very accurate, but there is no way of proving it.

The statisticians who evaluated Kinsey's methods felt that two of his findings might have been particularly subject to error: (1) generally high levels of sexual activity, and particularly the high incidence of homosexuality; and (2) a strong relationship between sexual activity and social class. These conclusions might have been seriously influenced by discrepancies between reported and actual behavior and by sampling problems, particularly Kinsey's tendency to seek out persons with unusual sexual practices.

Kinsey's associates felt that the most questionable statistic was the incidence of male homosexuality. Wardell Pomeroy commented, "The magic 37 percent of males who had one or more homosexual experiences was, no doubt, overestimated." (1972, p. 466).

In sum, it is impossible to say how accurate the Kinsey statistics are; they may be very accurate, or they may contain serious errors. Probably the single most doubtful figure is the high incidence of homosexuality. Also, at this point the Kinsey survey is more than 40 years old, and so we need to look to more recent research.

African American and Hispanic Youth

Kathleen Ford and Anne Norris (1991) conducted a survey on the sexual behavior of urban African American and Hispanic youth. Although the sample size was small (34 African American males and females and 30 Hispanic males and females), the authors were very careful about methodological issues and provide an extensive discussion of methodological points that must be kept in mind as researchers move beyond studying all or mostly white samples and focus increasingly on ethnic minorities in the United States.

Respondents were interviewed by an interviewer of the same gender and ethnic background. This practice is important for building rapport and establishing trust during the interview, both of which are critical in obtaining honest answers.

Language was another important issue in constructing the interview. Many people, Anglos included, do not know scientific terms for sexual concepts. Interviewers therefore have to be ready with a supply of slang terms so that they can switch to these if a respondent does not understand a question. The problem becomes more complex when interviewing people whose first language is not English. The interviewers who interviewed Hispanics were themselves fluent in Spanish and had a good knowledge of Spanish slang for sexual terms.

Cultural differences may mean that people from different ethnic groups attach different meanings to sexual concepts. An example is the apparently simple question, "Would you classify yourself as homosexual, heterosexual, or bisexual?" In Hispanic cultures, men who engage in anal intercourse with other men are typically not categorized as homosexual as long as they are the inserting partner (the receiving partner is definitely categorized as homosexual) (see Chapter 15). Therefore, a Hispanic male who frequently has sex with other men but is always the inserter, might quite truthfully answer that he does not classify himself as homosexual.

In this study, the Hispanic women presented some special challenges for the researchers. Hispanic culture is characterized by sharply defined gender roles, a high valuation on virginity for women, and protecting women from sexual discussions and sexual knowledge. In keeping with these cultural traditions, the Hispanic women in this sample seemed to have the least sexual knowledge of all the groups and were especially sensitive about sexual topics, making it difficult to interview them.

Among the many results of the study, let's consider one as an example. The researchers found that, among these 15- to 21-year-olds, 82 percent of the African American males and 100 percent of the African American females had engaged in vaginal intercourse, as had 80 percent of the Hispanic males but only 53 percent of the Hispanic females. The low percentage for Hispanic females is in keeping with the cultural norm of protecting and restricting female sexuality.

In conclusion, doing sex research with ethnic minorities in the United States requires more than just administering the same old surveys to samples of minorities. It also requires revisions to methodology that are culturally sensitive on issues such as the ethnicity of the interviewer, the language used in the interview, and the special sensitivity of some groups regarding some topics.

The Magazine Surveys

A number of large-scale surveys have been conducted through magazines. For example, *Psychology Today* included a 100-item sex questionnaire in its July 1969 issue. Over 20,000 readers responded, and the results were later published (Athanasiou et al.; 1970). *Redbook* included a questionnaire about female sexuality in its October 1974 issue (Levin & Levin, 1975). *Redbook* did another survey in February 1980, and *Ladies Home Journal* did one in June 1982. Let us consider, as a typical example, a survey by *McCall's*.

The *McCall's* Survey

McCall's magazine printed a survey on marriage, love, and sex in its August 1979 issue and reported the results in January 1980 (Gittelson, 1980).

In terms of sample size, the response was enormous; questionnaires were returned by more than 20,000 women. However, in sex research, as in some other aspects of sexuality, bigger is not always better. A carefully chosen probability sample of 1000 is much better than a highly selective sample of 20,000, and the *McCall's* sample gives evidence of having been such a selective sample. First, only *McCall's* readers were surveyed, and not every woman reads *McCall's*. Among others, this omits all women who cannot or do not read. Second, only those who voluntarily returned the questionnaire were included; presumably, women who felt very uncomfortable about sex or who were not married or in some other permanent relationship were less likely to respond. Confirming this argument, 82 percent of the respondents were married, whereas nationally the percentage is only 70.

As an example of the problems associated with selective samples, one of the questions asked what was most important to them. The leading response—from 61 percent—was "the feeling of being close to someone." Only 17 answered "my job." Should we infer from this that only 17 percent of U.S. women feel that their job is most important to them? Of course not. The likelier explanation is that happy housewives read *McCall's* and happy career women don't.

For these reasons, the statistics from the *McCall's* survey characterize only the 20,000 women who responded; it would not be legitimate to infer that they characterize U.S. women in general.

I could continue with more examples of magazine surveys, but the general conclusion should be clear by now. Although they may appear impressive because of the large number of respondents, they actually are poor in quality because the sample is seriously biased.

Probability Samples

As has been noted, one of the biggest problems with the major sex surveys is sampling. Recently several major studies have conquered this problem and have actually obtained probability samples in sex surveys. Examples are the studies of U.S. teenagers by Kantner and Zelnik (1972; Zelnik & Kantner, 1977), the National AIDS Behavioral Survey (Catania et al., 1992), Johnson's British study (Johnson et al., 1992), and the ACSF French study (ACSF, 1992).

The Kantner and Zelnik Survey

In 1971, John Kantner and Melvin Zelnik conducted a study based on a national probability sample of the 15- to 19-year-old female population of the United States. A total of 4611 young women were interviewed. The study provides particularly good information on premarital sexual behavior among females and on contraceptive use among young unmarried women (Kantner & Zelnik, 1972, 1973). It provides excellent data on differences between blacks and whites in sexual behavior, since 1479 blacks were interviewed. It also provides interesting analyses of how various social factors, such as social class and religion, are related to varying patterns of sexual behavior. Kantner and Zelnik conducted a parallel survey in 1976, and a comparison of the results of the two studies provides good information on increases in premarital sex and contraceptive use in the 1970s, during the sexual revolution (Zelnik & Kantner, 1977).

   The major virtue of these studies is that the sampling was excellent. The studies

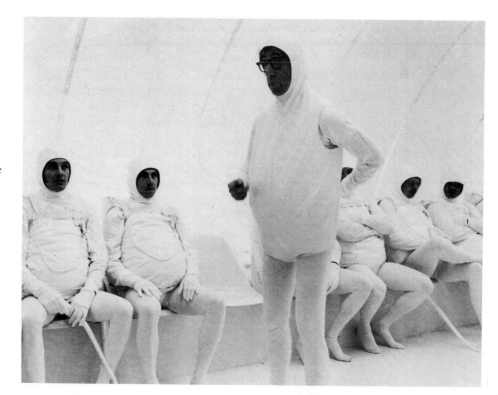

FIGURE 3.3
One visible sign of the sexual revolution of the 1960s and 1970s is the more open treatment of sexuality by the media. Here Woody Allen and fellow sperm await blast-off in the film Everything You Always Wanted to Know About Sex but Were Afraid to Ask.

had some limitations, however. Because only young women between the ages of 15 and 19 were interviewed, it was impossible to reach any conclusions about male-female differences or about people who are older or younger. This is a particular problem for the data on premarital sex, since some young women do not begin engaging in it before their twenties.

Another limitation is that the studies relied on self-reports. In the 1976 survey, however, Kantner and Zelnik used a new research method, called the *randomized response technique*. Space does not permit a detailed explanation; suffice it to say that it enables the researcher to estimate how accurate people are being in their self-reports. Kantner and Zelnik used this method on one of the most sensitive questions—and therefore the one likeliest to yield inaccurate self-reports—namely, whether the respondent had ever had intercourse. According to self-reports, 42 percent of the women had; the estimate of the true incidence, by use of the randomized response technique, was 44 percent. This result indicates that the self-reports were highly accurate. Perhaps we can, after all, place a good deal of confidence in self-report studies.

The National AIDS Behavioral Surveys

There are so few well-done sex surveys in the United States that it has been nearly impossible to obtain good estimates of the number of people who may be infected with HIV. To address this problem the National AIDS Behavioral Surveys were undertaken under the leadership of Joseph Catania of the Centers for Disease Control (Catania et al., 1992).

The data were collected in 1990 and 1991, using the technique of random-digit dialing of telephones to obtain a random sample. Random-digit dialing is an excellent technique and omits from the sample only those people who have no telephone. The researchers argued that telephone interviews are preferable to face-to-face interviews for collecting data on sexual behavior because the respondent feels more of a sense of anonymity. The response rate was 70 percent. Interviews were conducted in Spanish for those who requested them; 56 percent of Hispanic respondents preferred the Spanish interview.

The result was a survey of a total of 10,630 adults ranging in age from 18 to 75; 63 percent of the sample were married.

As of this writing, only early data analyses have been published, but these early results are interesting. For example, 7 percent of the sample was considered to be in an HIV-risk group because of having had multiple sexual partners (two or more) in the past 12 months.

The tragedy of AIDS has had at least some positive side benefits in that it has legitimized some major, well-done projects of this kind.

Sexual Behavior in France

Again stimulated by a need for far better information about sexual behavior in order to deal with the AIDS crisis, a team of French researchers, called the ACSF Investigators, conducted a major French sex survey (ACSF Investigators, 1992). The data were collected in 1991 and 1992. These researchers, too, chose the method of telephone interviews, preceded by a letter notifying potential respondents that they had been identified for the representative sample. The response rate was 76.5 percent. The result was a sample of 20,055 adults ranging in age from 18 to 69.

Again, at the time of this writing only preliminary results of the survey have been released. They indicate, for example, that 13 percent of French men, compared with 6 percent of French women, had multiple sex partners (two or more) in the past 12 months and therefore were at higher risk of HIV infection. Other results from this study will be discussed in later chapters of this book.

A similar British survey has been conducted by Anne Johnson and her colleagues (1992), yielding data for 18,876 men and women aged 16 to 59, living in England, Wales, and Scotland. The data indicated that, for the entire sample, 14 percent of the men and 7 percent of the women had multiple sex partners in the past 12 months, figures quite similar to the French survey. However, when one looks just at 16- to 24-year-olds, 27 percent of the men and 16 percent of the women had two or more partners in the past 12 months, a considerably greater number.

STUDIES OF SPECIAL POPULATIONS

In addition to the large-scale studies of the U.S. population discussed earlier, many studies of special populations have been done. Two examples are given here: the George and Weiler study of sexuality in middle and late life, and the Bell, Weinberg, and Hammersmith study of homosexuals and heterosexuals.

George and Weiler: Sexuality in Middle and Late Life

Linda George and Stephen Weiler of Duke University conducted an important study of the sexuality of middle-aged and elderly persons (George & Weiler, 1981). With the "graying of America," there is increased interest in the behavior, including the sexual behavior, of older persons. Previous research, such as Kinsey's, had shown substantial declines in sexual expression among the elderly.

George and Weiler studied a broadly based sample of volunteers from the community. One important feature of their study is that they used a longitudinal design to study developmental changes with aging. Developmental researchers typically use one of two kinds of designs: cross-sectional or longitudinal. With the *cross-sectional design,* one studies several samples of people of different ages, collecting all the data within a short period of time. There is a problem with the cross-sectional design, however. Suppose we find that the average frequency of intercourse is twice a month in a sample of 50-year-olds, and once a month in a sample of 80-year-olds. Can we conclude that sexual activity declines in that 30-year period? No, we can't. The reason is that we had two different samples of subjects at the two different ages. Those two samples may differ in many ways other than their age. For example, the 80-year-olds grew up 30 years before the 50-year-olds, and socialization about sexuality might have been much more rigid during childhood for the 80-year-olds. The way to overcome this problem is by doing *longitudinal research,* in which the same subjects are studied repeatedly over the years. Obviously this kind of research takes considerably more time than cross-sectional research, but it allows the investigator to reach conclusions about actual changes in people's lives as they age.

George and Weiler were also careful to restrict their sample to 278 people who were married throughout the four testing times of the study (1969, 1971, 1973, and 1975). This is an important control because widows often cease engaging in sexual intercourse simply because no partner is available.

George and Weiler's results indicated very little decline in sexual activity across the 6 years of the study, in contrast to the findings of previous researchers. Probably George and Weiler got different results because of their longitudinal design. On the other hand, they looked at only a 6-year period. If they had extended the study to 10 or 20 years (an ambitious project), they might have obtained different results.

3.2

Politics Versus Sex Research

Although major well-sampled surveys of adult sexual behavior have recently been published, we do not have comparable studies of teenage sexuality, and we need them. Many of the surveys we have tend to be out-of-date (the Kantner and Zelnik studies) or poorly sampled (studies of college students). The surveys that use good sampling techniques typically ask only a limited set of questions about sex, or are surveys of adults only. As a result, we have a knowledge gap. Scientists do not know with any degree of accuracy, for example, what percentage of teenage males in the United States have engaged in homosexual interactions. We cannot hope to educate people about sex, much less fight the AIDS epidemic, with such a glaring lack of information.

Recognizing this serious problem, the National Institutes of Health (NIH) decided to fund a major survey of teenage sexuality. The grant was won by a team of researchers from the University of North Carolina, headed by Dr. Ronald Rinfuss and co-directed by the eminent sex researcher Dr. Richard Udry. The research was a five-year project studying teenagers' sexual behavior, the focus of which was a survey of 24,000 children in grades 7 through 11

whose parents had given consent to participate. The project had been evaluated by scientific review panels at the NIH and had received glowing reviews. Funding was awarded in May 1991.

Then the Secretary of Health and Human Services (HHS), Louis Sullivan, a George Bush appointee, heard about the study, as did members of Congress. NIH is under the jurisdiction of Health and Human Services. Senator Jesse Helms (R-NC) and Representative William Dannemeyer (R-CA) quickly initiated legislation to force NIH to stop funding the study. Senator Helms said that the real purpose of the study "is to 'cook the books,' so to speak, in terms of presenting 'scientific facts'— in order to do what? To legitimize homosexual lifestyles of course." Meanwhile Sullivan, seeing the direction the political winds were blowing, terminated the study. This was the first time in the history of federal funding for scientific research that a political appointee, the Secretary of HHS, interfered with the scientific process and cancelled a study that had met the high standards of the scientific peer review process and been approved.

Bell, Weinberg, and Hammersmith: Homosexuals and Heterosexuals

Under the sponsorship of the Kinsey Institute at Indiana University, Alan Bell, Martin Weinberg, and Sue Hammersmith conducted a major survey of homosexuals and heterosexuals, reporting the results in their book *Sexual Preference* (1981). As the title of the book implies, their goal was to find out what factors determine people's sexual preference, whether heterosexual or homosexual.

The data came from face-to-face interviews with 979 homosexual women and men and 477 heterosexual women and men, all living in the San Francisco Bay Area. Although the sampling has an obvious geographical limitation, Bell and his col-

Card 11

97. Look at the sentences below and decide if you do that activity
    for your best female friend.

    A.   Encourage her to learn about sex.

        1   Yes.

        2   No.   72

    B.   Teach her things about sex.

        1   Yes.

        2   No.   73

    C.   Try to set sexual rules for her.

        1   Yes.

        2   No.   74

    D.   Encourage her to be more sexually active.

        1   Yes.

        2   No.   75

    E.   Encourage her to be less sexually active.

        1   Yes.

        2   No.   76

End Card 11

(a)

(b)

FIGURE 3.4
*(a) Dr. J. Richard Udry, co-director of the questionnaire study of teenage sexuality that was
canceled during the Bush administration by then-Secretary of Health and Human Services,
Louis Sullivan. (b) A section from the questionaire.*

These actions raise a number of serious questions.
How can we fight the AIDS epidemic when we lack
current, accurate information on teenagers' sexual
behavior? Can a federal agency arbitrarily terminate
a contract it has made with a university?

Should politicians be permitted to interfere with the
integrity of the scientific process?

Source: Charrow, Robert P. (1991). (November). Sex, politics, and science. *The Journal of NIH Research, 3,* 80–83.

leagues justified their choice of working in the Bay Area as permitting them to obtain
a large sample of homosexuals who could be open enough to cooperate and participate in the research. In order to contact prospective subjects, recruiters—half of
them gay themselves—visited locations such as gay bars; recruiting was also done
by posters, ads in local newspapers, television spots, and referral by persons already
interviewed for the study. Heterosexual subjects were obtained by a random sampling technique.

    The interview contained 200 questions and took three to five hours. The ques-
tions focused on a wide variety of events in the subject's childhood and adolescence,
the goal being to use the responses to test the various theories that have been
proposed to explain why people become homosexual—or heterosexual. In several

cases, two questions on the same topic appeared at different places in the interview, so that an individual's answers could be checked for reliability. Some of the respondents were reinterviewed six months after the original interview, again to check for the reliability of the self-reports. Bell and his colleagues reported no specific results of these reliability checks, but they appeared to be satisfied with the results.

They used a statistical technique called path analysis to analyze the data. I would have to go too far afield from our discussion of sexuality to explain path analysis here, but briefly, it is a statistical technique that allows one to make conclusions about causal factors from correlational data. Bell and his colleagues wanted to test various hypotheses about experiences and environmental factors that might cause homosexuality, yet their survey data were clearly correlational, so path analysis was a good solution. The results of this study will be discussed in detail in Chapter 15; to summarize them briefly here, they found that the usual environmental factors that have been used to explain homosexuality—parent-child relationship, parental identification, early heterosexual trauma—were not confirmed by their data.

In evaluating this study, one can see that it was done more carefully and according to better scientific standards than many other surveys. The interviewing seems to have met the same high standards as the earlier Kinsey report. There were internal checks for reliability, although the method of self-report was still used, and there might have been problems of memory for events that occurred years ago, in childhood. Although the sampling was done carefully, it is still problematic. The sample could not be considered random or representative of all gays in the United States. It omits all those who are outside the "San Francisco scene." And it omits covert gays, those who do not frequent bars or parties and are not willing to be open enough to participate in a research interview. This research raises the point that studies of special populations defined by their sexual behavior—such as homosexuals or bisexuals or fetishists—are essentially impossible to do in any kind of representative fashion. It is impossible to identify all the people in the population in the first place, and therefore it is impossible to sample them properly. In contrast, samples of the general population, such as Kinsey's, are more feasible to obtain, though not easy.

LABORATORY STUDIES USING DIRECT OBSERVATIONS OF SEXUAL BEHAVIOR

The numerous problems associated with using self-reports of sexual behavior in scientific research have been discussed. The major alternative to using self-reports is to make direct observations of sexual behavior in the laboratory. These direct observations overcome the major problems of self-reports: purposeful distortion, inaccurate memory, and inability of subjects to estimate correctly or describe certain aspects of their behavior. The pioneering example of this approach is Masters and Johnson's work on the physiology of sexual response. By the 1980s research of this kind was being conducted in many laboratories across the country (Rosen & Beck, 1988).

Masters and Johnson: The Physiology of Sexual Response

William Masters began his research on the physiology of sexual response in 1954 (Brecher & Brecher, 1966). No one had ever studied human sexual behavior in the laboratory before. Thus Masters had to develop all the necessary research techniques from scratch. He began by interviewing 118 female prostitutes (as well as 27 male prostitutes working for a homosexual clientele). They gave him important preliminary data in which they "described many methods for elevating and controlling sexual tensions and demonstrated innumerable variations in stimulative techniques," some of which were useful in the later program of therapy for sexual dysfunction.

Meanwhile, Masters began setting up his laboratory and equipping it with the necessary instruments: an electrocardiograph to measure changes in heart rate over the sexual cycle, an electromyograph to measure muscular contractions in the body during sexual response, and a pH meter to measure the acidity of the vagina during the various stages of sexual response.

Sampling

Masters made a major breakthrough when he decided that it was possible to recruit normal subjects from the general population and have them engage in sexual behavior in the laboratory, where their behavior and physiological responses could be carefully observed and measured. This approach had never been used before, as even the daring Kinsey had settled for subjects' verbal reports of their behavior.

Most of the subjects were obtained from the local community simply by word of mouth. Masters let it be known in the medical school and university community that he needed volunteer subjects for laboratory studies of human sexual response. Some subjects volunteered because of their belief in the importance of the research, and others were referred by their own physicians. Some, of course, came out of curiosity or because they were exhibitionists; they were weeded out in the initial interviews. Subjects were paid for their hours in the laboratory, as is typical in medical research, and so many young medical students and graduate students participated because it was a way to earn money. Some of the subjects were women who had been patients of Dr. Masters. When they heard he needed volunteers, they wanted to help, and they brought their husbands along as well.

Initially, all subjects were given detailed interviews by the Masters and Johnson team. Subjects who had histories of emotional problems or who seemed uncomfortable with the topic of sex either failed to come back after this interview or were eliminated even if they were willing to proceed. Subjects were also assured that the anonymity and confidentiality of their participation would be protected carefully.

In all, 694 people participated in the laboratory studies reported in *Human Sexual Response*. The men ranged in age from 21 to 89, while the women ranged from 18 to 78. A total of 276 married couples participated, as well as 106 women and 36 men who were unmarried when they entered the research program. The unmarried subjects were helpful mainly in the studies that did not require sexual intercourse, for example, studies of the ejaculatory mechanism in males and of the effects of sexual arousal on the positioning of the diaphragm in the vagina.

Certainly the group of people Masters and Johnson studied were not a random sample of the population of the United States. In fact, one might imagine that people who would agree to participate in such research would be rather unusual. The data indicate that they were more educated than the general population, and the sample was mostly white, with only a few blacks participating. Paying the subjects probably helped since this attracted some participants who simply needed the money. The sample omitted two notable types of people: those who are not sexually experienced or do not respond to sexual stimulation and those who are unwilling to have their sexual behavior studied in the laboratory. Therefore, the results Masters and Johnson obtained might not generalize to such people.

Just exactly how critical is this sampling problem to the validity of the research? Masters and Johnson were not particularly concerned about sampling because of their assumption that the processes they were studying are normative; that is, they work in essentially the same way in all people. This assumption is commonly made in medical research. For example, a researcher who is studying the digestive process does not worry that the sample is composed of all medical students, since the assumption is that digestion works the same way in all human beings. If this assumption is also true for the physiology of sexual response, then all people respond similarly, and it does not matter that the sample is not random. Whether this assumption is correct remains to be seen (see Chapter 9 for further critiques). The sampling problem, however, does mean that Masters and Johnson cannot make statistical conclusions on the basis of their research; for example they cannot say that X percent of all women have multiple orgasms. Any percentages they calculate would be specific to their subjects and could not be generalized to the rest of the population.

In defense of their sampling techniques, even if they had identified an initial probability sample, they would still almost surely have had a very high refusal rate, probably higher than in survey research, and the probability sample would have been ruined. At present, this seems to be an unsolvable problem in this type of research.

Data Collection Techniques

After they were accepted for the project, subjects then proceeded to the laboratory phase of the study. First, they had a "practice session," in which they engaged in sexual activity in the laboratory in complete privacy, with no data being recorded and with no researchers present. The purpose of this was to allow the subjects to become comfortable with engaging in sexual behavior in a laboratory setting. Interestingly, males had a higher "failure rate" (inability to have orgasm) under these conditions than females did.

The physical responses of the subjects were then recorded during sexual intercourse, masturbation, and "artificial coition." Masters and Johnson made an important technical advance with the development of the artificial coition technique. It involves the woman stimulating herself with an artificial penis constructed of clear plastic; it is powered by an electric motor, and the woman can adjust the depth and frequency of the thrust. There is a light and a recording apparatus inside the artificial penis, and thus motion picture records can be made of the changes occurring inside the vagina.

Measures such as these avoid problems of distortion possible in self-reports. They also answer much different questions. That is, it would be impossible from such measures to tell whether the person had had any homosexual experiences or how frequently he or she masturbated. Instead, they ascertain how the body responds to sexual stimulation, with a kind of accuracy and detail that would be impossible to obtain through self-reports.

Two problems also deserve mention. One has to do with the problems of laboratory studies: Do people respond the same sexually in the laboratory as they do in the privacy of their own homes?

Ethics

Masters and Johnson were attentive to the ethical implications of their research. They were careful to use the principle of informed consent. Potential subjects were given detailed explanations of the kinds of things they would be required to do in the research, and they were given ample opportunity at all stages to withdraw from the research if they so desired. Further, Masters and Johnson eliminated from the subject pool people who appeared too anxious or distressed during the preliminary interviews.

It is also possible that participating in the research itself might have been harmful in some way to the subjects, perhaps damaging their future ability to respond sexually. Masters and Johnson were particularly concerned with the long-term effects on their subjects of participating in the research. Accordingly, they made follow-up contacts with the subjects at five-year intervals. In no case did a subject report developing a sexual dysfunction (for example, impotence). In fact, many of the couples reported specific ways in which participating in the research enriched their marriages. Thus the available data seem to indicate that such research does not harm the subjects and may in some ways benefit them, not to mention the benefit to society that results from gaining information in such an important area.

In sum, direct observations of sexual behavior of the type done by Masters and Johnson have some distinct advantages but also some disadvantages, compared with survey-type research. The research avoids the problems of self-reports and is capable of answering much more detailed physiological questions than self-reports could. But the research is costly and time-consuming, making large samples impossible; further, a high refusal rate is probably inevitable, and thus probability samples are impossible.

Masters and Johnson: Homosexual Behavior

Even more innovative than the Masters and Johnson study of the physiology of sexual response was their study of homosexual behavior, *Homosexuality in Perspective* (1979). Essentially, they repeated the 1966 study, but this time with gays as subjects. That is, gay men and lesbian women volunteers came into the laboratory and engaged in sexual acts; their behavior was observed, and their physiological responses were recorded. The findings of this study are discussed in Chapter 15.

PARTICIPANT-OBSERVER STUDIES

Participant-observer study: A research method in which the scientist becomes part of the community to be studied and makes observations from inside the community.

A research method used by anthropologists and sociologists is the **participant-observer** technique. In this type of research, the scientist actually becomes a part of the community to be studied, and she or he makes observations from inside the community. In the study of sexual behavior, the researcher may be able to get direct observations of sexual behavior combined with interview data.

Examples of this type of research are studies of sexual behavior in other cultures, such as those done in Mangaia, Mehinaku, and Inis Beag, which were discussed in Chapter 1. Two other examples are Laud Humphreys's study of the tearoom trade and Bartell's study of swinging.

Humphreys: The Tearoom Trade

Sociologist Laud Humphreys (1970) did a participant-observer study of impersonal homosexual sex in public places such as rest rooms. The study is discussed in detail in Focus 15.2 in Chapter 15. Briefly, Humphreys acted as a lookout while men engaged in homosexual acts in public rest rooms ("tearooms"); his job was to sound a warning if police or other intruders approached. This permitted Humphreys to make direct observations of the sexual behavior. He also got the license-plate numbers of the men involved, traced them, and later interviewed them in their homes under the pretext of taking a routine survey.

Humphreys obtained a wealth of information from the study, but in so doing he violated most of the ethical principles of behavioral research. He had no informed consent from his subjects; they were never even aware of the fact that they were subjects in research, much less of the nature of the research. Thus this study has been quite controversial.

Bartell: Swinging

Anthropologist Gilbert Bartell (1970) did a participant-observer study of swinging (a married couple having sex with another person or another couple). He and his wife contacted swinging couples by responding to ads that swingers had placed in newspapers. They took the role of "baby swingers"—a couple who are swinging for the first time—but they also state that they did not misrepresent themselves and informed all subjects that they were anthropologists interested in knowing more about swinging. In addition, they attended a large number of swingers' parties and large-scale group sexual activities and made observations in that context.

Sampling is often a problem in studies of special groups such as this one, since it is difficult to get any kind of a random sample of people who engage in a particular kind of sexual behavior. In this particular case the problem was made somewhat less difficult because many such contacts are made through newspaper ads, to which the researchers could respond. This method permitted studying only current swingers; it did not allow sampling of people who had engaged in swinging but had stopped for one reason or another (Kirby, 1977). There is also some question as to how honest the respondents were, since swingers are doing something that they take great pains to hide; in fact, Bartell cited specific examples of distortion in reports of information on such things as age and interests.

Ethically, it was easy to preserve anonymity, since swingers go to great lengths to preserve their own anonymity; even with one another, they use first names only. Bartell obtained some kind of informed consent, since he told his subjects that he was doing research; in other, similar studies, however, researchers have posed as swingers, have not divulged the fact that data were being collected, and therefore have seriously misled their subjects.

EXPERIMENTAL SEX RESEARCH

All the studies discussed so far had one thing in common: they all were studies of people's sexual behavior as it occurs naturally, conducted by means of either self-reports or direct observations. Data obtained from such studies are correlational in nature; that is, at best they can tell us that certain factors are related. They cannot tell us what *causes* various aspects of sexual behavior.

Correlational study: A study in which the researcher does not manipulate variables but rather studies naturally occurring relationships (correlations) among variables.

As an example, Kinsey found that women who masturbated to orgasm before marriage were more likely to have a high consistency of orgasm in marriage than women who did not. From this it would be tempting to conclude that practice in masturbating to orgasm causes women to have more orgasms in heterosexual sex. Unfortunately, this is not a legitimate conclusion to draw from the data, since many other factors might also explain the results. For example, it could be that some women have a higher sex drive than others; this high sex drive causes them to masturbate and also to have orgasms in heterosexual sex. Therefore, the most we can conclude is that masturbation experience is related to (or correlated with) orgasm consistency in marital sex.

An alternative method in behavioral research that allows us to determine the causes of various aspects of behavior is the experiment. According to the technical definition of "experiment," one factor must be manipulated while all other factors are held constant. Thus any differences among the groups of people who received different treatments on that one factor can be said to be caused by that factor. For obvious reasons, most experimental research is conducted in the laboratory.

One example of experimental sex research is Julia Heiman's study of male and female responses to erotic materials, which is discussed in Chapter 14. As an example of experimental sex research here, let us consider a study of the effects of sex education about masturbation on masturbation attitudes, knowledge, and behavior (Lo Presto et al., 1985). In this study, 198 males who were high school sophomores enrolled in a biology course, were randomly assigned to participate in a 40-minute seminar on masturbation (the experimental group) or a seminar on a different topic (the control group). The faculty who taught the masturbation seminar stressed that masturbation is very common among teenagers, challenged myths about masturbation (e.g., that it is a sign of homosexuality), presented masturbation as an acceptable form of sexual expression that carries no risk of pregnancy or sexually transmitted disease, and so on. Two weeks later, the participants were asked to complete a survey that measured their attitudes toward masturbation, their factual knowledge about masturbation, their guilt feelings about masturbation, and their actual self-reported masturbation.

In the language of experimental design, the *independent variable* (manipulated variable) was the seminar to which students were assigned (on masturbation or another topic). There were actually four *dependent variables* (the measured variables): attitudes toward masturbation, knowledge of facts about masturbation, guilt about masturbation, and self-reported masturbation. Notice that, following principles for a good experimental design, the researchers held all other factors constant—for example, the students were all from the same school, were taking the same course, were approximately the same age, and were the same gender.

The results indicated that those in the experimental group (compared with the control group) had significantly more positive attitudes about masturbation following the seminar, and had significantly greater factual knowledge about masturbation. On the other hand, there were no differences between experimental and control groups in guilt about masturbation or in actual masturbation behavior. Because the research design was experimental, we can make causal inferences. That is, we can say that the seminar had an effect on attitudes and knowledge about masturbation. It had no effect on masturbation behavior.

Experimental sex research permits us to make much more powerful statements about the causes of various kinds of sexual phenomena and to address issues that have important implications for public policy. For example, those who oppose sex education in the schools often claim that telling students about a particular behavior will make them want to try it. The experiment described here refutes such a view because, although there were differences in attitudes and knowledge between the experimental and control groups, there were no differences in masturbation behavior. On the other hand, much of the experimental sex research, including the study described here, still relies on self-reports. Experimental sex research is time-consuming and costly, and it can generally be done only on small samples of subjects. Sometimes in their efforts to control all variables except the independent variable, researchers control too much; for example, in this experiment gender was controlled by using only male subjects. We are left not knowing the effects for females of instruction about masturbation, something I am rather curious about. As a remedy, the researchers could have included both males and females in their research and then made gender one of the factors in the design. Finally, experiments cannot address some of the most interesting, but most complex, questions in the field of sexual behavior, such as what factors cause people to develop heterosexual or homosexual orientations.

SOME STATISTICAL CONCEPTS

Kinsey pioneered the approach of using statistics to describe people's sexual behavior, an approach that is now quite common. Therefore, before you can understand the reports of sex research, you must understand some basic statistical concepts.

Average

Suppose we get data from a sample of married couples on how many times per week they have sexual intercourse. How can we summarize the data? One way to do this is to compute some average value for all the subjects; this will tell us how often, on the average, these people have intercourse. In sex research, the number that is usually calculated is either the mean or the median; both of these give us an indication of approximately where the average value for that group of subjects is. The **mean** is simply the average of the scores of all the subjects. The *median* is the score that splits the sample in half, with half the respondents falling below that score and half falling above.

Mean: The average of respondents' scores.

Variability

In addition to having an indication of the average for the sample of respondents, it is also interesting to know how much variability there was from one respondent to the next in the numbers reported. That is, it is one thing to say that the average

FIGURE 3.5
Two hypothetical graphs of the frequency of intercourse for married couples in a sample. In both, the average frequency is about 3 times per week, but in (a) there is little variability (almost everyone has a frequency between 2 and 4 times per week) whereas in (b) there is great variability (the frequency ranges from 0 to 15 or 20 times per week). The graph for most sexual behavior looks like (b); there is great variability.

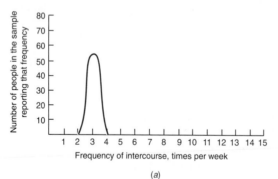

(a)

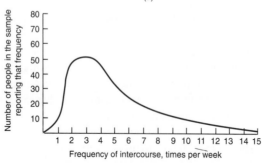

(b)

married couple in a sample had intercourse 3 times per week, with a range in the sample from 2 to 4 times per week, and it is quite another thing to say that the average was 3 times per week, with a range from 0 to 15 times per week. In both cases the mean is the same, but in the first there is little variability, and in the second there is a great deal of variability. These two alternatives are shown graphically in Figure 3.5. There is great variability in virtually all kinds of sexual behavior.

Average Versus Normal

It is interesting and informative to report the average frequency of a particular sexual behavior, but this also introduces the danger that people will confuse "average" with "normal." That is, there is a tendency, when reading a statistic like "The average person has intercourse twice per week," to think of one's own sexual behavior, compare it with that average, and then conclude that one is abnormal if one differs much from the average. If you read that statistic and your frequency of intercourse is only once a week, you may begin to worry that you are undersexed or that you are not getting as much as you should. If you are having intercourse seven times per week, you might begin worrying that you are oversexed or that you are wearing out your sex organs. Such conclusions are a mistake, first because they can make you miserable and second because there is so much variablity in sexual behavior that any behavior (or frequency or length of time) within a wide range is perfectly normal. Don't confuse average with normal.

Incidence Versus Frequency

Incidence: The percentage of people giving a particular response.

Frequency: How often a person does something.

In sex statistics, the terms "incidence" and "frequency" are often used. Incidence refers to the percentage of people who have engaged in a certain behavior. Frequency refers to how often people do something. Thus we might say that the incidence of masturbation among males is 92 percent (92 percent of all males masturbate at least once in their lives), while the average frequency of masturbation among males between the ages of 16 and 20 is about once per week.

A closely related concept is that of cumulative incidence (or accumulative incidence). If we consider a sexual behavior according to the age at which each person in the sample first engaged in it, the *cumulative incidence* refers to the percentage of people who have engaged in that behavior before a certain age. Thus the cumulative incidence of masturbation in males might be 10 percent by age 11, 25 percent by age 12, 80 percent by age 15, and 95 percent by age 20. Graphs of cumulative incidence always begin in the lower left-hand corner and move toward the upper right-hand corner. An example of a cumulative-incidence curve is shown in Figure 3.6.

FIGURE 3.6
A cumulative-incidence curve for masturbation in males. From the graph, you can read off the percentage of males who report having masturbated by a given age. For example, about 82 percent have masturbated to orgasm by age 15.

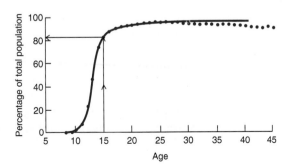

FIGURE 3.7

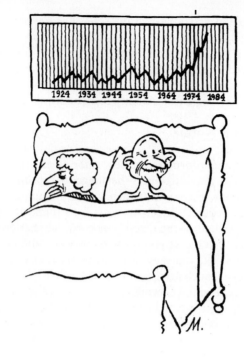

Correlation

In this chapter the concept of correlation has already been mentioned several times—for example, test-retest reliability is measured by the correlation between people's answer to a question with their answer to the same question a week or two later—and the concept of correlation will reappear in later chapters of the book.

The term "correlation" is used by laypeople in contexts such as the following: "There seems to be a correlation here between how warm the days are and how fast the corn is growing." But what do statisticians mean by the term "correlation"? A correlation is a number that measures the relationship between two variables. A correlation can be positive or negative. A positive correlation occurs when there is a positive relationship between the two variables, that is, people who have high scores on one variable tend to have high scores on the other variable; low scores go with low scores. A negative correlation occurs when there is an opposite relationship between the two variables; that is, people with high scores on one variable tend to have low scores on the other variable. We might want to know, for example, whether there is a correlation between the number of years a couple has been married and how frequently they have sexual intercourse. In this case we might expect that there would be a negative correlation, and that is just what researchers have found. That is, the *greater* the number of years of marriage, the *lower* the frequency of intercourse. As another example, we might want to know whether there is a correlation between people's sexual attitudes and their sexual behavior, specifically whether people who hold more permissive attitudes about premarital sex have more premarital partners. In this case we expect a positive correlation in the sense that the people who score high on the measure of permissive attitudes are expected to have more partners and that people who score low on the measure of permissiveness are expected to have few partners.

Correlations range between +1.0 and −1.0. A correlation of +1.0 indicates a perfect positive relationship between two variables, in the sense that the person in the sample who scores highest on one variable also has the highest score on the other

Correlation: A number that measures the relationship between two variables.

variable, the person with the second highest score on the first variable also has the second highest score on the other variable, and so on. A correlation of 0 indicates no relationship between the two variables. Knowing a person's score on one variable tells us nothing about whether the person will have a high or low score on the other variable. Positive correlations between 0 and +1.0—for example, +.62—say that the relationship is positive but not a perfect relationship. A correlation of −1.0 means that there is a perfect negative correlation between the two variables. That is, the person in the sample with the highest score on variable X has the lowest score on variable Y, the person with the second highest score on variable X has the second lowest score on variable Y, and so on.

Returning to the example of test-retest reliability discussed earlier in the chapter, suppose we administer a questionnaire to a sample of adults. One of the questions asks, "How many times did you masturbate to orgasm during the month of September?" We ask this question of the sample on October 1 and again on October 8. If each person in the sample gives us exactly the same answer on October 1 and on October 8, the correlation between the two variables (the number given on October 1 and the number given on October 8) would be +1.0 and the test-retest reliability would be a perfect +1.0. In fact, test-retest reliabilities for questions about sex typically range between +.60 and +.90, indicating that people's answers on the two occasions are not identical but are very similar.

Summary

This chapter reviewed the major methods that have been used in sex research and the problems and merits associated with each; the goal was to help readers better evaluate the sex research that has been done and to aid them in developing skills for understanding and evaluating the sex research that will be done in the future.

Ideally, sex research should employ random sampling or probability sampling techniques; this is generally not possible because some people refuse to participate in sex research.

Large-scale surveys of sexual behavior generally rely on subjects' self-reports, which may be inaccurate because of purposeful distortion, problems of memory, or inability to estimate some of the information requested. Direct observations of sexual behavior avoid these problems, but they lead to an even more restricted sample of subjects. They also answer questions that are somewhat different from those answered by surveys.

In all behavioral research, the ethical principles of informed consent and protection from harm must be observed, although historically some sex researchers have not done this.

One major sex survey was Kinsey's large-scale interview study of the sexual behavior of Americans, done during the 1940s. Other large surveys have been done, including one through *McCall's* magazine; the samples in magazine surveys, however, are so restricted that we cannot draw any general conclusions from them. Several surveys have used probability samples: the Kantner and Zelnik study of young unmarried women, the National AIDS Behavioral Surveys, and the ACSF French study.

Studies of special populations include George and Weiler's study of sexuality in later life and the Bell, Weinberg, and Hammersmith study of homosexuals and heterosexuals.

In participant-observer studies, the scientist becomes a part of the community to be studied, and he or she uses a combination of direct observations and interviewing. Examples are studies of sexual behavior in other cultures, Humphreys's study of the tearoom trade, and Bartell's study of swinging.

In experimental sex research, the goal is to discover what factors cause various aspects of sexual behavior. There is an independent variable and a dependent variable.

The following statistical terms were introduced: "average," "variability," "incidence," "frequency," and "correlation."

Review Questions

1. Random sampling or probability sampling is important in doing a good sex survey, but these techniques have been used in only a few studies. True or false?

2. Sex researchers can study only those subjects who agree to participate. This introduces the problem of _____.

3. Purposeful distortion and memory problems may create problems with the reliability of self-reports in sex research. True or false?

4. One alternative to self-reports that helps overcome some of their problems is the method of _____, which was used by Masters and Johnson.

5. Kinsey's sampling techniques were excellent; his interviewing techniques were also excellent. True or false?

6. The most questionable stastistic in the Kinsey report was the incidence of homosexuality. True or false?

7. Magazine surveys, such as those conducted by *Psychology Today* and *McCall's,* provide a good, rich source of information about human sexuality. True or false?

8. _____ is the term for the type of study in which the researcher becomes a part of the community being studied and thus observes it from the inside, as in the studies of swingers.

9. The ACSF Investigators' representative sample of French adults' sexuality would properly be termed an experiment. True or false?

10. If someone says "Approximately 67 percent of people engage in premarital intercourse," this is a statement about frequency. True or false?

(The answers to all review questions are at the end of the book, beginning on page 731)

Questions for Thought, Discussion, and Debate

1. Find a recent sex survey in a magazine. Evaluate the quality of the study, using concepts you have learned in this chapter.

2. Of the research techniques in this chapter—surveys, laboratory studies using direct observations, participant-observer studies, experiments—which do you think is best for learning about human sexuality? Why?

Suggestions for Further Reading

Byrne, Donn, & Kelley, Kathryn (Eds.). (1986). *Alternative approaches to the study of sexual behavior.* Hillsdale, NJ: Lawrence Erlbaum Publishers. This book provides up-to-date descriptions of current methods of sex research.

Catania, Joseph A., et al. (1990). Methodological problems in AIDS behavioral research: Influences on measurement error and participation bias in studies of sexual behavior. *Psychological Bulletin,* **108,** 339–362. This article takes up where the present chapter leaves off and offers an excellent analysis of methodological issues in sex research.

Harry, Joseph. (1986). Sampling gay men. *Journal of Sex Research,* **22,** 21–34. This article provides an interesting discussion of some of the methodological problems that occur when sampling special populations of subjects, such as gay men.

Sexual Anatomy

Chapter Highlights

As souls unbodied, bodies unclothed must be,
To taste whole joys. *

All the body image problems are just heightened when you narrow
your sights to your genitals. Even people who don't feel particularly
sensitive about how they look to the man on the street feel shy or
nervous when confronting their own or another's sexual anatomy.
The endless taboos on sex in this society and the misguided
romanticism of the airbrush mentality keep people from really
looking at their sex organs. . . . To integrate your sex into yourself in
a positive way, you have to have a clear picture of your external
genitals. You also have to know what goes on inside your body
sexually.†

One outgrowth of the feminist movement, the women's health movement, has emphasized that women need to know more about their bodies. Actually, that is a good principle for everyone to follow. The current trend is away from the elitist view that only a select group of people—physicians—should understand the functioning of the body and toward the view that everyone needs more information about his or her own body. The purpose of this chapter is to provide basic information about the structure and functions of the parts of the body that are involved in sexuality and reproduction. Some readers may anticipate that this will be a boring exercise. Everyone, after all, knows what a penis is and what a vagina is. But even today, we find some bright college students who think a woman's urine passes out through her vagina. And how many of you know what the epididymis and the seminiferous tubules are? If you don't know, keep reading. You may even find out a few interesting things about the penis and the vagina that you were not aware of.

FEMALE SEXUAL ORGANS

The female sexual organs can be classified into two categories: the *external organs* and the *internal organs*.

External Organs

The external genitals of the female consist of the clitoris, the mons pubis, the inner lips, the outer lips, and the vaginal opening (see Figure 4.1). Collectively, they are known as the **vulva** ("crotch"; other terms such as "cunt" and "pussy" may refer either to the vulva or to the vagina, and some ethnic groups use "cock" for the vulva—slang, alas, is not so precise as scientific language). "Vulva" is a wonderful term but, unfortunately, it tends to be underused—the term, that is.

The Clitoris

The clitoris *(klit'-or-is)* is a sensitive organ that is exceptionally important in female sexual response. It is a knob of tissue situated externally, in front of the vaginal opening and the urethral opening. Like the penis, the clitoris is composed of two parts: the *shaft* and the tip or *glans* (see Figure 4.2). The glans is visible, protruding like a small lump. The shaft disappears into the body beneath the *clitoral hood,* a sheath of tissue that passes around the clitoris and is an extension of the inner lips.

As will be discussed in Chapter 5, female sexual organs and male sexual organs develop from similar tissue before birth; thus we can speak of the organs of one gender as being *homologous* (in the sense of developing from the same source) to the organs of the other gender. The female's clitoris is homologous to the tip portion (glans) of the male's penis; that is, both develop from the same embryonic tissue.

Vulva (VULL-vuh): The collective term for the external genitals of the female.

Clitoris (KLIT-or-is): A small, highly sensitive sexual organ in the female, found in front of the vaginal entrance.

FIGURE 4.1
The vulva: The external genitals of the female.

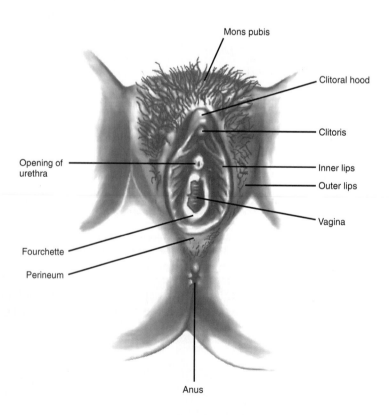

Mons pubis

Clitoral hood

Clitoris

Opening of urethra

Inner lips

Outer lips

Vagina

Fourchette

Perineum

Anus

FIGURE 4.2
*The position of the
Bartholin glands and the
nerve structure of the
clitoris.*

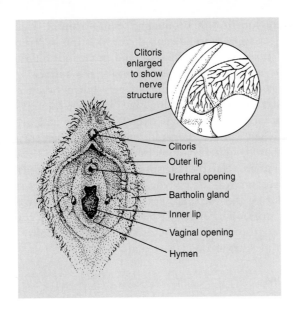

The clitoris has a structure similar to that of the penis in that both have a shaft and a glans. The clitoris varies in size from one woman to the next, much as the penis varies in size from man to man. Also, the clitoris, like the penis, is erectile. Its erection is possible because its internal structure contains *corpora cavernosa* that fill with blood, as the similar structures in the penis do. The corpora cavernosa and the mechanism of erection will be considered in more detail in the discussion of the male sexual organs. Like the penis, the clitoris has a rich supply of nerve endings, making it very sensitive to stroking (see Figure 4.2). It is more sensitive to erotic stimulation than any other part of the female body.

The clitoris is unique in that it is the only part of the sexual anatomy with no known reproductive function. All the other sexual organs serve dual sexual-reproductive functions. For example, not only is the vagina used for sexual intercourse, but it also receives the sperm and serves as the passageway through which the baby travels during childbirth. The penis not only produces sexual arousal and pleasure but also is responsible for ejaculation and impregnation. The clitoris clearly has an

FIGURE 4.3
*The shape of the vulva
varies widely from one
woman to the next.*

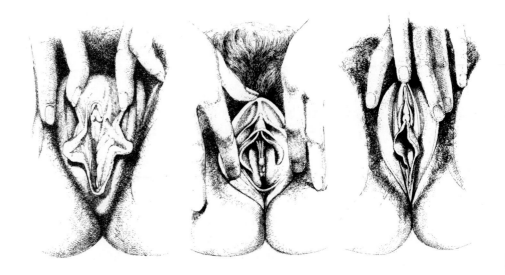

important function in producing sexual arousal. Unlike the other sexual organs, however, it appears to have no direct function in reproduction.

At various times in history and in various cultures, the clitoris has been subjected to mutilation. *Clitoridectomy*[1]—the surgical removal of the clitoris, also known as female circumcision—is rare but is practiced in the Middle East and in some parts of Africa and Indonesia (Lightfoot-Klein, 1989). A 1980s survey of 1150 Nigerian women found that over 90 percent had been circumcised in childhood, usually when 7 to 10 days old; and over 90 percent will continue the practice by having their daughters circumcised (Ebomoyi, 1987). Some experts believe that these mutilations are related to the spread of AIDS among African women (Hosken, 1988). Clitoridectomy was also advocated and practiced by some physicians in the United States during the Victorian era, ostensibly to cure women who were "compulsive masturbators." The existence of the practice in this country is a commentary on the repressive attitudes of the Victorians toward sexuality and their particularly repressive attitudes toward female sexuality.

Female circumcision: Amputation of the clitoris.

The Mons

In outward appearance, the more obvious parts of the vulva are the mons pubis, the inner lips, and the outer lips. The mons pubis (also called the *mons* or the *mons veneris,* for "mountain of Venus") is the rounded, fatty pad of tissue, covered with pubic hair, at the front of the body. It lies on top of the pubic bones (which come together in the center at a point called the *pubic symphysis*) and is the most visible part of the female sexual organs.

Mons pubis (PYOO-bis): The fatty pad of tissue under the public hair.

The Labia

The outer lips (or *labia majora,* for "major lips") are rounded pads of tissue lying along both sides of the vaginal opening; they are covered with pubic hair. The inner lips (or *labia minora,* for "minor lips") are two hairless folds of skin lying between the major lips and running right along the edge of the vaginal opening. Sometimes they are folded over, concealing the vaginal opening until they are spread apart. The inner lips extend forward and come together in front, forming the clitoral hood. The inner and outer lips are well supplied with nerve endings and thus are also important in sexual stimulation and arousal.

Outer lips: Fatty pads of tissue lying on either side of the vaginal entrance.

Inner lips: Thin folds of skin lying on either side of the vaginal entrance.

A pair of small glands, Bartholin glands, lie just inside the inner lips. Their functioning is relatively unimportant, and they are of interest only because they sometimes become infected.[2] *Skene's glands* are located nearby and, similarly, usually attract attention only when infected.

Bartholin glands: Two tiny glands located on either side of the vaginal entrance.

A few more landmarks should be noted (Figure 4.1). The place where the inner

---

[1] A related practice is *infibulation,* which refers to removal of the inner lips and sewing together of the outer lips so that the opening to the vagina is closed except for a small opening to allow the menstrual flow out. Intercourse is impossible. This ritual is practiced mainly in eastern Africa (Gregersen, 1983; Lightfoot-Klein, 1989).

[2] And there is a limerick about them:

> There was a young man from Calcutta
> Who was heard in his beard to mutter,
>   "If her Bartholin glands
>   Don't respond to my hands,
> I'm afraid I shall have to use butter."

Actually, there is a biological fallacy in the limerick. Can you spot it? If not, see Chapter 9.

Perineum (pair-ih-NEE-um): The skin between the vaginal entrance and the anus.

Introitus: Another word for the vaginal entrance.

lips come together behind the vaginal opening is called the *fourchette*. The area of skin between the vaginal opening and the anus is called the perineum. The vaginal opening itself is sometimes called the introitus. Notice also that the urinary opening lies about midway between the clitoris and the vaginal opening. Thus urine does not pass out through the clitoris (as might be expected from analogy with the male) or through the vagina, but instead through a separate pathway, the *urethra*, with a separate opening.

What You See Is What You Get

One important difference between the male sex organs and the female sex organs—and a difference that has some important psychological consequences—is that the female's external genitals are much less visible than the male's. A male can view his genitals directly either by looking down at them or by looking into a mirror while naked. Either of these two strategies for the female, however, will result at best in a view of the mons. The clitoris, the inner and outer lips, and the vaginal opening remain hidden. Indeed, many adult women have never taken a direct look at their own vulva. The mirror, however, makes this possible. The genitals can be viewed either by putting a mirror on the floor and squatting over it or by standing up and putting one foot on the edge of a chair, bed, or something similar and holding the mirror up near the genitals (see Figure 4.4). I recommend that all women use a mirror to identify on their own bodies all the parts shown in Figure 4.1. The female genitals need not remain mysterious to their owner.

The Hymen

Hymen (HYE-men): A thin membrane that may partially cover the vaginal entrance.

Before the internal structures are discussed, one other external structure deserves mention: the hymen. The hymen ("cherry," "maidenhead") is a thin membrane which, if present, is situated at the vaginal opening. The hymen may be one of a number of different types (see Figure 4.5), although it generally has some openings in it; otherwise the menstrual flow would not be able to pass out.[3] At the time of first intercourse, the hymen, if present, may be broken or stretched as the penis moves into the vagina. This may cause bleeding and possibly some pain. Typically, though, it is an untraumatic occurrence and goes unnoticed in the excitement of the

---

[3] The rare condition in which the hymen is a tough tissue with no opening is called *imperforate hymen* and can be corrected with fairly simple surgery.

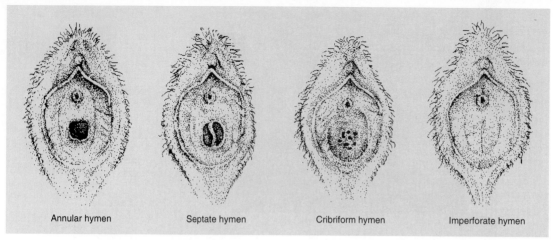

Annular hymen   Septate hymen   Cribriform hymen   Imperforate hymen

FIGURE 4.5
There are several types of hymens.

moment. For a woman who is very concerned about her hymen and what will happen to it at first coitus, there are two possible approaches. A physician can cut the hymen neatly so that it will not tear at the time of first intercourse, or the woman herself can stretch it by repeatedly inserting a finger into the vagina and pressing on it.

The hymen, and its destruction at first intercourse, has captured the interest of people in many cultures. In Europe during the Middle Ages, the lord might claim the right to deflower a peasant bride on her wedding night before passing her on to her husband (the practice is called *droit du seigneur* in French and *jus primae noctis* in Latin). The hymen has been taken as evidence of virginity. Thus bleeding on the wedding night was proof that the bride had been delivered intact to the groom; the parading of the bloody bed sheets on the wedding night, a custom of the Kurds of Arabia, is one ritual based on this belief. In other cultures the destruction of the mysterious hymen has been considered dangerous. In one Australian tribe, the task was accomplished by two old women a week before the wedding. If, at that time, the girl's hymen was discovered not to be in mint condition, she might be tortured or even killed.

These practices rest on the assumption that a woman without a hymen is not a virgin. However, we now know that this is not true. Some females are simply born without a hymen, and others may tear it in active sports such as horseback riding. Unfortunately, this means that some women have been humiliated unjustly for their lack of a hymen.

Internal Organs

The internal sex organs of the female consist of the vagina, the uterus, a pair of ovaries, and a pair of oviducts or fallopian tubes (see Figures 4.6 and 4.7).

The Vagina

Vagina (vuh-JINE-uh):
The barrel-shaped organ in the female into which the penis is inserted during coitus and through which a baby passes during birth.

The vagina is the organ into which the penis is inserted during coitus, and it receives the ejaculate. It is also the passageway through which the baby travels during birth, and so it is sometimes called the *birth canal*. In the resting state, the vaginal barrel is about 8 to 10 centimeters (3 to 4 inches) long and tilts slightly backward from the bottom to the top. At the bottom it ends in the vaginal opening, or *introitus*. At the top it connects with the cervix (the lower part of the uterus). It is a very flexible, tube-shaped organ that works somewhat like a balloon. In the "resting" state its

86

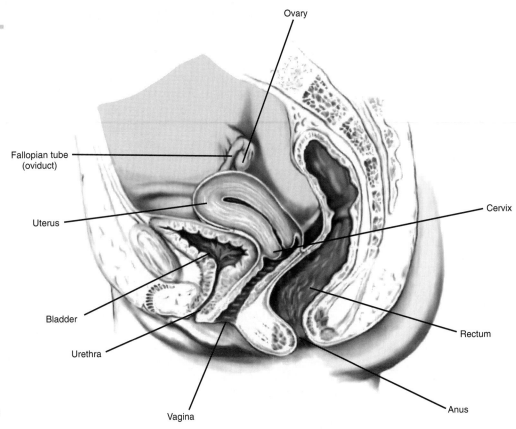

FIGURE 4.6
Internal sexual and reproductive organs of the female from a side view.

FIGURE 4.7
Internal sexual and reproductive organs of the female from a front view.

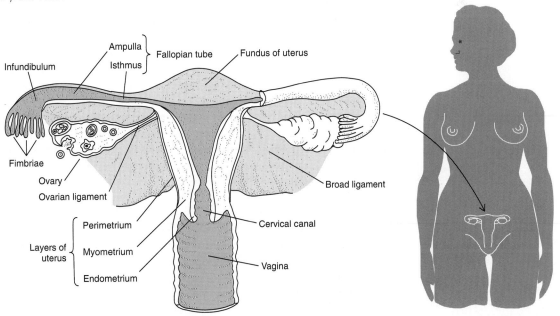

walls lie against each other like the sides of an uninflated balloon; during arousal it expands like an inflated balloon, allowing space to accommodate the penis.

The walls of the vagina have three layers. The inner layer, the *vaginal mucosa,* is a mucous membrane similar to the inner lining of the mouth. The middle layer is muscular, and the outer layer forms a covering. The walls of the vagina are extremely elastic and are capable of expanding to the extent necessary during intercourse and childbirth, although with age they become thinner and less flexible.

The nerve supply of the vagina is mostly to the lower one-third, near the introitus. That part is sensitive to erotic stimulation. The inner two-thirds of the vagina contains almost no nerve endings and is therefore very insensitive except to feelings of deep pressure. There is a spot on the front wall of the vagina that is more sensitive than the rest of the vagina, but even it is not nearly so sensitive as the inner lips, outer lips, or clitoris (Schultz et al., 1989). This spot is referred to by some as the G-spot.

The number of slang terms for the vagina (for example, "beaver," "cunt") and the frequency of their usage testify to its power of fascination across the ages. One concern has been with size: whether some vaginas are too small or too large. As has been noted, though, the vagina is highly elastic and expandable. Thus, at least in principle, any penis can fit into any vagina. The penis is, after all, not nearly so large as a baby's head, which manages to fit through the vagina.

The part of the vagina which is most responsible for the male's sensation that it is "tight," "too tight," or "too loose" is the introitus. One of the things that can stretch the introitus is childbirth; indeed, there is a considerable difference between the appearance of the vulva of a woman who has never had a baby *(nulliparous)* and the vulva of a woman who has *(parous)* (see Figure 4.8).

Surrounding the vagina, the urethra, and the anus is a set of muscles called the *pelvic floor muscles* (see Figure 4.9). One of these muscles, the **pubococcygeal muscle,** is particularly important. It may be stretched during childbirth, or it may simply be weak. However, it can be strengthened through exercise, and this is recommended by sex therapists (see Chapter 19) as well as by many popular sex manuals and magazines.

Because the introitus is highly sensitive, both to pleasure and pain, and because it is surrounded by muscles, it may reflect a woman's psychological response to sex. If a woman responds to arousal with fear or anxiety, the muscles may tighten, making it difficult for the penis to enter the vagina. In extreme cases, the muscles become so tight that intercourse is impossible, a condition known as *vaginismus* (see Chapter 19). On the other hand, a very expansive and relaxed introitus also has some disadvantages in that it may not produce enough sensation for the male. Exercising the pubococcygeal muscle should correct this problem.

The vagina has also provoked some anxieties. There are many myths among primitive peoples that the vagina is lined with teeth *(vagina dentata),* thorns, or other dangerous objects that can damage the penis. For example, the Pomo Indians of California have a myth in which a young girl has thorns surrounding her vagina, which her intended husband must break off before marrying her.

The Uterus

The **uterus** (womb) is about the size of a fist and is shaped somewhat like an upside-down pear. It is usually tilted forward and is held in place by ligaments. The narrow lower third is called the *cervix* and opens into the vagina. The top is the *fundus,* and the main part is the *body.* The entrance to the uterus through the cervix is very narrow, about the size of a straw, and is called the *os* (or cervical canal). The major function of the uterus is to hold and nourish the developing fetus.

Pubococcygeal muscle (pyoo-bo-cox-ih-GEE-ul): A muscle around the vaginal entrance.

Uterus (YOO-tur-us): The organ in the female in which the fetus develops.

FIGURE 4.8
Appearance of the vulva of a woman who is a virgin; a woman who has had intercourse but has not had a baby (nulliparous); and a woman who has had a baby (parous).

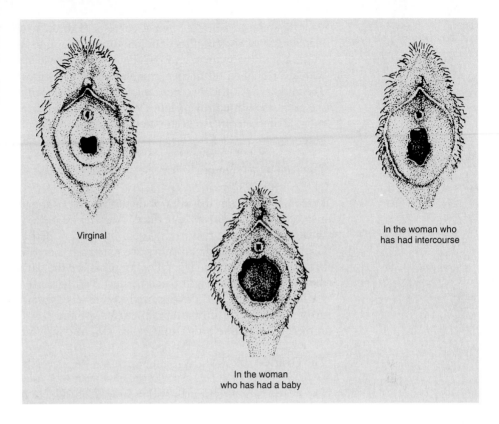

Virginal

In the woman who
has had intercourse

In the woman
who has had a baby

FIGURE 4.9
Muscles on the floor of the pelvis. Note particularly the pubococcygeal muscle, which women may want to exercise (see Chapter 19).

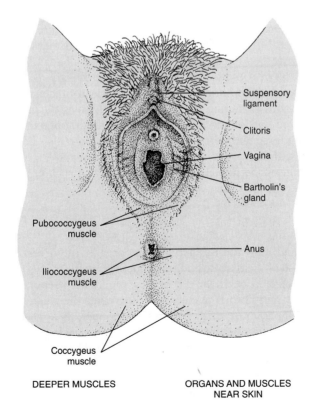

Suspensory
ligament

Clitoris

Vagina

Bartholin's
gland

Pubococcygeus
muscle

Anus

Iliococcygeus
muscle

Coccygeus
muscle

DEEPER MUSCLES

ORGANS AND MUSCLES
NEAR SKIN

The uterus, like the vagina, consists of three layers. The inner layer, or *endo-metrium,* is richly supplied with glands and blood vessels. Its state varies according to the age of the woman and the phase of the menstrual cycle. It is the endometrium which is sloughed off at menstruation and creates most of the menstrual discharge. The middle layer, the *myometrium,* is muscular. The muscles are very strong, creating the strong contractions of labor and orgasm, and are also highly elastic; they are capable of stretching to accommodate a nine-month-old fetus. The outer layer—the *perimetrium* or *serosa*—forms the external cover of the uterus.

The Fallopian Tubes

Fallopian tube (fuh-LOW-pee-un): The tube extending from the uterus to the ovary; also called the oviduct.

Extending out from the sides of the upper end of the uterus are the **fallopian tubes,** also called the *oviducts* ("egg ducts") or *uterine tubes* (see Figures 4.6 and 4.7). It is these tubes that are tied in the tubal ligation, a method of female sterilization (see Chapter 8). The fallopian tubes are extremely narrow and are lined with hairlike projections called *cilia.* The fallopian tubes are the pathway by which the egg leaves the ovaries and the sperm reach the egg. Fertilization of the egg typically occurs in the infundibulum, and the fertilized egg travels the rest of the way through the tube to the uterus. The infundibulum curves around toward the ovary; at its end are numerous fingerlike projections called *fimbriae* which extend toward the ovary.

The Ovaries

Ovaries: Two organs in the female that produce eggs and sex hormones.

The ovaries are two organs about the size and shape of an unshelled almond; they lie on either side of the uterus. The ovaries have two important functions: they produce eggs (ova), and they manufacture the female sex hormones, *estrogens* and *progesterone.*

Each ovary contains numerous follicles. A *follicle* is a capsule that surrounds an egg (not to be confused with hair follicles, which are quite different). It is estimated that a female is born with about 400,000 immature eggs. Beginning at puberty, one or several of the follicles mature during each menstrual cycle. When the egg has matured, the follicle moves to the surface of the ovary, bursts open, and releases the egg. The ovaries do not actually connect directly to the fallopian tubes. The egg is released into the body cavity and apparently reaches the tube as a result of some mysterious attraction for the fimbriae. If the egg does not reach the tube, it may be fertilized outside the tube, resulting in an abdominal pregnancy (see the section on ectopic pregnancy in Chapter 7). There have also been cases recorded of women who, although they are missing one ovary and the opposite fallopian tube, have nonetheless become pregnant. Apparently, in such cases the egg migrates to the tube on the opposite side.

The Breasts

Although they are not actually sex organs, the *breasts* deserve some mention here because of their erotic and reproductive significance. The breast consists of about 15 or 20 clusters of *mammary glands,* each with a separate opening to the nipple, and of fatty and fibrous tissue which surrounds the clusters of glands (see Figure 4.10). The nipple, into which the milk ducts open, is at the tip of the breast. It is richly supplied with nerve endings and therefore very important in erotic stimulation. The nipple consists of smooth muscle fibers; when they contract, the nipple becomes erect. The area surrounding the nipple is called the *areola.*

There is wide variation among women in the size and shape of the breasts. One thing is fairly consistent, though. Few women are satisfied with the size of their breasts. Most women think they are either too small or too large, and almost no

FIGURE 4.10
*The internal structure of
the breast.*

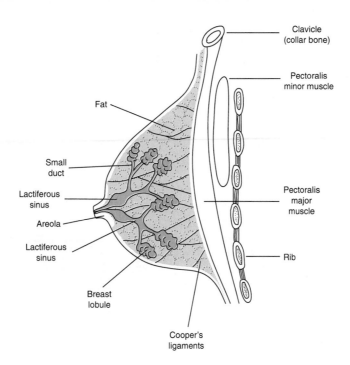

woman thinks hers are just right. It is well to remember that there are the same number of nerve endings in small breasts as in large breasts. It follows that small breasts are actually more erotically sensitive per square inch than large ones (McCary, 1973).

Breasts may take on enormous psychological meaning; they can be a symbol of femininity or a means of attracting men. Ours is a very breast-oriented culture, and men in the United States may develop a nearly overpowering interest in, and attraction to, women's breasts. The social definition of beauty is a powerful force; many women strive to meet the ideal and a few overadapt, going too far in their striving (Mazur, 1986). Breast augmentation surgery has increased steadily since the 1960s, while other women are undergoing breast reduction surgery, in both cases to meet a socially defined standard of beauty.

The Pelvic Exam

All adult women should have a checkup every year that includes a thorough pelvic exam. Among other things, such an exam is extremely important in the detection of cervical cancer, and early detection is the key to cure (see the last section of this chapter). Some women neglect to have the exam because they feel anxious or embarrassed about it or because they think they are "too young" or "too old"; however, having regular pelvic exams can be a matter of life and death. Actually, the exam is quite simple and need not cause any discomfort. The following is a description of the procedures in a pelvic exam (Boston Women's Health Book Collective, 1984).

First, the physician inspects the vulva, checking for irritations, discolorations, bumps, lice, adhesions to the clitoris, skin lesions, and unusual vaginal discharge. Then there is an internal check for *cystoceles* (bulges of the bladder into the vagina) and *rectoceles* (bulges of the rectum into the vagina), for pus in the Skene glands, for cysts in the Bartholin glands, and for the strength of the pelvic floor muscles and abdominal muscles. There is also a test for stress incontinence; the physician asks the patient to cough and checks to see whether urine flows involuntarily.

Next comes the speculum exam. The *speculum* is a plastic or metal instrument

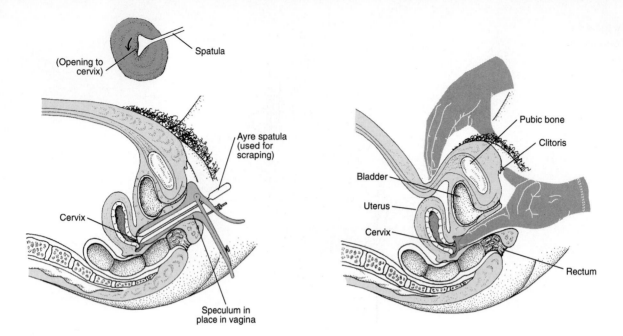

FIGURE 4.11
The pelvic exam. (a) The speculum in place for a pelvic exam. The Ayre spatula is used to get a sample of cells for the Pap test. (b) The bimanual pelvic exam.

that is inserted into the vagina to hold the vaginal walls apart to permit examination (see Figure 4.11). Once the speculum is in place (it should be prewarmed to body temperature if it is metal), the physician looks for any unusual signs, such as lesions, inflammation, or unusual discharge from the vaginal walls, and for any signs of infections or damage to the cervix. The physician then uses a small metal spatula to scrape a tiny bit of tissue from the cervix for the Pap test for cervical cancer. If done properly, this should be painless. A smear of discharge should also be taken to check for gonorrhea.

If the woman is interested in seeing her own cervix, she can ask the doctor to hold up a mirror so that she can view it through the speculum. Indeed, some women's groups advocate that women learn to use a speculum and give themselves regular exams with it; early detection of diseases would thus be much more likely. (For a more detailed description, see Boston Women's Health Book Collective, 1984.)

Next, the physician does a bimanual vaginal exam. She or he slides the index and middle fingers of one hand into the vagina and then, with the other hand, presses down from the outside on the abdominal wall (Figure 4.11). The physician then feels for the position of the uterus, tubes, and ovaries and for any signs of growths, pain, or inflammation.

Finally, the physician may also do a recto-vaginal exam by inserting one finger into the vagina and one into the rectum; this provides further information on the positioning of the pelvic organs and can include a test for colon cancer.

Once again, it is important to emphasize that these are not painful procedures and that having them performed regularly is extremely important to a woman's health.

MALE SEXUAL ORGANS

Externally, the most obvious parts of the male sexual anatomy are the penis and the scrotum, or scrotal sac, which contains the testes (see Figure 4.12).

FIGURE 4.12
*The male sexual and
reproductive organs from a
side view.*

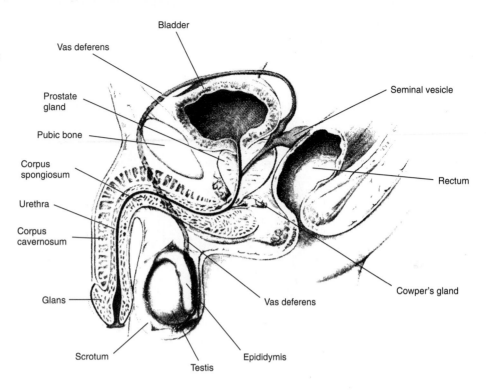

Bladder

Vas deferens

Prostate
gland

Pubic bone

Corpus
spongiosum

Urethra

Corpus
cavernosum

Glans

Scrotum

Testis

Epididymis

Vas deferens

Cowper's gland

Rectum

Seminal vesicle

The Penis

The penis (phallus, "prick," "cock," "johnson," and many other slang terms too numerous to list) serves important functions in sexual pleasure, reproduction, and elimination of body wastes by urination. It is a tubular organ with an end or tip called the *glans.* The opening at the end of the glans is the *meatus,* or *urethral opening,* through which urine and semen pass. The part of the penis that attaches to the body is called the *root,* and the main part of the penis is called the *body* or *shaft.* The raised ridge separating the glans from the body of the penis is called the *corona,* or *coronal ridge.* While the entire penis is sensitive to sexual stimulation, the glans and corona are by far the most sexually excitable region of the male anatomy.

Internally, the penis contains three long cylinders of spongy tissue running parallel to the *urethra,* which is the pathway through which semen and urine pass (see Figure 4.13). The two spongy bodies lying on top are called the corpora cavernosa, and the single one lying on the bottom of the penis is called the corpus spongiosum (the urethra runs through the middle of it). During erection, the corpus spongiosum can be seen as a raised column on the lower side of the penis. As the names suggest, these bodies are tissues filled with many spaces and cavities, much like a sponge. They are richly supplied with blood vessels and nerves. In the flaccid (unaroused, not erect) state, they contain little blood. *Erection,* or *tumescence,* occurs when they become filled with blood (engorged) and expand, making the penis stiff.

Contrary to popular belief, the penis does not contain a muscle, and no muscle is involved in erection. Erection is purely a vascular phenomenon; that is, it results entirely from blood flow. It is also commonly believed that the penis of the human male contains a bone. This is not true either. In some other species—for example, dogs—the penis does contain a bone, which aids in intromission (inserting the penis into the vagina). In human males, however, there is none, and a man must accomplish intromission purely on the strength of his own erection.

FIGURE 4.13
*The internal structure of
the penis.*

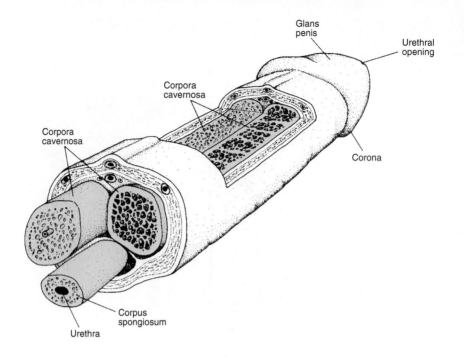

The skin of the penis usually is hairless and is arranged in loose folds, permitting expansion during erection. The foreskin, or *prepuce,* is an additional layer of skin which forms a sheathlike covering over the glans; it may be present or absent in the adult male, depending on whether he has been circumcised (see Figure 4.14). Under the foreskin are small glands (Tyson's glands) that produce a substance called *smegma,* which is cheesy in texture. The foreskin is easily retractable,[4] and its retraction is extremely important for proper hygiene. If it is not pulled back and the glans washed thoroughly, the smegma may accumulate, producing a very unpleasant smell.

Foreskin: A layer of skin covering the glans or tip of the penis in an uncircumcised male; also called the prepuce.

Circumcision refers to the surgical cutting away or removal of the foreskin. Circumcision is practiced widely throughout the world and, when parents so choose, is done to infants in the United States within a few days after birth.

Circumcision may be practiced for ritualistic and religious reasons. Circumcision has been a part of Jewish religious practice for thousands of years. It symbolizes the covenant between God and the Jewish people and is done on the eighth day after birth, according to scriptural teaching (Genesis 17:9–27). In some cultures circumcision may be done at puberty as an initiation ritual, or *rite de passage.* The ability of the young boy to stand the pain may be seen as a proof of manhood.

Circumcision: Surgical removal of the foreskin of the penis.

In the 1980s, an anticircumcision movement gained momentum in the United States. Its proponents argue that circumcision does not have any health benefits and that it does entail some health risk as well as psychological trauma. (For a statement of the anticircumcision position, see Wallerstein, 1980.) In fact, as early as 1971 the American Academy of Pediatrics had gone on record saying that there is no medical need for routine circumcision of newborn boys. Reflecting this advice and the growth

---

[4] In a rare condition, the foreskin is so tight that it cannot be pulled back; this is called *phimosis* and requires circumcision.

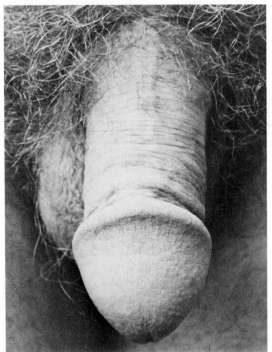

(a)

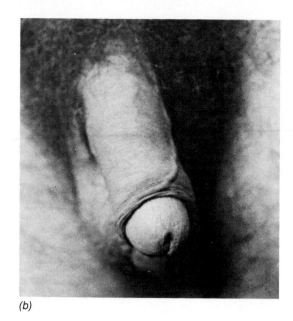

(b)

FIGURE 4.14
(a) A circumcised penis and
(b) an uncircumcised penis,
showing the foreskin.

of controversy about circumcision, only 59 percent of infant boys were circumcised in the United States in 1986, compared with 90 percent in 1970 (Lindsey, 1988).

In the last few years, however, new evidence has been accumulating, and in 1989 the American Academy of Pediatrics, changing its 1971 statement, declared that there are potential medical benefits and advantages to circumcision as well as some potential risks. The new evidence indicates, for example, that uncircumcised male babies are 11 times more likely to get urinary tract infections than circumcised babies (Wiswell et al., 1987). There is also some evidence that uncircumcised men have a greater chance of infection with the AIDS virus (Holmes, 1988; Touchette, 1991). In a study of different geographic and ethnic groups in Africa, some of which practice circumcision and some of which do not, it was found that HIV infection rates were very low among groups that practice circumcision and high among those that do not (Moses et al., 1990). Thus scientific evidence is beginning to swing toward the view that circumcision has some significant health benefits.

Other arguments have focused on whether the circumcised or the uncircumcised male receives more pleasure from sexual intercourse. In fact, Masters and Johnson (1966) found that there is no difference in excitability between the circumcised and the uncircumcised penis.

A particularly exotic manipulation of the penis occurs in a surgical ritual known as *subincision*. In this operation, which is common among primitive tribes, especially those in central Australia, a slit is made on the lower side of the penis along its entire length and to the depth of the urethra. Urine is then excreted at the base rather than at the tip.

To say the least, the penis has been the focus of quite a lot of attention throughout history. In some cultures, the attention has become so pronounced that the male genitals have actually become the object of religious worship (phallic worship). Not surprisingly, the male genitals were often seen as symbols of fertility and thus were worshipped for their powers of procreativity. In ancient Greece, phallic worship centered on Priapus, the son of Aphrodite (the goddess of love) and Dionysus (the god of fertility and wine). Priapus is usually represented as a grinning man with a huge penis.

In contemporary American society, phallic concern often focuses on the size of the penis. It is commonly believed that a man with a large penis is a better lover than the man with a small penis and can satisfy a woman more. Masters and Johnson (1966), however, have found that this is not true. While there is considerable variation in the length of the penis from one man to the next—the average penis is generally somewhere between 6.4 centimeters (2.5 inches) and 10 centimeters (4 inches) in length when flaccid (not erect)—there seems to be a tendency for the small penis to grow more in erection than the one that starts out large. As a result, there is little correlation between the length of the penis when flaccid and the length when erect. As the saying has it, "Erection is the great equalizer." The average erect penis is about 15 centimers (6 inches) long; as indicated, there tends to be somewhat less variation in the length of the erect penis than in the length of the flaccid one, although erect penises longer than 33 centimeters (13 inches) have been measured (Dickinson, 1949). Further, as noted earlier, the vagina has relatively few nerve endings and is relatively insensitive. Hence penetration to the far reaches of the vagina by a very long penis is not essential and may not even be noticeable. Research also shows that women are no more aroused by viewing a large penis than by viewing a smaller one (Fisher et al., 1983). Many other factors are more important than penis size in giving a woman pleasure (see Chapters 10 and 19).

Phallic concern has also included an interest in the variations in the shape of the penis when flaccid and when erect, as reflected in this famous limerick:

> There was a young man of Kent
> Whose kirp in the middle was bent.
> To save himself trouble
> He put it in double,
> And instead of coming, he went.

Phallic concern has also been expressed in psychological theory, the best example being in psychoanalytic theory. According to Freud, concern for the penis and a related castration anxiety are the key factors in male psychological development, leading to the resolution of the Oedipus complex, increased independence from parents, and increased psychological maturity. All this from such a small part of the body! (Indeed, the theory even says that the key factor in female psychological development is the *lack* of a penis.)

The Scrotum and Testes

Scrotum (SKROH-tum): The pouch of skin that contains the testes in the male.

The other major part of the external genitals in the male is the scrotum; this is a loose pouch of skin, lightly covered with hair, which holds the testes ("balls" or "nuts" in slang[5]). The testes themselves are considered part of the internal genitals.

---

[5] That reminds me of another limerick:

> There once was a pirate named Gates
> Who thought he could rhumba on skates.
>   He slipped on his cutlass
>   And now he is nutless
> And practically useless on dates.

Testes: The pair of glands in the scrotum that manufacture sperm and sex hormones.

Seminiferous tubules (sem-ih-NIFF-ur-us): Tubes in the testes that manufacture sperm.

Interstitial cells (int-er-STIH-shul): Cells in the testes that manufacture testosterone.

The testes[6] are the *gonads,* or reproductive glands, of the male, and thus they are analogous to the female's ovaries. Like the ovaries, they serve two major functions: they manufacture germ cells (sperm), and they manufacture the male sex hormone, *testosterone.* Both testes are about the same size, although the left one usually hangs lower than the right one.

In the internal structure of the testes, two parts are important: the seminiferous tubules and the interstitial cells (see Figure 4.15). The seminiferous tubules carry out the important function of manufacturing and storing sperm, a process called *spermatogenesis.* They are a long series of threadlike tubes curled and packed densely into the testes. There are about 1000 of these tubules, and it is estimated that if they were stretched out end to end, they would be several hundred feet in length.

The interstitial cells (or *Leydig's cells*) carry out the second important function of the testes, the production of the male sex hormone, testosterone. These cells are found in the connective tissue lying between the seminiferous tubules. The cells lie close to the blood vessels in the testes and pour the hormones they manufacture directly into the blood vessels. Thus the testes are endocrine glands.

Each testis is surrounded by a tight, whitish sheath (the *tunica albuginea*). In addition to encapsulating the testis, the sheath also extends into it, dividing it into sections, much like a grapefruit; each section is filled with seminiferous tubules. This sheath is responsible for the problem of sterility caused by mumps in the adult male. When the virus invades the testes, it causes them to swell. The tunica albuginea is tight, however, and does not permit expansion. The delicate tubules are thus crushed, which impairs their sperm-producing function. Mumps is not a problem in the female because the ovaries are not enclosed in a comparable tight sheath.

One of the clever tricks that the scrotum and testes perform, as any male will testify, is that they can move up and close to the body or down and away from the body. These changes are brought about mainly by temperature (although emotional factors may also produce them). If a man plunges into a cold lake, the scrotum will shrivel and move close to the body. If the man is working in an extremely hot place, the scrotum will hang down and away from the body. This mechanism is important

---

[6] "Testes" is from the Latin root meaning "witnesses" and comes from the same root as "testimony" does. It is derived from the ancient Roman custom of placing the hand on the genitals when taking an oath. Apparently Roman women were not considered important enough to take oaths, so there was no similar ritual for them. The singular of "testes" is "testis."

FIGURE 4.15
Schematic cross section of the internal structure of the testis.

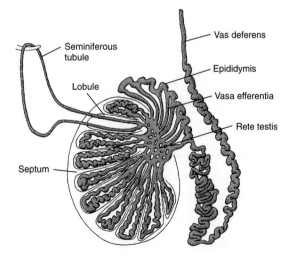

because the testes should remain at a fairly constant temperature, slightly lower than normal body temperature. This constancy of temperature is necessary to protect sperm, which may be injured by extremes of temperature. Thus if the air is cold, the testes move closer to the body to maintain warmth, but if the air is too hot, they move away from the body to keep cool. The mechanics of this movement are made possible by the *dartos muscle,* which forms the middle layer of the scrotum. It contracts or relaxes reflexively, thereby moving the testes up or down.

Many people believe that taking hot baths, wearing tight athletic supporters, or having a high fever can cause infertility. Indeed, in some countries the men take long, hot baths as a method of contraception. Such a practice has some basis in biological fact, because sperm can be destroyed by heat. However, as a method of contraception, this practice has not been particularly effective. In one study, it was found that the use of a special jockstrap raised the temperature of the scrotum by nearly 1°C (1.7°F) and that wearing the device daily for seven weeks caused about a 25 percent reduction in the number of sperm produced (Robinson and Rock, 1967). Thus such practices might decrease a man's fertility somewhat, but they are far from 100 percent effective as contraceptives. On the other hand, men with problems of infertility can sometimes cure them by getting out of their tight jockstraps and jockey shorts.

Sperm

Following initial cell division in the seminiferous tubules, the male germ cells go through several stages of maturation. At the earliest stage, the cell is called a *spermatogonium.* Then it becomes a *spermatocyte* (first primary and then secondary) and then a *spermatid.* Finally when fully mature, it is a *spermatozoan,* or sperm. *Spermatogenesis,* the manufacture of sperm, occurs continuously in the adult human male. An average ejaculate contains about 300 million sperm.

A mature sperm is very tiny—about 60 micrometers, or 60/10,000 millimeter (0.0024 inch), long—and consists of a head, a neck, a midpiece, and a tail. A normal sperm carries 23 chromosomes in the head. This 23 is half the normal number in the other cells of the human body. When the sperm unites with the egg, which also carries 23 chromosomes, the full complement of 46 for the offspring is produced. (See Chapter 7 for a discussion of the sperm's role in conception.)

Human cells contain two sex chromosomes: XX in the female and XY in the male (see Chapter 5). Because sperm cells contain only half of the full number, they contain only one sex chromosome. Thus each egg contains one X chromosome. A sperm may contain either an X chromosome or a Y chromosome.

After the sperm are manufactured in the seminiferous tubules, they proceed into the *rete testes,* a converging network of tubes on the surface of the testis toward the top. The sperm then pass out of the testis and into a single tube, the epididymis. The epididymis is a long tube (about 6 meters, or 20 feet, in length) coiled into a small crescent-shaped region on the top and side of the testis. The sperm may be stored in the epididymis, in which they ripen and mature, possibly for as long as six weeks.

At the end of the epididymis, the sperm pass into another tube, the vas deferens, or *ductus deferens* (it is the vas that is cut in a vasectomy—see Chapter 8). The vas passes up and out of the scrotum and then follows a peculiar circular path as it loops over the pubic bone, travels across beside the urinary bladder, and then turns downward toward the prostate. As the tube passes through the prostate, it narrows, and at this point is called the *ejaculatory duct.* The ejaculatory duct then opens into the *urethra,* which has the dual function of conveying sperm and conveying urine; sperm move, via the urethra, out through the penis.

Sperm: The mature male reproductive cell, capable of fertilizing an egg.

Epididymis (ep-ih-DIH-dih-mus): Highly coiled tubules located on the edge of the testis, where sperm mature.

Vas deferens: The tube through which sperm pass on their way from the testes and epididymis, out of the scrotum, and to the urethra.

Apparently sperm have little motility (capability of movement) of their own while in the epididymis and vas. Not until they mix with the secretions of the prostate and seminal vesicles are they capable of movement on their own. It is thought that up to this point, they are conveyed by the cilia and by contractions of the epididymis and vas.

Other Internal Structures

The *seminal vesicles* are two saclike structures which lie above the prostate, behind the bladder, and in front of the rectum. They produce about 70 percent of the seminal fluid, or ejaculate. The remaining 30 percent is produced by the prostate (Spring-Mills & Hafez, 1980). They empty their fluid into the ejaculatory duct to combine with the sperm.

Prostate: The gland in the male, located below the bladder, that secretes some of the fluid in semen.

The prostate lies below the bladder and is about the size and shape of a chestnut. It is composed of both muscle and glandular tissue. The prostate secretes a milky alkaline fluid which is part of the ejaculate. It is thought that the alkalinity of the secretion provides a favorable environment for the sperm and helps prevent their destruction by the acidity of the vagina. The prostate is fairly small at birth, enlarges at puberty, and typically shrinks in old age. It may become enlarged enough so that it interferes with urination, in which case surgery is required. Its size can be determined by rectal examination.

Cowper's glands: Glands that secrete substances into the male's urethra.

Cowper's glands, or the *bulbourethral glands,* are located just below the prostate and empty into the urethra. During sexual arousal, these glands secrete a small amount of a clear alkaline fluid, which appears as droplets at the tip of the penis before ejaculation occurs. It is thought that the function of this secretion is to neutralize the acidic urethra, allowing safe passage of the sperm. Generally it is not produced in sufficient quantity to serve as a lubricant in intercourse. The fluid often contains some stray sperm. Thus a woman may become pregnant from the sperm in this fluid though the man has not ejaculated.

CANCER OF THE SEX ORGANS

Breast Cancer

Cancer of the breast is the most common form of cancer in women. About 1 out of every 9 American women has breast cancer at some time in her life. Every year, 44,000 women in this country die of breast cancer (American Cancer Society, 1991). The risk is higher for women whose mother, sister, or grandmother has had breast cancer.

Diagnosis

Because of the statistics cited above, it is extremely important for women to do a breast self-exam regularly (see Focus 4.1). The exam should be done once a month, but not during the menstrual period, when there tend to be natural lumps in the breast. It is important to do the self-exam once a month because the earlier breast cancer is detected, the better the chances of a complete recovery with proper treatment.

Unfortunately, psychological factors can interfere with this process. Many women do not do the self-exam because they are afraid they will find a lump; thus one can go undetected for a long time, making recovery less likely. Some other women do the self-exam, but when they discover a lump, they become so frightened that they do nothing about it.

The Breast Self-Exam

(a) In the shower: Examine your breasts during a bath or shower; your hands glide more easily over wet skin. With your fingers flat, move your hand gently over every part of each breast. Use your right hand to examine the left breast, your left hand for the right breast. Check for any lump, hard knot, or thickening. *(b) Before a mirror:* Inspect your breasts with your arms at your sides. Next, raise your arms high overhead. Look for any changes in the contour of each breast, a swelling, a dimpling of the skin, or changes in the nipple. Then rest your palms on your hips and press down firmly to flex your chest muscles. The left and right breasts will not exactly match—few women's breasts do. Regular inspection shows what is normal for you and will give you confidence in your examination. *(c) Lying down:* To examine your right breast, put a pillow or folded towel under your right shoulder. Place your right hand behind your head—this distributes the breast tissue more evenly on the chest. With your left hand, fingers flat, press gently in small circular motions around an imaginary clock face. Begin at the outermost top of your right breast for 12 o'clock, then move to 1 o'clock and so on around the circle back to 12. A ridge of firm tissue in the lower curve of each breast is normal. Then move in an inch, toward the nipple. Keep circling to examine *every part of your breast,* including the nipple. This requires at least three more circles. Now slowly repeat the procedure on your left breast, with a pillow under your left shoulder and your left hand behind your head. Notice how your breast structure feels. Finally squeeze the nipple of each breast gently between your thumb and index finger. Any discharge, clear or bloody, should be reported to your doctor immediately.

Perhaps knowing a bit more about the realities of breast lumps and the surgery that is performed when they are discovered will help dispel some of the fears surrounding the subject of breast cancer. There are three kinds of breast lumps: *cysts* (fluid-filled sacs, also called *fibrocystic disease* or *cystic mastitis*), *fibroadenomas,* and *malignant tumors.* The important thing to realize is that 80 percent of breast lumps are cysts or fibroadenomas and are benign—that is, not dangerous. Therefore, if you find a lump in your breast, the chances are fairly good that it is not malignant; of course, you cannot be sure of this until a doctor has performed a biopsy.

Once you have discovered a lump, you should see a doctor immediately. One of several diagnostic procedures may then be carried out. One is *needle aspiration,* in which a fine needle is inserted into the breast; if the lump is a cyst, the fluid in the cyst will be drained out. If the lump disappears after this procedure, then it was a cyst; the cyst is gone, and there is no need for further concern. If the lump remains, it must be either a fibroadenoma or a malignant tumor. Other procedures can then be used to determine whether it is malignant: mammography and xeroradiography.

FIGURE 4.16
Techniques used in the
breast self-exam.

Basically, *mammography* involves taking an x-ray of the breast. *Xeroradiography* is a refinement of this technique; there is less exposure to x-rays, the test is processed more efficiently, and there is a higher degree of accuracy. Both of these x-ray techniques are highly accurate, although some errors are still made. Their major advantage, though, is that they are capable of detecting tumors that are so small that they cannot yet be felt; thus they can detect cancer in very early stages, making recovery more likely. For this reason, some experimental mass-screening programs, in which women were given yearly mammograms routinely, were begun a few years ago. In 1976, Dr. Lester Breslow of U.C.L.A. provided data suggesting that mammograms themselves may cause breast cancer (see also Breast Cancer, 1976). The question is: Which is more dangerous—having yearly mammography or not detecting breast cancer until a later stage? Experts have concluded that the benefits outweigh the risks. The American Cancer Society now says that a woman should have a baseline mammogram around age 35 and then should have one done regularly at one- or two-year intervals from age 40 to 49, and every year from age 50 on.

FIGURE 4.17
*Appearance of a breast
reconstructed after a
mastectomy.*

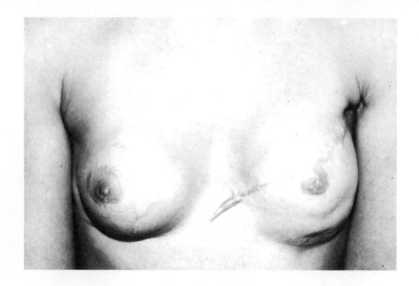

Most physicians feel that the only definitive way to differentiate between a fibroadenoma and a malignant tumor is to do an *excisional biopsy.* A small slit is made in the breast, and the lump is removed. A pathologist then examines it to determine whether it is cancerous. If it is simply a fibroadenoma, it has been removed, and there is no further need for concern.

Unfortunately, no one yet knows what causes breast cancer. The likeliest candidate currently seems to be a particular virus. There is also increasing evidence that the high-fat diet of Americans is a contributing factor; in countries such as Japan and Romania where the diet is low in fat, breast cancer rates are less than half those in the United States. A great deal of research is currently being focused on this problem.

Mastectomy

Several forms of surgery may be performed when the lump is malignant. Radiation therapy, chemotherapy, and hormone therapy may also be used. The most serious is radical mastectomy, in which the entire breast and the underlying muscle (pectoral muscle) and the lymph nodes are removed. Advocates of this procedure argue that if the cancer has spread to the adjoining lymph nodes, the procedure ensures that all the affected tissue is removed. The disadvantage of the procedure is that there may be difficulty in arm movement following removal of the pectoral muscles. In *modified radical mastectomy* the breast and lymph nodes, but not the muscles, are removed. In *simple mastectomy* only the breast (and possibly a few lymph nodes) is removed. In lumpectomy, only the lump itself and a small bit of surrounding tissues are removed. The breast is thus preserved. Current research indicates that in cases of early breast cancer, lumpectomy or quadrantectomy (removing the quarter of the breast containing the lump) followed by radiation therapy are as effective as the old-fashioned radical mastectomy (Veronesi et al., 1981; Henahan, 1984) and obviously much preferable. (See *Consumer Reports,* January 1981, for a discussion of the relative merits of various treatments.)

Treatments generally are highly effective. If the cancer has not spread beyond the breast, the survival rate is over 91 percent five years after treatment (American Cancer Society, 1991).

Radical mastectomy (mast-ECT-uh-mee): A surgical treatment for breast cancer in which the entire breast, as well as underlying muscles and lymph nodes, is removed.

Lumpectomy: A surgical treatment for breast cancer in which only the lump and a small bit of surrounding tissue are removed.

Psychological Aspects

A lot more is at stake with breast cancer and mastectomy than technical details about diagnosis and surgery. The psychological impact of breast cancer and mastectomy can be enormous (for an excellent review see Meyerowitz, 1980). There seem to be two sources of the trauma: Finding out that one has cancer of any kind is traumatic, and the amputation of the breast is additionally stressful.

The typical emotional response of the mastectomy patient is depression, often associated with anxiety and anger. These responses are so common that they can be considered normal. The woman must make a number of physical and psychological adaptations, including different positions for sleeping and lovemaking and a change to less revealing clothing. It is common for women to have difficulty showing their incisions to their sexual partners. Marital tensions and sexual problems may increase. The woman experiences a fear of recurring cancer and its treatment and of death, as well as concerns about the mutilation of mastectomy and loss of femininity. Our culture is very breast-oriented, and a woman who has defined her identity in terms of her beauty and voluptuous figure may have a more difficult time adjusting.

Often these emotional responses last for a year. However, long-term studies indicate that women gradually adapt to the stresses they have experienced and return to their precancer level of psychological functioning.

It is extremely important for a mastectomy patient and her husband or partner to have some form of counseling available to them. In many towns the American Cancer Society has organized support groups for mastectomy patients; these are composed of women who have themselves had mastectomies and who are willing to share their experiences and provide emotional support to mastectomy patients.

Cancer of the Cervix

Cancer of the cervix and other portions of the uterus is the third most common form of cancer in women; about 2 to 3 percent of all women develop it at some time in their lives. In 1987, 10,000 American women died of uterine cancer, and another 48,000 new cases were detected (American Cancer Society, 1987). It is encouraging to realize that the death rate from uterine cancer has decreased more than 70 percent in the last 40 years, mainly as a result of the Pap test and more regular checkups (American Cancer Society, 1987).

The exact causes of cervical cancer are unknown, but, as in the case of breast cancer, a virus is suspected. A number of pieces of data lead to this conclusion. There seems to be an association between heterosexual intercourse and cervical cancer; the greater the number of partners, the greater the chances of developing cervical cancer. Teenagers who start having intercourse very early seem especially susceptible, suggesting that the virus or viruses may be spread by intercourse (Sloane, 1985; Rotkin, 1962, 1973). Cervical cancer is unknown among nuns, and it is rare among other celibate women and among lesbians (F. Gagnon, 1950; Towne, 1955).

If detected in the early stages, cervical cancer is quite curable. Fortunately, there is a good, routine test to detect it, the *Pap test* (discussed earlier in this chapter), which is highly accurate and can detect the cancer long before the woman feels any pain from it. Every woman over the age of 20 should have one done annually.

Hysterectomy (his-tuh-REK-tuh-mee): Surgical removal of the uterus.

If cervical cancer is confirmed, the treatment is usually a complete hysterectomy, which involves the surgical removal of the entire uterus and cervix but not the ovaries (although in some cases, less radical procedures may be possible). The side effects of hysterectomy are minimal, except, of course, for the risks associated with any major surgery. A hysterectomy does not leave the woman "masculinized," with a beard growing and a deep voice developing, because hormone production is not affected; recall that it is the ovaries that manufacture hormones, and they are not removed (except in rare cases where there is evidence that the cancer has spread to them).

Other cancers of the female sexual-reproductive organs include uterine (endometrial) cancer, ovarian cancer, and cancer of the vulva, vagina, and fallopian tubes, but these are all rare in comparison with cervical cancer.

Cancer of the Prostate

Cancer of the prostate is the third most common form of cancer in men (the more common being lung cancer and skin cancer). It is not, however, a major cause of death because it generally affects older men (25 percent of men over 90 have prostate cancer) and because most of the tumors are small and spread only very slowly.

Early symptoms of prostate cancer are frequent urination (especially at night), difficulty in urination, and difficulty emptying the bladder (these are also symptoms of benign prostate enlargement). These symptoms result from the pressure of the prostate growth on the urethra. In the early stages, there may be frequent erections and an increase in sex drive; however, as the disease progresses, there are often problems with sexual functioning.

Preliminary diagnosis of prostate cancer is by a rectal examination, which is simple and causes no more than minimal discomfort. The physician (wearing a lubricated glove) simply inserts one finger into the rectum and palpates (feels) the prostate. All men over 40 should have a rectal exam at least once a year. If the rectal exam provides evidence of a tumor, further laboratory tests can be made as confirmation. The rectal exam has its disadvantages, though. Most men dislike the discomfort it causes, and it is not 100 percent accurate. A major advance came in 1991 with the announcement of a blood test that could routinely detect tumors, including ones far too small to be found by the rectal exam (Catalona et al., 1991).

Treatment often involves surgical removal of the prostate, plus some type of hormone therapy, radiation therapy, or anticancer drugs.

Cancer of the penis is another cancer of the male sexual-reproductive system, but it is rare compared with prostate cancer. It seems to be much more common among uncircumcised men than among circumcised men, suggesting that the accumulation of smegma under the foreskin may be related to its cause. Treatment may consist of surgery or radiation therapy.

Cancer of the Testes

Cancer of the testes is not a particularly common form of cancer. About 5500 new cases are diagnosed each year (2 per 100,000 men). However, it tends to be a disease of young men, and it is the most common form of cancer in men between the ages of 29 and 35. Rates for white men are about double that for black men, with rates for Hispanics, American Indians, and Asian Americans falling in between (American Cancer Society, 1988).

The first sign is usually a painless lump in the testes, or a slight enlargement or change in consistency of the testes. There may be pain in the lower abdomen or groin. Unfortunately, many men do not discover the tumor, or if they do, they do not see a physician soon, so that in most cases the cancer has spread (metastasized) to other organs by the time a physician is consulted. One study showed that when the lump was reported early to the physician, the chances for survival were better than 90 percent. However, when the man waited over three months to see a physi-

The Testicular Self-Exam

Do your self-examination after a warm bath or shower when the skin of the scrotum is relaxed. Examine each testicle gently with the fingers of both hands by rolling the testicle between the thumb and fingers to check for any hard lumps. If a lump or a nodule is found, it will usually be on the sides or front of the testicle and should not be confused with the epididymis, which is located on the top and back side of the testicle. The lump may not be malignant, but most lumps are found in men in their twenties and thirties, and thus you should see a physician promptly.

These are warning signals:

1. A small, hard lump, usually painless, on the front or side of the testicle
2. A heavy feeling in the testicle
3. Discomfort and/or pain in the groin
4. Swelling or tenderness in the breast
5. Accumulation of fluid in the scrotum
6. Enlarged lymph nodes.

See a physician promptly if you have any of these symptoms.

Source: American Cancer Society. (1988). *Facts on testicular cancer.*

FIGURE 4.18
The technique used in the testicular self-exam.

cian, the survival rate dropped to approximately 25 percent ("A Regular Check," 1980).

Diagnosis is made either by a physician's or by your examination of the testes (see Focus 4.2) and by x-rays. Final diagnosis involves surgical removal of the entire testis. This is also the first step in treatment. Fortunately, the other testicle remains, so that hormone production and sexual functioning can continue unimpaired. An artificial, gel-filled testicle can even be implanted.

The cause of testicular cancer is not known for certain. However, it is fairly certain that an undescended testis has a much greater risk of developing cancer. Also, one study found that excessive estrogens during embryonic development of the testes may increase the risk of developing testicular cancer (Henderson et al., 1978).

Summary

The important external organs of the female are the clitoris, the mons, the inner lips, the outer lips, and the vaginal opening. Collectively these are referred to as the vulva. The clitoris is an extremely sensitive organ and is very important in female sexual response. Another important external structure is the hymen, which has taken on great symbolic significance as a sign of virginity, although its absence is not a reliable indicator that a woman is not a virgin. The important internal structures are the vagina, which receives the penis during coitus; the uterus, which houses the developing fetus; the ovaries, which produce eggs and manufacture sex hormones; and the fallopian tubes, which convey the egg to the uterus. The breasts of the female also function in sexual arousal and may have great symbolic significance.

The important external sexual organs of the male are the penis and the scrotum. The penis contains three spongy bodies which, when filled with blood, produce an erection. Circumcision, or surgical removal of the foreskin of the penis, is a debated practice in the United States but may have some health advantages. The scrotum contains the testes, which are responsible for the manufacture of sperm (in the seminiferous tubules) and sex hormones (in the interstitial cells). The temperature of the testes is important and is regulated by the contraction and relaxation of the dartos muscle in the scrotum. Sperm pass out of the testes during ejaculation via the vas deferens, the ejaculatory duct, and the urethra. The seminal vesicles manufacture most of the fluid that mixes with the sperm to form semen. Cowper's glands and the prostate also contribute secretions.

Breast cancer is the most common form of cancer in women. All women should do a monthly self-exam because the earlier a lump is detected, the greater the chances of complete recovery. The Pap test is used to detect cervical cancer. Prostate cancer is the third most common form of cancer in men, but it generally affects only older men. Cancer of the testes, in contrast, although rare, is the most common cancer in men between the ages of 29 and 35. Men should do a monthly testicular self-exam, just as women should do the breast self-exam.

Review Questions

1. The most sexually sensitive organ in the female is the _____.

2. The _____ is a membrane stretching over the vaginal entrance in some virgins.

3. The pubococcygeal muscle is a muscle that supports the uterus, keeping it in place. True or false?

4. The inner layer of the uterus is termed the _____.

5. The ovaries manufacture the sex hormones _____ and _____.

6. The spongy bodies, the corpora cavernosa and the corpus spongiosum, run the length of the penis. True or false?

7. _____ is the term for the surgical removal of the foreskin or prepuce.

8. Testosterone is manufactured in the _____ in the testes.

9. After passing out of the testes and epididymis, sperm move to the vas deferens. True or false?

10. Approximately _____ percent of breast lumps are benign.

(The answers to all review questions are at the end of the book, beginning on page 731.)

Question for Thought, Discussion, and Debate

1. Form two groups of students to debate the following: Resolved: Circumcision should not be performed routinely. You can draw on many resources to provide evidence for your debate, including interviews with doctors and nurses, library materials (books and journal articles on the effects of circumcision), and interviews with parents of infants.

Suggestions for Further Reading

Boston Women's Health Book Collective. (1984). *The new our bodies, ourselves.* (3rd ed.) New York: Simon & Schuster. A good, easy-to-read source on female biology and sexuality.

Diagram Group. (1976). *Man's body: An owner's manual.* New York: Paddington Press (Bantam Books paperback). A comprehensive book on men's health, including sexuality.

Lightfoot-Klein, Hanny. (1989). *Prisoners of ritual: An odyssey into female genital circumcision in Africa.* New York: Haworth. An amazing story of the author's investigations into current female circumcision practices.

Weitzman, Sigmund, Kuter, Irene, & Pizer, H. F. (1987). *Confronting breast cancer. New options in detection and treatment.* New York: Vintage Books. A book that provides a good list of alternatives to consider when dealing with breast cancer so that one can make well-informed decisions.

5

Sex Hormones and Sexual Differentiation

Chapter Highlights

An Odd Gastropod

The snail is a hermaphrodite:
It has beneath its shell
The organs we ascribe to males,
And female parts as well.

When courting snails pair off for love,
Do they embrace as gays?
Or Lesbians? Or two of each
That join in wondrous ways?

The puzzle that I ponder most
Is, do their dual features
Provide them half or twice the fun
*Enjoyed by other creatures?**

One of the marvels of human biology is that the complex and different male and female anatomies—males with penis and scrotum; females with vagina, uterus, and breasts—arise from a single cell, the fertilized egg, which varies only in whether it carries two X chromosomes (XX) or one X and one Y (XY). Many of the structural differences between males and females arise before birth, during the prenatal period, in a process called *prenatal sexual differentiation*. Further differences also develop during puberty. This process of sexual differentiation—both prenatally and during puberty—will be examined in this chapter. First, however, another biological system, the endocrine (hormonal) system, needs to be considered; particular attention will be given to the sex hormones, which play a major role in the differentiation process.

> **Prenatal period (pree-NAY-tul):** The nine months from conception to birth.

* *Source:* Milton Hildebrand. (1979). *Laugh and love.* Hicksville, NY: Exposition Press, p. 134.

SEX HORMONES

Hormones: Chemical substances secreted by the endocrine glands into the bloodstream.

Testosterone: A hormone secreted by the testes in the male (and also present at lower levels in the female).

Androgens: The group of "male" sex hormones, one of which is testosterone.

Estrogens (ESS-troh-jens): The group of "female" sex hormones.

Progesterone (pro-JES-tur-ohn): A "female" sex hormone secreted by the ovaries.

Pituitary gland (pih-TOO-ih-tair-ee): A small endocrine gland located on the lower side of the brain next to the hypothalamus; the pituitary is important in regulating levels of sex hormones.

Hypothalamus (hy-poh-THAL-ah-mus): A small region of the brain that is important in regulating many body functions, including the functioning of the sex hormones.

Hormones are powerful chemical substances manufactured by the *endocrine glands* and secreted directly into the bloodstream. Because they go into the blood, their effects are felt fairly rapidly and at places in the body quite distant from the place in which they were manufactured. The most important sex hormones are **testosterone** (one of a group of hormones called **androgens**) in the male and **estrogens** and **progesterone** in the female. The thyroid, the adrenals, and the pituitary are examples of endocrine glands. We are interested here in the sex glands: the testes in the male and the ovaries in the female. The **pituitary gland** and a closely related region of the brain, the **hypothalamus**, are also important because the pituitary regulates the other glands, in particular the testes and ovaries. Because of its importance, the pituitary has been called the "master gland" of the endocrine system. The pituitary is a small gland, about the size of a pea, which hangs down from the lower side of the brain. It is divided into three lobes: the anterior lobe, the intermediary lobe, and the posterior lobe. The anterior lobe is the one that interacts with the gonads. The hypothalamus is a region at the base of the brain just above the pituitary (see Figure 5.1); it plays a part in regulating many vital behaviors such as eating, drinking, and sexual behavior,[1] and it is important in regulating the pituitary.

These three structures, then—hypothalamus, pituitary, and gonads (testes and ovaries)—function together. They influence such important sexual functions as the

---

[1] One psychologist summarized the functions of the hypothalamus as being the four F's: fighting, feeding, fleeing, and, ahem, sexual behavior.

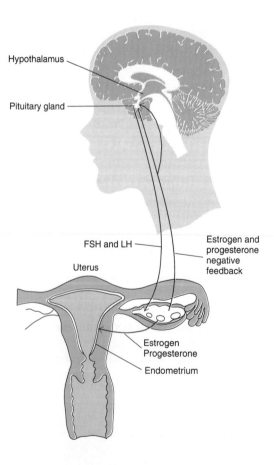

FIGURE 5.1
The hypothalamus-pituitary-gonad feedback loop in women, which regulates production of the sex hormones.

menstrual cycle, pregnancy, the changes of puberty, and sexual behavior. Because these systems are, not surprisingly, somewhat different in males and in females, the sex hormone systems in the male and in the female will be discussed separately.

Sex Hormone Systems in the Male

The pituitary and the testes both produce hormones. The important hormone produced by testes is *testosterone*. Testosterone, a "male" or masculinizing sex hormone, has important functions in stimulating and maintaining the secondary sex characteristics (such as beard growth), maintaining the genitals and their sperm-producing capability, and stimulating the growth of bone and muscle.

The pituitary produces several hormones, two of which are important in this discussion: follicle-stimulating hormone (FSH) and luteinizing hormone (LH). These hormones affect the functioning of the testes. LH controls the amount of testosterone production, and FSH controls sperm production.

Testosterone levels in males are relatively constant. These constant levels are maintained because the hypothalamus, pituitary, and testes operate in a negative feedback loop (Figure 5.2). The levels of testosterone are regulated by a substance called Gn-RH (gonadotropin-releasing hormone), which is secreted by the hypothalamus. (FSH levels are similarly regulated by Gn-RH.) The system comes full circle because the hypothalamus is sensitive to the levels of testosterone present, and thus testosterone influences the output of Gn-RH.

This negative feedback loop operates much like a thermostat-furnace system. If a room is cold, certain changes occur in the thermostat, and it signals the furnace to turn on. The action of the furnace warms the air in the room. Eventually the air becomes so warm that another change is produced in the thermostat, and it sends a signal to the furnace to turn off. The temperature in the room then gradually falls until it produces another change in the thermostat, which then turns on the furnace, and the cycle is repeated. This is a *negative* feedback loop because *rises* in temperature turn *off* the furnace, whereas *decreases* in temperature turn *on* the furnace.

Follicle-stimulating hormone (FSH): A hormone secreted by the pituitary; it stimulates follicle development in females and sperm production in males.

Luteinizing hormone (LH): A hormone secreted by the pituitary; it regulates estrogen secretion and ovum development in the female.

Gn-RH (gonadotropin-releasing hormone): A hormone secreted by the hypothalamus that regulates the pituitary's secretion of hormones.

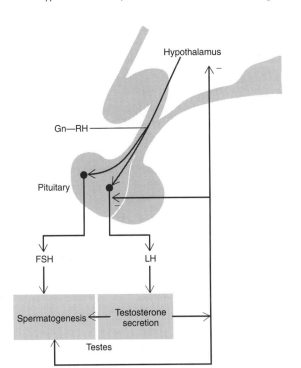

FIGURE 5.2
Schematic diagram of hormonal control of testosterone secretion and sperm production by the testes. The negative signs indicate that testosterone inhibits LH production, both in the pituitary and in the hypothalamus.

The hypothalamus, pituitary, and testes form a similar negative feedback loop, ensuring that testosterone is maintained at a fairly constant level, just as the temperature of a room is kept fairly constant. The pituitary's production of LH stimulates the testes to produce testosterone. But when testosterone levels get high, the hypothalamus reduces its production of Gn-RH; the pituitary's production of LH is then reduced, and the production of testosterone by the testes consequently decreases. When it has fallen, the hypothalamus again increases production of Gn-RH, and the process starts again.

While the level of testosterone in men is fairly constant, there is probably some cycling, with variations according to the time of the day and possibly according to the time of the month (see Chapter 6).

Although it has been clear for some time that there is a negative feedback loop between testosterone levels and LH levels, it has not been clear what regulates FSH levels. Inhibin is a substance produced in the testes (by cells called the Sertoli cells) which serves exactly that function—it acts to regulate FSH levels in a negative feedback loop (Hafez, 1980; Moodbidri et al., 1980).

Inhibin: A substance secreted by the testes, which regulates FSH levels.

Interest in inhibin has been great not only because it is a kind of "missing link" in our understanding of sex hormone control but also because it shows great promise, at least theoretically, as a male contraceptive. That is, because inhibin suppresses FSH production, sperm production in turn is inhibited. Developments in this field in the 1990s should be interesting.

Sex Hormone Systems in the Female

The ovaries produce two important hormones, *estrogen*[2] and *progesterone*. The functions of estrogen include bringing about many of the changes of puberty (stimulating the growth of the uterus and vagina, enlarging the pelvis, and stimulating breast growth). Estrogen is also responsible for maintaining the mucous membranes of the vagina and stopping the growth of bone and muscle, which accounts for the smaller size of females as compared with males.

In adult women the levels of estrogen and progesterone fluctuate according to the various phases of the menstrual cycle (see Chapter 6) and during various other stages such as pregnancy and menopause. The levels of estrogen and progesterone are regulated by the two pituitary hormones, FSH and LH. Thus the levels of estrogen and progesterone are controlled by a negative feedback loop of the hypothalamus, pituitary, and ovaries, similar to the negative feedback loop in the male (see Figure 5.3). For example, as shown on the right side of Figure 5.3, increases in the level of Gn-RH increase the level of LH, and the increases in LH eventually produce increases in the output of estrogen; finally, the increases in the level of estrogen inhibit (decrease) the production of Gn-RH and LH.

The pituitary produces two other hormones, *prolactin* and *oxytocin*, which play roles in stimulating secretion of milk by the mammary glands after a woman has given birth to a child.

The female sex hormone system functions much like the male sex hormone system, except that the female system is, in two senses, somewhat more complex: the ovaries produce two major hormones (unlike the testes, which produce only one), and the levels of hormones fluctuate in females, whereas levels are fairly constant in males.

The functioning of the female sex hormone system and the menstrual cycle will be considered in more detail in Chapter 6.

---

[2] "Estrogen" actually refers to a group of hormones and might more properly be called "estrogens," much as we refer to "androgens."

FIGURE 5.3
Schematic diagram of
hormonal control of
estrogen secretion and
ovum production by the
ovaries (during the
follicular phase of the
menstrual cycle). Note how
similar the mechanism is to
the one in the male (Figure
5.2).

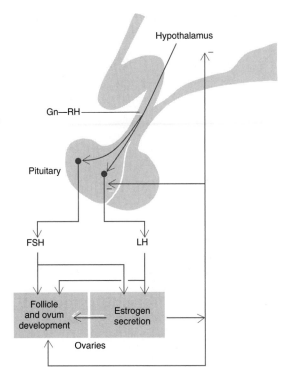

PRENATAL SEXUAL DIFFERENTIATION

Sex Chromosomes

As noted above, at the time of conception the future human being consists of only a single cell, the fertilized egg. The only difference between the fertilized egg that will become a female and the fertilized egg that will become a male is the sex chromosomes carried in that fertilized egg. If there are two X chromosomes, the result will normally be a female; if there is one X and one Y, the result will normally be a male. Thus, while incredibly tiny, the sex chromosomes carry a wealth of information which they transmit to various organs throughout the body, giving them instructions on how to differentiate in the course of development. The Y chromosome, because it is smaller, carries less information than the X.

Occasionally, individuals receive at conception a sex chromosome combination other than XX or XY. Such abnormal sex chromosome complements may lead to a variety of clinical syndromes, such as Klinefelter's syndrome. In this syndrome, a genetic male has an extra X chromosome (XXY). As a result, the testes are abnormal, no sperm are produced, and testosterone levels are low.

The single cell divides repeatedly, becoming a two-celled organism, then a four-celled organism, than an eight-celled organism, and so on. By the time the embryo is 28 days of age (postconception), it is about 1 centimeter (less than ½ inch) long, but the male and female embryo are still identical, save for the sex chromosomes; that is, the embryo is still in the undifferentiated state. However, by the fifth or sixth week after conception, some basic structures have been formed that will eventually become either a male or a female reproductive system. At this point, the embryo has a pair of gonads (each gonad has two parts, an outer cortex and an inner medulla), two sets of ducts (the *Müllerian ducts* and the *Wolffian ducts*), and rudimentary external genitals (the *genital tubercle,* the *genital folds,* and the *genital swelling*) (see Figure 5.4).

FIGURE 5.4
*Development of the male
and female external
genitals from the
undifferentiated stage. This
occurs during prenatal
development. Note
homologous organs in the
female and male.*

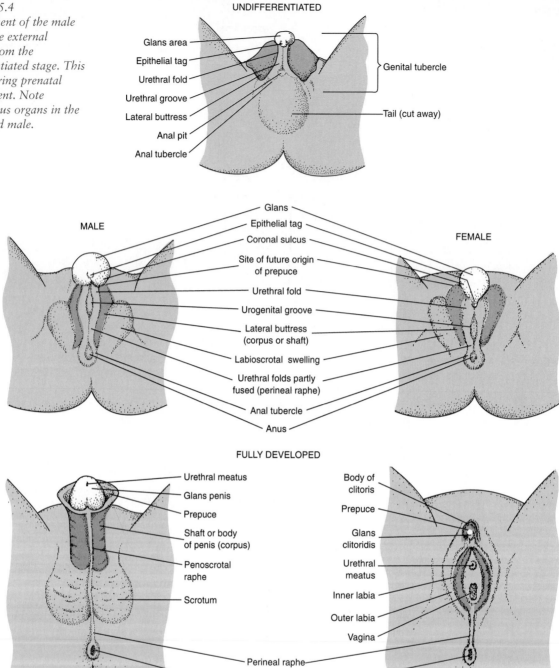

UNDIFFERENTIATED

Glans area
Epithelial tag
Urethral fold
Urethral groove
Lateral buttress
Anal pit
Anal tubercle

Genital tubercle
Tail (cut away)

MALE **FEMALE**

Glans
Epithelial tag
Coronal sulcus
Site of future origin
of prepuce
Urethral fold
Urogenital groove
Lateral buttress
(corpus or shaft)
Labioscrotal swelling
Urethral folds partly
fused (perineal raphe)
Anal tubercle
Anus

FULLY DEVELOPED

Urethral meatus
Glans penis
Prepuce
Shaft or body
of penis (corpus)
Penoscrotal
raphe
Scrotum

Body of
clitoris
Prepuce
Glans
clitoridis
Urethral
meatus
Inner labia
Outer labia
Vagina

Perineal raphe
Perianal tissues including
external sphincter

Gonads

In the seventh week after conception, the sex chromosomes direct the gonads to begin differentiation. In the male, the undifferentiated gonad develops into a testis at about 7 weeks. In the female, the process occurs somewhat later, with the ovaries developing at around 11 or 12 weeks.

An exciting development was reported in 1986, when researchers located the gene that directs male or female development (Kolata, 1986; Page et al., 1987). The gene, located on the Y chromosome, is called **testis-determining factor,** or TDF. If present, testes differentiate and male development occurs; if not, ovaries differentiate and female development occurs. The researchers discovered the gene by studying cases of abnormal development—for example, adult women who had XY sex chromosomes and were infertile. The researchers found that these individuals were missing a section of the Y chromsome, precisely the section containing the TDF gene.

Prenatal Hormones and the Genitals

Once the ovaries and testes have differentiated, they begin to produce different sex hormones, and these hormones then direct the differentiation of the rest of the internal and external genital system (see Figure 5.4).

In the female the Wolffian ducts degenerate, and the **Müllerian ducts** turn into the fallopian tubes, the uterus, and the upper part of the vagina. The tubercle becomes the clitoris, the folds become the inner lips, and the swelling develops into the outer lips.

In the male the testes secrete *Müllerian inhibiting substance,* which causes the Müllerian ducts to degenerate, and the **Wolffian ducts** turn into the epididymis, the vas deferens, and the ejaculatory duct. The tubercle becomes the glans penis, the folds form the shaft of the penis, and the swelling develops into the scrotum.

The mechanism by which the internal and external genitals differentiate has been the subject of much research. The principle seems to be parallel to that for differentiation of gonads; it appears that the presence or absence of the testes and their hormone production is critical. The testes of the male fetus secrete androgens, which stimulate the development of male structures, and a second substance, the Müllerian inhibiting substance which suppresses the development of the Müllerian ducts. Thus if the hormonal output of the testes is present, male structures develop. If it is absent, female structures develop.

By four months after conception, the gender of the fetus is clear from the appearance of the external genitals (Figure 5.4).

Descent of the Testes and Ovaries

As the developmental changes are taking place, the ovaries and testes are changing in shape and position. At first, the ovaries and testes lie near the top of the abdominal cavity. By the tenth week they have grown and have moved down to the level of the upper edge of the pelvis. The ovaries remain there until after birth; later they shift to their adult position in the pelvis.

The male testes must make a much longer journey, down into the scrotum via a passageway called the *inguinal canal.* Normally this movement occurs around the seventh month after conception. After the descent of the testes, the inguinal canal is closed off.

Two problems in this process may occur. First, one or both testes may have failed to descend into the scrotum by the time of birth, a condition known as *undescended testes,* or cryptorchidism. This occurs in about 2 percent of all males. In most of these cases, the testes do descend by puberty, and so only about 1 in 500 adult men has undescended testes. If the testes do not descend spontaneously, however, the condition must be corrected by surgery or hormonal therapy. The optimum time for doing this is before age 5. Otherwise, if both testes have failed to descend, the man would be sterile because, as was discussed in Chapter 4, the high temperature

FIGURE 5.5
The death, in 1980, of Stella Walsh, aged 69, attracted widespread publicity. Walsh had been a star in women's track competition in the 1930s, winning five gold, one bronze, and three silver medals in international competition. She won the gold medal in the 100-meter dash in the 1932 Olympics, running it in a record 11.9 seconds. She continued on in many events, winning the national pentathlon championship in 1954 at the age of 43. The coroner's report at her death revealed some startling findings, however. Genetically, she was a mosaic—that is, some of the cells in her body contained the male sex chromosome combination (XY) and some contained the female sex chromosomes (XX). Anatomically, she had male sex organs, but they were nonfunctional. Her hair was balding. Yet she had been raised and lived as a female. Unfortunately, the research and treatments of John Money and others were not available in her childhood and certainly her case would be handled differently today. She was married to a man in 1956 for two months. Her former husband, in an interview, said that they had sex a couple of times, always with the lights out. At the time of her death, Walsh was employed by the city of Cleveland in a coaching-type job for the recreation department at a salary of $10,000, the highest one she ever attained.

of the testes inside the body would inhibit the production of sperm. Undescended testes are also more likely to develop cancer.

The second possible problem occurs when the inguinal canal does not close off completely. It may then reopen later in life, creating a passageway through which loops of the intestine may enter the scrotum. This condition is called *inguinal hernia* and can be remedied by simple surgery.

Brain Differentiation

There are some differences between male and female brains (MacLusky & Naftolin, 1981). Some of the major differences are found in the hypothalamus, and they result from a differentiation process in prenatal development much like the differentiation process that creates reproductive-system differences (Money & Ehrhardt, 1972). Once the gonads have differentiated, if testosterone is produced, the hypothalamus differentiates in the male direction; if testosterone is absent, the differentiation is in the female direction.

Anatomically, the consequences of this differentiation are that the cells and the neural circuits of the hypothalamus differ somewhat for males and females. Physiologically, an important consequence is that beginning in puberty, the female hypothalamus directs a cyclic secretion of sex hormones, creating the menstrual cycle; the male hypothalamus directs a relatively acyclic, or constant, production of sex hormones.

The brain differentiation probably also has some consequences in terms of behavior, most notably sexual behavior, and aggressive behavior and possible other behaviors as well. Unfortunately, most of the research on this point has been done with animals, and so there is some debate over whether the effects also occur in humans. This research will be discussed in detail in Chapter 9.

Homologous Organs

The preceding discussion of sexual differentiation highlights the fact that although adult men and women appear to have very different reproductive anatomies, their reproductive organs have similar origins. When an organ in the male and an organ in the female both develop from the same embryonic tissue, the organs are said to be homologous. When the two organs have similar functions, they are said to be analogous. Table 5.1 summarizes the major homologies and analogies of the male and female reproductive systems. For example, ovaries and testes are both homologous (they develop from an indifferent gonad) and analogous (they produce gametes and sex hormones).

Homologous organs (huh-MOLL-uh-gus): Organs in the male and female that develop from the same embryonic tissue.

Analogous organs: Organs in the male and female that have similar functions.

JOHN MONEY, HERMAPHRODITES, AND THE EIGHT VARIABLES OF GENDER

Gender is not a simple matter, a fact that is apparent from the preceding discussion. Most people, however, assume that it is. That is, people typically assume that if a person is female, she will be feminine; will think of herself as a woman; will be

Table 5.1
Homologous and Analogous Organs of the Male and Female Reproductive Systems

| Embryonic Source | Homologous Organs | | Analogous Organs | |
	In the Adult Male	In the Adult Female	In the Adult Male	In the Adult Female
Gonad (medulla plus cortex)	Testes (from medulla)	Ovaries (from cortex)	Testes (from medulla)	Ovaries (from cortex)
Genital tubercle	Glans penis	Clitoris	Glans penis	Clitoris
Genital swelling	Scrotum	Outer lips		
Müllerian duct	Degenerates, leaving only remnants	Fallopian tubes, uterus, part of vagina		
Wolffian duct	Epididymis, vas deferens, seminal vesicles	Degenerates, leaving only remnants		
Urethral primordia	Prostate, Cowper's glands	Skene's glands, Bartholin's glands	Prostate, Cowper's glands	Skene's glands, Bartholin's glands

sexually attracted to men; will have a clitoris, vagina, uterus, and ovaries; and will have sex chromosomes XX. The parallel assumption is that all males are masculine; think of themselves as male; are sexually attracted to women; have a penis, testes, and scrotum; and have sex chromosomes XY.

A major research program of the last several decades, conducted at Johns Hopkins University by the psychologist John Money and his colleagues, challenges these assumptions and provides a great deal of information about sexuality and gender and their development. (For an excellent summary of this research, see Money & Ehrhardt, 1972.) Before the results of this research are discussed, however, some background information is necessary.

First, Money (1987) distinguishes among the eight variables of gender.[3]

1. *Chromosomal gender*   XX in the female; XY in the male
2. *Gonadal gender*   Ovaries in the female; testes in the male
3. *Prenatal hormonal gender*   Estrogen and progesterone in the female; testosterone in the male before birth
4. *Internal accessory organs*   Uterus and vagina in the female; prostate and seminal vesicles in the male
5. *External genital appearance*   Clitoris and vaginal opening in the female; penis and scrotum in the male
6. *Pubertal hormonal gender*   At puberty, estrogen and progesterone in the female; testosterone in the male
7. *Assigned gender*   The announcement at birth, "It's a girl" or "It's a boy," based on the appearance of the external genitals; the gender the parents and the rest of society believe the child to be; the gender in which the child is reared
8. *Gender identity*   The person's private, internal sense of maleness or femaleness—which is expressed in personality and behavior—and the integration of this sense with the result of the personality and with the gender roles prescribed by society.

These variables might be subdivided into biological variables (the first six) and psychological variables (the last two).

In most cases, of course, all the variables are in agreement in an individual. That is, in most cases the person is a "consistent" female or male. If the person is a female, she has XX chromosomes, ovaries, a uterus and vagina, and a clitoris; she is reared as a female; and she thinks of herself as a female. If the person is a male, he has the parallel set of appropriate characteristics.

However, as a result of a number of "accidents" during the course of prenatal sexual development and differentiation, the gender indicated by one or more of these variables may disagree with the gender indicated by others. When the contradictions are among several of the biological variables (1 through 6), the person is called a **pseudohermaphrodite** or a *hermaphrodite*.[4] Biologically, the gender of such a person is ambiguous; the reproductive structures may be partly male and partly female, or they may be incompletely male or incompletely female. Money's research is based on these individuals.

A number of syndromes can cause pseudohermaphroditism, some of the most

Pseudohermaphrodite: An individual who has a mixture of male and female reproductive structures, so that it is not clear whether the individual is a male or a female.

---

[3]   The distinction between the terms "gender" and "sex," discussed in Chapter 1, is being maintained here.

[4]   The term "hermaphrodite" is taken from Hermaphroditos, the name of the mythological son of Hermes and Aphrodite. The latter was the Greek goddess of love.

common being the adrenogenital syndrome, progestin-induced hermaphroditism, and the androgen insensitivity syndrome. In *congenital adrenal hyperplasia* (also called "adrenogenital syndrome"), a genetic female develops ovaries normally as a fetus; later in the course of prenatal development, however, the adrenal gland begins to function abnormally (as a result of a recessive genetic condition unconnected with the sex chromosomes), and an excess amount of androgens is produced. Prenatal sexual differentiation then does not follow the normal female course. As a result, the external genitals are partly or completely male in appearance; the labia are partly or totally fused (and thus there is no vaginal opening), and the clitoris is enlarged to the size of a small penis (see Figure 5.6). Hence at birth these genetic females are often identified as males. *Progestin-induced hermaphroditism* is a similar syndrome which resulted from a drug, progestin, that was at one time given to pregnant women to help them maintain the pregnancy if they were prone to miscarriage. (The drug is no longer prescribed because of the following effects.) As the drug circulated in the mother's bloodstream, the developing fetus was essentially exposed to a high dose of androgens. (Progestin and androgens are quite similar biochemicals, and in the body the progestin acted like androgen.) In genetic females this produced an abnormal, masculinized genital development similar to that found in the adrenogenital syndrome. The reverse case occurs in *androgen insensivity syndrome*. In this syndrome a genetic male produces normal levels of testosterone; however, as a result of a genetic condition, the body tissues are insensitive to the testosterone, and prenatal development is feminized. Thus the individual is born with the external appearance of a female: a small vagina (but no uterus) and undescended testes.

Several findings have emerged from Money's studies of these individuals. First, the research provides good evidence of the great complexity of sex and gender and their development. Many variables are involved in gender and sex, and there are many steps in gender differentiation, even before birth. Because the process is complex, it is very vulnerable to disturbances, creating conditions such as hermaphroditism. Indeed, the research serves to question our basic notions of what it means to be male or female. In the adrenogenital syndrome, is the genetic female who is born with male external genitals a male or a female? What makes a person male or female? Chromosomal gender? External genital appearance? Gender identity?

A second important result from this research has to do with gender identity and how it develops. There has been a debate over whether gender identity is biologically programmed in an individual or environmentally produced through learning. Money argues a biology-environment interaction position. As evidence, he cites cases of matched pairs of pseudohermaphrodites (see Focus 5.1). If such a child is assigned to be a female and is reared as a female (with appropriate corrective surgery and hormone therapy), she adjusts well in the female role and has a female gender identity. If a child with the identical syndrome at birth is assigned to be a male and is reared accordingly (once again with surgical and hormonal treatment), he adjusts well to the male role and has a male gender identity. These outcomes provide evidence of the importance of environment in the development of gender identity. However, in all the cases, gender reassignment was supplemented by appropriate surgical or hormonal therapy. Thus biological factors also contributed to the success of the outcome—that is, biology and environment interact.

There do seem to be some limitations to the arbitrariness with which gender can be assigned or reassigned by the environment. Gender reassignment can be done very successfully, as the case histories indicate, up to the age of about 18 months. After that time, reassignment is difficult (and in most cases impossible) and causes serious problems of adjustment, apparently because the child begins forming a strong concept of his or her own identity at around 18 months of age (Kohlberg, 1966; Money & Ehrhardt, 1972). Once this basic concept is formed, it is essentially irreversible. Attempts at reassignment are futile.

Two Case Histories from the Johns Hopkins Clinic

The two individuals discussed below are interesting because both are genetic females (both with the adrenogenital syndrome), and yet one eventually became a female with a female gender identity, while the other eventually become a male with a male gender identity.

The first member of the pair was reared as a girl but was actually announced as a boy at birth because of the appearance of the genitals (Figure 5.6). The correct diagnosis was established by the age of 2 months, and a sex reannouncement was decided upon. The parents were counseled on how to make such an announcement within the family and the community, and they accomplished this successfully. Today it is known that the first stage of surgical feminization could have been done immediately, but at the time it was delayed until the age of 2 years as a precaution against surgically induced trauma. After the surgery, the child had an unremarkable childhood medically, except for the fact that she took cortisone pills daily. Her breast development began at the age of 13, and menstruation did not begin until age 20.

During childhood, she developed behaviorally as a girl with tomboyish tendencies. In adolescence, academic and career interests had priority over dating and romance. There was no romantic inclination toward either boys or girls, but rather a projection of boyfriends and marriage into the future. The girl was attractive and feminine.

The second member of the pair was diagnosed at birth as a male with a hypospadiac phallus and undescended testes. Three stages of surgical masculination ended in failure because urine backed up into the internal vagina and caused infection. At age 3½ a correct diagnosis was made, and the case was referred to Johns Hopkins. At this time, being in a hospital again terrified the child. He said that a nurse would cut off his "wee-wee" and that his baby sister had had hers cut off. His terror abated when, with clay and water, he was shown how an imperfect penis could be repaired.

It was decided to allow him to continue living as a boy. The appropriate surgery was done, and he was given cortisone therapy during childhood. At the time of puberty, masculination was induced by androgen therapy. Artificial testes were implanted in the empty scrotum.

Unfortunately, as the boy approached adolescence, his family life was tortured. His parents

One criticism of Money's research and conclusions should be raised. It is difficult to know how relevant the abnormal cases that Money studied are to an understanding of the normal process of acquiring a gender identity.

Nonetheless, Money's data do provide interesting evidence on abnormalities of prenatal sexual differentiation, on the complexity of sex and gender, and on the environmental and biological determinants of gender identity.

Diamond's Biased Interaction Model

Reproductive biologist Milton Diamond (1965, 1979, 1982) has proposed a model in opposition to Money's interaction theory of the determination of gender identity. According to Diamond's *biased interaction model,* gender identity and sexuality are influenced by environmental forces, but this influence is significantly affected by

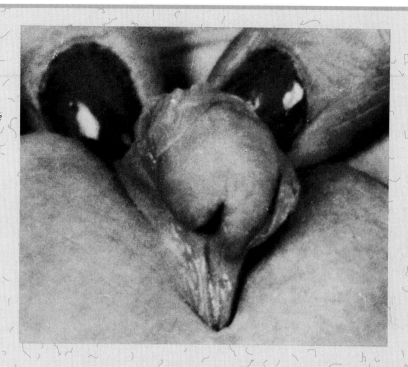

fought. The mother won points by reminding her husband that he was not the father of this particular child, and the boy heard what she said.

In adolescence the boy was an academic under-achiever, and he tended to seek the company of quasi-delinquents, with whom he could achieve status as a rebel. He was accepted by the other boys as one of them. He was not overly aggressive. Psychosexually, all his romantic feelings and approaches were directed toward girls, despite his trepidation at the prospect of attempting intercourse with a penis that was too small and with prosthetic testes that could be recognized on touching as not soft enough.

Thus, although both members of the pair were genetically and anatomically identical at birth, one eventually became a female functioning adequately in the female role, while the other became a male functioning adequately in the male role.

Source: John Money and Anke Ehrhardt. *Man and woman, boy and girl.* Baltimore: Johns Hopkins, 1972, pp. 154–156.

the individual's biological makeup, specifically genes and hormones. Diamond does not deny environmental forces. Rather, he claims that gender identity and sexuality are an outcome of an interaction between biology and environment, with biology biasing the interaction. Thus, according to his position, it is not surprising that the vast majority of people have a gender identity that agrees with their genetic gender and their hormonal gender.

Diamond cites as evidence both animal studies and human studies indicating the effect of biological factors in determining gender identity. One classic study was of an accidental experiment in a small community in the Dominican Republic (Imperato-McGinley et al., 1974). These people are called the Guevodoces. Due to a genetic-endocrine problem, a large number of genetic males were born who, at birth, appeared to be females. (The syndrome is called 5-Alpha Reductase Syndrome of male hermaphroditism.) They had a vaginal pouch instead of a scrotum and a clitoris-sized penis. The uneducated parents were unaware that there were any problems, and these genetic males were treated as typical females. At puberty, a spontaneous biological change causes a penis to develop. Significantly, their psychological orientation also changed. Despite rearing as females, their gender identity switched to male, and they developed heterosexual interests. Thus all the forces of environment to that point had no effect when biology changed. Biology definitely biased the outcome of their gender identity, just as Diamond's biased interaction model would predict. (For a rebuttal, see Money, 1987; Herdt, 1990.)

PUBERTY

Puberty is not a point in time, but rather a process during which there is further sexual differentiation. It is the stage in life during which the body changes from that of a child into that of an adult, with secondary sexual characteristics and the ability to reproduce sexually. **Puberty** can be scientifically defined as the time during which there is sudden enlargement and maturation of the gonads, other genitalia, and secondary sex characteristics, leading to reproductive capacity (Tanner, 1967). It is the second important period—the other being the prenatal period—during which sexual differentiation takes place. Perhaps the most important single event in the process is the first ejaculation for the male and the first menstruation for the female, although the latter is not necessarily a sign of reproductive capability since girls typically do not produce mature eggs until a year or two after the first menstruation.

> **Puberty:** The time during which there is sudden enlargement and maturation of the gonads, other genitalia, and secondary sex characteristics, so that the individual is capable of reproduction.

The physiological process which underlies puberty in both genders is a marked increase in level of sex hormones. Thus the hypothalamus, pituitary, and gonads control the changes.

Adolescence is a socially defined period of development which bears some relationship to puberty. Adolescence represents a psychological transition from the behavior and attitudes of a child to the behavior, attitudes, and responsibilities of an adult. In the United States it corresponds roughly to the teenage years. Modern American culture has an unusually long period of adolescence. A century ago, adolescence was much shorter; the lengthening of the educational process has served to prolong adolescence. In some cultures, in fact, adolescence does not exist; the child shifts to being an adult directly, with only a *rite de passage* in between.

Before describing the changes that take place during puberty, two points should be noted. First, the timing of the pubertal process differs considerably for males and females. Girls begin the change around 8 to 12 years of age, while boys do so about two years later. Girls reach their full height by about age 16, while boys continue growing until about age 18 or later. Mother Nature's capriciousness in allowing males and females to be out of step with each other at this stage creates no small number of crises for the adolescent. Girls are interested in boys long before boys are aware that girls exist. A girl may be stuck with a date who barely reaches her armpits, while the boy may have to cope with someone who is better qualified to be on the basketball team than he is.

Second, there are large individual differences (differences from one person to the next) in the age at which the processes of puberty take place. Thus there is no "normal" time to begin menstruating or growing a beard. Accordingly, age ranges are given in describing the timing of the process.

Changes in the Female

A summary of the physical changes of puberty in males and females is provided in Table 5.2. The first sign of pubescence in the female is the beginning of breast

Table 5.2
Summary of the Changes of Puberty and Their Sequence

	Girls			Boys	
Characteristic	Age of First Appearance (Years)	Major Hormonal Influence	Characteristic	Age of First Appearance (Years)	Major Hormonal Influence
1. Growth of breasts	8–13	Pituitary growth hormone, estrogens, progesterone, thyroxine	1. Growth of testes, scrotal sac	10–13.5	Pituitary growth hormone, testosterone
2. Growth of pubic hair	8–14	Adrenal androgens	2. Growth of pubic hair	10–15	Testosterone
3. Body growth	9.5–14.5	Pituitary growth hormone, adrenal androgens, estrogens	3. Body growth	10.5–16	Pituitary growth hormone, testosterone
4. Menarche	10–16.5	Hypothalamic releasing factors, FSH, LH, estrogens, progesterone	4. Growth of penis	11–14.5	Testosterone
			5. Change in voice (growth of larynx)	About the same time as penis growth	Testosterone
5. Underarm hair	About two years after pubic hair	Adrenal androgens	6. Facial and underarm hair	About two years after pubic hair	Testosterone
6. Oil- and sweat-producing glands (acne occurs when glands are clogged)	About the same time as under-arm hair	Adrenal androgens	7. Oil- and sweat-producing glands, acne	About the same time as under-arm hair	Testosterone

Source: After B. Goldstein. (1976). *Introduction to human sexuality.* New York: McGraw-Hill, pp. 80–81.

development, which generally starts at around 8 to 13 years of age. The ducts in the nipple area swell, and there is a growth of fatty and connective tissue, causing the nipples to project forward and the small, conical buds to increase in size. These changes are produced by increases in the levels of the sex hormones by a mechanism that will be described below.

As the growth of fatty and supporting tissue increases in the breasts, a similar increase takes place at the hips and buttocks, leading to the rounded contours that distinguish adult female bodies from adult male bodies. Individual females have unique patterns of fat deposit, and so there are also considerable individual differences in the resulting female shapes.

Another visible sign of pubescence is the growth of pubic hair, which occurs shortly after breast development begins. About two years later, axillary (underarm) hair appears.

Body growth increases sharply during pubescence, approximately during the age range of 9.5 to 14.5 years. The growth spurt for girls occurs about two years before the growth spurt for boys (Figure 5.7). This is consistent with girls' general pattern of maturing earlier than boys. Even prenatally, girls show an earlier hardening of the structures that become bones. One exception to this pattern is in fertility; boys produce mature sperm earlier than girls produce mature ova.

Estrogen eventually applies the brakes to the growth spurt in girls; the presence of estrogen also causes the growth period to end sooner in girls, thus accounting for the lesser height of adult women as compared with adult men.

At about 13 years of age, the menarche (first menstruation) occurs. The girl, however, is not capable of becoming pregnant until ovulation begins, typically about two years after the menarche. The first menstruation is not only an important biological event but also an important psychological one. Various cultures have ceremonies recognizing its importance. In some families, it is a piece of news that spreads quickly to the relatives. Girls themselves display a wide range of reactions to the event, ranging from negative ones, such as fear, shame, or disgust, to positive ones, such as a sense of pride, maturity, and womanliness. Some of the most negative reactions occur when the girl has not been prepared for the menarche, which is still the case surprisingly often.

Parents who are concerned about preparing their daughters for the first menstruation should remember that there is a wide range in the age at which it occurs. It is not unusual for a girl to start menstruating in the fifth grade, and instances of the menarche during the fourth grade, while rare, do occur.

What determines the age at which a girl first menstruates? One explanation is the *percent body fat hypothesis* (Fishman, 1980; Frisch & McArthur, 1974; Hopwood et al., 1990). During puberty, deposits of body fat increase in females. According to the percent body fat hypothesis, the percentage of body weight that is fat has to rise to a certain level for menstruation to occur for the first time and for it to be maintained. Thus very skinny adolescent girls would tend to be late in the timing of first menstruation. The percent body fat hypothesis also helps to make sense of two related phenomena: the cessation of menstruation in anorexics and the cessation of menstruation in women distance runners. *Anorexia nervosa* refers to a condition in which the person—most commonly an adolescent girl—engages in compulsive, extreme dieting, perhaps to the point of starving herself to death. As anorexia

Menarche (MEN-ar-key): First menstruation.

FIGURE 5.7
The adolescent spurt of growth for boys and girls. Note that girls experience their growth spurt earlier than boys do.

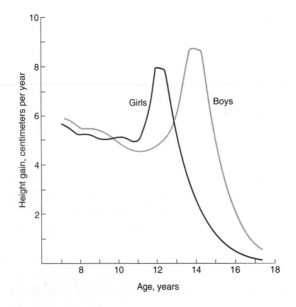

FIGURE 5.8
There is great variability in the onset of puberty and its growth spurt. (a) Both girls are 12-year-old seventh graders. (b) All boys are 13 years old.

progresses, the percentage of body fat declines and menstruation ceases. It is also fairly common for women who are runners, and all women who exercise seriously to the point where their body fat is substantially reduced, to cease menstruating. For both anorexics and female runners, it seems that when the percentage of body fat falls below a critical value, the biological mechanisms controlling the menstrual cycle shut off the functions producing menstruation.[5]

Before we leave the topic of running, I should note that there is some evidence that serious exercise also affects the male reproductive system. One study of male distance runners found that their testosterone levels were only about 68 percent as high, on the average, as a control group's testosterone levels (Wheeler et al., 1984). There are some reports of male long-distance runners complaining of a loss of sex drive, but it is unclear whether it results from reduced testosterone levels or from the perpetual feelings of fatigue they have from their intensive training (Wheeler et al., 1984).

Other body changes during puberty include a development of the blood supply to the clitoris, a thickening of the walls of the vagina, and a rapid growth of the uterus, which doubles in size between the tenth and the eighteenth years. The pelvic bone structure grows and widens, contributing to the rounded shape of the female and creating a passageway large enough for an infant to move through during birth. Once again, there are large individual differences in the shape of the pelvis, and it is important for the physician to identify shapes that may lead to problems in childbirth.

The dramatic changes that occur during pubescence are produced, basically, by the endocrine system and its upsurge in sex hormone production during puberty. The process begins with an increase in secretion of FSH by the pituitary gland. FSH

[5] On the other hand, programs of moderate, regular aerobic exercise have been shown to reduce menstrual problems such as cramps (Golub, 1992; Israel et al., 1985).

Adrenal gland (uh-DREE-nul): An endocrine gland located just above the kidney; in the female, it is the major producer of androgens.

in turn stimulates the ovaries to produce estrogen. Estrogen is responsible for many of the changes that occur; it stimulates breast growth and the growth of the uterus and vagina.

Another endocrine gland involved in puberty is the adrenal gland, which is located just above the kidney. In the female, the adrenal gland is the major producer of androgens (male sex hormones), which exist at low levels in females. Adrenal androgens stimulate the growth of pubic and axillary hair and may be related to the female sex drive. They also may be related to the development of *acne,* a distressing problem of adolescence that is caused by a clogging of the sebaceous (oil-producing) glands, resulting in pustules, blackheads, and redness on the face and possibly the chest and back. Generally it is not severe enough to be a medical problem, although its psychological impact may be great. In order to avoid scarring, severe cases should be treated by a physician, the treatment typically being ultraviolet light and/or antibiotics. A new drug, Accutane, has recently been developed and is highly effective for severe cases. However, it must be used cautiously because it may have serious side effects, including birth defects if taken by a pregnant woman.

Another problem for some girls during puberty is a temporary period of overweight or obesity. If the weight gain is not excessive and lasts for only a short period, there is no cause for concern.

Changes in the Male

As noted above, puberty begins at about 10 or 11 years of age in boys, about two years later than it does in girls.

The physical causes of puberty in boys parallel those in girls. They are initiated by increased production of FSH and LH by the pituitary. At the beginning of puberty, the increase in LH stimulates the testes to produce testosterone, which is responsible for most of the changes of puberty in the male.

The first noticeable pubertal change in males is the growth of the testes and scrotal sac, which begins at around 10 to 13 years of age as a result of testosterone stimulation. The growth of pubic hair begins about the same time. About a year later the penis begins to enlarge, first thickening, and then lengthening. This change also results from testosterone stimulation. Then as the testes enlarge, their production of testosterone increases even more; thus there is rapid growth of the penis, testes, and pubic hair at ages 13 and 14.

The growth of facial and axillary hair begins about two years after the beginning of pubic-hair growth. The growth of facial hair begins with the appearance of fuzz on the upper lip; adult beards do not appear until two or three years later. Indeed, by age 17, 50 percent of American males have not yet shaved. These changes also result from testosterone stimulation, which continues to produce growth of facial and chest hair beyond 20 years of age.

Erections increase in frequency. The organs that produce the fluid of semen, particularly the prostate, enlarge considerably at about the same time the other organs are growing. By age 13 or 14 the boy is capable of ejaculation.[6] By about age 15, the ejaculate contains mature sperm, and the male is now fertile. The pituitary hormone FSH is responsible for initiating and maintaining the production of mature sperm.

Beginning about a year after the first ejaculation, the boy begins having nocturnal emissions, or "wet dreams." For the boy who has never masturbated, a wet dream may be his first ejaculation.

---

[6] Note that orgasm and ejaculation are two separate processes, even though they generally occur together, at least in males after puberty. But orgasm may occur without ejaculation, and ejaculation may occur without orgasm.

At about the same time penis growth occurs, the larynx ("voice box") begins to grow in response to testosterone. As the larynx enlarges, the boy's voice drops, or "changes." Typically the transition occurs at around age 13 or 14. Because testosterone is necessary to produce the change in voice, castration before puberty results in a male with a permanently high voice. This principle was used to produce the castrati, who sang in the great choirs of Europe during the eighteenth century. They began as lovely boy sopranos, and their parents or the choirmaster, hating to see their beautiful voices destroyed at puberty, had them castrated so that they remained permanent sopranos. Female bodies are not the only ones that have been mutilated for strange reasons! Contrary to popular belief, castration in adulthood will not produce a high voice because the larynx has already grown.

A great spurt of body growth begins in males at around 11 to 16 years of age (Figure 5.7). Height increases rapidly. Body contours also change. While the changes in girls involve mainly the increase in fatty tissue in the breasts and hips, the changes in boys involve mainly an increase in muscle mass. Eventually testosterone brings the growth process to an end, although it permits the growth period to continue longer than it does in females.

Puberty brings changes and also problems. As noted previously, one of them is acne, which affects boys more frequently than girls. Gynecomastia (breast enlargement) may occur temporarily in boys, creasing considerable embarrassment. About 80 percent of boys in puberty experience this problem, which is probably caused by small amounts of female sex hormones produced by the testes. Obesity may also be a temporary problem, although it is more frequent in girls than boys.

In various cultures around the world, puberty rites are performed to signify the boy's passage to manhood. In the United States the only remaining vestiges of such ceremonies are the Jewish bar mitzvah and, in Christian churches, confirmation. In a sense, it is unfortunate that we do not give more formal recognition to puberty. Puberty rites probably serve an important psychological function in that they are a formal, public announcement of the fact that the boy or girl is passing through an important and difficult period of change. In the absence of such rituals, the young person may think that his or her body is doing strange things and may feel very much alone. This might be particularly problematic for boys, who lack an obvious sign of puberty like the first menstruation (the first ejaculation is probably the closest analogy) to help them identify the stage they are in.

Summary

The sex hormone systems in males and females were discussed in the first section. The major sex hormones are testosterone, which is produced by the male's testes, and estrogen and progesterone, which are produced by the female's ovaries. Levels of the sex hormones are regulated by two hormones secreted by the pituitary: FSH (follicle-stimulating hormone) and LH (luteinizing hormone). The gonads, pituitary, and hypothalamus regulate one another's output through a negative feedback loop. Inhibin is a recently discovered substance that regulates FSH levels.

Next the process of prenatal sexual differentiation was considered. At conception males and females differ only in the sex chromosomes (XX in females and XY in males). As the fetus grows, the TDF gene on the Y chromosome directs the gonads to differentiate into the testes or ovaries. Different hormones are then produced by the gonads, and these stimulate further differentiation of the internal and external reproductive structures as well as differentiation of the hypothalamus. A male organ and a female organ which derive from the same embryonic tissue are said to be homologous to each other.

An important distinction between the eight variables of gender arises from John Money's research on hermaphrodites. Pseudohermaphroditism is generally the result of various accidents that occur during the course of prenatal sexual differentiation. Money's work has important implications for an understanding of the environmental and biological determinants of the development of gender identity. Diamond has proposed an alternative biased interaction model.

Finally, the other great period of sexual differentiation, puberty, was considered. Puberty is initiated and characterized by a great increase in the production of sex hormones. Pubertal changes in both males and females include body growth, the development of pubic and axillary hair, and increased output from the oil-producing glands. Changes in the female include breast development and the beginning of menstruation. Changes in the male include growth of the penis and testes, the beginning of ejaculation, and a deepening of the voice.

Review Questions

1. The _____ is the region of the brain that works together with the pituitary and gonads to regulate sex hormone levels.
2. FSH and LH are manufactured by the _____.
3. The hypothalamus produces Gn-RH. True or false?
4. In the female, during prenatal sexual differentiation, the Müllerian ducts degenerate, leaving the Wolffian ducts. True or false?
5. Differences between male and female brains are found in the _____.
6. The testes in the male are homologous to the _____ in the female.
7. The adrenogenital syndrome results in hermaphroditism. True or false?
8. From his research, John Money has concluded that gender identity is determined by genetic and hormonal factors. True or false?
9. "Menarche" refers to a teenage girl who has stopped menstruating. True or false?
10. The percent body fat hypothesis has been used to explain the age at which a girl first menstruates. True or false?

(The answers to all review questions are at the end of the book, beginning on page 731.)

Question for Thought, Discussion, and Debate

1. Of the physical changes of puberty, which are the most difficult to cope with?

Suggestions for Further Reading

Bancroft, John, and Reinisch, June M. (Eds.) (1990). *Adolescence and puberty*. New York: Oxford University Press. A collection of chapters presenting the most recent research on biological, psychological, and social aspects of puberty.

Money, John, and Ehrhardt, Anke. (1972). *Man and woman, boy and girl*. Baltimore: Johns Hopkins. An excellent, detailed summary of John Money's important research. Also contains a great deal of other information on sexuality.

Wilson, Jean D., and Foster, Daniel W. (1991). *Williams textbook of endocrinology*. Philadelphia: Saunders. An outstanding endocrinology text, with a particularly good chapter on sexual differentiation.

Menstruation and Menopause

Chapter Highlights

It [menstruation] makes me very much aware of the fact that I am a woman, and that's something very important to me. . . . It's also a link to other women. I actually enjoy having my period. I feel like I've been cleaned out inside.

—M. P. W.

Menstruation is a pain in the vagina.

—S. B. P.

Menopause, can I get through it without collapse? Men don't have that damned inconvenience and discomfort. God must have been a man—a woman would have done a better job on women's bodies.

—B. B. W.

Menopause, it's the best form of birth control. Face it graciously and brag about it. It's great.

*—S. F.**

Women's sexual and reproductive lives have a rhythm of changes much like that of the seasons. And, as is true of the seasons, there are some tangible signs that mark the shifts, the two most notable being menstruation and menopause. As the women quoted above testify, these events are not only biological but psychological as well, and the psychological responses to them may range from very positive to very negative. This chapter deals with the biology and psychology of menstruation and menopause, as well as with biological cycles in men, including a discussion of "male menopause."

* *Source:* Paula Weideger. (1976). *Menstruation and menopause.* New York: Knopf, pp. 4–5.

BIOLOGY AND THE MENSTRUAL CYCLE

The menstrual cycle is regulated by fluctuating levels of sex hormones which produce certain changes in the ovaries and uterus. The hormone cycles are regulated by means of the negative feedback loops discussed in Chapter 5.

It is important to note that humans are nearly unique among species in having a menstrual cycle. Only a few other species of apes and monkeys also have menstrual cycles. All other species of mammals (for example, horses and dogs) have *estrous* cycles. There are several differences between estrous cycles and menstrual cycles. First, in animals that have estrous cycles, there is no menstruation; there is either no bleeding or only a slight spotting (as in dogs), which is not a real menstruation. Second, the timing of ovulation in relation to bleeding (if there is any) is different in the two cycles. For estrous animals, ovulation occurs while the animal is in "heat," or estrus, which is also the time of slight spotting (that is, there are spots of blood, but not a real flow). Dogs ovulate at about the time of bleeding. In the menstrual cycle, however, ovulation occurs about midway between the periods of menstruation. A third difference is that female animals with estrous cycles engage in sexual behavior only when they are in heat, that is, during the estrous phase of the cycle. Females with menstrual cycles are capable of engaging in sexual behavior throughout the cycle. It is important to note these differences because some people mistakenly believe that women's cycles are like those of a dog or cat, when in fact the cycles are quite different.

The Phases of the Menstrual Cycle

The menstrual cycle has four phases, each characterized by a set of hormonal, ovarian, and uterine changes (see Figure 6.1). Because menstruation is the easiest phase to identify, it is tempting to call it the first phase; biologically, though, it is actually the last phase (although in numbering the days of the menstrual cycle, day 1 is counted as the first day of menstruation because it is the most identifiable day of the cycle).

Hormones and What Happens in the Ovaries

Follicular phase (fuh-LIK-you-lur): The first phase of the menstrual cycle, beginning just after menstruation, during which an egg matures in preparation for ovulation.

The first phase of the menstrual cycle is called the **follicular phase** (it is sometimes called the *proliferative phase* or the *preovulatory phase*). At the beginning of this phase, the pituitary secretes relatively high levels of FSH (follicle-stimulating hormone). As the name of this hormone implies, its function is to stimulate follicles in the ovaries. At the beginning of the follicular phase, it signals one follicle (occasionally more than one) in the ovaries to begin to ripen and bring an egg to maturity. At the same time, the follicle secretes estrogen. As the egg matures, it moves, enclosed in the follicle, toward the surface of the ovary.

Ovulation: Release of an egg from the ovaries; the second phase of the menstrual cycle.

The second phase of the cycle is **ovulation**, which is the phase during which the follicle ruptures open, releasing the ripened egg. By this time, estrogen has risen to a high level, which inhibits FSH production, and so FSH has fallen back to a low level. The high levels of estrogen also stimulate the hypothalamus to produce Gn-RH, which causes the pituitary to begin production of LH (luteinizing hormone).[1] A surge of LH and FSH causes ovulation.

---

[1] This may seem to contradict a statement made in Chapter 5, that high estrogen levels cause a decline in LH. It appears that both of these effects may occur, but at different times in the menstrual cycle (Vander et al., 1975). There seems to be two centers in the hypothalamus, one of which produces a negative feedback between estrogen and LH, the other of which produces a positive feedback between the two.

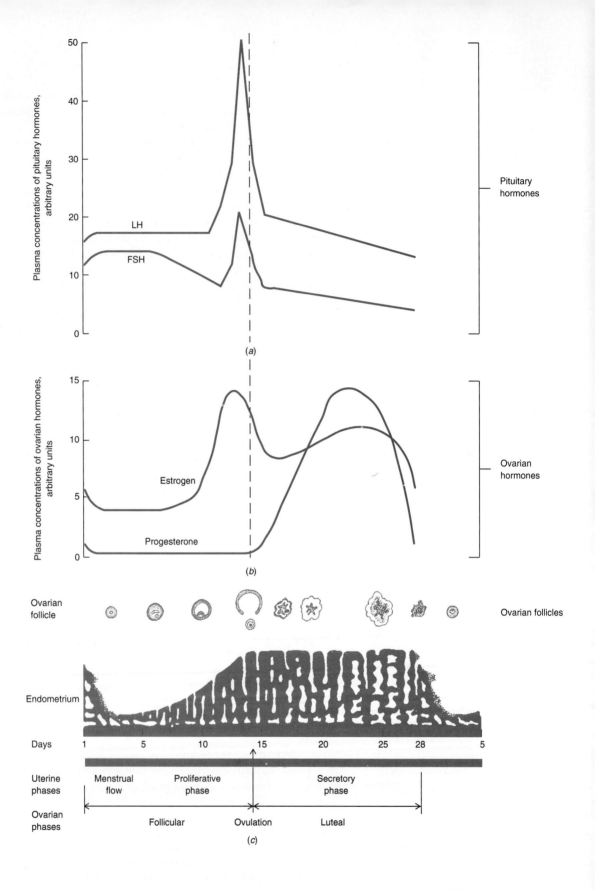

Plasma concentrations of pituitary hormones, arbitrary units

50
40
30
20
10
0

LH

FSH

Pituitary hormones

(a)

Plasma concentrations of ovarian hormones, arbitrary units

15
10
5
0

Estrogen

Progesterone

Ovarian hormones

(b)

Ovarian follicle

Ovarian follicles

Endometrium

Days
1   5   10   15   20   25   28   5

Uterine phases

Menstrual flow   Proliferative phase   Secretory phase

Ovarian phases

Follicular   Ovulation   Luteal

(c)

Luteal phase (LOO-tee-uhl): The third phase of the menstrual cycle, following ovulation.

Corpus luteum: The mass of cells of the follicle remaining after ovulation; it secretes progesterone.

Menstruation: The fourth phase of the menstrual cycle, during which the endometrium of the uterus is sloughed off in the menstrual discharge.

Toxic shock sydrome: A sometimes fatal disease associated with tampon use during menstruation.

The third phase of the cycle is called the luteal phase (sometimes also called the *secretory phase* or the *postovulatory phase*). After releasing an egg, the follicle, under stimulation of LH, turns into a glandular mass of cells called the corpus luteum[2] (hence the names "luteal phase" and "luteinizing hormone"). The corpus luteum manufactures progesterone; thus progesterone levels rise during the luteal phase. But high levels of progesterone also inhibit the pituitary's secretion of LH, and as LH levels decline, the corpus luteum degenerates. Thus the corpus luteum's output leads to its own eventual destruction. And with this degeneration also comes a sharp decline in estrogen and progesterone levels at the end of the luteal phase. The falling levels of estrogen stimulate the pituitary to begin production of FSH, and the whole cycle begins again.

The fourth and final phase of the cycle is menstruation. Physiologically, menstruation is a shedding of the inner lining of the uterus (the endometrium), which then passes out through the cervix and the vagina. During this phase, estrogen and progesterone levels are low, and FSH levels are rising. Menstruation is triggered by the sharp decline in estrogen and progesterone levels at the end of the luteal phase.

What Happens in the Uterus

This brings us to the changes that have been occurring in the uterus while the ovaries and endocrine system were going through the four phases described above. During the first, or follicular, phase, the high levels of estrogen stimulate the endometrium of the uterus to grow, thicken, and form glands that will eventually secrete substances to nourish the embryo; that is, the endometrium proliferates (hence the alternative name for this first phase, the "proliferative phase"). During the luteal phase, the progesterone secreted by the corpus luteum stimulates the glands of the endometrium to start secreting the nourishing substances (hence the name "secretory phase"). If the egg is fertilized and the timing goes properly, about six days after ovulation the fertilized egg arrives in a uterus that is well prepared to cradle and nourish it.

The corpus luteum will continue to produce estrogen and progesterone for about 10 to 12 days. If pregnancy has not occurred, its hormone output declines sharply at the end of this period. The uterine lining thus cannot be maintained, and it is shed, resulting in menstruation. Immediately afterward, a new lining starts forming in the next follicular phase.

The menstrual fluid itself is a combination of blood (from the endometrium), degenerated cells, and mucus from the cervix and vagina. Normally the discharge for an entire period is only about 2 ounces (4 tablespoons). Most commonly the fluid is absorbed with sanitary napkins, which are worn externally, or tampons, which are worn inside the vagina.

Toxic shock syndrome (Todd et al., 1978), sometimes abbreviated TSS, is caused by the bacterium *Staphylococcus aureus*. In 1980 a disturbing discovery was made that TSS was associated with tampon use (Price, 1981). It was particularly associated with Rely brand tampons, and they were withdrawn from the market.

---

[2] *Corpus luteum* is Latin for "yellow body." The corpus luteum is so named because the mass of cells is yellowish in appearance.

FIGURE 6.1
The biological events of the menstrual cycle. (a) Levels of hormones produced by the pituitary. (b) Hormones produced by the ovaries. (c) Changes in follicles in the ovary and the endometrium of the uterus.

Tampon use seems to encourage an abnormal growth of the bacteria. Symptoms of toxic shock syndrome include high fever (102°F or greater) accompanied by vomiting or diarrhea; any woman who experiences these symptoms during her period should discontinue tampon use immediately and see a doctor. Toxic shock syndrome leads to death in approximately 10 percent of cases, although its incidence is low and has decreased, apparently in part with a decline in the number of women using tampons as a result of publicity over TSS. It is now recommended that women change tampons frequently, at least every six to eight hours during their periods (although the effectiveness of this is debated), and that they not use tampons continuously throughout a menstrual period.

Length and Timing of the Cycle

How long is a normal menstrual cycle? Generally anywhere from 20 to 36 or 40 days is considered within the normal range. The average is about 28 days, but somehow this number has taken on more significance than it deserves. There is enormous variation from one woman to the next in the average length of the cycle, and for a given woman there can be considerable variation in length from one cycle to the next.

What is the timing of the various phases of the cycle? In a perfectly regular 28-day cycle, menstruation begins on day 1 and continuous until about day 4 or 5. The follicular phase extends from about day 5 to about day 13. Ovulation occurs on day 14, and the luteal phase extends from day 15 to the end of the cycle, day 28 (see Figure 6.1). But what if the cycle is not one of those perfect 28-day ones? In cycles that are shorter or longer than 28 days, the principle is that the length of the *luteal* phase is relatively constant. That is, the time from ovulation to menstruation is always 14 days, give or take only a day or two. It is the follicular phase which is of variable length. Thus, for example, if a woman has a 44-day cycle, she ovulates on about day 30. If she has a 22-day cycle, she ovulates on about day 8.

Some women report that they can actually feel themselves ovulate, a phenomenon called *Mittelschmerz* ("middle pain"). The sensation described is a cramping on one or both sides of the lower abdomen, lasting for about a day, and it is sometimes confused with appendicitis.

It is also true that ovulation does not occur in every menstrual cycle. That is, menstruation may take place without ovulation. When this happens the woman is said to have an *anovulatory cycle*. Such cycles occur once or twice a year in women in their twenties and thirties and are fairly common among girls during puberty and among women during the menopausal period.

Other Cyclic Changes

Two other physiological processes that fluctuate with the menstrual cycle also deserve mention: the cervical mucus cycle and the basal body temperature cycle. The cervix contains glands that secrete mucus throughout the menstrual cycle. One function of the mucus is to protect the entrance to the cervix, helping to keep bacteria out. These glands respond to the changing levels of estrogen during the cycle. As estrogen increases at the start of a new cycle, the mucus is alkaline, thick, and viscous. When LH production begins, just before ovulation, the cervical mucus changes markedly. It becomes even more alkaline, thin, and watery. Thus the environment for sperm passage is most hospitable just at ovulation. After ovulation, the mucus returns to its former viscous, less alkaline state. If a sample of mucus is taken just before ovulation and is allowed to dry, the dried mucus takes on a fern-shaped pattern.

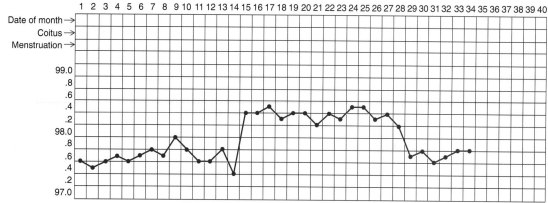

FIGURE 6.2
A basal body temperature graph. Note the dip in temperature, indicating ovulation on day 14.

After ovulation, during the luteal phase, the fernlike patterning will not occur. Thus the "fern test" is one method for detecting ovulation.

A woman's *basal body temperature,* taken with a thermometer, also flutuates with the phases of the menstrual cycle. Basically, the pattern is the following: The temperature is low during the follicular phase and may take a dip on the day of ovulation; on the day after ovulation it rises noticeably, generally by 0.4°F or more, and then continues at the higher level for the rest of the cycle (Figure 6.2). Progesterone raises body temperature, and the higher temperature during the luteal phase is due to the increased production of progesterone during that time. As the saying goes, "Where there's progesterone, there's heat." This change in basal body temperature is important when a couple are using the rhythm method of birth control (Chapter 8), and also when a woman is trying to determine the time of ovulation so that she may become pregnant (Chapter 7).

Menstrual Problems

Dysmenorrhea (dis-men-oh-REE-uh): Painful menstruation.

The most common menstrual problem is **dysmenorrhea** (painful menstruation). Almost every woman experiences at least some menstrual discomfort at various times in her life, but the frequency and severity of the discomfort vary considerably from one woman to the next. Cramping pains in the pelvic region are the most common symptom, and other symptoms may include headaches, backaches, nausea, and a feeling of pressure and bloating in the pelvis.

Prostaglandins: Chemicals secreted by the uterus that cause the uterine muscles to contract; they are a likely cause of painful menstruation.

Although the exact causes of dysmenorrhea are unknown, the current leading theory involves **prostaglandins,** hormonelike substances produced by many tissues of the body, including the lining of the uterus (Budoff, 1980). Prostaglandins can cause smooth muscle to contract and can affect the size of blood vessels. Women with severe menstrual pain have unusually high levels of prostaglandins. The high levels cause intense uterine contractions, which in turn choke off some of the uterus's supply of oxygen-carrying blood. Prostaglandins may also cause greater sensitivity in nerve endings. The combination of the uterine contractions, lack of oxygen, and heightened nerve sensitivity produces menstrual cramps.

Household remedies for painful menstruation are available and may be helpful to some women. Aspirin appears to be the best, and cheapest, painkiller available, and it can help to relieve menstrual pain. Exercise and keeping in good shape also help (Golub, 1992). A somewhat more provocative remedy suggested by, among others, Masters and Johnson is masturbation. This makes good physiological sense because part of the discomfort of menstruation—the pressure and bloating—results from pelvic edema (a congestion of fluids in the pelvic region). During sexual arousal and orgasm, pelvic congestion increases. After orgasm, the congestion dissipates (see Chapter 9). Thus orgasm, whether produced by masturbation or some other means, should help to relieve the pelvic edema which causes menstrual discomfort. And it's a lot more fun than taking medicine!

The FDA has approved mefenamic acid (an antiprostaglandin drug) for use in the treatment of menstrual pain. The drug is sold with brand names such as Naprosyn and Anaprox. Of the women tested so far, 85 percent have reported significant relief from menstrual pain and symptoms such as nausea, vomiting, dizziness, and weakness (Budoff, 1980). Interestingly, a traditional cure for cramps, aspirin, is also an antiprostaglandin.

Endometriosis: A condition in which the endometrium grows abnormally outside the uterus; the symptom is usually painful periods with excessive bleeding.

A menstrual problem which may be mistaken for dysmenorrhea is endometriosis. As noted previously the endometrium is the lining of the uterus; it grows during each menstrual cycle and is sloughed off in menstruation. Endometriosis occurs when the endometrium grows in a place other than the uterus. The place may be the ovaries, fallopian tubes, rectum, bladder, vagina, vulva, cervix, or lymph glands. The symptoms vary, depending on the location of the growth, but very painful periods that last an unusually long time are the most common. Endometriosis is fairly serious and should be treated by a physician; if left untreated, it may lead to sterility. Hormones are generally used in treatment, but if the problem is severe, surgery may be required. Laser surgery is a new, experimental treatment.

Amenorrhea: The absence of menstruation.

Another menstrual problem is amenorrhea, or the absence of menstruation. It is called *primary amenorrhea* if the girl has not yet menstruated by about age 18. It is called *secondary amenorrhea* if she has had at least one period. Amenorrhea has received considerable attention from physicians because, while rare, it is a symptom of infertility. Some of the causes of amenorrhea include pregnancy, congenital defects of the reproductive system, hormonal imbalance, cysts or tumors, disease, stress, and emotional factors related to puberty. Amenorrhea resulting from programs of strenuous exercise and from anorexia was discussed in Chapter 5.

PSYCHOLOGICAL ASPECTS OF THE MENSTRUAL CYCLE

"Why do I get so emotional?" screams the ad for Midol PMS in *Teen* magazine. It is part of the folk wisdom of our culture that women experience fluctuations in mood over the phases of the menstrual cycle. In particular, women are supposed to be especially cranky and depressed just before and during their periods. In France, if a woman commits a crime during her premenstrual period, she may use the fact in her defense, claiming "temporary impairment of sanity."

What is the scientific evidence concerning the occurrence of such fluctuations in mood, and, if they do occur, what causes them?

Fluctuations in Mood: Do Women Get Extra Emotional?

In 1931, R. T. Frank gave the name "premenstrual tension" to the mood changes that may occur during the three or four days immediately preceding menstruation (about days 24 to 28 of the cycle). Symptoms of premenstrual tension include depression, anxiety, irritability, fatigue, headaches, and low self-esteem. Since the time of Frank's early work, a great many data have been collected on moods during the premenstrual period and on whether moods fluctuate during the cycle.

The results seem to indicate a basic pattern. On the average, mood is positive around the time of ovulation (mid-cycle) and is negative premenstrually. For example, in one study, mood was measured by means of a projective technique in which subjects told stories at regular intervals throughout the cycle; the stories were then scored for the amount of anxiety shown in them (Bardwick, 1971; Ivey & Bardwick, 1968). The results indicated that self-confidence and self-esteem are high at ovulation, while anxiety is high premenstrually. The following examples illustrate these shifts.

One woman at ovulation said:

> We took our skis and packed them on top of the car and then we took off for up north. We used to go for long walks in the snow, and it was just really great, really quiet and peaceful.

The same woman showed anxiety in this story told premenstrually:

> [The car] came around a curve and did a double flip and landed upside down. I remember this car coming down on my hand and slicing it right open and all this blood was all over the place. Later they thought it was broken because every time I touched the finger, it felt like a nail was going through my hand.

Another woman expressed a positive mood at ovulation in this story:

> Talk about my trip to Europe. It was just the greatest summer of my life. We met all kinds of terrific people everywhere we went, and just the most terrific things happened.

But the same woman showed hostility premenstrually:

> Talk about my brother and his wife. I hated her. I just couldn't stand her. . . . I used to do terrible things to separate them.

Premenstrual syndrome (PMS): A combination of severe physical and psychological symptoms, such as depression and irritability, occurring just before menstruation.

The term premenstrual syndrome (PMS) is used to refer to those cases in which the woman has a particularly severe combination of physical and psychological symptoms premenstrually; these symptoms may include tension, depression, irritability, backache, and water retention (Dalton, 1979).

Evidence of the premenstrual syndrome comes from statistics indicating that a large proportion of the criminal acts of violence and suicides committed by women take place during the four premenstrual and four menstrual days of the cycle (Dalton, 1964). It has been found that 46 percent of the women admitted to psychiatric care are admitted on one of these eight days; also, 52 percent of female accident-emergency admissions occur during the eight premenstrual and menstrual days. In addition, 54 percent of the children brought to a clinic with minor colds were brought during their mother's eight premenstrual and menstrual days, perhaps indicating an increase in the mother's anxiety at this time (Dalton, 1966).

The evidence concerning mood fluctuation and the premenstrual syndrome has not been accepted without challenge. Of the numerous criticisms that have been made (Parlee, 1973), three deserve special mention here. First, much of the evidence depends on subjective reports of mood and symptoms, which are probably not very reliable. Second, the research has not given sufficient consideration to coping mechanisms; most women do not dissolve into tears and confine themselves to bed for the eight premenstrual and menstrual days of each month. It seems likely that women develop mechanisms for coping with the symptoms. Third, the interpretation of the direction of the differences might be questioned. The typical interpretation is that women show a psychological "deficit" premenstrually, as compared with the "normal" state at ovulation and during the rest of the cycle. However, the opposite interpretation might also be made: that women are "normal" premenstrually and are unusually well-adjusted psychologically at mid-cycle. What defines "normal" or "average" mood, then? Men's moods? Support for a reinterpretation might come from the statistics on violent crimes committed by women. While it is true that women are somewhat more likely to commit crimes during the eight premenstrual and menstrual days, even during this period they are far less likely to commit crimes than men are. Thus women might be considered to experience "normal" or typical moods (comparable to men's moods) during the premenstrual and menstrual days and to have feelings of unusual well-being around ovulation (see also Sommer, 1973).

Taking into account the criticisms and available evidence, it seems reasonable to conclude the following:

1. Women do, on the average, experience some fluctuations in mood over the phases of the menstrual cycle.
2. Present evidence does not clearly indicate how the direction of the shifts should be interpreted—whether women are unusually "low" premenstrually or unusually "high" around the time of ovulation.
3. There is a great deal of variation from one woman to the next in the size of these shifts and the way they are expressed. Some women experience no shifts or shifts so slight that they are not noticeable, while others may experience large shifts. It would be interesting to know how many do show mood fluctuations and how many do not. Unfortunately, the studies that have tried to provide this information themselves show substantial variation in their conclusions (Hyde, 1985). It appears that about 50 to 75 percent of all women show some mood fluctuation, while at least 25 percent show no fluctuation. It is important to make a distinction between women who have full-blown PMS and women who experience no fluctuation or only moderate fluctuations in mood over the cycle.

Katharina Dalton (1979), an expert in treating menstrual problems, advocates the use of *progesterone therapy* in the treatment of PMS. The effectiveness of progesterone in treating PMS is being debated in the medical community. Those studies that are well-controlled show progesterone to be no more effective than a placebo (sugar pill) (Abplanalp, 1983). Currently, then, there is no known medical cure for PMS (Abplanalp, 1983).

Fluctuations in Performance:
Can a Woman Be President?

So far the discussion has concentrated on fluctuations in psychological characteristics such as depression, anxiety, and low self-confidence. However, in some situations performance is of more practical importance than mood. For example, is a woman secretary's clerical work less accurate premenstrually and menstrually? Is a female athlete's coordination or speed impaired during the premenstrual-menstrual period?

The available data do not provide evidence of fluctuations in performance on tasks such as cognitive ability tests with the phases of the menstrual cycle (Golub,

1992; Sommer, 1973). In one study, women were asked if they thought their ability to concentrate declined during menstruation; about 20 percent thought it did (Golub, 1976). When these same women were given a test measuring concentration, they showed no actual impairment. In another study, 31 percent of female athletes said they believed that they experienced performance decrements during the premenstrual or menstrual phases; yet when their actual performance was measured, they showed no deficits in strength (weight lifters) or swimming speed (swimming team members) (Quadagno, et al., 1991). Thus there is no substantial evidence indicating that the kinds of performance required in a work situation or an athletic competition fluctuate over the menstrual cycle.

Fluctuations in Sex Drive

Another psychological characteristic that has been investigated for fluctuations over the cycle is women's sex drive or arousability. Observations of female animals that have estrous cycles indicate that sexual behavior depends a great deal on cycle phase and the corresponding hormonal state. Females of these species engage in sexual behavior enthusiastically when they are in the estrous, or "heat," phase of the cycle and do not engage in sexual behavior at all during any other phase. This makes good biological sense, since the females engage in sex precisely when they are fertile.

Human females, of course, engage in sexual behavior throughout the menstrual cycle. But might there still remain some subtle cycling in drive, expressed, perhaps, in fluctuations in frequency of intercourse? Generally there seem to be two peaks in the frequency of intercourse, one just before menstruation and one just after menstruation (Udry & Morris, 1968; Gold & Adams, 1981). Of course, these fluctuations may have nothing to do with hormones; rather, the high frequency of intercourse just after menstruation may be a compensation for deprivation during menstruation (Gold & Adams, 1981), and the high frequency before menstruation might result from anticipated deprivation. Also, one should be cautious about using frequency of intercourse as a measure of a woman's sex drive. Intercourse requires some agreement between the female and the male, and thus reflects not only her desires but his as well. One study investigated autosexual activity (masturbation, fantasy, and so on) in addition to intercourse and found that the frequency of autosexual activity actually increased during menstruation, while the frequency of intercourse decreased (Gold & Adams, 1981). Two other studies examined women's sexual arousability to erotic films at the different phases of the cycle, measuring both physiological arousal and self-ratings of arousal (Morrell et al., 1984; Hoon et al., 1982). Both studies concluded that there were no differences in arousability at the different phases. Thus there seems to be little correspondence between hormonal fluctuations over the menstrual cycle and fluctuations in sex drive or arousability.

What Causes the Fluctuations in Mood:
Why Do Women Get Emotional?

The answer to the question of what causes mood fluctuations during the menstrual cycle (if such fluctuations do occur) touches off a nature-nurture, or biology-environment, controversy. That is, some investigators argue that the mood fluctuations are caused primarily by biological factors—in particular, fluctuation in levels of hormones—while others argue that environmental factors such as menstrual taboos and cultural expectations are the primary cause.

On the biology side, changes in mood appear to be related to changes in hormone levels during the cycle. The fact that depression is more frequent in women premenstrually, at menopause, and postpartum (after having a baby) and among those using birth control pills suggests that there is at least some relationship between sex hormones and depression (S. L. Smith, 1975). The exact hormone-mood relationship is not known, though. Theories of hormonal causes of premenstrual tension involving the following factors have been proposed: (1) absolute amount of estrogen; (2) absolute amount of progesterone; (3) the estrogen-progesterone ratio or estrogen-progesterone balance; (4) hypersensitivity of some individuals to estrogen levels; and (5) withdrawal reactions to either estrogen or progesterone (during all the premenstrual, postpartum, and menopausal periods, hormone levels are dropping rapidly). Research has not determined which, if any, of these factors is the real cause, though each has some data in its favor. Neither is it known exactly what the mechanism is by which hormones influence mood. The likeliest explanation would involve the effects of estrogen and progesterone on brain neurotransmitters (substances that are involved in the the transmission of nerve impulses) such as norepinephrine and dopamine (for a review, see Ruble et al., 1980).

Critics of the hormone point of view note that causality is being inferred from correlational data. That is, the data show a correlation between cycle phase (hormone levels) and mood. From this, it is unwarranted to infer that the hormone levels cause the mood shifts. Another equally reasonable interpretation of the data might be that moods influence hormone levels and cycle phase. For example, a bout of depression might bring on menstruation.

A study that answers this objection partially was done by psychologist Karen Paige (1971). She used a manipulation of hormone levels—birth control pills—and studied mood fluctuations resulting from the manipulation. The spoken stories of 102 married women were obtained on days 4, 10, and 16 and 2 days before menstruation during one cycle, and they were scored using the technique mentioned previously. The subjects fell into three groups: (1) those who were not taking oral contraceptives and never had; (2) those who were taking a combination pill (combination pills provide a steady high dose of both estrogen and progestin, a synthetic progesterone, for 20 or 21 days—see Chapter 8 for a more complete discussion); and (3) those who were taking sequential pills (which provide 15 days of estrogen followed by 5 days of estrogen plus progestin, which is a fluctuation similar to the natural cycle but at higher levels). The hormone levels across the cycles of the women in these three groups are shown in Figure 6.3. Paige found that the nonpill women experienced statistically significant variation in their anxiety and hostility levels over the menstrual cycle, which was in agreement with findings from previous studies. Women taking the sequential pill showed the same mood change that nonpill women did. This agrees with the predicted outcome, since their artificial hormone cycle is similar to the natural one. Most important, combination-pill women, whose hormone levels are constant over the cycle, showed *no* mood shifts over the cycle; their hostility and anxiety levels were constant. This study therefore provides evidence that fluctuations in hormone levels over the menstrual cycle cause mood fluctuations and that when hormone levels are constant, mood is constant.

Those arguing the other side—that the fluctuations are due to cultural forces—note the widespread cultural expectations and taboos surrounding menstruation (for reviews, see Novell, 1965; Stephens, 1961; Weideger, 1976). In many nonindustrialized cultures, women who are menstruating are isolated from the community and may have to stay in a menstrual hut at the edge of town during their period. Often the menstrual blood itself is thought to have supernatural, dangerous powers, and the woman's isolation is considered necessary for the safety of the community. Among the Lele of the Congo, for example:

> A menstruating woman was a danger to the whole community if she entered the forest. Not only was her menstruation certain to wreck any enterprise in the forest

FIGURE 6.3
Hormone levels over the menstrual cycle for the three groups of women in Paige's study (see text for further explanation).

Group 1: Nonpill women

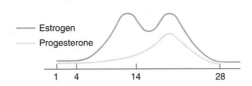

Group 2: Combination pill

Group 3: Sequential pill

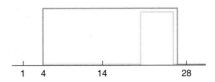

that she might undertake, but it was thought to produce unfavorable conditions for men. Hunting would be difficult for a long time after, and rituals based on forest plants would have no efficacy. Women found these rules extremely irksome, especially as they were regularly short-handed and later in their planting, weeding, harvesting, and fishing. (Douglas, 1970, p. 179)

Lest one think that such practices occur only among non-Western people, it should be noted that there is a history of similar practices in our own culture as well. For example, the following passage is from the book of Leviticus in the Bible:

When a woman has a discharge of blood which is her regular discharge from her body, she shall be in her impurity for seven days, and whoever touches her shall be unclean until the evening. . . . And whoever touches her bed shall wash his clothes, and bathe himself in water, and be unclean until the evening; whether it is the bed or anything upon which she sits, when he touches it he shall be unclean until the evening. (Leviticus 15:19–23)

Even closer to home, the U.S. Parks Department issued the following warning:

Special precautions apply to women. For their protection, women should refrain from wilderness travel during their menstrual periods. Bears and other large carnivores have attacked women in this physiological condition. (Weideger, 1976, p. 226)

Among the most common menstrual taboos are those prohibiting sexual intercourse with a menstruating woman. For example, the continuation of the passage from Leviticus quoted above is:

And if any man lies with her, and her impurity is on him, he shall be unclean seven days; and every bed on which he lies shall be unclean. (Leviticus 15:24)

Couples who violated the taboo could be stoned. To this day, Orthodox Jews abstain from sex during the woman's period and for seven days afterward. At the end of

Erica's "Come as you are During PMS" party turns out to be less than successful.

FIGURE 6.4
PMS. *(a) A cartoonist's view. (b) The media, from drug ads to teen magazine articles, have created negative stereotypes about women and PMS.*

this time the woman goes to the mikvah (ritual bath) to be cleansed, and only after this cleansing may she resume sexual relations.

There is evidence that these "primitive" or "archaic" practices are actually widespread in our modern culture as well. For example, a 1972 survey of 960 California families showed that half the men and women had *never* had coitus during the woman's menstrual period (Paige, 1973). No wonder women get depressed around the time of menstruation!

Advocates of the cultural explanation argue, then, that women become anxious and depressed around the time of menstruation because of the many cultural forces, such as menstrual taboos, that create negative attitudes toward menstruation. Further, women's expectations may play a role. It is a well-documented phenomenon that people's expectations can influence their behavior. Our culture is filled with teachings that women are supposed to behave strangely just before and during their periods—for example, the drug company ads that ask "Why am I so emotional?" Thus, according to this line of reasoning, women are taught that they should be depressed around the time of menstruation, and because they expect to become depressed, they become depressed. Psychologist Elaine Blechman (1988) has proposed an additional role for expectations. Women who experience painful cramps may well spend the several days before they know their period is due anticipating the pain, which makes them feel anxious and depressed.

Surely such forces do exist in our culture. But is there any evidence that they really do have an effect on women's moods and behavior? Psychologist Diane Ruble (1977) did a clever experiment to determine whether subjects' culturally induced expectations influence their reporting of premenstrual symptoms. College students were tested on the sixth or seventh day before the onset of their next menstrual perod. They were told that they would participate in a study on a new technique for predicting the expected date of menstruation using an electroencephalogram (EEG), a method that had already been successfully tested with older women. After the EEG had been run (it actually wasn't), the subject was informed of when her next period was to occur, depending on which of three experimental groups she had randomly been assigned to: (1) the subject was told she was "premenstrual" and her period was due in 1 or 2 days; (2) the subject was told she was "intermenstrual" or "mid-cycle" and her period was not expected for at least a week to 10 days; or (3) she was given no information at all about the predicted date of menstruation (control group). The women then completed a self-report menstrual distress questionnaire. The results indicated that subjects who had been led to believe they were in the premenstrual phase reported significantly more water retention, pain, and changes in eating habits than did subjects who had been led to believe they were around mid-cycle. (In fact, subjects in these groups did not differ significantly in when their periods actually arrived.) There were no significant differences between the groups in ratings of negative moods, however. This study indicates that probably because of learned beliefs, women overstate the changes in body states that occur over the menstrual cycle. When they think they are in the premenstrual phase, they report more problems than when they think they are at mid-cycle.

This nature-nurture argument will not be easily resolved, particularly because there is good evidence for both points of view. Perhaps the best solution is to say that some women probably do experience mood shifts caused by hormonal and possibly other physical factors and that for many others, slight biological influences are magnified by psychological and cultural influences. Premenstrual hormonal state may act as a sort of "trigger." It may, for example, provide a state conducive to depression; and if the environment provides further stimuli to depression, the woman becomes depressed.

CYCLES IN MEN

The traditional assumption, of both laypeople and scientists, has been that monthly biological and psychological cycles are the exclusive property of women. The corollary assumption has been that men experience no such monthly cycles. These assumptions are made, at least in part, because men have no obvious signs like menstruation to call attention to the fact that some kind of periodic change is occurring.

Recently there has been an interest in discovering whether men might not experience subtle monthly hormone cycles and corresponding psychological cycles. As early as 1897, it had been observed that bleeding from lung hemorrhages, hemorrhoids, and hyperemia of the liver is periodic, in both women and men (cited in Delaney et al., 1976, pp. 212–213). Epileptic attacks appear to follow a monthly cycle in men (Delaney et al., 1976, p. 213).

In one early study, male industrial workers did appear to have periodic emotional cycles, with an average cycle length of about five weeks. Individual cycle lengths varied from three to nine weeks and were remarkably consistent (Hersey, 1931).

One interesting applied study found some evidence of behavioral cycles in men (cited in Ramey, 1972). The Omi Railway Company of Japan operates more than

700 buses and taxis. In 1969 the directors became concerned about the high losses resulting from accidents. The company's efficiency experts studied each man working for the company to determine his monthly cycle pattern of mood and efficiency. Then schedules were adjusted to coincide with the best times for the drivers. Since then, the accident rate has dropped by one-third.

In another study, the testosterone levels of 20 men were studied for a period of 60 days (Doering et al., 1975). The majority of the men had identifiable testosterone cycles ranging in length from 3 to 30 days, with many clustered around 21 to 23 days. A psychological test to measure the men's moods was also administered (Doering et al., 1978). Although testosterone levels were not correlated with several kinds of moods such as anxiety, high testosterone levels were correlated with depression. Other researchers have also found cycles in men's emotional states (Parlee, 1978). Thus, the preliminary evidence indicates that men do experience mood cycles. Undoubtedly there will be increased research on this topic in the next decade.

MENOPAUSE

Biological Changes

The *climacteric* is a period lasting about 15 or 20 years (from about ages 45 to 60) during which a woman's body makes the transition from being able to reproduce to not being able to reproduce; the climacteric is marked particularly by a decline in the functioning of the ovaries. But climacteric changes occur in many other body tissues and systems as well. Menopause (the "change of life," the "change") refers to one specific event in this process, the cessation of menstruation; this occurs, on the average, during a two-year period beginning at around age 47 (with a normal menopause occurring anywhere between the ages of 35 and 60).

Biologically, as a woman grows older, the pituitary continues a normal output of FSH and LH; however, as the ovaries age, they become less able to respond to the pituitary hormones. Thus the major biological change during the climacteric is the aging of the ovaries with an accompanying decline in the output of their two major products: eggs and the sex hormones estrogen and progesterone. More specifically, the ovaries become less capable of responding to FSH by maturing and releasing an egg. The hormonal changes of menopause involve a decline in estrogen and progesterone levels and hormonal imbalance.

Physical symptoms of menopause include "hot flashes" or "hot flushes," headaches, dizziness, heart palpitations, and pains in the joints. A probable long-range effect of the decline in estrogen levels is *osteoporosis* (porous and brittle bones, which may lead to "dowager's hump"). The hot flash is probably the best known of the symptoms. Typically it is described as a sudden wave of heat from the waist up. The woman may get red and perspire a lot; when the flush goes away, she may feel chilled and sometimes may shiver. The flashes may last from a few seconds to half an hour and may occur several or many times a day. They may also occur at night, causing insomnia, and the resulting perspiration can actually soak the sheets.

Do all women experience these menopausal symptoms? In a survey of 638 women aged 45 to 55, conducted in London in 1964–1965, 30 to 50 percent of the women reported experiencing dizziness, palpitations, insomnia, depression, headache, or weight gain, and most of these women reported experiencing several of these symptoms rather than just one. About 50 percent of the women experienced hot flashes, and half of the 50 percent said the flashes were acutely uncomfortable (McKinlay and Jeffreys, 1974). It is generally estimated that only about 10 percent of all women suffer severe distress at menopause. Thus it might be concluded that

Menopause: The cessation of menstruation in middle age.

at least as many as 50 percent (perhaps 80 to 90 percent) of all women suffer some of these uncomfortable menopausal symptoms, only about 10 percent are severely affected, and a sizable proportion—at least 10 percent and perhaps as many as 50 percent—display none of these symptoms.

Estrogen-replacement therapy (ERT) is available and may be helpful to many menopausal women, particularly for relief of physical discomfort such as hot flashes. The treatment today often includes both estrogen and progesterone. However, the therapy needs to be carefully administered by a physician, and its benefits need to be weighed against its potential risks (for a good review and evaluation, see Hammond and Maxson, 1982). There is some evidence linking it to breast cancer (Steinberg et al., 1991). On the other hand, estrogen replacement protects women from osteoporosis, which may cause broken hips, which may lead to death. More elderly women die annually from broken hips than from endometrial cancer (Budoff, 1981). In one study, women aged 40 to 69 were followed yearly for five years; the women taking replacement estrogen had a death rate much *lower* than those not taking estrogen (Bush et al., 1983). Thus, on balance, estrogen replacement may be relatively safe.

Sexuality and Menopause

During the climacteric, physical changes also occur in the vagina. The lack of estrogen causes the vagina to become less acidic, which leaves it more vulnerable to infections. Estrogen is also responsible for maintaining the mucous membranes of the vaginal walls. With a decline in estrogen, there is a decline in vaginal lubrication during arousal, and the vaginal walls become less elastic. Either or both of these may make intercourse painful for the woman. Several remedies are available, including estrogen-replacement therapy and the use of artificial lubricants. Unfortunately, some women do not communicate their discomforts to their partners or physician and instead suffer quietly and develop an aversion to sex. On the other hand, some women report that intercourse is even better after menopause, when the fear of pregnancy no longer inhibits them.

One sex researcher, having reviewed the research on women's sexuality during and after menopause, reached the following conclusions (Morokoff, 1988): (1) The majority of women continue to engage in sexual activity and enjoy it both during and after menopause. (2) There is some decline in sexual functioning, on the average, during menopause and particularly after the last period. (3) Estrogen may be related to the decline in sexual functioning, although it isn't exactly clear how the effect occurs. There is at least some evidence that higher estrogen levels are associated with better sexual functioning. (4) Testosterone is also important, and a woman's sexual functioning may decline if her levels of testosterone have been reduced because the ovaries were removed in a hysterectomy. Testosterone replacement therapy may be helpful in such cases.

The topic of sexuality and the elderly will be discussed in more detail in Chapter 12.

Psychological Changes

Psychological problems of menopause include depression, irritability, anxiety, nervousness, crying spells, inability to concentrate, and feelings of suffocation. In rare cases, the depression may be extremely severe *(involutional melancholia)* in a woman who has no previous history of mental problems. It is estimated that about 10 percent of women suffer from serious depression during menopause.

These psychological symptoms, though, involve a subtle problem of interpretation similar to the one mentioned in conjunction with the premenstrual-tension syndrome. Women are said to have "more" problems during menopause. More than what? More than men? More than at other times in their own lives? Investigating the latter question, psychologists Bernice Neugarten and Ruth Kraines (1965) studied symptoms among women of different age groups. They found that adolescents and menopausal women reported the largest number of problematic symptoms. Post-menopausal women reported the smallest number of problematic symptoms; apparently, menopause does not permanently "wreck" a woman. Among the adolescents, psychological symptoms were the most common (for example, tension), while among the menopausal women, physical symptoms such as hot flashes were most common. Menopausal women showed an increase in only five categories of psychological symptoms: headache, irritability, nervousness, feeling blue, and feelings of suffocation (the latter being associated with hot flashes). Thus menopause may not be the worst time of a woman's life psychologically; probably it is not so bad as adolescence.

What Causes the Symptoms?

The difficulties associated with menopause are attributed to biology (in particular, hormones) by some and to culture and its expectations by others.

From the biological perspective, the symptoms of menopause appear to be due to the woman's hormonal state. In particular, the symptoms appear to be related either to low estrogen levels or to hormonal imbalance. The former hypothesis, called the *estrogen-deficiency theory,* has been the subject of the most research. Proponents of this theory argue that the physical symptoms, such as hot flashes, and the psychological symptoms, such as depression, are caused by declining amounts of estrogen in the body.

The best evidence for the estrogen-deficiency theory comes from the success of estrogen-replacement therapy. It is effective in relieving low-estrogen menopausal symptoms like hot flashes, sweating, cold hands and feet, and osteoporosis. It also keeps the vagina "young," maintaining the elasticity of its walls and the capacity for lubrication, as well as reducing the risk of vaginitis (Walling et al., 1990). The success of this therapy suggests that low estrogen levels cause menopausal symptoms and that raising estrogen levels relieves the symptoms.

On the other hand, there is a strong cultural bias toward expecting menopausal symptoms. Thus any quirk in a middle-aged woman's behavior is attributed to the "change." It simultaneously becomes the cause of, and explanation for, all the problems and complaints of the middle-aged woman. Given such expectations, it is not surprising that the average person perceives widespread evidence of the pervasiveness of menopausal symptoms. Ironically, idiosyncrasies in women of childbearing age are blamed on menstruation, while problems experienced by women who are past that age are blamed on the *lack* of it.

There is also a cultural stereotype that women suffer from an "empty-nest syndrome" in the middle years—that is, that they become depressed when all their children have left home and the mother role is at an end for them. However, sociologist Lillian B. Rubin (1979) has challenged the whole notion of the empty-nest syndrome and questions whether there is substantial depression in the mid-life period for women. Her results are based on a study of 160 women, a cross section of white mothers aged 35 to 54, from the working, middle, and professional classes. To be included in the sample, they had to have given up work or careers after a minimum of 3 years and to have assumed the traditional role of housewife and mother for at least 10 years after the birth of their first child. Therefore this group should be most prone to the empty-nest syndrome. Typically these women said, "My career was my

FIGURE 6.5

child." Contrary to the notion of the empty nest, Rubin found that although some women were momentarily sad, lonely, or frightened, they were not depressed in response to the departure of their children. The predominant feeling of every woman except one was a feeling of relief. As one woman put it,

> Lonesome? God, no! From the day the kids are born, if it's not one thing, it's another. After all these years of being responsible for them, you finally get to the point where you want to scream: "Fall out of the nest already, you guys, will you? It's time." (Rubin, 1979, p. 13)

Rather than experiencing an immobilizing depression, most of the women found new jobs and reorganized their daily lives. This research leads one to question whether women do have substantial problems with depression around mid-life or the time of menopause.

In agreement with Rubin's thesis, one authoritative review concluded that there was good evidence that menopause does *not* increase the rate of depression (Weissman & Klerman, 1977).

In summary, the evidence indicates that some, though not all, women experience physical problems such as hot flashes during menopause. These physical symptoms seem to be most related to declining estrogen levels and are relieved for many women by estrogen-replacement therapy. On the other hand, there is little evidence that the menopausal years are a bad time psychologically, and so we needn't waste our time trying to figure out the causes of psychological problems during that period.

147

MALE MENOPAUSE

Biological Changes

In the technical sense, men do not experience a "menopause"; never having menstruated, they can scarcely cease menstruating. However, men do experience a very gradual decline in the manufacture of both testosterone and sperm by the testes, a mild version of the climacteric process in women, although viable sperm may still be produced at age 90.

One of the most common physical problems for men at this age is enlargement of the prostate gland, which is believed to be related to changes in hormone levels. Prostate enlargement occurs in 10 percent of men by age 40, and 50 percent of men who reach age 80. Enlargement of the prostate causes urination problems; there is difficulty in voluntarily initiating urination, as well as frequent nocturnal urination. These symptoms are usually remedied by surgery to remove the part of the gland pressing against the urethra. Nonsurgical treatment is not effective. Administration of female sex hormones causes shrinkage of prostate cancer but does not reduce benign (noncancerous) prostate enlargement. Contrary to a number of myths, prostate enlargement is not caused by masturbation or excessive sexual activity. The infection and inflammation resulting from sexually transmitted diseases, though, can cause prostate enlargement.

Psychological Changes

Research in the last two decades has focused on the notion of a "male mid-life crisis," whether men experience one in their forties, and what its nature is (Levinson, 1978; Lowenthal et al., 1975; see review by Brim, 1976). Major themes that emerge from that research are discussed below.

One theme is the *aspiration-achievement gap*. Most human beings have a desire to feel good about themselves based on their achievements. For men, this positive sense of self comes mainly from their job or career. Around age 40 many men recognize that there is an aspiration-achievement gap, that is, that their achievements have not matched the high aspirations and goals they set for themselves when they were in their twenties. How does the man resolve this aspiration-acheivement gap for himself? For many, perhaps the majority, there is a gradual reconciliation, with aspirations being reduced until they are at a realistic, attainable level, and the man emerges feeling good about himself. For some, the reconciliation is not easy and there is a crisis and depression.

According to Erik Erikson (1950), one of the major tasks of adult development is a resolution of the *stagnation versus generativity* conflict. Most people seem to have a deep-seated desire to feel a sense of personal growth, or generativity, in their lives. At age 40, when the only thing that seems to be growing is the waistline, it may be difficult to feel a sense of generativity, and stagnation may set in. This crisis may be resolved positively by having a continual sense of generativity in adulthood, often by finding growth in other sources, such as the growth of one's children or grandchildren. Single men or gay men with no children can gain a sense of generativity in many other ways, such as taking an interest in fostering the careers of their younger coworkers.

Relationships within the man's family shift during the mid-life period (Brim, 1976). The children grow and leave home, leaving the husband and wife alone together. Although it is a popular stereotype that this is a difficult time in marriage, causing many divorces, the data actually indicate that married couples on the average rate the postparental period as one of the happiest in their lives (Brim, 1976). The

man's own parents may become increasingly dependent on him, requiring a transformation of that relationship. And the man's wife, free from child-care responsibilities, may seek education, a career, or a more active involvement in a job she already has, once again requiring renegotiation of the marital relationship.

Systematic, well-sampled research indicates that men in their forties—compared with groups of men aged 25 to 39 and 50 to 69—do show significantly higher depression scores and more alcohol and drug use; on the other hand, their levels of anxiety are no higher, and they report no less life satisfaction or happiness (Tamir, 1982). Thus it seems that men in their forties have some problems, but the problems are probably not much worse than the problems men face at other ages.

It is important that the complaints of middle-aged men and women be recognized and that they be considered legitimate complaints. It is also important to note how many of these crises of middle age lead to satisfactory resolution, in which the person makes a positive alteration in her or his life.

Summary

Biologically, the menstrual cycle is divided into four phases: the follicular phase, ovulation, the luteal phase, and menstruation. Corresponding to these phases, there are changes in the levels of pituitary hormones (FSH and LH) and in the levels of ovarian hormones (estrogen and progesterone), as well as changes in the ovaries and the uterus. A fairly common menstrual problem is dysmenorrhea, or painful menstruation. Toxic shock syndrome has been found to be associated with the use of tampons during the menstrual period.

Research indicates that some, though probably not all, women experience changes in mood over the phases of the menstrual cycle. For those who experience such changes, mood is generally positive around the middle of the cycle (i.e., around ovulation), while negative moods characterized by depression and irritability are more likely just before and during menstruation. These negative moods and physical discomforts are termed the premenstrual syndrome. On the other hand, research indicates that there are no fluctuations in performance over the cycle. There is evidence suggesting that fluctuations in mood are related to changes in hormone levels, but data are also available suggesting that mood fluctuations are related to cultural factors. Research attempting to document whether men experience monthly biological and/or psychological cycles is now in progress.

The climacteric is the period in middle age during which the functioning of the ovaries (both hormone and egg production) declines gradually. One symptom of this process is menopause, the cessation of menstruation. Physical symptoms, such as hot flashes, during this period probably result from declining levels of estrogen, and may be relieved by estrogen-replacement therapy; psychological problems, such as depression, may not be so common as is generally believed.

Men experience a much more gradual decline in the functioning of their gonads. They may experience a psychological transition in middle age parallel to that of women.

Review Questions

1. The phase of the menstrual cycle following ovulation is called the _____.

2. Toxic shock syndrome is caused by an abnormal growth of a *Staphylococcus* bacterium in the vagina. True or false?

3. A woman's basal body temperature generally takes a dip on the day of ovulation and then shows a noticeable rise on the day after ovulation. True or false?

4. _____ are the hormonelike substances that are thought to be responsible for menstrual cramps.

5. The premenstrual syndrome consists of physical and psychological symptoms, including tension, depression, irritability, backache, and headache. True or false?

6. Well-controlled scientific studies show that progesterone is highly effective in curing PMS. True or false?

7. Research indicates that some women experience mood shifts over the phases of the menstrual cycle, but other women do not experience such mood shifts. True or false?

8. _____ has been shown to be effective in treating the physical symptoms of menopause, as well as protecting women from osteoporosis.

9. Challenging the notion of the empty-nest syndrome, one sociologist found in interviews with middle-aged women that their predominant feeling about the departure of their children was relief. True or false?

10. One major theme of the male mid-life crisis is the aspiration-achievement gap. True or false?

(The answers to all review questions are at the end of the book, beginning on page 731.)

Questions for Thought, Discussion, and Debate

1. Are women's fluctuations in mood over the menstrual cycle caused by biological factors or by environmental/cultural factors?

2. Is there a male mid-life crisis? If so, what are its "symptoms," and what causes it?

Suggestions for Further Reading

Golub, Sharon (1992). *Periods: From menarche to menopause*. Newbury Park, CA: Sage. This book, by a well-known researcher in the field, tells you everything you always wanted to know about menstruation and menopause.

Parlee, Mary B. (April 1978). The rhythms in men's lives. *Psychology Today*, 82–91. An article that discusses research on possible monthly cycles in men's moods.

Ransohoff, Rita M. (1987). *Venus after forty*. New York: Macmillan. A book that aims to shatter myths about menopause and about "sexless" older women.

Rubin, Lillian B. (1979). *Women of a certain age: The midlife search for self*. New York: Harper & Row. A description of Rubin's provocative research and her conclusion that the empty nest is more pleasure than pain.

7

Conception, Pregnancy, and Childbirth

Chapter Highlights

I was laying on my stomach and felt—something, like someone lightly touching my deep insides. Then I just sat very still and for an alive moment felt the hugeness of having something living growing in me. Then I said no, it's not possible, it's too early yet, and then I started to cry. . . . That one moment was my first body awareness of another living thing inside me.

I thought it would never end. I was enormous. I couldn't bend over and wash my feet. And it was incredibly hot.*

Chapter 5 described the remarkable biological process by which a single fertilized egg develops into a male or a female human being. This chapter is about some equally remarkable processes involved in creating human beings: conception, pregnancy, and childbirth.

CONCEPTION

Sperm Meets Egg: The Incredible Journey

On about day 14 of an average menstrual cycle the woman ovulates. The egg is released from the ovary into the body cavity. Typically it is then picked up by the fimbriae (long fingerlike structures at the end of the fallopian tube—see Figure 7.1) and enters the fallopian tube. It then begins a leisurely trip down the tube toward the uterus, reaching it in about five days, if it has been fertilized. Otherwise, it disintegrates in about 48 hours. The egg, unlike the sperm, has no means of moving itself and is propelled by the cilia (hairlike structures) lining the fallopian tube. The egg has begun its part of the journey toward conception.

---

* *Source:* Boston Women's Health Book Collective. (1984). *The new our bodies, ourselves.* New York: Simon and Schuster, pp. 344–351.

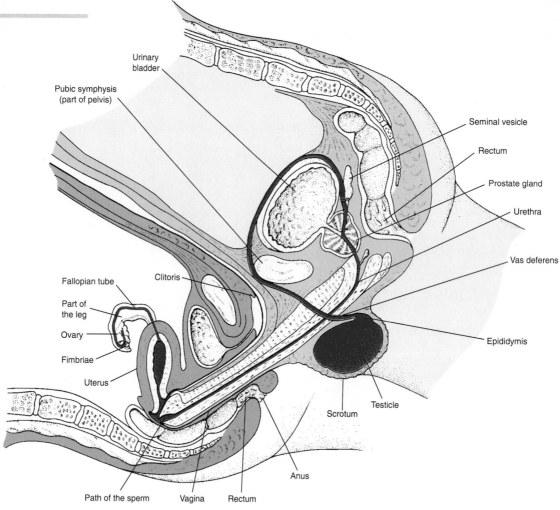

Urinary
bladder

Pubic symphysis
(part of pelvis)

Seminal vesicle

Rectum

Prostate gland

Urethra

Vas deferens

Fallopian tube

Clitoris

Part of
the leg

Ovary

Fimbriae

Uterus

Epididymis

Testicle

Scrotum

Anus

Path of the sperm   Vagina   Rectum

FIGURE 7.1
Sexual intercourse in the
man-on-top position
showing the pathway of
sperm and egg from
manufacture in the testes
and ovary to conception,
which typically occurs in
the fallopian tube.

Meanwhile, the couple have been having intercourse. The man has an orgasm and ejaculates inside the woman's vagina. The sperm are deposited in the vagina, there to begin their journey toward the egg. Actually they have made an incredible trip even before reaching the vagina. Initially they were manufactured in the seminiferous tubules of the testes (see Chapter 4). They then collected and were stored in the epididymis. During ejaculation they moved up and over the top of the bladder in the vas deferens; then they traveled down through the ejaculatory duct, mixed with seminal fluid, and went out through the urethra.

The sperm is one of the tiniest cells in the human body. It is composed of a *head,* a *midpiece,* and a *tail* (see Figure 7.2). The head is about 5 micrometers long, and the total length, from the tip of the head to the tip of the tail, is about 60 micrometers (about 2/1000 inch, or 0.06 millimeter). The chromosomal material, which is the sperm's most important contribution when it unites with the egg, is contained in the nucleus, which is in the head of the sperm. The *acrosome,* a chemical reservoir, is also in the head of the sperm. The midpiece contains mitochondria, which are tiny structures in which chemical reactions occur that provide energy. This energy is used when the sperm lashes its tail back and forth. The lashing action (called *flagellation*) propels the sperm forward.

A typical ejaculate has a volume of about 3 milliliters, or about a teaspoonful,

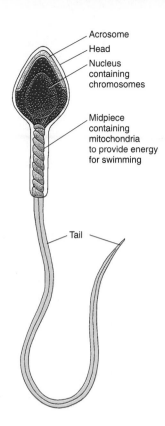

FIGURE 7.2
The structure of a mature human sperm.

Acrosome
Head
Nucleus containing chromosomes
Midpiece containing mitochondria to provide energy for swimming
Tail

contains about 300 million sperm. Although this might seem to be a wasteful amount of sperm if only one is needed for fertilization, the great majority of the sperm never even get close to the egg. Some of the ejaculate, together with the sperm in it, may flow out of the vagina as a result of gravity. Other sperm may be killed by the acidity of the vagina, to which they are very sensitive. Of those that make it safely into the uterus, half swim up the wrong fallopian tube (the one containing no egg).

But here we are, several hours later, with a hearty band of sperm swimming up the fallopian tube toward the egg, against the currents that are bringing the egg down. Sperm are capable of swimming 1 to 3 centimeters (about 1 inch) per hour, although it has been documented that sperm may arrive at the egg within 1 to $1\frac{1}{2}$ hours after ejaculation, which is much sooner than would be expected, given their swimming rate. It is thought that muscular contractions in the uterus may help speed them along. By the time a sperm reaches the egg, it has swum approximately 3000 times its own length. This would be comparable to a swim of over 3 miles for a human being.

Contrary to the popular belief that conception occurs in the uterus, typically it occurs in the outer third (the part near the ovary) of the fallopian tube. Of the original 300 million sperm, only about 2000 reach the tube containing the egg. The egg is surrounded by a thin, gelatinous layer called the *zona pellucida*. It is thought that the sperm swarm around the egg and secrete an enzyme called hyaluronidase (produced by the acrosome located in the head of the sperm—see Figure 7.2); this enzyme dissolves the zona pellucida, permitting one sperm to penetrate the egg.[1] Conception has occurred.

Hyaluronidase: An enzyme secreted by the sperm that allows one to penetrate the egg.

---

[1] Thus while only one sperm is necessary to accomplish fertilization, it appears that it is important for him to have a lot of his buddies along to help him get into the egg. Therefore, maintaining a high sperm count seems to be important for conception.

The fertilized egg, called the zygote, continues to travel down the fallopian tube. About 36 hours after conception, it begins the process of cell division, by which the original one cell becomes a mass of two cells, then four cells, then eight cells, and so on. About five to seven days after conception, the mass of cells implants itself in the lining of the uterus, there to be nourished and grow. For the first eight weeks of gestation the *conceptus* (product of conception) is called an *embryo;* from then until birth it is called a *fetus.*

Improving the Chances of Conception: Making a Baby

While this topic may seem rather remote to a 20-year-old college student, whose principal concern is probably *avoiding* conception, some couples do want to have a baby. The following are points for them to keep in mind.

The whole trick, of course, is to time intercourse so that it occurs around the time of ovulation. To do this, it is necessary to determine when the woman ovulates. If she is that idealized woman with the perfectly regular 28-day cycle, then she ovulates on day 14. But for the vast majority of women, the time of ovulation can best be determined by keeping a *basal body temperature chart.* To do this, the woman takes her temperature every morning immediately upon waking (that means before getting up and moving around or drinking a cup of coffee). She then keeps a graph of her temperature (like the one shown in Figure 6.2). During the preovulatory phase, the temperature will be relatively constant (the temperature is below 98.6°F because temperature is low in the early morning). On the day of ovulation the temperature drops, and on the day following ovulation it rises sharply, by 0.4°F to 1.0°F above the preovulatory level. The temperature should then stay at that high level until just before menstruation. The most reliable indicator of ovulation is the rise in temperature the day after it occurs. From this, the woman can determine the day of ovulation, and that determination should be consistent with menstruation occurring about 14 days later. After doing this for a couple of cycles, the woman should have a fairly good idea of the day in her cycle on which she ovulates.

Sperm live inside the woman's body for about 48 hours.[2] The egg is capable of being fertilized for about the first 12 to 24 hours after ovulation. Allowing the sperm some swimming time, this means that intercourse should be timed right at ovulation or one or two days before.

Assuming you have some idea of the time of ovulation, how frequent should intercourse be? While more may be merrier, more is not necessarily more effective. The reason for this is that it is important for the man's sperm count to be maintained. It takes a while to manufacture 300 million sperm—at least 24 hours. And, as was discussed earlier, maintaining a high sperm count appears to be important in accomplishing the task of fertilizing the egg. For purposes of conceiving, then, it is probably best to have intercourse about every 24 to 48 hours, or about four times during the week in which the woman is to ovulate.

It is also important to take some steps to ensure that once deposited in the vagina, the sperm get a decent chance to survive and to find their way into the fallopian tubes. Position during and after intercourse is important. For purposes of conceiving, the best position for intercourse is with the woman on her back (man-on-top, or "missionary," position—see Chapter 10). If the woman is on top, much of the ejaculate may run out of the vagina because of the pull of gravity. After intercourse, she should remain on her back, possibly with her legs pulled up and a

[2] But do not assume this if you are concerned with *contraception.* A few reports indicate that they may survive for 5 or even 10 days.

pillow under her hips, preferably for about a half hour to an hour. This allows the semen to remain in a pool in the vagina, which gives the sperm a good chance to swim up into the uterus. Because sperm are very sensitive to the pH (acidity-alkalinity) of the vagina, this factor also requires some consideration. Acidity kills sperm. Douching with commercial preparations or with acidic solutions (such as vinegar) should be avoided. If anything, the woman may want to douche before intercourse with a slightly basic solution made by adding two or three tablespoons of baking soda to a quart of water. Finally, lubricants and/or suppositories should not be used; they may kill sperm or block their entrance into the uterus.

DEVELOPMENT OF THE CONCEPTUS

For the nine months of pregnancy, two organisms—the conceptus and the pregnant woman—undergo parallel, dramatic changes. The changes that occur in the developing conceptus will be discussed in this section; a later section will be about the changes that take place in the pregnant woman.

Typically the nine months of pregnancy are divided into three equal periods of three months, each called *trimesters*. Thus the first trimester is months 1 to 3, the second trimester is months 4 to 6, and the third (or last) trimester is months 7 to 9.

The Embryo and Its Support Systems

We left the conceptus, which began as a single fertilized egg cell, dividing into many cells as it passed down the fallopian tube, finally arriving in the uterus and implanting itself in the uterine wall.

During the embryonic period of development (the first eight weeks), most of the fetus's major organ systems are formed in processes that occur with amazing speed. The inner part of the ball of cells implanted in the uterus now differentiates into two layers, the endoderm and the ectoderm. Later a third layer, the mesoderm, forms between them. The various organs of the body differentiate from these layers. The *ectoderm* will form the entire nervous system and the skin. The *endoderm* differentiates into the digestive system—from the pharynx, to the stomach and intestines, to the rectum—and the respiratory system. The muscles, skeleton, connective tissues, and reproductive and circulatory systems derive from the *mesoderm*. Fetal development generally proceeds in a cephalocaudal order. That is, the head develops first, and the lower body last. For this reason, the head of the fetus is enormous compared with the rest of the body (see Figure 7.3).

Meanwhile, another group of cells has differentiated into the *trophoblast*, which has important functions in maintaining the embryo and which will eventually become the placenta.

The placenta is the mass of tissues that surrounds the conceptus early in development and nurtures its growth. Later it moves to the side of the fetus. The placenta has a number of important functions, perhaps the most important of which is that it serves as a site for the exchange of substances between the woman's blood and the fetus's blood. It is important to note that the woman's circulatory system and the fetus's circulatory system are completely separate. That is, with only rare exceptions, the woman's blood never circulates inside the fetus; nor does the fetus's blood circulate in the woman's blood vessels. Instead, the fetus's blood passes out of its body through the umbilical cord to the placenta. There it circulates in the numerous *villi* (tiny fingerlike projections in the placenta). The woman's blood circulates around the outside of these villi. Thus there is a membrane barrier between the two blood systems. Some substances are capable of passing through this barrier,

Placenta (plah-SEN-tuh): An organ formed on the wall of the uterus through which the fetus receives oxygen and nutrients and gets rid of waste products.

while others are not. Oxygen and nutrients can pass through the barrier, and thus the woman's blood supplies oxygen and nutrients to the fetus, providing substitutes for breathing and eating. Carbon dioxide and waste products similarly pass back from the fetal blood to the woman's blood. Some viruses and other disease-causing organisms can pass through the barrier, including those for German measles (rubella) and syphilis. But other organisms cannot pass through the barrier; thus the woman may have a terrible cold, but the fetus will remain completely healthy. Various drugs can also cross the placental barrier, and the woman should therefore be careful about drugs taken during pregnancy (see the section on drugs during pregnancy, later in this chapter).

Another major function of the placenta is that it secretes hormones. The placenta produces large quantities of estrogen and progesterone. Many of the physical symptoms of pregnancy may be caused by these elevated levels of hormones. Another hormone manufactured by the placenta is **human chorionic gonadotropin** (HCG). HCG is the hormone that is detected in pregnancy tests.

The **umbilical cord** is formed during the fifth week of embryonic development. The fully developed cord is about 55 centimeters (20 inches) long. Normally, it contains three blood vessels: two arteries and one vein. Some people believe that the fetus's umbilical cord attaches to the woman's navel; actually, the umbilical cord attaches to the placenta, thereby providing for the interchanges of substances described above.

Two membranes surround the fetus, the *chorion* and the *amnion,* the amnion being the innermost. The amnion is filled with a watery liquid called **amniotic fluid,** in which the fetus floats and can readily move. It is the amniotic fluid that is sampled when an amniocentesis is performed (see below). The amniotic fluid maintains the fetus at a constant temperature and, most important, cushions the fetus against possible injury. Thus the woman can fall down a flight of stairs, and the fetus will remain undisturbed. Indeed, the amniotic fluid might be considered the original waterbed.

Fetal Development During the First Trimester

In a sense, the development of the fetus during the first trimester is more remarkable than its development during the second and third trimesters, for it is during the first trimester that the small mass of cells implanted in the uterus develops into a fetus with most of the major organ systems present and with recognizable human features.

By the third week of gestation, the embryo appears as a small bit of flesh and is about 0.2 centimeters ($\frac{1}{12}$ inch) long. During the third and fourth weeks, the head undergoes a great deal of development. The central nervous system begins to form, and the beginnings of eyes and ears are visible. The backbone is constructed by the end of the fourth week. A "tail" is noticeable early in embryonic development but has disappeared by the eighth week.

From the fourth to the eighth weeks, the external body parts—eyes, ears, arms, hands, fingers, legs, feet, and toes—develop (see Figure 7.3*c*, following page 162). By the end of the tenth week they are completely formed. Indeed, by the tenth week, the embryo has not only a complete set of fingers but also fingernails.

By the end of the seventh week, the liver, lungs, pancreas, kidneys, and intestines have formed and have begun limited functioning. The gonads have also formed, but the gender of the fetus is not clearly distinguishable until the twelfth week.

At the end of the twelfth week (end of the first trimester) the fetus is unmistakably human and looks like a small infant. It is about 10 centimeters (4 inches) long

Human chorionic gonadotropin (HCG): A hormone secreted by the placeta; it is the substance detected in pregnancy tests.

Umbilical cord: The tube that connects the fetus to the placenta.

Amniotic fluid: The watery fluid surrounding a developing fetus in the uterus.

and weighs about 19 grams ($\frac{2}{3}$ ounce). From this point on, development consists mainly of enlargement and differentiation of structures that are already present.

Fetal Development During the Second Trimester

Around the end of the fourteenth week, the movements of the fetus can be detected ("quickening"). By the eighteenth week, the woman has been able to feel movement for two to four weeks, and the physician can detect the fetal heartbeat. The latter is an important point, because it helps the physician determine the length of gestation. The baby should be born about 20 weeks later.

The fetus first opens its eyes around the twentieth week. By about the twenty-fourth week, it is sensitive to light and can hear sounds in utero. Arm and leg movements are vigorous at this time, and the fetus alternates between periods of wakefulness and sleep.

Fetal Development During the Third Trimester

At the end of the second trimester the fetus's skin is wrinkled and covered with downlike hair. At the beginning of the third trimester, fat deposits form under the skin; these will give the infant the characteristic chubby appearance of babyhood. The downlike hair is lost.

During the seventh month the fetus turns in the uterus to assume a head-down position. If this turning does not occur by the time of delivery, there will be a *breech presentation.* Women can do certain exercises to aid the turning (Boston Women's Health Book Collective, 1984).

The fetus's growth during the last two months is rapid. At the end of the eighth month it weighs an average of 2500 grams (5 pounds, 4 ounces). The average full-term baby weighs 3300 grams (7.5 pounds) and is 50 centimeters (20 inches) long.

THE STAGES OF PREGNANCY

The First Trimester (The First 12 Weeks)

Symptoms of Pregnancy

For most women, the first symptom of pregnancy is a missed menstrual period. Of course, there may be a wide variety of reactions to this event. For the teenager who is not married or for the married woman who feels that she already has enough children, the reaction may be negative—depression, anger, and fear. For the woman who has been trying to conceive for several months, the reaction may be joy and eager anticipation.

In fact, there are many other reasons besides pregnancy for a woman to have a late period or miss a period; illness or emotional stress may delay a period, and women occasionally skip a period for no apparent reason.

It is also true that a woman may continue to experience some cyclic bleeding or spotting during pregnancy. It is not particularly a danger sign, except that in a few cases it is a symptom of a miscarriage.

If the woman has been keeping a basal body temperature chart, this can provide a very early sign that she is pregnant. If her temperature rises abruptly at about the time ovulation would normally occur and then stays up for more than two weeks—

say, about three weeks—the chances are fairly good that she is pregnant. The increased temperature results from the high level of progesterone manufactured by the corpus luteum and, later, the placenta.

Other early symptoms of pregnancy are tenderness of the breasts—a tingling sensation and special sensitivity of the nipples—and nausea and vomiting (called "morning sickness," although these symptoms may actually happen anytime during the day). More frequent urination, feelings of fatigue, and a need for more sleep are other early signs of pregnancy.

Pregnancy Tests

A pregnancy test may be done by a physician, at a Planned Parenthood or family planning clinic, or at a medical laboratory.

A widely used pregnancy test is an immunologic test based on detecting the presence of HCG (human chorionic gonadotropin, secreted by the placenta) in the woman's urine. It can be done in a matter of minutes to a few hours and is very accurate. It involves mixing a drop of urine with certain chemicals, either on a slide or in a tube. If HCG is present, the mixture will coagulate and the test for pregnancy is positive (the woman is pregnant).

The laboratory tests for pregnancy are 99 percent accurate. A laboratory test may produce a false negative (tell the woman she is not pregnant when she really is) if it is done too early or if errors are made in processing. Also, some women simply do not show positive signs in the tests or do not do so until the second or third test. The presence of HCG can be detected as early as the third week of pregnancy (one week after the missed period), but the tests are not highly accurate until the sixth or eighth week of pregnancy.

A newer test, called the *beta subunit HCG radioimmunoassay,* is 99 percent accurate. It measures HCG in a blood sample and is sensitive enough to detect a pregnancy eight days after conception or five days *before* the missed period. It is highly accurate and is becoming increasingly available.

It is important that early, accurate pregnancy tests be available and that women make use of them. This is true for several reasons. A woman needs to know that she is pregnant as early as possible so that she can see a physician and begin getting good prenatal care. She also needs to know so that she can get the nutrition she requires during pregnancy (see the section on nutrition, below). And if she does not want to carry the baby to term, she needs to know as soon as possible, because abortions are much safer and simpler when performed in the first trimester than when done in the second trimester.

Home pregnancy tests are also available, sold under various brand names as e.p.t. (for "early pregnancy test"), AcuTest, Answer, and Predictor. These are all urine tests designed to measure the presence of HCG; they cost around $15. They can be used about nine days after a missed menstrual period. Their charm lies in their convenience and the privacy of getting the results. The major problem with them is that they have a very high rate—between 25 and 38 percent—of false negatives, that is, telling the woman she is not pregnant when she actually is (Hart, 1990; Doski, 1986). This compares with an error rate of 1 percent for laboratory tests. The home pregnancy tests also have a 16 percent rate of false positives. To guard against false negatives, the manufacturers recommend repeating the test one week later if the results are negative the first time, although this doubles the cost. The reason that a high rate of false negatives is so serious is that it leads a pregnant woman to think she is not pregnant, and thus she might take drugs that would harm the fetus, and she will not begin getting prenatal care; such dangerous conditions as ectopic pregnancy might therefore go undetected. The tests also require a certain amount of coordination and care in performing. All in all, they are probably not as good an idea as they seem, although they may be improved in the future.

The signs of pregnancy may be classified as *presumptive signs, probable signs,* and *positive signs.* Amenorrhea, breast tenderness, nausea, and so on, are presumptive signs. The pregnancy tests discussed above all provide probable signs. Three signs are interpreted as positive signs, that is, as definite indications of pregnancy: (1) beating of the fetal heart, (2) active fetal movement, and (3) detection of a fetal skeleton by ultrasound. These signs cannot be detected until the fourth month, with the exception of ultrasound, which can be used in the first trimester.

Once the pregnancy has been confirmed, the woman generally is very interested in determining her expected delivery date (called EDC for a rather antiquated expression, "expected date of confinement"). The EDC is calculated using *Nägele's rule.* The rule says to take the date of the first day of the last menstrual period, subtract three months, add seven days, and finally add one year. Thus if the first day of the last menstrual period was September 10, 1993, the expected delivery date would be June 17, 1994: subtracting three months from September 10 gives June 10, adding seven days yields June 17, and adding one year gives June 17, 1994.

Physical Changes

The basic physical change that takes place in the woman's body during the first trimester is the large increase in the levels of hormones, especially estrogen and progesterone, which are produced by the placenta. Many of the other physical symptoms of the first trimester arise from these endocrine changes.

The breasts swell and tingle. This results from the development of the mammary glands, which is stimulated by hormones. The nipples and the area around them (areola) may darken and broaden.

There is often a need to urinate more frequently. This is related to changes in the pituitary hormones that affect the adrenals, which in turn change the water balance in the body so that more water is retained. The growing uterus also contributes by pressing against the bladder.

Some women experience morning sickness—feelings of nausea, perhaps to the point of vomiting, and of revulsion toward food or its odor. The nausea and vomiting may occur on waking or at other times during the day. The exact cause of this is not known. One theory is that the high levels of estrogen irritate the stomach. The rapid expansion of the uterus may also be involved. While these symptoms are quite common, it is also true that about 25 percent of pregnant women experience no vomiting at all.

Vaginal discharges may also increase at this time, partly because the increased hormone levels change the pH of the vagina and partly because the vaginal secretions are changing in their chemical composition and quantity.

The feelings of fatigue and sleepiness are probably related to the high levels of progesterone, which is known to have a sedative effect.

Psychological Changes

Our culture is full of stereotypes about the psychological characteristics of pregnant women. It is supposed to be a time of happiness and calm; radiant contentment is said to emanate from the woman's face, making this a good time for her to be photographed. Pregnant women are also seen as somewhat irrational, demanding, and dependent—capable, for example, of sending their husbands to the refrigerator for dill pickles and ice cream at midnight.

Actually, the data suggest that the situation is much more complex than this.

A woman's emotional state during pregnancy appears to vary according to a number of factors: her attitude toward the pregnancy (whether she wanted to be pregnant), her social class, her general life adjustment, conflict in the marriage, and stage of pregnancy. The positive emotions noted above are probably a result of the traditional assumption in our culture that all babies are wanted and that all women want babies. However, with increased concern over population size, growing acceptance of contraception, and decreased emphasis on fertility, it has become increasingly recognized that pregnancy may not always be a good thing. These changes in values may make pregnant women feel freer to acknowledge their negative feelings.

Depression and fatigue are not at all uncommon during the first trimester; they may be partly the result of morning sickness. But there is great variation in pregnant women's emotional state. Happiness is more common among those who want to be pregnant, whereas depression is more common among those who do not. Women of lower socieconomic status are more likely to have negative feelings (although this may be explained by the fact that there are more unwanted pregnancies among low-income women). Women who have made a generally good life adjustment tend to feel more positive at this time than women with a history of adjustment problems. Finally, negative emotions are commoner when there is a conflict in the marriage.

Myra Leifer (1980) did an intensive study of 19 women, all pregnant for the first time. They were interviewed once during each trimester of pregnancy, on the third day after giving birth, and at six to eight weeks postpartum, and a questionnaire was mailed to them at seven months postpartum. Her general findings were that rather than being a time of calm and bliss, pregnancy was, for most of the women in her sample, difficult and turbulent. She also found that emotional changes during pregnancy and postpartum were strongly related to the emotional support and help the women received from her husband. The women tended to be emotionally labile (have mood shifts) and to have anxieties. Specifically, in the first trimester anxieties centered on worries about miscarriage. In the first trimester, only the four women for whom the pregnancy was unplanned expressed overall negative emotions. The other women were either positive or ambivalent (had mixed feelings).

The Second Trimester (Weeks 13 to 26)

Physical Changes

During the fourth month, the woman becomes aware of the fetus's movements ("quickening"). Many women find this to be a very exciting experience.

The woman is made even more aware of the pregnancy by her rapidly expanding belly. There are a variety of reactions to this. Some women feel that it is a magnificent symbol of womanhood, and they rush out to buy maternity clothes and wear them before they are even necessary. Other women feel awkward and resentful of their bulky shape and may begin to wonder whether they can fit through doorways and turnstiles.

Most of the physical symptoms of the first trimester, such as morning sickness, disappear, and discomforts are at a minimum. Physical problems at this time include constipation and nosebleeds (caused by increased blood volume). Edema—water retention and swelling—may be a problem in the face, hands, wrists, ankles, and feet; it results from increased water retention throughout the body.

By about mid-pregnancy, the breasts, under hormonal stimulation, have essentially completed their development in preparation for nursing. Beginning about the nineteenth week, a thin amber or yellow fluid called colostrum may come out of the nipple, although there is no milk yet.

Edema (eh-DEE-muh): Excessive fluid retention and swelling.

Colostrum: A watery substance that is secreted from the breast at the end of pregnancy and during the first few days after delivery.

FIGURE 7.3
These micrographs show the remarkable biology of human reproduction.

(a) Ovulation, showing the egg bursting forth from the wall of the ovary.

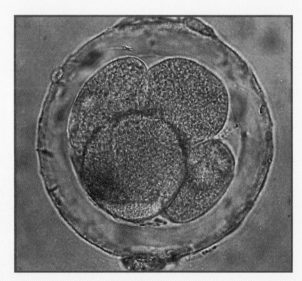

(b) The egg is fertilized by one sperm as many sperm cluster about.

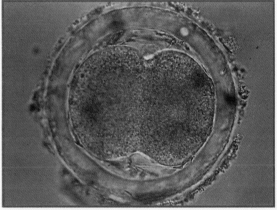

(c) A fertilized human zygote at the time of the first cell division.

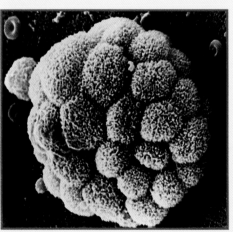

(d) This embryo has divided into four cells and would still be travelling down the fallopian tube.

(e) The blastula at about the 64-cell stage. The blastula can implant itself into the endometrium of the uterus.

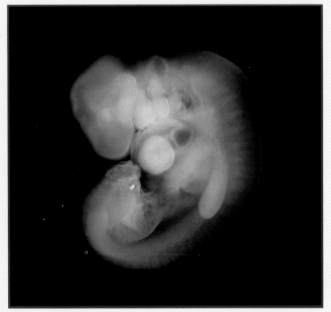

(f) The embryo after 4 weeks of development. The major organs are forming, the bright red, blood-filled heart is just below the lower jaw.

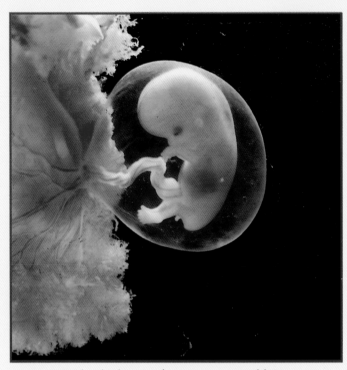

(g) At 9 weeks the human form is recognizable as a primate. Limbs have formed and ears are clearly visible.

(h) By about 3 months the fetus is approximately 8 centimeters long and weighs about 28 grams. Muscles have formed and they move the limbs and body.

(i) By 4 months the fetus is about 16 centimeters long, weighs 200 grams, and has begun the rapid growth that occurs before birth.

Psychological Changes

While the first trimester can be relatively tempestuous, particularly with morning sickness, the second trimester is generally a period of relative calm and well-being. The discomforts of the first trimester are past, and the tensions associated with the close approach of delivery are not yet present. Leifer (1980) found that the second trimester was the high point psychologically—there was the most happiness and pride in pregnancy. Fears of miscarriage diminished as the women could feel fetal movements, and there was an intense feeling of relief that the fetus was alive.

The Third Trimester (Weeks 27 to 38)

Physical Changes

The uterus is very large and hard now. The woman is increasingly aware of her size and of the fetus, which is becoming more and more active. In fact, some women are kept awake at night by its somersaults and hiccups.

The extreme size of the uterus puts pressure on a number of other organs, causing some discomfort. There is pressure on the lungs, which may cause shortness of breath. The stomach is also being squeezed, and indigestion is common. The navel is pushed out. The heart is being strained because of the large increase in blood volume. Most women feel low in energy (Leifer, 1980).

The weight gain of the second trimester continues. Most physicians recommend about 22 to 27 pounds of weight gain during pregnancy. The average infant at birth weighs 7.5 pounds; the rest of the weight gain is accounted for by the placenta (about 1 pound), the amniotic fluid (about 2 pounds), enlargement of the uterus (about 2 pounds), enlargement of the breasts (1.5 pounds), and the additional fat and water retained by the woman (8 or more pounds). Physicians restrict the amount of weight gain because the incidence of complications such as high blood pressure and strain on the heart is much higher in women who gain an excessive amount of weight. Also, excessive weight gained during pregnancy can be very hard to lose afterward.

The woman's balance is somewhat disturbed because of the large amount of weight that has been added to the front part of her body. She may compensate for this by adopting the characteristic "waddling" walk of the pregnant woman, which can result in back pains.

Braxton-Hicks contractions: Contractions of the uterus during pregnancy that are not part of actual labor.

The uterus tightens occasionally in painless contractions called Braxton-Hicks contractions; these are not part of labor. It is thought that these contractions help to strengthen the uterine muscles, preparing them for labor.

In a first pregnancy, around two to four weeks before delivery the baby turns, and the head drops into the pelvis. This is called *lightening, dropping,* or *engagement.* Engagement usually occurs during labor in women who have had babies before.

Some women are concerned about the appropriate amount of activity during pregnancy—whether some things constitute "overdoing it." Traditionally physicians and textbooks warned of the dangers of physical activities and tried to discourage them. It appears now, however, that such restrictions were based more on superstition than on scientific fact. Current thinking holds that for a healthy pregnant woman, moderate activity is not dangerous and is actually psychologically and physically beneficial. Modern methods of childbirth encourage sensible exercise for the pregnant woman so that she will be in shape for labor (see the section on natural childbirth, below). The matter, of course, is highly individual. But one Olympic swimmer placed third in her event while 3½ months pregnant, and it was reported that 10 of the 25 Soviet women Olympic champions of the Sixteenth Olympiad in Melbourne, Australia, were pregnant (Bruser, 1969).

Psychological Changes

While the second trimester is relatively sunny, the third trimester may be somewhat stressful psychologically. The incidence of depression increases (O'Hara, 1986). During the last month women often become very impatient, feeling as if they are in a state of suspended animation and really wanting to get on with it.

The birth of the baby becomes an ever-nearer reality. With that comes some anxieties. Notable among these are worries that the baby will be deformed or defective in some way; the woman may also wonder, especially if it is a first child, whether she will be a good mother and whether labor will be difficult (Entwisle & Doering, 1981). Leifer (1980) found increases during the third trimester in anxiety about the delivery and about possible deformity of the baby.

The Father's Role in Pregnancy

Couvade and Sympathetic Pregnancy

Occasionally some men experience nausea and vomiting along with the pregnant woman. This reaction is called *sympathetic pregnancy*.

In some cultures this phenomenon takes a more dramatic form, known as *couvade*. In the couvade, the husband retires to bed while his wife is in labor. He suffers all the pains of delivery, moaning and groaning as she does. Couvade is still practiced in parts of Asia, North and South America, and Oceania (Mead & Newton, 1967).

The Father-to-Be

In modern American culture many men expect to devote substantial amounts of time and energy to fathering, unlike the distant fathers of yesteryear. In fact, it has even been claimed that there is a "father instinct" (Biller & Meredith, 1975). Although some men choose to remain in the background, many choose to be actively involved in the pregnancy and the parenting (Antle, 1978). Early in the pregnancy, first-time fathers may recall their own childhood and relationship to their father, and may

FIGURE 7.4
Dad changes his daughter's diaper at a "Bootee Camp" in Irvine, California, that helps new or prospective fathers adjust to their new role.

need to resolve any mixed emotions they still have about their relationship. In one study, 70 percent of expectant fathers were initially ambivalent about fathering, but their feelings gradually became more positive, in anticipation of satisfactions to be derived from being fathers (Obzrut, 1976). In the same study, the fathers reported engaging in many activities in preparation for becoming fathers. Many reported attending parenting classes, planning father-child activities, observing and talking to other fathers, and daydreaming about the baby. Most of these activities, of course, parallel those done by expectant mothers. It has been theorized that men who display this active involvement will do best in the father role after the baby is born (Antle, 1978).

Diversity

There are lots of family contexts in which women have babies these days besides the traditional one of being married to the baby's father. These include living in a stable relationship with the baby's father but not being married; not being married to or living with the baby's father but seeing him regularly; being a single mother-to-be who has no contact with the baby's father; being a single mother-to-be who is pregnant as a result of artificial insemination or other reproductive technologies; and being a woman in a stable relationship with another woman, who is pregnant as a result of artificial insemination or other technologies. Because it is too complicated to mention these alternatives constantly, in the sections that follow my language will be based on a situation in which the woman is married to the baby's father, which is still statistically the most common context in which babies are born in the United States. Readers should keep in mind all these other possible family scenarios, though.

SEX DURING PREGNANCY

Many women are concerned about whether it is safe or advisable for them to have sexual intercourse while they are pregnant, particularly during the latter stages of the pregnancy. Traditionally, physicians were concerned that intercourse might (1) cause an infection or (2) precipitate labor prematurely or cause a miscarriage (for a review on sexuality and pregnancy, see White & Reamy, 1982).

Masters and Johnson (1966) investigated sexual intercourse during pregnancy. They state emphatically that given a normal, healthy pregnancy, intercourse can continue safely at least until four weeks before the baby is due. (This is an individual matter, however, and should be decided in consultation with a physician; some women are clearly high-risk cases for whom intercourse is inadvisable.) Masters and Johnson find that the woman is usually sufficiently recovered three weeks after birth for coitus to be safe, and the woman's sexual interest also generally returns at about that time.

However, an analysis of 27,000 pregnancies occurring between 1959 and 1966 indicated that infections of the amniotic fluid and subsequent death of the baby were more frequent among women who had intercourse in the month before delivery compared with those who abstained (Naeye, 1979). Criticisms of the study have been made, and one should probably not rush out to urge abstinence by pregnant women. A reasonable recommendation is for women who have a history of miscarriage or whose cervix has begun to dilate to avoid intercourse and orgasm during the last trimester (Herbst, 1979).

Physicians' pronouncements aside, the available data indicate that women continue to have intercourse, and do so at a near-normal rate, until well into the third trimester. As the data in Table 7.1 indicate, intercourse continues through the second

Table 7.1
Percentage of Women Having Various Frequencies of Coitus at Different Stages of Pregnancy

Number of Acts of Coitus per Week	Baseline Prepregnancy, %	12 Weeks Pregnant, %	24 Weeks Pregnant, %	36 Weeks Pregnant, %
None	0	11	8	36
<1	7	24	25	26
1–3	54	52	55	33
4 or more	40	14	13	5

Source: R. Kumar, H. A. Brant, and K. M. Robson. (1981). Childbearing and maternal sexuality: A prospective study of 119 primiparae. *Journal of Psychosomatic Research, 25,* 373–383.

trimester with essentially the same frequency as before pregnancy. Not until the last month do substantial numbers of women report abstaining from intercourse.

Of course, during the latter stages of pregnancy, the woman's shape makes intercourse increasingly awkward. The missionary position is probably best abandoned at this time. The side-to-side position (see Chapter 10) is probably the position best suited to the special problems of intercourse during the late stages of pregnancy. Couples should also remember that there are many ways of experiencing sexual pleasure and orgasm besides having intercourse—hand-genital stimulation or oral-genital sex[3] may be good alternatives for the very pregnant woman.

One of the best guides in this matter is the woman's own feelings. If intercourse becomes uncomfortable for her, it should be discontinued until it feels more comfortable.

NUTRITION

During pregnancy, another living being is growing inside the woman, and she needs lots of energy, protein, vitamins, and minerals at this time. Therefore, diet during pregnancy is extremely important. If the woman's diet is good, she has a much better chance of remaining healthy during pregnancy and of bearing a healthy baby; if her diet is inadequate, she stands more of a chance of developing one of a number of diseases during pregnancy herself and of bearing a child whose weight is low at birth. Babies with low birth weights do not have as good a chance of survival as babies with normal birth weights. According to a study done in Toronto, mothers in a poor-diet group had four times as many serious health problems during pregnancy as a group of mothers whose diets were supplemented with highly nutritious foods. Those with the poor diets had seven times as many threatened miscarriages and three times as many stillbirths; their labor lasted five hours longer on the average (Newton, 1972).

It is particularly important that a pregnant woman get enough protein, folic acid, iron, calcium, and vitamins A, B, C, D, and E. Protein is important for building new tissues. Folic acid is also important for growth; symptoms of folic acid deficiency are anemia and fatigue. Iron is important for the blood that circulates to the placenta, from which the fetus draws off additional iron for itself. Muscle cramps, nerve pains,

---

[3] There is, however, some risk associated with cunnilingus for the pregnant woman, as discussed in Chapter 10.

uterine ligament pains, sleeplessness, and irritability may all be symptoms of a calcium deficiency. Sometimes even an excellent diet does not provide enough iron, calcium, or folic acid, in which case the pregnant woman's intake should be implemented with pills.

EFFECTS OF DRUGS TAKEN DURING PREGNANCY

We are such a pill-popping culture that we seldom stop to think about whether we should take a certain drug. The pregnant woman, however, needs to know that when she takes a drug, not only does it circulate through her body, but it may also circulate through the fetus. Because the fetus develops so rapidly during pregnancy, drugs may have severe consequences, including producing serious malformations. Drugs that produce such defects are called **teratogenic**.[4] An example that attracted much attention in the early 1960s was the drug thalidomide, a tranquilizer; if taken early in pregnancy, it resulted in babies with grotesque deformities such as flipperlike appendages where there should have been arms and legs. Of course, not all drugs can cross the placental barrier, but many can. The drugs that pregnant women should be cautious in using are discussed below.

Teratogenic: Producing defects in the fetus.

Antibiotics

Long-term use of antibiotics by the woman may cause damage to the fetus. Tetracycline may cause stained teeth and bone deformities. Gentamycin, kanamycin, neomycin, streptomycin, and vincomycin all may cause deafness. Nitrofurantoin may cause jaundice. A new drug, Accutane (isotretinoin) is used to treat acne, replacing earlier antibiotic treatments in some cases. It can cause severe birth defects if taken by a pregnant woman. Some drugs taken by diabetics may cause various fetal anomalies.

Alcohol and Other Addictive Drugs

Alcohol consumed by the woman circulates through the fetus. Alcoholic women can give birth to babies who have alcohol on their breath; the babies then have withdrawal symptoms for the first few days after they are born—scarcely a pleasant introduction to life outside the womb. Excessive amounts of alcohol lead to vitamin depletion and biochemical imbalance, and to low-birth-weight babies, premature birth, or even intrauterine death.

Fetal alcohol syndrome (FAS): Serious disease in the newborn of an alcoholic mother.

The pattern of physical malformations that occur in the offspring of women who abuse alcohol during pregnancy has been termed the **fetal alcohol syndrome (FAS)** (for reviews, see Abel, 1984; Clarren & Smith, 1978). Among the characteristics of the syndrome are both prenatal and postnatal growth deficiencies, a small brain, small eye openings, and joint, limb, and heart malformations. Perhaps the most serious effect is mental retardation. About 85 percent of children with the FAS score two or more standard deviations below the mean on intelligence tests—that would be an IQ of about 70 or below. Indeed, two experts concluded that "maternal abuse of alcohol during gestation . . . appears to be the most frequent known teratogenic cause of mental deficiency in the Western world" (Clarren & Smith, 1978, p. 1066).

---

[4] "Teratogenic" is from the Greek words *teras*, meaning "monster," and *genic*, meaning "cause."

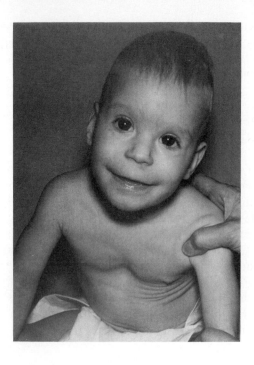

FIGURE 7.5
A child born with fetal
alcohol syndrome.

Current research indicates that the fetus is at risk for the FAS if the mother's consumption of alcohol is six or more drinks per day. It is also clear that women who drink moderately may have children who are affected to some degree (Abel, 1980). The effects have even been documented in the children when they reach adulthood (Streissguth et al., 1989). Unfortunately, "safe" limits for alcohol consumption during pregnancy have not been established, so probably the best advice for pregnant women about drinking is "Don't."

Heroin addiction and morphine addiction lead to similar problems (Householder et al., 1982). The babies are born smaller than average and undergo withdrawal symptoms after birth. In infancy their symptoms include irritability, hyperactivity, and sleep and feeding disturbances. The psychological problems persist into childhood. Methadone can also cause problems in the baby.

Cocaine became a popular drug in the 1980s and 1990s, raising concerns about its use by pregnant women. Research shows that cocaine abuse during pregnancy increases the number of low-birth-weight babies, stillbirths, and birth defects (Bingol et al., 1987; Little et al., 1989). For example, in one study of pregnant women who used cocaine, 36 percent gave birth to preterm, low-birth-weight babies (<2500 grams), 31 percent of the babies had neurological problems, and 17 percent had a birth defect. On the other hand, there are methodological complications in most of these studies, and the media hysteria over the effects may be out of proportion to the evidence (Mayes et al., 1992). For example, a high percentage of women who abuse cocaine during pregnancy are multiple drug users, including a high rate of cigarette smoking and alcoholism. The effects of cigarettes and alcohol prenatally are well documented. The question then becomes, Does cocaine have adverse effects over and above the effects of the other drugs the women are using?

Steroids

Synthetic hormones such as progestin can cause masculinization of a female fetus, as discussed in Chapter 5. Corticosteroids are linked with jaundice, low birth weights, cleft palate, and stillbirth. Excessive amounts of vitamin A are associated with cleft palate. Excesses of vitamins D, B_6, and K have also been associated with fetal defects. A potent estrogen, diethylstilbestrol (DES), has been shown to cause cancer of the vagina in girls whose mothers took the drug while pregnant (Herbst, 1972). (DES pops up in a number of places. It is used in the "morning-after" pill and as a diet supplement to fatten cattle, the latter use having been prohibited because of the possible dangers of ingesting too much DES.)

Other Drugs

According to the U.S. Public Health Service, maternal smoking during pregnancy exerts a retarding influence on fetal growth indicated by decreased infant birth weight and increased incidence of prematurity (for a review, see Coleman et al., 1979). A study of 28,000 children found that those children whose mothers smoked heavily during pregnancy were almost twice as likely to be hyperactive and impulsive when they were 6 years old than were the children of nonsmoking mothers; the children of smoking mothers also had lower IQs and less developed motor skills (Dunn et al., 1977).

Some antihistamines may produce malformations. Even plain aspirin may cause blood problems (Cunningham et al., 1989).

Although not classified as a drug, x-rays deserve mention here since they can damage the fetus, particularly during the first 42 days after conception.

The psychoactive chemical in marijuana crosses the placental barrier (Harbison & Mantilla-Plata, 1972; Idänpään-Heikkilä et al., 1969). There is some evidence that marijuana inhibits ovulation (Abel, 1985); thus its use might make it more difficult to become pregnant. In one Canadian study, women who used marijuana during pregnancy were compared with a control group of nonusers. There were no differences between the two groups in rate of miscarriage, complications during birth, or incidence of birth defects. However, the newborns of the marijuana users had more tremors and had a higher rate of visual problems in the preschool years (Fried, 1986).

Probably the best rule for the pregnant woman considering using a drug is, "When in doubt, don't."

Dads and Drugs

Most research has focused on the effects of drugs taken by the pregnant woman. However, new theorizing suggests that drugs taken by men before a conception may also cause birth defects, probably because the drugs damage the sperm and their genetic contents (Narod et al., 1988). In addition, one recent study found evidence that mother's smoking during the first trimester of pregnancy increased her offspring's risk of cancer in childhood; but father's smoking during the pregnancy in the absence of mother's smoking also increased the risk of childhood cancer (John et al., 1991). In the future we will surely see more concern and research on the effects of fathers' use of drugs on their children.

BIRTH

The Beginning of Labor

The signs that labor is about to begin vary from one woman to the next. There may be a discharge of a small amount of bloody mucus (the "bloody show"). This is the mucus plug that was in the cervical opening during pregnancy, its purpose being to prevent germs from passing from the vagina up into the uterus. In about 10 percent of all women the membranes containing the amniotic fluid rupture (the bag of waters bursts), and there is a gush of warm fluid down the woman's legs. Labor usually begins within 24 hours after this occurs. More commonly, though the amniotic sac does not rupture until the end of the first stage of labor. The Braxton-Hicks contractions may increase before labor and actually may be mistaken for labor. Typically they are distinct from the contractions of labor in that they are very irregular.

The biological mechanism that initiates and maintains labor is not completely understood. Currently it is thought that *prostaglandins* are the critical substance. They are known to cause strong uterine contractions at any time during pregnancy; and aspirin, which inhibits prostaglandin manufacture, can delay the onset of labor (Pritchard & MacDonald, 1980).

The Stages of Labor

Labor is typically divided into three stages, although the length of the stages may vary considerably from one woman to the next. The whole process of childbirth is sometimes referred to as *parturition.*

First-Stage Labor

First-stage labor begins with the regular contractions of the muscles of the uterus. These contractions are responsible for producing two changes in the cervix, both of which must occur before the baby can be delivered. These changes are called effacement (thinning out) and dilation (opening up). The cervix must dilate until it has an opening 10 centimeters (4 inches) in diameter before the baby can be born.

First-stage labor itself is divided into three stages: early, late, and transition. In *early first-stage labor,* contractions are spaced far apart, with perhaps 15 to 20 minutes between them. A contraction typically lasts 45 seconds to a minute. This stage of labor is fairly easy, and the woman is quite comfortable between contractions. Meanwhile, the cervix is effacing and dilating.

Late first-stage labor is marked by the dilation of the cervix from 5 to 8 centimeters (2 to 3 inches). It is generally shorter than the early stage, and the contractions are more frequent and more intense.

The final dilation of the cervix from 8 to 10 centimeters (3 to 4 inches) occurs during the transition phase, which is both short and difficult. The contractions are very strong, and it is during this stage that women report pain and exhaustion.

The first stage of labor can last anywhere from 2 to 24 hours. It averages about 12 to 15 hours for a first pregnancy and about 8 hours for later pregnancies. (In most respects, first labors are the hardest, and later ones are easier.) The woman is usually told to go to the hospital when the contractions are 4 to 5 minutes apart. Once there, she is put in the labor room or birthing room for the rest of first-stage labor.

Second-Stage Labor: Delivery

The second stage of labor begins when the cervix is fully dilated and the baby's head (or whichever part comes first, if the baby is in some other position) begins to move into the vagina, or birth canal. It lasts from a few minutes to a few hours and is generally much shorter than the first stage.

Effacement: A thinning out of the cervix during labor.

Dilation: An opening up of the cervix during labor; also called dilatation.

First-stage labor: The beginning of labor during which there are regular contractions of the uterus; the stage lasts until the cervix is dilated 8 centimeters (3 inches).

Transition: The difficult part of labor at the end of the first stage, during which the cervix dilates from 8 to 10 centimeters (3 to 4 inches).

Second-stage labor: The stage during which the baby moves out through the vagina and is delivered.

Episiotomy (ih-PEE-see-ah-tuh-mee): An incision made in the skin just behind the vagina, allowing the baby to be delivered more easily.

During this stage, many women feel an urge to push or bear down, and if done properly, this may be of great assistance in pushing the baby out. With each contraction the baby is pushed farther along.

When the baby's head has traversed the entire length of the vagina, the top of it becomes visible at the vaginal entrance; this is called *crowning*. It is at this point that many physicians perform an episiotomy (see Figure 7.6), in which an incision or slit is made in the perineum, the skin just behind the vagina. Most women do not feel the episiotomy being performed because the pressure of the baby against the pelvic floor provides a natural anesthetic. The incision is stitched closed after the baby is born. The reasons physicians give for performing the episiotomy is that if it is not done, the baby's head may rip the perineum; a neat incision is easier to repair than a ragged tear, and the tear may go much deeper and damage more tissue. But the use of the episiotomy has been questioned by feminists, who claim that it is unnecessary and is done merely for the doctor's convenience, while causing the woman discomfort later as it is healing. They note that episiotomies are usually not performed in western European countries, where delivery still takes place quite nicely.

The baby is finally eased completely out of the mother's body. At this point, the baby is still connected to the mother by the umbilical cord, which runs from the baby's navel to the placenta, and the placenta is still inside the mother's uterus. As the baby takes its first breath of air, the functioning of its body changes dramatically. Blood begins to flow to the lungs, there to take on oxygen, and a flap closes between the two atria (chambers) in the heart. This process generally takes a few minutes, during which time the baby changes from a somewhat bluish color to a healthy, pink hue. At this point, the baby no longer needs the umbilical cord, which is clamped and cut off about 7 centimeters (3 inches) from the body. The stub gradually dries up and falls off.

To avoid the possibility of transmitting gonorrhea or other eye infections from the mother to the baby, drops of silver nitrate or a similar drug are placed in the baby's eyes (see Chapter 20).

FIGURE 7.6
Episiotomy.

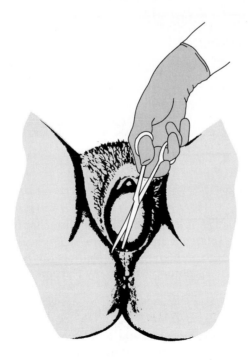

FIGURE 7.7
*Second-stage labor. (a)
Baby's head crowning and
(b) then moving out.*

(a)

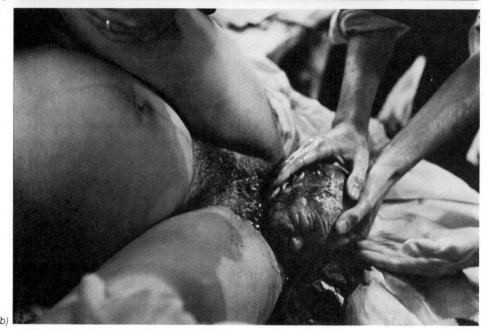

(b)

Third-Stage Labor

Third-stage labor: The
stage during which the
afterbirth is expelled.

During the third stage of labor, the placenta detaches from the walls of the uterus, and the afterbirth (placenta and fetal membranes) is expelled. This stage may take from a few minutes to an hour. Several contractions may accompany the expulsion of the placenta. The episiotomy and/or any tears are sewn up.

Positions of the Fetus

As was noted earlier, in most cases the fetus rotates into a head-down position inside the uterus during the last trimester of pregnancy, and the head emerges first at birth.

Cesarean section (C section): A method of delivering a baby surgically, by an incision in the abdomen.

Such normal presentations occur most often, but the baby may also be born in a number of other positions (see Figure 7.8).

Cesarean Section (C Section)

Cesarean section is a surgical procedure for delivery; it is used when normal vaginal birth is impossible or undesirable. Cesarean section may be required for a number of different reasons: if the baby is too large or if the mother's pelvis is too small to allow the baby to move into the vagina; if the labor has been very long and hard and the cervix is not dilating or if the mother is nearing the point of total exhaustion; if the umbilical cord *prolapses* (moves into a position such that it is coming out through the cervix ahead of the baby); if there is an Rh incompatibility (see below); or if there is excessive bleeding or the mother's or the infant's condition takes a sudden turn for the worse.

In the cesarean section, an incision is made through the abdomen and through the wall of the uterus. The physician lifts out the baby and then sews up the uterine wall and the abdominal wall.

Cesarean delivery rates increased steadily in the United States in the 1970s and 1980s, leveling off at 24 percent in 1989 (Taffel et al., 1991), which is a rate considerably higher than in most western European countries. For example, the cesarean rate is 10 percent of deliveries in the Netherlands, 12 percent of deliveries in Norway, and 10 percent of deliveries in England and Wales (Notzon, 1990). Contrary to popular opinion, it is not true that once a woman has had one delivery by cesarean she must have all subsequent deliveries by the same method. Normal vaginal births are possible after cesareans (Taffel et al., 1991), although often the same conditions are present in later deliveries that necessitated the first cesarean, making it necessary again in the later deliveries. Here, too, the United States has different statistics from other countries. In the United States, only 7 percent of women having another delivery following a cesarean have a vaginal delivery, compared with 39 percent of women in Scotland and 47 percent of women in Norway (Notzon, 1990). It is also quite possible for a woman to have two or three cesarean deliveries.

There is concern about the high U.S. cesarean rates. Reasons that have been proposed to explain them include the following: (a) Physicians make more money performing cesareans. (b) There are more older women giving birth; they may have more difficult labors necessitating cesareans. (c) There are more births to teenagers, who also are at risk for difficult deliveries. (d) Fetal monitors are used increasingly;

FIGURE 7.8
Possible positions of the fetus during birth. (a) A breech presentation (4 percent of births). (b) A transverse presentation (less than 1 percent). (c) A normal, head-first or cephalic presentation (96 percent of births).

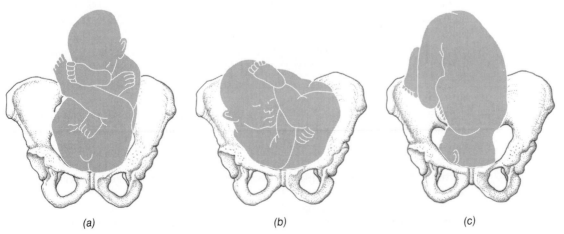

(a)   (b)   (c)

they can give the physician early warning if the fetus is in distress, necessitating a cesarean to save the fetus.

With modern surgical techniques, the rate of complications from such a delivery is extremely low. The recovery period, of course, is somewhat longer than that after a vaginal birth, usually requiring five or six days in the hospital, compared with one or two for a normal vaginal delivery.

NATURAL CHILDBIRTH

The term "natural childbirth" was coined by the English obstetrician Grantly Dick-Read in his book *Childbirth Without Fear,* published in 1932. He postulated that fear causes tension and that tension causes pain. Thus to eliminate the pain of childbirth, he recommended a program consisting of education (to eliminate the woman's fears of the unknown) and the learning of relaxation techniques.

Another, similar method—more properly called *prepared childbirth* or the Lamaze method—has become extremely popular in the United States.

Lamaze method: A method of "prepared" childbirth.

The Lamaze Method

A French obstetrician, Fernand Lamaze, developed a childbirth technique after observing women in Russia undergoing labor with apparently no pain. The method has become very popular in the last two decades in the United States, and prepared childbirth classes are now offered in most areas of the country.

The two basic techniques taught in the Lamaze approach are *relaxation* and *controlled breathing.* The woman learns to relax all the muscles in her body. Knowing how to do this has a number of advantages, including conservation of energy during an event that requires considerable endurance and, more important, avoidance of the tension that increases the perception of pain. The woman also learns a series of controlled breathing exercises, which she will use to help her get through each contraction.

Some other techniques are taught as well. One, called *effleurage* (Figure 7.9), consists of a light, circular stroking of the abdomen with the fingertips. There are also exercises to strengthen specific muscles, such as the leg muscles, which undergo considerable strain during labor and delivery. Finally, because the Lamaze method is based on the idea that fear and the pain it causes are best eliminated through education, the Lamaze student learns a great deal about the processes involved in pregnancy and childbirth.

One other important component of the Lamaze method is the requirement that the woman be accompanied during the classes and during childbirth itself by her husband (or by some other person who serves as "coach"). The husband or coach serves an important function and plays an integral role in the woman's learning of the techniques and her use of them during labor. He (we shall assume that it is the father) is present during labor and delivery. He times contractions, checks on the woman's state of relaxation and gives her feedback if she is not relaxed, suggests breathing patterns, helps elevate her back as she pushes the baby out, and generally provides encouragement and moral support. Aside from the obvious benefits to the woman, this principle of the Lamaze method represents real progress in that it allows the man to play an active role in the birth of his own child and to experience more fully one of the most basic and moving of all human experiences, a privilege men have been denied too long.

One common misunderstanding about the Lamaze method is that it is "natural" childbirth; that is, that the use of anesthetics is prohibited. In fact, the Lamaze

FIGURE 7.9
*Practice and concentration
are essential in preparing
for a Lamaze childbirth.
This woman is practicing
effleurage.*

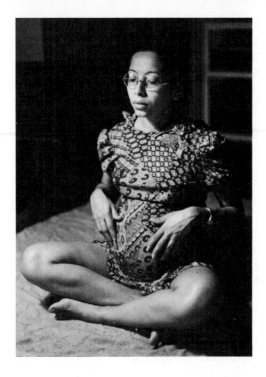

method is more flexible than that. Its goal is to teach each woman the techniques she needs to control her reactions to labor so that she will not need an anesthetic; however, her right to have an anesthetic if she wants one is affirmed. The topic of anesthetics in childbirth, which has become quite controversial in recent years, is discussed below.

A number of studies indicate that childbirth training, such as Lamaze, has several desirable results, including reduction in the length of labor, decreased incidence of birth complications, a decrease in the use of anesthetics, a more positive attitude after birth, increased self-esteem, and an increased sense of being in control (e.g., Felton & Segelman, 1978; Zax et al., 1975).

There is no doubt that the Lamaze method has improved the childbirth experiences of thousands of women and men. On the other hand, some Lamaze advocates are so idealistic that they may create unrealistic expectations about delivery, especially for women having their first baby (**primiparas**). Psychologist Ronald Melzack, a leading authority on pain, has found that the use of the Lamaze method reduces pain in childbirth but does not eliminate it completely (Warga, 1987). He found that many Lamaze women still requested some anesthesia during labor, but then felt guilty or like a failure for having done so. For primiparas, there is often a discrepancy between their positive expectations for delivery and the actual outcomes (Booth & Meltzoff, 1984). Thus, while the Lamaze method produces excellent outcomes and helps women control pain, childbirth still involves some pain, as well as unexpected complications in some cases.

Primipara: A woman having her first baby.

The Use of Anesthetics in Childbirth

Throughout most of human history, childbirth has been "natural"; that is, it has taken place without anesthetics and in the woman's home or other familiar surroundings. The pattern in the United States began to change about 200 years ago, at the time of the Revolutionary War, when male physicians rather than midwives started to assist during birth (Wertz & Wertz, 1977). The next major change came around the middle of the nineteenth century, with the development of anesthetics for use in surgery. When their use in childbirth was suggested, there was some opposition from physicians, who felt they interfered with "natural" processes, and some opposition from the clergy, who argued that women's pain in childbirth was prescribed in the Bible, quoting Genesis 3:16: "In sorrow thou shalt bring forth children." Opposition to the use of anesthetics virtually ceased, however, when Queen Victoria gave birth to a child under chloroform anesthesia in 1853. Since then, the use of anesthetics has become routine (too routine, according to some) and effective. Before discussing the arguments for and against the use of anesthetics, let us briefly review some of the common techniques of anesthesia used in childbirth.

Tranquilizers (such as Valium) or narcotics may be administered when labor becomes fairly intense. They relax the woman and take the edge off the pain. Barbiturates (Nembutal or Seconal) are administered to put the woman to sleep. Scopolamine may sometimes be used for its amnesic effects; it makes the woman forget what has happened, and thus she has no memory afterward of any pain during childbirth. Regional and local anesthetics, which numb only the specific region of the body that is painful, are used most commonly. An example is the pudendal block (named for the pudendum, or vulva), in which an injection numbs only the external genitals. Other examples are spinal anesthesia (a "spinal"), in which an injection near the spinal cord numbs the entire birth area, from the waist down, and the caudal block and epidural anesthesia, which are both administered by injections in the back and produce regional numbing from the belly to the thighs.

The routine use of anesthetics has been questioned by some. Proponents of the use of anesthetics argue that with modern technology, women no longer need to experience pain during childbirth and that it is therefore silly for them to suffer unnecessarily. Opponents argue that anesthetics have a number of well-documented dangerous effects on both mother and infant. All anesthetics in the mother's body pass thrugh the placenta to the infant. Thus while they have the desired effect of depressing the mother's central nervous system, they also depress the infant's nervous system. Research indicates that babies born under anesthesia have poor sucking ability and retarded muscular and neural development in the first four weeks of life compared with infants born with no anesthesia (Boston Women's Health Book Collective, 1984; MacFarlane et al., 1978). Thus the effects on the infant are moderately to extremely harmful. There are also negative effects on the mother. Anesthetics prevent her from using her body as effectively as she might to help push the baby out. If administered early in labor, anesthetics may inhibit uterine contractions, slow cervical dilation, and prolong labor. They also numb a woman to experiencing one of the most fundamental events of her life.

Perhaps the best resolution of this controversy is to say that a pregnant woman should participate in prepared childbirth classes and should use the techniques during labor. If, when she is in labor, she discovers that she cannot control the pain and wants an anesthetic, she should feel free to request it and to do so without guilt; the anesthetic should then be administered with great caution.

Home Birth Versus Hospital Birth

In the last two decades, home birth has become increasingly popular. Either a physician or a nurse-midwife may assist in a home birth. Advocates of home birth argue that the atmosphere in a hospital—with all of its forbidding machines, rules and regulations, and general lack of comfort and "homeyness"—is stressful to the woman and detracts from what should be a joyous, natural human experience. Further,

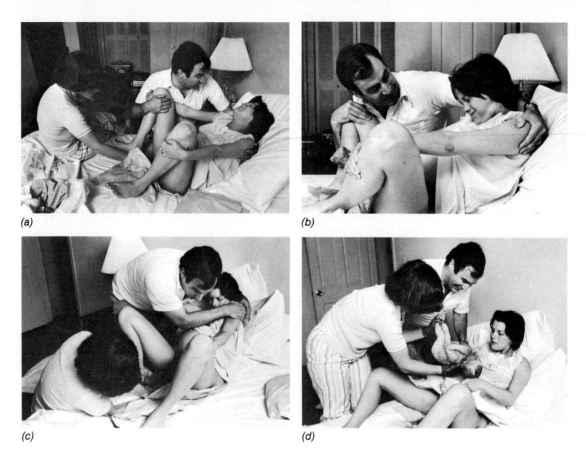

(a) (b)

(c) (d)

FIGURE 7.10
A home birth.

hospitals are meant to deal with illness, and the delivery of a baby should not be viewed as illness; hospital births encourage the use of procedures such as forceps deliveries and episiotomies that are themselves dangerous. Birth at home should be more relaxed and less stressful; friends and other children are allowed to be present. There are some studies that indicate that—for uncomplicated pregnancies—home delivery is as safe as hospital delivery (Hahn & Paige, 1980; for a detailed discussion, see Hoff & Schneiderman, 1985).

On the other side of the argument, if unforeseen emergency medical procedures are necessary, home birth may be downright dangerous for the mother, the baby, or both. Further, hospital practices in labor and delivery have changed radically in the last decade, particularly with the increased popularity of the Lamaze method; thus hospitals are not the forbidding, alien environments they once were. Most hospitals, for example, allow fathers to be present for the entire labor and delivery, and many allow the father to be present in the operating room during cesarean deliveries. Many hospitals have created birthing centers which contain a set of homelike rooms, with comfortable beds and armchairs, that permit labor and delivery to occur in a relaxed atmosphere, while being only a minute away from emergency equipment if it is required.

For a woman who wants to have a home birth, careful medical screening is essential. Only women with normal pregnancies and anticipated normal deliveries should attempt a home birth. A qualified physician or nurse-midwife must be part of the planning. Finally, there must be access to a hospital in case of an unanticipated emergency.

AFTER THE BABY IS BORN: THE POSTPARTUM PERIOD

Physical Changes

With the birth of the baby, the woman's body undergoes a drastic physiological change. During pregnancy the placenta produces high levels of both estrogen and progesterone. When the placenta is expelled, the levels of these hormones drop sharply, and thus the postpartum period is characterized by low levels of both estrogen and progesterone. The levels of these hormones gradually return to normal over a period of a few weeks to a few months. Other endocrine changes include an increase in hormones associated with breast-feeding (discussed below).

In addition, the body undergoes considerable stress during labor and delivery, and the woman may feel exhausted. Discomfort from the episiotomy is common in the first postpartum weeks (Leifer, 1980).

Psychological Changes

For the first one or two days after parturition, the woman typically remains in the hospital, although there is an increasing national trend toward leaving the hospital less than 24 hours after delivery. For the first two days, women often feel elated; the long pregnancy is over, they have been successful competitors in a demanding athletic event and are pleased with their efforts, and the baby is finally there, to be cuddled and loved.

Within a couple of days after delivery, many women experience depression and periods of crying. These mood swings range from mild to severe. In the mildest type, *maternity blues* or "baby blues," the woman experiences sadness and periods of crying, but this mood lasts only 24 to 48 hours (Hopkins et al., 1984). Between 50 percent and 80 percent of women experience mild baby blues postpartum. Mild to moderate postpartum depression is experienced by approximately 20 percent of women and typically lasts 6 to 8 weeks (Hopkins et al., 1984). Postpartum depression is characterized by a depressed mood, insomnia, tearfulness, feelings of inadequacy and inability to cope, irritability, and fatigue. Finally, the most severe disturbance is *postpartum depressive psychosis;* fortunately, it is rare, affecting only 0.01 percent of women following birth (Hopkins et al., 1984).

Postpartum depression: Mild to moderate depression in women following the birth of a baby.

It appears that many factors contribute to this depression (see, for example, R. E. Gordon et al., 1965). Being in a hospital in and of itself is stressful, as noted previously. Once the woman returns home, another set of stresses faces her. She has probably not yet returned to her normal level of energy, and yet she must perform the exhausting task of caring for a newborn infant. For the first several weeks or months she may not get enough sleep, rising several times during the night to tend to a baby that is crying because it is hungry or sick, and she may become exhausted. Clearly she needs help and support from her husband and friends at this time. Some stresses vary depending on whether this is a first child or a later child. The first child is stressful because of the woman's inexperience; while she is in the hospital she may become anxious, wondering whether she will be capable of caring for the infant when she returns home. In the case of later-born children, and some first-borns, the mother may become depressed because she did not really want the baby. It is hoped that with the improvement of contraceptive technology the percentage of undesired pregnancies will decline.

Of course, physical stresses are also present during the postpartum period; hormone levels have declined sharply, and the body has been under stress. Thus it appears that postpartum depression is caused by a combination of physical and social factors.

Another view of the psychological aspects of pregnancy and the postpartum period has been proposed by psychoanalyst Grete Bibring and her colleagues (1961), who studied pregnant women over a 10-year period. Bibring and her colleagues see the pregnancy-postpartum period as a developmental stage, a time of maturational crisis, the resolution of which leads to emotional growth. Perhaps, then, we should begin to think of pregnancy and the postpartum period as normal parts of the process of adult development.

Attachment to the Baby

While much of the traditional psychological research focused on the baby's developing attachment to the mother, more recent interest has been about the development of the mother's attachment (bond) to the infant. Leifer's study (1980) showed clearly that this process begins even before the baby is born; during pregnancy, most women in her sample developed an increasing sense of the fetus as a separate individual and developed an increasing emotional attachment to it. In this sense, pregnancy is something of a psychological preparation for motherhood.

In the 1970s, pediatricians Marshall Klaus and John Kennell popularized the idea that there is a kind of "critical period" or "sensitive period" in the minutes and hours immediately after birth, during which the mother and infant should "bond" to each other (Klaus & Kennell, 1976). These ideas have enthusiastically been incorporated into hospital practices, so that in many progressive hospitals the infant is given to the mother to hold immediately after birth. Ironically, scientists later concluded that there is little or no evidence for the sensitive-period-for-bonding hypothesis (e.g., Goldberg, 1983; Lamb, 1982; Lamb & Hwang, 1982; Myers, 1984). That outcome is fortunate. Otherwise, mothers who give birth by cesarean section (and may therefore be asleep under a general anesthetic for an hour or more after the birth) and adoptive parents would have to be presumed to have inadequate bonds with their children. We know that, in both cases, strong bonds of love form between parents and children despite the lack of immediate contact following birth. The hospital policy of immediate mother-infant and father-infant contact is still a good one, if for no other reason than it is intensely pleasurable and satisfying.

Baby Blues for Dads?

Fathers, too, sometimes experience depression after the birth of a baby. In one study, 89 percent of the mothers and 62 percent of the fathers had experienced the blues during the three months after the birth (Zaslow et al., 1985). The research indicates that less depressed fathers are more likely to be involved with the infant and the parenting role.

BREAST-FEEDING

Biological Mechanisms

Two hormones, both secreted by the pituitary, are involved in lactation (milk production). One, *prolactin*, stimulates the breasts to produce milk. Prolactin is produced fairly constantly for whatever length of time the woman breast-feeds. The other hormone, *oxytocin*, stimulates the breasts to eject milk. Oxytocin is produced reflexively by the pituitary in response to the infant's sucking of the breast. Thus sucking stimulates nerve cells in the nipple; this nerve signal is transmitted to the brain, which then relays the message to the pituitary, which sends out the messenger oxytocin, which stimulates the breasts to eject milk. Interestingly, research with animals indicates that oxytocin stimulates maternal behavior (Jenkins & Nussey, 1991).

Actually, milk is not produced for several days after delivery. For the first few days, the breast secretes colostrum, discussed earlier, which is high in protein and is believed to give the baby a temporary immunity to infectious diseases. Two or three days after delivery, true lactation begins; this may be accompanied by discomfort for a day or so because the breasts are swollen and congested.

It is also important to note that, much as in pregnancy, substances ingested by the mother may be transmitted through the milk to the infant. The nursing mother thus needs to be cautious about using alcohol and other drugs.

Psychological Aspects

Although bottles for artificially feeding babies were known in Egypt and a few other places as early as the first century, they were used by only a small minority of very wealthy women. Thus throughout most of human history, the vast majority of babies have been breast-fed. By the 1950s and 1960s, however, the majority of babies in the United States were bottle-fed.

Public health officials viewed the decline in breast-feeding with alarm, because breast milk is the ideal food for a baby and has even been termed the "ultimate health food." It provides the baby with the right mixture of nutrients, it contains antibodies that protect the infant from some diseases, it is free from bacteria, and it is always the right temperature. Thus there is little question that it is superior to cow's milk and commercial formulas.

The evidence indicates that the percentage of infants who were breast-fed rose steadily during the 1970s. It peaked in 1984 and then declined somewhat in the late 1980s, so that in 1989, 52 percent were breast-fed initially and 18 percent were still breast-fed at five to six months of age (Ryan et al., 1991). This contrasts with 1971, when only 5 percent of babies were still breast-fed at five to six months of age. These

FIGURE 7.11
Breast-feeding.

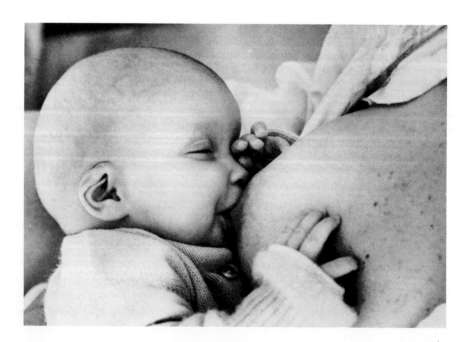

statistics vary as a function of ethnicity, with 59 percent of Anglo mothers, 48 percent of Hispanic mothers, and 23 percent of black mothers breast-feeding (Ryan et al., 1991).

From the mother's point of view, breast-feeding has several advantages. Women who breast-feed find that their sexual responsiveness returns sooner after childbirth, compared with women who do not breast-feed (Masters & Johnson, 1966).[5] Some women report sexual arousal during breast-feeding, and a few even report having orgasms. Unfortunately, this sometimes produces anxiety in the mother, leading her to discontinue breast-feeding. However, there is nothing "wrong" with this arousal, and it appears to stem from activation of hormonal mechanisms. Clearly, from an adaptive point of view, if breast-feeding is important to the infant's survival, it would be wise for Nature to design the process so that it is rewarding to the mother.

Other advantages from the mother's point of view include a quicker shrinking of the uterus to its normal size and reduced likelihood of becoming pregnant again immediately. The return of normal menstrual cycles is delayed, on the average, in women who breast-feed, compared with those who do not. This provides some period of rest between pregnancies. However, it is important to note that a woman can become pregnant again after parturition but before she has had her first menstrual period. As was discussed in Chapter 6, ovulation precedes menstruation; thus a woman may ovulate and conceive without having a period. Therefore, a woman should not count on breast-feeding as a means of contraception.

The La Leche League, an organization devoted to breast-feeding, has done much to encourage women to breast-feed their babies and has helped to spread information on breast-feeding. The organization tends to be a bit militant in its advocacy of breast-feeding, however. A few women are physically unable to breast-feed, while some others feel psychologically uncomfortable with the idea. And breast-feeding can be very inconvenient for the woman who works full-time. While breast-feeding has some of the important advantages noted above, long-term studies comparing breast-fed children with bottle-fed children have found no significant differences between them (Schmitt, 1970). What appears to be more important than the method of feeding is the quality of the relationship between the mother and infant and feelings that the mother communicates to the baby:

> A baby raised in a loving home can grow up to be a healthy, psychologically secure individual no matter how he receives his nourishment. While successful nursing is a beautiful, happy experience for both mother and child, the woman who nurses grudgingly because she feels she *should* will probably do more harm to her baby by communicating her feelings of resentment and unhappiness, than she would if she were a relaxed, loving, bottle-feeding mother. (Olds & Eiger, 1973, p. 18)

PROBLEM PREGNANCIES

Ectopic Pregnancy

Ectopic pregnancy: A pregnancy in which the fertilized egg implants somewhere other than the uterus.

Ectopic (misplaced) pregnancy occurs when the fertilized egg implants someplace other than the uterus. Most commonly, ectopic pregnancies occur when the egg

[5] If you are a psychology student, you might want to note that these data are correlational. In view of this, can you infer that breast-feeding *causes* a quicker return of sexual desire? How else might one interpret the data? Why are the data correlational rather than experimental?

implants in the fallopian tube (tubal pregnancy; Schenker & Evron, 1983). In rare cases, implantation may also occur in the abdominal cavity, the ovary, or the cervix.

Tubal pregnancy may occur if, for one reason or another, the egg is prevented from moving down the tube to the uterus, as when the tubes are obstructed as result of a gonorrheal infection, for example. Early in a tubal pregnancy, the fertilized egg implants in the tube and begins development, forming a placenta and producing the normal hormones of pregnancy. The woman may experience the early symptoms of pregnancy, such as nausea and amenorrhea, and think she is pregnant; or she may experience some bleeding which she mistakes for a period, and think that she is not pregnant. It is therefore quite difficult to diagnose a tubal pregnancy early.

A tubal pregnancy may end in one of two ways. The embryo may spontaneously abort and be released into the abdominal cavity, or the embryo and placenta may continue to expand, stretching the tube until it ruptures. Symptoms of a rupture include sharp abdominal pain or cramping, dull abdominal pain and possibly pain in the shoulder, and vaginal bleeding. Meanwhile, hemorrhaging is occurring, and the woman may go into shock and, possibly, die; thus it is extremely important for a woman displaying these symptoms to see a doctor quickly.

The rate of ectopic pregnancy more than doubled in the United States from 1972 to 1985, going from 6.3 cases per 1000 reported pregnancies to 15.2 per 1000 pregnancies (Cunningham et al., 1990). Similar increases have been observed in a number of western European nations. It is thought that these changes are due to (1) increased rates of sexually transmitted diseases, some of which lead to blocking of the fallopian tubes; and (2) increased use of contraceptives such as the IUD and progestin-only methods that prevent implantation in the uterus but do not necessarily prevent conception.

Pseudocyesis (False Pregnancy)

Pseudocyesis: False pregnancy, in which the woman displays the signs of pregnancy but is not actually pregnant.

In pseudocyesis, or *false pregnancy,* the woman believes that she is pregnant and shows the signs and symptoms of pregnancy without really being pregnant. She may stop menstruating and having morning sickness. She may begin gaining weight, and her abdomen may bulge. The condition may persist for several months before it goes away, either spontaneously or as a result of psychotherapy. In rare cases it persists until the woman goes into labor and delivers nothing but air and fluid.

Toxemia

Toxemia: A serious disease of pregnancy, marked by severe edema and high blood pressure.

Metabolic toxemia of late pregnancy is a disease with several stages. The first is called *preeclampsia.* The symptoms of mild preeclampsia are severe edema (fluid retention and swelling), high blood pressure, and protein in the urine. Toxemia usually does not appear until after the twentieth to twenty-fourth week of pregnancy, that is, late in pregnancy. In severe preeclampsia, the earlier symptoms persist, blood pressure is dangerously high, and the woman also experiences vision problems, abdominal pains, mental dullness, and severe headaches. In the most severe stage, *eclampsia,* the woman has convulsions, goes into a coma, and may die.

It seems likely that toxemia results from malnutrition, although no one really knows what causes it. Toxemia seems to be related to socioeconomic factors, which probably determine whether a pregnant woman receives adequate nutrition (Eastman, 1968). This argues for the importance of proper diet during pregnancy. It also emphasizes the importance of proper medical care during pregnancy, because toxemia can be managed well during its early stages and death typically occurs only when the woman is receiving no medical care.

Illness During Pregnancy

As was discussed in a previous section, certain substances such as drugs can cross the placental barrier from the woman to the fetus, causing damage. Similarly, certain viruses may pass from the woman to the fetus and cause considerable harm, particularly if the illness occurs during the first trimester of pregnancy. The best-known example is rubella, or German measles. If a woman gets German measles during the first month of pregnancy, there is a 50 percent chance that the infant will be born deaf or mentally deficient or with cataracts or congenital heart defects. The risk then declines, and by the third month of pregnancy the chance of abnormalities is about 10 percent. While most women have an immunity to rubella because they had it when they were children, a woman who suspects that she is not immune can receive a vaccination that will give her immunity; she should do this well before she becomes pregnant.

Herpes simplex is also *teratogenic,* that is, capable of producing defects in the fetus. Symptoms of herpes simplex are usually mild: cold sores or fever blisters. Genital herpes (see Chapter 20) is a form of herpes simplex in which sores may appear in the genital region. Usually the infant contracts the disease by direct contact with the sore; delivery by cesarean section can prevent this. Women with herpes genitalis also have a high risk of spontaneously aborting.

Birth Defects

As has been noted, a number of factors, such as drugs taken during pregnancy and illness during pregnancy, may cause defects in the fetus. Other causes include genetic defects [for example, phenylketonuria (PKU), which causes retardation] and chromosomal defects (for example, Down syndrome, which causes retardation).

About 3 percent of all babies born in the United States have a significant birth defect. The incidence is considerably higher among miscarriages.

In most cases, families have simply had to learn, as best they could, to live with a child who had a birth defect. Now, however, amniocentesis (combined with abortion) and genetic counseling are available to help prevent some of the sorrow, provided that abortion is ethically acceptable to the parents.

Amniocentesis (am-nee-oh-sen-TEE-sus): A test done to determine whether a fetus has birth defects; done by inserting a fine tube into the woman's abdomen in order to obtain a sample of amniotic fluid.

The technique of amniocentesis (see Figure 7.12) involves inserting a fine tube through the pregnant woman's abdomen and removing some amniotic fluid, including cells sloughed off by the fetus, for analysis. The technique is capable of providing an early diagnosis of most chromosomal abnormalities, some genetically produced biochemical disorders, and sex-linked diseases carried by females but affecting males (hemophilia and muscular dystrophy), although it cannot detect all defects. If a defect is discovered, the woman may then decide to terminate the pregnancy with an abortion.

Amniocentesis should be performed between the fourteenth and sixteenth weeks of pregnancy. This timing is important for two reasons. First, if a defect is discovered and an abortion is to be performed, it should be done as early as possible (see Chapter 8). Second, there is a 1 percent chance that the amniocentesis itself will cause the woman to lose her baby, and the risk becomes greater as the pregnancy progresses.

Because amniocentesis itself involves some risk, it is generally thought (although the matter is controversial) that it should be performed only on women who have a high risk of bearing a child with a birth defect. A woman is in that category (1) if she has already had one child with a genetic defect; (2) if she believes that she is a carrier of a genetic defect, which can usually be established through genetic counseling; and (3) if she is over 40, in which case she has a greatly increased chance of bearing a child with a chromosomal abnormality.

FIGURE 7.12
Amniocentesis. The needle collects a sample of amniotic fluid, containing cells sloughed off by the fetus which can then be analyzed for indicators of genetic birth defects.

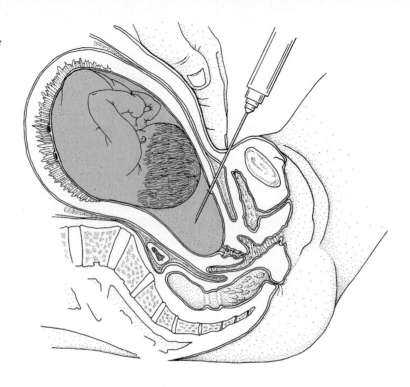

Of course, amniocentesis (when followed by abortion) raises a number of serious ethical questions, some of which will be discussed in later chapters. However, it is important to note the extreme psychological stress to which families of children with birth defects are often subjected.

Chorionic villus sampling (CVS) is a new technique that may replace amniocentesis for prenatal diagnosis of genetic defects (Doran, 1990; Kolker, 1989). A major problem with amniocentesis is that it cannot be done until the second trimester of pregnancy; if genetic defects are discovered, there may have to be a late abortion. Chorionic villus sampling, in contrast, can be done in the first trimester of pregnancy, usually around 9 to 11 weeks postconception. Chorionic villus sampling can be performed in one of two ways: transcervically, in which a catheter is inserted into the uterus through the cervix; and transabdominally, in which a needle (guided by ultrasound) is inserted through the abdomen. In either case a sample of cells is taken from the chorionic villi (the chorion is the outermost membrane surrounding the fetus, the amnion, and the amniotic fluid), and these cells are analyzed for evidence of genetic defects. The studies are very new but seem to indicate that CVS is as accurate as amniocentesis. Like amniocentesis, it carries with it a slight risk of fetal loss (due, for example, to miscarriage). For amniocentesis, the fetal loss rate is around 1 percent; for CVS it is around 2 percent (Wass et al., 1991).

Rh Incompatibility

The Rh factor is a substance in the blood; if it is present, the person is said to be Rh positive (Rh +); if it is absent, the person is said to be Rh negative (Rh −). The Rh factor is genetically transmitted, with Rh + being dominant over Rh −.

The presence or absence of the Rh factor does not constitute a health problem except when an Rh − person receives a blood transfusion and when an Rh − woman is pregnant with an Rh + fetus (which can happen only if the father is Rh +). A blood test is done routinely early in pregnancy to determine whether a woman is

Chorionic villus sampling (CVS): A new technique that may replace amniocentesis as a method for prenatal diagnosis of birth defects.

Rh−. Fortunately, about 85 percent of whites and 93 percent of blacks are Rh+; thus the problems associated with being Rh− are not very common.

If some Rh+ blood gets into Rh− blood, the Rh− blood forms antibodies as a reaction against the Rh factor in the invading blood. Typically, as has been noted, there is little interchange between the woman's blood and the fetus's; the placenta keeps them separate. However, during parturition there can be considerable mixing of the two. Thus during birth, the blood of an Rh+ baby causes the formation of antibodies in an Rh− woman's blood. During the next pregnancy, some of the woman's blood enters the fetus, and the antibodies attack the fetus's red cells. The baby may be stillborn, severely anemic, or retarded. Thus there is little risk for an Rh− woman with the first pregnancy because antibodies have not yet formed; however, later pregnancies can be extremely dangerous.

Fortunately, techniques for dealing with this situation have been developed. An injection of a substance called *Rhogam* prevents the woman's blood from producing antibodies. If necessary the fetus or newborn infant may get a transfusion.

Miscarriage (Spontaneous Abortion)

Miscarriage: When a pregnancy terminates before the fetus is viable, as a result of natural causes (not medical intervention).

Miscarriage, or *spontaneous abortion,* occurs when a pregnancy terminates through natural causes, before the conceptus is viable (capable of surviving on its own). It is not to be confused with *induced abortion,* in which a pregnancy is terminated by mechanical or medicinal means (what is commonly called *abortion*—see Chapter 7), or with *prematurity,* in which the pregnancy terminates early, but after the infant is viable.

It is estimated that 10 percent of all pregnancies end in spontaneous abortion (Pritchard et al., 1985). This is probably an underestimate, since very early spontaneous abortions may not be detected. The woman may not know that she is pregnant, and the products of the miscarriage are mistaken for a menstrual period. Thus the true incidence may be closer to 40 percent (Cunningham et al., 1990). Most spontaneous abortions (75 percent) occur during the first trimester of pregnancy.

Studies indicate that most spontaneous abortions occur because the conceptus was defective. Studies of spontaneously aborted fetuses indicate that about 50 percent showed abnormalities that were incompatible with life; for example, many had gross chromosomal abnormalities. Thus, contrary to popular belief, psychological and physical traumas are not common causes of miscarriage. In fact, spontaneous abortions seem to be functional in that they naturally eliminate many defective fetuses.

Prematurity

A major complication during the third trimester of pregnancy is premature labor and delivery of the fetus. Because the date of conception cannot always be accurately determined, prematurity (or preterm birth) is usually defined in terms of the birth weight of the infant; an infant weighing less than 2500 grams ($5\frac{1}{2}$ pounds) is considered to be in the low-birth-weight category. However, physicians have recently become concerned more with the functional development of the infant than with the weight. It is estimated that about 7 percent of the births in the United States are premature.

Preterm birth is a cause for concern because the premature infant is much less likely to survive than the full-term infant. It is estimated that more than half of the deaths of newborn babies in the United States are due to preterm birth. Preterm infants are particularly susceptible to respiratory infections, and they must receive expert care. Advances in medical techniques have improved survival rates for preterm infants considerably. Currently 99 percent of infants weighing 2500 grams at birth survive, as do 64 percent of those weighing 1000 grams (Cunningham et al., 1990). However, prematurity may cause damage to an infant who survives.

Maternal factors such as poor health, poor nutrition, heavy smoking, and syphilis are associated with prematurity. Young teenage mothers, whose bodies are not yet ready to bear children, are also very susceptible to premature labor and delivery. However, in over 50 percent of the cases, the cause of prematurity is unknown (Pritchard et al., 1985).

INFERTILITY

It is estimated that 14 percent of all couples in the United States have an infertility problem at some time (Sciarra, 1991). When fertile couples are purposely attempting to conceive a child, about 20 percent succeed in the first month, and about 50 percent succeed in the first six months (Hatcher et al., 1990). Most doctors consider a couple infertile if they have not conceived after a year of "trying." The term "sterility" refers only to an individual who has an absolute factor preventing procreation.

Causes of Infertility

Contrary to popular opinion, a couple's infertility is not always caused by the woman; it is estimated that in about 40 percent of infertile couples, male factors are responsible (for a detailed discussion of infertility, see Liebmann-Smith, 1987).

Causes in the Female

The most common causes of infertility in the female are (1) failure to ovulate, (2) blockage of the fallopian tubes, and (3) cervical mucus, called "hostile mucus," that does not permit the passage of sperm. Age may also be a factor; fertility declines in woman after 35 years of age, the decline being especially sharp after age 40. Some cases of infertility in women can be successfully treated using "fertility drugs" such as Clomid.

Causes in the Male

The most common causes of infertility in the male are (1) low sperm count (often due to varicoceles, which are varicose veins in the testes and can generally be remedied by surgery) and (2) low motility of the sperm, which means that the sperm are not good swimmers.

Combined Factors

In some situations a combination of factors in both the man and the woman causes the infertility. For example, there may be an immunologic response. The woman may have an allergic response to the man's sperm, causing her to produce antibodies that destroy the sperm, or the man may produce the antibodies himself. A couple may also simply lack knowledge; they may not know how to time intercourse correctly so that conception will take place, or they may lack other important information.

Psychological Aspects

It is important to recognize the psychological stress to which an infertile couple may be subjected (Liebmann-Smith, 1987). Their marriage may be strained. Because the male role is defined partly in our society by the ability to father children, the man may feel that his masculinity or virility is in question. Similarly, the female role is defined largely by the ability to bear children and be a mother, and the woman may feel inadequate in her role as a woman. Historically, in most cultures fertility has been encouraged, and indeed demanded; hence pressures on infertile couples were high, leading to more psychological stress. As emphasis on population control increases in our society, and as childlessness[6] becomes an acceptable and more recognized option in marriage, some of the psychological stresses on the infertile couple may lessen.

Treatment of Infertility

If the infertility problem is a result of the woman not ovulating, the treatment may be by the use of so-called "fertility drugs." The drug of first choice is clomiphene (Clomid). It stimulates the pituitary to produce LH and FSH, thus inducing ovulation. The treatment produces a pregnancy in about half the women who are given it. Contrary to flashy media reports of quintuplets and other multiple births resulting from the use of fertility drugs, multiple births occur only about 8 percent of the time with Clomid, compared with 1.2 percent with natural pregnancies. If treatment with Clomid is not successful, a second possibility is injections with HMG (human menopausal gonadotropin).

If the infertility is caused by blocked fallopian tubes, delicate microsurgery can sometimes be effective in removing the blockage.

If the infertility is caused by varicoceles in the testes, the condition can usually be treated successfully by a surgical procedure known as varicocelectomy.

Finally, a number of new reproductive technologies, such as in vitro fertilization, are now available for those with fertility problems, as discussed in the next section.

A Canadian study is helpful in putting issues of the treatment of infertility into perspective. Among infertile couples seeking treatment, 65 percent subsequently achieved a pregnancy with *no treatment* (Rousseau et al., 1983). For some couples it just takes a bit longer. Thus the risks associated with treatments need to be weighed against the possibility that a pregnancy can be achieved without treatment.

NEW REPRODUCTIVE TECHNOLOGIES

Reproductive technologies developed in the last two decades mean that there are many ways to conceive and birth babies besides old-fashioned sexual intercourse and pregnancy.

Artificial Insemination

Artificial insemination: Procedure in which sperm are placed into the vagina by a physician.

Artificial insemination involves artificially placing semen in the vagina to produce a pregnancy; thus it is a means of accomplishing reproduction without having sexual intercourse. Artificial insemination in animals was first done in 1776. In 1949, when British scientists successfully froze sperm without any apparent damage to them, a new era of reproductive technology for animals began. Today cattle are routinely bred by artificial insemination.

In humans, there are two kinds of artificial insemination: artificial insemination

---

[6]   Semantics can make a big difference here. Many couples who choose not to have children prefer to call themselves "child-free" rather than "childless."

by the husband (AIH) and artificial insemination by a donor (AID, not to be confused with the disease AIDS). AIH can be used when the husband has a low sperm count. Several samples of his semen are collected and pooled to make one sample with a higher count. This sample is then placed in the woman's vagina at the time of ovulation. AID is used when the husband is sterile. A donor provides semen to impregnate the wife. Estimates are that between 10,000 and 20,000 babies are born every year in the United States as a result of AID.

Sperm Banks

Because it is now possible to freeze sperm, it is possible to store it, and that is just what some people are doing: using frozen human *sperm banks*. The sperm banks open up many new possibilities for various life choices. For example, suppose that a couple decide, after having had two children, that they want a permanent method of contraception. The husband then has a vasectomy. Two years after he has the vasectomy, however, one of their children dies, and they very much want to have another baby. If the man has stored semen in a sperm bank, they can.

Young men can use sperm banks to store sperm before they undergo radiation therapy for cancer. They can later father children without fearing that they will transmit damaged chromosomes (as a result of the radiation) to their offspring.

One of the flashiest projects in this area is that of Robert K. Graham, a wealthy California businessman (*Time,* March 10, 1980). He started a sperm bank to collect "superior" sperm from scientists who have won a Nobel prize. He offers the sperm to young women who have a high IQ. At least five Nobel prizewinners have given donations, including physicist William Shockley. Graham provides a description of each scientist, and bright women applicants may choose whose sperm they want. Some Nobel winners are not amused, however. Burton Richter of Stanford, who

FIGURE 7.13

"I ALREADY KNOW ABOUT THE BIRDS AND THE BEES, MOM;
I WANT TO KNOW ABOUT ARTIFICIAL INSEMINATION, IN-
VITRO FERTILIZATION AND SURROGATE MOTHERING!"

FIGURE 7.14
The new technologies of sex.

received a Nobel prize in physics, reported that his students have asked him if he supplements his salary with stud fees.

Embryo Transfer

Embryo transfer: Procedure in which an embryo is transferred from the uterus of one woman into the uterus of another.

With **embryo transfer**, a fertilized, developing egg (embryo) is transferred from the uterus of one woman to the uterus of another woman. Dr. John Buster of UCLA perfected the technique for use with humans, and the first two births resulting from the procedure were announced in 1984 (Brotman, 1984; Associated Press, 1984).

This technique may enable a woman who can conceive but who always miscarries early in the pregnancy to transfer her embryo to another woman who serves as the *surrogate mother,* that is, the person who provides the uterus in which the fetus grows (called, somewhat callously, by the media "rent-a-womb"). The embryo transfer procedure also essentially can serve as the opposite of artificial insemination. That is, if a woman produces no viable eggs, her husband's sperm can be used to artificially inseminate another woman (who donates her egg), and the fertilized egg is then transferred from the donor to the mother.

Test-Tube Babies

In vitro fertilization: A procedure in which an egg is fertilized by sperm in a laboratory dish.

It is possible for scientists to make sperm and egg unite outside the human body (in a "test tube"). The scientific term for this procedure is in vitro fertilization or IVF (*in vitro* is Latin for "in glass"). The fertilized egg or embryo can then be implanted in the uterus of a woman and carried to term. This technique can be of great benefit to couples who are infertile because the woman's fallopian tubes are blocked, which is a fairly common cause of infertility.

A milestone was reached with the birth of Louise Brown in England on July 25, 1978. Obstetrician Patrick Steptoe and physiologist Robert Edwards had fertilized the mother's egg with her husband's sperm in a laboratory dish and implanted the embryo in the mother's uterus. The pregnancy went smoothly, and Louise was born healthy and normal, the first test-tube baby. The procedure is now performed in a number of countries, with 70 clinics in the United States alone.

Successful IVF centers generally obtain a pregnancy rate of about 15 to 25 percent per "try." The procedure is expensive, around $6000 per attempt, not counting preliminary procedures. It is estimated that the average IVF baby costs between $9000 and $18,000 to produce.

FIGURE 7.15
*Louise Brown, the first
test-tube baby, was born in
1978. She is shown here on
her tenth birthday.*

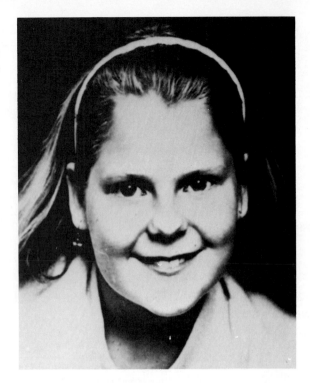

It is also possible to freeze eggs that have been fertilized in vitro, resulting in frozen embryos. This procedure creates the possibility of donated embryos; the birth of a baby resulting from this procedure was first announced in 1984 in Australia. The legal and moral status of the frozen embryo is a difficult question, and some worry about "embryo wastage."

GIFT

GIFT: Gamete intra-fallopian transfer, a procedure in which sperm and eggs are collected and then inserted together into the fallopian tube.

GIFT (for *gamete intra-fallopian transfer*) is an improvement, in some cases, over IVF. Sperm and eggs (gametes) are collected and then inserted together into the fallopian tube, where natural fertilization can take place, followed by natural implantation. This method has a higher success rate than IVF, probably because it allows natural implantation of an embryo rather than the mechanical and somewhat rough method of squirting the embryo into the uterus in IVF.

Yet another improvement is ZIFT (zygote intra-fallopian transfer), which involves fertilizing the egg with sperm in a laboratory dish and then placing the developing fertilized egg (zygote) into the fallopian tube, again allowing natural implantation. In cases in which the man's sperm are of good quality, a single GIFT or ZIFT cycle can result in a 40 to 50 percent pregnancy rate.

Cloning

Cloning is the reproduction of an individual from a single cell taken from a "donor" or "parent." The technique involves replacing the nucleus of an ovum with the nucleus from a donor, thus producing an embryo that is genetically identical to the donor. Normally, of course, a child has only half of its genes in common with the mother; the other half come from the father. Therefore, children are never genetically identical to either parent. But in cloning, no sperm is necessary and the result is an individual who is genetically identical to the donor.

The concept of cloning raises ugly possibilities in the mind of the general public,

(a)

(b)

FIGURE 7.16
New reproductive technologies. (a) With in vitro fertilization, conception is more likely if the egg is scratched, allowing the sperm to enter more easily. (b) Donor and patient sperm to be used in IVF and other infertility procedures are stored using liquid nitrogen.

such as an army of 100,000 genetically identical individuals. At present, cloning is on the brink of becoming scientifically feasible (Galston, 1975). A breakthrough came with the first successful cloning of mice in 1981 (*Time,* January 19, 1981). The difficulties in doing this by now are mostly technical: The eggs of most mammals are so tiny that it is difficult to manipulate them in the ways necessary to achieve cloning. As an example, the human egg is approximately the size of the period at the end of this sentence.

Gender Selection

There is much interest in techniques that will allow couples to choose whether to have a boy or a girl. Such a technology would be useful to parents who have six girls and really want a boy, or for people who would like to have two children, one of each gender. Problems might arise, though. Some scientists fear that the result of being able to choose gender would be a great imbalance in our population, with many more males than females, because many couples prefer their first child to be a boy.

The commercial aspects of this concept are being capitalized on with the marketing, through drugstores, of a kit called Gender Choice, although there is no scientific evidence that the procedure it uses is effective. Various home methods, such as douching with vinegar before intercourse, have been discredited. At this point there is no proven method of gender selection.

The technologies discussed here raise complex legal questions (discussed in detail in Chapter 22) and ethical questions (discussed in detail in Chapter 21). While the answers to these questions remain uncertain, one thing is certain: The technologies are here already.

Summary

The first section traced the journey of the sperm, which are manufactured in the testes and ejaculated out through the vas deferens and urethra into the vagina. Then they begin their swim through the cervix and uterus and up a fallopian tube to meet the egg, which has already been released from the ovary. When the sperm and egg unite in the fallopian tube, conception occurs. The single fertilized egg cell then begins dividing as it travels down the tube, and finally it implants in the uterus. Techniques for improving the chances of conception were suggested.

The development of the fetus was traced during the nine months of prenatal development. The placenta, which is important in transmitting substances between the woman and the fetus, develops early. The most remarkable development of the fetus occurs during the first trimester (first three months), when most of the major organ systems are formed and when human features develop.

Next, pregnancy was considered from the woman's point of view. Early signs of pregnancy include amenorrhea, tenderness of the breasts, and nausea. The most common pregnancy test is designed to detect HCG in the urine. Physical changes during the first trimester are mainly the result of the increasing levels of estrogen and progesterone produced by the placenta. Despite cultural myths about the radiant contentment of the pregnant woman, some women do have negative feelings during the first trimester. During the second trimester the woman generally feels better, both physically and psychologically.

Despite many people's concerns, sexual intercourse is generally quite safe during pregnancy.

Nutrition is exceptionally important during pregnancy because the woman's body has to supply the materials to create another human being. Pregnant women also must be very careful about ingesting drugs because some can penetrate the placental barrier and enter the fetus, possibly causing damage.

Labor is typically divided into three stages. During the first stage, the cervix undergoes effacement and dilation. During the second stage, the baby moves out through the vagina. The placenta is delivered during the third stage. Cesarean section is a surgical method of delivering a baby.

The Lamaze method of "natural" childbirth has become very popular; it emphasizes the use of relaxation and controlled breathing to control contractions and minimize the woman's discomfort. Anesthetics may not be necessary, which seems desirable, since they are potentially dangerous to the infant.

During the postpartum period, hormone levels are very low, and postpartum depression may arise from a combination of this hormonal state and the many environmental stresses on the woman at this time.

Two hormones are involved in lactation: prolactin and oxytocin. Breast-feeding has a number of psychological as well as health advantages, although the nature of the relationship between mother and infant appears to be more important than whether the baby is bottle-fed or breast-fed.

Problems of pregnancy were discussed: ectopic (misplaced) pregnancy, pseudocyesis (false pregnancy), toxemia, illness (such as German measles), a defective conceptus, Rh incompatibility, spontaneous abortion, and prematurity.

The causes of infertility, both in men and in women, were discussed.

New reproductive technologies include artificial insemination, frozen sperm banks, embryo transplants, in vitro fertilization (test-tube babies), and GIFT, all of which are now a reality.

Review Questions

1. If an egg is not fertilized, it disintegrates about 10 days after ovulation. True or false?

2. It is possible for several sperm to penetrate the egg and fertilize it simultaneously, which is how twins and triplets occur. True or false?

3. The _____ is the mass of tissue lying beside the fetus that serves important functions in allowing nutrients and oxygen to pass from the mother's blood to the baby's blood.

4. During pregnancy, the placenta manufactures a hormone called _____, which is the substance detected in pregnancy tests.

5. Most of the major organ systems of the body develop during the first three months of fetal development. True or false?

6. Drugs taken during pregnancy—including aspirin, antibiotics, and alcohol—may cause damage to the developing fetus. True or false?

7. The _____ is a method of prepared childbirth in which the woman learns relaxation techniques and controlled breathing to help control the pain of childbirth.

8. Approximately 90 percent of cases of infertility are caused by problems with the woman's reproductive system. True or false.?

9. The technique in which egg and sperm are mixed outside the body in a laboratory dish, in the hope of creating a conception, is called _____.

10. _____ refers to a doctor inserting eggs and sperm into the fallopian tube, where natural fertilization may occur, followed by implantation.

(The answers to all review questions are at the end of the book, beginning on page 731.)

Questions for Thought, Discussion, and Debate

1. Taking the point of view of a pregnant woman, which would you prefer to have, a home birth or a hospital birth? Why?

2. For those readers who are men, what role would you envision for yourself in parenting if you had a child? Do you feel that you are adequately prepared for that role? For those readers who are women, what role would you ideally like an imaginary husband to take in the parenting of your imaginary children?

Suggestions for Further Reading

Dorris, Michael. (1989). *The broken cord.* New York: Harper & Row. The true story of a man and the child he adopted, who turned out to have fetal alcohol syndrome and all the behavior disturbances that go with it.

Kane, Elizabeth. (1988). *Birth mother: The story of America's first legal surrogate mother.* San Diego: Harcourt Brace Jovanovich. An insightful, first-person account by the woman who was the first to have a contract to bear a child for another couple but later developed serious misgivings.

Liebmann-Smith, Joan. (1987). *In pursuit of pregnancy: How couples discover, cope with, and resolve their fertility problems.* New York: Newmarket Press. More couples than ever have problems with infertility, and this book provides a wealth of information for them.

Nilsson, A. L., et al. (1986). *A child is born.* New York: Dell. Contains exceptional photographs of prenatal development.

Singer, Peter, and Wells, Deane. (1985). *Making babies: The new science and ethics of conception.* New York: Charles Scribner's Sons. A fascinating account of the new reproductive technologies such as in vitro fertilization, with a consideration of ethical issues. The authors are very confident about their position on the ethics (not to worry about all this technology), but the book is nonetheless very informative.

8

Contraception and Abortion

Chapter Highlights

*For a short time I worked in an abortion clinic. One day I was counseling a woman who had come in for an abortion. I began to discuss the possible methods of contraception she could use in the future (she had been using rhythm), and I asked her what method she planned to use after the abortion. "Rhythm," she answered. "I used it for eleven months and it worked!"**

The average student of today grew up in the pill era and simply assumes that highly effective methods of contraception are available. It is sometimes difficult to remember that this has been true only for about the last three decades and that previously contraception was a hit-or-miss affair at best. Contraception is less controversial than it once was (except for the issue of side effects), and yet as recently as 1965 the use of contraceptives was illegal in Connecticut (see the Supreme Court decision in the case of *Griswold v. Connecticut*, 1965, discussed in Chapter 22).

Today there are a variety of reasons for an individual's use of contraceptives. Many women desire to space pregnancies at least two years apart, knowing that that pattern is better for their health and for the health of their babies. Most couples want to limit the size of their family—usually to one or two children. Unmarried persons typically wish to avoid pregnancy. In some cases a couple know, through genetic counseling, that they have a high risk of having a child with a birth defect and they therefore wish to prevent pregnancy. And in this era of successful career women, many women feel that it is essential to be able to control when and if they have children.

At the level of society as a whole, there are also important reasons for encouraging the use of contraceptives. There are approximately 1 million adolescent pregnancies annually in the United States, and they constitute a major social problem. On the global level, the problem of overpopulation is serious; most experts believe that we must limit the size of the American population as well as assist other countries in limiting theirs.

* *Source:* Paula Weideger. (1976). *Menstruation and menopause.* New York: Knopf, p. 42.

FIGURE 8.1
*The growth of the world
population from 6000* B.C.
to A.D. *1985, with a
projection to the year 2000
(David, 1986). Reducing
the population problem is
one major reason for using
birth control.*

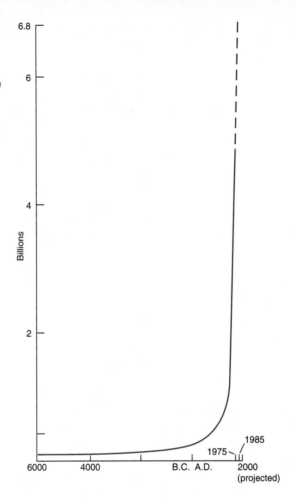

In this chapter we discuss various methods of birth control, how each works, how effective they are, what side effects they have, and their relative advantages and disadvantages.

THE PILL

With combination birth control pills (sometimes also called *oral contraceptives*) such as Ortho-Novum, Loestrin, and Ovcon, the woman takes a pill that contains an estrogen and progestin (a synthetic progesterone), both at doses higher than natural levels, for 20 or 21 days. Then she takes no pill or a placebo for seven days, after which she repeats the cycle. Today's combination pills are sometimes referred to as "lower-dose pills" because their levels of estrogen and progestin are considerably lower than those of the original pill of the 1960s.

How It Works

The pill works mainly by preventing ovulation. Recall that in a natural menstrual cycle, the low levels of estrogen during and just after the menstrual period trigger the pituitary to produce FSH, which stimulates the process of ovulation (see Chapter 6). The woman starts taking the birth control pills on about day 5 of the cycle. Thus just when estrogen levels would normally be low, they are artificially made high.

This high level of estrogen inhibits FSH production, and the message to ovulate is never sent out. The high level of progesterone inhibits LH production, further preventing ovulation.

The progestin provides additional backup effects. It keeps the cervical mucus very thick, making it difficult for sperm to get through, and it changes the lining of the uterus in such a way that even if a fertilized egg arrived, implantation would be unlikely.

When the estrogen and progestin are withdrawn after day 21, the lining of the uterus disintegrates, and withdrawal bleeding or menstruation occurs, although the flow is typically reduced because the progestin has inhibited development of the endometrium.

Hormonally, the action of the pill produces a condition much like pregnancy, when hormone levels are also high, preventing further ovulation and menstrual periods. Thus it is not too surprising that some of the side effects of the pill are similar to the symptoms of pregnancy.

Effectiveness

Before the effectiveness of the pill is discussed, several technical terms that are used in communicating data on effectiveness need to be defined. If 100 women use a contraceptive method for one year, the number of them who become pregnant during that first year of use is called the **failure rate** or *pregnancy rate*. That is, if 5 women out of 100 become pregnant during a year of using contraceptive A, then A's failure rate is 5 percent. *Effectiveness* is 100 minus the failure rate; thus contraceptive A would be said to be 95 percent effective. We can also talk about two kinds of failure rate; the *lowest observed failure rate* and the *failure rate for typical users*. The lowest observed failure rate refers to studies of the best possible use of the method—for example, when the user has been well-taught about the method, uses it with perfect consistency, and so on. The failure rate for typical users is just that—the failure rate when people actually use the method, perhaps imperfectly when they forget to take a pill or do not use a condom every time. The good news is that if you are very responsible about contraception, you can anticipate close to the lowest failure rate for yourself.

Failure rate: The pregnancy rate occurring using a particular contraceptive method; the percentage of women who will be pregnant after a year of use of the method.

The use of combination pills is the most effective method of birth control short of sterilization. The lowest failure rate is 0.1 percent (that is, the method is essentially 100 percent effective), and the typical failure rate is 3 percent (Hatcher et al., 1990). Failures occur primarily as a result of forgetting to take a pill for two or more days. If a woman forgets to take a pill for one day, she should simply take two the next day; this does not appear to increase the pregnancy risk appreciably. If she forgets for two days, she should take two pills on each of the next two days; however, the chances of pregnancy are now increased. If she forgets for three or more days, she should switch to some other method of birth control for the remainder of that cycle.

Side Effects

You may have seen various reports in the media on the dangerous side effects of birth control pills. Some of these reports are no more than scare stories with little or no evidence behind them. On the other hand, there are some well-documented risks associated with the use of the pill, and women who are using it or who are contemplating using it should be aware of them.

Among the serious side effects associated with use of the pill are slight but significant increases in certain diseases of the circulatory system. One of these is problems of blood clotting (thromboembolic disorders). Women who use the pill

Margaret Sanger—Birth Control Pioneer

Margaret Higgins Sanger (1883–1966) was a crusader for birth control in the United States; to reach her goals, she had to take on a variety of opponents, including the United States government, and she served one jail term.

She was born in Corning, New York, the daughter of a tubercular mother who died young after bearing 11 children. Her father was a free spirit who fought for women's suffrage. After caring for her dying mother, she embarked on a career in nursing and married William Sanger in 1900.

She became interested in women's health and began writing articles on the subject. Later these were published as books entitled *What Every Girl Should Know* (1916) and *What Every Mother Should Know* (1917).

Perhaps her strongest motivation came from her work as a nurse. Her patients were poor maternity cases on New York's Lower East Side. Among these women, pregnancy was a "chronic condition." Margaret Sanger saw them, weary and old at 35, resorting to self-induced abortions, which were frequently the cause of their deaths. Frustrated at her inability to help them, she renounced nursing:

I came to a sudden realization that my work as a nurse and my activities in social service were entirely palliative and consequently futile and useless to relieve the misery I saw all about me.

She determined, instead, to "seek out the root of the evil." Though she was often accused of wanting to lower the birthrate, she instead envisioned families, rich and poor alike, in which children were wanted and given every advantage.

Impeding her work was the Comstock Act of 1873 (see Chapter 22), which classified contraceptive information as obscene and made it illegal to send it through the mail. In 1914 she founded the National Birth Control League, launching the birth control movement in the United States. Though her magazine, *Woman Rebel,* obeyed the letter of the law and did not give contraceptive information, she was nonetheless indicted on nine counts and made liable to a prison term of 45 years.

Margaret Sanger left the United States on the eve of the trial. She toured Europe, and in Holland she visited the first birth control clinics to be estab-

have a higher chance than nonusers of developing blood clots (thrombi). Often these form in the legs, and they may then move to the lungs. There may also be clotting or hemorrhaging in the brain (stroke). The clots may lead to pain, hospitalization, and (in rare cases) death. The risk of death is somewhat less than 3 per 100,000 per year for women on the pill, as compared with 0.4 per 100,000 women per year among nonusers. Symptoms of blood clots are severe headaches, sudden blurring of vision, severe leg or chest pains, and shortness of breath. For some women, the pill can cause high blood pressure; thus it is important to have regular checkups so that this can be detected if it occurs. There are also slight increases in the risk of heart attack and stroke with pill use (Wharton & Blackburn, 1988). Unfortunately, most of the studies of these side effects were done with women using the old, high-dose pill, so they may overestimate the risk. It seems likely that current lower-dose pills

FIGURE 8.2
Margaret Sanger, a pioneer of the birth control movement.

down allowing doctors to give contraceptive information to women for the "cure and prevention of disease."

The birth control movement was gaining followers, and the first National Birth Control Conference was held in 1921 in New York; it was attended by doctors, scientists, and lay supporters. In 1931, the Pope approved the rhythm method for use by Roman Catholics.

Women in Canada were also at the forefront of the birth control movement in that country. In Hamilton, Ontario, Mary Elizabeth Hawkins organized the Hamilton Birth Control Society in 1932. Dr. Elizabeth Bagshaw, one of Hamilton's few female physicians at the time, served the clinic for the next thirty-odd years. Providing information about birth control was technically illegal in Canada, too, at the time, unless it served "the public good," and an Ottawa social worker was actually charged (and acquitted in 1937) for her family planning activity.

Margaret Sanger's role in getting birth control information to American women and in making it legal for them to use the information is unquestioned. Heywood Broun once remarked that Margaret Sanger had no sense of humor. She replied, "I am the protagonist of women who have nothing to laugh at."

lished anywhere. There she got the idea of opening birth control clinics in the United States. Meanwhile, the charges against her had been dropped.

She returned to the United States and, in 1916, opened a birth control clinic in Brooklyn. The office was closed by the police after nine days of operation, and Margaret Sanger was put in jail for 30 days. However, on appeal, her side was upheld by the courts, and in 1918 a decision was handed

Sources: Current Biography, (1944). P. Van Preagh. (1982). The Hamilton birth control clinic: In response to need. News/ Nouvelles, Journal of Planned Parenthood Federation of Canada, 3(2).

have lower risks of these side effects, but they have been in use a relatively short time so there is less research on them.

There have been many emotional reports in the media of the pill causing cancer; the scientific data, however, do not provide evidence that the pill causes cancer of the cervix, uterus, or breast. The good news is that the pill actually protects women from endometrial cancer and ovarian cancer (Wharton & Blackburn, 1988). However, the pill may aggravate already existing cancer. And while some of the studies have looked at effects after fairly long periods of time, there is a need for studies of even longer-term effects, since it is known that cancer-causing agents (carcinogens) may not show their effects for as much as 20 years.

The pill increases the risk of gallbladder disease. For women who have taken it more than five years, the risk of benign liver tumors increases (Hatcher et al.,

FIGURE 8.3
Birth control devices: (a)
birth control pills, (b)
diaphragm and spermicidal
jelly, (c) contraceptive foam
with applicator, (d)
condoms.

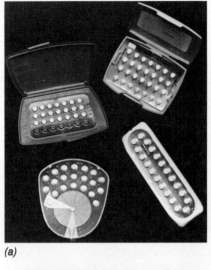

(a)

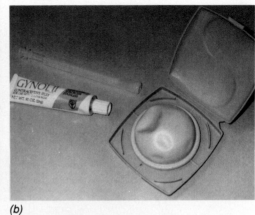

(b)

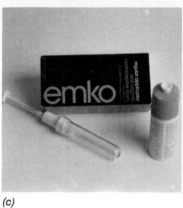

(c)

(d)

1990). These tumors can cause death due to bleeding if they rupture. Although these problems are relatively rare, they underline the importance of the doctor's giving a thorough examination before prescribing birth control pills and of the woman's having regular checkups while using them.

The pill increases the amount of vaginal discharge and the susceptibility to vaginitis (vaginal inflammations such as monilia and trichomonas—see Chapter 20) because it alters the chemical balance of the lining of the vagina. Women on the pill have an increased susceptibility to gonorrhea, probably for similar reasons, as well as the fact that they are unlikely to be using condoms or other methods that protect against sexually transmitted diseases. Nonetheless, in one study women using the pill had a 73 percent higher rate of acquiring chlamydia and a 70 percent higher rate of acquiring gonorrhea than did comparison groups of women using sterilization or an IUD (Louv et al., 1989).

The pill may cause some nausea, although this almost always goes away after the first month or two of use. Some brands of pills can also cause weight gain, by increasing appetite or water retention, but this can often be reversed by switching to another brand.

Finally, there may be some psychological effects. About 20 percent of women on the pill report increased irritability and depression, which become worse with length of time used. These side effects are probably related to the progesterone in the pill; switching to a different brand may be helpful. There may also be changes in sexual desire. Some women report an increase in sexual interest, mainly because they are now free of the fear of pregnancy. But other women report a decrease in sexual desire as well as a decrease in vaginal lubrication, a loss of sensitivity of the vulva, and decreased ability to have orgasms. Once again, switching brands may be helpful.

Because of the side effects discussed above, the following women should *not* use the pill (Hatcher et al., 1990): those with poor blood circulation or blood clotting problems; those who have had a heart attack or who have coronary artery disease; those with liver tumors; those with undiagnosed abnormal genital bleeding; those with cancer of the breast; those with sickle-cell disease (the latter because of the blood-clotting problems); nursing mothers (the pill tends to dry up the milk supply, and the hormones may be transmitted through the milk to the baby); pregnant women (prenatal doses of hormones, as has been noted, can damage the fetus); and women over 40 if they are cigarette smokers (because the risk of heart attack is considerably higher in this group). However, most women in the last category probably plan on having no more babies anyway. A better alternative would probably be some form of sterilization, either a tubal ligation for her or a vasectomy for her husband. Neither should the pill be prescribed for teenagers with infrequent menstrual periods because interfering with natural cycling before it is well established seems to lead to infertility problems later on. With the exception of women over 40 who smoke, there are no age limits for use of the pill (Kaeser, 1989).

Well, after all this discussion, just how dangerous is the pill? It seems that this depends on who you are and on how you look at it. If you have blood-clotting problems, the pill is extremely dangerous to you; if you have none of the contraindications listed above, it is very safe. One's point of view and standard of comparison also matter. While a death rate of 3 per 100,000 from clotting disorders sounds high, it is important to consider that one alternative to the pill is intercourse with no contraceptive, and that can mean pregnancy, which has a set of side effects and a death rate all its own. Thus while the death rate for the pill is 3 per 100,000, the death rate for pregnancy and delivery is 10 per 100,000 (Hatcher et al., 1988). And while the pill may precipitate diabetes, diabetes may also be precipitated by pregnancy. Thus in many ways the pill is no more dangerous than the alternative, pregnancy, and may even be safer. Another possible standard of comparison is drugs that are commonly taken for less serious reasons. Aspirin, for example, is routinely used for headaches. Recent reports indicate that aspirin has side effects, and thus the birth control pill may be no more dangerous than drugs we take without worrying much.

A study of 16,638 women from 1969 to 1977 indicates that the pill may be even less dangerous than previous studies indicated (Ramcharan et al., 1980). In particular, there was no significant difference in death rates for pill users and nonusers. How can one reconcile these findings with the earlier discussions of increased risk for certain problems? Perhaps the pill protects one against as many problems as it creates. And the risk of the serious problems—such as thromboembolisms, high blood pressure, and gallbladder disease—is still so low even while taking the pill that it does not produce any significant effects even in a study of 16,000 women.

The pill does have some serious potential dangers, particularly for high-risk individuals, but for many others it is an extremely effective means of contraception that poses little or no danger.

Advantages and Disadvantages

The pill has a number of advantages. It is close to 100 percent effective if used properly. It does not interfere with intercourse, as some other methods—the diaphragm, the condom, and foam—do. It is not messy. Some of its side effects are also advantages; it reduces the amount of menstrual flow and thus reduces premenstrual tension and cramps. Indeed, it is sometimes prescribed for the noncontraceptive purpose of regulating menstruation and eliminating cramps. Iron-deficiency anemia is also less likely to occur among pill users. It can clear up acne. And the pill has a protective effect against some rather serious things, including pelvic inflammatory disease (PID), and ovarian and endometrial cancer (Hatcher et al., 1988; Ory, 1982).

The side effects of birth control pills, discussed above, are of course major disadvantages. Another disadvantage is the cost, which is about $19 a month (or as little as $2 to $4 per month through a Planned Parenthood clinic) for as long as they are used. They also place the entire burden of contraception on the woman. In addition, taking them correctly is a little complicated; the woman must understand when they are to be taken, and she must remember when to take them and when not to take them. This would not be too taxing for the average college student, but for an illiterate peasant woman in a developing nation who thinks the pills are to be worn like an amulet on a chain around the neck or for the mentally retarded (they need contraceptives too), presently available birth control pills are too complicated.

One other criticism of the pill is that for a woman who has intercourse only infrequently (say, once or twice a month or less), it represents contraceptive "over-kill"; that is, the pill makes her infertile every day of the month (with the side effects of taking it every day), and yet she needs it only a few days each month. Women in this situation might consider a method, such as the diaphragm, that is used only when needed.

Finally, it is important to recognize that, although it is an excellent contraceptive, the pill provides absolutely no protection against sexually transmitted diseases.

Reversibility

When a woman wants to become pregnant, she simply stops taking pills after the end of one cycle. Among people who do this, 40 percent become pregnant within a year, and 93 percent become pregnant within two and a half years (Liskin, 1984; Vessey et al., 1978). This is essentially the same rate as for women who have never taken the pill. Therefore, the pill does not seem to affect the fertility of a woman after she stops taking it.

Drug Interactions

If you are taking birth control pills, you are taking a prescription drug and there may be interactions with other prescription drugs you take (Hatcher et al., 1990; Wharton & Blackburn, 1988). There is some evidence that taking antibiotics such as ampicillin and tetracycline reduces the effectiveness of the pill. Women in this situation may either switch to a higher-dose pill while on the antibiotic, or may use a backup method in addition, such as rhythm, condoms, or foam.

The pill may also increase the metabolism of some drugs, making them more potent (Wharton & Blackburn, 1988). Examples include some antianxiety drugs, corticosteroids used for inflammations, and theophylline (a drug used for asthma). Therefore, women using the pill may require lower doses of these drugs.

Other Kinds of Pills

To this point, the discussion has centered chiefly on the *combination pill,* so named because it contains both estrogen and progestin. This variety of pill is the most widely used, but there are many kinds of combination pills and several kinds of pills other than combination ones.

Combination pills vary from one brand to the next in the dosages of estrogen and progestin. The dose of estrogen is important because higher doses are more likely to induce blood-clotting problems. Most women do well on pills containing no more than 30 to 50 micrograms of estrogen; brands fulfilling that requirement include Ortho-Novum 1/35, Norinyl 1/50, Demulen, Norlestrin, Ovral, and Ovcon 50 (Hatcher et al., 1988). Because of concerns about side effects due to the estrogen in the pill, current pills have considerably lower levels of estrogen than early pills; for example, Ortho-Novum 1/35 has one-third the amount of estrogen of the early pill Enovid 10. High-progestin brands are related to symptoms such as vaginitis and depression. Thus, depending on what side effects the woman wants to avoid, she can choose a brand for its high or low estrogen or progesterone level. (See Hatcher et al., 1986, pp. 153–155, for a list of symptoms related to dosages of estrogen and progestin.)

Another variation of the combination pill is the 28-day pill. There are 28 pills in every package. The first 21 pills that the woman takes are regular combination pills, and the last 7 are placebos (they contain no drugs). The purpose of this is simply to help the woman use the pills properly, the idea being that it is easier to remember to take a pill every day than to remember to take one each day for 21 days and then none for 7 days; also, the seven placebos eliminate confusion about when to start taking pills again.

> **Biphasic pill:** A birth control pill containing a steady level of estrogen and two phases of progesterone, one at a low level and one at a high level. Intended to mimic more closely women's natural hormonal cycles.

A **biphasic pill** (Ortho-Novum 10/11) was introduced in 1982. It contains a steady level of estrogen like the combination pill does, but there are two phases in the levels of progesterone, a lower level for the first 10 days, followed by a higher level for the last 11 days. The idea is to reduce total hormone exposure and provide a cycle more similar to the natural one. It is too early to know much about the effectiveness or side effects of the biphasic pill. *Triphasic pills* (e.g., Ortho-Novum 7-7-7) were introduced in 1984.

Progestin-only pills (such as Micronor, Nor-Q-D, and Ovrette) have also been developed. They are sometimes called *mini-pills*. The pills contain only a low dose of progestin and no estrogen, and they were designed to avoid the estrogen-related side effects of the standard pills. The woman takes one beginning on the first day of her period and every day thereafter, at the same time each day. Although no one is exactly sure how they work, hypotheses include the following: changes in the cervical mucus such that sperm cannot get through, inhibition of the egg's ability to travel down the tube, inhibition of the sperm's ability to penetrate the egg, inhibition of implantation, and inhibition of ovulation (although while taking mini-pills, about 40 percent of women ovulate consistently). Progestin-only pills have a typical user failure rate of 2.5 percent, which is higher than that of combination pills, although much of the failure occurs during the first six months of use. They were originally developed to avoid the side effects of the estrogen in combination pills; their major side effect seems to be that they produce very irregular menstrual cycles. The mini-pill is probably most useful for women who cannot take combination pills—for example, women over 35 who smoke, or women with a history of high blood pressure or blood-clotting problems.

Progestin-only pills are also useful for women who are breast-feeding and cannot use combination pills because they reduce milk production. Probably neither kind of pill should be used in the first 4 months after birth when breast-feeding, because trace amounts of the hormones can reach the infant through the breast milk. After that time, though, progestin-only pills are a good choice.

> **Morning-after pill:** A pill containing a high dose of DES, which can be used in emergency situations for preventing pregnancy after intercourse has occurred.

The **morning-after pill** is used in cases of emergency (for example, after a rape). It contains a high dose (25 milligrams) of a potent estrogen, diethylstilbestrol (DES), and is taken twice a day for five days, beginning no more than 72 hours after the act of intercourse and preferably within 24 hours. It should be stressed that it is for emergency use only, because of its serious side effects; about 16 percent of women taking it develop severe nausea and vomiting. Possible side effects if it is taken by a pregnant woman were noted in Chapter 7. Therefore it cannot be considered a method of birth control for regular use.

IMPLANTS AND INJECTIONS

The first introduction of a major new method of contraception in the United States in years came in 1990 with the introduction of Norplant, a progestin-only implant that lasts for five years.

Norplant comes in six rod-shaped silicone capsules, each about the size of a matchbook match. They are implanted by a medical professional using a minor surgical procedure under local anesthetic (see Figure 8.4). They are usually placed in a fan-shaped configuration on the inside of the woman's upper arm. Once in place, the progestin diffuses slowly but steadily into the body, and the implant lasts for five years.

How It Works

Norplant, like other progestin-only contraceptives (progestin-only pills and injections) seems to work in several ways. It inhibits ovulation; it thickens the cervical mucus, making it difficult for sperm to get through; and it creates a puny endometrium in the uterus so that if a fertilized egg did arrive, it would not have much to implant in.

Effectiveness

Norplant is the most effective method of contraception now available (with the exception of sterilization). In fact, it is more effective than the combination pill. The failure rate in the first year of use is only 0.04 percent (Hatcher et al., 1990). That

FIGURE 8.4
Norplant, a progestin contraceptive implanted in the woman's upper arm, is the most exciting new development in contraception of the last 10 years. It is the first major new method of contraception to be introduced in the United States in a decade. It is implanted using a minor surgical procedure shown here.

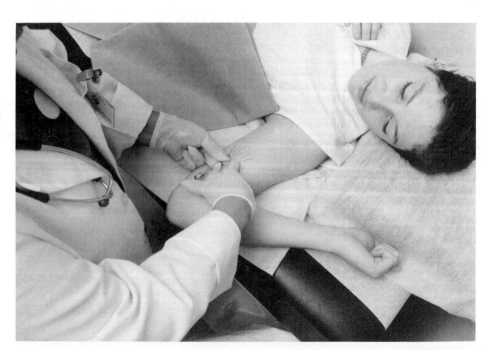

is, it is essentially 100 percent effective. Failure rates go up substantially after five years, but it is only a five-year implant and a new implant must be obtained after that time has elapsed.

Side Effects

The side effects found so far with Norplant can be regarded as minor rather than major. Menstrual cycle irregularities are the most common side effect. These vary from woman to woman and may include prolonged menstruation during the first few months of use, spotting between periods, and amenorrhea (Darney et al., 1990).

At this point there is no evidence of circulatory system side effects (for example, blood-clotting disorders) with Norplant use such as those that have been found with birth control pills. However, Norplant has been introduced so recently that the number of women who have used it is still relatively small, and none have used it for a long period of time. Therefore, future research may document side effects involving cancer or the circulatory system. However, it seems unlikely that these side effects will be very frequent because most of the side effects of combination pills are due to the estrogen, and Norplant uses only progestin.

At the current time, it is recommended that women in the following categories not use Norplant: pregnant women and those with acute liver disease; jaundice; unexplained vaginal bleeding; a history of blood clots in the legs, lung, or eyes; or a history of heart attack or stroke. In the unlikely event that a woman becomes pregnant while using Norplant, the capsules should be removed because it is unwise to expose the fetus to hormones, even at the low dose found in Norplant.

Advantages and Disadvantages

The big advantage of Norplant is that it does not require memory to use it properly. There are no failures due to forgetting to take a pill. In addition, it has all the advantages of the pill, particularly the fact that it does not intrude in lovemaking. Its extremely high effectiveness is another major advantage. Because it contains no estrogen, it has no estrogen-related side effects.

One disadvantage is the high initial cost ($550 for a full-paying client at Planned Parenthood, but less for someone on a smaller income). However, when the cost is considered over five years of use, it reduces to slightly over $100 per year, which is about the same as birth control pills, and is certainly cheaper than having a baby. The implants may be slightly visible. Menstrual irregularities are a disadvantage for some women. Finally, Norplant must be inserted and removed by a trained medical professional, so it cannot be used on the spur of the moment.

It is a method best suited for a woman who wants long-term contraception. It is not sensible for someone needing contraception for only a short period of time.

Reversibility

If the woman desires to become pregnant any time during the five years of use, she simply has a trained medical professional remove the capsules. Progestin levels quickly go down, and the woman can become pregnant.

Depo-Provera Injections

Depo-Provera (DMPA) is a progestin administered by injection. Injections must be repeated every three months for maximum effectiveness. Depo-Provera has been available for more than a decade and is currently in use in more than 80 nations worldwide (Hatcher et al., 1990). It is available in the United States, but it has not achieved as much popularity as the pill.

Depo-Provera works like the other progestin-only methods, by inhibiting ovulation, thickening cervical mucus, and inhibiting the growth of the endometrium.

Depo-Provera has many advantages. It does not interfere with lovemaking. It requires far less reliance on memory than birth control pills do, although the woman must remember to have a new injection every three months. It is available for women who cannot use the combination pill, such as those over 40 who smoke and those with blood pressure problems. Compared with Norplant, it has a lower initial cost, although the two are probably about equal in cost over a long period of time.

A disadvantage of Depo-Provera is that most users experience amenorrhea (no menstrual periods). However, this may also be an advantage. It can relieve anemia due to heavy menstrual periods, and Depo-Provera can be used in the treatment of endometriosis.

No lethal side effects of Depo-Provera have been found, although long-term studies have not yet been done (Hatcher et al., 1990).

The method is reversible simply by not getting another injection. Many women are infertile for 6 to 12 months after stopping its use. However, over 80 percent of women who stop using Depo-Provera to become pregnant succeed within one year (Hatcher et al., 1990).

THE IUD

Intrauterine device (IUD): A plastic device sometimes containing metal or a hormone that is inserted into the uterus for contraceptive purposes.

The **intrauterine device, or IUD** [sometimes also called *intrauterine contraceptive device* (IUCD)], is a small piece of plastic; it comes in various shapes. Metal or a hormone may also be part of the device. An IUD is inserted into the uterus by a doctor or nurse practitioner and then remains in place until the woman wants to have it removed. One or two plastic strings hang down from the IUD through the cervix, enabling the woman to check to see whether it is in place.

The basic idea for the IUD has been around for some time. In 1909 Richter reported on the use of an IUD made of silkworm gut. In the 1920s the German physician Ernst Grafenberg reported data on 2000 insertions of silk or silver wire rings. In spite of the high effectiveness he reported (98.4 percent), his work was poorly received. Not until the 1950s, with the development of plastic and stainless-steel devices, did the method gain much popularity. In the 1980s the use of the IUD in the United States was sharply reduced by numerous lawsuits against manufacturers by persons claiming to have been damaged by the device. Some companies stopped producing IUDs, and others were forced into bankruptcy. As a result, only two IUDs are available in the United States today. Both are T-shaped; one contains copper (the copper T or TCU-380A, shown in Figure 8.5), and the other contains progesterone (Progestasert). On the other hand, currently 60 million women worldwide are using IUDs, 40 million of them in the People's Republic of China (Population Information Program, 1982). For a summary of contraceptive practices around the world, see Table 8.1.

How It Works

No one is really sure how the IUD works, but the data clearly show that it does. The leading hypothesis is that it produces a continual slight inflammation in the uterus, and in this environment, sperm that reach the uterus are either destroyed or immobilized and cannot move into the fallopian tube (Hatcher et al., 1990; Sivin, 1989).

One of the few IUDs left on the market in the United States, the Progestasert, releases progesterone directly into the uterus. One effect is to reduce the endometrium. This results in reduced menstrual flow and reduced risk of anemia, thus overcoming two undesirable side effects of other IUDs.

The small amount of copper that is added to some of the devices (for example, the copper "T") is thought to have an additional contraceptive effect. It seems to alter the functioning of the enzymes involved in implantation. A new copper T (T-380A) was introduced in the United States in 1988, the first new IUD in years (see Figure 8.5). Preliminary studies show that it has a failure rate as low as that of the pill (Thomas, 1988).

Effectiveness

The IUD is extremely effective; it is third behind Norplant and the pill (and sterilization) in effectiveness. Pregnancy rates for the two types now in use in the United States are 3 percent. The copper devices have a lower pregnancy rate. The failure

Table 8.1

Contraception Around the World, Reported by Currently Married Women (The great variations reflect differences among cultures in such factors as availability of medical service, people's education about contraception, and gender roles.)

Region, Country	Voluntary Sterilization		Pill	IUD	Condom	Injectables	Vaginal Methods[†]	Rhythm
	Male	Female						
North America								
United States	10	17	13	5	10	0	7	3
Europe								
Netherlands	11	8	38	10	7	NA	NA	NA
Italy	NA	1	14	2	13	NA	2	9
Norway	2	4	13	28	16	NA	2	3
Africa								
Botswana	0	4	16	6	1	6	0	0
Nigeria	0	0	1	1	0	1	0	1
Asia								
Korea	11	37	3	7	10	NA	2	NA
Thailand	6	22	20	7	1	9	0	1
Latin America								
El Salvador	1	30	8	2	2	1	0	2
Mexico	1	18	11	11	2	3	1	5
Middle East and North Africa								
Egypt	0	1	16	17	3	0	0	1
Jordan	0	6	5	15	1	0	1	4

Percentage Using Contraception

NA: Statistics not available.

* Includes injections such as Depo-Provera.

† Includes diaphragm, cervical cap, and spermicides.

Sources: Bryant Robey et al. (1992). The reproductive revolution: New survey findings. *Population Reports,* Series M, Number 11. Baltimore: Johns Hopkins University, Population Information Program. Kathy A. London et al. (1985). Fertility and family planning surveys: An update. *Population Reports,* Series M, Number 8, M-291–M-348. Baltimore: Johns Hopkins University, Population Information Program.

FIGURE 8.5
Copper-T IUD.

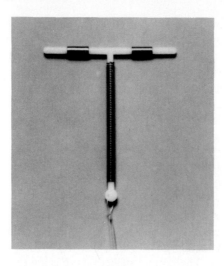

rates are for the first year of use; after that, the failure rate is lower. Most failures occur during the first three months of use, either because the IUD is expelled or for other, unknown reasons. Expulsion is most likely in women who have had no children, in younger women, and in women during menstruation. The expulsion rate is about 5 to 7 percent during the first year.

The IUD can be made essentially 100 percent effective when combined with another method such as a contraceptive foam or a condom.

Side Effects

There are two possible serious side effects of the IUD. One is uterine perforation. This occurs in only about 1 woman in 2500 (Hatcher et al., 1986), but it can be fatal. It is caused mainly by improper insertion, and thus women should exercise care in choosing a physician or clinic when obtaining an IUD. The other serious side effect is **pelvic inflammatory disease** (PID—e.g., uterine or tubal infection). The IUD aggravates already existing pelvic infections, and so it should not be used by a woman who has such an infection or a history of such infections. PID may create a blocking of the fallopian tubes, thus causing infertility. The risk of infertility due to blocked fallopian tubes among women who have never had a baby is 2.6 times higher in women who have used an IUD than in women who have never used one (Daling et al., 1985). The risk is particularly high—nearly 7 times as great—in women who have used the Dalkon Shield (now withdrawn from the market). The use of copper-containing IUDs does not seem to increase the rate of infertility.

The most common side effects of IUDs are cramping and abdominal pain, irregular bleeding, and increased menstrual flow. Anemia may result. These symptoms occur in 10 to 20 percent of women using IUDs and are most likely immediately after insertion. These side effects are a major reason for requests for IUD removal.

There is no evidence that the IUD causes cancer.

Because of the possible side effects, women with the following conditions should not use an IUD: pregnancy, endometriosis, vaginal or uterine infection (including gonorrhea or chlamydia), or pelvic inflammatory disease.

Advantages and Disadvantages

All the side effects discussed above are disadvantages of the IUD. Another disadvantage is the cost; some private physicians in large cities charge $200 or more for an

Pelvic inflammatory disease (PID): Infection of the pelvic organs such as the fallopian tubes.

IUD plus insertion. Planned Parenthood clinics generally charge much less, and fees are based on the ability to pay. Even at the high rates, though, the IUD is a cheap means of contraception over a long period of use, since the cost is incurred only once (except in the case of devices containing copper or progesterone, which must be replaced every year or two).

Although the failure rate of the IUD is low, it is not zero, and this is another major disadvantage. In a group of 100 women using the IUD for a year, about three will become pregnant. Those women who absolutely do not want to become pregnant should use either a backup method, at least around the time of ovulation, or a different method entirely.

Once inserted, the IUD is perfectly simple to use. The woman has only to check periodically to see that the strings are in place. Thus it has an advantage over methods like the diaphragm or condom in that it does not interrupt intercourse in any way. It has an advantage over the pill in that the woman does not have to remember to use it. For these reasons, it has been very popular in developing nations such as China.

Contrary to what some people think, the IUD does not interfere with the use of a tampon during menstruation; nor does it have any effect on intercourse.

Reversibility

When a woman who is using an IUD wants to become pregnant, she simply has a physician remove the device. She can become pregnant immediately.

THE DIAPHRAGM AND THE CERVICAL CAP

Diaphragm: A cap-shaped rubber contraceptive device that fits inside a woman's vagina over the cervix.

The diaphragm is a circular, dome-shaped piece of thin rubber with a rubber-covered rim of flexible metal (see Figure 8.6). It is inserted into the vagina and, when properly in place, fits snugly over the cervix. In order for it to be used properly, a contraceptive cream or jelly (such as Delfen) must be applied to the diaphragm. The cream is spread on the rim and the inside surface (the surface that fits against the cervix). The diaphragm may be inserted up to 6 hours before intercourse; it must be left in place for at least 6 hours afterward and may be left in for as long as 12 hours. Keeping it in place longer than that is thought to increase the risk of toxic shock syndrome.

Use of the diaphragm was the earliest of the highly effective methods of contraception for women. It was popularized in a paper in 1882 by the German researcher Mensinga. In 1925, Margaret Sanger's husband funded the first U.S. company to manufacture them, and they were the mainstay of contraception until about 1960. Many readers may safely assume that their own parents managed to limit their number of children to two or three by careful use of the diaphragm.

How It Works

The primary action of the diaphragm itelf is mechanical; it blocks the entrance to the uterus so that sperm cannot swim up into it. The spermicidal cream kills any sperm that manage to get past the barrier. Any sperm remaining in the vagina die after about eight hours (for this reason, the diaphragm cannot be removed until at least six hours after intercourse).

Effectiveness

The typical failure rate of the diaphragm has been estimated to be about 18 percent. Most failures are due to improper use; the woman may not use it every time, she

FIGURE 8.6
The proper use of a diaphragm. (a) Spermicide is applied (about 1 tablespoon in center and around the rim). (b) The edges are held together to permit easier insertion. (c) The folded diaphragm is inserted up through the vagina. (d) The diaphragm is placed properly, covering the cervix. To check for proper placement, feel the cervix to be sure that it is completely covered by the diaphragm.

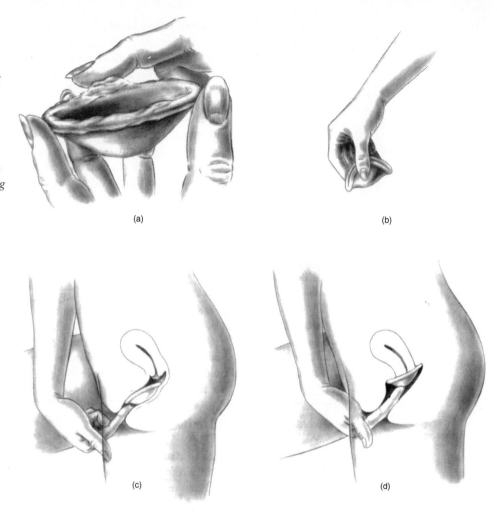

(a)

(b)

(c)

(d)

may not leave it in long enough, or she may not use cream or jelly. Even with perfectly proper use, there is still a failure rate. For example, Masters and Johnson have shown that expansion of the vagina during sexual arousal (see Chapter 9) may cause the diaphragm to slip. To get closer to 100 percent effectiveness, the diaphragm can be combined with a condom around the time of ovulation or throughout the cycle.

Failure rates for the diaphragm, cervical cap, and sponge (discussed later) are often stated as ranges, for example, 17 to 25 percent. This is done because failure rates for these methods depend so much on the fertility characteristics of the user. For example, a woman under 30 who has intercourse four or more times weekly has twice the average failure rate of a woman over 30 who has intercourse less than four times a week.

Because the fit of the diaphragm is so important to its effectiveness, it is important that the woman be individually fitted for one by her physician. She must be refitted after the birth of a child, an abortion, extreme weight gain or loss, or any similar occurrence that would alter the shape and size of the vagina.

Side Effects

The diaphragm has few side effects, one being the possible irritation of the vagina or the penis; this is caused by the cream or jelly and can be relieved by switching to another brand. Another side effect is the rare occurrence of toxic shock syndrome (TSS) that has been reported in women who left the diaphragm in place for more than 24 hours. Therefore users shoud be careful not to leave the diaphragm in place for much more than the necessary six to eight hours, especially during menstruation.

Advantages and Disadvantages

Some people feel that the diaphragm is undesirable because it must be inserted before intercourse and therefore ruins the "spontaneity" of sex. People with this attitude, of course, should not use the diaphragm as a means of birth control, since they probably will not use it all the time, in which case it will not work. However, a student of mine told me that she and her partner made the preparation and insertion of the diaphragm a ritual part of their foreplay; he inserts it, and they both have a good time! Couples who maintain this kind of attitude are much more likely to use the diaphragm effectively.

Some women dislike touching their genitals and sticking their fingers into their vagina. Use of the diaphragm is not a good method for them.

The diaphragm requires some thought and presence of mind on the woman's part. She must remember to have it with her when she needs it and to have a supply of cream or jelly. She also needs to avoid becoming so carried away with passion that she forgets about it or decides not to use it.

A disadvantage is that the cream or jelly may leak out after intercourse.

The cost of a diaphragm is about $10 plus the cost of the office visit and the cost of the spermicidal cream. With proper care, a diaphragm should last about two years, and thus it is not expensive.

The major advantages of the diaphragm are that it has few side effects and, when used properly, is very effective. For this reason, women who are worried about the side effects of the pill or the IUD should seriously consider the diaphragm as an alternative. There is also evidence of a reduction in the rate of cervical cancer among long-time users of the diaphragm.

Reversibility

If a woman wishes to become pregnant, she simply stops using the diaphragm. Its use has no effect on her later chances of conceiving.

The Cervical Cap

Cervical cap: A method of birth control involving a rubber cap that fits snugly over the cervix.

The cervical cap was approved by the FDA in 1988. It is similar to the diaphragm but is somewhat different in shape, fitting more snugly over the cervix (see Figure 8.7). Like the diaphragm, it should be used with a spermicidal cream. One advantage is that it can be left in place longer than the diaphragm. It can remain in place for 48 hours, but experts advise aginst leaving it in longer because of problems with odors and increased risk of toxic shock syndrome (Hatcher et al., 1986). One potential risk is that it may irritate the cervix by pressing or rubbing on it, but the device has not been in use long enough to assess whether that risk is serious. The cervical cap has approximately the same effectiveness as the diaphragm; that is, it has a typical user failure rate around 18 percent.

Protection from STDs

One advantage of both the diaphragm and the cervical cap is that they probably lower the risk of transmission of sexually transmitted diseases, in part because spermicides are fairly effective at killing the organisms causing these diseases.

FIGURE 8.7
The cervical cap.

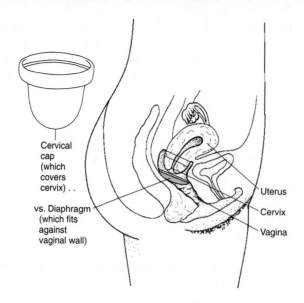

Cervical cap (which covers cervix) . .

vs. Diaphragm (which fits against vaginal wall)

Uterus

Cervix

Vagina

THE CONDOM

Condom: A male contraceptive sheath that is placed over the penis.

The condom ("rubber," "prophylactic," "safe") is a thin sheath that fits over the penis. It comes rolled up in a little packet (see Figure 8.3) and must be unrolled before use. It may be made of latex ("rubber") or of the intestinal tissue of lambs ("skin"). The widespread use of the modern condom, both for contraception and for protection against venereal disease (VD), dates from about 1843, when vulcanized rubber was developed; however, the use of a sheath to cover the penis has been known throughout most of recorded history.[1] Casanova (1725–1798) was one of the first to popularize it for its contraceptive value as well as its protective value. Condoms became increasingly popular in the 1980s because they help protect against sexually transmitted diseases such as AIDS.

To be effective, the condom must be used properly. It must be unrolled onto the erect penis before the penis ever enters the vagina—*not* just before ejaculation, since long before then some drops containing a few thousand sperm may have been produced. Condoms come in two shapes: those with plain ends and those with a protruding tip that catches the semen. If a plain-ended one is used, about $1/2$ inch of air-free space should be left at the tip to catch the ejaculate. Care should be taken that it does not slip during intercourse. After the man has ejaculated, he must hold the rim of the condom against the base of the penis as he withdraws. It is best to withdraw soon after ejaculation, while the man still has an erection, in order to minimize the chances of slippage.

Condoms may be either lubricated or unlubricated. Some further lubrication for intercourse may be necessary. A contraceptive foam or jelly works well and

---

[1] Condoms have also been the stimulus for humor throughout history, an example being this limerick:

There was a young man of Cape Horn
Who wished he had never been born
   And he wouldn't have been
   If his father had seen
That the end of the rubber was torn.

provides additional protection. A sterile lubricant such as K-Y jelly may also be used. Ramses Extra, a condom coated on the inside and outside with spermicide, was introduced in 1982. LifeStyles condoms are also lubricated on the inside and outside with the spermicide nonoxynol, which is relatively effective in killing the AIDS virus.

How It Works

The condom simply catches the semen and thus prevents it from entering the vagina. For condoms coated with a spermicide, the spermicide kills sperm and thus provides double protection.

Effectiveness

Condoms are actually much more effective as a contraceptive than most people think. The lowest failure rate is about 2 percent. The typical failure rate is about 12 percent, but many failures result from improper or inconsistent use. The FDA controls the quality of condoms carefully, and thus the chances of a failure due to a defect in the condom itself are small. However, the FDA regulates only condoms manufactured in the United States; you can't be quite as sure about imports.

Combined with a contraceptive foam or cream or a diaphragm, the condom is close to 100 percent effective.

Side Effects

The condom has no side effects.

Advantages and Disadvantages

One disadvantage of the condom is that it must be used at the time of intercourse, raising the old "spontaneity" problem again. If the couple can make an enjoyable ritual of putting it on together, this problem can be minimized.

Some men complain that the condom reduces their sensation and thus lessens their pleasure in intercourse ("It's like taking a shower with a raincoat on"). This can be a major disadvantage. The reduction in sensation, however, may be an advantage for some; for example, it may help the premature ejaculator.

There are several advantages to condoms. Their use is the only contraceptive method presently available for men except sterilization. They are cheap (around $1.00 to $1.50 for three), they are readily available without prescription at a drugstore, and they are fairly easy to use, although the man (or woman) must plan ahead so that one will be available when it is needed. Finally, it is one of the few contraceptive devices that also provide protection against sexually transmitted diseases, an important consideration in our epidemic era. Research indicates that, used consistently and correctly, condoms are highly effective in preventing the transmission of most STDs (Hatcher et al., 1990). Latex condoms coated with spermicides are particularly effective. On the other hand, animal skin condoms allow the HIV virus to pass through and so are not effective.

Reversibility

The method is easily and completely reversible. The man simply stops using them if conception is desired.

Innovations

With the increased popularity of condoms in the 1980s, several innovations have occurred. The new Mentor brand has an adhesive inner surface, the idea being to reduce the risk of slippage and spillage. The marketing of condoms has also changed dramatically. Promotion efforts are now directed increasingly toward women, and there is a new openness in marketing and purchasing. Brands such as Lady Trojan can be found packaged in attractive pastel wrappers in the women's health sections of drugstores (see Figure 8.3). *Consumer Reports* (March, 1989) reviewed the wide variety of brands now available.

SPERMICIDES

Spermicide (SPERM-ih-side): A substance that kills sperm.

Contraceptive foams (Delfen, Emko), creams, and jellies are all classified as spermicides, that is, sperm killers. They come in a tube or a can, along with a plastic applicator. The applicator is filled and inserted into the vagina; the spermicide is then pushed out into the vagina near the cervix with the plunger. Thus it is inserted much as a tampon is. It must be left in for six to eight hours after intercourse. One application provides protection for only one act of intercourse.

Spermicides are not to be confused with the various feminine hygiene products (vaginal deodorants) on the market. The latter are not effective as contraceptives.

How They Work

Spermicides consist of a spermicidal chemical in an inert base, and they work in two ways: chemical and mechanical. The chemicals in them kill sperm, while the inert base itself mechanically blocks the entrance to the cervix so that sperm cannot swim into it.

Effectiveness

Actual failure rates for spermicides can be as high as 25 percent. Put simply, they are not very effective. Foams tend to be more effective, and creams and jellies less so. Spermicidal tablets and suppositories are also available, and they are the least effective. Spermicides are highly effective only when used with a diaphragm or a condom.

Side Effects

Most evidence indicates that spermicides have no side effects except that they may occasionally irritate the vagina or penis, and some women are allergic to them.

Advantages and Disadvantages

The major advantage of spermicides is that they are readily available, without a prescription, in any drugstore. Thus they can be used as a stopgap method until the woman can see a physician and get a more effective contraceptive. Their failure rate is so high, though, that I cannot recommend using them by themselves; always combine them with a second method such as a condom. Foam and some brands of creams and jellies also help prevent sexually transmitted diseases.

Their major disadvantage is that by themselves, they are not very effective. They also interrupt the spontaneity of sex, although only very briefly. Some women

FIGURE 8.8
*Male responsibility is a key
issue in birth control.*

dislike the sensation of the spermicide leaking out after intercourse, and some are irritated by the chemicals. Finally, some people find that they taste terrible, and so their use interferes with oral sex.

THE SPONGE

Contraceptive sponge: A
polyurethane sponge
containing a spermicide,
which is placed in the
vagina for contraceptive
purposes.

The vaginal **contraceptive sponge** was approved by the FDA in 1983. It is marketed under the brand name Today. It is made out of polyurethane and is shaped rather like a large mushroom cap (see Figure 8.9). It is inserted into the vagina in a similar way to the diaphragm. The hollow side fits gainst the cervix, and the side with the woven loop is on the outside so that the loop can be used for removing it. It must be moistened with water before insertion, and it can be left in place for up to 24

FIGURE 8.9
The contraceptive sponge.

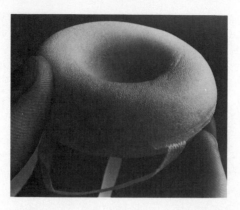

hours. It provides protection if there are multiple acts of intercourse while it is in place. After use it is discarded. It comes in a single size and is available over the counter without a prescription.

How It Works

The sponge works in three ways. First, it contains a spermicide, which kills sperm. Second, because it fits over the cervix, it provides a mechanical barrier to sperm swimming into the uterus. Finally, as a sponge, it soaks up semen, trapping sperm inside it.

Effectiveness

The typical failure rate of the sponge is between 17 and 25 percent (Hatcher et al., 1990), making it somewhat less effective than the diaphragm.

Side Effects

Some women are allergic to the spermicide in the sponge. About 6 percent of women in a U.S. study had such difficulty removing the sponge that they discontinued using it, and a few found it uncomfortable (Edelman et al., 1984). Some women also find that it absorbs their vaginal lubrication so that they have a problem with vaginal dryness during sexual intercourse. Finally, the sponge slightly increases the risk of toxic shock syndrome.

Advantages and Disadvantages

The main advantage of the sponge is that it is available over the counter, without a prescription, and thus it is a good stopgap method until a woman can see a physician for a more effective, prescription contraceptive. It can be inserted well before intercourse, so it does not interrupt lovemaking. Because it contains a spermicide, it provides some protection from sexually transmitted diseases.

The major disadvantage is its high failure rate. Also, costing about $1 per sponge, it is a rather expensive method for a woman who has intercourse frequently.

Douching (DOOSH-ing): Flushing out the inside of the vagina with a liquid.

DOUCHING

Some people believe that **douching** (flushing the vagina with a liquid) with any one of a variety of solutions is an effective contraceptive technique. A popular rumor among teenagers is that douching with Coca-Cola will prevent pregnancy. Unfortunately, while it is true that acidic solutions will kill sperm, it takes only seconds for some of the sperm to reach the cervical mucus; once there, they are free to continue moving up into the uterus, and no douching solution will reach them. The woman would have to be a championship sprinter to get herself up and douched soon enough. And the douche itself may even push some sperm up into the uterus. Douching, therefore, is just not effective as a contraceptive method.

WITHDRAWAL

Withdrawal: A method of birth control in which the man withdraws his penis from the vagina before he has an orgasm.

Withdrawal (coitus interruptus, "pulling out") is probably the most ancient form of birth control. (A reference to it is even found in Genesis 38:8–9, in the story of Onan; hence it is sometimes called *onanism,* although this term is also sometimes used for masturbation.) Withdrawal is still widely used throughout the world. The man withdraws his penis from the vagina before he has an orgasm and thus ejaculates outside the vagina. To be effective as contraception, the ejaculation must occur completely away from the woman's vulva.

Effectiveness

Withdrawal is not very effective as a method of birth control. The failure rate is somewhere around 20 percent. Failures occur for several reasons: The few drops of fluid that come out of the penis during arousal may carry enough sperm for conception to occur; if ejaculation occurs outside the vagina but near or on the vulva, sperm may still get into the vagina and continue up into the uterus; and sometimes the man simply does not withdraw in time.

Side Effects

Withdrawal produces no direct physical side effects. However, over long periods of time, it may contribute to producing sexual dysfunctions in the man, such as premature ejaculation, and also sexual dysfunction in the woman.

Advantages and Disadvantages

The major advantage of withdrawal is that it is the only last-minute method; it can be used when nothing else is available, although if the situation is this desperate, one might consider abstinence or some other form of sexual expression such as mouth-genital sex as alternatives. Obviously, withdrawal requires no prescription, and it is completely free.

One major disadvantage is that withdrawal is not very effective. In addition, it requires exceptional motivation on the part of the man, and it may be very psychologically stressful to him. He must constantly maintain a kind of self-conscious control. The woman may worry about whether he really will withdraw in time, and the situation is certainly less than ideal for her to have an orgasm.

Rhythm method: A method of birth control that involves abstaining from intercourse around the time the woman ovulates.

FERTILITY AWARENESS METHODS (RHYTHM)

Rhythm (fertility awareness) is the only form of "natural" birth control and is therefore the only method officially approved by the Roman Catholic Church. It requires abstaining from intercourse during the woman's fertile period (around ovulation). There are actually several rhythm methods, depending on how the woman's fertile period is determined.

The Calendar Method

The calendar method is the simplest rhythm method. It is based on the assumption that ovulation occurs about 14 days before the onset of menstruation. It works best for the woman with the perfectly regular 28-day cycle. She should ovulate on day 14, and almost surely on one of days 13 to 15. Three days are added in front of that period (previously deposited sperm may result in conception), and 2 days are added after it (to allow for long-lasting eggs); thus the couple must abstain from day 10 to day 17. Therefore even for the woman with perfectly regular cycles, 8 days of abstinence are required in the middle of each cycle.

The woman who is not perfectly regular must keep a record of her cycles for at least 6 months, and preferably a year. From this she determines the length of her shortest cycle and the length of her longest cycle. The preovulatory safe period is then calculated by subtracting 18 from the number of days in the shortest cycle, and the postovulatory safe period is calculated by subtracting 11 from the number of days in the longest cycle (see Table 8.2). Thus for a woman who is somewhat irregular—say, with cycles varying from 26 to 34 days in length—a period of abstinence from day 8 to day 23 (a total of 16 days) would be required.

The Basal Body Temperature Method

A somewhat more accurate method for determining ovulation is the basal body temperature (BBT) method. The principle behind this was discussed in Chapters 6

Table 8.2
Determining the Fertile Period Using the Calendar Method*

Shortest Cycle (Days)	Day Fertile Period Begins	Longest Cycle (Days)	Day Fertile Period Ends
22	4	23	12
23	5	24	13
24	6	25	14
25	7	26	15
26	(8)	27	16
27	9	28	17
28	10	29	18
29	11	30	19
30	12	31	20
31	13	32	21
32	14	33	22
		34	(23)
		35	24

Example: If a woman's cycles vary in length from 26 days to 34 days, she can be fertile any time between days 8 and 23 of the cycle, and she must therefore abstain from day 8 to day 23.

* See text for further explanation.
Source: After E. Havemann (1967). Birth control. New York: Time-Life, p. 23.

and 7. The woman takes her temperature every day immediately upon waking. During the preovulatory phase her temperature will be at a fairly constant low level. On the day of ovulation it drops (although this does not always occur), and on the day after ovulation it rises sharply, staying at that high level for the rest of the cycle. Intercourse would be safe beginning about three days after ovulation. Some of the psychological stresses involved in using this method have been noted previously. As a form of contraception, the BBT method has a major disadvantage in that it determines safe days only *after* ovulation; theoretically, according to the method, there are no safe days before ovulation. Thus the BBT method is probably best used in combination with the calendar method, which determines the preovulatory safe period; the BBT method determines the postovulatory safe period.

The Cervical Mucus (Ovulation) Method

Cervical mucus method: A type of rhythm method of birth control in which the woman determines when she ovulates by checking her cervical mucus.

Another rhythm method was deveoped by Evelyn and John Billings (Billings et al., 1974). Their method is based on variations over the cycle in the mucus produced by the cervix. It works in the following way:

There are generally a few days just after menstruation during which no mucus is produced and there is a general sensation of vaginal dryness. This is a relatively safe period. Then there are a number of days of mucus discharge around the middle of the cycle. On the first days, the mucus is white or cloudy and tacky. The amount increases, and the mucus becomes clearer, until there are one or two *peak days*, when the mucus is like raw egg white—clear, slippery, and stringy. There is also a sensation of vaginal lubrication. Ovulation occurs within 24 hours after the last peak day. Abstinence is required from the first day of mucus discharge until four days after the peak days. After that the mucus, if present, is cloudy or white, and intercourse is safe.

The Billingses believe that women can be taught to use this method very effectively.

The Sympto-Thermal Method

Sympto-thermal method: A type of rhythm method of birth control combining both the basal body temperature and the cervical mucus method.

The sympto-thermal method combines two rhythm methods in order to produce better effectiveness. The woman records changes in her cervical mucus (symptoms) as well as her basal body temperature (thermal). The combination of the two should give a more accurate determination of the time of ovulation.

Effectiveness

The effectiveness of the rhythm method varies considerably, depending on a number of factors, but basically it is not a very effective method (giving rise to its nickname, "Vatican roulette," and a number of old jokes like, "What do they call people who use the rhythm method?" Answer: "Parents"). The typical failure rate is about 20 percent; there tend to be fewer failures when the woman's cycle is very regular and when the couple are highly motivated and have been well instructed in the methods.

On the other hand, the effectiveness of the rhythm method depends partly on one's purpose in using it: whether for preventing pregnancy absolutely or for spacing pregnancies. If absolute pregnancy prevention is the goal (as it would be, for example, for an unmarried teenager), the method is just not effective enough. But if the couple simply wish to space pregnancies farther apart than would occur naturally, the method will probably accomplish this. Knowing when the woman's fertile times occur can also improve the effectiveness of other methods of contraception.

For many users of the rhythm method, its main advantage is that it is considered an acceptable method of birth control by the Roman Catholic Church.

The method has no side effects except possible psychological stress, and it is cheap. It is easily reversible. It also helps the woman become more aware of her body's functioning. Finally, the method requires cooperation from both partners, which may be considered either an advantage or a disadvantage.

Its main disadvantages are its high failure rate and the psychological stress it may cause. Periods of abstinence of at least eight days, and possibly as long as two or three weeks, are necessary, which is an unacceptable requirement for many couples. Actually, the rhythm method would seem best suited to people who do not like sex very much.

A certain amount of time, usually at least six months, is required to collect the data needed to make the method work. Thus one cannot simply begin using it on the spur of the moment.

Finally, a risk associated with the method has been discovered. Some research shows that when the method fails and a pregnancy occurs, there is a higher percentage of babies with birth defects born as a result (Berger, 1980; Iffy & Wingate, 1970). Apparently this occurs because such pregnancies are a resut of intercourse *after* the "safe" period, and thus an overripe egg is fertilized; this may create a higher incidence of chromosomal defects and abnormal development. The evidence on this point is mixed, however.

STERILIZATION

Sterilization: A surgical procedure by which an individual is made sterile, that is, incapable of reproducing.

Sterilization is a surgical procedure whereby an individual is made permanently sterile, that is, unable to reproduce. Sterilization is a rather emotion-laden topic for a number of reasons. It conjures up images of government-imposed programs of *involuntary* sterilization in which groups of people—possibly the mentally retarded, criminals, or members of some minority group—are sterilized so that they cannot reproduce. (The following discussion deals only with voluntary sterilization used as a method of contraception for those who want no more children or who want no children at all.) Some people confuse sterilization with castration, though the two are quite different. This is also an emotional topic because sterilization means the end of one's capacity to reproduce, which is very basic to gender roles and gender identity. The ability to impregnate and the ability to bear a child are very important in cultural definitions of manhood and womanhood. It is hoped that as gender roles beome more flexible in our society and as concern about reproduction is replaced by a concern for limiting population size, the word "sterilization" will no longer be so frightening.

Most physicians are conservative about performing sterilizations; they want to make sure that the patient has made a firm decision on his or her own and will not be back a couple of months later wanting to have the procedure reversed. The physician has an obligation to follow the principle of "informed consent." This means explaining the procedures involved, telling the patient about the possible risks and advantages, discussing alternative methods, and answering any questions the patient has. Only after the patient has been so informed should the doctor obtain her or his written consent to have the surgery performed.

Despite this conservatism, both male sterilization and female sterilization have become increasingly popular as methods of birth control, and the number performed per year rose phenomenally beginning in the 1970s. Among white couples married

15 to 19 years, 4 percent had vasectomies in 1965, compared with 20 percent in 1975 (Westoff & Jones, 1977). Sterilization is the most common method of birth control for married couples in the United States (Pratt et al., 1984). Currently 30 percent of married white women and 20 percent of married white men are sterilized, as are 48 percent of married black women and 2 percent of married black men (Mosher, 1990).

Male Sterilization

Vasectomy (vas-EK-tuh-mee): A surgical procedure for male sterilization involving severing of the vas deferens.

The male sterilization operation is called a vasectomy, so named for the vas deferens, which is tied or cut (see Figure 8.10). It can be done in a physician's office under local anesthesia and requires only about 20 minutes to perform. The physician makes a small incision on one side of the upper part of the scrotum. The vas is then separated from the surrounding tissues, tied off, and cut. The procedure is then repeated on the other side, and the incisions are sewn up. For a day or two the man may have to refrain from strenuous activity and be careful not to pull the incision apart. A new *no-scalpel vasectomy* procedure has been deveoped recently (Liskin et al., 1992).

FIGURE 8.10
The procedure for doing a vasectomy.

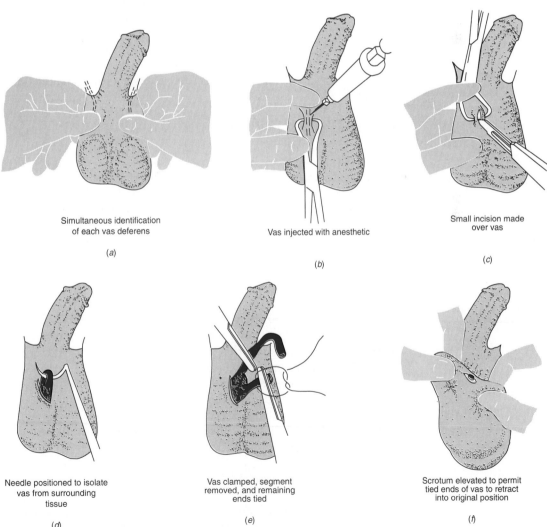

Simultaneous identification
of each vas deferens

(a)

Vas injected with anesthetic

(b)

Small incision made
over vas

(c)

Needle positioned to isolate
vas from surrounding
tissue

(d)

Vas clamped, segment
removed, and remaining
ends tied

(e)

Scrotum elevated to permit
tied ends of vas to retract
into original position

(f)

It involves making just a tiny pierce in the scrotum and has an even lower rate of complications than a standard vasectomy.

Typically, the man can return to having intercourse within a few days. It should not be assumed that he is sterile yet, however. There may still be some stray sperm lurking in his ducts beyond the point of the incision. All sperm are generally gone after 10 ejaculations, and their absence should by confirmed by semen analysis. Until this confirmation is made, an additional method of birth control should be used.

Misunderstandings about the vasectomy abound. In fact, a vasectomy creates no physical changes that interfere with erection. Neither does it interfere in any way with sex hormone production; the testes continue to manufacture testosterone and secrete it into the bloodstream. Men with vasectomies will not develop high-pitched voices! Neither does a vasectomy interfere with the process or sensation of ejaculation. As was noted earlier, virtually all the fluid of the ejaculate is produced by the seminal vesicles and prostate, and the incision is made long before that point in the duct system. Thus the ejaculate is completely normal, except that it does not contain any sperm.

How It Works

The vasectomy makes it impossible for sperm to move beyond the cut in the vas. Thus the vasectomy prevents sperm from being in the ejaculate.

Effectiveness

The vasectomy is essentially 100 percent effective; it has a failure rate of 0.1 percent. Failures occur because stray sperm are still present during the first few ejaculations after surgery, because the physician did not successfully sever the vas, or because the ends of the vas have grown back together.

Side Effects

The physical side effects of the vasectomy are minimal. In about 5 percent of cases, there is a minor complication from the surgery, such as inflammation of the vas (Gould, 1974).

Some psychologically based sexual problems such as impotency may arise. Thus the man's attitude toward having a vasectomy is extremely important.

Reversibility

Quite a bit of effort has been devoted to developing techniques for reversing vasectomies (the surgical procedure for reversal is termed *vasovasostomy*) and to developing vasectomy techniques that are more reversible. At present, using sophisticated microsurgery techniques, pregnancy rates are around 50 percent (Hatcher et al., 1990; Yarbro & Howards, 1987). In making a decision about whether to have a vasectomy, though, it should be assumed that it is irreversible.

It appears that after a vasectomy some men begin forming antibodies to their own sperm. Because these antibodies destroy sperm, they might contribute further to the irreversibility of the vasectomy.

Advantages and Disadvantages

The major advantages of the vasectomy are its effectiveness and its minimal health risks. Once performed, it requires no further thought or planning on the man's part. As a permanent, long-term method of contraception, it is very cheap. The operation itself is simple—much simpler than the female sterilization procedures—and requires no hospitalization or absence from work. Finally, it is one of the few methods that allow the man to assume contraceptive responsibility.

The permanency of the vasectomy may be either an advantage or a disadvantage. If permanent contraception is desired, the method is certainly much better than something like birth control pills, which must be used repeatedly. But if the couple change their minds and decide that they want to have another child, the permanency is a distinct disadvantage. Some men put several samples of their sperm in a frozen sperm bank so that artificial insemination can be performed if they do decide to have another child after a vasectomy.

Another disadvantage of the vasectomy is the various psychological problems that might result if the man sees sterilization as a threat to his masculinity or virility. However, long-term studies of vasectomized men provide no evidence of such psychological problems (Population Information Program, 1983). In studies done around the world, the majority of vasectomized men say that they have no regrets about having had the sterilization performed, that they would recommend it to others, and that there has been no change or else an improvement in their happiness and sexual satisfaction in marriage. Fewer than 5 percent of vasectomized men report psychological problems such as decreased libido or depression, and this rate is no higher than in control samples of unvasectomized men.

Finally, if a married couple use the vasectomy as a permanent method of birth control, the woman is not protected if she has intercourse with someone other than her husband.

Female Sterilization

Two surgical techniques are used to sterilize a woman: minilaparotomy and laparoscopy (tubal ligation or "having the tubes tied" are terms that are also heard). These techniques differ in terms of the type of procedure used. Both are performed under local or general anesthesia, and both involve blocking the fallopian tubes in some way so that sperm and egg cannot meet.

Minilaparotomy: A method of female sterilization.

In a *minilaparotomy* ("minilap"), a small incision (less than 3 centimeters, or about 1 inch long) is made in the abdomen. Each fallopian tube is in turn gently pulled to the opening. Each tube is blocked either by cutting and tying off the ends or by applying a small clip; the tubes are then allowed to slip back into place. With

FIGURE 8.11
Two methods for performing a tubal ligation or minilaparotomy. In (a) the fallopian tubes are tied off and the loop is cut: the cut ends then scar over. In (b) the tubes are tied in two places and the section between is cut and removed.

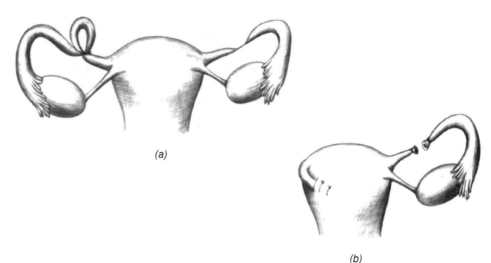

(a)

(b)

the *laparoscopy,* a magnifying instrument is inserted into the abdomen. The doctor uses it to identify the fallopian tubes and then blocks them by electrocoagulation or by clips. Either procedure takes only about 10 to 20 minutes and does not require that the woman spend the night in the hospital.

These female sterilization procedures do not interfere with the ovaries, and therefore the production of sex hormones continues normally; thus a tubal ligation does not bring on premature menopause or cause the woman to grow a beard. Some of the misunderstandings concerning female sterilization procedures arise from confusion of these procedures with hysterectomy (surgical removal of the uterus) or oophorectomy (surgical removal of the ovaries, which does impair hormonal functioning). These latter two operations do produce sterility, but they are generally performed for purposes other than sterilization, for example, removal of tumors.

How It Works

Female sterilization procedures make it impossible for the egg to move down the fallopian tube toward the uterus. They also prevent sperm from reaching the egg.

Effectiveness

These procedures are essentially 100 percent effective. The failure rate of 0.4 percent is due to an occasional rejoining of the ends of the fallopian tubes.

Side Effects

Occasionally there are side effects arising from the surgery, such as infections, hemorrhaging, and problems related to the anesthetic. Generally, only 1 to 2 percent of women undergoing the surgery experience complications. A small percentage of women have long-term side effects including menstrual problems (dysmenorrhea or irregular cycles) or benign breast lumps (Vorherr et al., 1983).

Reversibility

Highly refined microsurgery techniques make it possible to reverse female sterilization in some cases. The success rate varies considerably depending on the method used to perform the sterilization. Pregnancy rates range between 45 percent and 80 percent (Hatcher et al., 1990). However, in deciding whether to have sterilization surgery, a woman should assume that it is irreversible.

Advantages and Disadvantages

Female sterilization has some of the same advantages as male sterilization in terms of effectiveness, permanence, and cheapness when used for long-term contraception.

Compared with male sterilization methods, the methods of female sterilization are somewhat more complex. A hospital stay may be required, although generally the procedures can be performed on an outpatient basis.

PSYCHOLOGICAL ASPECTS: ATTITUDES TOWARD CONTRACEPTION

It is a favorite old saying among Planned Parenthood workers that contraceptives are only as effective as the people who use them. That is, no contraceptive method is effective if it is not used or if it is used improperly. Thus the user is at least as important as all the technology of contraception.

Each year in the United States 1 million teenagers (mostly unmarried) become pregnant; 30,000 of those pregnancies happen to girls 15 years of age and younger (Byrne, 1983). Approximately 16 percent of teenage women become premaritally pregnant (Zelnik & Kanter, 1980). It is not an overstatement, then, to say that teenage pregnancy is at epidemic proportions. Approximately 30 to 40 percent of these unwanted pregnancies are terminated by abortion (Stevens-Simon & White, 1991), 50 percent result in live births (to single teenagers or to couples joined in "shotgun" matrimony), and the remainder end in miscarriage.

The great majority of these unwanted pregnancies are the result of the failure of sexually active persons to use contraceptives responsibly. For example, in one well-sampled study it was found that 26 percent of sexually active 15- to 19-year-old girls never used contraception, and an additional 45 percent did so only sometimes (Zelnik & Kanter, 1977). That is, 71 percent never used contraception or did so inconsistently.

If we are to understand this problem and take effective steps to solve it, we must understand the psychology of contraceptive use and nonuse. Many researchers have been investigating this issue.

When adolescents are asked why they do not use contraceptives, the reasons they give tend to fall into the following categories (Morrison, 1985):

1. Beliefs about their own fertility. "I thought I (or my partner) couldn't get pregnant."

2. Wanting to become pregnant, or at least not minding if they did become pregnant.

3. Problems in obtaining contraception. Many factors may be involved, such as not knowing where to get contraceptives, feeling that it is a "hassle" to get contraceptives, or expecting that they would be too expensive to buy.

4. Intercourse is unplanned, and therefore contraception is not planned.

5. Negative attitudes and feelings about contraception. For example, some feel that contraceptives are messy or embarrassing; others have religious objections; and some believe that contraceptives are dangerous.

Social scientists have developed several theories to explain teenagers' use and nonuse of contraceptives. These theories tend to fall into one of three categories: (1) those theories that view contraceptive behavior as a result of a decision-making process (an example of such a theory is provided in Focus 8.2); (2) those theories that view contraceptive behavior as the outcome of psychological development; and (3) those theories that focus on personality and emotions, such as Donn Byrne's work on erotophobia. Let us look first at the developmental theories, and then at Byrne's theory.

Developmental models look at the process of psychological development during adolescence (e.g., Jorgensen, 1980; Morrison, 1985). Teenagers may find their values to be firmly in line with their parents' values, but their behavior increasingly conforms to the norms of their peer group. A conflict between values and behavior results (Zabin et al., 1984). More specifically, teenagers may hold their parents' conservative values about premarital sex, which prize abstinence and therefore nonuse of contraceptives. Meanwhile, their actual behavior conforms to that of the peer group and they engage in premarital intercourse. The hope is that as adolescents mature, their behavior and values will become more consistent with each other.

Social psychologist Donn Byrne (1983; Fisher et al., 1988) focuses on a dimen-

The Social Psychology of Contraception: Taking Chances

Nearly one-third of all pregnant women in the United States terminate the pregnancy with an abortion (Henshaw, 1990). This raises the following question: Why should women who have readily available, highly effective contraceptives as an option choose not to use them and instead undergo the expensive and possibly humiliating or traumatic experience of abortion, or of unwanted pregnancy? Sociologist Kristin Luker set out to answer this question. To do so, she collected data at an abortion clinic in northern California, analyzing the medical records of 500 women seen at the clinic and doing in-depth interviews with 50 women undergoing abortions at the clinic. As a result, she developed a theory of the social psychology of contraceptive use (and nonuse) among women.

Prior to Luker's work, there were two prevailing theories about why women have unwanted pregnancies. The first theory, held widely by family planning agencies, is that women have unwanted pregnancies because they lack knowledge about or access to contraceptives. The second theory, growing out of psychoanalytic thought, holds that women have adequate contraceptive skills but fail to use them because of internal psychological conflict. The first theory was inadequate to explain the cases of the women Luker studied, since over half of them had previously used a prescription method (usually the pill), and 86 percent had used some method of birth control in the past; further, the majority of

them displayed some or considerable birth control information when interviewed. Clearly the women had skills that they did not use. This makes the second theory seem more reasonable. However, Luker also rejected that theory. First, she argued that the data upon which this theory is based are biased, since the psychiatrist typically sees only the unwanted pregnancies that lead to severe disturbance. Second, this theory ignores social influences on contraceptive behavior, which are enormous.

As an alternative, Luker developed a theory in which unwanted pregnancy results from "contraceptive risk-taking" behavior which is the result of a conscious decision-making process. As such, the unwanted pregnancy is not indicative of neurotic conflict or irrationality; instead, it becomes an analyzable process much like the decision not to fasten one's seat belt when driving. According to Luker's theory, the woman engages in a cost-benefit analysis (although she might not be able to articulate it) in which she weighs the costs and benefits of contraception, the costs of pregnancy, and the possible benefits of pregnancy. The woman must assess the probability of pregnancy (which is actually unknown, even to the scientist), and she generally decides that it is very low. Thus if there are many costs associated with contraception, or many benefits associated with pregnancy, the woman begins to engage in risk taking.

sion of personality he calls erotophobia-erotophilia. According to his analysis there are five steps in effective contraception:

1. The person must acquire and remember accurate information about contraception.

2. The person must acknowledge that there is a likelihood of engaging in sexual intercourse. Contraceptive preparation, of course, makes sense only if one has

What are the costs of contraception? First there are a number of social-psychological costs. Using, and planning to use, contraceptives involves acknowledging that one is a sexually active woman, and this is difficult for many women, even today. Using a contraceptive such as the pill signals that one is always sexually available, and this decreases the woman's right to say "no." Some methods, particularly using foam and using the diaphragm, decrease the spontaneity of sex, and this is a psychological cost. Second, there are structurally created costs—women must call for an appointment with a physician for some methods, and they may be told that no appointments are available for several weeks. They are expected to have high motivation and use abstinence, or call repeatedly for appointments. Even the "drugstore" methods (foam, condoms) involve going into the store and openly acknowledging to the world—or at least the people in the store—that one is sexually active. Third, there may be costs to the relationship—the woman may fear negative reaction from the man if she uses a contraceptive such as foam or a diaphragm, or rejection if she asks him to use a condom. Finally, there are biological-medical costs, particularly fears of side effects from the pill. The most frequent concern of women in the study was potential weight gain from using the pill.

Luker also points out that benefits to pregnancy may be anticipated. Pregnancy is proof of womanhood, and this may be particularly important in a society with a fluctuating view of gender roles. Pregnancy may enhance one's feeling of self-worth, proving that one is a valuable person who can produce children. Unarguably, pregnancy is a proof of fertility, and some women may feel a need for this proof—fully two-thirds of the women interviewed said that their gynecologists had told them they would have trouble getting pregnant because of problems in their reproductive system. Pregnancy can be a way of accomplishing things with significant others such as parents, perhaps rebelling against them or gaining independence. Pregnancy may force the man to define the relationship more clearly—perhaps going from living together to marriage. Finally, the pure excitement of risk taking itself may be fun for some—the Evel Knievels of contraception.

Given all this, the woman, according to Luker, weighs the costs and benefits and often decides to take risks. The costs and benefits, of course, vary from one woman to the next at different times in a woman's life. The costs of pregnancy to a single college student are probably far greater than they are to a married woman with two children who would rather have no more. Risk taking, if successful, may foster more risk taking—"If I got away with it once, I surely can again." And so the cycle goes, eventually ending in an unwanted pregnancy. But the costs of this failure are not terribly high now, with the legalization and availability of abortion. Accordingly, some women leave the abortion clinic with no plans to use an effective method in the future, and the risk taking begins again.

On a more hopeful note, Luker argues that the more aware women become of their decision-making process, the more effective they will become in using contraceptives to achieve the goals they truly desire.

Source: Kristin Luker. (1975). *Taking chances: Abortion and the decision not to contracept*. Berkeley: University of California Press.

some expectations of having intercourse. Gender-role socialization has made it particularly difficult for women to acknowledge such expectations.

3. The person must obtain the contraceptive. This may involve a visit to a doctor or to a drugstore or Planned Parenthood clinic.

4. The person must communicate with his or her partner about contraception. Otherwise, both may assume that the other will take care of things.

5. The person must actually use the method of contraception.

Erotophobia: Feeling guilty and fearful about sex.

Erotophilia: Feeling comfortable with sex, lacking in feelings of guilt and fear about sex.

According to Byrne's analysis, a number of psychological factors can intervene in any of these five steps, making the person either more likely or less likely to use contraceptives effectively. These factors include attitudes and emotions, information, expectations, and fantasies.

Attitudes and emotions play an important role. One particular dimension is *erotophilia-erotophobia* (Byrne, 1983; Fisher et al., 1983; Byrne, 1977). Erotophobes don't discuss sex, have sex lives that are influenced by guilt and fear of social disapproval, have intercourse infrequently with few partners, and are shocked by sexually explicit films. Erotophiles are just the opposite—they discuss sex, they are relatively uninfluenced by sex guilt, they have intercourse more frequently with more partners, and they find sexually explicit films to be arousing. Research shows that erotophiles are more likely to be consistent, reliable contraceptive users. At every one of the five steps of contraceptive use, the erotophobes are more likely to fail. Research shows that they have less sex information than erotophiles do, and that, when exposed to the same sex information, erotophobes learn less than erotophiles do (Fisher et al., 1983). Because of their fearfulness, erotophobes are less likely to acknowledge that intercourse may occur, which makes contraceptive planning difficult (although extreme erotophobes are likely to abstain from sex completely, which definitely reduces the risk of unwanted pregnancy). Erotophobes also have more difficulty going to a doctor or a drugstore to obtain contraceptives. Erotophobes don't discuss sex or contraception very much, and therefore effective communication with their partner is unlikely to occur. And finally, erotophobes have trouble with the final step of actually using the contraceptive. An erotophobic male isn't going to be thrilled about pulling out a condom. An erotophobic female won't be thrilled with inserting a diaphragm or thinking about sex every day as she takes her pill.

Information is also an important factor in contraceptive use and nonuse. People who lack information about contraceptives and their correct use can scarcely use them effectively.

Expectations play an important role. When thinking about sex and contraception, people have some expectations about how likely it is that intercourse will result in pregnancy. Research shows that many people think that the chance is zero or close to it, expressing the expectation that "It can't happen to me" (see Focus 8.2). People with that expectation are unlikely to use contraceptives.

Although it is generally recognized that *fantasy* is an important part of sexual expression, only recently have scientists realized that fantasy may play an important role in contraceptive behavior (Byrne, 1983). Most of us have fantasies about sexual encounters, and we often try to make our real-life sexual encounters turn out like the "scripts" of our fantasies. An important shaper of our fantasies is the media. Through movies, television, and romance novels, we learn idealized techniques for kissing, holding, lovemaking. But the media's idealized versions of sex almost never include a portrayal of the use of contraceptives. When obstetrician Cliff Huxtable and lawyer Claire Huxtable of *Cosby* hop into bed together, they never show Cliff reaching for a condom or Claire's nightly routine of taking her pill. Thus our fantasy sex, shaped by the media, lacks contraception as part of the script. One exception occurred in the movie *Saturday Night Fever*. John Travolta, lying on top of a willing young woman in the back seat of a car, asks her if she is using a contraceptive. When she replies that she isn't, he zips his pants up and leaves. If teenagers saw lots of instances of their heroes and heroines behaving responsibly about contraception, it would probably influence their behavior. But right now that is not what the media gives them.

What are the solutions? Can this research and theorizing on the social psychology of contraceptive use be applied to reducing the teenage pregnancy problem? The most direct solution would be to have better programs of sex education in the schools. Many districts have no sex education programs, and those that do often skip the important issue of contraception, fearing that it is too controversial. Sex education programs would need to include a number of components that are typically missing (Gross & Bellew-Smith, 1983). These include legitimizing presex communication about sex and contraception (Milan & Kilmann, 1987); legitimizing the purchase and carrying of contraceptives; discussing how one weighs the costs and benefits of pregnancy, contraception, and abortion; legitimizing noncoital kinds of sexual pleasure, such as masturbation and oral-genital sex; and encouraging males to accept equal responsibility for contraception.

ABORTION

Abortion: The termination of a pregnancy.

In the past two decades, abortion (the termination of a pregnancy) has been a topic of considerable controversy in North America. Feminist groups talk of the woman's right to control her own body, while members of Right-to-Life groups speak of the fetus's rights. In 1973, the United States Supreme Court made two landmark decisions (*Roe v. Wade* and *Doe v. Bolton*) that essentially decriminalized abortion by denying the states the right to regulate early abortions. Since then, the number of abortions performed each year has risen steadily. However, the conservative Supreme Court of the 1990s has made some rulings that partly reverse the earlier decisions (see Chapter 22).

In other countries, policies on abortion vary widely. It is legal and widely practiced in Russia and Japan, parts of eastern and central Europe, and South America. The use of abortion in the developing nations of Africa and Asia is limited because of the scarcity of medical facilities.

This section will be about methods of abortion and the psychological aspects of abortion; the ethical and legal aspects will be discussed in Chapters 21 and 22.

Abortion Procedures

There are several methods of abortion; which one is used depends on how far the pregnancy has progressed.

Vacuum Curettage

Vacuum curettage: A method of abortion that is performed during the first trimester.

The vacuum curettage method (also called *vacuum suction,* and *vacuum aspiration*) can be performed during the first trimester of pregnancy and up to 18 weeks from the beginning of the last menstrual period (LMP). It is done on an outpatient basis with a local anesthetic. The procedure itself takes only about 10 minutes, and the woman stays in the doctor's office, clinic, or hospital for a few hours. It is the most widely used abortion procedure in the United States today, accounting for 94 percent of abortions (Koonin et al., 1991b).

The woman is prepared as she would be for a pelvic exam, and an instrument is inserted into the vagina; the instrument dilates (stretches open) the opening of the cervix. A tube is then inserted into this opening until one end is in the uterus. The other end is attached to a suction-producing apparatus, and the contents of the uterus, including the fetal tissue, are sucked out.

The vacuum curettage has become the most common method of early (first-trimester) abortion because it is simple and entails little risk. There are minor risks of uterine perforation, infection, hemorrhaging, and failure to remove all the fetal material.

FIGURE 8.12
A vacuum curettage
abortion.

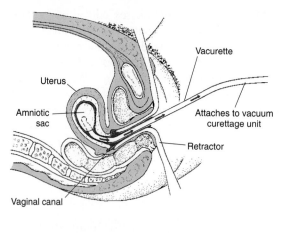

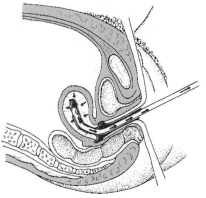

Dilation and Curettage

The *dilation and curettage* (D and C), or *dilatation and curettage,* is similar to the vacuum curettage, but it must be done in a hospital under a general anesthetic. It is also done from 8 to 20 weeks LMP.

As in the vacuum curettage, the cervical opening is dilated. Then a sharp metal loop, attached to the end of a long handle (the curette), is inserted into the uterus; it is used to scrape out the uterine contents.

The D and C is now rarely used in the United States because it requires hospitalization (and is therefore more expensive) and a general anesthetic. It also causes more discomfort, and the risks of complications such as uterine perforation, infection, and hemorrhaging are greater.

Yet a third procedure is the D and E (*dilation and evacuation*). It is used especially from 15 to 20 weeks LMP. It is somewhat similar to the D and C and vacuum curettage, except that the procedures are a bit more complicated because the fetus is relatively large by 15 to 20 weeks LMP.

Induced Labor

Saline-induced abortion: A method of abortion done in the late second trimester, involving inducing labor by injecting a saline solution into the amniotic sac.

During the late part of the second trimester, abortion is usually performed by inducing labor and a miscarriage. The most commonly used version of this method is the saline-induced abortion. A fine tube is inserted through the abdomen into the amniotic sac inside the uterus. Some amniotic fluid is removed through the tube, and an equal amount of saline solution is injected into the amniotic sac. Within several hours, the solution has caused labor to begin. The cervix dilates, and the fetus is expelled through the contractions of labor. A variation on this technique is the prostaglandin method. Prostaglandins (hormonelike substances that cause contractions) are injected into the amniotic sac (or intravenously or by means of a vaginal suppository) and cause labor.

Induced labor is used only for abortion if pregnancy has progressed late into the second trimester and accounts for only 1 percent of abortions in the United States (Koonin, 1991b). This method is both more hazardous and more costly ($350 to $750) than the previous methods. The most serious complications of the saline-induced method are shock and possibly death (if the technique is done carelessly and the saline solution gets into a bood vessel) and a bleeding disorder, although these are rare. The prostaglandin method has several advantages over the saline method: it induces labor more quickly, and the labor itself is shorter. The chances of excessive bleeding and retained placenta are higher with the prostaglandin method, however, and there is also the risk that the cervix may tear as a result of too rapid dilation. There is also some chance that a live fetus will be expelled. Less serious side effects such as nausea, vomiting, and diarrhea are more common with the prostaglandin method.

Traditionally it was thought that abortions should not be performed during weeks 13 to 15 because the uterus was too soft and the procedure was dangerous; the recommended procedure from 16 weeks on was saline-induced abortion. However, data indicate that the D and E is safe through weeks 13 to 15 and is safer than saline-induced abortion through week 20 (Centers for Disease Control, 1976).

Hysterotomy

Hysterotomy: A surgical method of abortion done in the late second trimester.

Hysterotomy is a surgical method of abortion that can be done from 16 to 24 weeks LMP. Essentially, a cesarean section is performed, and the fetus is removed. Hysterotomy is more serious and more expensive (around $1000) than the other methods, and there is greater risk of complications. It is done only rarely, but it may be useful if the pregnancy has progressed to the late second trimester and the woman's health is such that the induction methods should not be used.

A summary of statistics on death rates associated with the various methods of abortion is shown in Table 8.3.

Table 8.3
Summary of Death Rates Associated with Legal Abortion and with Normal Childbirth

Deaths per 100,000 legal abortions*	
Suction methods	0.5
Induced labor	4.0
Hysterotomy	58.9
Deaths per 100,000 normal childbirths	9.1
Blacks	22.0
Whites	6.5
Others	9.8

* Based on 4,500,000 abortions, Centers for Disease Control, 1985.
Sources: Centers for Disease Control. (1985). *Abortion surveillance report, 1981;* Tietze (1984); Koonin et al. (1991b).

Other Methods

There are several other abortion methods, but they are not widely used in North America either because they are still in the developmental stages or because they have not gained acceptance here.

Several mechanical methods of stimulating the uterus to induce abortion have been developed and are used widely in Japan (Manabe, 1969). They are simple to perform and inexpensive, but they have not become popular in the United States because they are associated with more blood loss and a greater chance of infection.

Menstrual regulation (also called *endometrial aspiration, preemptive abortion,* and *menstrual extraction*) is another technique. The uterine contents are sucked out before the period is due and before pregnancy has been confirmed.

Psychological Aspects

The discovery of an unwanted pregnancy sets off a complicated set of emotions, as well as a complex decision-making process. Initially women tend to feel anger and some anxiety (Shusterman, 1979). They then embark on a decision-making process studied by psychologist Carol Gilligan (1982). In this process women essentially weigh the need to think of themselves and protect their own welfare against the need to think of the welfare of the fetus. Even focusing only on the welfare of the fetus can lead to conflicting conclusions: Should I complete the pregnancy because the fetus has a right to life, or should I have an abortion because the fetus has a right to be born into a stable family with married parents who have completed their education and can provide good financial support? Many women in Gilligan's study showed

Table 8.4
Abortion Rates Around the World*

Country	No. of Abortions per Year	Abortion Rate	Abortion Ratio
Australia (1988)	63,200	16.6	20.4
Bulgaria (1987)	119,900	64.7	50.7
Canada (1987)	63,600	10.2	14.7
China (1987)	10,394,500	38.8	31.4
India (1987)[†]	588,400	3.0	2.2
Israel (1987)[†]	15,500	16.2	13.5
Italy (1987)[†]	191,500	15.3	25.7
Japan (1987)[†]	497,800	18.6	27.0
South Korea (1984)	528,000	53	43
Sweden (1987)	34,700	19.8	24.9
USSR (1987)[†]	6,818,000	111.9	54.9
U.S. (1985)	1,588,600	28.0	29.7
Vietnam (1980)[†]	170,600	14.6	8.2

* "Abortion rate" is the number of abortions per 1000 women aged 15 to 44. "Abortion ratio" is the number of abortions per 100 known pregnancies.
[†] Data are of unknown accuracy.
Source: Stanley K. Henshaw. (1990). Induced abortion: A world review, 1990. *Family Planning Perspectives,* 22(2), 76–89.

considerable psychological growth over the period in which they wrestled with these issues and made their decision.

The best scientific evidence indicates that most women do not experience severe negative psychological responses to abortion (Adler et al., 1990). When women are interviewed a year or so after their abortion, most show good adjustment (Burnell & Norfleet, 1987; Shusterman, 1979). Typically they do not feel guilt or sorrow over the decision. Instead, they report feeling relieved, satisfied, and relatively happy, and say that if they had the decision to make over again, they would do the same thing. Nonetheless, some women benefit from talking about their experience, and it is important that postabortion support groups be available (Lodl et al., 1984).

Research in this area raises many interesting questions. Women generally show good adjustment after having an abortion, but good adjustment compared with what? That is, what is the appropriate control or comparison group? One comparison group that could be studied is women who requested an abortion but were denied it. It would be important to know the consequences for their adjustment.

One group that has been studied is children who were born because an abortion request was denied. It is impossible to do this research in the United States now because abortion has been legal since 1973. However, in some other countries access to abortion depends upon obtaining official approval. One such country is Czechoslovakia. Researchers followed up 220 children born to women denied abortion (the "study group") and 220 children born to women who had not requested abortion; the children were studied when they were 9 years old and again when they were 14 to 16 years old (David, 1992; David & Matejcek, 1981). By age 14, 43 children from the study group, but only 30 of the controls, had been referred for counseling. Although there were no differences between the groups in tested intelligence, children in the study group did less well in school and were more likely to drop out. Teachers described them as less sociable and more hyperactive compared with the control group. At age 16, the boys (but not the girls) in the study group more frequently rated themselves as feeling neglected or rejected by their mothers, and felt that their mothers were less satisfied with them. By their early twenties, the study group reported less job satisfaction, more conflicts with coworkers and supervisors, and fewer and less satisfying friendships. Several other studies have found results similar to the Czechoslovakian one (David et al., 1988). These results point to the serious long-term consequences for children whose mothers would have preferred to have an abortion.

Men and Abortion

Only women become pregnant, and only women have abortions, but where do men enter the picture? Do they have a right to contribute to the decision to have an abortion? What are their feelings about abortion?

Sociologist Arthur Shostak and his colleagues (1984) surveyed 1000 male "abortion veterans." The most common reaction from the men was a sense of helplessness. Although most men are used to being in control, in this situation they are not, and the feeling of powerlessness is difficult for them. Most of the men also felt isolated, angry at themselves and their partners, and fearful of emotional and physical damage to the woman. Most of them tried to hide their stress and remain unemotional. Nonetheless, 26 percent thought of abortion as murder, and 81 percent said they thought about the child who might have been born. However, few men wanted to be able to overrule the woman's decision; they only wanted to share in it.

Although counseling for women undergoing abortion is a standard procedure, counseling is rarely available for the men who are involved. Given Shostak's findings, it is clear that such counseling is badly needed.

8.3

A Brief Summary of the Development of Sophisticated Methods of Contraception

Late 1700s	Casanova (1725–1798) popularizes and publicizes use of the sheath, or "English riding coat."
1798	Malthus urges "moral restraint" or abstinence.
1840s	Goodyear vulcanizes rubber. Production of rubber condoms soon follows.
1883	Mensinga invents the diaphragm.
1893	Harrison performs the first vasectomy.
1909	Richter uses the intrauterine silkworm gut.
1910–1920	Margaret Sanger pioneers in New York City; the term "birth control" is coined.
1930	Graffenberg publishes information documenting his 21 years of experience with the ring (silver and copper) and catgut as IUDs.
1930–1931	Knaus and Ogino elucidate "safe and unsafe" periods of the woman's menstrual cycle: the rhythm method.
1934	Corner and Beard isolate progesterone.
1937	Makepeace demonstrates that progesterone inhibits ovulation.
1950s	Abortions are utilized extensively in Japan.
1950–1960	Hormonal contraceptive research results in FDA approval of the use of the pill as a contraceptive in 1960.
1960s	Many Western nations liberalize abortion laws. Modern IUDs become available. Contraceptive sterilization becomes more acceptable. The laparoscopic tubal ligation technique is developed.
1973	The United States Supreme Court rules on abortion. The first "minipill," or low-dose progestin pill, wins FDA approval. The Shot is provided in over 50 nations.

Source: Robert A. Hatcher et al. (1976). *Contraceptive technology, 1976–1977* (8th ed.). New York: Irvington.

NEW ADVANCES

According to some, a really good method of contraception is not yet available. The highly effective methods either are permanent (sterilization) or have associated health risks (the pill). Other, safer methods (such as the condom and the diaphragm) have appreciable failure rates. Most of the methods are for women, not men. Because of the dissatisfaction with the currently available methods, contraception research continues. A few of the more promising possibilities for the future are discussed below.

Male Methods

Several possibilities for male contraception are being explored (Goldstein, 1986; Hatcher et al., 1990). One is the use of hormones in a "male pill" that would stop spermatogenesis (much as the pill inhibits ovulation in women). Gn-RH accomplishes this. Unfortunately, it inhibits not only sperm production but also sex drive, and therefore is considered unacceptable. The addition of androgens counters this side effect. Theoretically at least, sperm production and hormone production are separate processes, so it should be possible to stop sperm production without affecting sex drive.

Chinese scientists have done large-scale studies on the use of *gossypol* as a male contraceptive (National Coordinating Group on Male Antifertility Agents, 1978; Peyster, 1979). Gossypol is derived from the cotton plant. The Chinese accidentally discovered in the 1950s that cooking with cottonseed oil could cause infertility and that the effect seemed to be stronger in men. Gossypol appears to be capable of reducing the sperm count to zero, and a study of 4000 men over a period of six months indicated that it was 99.89 percent effective in preventing pregnancy. Unfortunately, by U.S. standards the drug is rather toxic (it has been used as a pesticide), so it is unlikely that the FDA will approve it for use in the United States.

Ultrasound applied to the testes has been shown to inhibit sperm production in several species including humans, so this possibility is also being explored.

Female Methods

A *vaginal ring*, shaped like a diaphragm and containing hormones, should be on the market shortly (Hatcher et al., 1986). When it contains progestin, it apparently does not suppress ovulation but rather affects the cervical mucus, making it impenetrable to sperm. Other rings contain both estrogen and progestin. Clinical trials indicate that the ring has a typical failure rate of 3.7 percent, making it about as effective as the combination pill (Turner, 1990).

Analogous to the reversible valve in the vas, the possibility of improved reversibility of the female sterilization procedure is being explored. One promising lead is to inject a fast-setting latex substance into the tubes to block them; a line is attached to this "plug" so that it can be pulled out if it is desired for the woman to become pregnant.

A female condom underwent field trials in the United States in 1991 and was expected to be available over the counter by late 1992. It is made of polyurethane and resembles a clear balloon (see Figure 8.13). There are two rings in it, at either end. One ring is inserted into the vagina much like a diaphragm, while the other is spread over the vaginal entrance. Field trials indicate that it is approximately as effective as standard male condoms for contraceptive purposes and that it has a lower tear rate. It is likely to be more effective than male condoms at protecting women from sexually transmitted diseases, including AIDS (Millenson, 1992).

In 1986 French researchers announced the development of a new drug called RU 486 (mifepristone) (Couzinet et al., 1986; Ulmann et al., 1990). It can be regarded as a postcoital pill; that is, it can be used after intercourse when there is a fear that pregnancy has occurred. It has a powerful antiprogesterone effect, causing the endometrium of the uterus to be sloughed off, bringing about a very early abortion. It is administered as a tablet followed 2 days later by a small dose of prostaglandin, which increases contractions of the uterus, helping to expel the embryo. It is used within 10 days of an expected but missed menstrual period. In initial studies it was effective in 80 to 85 percent of the cases. When combined with prostaglandin, the success rate rose to 96 percent (Silvestre, et al., 1990; Ulmann et al., 1990). Early research has found little evidence of side effects.

In France today, more than a quarter of women who decide to terminate an

RU 486: The newly developed "abortion pill."

FIGURE 8.13
*A new condom for women,
designed to line the vagina.*

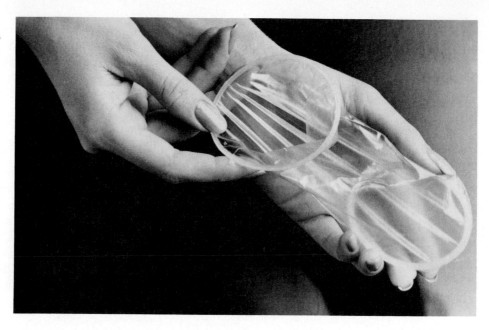

early pregnancy choose RU 486 rather than conventional abortion methods (Ulmann et al., 1990). However, the drug is not available in the United States. It is highly controversial because antiabortion groups classify it as a method of abortion, and their political pressures have blocked its entry into the United States. Scientists who developed the drug, as well as prochoice groups, prefer not to call it an abortion method, but rather a method for the induction of menstruation or a contragestational drug—it cannot properly be called a contraceptive because it does not prevent conception, but it does prevent gestation. While the argument rages on, American women do not have the option of choosing it.

Ironically, given the controversy, RU 486 was not developed in a contraceptive research program but rather in a basic research program, and it has many potential applications unrelated to the termination of pregnancy. For example, it might be used to treat cancers that are progesterone-related. It is currently being tested in Canada for the treatment of breast cancer (Stephens, 1992). Yet research on these possibilities cannot proceed in the United States because of the political pressure of antiabortion groups.

Methods for Either Men or Women

An immunologic approach might be used on either women or men. Since some cases of infertility are caused by the formation of antibodies that destroy sperm (see Chapter 7), it would seem that if antibody formation could be stimulated, it would work as a contraceptive, although it would probably be a permanent method. Other immunologic methods, such as immunizing the woman against placental hormones so that implantation will not occur, are also being explored (Hatcher et al., 1986).

A contraceptive nasal spray for either men or women is being investigated (Bergquist et al., 1979). The spray contains a hypothalamic releasing factor (Gn-RH). It reduces the production of gonadotropins (pituitary hormones) and thus prevents ovulation in women and, speculatively, sperm production in men. Perhaps a common question of the future between men and women will be, "Did you take a sniff today?

FIGURE 8.14
The controversy over RU-486. (a) Prolife forces protest against RU-486. (b) July, 1992. An American woman identified only as Leona (left) is led away in tears by her physician, Dr. Louise Tyrer, after the stress of a news conference in New York. Leona, who is pregnant, tried to bring the abortion pill, RU-486, into the United States from Britain. Because the pill was banned in the United States, it was seized by customs officials at J. F. Kennedy Airport.

(a)

(b)

Table 8.5
Summary of Information on Methods of Contraception and Abortion

Method	Effectiveness Rating	Lowest Failure Rate, %	Typical Failure Rate, %	Death Rate (per 100,000 Women)	Yearly Costs, $*	Advantages	Disadvantages
Combined birth control pills	Excellent	0.1	3	1.6–6.3	117	Highly effective, not used at time of coitus, improved menstrual cycles	Cost, possible side effects, must be taken daily
Progestin-only pills	Excellent	0.5	2.5	—	117		
Implant (Norplant)	Excellent	—	0.04	—	110[†]	Highly effective, does not require memory, not used at time of coitus	Cost, side effects yet to be documented
IUD	Excellent	0.8	3	1.0	175[‡]	Requires no memory or motivation	Side effects, may be expelled
Condom	Very good	4	12	1.7[§]	50	Easy to use, protection from STDs	Interference with coitus, continual expense
Diaphragm with cream or jelly	Good	2	18	2.0[§]	75	No side effects, inexpensive	Aesthetic objections
Cervical cap with spermicide	Good	8	18	2.0[§]	100	—	—
Sponge	Fair	14–28	17–25	2.0[§]	150	Availability	Continual expense
Vaginal foam	Fair	3	21	2.0[§]	50	Easy to use, availability	Messy, continual expense
Withdrawal	Poor to fair	4	18	2.0[§]	None	No cost	Requires high motivation
Rhythm	Poor to fair	2–9	20	2.5[§]	None	No cost, accepted by Roman Catholic Church	Requires high motivation, prolonged abstinence, not all women can use
Unprotected intercourse	Poor	90	90	10[§]	None[¶]		
Legal abortion, first trimester	Excellent	0	0	0.5	200–400	Available when other methods fail	Expense, moral or psychological unacceptability
Sterilization, male	Excellent	0	0.1	0.3	250**	Is permanent and highly effective	Is permanent
Sterilization, female	Excellent	0	0.4	3.0	850**	Is permanent and highly effective	Is permanent, expense

* Based on 150 acts of intercourse. Prices are provided by Wisconsin Planned Parenthood, 1992, for full-paying clients. Prices are reduced for those with low incomes. Prices are higher for private physicians.

† Based on a cost of $550 for Norplant and insertion and use for five years.

‡ Based on a cost of $150 for the IUD plus the cost of the insertion by the physician, and the assumption that the IUD will be used for one year.

§ Based on the death rate for pregnancies resulting from the method.

¶ But having a baby is expensive.

** These are one-time-only costs.

Source: R. A. Hatcher et al. (1990). Contraceptive technology, 1990–1992. New York Irvington.

Summary

Table 8.5 provides a comparative summary of the various methods of birth control discussed in this chapter.

Review Questions

1. Combination birth control pills contain the hormones _____ and _____.
2. The birth control pill works mainly by preventing ovulation. True or false?
3. Cancer is the major health risk associated with the use of the birth control pill. True or false?
4. The female sterilization technique in which each fallopian tube is in turn drawn to a small incision and then blocked off is called the _____.
5. The actual failure rate of the IUD is about 25 percent. True or false?
6. In order to be highly effective, the diaphragm must be used with a spermicidal cream or jelly. True or false?
7. The contraceptive sponge is 99 percent effective in preventing pregnancy. True or false?
8. The calendar method, the basal body temperature method, and the cervical mucus method are all variations on the _____ method of birth control.
9. Two highly effective methods of birth control that can be used by men are _____ and _____.
10. According to the research of Byrne, erotophobes are more likely than erotophiles to be consistent, reliable users of contraceptives. True or false?

(The answers to all review questions are at the end of the book, beginning on page 731.)

Questions for Thought, Discussion, and Debate

1. Do you think you are an erotophobe or an erotophile? In what ways do you think your erotophobia or erotophilia has affected or will affect your use of birth control?
2. Debate the following topic. Resolved: The birth control pill is a safe and effective method of birth control for most women.
3. In the United States, IUDs have become nearly unavailable because of lawsuits against companies that make them and concern over possible health risks. In contrast, in the People's Republic of China they are the mainstay of contraception, with 40 million in use. Which country has the better policy?
4. On your campus, as on all campuses, students probably are inconsistent in their use of birth control or use nothing even though they are sexually active. Design a program to improve birth control practices on your campus.

Suggestions for Further Reading

Gordon, Linda. (1990). *Woman's body, woman's right.* 2nd ed. New York: Penguin Books. This book provides a fascinating and enlightening social history of the development of birth control in America, from the outlawing of contraceptive methods in the early 1800s, to the pioneering efforts of Margaret Sanger, to the influences of the modern women's movement.

Hatcher, Robert A., et al. (1990). *Contraceptive technology 1990–1992.* New York: Irvington. This authoritative book is updated every two years and provides the most recent information on all methods of contraception.

Luker, Kristin. (1984). *Abortion and the politics of motherhood.* Berkeley, University of California Press. A sociological analysis of the women who are in the pro-choice and prolife camps of the abortion debate. The book is both sympathetic and insightful.

Goldstein, Marc, and Feldberg, Michael. (1982). *The vasectomy book: A complete guide to decision making.* Los Angeles: J. P. Tarcher (distributed by Houghton Mifflin). This book is a model of clarity, and written for the lay public. It is especially aimed at men who are considering vasectomy and their partners; it provides all the essentials for making a well-informed decision.

Ulmann, André, Teutsch, Georges, and Philibert, Daniel (June 1990). RU 486. *Scientific American, 262,* 42–48. An interesting, behind-the-scenes article by three of the French scientists involved in the development of RU 486.

9

The Physiology of Sexual Response

Chapter Highlights

Here are some colors of different people's orgasms: champagne, all colors and white and gray afterward, red and blue, green, beige and blue, red, blue and gold. Some people never make it because they are trying for plaid. *

This chapter is about the way the body responds during sexual arousal and orgasm and the mechanisms behind these responses. This information is very important in developing good techniques of lovemaking (see Chapter 10) and in analyzing and treating sexual dysfunctions such as premature ejaculation (see Chapter 19). Important though the topic is, it had not been investigated scientifically before the work of Masters and Johnson.

THE FOUR STAGES OF SEXUAL RESPONSE

The Masters and Johnson research on the physiology of sexual response began in 1954 and culminated in 1966 with the publication of *Human Sexual Response,* which reported data on 382 women and 312 men observed in over 10,000 sexual cycles of arousal and orgasm. (A discussion and critique of the Masters and Johnson research techniques were presented in Chapter 3.)

According to Masters and Johnson, there are four stages of sexual response, which they call *excitement, plateau, orgasm,* and *resolution.*

The two basic physiological processes that occur during these stages are vasocongestion and myotonia. Vasocongestion occurs when a great deal of blood flows into the blood vessels in a region, in this case the genitals, as a result of dilation of the blood vessels in the region. Myotonia occurs when muscles contract, not only in the genitals but also throughout the body. Let us now consider in detail what occurs in each of the stages.

Vasocongestion (vay-so-con-JES-tyun): An accumulation of blood in the blood vessels of a region of the body, especially the genitals; a swelling or erection results.

Myotonia (my-oh-TONE-ee-ah): Muscle contraction.

* *Source:* Eric Berne. (1970). *Sex in human loving.* New York: Simon & Schuster, p. 238.

Excitement

The excitement phase is the beginning of erotic arousal. The basic physiological process that occurs during excitement is vasocongestion. This produces the obvious arousal response in the male, erection. Erection results when the corpora cavernosa and the corpus spongiosum fill (becoming engorged) with blood (see Figure 9.1). Erection may be produced by direct physical stimulation of the genitals, by stimulation of other parts of the body, or by erotic thoughts. It occurs very rapidly, within a few seconds of the stimulation, although it may take place more slowly as a result of a number of factors including age, intake of alcohol, and fatigue.

An important response of females in the excitement phase is lubrication of the vagina. Although this response might seem much different from the male's, actually they both result from the same physiological process: vasocongestion. Masters and Johnson found that vaginal lubrication results when fluids seep through the semipermeable membranes of the vaginal walls, producing lubrication as a result of vasocongestion in the tissues surrounding the vagina. This response to arousal is also rapid, though not quite so fast as the male's; lubrication begins 10 to 30 seconds after the onset of arousing stimuli.[1] Some sex manuals advise that the appearance of lubrication serves as a good indicator to the man that the woman is "ready" for intercourse; the lubrication, however, signals only the beginning of arousal. Many other changes must also occur before the woman is ready for intercourse or close to orgasm. Like male sexual response, female responding can be affected by factors such as intake of alcohol and fatigue.

Several other physical changes occur in women during the excitement phase. The glans of the clitoris (the tip) swells. This results from engorgement of its corpora cavernosa and corpus spongiosum and thus is quite similar to erection in the male. The clitoris can be felt as larger and harder than usual.

The nipples become erect; this results from contractions of the muscle fibers (myotonia) surrounding the nipple. The breasts themselves swell and enlarge somewhat in the late part of the excitement phase (a vasocongestion response). Thus the nipples may not actually look erect but may appear somewhat flatter against the breast because the breast has swollen. Many males also have nipple erection during the excitement phase.

In the unaroused state the inner lips are generally folded over, covering the entrance to the vagina, and the outer lips lie close to each other. During excitement the inner lips swell and open up (a vasocongestion response). The outer lips move apart a bit and flatten out.

The vagina shows an important change during excitement. Think of the vagina as being divided into two parts, an upper (or inner) two-thirds and a lower (or outer) one-third. In the unaroused state the walls of the vagina lie against each other, much like the sides of an uninflated balloon. During the excitement phase, the upper two-thirds of the vagina expands dramatically in what is often called a "ballooning" response; that is, it becomes more like an inflated balloon (see Figure 9.2). This helps to accommodate the entrance of the penis. As part of the ballooning, the cervix and uterus pull up, creating a "tenting effect" in the vaginal walls (Figure 9.2) and making a larger opening in the cervix, which probably allows sperm to move into the uterus more easily.

---

[1] Before the Masters and Johnson research, it was thought that the lubrication was due to secretions of Bartholin's glands, but it now appears that these glands contribute little if anything. At this point, you might want to go back to the limerick about Bartholin's glands in Chapter 4 and see whether you can spot the error in it.

FIGURE 9.1
Changes during the sexual response cycle in the male.

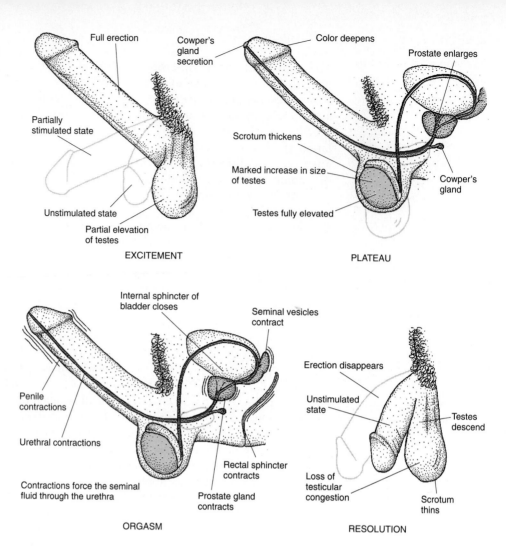

Full erection
Cowper's gland secretion
Partially stimulated state
Unstimulated state
Partial elevation of testes
EXCITEMENT

Color deepens
Prostate enlarges
Scrotum thickens
Marked increase in size of testes
Cowper's gland
Testes fully elevated
PLATEAU

Internal sphincter of bladder closes
Seminal vesicles contract
Penile contractions
Urethral contractions
Contractions force the seminal fluid through the urethra
Rectal sphincter contracts
Prostate gland contracts
ORGASM

Erection disappears
Unstimulated state
Testes descend
Loss of testicular congestion
Scrotum thins
RESOLUTION

During excitement a "sex flush" may appear on the skin of both men and women, though more commonly of women. The sex flush resembles a measles rash; it often begins on the upper abdomen and spreads over the chest. It may also appear later in the sexual response cycle.

Other changes that occur in both men and women include an increase in pulse rate and in blood pressure.

In men, the skin of the scrotum thickens. The scrotal sac also tenses, and the scrotum is pulled up and closer to the body (Figure 9.1). The spermatic cords shorten, elevating the testes.

Plateau: The second stage of sexual response, just before orgasm.

Plateau

During the plateau phase, vasocongestion reaches its peak. In men, the penis is completely erect, although there may be fluctuations in the firmness of the erection. The glans swells. The testes are so engorged with blood that they may be 50 percent larger than in the unaroused state. They are pulled up even higher and closer to the body. A few drops of fluid (for some men, quite a few), secreted by the Cowper's glands, appear at the tip of the penis. Although they are not the ejaculate, they may contain active sperm.

FIGURE 9.2
Changes during the sexual response cycle in the female.

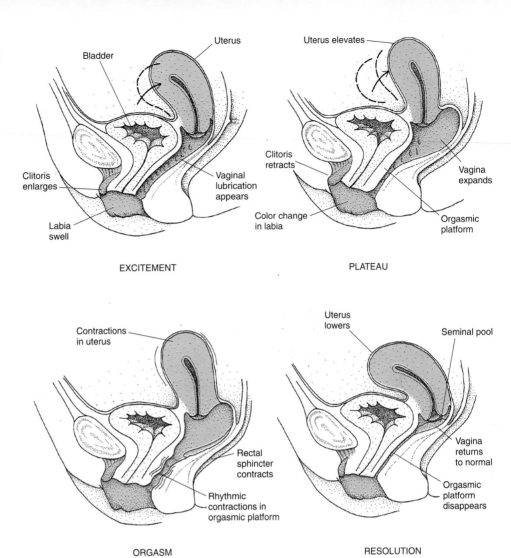

EXCITEMENT

Bladder
Uterus
Clitoris enlarges
Vaginal lubrication appears
Labia swell

PLATEAU

Uterus elevates
Clitoris retracts
Vagina expands
Color change in labia
Orgasmic platform

ORGASM

Contractions in uterus
Rectal sphincter contracts
Rhythmic contractions in orgasmic platform

RESOLUTION

Uterus lowers
Seminal pool
Vagina returns to normal
Orgasmic platform disappears

In both women and men there is a further increase in the rate of breathing, in pulse rate, and in blood pressure.

In females, the most notable change during the plateau phase is formation of the **orgasmic platform**. This is a swelling or thickening of the tissues surrounding the outer third of the vagina (Figure 9.2). Thus the size of the vaginal entrance actually becomes smaller, and there may be a noticeable increase in gripping of the penis.

Another change is the elevation of the clitoris. The clitoris essentially retracts or draws up into the body.

Other changes include a further swelling of the breasts and an enlargement of the uterus. Finally, the color of the inner lips changes, from bright red to a deep wine color in women who have had children and from pink to bright red in women who have not. This last change indicates that orgasm is close. If proper stimulation continues and other conditions are right, the woman will have an orgasm soon after the color change.

Essentially, then, the processes of the plateau phase are a continuation of the basic processes—vasocongestion and myotonia—of the excitement phase. Both processes continue to build until there is sufficient tension for orgasm.

Orgasmic platform: The thickening of the walls of the outer third of the vagina that occurs during the plateau stage of sexual response.

Orgasm

In the male, orgasm consists of a series of rhythmic contractions of the pelvic organs at 0.8-second intervals. Actually, male orgasm occurs in two stages. In the preliminary stage, the vas, seminal vesicles, and prostate contract, forcing the ejaculate into a bulb at the base of the urethra (Figure 9.1). Masters and Johnson call the sensation in this stage one of "ejaculatory inevitability" ("coming"); that is, there is a sensation that ejaculation is just about to happen and cannot be stopped. And, indeed, it cannot be, once the man has reached this point. In the second stage the urethral bulb and the penis itself contract rhythmically, forcing out the semen.

In both males and females, there are sharp increases in pulse rate, blood pressure, and breathing rate during orgasm.[2] Muscles contract throughout the body. The face may be contorted in a grimace; the muscles of the arms, legs, thighs, back, and buttocks may contract; and the muscles of the feet and hands may contract in "carpopedal spasms." Generally, of course, in the passion of the moment, one is not really aware of these occurrences, but an aching back or buttocks may serve as a reminder the next day.

The process of orgasm in females is basically similar to that in males. It is a series of rhythmic muscular contractions of the orgasmic platform. The contractions generally occur at about 0.8-second intervals; there may be three or four in a mild orgasm or as many as a dozen in a very intense, prolonged orgasm. The uterus also contracts rhythmically, with the contractions moving in waves from the top of the uterus down toward the cervix. Other muscles, such as those around the anus, may also contract rhythmically.

Female orgasm is a funny thing. As with love, you can almost never get anyone to give you a solid definition of what it is. Instead, people usually fall back on, "You'll know what it is when you have one." This evasiveness is probably related to several factors, most notably that female orgasm leaves no tangible evidence of its occurrence like ejaculation; indeed, the very existence of female orgasm has sometimes been questioned (for a clever satire on this point, see Raphael, 1973). Also, women often do not reach orgasm as quickly as men do, a point to be discussed in more detail in Chapter 14. In fact, some women, particularly young women, may think they are having an orgasm when they are not; they have never had an orgasm, and they mistake intense arousal for orgasm.

Just what does orgasm in the female feel like? The main feeling is a spreading sensation that begins around the clitoris and then spreads outward through the whole pelvis. There may also be sensations of falling or opening up. The woman may be able to feel the contraction of the muscles around the vaginal entrance. The sensation is very intense and is more than just a warm glow or a pleasant tingling. In one study, college men and women gave written descriptions of what an orgasm felt like to them (Vance & Wagner, 1976). Interestingly, a panel of experts (medical students, obstetrician-gynecologists, and clinical psychologists) could not reliably figure out which of the descriptions were written by women and which by men. This suggests that the sensations are quite similar for males and females.

Some of the men in my classes have asked me how they can tell whether a woman has really had an orgasm. Their question in itself is interesting. In part it reflects a cultural skepticism about female orgasm. There is usually obvious proof of male orgasm: ejaculation. But there is no similar proof of female orgasm. The question also reflects the fact that men know that women sometimes "fake" orgasm.

---

[2] With all the current attention to aerobics and exercising the heart, I have yet to hear anyone suggest orgasm aerobics. It seems to me that it should work. Jazzercise, watch out. Here comes sexercise!

Faking orgasm is a complex issue. Basically, it probably is not a very good idea, because it is dishonest. On the other hand, one needs to be sympathetic to the variety of reasons women do it. It is often difficult for women to reach orgasm, and our culture currently places a lot of emphasis on everyone's having orgasms. Thus the woman may feel that she is expected to have an orgasm, and realizing that it is unlikely to happen this time, she "fakes" it in order to meet expectations. She may also do it to please her partner.[3] But back to the question: How can one tell? There really is not any very good way. From a scientific point of view, a good method would be to have the woman hooked up to an instrument that registers pulse rate; there is a sudden sharp increase in the pulse rate at orgasm, and that would be a good indicator. I doubt, though, that most men have such equipment available, and I am even more doubtful about whether most women would agree to be so wired up. Probably rather than trying to check up on each other, it would be better for partners to establish good, honest communication and avoid setting up performance goals in sex, points that will be discussed further in later chapters.

Resolution

Resolution: The fourth stage of sexual response, in which the body returns to the unaroused state.

Following orgasm is the resolution phase, during which the body returns physiologically to the unaroused state. Orgasm triggers a massive release of muscular tension and of blood from the engorged blood vessels. These are the basic processes that occur during resolution. Resolution, then, represents a reversal of the processes that build up during the excitement and plateau stages.

The first change in women is a reduction in the swelling of the breasts. As a result, the nipples may appear to become erect, since they seem to stand out more as the surrounding flesh moves back toward the unstimulated size. In women who develop a sex flush during arousal, this appears rapidly following orgasm. In the 5 to 10 seconds after the end of the orgasm, the clitoris returns to is normal position, although it takes longer for it to shrink to its normal size. The orgasmic platform relaxes and begins to shrink. The ballooning of the vagina diminishes, and the uterus shrinks.

The resolution phase generally takes 15 to 30 minutes, but it may take much longer—as much as an hour—in women who have not had an orgasm. This latter fact helps to account for the chronic pelvic congestion that Masters and Johnson observed in prostitutes (see Chapter 4). The prostitutes frequently experienced arousal without having orgasms. Thus there were repeated buildups of vasocongestion without the discharge of it brought about by orgasm. The result was a chronic vasocongestion in the pelvis. A mild version of this occurs in some women who engage in sex but are not able to have orgasms, and it can be quite uncomfortable.

In both males and females, there is a gradual return of pulse rate, blood pressure, and breathing rate to the unaroused levels during resolution.

In men, the most obvious occurrence in the resolution phase is the loss of erection in the penis. This happens in two stages, the first occurring rapidly but leaving the penis still enlarged (this first loss of erection results from an emptying of the corpora cavernosa) and the second occurring more slowly, as a result of the slower emptying of the corpus spongiosum and the glans. The scrotum and testes return to their unstimulated size and position.

---

[3] Indeed, many of the old sex manuals, as well as physicians' textbooks, counseled women to fake orgasm. For example: "It is good advice to recommend to the women the advantage of innocent stimulation of sex responsiveness, and as a matter of fact many women in their desire to please their husbands learned the advantage of such innocent deception" (Novak & Novak, 1952, p. 572).

William Masters and Virginia Johnson

William Howell Masters was born in Cleveland in 1915. He attended Hamilton College in Clinton, New York, graduating in 1938 with a B.S. degree. At Hamilton he specialized in science courses, and yet he managed to play on the varsity football, baseball, basketball, and track teams and to participate in the Debate Club. The college yearbook called him "a strange, dark man with a future. . . . Has an easy time carrying three lab courses but a hard time catching up on lost sleep. . . . Bill is a boy with purpose and is bound to get what he is working for." His devotion to athletics persisted, and in 1966 a science writer described him as "a dapper, athletically trim gynecologist who starts his day at 5:30 with a two-mile jog."

He entered the University of Rochester School of Medicine in 1939, planning to train himself to be a researcher rather than a practicing physician. In his first year there he worked in the laboratory of the famous anatomist Dr. George Washington Corner. Corner was engaged in research on the reproductive system in animals and humans, which eventually led to important discoveries about hormones and the reproductive cycle. He had also published *Attaining Manhood: A Doctor Talks to Boys About Sex* and the companion volume, *Attaining Womanhood.*

The first-year research project that Corner assigned to Masters was a study of the changes in the lining of the uterus of the rabbit during the reproductive cycle. Thus his interest was focused early on the reproductive system.

Masters was married in 1942 and received his M.D. in 1943. He and his wife had two children, born in 1950 and 1951.

After Masters received his degree, he had to make an important decision: To what research area should he devote his life? Apparently his decision to investigate the physiology of sex was based on his shrewd observation that almost no prior research had been done in the area and that he thus would have a good opportunity to make some important scientific discoveries. In arriving at the decision, he consulted with Dr. Corner, who was aware of Kinsey's progress and also of the persecution he had suffered; thus Corner advised Masters not to begin

---

Refractory period (ree-FRAK-toh-ree): The period following orgasm during which the male cannot be sexually aroused.

During the resolution phase, men enter into a refractory period, during which they are refractory to further arousal; that is, they are incapable of being aroused again, having an erection, or having an orgasm. The length of this refractory period varies considerably from one man to the next; in some it may last only a few minutes, and in others it may go on for 24 hours. The refractory period tends to become longer as men grow older.

Women do not enter into a refractory period, making possible the phenomenon of multiple orgasm in women, to be discussed in the next section.

OTHER FINDINGS OF THE MASTERS AND JOHNSON RESEARCH

A number of other important findings on the nature of sexual response have emerged from the Masters and Johnson research, two of which will be discussed here.

FIGURE 9.3
Virginia Johnson and William H. Masters.

the study of sex until he had established himself as a respected researcher in some other area, was somewhat older, and could conduct the research at a major university or medical school.

Masters followed the advice. He completed his internship and residency and then established himself on the faculty of the Washington University School of Medicine in St. Louis. From 1948 to 1954 he published 25 papers on various medical topics, especially on hormone-replacement therapy for postmenopausal women.

In 1954 he began his research on sexual response at Washington University, supported by grants from the U.S. Public Health Service. The first paper based on that research was published in 1959, but the research received little attention until the publication, in 1966, of *Human Sexual Response*

and, in 1970, of *Human Sexual Inadequacy* (to be discussed in Chapter 19), both of which received international acclaim.

In 1964 he founded the Reproductive Biology Research Foundation, now called the Masters and Johnson Institute, near the medical school, where the research continues today.

Virginia Johnson was born Virginia Eshelman in 1925 in the Missouri Ozarks. She was raised with the realistic attitude toward sex that rural children often have, as well as many of the superstitions that have grown up in that area. She began studying music at Drury College but transferred to Missouri University, where she studied psychology and sociology. She was married in 1950 and had two children, one in 1952 and the other in 1955. Shortly after that, she and her husband separated, and she went to the Washington University placement office to find a job. Just at that time, Masters had put in a request for a woman to assist him in research interviewing, preferably a married woman with children who was interested in people. Mrs. Johnson was sent over to him, and she has been a member of the research team and therapy team since 1957.

Following the divorce of Masters and his first wife, he and Virginia Johnson were married. Then in 1992 Masters and Johnson announced that they would divorce.

Source: Ruth Brecher & Edward Brecher (Eds.). (1966). *An analysis of human sexual response*. New York: Signet Books, New American Library.

Clitoral Orgasm Versus Vaginal Orgasm

Clitoral orgasm: Freud's term for orgasm in the female resulting from stimulation of the clitoris.

Vaginal orgasm: Freud's term for orgasm in the female resulting from stimulation of the vagina in heterosexual intercourse; Freud considered vaginal orgasm to be more mature than clitoral orgasm.

Some people believe that women can have two kinds of orgasm: **clitoral orgasm** and **vaginal orgasm**. The words "clitoral" and "vaginal" are not meant to imply that the clitoris has an orgasm or that the vagina has an orgasm. Rather, they refer to the locus of stimulation: an orgasm resulting from clitoral stimulation versus an orgasm resulting from vaginal stimulation. The whole notion of the distinction was originated by Sigmund Freud. Freud believed that in childhood little girls masturbate and thus have orgasms by means of clitoral stimulation, or clitoral orgasms. He thought that as women grow older and mature, they ought to shift from having orgasms as a result of masturbation to having them as a result of heterosexual intercourse, that is, by means of vaginal stimulation. (Freud's self-interest as a male in this matter is rather transparent!) Thus the vaginal orgasm was considered "mature" and the clitoral orgasm "immature" or "infantile," and not only did there come to be two kinds of orgasm, but also one was "better" (that is, more mature) than the other. (For a review of the clitoral orgasm—vaginal orgasm controversy, see Brown, 1966.)

Freud's formulation is of more than theoretical interest, since it has had an impact on the lives of many women. Many have undertaken psychoanalysis and spent countless hours agonizing over why they were not able to achieve the elusive vaginal orgasm and why they enjoyed the immature clitoral one so much. Women who could have orgasm only through clitoral stimulation were called "vaginally frigid" or "fixed" at an infantile stage.

According to the results of Masters and Johnson's research, though, the distinction beteen clitoral and vaginal orgasms does not make sense. This conclusion is based on two findings. First, their results indicate that all female orgasms are physiologically the same, regardless of the locus of stimulation. That is, an orgasm always consists of contractions of the orgasmic platform and the muscles around the vagina, whether the stimulation is clitoral or vaginal. Indeed, they found a few women who could have orgasm purely through breast stimulation, and that orgasm was the same as the other two, consisting of contractions of the orgasmic platform and the muscles around the vagina. Thus physiologically there is only one kind of orgasm. (Of course, this does not mean that psychologically there are not different kinds; the experience of orgasm during intercourse may be quite different from the experience of orgasm during masturbation.) Second, Masters and Johnson found that clitoral stimulation is almost always involved in producing orgasm. Because of the way in which the inner lips connect with the clitoral hood, the movement of the penis in and out of the vagina creates traction on the inner lips, which in turn pull the clitoral hood so that it moves back and forth, stimulating the clitoris. Thus even the purely "vaginal" orgasm results from quite a bit of clitoral stimulation.

It seems that clitoral stimulation is usually the "trigger" to orgasm and that the orgasm itself occurs in the vagina and surrounding tissues.

It is unfortunate that the distinction between clitoral and vaginal orgasms persists, since it has no scientific basis. That is, there is no physiological difference between orgasms occurring during intercourse and those occurring as a result of clitoral stimulation during masturbation.

Multiple Orgasm

Traditionally it was believed that orgasmically, women behaved like men in that they could have one orgasm and then would enter into a refractory period before they could have another. According to the Masters and Johnson research, however, this is not true; rather, women do not enter into a refractory period, and they can have **multiple** orgasms within a short period of time. Actually, women's capacity for multiple orgasms was originally discovered by Kinsey in his interviews with women (Kinsey et al., 1953; see also Terman et al., 1938). The scientific establishment, however, dismissed these reports as another instance of Kinsey's unreliability.

Kinsey estimated that about 13 percent of all women have multiple orgasms. The Masters and Johnson research, though, suggests that many more women, perhaps most, are capable of having multiple orgasms if properly stimulated (though the Masters and Johnson data are not good for estimating percentages—see Chapter 3).

The term "multiple orgasm," then, refers to having one orgasm after another within a short period of time. They do not differ physiologically from simple orgasms except that there are many of them. Each is a "real" orgasm, and they are not minor experiences. One nice thing, though, is that the later ones generally require much

Multiple orgasm: Having several orgasms within a short period of time.

less effort than the first one. The first one may require quite a bit of stimulation, but subsequent ones can often be triggered by less than a minute of stimulation.

How does multiple orgasm work physiologically? Immediately following an orgasm, both males and females move into the resolution phase. In this phase, the male enters into a refractory period, during which he cannot be aroused again. But the female does not enter into a refractory period. That is, if she is stimulated again, she can immediately be aroused and move back into the excitement or plateau phase and have another orgasm.

Multiple orgasm, of course, is more likely to result from hand-genital or mouth-genital stimulation than from intercourse, since most men do not have the endurance to continue thrusting for such long periods of time. Regarding capacity, Masters and Johnson found that women in masturbation might have 5 to 20 orgasms. In some cases, they quit only when physically exhausted. When using a vibrator, less effort is required, and some women were capable of having 50 orgasms.

It should be noted that some women who are capable of multiple orgasms are completely satisfied with one, particularly in intercourse, and do not wish to continue. We should be careful not to set multiple orgasm as another of the many goals in sexual performance.

In one sample of adult women, all of whom were nurses (and therefore presumably had a good understanding of the anatomy and physiology involved), 43 percent reported that they usually experienced multiple orgasms (Darling et al., 1991). Among these women, 40 percent reported that each successive orgasm was stronger than the previous one, 16 percent said that each successive one was weaker than the one before, and the remainder said that the orgasms varied or there were no differences in intensity among them. Women who had multiple orgasms were more likely, compared with women who had single orgasms, to have their orgasm before their partner did.

There is increasing evidence that some men are capable of having multiple orgasms (e.g., Zilbergeld, 1978; Hartman & Fithian, 1984; Robbins & Jensen, 1978). In one study, 21 men were interviewed, all of whom had volunteered for research on multiply orgasmic men (Dunn & Trost, 1989). Some of the men reported having been multiply orgasmic since their sexual debut, whereas others had developed the pattern later in life, and still others had worked actively to develop the capacity after reading about the possibility. The respondents reported that multiple orgasm did not occur every time they engaged in sexual activity. For these men, detumescence did not always follow an orgasm, allowing for continued stimulation and an additional orgasm. Some reported that some of the orgasms included ejaculation and others in the sequence did not. This study cannot tell us the incidence of multiply orgasmic men in the general population, but it does provide some evidence that multiply orgasmic men exist.

ALTERNATIVES TO THE MASTERS AND JOHNSON MODEL

Some experts on human sexuality are critical of Masters and Johnson's four-stage model. One important criticism is that the Masters and Johnson model ignores the cognitive and subjective aspects of sexual response (Zilbergeld & Ellison, 1980). That is, Masters and Johnson focused almost entirely on the physiological aspects of the response, ignoring what the person is thinking and feeling emotionally. There is no desire or passion in the model. This omission in their model would not be such a problem except that there can be major discrepancies between physiological response and subjective feelings. Men can have erections without feeling the least bit aroused sexually. People can also feel a high level of sexual desire, yet have no erection or vaginal lubrication.

A second important criticism concerns how subjects were selected for the research and how this process may have created a self-fulfilling prophecy for the outcome (Tiefer, 1991). To participate in the research, subjects were required to have a history of orgasm both through masturbation and through coitus. Essentially, anyone whose pattern of sexual response did not include orgasm—and therefore did not fit Masters and Johnson's model—was excluded from the research. As such, the model cannot be generalized to the entire population. Masters and Johnson themselves commented that every one of their subjects was characterized by high and consistent levels of sexual desire. Yet sexual desire is certainly missing among some members of the general population, or it is present sometimes and absent other times. It is not surprising that sexual desire was omitted from Masters and Johnson's model when the subjects were preselected to be uniform in their high levels of desire. The research, in short, claims to be objective and universal when it is neither (Tiefer, 1991).

Once these difficulties with the Masters and Johnson research and model of sexual response were recognized, several alternative models were proposed. We will examine two of them here.

Kaplan: Triphasic Model

On the basis of her work on sex therapy (discussed in Chapter 19), Helen Singer Kaplan (1974; 1979) has proposed a **triphasic model** of sexual response. Rather than thinking of the sexual response as having successive stages, she prefers to conceptualize it as having three relatively independent phases or components: *vasocongestion* of the genitals, the reflex *muscular contractions* of the orgasm phase, and *sexual desire*. Notice that two of the components (vasocongestion and muscular contractions) are physiological, whereas the other (sexual desire) is psychological.

There are a number of justifications for this approach. First, the two physiological components are controlled by different parts of the nervous system. Vasocongestion—producing erection in the male and lubrication in the female—is controlled by the parasympathetic division of the autonomic nervous system. In contrast, ejaculation (and presumably orgasm in the female) is controlled by the sympathetic division. Second, the two phases or components involve different anatomical structures, blood vessels for vasocongestion and muscles for the contractions of orgasm. Third, vasocongestion and orgasm differ in their susceptibility to being disturbed by injury, drugs, or age. For example, the refractory period following orgasm in the male lengthens with age. Accordingly, there is a decrease in the frequency of orgasm with age. In contrast, the capacity for erection is relatively unimpaired with age, although the erection may be slower to make its appearance. An elderly man may have nonorgasmic sex several times a week, with a firm erection, although he may have an orgasm only once a week. Fourth, the reflex of ejaculation in the male can be brought under voluntary control by most men, but the erection reflex generally cannot. Finally, the impairment of the vasocongestion response and impairment of the orgasm response produce different disturbances (sexual dysfunctions). Erection problems in the male are caused by an impairment of the vasocongestion response, whereas premature ejaculation and retarded ejaculation are disturbances of the orgasm response. Similarly, many women show a strong arousal and vasocongestion response yet have trouble with the orgasm component of their sexual response.

Triphasic model: Kaplan's model of sexual response in which there are three phases: vasocongestion, muscular contractions, and sexual desire.

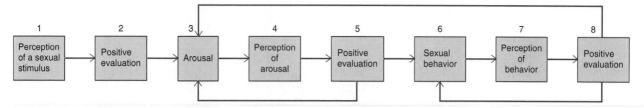

FIGURE 9.4
Walen and Roth's cognitive model showing the feedback loop that produces a positive sexual experience.

Kaplan's triphasic model seems to be useful both for understanding the nature of sexual response and for understanding and treating disturbances in it. Her writing on the desire phase is particularly useful in understanding disorders of sexual desire, to be discussed in Chapter 19.

Walen and Roth: A Cognitive Model

As noted earlier, an important criticism of the Masters and Johnson model is that it ignores the cognitive and subjective aspects of sexual response (Zilbergeld & Ellison, 1980). In Chapter 2 we discussed the importance of cognitive approaches in understanding the psychology of human sexuality. Susan R. Walen and David Roth (1987) have applied this approach to understanding the sexual response. Their model is shown in Figure 9.4.

Recall from Chapter 2 that according to the cognitive approach, how we feel depends tremendously on what we are thinking: how we perceive what is occurring and how we evaluate it. Thus the first step in the cognitive model is *perception*: the perception of a stimulus as sexual. What we perceive to be sexy stimuli (whether they are visual stimuli, touch stimuli, or odors) depends a great deal on the culture in which we've grown up and our prior learning. If you've just begun a sexual relationship with someone, the very sight of that person may make you feel turned on, whereas looking at 10 other people in the same room produces no turn-on. To a fetishist, the sight of black leather, high-heeled women's boots may produce instant arousal. According to the model, perception is the first step.

The second step in the cognitive model is *evaluation*. If we feel positive about the sexual stimulus, that will lead to the next step, arousal, but if our evaluation of the stimulus is negative, the arousal cycle stops. For example, if you are a married woman and your husband, with whom you normally have a great sex life, begins to kiss you when his breath smells of a cigarette he has just smoked, your evaluation of the sexual stimulus is likely to be negative and you will not feel aroused.

Let's suppose, though, that the evaluation of the sexual stimulus is positive. Physiological *arousal*—as described in the Masters and Johnson model discussed earlier in this chapter—is the next step. But again, the cognitive approach says that it is not so much what happens physically, but how we perceive it, that counts. So the *perception of arousal*, step 4, is critical. For example, some research shows that women, probably because vaginal lubrication can be a rather subtle response, are sometimes not aware of their own physical arousal (Heiman, 1975, discussed in Chapter 14). Or a man might pay so much attention to whether his technique is pleasing his partner that he fails to perceive his own arousal and thus does not experience as much sexual pleasure as he might. People can create sexual problems for themselves if they set too high criteria for deciding that they are aroused. How much lubrication, or how firm an erection, is "enough?" You can augment your sexual response by perceiving even a little bit of lubrication, or a bit of erection, or other signs (such as increased heart rate) as indications of arousal.

Again, the cognitive approach argues that it is not only the perception of arousal, but a positive evaluation of the arousal, that is important if the sexual response cycle is to increase; thus *evaluation* is the next step. As before, if the evaluation is negative, the response cycle stops. An example would be an adult who feels himself becoming aroused when looking at a child. He realizes that this response is totally inappropriate, evaluates the arousal negatively, and feels anxiety rather than arousal. If the evaluation of the arousal is positive, though—you like the feeling of being turned on in this situation—there is feedback to step 3, so that physical arousal increases further. Essentially, feeling good about being turned on makes you feel even more turned on.

All this propels you to the next step, *sexual behavior*. Again, cognitive psychologists believe that two further steps—*perception of the behavior* and a *positive evaluation* of it—are critical for the arousal cycle to continue. If the evaluation is positive, two kinds of feedback occur: the sexual behavior is likely to continue, and arousal increases.

In sum, the cognitive model of the sexual response cycle stresses the importance of our perception and evaluation of sexual events. It's a testimony to the power of positive thinking, although in a context that Normal Vincent Peale probably didn't intend. As another saying has it, the greatest erogenous zone is the brain.

HORMONAL AND NEURAL CONTROL OF SEXUAL BEHAVIOR

Up to this point we have focused on the cognitive and genital responses that occur during sexual activity. We have not yet considered the neural and hormonal mechanisms that make this possible; they are the topic of the following section.

The Brain, the Spinal Cord, and Sex

The brain and the spinal cord both have important interacting functions in sexual response. First, the relatively simple spinal reflexes involved in sexual response will be discussed; then the more complex brain mechanisms will be considered.

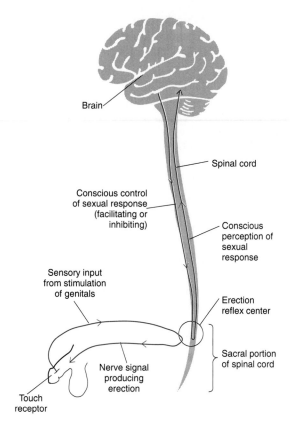

Brain

Spinal cord

Conscious control of sexual response (facilitating or inhibiting)

Conscious perception of sexual response

Sensory input from stimulation of genitals

Erection reflex center

Sacral portion of spinal cord

Nerve signal producing erection

Touch receptor

Spinal Reflexes

Several important components of sexual behavior, including erection and ejaculation, are controlled by fairly simple spinal cord reflexes (see the lower part of Figure 9.6). A reflex has three basic components: the *receptors,* which are sense organs that detect stimuli and transmit the message to the spinal cord (or brain); the *transmitters,* which are centers in the spinal cord (or brain) that receive the message, interpret it, and send out a message to produce the appropriate response; and the *effectors,* which are organs that respond to the stimulation. The reflex jerking away of the hand when it touches a hot object is a good example.

Mechanism of Erection

Erection is produced by a spinal reflex with a similar mechanism. Tactile stimulation (stroking or rubbing) of the penis (the receptor) or nearby regions such as the scrotum or inside of the thighs produces a neural signal which is transmitted to an "erection center" in the sacral, or lowest, part of the spinal cord (there may also be another erection center higher in the cord). This center then sends out a message via the parasympathetic division of the autonomic nervous system to the muscles (the effectors) around the walls of the arteries in the penis. In response to the message, the muscles relax; the arteries then expand, permitting a large volume of blood to flow into them, and erection results. Further, the valves in the veins and the compression of the veins caused by the swelling in the tissue around them reduce the blood flow out of the penis (Weiss, 1973).

The existence of this reflex is confirmed by the responses of men who have had their spinal cords severed, as a result of accidents, at a level above that of the reflex center. They are capable of having erections and ejaculations produced by rubbing their genitals, although it is clear that no brain effects can be operating, since signals from the brain cannot move past the point at which the spinal cord was severed. (In fact, they cannot "feel" anything because neural signals cannot be transmitted up the spinal cord either.) Thus erection can be produced simply by tactile stimulation of the genitals, which triggers the spinal reflex.

Erection may also be produced by conditions other than tactile stimulation of the genitals; for example, fantasy or other purely psychological factors may produce erection. This points to the importance of the brain in producing erection, a topic that will be discussed in more detail below.

Mechanism of Ejaculation

The ejaculation reflex is much like the erection reflex, except that the ejaculation center is located higher in the spinal cord, the sympathetic division of the nervous system is involved (as opposed to the parasympathetic division in the erection reflex), and the response is muscular, with no involvement of the blood vessels. In the ejaculation reflex, the penis responds to stimulation by sending a message to the "ejaculation center," which is located in the lumbar portion of the spinal cord. A message is then sent out via the nerves in the sympathetic nervous system, and this message triggers the contractions of the muscles in the internal organs involved in ejaculation.

Ejaculation can often be controlled voluntarily. This fact highlights the importance of brain influences on the ejaculation reflex.

The three main problems of ejaculation are premature ejaculation, retarded ejaculation, and retrograde ejaculation. Premature ejaculation, which is by far the most common problem, and retarded ejaculation will be discussed in Chapter 19.

FIGURE 9.7
How a retrograde ejaculation occurs.

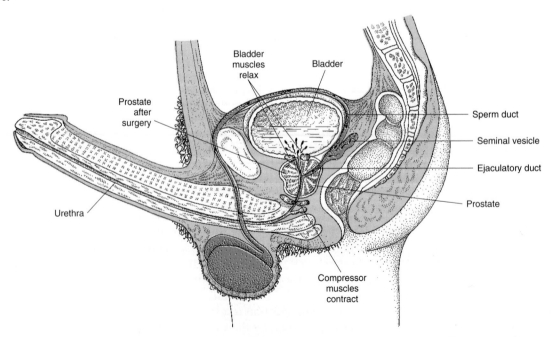

Retrograde ejaculation occurs when the ejaculate, rather than going out through the tip of the penis, empties into the bladder (Greene et al., 1970). A "dry orgasm" results, since no ejaculate is emitted. This problem can be caused by some illnesses, by tranquilizers and drugs used in the treatment of psychoses, and by prostate surgery. The mechanism that causes it is fairly simple (see Figure 9.7). Two sphincters are involved in ejaculation: an internal one, which closes off the entrance to the bladder during a normal ejaculation, and an external one, which opens during a normal ejaculation, allowing the semen to flow out through the penis. In retrograde ejaculation, the action of these two sphincters is reversed; the external one closes, and thus the ejaculate cannot flow out through the penis, and the internal one opens, permitting the ejaculate to go into the bladder. The condition itself is quite harmless, although some men are disturbed by the lack of sensation of emitting semen.

Mechanisms in Women

Unfortunately there is no comparable research on similar reflex mechanisms of arousal in women. Generally it is assumed that since the basic processes of sexual response (vasocongestion and myotonia) are similar in males and females and since their genital organs are derived from the same embryonic tissue (and thus have similar nerve supplies), reflexive mechanisms in women are similar to those in men. That is, since the lubrication response in women results from vasocongestion, it is similar to erection in the male, and thus it might be expected to be controlled by a similar spinal reflex. This is purely speculative, though, since there is no research on the subject.

Some research suggests the possibility that there is such a thing as *female ejaculation* (Perry & Whipple, 1981; Addiego et al., 1981; Belzer, 1981). The research discovered fluid spurting out of the urethra during orgasm; chemically, the fluid in one study was like the seminal fluid of vasectomized men—that is, semen without the sperm. The organ responsible seems to be the Gräfenberg spot (or *G-spot*), also called the female prostate. It is located on the top side of the vagina (with the woman lying on her back, which is the best position for finding it), about halfway between the pubic bone and the cervix (see Figure 9.8). Stroking it produces an urge to urinate, but if the stroking continues for a few seconds more, it begins to produce sexual pleasure. Perry and Whipple argue that continued stimulation of it produces a *uterine orgasm,* characterized by deeper sensations of uterine contractions than the clitorally induced vulvar orgasm investigated in the Masters and Johnson research. Their ideas raise the whole clitoral-vaginal orgasm controversy again, al-

*FIGURE 9.8
G-spot: Hypothesized to produce ejaculation in some women.*

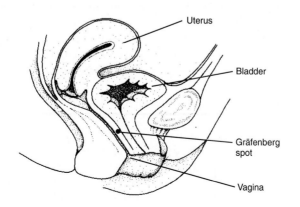

though from a different research base. Perry and Whipple found that not every woman ejaculates, but it is important to recogize that some women do. Our firm notions of male-female differences are constantly challenged!

But Perry and Whipple's results have also been challenged. In their book, Perry and Whipple claimed to have examined over 400 women and found a G-spot in every one (Ladas, Whipple, & Perry, 1982). Yet in one study, two gynecologists examined 11 women, 6 of whom said they were ejaculators (Goldberg et al., 1983). The gynecologists found an area fitting the description of the G-spot in only 4 of the women, and 2 of them were ejaculators and 2 were not. Chemical analysis of the fluid ejaculated by the 6 ejaculators did not find it to be chemically like male semen; chemically it was like urine. Thus the study gave some support to the existence of a G-spot, but it gave no support to the hypothesis that some females ejaculate. On the other hand, in one survey of 1289 adult women, 40 percent reported having experienced ejaculation at the time of orgasm at least once, and 66 percent reported having an especially sensitive area on the front wall of the vagina (Darling et al., 1990). (For other mixed evidence, see Alzate & Londono, 1984.) In my judgment, it will take another 10 years of research, by many independent investigators, before we will really be able to sort out whether there is a G-spot and, if so, what it does (Rosen & Beck, 1988).

Brain Control

As was noted above, it is clear that sexual responses are controlled by more than simple spinal reflexes. Sexual responses may be brought under voluntary control, and they may be initiated by purely psychological forces, such as fantasy. Environmental factors, such as having been taught as a child that sex is dirty and sinful, may also affect one's sexual response. All these phenomena point to the critical influence of the brain and its interaction with the spinal reflexes in producing sexual response (see Figure 9.6).

Brain control of sexual response is complex and only partly understood at the present time. It appears that the most important influences come from a set of structures called the **limbic system** (see Figure 9.9) (MacLean, 1962). The limbic system forms a border between the central part of the brain and the outer part (the cerebral cortex); it includes the amygdala, the hippocampus, the cingulate gyrus, the fornix, and the septum. The thalamus, the hypothalamus, the pituitary, and the reticular formation are not properly part of the limbic system, but they are closely connected to it.

Several lines of evidence point to the importance of the limbic system in sexual behavior. In experiments with monkeys, an electrode was inserted into various regions of the brain to deliver electrical simulation. It was discovered that stimulation of some areas of the brain would produce an erection. In particular, three "erection centers" were found in the limbic system, including one in the septal region. For obvious reasons, little of this research has been done with humans. But in one study, stimulation of the septal region of the limbic system produced orgasm in two human subjects (Heath, 1972).

The existence of a phenomenon called the **Klüver-Bucy syndrome** provides further evidence of the importance of the limbic system in sexuality. If the temporal lobes of the brain (the lobes at the side of the brain) of monkeys are destroyed, they become highly erotic and hypersexual (as well as very tame); this is the Klüver-Bucy syndrome. When the temporal lobes are destroyed, the amygdala and the hippocampus, among other things, are destroyed; since they are important structures in the limbic system, the hypersexuality that results from their destruction further implicates the limbic system in the control of sexual response.

Limbic system: A set of structures in the interior of the brain, including the amygdala, hippocampus, and fornix; believed to be important for sexual behavior in both animals and humans.

Klüver-Bucy syndrome: A syndrome of hypersexuality discovered in monkeys that had had the temporal lobes of the brain destroyed.

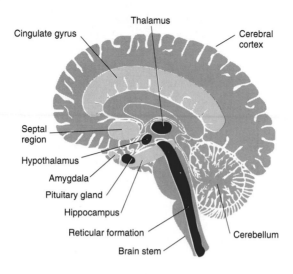

FIGURE 9.9
The limbic system of the brain, which is important in sexuality.

The important work of the physiological psychologist James Olds (Olds, 1956; Olds & Milner, 1954) established the existence of "pleasure centers" in the brain. Electrodes were implanted in various regions of the brains of rats and were wired so that a rat could stimulate its own brain by pressing a lever. When the electrodes were placed in certain regions—in particular, the septal region and the hypothalamus—the rats would press the lever thousands of times per hour and would forgo food and sleep and endure pain in order to stimulate these regions. The location of these pleasure centers so close to the sex centers may explain why sexual experiences are so intensely pleasurable.

The study of humans noted above also points to an association between the sex centers and the pleasure centers (Heath, 1972). Electrodes were placed in the brains of two human subjects for therapeutic purposes (one male psychiatric patient and one female epileptic). When the stimulation was to certain areas, the subjects reported it as being very pleasurable; these areas were essentially the same as the pleasure centers found in the brains of animals. When the stimulation was delivered to the septal region or the amygdala (both in the limbic system), the pleasure was sexual in nature. In addition to the subjects' reports of sexual arousal and pleasurable sexual feelings, the male subject stimulated himself almost insatiably (as many as 1500 times per hour) and begged to be allowed to stimulate himself a few more times whenever the apparatus was taken away.

There are also "rage," or "aggression," centers in the brain, the stimulation of which throws the animal into a rage so that it will attack any object in the cage. These centers are located in the hypothalamus and, like the pleasure centers, are close to the sex centers; the closeness of the two may explain the association of sex and aggression in phenomena such as rape, competition over mates, and sado-masochism (MacLean, 1962).

The brain centers for sex are also close to the olfactory centers. This brings us to the topic of pheromones and their role in sexual behavior, which will be discussed later in the chapter.

Hormones and Sex

The sex hormones are another important physiological force that interacts with the nervous system to influence sexual response.

Organizing effects of hormones: Effects of sex hormones early in development, resulting in a permanent change in the brain or reproductive system.

Activating effects of hormones: Effects of sex hormones in adulthood, resulting in the activation of behaviors, especially sexual behaviors and aggressive behaviors.

Endocrinologists generally make a distinction between the organizing effects of hormones and the activating effects of hormones (Feder, 1984). As was seen in Chapter 5, hormones present during prenatal development may have important influences on the hypothalamus and on the genitals (creating male or female genitals). Hormone effects such as these are called organizing effects because they cause a relatively permanent change in the organization of some structure, whether in the nervous system or in the reproductive system. Typically there are "critical periods" during which these hormones effects may occur.

It has also been known for some time that if an adult male mouse or cat is castrated (has the testes removed, which removes the source of testosterone), it will cease engaging in sexual behavior (and also will be less aggressive). If that animal is then given injections of testosterone, it will start engaging in sex again. Hormone effects such as these are called activating effects because they activate (or deactivate) certain behaviors.

The organizing effects of sex hormones on sexual behavior have been well documented. In a classic experiment, testosterone was administered to pregnant female guinea pigs. The female offspring that had been exposed to testosterone prenatally[4] were, in adulthood, incapable of displaying female sexual behavior (in particular, lordosis, which is a sexual posturing involving arching of the back and raising of the hindquarters so that the male's intromission is possible) (Phoenix et al., 1959). It is thought that this occurred because the testosterone "organized" the brain tissue (particularly the hypothalamus) in a male fashion. These female offspring were also born with masculinized genitals, and thus their reproductive systems had also been organized in the male direction. But the important point here is that the prenatal doses of testosterone had masculinized their sexual behavior. Similar results have been obtained in experiments with many other species as well.

These hormonally masculinized females in adulthood displaying mounting behavior, a male[5] sexual behavior. When they were given testosterone in adulthood, they showed about as much mounting behavior as males did. Thus the testosterone administered in adulthood *activated* male patterns of sexual behavior.

The analogous experiment on males would be castration at birth, followed by administration of ovarian hormones in adulthood. When this was done with rats, female sexual behavior resulted; these males responded to mating attempts by other males essentially in the same way females do (Harris & Levine, 1965). Apparently their brain tissue had been organized in a female direction during an early, critical period when testosterone was absent, and the female behavior patterns were activated in adulthood by administration of ovarian hormones.

It thus seems that males and females initially have capacities for both male and female sexual behaviors; if testosterone is present early in development, the capacity for exhibiting female behaviors is suppressed. Sex hormones in adulthood then activate the behavior patterns that were differentiated early in development.

---

[4]   Note the similarity of these experiments to John Money's observations of human hermaphrodites (Chapter 5).

[5]   The term "male sexual behavior" is being used here to refer to a sexual behavior that is displayed by normal males of the species and either is absent in females of that species or is present at a much lower frequency. Normal females do mount, but they do so less frequently than males do. "Female sexual behavior" is defined similarly.

One question that might be raised is: How relevant is this research to humans? Generally the trend is for the behavior of lower species to be more under hormonal control and for the behavior of higher species to be more under brain (neural) control. Thus human sexual behavior is less under hormonal control than rat sexual behavior; human sexual behavior is more controlled by the brain, and thus learning and past experiences, which are stored in the brain, are more likely to have a profound effect. For example, it is estimated that only about 20 to 50 percent of cases of human sexual dysfunction (e.g., impotence) are caused by physical factors; the rest are due to psychological factors (see Chapter 19).

Let us now consider in more detail the known activating effects of sex hormones on the sexual behavior of adult humans.

Testosterone and Libido

Testosterone has well-documented effects on libido in humans (Carani et al., 1990; Everitt & Bancroft, 1991). In men deprived of their main source of testosterone by castration or by illness, there is a dramatic decrease in sexual behavior in some, but not all, cases (Feder, 1984). Libido and potency are rapidly lost if a man is given an antiandrogen drug. Thus testosterone seems to have an activating effect in maintaining sexual desire in the adult male. However, in cases of castration, sexual behavior may decline very slowly and may be present for several years after the source of testosterone is gone; this points to the importance of experience and brain control of sexual behavior in humans.

It has also been demonstrated that levels of testosterone are correlated with sexual behavior in boys around the time of puberty (Udry et al., 1985). Boys in the eighth, ninth, and tenth grades filled out a questionnaire about their sexual behavior and gave blood samples from which their level of testosterone could be measured. Among those boys whose testosterone level was in the highest quartile (25 percent of the sample), 69 percent had engaged in sexual intercourse, whereas only 16 percent of the boys whose testosterone level was in the lowest quartile had engaged in intercourse. Similarly, of those boys with testosterone levels in the highest quartile, 62 percent had masturbated, compared with 12 percent for the boys in the lowest quartile. These effects were uncorrelated with age, so it wasn't simply a matter of the older boys having more testosterone and more sexual experience. The authors concluded that at puberty, testosterone affects sexual motivation directly.

Recently it has been demonstrated that androgens, not estrogen, are related to libido in women also, although the evidence is somewhat conflicting (Sherwin, 1991; Feder, 1984; Bancroft, 1987). If all sources of androgen in women are removed (the adrenals and the ovaries), women lose sexual desire. On the other hand, androgens are sometimes used in the treatment of low-libido states in women, although their use is limited by their tendency to have masculinizing side effects.[6]

PHEROMONES

Pheromones (FARE-oh-mones): Biochemicals secreted outside the body that are important in communication between animals and that may serve as sex attractants.

There has been a great deal of interest recently in the role that pheromones play in sexual behavior. Pheromones are somewhat like hormones. Recall that hormones

[6] Lest the reader be distressed by the thought that women's considerably lower levels of testosterone might mean that they have lower sex drives, it should be noted that the sensitivity of cells to hormone levels is critical. Women's cells may be more sensitive to testosterone than men's are. Thus for women, a little testosterone may go a long way.

Sexuality and Disability

It is commonly believed that a person in a wheel-chair is sexless. The physically disabled are thought not to be interested in sex, much less to be capable of engaging in sexual activity. Contrast those stereotypes with the following ideas:

> A stiff penis does not make a solid relationship, nor does a wet vagina. . . .
>
> Absence of sensation does not mean absence of feelings. . . .
>
> Inability to move does not mean inability to please. . . .
>
> (Cole & Cole, 1978, p. 118)

About 10 percent of adults in the United States have a physical handicap that imposes a substantial limitation on their activities. Given a chance to express themselves, these people emphasize the importance of their sexuality and sex drive, which may be unaltered by their disability (Richardson, 1972).

Just what can handicapped people do sexually? Space does not permit a complete listing of all types of disabilities and their consequences for sexuality. Instead, the discussion will concentrate on two illustrative examples: spinal-cord injury and mental retardation.

Spinal Cord Injury

Paraplegia (paralysis of the lower half of the body on both sides) and quadriplegia (paralysis of the body from the neck down) are both caused by injuries to the spinal cord. Many able-bodied people find it difficult to understand what it feels like to be paralyzed. Imagine that your genitals and the region around them have lost all sensation. You would not know they were being touched unless you saw it happen. Further, there is loss of bladder and bowel

control, which may produce embarrassing problems if sexual activity is attempted.

The capacity of a spinal-cord-injured man to have erections depends on the level of the spinal cord at which the injury (lesion) occurred, and whether the spinal cord was completely or only partially severed. According to most studies, a majority of spinal-cord-injured men are able to have erections. In some cases only reflex erections are possible, that is, erections produced by direct stimulation of the genitals, even though the man cannot feel the sensation. In a few cases, particularly if the injury was not severe, the man is able to produce an erection by erotic thoughts, but this capacity is typically lost with spinal-cord injury. When the injury is severe, the man is not able to ejaculate, although ejaculation may be possible if the cord was only partially severed. Generally men's fertility is impaired by spinal-cord injury. In sum, many spinal-cord-injured men experience the same sexual responses as able-bodied men—including erection, elevation of the testes, and increases in heart rate—except that they generally cannot ejaculate, nor can they feel the physical stimulation.

The data on women with spinal-cord injuries, interestingly, generally do not focus on their capacity for vaginal lubrication and orgasm, but rather on their menstrual cycles and capacity for pregnancy. Women typically have amenorrhea (absence of menstruation) immediately following a spinal-cord injury, although normal menstrual cycling generally returns within six months. After that time, their ability to conceive a baby is normal. The pregnancy generally proceeds normally, although there is a higher risk of some complications such as cystitis (bladder infection), anemia, premature labor, and autonomic hyperreflexia (an exaggerated response of the autonomic nervous system, in which the woman

(a)

(b)

(c)

FIGURE 9.10

(a) and (b) In the 1980s and 1990s we have become more aware of disabled people's capacity for sexual expression and of the need for sex education for disabled children. (c) Ellen Stohl, the first disabled woman to appear in Playboy *(October, 1987). She is a quadriplegic, having suffered several broken bones in the neck in an automobile accident. She was completely paralyzed initially, although she gradually recovered some use of her arms. She has some sensitivity in her legs and is hypersensitive in the genitals. She enjoys sex very much and is orgasmic.*

experiences a great deal of sweating, abnormally rapid heartbeat, and anxiety). Normal vaginal deliveries are usually possible, and they can be done without anesthetic because the woman feels no sensation in the pelvic region. The fertility of spinal-injured women means that contraception is an important consideration for them.

Spinal-cord-injured women generally experience many of the same sexual responses as able-bodied women, including engorgement of the clitoris and labia, erection of the nipples, and increases in heart rate. However, vaginal lubrication and orgasm generally do not occur, although they may in some cases. It is interesting to note that some spinal-cord-injured women develop a capacity for orgasm from stimulation of the breasts or lips.

Because sexuality in our culture is currently so orgasm-oriented, orgasm problems among spinal-cord-injured people may appear to be devastating. But many of these handicapped people report that they have been able to cultivate a kind of "psychological orgasm" that is as satisfying as the physical one. Fantasy is a perfectly legitimate form of sexual expression that has not been ruled out by their injury.

Mental Retardation

Persons with IQs below 70 are generally classified as retarded. There is a great range in the capacities of

(continued on next page)

(continued)

retarded individuals, from some who require institutionalization and constant care, to those who function quite normally in the community, who can read and write and hold simple jobs. It is important to recognize that the great majority of retarded persons are only moderately retarded (IQs between 50 and 70) and are in the latter category of near-normal functioning.

Three issues are especially important when considering the sexuality of mentally retarded persons: their opportunity for sexual expression, the need for sex education, and the importance of contraception.

Retarded persons have normal sexual desires and seek to express them. Unfortunately, because retarded children are often slower to learn the norms of society, they may express themselves sexually in ways that may shock others, such as masturbating in public. For this reason and others, careful sex education for retarded persons is essential. They must be taught about the norms of privacy for sexuality. At the same time, they must be allowed a right to their own privacy, something that institutions often fail to recognize.

It is important that retarded individuals be educated about contraception and that contraceptives be made available to them. Because the retarded have normal sexual desires, they may engage in sexual intercourse but, if they are lacking sex education, they may not realize that pregnancy can result. An unwanted pregnancy for a retarded woman or couple may be a difficult situation; they may be able to function well when taking care of themselves, but they are unable to function with the added burden of a baby. On the other hand, some retarded persons function sufficiently well to care for a child. The important thing is that they make as educated a decision as possible and that they have access to contraceptives. Many experts recommend the IUD for retarded women, because it does not require memory and forethought for effective use.

The topic of contraception and the retarded raises the ugly issue of involuntary sterilization. Until the mid-1950s, retarded persons in institutions were routinely sterilized, although certainly not with their informed consent. We now view this as a violation of the rights of retarded persons, especially if they are only mildly retarded. Legally it is now very difficult to gain permission to sterilize a retarded person.

In summary, there are three general points to be made about sexuality and handicapped persons: (1) They generally do have sexual needs and desires; (2) they are often capable of sexual response quite similar to that of able-bodied people of average intelligence; and (3) there is a real need for more information—and communication—about what people with various disabilities can and cannot do sexually.

Sources: Cole (1975); Higgins (1978); Young et al. (1983); Allen & Allen (1979); Stewart (1979); Willmuth (1987).

are biochemicals that are manufactured in the body and secreted into the bloodstream to be carried to the organs that they affect. Pheromones, on the other hand, are biochemicals that are secreted outside the body. Thus, through the sense of smell, they are an important means of communication between animals. Often the pheromones are contained in the animal's urine. Thus the dog that does "scent marking" is actually depositing pheromones. Some pheromones appear to be important in sexual communication, and some have even been called "sex attractants."

Much of the research on pheromones has been done with mice and demonstrates the importance of pheromones in sexual and reproductive functioning. For example, exposure to the odor of male urine induces estrus (ovulation and sexual behavior) in female mice (the *Whitten effect*). If a female mouse copulates with a male and conceives and is then exposed to the odors of a strange male mouse, the pregnancy is aborted, presumably because implantation is prevented (the *Bruce effect*).

It appears that testosterone is critical to the male pheromones' ability to have these effects on females. If a male mouse is castrated, its urine will not induce estrus or block pregnancy (Bruce, 1969).

Pheromones present in female urine also have an influence on male sexual behavior. An early study demonstrated that male rats can tell the difference between the odor of estrous females and that of females not in estrus and that the males prefer estrous females (LeMagnen, 1952). Similar phenomena have been demonstrated in male dogs, stallions, bulls, and rams (Michael & Keverne, 1968). The ovarian hormones estrogen and progesterone are critical to the female pheromones' ability to have an effect on males (Beach & Merari, 1970).

The sense of smell (olfaction) seems to be essential in order for pheromone effects to occur. Removal of the olfactory bulbs (a part of the brain important in olfaction) severely inhibits sexual behavior in both males and females (Bronson, 1968).

Some research has been done on pheromones in monkeys. It has been found, for example, that estrogen treatment of a female rhesus monkey sexually excites the males in her cage (Herbert, 1966). If the males' sense of smell is blocked, they no longer are sexually excited.

What relevance does all this have for humans? Humans are not, by and large, "smell animals." Olfaction is not particularly important for us, especially compared with other species. We tend to rely mostly on vision and, secondarily, hearing. Compare this with a dog's ability to get a wealth of information about who and what has been in a park simply by sniffing around for a few minutes. Does this mean that pheromones have no influence on our sexual behavior?

Researchers are now speculating that human pheromones exist and that they play an important role in sexual behavior (Comfort, 1971). Indeed, pheromones may be exactly the "body chemistry" that attracts people to each other. It has been speculated that human pheromones are produced by the sweat glands of the armpits and by the prepuce of the male's penis and the female's clitoris. Perfumes with musky scents have become quite popular and presumably increase sexual attractiveness, perhaps because they smell like pheromones. The perfume industry has eagerly tried to capitalize on the pheromone research; indeed, there is a perfume on the market called "Pheromone."

One exciting advance in this research has been the identification, in the vaginal secretions of 50 women, of chemicals known to be sex-attractant pheromones in monkeys (Michael et al., 1974). The peak in production of these volatile fatty acids is just before and during ovulation. In another study, subjects rated the pleasantness of the odor of vaginal secretions at various stages of the menstrual cycle (Doty et al., 1975). The results indicate that the secretions are more pleasant around ovulation. In sum, it appears that there are the most pheromones around ovulation and that pheromones have the pleasantest smell around ovulation, exactly when it would be expected from an evolutionary perspective. That is exactly when the pheromones would promote intercourse, which would encourage reproduction, and that is exactly what natural selection tries to encourage. At the very least, it seems clear that humans do produce pheromones.

An interesting series of experiments seems to demonstrate the influence of pheromones in the human menstrual cycle (Cutler et al., 1986; Preti et al., 1986). Men and women "donors" wore cotton pads under their armpits. These pads col-

9.3

Castration or Incarceration

In 1983, Judge C. Victor Pyle delivered a controversial sentence in a rape case: The defendants could choose 30 years in prison or castration. The three men had been convicted of a brutal gang rape of an 80-pound woman, after which she required a transfusion of 4 pints of blood and five days of hospitalization. The issue was raised again in 1992 when a young man, who was on probation for molesting a 7-year-old and had just been arrested for raping a 13-year-old girl, volunteered to be castrated rather than being jailed.

These cases raise a host of questions, some of them legal, some within the province of the sciences. Legally, the castration sentence could be protested on the grounds that it is cruel and unusual punishment. What purpose did Judge Pyle have in mind when he assigned the castration sentence? Was he simply being punitive and letting the punishment fit the crime? Or did he view castration as a solution that would ensure that the men would never commit rape again? The scientific data become pertinent in addressing this last point.

Would castration (surgical removal of the testes, technically known as *bilateral orchidectomy*) prevent a man from committing rape? When the tes-

tes are removed, the man is left with little or no natural testosterone in his body. Numerous experiments with lower animals have demonstrated that the effect of this level of testosterone is a sharply reduced sex drive and the virtual elimination of sexual behavior. However, the effects in humans are not so clear, because we are not as hormone-dependent as other species. There are documented cases of castrated men continuing to engage in sexual intercourse for years after the castration. Thus, castration may reduce sexual behavior in humans, but the effects are not completely predictable. Further, testosterone is available artificially, either by pill or by injection, so that the men might secretly obtain replacement testosterone even when their natural testosterone had been removed.

The discussion up to this point has focused on rape as a form of sexual behavior. Yet many experts believe that rape is better conceptualized as an aggressive or violent crime that happens to be expressed sexually. Thus, the scientific question may be restated from "Does castration eliminate sexual behavior?" to "Does castration eliminate aggressive behavior?" Here, too, there are numerous experiments documenting—in other species—that castra-

lected axillary (underarm) secretions, including, presumably, pheromones. The secretions were then extracted from the cotton pads, producing "male extract" and "female extract" (it reminds one a bit of vanilla extract). In one of the experiments, a group of volunteer women were exposed to female extract collected at regular intervals across the menstrual cycle. The recipient women showed significant shifts toward having their cycles at the same time (the menstrual synchrony phenomenon was first discovered by McClintock in 1971). In another experiment, women with "abnormal" menstrual cycles (defined as cycles shorter than 26 days or longer than 32 days) were exposed to male extract. These women showed a reduction in the proportion of their cycles that were aberrant in length.

FIGURE 9.11
Judge C. Victor Pyle

tion, by lowering testosterone levels, greatly reduces aggressive behavior. But once again, the hormone effects are not as clear or consistent in humans. Thus, castration might be effective in reducing sexual or aggressive behaviors and thus might reduce the chance of the men committing rape again, but such effects cannot be guaranteed.

Other biological treatments for rapists are being explored. One is injections of the drug **Depo-**

Provera, which has also been used experimentally as a form of birth control for women. In male sex offenders, Depo-Provera is thought to be a kind of "chemical castration" because its effect is to reduce sharply the levels of testosterone in the body. It seems clear that Depo-Provera should be only part of the treatment, which should also include intensive psychotherapy. In one treatment program combining Depo-Provera and psychotherapy, after three and a half years only 15 percent of the men had repeated their offense, compared with rates as high as 85 percent for men who are only imprisoned. Yet some authorities believe that Depo-Provera is dangerous, possibly increasing the risk of cancer and suicidal depression.

Two questions remain for scientists. What role does testosterone play in sexual behavior and in aggressive behavior in humans? And, will biological therapies be effective in stopping rapists from repeating their crime?

Sources: Michael S. Serrill. (1983, Dec. 12). Castration or incarceration? *Time*, p. 70. Nikolaus Heim. (1981). Sexual behavior of castrated sex offenders. *Archives of Sexual Behavior*, 10, pp. 11–20. Robert T. Rubin, June M. Reinisch, & Roger F. Haskett. (1981). Postnatal gonadal steroid effects on human behavior. *Science*, 211, pp. 1318–1324. Robert Lacayo (1992, Mar. 23). Sentences inscribed on flesh. *Time*, 54.

Depo-Provera (DEH-poh-proh-VARE-uh): A drug containing synthetic hormones; used as an experimental form of birth control in women, as well as in treating male sex offenders.

It should be noted that the smell of pheromones would not necessarily have to be consciously perceived in order for it to have an effect. The olfactory system can respond to odors even when they are not consciously perceived. Thus, pheromones that we are not even aware of may have important influences.

If these speculations about the effects of pheromones on human sexual behavior are correct, our "hyperclean" society may be destroying the scents that attract people to each other. The normal genital secretions (assuming reasonable cleanliness to eliminate bacteria) may contain sex attractants. The feminine hygiene deodorants may destroy precisely the odors that "turn men on."

Future research on human pheromones should be interesting indeed.

(a)

(b)

FIGURE 9.12
Pheromones.
(a) Pheromones are a
major means of
communication between
animals. (b) Are there
human pheromones that
are sex attractants?

Summary

William Masters and Virginia Johnson conducted an important program of research, beginning in the 1950s, on the physiology of human sexual response. They found that two basic physiological processes occur during arousal and orgasm: vasocongestion and myotonia. They divide the sexual response cycle into four stages: excitement, plateau, orgasm, and resolution.

Their research indicates that there is no physiological distinction between clitoral and vaginal orgasms in women, which refutes an early idea of Freud's. They have also provided convincing evidence of the existence of multiple orgasm in women.

Criticisms of Masters and Johnson's model are that (1) they ignored cognitive factors, and (2) their selection of subjects may have led to a self-fulfilling prophecy in their results.

Alternatives to Masters and Johnson's model are Kaplan's three component (vasocongestion, muscular contraction, and desire) model and Walen and Roth's model, which emphasizes cognitive aspects of sexual response (perception and evaluation).

The nervous system and sex hormones are important in sexual response. The nervous system functions in sexual response by a combination of spinal reflexes (best documented for erection and ejaculation) and brain influences (particularly of the limbic system). There is controversial evidence that some women ejaculate. Hormones are important to sexual behavior, both in their influences on prenatal development (organizing effects) and in their stimulating influence on adult sexual behavior (activating effects). Testosterone seems to be important for maintaining libido in both men and women.

Pheromones are biochemicals secreted outside the body that play an important role in sexual communication and attraction.

Review Questions

1. According to Masters and Johnson, the four stages of sexual response are, in order, _____, _____, _____, and _____.

2. According to Masters and Johnson, the two basic physiological processes that occur during sexual arousal are _____ and myotonia.

3. According to Masters and Johnson, vaginal lubrication in the female is caused by vasocongestion. True or false?

4. Masters and Johnson's model of sexual response has been criticized because they ignored _____ factors such as sexual desire.

5. Only men are capable of multiple orgasm. True or false?

6. Erection in the male is produced by a simple spinal reflex. True or false?

7. It has been hypothesized that a small organ, called the _____, is responsible for ejaculation in some women.

8. If female guinea pig fetuses are exposed to testosterone prenatally, they are born with masculinized genitals and hypothalamus and show male sexual behaviors; this demonstrates the _____ effects of hormones.

9. _____ are biochemicals secreted outside the body that may serve a role as sex attractants.

10. When Judge Pyle sentenced three convicted rapists to prison or castration, he made a wise decision because research has proven that castration prevents men from commiting rape in the future. True or false?

(The answer to all review questions are at the end of the book, beginning on page 731.)

Question for Thought, Discussion, and Debate

1. Debate the following topic. Resolved: Castration is an approporiate and effective treatment for convicted rapists.

Suggestions for Further Reading

Comfort, Alex. (1978). *Sexual consequences of disability*. Philadelphia: George F. Stickley Company. This is an outstanding collection of articles put together by the noted sexologist Alex Comfort (of *The Joy of Sex*). A broad range of topics are covered, including sex problems of those with multiple sclerosis, arthritis, diabetes, kidney problems requiring hemodialysis, heart disease, and stroke, and sex education for children with disabilities.

Rosen, Raymond C., & Beck, Gayle. (1988). *Patterns of sexual arousal: Psychophysiological processes and clinical applications*. New York: Guilford. A thorough analysis of physiological influences on sexual behavior, using new advances in psychophysiology research.

White, David. (1981, Sept.) Pursuit of the ultimate aphrodisiac. *Psychology Today, 15,* 9–12. An evaluation of current scientific evidence on human pheromones.

Techniques of Arousal and Communication

Seeking sexual satisfaction is a basic desire, and masturbation is our first natural sexual activity. It's the way we discover our eroticism, the way we learn to respond sexually, the way we learn to love ourselves and to build self-esteem. Sexual skill and the ability to respond are not "natural" in our society. "Doing what comes naturally," is to be sexually inhibited. Sex, like any other skill, has to be learned and practiced. *

We live in the era of sex manuals. Books like *Everything You Always Wanted to Know about Sex . . .*, *The New Joy of Sex*, *The Sensuous Woman*, and *The Sensuous Man*, as well as numerous feature articles and advice columns in magazines like *Playboy*, give us information on how to produce bigger and better orgasms in ourselves and our partners. The "read-all-about-it" boom has produced not only benefits but also problems. It may turn our attention so much to mechanical techniques that we forget about love and the emotional side of sexual expression. The sex manuals may also set up impossible standards of sexual performance that none of us can meet. On the other hand, we live in a society that has a history of leaving the learning of sexual techniques to nature or to chance, in contrast to some "primitive" societies in which adolescents are given explicit instruction in methods for producing sexual pleasure. For human beings, sexual behavior is a lot more than "doin' what comes naturally"; we all need some means for learning about sexual techniques, and the sex manuals may help to fill that need.

The purpose of this chapter is to provide information on techniques of arousal, while attempting to avoid making sex too mechanical or setting up unrealistic performance standards. It also focuses on skills for communicating in a relationship. As you build a sexual relationship with another person, three components are important: (1) building a loving attachment, (2) building the sexual part of the relationship, and (3) developing good communication. This chapter focuses on items 2 and 3. Love in relationships will be discussed in Chapter 13.

* *Source:* Betty Dodson. (1987). *Sex for One*, (p. 36). New York: Harmony Books (Crown Publishers).

EROGENOUS ZONES

Erogenous zones (eh-RAH-jen-us): Areas of the body that are particularly sensitive to sexual stimulation.

While the notion of erogenous zones originated in Freud's work, the term is now part of our general vocabulary and refers to parts of the body which are sexually sensitive; stroking them or otherwise stimulating them produces sexual arousal. The genitals and the breasts are good examples. The lips, neck, and thighs are generally also erogenous zones. But even some rather unlikely regions—such as the back, the ears, the stomach, and the feet—can also be quite erogenous. One person's erogenous zones can be quite different from another person's. Thus it is impossible to give a list of sure "turn-ons." The best way to find out is to communicate with your partner, either verbally or nonverbally.

ONE-PERSON SEX

It does not necessarily take two to have sex. One can produce one's own sexual stimulation. Sexual self-stimulation is called **autoeroticism**.[1] The best examples are masturbation and fantasy.

Autoeroticism: Sexual self-stimulation; for example, masturbation.

[1] For those of you who are interested in the roots of words, "autoeroticism" does not refer to sex in the back seat of a car. The prefix "auto" means "self" (as in "autobiography"); hence self-stimulation is autoeroticism.

FIGURE 10.1
Erotic miniature painting from India (eighteenth century) showing the sensitive parts of the female body, which were believed to vary during each day of the lunar month.

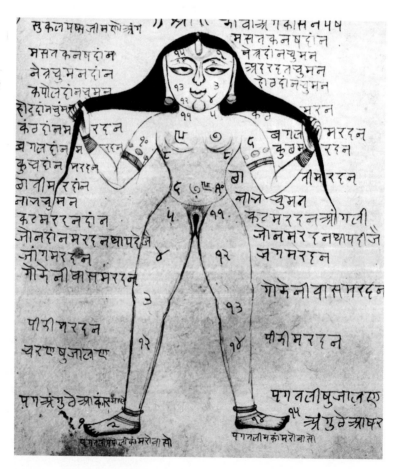

Masturbation

Masturbation: Hand
stimulation of one's own
genitals.

The term masturbation can refer either to hand stimulation of one's own genitals or to hand stimulation of another's genitals. Here the term "hand-genital stimulation" will be reserved for stimulation of another's genitals and the term "masturbation" for self-stimulation, either with the hand or with some object, such as a pillow or a vibrator. Masturbation is a very common sexual behavior; almost all men and the majority of women masturbate to orgasm at least a few times during their lives, and many do so frequently. The techniques used by males and females in masturbation are interesting in part because they provide information to their partners concerning the best techniques to use in lovemaking.

Techniques of Female Masturbation

Most commonly women masturbate by manipulating the clitoris and the inner lips (Hite, 1976; Kinsey et al., 1953, pp. 158, 189). They may rub up and down or in a circular motion, sometimes lightly and sometimes applying more pressure to the clitoris. Some prefer to rub at the side of the clitoris, while a few stimulate the glans of the clitoris directly. The inner lips may also be stroked or tugged. One woman described her technique as follows:

> I use the tips of my fingers for actual stimulation, but it's better to start with patting motions or light rubbing motions over the general area. As excitement increases I begin stroking above the clitoris and finally reach a climax with a rapid, jerky circular motion over the clitoral hood. Usually my legs are apart, and occasionally I also stimulate my nipples with the other hand. (Hite, 1976, p. 20)

This finding is in distinct contrast to what many men imagine to be the techniques of female masturbation; the male pictures the woman inserting a finger, a banana, or a similar object into the depths of the vagina (Kinsey et al., 1953). In fact, this is not often done; by far the most common method is clitoral and labial manipulation. Of the women in Kinsey's sample who masturbated, 84 percent used clitoral and labial manipulation; inserting fingers or objects into the vagina was the second most commonly used technique, but it was practiced by only 20 percent of the women.

Other techniques used by women in masturbation include breast stimulation, thigh pressure exerted by crossing the legs and pressing them together rhythmically to stimulate the clitoris, and pressing the genitals against some object, such as a pillow, or massaging them with a stream of water while in the shower. A few women (about 2 percent in Kinsey's sample) are capable of using fantasy alone to produce orgasm.

Techniques of Male Masturbation

Almost all males report masturbating by hand stimulation of the penis. For those interested in speed, an orgasm can be reached in only a minute or two (Kinsey et al., 1948, p. 509).

Most men use the technique of circling the hand around the shaft of the penis and using an up-and-down movement to stimulate the shaft and glans. Because the penis produces no natural lubrication of its own, some men like to use a form of lubrication, such as soapsuds while showering. The tightness of the grip, the speed of movement, and the amount of glans stimulation vary from one man to the next. Most increase the speed of stimulation as they approach orgasm, slowing or stopping

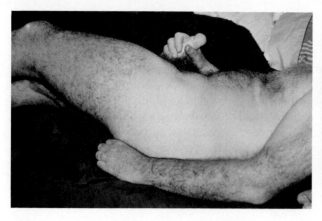
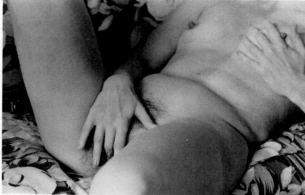

FIGURE 10.2
(a) Male masturbation.
(b) Female masturbation.

the stimulation at orgasm because further stimulation would be uncomfortable (Masters & Johnson, 1966). At the time of ejaculation, they often grip the shaft of the penis tightly. Immediately after orgasm, the glans and corona are hypersensitive, and the man generally avoids further stimulation of the penis at that time (Sadock & Sadock, 1976).

Fantasy

Fantasy: Mental images that are usually pleasant and unrestrained by reality.

Fantasies are another form of self-stimulation, or autoeroticism. Sexual fantasies can occur while daydreaming or during masturbation or sexual intercourse with another person. In one study, 88 percent of respondents indicated that they had experienced sexual fantasies (Davidson & Hoffman, 1986).

Fantasy During Masturbation

Approximately 59 percent of men and 12 percent of women who masturbate fantasize every time they do so (Jones & Barlow, 1990). An additional 41 percent of males and 64 percent of females fantasize at least some of the time. Such fantasies are, therefore, quite common.

The exact content of fantasies is highly individual, but some general themes are quite common. Table 10.1 summarizes some of the themes of fantasies during masturbation that were reported by the respondents in one survey. Common themes include having intercourse with a loved one or with a stranger (sometimes a movie or TV star such as Tom Cruise or Cindy Crawford), engaging in group sex, being forced to or forcing someone to have sex, or doing other things that would not happen in reality. Heterosexuals typically have heterosexual fantasies, and homosexuals have homosexual fantasies, but there may be some crossing over; for example, a heterosexual may sometimes have homosexual fantasies.

As Table 10.1 indicates, the themes of fantasies differ somewhat for males and females, though there are considerable similarities. The differences might be summarized as follows: Males' fantasies tend to involve situations in which they are powerful and aggressive and are engaged in impersonal sex, while females' fantasies are more likely to involve romance or being forced to have sex (Barclay, 1973; DeLora & Warren, 1977; Shope, 1975). Here is an adolescent male's description of one of his favorite fantasies during masturbation:

Table 10.1
Common Themes of Fantasies While Masturbating

Theme of Fantasy	Percentage of People Having That Type of Fantasy	
	Males	Females
1. Having intercourse with a loved one	75	80
2. Having intercourse with a stranger	47	21
3. Having sex with more than one person at the same time	33	18
4. Doing sexual things one would never do in reality	19	28
5. Being forced to have sex	10	19
6. Forcing someone to have sex	13	3
7. Having sex with someone of the same gender	7	11

Source: Morton Hunt. (1974). *Sexual Behavior in the 1970s.* Chicago. Playboy Press, pp. 91–93.

> We would be riding in the back seat of the car, and I would reach over and fondle her breasts. She would reach into my pants and begin to caress my penis and finally suck me off. (Jensen, 1976a, p. 144)

This is the fantasy of one college woman as she imagines the seduction of her French teacher:

> At exactly 8:00 I knocked on the door. When this guy saw what I was wearing I thought his eyes were going to pop out. Calmly he asked me to come in and sit down. . . .
> "Please call me Jim." Now I was getting somewhere. . . . I slipped out of my shoes and loosened my dress. When Jim returned I was ready and waiting. . . . Well the man finally got the hint; he reached around and unzipped my dress. While I was slowly undoing his zipper, he buried his head between my breasts. As his mouth slowly descended down my body I could feel the heat rising from between my legs. . . . To add to my desire he started speaking French to me. You didn't have to be fluent to understand this. As his mouth continued to nibble away, his tongue zeroed in on my clit and sent me to a mind boggling orgasm. As my pleasure subsided I began to return the favor. . . . Although I had enjoyed several orgasms by now the night was far from over. Jim then got on top of me and made love to me for what seemed like an eternity. . . . (Moffatt, 1989, pp. 190–191)

The content of male and female sexual fantasies seems to be influenced by cultural stereotypes of male and female sexuality.

Fantasy During Two-Person Sex

Fantasies are also a means of self-stimulation to heighten the experience of sex with another person. Particularly in a long-term, monogamous relationship, sexual monotony can become a problem; fantasies are one way to introduce some variety and excitement without violating an agreement to be faithful to the other person. It is important to view such fantasies in this way, rather than as a sign of disloyalty to, or dissatisfaction with, one's sexual partner.

Fantasies during two-person sex are generally quite similar to the ones people have while masturbating. In one study, 84 percent of males and 82 percent of females reported that they fantasized at least some of the time during intercourse (Cado & Leitenberg, 1990). This kind of fantasizing is quite common.

Fantasies are not a sign of poor marital relations; in one study the women who fantasized reported better sexual relationships with their husbands than the women who did not fantasize (Hariton, 1973). Diane is an example:

> Diane is happily married. Yet she finds sexual foreplay with her husband more exciting if she imagines herself a harem slave displaying her breasts to an adoring sheik. While having intercourse, she sometimes envisions making love in the back seat of a car or in an old-fashioned house during a group orgy. She likes to imagine being forced by one man after another. In one favorite scene she goes to a drive-in movie and is raped by a masculine figure whose face is a "blur." (Hariton, 1973, p. 39)

Some couples also enjoy sharing their sexual fantasies with each other.

Vibrators, Dildos, and Such

Various sexual devices, such as vibrators and dildos, are used by some people in masturbation or by couples as they have sex together.

Dildo: An artificial penis.

Both male and female artificial genitals can be purchased. A dildo is an artificial penis; it can be inserted into the vagina or the anus. Dildos are used by women in masturbation (although, as was noted in the previous section, this is not very common), by lesbians, by male homosexuals or heterosexuals, and by heterosexual couples. Artificial vaginas, and even inflatable replicas of the entire female body, can also be purchased.

Some *vibrators* are shaped like a penis and others are not; there are models with a cord that plugs into an electric socket and also battery-operated, cordless models. Women may use them to masturbate, stimulating the clitoral and mons area, or they may insert them into the vagina. Males may use them to stimulate the genitals or the anus. They are used either in masturbation or during sex with another person. They can be purchased in "respectable" stores (where they are sometimes euphemistically called "face massagers"), in sex supermarkets, and by mail.

Body oils are also popular for sexual use. In fact, their use has been encouraged by experts in the field; for example, Masters and Johnson and other sex therapists recommend them for the touching or sensate focus exercises that they prescribe for their patients in sex therapy (see Chapter 19). Oils have a sensuous quality that heightens erotic feelings. Further, if you are being stroked or massaged for any extended period of time, the oil helps ensure that the part of your body that is being stimulated will not end up feeling like a piece of wood that has been sandpapered. Oils can be used either while masturbating or while having sex with another person. The sex stores sell them in a variety of exotic scents, but plain baby oil will also do nicely.

TWO-PERSON SEX

When most of us think of techniques of two-person sex, the image that flashes across our mind generally reflects several assumptions. One assumption is that one of the people is a male and the other a female, that is, that the sex is heterosexual. This reflects a belief that heterosexual sex is normative. Further, we tend to assume that the male is supposed to do certain things during the act and that the female is supposed to do certain other things, reflecting the sexual scripts of our culture. He, for example, is supposed to take the initiative in deciding what techniques are used, while she is to follow his lead. Although there is nothing particularly evil in these assumptions, they do tend to impose some limitations on our own sexual expression and to make some people think that their own sexual behavior is "not quite right." Therefore, an attempt to avoid these assumptions will be made in the sections that follow.

Kissing

Kissing (or what we might call, technically, "mouth-to-mouth stimulation") is an activity that virtually everyone in our culture has engaged in (DeLamater & MacCorquodale, 1979). In simple kissing, the partners keep their mouths closed and touch each other's lips. In deep kissing ("French kissing"), both people part their lips slightly and insert their tongues into each other's mouths (somehow these clinical descriptions do not make it sound like as much fun as it is). There are endless variations on these two basic approaches, such as nibbling at the partner's lips or tongue or sucking at the lips; they depend only on your imagination and personal preference. There are also plenty of other regions of the body to kiss: the nose, the forehead, the eyelids, the earlobes, the neck, the breasts, the genitals, and even the feet, to give a few examples.

Touching

Enjoying touching and being touched is essential to sexual pleasure. Caressing or massaging, applied to virtually any area of the body, can be exciting. The regions that are exciting vary a great deal from one person to the next and depend on how the person is feeling at the moment; thus it is important to communicate what sort of touching is most pleasurable to you. (For specific exercises on touching and being touched, see Chapter 19).

As was noted earlier, one of the best ways to find out how to use your hand in stimulating the genitals of another person is to find out how that person masterbates.

Hand Stimulation of the Male Genitals

As a technique of lovemaking, hand stimulation of the male genitals can be used as a pleasurable preliminary to intercourse, as a means of inducing orgasm itself, or as a means of producing an erection after the man has had one orgasm and wants to continue for another round of lovemaking ("rousing the dead").

Alex Comfort, in *The Joy of Sex,* recommends the following technique:

> If he isn't circumcised, she will probably need to avoid rubbing the glans itself, except in pursuit of very special effects. Her best grip is just below the groove, with the skin back as far as it will go, and using two hands—one pressing hard near the root, holding the penis steady, or fondling the scrotum, the other making a thumb-and-first-finger ring, or a whole hand grip. She should vary this, and, in prolonged masturbation, change hands often. (1972, p. 118)

As a good technique for producing an erection he also mentions rolling the penis like dough between the palms of the hands. Firm pressure with one finger midway between the base of the penis and the anus is another possibility.

One of the things that make hand stimulation most effective is for the man's

FIGURE 10.3
Hand stimulation
of the penis.

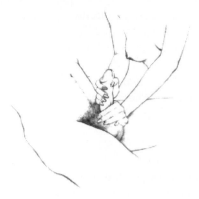

partner to have a playful delight in, and appreciation of, the man's penis. Most men think their penis is pretty important. If the partner cannot honestly appreciate it and enjoy massaging it, hand stimulation might as well not be done.

Hand Stimulation of the Female Genitals

The hand can be used to stimulate the woman's genitals to produce orgasm, as a preliminary method of arousing the woman before intercourse, or simply because it is pleasurable.

Generally it is best, particularly if the woman is not already aroused, to begin with gentle, light stroking of the inside of the thighs and the inner and outer lips, moving to light stroking of the clitoris. As she becomes more aroused, the stimulation of the clitoris can become firmer. There are several rules for doing this, though. First, remember that the clitoris is very sensitive and that this sensitivity can be either exquisite or painful. Some care has to be used in stimulating it; it cannot be manipulated like a piece of Silly Putty. Second, the clitoris should never—except, perhaps, for some light stroking—be rubbed while it is dry, for the effect can be more like sandpaper stimulation than sexual stimulation. If the woman is already somewhat aroused, lubrication can be provided by touching the fingers to the vaginal entrance and then spreading the lubrication on the clitoris. If she is not aroused or does not produce much vaginal lubrication, saliva works well too. Moisture makes the stimulation not only more comfortable but also more sensuous. Third, some women find direct stimulation of the clitoral glans to be painful in some states of arousal. These women generally prefer stimulation on either side of the clitoris instead.

With these caveats in mind, the clitoris can be stimulated with circular or back-and-forth movements of the finger. The inner and outer lips can also be stroked, rubbed, or tugged. These techniques, if done with skill and patience, can bring the woman to orgasm. Another technique that can be helpful in producing orgasm is for the partner to place the heel of the hand on the mons, exerting pressure on it while moving the middle finger in and out of the vaginal entrance. Another rule should also be clear by now: The partner needs to have close-trimmed nails that do not have any jagged edges. This is sensitive tissue we are dealing with.

The Other Senses

So far, this chapter has been focused on tactile (touch) sensations in sexual arousal. However, the other senses—vision, smell, and hearing—can also make contributions.

Sights

The things that you see while making love can contribute to arousal. Men seem, in general, to be more turned on by visual stimuli; many men have mild fetishes (see

Chapter 16 for more detail on fetishes) and like to see their partners wearing certain types of clothing. Perhaps as female sexuality becomes more liberated, women will become more interested in visual turn-ons. A good rule here, as elsewhere, is to communicate with your partner to find out what he or she would find arousing.

The decor of the room can also contribute to visual stimulation. Furry rugs, placed on the floor or used as a bedspread, are sensuous both visually and tactilely. Large mirrors, hung either behind the bed or on the ceiling above it, can be a visual turn-on, since they allow you to watch yourself make love. Candlelight is soft and contributes more to an erotic atmosphere than an electric light, which is harsh, or complete darkness, in which case there is no visual stimulation at all.

Perhaps the biggest visual turn-on comes simply from looking at your own body and your partner's body.

Smells

Odors can be turn-ons or turn-offs. The odors of a body that is clean, having been washed with soap and water, are themselves natural turn-ons. They do not need to be covered up with anything like "intimate deodorants."[2] In a sense, the odor of your skin, armpits, and genitals is your "aroma signature," and these natural odors can be quite arousing (Comfort, 1972).

A body that has not been washed or a mouth that has not been cleaned or has recently been used for smoking can be a real turn-off. Ideally, the communication between partners is honest and trusting enough so that if one offends, the other can simply request that the appropriate clean-up be done.

Sounds

Music—whether your preference is for rock or Brahms's Fourth—can contribute to an erotic atmosphere. Another advantage of playing music is that it helps muffle the sounds of sex, which can be important if you live in an apartment with thin walls or if you are worried about your children hearing you.

Genital-Genital Stimulation: Positions of Intercourse

One of the commonest heterosexual techniques involves the insertion of the penis into the vagina; this is called coitus[3] or *sexual intercourse*.

The couple may be in any one of a number of different positions while engaging in this basic sexual activity. Ancient love manuals and other sources illustrate many positions of intercourse (see Figure 10.4).

Some authorities state that there are only four positions of intercourse. Personally, I prefer to believe that there are an infinite number. Consider how many different angles your arms, legs, and torso may be in, in relation to those of your partner, and all the various ways in which you can intertwine your limbs—that's a lot of positions. I trust that given sufficient creativity and time, you can discover them all for yourselves. I would agree, though, that there are a few basic positions and a few basic

Coitus: Sexual intercourse; insertion of the penis into the vagina.

---

[2] With the increased popularity of mouth-genital sex, some women worry that the scent of their genitals might be offensive. The advertisements for feminine hygiene deodorant sprays prey upon those fears. These sprays should not be used because they may irritate the vagina (*Consumer Reports,* January 1972). And besides, there is nothing offensive about the scent of a vulva that has been washed; some people, in fact, find it arousing.

[3] From the Latin word *coire,* meaning "to go together."

FIGURE 10.4
*Erotic sculptures at the
Temple of Kandariya
Mahadevo, India, built in
A.D. 1000.*

dimensions along which positions can vary. One basic variation depends on whether
the couple face each other (face-to-face position) or whether one partner faces the
other's back (rear-entry position); if you try the other obvious variation, a back-to-
back position, you will quickly find that you cannot accomplish much that way. The
other basic variation depends on whether one partner is on top of the other or
whether the couple are side by side. Let us consider four basic positions that illustrate
these variations. As Julia Child does, I'll give you the basic recipes and let you decide
on the embellishments.

Man on Top

The face-to-face, man-on-top position ("missionary" position—see Figure 10.5) is
the one used most frequently by couples in the United States. Indeed, Kinsey, commenting from his 1940s perspective, said:

> Nearly all coitus in our English-American culture occurs with the partners lying
> face to face, with the male above the female. There may be as much as 70 percent
> of the population which has never attempted to use any other position in inter-
> course. (Kinsey et al., 1948, p. 578)

Beginning in the 1970s, however, people began to use much more of a variety of
positions (Hunt, 1974).

FIGURE 10.5
*The man-on-top position
of intercourse.*

In the man-on-top position (which used to be called "male-superior," an unacceptable term today) the man and woman stimulate each other until they are aroused, he has an erection, and she is producing vaginal lubrication. Then he moves on top of her as she spreads her legs apart, either he or she spreads the vaginal lips apart, and he inserts his penis into her vagina. He supports himself on his knees and hands or elbows and moves his penis in and out of the vagina (pelvic thrusting). Some men worry that their heavy weight will crush the poor woman under them; however, because the weight is spread out over so great an area, most women do not find this to be a problem at all, and many find the sensation of contact to be pleasurable.

The woman can have her legs in a number of positions that create variations. She may have them straight out horizontally, a position that produces a tight rub on the penis but does not permit it to go deeply into the vagina. She may bend her legs and elevate them to varying degrees, or she may hook them over the man's back or over his shoulders. The last approach permits the penis to move deeply into the vagina. The woman can also move her pelvis, either up and down or side to side, to produce further stimulation.

The man-on-top position has some advantages and some disadvantages. It is the best position for ensuring conception, if that is what you want to ensure. It leaves the woman's hands free to stroke the man's body (or her own, for that matter). The couple may feel better able to express their love or to communicate other feelings, since they are facing each other. This position, however, does not work well if the woman is in the advanced stages of pregnancy or if either she or the man is extremely obese. Sex therapists have also found that it is not a very good position if the man wants to control his ejaculation; the woman-on-top position is better for this (see Chapter 19).

Woman on Top

There are a number of ways of getting into the woman-on-top position (Figure 10.6). You can begin by inserting the penis into the vagina while in the man-on-top position

FIGURE 10.6
The woman-on-top
position of intercourse.

and then rolling over. Another possibility is to begin with the man on his back; the woman kneels over him, with one knee on either side of his hips. Then his hand or her hand guides the erect penis into the vagina as she lowers herself onto it. She then moves her hips to produce the stimulation. Beyond that, there are numerous variations, depending on where she puts her legs. She can remain on her knees, or she can straighten out her legs behind her, putting them outside his legs or between them. Or she can even turn around and face toward his feet.

This position has a number of advantages. It provides a lot of clitoral stimulation, and the woman can control the kind of stimulation she gets; thus many women find it the best position for them to have an orgasm. It is also a good position for the man who wants to delay his ejaculation, and for this reason it is used in sex therapy. This position is also a good one if the man is tired and it seems advisable for the woman to supply most of the movement. Further, the couple face each other, facilitating better communication, and each has the hands free to stroke the other.

Rear Entry

In the rear-entry position, the man faces the woman's back. One way to do this is to have the woman kneel with her head down; the man kneels and inserts his penis into her vagina (Figure 10.7). (This is sometimes called the "doggie position," because it is the manner in which dogs and most other animals copulate.) Another possibility is for the woman to lie on her stomach, raising her hips slightly so that the man can insert his penis while kneeling over her. Rear entry can also be accomplished when the couple are in the side-to-side position (see below).

FIGURE 10.7
The rear-entry position of intercourse.

In this position the man's hands are free to stimulate the woman's clitoris or any other part of her body. The couple, however, do not face each other, and some couples dislike this aspect of the position. A small amount of air may enter the vagina when this position is used, producing interesting noises when it comes out.

Side to Side

In the side-to-side position, the man and woman lie beside each other, either face to face or in a rear-entry position (Figure 10.8). There are many variations beyond this, depending on where the arms and legs go—so many, in fact, that no attempt will be made to list them. One should be aware, though, that in this position an arm or a leg can get trapped under a heavy body and begin to feel numb, and shifting positions is sometimes necessary.

The side-to-side position is good for leisurely or prolonged intercourse or if one or both of the partners are tired. It is also good for the pregnant and the obese. At least some hands are free to stimulate the clitoris, or whatever.

FIGURE 10.8
The side-to-side position of intercourse.

Other Variations

Aside from the variations in these basic positions that can be produced by switching the position of the legs, there are many other possibilities for variations. For example, the man-on-top position can be varied by having the woman lie on the edge of a bed with her feet on the floor while the man kneels on the floor. Or the woman can lie on the edge of a table while the man stands (don't forget to close the curtains first). Both these positions produce a somewhat tighter vagina and therefore more stimulation for the penis. Or the man can sit on a chair and insert the penis as the woman sits on his lap, using either a face-to-face or a rear-entry approach. Or, with both partners standing, the man can lift the woman onto his erect penis as she wraps her legs around his back, or she can put one leg over his shoulder (you have to be pretty athletic to manage this one, however).

Mouth-Genital Stimulation

One of the most striking features of the sexual revolution of the last few decades is the increased popularity of mouth-genital, or oral-genital, techniques (Hunt, 1974). There are two kinds of mouth-genital stimulation ("going down on" one's partner): cunnilingus and fellatio.

Cunnilingus

Cunnilingus (cun-ih-LING-us): Mouth stimulation of the female genitals.

In cunnilingus, or "eating" (from the Latin words *cunnus,* meaning "vulva," and *lingere,* meaning "to lick"), the woman's genitals are stimulated by her partner's mouth. Generally the focus of stimulation is the clitoris, and the tongue stimulates it and the surrounding area with quick darting or thrusting movements, or the mouth can suck at the clitoris. A good prelude to cunnilingus can be kissing of the inner thighs or the belly, gradually moving to the clitoris. The mouth can also suck at the inner lips, or the tongue can stimulate the vaginal entrance or be inserted into the vagina. During cunnilingus, some women also enjoy having a finger inserted into the vagina or the anus for added stimulation. The best way to know what she wants is through communication between partners, either verbally or nonverbally.

Many women are enthusiastic about cunnilingus and say that it is the best way,

284

or perhaps the only way, for them to have an orgasm. Such responses are well within the normal range of female sexuality. As one woman put it:

> A tongue offers gentleness and precision and wetness and is the perfect organ for contact. And, besides, it produces sensational orgasms. (Hite, 1976, p. 234)

Cunnilingus (like fellatio) can transmit some sexually transmitted diseases such as gonorrhea. Therefore, you need to be as careful about whom you engage in mouth-genital sex with as about whom you would engage in intercourse with. A small sheet of plastic, called a dental dam, can be placed over the vulva for those wanting to practice safer sex. One other possible problem should be noted, as well. Some women enjoy having their partner blow air forcefully into the vagina. While this technique is not dangerous under normal circumstances, when used on a pregnant woman it has been known to cause death (apparently as the result of air getting into the uterine veins), damage to the placenta, and embolism (Sadock & Sadock, 1976). Thus it should not be used on a pregnant woman.

Cunnilingus can be performed by either heterosexuals or lesbian couples.

Fellatio

Fellatio (feh-LAY-shoh): Mouth stimulation of the male genitals.

In fellatio[4] ("sucking," "a blow job") the man's penis is stimulated by his partner's mouth. The partner licks the glans of the penis, its shaft, and perhaps the testicles. The penis is gently taken into the mouth. If it is not fully erect, an erection can generally be produced by stronger sucking combined with hand stimulation along the penis. After that, the partner can produce an in-and-out motion by moving the lips down toward the base of the penis and then back up, always being careful not to scrape the penis with the teeth. Or the tongue can be flicked back and forth around the tip of the penis or along the corona.

To bring the man to orgasm, the in-and-out motion is continued, moving the penis deeper and deeper into the mouth and perhaps also using the fingers to encircle the base of the penis and give further stimulation. Sometimes when the penis moves deeply toward the throat, it stimulates a gag reflex, which occurs anytime something comes into contact with that part of the throat. To avoid this, the partner should concentrate on relaxing the throat muscles while firming the lips to provide more stimulation to the penis.

When a couple are engaged in fellatio, the big question in their minds may concern ejaculation. The man may, of course, simply withdraw his penis from his partner's mouth and ejaculate outside it. Or he may ejaculate into it, and his partner may even enjoy swallowing the ejaculate. The ejaculate resembles partially cooked egg white in texture; it does not have a very distinctive flavor but often leaves a salty aftertaste. Because some people have mixed feelings about having the semen in their mouths, it is probably a good idea for the couple to discuss ahead of time (or during the activity) what they plan to do, particularly because ejaculation into the mouth is not a "safer sex" practice in the AIDS era (see Chapter 20).

Most men find fellatio to be a highly stimulating experience, which no doubt accounts for the high frequency with which prostitutes are asked to do it. Enjoyment of fellatio is certainly within the normal range of male sexuality.

Fellatio can be performed by either heterosexuals or male homosexual couples.

---

[4] "Fellatio" is from the Latin word *fellare,* meaning "to suck." Women should not take the "sucking" part too literally. The penis, particularly at the tip, is a delicate organ and should not be treated like a straw in an extra-thick milkshake.

Sixty-Nining

Fellatio and cunnilingus can be performed simultaneously by both partners. This is often called sixty-nining[5] because the numerals "69" suggest the position of the two bodies during simultaneous mouth-genital sex. Sixty-nining may be done either side to side or with one person on top of the other, each with the mouth on the other's genitals (Figure 10.9).

Simultaneous mouth-genital sex allows both people to enjoy the pleasure of that stimulation at the same time. It can give a feeling of total body involvement and total involvement between partners. Some couples, however, feel that this technique requires doing too many things at once and is more complicated than enjoyable. For example, the woman may be distracted from enjoying the marvelous clitoral stimulation she is receiving because she has to concentrate at the same time on using her mouth to give good stimulation to the penis. If sixty-nining is done in the man-on-top position, some women also feel that they have no control over the movement and that they may be choked.

Anal Intercourse

In anal intercourse the man inserts his penis into his partner's rectum (Morin, 1981). In legal terminology it is sometimes called sodomy (although this term may also refer to other things such as intercourse with animals), and it is sometimes referred to as having sex "Greek style." It may be done by either heterosexual couples or male homosexual couples.

Anal intercourse is somewhat more difficult than penis-in-vagina intercourse because the rectum has no natural lubrication and because it is surrounded by fairly tight muscles. The man should therefore begin by moistening the partner's anus, either with saliva or with a sterile surgical lubricant such as K-Y jelly (*not* Vaseline). He should also lubricate his penis. He then inserts it gently into the rectum and begins controlled pelvic thrusting. It is typically done in the rear-entry position or in

---

[5] If you want to be elegant and impress your friends, you can call it *soixante-neuf*, which is just "sixty-nine" in French.

FIGURE 10.9 Simultaneous mouth-genital stimulation in the sixty-nine position.

the man-on-top position. The more the partner can relax, the less uncomfortable it is; if it is done properly, it need involve no pain. While some heterosexual couples find the idea repulsive, others delight in it. Some women report orgasm during anal intercourse, particularly when it is accompanied by hand stimulation of the clitoris. Gay men also report orgasms from anal intercourse, primarily due to stimulation of the prostate.

Anal intercourse may be chosen if the woman is having a particularly heavy menstrual flow, if her vagina is loose and the man wants more stimulation, or simply if more variety in sexual techniques is desired.

There are some health risks associated with anal intercourse. The AIDS virus can be transmitted through anal intercourse. Thus "safer sex" consists of either refraining from engaging in anal intercourse, or using a condom if one does (or doing it only in a monogamous relationship with an uninfected partner). Further, for heterosexuals the penis should never be inserted into the vagina after anal intercourse unless it has been washed thoroughly. The reason for this is that the rectum contains bacteria that do not belong in the vagina and that can cause a dandy case of vaginitis if they happen to get there.

Another variation is anilingus (*feuille de rose* in French, "rimming" in slang), in which the tongue and mouth stimulate the anus. The anus may also be stimulated by the hand, and some people report that having a finger inserted into the rectum near the time of orgasm provides a heightened sexual sensation. Anilingus carries with it some risk of getting AIDS, hepatitis, or *E. coli* infections.

Anilingus (AY-nih-ling-us): Mouth stimulation of the partner's anus.

Techniques of Lesbians and Gays

Some people have difficulty imagining exactly what gays do in bed; after all, the important ingredients for sex are one penis and one vagina, aren't they?

The preliminaries consist, as they do for heterosexuals, of kissing, hugging, and petting. Male homosexuals engage in mutual masturbation, oral-genital sex (fellatio), and, less frequently, anal intercourse (also called *sodomy* in legal terminology in the United States and *buggery* in England). Male homosexuals sometimes also engage in interfemoral intercourse, in which one man's penis moves between the thighs of the other. Lesbians engage in mutual masturbation, oral-genital sex (cunnilingus), and a practice called tribadism ("dry hump"), in which heterosexual intercourse is imitated, with one partner lying on top of the other and making thrusting movements so that both receive genital stimulation. According to *The Gay Report,* this is a common practice (Jay & Young, 1979). A rare practice is the use of an artificial penis, or dildo, by one person to stimulate the other. Of course, dildos are also used by heterosexual women in masturbation, although they probably appear much more frequently in men's fantasies than they do in women's hands.

Interfemoral intercourse: A sexual technique used by male homosexuals in which one man moves his penis between the thighs of the other.

Tribadism (TRY-bad-izm): A sexual technique in which one woman lies on top of another and moves rhythmically in order to produce sexual pleasure, particularly clitoral stimulation.

An important point to note about these practices is that they are all behaviors in which heterosexuals also engage. That is, homosexuals do the same things sexually that heterosexuals do. The only thing that is distinctive about the homosexual act is that both partners are of the same gender.

Masters and Johnson (1979), in their laboratory studies, have done direct observations of the lovemaking techniques of gays, and compared them with those of straights. They found that, in masturbation techniques, there were no differences. However, in couple interactions there were some substantial differences. The major one was that homosexuals "took their time"—that is, they seemed not to have any goal orientation. Heterosexual couples, on the other hand, seemed to be performance-oriented—they seemed to strive toward a goal of orgasm for each. In the initial approach to stimulating the female, heterosexuals and lesbians began with holding and kissing, but this only lasted about 30 seconds for the heterosexuals, who quickly moved on to genital stimulation. Lesbians, on the other hand, spent more time in holding and kissing and then went on to a long period of breast stimulation, which sometimes resulted in orgasm in the absence of genital stimulation. This breast stimulation was a major difference between heterosexual and homosexual techniques. Lesbians also appeared to communicate more with each other. In the initial approach to stimulating the male, gays did extensive stimulation of the nipples, generally producing erection; such a technique was rare among heterosexuals (only with 3 of 100 couples). Homosexuals were also much more likely to stimulate the frenulum (the area of the penis on the lower side, just below the corona). Homosexuals also used a "teasing technique" in which the man brings his partner near orgasm, then relaxes the stimulation, then increases the stimulation again, and so on, essentially prolonging the pleasure. Among heterosexuals, the husband's most frequent complaint was that the wife did not grasp the shaft of the penis tightly enough. Masters and Johnson argue that heterosexuals can learn from homosexuals; the technique of gays benefits from stimulating another body like their own.

APHRODISIACS

Is There a Good Aphrodisiac?

Aphrodisiac (ah-froh-DIZ-ih-ak): A substance that increases sexual desire.

An aphrodisiac is something—such as a food, a drug, or a perfume—that excites sexual desire. Throughout history people have searched for the "surefire" aphrodisiac. Before arousing your hopes, I should note that the search has been unsuccessful; there is no known substance that works well as an aphrodisiac.

One popular idea is that oysters are an aphrodisiac. This notion appears to be an example of the idea that foods that resemble sexual organs have sexual powers. For example, bananas resemble the penis and have been thought to be aphrodisiacs. Another example is the Asian belief that powdered rhinoceros horn is an aphrodisiac (perhaps this is also the origin of the term "horny") (Taberner, 1985). Perhaps oysters are thought to have such powers because of their resemblance to the testes (MacDougald, 1961). Oysters, however, contain no substances that can in any way influence sexual functioning (Neiger, 1968).

Doubtless some substances gain a continued reputation as aphrodisiacs because simply believing that something will be arousing can itself be arousing. Thus the belief that a bull's testicles ("prairie oysters") or peanuts or clams have special powers may produce a temporary improvement of sexual functioning, not because of the chemicals contained in them but because of a belief in them (McCary, 1973).

Alcohol also has a reputation as an aphrodisiac. The effects of alcohol on sexual functioning will be discussed in Chapter 19. Briefly, drinking small quantities of alcohol may, for some people, decrease psychological inhibitions and therefore increase sexual desire. Moderate to large quantities, however, rapidly lead to an inability to function sexually.

Users of marijuana report that it acts as a sexual stimulant. Probably this is due, in part, to the fact that marijuana produces the sensation that time is being stretched out, thus prolonging and intestifying sensations, including sexual sensations. There is no scientific documentation of the aphrodisiac effects of marijuana except for the reports of users. Possible negative effects of marijuana on sexual functioning are discussed in Chapter 19.

Unfortunately, some of the substances that are thought to enhance sexual functioning are quite dangerous. For example, cantharides (Spanish fly) has a reputation as an aphrodisiac, but it is poisonous (Kaplan, 1974; Leavitt, 1974; Taberner, 1985).

Amyl nitrite ("poppers") is popular among some homosexuals and some heterosexuals. Because it relaxes the sphincter muscle of the anus, it is used by those engaging in anal intercourse (Taberner, 1985). Users report that it produces heightened sensations during orgasms (Everett, 1975). Probably it acts by dilating the blood vessels in the genitals. It may, however, have side effects, including dizziness, headaches, fainting, and, in rare cases, death; thus it can be dangerous (Taberner, 1985).

Butyl nitrite—sold under such trade names as Rush, Locker Room, and Climax—is a chemical relative of amyl nitrite. It is used to heighten sexual pleasure. Although no deaths have been reported from inhaling it, there are two reported deaths from swallowing it (UPI, 1981).

Anaphrodisiacs

Anaphrodisiac (an-ah-froh-DIZ-ih-ak): A substance that decreases sexual desire.

Just as people have searched for aphrodisiacs, so they have sought anaphrodisiacs, substances or practices that would diminish sexual desire. Cold showers are reputed to have such effects, as is potassium nitrate (saltpeter). The latter contains nothing that decreases sexual drive, but it does act as a diuretic; it makes the person want to urinate frequently, which may be distracting enough so that he or she is not much interested in sex.

There has been some medical interest in finding drugs that would decrease sex drive for use in treating aggressive sexual offenders. One such drug is cyproterone acetate, which is an antiandrogen (Taberner, 1985). Within about two weeks of use, it causes a reduction of libido; the sperm count declines substantially and testosterone levels fall to 20 to 30 percent of normal.

Other drugs that may lead to a loss of sexual functioning are discussed in Chapter 19.

ARE INTERCOURSE AND ORGASM THE GOAL?

Traditionally in our culture it has been the belief that a sexual encounter should "climax" with intercourse and orgasm, at least orgasm for the man. In our modern era of multiple orgasms for women and general sexual liberation, the view that intercourse is the important part of sex and that orgasm is the goal toward which both must strive is pervasive. This belief system is reflected in the term "foreplay," which implies that activities like hand stimulation of the genitals, kissing, and mouth-genital sex are only preliminaries that take place before intercourse, the latter being "real sex." Similar beliefs are reflected in a commonly used phrase, "achieving orgasm," as if orgasm were something to be achieved like a promotion on the job.[6]

Psychologist Rollo May feels that men particularly, by concentrating on "achieving" orgasm and *satisfying* their desire, miss out on the more important part of the sexual experience: prolonging the feeling of desire and pleasure, building it higher and higher. As he puts it:

> The pleasure in sex is described by Freud and others as the reduction of tension [orgasm]; in eros, on the contrary, we wish not to be released from the excitement but rather to hang on to it, to bask in it, and even to increase it. (1974, pp. 71–72)

Marc Feigen Fasteau, a men's liberation leader, argues that although orgasm is good, a large part of pleasure is building up to orgasm:

> What the masculine disdain for feeling makes it hard for men to grasp is that the state of desire . . . is one of the best, perhaps *the* best, part of the experience of love. (1974, p. 31)

Another one of the "goals" of sex that has emerged recently is the simultaneous orgasm. Some people consider this an event to be worked for rather than a pleasant thing that sometimes happens.

The legacy of the Protestant ethic in our culture is that our achievement drives now seem to be channeled into our sexual behaviors (see Focus 10.1). There is nothing intrinsically wrong with expressing achievement drives in sex, except that anytime there is an achievement situation, there is also the potential for a failure. If she does not have an orgasm or if he cannot get an erection, the couple feel as if the whole experience was a disaster. The problem with setting up sexual goals, then, is that the possibility of sexual failures or sexual dysfunctions is also being set up.

The best approach is to enjoy all the various aspects of lovemaking for themselves, rather than as techniques for achieving something, and to concentrate on sex as a feast of the senses, rather than as an achievement competition.

FROM INEXPERIENCE TO BOREDOM

Some people, after an initial lack of experience with sex, shift rather quickly to becoming bored with it, with perhaps only a brief span of self-confident, pleasurable sexuality in between. Most of us, of course, are sexually inexperienced early in our

---

[6] To avoid this whole notion, I never use the phrase "to achieve orgasm" in this book. Instead, I prefer "to have an orgasm" or simply "to orgasm." Why not turn it into a verb so that we will not have to work at achieving it?

The Protestant Ethic: Sex as Work

Sociologist Philip Slater has argued that the old Protestant ethic—work hard and become successful—is alive and well in modern American sexual attitudes. According to him, we turn sex into work and then work hard to become successful at it.

Our discussions of sex tend to focus on orgasm rather than on pleasure in general. Orgasm is the observable "product," and we are concerned with how many orgasms we can produce or have, much as a plant manager is concerned with how many cans of soup are produced on the assembly line each day.

The emphasis on "simultaneous orgasm" may express how clock-oriented we are. It is important for us to have things running on schedule and happening at exactly the right time, and so orgasms must also be timed perfectly.

We tend to use the term "adequacy" in relation to sex and to set standards of sexual performance, much as we would set standards of work performance on the job. Ironically, according to current definitions of "adequacy," a man is considered adequate if he can delay his orgasm, whereas a woman is considered adequate if she can make hers happen faster. Why does the same standard not apply to both? The answer has to do with our concept of orgasm as a "product" and with our concern about timing.

Slater also argues that work (on the job) and

sex are natural enemies. The more a person becomes dedicated to work and the more time she or he spends on it, the greater the inroads on the sex life. This is substantiated in a study of successful executives, government officials, and professionals (*Sex and the Significant Americans*, by John Cuber and Peggy Harroff). For those in the study, sex was brief and perfunctory. Their commitment to work left little time for, or interest in, sex.

One might even speculate that the more we see sex as work and apply performance standards to it, the more "failures"—sexual dysfunctions—we shall have.

As Slater put it:

> The preoccupation in Western sexual literature with orgasm seems to be a natural extension of the Protestant work ethic in which nothing is to be enjoyed for its own sake except striving.
> The antithetical attitude would be to view orgasm as a delightful interruption in an otherwise continuous process of generating pleasurable sensations. (1973, p. 134)

Source: P. E. Slater. (1973, Dec.). Sexual adequacy in America. *Intellectual Digest,* pp. 132–135. See also George W. Albee. (1977). The Protestant ethic, sex, and psychotherapy. *American Psychologist,* **32,** pp. 150–161.

lives, and most of us feel bored with the way we are having sex at times. How do we deal with these problems?

Sexual Inexperience

In our culture we expect men to be "worldly" about sex—to have had experience with it and to be skillful in the use of sexual techniques. A man or a boy who is sexually inexperienced (perhaps a virgin) or who has had only a few sexual experiences, with little opportunity to practice, may have a real fear about whether he will be able to "perform" (the achievement ethic again) in a sexual encounter. With the sexual revolution has come an increasing expectation that women also should have a bag of sexual tricks ready to use, and so they, too, are increasingly expected to be experienced.

How can one deal with this problem of inexperience? First, it is important to question society's assumption that one should be experienced (see, for example, Glassberg, 1970). Everyone has to begin sometime, and there is absolutely nothing wrong with inexperience. Second, there are many good books and articles on sexual techniques that are definitely worth reading, although it is important to be selective, since a few of these may be more harmful than helpful. This chapter should be a good introduction; you also might want to consult *The New Joy of Sex* or any of the self-help manuals listed at the end of Chapter 19. Do not become slavishly attached to the techniques you read about in books, though; they should serve basically as a stimulus to your imagination, not as a series of steps that must be followed. Third, communicate with your partner. Because individual preferences vary so much, no one, no matter how experienced, is ever a sexual expert with a new partner. The best way to please a partner is to find out what that person likes, and communication may accomplish this better than prior experience. A later section in this chapter gives some specific tips on communication. Interestingly, one study found that the best sexual predictor of relationship satisfaction was not frequency of sex or techniques but mutual agreement on sexual issues (Markman, personal communication).

Boredom

The opposite problem to inexperience is the feeling of boredom in a long-term sexual relationship. Boredom, of course, is not always a necessary consequence of having sex with the same person over a long period of time. Certainly there are couples who have been married for 40 or 50 years and who continue to find sexual expression exciting. Unfortunately, the major sex surveys have not inquired about the phenomenon of boredom, and thus it is not possible to estimate the percentage of people who eventually become bored or who experience occasional fits of boredom. However, such experiences are surely common. As someone once said, a rut is no place to be making love. How can we deal with the problem of boredom?

Communication can help in this situation, as it can in others. Couples sometimes evolve a routine sexual sequence that leads to boredom, and sometimes that sequence is not really what either person wants. By communicating to each other what they really would like to do and then doing it, two people can introduce some variety into their relationship. The various love manuals can also give ideas on new techniques. Finally, a couple's sexual relationship often mirrors the other aspects of their relationship, and sexual boredom may sometimes mean that they are generally bored with each other. Rejuvenating the rest of the relationship—perhaps taking up a hobby or a sport together or going on a good vacation, during which they really try to build their relationship in general—may do wonders for their sexual relationship.

One might also question the meaning of "boredom." Perhaps our expectations for sexual experience are too high. Encouraged by the media, we tend to believe that every time we have intercourse, the earth should move. We do not expect that every meal we eat will be fantastic or that we will always have a huge appetite and enjoy every bite. Yet we do tend to have such expectations with regard to sexuality. Perhaps when boredom seems to be a problem, it is not the real issue; rather, the problem may be unrealistically high expectations.

COMMUNICATION AND SEX

Consider the following situation:

> Sam and Donna have been married for about three years. Donna had had intercourse with only one other person before Sam, and she had never masturbated. Since they've been married, she has had orgasms only twice during intercourse, despite the fact that they make love three or four times per week. She has been reading some magazine articles about female sexuality, and she is beginning to think that she should be experiencing more sexual satisfaction. As far as she knows, Sam is unaware that there is any problem. Donna feels lonely and a bit sad.

What should Donna do? She needs to communicate with Sam. They apparently have not communicated much about sex in the last three years, and they need to begin. The following sections will discuss the relationship between sex, communication, and relationships and provide some suggestions on how to communicate effectively.

Communication and Building a Good Relationship

A good deal of research has looked at differences in communication patterns between nondistressed (happy) married couples and distressed (unhappy, seeking marital counseling) married couples. This research shows, in general, that distressed couples tend to have communication deficits (Markman & Floyd, 1980; Noller, 1984). Research also shows that couples seeking therapy for sex problems have poor communication patterns compared with nondistressed couples (Zimmer, 1983). Of course, there are many other factors that contribute to marital or relationship conflict or sex problems, but poor communication patterns are certainly among them. The problem with this research is that it is correlational (see Chapter 3 for a discussion of this problem in research methods)—in particular, we cannot tell whether poor communication causes unhappy marriages or whether unhappy marriages create poor communication patterns.

An elegant longitudinal study designed to meet this problem provides evidence that unrewarding, ineffective communication precedes and predicts later relationship problems (Markman, 1979; 1981). Dating couples who were planning marriage were studied for $5\frac{1}{2}$ years. The more positively couples rated their communication interactions at the beginning of the study, the more satisfaction they reported in their relationship when they were followed up $2\frac{1}{2}$ years later and $5\frac{1}{2}$ years later.

On the basis of this notion that communication deficits cause relationship problems, marriage counselors and marital therapists often work on teaching couples better communication skills. Research shows that this training is effective (e.g., Jacobson, 1978; Wampler, 1982). After training to improve communication skills, couples show improved communication and report more satisfaction in their relationships.

One such program is Relationship Enhancement Therapy (Guerney, 1977). The purpose of RE programs is to increase the psychological and emotional satisfaction that can be derived from intimate relationships; this is accomplished in large part by communication skills training. The goal is to develop an empathic relationship in which the participants have compassionate understanding of their own and the other's thoughts, needs, and feelings, and good communication is essential to doing so. RE programs are probably better viewed as education rather than therapy, and they can be used for enrichment with happily married couples, for therapy with distressed couples, and for "preventive medicine" training with premarital couples (Ginsberg & Vogelsong, 1977). The goal of communication skills training with premarital couples is to establish good communication early in the relationship, trying to prevent relationship problems later on (Markman & Floyd, 1980).

All in all, it is clear that good communication patterns are important in developing and maintaining good intimate relationships. The sections that follow will describe some of the skills that are involved in good communication. They are techniques that are often recommended by therapists. These ideas arise from extensive programs of research comparing distressed and nondistressed couples (e.g., Gottman et al., 1976) to see exactly how the happy, nondistressed couple communicate differently from the unhappy one; the ideas are also based on the experiences of marital theapists.

Being an Effective Communicator

Back to Donna and Sam: One of the first things to do in a situation like Donna's is to decide to talk to one's partner, admitting that there is a communication gap. Then the issue is to resolve to communicate, and particularly to be an *effective* communicator. Suppose Donna begins by saying,

You're not giving me any orgasms when we have sex. (1)

Intent: What the speaker means.

Impact: What someone else understands the speaker to mean.

Effective communicator: A communicator whose impact matches his or her intent.

Sam gets angry and walks away. Donna meant to communicate that she wasn't having any orgasms, but Sam thought she meant that he was a lousy lover. It is important to recognize the distinction between intent and impact in communicating (Gottman et al., 1976). Intent is what you mean. Impact is what the other person thinks you mean. A good communicator is one whose impact matches her or his intent. Donna wasn't an effective communicator in the above example because the impact on Sam was considerably different from her intent.

Many people value spontaneity in sex, and this attitude may extend to communicating about sex. It is best to recognize that to be an effective communicator, it may be necessary to plan your strategy (Langer & Dweck, 1973). It often takes some thinking to figure out how to make sure that your impact matches your intent. Planning also allows you to make sure that the timing is good—that you are not speaking out of anger, or that your partner is not tired or preoccupied with other things (Brenton, 1972).

FIGURE 10.11

Finally, we ought to recognize that it is going to be harder for Donna to broach this subject than it would be to ask Sam why he didn't take out the garbage as he had promised. It is hard for most people to talk about sex, particularly sexual problems, with their partners.[7] Ironically, in the last few decades public communication about sex has become relatively open, but private communication remains difficult (Brenton, 1972). That doesn't mean that Donna can't communicate. But she shouldn't feel guilty or stupid because it is difficult for her. And she will be better off if she uses some specific communication skills and has some belief that they will work. The sections that follow suggest some skills that are useful in being an effective communicator and how to apply these to sexual relationships.

Leveling and Editing

Leveling: Telling your partner what you are feeling by stating your thoughts clearly, simply, and honestly.

Leveling means that you tell your partner what you are feeling by stating your thoughts clearly, simply, and honestly (Gottman et al., 1976). It is the first step in communication and is often the hardest. In leveling keep in mind that the purposes are:

1. To make communication clear
2. To clear up what partners expect of each other
3. To clear up what is pleasant and what is unpleasant
4. To clear up what is relevant and what is irrelevant
5. To notice things that draw you closer or push you apart (Gottman et al., 1976)

Editing: Censoring or not saying things that would be deliberately hurtful to your partner or that are irrelevant.

When you begin to level with your partner, you also need to do some editing. Editing involves censoring (not saying) things that would be deliberately hurtful to your partner or that would be irrelevant. You must take responsibility for making your communication polite and considerate. Leveling, then, should not mean a "no holds barred" approach. Ironically, research indicates that married people are ruder to each other than they are to strangers (Gottman et al., 1976).

Donna may be so disgruntled about her lack of orgasms that she's thinking of having an affair to jolt Sam into recognizing her problem, or perhaps in order to see if another man would stimulate her to orgasm. Donna is probably best advised to edit out this line of thought and concentrate on the specific problem: her lack of orgasms. If they can solve that, she won't need to have the affair anyway.

The trick is to balance leveling and editing. If you edit too much, you may not level at all, and there will be no communication. If you level too much and don't edit, the communication will fail because your partner will respond negatively, and things may get worse rather than better.

Good Messages

"I" language: Speaking for yourself, using the word "I"; not mind reading.

One tip that couples communication experts give is to use I language (e.g., Brenton, 1972). That is, speak for yourself, not your partner (Miller et al., 1975). By doing this you focus on what you know best—your own thoughts and feelings. "I" lan-

---

[7] In fact, a survey of students in human sexuality courses at two universities indicated that sexual "pleases" and "displeases" are the most difficult topics to talk about with one's partner. Further, women seem more aware of problems in this aspect of the relationship than men are (Markman, personal communication).

FIGURE 10.12

guage is less likely to make your partner defensive. If Donna were to use this technique, she might say,

> I feel a bit unhappy because I don't have orgasms very often when we make love. **(2)**

Notice that she focuses specifically on herself. There is less cause for Sam to get angry than there was in message 1.

One of the best things about "I" language is that it avoids mind reading (Gottman et al., 1976). Suppose Donna says,

> I know you think women aren't much interested in sex, but I really wish I had more orgasms. **(3)**

Mind reading: Making assumptions about what your partner thinks or feels.

She is engaging in **mind reading**. That is, she is making certain assumptions about what Sam is thinking. She assumes that Sam believes women aren't interested in sex or having orgasms. Research shows that mind reading is more common among distressed couples than among nondistressed couples (Gottman et al., 1977). Worse, she doesn't *check out* her assumptions with Sam. The problem is that she may be wrong, and Sam may not think that at all. "I" language helps avoid this by focusing on me and what I feel rather than on what my partner is doing or failing to do. Another important way to avoid mind reading is by giving and receiving feedback, a technique to be discussed in a later section.

Documenting is another important component of giving good messages (Brenton, 1972). In documenting you give specific examples of the issue. This is not quite so relevant in Donna's case, because she is talking about a general problem, but even here, specific documenting can be helpful. Once Donna has broached the subject, she might say,

> Last night when we made love, I enjoyed it and felt very aroused, but then I didn't
> have an orgasm, and I felt disappointed. (4)

Now she has gotten her general complaint down to a specific situation that Sam can remember.

Suppose further that Donna has some idea of what Sam would need to do to bring her to orgasm: he would have to do more hand stimulation of her clitoris. Then she might do specific documenting as follows:

> Last night when we made love, I enjoyed it, but I didn't have an orgasm, and
> then I felt disappointed. I think what I needed was for you to stimulate my clitoris
> with your hand a bit more. You did it for a while, but it seemed so brief. I think
> if you had kept doing it for two or three minutes more, I would have had an
> orgasm. (5)

Now she has not only documented to Sam exactly what the problem was, but she has given a specific suggestion about what could have been done about it, and therefore what could be done in the future.

Another technique in giving good messages is to offer *limited choices* (Langer & Dweck, 1973). Suppose Donna begins by saying,

> I've been having trouble with orgasms. Could we discuss it? (6)

The trouble with this approach is that a "no" from Sam is not really an acceptable answer to her because she definitely wants to discuss the problem. Yet she set up the question so that he could answer by saying "no." To use the technique of limited choices she might say,

> I've been having trouble with orgasms when we make love. Would you like to
> discuss it now, or would you rather wait until tomorrow night? (7)

Now, either answer he gives will be acceptable to her; she has offered a set of acceptable limited choices.[8] She has also shown some consideration for him by recognizing that he might not be in the mood for such a discussion now and would rather wait.

---

[8] The technique of limited choices is useful in a number of other situations, including dealing with children. For example, when my daughter was a 2-year-old and she had finished watching *Sesame Street* and I wanted the TV turned off, I didn't say, "Would you turn the TV off?" (she might say "no") but, rather, "Do you want to turn off the TV, or would you like me to?" Of course, sometimes she evaded my efforts and said "no" anyway, but most of the time it works.

Breaking the Ice: Sex Manuals

As we have already noted, one of the most difficult things about situations like Donna and Sam's is just getting the communication started—breaking the ice. One possible approach is to suggest reading a sex manual together as an icebreaker. For example, Donna could go out and buy a copy of *The New Joy of Sex* (or Raley's *Making Love,* or *Making Love Better*), bring it home, and suggest to Sam that they read and discuss it together. When they get to the section on hand stimulation, it may be easier for Donna to raise the subject of her own desire for hand stimulation of the clitoris.

A side benefit of this approach is that Donna and Sam may find out about some techniques that they weren't aware of or had been afraid to do. For example, Donna may have secret thoughts that cunnilingus would be nice and might help her to have orgasms, but she is afraid to mention it to Sam because she thinks he would be repulsed by the idea. Sam might be thinking that Donna might enjoy cunnilingus, but he is afraid to bring up the subject, fearing that she may be shocked. Note that they have both been doing some mind reading. When they get to the section on mouth-genital sex in the manual, their discussion may be able to clear up some of their assumptions. And Donna may be able to learn some more about what Sam would like sexually.

Self-Disclosure

Self-disclosure: Telling personal things about yourself.

Self-disclosure involves telling your partner some personal things about yourself. It may range from telling your partner about something embarrassing that happened to you at work today, to disclosing a very meaningful event that happened between you and your parents 15 years ago. Social psychologists believe that self-disclosure helps a relationship to progress (e.g., Altman & Taylor, 1973).

Self-disclosure is also related to satisfaction with the relationship. Research shows that there is a positive correlation between the extent of a couple's self-disclosure and their satisfaction with the relationship—that is, couples that practiced more self-disclosure were more satisfied (Hendrick, 1981).

Research consistently shows that self-disclosure leads to reciprocity (Berg & Derlega, 1987; Hendrick & Hendrick, 1992). That is, if one member of the couple self-discloses, it seems to prompt the other partner to self-disclose also. Self-disclosure by one member of the couple can essentially get the ball rolling. Psychologists have proposed a number of reasons why this occurs (Hendrick & Hendrick, 1992). First, disclosure by our partner may make us like and trust that person more. Second, as social learning theorists would argue, simple modeling and imitation may occur. That is, one partner's self-disclosing serves as a model for the other partner. Norms of equity may also be involved (see Chapter 12 for a discussion of equity theory). After one partner has self-disclosed, the other person may follow suit in order to maintain a sense of balance or equity in the relationship.

Not only does self-disclosure seem to help a relationship progress, but patterns of self-disclosure can actually predict whether a couple stays together or breaks up. Research in which couples are followed for periods ranging from two months to four years shows that the greater the self-disclosure, the greater the likelihood that the relationship will continue, and the less the self-disclosure, the greater the likelihood of breakup (Hendrick et al., 1988; Sprecher, 1987).

It is important to use some good judgment in self-disclosure, of course. As we discussed earlier in the section on leveling and editing, it is probably best not to self-disclose absolutely everything. Some things just need to be edited.

Body Talk: Nonverbal Communication

Often the precise words we use are not so important as the way we say them. Tone of voice, expression on the face, position of the body, whether you touch the other person—all are important in conveying the message.

As an example, take the sentence "So you're here." If it is delivered "So *you're* here" in a hostile tone of voice, the message is that the speaker is very unhappy that you're here. If it is delivered "So you're *here*" in a pleased voice, the meaning may be that the speaker is glad and surprised to see you here in Wisconsin, having thought you were in Europe. "So you're here" with a smile and arms outstretched to initiate a hug might mean that the speaker has been waiting for you and is delighted to see you.

Suppose that in Donna and Sam's case, the reason Donna doesn't have more orgasms is that Sam simply doesn't stimulate her vigorously enough. During sex, Donna has adopted a very passive, nearly rigid posture for her body. Sam doesn't stimulate her more vigorously because he is afraid that he might hurt her, and he is sure that no lady like his wife would want such a vigorous approach. The response (or rather nonresponse) of her body confirms his assumptions. Her body is saying "I don't enjoy this. Let's get it over with." And that's exactly what she's getting. To correct this situation, she might adopt a more active, encouraging approach. She might take his hand and guide it to her clitoris, showing him the kind of firm way she likes to have it rubbed. She might place her hands on his hips and press to indicate how deep and forceful she would like the thrusting of his penis in her vagina to be. She might even take the daring approach of using some verbal communication and saying "That's good" when he becomes more vigorous.

The point is that in communicating about sex, we need to be sure that our nonverbal signals help to create the impact we intend rather than one we don't intend. It is also possible that nonverbal signals are confusing communication and need to be straightened out. Checking out is a technique for doing this which will be discussed in a later section.

Interestingly, research shows that distressed couples differ from nondistressed couples more in their nonverbal communication than in their verbal communication (Gottman et al., 1977; Vincent et al., 1979). For example, even when a person from a distressed couple is expressing agreement with his or her spouse, that person is more likely to accompany the verbal expressions of agreement with negative nonverbal behavior. Distressed couples are also more likely to be negative listeners—while listening the individuals are more likely to display frowning, angry, or disgusted facial expressions, or tense or inattentive body postures. In contrast, harmonious marriages are characterized by closer physical distances and more relaxed postures than are found in distressed couples (Beier & Sternberg, 1977). Once again, it is not only what we say verbally but how we say it, and how we listen nonverbally, that makes the difference.

Listening

Up to this point, we have been concentrating on techniques for you to use in sending messages about sexual relationships. But, of course, communication is a two-way street, and you and your partner will exchange responses. It is therefore important for you and your partner to gain some skills in listening and responding constructively to messages. The following discussion will suggest such techniques.

One of the most important things is that you must really *listen*. That means more than just removing the headphones from your ears. It means actively trying to

(a)

(b)

FIGURE 10.13
(a) A couple with good body language (good eye contact and body position). (b) A couple with poor body language (poor eye contact and body position).

Paraphrasing: Saying, in your own words, what you thought your partner meant.

understand what the other person is saying. Often people are so busy trying to think of their next response that they hardly hear what the other person is saying. Good listening also involves positive nonverbal behaviors, such as maintaining eye contact with the speaker and nodding one's head when appropriate.

The next step, after you have listened carefully, is to give *feedback*. This often will involve the technique of paraphrasing, that is, repeating in your own words what you thought your partner meant. Suppose, in response to Donna's initial statement, "You're not giving me any orgasms when we have sex," Sam hadn't walked away angrily. Instead, he tried to listen and then gave her feedback by paraphrasing. He might have responded,

> I hear you saying that I'm not very skillful at making love to you, and therefore you're not having orgasms. (8)

At that point, Donna would have had a chance to clear up the confusion she had created with her initial message, because Sam had given her feedback by paraphrasing his understanding of what she said. At that point she could have said, "No, I think you're a good lover, but I'm just not having any orgasms, and I don't know why. I thought maybe we could figure it out together." Or perhaps she could have said, "No, I think you're a good lover. I just wish you'd do some of the things you do more, like rubbing my clitoris."

It's also a good idea to *ask for feedback* from your partner, particularly if you're not sure whether you're communicating clearly.

Just as it is important to be a good listener to your partner's verbal messages, so too is it important to be good at "reading" your partner's nonverbal messages. There's nothing quite so frustrating as turning your back on another person in order to express anger and having the person miss the signal. In technical language, the ability to comprehend another's nonverbal signals is termed "decoding" nonverbal communication; the opposite process, sending the nonverbal message, is called "encoding." Some research shows that it is the wife's skill in this area that is most important (Sabatelli, Buck, & Dreyer, 1982). Wives who are good encoders (their signals are easy to understand) have husbands with few marital complaints. Other research, though, shows that the husband's ability to decode his wife's nonverbal messages correlates more with the degree of marital happiness than the wife's ability to decode his messages (Gottman & Porterfield, 1981). Probably the best scenario is when both partners are good at encoding and decoding and are committed to such accurate and sensitive nonverbal communication.

Checking Out Sexy Signals

One of the problems with verbal and nonverbal sexual communications is that they are often ambiguous. It is therefore important to check them out—ask the communicator exactly what she or he means—before proceeding.

Sue is at the office party. While she is in conversation with three people, one of them, Howard, puts his arm around her shoulder and gives her a quick hug. How should she interpret that? Is it a gesture of camaraderie and goodwill? Is he being patronizing, putting his arm around her shoulder as if she were a little girl? Or is he issuing an invitation to have sex at his place after the party? And what will it mean if she gives him a hug back? Is she spreading more cheer, or is she saying, "Sure, I'd like to go back to your place."

The problem is that most of us are very reticent about checking out the meaning in situations like this. Somehow we assume that we ought to know exactly what the person meant, and we are dumb or naive if we don't. It is important to recognize that many "sexy signals" like putting an arm around someone's shoulder are ambiguous; we need to make some effort to clear them up. But probably Sue would feel awkward saying, "Excuse me, did that hug mean you want to have sex, or are you just being friendly?"

Probably Sue's best bet in this case is to ignore the hug. But what if Howard continues to keep close to her for the next hour and starts raising his eyebrows? At that point she had better do some explicit checking out of his meaning. It's important for her to do that before she says "OK—let's go to your place now" because Howard may just be too shy to talk to anyone else and may have a muscle twitch around his eyebrows. It's also important for her to do some checking out before she gets angry at Howard for propositioning her if she's a married woman. The best rule here is not to make any assumptions about the meaning of ambiguous messages unless you have checked them out with the sender.

Validating

Validation: Telling your partner that, given his or her point of view, you can see why he or she thinks a certain way.

One good technique in communication is **validation** (Gottman et al., 1976). This means that you communicate to your partner that, given his or her point of view, you can see why he or she thinks a certain way. It doesn't meant that you agree with your partner or that you're giving in. It simply means that you recognize your partner's point of view as legitimate, given his or her set of assumptions, which may be different from yours.

Suppose that Donna and Sam have gotten into an argument about cunnilingus. She wants him to do it and thinks it would bring her to orgasm. He doesn't want to do it because he finds the idea repulsive and because he believes no real man would do such a thing. If Donna tried to validate Sam's feelings, she might say,

> I can understand the way you feel about cunnilingus, especially given the way you were brought up about sex. (9)

Sam might validate Donna's feelings by saying,

> I understand how important it is for you to have an orgasm. (10)

Validating hasn't solved their disagreement, but it has left the door pleasantly open so that they can now make some progress.

Drawing Your Partner Out

Suppose it is Sam who initiates the conversation rather than Donna. Sam has noticed that Donna doesn't seem to get a lot of pleasure out of sex, and he would like to find out why and see what they can do about it. He needs to draw her out. He might begin by saying,

> I've noticed lately that you don't seem to be enjoying sex as much as you used to. Am I right about that? **(11)**

That much is good because he's checking out his assumption. Unfortunately, he's asked a question that leads to a "yes" or "no" answer, and that can stop the communication. So, if she replies "yes," he'd better follow it up with an *open-ended* question like

> Why do you think you aren't enjoying it more? **(12)**

If she can give a reasonable answer, good communication should be on the way. One of the standard—and best—questions to ask in a situation like this is

> What can we do to make things better? **(13)**

Fighting Fair

Even if you use all the techniques described above, you may still get into arguments with your partner. Arguments are a natural part of a relationship and are not necessarily bad. Given that there will be arguments in a relationship, it is useful if you and your partner have agreed to a set of rules called fighting fair (Bach & Wyden, 1969) so that the arguments may help and won't hurt.

Here are some of the basic rules for fighting fair that may be useful to you (Brenton, 1972; Creighton, 1992).

Fighting fair: A set of rules designed to make arguments constructive rather than destructive.

1. Don't make sarcastic or insulting remarks about your partner's sexual adequacy. It generates resentment, opens you to counterattack, and is just a dirty way to fight.

2. Don't bring up the names of former spouses, lovers, boyfriends, or girlfriends to illustrate how all these problems didn't happen with them. Stick to the issue: your relationship with your partner.

3. Don't play amateur psychologist. Don't say things like "The problem is that you're a compulsive personality" or "You acted that way because you never resolved your Oedipus complex." You really don't have the qualifications (even after reading this book) to do that kind of psychologizing. Even if you did, your partner would not be apt to recognize your expertise in the middle of an argument, thinking, quite rightly, that you're probably biased at the moment.

4. Don't threaten to tell your parents or run home. This involves ganging up on your partner or retreating like a child.

5. If you have children, don't bring them into the argument. It is too stressful emotionally to force them to take sides between you and your spouse.

FIGURE 10.14
*Arguments are not
necessarily bad for a
relationship, but it is
important to observe the
rules for "fighting fair."*

6. Don't engage in dumping. Don't store up gripes for six months and then dump them on your partner all at one time.

7. Don't hit and run. Don't bring up a serious negative issue when there is no opportunity to continue the discussion, such as when you're on the way out the door going to work or when guests are coming for dinner in five minutes.

8. Don't focus on who's to blame. Focus on solutions, not on who's at fault. If you avoid blaming, it lets both you and your partner save face, which helps both of you feel better about the relationship.

Taking Responsibility for Your Own Pleasure

Self-awareness is essential to good couple communication (Miller et al., 1975). Up to this point, we have been assuming that if only Sam would change his technique a little bit, Donna would have her orgasm. The problem with this is that Donna is not taking responsibility for her own sexual pleasure; instead, she is expecting Sam to produce her orgasm for her. This isn't very effective, and it isn't fair to Sam.

The first step in taking responsibility for your own sexual pleasure is to get to know your own body and its responsiveness better. The exercise in Focus 10.2 is designed to help you do that. Once you have this knowledge, your responsiblity is to communicate it to your partner.

Positive Communication

We have been concentrating on negative communications, that is, communications where some problem or complaint needs to be voiced. It is also important to communicate positive things about sex (Miller et al., 1975). If that was a great episode of lovemaking, or the best kiss you've ever experienced, say so. A learning theorist would say that you're giving your partner some positive reinforcement. Social psychologists' research shows that we tend to like people better who give us positive reinforcements (see Chapter 13). Recognition of the strengths in a relationship offers

10.2

A Personal Growth Exercise: Getting to Know Your Own Body

Most experts on sexual communication agree that before you can begin to communicate your sexual needs to your partner, you must get to know your own body and its sexual responsiveness. This exercise is designed to help you do that. Set aside some time for yourself, preferably 30 minutes or more. You'll need privacy and a mirror, preferably a full-length mirror.

1. Undress and stand in front of the mirror. Relax your body completely.

2. Take a good look at your body, top to bottom. Look at the colors, the curves, the textures. Take your time doing this. Try to discover things you haven't noticed before. What pleases you about your body? What don't you like about your body? Can you say these things aloud?

3. Look at your body. What parts of it influence how you feel about yourself sexually?

4. Run your fingers slowly over your body, head to toe. How does it feel to you? Are some parts soft? Are some sensitive? Are you hurrying over some places? Why? How do you feel about doing this?

5. Explore your genitals. *If you're a man,* look at them. Do you like the way they look? Now explore your genitals with your fingers. Gently stroke your penis, scrotum, and the area behind the scrotum. Pay close attention to the various sensations you're producing. Which areas feel particularly good when they're stroked? Try different kinds of touching—light, hard, fast, slow. Which kind feels best? If you get an erection, that's OK. Just take your time and learn as much as you can. Are there differences in sensitivities between the aroused state and the unaroused state? *If you're a woman,* take a hand mirror and look at your genitals. Do you like the way they look? Now explore your genitals with your fingers. Touch your outer lips, inner lips, clitoris, vaginal entrance. Which areas feel particularly good? Try different kinds of touching—light, hard, fast, slow. Which kind feels best? If you get aroused, that's OK. Are there differences in sensitivities between the aroused state and the unaroused state? Just take your time and learn as much as you can.

6. Now you're ready to communicate some new information to your partner!

For more exercises like this, see Zilbergeld's *The New Male Sexuality* (1992) and Heiman, LoPiccolo, and LoPiccolo's *Becoming Orgasmic: A Sexual Growth Program for Women* (1976).

Sources: Myron Brenton. (1972). *Sex Talk.* New York: Stein & Day. Julia Heiman, Leslie LoPiccolo, & Joseph LoPiccolo. (1976). *Becoming Orgasmic: A Sexual Growth Program for Women.* Englewood Cliffs, NJ: Prentice-Hall. Bernie Zilbergeld. (1992). *The New Male Sexuality.* New York: Bantam Books.

the potential for enriching it (e.g., Miller et al., 1975; Otto, 1963). And if you make a habit of positive communications about sex, it will be easier to initiate the negative ones, and they will be better received.

Most communication during sex is limited to muffled groans, or "Mm-m's," or an occasional "Higher, Harry" or "Did you, Diane?" It might help your partner greatly if you gave frequent verbal and nonverbal feedback such as "That was great" or "Let's do that again." That would make the positive communications and the negative ones far easier.

Research shows that nondistressed couples make more positive and fewer negative communications than distressed couples (Birchler et al., 1975; Billings, 1979). Not only do the happy couples make more positive communications; they are more likely to respond to a negative communication with something positive (Billings, 1979). Distressed couples, on the other hand, are more likely to respond to negative communication with more negative communicating, escalating into conflict. We might all take a cue from the happy couples and make efforts not only to increase our positive communications but even to make them in response to negative comments from our partner.

A Symmetrical Communicating Relationship

Symmetrical communicating relationship: A relationship in which both partners take equal responsibility for communication.

Research shows that a symmetrical communicating relationship and a symmetry or equality in other areas of the relationship between partners is related to satisfaction and growth in the relationship (Miller et al., 1975). In particular:

1. Couples in which both husband and wife use high levels of disclosure (leveling) in communicating report higher levels of marital satisfaction than couples in which one or both partners use low disclosure (Corrales, 1974).
2. Couples in which both members are highly accurate at understanding the other's view on a number of issues are more satisfied than couples in which one or both partners are low in accuracy (Corrales & Miller, cited in Miller et al., 1975).
3. A number of studies show that couples with egalitarian power structures rate higher in marital satisfaction than couples with other kinds of power structures (Blood & Wolfe, 1960; Rainwater, 1965; Corrales, 1974).

In a word, if communication is to be good, it must be mutual.

Summary

Sexual pleasure is produced by stimulation of various areas of the body; these are the erogenous zones.

Sexual self-stimulation, or autoeroticism, includes masturbation and sexual fantasies. Women typically masturbate by rubbing the clitoris and surrounding tissue and the inner and outer lips. Men generally masturbate by circling the hand around the penis and using an up-and-down movement to stimulate the shaft. Many people have sexual fantasies while masturbating. Common themes of these fantasies are having intercourse with a loved one or a stranger and having sex with several people simultaneously. Similar sexual fantasies are also common while having intercourse.

An important technique in two-person sex is hand stimulation of the partner's genitals. A good guide to technique is to find out how the partner masturbates. Touching other areas of the body and kissing are also important. The other senses—sight, smell, and hearing—can also be used in creating sexual arousal.

While there are infinite varieties in the positions in which one can have intercourse, there are four basic positions: man on top (the "missionary" position), woman on top, rear entry, and side to side.

There are two kinds of mouth-genital stimulation: cunnilingus (mouth stimulation of the female genitals) and fellatio (mouth stimulation of the male genitals). Both are engaged in frequently today and are considered highly pleasurable by many people. Lesbians and gays use techniques similar to those of straights (e.g., hand-genital stimulation and oral-genital sex). Homosexuals, though, seem less goal-oriented, take their time more, and communicate more than heterosexuals do.

Anal intercourse involves inserting the penis into the rectum.

An aphrodisiac is a substance that arouses sexual desire. There is no known reliable aphrodisiac, and some of the substances that are popularly thought to act as aphrodisiacs can be dangerous to one's health.

We have a tendency in our culture, perhaps a legacy of the Protestant ethic, to view sex as work and to turn sex into an achievement situation, as witnessed by expressions such as "achieving orgasm." Such attitudes make sex less pleasurable and may set the stage for sexual failures or sexual dysfunctions.

Some specific tips for being a good communicator were given: leveling and editing, using "I" language, avoiding mind reading, documenting your points with specific examples, offering limited-choice questions, breaking the ice by using sex manuals, self-disclosing, being aware of nonverbal communication, listening carefully, giving feedback by paraphrasing, checking out sexy signals, and validating. It is important to draw your partner out and to fight fair. Taking responsibility for your own sexual pleasure and emphasizing positive communications are other good techniques. An equal pattern of communication between partners is related to marital satisfaction.

Review Questions

1. The most common technique of female masturbation involves inserting a dildo or similar object into the vagina. True or false?

2. The majority of both men and women fantasize while they masturbate. True or false?

3. The man-on-top position of intercourse works well for a woman in the late stages of pregnancy. True or false?

4. The scientific term for mouth stimulation of the female genitals is _____.

5. There are no health risks associated with anal intercourse. True or false?

6. Masters and Johnson, in their research on the lovemaking techniques of homosexuals and heterosexuals, found that the gays took their time and were less goal-oriented. True or false?

7. Research shows that couples seeking therapy for sex problems have poor communication patterns compared with nondistressed couples. True or false?

8. _____ is the term for telling your partner what you are feeling by stating your thoughts clearly, simply, and honestly.

9. The use of "I" language is considered to be a poor technique in couple communication. True or false?

10. Communicating to your partner that, given his or her point of view, you can see why he or she thinks a certain way, is termed _____.

(The answers to all review questions are at the end of the book, beginning on page 731.)

Questions for Thought, Discussion, and Debate

1. If you are in a long-term relationship, think about the kind of communication pattern you have with your partner. Do you use the methods of communication

recommended in this chapter? If not, do you think that there are areas in which you could change and improve? Would your partner cooperate in attempts to improve your communication pattern?

2. What do you think about sexual fantasizing? Is it harmful, or is it a good way to enrich one's sexual expression? Are your ideas consistent with the results of the research discussed in this chapter?

Suggestions for Further Reading

Comfort, Alex (1991). *The new joy of sex: A gourmet guide to lovemaking for the nineties*. New York: Crown. Alex Comfort has rewritten his bestseller to maintain the joy of sex while recognizing the risk of AIDS.

Dodson, Betty. (1987). *Sex for one: The joy of self-loving*. New York: Harmony Books (Crown Publishers). An inspiring ode to masturbation.

Gibbons, Boyd. (1986). The intimate sense of smell. *National Geographic Magazine,* **170,** 324–361. A fascinating discussion of the sense of smell, including its role in sexual interactions.

Gottman, John, Notarius, Cliff, Gonso, Jonni, & Markman, Howard. (1976). *A couple's guide to communication*. Champaign, Ill.: Research Press. Offers a good, complete guide and specific suggestions to help couples enhance their communication.

Tannen, Deborah. (1986). *That's not what I meant: How conversational style makes or breaks relationships*. New York: Ballatine Books. Tannen, a communications expert and author of very popular books, provides excellent tips for improving communication.

Sexuality and the Life Cycle: Childhood and Adolescence

Chapter Highlights

My friend said to me, "If you show me yours, I'll show you mine." I said, "All right," but that we should go into the garage where no one would see us. I knew or thought that if someone caught us, we'd both be in real trouble. I don't remember what brought on this fear, but he seemed to have the same idea. So we went into the garage, and that was the first time I ever remember seeing a boy's penis. Many more incidents of sexual interest and exploration took place with this same playmate. . . .*

Stop for a moment and think of the first sexual experience you ever had. Some of you will think of the first time you had sexual intercourse, while others will remember much earlier episodes, like "playing doctor" with the other kids in the neighborhood. Now think of the kind of sex life you had, or expect to have, in your early twenties. Finally, imagine yourself at 65 and think of the kinds of sexual behavior you will be engaging in then.

In recent years, scientists have begun thinking of human development as a process that occurs throughout the lifespan. This represents a departure from the Freudian heritage, in which the crucial aspects of developments were all thought to occur in childhood. This chapter and Chapter 12 are based on the newer lifespan or "life-cycle" approach to understanding the development of our sexual behavior throughout the course of our lives. The things you were asked to remember and imagine about your own sexual functioning at the beginning of this chapter will give you an idea of the sweep of this development.

Lifespan development: Development from birth through old age.

DATA SOURCES

What kinds of scientific data are available on the sexual behavior of people at various times in their lives? One source we have is the Kinsey report (Kinsey et al., 1948,

---

* *Source*: Female respondent quoted in Eleanor S. Morrison et al. (1980). *Growing up sexual*. New York: Van Nostrand.

1953). The scientific techniques used by Kinsey were discussed and evaluated in Chapter 3; since there are limitations to them, your evaluation of them may affect how much you are willing to accept the data presented in this chapter and in Chapter 12.

In the Kinsey study, adult subjects were questioned about their childhood sexual behavior, and their responses form some of the data to be discussed in this chapter. These responses may be even more problematic than some of the other kinds of data from those studies, though. For example, a 50- or 60-year-old man is asked to report on his sexual behavior at age 10. How accurately will he remember things that happened 40 or 50 years ago? Surely there will be some forgetting. Thus the data on childhood sexual behavior may be subject to errors that result from adults being asked to recall things that happened a very long time ago.

An alternative would be to interview children about their sexual behavior or perhaps even to observe their sexual behavior. Few researchers have done either. The reasons are obvious; such a study would be exceptionally difficult and would raise serious ethical questions. Might a child be harmed by being interviewed about his or her sexual behavior? Could a child truly give informed consent to participate in such a study?

In a few studies children have been questioned directly about their sexual behavior. Kinsey interviewed 432 children, aged 4 to 14, and the results of the study were published after his death by Elias and Gebhard (1969).

Many studies of adolescent sexual behavior have also been done. Particularly notable is the survey done by Sorensen (1973), popularly known as the "Sorensen report," the well-done study by Kantner and Zelnik of young unmarried women (1972, 1973; Zelnik & Kantner, 1980), and Coles and Stokes's report, *Sex and the American Teenager* (1985). Sociological studies of premarital sexual behavior have been done by Ira Reiss (1967) and by John DeLamater and Patricia MacCorquodale (1979; see Focus 11.1). Increasingly we have available well-sampled studies of adolescent sexuality, and we can have the most confidence in their statistics.

The studies of child and adolescent sexual behavior have all been surveys, and they have used either questionnaires or interviews. No one has made systematic, direct observations of children's sexual behavior.

INFANCY (0 to 2 YEARS)

A century ago it was thought that sexuality was something that magically appeared at puberty. Historically, we owe the whole notion that children—in fact, infants—have sexual urges and engage in sexual behavior to Sigmund Freud.

The capacity of the human body to show a sexual response is present from birth. Male infants, for example, get erections. Indeed, boy babies are sometimes born with erections. Ultrasound studies indicate that reflex erections occur in the male fetus for several months before birth (Masters et al., 1982). Vaginal lubrication has been found in baby girls in the 24 hours after birth (Masters et al., 1982).

Masturbation

Infants have been observed masturbating, that is, fondling their own genitals. There is some question as to how conscious they are of what they are doing, but at the least they seem to be engaging in some pleasurable, sexual self-stimulation. The capacity for masturbation emerges between the first and third birthdays (Martinson, 1981). Ford and Beach (1951), on the basis of their survey of sexual behavior in other cultures, noted that if permitted, most boys and girls will progress from ab-

FIGURE 11.1
Infant masturbation.

sentminded fingering of their genitals to systematic masturbation by ages 6 to 8. In fact, in some cultures adults fondle infants' genitals to keep them quiet, a remarkably effective pacifier.

Orgasms from masturbation are possible even at this early age, although before puberty boys are not capable of ejaculation. Masturbation is a normal, natural form of sexual expression in infancy. It is definitely not a sign of pathology, as some previous generations believed. Indeed, in one study comparing infants who had optimal relationships with their mothers and infants who had problematic relationships with their mothers, it was the infants with the optimal maternal relationships who were more likely to masturbate (Spitz, 1949).

Infant-Infant Sexual Encounters

Infants and young children are very self-centered (what the psychologist Jean Piaget called *egocentric*). Even when they seem to be playing with another child, they may simply be playing alongside the other child, actually in a world all their own. Their sexual development parallels the development of their other behaviors. Thus their earliest sex is typically one-person sex—masturbation. Not until later do they develop social, two-person sex, either heterosexual or homosexual.

Nonetheless, particularly in later infancy, there may be some infant-infant encounters, either affectionate or sexual.

Nongenital Sensual Experiences

Many of the sensual experiences that infants and young children have are diffuse and not easily classified as masturbation or as heterosexual or homosexual activity. For example, as Freud noted, infants delight in putting things in their mouths. Thus sucking at the mother's breast, or sucking on his or her own fingers, may be a sensuous experience for the infant.

Being cuddled or rocked can be a warm, sensuous experience. Indeed, the infant's experiences in such early intimate encounters might influence her or his reactions to intimacy and cuddling in adulthood. It seems that some infants are cuddlers and some are noncuddlers (Schaffer & Emerson, 1964). Cuddlers enjoy physical contact. Noncuddlers, unlike cuddlers, show displeasure and restlessness when they are handled or held. As soon as they are old enough to do so, they show resistance to such situations or crawl or walk away from them. Cuddling and non-cuddling seem to be basically different personality patterns. It would be interesting to know whether these patterns remain consistent into adulthood.

Attachment

Attachment: A psychological bond that forms between an infant and the mother, father, or other care giver.

The quality of the relationship with the parents at this age can be very important to the child's capacity for later sexual and emotional relationships. In psychological terms, an **attachment** (or bond) forms between the infant and the mother, father, or other care giver. The bond begins in the hours immediately following birth and continues throughout the period of infancy (Higham, 1980). Later, other attachments form to other familiar people. These are the individual's earliest experiences with love and emotional attachment. It seems likely that the quality of these attachments—whether they are stable, secure, and satisfying or unstable, insecure, and frustrating—affects the person's capacity for emotional attachments in adulthood.

We have little direct evidence supporting this last point. However, a classic study of attachment in infant monkeys by Harlow (1959) provides some suggestive evidence. Infant monkeys were reared not by their own mothers but by cloth or wire dolls. In adulthood, these monkeys showed seriously disturbed sexual behavior. Presumably their early lack of attachment to their mother had severe consequences for their later sexuality. And recent research with humans (discussed in Chapter 13) suggests that adults have similar styles of romantic attachment to the kind of attachment they remember having with their parents in childhood.

Knowing About Boy-Girl Differences

By age 2 or 2½, children know what gender they are (see Chapter 14). They know that they are like the parent of the same gender and different from the parent of the

FIGURE 11.2
Harlow's study of infant monkeys reared not by their own mothers but by dolls is a classic. In adulthood, these monkeys showed disturbed sexual behavior, presumably as a result of being deprived of an early attachment to their mothers.

opposite gender and from other children of the opposite gender. At first, infants think that the difference between girls and boys is a matter of clothes or haircuts. But by age 2½ there may be at least some vague awareness of differences in the genital region and differences in positions during urination (Martinson, 1973).

EARLY CHILDHOOD (3 to 7 YEARS)

Between the ages of 3 and 7, there is a marked increase in sexual interest and activity, just as there is an increase in activity and interest in general.

Masturbation

Children increasingly gain experience with masturbation during childhood, although certainly not all children masturbate during this period. In a study of college students, 15 percent of the males and 20 percent of the females recalled that their first masturbation experiences occurred between ages 5 and 8 (Arafat and Cotton, 1974). In a Norwegian study, kindergarten teachers reported that between one-half and one-third of their pupils engaged in some masturbation (Langfeldt, 1981).

Children also learn during this period that masturbation is something that one does in private.

FIGURE 11.3
Between the ages of 3 and 7 there is a marked increase in sexual interest.

Heterosexual Behavior

By the age of 4 or 5, children's sexuality has become more social. There is some heterosexual play. Boys and girls may hug each other or hold hands in imitation of adults. "Playing doctor" can be a popular game at this age (Gundersen et al., 1981). It generally involves no more than exhibiting one's own genitals, looking at those of others, and perhaps engaging in a little fondling or touching. As one man recalled,

> When I was six years old, I consciously experienced my first erection with a neighborhood girl of the same age. My curiosity increased when I saw only a small glimpse of her genital area when we played "doctor" and my desire to know more about the female sex increased tremendously. One day after school, the girl came over to my house. We proceeded up to my bedroom where I told her, "You can see me if I can see you." After she agreed, we both pulled down our pants. She asked me what my penis was. I told her that it was my "weiner," and that she didn't have one—only boys had "weiners." I then proceeded to touch my "weiner" to her "doop" (rear). This contact lasted for only a short time, yet I noticed for the first time that my penis was stiff. I had previously seen my friend's penis become erect as we played "doctor," but my penis becoming stiff was something I had never consciously experienced before. (Martinson, 1973, p. 31)

By about the age of 5, children have formed a concept of marriage—or at least of its nongenital aspects. They know that a member of the opposite gender is the appropriate marriage partner, and they are committed to marrying when they get older (Broderick, 1966). They practice marriage roles as they "play house."

Homosexual Behavior

During late childhood and preadolescence, sexual play with members of one's own gender may be more common than sexual play with members of the other gender (Martinson, 1973). Generally the activity involves no more than touching the other's genitals (Broderick, 1966a). One girl recalled:

> I encountered a sexual experience that was confusing at kindergarten age. . . . Some afternoons we would meet and lock ourselves in a bedroom and take our pants off. We took turns lying on the bed and put pennies, marbles, etc. between our labia. . . . As the ritual became old hat, it passed out of existence. (Martinson, 1973, p. 39)

Sex Knowledge and Interests

At age 3 or 4, children begin to have some notion that there are genital differences between males and females, but their ideas are very vague. By age 7, 30 percent of American children understand what the differences are (Goldman & Goldman, 1982). Children generally react to their discovery of genital differences calmly, though of course there are exceptions.

At age 3, children are very interested in different postures for urinating. Girls attempt to urinate while standing. Children are also very affectionate at this age. They enjoy hugging and kissing their parents and may even propose marriage to the parent of the opposite gender (Martinson, 1973).

At age 4, children are particularly interested in bathrooms and elimination. Games of "show" are also common at this age.

Games of show become less common at age 5, as children become more modest.

Generally children have well-developed principles of modesty and privacy by age 6 or 7. Children at this age are also becoming aware of the social restrictions on sexual expression. A woman recalled:

> When I was six years old I climbed up on the bathroom sink and looked at myself naked in the mirror. All of a sudden I realized I had three different holes. I was very excited about my discovery and ran down to the dinner table and announced it to everyone, "I have three holes!" Silence. "What are they for?" I asked. Silence even heavier than before. I sensed how uncomfortable everyone was and answered for myself. "I guess one is for pee-pee, the other for doo-doo and the third for ca-ca." A sigh of relief; no one had to answer my question. But I got the message— I wasn't supposed to ask "such" questions, though I didn't fully realize what "such" was about at that time (Boston Women's Health Book Collective, 1976, p. 40)

It is important to remember that children's sex play at this age is motivated largely by curiosity and is part of the general learning experiences of childhood. One man illustrated this well as he recalled:

> As a child I experienced several incidents of homosexual exhibitions, many heterosexual exhibitions, and several instances of heterosexual play. This exploratory stage was experienced chiefly between the ages of four to seven. A secluded spot would be secured for purposes of observing and touching the opposite sex's genitals. This happened repeatedly with two girls, one older and one younger. Initiation for each experience seemed to be about fifty percent my effort. . . . At the age of six or seven my friend (a boy) and I had a great curiosity for exploring the anus. It almost seemed *more like scientific research*. (Martinson, 1973, p. 40, italics added)

PREADOLESCENCE (8 to 12 YEARS)

Preadolescence is a period of transition between the years of childhood and the years of puberty and adolescence.

Freud used the term "latency" to refer to the preadolescent period following the resolution of the Oedipus complex. He believed that the sexual urges go "underground" during latency and are not expressed. The evidence indicates, however, that Freud was wrong and that children's interest in and expression of sexuality remain lively throughout this period, perhaps more lively than their parents are willing to believe. For many, "sexual awakening" does not occur until the teens, but for others, it is a very real and poignant part of preadolescence (Martinson, 1973).

At around age 9 or 10, the first bodily changes of puberty begin: the formation of breast buds in girls and the growth of pubic hair. An increased self-consciousness about the body develops, to the point where the child may feel uncomfortable about being seen nude by the parent of the opposite gender. All this marks the transition to adolescence.

Masturbation

During preadolescence, more and more children gain experience with masturbation. In a sample of college women, 32 percent recalled masturbating to orgasm by age 13.[1] The comparable figures for males are 49 percent by age 13 (Arafat & Cotton,

---

[1] These are cumulative-incidence figures, to use the terminology introduced in Chapter 3.

1974). These data, as well as those on adolescence, indicate that boys generally start masturbating earlier than girls do.

Interestingly, boys and girls learn about masturbation in different ways. Typically boys are told about it by their male peers, they see their peers doing it, or they read about it; girls, on the other hand, most frequently learn about masturbation through accidental self-discovery (Langfeldt, 1981). One man recalled:

> An older cousin of mine took two of us out to the garage and did it in front of us. I remember thinking that it seemed a very strange thing to do, and that people who were upright wouldn't do it, but it left a powerful impression on me. A couple of years later, when I began to get erections, I wanted to do it, and felt I shouldn't, but I remembered how he had looked when he was doing it, and the memory tempted me strongly. I worried, and held back, and fought it, but finally I gave in. The worry didn't stop me, and doing it didn't stop my worrying. (Hunt, 1974, p. 79)

Heterosexual Behavior

There is generally little heterosexual behavior during the preadolescent period, mainly because of the social division of males and females into separate groups.

However, children commonly hear about sexual intercourse for the first time during this period. For example, in a sample of adult women, 61 percent recalled having learned about intercourse by age 12 (Wyatt et al., 1988). Children's reactions to this new information are an amusing combination of shock and disbelief—particularly disbelief that their parents would do such a thing. A college woman recalled:

> One of my girlfriends told me about sexual intercourse. It was one of the biggest shocks of my life. She took me aside one day, and I could tell she was in great distress. I thought she was going to tell me about menstruation, so I said that I already knew, and she said, "No, this is *worse!*" Her description went like this: "A guy puts his thing up a girl's hole, and she has a baby." The hole was, to us, the anus, because we did not even know about the vagina and we knew that the urethra was too small. I pictured the act as a single, violent and painful stabbing at the anus by the penis. Somehow, the idea of a baby was forgotten by me. I was horrified and repulsed, and I thought of that awful penis I had seen years ago. At first I insisted that it wasn't true, and my friend said she didn't know for sure, but that's what her cousin told her. But we looked at each other, and we knew it was true. We held each other and cried. We insisted that "my parents would never do that," and "I'll never let anyone do it to me." We were frightened, sickened, and threatened by the idea of some lusty male jabbing at us with his horrid penis. (From a student essay)

For some preadolescents, too, heterosexual activity occurs in an incestuous relationship, whether brother-sister or parent-child. This topic is discussed in detail in Chapter 17.

Homosexual Behavior

Homosocial: A general form of social groupings in which males play and associate with other males, and females play and associate with other females; that is, the genders are separate from each other.

It is important to understand homosexual activity as a normal part of the sexual development of children. In preadolescence, children have a social organization that is essentially **homosocial**. That is, boys play separately from girls, and thus children socialize mainly with members of their own gender. This separation begins at around age 8. According to one study of children's friendship patterns, the segregation reaches a peak at around 10 to 12 years of age. At ages 12 to 13 children are simultaneously the most segregated by gender and the most interested in members of the opposite gender (Broderick, 1966b). Some of the social separation of the genders during preadolescence is actually comical; boys, for example, may have been convinced that girls have "cooties" and that they must be very careful to stay away from them. Given that children are socializing almost exclusively with other members of their own gender, sexual exploring at this age is likely to be homosexual in nature.

These homosexual activities generally involve masturbation, exhibitionism, and the fondling of other's genitals. Boys, for example, may engage in a "circle jerk," in which they masturbate in a group.

Girls do not seem so likely to engage in such group homosexual activities, perhaps because the spectacle of them masturbating is not quite so impressive or perhaps because they already sense the greater cultural restrictions on their sexuality and are hesitant to discuss sexual matters with other girls. In any case, as noted above, boys seem to do their sexual exploring with a gang, while girls do it alone (Kinsey et al., 1953).

Dating

There is some anticipation of adolescent dating in the socializing patterns of preadolescents.

Group dating and heterosexual parties emerge first among preadolescents. Boys, particularly, are slow in adjusting to the behavior expected of them, and they may be more likely to roughhouse than to ask a girl to dance.

Kissing games are popular at parties, reaching their peak of popularity among children aged about 10 to 13 (Broderick, 1966b). There may also be some pairing off for "making out," which generally involves no more than kissing at this age. Genital fondling is not common (Martinson, 1973).

The first paired dating generally begins around the age of 12 or 13. It may consist simply of walking to a movie or going bowling together. At age 12, 48 percent of the boys and 57 percent of the girls in one study were dating (Broderick, 1966b). At age 13, the figure was 69 percent for both. Typically, though, boys and girls at this age date only a few times a year.

FIGURE 11.4
Girls' earlier growth spurts make for amusing height combinations in pre-adolescent and adolescence. Both children are fifth graders.

Going steady also starts at this age, although often the activity centers more on symbols, such as an exchange of rings or bracelets, than it does on any real dating (Martinson, 1973).

Of course, these patterns are averages for American preadolescents. There is great variability within American culture, and in some other cultures boys and girls may already be married by age 13.

Sexual Values

Preadolescents tend to be sexually conservative, while adolescents become increasingly liberal (Schoof-Tams et al., 1976). For example, in regard to premarital intercourse, 11-year-olds generally favor abstinence; they see intercourse as proper in marriage. Later in adolescence, the precondition for intercourse will shift to love rather than marriage.

ADOLESCENCE (13 to 19 YEARS)

A surge of sexual interest occurs around puberty and continues through adolescence (which is equated here roughly with the teenage years, ages 13 to 19). This heightened sexuality may be caused by a number of factors, including bodily changes and an awareness of them, rises in levels of sex hormones, and increased cultural emphasis on sex and rehearsal for adult gender roles. We can see evidence of this heightened sexuality particularly in the data on masturbation. But before examining those data, let's consider some theoretical ideas about how hormones and social forces might interact as influences on adolescent sexuality.

Sociologist J. Richard Udry (1988) has proposed a theoretical model that recognizes that both sociological factors and biological factors are potent in adolescent sexuality. He studied eighth-, ninth-, and tenth-graders (13 to 16 years old), measuring their hormone levels (testosterone, estrogen, and progesterone), and a number of sociological factors (for example, whether they were in an intact family, parents' educational level, the teenager's response to a scale measuring sexually permissive attitudes, and the teenager's attachment to conventional institutions such as involvement in school sports and church attendance). Thirty-five percent of the males had engaged in sexual intercourse, as had 14 percent of the females.

For boys, testosterone levels had a very strong relationship to sexual activity (including coitus, masturbation, and extent of feeling sexually "turned on"). For girls, the relationship between testosterone levels and sexual activity was not as strong as it was for boys, but it was a significant relationship, and it was testosterone—not estrogen or progesterone—that was related to sexuality. Among the social variables, sexually permissive attitudes were related to sexuality for boys, although they had a much smaller effect than that of testosterone. For girls, pubertal development (developing a "curvy" figure) had an effect, probably by increasing the girl's attractiveness. And the effects of testosterone were accentuated among girls in father-absent families. When asked to rate their future plans about sexuality, testosterone levels were an important predictor of their ratings, as were the social variables of permissive attitudes and church attendance.

The bottom line on this study is that it shows testosterone levels to have a substantial impact on the sexuality of adolescent boys and girls. Social variables (such as permissive attitudes, father absence for girls, and church attendance) then interact with the biological effects, in some cases magnifying them (father absence for girls) and in some cases suppressing them (church attendance).

Masturbation

According to the Kinsey data, there is a sharp increase in the incidence of masturbation for boys between the ages of 13 and 15. This is illustrated in Figure 11.5. Note that the curve is steepest between the ages of 13 and 15, indicating that most boys begin masturbating to orgasm during that period. By age 15, 82 percent of the boys in Kinsey's study had masturbated. Many girls also begin masturbating at around that age, but note that the curve on the graph is flatter for them, indicating that many girls do not begin masturbating until later. Thus the increase in their masturbation behavior is much more gradual than boys' and continues past adolescence.

More recent data suggest that children and adolescents begin to masturbate earlier today, and thus the Kinsey data probably need to be pushed back about one or two years. However, the general shape of the curves still seems to hold.

Boys typically masturbate two or three times per week, whereas girls do so about once per month (Hass, 1979).

One man recalled his adolescent experiences with masturbation and the intense feelings involved as follows:

> When I was fourteen I was like Portnoy—always rushing off to the bathroom when the urge came over me. I did it so much that my dick would get swollen and sore, but even that didn't stop me. By the time I was nineteen I was screwing, but there'd be times when I wouldn't be able to get anything, and I'd go back to jacking off—and then I felt really guilty and ashamed of myself, like I was a failure, like I had a secret weakness. (Hunt, 1974, p. 95)

Interestingly, the frequency of masturbation among boys decreases during periods when they are having sexual intercourse; among girls, however, this situation is accompanied by an increased frequency of masturbation (Sorensen, 1973).

Attitudes Toward Masturbation

Attitudes toward masturbation have undergone a dramatic change in this century. As a result, adolescents are now given much different information about masturbation, and this may affect both their behavior and their feelings about masturbation.

For example, a popular handbook, *What a Boy Should Know,* written in 1913 by two doctors, advised its readers:

> Whenever unnatural emissions are produced . . . the body becomes "slack." A boy will not feel so vigorous and springy; he will be more easily tired. . . . He will probably look pale and pasty, and he is lucky if he escapes indigestion and

FIGURE 11.5
Cumulative incidence of males and females who have masturbated to orgasm, according to Kinsey's data.

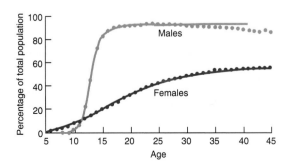

getting his bowels confined, both of which will probably give him spots and pimples on his face. . . .

The results on the mind are the more severe and more easily recognized. . . . A boy who practices this habit can never be the best that Nature intended him to be. His wits are not so sharp. His memory is not so good. His power of fixing his attention on whatever he is doing is lessened. . . . A boy like this is a poor thing to look at. . . .

. . . The effect of self-abuse on a boy's character always tends to weaken it, and in fact, to make him untrustworthy, unreliable, untruthful, and probably even dishonest. (Schofield and Vaughan-Jackson, 1913, pp. 30–42)

Masturbation, in short, was believed to cause everything from warts to insanity.[2]

Attitudes toward masturbation are now considerably more positive, and few people would now subscribe to notions like those expressed above. By the 1970s only about 15 percent of young people believed that masturbation is wrong (Hunt, 1974, p. 74). Indeed, masturbation is now recommended as a remedy in sex therapy. As psychiatrist Thomas Szasz said, the shift in attitudes toward masturbation has been so great that in a generation it has changed from a disease to a form of therapy.

While approval of masturbation is now explicit, people can still have mixed feelings about it. An example of a lingering negative attitude is that of the man quoted previously who likened his adolescent masturbation to Portnoy's,[3] accompanied as it was by feelings of guilt and shame. Among the adolescents interviewed by Sorensen (1973), few felt guilty about masturbation, but many felt defensive or embarrassed about it.

Homosexual Behavior

About 11 percent of adolescent males and 6 percent of adolescent females report having had homosexual experiences, and 25 percent say they have been approached for a homosexual experience. Of those who have had homosexual experiences, 24

---

[2] In case you're wondering why boys' advice books were saying such awful things, there is a rather interesting history that produced those pronouncements (Money, 1986). The Swiss physician Simon André Tissot (1728–1797) wrote an influential book, *Treatise on the Diseases Produced by Onanism,* taking the term from the biblical story of Onan (Genesis 38:9). In this work he articulated a degeneracy theory, in which loss of semen was believed to weaken a man's body; Tissot had some very inventive physiological explanations for his idea. The famous American physician of the 1800s Benjamin Rush was influenced by Tissot and spread degeneracy theory in the United States. The theory became popularized by Sylvester Graham (1794–1851), a religious zealot and health reformer, who was a vegetarian and whose passion for health foods gave us the names for Graham flour and Graham crackers. To be healthy, according to Graham, one needed to follow the Graham diet and practice sexual abstinence. Then John Harvey Kellogg (1852–1943) of—you guessed it—cornflakes fame entered the story. He was an ardent follower of Graham and his doctrines of health food and sexual abstinence. While experimenting with healthful foods he invented cornflakes. His younger brother Will Keith Kellogg thought to add sugar and made a fortune. John Harvey Kellogg contributed further to public fears about masturbation by writing (during his honeymoon, no less) *Plain Facts for Old and Young: Embracing the Natural History and Hygiene of Organic Life,* which provided detailed descriptions of the horrible diseases supposedly caused by masturbation. These ideas then found their way into the advice books for boys of the early 1900s.

[3] Of the novel *Portnoy's Complaint,* which poignantly and humorously describes an adolescent male's masturbation.

percent had their first experience with a younger person, 39 percent with someone of their own age, 29 percent with an older teenager, and 8 percent with an adult (Sorensen, 1973). Thus there is no evidence that adolescent homosexual experiences result from being seduced by adults; most such encounters take place between peers. In many cases the person has only one or a few homosexual experiences, partly out of curiosity, and the behavior is discontinued. Such adolescent homosexual behavior does not seem to be predictive of adult homosexual orientation.

The data indicate that there has been no increase in the incidence of premarital homosexual behavior in recent years (DeLamater & MacCorquodale, 1979). It seems safe to conclude from various studies, taken together, that about 10 percent of adolescents have homosexual experiences, with the percentages being somewhat higher for boys than for girls.

Teenagers can be quite naive about homosexual behavior and societal attitudes toward it. In some cases, they have been taught that heterosexual sex is "bad"; having been told nothing about homosexual sex, they infer that it is permissible. In some cases, homosexual relationships naively develop from a same-gender friendship of late childhood and adolescence. One woman recalled:

> When I was a junior and senior in high school I had an intense friendship with Jan, a girl in my school. We wrote notes and went on walks and climbed trees, sharing dreams, reciting poems that we liked, and talking about coming back to the school in later years to teach together. We vowed lifelong love and friendship, but physically we could express the energy that was between us only by clowning around, bumping into each other—and once when she was asleep I kissed her hair. The intensity of my friendship with Jan made my family uneasy—I remember

*FIGURE 11.6
Sexuality in early
adolescence is often playful
and unsophisticated.*

comments about seeing too much of one person. Their uneasiness got to me a little, because I was a bit uncomfortable with my strong pit-of-the-stomach feelings about her anyway. I remember being shy about undressing with her in the room, although I undressed with other friends without thinking about it. Then during the summer after we graduated, having not seen Jan for several weeks, I was leafing through a psychology book and found a section that talked about the intense, bordering-on-homosexual friendship of young girls.

Before long I had labeled it as a silly, childishly intense friendship. I made no efforts to see her when we both went to college, for I figured we had nothing in common.

I think our feelings grew more intense as we tried to repress their sexual side. So I pulled away from Jan because I couldn't handle the natural sexual part of my feelings and affection for her. (Boston Women's Health Book Collective, 1976, p. 64)

Heterosexual Behavior

Toward the middle and end of the adolescent years, more and more young people engage in heterosexual sex, with more and more frequency. Thus heterosexual behavior gains prominence and becomes the major source of sexual outlet.

In terms of the individual's development, the data indicate that there is a very regular progression from kissing, through French kissing and breast and genital fondling, to intercourse and oral-genital contact; this generally occurs over a period of four or more years (DeLamater & MacCorquodale, 1979). To use terminology introduced in Chapter 2, these behaviors tend to follow a sexual script.

PREMARITAL SEX[4]

One of the most dramatic changes to occur in sexual behavior and attitudes in recent decades is in the area of premarital sexual behavior.

How Many People Have Premarital Intercourse?

On the basis of his data collected in the 1940s, Kinsey concluded that about 33 percent of all females and 71 percent of all males have had premarital intercourse by the age of 25. More recent studies show that the incidence is now higher, particularly for females (see Table 11.1), so that the gender gap has narrowed. Now, about three-fourths of Americans engage in premarital sex, with the percentage being somewhat higher for males and somewhat lower for females.

In the United States, patterns of premarital intercourse vary substantially according to ethnic group. Table 11.2 shows data on this point from a survey of 16- to 25-year-olds conducted in the greater Los Angeles area (Moore & Erickson, 1985). Notice first that there is essentially no gender difference: approximately two-thirds

---

[4] Note that the very term "premarital sex" contains some hidden assumptions, most notably that marriage is normative and that proper sex occurs in marriage. Thus, sex among never-married (young) persons is considered premarital—something done before marrying. A more neutral term would be "nonmarital sex," although it fails to distinguish between premarital sex, extramarital sex, and postmarital sex.

Table 11.1
Percentages of People Who Had Engaged in Premarital Intercourse, According to Four Surveys

	Males	Females
Kinsey (1948, 1953), by age 25	71	33
Zelnik & Kantner (1980), by age 19		59
Robinson & Jedlicka (1982), college students	77	64
Forrest & Singh (1990), by age 19		74

of both males and females in this sample had engaged in premarital intercourse. The incidence of premarital intercourse is highest among blacks and whites and lowest among Asians. Blacks, on the average, begin engaging in sexual intercourse approximately two years earlier than whites and Asians do.

There are also substantial variations in patterns of premarital intercourse in different cultures around the world, as the data in Table 11.4 indicate (see page 326). Several interesting points emerge from the data in that table. First, in all societies except perhaps the United States, males are more likely than females to engage in premarital intercourse. On the other hand, the extent of this gender gap varies considerably, from a small one in the United States to an enormous one in Mexico, where the virginity of adolescent girls is closely guarded. And in Japan, the incidence of premarital intercourse is low for both males and females.

In many countries around the world, the incidence of premarital intercourse has risen in the last few decades. Around the globe, especially where modernization has been rapid, adolescents are less and less under the influence of family and community and more and more responsive to peers and the mass media (Liskin, 1985).

To summarize, the trends in premarital intercourse in the last two decades are in the direction of: (1) both in the United States and in most other countries, more adolescents engaging in premarital intercourse; (2) in the United States, a greater increase in incidence for females, thereby narrowing the gap between males and females; (3) first intercourse occurring at somewhat earlier ages; (4) moderately large

Table 11.2
Ethnicity and Premarital Intercourse in a Sample of Adolescents and Young Adults (ages 16 to 25) in the Los Angeles Area

Subgroup	Percentage Having Had Intercourse	Mean Age of First Intercourse
Males (all ethnic groups combined)	64	14.9
Females (all ethnic groups combined)	67	15.9
Whites	79	16.2
Blacks	81	14.4
Hispanics	61	15.3
Asians	32	16.4

Source: D. A. Moore & P. I. Erickson. (1985, Nov.). Age, gender, and ethnic differences in sexual and contraceptive knowledge, attitudes, and behaviors. *Family & Community Health,* 8(3), 38–51.

A Sociological Analysis of Premarital Sexual Behavior

Sociologists John DeLamater and Patricia MacCorquodale (1979) conducted a large-scale survey and detailed analysis of patterns of premarital sexuality. They interviewed both students and nonstudents between the ages of 18 and 23 in Madison, Wisconsin. They obtained an initial random sample of 1141 students at the University of Wisconsin. They attempted to interview all these people, obtaining an 82 percent response rate. Nonstudents were contacted by a probability sample of residences in the telephone directly; they had a 63 percent response rate. Data for a total of 1376 respondents were analyzed. The study is notable because it included both students and nonstudents, and because it used excellent sampling techniques and had a good response rate, except that the nonstudent response rate was a bit lower than would be desirable. It is difficult to know to what extent the results are limited to Madison, Wisconsin, and whether they would be generalizable to other areas of the country.

The data on the sexual experience of the respondents are summarized in Table 11.3.

Respondents also answered a number of other questions, and analyses of the answers permitted the authors to come to some conclusions regarding what factors are most strongly related to premarital sexual expression.

One of the most important factors appeared to be sexual ideology or attitudes. That is, those with the most liberal attitudes had the most premarital sexual experience. DeLamater and MacCorquodale argued that this occurs because ideology forms the basis for self-control. That is, the individual's standards specify the type of relationship, in terms of emotional commitment, which is necessary before particular behaviors are appropriate. Confirming this notion, the variable most closely related to the respondents' current behavior has the emotional quality of their current relationship.

How are the person's attitudes shaped? DeLamater and MacCorquodale found that parents, and sometimes religion, are early shapers of ideology. Later, close friends and dating partners become more important, while the influence of parents wanes. As peers become more important influences, the young person's standards typically become more permissive.

ethnic-group variations in the United States; and (5) substantial variations from one country to another (Hopkins, 1977; Liskin, 1985; Moore & Erickson, 1985).

First Intercourse

The adolescents in the Coles and Stokes (1985) report described their emotional reactions to their first act of intercourse. Positive reactions—feeling glad—were more than twice as common among boys (60%) as among girls (23%). Girls more often said they felt such emotions as sadness, ambivalence, and disappointment. Most

Table 11.3
Percentages of Respondents Who Had Ever Engaged in Various Sexual Behaviors

	Male		Female	
	Student	Nonstudent	Student	Nonstudent
Necking	97	98	99	99
French kissing	93	95	95	95
Breast fondling	92	92	93	93
Male fondling of female genitals	86	87	82	86
Female fondling of male genitals	82	84	78	81
Genitals touching	77	81	72	78
Intercourse	75	79	60	72
Male mouth contact with female genitals	60	68	59	67
Female mouth contact with male genitals	61	70	54	63

Contrary to what one might expect, the results indicated that a number of psychological variables—self-image, self-esteem, body image, sense of internal or external control, and gender-role definitions—were *un*related to premarital sexual behavior.

Finally, the results indicated increased similarities between women and men and a decline of the double standard, as other recent surveys have found. One of the few differences that remain, though, is that women still require greater emotional commitment before they are accepting of premarital intercourse. This may cause conflicts in some relationships.

DeLamater and MacCorquodale concluded that it is the couple and the nature of their relationship—rather than variables such as social class or religion—that are essential to understanding premarital sexuality.

It is tempting to make causal inferences from these data—for example, that permissive attitudes *cause* increased premarital sexual experience. It is important to remember that these data are correlational in nature and that causality cannot be inferred. Nonetheless, this study provides good evidence of what factors are most related to premarital sexual patterns, and these findings can be confirmed by later research.

Source: John DeLamater and Patricia MacCorquodale. (1979). *Premarital sexuality: Attitudes, relationships, behavior.* Madison: University of Wisconsin Press.

typically, the immediate reaction of males was to feel excitement, while females typically felt afraid. Unfortunately, the boy usually does not realize that the girl is having a negative reaction (Sorensen, 1973).

The typical female reaction to intercourse has been described as the Peggy Lee syndrome (named for her song "Is That All There Is?"). Despite our culture's romanticized high expectations that the first intercourse experience will be like firecrackers popping on the Fourth of July, it turns out to be much less thrilling than that for most females. For example, a sample of college women, recalling their experience of first intercourse, on the average gave it only a 3.9 on a pleasure scale

Peggy Lee syndrome: The feelings of disappointment experienced by teenage girls at first intercourse when it is not as thrilling as they expected.

Table 11.4
A Global Perspective on Premarital Intercourse

Country and Year	Age of Respondents	Percentage Having Had Intercourse		Mean Age of First Coitus	
		Females	Males	Females	Males
Africa					
Liberia 1984	18–21	82	93		
Nigeria 1982	19	63	86	17 years	16 years
Latin America					
Mexico 1985	15–19	13	44	17 years	16 years
Developed countries					
Israel 1978	16–17	16	46		
Japan 1974	16–21	7	15	17 years	18 years
United States 1979	21		71		
	19	69			

Source: L. Liskin. (1985, Nov.–Dec.) Youth in the 1980s: Social and health concerns. *Population Reports,* Vol. XIII, No. 5.
B. Robey, S. O. Rutstein, L. Harris, & R. Blackburn (1992, Dec.) The reproductive revolution: New survey findings. *Population Reports,* Series M., No. 11.

(1 = didn't experience pleasure at all, 7 = strongly experienced pleasure) (Weis, 1983).

Sex with a Prostitute

A generation ago, premarital sex with a prostitute was fairly common among males, and many young men received their sexual initiation in this manner. Among the noncollege men over age 35 in the Hunt study 20 percent had had their first intercourse with a prostitute (Hunt, 1974, p. 145). Now, however, having premarital sex with a prostitute is much less common. This can be seen by comparing the percentages of men under 35 in Hunt's study who had ever had sex with a prostitute with the percentages of men over 35 who had ever done so (see Table 11.5). From these data it appears that only about half as many men now have premarital sex with prostitutes as was the case a generation ago. Further, those who do have such contacts have far fewer of them. Sex with prostitutes is one of the few sexual behaviors to show a decline between the time of the Kinsey study and the present.

Techniques in Premarital Sex

Paralleling the increase in the incidence of premarital intercourse is an increase in the variety of techniques that are used in premarital sex. One of the most dramatic changes has been the increased use of oral-genital techniques. In the Kinsey sample, 33 percent of the males had experienced fellatio premaritally and 14 percent had engaged in cunnilingus. In the DeLamater survey, 65 percent of the males had engaged in fellatio premaritally and 64 percent had performed cunnilingus (DeLamater & MacCorquodale, 1979). In my classes, I generally find that about 5 percent of the women students have engaged in fellatio and/or cunnilingus but not in intercourse—I suspect because some have discovered that mouth-genital sex cannot cause pregnancy. Young people today also use a greater variety of positions, not just the standard man on top.

Table 11.5
Percentages of Married Males Who Had Ever
Had Premarital Intercourse with a Prostitute

	Percentage	
Education of Respondents	Under 35 Years Old	35 Years and Over
High school or less	30	61
Some college or more	19	52

Source: Morton Hunt. (1974). *Sexual behavior in the 1970s.* Chicago: Playboy Press, p. 144.

Doubtless some of this increased variety in techniques is a result of today's "performance ethic" in sexual relations, which was discussed in Chapter 10. Adolescents and young adults may feel pressured to be gold medalists in the sexual Olympics. One man said:

> Sometimes I'm really good; I can make a girl have orgasms until she's about half dead. But if I don't like the girl, or if I'm not feeling confident, it can be hard work—and sometimes I can't even cut the mustard, and that bothers me a lot when that happens. (Hunt, 1974, p. 163)

Attitudes Toward Premarital Intercourse

Attitudes toward premarital intercourse have also undergone marked changes, particularly among young people.

Sociologist Ira Reiss (1960) has distinguished between four kinds of standards for premarital coitus:

1. **Abstinence** Premarital intercourse is considered wrong for both males and females, regardless of the circumstances.
2. **Permissiveness with affection** Premarital intercourse is permissible for both males and females if it occurs in the context of a stable relationship that involves love, commitment, or being engaged.
3. **Permissiveness without affection** Premarital intercourse is permissible for both males and females, regardless of emotional commitment, simply on the basis of physical attraction.
4. **Double standard** Premarital intercourse is acceptable for males but is not acceptable for females. The double standard may be either "orthodox" or "transitional." In the orthodox case, the double standard holds regardless of the couple's relationship, while in the transitional case, sex is considered acceptable for the woman if she is in love or if she is engaged.

Historically in the United States, the standard has been either abstinence or the double standard. However, today, particularly among young people, the standard is one of permissiveness with affection.

We can see evidence of this new standard, and of the shift it represents from previous generations, by comparing the data on current attitudes toward premarital intercourse with those from previous decades, as shown in Table 11.6. Note that in surveys conducted in 1937, 1959, and 1969, few people approved of premarital intercourse. However, by 1991 more people approved than disapproved, representing a real shift in norms.

Abstinence: A standard in which premarital intercourse is considered wrong, regardless of the circumstances.

Permissiveness with affection: A standard in which premarital intercourse is considered acceptable if it occurs in the context of a loving, committed relationship.

Permissiveness without affection: A standard in which premarital intercourse is acceptable even if there is no emotional commitment.

Double standard: A standard in which premarital intercourse is considered acceptable for males but not for females.

Table 11.6
Percentages of People Agreeing That Premarital Intercourse Is Acceptable, 1937, 1959, 1969, 1978, 1991

Do you think it is all right for either or both parties to a marriage to have had previous sexual intercourse?

	1937, %	1959, %
All right for both	22	22
All right for men only	8	8
All right for neither	56	54
Don't know or refused to answer	14	16

Do you think it is wrong for a man and a woman to have sex relations before marriage or not?

	1969, %	1978, %	1991, %
Yes, it is wrong	68	50	40
No, it is not wrong	21	41	54
Don't know	11	9	6

Source: Gallup Poll, 1969; Gallup Poll, 1978; Gallup Poll, 1991. Morton Hunt. (1974). *Sexual behavior in the 1970s.* Chicago: Playboy Press, pp. 115–116.

Motives for Having Premarital Intercourse

The adolescent respondents in the Sorensen study (1973) commonly mentioned a need to search for new experience and a desire to escape from tensions as reasons for engaging in premarital coitus. Other reasons included using it as a means of communication, as a sign of maturity, and as a way of handing out rewards or punishments (perhaps rewarding a boyfriend or punishing parents—recall the non-sexual uses of sexual behavior). Some respondents said they engaged in premarital intercourse simply because it was expected by the peer group. Challenging parents or society and deriving physical pleasure were not commonly mentioned as reasons for engaging in premarital intercourse. As homosexuality receives more publicity and as adolescents become anxious about it, having premarital sex may also be a means of "proving" one's heterosexuality.

Nonetheless, one should not overestimate the importance teenagers attach to sex. When asked to rank what was most important to them, teenagers listed doing well in school and friendships first and second, and sex sixth in a list of six (Hass, 1979).

Dating, Going Steady, Getting Engaged

The social forces that have produced changes in premarital sexual behavior and standards are complex. But among them seems to be a change in courtship stages—in the process of dating, going steady, and getting engaged. Dating and going steady occur much earlier now than in previous generations. Dating earlier and going steady earlier create both more of a demand for premarital sex and more of a legitimacy for it. For many, sexual intimacy is made respectable by going steady (R. R. Bell, 1966). As Ira Reiss noted, "No other dating custom is quite so central to the understanding of teen-age sexual codes as going steady."

Sorensen (1973) found the most common premarital sexual pattern to be serial monogamy without marriage. In such a relationship there is an intention of being faithful, but the relationship is of uncertain duration. Of those in the sample who had premarital intercourse, 40 percent were serial monogamists. Though they averaged about four partners, nearly half of them had had only one partner, and about half of them had been involved in their current relationship for a year or more. Current data indicate that about 25 percent of all women have only one partner premaritally (26 percent for white women, 21 percent for black women); but 23 percent have six or more partners (24 percent of white women, 17 percent of black women) (Tanfer & Schoorl, 1992).

Conflicts

We are currently in an era in which there are tensions between a restrictive sexual ethic and a permissive one. In such circumstances, conflicts are bound to arise. One is between parents and children, as parents hold fast to conservative standards while their children adopt permissive ones.

These conflicts within our society are mirrored in the messages of the mass media. As Albert Ellis describes the situation:

> Premarital sex relations today are widely believed to be bad, silly and pointless; *but* thoroughly enjoyable; *but* normal and natural; *but* necessary for healthful living; *but* smart and sophisticated; *but* romantically permissible and thrilling; *but* adventurous and exciting; *but* inevitable in this all-too-fleshy world, and so on. (1962, p. 29)

Listening to such messages while growing up, it is no wonder adolescents may sometimes feel conflicts about premarital sex.

Young people may also experience conflicts between their own behaviors and their attitudes or standards. Behaviors generally change faster than attitudes do. As a result, people may engage in premarital sex while still disapproving of it. For example, in one study of inner-city junior high and senior high school students, of those who were sexually active, 83 percent gave an ideal age for first intercourse that was older than when they first had had intercourse (Zabin et al., 1984). And among those who had engaged in premarital intercourse, 25 percent believed that premarital sex is wrong. These inconsistencies between behavior and attitudes can create feelings of conflict.

THE SEXUAL REVOLUTION:
IS IT OVER?

In 1984 *Time* magazine ran a cover story entitled "Sex in the '80s: The revolution is over." The writer argued that the sexual revolution of the 1960s and 1970s— which tried to free people from repressive, Victorian standards, while maintaining that premarital sex, and even extramarital sex and vibrator sex were groovy—has come to a grinding halt. According to the authors, the trend for the 1980s and 1990s is toward long-term, committed relationships. People are more interested in committing themselves to a single partner than in finding 10 new partners with whom to have casual sex. Commitment, intimacy, and working at relationships are the new goals. Some evidence supporting *Time*'s claims comes from a survey given repeatedly at a large state university (the University of Texas) (Gerrard, 1987). In 1973–1974, 35 percent of these college women were sexually active (defined as having sexual

Teen Pregnancy

Each year in the United States, more than 1 million young women under 20 years of age, or 1 of every 10 teenage girls, becomes pregnant (Stevens-Simon & White, 1991). Although rates are higher for black teenagers than for white teenagers, U.S. whites still have the highest teenage pregnancy rate of any Western nation; white U.S. teenagers are twice as likely to become pregnant as Canadian teenagers and four times as likely as Swedish teenagers. There are excessive costs associated with these teen pregnancies: costs to the girls or women themselves, costs to their offspring, and costs to society at large.

Sociologist Frank Furstenberg and his colleagues Jeanne Brooks-Gunn and Philip Morgan have done an important study of teenage pregnancy that gives essential information on its effects on the mother and her child. The study is particularly impressive because they recently followed up the women and their children in 1984, 17 years after the women were initially interviewed while pregnant in 1966–1967. There were approximately 400 respondents, most of them black, all of them initially residing in Baltimore.

Furstenberg and his colleagues concluded that although there are many negative consequences to teenage childbearing, the negative consequences have been exaggerated and there has not been enough attention paid to those women who, despite the odds against them, nonetheless manage to cope and succeed.

Let's focus first on the findings for the mothers. When they were first followed up 5 years after the pregnancy, they looked very disadvantaged. For example, 49 percent had not graduated from high school. Approximately one-third of them were on welfare at some point during the 17 years of the study. However, by the time of the 1984 follow-up, an impressive proportion of women had staged a substantial recovery. At that point, an additional 38 percent had graduated from high school, an additional 25 percent had some education beyond high school, and 5 percent had graduated from college. Of those who had been on welfare at some time during the study, two-thirds had managed to get off it by 1984; 67 percent were employed, and fully a quarter had incomes in excess of $25,000 per year.

The study shows clearly that there is great diversity in the outcomes for adolescent mothers. Some remain locked in poverty for the rest of their lives, whereas others manage to succeed despite their circumstances. Furstenberg and his colleagues feel that it is important to understand the routes to success that some women find. The most important factor is differential resources. Women with more educated parents who have more income tend to do better because they have more resources on which to

intercourse once per month or more). In the 1978–1979 sample, the percentage had risen to 51 percent, but for the 1983–1984 sample, it was 37 percent. That is, the sexual activity of these unmarried college women in the 1980s had returned to earlier, more conservative patterns.

Another survey given repeatedly at a different southern university found quite different results (Robinson et al., 1991). The results are shown in Figure 11.7. The incidence of premarital intercourse increased for men and for women between 1965 and 1985, although the increase was greater for women, narrowing the gender gap.

draw. The second most important factor is competence and motivation. Those women who were doing well in school at the time of the pregnancy and had high educational aspirations were more likely to do well following the birth. A third factor is intervention programs such as special schools for pregnant teenagers and hospital intervention programs. When these programs are successful, they help the women complete high school and postpone other births, two factors that are crucial to recovering from the adverse circumstances of a teenage pregnancy. If there are additional births soon after the first, the woman essentially becomes locked out of the job market, but she can successfully build a career if she has only one child to manage.

Turning now to the children, the results indicate that they are at risk in many ways. At birth, 11 percent were low birth weight (2500 grams or less), which puts them at risk for a variety of other problems (see Chapter 7). However, it seems that the excess of low-birth-weight babies is more a function of the adequacy or inadequacy of medical care during pregnancy than it is a function of the mother being a teenager. By 1984 the school record showed evidence of academic failure and behavior problems. Half of the children had had to repeat at least one grade. Thirty-five percent had had to bring their parents to school in the last year because of a behavioral problem, and 44 percent had been suspended or expelled in the past 5 years. The study sample was also more sexually active than randomly chosen national samples. By age 16, 78 percent (84 percent of the boys, 60 percent of the girls) had engaged in sexual intercourse. By age 17, 26 percent of the girls reported having been pregnant. Thus the cycle of teen pregnancy and poverty tends to perpetuate itself.

Teenage pregnancy in the United States is a serious problem, both because of the large numbers of people affected and because the consequences can be so serious. What can be done?

The strategy of Furstenberg and his colleagues is to look at the success stories—those women who manage to rise out of poverty to make successful and happy lives for themselves. Once the factors that were crucial to their success are identified, social programs can be designed to provide similar resources or experiences to more teenage mothers, thereby breaking the cycle of poverty and teen pregnancy. Two critical factors to success, for example, are finishing high school (and preferably getting even more education) and postponing other births. Social programs need to be set up to assist adolescent mothers in finishing high school (including special schools for pregnant teenagers, and child care for mothers while attending school). Information on and access to contraception is essential. Programs such as Head Start that help prepare these children for school are critical, because they are at risk for academic failure. Marriage to a man with some financial resources was also a route to success for some women in this study. However, the high rate of unemployment among young, black, urban men makes such marriages less likely. This points out the importance of social programs aimed at males as well as females.

In summary, teenage pregnancy is a serious problem, but not an unsolvable one. By studying those women who stage a recovery from the experience, we can gain important insights into how we can break the cycle of poverty and teen pregnancy.

Source Frank F. Furstenberg, Jr., J. Brooks-Gunn, & S. Philip Morgan. (1987). *Adolescent mothers in later life.* New York: Cambridge University Press.

But the incidence of premarital intercourse was just as high in 1985—well into the AIDS and herpes era—as it had been in 1980, and higher than it had been in 1975. These data provide no evidence of a lowering of the incidence of premarital intercourse. Unfortunately, this study did not report on what may be more important than the incidence of premarital sex—that is, the number of premarital partners. An end to the sexual revolution might not be revealed by how many people engage in premarital intercourse but rather by whether they restrict themselves to a single partner.

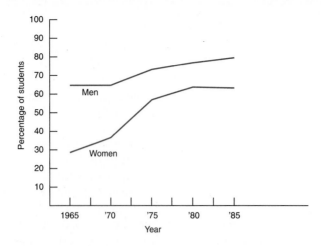

FIGURE 11.7
Is the revolution over?
Incidence of premarital
intercourse among college
students, 1965–1985.
(Robinson et al., 1991)

This same survey also inquired about attitudes. Here they did find increasing conservatism. In response to the statement "A man who has had sexual intercourse with a great many women is immoral," 35 percent of males and 57 percent of females agreed in 1965. By 1975, those percentages had fallen to 20 percent and 30 percent. But then in 1985 they had again risen to 32 percent of male respondents agreeing and 52 percent of females agreeing. In sum, then, there is increasing disapproval of casual sex with multiple partners. Interestingly, when the statement referred to a woman having sexual intercourse with a great many men, 51 percent of males and 64 percent of females agreed in the 1985 data. That is, there is more disapproval of this behavior when it is a woman who engages in it.

I do similar surveys each year in my own human sexuality class. I see no trend toward sexual conservatism there. The incidence of premarital intercourse has been fairly steady for many years, for both males and females, ranging around 80 to 85 percent. If anything, there is an increasing trend toward having multiple premarital sexual partners. Generally around 20 percent of the students report 6 to 10 partners, and a few report 11 or more. Of course, it is true that students taking a human sexuality course are not a random sample of college students, much less a random sample of all people in their age group. They are more sexually experienced and sexually liberal. But if there is a trend toward sexual conservatism, it should show up among this group as well as among others.

Perhaps the best evidence comes from the National Survey of Family Growth, in which a probability sample of American women of reproductive age were interviewed, once in 1982 and again in 1988 (Forrest & Singh, 1990). The relevant results are shown in Table 11.7. Notice that, among 18- to 19-year-olds, 64 percent had engaged in sexual intercourse in 1982, compared with 74 percent of 18- to 19-year-olds in 1988. Again, the incidence of premarital intercourse is increasing, not declining.

What is the answer to the question, Is the sexual revolution over? The weight of the evidence says no. Rates of premarital intercourse continued to climb in the 1980s. If there is a return to more conservative attitudes, this change in attitudes seems not to be reflected in behavior.

HOW SEXUALITY AIDS IN PSYCHOLOGICAL DEVELOPMENT

Erik Erikson, whose work represents a major revision of Freudian theory, has postulated a theory of psychosocial development according to which we experience

Table 11.7
Percentage of Women Aged 18 to 19 Who Have Ever Engaged in Sexual Intercourse, According to a Well-Sampled Survey

Race or Ethnicity	1982	1988
Total	64	74
White, non-Hispanic	61	74
Black, non-Hispanic	79	78
Hispanic	70	70

Source: J. D. Forrest & S. Singh. (1990). The sexual and reproductive behavior of American women, 1982–1988. *Family Planning Perspectives, 22*(5), 206–24.

crises at eight different stages of our lives (Erikson, 1950, 1968). Each one of these crises may be resolved in one of two directions. Erikson notes that social influences are particularly important in determining the outcomes of these crises.

The stages postulated by Erikson are listed in Table 11.8. Note that the outcomes of several of them may be closely linked to sexuality. For example, in early childhood there is a crisis between autonomy and shame, and later between initiative and guilt. The child who masturbates at age 5 is showing autonomy and initiative. But if the parents react to this activity by severely punishing the child, their actions may produce shame and guilt. Thus they may be encouraging the child to feel ashamed and consequently to suffer a loss of self-esteem.

In adolescence, the crisis is between identity and role confusion. Gender roles are among the most important; in later adolescence the person may emerge with a stable, self-confident sense of manhood or womanhood or, alternatively, may feel in conflict about gender roles. A choice of career is extremely important in this developing sense of identity, and gender roles influence career choice. A sexual identity also emerges—whether, for example, one is heterosexual or homosexual, popular or unpopular.

In young adulthood, the crisis is between intimacy and isolation. Sexuality, of course, can function in an important way as people develop their capacity for intimacy.

For adolescents particularly, sexuality is related to accomplishing important developmental tasks (A. P. Bell, 1974a). Among these are:

1. Becoming independent of parents. Sexuality is a way of expressing one's autonomy and one's independence from parents. The adolescent boy who mas-

Table 11.8
Erikson's Stages of Psychosocial Development

Approximate Stage in the Life Cycle	Crisis
Infancy	Basic trust vs. mistrust
Ages 1½ to 3 years	Autonomy vs. shame and doubt
Ages 3 to 5½ years	Initiative vs. guilt
Ages 5½ to 12 years	Industry vs. inferiority
Adolescence	Identity vs. role confusion
Young adulthood	Intimacy vs. isolation
Adulthood	Generativity vs. stagnation
Maturity	Ego integrity vs. despair

turbates, for example, may be expressing a need to cut the apron strings that tie him to his mother—as you know if you have read *Portnoy's Complaint.*

2. Establishing a viable moral system of one's own. For many adolescents, some of the most critical moral decisions of their lives made independently of parents are in the area of their own sexual conduct. A personal ethical system emerges.

3. Establishing an identity—in particular, a sexual identity.

4. Developing a capacity for establishing an intimate relationship with another person and sustaining it.

Thus we can see that sexuality is an integral part of our psychological development.

Summary

A capacity for sexual response is present from infancy. According to Kinsey's data, about 10 percent of children have masturbated to orgasm by age 10, although recent studies indicate that children begin masturbating at somewhat earlier ages now than a generation or so ago. Children also engage in some heterosexual play, as well as some homosexual activity.

During adolescence there is an increase in sexual activity. According to one theory, this activity is influenced by the interaction of biological factors (increasing testosterone levels) and social and psychological factors (for example, sexually permissive attitudes). By age 15, nearly all boys have masturbated. Girls tend to begin masturbating somewhat later than boys, and fewer of them masturbate. Attitudes toward masturbation are considerably more permissive now than they were a century ago. About 10 percent of adolescents have homosexual experiences to orgasm, with this figure being slightly higher for boys than for girls.

Today the majority of males and the majority of females have premarital sex. This is a considerable increase over the incidence reported in the Kinsey studies, done 50 years ago. Adolescents today are considerably more likely to use a variety of sexual techniques, including mouth-genital sex. There is variation in the incidence of premarital intercourse among various racial and ethnic groups in the United States, and there is even greater variability from one country to another.

The predominant sexual standard today is one of "permissiveness with affection"; that is, sex is seen as acceptable outside marriage, provided there is an emotional commitment between the partners.

Following Erik Erikson's theory, experiences with sexuality can serve important functions in a person's psychological development. They may be important, for example, in the process of becoming independent of parents and in establishing a viable moral system.

Review Questions

1. The physical capacity for erection in the male and vaginal lubrication in the female are present as early as _____ (age).

2. Children do not begin masturbating until 10 or 11 years of age. True or false?

3. The results of Harlow's experiments indicate that monkeys that did not have normal attachments to their mothers in infancy showed seriously disturbed sexual behavior in adulthood. True or false?

4. The majority of both males and females in the United States engage in premarital intercourse. True or false?

5. One of the few sexual behaviors to show a decline in incidence in the last few decades is sex with a prostitute. True or false?

6. DeLamater and MacCorquodale, in their sociological analysis of premarital sexual behavior, concluded that the particular couple and the nature of their relationship are the most important factors determining whether people engage in premarital intercourse. True or false?

7. According to sociologist Ira Reiss, the current standard under which most adolescents believe that intercourse is acceptable is termed "permissiveness without affection." True or false?

8. According to Udry's theory, the biological factor of _____ interacts with social psychological factors as influences on adolescent sexuality.

9. According to Furstenberg's study, 95 percent of teen mothers remain below the poverty line throughout adulthood. True or false?

10. Sexuality may aid in psychological development, including establishing a moral system of one's own and establishing an intimate relationship with another person. True or false?

(The answers to all review questions are at the end of the book, beginning on page 731.)

Questions for Thought, Discussion, and Debate

1. Do you see evidence of conservative trends in sexual attitudes and behaviors, reversing the sexual revolution?

2. Does "permissiveness with affection" characterize the standard for premarital intercourse among the 18- to 22-year-olds you know?

Suggestions for Further Reading

Marin, Peter. (1983, July). A revolution's broken promises. *Psychology Today,* 17(7), 50–57. Some second thoughts on the sexual revolution.

McCormick, Naomi B. (1979). Come-ons and put-offs: Unmarried students' strategies for having and avoiding intercourse. *Psychology of Women Quarterly,* 4, 194–211. An interesting discussion of college students' reported techniques for inviting or avoiding intercourse, and how these techniques relate to gender-role stereotypes.

Morrison, Eleanor S., et al. (1980). *Growing up sexual.* New York: Van Nostrand. A fascinating view of sexual development with many first-person quotes, based on student autobiographies for a human sexuality course.

Stark, Elizabeth. (1986, Oct.). Young, innocent, and pregnant. *Psychology Today,* 28–35. Discusses psychologists' most recent research on teen pregnancy.

Sexuality and the Life Cycle: Adulthood

Grow old along with me!
The best is yet to be.*

This chapter will continue to trace the development of sexuality across the lifespan by considering sexuality in adulthood. First we will look at a theory of the development of sexuality in adulthood. Then we will look at various aspects of sexuality in adulthood: marital sexuality, extramarital sex, the sexual expression of single persons, and sex among the elderly.

SEXUAL TURNING POINTS: STAGES OF ADULT SEXUALITY

Yale sex educators and therapists Lorna and Philip Sarrel (1984) have formulated a theory of human sexual development in adulthood. It is helpful because it describes common changes and transitions in sexual patterns. Knowing about these typical patterns is often reassuring to people who are themselves experiencing a transition and wonder whether it is "normal." On the other hand, it is important to remember that there is great variability in sexual experiences in adulthood, and therefore not every adult will go through every one of the stages specified by the Sarrels. For example, not everyone goes through a divorce and so not everyone will experience Stage 6. Not everyone has children, so not everyone will experience Stage 4. With that caveat in mind, let us consider the stages they have postulated.

Stage 1: Sexual Unfolding—Taking the First Steps Toward Adult Sexuality

The adolescent years represent a time of sexual unfolding, a discovery of sexuality that prepares one for mature, adult sexuality. Many developmental changes occur

*Source: Robert Browning. Rabbi Ben Ezra (1864).

during adolescence, and we have discussed them in detail in earlier chapters. The trick is for the young person to adapt to them successfully so that he or she emerges into adulthood with a sense of confidence and pleasure in sexuality.

There is a major growth spurt. Some teens have theirs earlier than others, and girls usually have theirs earlier than boys. All must adapt to a larger size. The penis grows. Breasts grow, some more than others. Wet dreams begin, and so does menstruation. The developmental task is to adapt positively to all these changes.

In the psychological realm, feelings of shame and guilt about sex may have been learned in childhood. As the body longs more for sexual expression, these negative feelings must be dealt with. In childhood, emotional attachments were directed primarily toward parents; in adolescence they shift to peers. Adolescence is also a time when there is a need to deal with issues of sexual orientation and define one's sexual identity. Heterosexuality is the overwhelming norm in our society and some people slip into it easily without much thought. Others sense that their orientation is homosexual and must struggle with society's negative messages about lesbians and gays. Still others feel that their orientation is heterosexual, but wonder why they experience something like homosexual fantasies, thinking that a person's sexual orientation must be perfectly consistent in all areas (research actually shows that heterosexuals sometimes have homosexual fantasies, and vice versa). These struggles over sexual orientation seem to be more difficult for males than for females because hyperheterosexuality is such an important cornerstone of the male role (Chapter 14).

Another step toward maturity is learning our sexual likes and dislikes and learning to communicate them to a partner.

First intercourse is another important developmental step. Statistically it is now most likely that that event will occur before the person has ever married. Some seek it out eagerly, knowing they will then be a "man" or a "woman." For some the experience is positive, while for others it is a disappointment.

Two more issues are important in achieving sexual maturity: becoming responsible about sex, and developing a capacity for intimacy. Taking responsibility includes being careful about contraception and sexually transmitted diseases, being responsible for yourself and for your partner. Intimacy (see Chapter 13) involves a deep emotional sharing between two people that goes beyond casual sex or manipulative sex. And that brings us to the next stage.

Stage 2: Making (or Breaking) Commitments

In early adulthood, it is common for couples to experiment with various levels of commitment, such as an exclusive dating relationship or living together. Even when living together, there are different levels of commitment, from "some days and nights" to "all the time." Living together is an important turning point not only because it represents commitment but because it is a public declaration of a sexual relationship. It is rare for a man and woman to live together just because it will save on rent. Cohabiting is an opportunity to try out marriage, at least to some extent.

Sometimes there are conflicts between the partners regarding the level of commitment. Some people have difficulty making an emotional commitment to a partner. There are many possible reasons. There has been so much media publicity about the high divorce rate that commitments may seem doomed to failure. Some find the feeling of intimacy and emotional vulnerability to be frightening. Others imagine glamorous benefits to being single.

Stage 3: Marriage—for Better or Worse (in Bed)

Marriage is a sexual turning point for a number of reasons. The decision to get married is a real decision these days, in contrast to previous decades when everyone assumed that they would marry, and the only question was to whom. Today, most couples have had a full sexual relationship, sometimes for years, before they marry. Some psychological pressures seem to intensify with marriage, and these pressures may result in sex problems where there were none previously. Marriage is a tangible statement that one has left the family of origin (the family in which you grew up) and shifted to the family of procreation (in which you become the parents rearing children); for some, this separation from parents is difficult. For some, there seem to be more intense pressures for sexual performance once married; when just living together, we can always say to ourselves that if things don't work out in bed, we can simply switch to another partner. And finally, marriage still today carries with it an assumption of fidelity or faithfulness, a promise that is hard for some to keep.

In marriage, there is a need to work out issues of gender roles. Who does what? Some of the decisions are as tame as who cooks supper. But who initiates sex is far more sensitive, and who has the right to say "no" to sex is even more so.

This is the era of two-career couples, or at least dual-earner couples. There are issues here of finding time for sex and for just being with each other.

As a marriage progresses, it can't stay forever as blushingly beautiful as it seemed on the day of the wedding. The nature of love changes (see Chapter 13), and for some couples there is a gradual disenchantment with sex. Couples need to take steps to avoid boredom in the bedroom. Sexual dysfunctions (see Chapter 19) occur in many marriages, and couples need to find ways to resolve them.

Finally, in some marriages one or the other partner may have an extramarital

(a)

(b)

FIGURE 12.1
Sexual turning points. (a) Stage 3: Marriage and the commitment it represents is a turning point. (b) Stage 4: The birth of a baby is a turning point that can have a negative impact on sexual aspects of the relationship, but couples who are aware of this can work to overcome these problems and keep the romance going.

affair. For some, the extramarital affair is a sexual turning point, perhaps ending a marriage or leading a person to a new view of himself or herself as a sexual being. In other cases the extramarital affair has little impact on the participants or on the marriage.

Stage 4: Making Babies, Making Love

Having a baby—what researchers call the transition to parenthood—has an impact on a marriage and on the sexual relationship of the couple. There is an issue of increased commitment—to each other and to the child. Trying to get pregnant and the threat of infertility, which is so much publicized, can be potent forces on one's identity as a sexual being. Pregnancy itself can influence a couple's sexual interactions, particularly in the last few months (see Chapter 7).

For the first few weeks after the baby is born, intercourse is typically uncomfortable for the woman. While estrogen levels are low—which lasts longer when breastfeeding—the vagina does not lubricate well. Then, too, the mother and sometimes the father feel exhausted with 2 A.M. feedings. The first few months after a baby is born are usually not the peak times in a sexual relationship, and so that, too, must be negotiated between partners.

Stage 5: Parenting—New Roles, New Challenges

As the Sarrels put it, "Being Mommy and Daddy is antierotic" (1984, p. 199). The problem is not only that there is too little time and too little privacy for sex, but that there is too little time for emotional intimacy with each other.

Parenting is a turning point also because it means dealing with our children's sexuality. Is it to be turned off, ignored, or discussed directly and honestly?

Stage 6: Making Love the Second Time Around

This stage is for those who divorce and then resume sexual relations. The divorce itself, of course, is probably surrounded by a deteriorating sexual relationship, and that can have an impact on one's sexual sense of self. As a later section in this chapter details, there is usually a phase of dating following a divorce, then a period of new sexual relationships, and then the contemplation of making a new emotional commitment.

From the point of view of developmental psychologists, the sexual relationship in a second marriage is especially interesting. In what ways is it the same and how does it differ from the sexual relationship in the first marriage? It represents the blending of things that are unique and consistent about the person with those things that are unique to the new situation and new partner. As we develop sexually throughout the lifespan, those two strands continue to be intertwined—the developmental continuities (those things that are us and always will be) and developmental changes (things that differ at various times in our lives, either because we are older or have experienced more, or because our partner or the situation is different).

Stage 7: Keeping Sex Alive (and Lively)

Some physical changes occur from middle adulthood to old age that can affect sexual expression (see Chapter 6). Menopause occurs gradually, caused by declining levels of estrogen production. Erections happen more slowly. Psychological transitions occur as well, and the male mid-life crisis has nearly become a national ritual. One's spouse may die, creating an at least temporary lack of a sexual partner. There is a "widowers' syndrome," in which a man, usually following his wife's prolonged illness and resulting lack of sexual activity, and then her death, finally attempts intercourse with someone and has a sexual dysfunction such as an erection problem. Whether this is due to psychological factors such as grief and depression, or physical factors (widowers are more prone to heart disease and tend to increase their consumption of alcohol, for example) is being debated.

The death of a spouse is a sexual turning point. It may mean the end of sexual activity, or it may mark the beginning of a new stage of sexual expression, depending on the person.

Many individuals and couples continue to have active and fulfilling sex lives well into their eighties and nineties. How do they do it? You should have a better idea by the end of this chapter.

Having considered the Sarrels' theory of adult sexual development, we will now look in more detail at the data on various kinds of sexual expression in adulthood.

MARITAL SEX

Despite all the talk in the 1970s about the end of the institution of marriage, it is clear from a 1990s perspective that the institution has survived, although perhaps now in more varied forms; indeed, there is a reawakening of interest in intimacy and forming relationships (Scanzoni, 1982).

About 90 to 95 percent of all people in the United States marry (Bureau of the Census, 1990). Of those who divorce, a high percentage—80 percent—remarry (Norton, 1987). In our society, marriage is also the context in which sexual expression has the most legitimacy. Therefore, sex in marriage is one of the commonest forms of sexual expression for adults.

Frequency of Marital Intercourse

It appears that the average American couple have coitus about two or three times per week when they are in their twenties, with the frequency gradually declining to about once per week for those aged 45 and over.

The data on this point from the Hunt, Kinsey, and Westoff studies are shown in Table 12.1. Several things can be noted from that table. First, there has been an increase in the frequency of marital sex since the 1940s. In every age group, the people in Hunt's study reported a higher average frequency of intercourse than the people in Kinsey's study. Second, the frequency of intercourse declines with age; however, even among those over 55, the frequency is still about once per week.

It is important to note that there is wide variability in these average frequencies. For example, about 8 to 12 percent of couples in their twenties report not engaging in intercourse at all, and another 5 to 10 percent report doing so less than once per month (Wilson, 1975). Data from a major 1980s survey of American couples also confirm this wide variability, as shown in Figure 12.2 (Blumstein & Schwartz, 1983).

As was noted in Chapter 3, there are problems with the Kinsey and Hunt data because of inadequacies in the sampling methods used. In contrast, Westoff's (1974) study of married women used a probability sample and therefore provides better data. Note in Table 12.1 that the frequencies reported by the women in Westoff's

Table 12.1
Marital Coitus: Frequency per Week (Male and Female Estimates Combined), 1938–1949 and 1970s

1938–1949 (Kinsey)		1972 (Hunt)		1970 (Westoff)	
Age	Median Frequency per Week	Age	Median Frequency per Week	Age	Mean Frequency per Week
16–25	2.45	18–24	3.25	20–24	2.5
26–35	1.95	25–34	2.55	25–34	2.1
36–45	1.40	35–44	2.00	35–44	1.6
46–55	0.85	44–54	1.00		
56–60	0.55	55 and over	1.00		

Sources: Morton Hunt. (1974). *Sexual behavior in the 1970s.* Chicago: Playboy Press, Table 30, p. 191. Charles Westoff. (1974). Coital frequency and contraception. *Family Planning Perspectives,* **6**(3), pp. 136–141.

study are generally lower than those reported by the people in Hunt's study, although the data were collected only two years apart. This suggests that Hunt's sample may indeed have been biased toward including people who were more sexually active than the general population.

Techniques in Marital Sex

Married couples now use—or at least say they use—a greater variety of sexual techniques than couples did before the sexual revolution (Hunt, 1974). The average duration of foreplay is about 15 minutes (Hunt, 1974, p. 201). The reported duration of actual coitus (from insertion of the penis to the male's orgasm) averaged about 10 minutes in the Hunt study.

FIGURE 12.2
There is a wide variety in the frequency of married couples having sex (Blumstein & Schwartz, 1983).

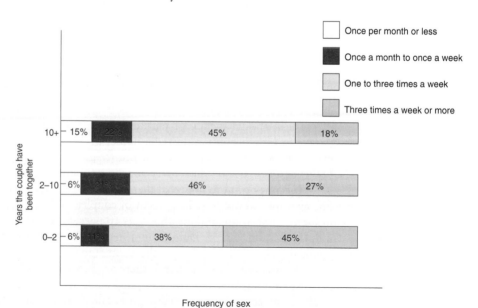

Married couples today use a wider variety of positions during coitus than couples in past decades. For example, the female-on-top position is now used, at least occasionally, by about 75 percent of married couples, as compared with about 35 percent in Kinsey's sample (Hunt, 1974, p. 202).

The increased popularity of mouth-genital techniques is one of the most dramatic changes in marital sex to have occurred since the time of the Kinsey study. By the 1970s cunnilingus and fellatio were used in the majority of marriages and were particularly common among the college-educated. According to a 1980s survey, 90 percent of married couples engage in fellatio and 93 percent engage in cunnilingus (Blumstein & Schwartz, 1983).

One author noted that there has been a comparable change in attitudes toward various sex techniques that is particularly noticeable among younger respondents:

> Among our older interviewees there were a number who, after a party at which they drank a great deal, or after some erotically stimulating event, might occasionally use fellatio, cunnilingus or even anal play, though ordinarily they felt squeamish about such acts or hesitant about suggesting them to their spouses. In contrast, most of the younger interviewees spoke as if they thoroughly enjoyed oral practices and took them as a matter of course, including them very frequently and naturally in their foreplay. (Hunt, 1974, p. 200)

Negotiations

Before these techniques themselves are executed, there is typically a "mating dance" between the man and the woman. Sexual scripts are played out in marriages as in other aspects of sex (J. H. Gagnon, 1977, pp. 208–209). Deciding to have intercourse involves some preliminary negotiations, which are often phrased in indirect or euphemistic language, in part so that the person's feelings can be salvaged if her or his partner is not interested. For example, the husband may say, "I think I'll go take a shower" or "I think I'll go take a nap" (that means "I want to, do you?"). The wife may respond with, "I think I'll take one too" (that means "yes") or "The kids will be home any moment" or "I have a headache" (that means "no"). Or conversely, she may put on a lot of his favorite perfume and parade around in front of him (that is *her* offer). He may respond with, "I had an exhausting day at work" (his "no") or "I'll meet you upstairs" (his "yes"). To avoid some of the risk of rejection inherent in such negotiations, some couples ritualize sex so they both understand when it will and when it will not occur—Thursday night may be their time, or perhaps Sunday afternoon.

A survey of married couples found that for 33 percent of them the husband and wife are about equally likely to initiate sex; for 51 percent the husband is more likely to be the initiator, and in only 16 percent of the couples is the wife usually the initiator (Blumstein & Schwartz, 1983). Thus there is some evidence of liberation (the couples where both are initiators), but traditional roles persist, with the majority of couples having the male in the initiating role. Women seem to be particularly careful not to initiate sex when they believe their spouse is feeling psychologically vulnerable. The traditional gender-typing of initiation patterns may also be related to how people deal with a refusal. If the man initiates and the woman refuses, he can simply attribute it to her lesser sexual appetite, according to traditional stereotypes. If the woman initiates and the man refuses, she has no stereotype to rescue her, and she is likely to conclude that he is not interested in *her* (Blumstein & Schwartz, 1983). Therefore men may have easier ways of dealing with refusal.

Many adults continue to masturbate even though they are married and have ready access to heterosexual sex. This behavior is perfectly normal, although it often evokes feelings of guilt and may be done secretly.

Data indicate that about 72 percent of young husbands masturbate, with an average frequency of about twice a month. About 68 percent of young wives do so, with an average frequency of slightly less than once a month (Hunt, 1974, p. 86).

Masturbation in marriage, of course, can serve a variety of distinctly nonsexual purposes. For example, it can be used as an expression of anger or hostility toward a spouse who has not furnished the expected sexual satisfaction.

But masturbation can also serve very legitimate sexual needs in marriage. It can be a way of remaining faithful to a spouse when husband and wife are separated or cannot have sex for some reason such as illness.[1] As one man expressed it:

> Whenever I travel, it takes about a week until I can't stand it anymore. I lie there at night trying to sleep, and the damn thing won't go away, and I tell myself, "It's either do it or go out on the town." But I'm not that kind of guy, so I do it, and I feel better—and also a little worse. (Hunt, 1974, p. 96)

Masturbation can also be a pleasant adjunct to marital sex. One young man said:

> My wife and I have a great sex relationship, and always have had since before we were married. But we both still masturbate, because it seems a pleasant thing to do and because sometimes the urge comes over each one of us at times when we're alone—I'm away most of the day in the laboratory or the library, and she works at the (TV) studio until after midnight. I may suddenly have a momentary desire to ejaculate, and I run into the bathroom and do it. Or I may read something and it makes me fantasize having sex with some strange voluptuous woman—a belly dancer maybe. Incidentally, I never have had intercourse with any woman other than my wife, so I enjoy these fantasies. There's nothing secret about it—I tell my wife if I've done it during the day, and she tells me if she has. It doesn't diminish our lovemaking at all, although sometimes one or the other of us isn't as eager as we might be—but then, sometimes it does just the opposite, because we try out with each other some of the exotic things we've been fantasizing. (Hunt, 1974, p. 98)

Attitudes Toward, and Satisfaction with, Marital Sex

The majority of married people today express satisfaction with their marital sex.

In one survey, 69 percent of husbands and 71 percent of wives expressed satisfaction with the quality of their sex life (Blumstein & Schwartz, 1983). Satisfaction varies considerably as a function of the frequency of sexual intercourse. For example, among wives who have intercourse three times a week or more, 89 percent are satisfied with their sex life, compared with 32 percent among those who have sex once a month or less. Of course, it is important to remember that these are correlational data, and it is not clear whether the satisfaction is the effect or the cause of the frequency of marital sex.

---

[1] An old Navy saying has it, "If your wife can't be at your right hand, let your right hand be your wife."

Sexual Patterns in Marriage

Sexual patterns can change during the course of a marriage: After 10 or 20 years of marriage they may be quite different from what they were during the first year. One stereotype is that sex becomes duller as marriage wears on, and certainly there are some marriages in which that happens. But there are also those in which the process is exactly the opposite—in which there is a gradual awakening of the sexuality of both partners over the course of the marriage. In other marriages, sexual patterns remain remarkably constant over the years. The following descriptions illustrate the diversity of patterns. First, the words of a man for whom marital sex has become less intense than it apparently once was:

> We do it maybe once a week now, or less. The underlying reason for the slowdown is that we're both pretty busy. It's not that we don't enjoy sex. We do, but I have a lot of meetings, and I get home late and she's asleep, and anyway I'm tired. I would perhaps enjoy a bit more activity, but I'm not discontented about it in any way. . . . Mostly, she does have orgasm—not that we ever discuss it, but I feel pretty sure she does. . . . Our typical sex act is about like this: I'll roll over and decide I'd like a little action. Sometimes it's very rapid—a minute or so—but sometimes it goes on longer, ten minutes, say, half before I put it in, half inside. (Hunt, 1974, p. 220)

A woman described the growth of sexuality in her marriage as follows:

> After we'd been married a while, we felt there was a lot happening that we didn't understand, so I asked my husband if him and I should try to read up on it. So we went out and bought three books, and through them we found all different ways of caressing, and different positions, and it was very nice because we realized that these things weren't dirty. Like I could say to my husband, "Around the world in eighty days" and he'd laugh and we'd really go at it, relaxed and having fun. (Hunt, 1974, p. 183)

Finally, a middle-aged man described a consistent pattern of excitement in marital sex:

> I love my sex, and I've got a wife that loves it just as much as me. Our first five years of married life it was every day with us, and sometimes twice a day because my job would allow me to stop off at home at lunchtime for a quickie. Nowadays, even after twenty years of marriage, it's still about three times a week—and with the kids finally all in school, we've even started up again on the lunchtime business once in a while. Most of the time, naturally, it's in the evening, after the kids are in bed. My wife puts some of that damned perfume on and I know right away that she wants it tonight, and that really gets me going. . . . She can wiggle that ass of hers around like you wouldn't believe, and any position I want to use, she couldn't care less. . . . And sometimes I kid her about stuff I've seen in some stag movie the boys have been showing down at the garage, and would you believe she often wants me to *show* her how it went? After all these years? (Hunt, 1974, pp. 225–226)

Sex and the Two-Career Family

In our busy, achievement-oriented society, is it possible that work commitments—particularly with the increased incidence of wives holding jobs—may interfere with

a couple's sex life? One couple, both of whom are professionals, commented to me that they actually have to make an appointment with each other to make love.

While there has been little scientific research on this topic, there is some evidence that pattens of marital sexuality are related to the wife's working (Westoff, 1974). As it turns out, the couple's frequency of intercourse is related not only to the fact that the woman has a job but also to her motivation for having it. Women who work for reasons other than money have a higher frequency of coitus than women who do not work or who work mainly to earn money. Career-motivated women have the highest frequency of coitus of any of the groups of women. Thus there is no evidence that a woman's commitment to a career will damage the expression of marital sexuality.

In the 1980s and 1990s we have witnessed the emergence of a new phenomenon with the yuppies: two-profession couples, both members committed to working 60 to 80 hours per week. They truly don't have much time for sex. The issue with couples of this type is not so much whether the wife (or husband) has a career, but rather it is workaholism (Sarrel & Sarrel, 1984). An addiction to one's work can spell the death of sex just as much as addiction to a drug can.

EXTRAMARITAL SEX

The term extramarial sex refers to sex between a married person and someone other than that person's spouse.[2] We can distinguish between three types of extramarital sex, each of which has different implications for the people involved (Clanton, 1973): (1) clandestine extramarital sex, in which the extramarital relationship is concealed from the spouse ("clandestine" means "secret"); (2) consensual extramarital sex, in which the spouse knows about the extramarital activity and may even approve of it ("consensual" means "by mutual consent"); and (3) ambiguous extramarital sex, in which the spouse knows about the extramarital relationship but pretends not to know. Consensual extramarital sex is relatively rare in our culture, as will be seen below, and most extramarital sex is either clandestine or ambiguous.

Extramarital sex: Sex between a married person and someone other than that person's spouse; adultery.

Clandestine (klan-DES-tin) extramarital sex: An extramarital relationship that is concealed from the spouse.

Consensual (kun-SEN-shoo-ul) extramarital sex: Extramarital sexual activity in which the spouse knows about the activity and may even approve of it.

Ambiguous extramarital sex: Extramarital sex in which the spouse knows about the activity but pretends not to.

[2] The traditional—and nastier—term for this is "adultery."

How Many People Engage
in Extramarital Sex?

Approximately one-half of all married men have extramarital sex at some time in their lives, compared with about one-quarter of all women. The relevant data are shown in Table 12.2. Several points should be noted from the table:

1. Men are more likely to report engaging in extramarital sex than women are.
2. Approximately 50 percent of all males and about 25 percent of all females engage in extramarital sex at least once.
3. Although the incidence of extramarital sex for males seems to be holding constant, there is some indication that the incidence for females increased in the 1970s and 1980s, and some experts believe that the rate for females is approaching the rate for males (Thompson, 1983).

A 1980s survey confirms this trend for increasing numbers of females to engage in extramarital sex, finding a higher incidence of extramarital sex in the youngest group of wives (Blumstein & Schwartz, 1983). This may be due to their rejection of the double standard; the young woman of today may believe that if extramarital sex is all right for her husband, it is for her, too.

How are we to evaluate the incidence figures shown in Table 12.2? Some—particularly the 69 percent of female readers of *Cosmopolitan* having extramarital sex—clearly suffer from sampling bias. Female readers of *Cosmo* are a highly select group. However, if one discounts the magazine-sample surveys, the remaining figures are probably best regarded as minimums, because of the problems of self-reports.

Table 12.2
Incidence of Extramarital Sex in 11 Studies

Study	Married Men, %	Married Women, %
Kinsey (1948, 1953)	50	26
Athanasiou et al. (1970)*	40	36
Johnson (1970)	20	10
Hunt (1974)	41	18
Bell et al. (1975)	—	26
Tavris and Sadd (1975)†	—	39
Maykovich (1976)	—	32
Pietropinto and Simenauer (1976)	47	—
Yablonsky (1979)	47	—
Wolfe (1980)‡	—	69
Blumstein & Schwartz (1983)	26	21

* Sample of *Psychology Today* readers.
† Sample of married female *Redbook* readers.
‡ Sample of married female *Cosmopolitan* readers.
§ Based on a national probability sample of adults in the United States.
Source: Anthony P. Thompson. (1983). Extramarital sex: A review of the research literature. *Journal of Sex Research,* **19,** Table 1. pp. 5–6.

Extramarital sex is one of those socially disapproved behaviors that people are likely not to report in a survey. For example, in one study 30 percent of the subjects initially reported extramarital sex, but during intensive psychotherapy an additional 30 percent revealed extramarital sexual activities (Green et al., 1974).

As I noted above, most extramarital sex tends to be clandestine or ambiguous. Swinging, which is a form of consensual extramarital sex, was reported by only 2 percent of the males and less than 2 percent of the females in the Hunt study (1974, p. 271); even in the *Redbook* survey, which generally reported very high levels of sexual activity, only 4 percent of the women said they had engaged in swinging (Levin & Levin, 1975, p. 44).

For women, at least, there is no indication that extramarital sex is casual or promiscuous. In one survey, of those married women who had had extramarital sex, 43 percent had done so with only one partner (Blumstein & Schwartz, 1983).

Attitudes Toward Extramarital Sex

While attitudes toward premarital sex have changed substantially during the last several decades, attitudes toward extramarital sex have apparently remained relatively unchanged; most people in the United States disapprove of extramarital sex. According to a well-sampled 1991 survey of adult Americans, 75 percent believe it is always wrong for a married person to have sex with someone other than the marriage partner; this statistic is relatively unchanged from 1973, when it was 69 percent (Davis & Smith, 1991).

One of the best predictors of extramarital sexual permissiveness is premarital sexual permissiveness (Thompson, 1983). That is, the person who has a liberal or approving attitude about premarital sex is also likely to hold a liberal or approving attitude toward extramarital sex. On the other hand, attitudes toward extramarital sex are not very good predictors of extramarital sexual behavior (Thompson, 1983). That is, the person who approves of extramarital sex is not more likely to actually engage in extramarital sex than the person who disapproves of it. Therefore, we have to look to factors other than attitudes in trying to understand why people engage in extramarital sex; some of these other factors are discussed later in this section.

Because our society condemns extramarital sex, the individual who engages in it typically has confused, ambivalent feelings. A 45-year-old physician described his extramarital affair and the complex emotions it involved:

> She was twenty years younger than I and very seductive, and she had this fantastic, longlegged, high-breasted body. She took the initiative one afternoon when she was the last one in my office, and I couldn't stop myself; it just happened, right then and there, on the waiting-room couch—the first time for me, after fifteen years of marriage. At first I was all torn up about it, but I couldn't give it up. It made me feel totally different—younger and more attractive than I had in twenty years, completely reawakened inside. A young girl, so sexy and so marvelous to look at and touch, wanting me! It went on for months. I'd meet her and have relations with her at least once or twice a week, usually at her place, sometimes at my office after hours. And now listen to the funny part—she was *no* good at all, sexually. Despite all her sexiness, she was frigid, and she'd lie there obviously getting nothing out of it. So even though I'd enjoy the whole situation and the buildup, when it came to the actual act I'd do it in a minute or two and get it over with. And still, for months I couldn't break it off; I felt as if I were hooked on some drug. (Hunt, 1974, p. 286)

Swinging

One form of consensual extramarital sex is swinging, in which married couples exchange partners with other married couples, with the knowledge and consent of all involved.[3]

Swingers may find their partners in several ways. Most commonly they advertise, either in a sensational tabloid, such as the *National Enquirer,* or in a swinger's magazine, such as *Swinger's Life* or *Kindred Spirits.* The following is an example:

> New Orleans, young couple, 28 and 32. She a luscious red head, 5'7", 36-26-38. He, 5'9", 175, well built. Enjoy all cultures.[4] Attractive couple main interest, but will consider extremely attractive single girls and men. Photo required to reply. (Bartell, 1970, p. 115)

The descriptions in such advertisements are not always accurate; generally they tend to minimize age and maximize the mammary measurement of the woman (Bartell, 1970). Swingers may also meet partners at swingers' bars or "sodalities"—clubs or organizations of swingers. In some cases, couples are referred by other couples. Finally, in rare cases, a couple may try to convert a nonswinging couple.

There are three forms of swinging: simple swinging with another couple (either open or closed), swinging at parties (open or closed), and three-way swinging (Bartell, 1970; for a critique of the Bartell study, see Chapter 3). In *closed swinging,* the two couples meet and exchange partners, and each pair goes off separately to a private place to have intercourse, returning to the meeting place at an agreed-upon time. In *open swinging,* the pairs get back together for sex in the same room for at least part of the time. In 75 percent of the cases, this includes the two women having sex with each other, although male homosexual sex almost never occurs (Bartell, 1970; Gilmartin, 1975).

Finally, a couple may sometimes swing with just one other person rather than another couple. In the majority of cases, the extra person is a female (Bartell, 1970).

Swingers may vary from those seeking purely sexual experiences to those wanting to form lasting relationships or friendships (Gilmartin, 1975). However, most swingers stress emotional noninvolvement with the other couple, and the norm is not to engage in sex with the same couple more than once (Bartell, 1970; Gilmartin, 1975). Swinging couples typically engage in swinging only about once every two weeks, and thus it is scarcely an obsession (Gilmartin, 1975).

What kind of people are swingers? In the nonsexual areas of their lives, they are quite ordinary—perhaps even dull. Although they describe themselves in their ads as exciting people with many interests, in fact they engage in few activities and have few hobbies. As one researcher observed, "These people do nothing other than swing and watch television" (Bartell, 1970, p. 122). Although one might expect them to be politically liberal, in one study the greatest number were Republicans, and only 27 percent described themselves as politically liberal—the rest were moderate or conservative (Jenks, 1985). And in this same sample, 93 percent were white; African Americans and other minorities are rare among swingers.

What sort of people become swingers? In a study of 406 swingers and a control

---

[3] Swinging was originally called "wife-swapping." However, because of the sexist connotations of that term and the fact that women were often as eager to swap husbands as men were to swap wives, the more equitable "mate-swapping" or "swinging" was substituted.

[4] In this context, "cultures" refers to various sexual techniques. Mouth-genital sex, for example, would be "French culture."

group of 340 nonswingers, it was found that a key factor for swingers was a low degree of jealousy (Jenks, 1985). Swingers also tend to have tolerant attitudes toward various forms of "exotic" sexuality, and they have a strong interest and involvement in sex.

Husbands tend to initiate swinging, but wives typically become the enthusiasts (Bartell, 1970; Gilmartin, 1975). Particularly in swinging at parties, the man's biological sexual capacity may limit him, compared with a woman. He goes to a party, and suddenly he is in a situation that he may have fantasized about since his youth— a roomful of naked women with whom he is permitted to have intercourse. But the pressure is on him to "perform," which may cause anxiety, and the anxiety may cause failure. Even if he "succeeds" with the first few women, he will eventually run out of steam long before the women do. Thus by the end of a swinging party, the only activity still going on may be homosexual activity between the women; 65 percent of the women in one study said they enjoyed their homosexual encounters with other women to the point where they preferred them to heterosexual encounters with males (Bartell, 1970). Thus some men can have negative experiences at a swinging party.

Equity and Extramarital Sex

Equity theory: A theory in social psychology that argues that people mentally calculate the benefits and costs for them in a relationship and thereby feel that the relationship is equitable or inequitable; their behavior is then affected by whether they feel there is equity or inequity and they will act to restore equity if there is inequity.

Equity theory is a social-psychological theory designed to predict and explain many kinds of human relations (Hatfield, Walster, & Berscheid, 1978). In particular, it has been applied to predicting patterns of extramarital sex (Hatfield, 1978).

The basic idea in equity theory is that in a relationship, people mentally tabulate their inputs to it and what they get out of it (benefits or rewards); then they calculate whether these are equitable or not. In an equitable relationship between person A and person B, it would be true that

$$\text{Rewards}_A - \text{Inputs}_A = \text{Rewards}_B - \text{Inputs}_B$$

In a traditional marriage, the wife's inputs might include her beauty, keeping a charming house, cooking good meals, and so on. The husband's inputs might include his income and his pleasant temperament. His rewards from the relationship might include feeling proud when he is accompanied by his beautiful wife, enjoying her cooking, and so on. Notice that this is not an egalitarian relationship in the modern sense; however, it is an equitable relationship (as defined by equity theory) because both partners derive equal benefits from it.

According to equity theory, if individuals perceive a relationship as inequitable (they feel they are not getting what they deserve), they become distressed. The more inequitable the relationship, the more distressed they feel. In order to relieve the distress, they make attempts to restore equity in the relationship. For example, people who feel they are putting too much into a relationship and not getting enough out of it might let their appearance go, or not work as hard to earn money, or refuse sexual factors, or refuse to contribute to conversations. The idea is that such actions will restore equity.

If these equity processes do occur, it seems logical that they might help to explain patterns of extramarital sex. That is, engaging in extramarital sex would be a way of restoring equity in an inequitable relationship. Social psychologist Elaine Hatfield (1978) tested this notion. Her prediction was that people who felt under-benefited in their marriages (that is, they felt that there was an inequity and that they were not getting as much as they deserved) would be the ones to engage in extramarital sex. Confirming this notion, subjects who felt they were underbenefited began engaging in extramarital sex earlier in their marriages and had more extramarital partners than did people who felt equitably treated or overbenefited. Apparently, feeling that one is not getting all one deserves in a marriage is related to engaging in extramarital sex. (As an aside, equitable marriages were rated as happier than inequitable ones.)

The more interesting point, deserving of further research, is that whether we feel a relationship is equitable or not may affect our patterns of sexual activity both in and out of the relationship.

SEX AND THE SINGLE PERSON

Although most adults in our society do marry, there are still many single adults—the never-married, the divorced, and the widowed—who have sexual needs and seek to express them.

The Never-Married

The person who passes age 25 without getting married gradually enters a new world (J. H. Gagnon, 1977). The social stuctures that supported dating—such as college—are gone, and most people of the same age are married. Dating and sex are no longer geared to mate selection, and by the time a person is 25 or 30, it no longer seems reasonable to call her or his sexual activity "premarital sex."

The attitudes of singles about their status vary widely. Some plan never to get married; they find their lifestyle exciting and enjoy its freedom. Others are desperately searching for a spouse, with the desperation increasing as the years wear on.

At one extreme, there is the *singles scene*. It is institutionalized in such form as singles' apartment complexes and single's bars. Health clubs and fitness centers provide the latest opportunities for meeting others. The singles group, of course, is composed of the never-married as well as the divorced and the widowed. The singles' bar is a visible symbol of the singles scene. It functions in many ways like a gay bar

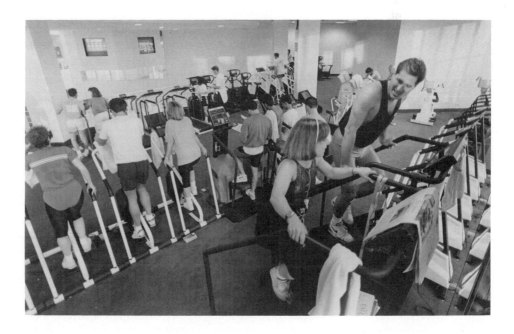

FIGURE 12.4
Fitness clubs are the current alternative to singles bars for people wanting to meet Mr. or Ms. Right.

(J. H. Gagnon, 1977). Everyone is there for a similar purpose: to meet Mr. or Ms. Right. However, most will settle for a date, and it is fairly well understood that coitus will be a part of the date. The singles' bar is somewhat like a meat market; the people there try to display themselves to their best advantage and are judged and chosen on the basis of their physical appearance—and perhaps rejected for too high a percentage of fat.

Many singles, however, do not go to singles' bars. Some are turned off by the idea; some feel that they cannot compete, that they are too old, or that they are not attractive enough; and some live in rural areas where they have no access to such places.

Unfortunately, the major studies of sexual behavior have focused primarily on premarital sexual behavior and only to a lesser extent on postmarital sexual behavior. Researchers have neglected the never-married adult, who deserves more attention in future studies.

The Divorced and the Widowed

Divorced and widowed people are in a somewhat unusual situation in that they are used to regular sexual expression and suddenly find themselves in a situation in which the socially acceptable outlet for that expression—marital sex—is no longer available. Partly recognizing this dilemma, our society places few restrictions on postmarital sexual activity, although it is not as approved as marital sex (Gebhard, 1968).

Most divorced women, but fewer widowed women, return to having an active sex life. In one well-sampled study, the percentage of formerly married women who had had intercourse in the last 3 months ranged between 50 percent and 67 percent, depending on the age group (Forrest & Singh, 1990). In another study, 86 percent of the widowed had been sexually abstinent in the last year, compared with 26 percent of the divorced (Smith, 1991).

The lower incidence of postmarital sex among widows, compared with divorced women, is due in part to the fact that widows are, on the average, older than divorced women, but even when matched for age, widows are still less likely to engage in postmarital sex. There are probably several reasons for this (Gebhard, 1968). Widows are more likely to be financially secure than divorced women and therefore have less motivation for engaging in sex as a prelude to remarriage. They have the continuing social support system of in-laws and friends, and so they are less motivated to seek new friendships. There is also a belief that a widow should be loyal to her dead husband, and having a sexual relationship with another man is viewed as disloyalty. Many widows believe this or tell themselves that they will "never find another one like him."

Most widowed or divorced women who have postmarital sex begin such relationships within a year after the death or divorce. Most women who engage in postmarital sex have multiple partners. In one study only 16 percent of widowed and 12 percent of divorced women had had sex with only the fiancé (Gebhard, 1968). On the other hand, the pattern is scarcely one of orgies. In a well-sampled survey, divorced women averaged one partner in the previous year (Stack & Gundlach, 1992).

Divorced and widowed women who return to having an active sex life generally express great satisfaction with it. Indeed, these women have a higher frequency of orgasm in postmarital sex than they did in marital sex (Hunt, 1974).

Virtually all divorced and widowed men return to an active sex life (Stack & Gundlach, 1992; Hunt, 1977). Although divorced men have slightly more partners than divorced women do—the typical pattern is one to two partners in the last year (Stack & Gundlach, 1992)—again the pattern today is scarcely an orgy.

For both women and men, there is a higher probability of being sexually active postmaritally for those who are younger (under 35) and those who have no children in the home (Stack & Gundlach, 1992).

In summary, virtually all divorced women and somewhat fewer widowed women engage in postmarital sex; virtually all divorced and widowed men do so, with little distinction between the divorced and widowed.

The Divorce Subculture

Morton and Bernice Hunt (1977) did an intensive study of the divorce experience, based on questionnaires completed by 984 people, plus 200 in-depth interviews. We will focus on their findings about sexual relationships here.

Within a couple of months of the divorce, the divorced person typically goes out on the "first date." Although divorced individuals may be in their thirties or forties and think of themselves as mature, the first date makes them strangely anxious. Essentially, they are "second-time beginners." The problem is that they do not know the rules of the dating game among formerly marrieds (FMs). They have never been an FM before. And worse, rules for dating and sex have changed a great deal since they were dating as teenagers.

Anxiety-provoking though this early dating is, it serves two important functions. First, it socializes the individuals into the norms of the FM world. They quickly learn the rules and expectations. Second, early dating fosters an important kind of self-appraisal. Having been married for a number of years, the individuals have no idea how they will be responded to by potential dates. How will they do in the dating market? Most make positive, self-affirming discoveries about themselves. Demoralized by the divorce, they find that members of the other gender do find them attractive.

They typically move into a phase of "dating around," which is the norm among FMs. Most quickly discover, to their surprise, that the sexual scene among FMs is even more open and fast-paced than it is among young singles. Most are surprised at how common it is for men to suggest intercourse with a woman they know only casually and are dating for only the first or second time. About 60 percent of the women surveyed said that most men they had dated made some kind of serious sexual approach on the first or second date. The median frequency of intercourse is about twice per week.

It seems, from the Hunts' work, that dating around (and sleeping around) is essentially a developmental stage after divorce. The individuals eventually move out of it into a reconstruction phase, in which they again form a deeper, more committed relationship and begin to reintegrate sex with emotion. Once again, we see that sex can serve important developmental functions.

SEX AND THE SENIOR CITIZEN

When Freud suggested that young children, even infants, have sexual thoughts and feelings, his ideas met with considerable resistance. When, 50 years later, researchers began to suggest that elderly men and women also have sexual thoughts and feelings, there was similar resistance (Pfeiffer et al., 1968). This section deals with the sexual behavior of elderly men and women, the physical changes they undergo, and the attitudes that influence them.

Have Adults Changed Their Sexual Behavior in the AIDS Era?

Time magazine, in a cover story, called it "The Big Chill—How Heterosexuals Are Coping with AIDS." In the late 1980s the media were deluged with stories on AIDS, including its risks and recommendations for safer sex practices. Has there been any impact on people's sexual behavior, or do people continue with high-risk practices? (See Chapter 20 for a discussion of high-risk and safer sex practices.)

In one survey of single heterosexual men in San Francisco, the men averaged 2.8 female partners per man in 6 months in 1984, but that number had decreased to 1.8 partners in 1986 (Winkelstein et al., 1987c). Thus heterosexual men, on the average, do seem to be reducing the number of their sexual partners, which is one way to reduce the risk of AIDS infection.

The comparable figures for the homosexual men in that study were 10.8 partners per man in 6 months in 1984, and 4.2 partners in 1986, an even more dramatic reduction.

In another survey, gay men were recruited either as a high-risk group (recruited as they left bathhouses or bars) or a lower-risk group (those in a primary relationship with another man) (McKusick et al., 1985). There was a reported decline in the number of partners from 6.3 per month in 1982 to 3.9 per month in 1984. Sexual practices had also changed. In 1982, on the average, the men had engaged in anal intercourse without a condom 3.3 times per month, compared with 2.3 times per month in 1984.

Research indicates that gay men, as a group, have shown the greatest behavior change in the AIDS era (Ehrhardt et al., 1991). By now there are numerous studies showing that gay men have reduced the number of sex partners, have fewer anonymous sexual encounters, and engage less in anal

intercourse or use condoms consistently. Data also indicate that the rate of infection with sexually transmitted diseases such as gonorrhea and syphilis has declined dramatically in this group since 1984, presumably as a result of increased use of safer sex practices.

Despite these overall changes, there are still some men who have not reduced their number of partners or switched to safer sex practices. The challenge to researchers is to try to understand this group better so that effective educational programs can be targeted toward them.

Turning to the data on women, one study of college women found an increase in condom use from 12 percent in 1975 to 50 percent in 1989 (DeBuono et al., 1990). However, when these women felt they were in committed sexual relationships, they were likely to engage in unprotected sexual behaviors; for many of these women, a perception of commitment in the relationship made them feel that the sex was safe—which it wasn't, of course, if the partner was infected. Furthermore, data from student health clinics indicate that infection with the HPV virus (which causes genital warts) is very common among college women, implying a failure to practice safer sex.

In sum, both heterosexual and homosexual men modified their sexual practices in the 1980s, primarily by reducing the number of sexual partners. There is less evidence on women; it seems to indicate some behavior change toward increased use of condoms, but there is probably still widespread practice of risky sexual behaviors.

Sources: McCusick et al. (1985); Winkelstein et al. (1987); Ehrhardt et al. (1991); DeBuono et al. (1990)

FIGURE 12.5
*Affection, romance, and
sex are not just for the
young.*

Physical Changes

Changes in the Female

There is a gradual decline in the functioning of the ovaries around menopause, and with this comes a gradual decline in the production of estrogen (see Figure 12.6). Because of the decline in estrogen, several changes take place in the sexual organs. The walls of the vagina, which are thick and elastic during the reproductive years, become thin and inelastic. Because the walls of the vagina are thinner, they cannot absorb the pressures from the thrusting penis as they once did, and thus nearby structures—such as the bladder and the urethra—may be irritated. As a result, elderly women may have an urgent need to urinate immediately after intercourse. Further, the vagina shrinks in both width and length, and the labia majora also shrink; thus there is a constriction at the entrance to the vagina, which may make penile insertion somewhat more difficult, and the vagina may be less able to accommodate the size of a fully erect penis. By about five years after menopause, the amount of vaginal lubrication has decreased noticeably. Intercourse can then become somewhat more difficult and painful.

Because of hormonal imbalance, the contractions of the uterus that occur during orgasm can become painful, to the point where the woman avoids intercourse. Nonetheless, the woman has the same physical capacity for orgasm at 80 that she did at 30.

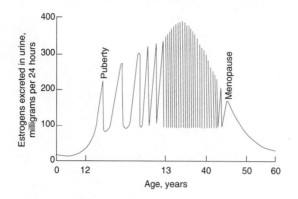

FIGURE 12.6
*Levels of estrogen
production in women
across the lifespan.*

Lest these changes sound discouraging, it is important to realize that there are a number of ways to deal with them successfully. Some women's physicians prescribe estrogen-replacement therapy for them after menopause; with these added doses of estrogen, the changes described above are minimized or may not occur at all. A simple measure is to use a sterile lubricant as a substitute for vaginal lubrication.

It also appears that these changes are related in part to sexual activity or, rather, to the lack of it. Among the women in the Masters and Johnson study, those who had intercourse infrequently (once a month or less) and who did not masturbate regularly had difficulty accommodating the penis when they attempted intercourse. The three women over 60 in their studies whose vaginas expanded well to accommodate the penis and who produced adequate lubrication had all maintained regular intercourse once or twice a week. For this reason and others, Masters and Johnson stress the importance of regular sexual activity in maintaining an active sex life among the elderly, a point which will be discussed in more detail later.

Thus it appears that the continuing of sexual activity depends more on the opportunity for such activity and on various psychological factors than it does on any physical changes, a point that holds true for both men and women.

Some people believe that a hysterectomy means the end of a woman's sex life. In fact, sex hormone production is not affected as long as the ovaries are not removed (surgical removal of the ovaries is called oophorectomy or ovariectomy). The majority of women report that hysterectomy has no effect on their sex life. However, approximately one-third of women who have had hysterectomies report problems with sexual response (Zussman et al., 1981). There are two possible physiological causes for these problems. If the ovaries have been removed, hormonal changes may be responsible; specifically, the ovaries produce androgens, and they may play a role in sexual response. The other possibility is that the removal of the cervix, and possibly the rest of the uterus, is an anatomical problem if the cervix serves as a trigger for orgasm.

Hysterectomy (hiss-tur-EK-tuh-mee): Surgical removal of the uterus.

Oophorectomy (OH-uh-fuh-REK-tuh-mee): Surgical removal of the ovaries.

Changes in the Male

Testosterone production declines gradually over the years (Schiavi, 1990) (see Figure 12.7). Vascular diseases such as hardening of the arteries are increasingly common with age in men, but good circulation is essential to erection (Riportella-Muller, 1989). A major change is that erections occur more slowly. It is important for men to know that this is a perfectly natural slowdown so that they will not jump to the conclusion that they are developing an erection problem. It is also important for women to know about this so that they will use effective techniques of stimulating the man and so that they will not mistake slowness for lack of interest.

Morning erections also become less frequent, declining from about two per

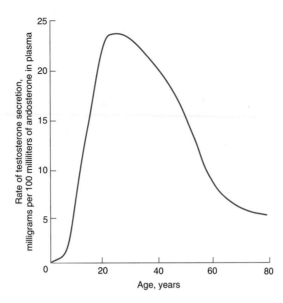

FIGURE 12.7
Levels of testosterone
production in men across
the lifespan.

*Rate of testosterone secretion,
milligrams per 100 milliliters of andosterone in plasma*

Age, years

week in the early thirties to about 0.5 per week at age 70 (Kinsey et al., 1948, p. 230).

For men, the refractory period lengthens with age; thus for an elderly man, there may be a period of 24 hours after an orgasm during which he cannot get an erection. (Note that women do not undergo a similar change; most women do not enter into a refractory period and are still capable of multiple orgasm at age 80.) Other signs of sexual excitement—the sex flush and muscle tension—diminish with age.

The volume of the ejaculate gradually decreases, and the force of ejaculation lessens. The testes become somewhat smaller, but viable sperm are produced by even very old men. Ninety-year-old men have been known to father children.

One advantage is that middle-aged and elderly men may have better control over orgasm than young men; thus they can prolong coitus and may be better sexual partners.

Despite these physical changes, though, Masters and Johnson conclude that there need be no time limit on sexual expression for either men or women.

Some people believe that prostate surgery or removal of the prostate (prostatectomy) means the end of a man's sex life. It is true that the volume of the ejaculate will decrease. Prostatectomy can cause damage to the nerves supplying the penis, creating erection problems. In other cases, retrograde ejaculation may result. Whether there are such problems depends on which of several available methods of surgery is used.

Prostatectomy (pros-tuh-TEK-tuh-mee): Surgical removal of the prostate.

Attitudes About Sex and the Elderly

Our society has a negative attitude toward sexual expression among the elderly. Somehow it seems indecent for two 70-year-old people to have sex with each other, and even more indecent for a 70-year-old to masturbate. These negative attitudes become particularly obvious in nursing homes, where staff members may frown on sexual activity among the residents. Somehow what is "virility" at 25 becomes "lechery" at 65 (I. Rubin, 1965).

Cross-cultural research indicates that the sexual behavior of the elderly is related to these cultural expectations (Winn & Newton, 1981). The elderly continue to be sexually active in 70 percent of societies and in precisely those societies where they are expected to be sexually active. Indeed, in 22 percent of societies, women are expected to become more uninhibited about sexuality when they become old.

Why does our society have such negative attitudes toward sex among the elderly? In part, these attitudes are due to the fact that ours is a youth-oriented culture. We value youth, and the physical characteristics that are considered "sexy" are youthful ones, such as a trim, firm body and smooth skin. It is therefore hard to believe that someone with old, wrinkled skin could be sexually active. Our negative attitudes may be a holdover from the belief that sex was for reproductive purposes only—those past the age of reproduction should therefore not engage in it (Pfeiffer, 1975). The incest taboo may also be involved in our negative attitudes. We tend to identify old people with our parents or grandparents, and we find it hard to think of them as sexual beings. This factor is made worse because many parents take great pains to hide their sexual activity from their children.

These attitudes affect the way elderly people are treated, and the elderly may even hold such attitudes themselves. One remedy that has been proposed for these negative attitudes is a "coming out of the closet"; as one 67-year-old commented.

> The common view that the aging and aged are nonsexual, I believe, can only be corrected by a dramatic and courageous process—the *coming-out-of-the-closet* of sexually active older women and men, so that people can see for themselves what the later years are really like. (Brecher, 1984, p. 21)

Various specific misunderstandings may influence sexuality. For example, a man may believe that sex will precipitate a heart attack or, if he has already had a heart attack, that it will bring on another one. Of patients who were sexually active before a heart attack, only 25 percent resumed sexual activity after the heart attack (Papadopoulos, 1978). The lack of sexual activity was caused by medical or physiological factors in only a few cases; in most, it was created by fears and misinformation. Most authorities agree, though, that the benefits of sexual activity for the cardiac patient outweigh any potential dangers (Hellerstein & Friedman, 1969).

Although Masters and Johnson found that the heart rate accelerated during sexual intercourse, another study showed that the mean heart rate during orgasm was only 117 beats per minute, which is about that attained during many common forms of daily exercise (Hellerstein & Friedman, 1969). It is about the equivalent of climbing two flights of stairs at a moderate pace. Thus the demands on the heart are not unreasonable. Unfortunately, many physicians neglect to discuss the issue with cardiac patients, who then may simply assume that sex is dangerous or forbidden. Even more unfortunate is the fact that there are only three or four studies on the potential problem of the "coital coronary" (see review by Derogatis & King, 1981), so physicians have little solid evidence to convey to their patients.

One interesting study of male coronary patients found that two-thirds had a sexual dysfunction (most commonly erectile dysfunction) *before* the heart attack (Wabrek & Burchell, 1980). This puts the incidence of dysfunction after a heart attack in better perspective. The authors suggested that there might be complex interactions among sexual dysfunction, stress, and heart attacks. That is, severe stress might precipitate both a sexual dysfunction and a heart attack. Or a bout of sexual dysfunction might be the stress that precipitated the heart attack. We need more research on the relationship between coronary problems and sex problems.

Some men also mistakenly believe that sexual activity saps their "vital strength." In some cases men may believe that they can have only a fixed number of orgasms during their life (as a woman has a fixed number of ova) and therefore adopt a strategy of saving them now so that they will have some left later on. One woman wrote:

> My husband has reached the age of sixty-five. He has decided that, in order to ensure a longer life and health, he will no longer engage in sex activity. He is convinced that intercourse and the emission of semen are quite debilitating, particularly in his years. (I. Rubin, 1966, p. 258)

Ideas such as this, as well as factors such as illness or hospitalization, may lead to a period of sexual inactivity. But being sexually inactive is one of the most effective ways of diminishing sexuality. In one study of elderly people, 75 percent were sexually inactive. When they were reinterviewed 3 to 4 years later, only 14 percent of the inactive group had returned to sexual activity; the rest had remained inactive (Pfeiffer et al., 1968). Thus it seems unlikely that an old person will return to sexual activity after a period of inactivity.

In agreement with these findings, Masters and Johnson emphasize that two factors are critical in maintaining sexual capacity in old age.

1. *Good physical and mental health* An excellent study confirms this notion (Persson, 1980). A representative sample of 70-year-olds in one town in Sweden were selected, and 85 percent agreed to participate in the detailed interviews. In the entire sample, 46 percent of the men and 16 percent of the women still had sexual intercourse; when only those who were currently married were considered, the figures rose to 52 percent for men and 36 percent for women. For both men and women, those who continued to have sexual intercourse had better mental health as rated by a psychiatrist and more positive attitudes toward sexual activity among the aged.

2. *Regularity of sexual expression* As was noted earlier, they even have evidence that some physical changes of the sex organs in old age are related to sexual inactivity. As the saying goes, "If you don't use it, you lose it."

Apparently some elderly people have caught on to this fact. As one 80-year-old husband said of his relationship with his 75-year-old wife,

> My wife and I both believe that keeping active sexually delays the aging process . . . if we are troubled with an erection or lubrication, we turn to oral methods or masturbation of each other. We keep our interest alive by a great deal of caressing and fondling of each other's genitals. We feel it is much better to wear out than to rust out. (Brecher, 1984, p. 33)

Women's beliefs about menopause may influence their sexuality in the later years. Some believe that menopause means the end of sex. Certainly such attitudes could lead to a diminishing, or even a cessation, of sexual activity. Probably in a few cases, women who never really enjoyed sex use menopause as an excuse to stop having intercourse. On the other hand, some women who spent their younger years worrying about getting pregnant find menopause to be a liberating experience; their sexual activity may actually increase.

Reformers urge us to change our attitudes about sex and the senior citizen. Nursing homes particularly need to revise their practices; even such simple changes as knocking before entering a patient's room would help (people masturbate, you know). Other reforms would include making provisions for spouses to stay overnight and allowing married—or unmarried—couples to share a bedroom. Indeed, some experts even advocate sex as a form of therapy for persons in nursing homes (Rice, 1974):

> Sex relations can provide a much needed and highly effective resource in the later years of life, when so often men face the loss of their customary prestige and self-confidence and begin to feel old, sometimes long before they have begun to age significantly. The premature cessation of sexual functioning may accelerate physiological and psychological aging since disuse of any function usually leads to concomitant changes in other capacities. After menopause, women may find that continuation of sexual relations provides a much needed psychological reinforcement, a feeling of being needed and of being capable of receiving love and affection and renewing the intimacy they earlier found desirable and reassuring. (L. K. Frank, 1961, pp. 177–178)

Sexual Behavior of the Elderly

While sexual behavior and sexual interest do decline somewhat with age, there are still substantial numbers of elderly men and women who have active sex lives, even when in their eighties.

In interviews, 40 to 65 percent of a group of active, healthy people between the ages of 60 and 71 reported engaging in sexual intercourse with some frequency (Pfeiffer et al., 1968). In a sample of healthy 80- to 102-year-olds, 62 percent of the men and 30 percent of the women reported that they still engaged in sexual intercourse (Bretschneider & McCoy, 1988). There does not seem to be any age beyond which all people are sexually inactive.

Some elderly people do, for various reasons, stop having intercourse after a certain age. For women, this occurs most often in the late fifties and early sixties, while it occurs somewhat later for men (Pfeiffer et al., 1968). Contrary to what one might expect, though, when a couple stop having intercourse, the husband is most frequently the cause; both wives and husbands agree that this is true. In some cases, the husband has died (and we can hardly blame him for that), but even excluding those cases, the husband is still most frequently the cause. Thus the decline in female sexual expression with age may be directly related to the male's decline. Death of the spouse is more likely to put an end to intercourse for women than it is for men, in part because women are less likely to remarry (Riportella-Muller, 1989).

One of the most important influences on sexuality in the elderly, then, is that there are far more elderly women than elderly men. Because of both men's earlier mortality and their preference for younger women, elderly women are more likely to be living alone and to have less access to sexual partners. For example, in 1990, among those 85 and over, 47 percent of the men were married and living with their spouse, compared with only 10 percent for women (Bureau of the Census, 1990). Some innovative solutions have been proposed, such as elderly women forming lesbian relationships.

A recent survey—the largest one to date on sexuality and the elderly—provides rich detail on sexual patterns among the elderly (Brecher et al., 1984). The study was sponsored by Consumers Union, the nonprofit organization that publishes the magazine *Consumer Reports*. In the November 1977 issue of *Consumer Reports,* a notice appeared requesting cooperation from men and women born before 1928, and thus over 50 years of age at the time. Readers were asked to write in to obtain a questionnaire on personal relationships—family, social, and sexual—during the later years of life. Over 10,000 questionnaires were mailed out in response, and 4246 were returned. Although earlier, in Chapter 3, I concluded that magazine surveys are of little value because of severe problems of sampling bias, I view this study as an exception. It is one of the few important sources of information concerning sex

Table 12.3
Sexual Activity in a Sample of Elderly Persons

	In Their 50s	In Their 60s	70 and Over
Women			
Orgasms when asleep or while waking up	26%	24%	17%
Women who masturbate	47%	37%	33%
Frequency of masturbation among women who masturbate	0.7/week	0.6/week	0.7/week
Wives having sex with their husbands	88%	76%	65%
Frequency of sex with their husbands	1.3/week	1.0/week	0.7/week
Men			
Orgasms when asleep or while waking up	25%	21%	17%
Men who masturbate	66%	50%	43%
Frequency of masturbation among men who masturbate	1.2/week	0.8/week	0.7/week
Husbands having sex with their wives	87%	78%	59%
Frequency of sex with their wives	1.3/week	1.0/week	0.6/week

Source: Edward M. Brecher and the Editors of Consumer Reports Books. (1984). *Love, Sex, and Aging.* Mount Vernon, NY: Consumers Union, p. 316.

and the elderly, a topic about which there is a real shortage of knowledge. The problem of a nonrandom and volunteer-biased sample remains. Specifically, elderly people who are sick or in nursing homes, or whose sight has failed so that they cannot read, are highly unlikely to have responded to the survey. Thus we must regard this as a survey of elderly people who are above average in health, activity, and intelligence and who are doubtless more sexually active than sick or disabled persons.[5] In a sense, the survey gives a view of the richest potential of sexuality in the later years.

Some statistics from the survey are summarized in Table 12.3. Notice that even among respondents over 70 years of age, 33 percent of the women and 43 percent of the men still masturbate (see also Catania & White, 1982). And 65 percent of the married women and 59 percent of the married men over 70 years old report that they continue to have sex with their spouse.

The questionnaire also contained questions about patterns of extramarital sexuality and homosexuality. The results indicated that 8 percent of the wives and 24 percent of the husbands had engaged in extramarital sex at least once after age 50. For the entire sample 13 percent of the men and 8 percent of the women had had a homosexual experience at some time in their lives, and 4 percent of the men and 2 percent of the women had engaged in homosexual activity after the age of 50.

What we see from this survey, then, is that among older people who are healthy and active and have regular opportunities for sexual expression, sexual activity in all forms—including masturbation and homosexual behavior—continues past 70 years of age. The sexuality of the elderly has indeed come out of the closet.

---

[5] For a discussion of sexuality among residents of nursing homes, see White (1982).

Summary

The Sarrels' theory of adult sexual development postulates seven stages: (1) sexual unfolding; (2) making (or breaking) commitments; (3) marriage; (4) making babies, making love; (5) parenting; (6) making love the second time around; and (7) keeping sex alive.

Married couples today report engaging in sexual intercourse more frequently than couples several decades ago. Currently, couples in their twenties have sex about two or three times a week, on the average, with the frequency declining to about once per week for those aged 45 and over. Married couples today also tend to use a wide variety of techniques other than intercourse in the man-on-top position, including intercourse in other positions and oral-genital sex. Many people continue to masturbate even though they are married. Most people today—both women and men—express general satisfaction with their marital sex life. Sexual patterns in marriage, however, show great variability.

About 50 percent of all married men and 25 percent of all married women engage in extramarital sex at some time. Extramarital sex is disapproved of in our society and is generally carried on in secrecy. In a few cases, it is agreed that both husband and wife can have extramarital sex, as in open marriage and swinging. Equity theory may be helpful in understanding patterns of extramarital sex.

Single adults—whether never-married, widowed, or divorced—generally do engage in sexual activity. Virtually all widowed and divorced men return to an active sex life, as do most divorced women and about half of widowed women. A particular set of sexual norms characterizes the divorce subculture.

Research indicates that both single heterosexual and homosexual men have modified their sexual practices somewhat in the AIDS era. Both groups have reduced their number of partners and have shifted away from risky sex practices. For women, there is some evidence of increased condom use, but there is also evidence of continued unsafe sex.

While sexual activity declines somewhat with age, it is perfectly possible to remain sexually active into one's eighties or nineties. Problems with sex or the cessation of intercourse may be related to physical factors. In women, declining estrogen levels result in a thinner, less elastic vagina and less lubrication; in men, there is lowered testosterone production and increased vascular disease, combined with slower erections and longer refractory periods. Psychological factors can also be involved, such as the belief that the elderly cannot or should not have sex. Masters and Johnson emphasize that two factors are critical to maintaining sexuality in old age: good physical and mental health and regularity of sexual expression. The Consumers Union survey indicates that all sexual behaviors—including heterosexual intercourse, masturbation, and homosexual behaviors—continue past age 70.

Review Questions

1. According to the Sarrels' theory, the birth of a baby is a sexual turning point for a couple. True or false?

2. In general, the frequency of marital intercourse declines with age. True or false?

3. One of the greatest changes in marital sex during the last few decades is the increased popularity of mouth-genital sex. True or false?

4. Masturbation is rare among married adults—only about 10 percent of husbands and wives report that they still engage in masturbation. True or false?

5. People's attitudes toward extramarital sex have changed in the last several

decades, so that by the 1990s a majority of Americans approved of extramarital sex. True or false?

6. _____ refers to married couples exchanging sexual partners with other married couples, with the knowledge and consent of all involved.

7. According to _____, people who feel they are in equitable marriages are more likely to engage in extramarital sex than those who are in inequitable marriages.

8. Most divorced women, but fewer widowed women, return to having an active sex life. True or false?

9. According to cross-cultural research, in societies in which the elderly are expected to be sexually active, they are. True or false?

10. According to Masters and Johnson, the most important factors in maintaining sexual capacity in old age are good physical and mental health and _____.

(The answers to all review questions are at the end of the book, beginning on page 731.)

Questions for Thought, Discussion, and Debate

1. What is your response when you see an elderly couple expressing affection physically with each other, perhaps kissing or holding hands? Why do you think you respond that way?

2. What is your opinion about extramarital sex? Is it ethical or moral? What are its effects on a marriage—does it destroy marriage or improve it, or perhaps have no effect?

3. If you are currently in a relationship, apply equity theory to your relationship. Do you feel that it is equitable or inequitable? If you view it as inequitable, what effects does that have on your behavior?

Suggestions for Further Reading

Brecher, Edward M. (1984). *Love, sex, and aging.* Mount Vernon, NY: Consumers Union. This large-scale survey offers a liberated view of sexuality in the elderly,

Sarrel, Lorna, & Sarrel, Philip. (1984). *Sexual turning points: The seven stages of adult sexuality.* New York: Macmillan. This book, written for a general audience, provides an interesting theory of adult sexual development.

13

Attraction, Love, and Intimacy

Chapter Highlights

To be in love is merely to be in a state of perceptual anesthesia—to mistake an ordinary young man for a Greek god or an ordinary young woman for a goddess. *

We made love, Your Honor. He didn't have any and neither did I. So we made some. It was good.†

The lyrics to the old song, "Love and marriage, love and marriage, go together like a horse and carriage," might today be rewritten as "Love and sex, love and sex, go together. . . ." The standard of today for many is that sex is appropriate if one loves the other person (see Chapter 11), and sex seems to be the logical outcome of a loving relationship. Therefore, it is important in a text on sexuality to spend some time considering the emotion we link so closely to sex: love.

This chapter is organized in terms of the way relationships usually progress—if they progress. That is, we begin by talking about attraction, what brings people together in the first place. Then we consider love and intimacy, which develop as relationships develop.

ATTRACTION

What causes you to be attracted to another person? Social psychologists have done extensive research on interpersonal attraction. The major results of this research are discussed below.

* *Source:* H. L. Mencken. (1919). *Prejudices.* (First Series). New York: Knopf, p. 16.

† *Source:* Julie, in Lois Gould. (1988). *Such good friends.* New York: Farrar, Straus, Giroux, p. 161.

FIGURE 13.1
*Communicating about love
is often difficult.*

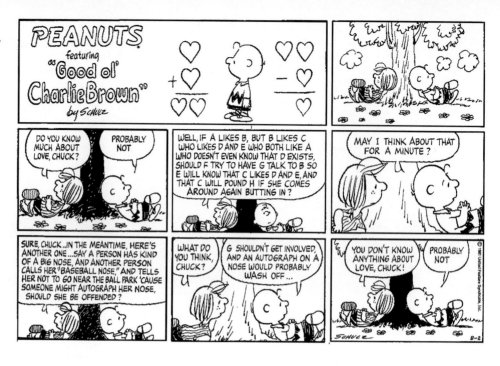

Birds of a Feather

We tend to like people who are similar to us. We are attracted to people who are approximately the same as we are in terms of economic and social status, ethnicity, intelligence, attractiveness, and attitudes (Byrne, 1971; Feingold, 1988; Vandenberg, 1972). This is sometimes called the matching phenomenon.

Social psychologist Donn Byrne (1971) has done numerous experiments demonstrating that we are attracted to people whose attitudes and opinions are similar to ours. In these experiments, Byrne typically has subjects fill out an opinion questionnaire. They are then shown a questionnaire that was supposedly filled out by another person and are asked to rate how much they think they would like that person. In fact, the questionnaire was filled out to show either high or low agreement with the subject's responses. Subjects report more liking for a person whose responses are similar to theirs than for one whose responses are quite different.

There are a number of reasons why we are attracted to a person who is similar to us in, say, attitudes (Huston & Levinger, 1978). We get positive reinforcement from that person agreeing with us. The other person's agreement bolsters our sense of rightness. And we anticipate positive interactions with that person.

Folk sayings are sometimes wise and sometimes foolish. The interpersonal-attraction research indicates that the saying "Birds of a feather flock together" contains some truth.

"Hey, Good-Lookin' "

We also tend to be attracted to people who are physically attractive, that is "good-looking" (Berscheid & Walster, 1974; Hatfield & Sprecher, 1986). For example, in one study snapshots were taken of college men and women (Berscheid et al., 1971). A dating history of each subject was also obtained. Judges then rated the attractiveness of the men and women in the photographs. For the women there was a fairly strong relationship between attractiveness and popularity; the women judged attrac-

Matching phenomenon:
The tendency for men and women to choose as partners people who match them, i.e., who are similar in attitudes, intelligence, and attractiveness.

366

tive had had more dates in the last year than the less attractive women. There was some relationship between appearance and popularity for men, but it was not so marked as it was for women. This phenomenon has even been found in children as young as 3 to 6 years of age, who are more attracted to children with attractive faces (Dion, 1977; 1973).

In general, then, we are most attracted to good-looking people. However, this effect depends on gender to some extent; physical attractiveness is more important to males evaluating females than it is to females evaluating males (Feingold, 1990). And this phenomenon is somewhat modified by our own feelings of personal worth, as will be seen in the next section.

The Interpersonal Marketplace

Although this may sound somewhat callous, whom we are attracted to and pair off with depends a lot on how much we think we have to offer and how much we think we can "buy" with it (see, for example, Rubin, 1973, pp. 67ff; Murstein, 1976). Generally, the principle seems to be that women's worth is based on their physical beauty, whereas men's worth is based on how successful they are. There is a tendency, then, for beautiful women to be paired with wealthy, successful men.

Data from many studies document this phenomenon. In one study, high school yearbook pictures of 601 males and 745 females were rated for attractiveness (Udry & Eckland, 1984). The subjects were followed up 15 years after graduation, and measures of education, occupation status, and income were obtained. Females who were rated the most attractive in high school were significantly more likely to have husbands who had high incomes and were highly educated (see also Elder, 1969). Interestingly, for males, the relationship was the reverse; the least attractive males had the most education and the highest occupational status.

In another study, women students were rated on their physical attractiveness (Rubin, 1973, p. 68). They were then asked to complete a questionnaire about what kinds of men they would consider desirable dates. A man's occupation had a big effect on his desirability as a date. Men in high-status occupations—physician, lawyer, chemist—were considered highly desirable dates by virtually all the women. Men in low-status occupations—janitor, bartender—were judged hardly acceptable by most of the women. A difference emerged between attractive and unattractive women, however, when rating men in middle-status occupations—electrician, bookkeeper, plumber. The attractive women did not feel that these men would be acceptable dates, whereas the unattractive women felt that they would be at least moderately acceptable. Here we see the interpersonal marketplace in action. Men with more status are more desirable. But how desirable the man is judged to be depends on the woman's sense of her own worth. Attractive women are not much interested in middle-status men because they apparently think they are "worth more." Unattractive women find middle-status men more attractive, presumably because they think such men are reasonably within their "price range."

From the Laboratory to Real Life

The phenomena discussed so far—feelings of attraction to people who are similar to us and who are good-looking—have been demonstrated mainly in psychologists' laboratories. Do these phenomena occur in the real world?

Donn Byrne and his colleagues (1970) did a study to find out whether these results would be obtained in a real-life situation. They administered an attitude and personality questionnaire to 420 college students. Then they formed 44 "couples." For half of the couples, both people had made very similar responses on the questionnaire; for the other half of the couples, the two people had made very different responses. The two people were then introduced and sent to the student union on a brief date. When they returned from the date, an unobtrusive measure of attraction was taken—how close they stood to each other in front of the experimenter's desk. The subjects also evaluated their dates on several scales.

The results of the study confirmed those from previous experimental work. The couples who had been matched for similar attitudes were most attracted to each other, and those with dissimilar attitudes were not so attracted to each other. The students had also been rated as to their physical attractiveness both by the experimenter and by their dates, and greater attraction to the better-looking dates was reported. In a follow-up at the end of the semester, those whose dates were similar to them and were physically attractive were more likely to remember the date's name and to express a desire to date the person again in the future. Thus in an experiment that was closer to real life and real dating situations, the importance of similarity and physical appearance was again demonstrated.

The Girl Next Door

There is also evidence that we tend to be more attracted to people with whom we have had contact many times than we are to people with whom we have had little contact (Rubin, 1973). This has been demonstrated in laboratory studies in which the amount of contact between subjects was varied. At the end of the session, subjects gave higher "liking" ratings to those with whom they had had much contact and lower ratings to those with whom they had had little contact (Saegert et al., 1973). There is a mere-exposure effect; repeated exposure to someone seems to make us like that person (Bornstein, 1989). Thus, there does seem to be a "girl-next-door" or "boy-next-door" phenomenon; we tend to be attracted to people with whom we have had much contact, to whom we have been exposed, and with whom we are familiar.

Mere-exposure effect: The tendency for us to like people more if we have repeatedly been exposed to them.

Playing Hard to Get

The traditional advice that has been given to girls—by Ann Landers and others—is that boys will be more attracted to them if they play hard to get. Is there any scientific evidence that this is true?

In fact, two experiments provide no support for this kind of strategy; according to these experiments, playing hard to get does not work (Walster et al., 1973). In one of these experiments, college men were recruited for a computer-dating program. They were given the phone number of their assigned date and were told to phone her and arrange a date from the experimenters' laboratory; after they phoned her, they assessed their initial impression of her. In fact, all the men were given the same telephone number—that of an accomplice of the experimenters. For half of the men, she played easy to get; she was delighted to receive the phone call and to be asked out. With the other half of the men, she played hard to get; she accepted the date with reluctance and obviously had many other dates. The results failed to support the hard-to-get strategy: the men had equally high opinions of the hard-to-get and easy-to-get woman.

The same experimenters reported an ingenious field experiment in which a prostitute played either hard to get or easy to get with her clients and then recorded the clients' responses, such as how much they paid her. Once again, the hard-to-get hypothesis was not supported; the men seemed to like the easy-to-get and the hard-to-get prostitute equally well.

The experimenters were faced with the bald fact that a piece of folk wisdom just did not seem to be true. They decided that they needed a somewhat more complex hypothesis. They hypothesized that it is not the woman who is generally hard to get or generally easy to get who is attractive to men but rather the one who is *selectively hard to get*. That is, she is easy to get for you, but she is hard to get for other men or unavailable to them. A computer-dating experiment supported this notion; the selectively hard-to-get woman was the most popular with men.

In practical terms, this means that if a woman is going to use hard-to-get strategies, she had better use them in a skillful way. It seems that the optimal strategy would be to give the impression that she has many offers for dates with others but refuses them, while being delighted to date the young man in question.

Interestingly, in all the research discussed, it is always the woman who is playing hard to get and the man who is rating her. This reflects cultural gender-role stereotypes, in which it is the woman's role to do things like play hard to get. What we do not know is how men's use of hard-to-get strategies would affect the way women perceive them.

Byrne's Law of Attraction

It is a rather commonsense idea—and one that psychologists agree with—that we tend to like people who give us reinforcements or rewards and to dislike people who give us punishments. Social psychologist Donn Byrne (cited in Hatfield & Walster, 1978) has actually formulated this mathematically:

$$Y = m \left(\frac{\Sigma R}{\Sigma R + \Sigma P} \right) + k$$

The Y stands for attraction, R for reinforcements, and P for punishments; m and k are just constants. Essentially what the formula says is that our attraction to another person is proportionate to the number of reinforcements that person gives us relative to the total number of reinforcements plus punishments the person gives us. Or, simplified even more, we like people who are frequently nice to us and seldom nasty.

These effects also work if we even *associate* another person with reinforcements or punishments. In one study, young people were asked to meet a stranger (Griffitt, 1970). In half the meetings, the couple met in a cool, comfortable room. In the other half, they met in an uncomfortably hot room. Those who met in the comfortable surroundings later liked each other more than did those who met in the unpleasant environment.

These findings have some practical implications (Hatfield & Walster, 1978). If you are trying to get a new relationship going well, make sure you give the other person some positive reinforcement. Also, make sure that you have some good times together, so that you *associate* each other with rewards. Do not spend all your time stripping paint off old furniture or cleaning out the garage. And do not forget to keep the positive reinforcements (or "strokes," if you like that jargon better) going in an old, stable relationship.

Evaluating the Interpersonal-Attraction Research

Much of the research discussed in this section is an investigation not so much of love as of first impressions, or of attraction in the early stages of a relationship. Thus many of the results might not be true of long-term, deeply committed relationships. On the other hand, first impressions have a lot to do with casual dating, and casual dating is the usual prelude to serious relationships. In this way, first impressions may influence whom we eventually come to love.

LOVE VOCABULARY

Love is one of those things that people seem to feel uncomfortable about defining. Perhaps when you were an adolescent, you were curious about love and asked an adult, "What is love?" or "How can you tell when you're in love?" Adults in this situation have a tendency to give answers like "It's not something you can define, but you'll know when you're in it." Such a response is not very enlightening. In the last two decades, though, psychologists have done some important research and theorizing on love that is helpful in understanding this powerful yet mysterious human emotion. But first, let's talk about some love words.

The Greeks

One problem we face immediately in talking about love is that the English language is rather limited; we have only one word, "love," to express a wide variety of feelings and relationships. "Love" can mean everything from a mother's love for her child to the kind of love that leads quickly to an intense affair that burns itself out after a week. Sometimes we seek to express these various kinds of love by adding modifiers, such as "platonic" love or "passionate" love.

The ancient Greeks had a much richer vocabulary that allowed them to express more precisely the different kinds of love that exist. They had four different words, all of which translate to "love": eros (AIR-ohs), agape (AH-gah-pay), philia (FIL-ee-ah), and storge (STORE-gay).

Eros refers to passionate love or erotic love; it is the kind of love we refer to when we say that we are "in love." Storge means affection, particularly the kind of affection that parents feel toward their children or that children feel toward their parents. Philia means solid friendship. Agape refers to a kind of selfless, giving love.

Maslow: B-love and D-love

The psychologist Abraham Maslow, founder of humanistic psychology, distinguishes between B-love and D-love (1968). B-love (short for Being love) is an unneeding, unselfish love for another. In contrast, D-love (short for Deficiency love) is a need for love, a selfish love. Maslow clearly believes that B-love is better than D-love. As he says, "B-love is, beyond the shadow of a doubt, a richer, 'higher,' more valuable subjective experience than D-love" (1968, p. 43).

Maslow believes that some people are B-lovers and some are D-lovers. He views B-lovers as far healthier and more self-actualizing.

> B-lovers are more independent of each other, more autonomous, less jealous or threatened, less needful, more individual, more disinterested, but also simultaneously more eager to help the other toward self-actualization, more proud of his triumphs, more altruistic, generous and fostering. (1968, p. 43)

Thus D-love is the kind of love that arises between two people because of their psychological needs; each seems to satisfy some needs that the other has. B-love

Eros (AIR-ohs): The Greeks' term for passionate or erotic love.

Agape (AH-gah-pay): The Greeks' term for a giving, self-sacrificing love.

Philia (FILL-ee-uh): The Greeks' term for friendship or liking.

Storge (STORE-gay): The Greeks' term for affection.

B-love (Being-love): Maslow's term for an unneeding, unselfish love between two self-actualized people.

D-love (Deficiency-love): A selfish love between two people that arises because of their psychological needs.

occurs between two self-actualized people who are independent and yet appreciative of each other.

THEORIES OF LOVE

Sternberg's Theory of Love

Yale psychologist Robert Sternberg (1986) has formulated a theory of the nature of love. According to his theory, there are three fundamental components of love: intimacy, passion, and commitment.

Intimacy

Intimacy is the emotional component of love. It includes our feelings of closeness or bondedness to the other person. The feeling of intimacy usually involves a sense of mutual understanding with the loved one; a sense of sharing one's self; intimate communication with the loved one, involving a sense of having the loved one hear and accept what is shared; and giving and receiving emotional support to and from the loved one.

Intimacy, of course, is present in many loving relationships besides romantic ones. Intimacy here is definitely *not* a euphemism for sex (as when someone asks "Have you been intimate with him?"). The kind of emotional closeness involved in intimacy may be found between best friends, and between parents and children, just as it is between lovers.

Passion

Passion is the motivational drive component of love. It includes physical attraction and the drive for sexual expression. Physiological arousal is an important part of passion. Passion is the component that differentiates romantic love from other kinds of love, such as the love of best friends or the love between parents and children. Passion is generally the component of love that is faster to arouse, but, in the course of a long-term relationship, it is also the component that fades most quickly.

Intimacy and passion are often closely intertwined. In some cases passion comes first, when a couple experience an initial powerful physical attraction to each other; emotional intimacy may then follow. In other cases, people know each other only casually, but as emotional intimacy develops, passion follows. Of course, there are also cases where intimacy and passion are completely separate. For example, in cases of casual sex, passion is present but intimacy is not.

Decision or Commitment

The third component of love, in Sternberg's theory, is the cognitive component, decision or commitment. This component actually has two aspects. The short-term aspect is the decision that one loves the other person. The long-term aspect is the commitment to maintain that relationship. Commitment is what makes relationships last. Passion comes and goes. All relationships have their better times and their worse times, their ups and their downs. When the words of the traditional marriage service ask whether you promise to love your spouse "for better or for worse," the promise is the promise of commitment.

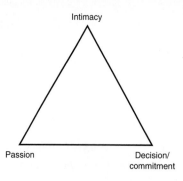

FIGURE 13.2
The triangle in Sternberg's triangular theory of love.

Intimacy

Passion

Decision/
commitment

The Triangle Theory

Sternberg (1986) calls his theory a triangular theory of love. Figure 13.2 shows Sternberg's love triangle.[1] The top point of the triangle is intimacy, the left point is passion, and the right point is decision or commitment.

This triangle metaphor allows us to show how the two people in a couple can be well matched or mismatched in the love they feel toward each other (see Figure 13.3). In Figure 13.3(*a*), Elizabeth feels as much intimacy toward Robert as he does toward her, they both feel equal levels of passion, and they both have the same level of commitment. According to Sternberg's theory, that is a perfect match. Figure 13.3(*b*) shows a situation in which a couple are slightly mismatched, but not seriously. Figure 13.3(*d*) shows a situation in which there is a severe mismatch. Both partners are equally committed, but one feels significantly more intimacy and passion that the other.

Sternberg's research indicates that when there is a good "match" [as shown in Figure 13.3(*a*) or (*b*)] between the two partners' love, the partners tend to feel satisfaction with the relationship. When there is a mismatch in the triangles, there is dissatisfaction with the relationship.

Thinking about practical applications of Sternberg's theory, if a relationship seems to be in trouble, it may be because there is a mismatch of the triangles. One could analyze the love in the relationship in terms of the three components (intimacy, passion, and commitment) to see where the partners are mismatched. It could be that they are well matched for passion, but that one feels and wants more intimacy or commitment than the other person does.

Sternberg has found that the best predictor of satisfaction with a relationship is the difference between your ideal for your partner's feelings and your perception of what your partner feels. If the difference is small (there is a close match between your ideal and your perception of your partner), then there tends to be great satisfaction. A great discrepancy between ideal and perception is related to dissatisfaction. So, for example, if you think your partner is overinvolved (you perceive him or her as more committed than you ideally would like), you will probably feel dissatisfied with the relationship and draw away. That, in turn, may make the other person try even harder to win you, generating a greater discrepancy for you between ideal and perception, making you draw further away, and so on.

[1] This terminology should not be confused with the popular use of the term "love triangle," which refers to a situation in which three people are involved in love, but the love is not reciprocated and so things don't work out quite right. For example, A loves B, B loves C, and C loves A, but A doesn't love C and B doesn't love A. Alas.

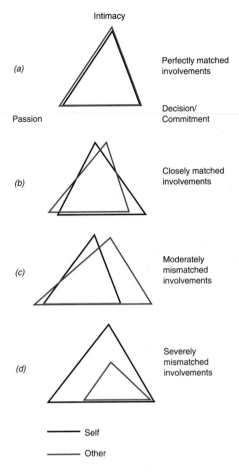

FIGURE 13.3
Partners can be well matched or mismatched, depending on whether their levels of intimacy, passion, and decision/commitment match.

Intimacy

(a)   Perfectly matched involvements

Passion   Decision/ Commitment

(b)   Closely matched involvements

(c)   Moderately mismatched involvements

(d)   Severely mismatched involvements

——— Self

——— Other

Love in Action

Sternberg also argues that each of the three components of love must be translated into action. The intimacy component is expressed in actions such as communicating personal feelings and information, offering emotional (and perhaps financial) support, and expressing empathy for the other. The passion component is expressed in actions such as kissing, touching, and making love. The decision or commitment component is demonstrated by actions such as saying "I love you," marriage, and sticking to a relationship through times when it isn't particularly convenient.

As the great psychoanalyst Erich Fromm wrote in his book *The Art of Loving* (1956), love is something one *does*, not a state one is *in*. Fromm believed that loving is an art, something that one must learn about and practice. And as Sternberg says, "Without expression, even the greatest of loves can die" (1986, p. 132). Love must be translated into actions.

Evidence for Sternberg's Triangular Theory of Love

Sternberg's theory is so new that there isn't a nice set of experiments testing it. However, many of the phenomena that are extensively documented in the research on attraction, discussed earlier in this chapter, are consistent with Sternberg's theory.

Jealousy

Jealousy—the green-eyed monster—is an unpleasant emotion that is often associated with love and with sexual relationships. Traditionally in the United States, jealousy has been considered a normal, even necessary, emotion; it has been viewed as strengthening monogamy and marriage.

Psychologists Gregory White and Paul Mullen have proposed a model for understanding jealousy. They see jealousy as a constellation including thoughts, emotions, and actions. Two situations, according to their research, activate jealousy. One is a situation in which there is a threat to our self-esteem. For example, in a good relationship, our romantic partner helps us feel good about ourselves—makes us feel attractive or fun to be with, for example. If a rival appears and our partner shows interest, we may think things like "He finds her more attractive than me" or "She finds him more fun to be with than me." We then feel less attractive or less fun to be with—that is, our self-esteem is threatened.

The second situation that activates jealousy is a threat to the relationship. If a rival appears on the scene, we may fear that our partner will separate from us and form a new relationship with the rival. Jealousy is activated because of our negative thoughts and feelings about the loss of a relationship that has been good for us and the loss of all the pleasant things that go along with that relationship, such as companionship and sex.

According to White and Mullen, we go through several stages in the jealousy response, sometimes very quickly. The first is cognitive, in which we make an initial appraisal of the situation and find that there is a threat to self-esteem or to the relationship. Next we experience an emotional reaction which intself has two phases. The first is a rapid stress response, the "jealous flash." To use the terminology of the two-component theory of love discussed earlier in this chapter, this stress response is the physiological component of the jealous emotion. The second phase of emotional response occurs as we reappraise the situation and decide how to cope with it. In the reappraisal stage, we may shift from seeing the situation as a threat to seeing it as a challenge, for example. The intense initial emotions quiet down and may be replaced by feelings of moodiness. We continue to make efforts to cope, and these in turn, if successful, should calm our emotions.

Psychologists Gordon Clanton and Lynn Smith believe that we have a choice in coping with our

For example, we saw that in forming initial attractions to people when we first meet them, the most important factor is physical appearance. This is consistent with Sternberg's theory, which specifies that the passion component—which is strongly affected by physical attraction and thus by physical appearance—is aroused most quickly at the beginning of a relationship. Another well-established finding is that similarities (in attitudes, intelligence, and appearance) cause initial attraction as well as being a predictor of long-term, stable relationships. In Sternberg's theory, it would be predicted that people with similar attitudes—about life and about relationships—would have very similar love triangles, and matching love triangles are related to satisfaction in the relationship.

FIGURE 13.4
One situation that activates jealousy is a perceived threat to the relationship.

own jealousy: We can react in an insecure, defensive manner, or we can react in a secure, constructive way. The following two reactions illustrate the difference. The first one is defensive:

> His interest in her confirms my suspicion that he is on the make. I never did trust him. Her interest in him shows she is dissatisfied with me. He's quite attractive. I guess she's grown tired of me. And he's so attentive to her, so appreciative. I guess I've come to take her for granted. No wonder's she so turned on by his courtesies. They want to go to the opera together, and I feel left out. I wonder what other excuses they'll find to spend time together. Maybe she'll take time away from me to be with him. Maybe I'll have to cook dinner and take care of the kids while she's off at the "opera." If I can't count on my own wife, what the hell can I count on?

This is a constructive reaction:

> His interest in her confirms her attractiveness. I'm proud of her. Her interest in him shows she is alert and alive. I'm glad for that. An inert partner, no matter how secure the relationship, is a bad deal. He's like me in some ways, so I am affirmed by her choice of him. He's different from me in some ways, which suggests she has some needs that I don't meet. I must consider these needs carefully and try to find out if I could do a better job of meeting them. But I realize I cannot meet all of her needs without violating my own autonomy, so I must work to become glad she has other friends who can fulfill her in ways I do not and would rather not. Thank God, she's found someone who wants to go to the opera with her. I want to be reassured that our relationship means as much to her as it does to me, but I won't demand that she renounce all others in order to demonstrate that to me.

Sources: Gregory L. White & Paul E. Mullen (1989). *Jealousy: Theory, research, and clinical strategies.* New York: Guilford Press. Gordon Clanton & Lynn G. Smith (1977). The self-inflicted pain of jealousy. *Psychology Today,* **10**(10), p. 44.

Attachment Theory of Love

In Chapter 11 we discussed the earliest attachment that humans experience, the attachment between infant and parent. One hypothesis is that the quality of this early attachment—whether secure and pleasant or insecure and unpleasant—profoundly affects us for the rest of our lives, and particularly affects our capacity to form loving attachments to others when we are adults.

The *attachment theory of love* is based on these ideas (Hazan & Shaver, 1987; Simpson, 1990). According to the attachment theory, adults are characterized, in their romantic relationships, by one of three styles. *Secure lovers* are people who find it easy to get close to others and are comfortable having others feel close to them. Mutual dependency in a relationship (depending on the partner and the partner depending on you) feels right to them. Secure lovers do not fear abandonment. In contrast, *avoidant lovers* are uncomfortable feeling close to another person or having that person feel close to them. It is difficult for them to trust or depend on a partner. The third type, *anxious-ambivalent lovers,* want desperately to get close to a partner, but often find the partner does not reciprocate the feeling, perhaps because anxious-ambivalent lovers scare away others. They are insecure in the relationship, worrying that the partner does not really love them. Research shows that about 53 percent of adults are secure, 26 percent are avoidant, and 20 percent are anxious-ambivalent (Hazan & Shaver, 1987). This research also shows that separation from a parent in childhood—perhaps because of divorce or death—is not related to adult attachment styles. That is, children of divorced parents are no more or less likely to be secure lovers than children from intact marriages (a finding that is probably fortunate, given the high divorce rate we currently have in the United States). What did predict adult attachment style was the person's perception of the *quality* of the relationship with each parent.

This research has some important implications. First, it helps us understand that adults bring to any particular romantic relationship their own personal history of love and attachment. The forces of that personal history can be strong, and one good and loving partner may not be able to change an avoidant lover into a secure lover. Second, it helps us understand that conflict in some relationships may be caused by a mismatch of attachment styles. A secure lover, who wants a close, intimate relationship, is likely to feel frustrated and dissatisfied with an avoidant lover, who is uncomfortable with feeling close. Finally, this theory provides some explanation for jealousy, which is most common among anxious-ambivalent lovers (although present among the others) because of their early experience of feeling anxious about their attachment to their parents.

RESEARCH ON LOVE

Measuring Love

So far the discussion has focused on theoretical definitions of various kinds of love. As we noted earlier, different people may mean different things when they use the word "love." One of the ways that psychologists define terms is by using an operational definition. In an operational definition a concept is defined by the way it is measured. Thus, for example, "IQ" is sometimes defined as the kinds of abilities that are measured by IQ tests. "Job satisfaction" can be defined as a score on a questionnaire that measures one's attitudes toward one's job. Operational definitions are very useful because they are precise and because they help clarify exactly what a scientist means by a complex term such as "love" or "aggression."

Psychologist Zick Rubin (1970) used the operational-definition approach to study love. That is, he constructed a paper-and-pencil test to measure romantic love. (He also constructed another test to measure "liking.") Basically, Rubin sees love as an attitude one has toward another person. Thus the items on the scale involve reporting feeings about a specific person. Subjects rate each item on a scale from 1 to 9 to indicate how much they agree with it. If you feel that you are in love with someone, you might want to think of how you would answer the questions, keeping that person in mind.

The content of the love items seems to imply that there are three major components of romantic love:

Operational definition: Defining some concept or term by how it is measured, for example, defining intelligence as those abilities that are measured by IQ tests.

FIGURE 13.5

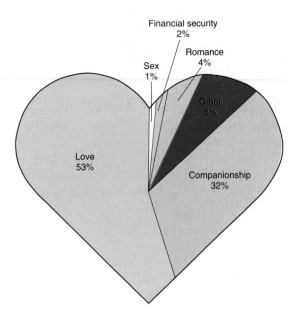

What do you look for in your relationship
with your partner?

Financial security
2%

Romance
4%

Sex
1%

Other
6%

Love
53%

Companionship
32%

1. *Affiliative and dependency needs* For example, "If I could never be with _____, I would feel miserable."

2. *A predisposition to help* For example, "I would do almost anything for _____."

3. *Exclusiveness and absorption* For example, "I feel very possessive toward _____."

In contrast, liking seems to involve respect and admiration.

Rubin administered the questionnaire to a group of dating couples at the University of Michigan. He found that loving and liking were only moderately correlated. That is, we seem to have some tendency to like the person we love, but not a very strong tendency. Love scores did, however, tend to be highly correlated with subjects' estimates of the likelihood that they would eventually marry this dating partner. Rubin also found that the love scores of men (for their girlfriends) were almost identical to the love scores of women (for their boyfriends). That is, there was no evidence that either men or women had a stronger tendency to feel more loving toward their partners. There was, however, a tendency for women to like their boyfriends more than men liked their girlfriends.

Using this instrument, Rubin was able to do further investigations of love relationships. For example, he found that couples who were strongly in love (both had high scores on the love scale) spent more time gazing into each other's eyes than couples who were only weakly in love (both had low scores on the love scale).

Rubin (1973) found some evidence that interfaith couples loved each other more strongly than same-faith couples. This may be an example of the "Romeo and Juliet effect" (R. Driscoll et al., 1972): The more parents object to a relationship, the stronger the love becomes.

Rubin's research is a good example of the way psychologists study an important but complex topic—such as love—scientifically.

Love as a Relationship Develops

As a romantic relationship progresses, the nature of the love typically changes. The early part of a relationship is generally characterized by passionate love, but there is a gradual switch to companionate love (Driscoll et al., 1972; Cimbalo et al., 1976). The transformation tends to occur when the relationship is between 6 and 30 months old (Hatfield & Walster, 1978). To use Sternberg's terminology, there is a shift from passion to intimacy and commitment.

Some may find this a rather pessimistic commentary on romantic love. But it may be, instead, that this is a good way for relationships to develop. Passionate love is probably necessary to hold a relationship together in the early stages, while conflicts are being resolved. But once we move past that, most of us find that what we really need is a friend—someone who shares our interests, who is happy when we succeed, and who sympathizes when we fail—and that is just what we get with companionate love.

Gender Differences

The stereotype is that women are the romantics—they yearn for love, fall in love more easily, cling to love. Do the data support this idea?

In fact, research measuring love in relationships indicates that just the opposite is true. Men hold a more romantic view of male-female relations than women do (Hobart, 1958). They fall in love earlier in a relationship (Kanin et al., 1970; Rubin et al., 1981). Men also cling longer to a dying love affair (Hill et al., 1976; Rubin et al., 1981). Indeed, three times as many men as women commit suicide after a disastrous love affair (Hatfield & Walster, 1978).

In a word, it seems that men are the real romantics.

Two decades ago, men and women held very different views of the importance of romantic love in marriage (Kephart, 1967). In response to the question, "If (someone) had all the other qualities you desired, would you marry this person if you were not in love?" about 30 percent of women said they would refuse to marry, compared with over 60 percent of men. That is, men were more likely to view love as an essential requirement for marriage. However, those patterns have changed. This survey was repeated in 1976 and again in 1984 (Simpson et al., 1986). The gender differences had disappeared, and love is now considered more essential to marriage than it was two decades ago. Over 80 percent of both men and women would refuse to marry under the conditions stated in the question. The researchers interpreted this dramatic shift as being a result of great changes in the social roles of men and women. In particular, women are more likely to hold paid employment and to be more economically independent of men. Therefore, they feel less need to be in a marriage—whether in love or not—in order to be financially supported. Consequently, love can be a necessary requirement for them, too. It is ironic that the sexual revolution—which stressed the right to liberated, even casual sex—has been accompanied by an increased, not a decreased, emphasis on love.

Love and Adrenaline

Two-component theory of love: Berscheid and Walster's theory that two conditions must exist simultaneously for passionate love to occur: physiological arousal and attaching a cognitive label ("love") to the feeling.

Social psychologists Ellen Berscheid and Elaine Walster (1974) have proposed a **two-component theory** of love. According to their theory, passionate love occurs when two conditions exist simultaneously: (1) the person is in a state of intense *physiological arousal,* and (2) the situation is such that the person applies a particular *label*—"love"—to the sensations being experienced. Their theory is derived from an important theory and experiment conducted by psychologist Stanley Schachter (1964); it will be described first.

The Schachter and Singer Study

Suppose that your heart is pounding and your palms are sweating. What emotions are you experiencing? Love? Anger? Fear? Embarrassment? Sexual arousal? As it turns out, it may be any of these. Psychologists have discovered that a wide variety of strong emotions produce similar physiological states (pounding heart and sweating palms) and that what differentiates these emotions is the way we interpret or label what we are experiencing. Schachter's (1964) two-component theory of emotion says just this: that an emotion consists of a physiological state of arousal plus a cognitive or mental labeling of it as a particular emotion.

Schachter and Singer (1962) demonstrated this phenomenon in a classic experiment in which they manipulated both the physiological arousal of subjects and the labeling of emotions. Male college-student volunteers were the subjects. When they arrived at the laboratory, they were told that they were participating in a study designed to measure the effects of a new vitamin, Suproxin, on vision. Physiological arousal was manipulated using the drug epinephrine (adrenaline). Epinephrine stimulates the sympathetic nervous system, producing an arousal state including increased heart rate and increased rate of breathing. Subjects were in one of four groups (see Table 13.1). Subjects in the *informed group* received an injection of Suproxin (really adrenaline) and were told to expect the exact effects of adrenaline: pounding heart, flushed face, and so on. Subjects in the *misinformed group* also received the adrenaline injection, but they were told to expect a wrong set of side effects: numbness, itching, and a slight headache. Subjects in the *ignorant group* received the injection of adrenaline but were given no information about the side effects. Finally, subjects in the *placebo group* were given an injection that contained no drug and were told nothing about side effects.

After receiving the injections, the subjects were put in a waiting room for 20 minutes. An accomplice of the experimenters was also in the waiting room. It was his job to create a situation that would lead the subjects to apply a certain label to their feelings of arousal. Half of the subjects were in the *euphoria* condition. The accomplice behaved in a deliriously happy way; among other things, he shot paper

Table 13.1
The Schachter-Singer Experiment

Group	Injection	Expectations	Resulting State	Model	Effects
Informed	Adrenaline	Told precise side effects of adrenaline	Not bewildered Aroused	Euphoric Angry	No effect No effect
Ignorant	Adrenaline	Told nothing about side effects	Bewildered Aroused	Euphoric Angry	Euphoric Angry
Misinformed	Adrenaline	Misled about side effects	Bewildered Aroused	Euphoric	Euphoric
Placebo	Neutral solution	Told nothing about side effects	Not bewildered Not aroused	Euphoric Angry	No effect No effect

airplanes and danced wildly with a hula hoop. The other half of the subjects were in the *anger* condition. The accomplice and the subjects were asked to fill out forms. The questions began innocuously but gradually became insulting. The accomplice became increasingly angry; finally he threw the questionnaire on the floor and stomped out, shouting, "I'm not wasting any more time. I'm getting my books and leaving."

The experimenters watched the interaction from behind a one-way mirror and rated the kind of emotion the subjects expressed. The subjects also rated themselves as to the kind of emotions they felt.

Schachter and Singer made the following predictions for the outcomes of the study: Subjects in the informed group are aroused, but they can easily explain it, and so they should not be susceptible to the accomplice's suggestions of emotion. Subjects in the misinformed and ignorant groups, however, are aroused, but they have no easy way to explain it. These subjects should seek a label for their emotional state and will use the one provided by the accomplice. Finally, subjects in the placebo group are not aroused, and so they are not likely to think they are experiencing strong emotions, regardless of the accomplice's behavior.

The results turned out exactly as predicted (Table 13.1). Subjects in the misinformed and ignorant groups felt either euphoric or angry, depending on the accomplice's behavior. Subjects in the informed and placebo groups were unaffected by the accomplice.

On the basis of these results, Schachter (1964) proposed his two-component theory of emotion: that an emotion consists of a physiological arousal state plus the labeling of it as a particular emotion (for a critical evaluation of the theory, see Reisenzein, 1983). Berscheid and Walster have applied this to the emotion of "love." What they suggest is that we feel passionate love when we are aroused and when conditions are such that we believe it is love that we are feeling.

Evidence on Berscheid and Walster's Theory

Several experiments provide evidence for Berscheid and Walster's two-component theory of love.

In one study, male subjects exercised vigorously by running in place; that produced the physiological arousal response of pounding heart and sweaty palms (White et al., 1981). Afterward they rated their liking for an attractive woman, who actually was a confederate of the experimenters. Subjects in the running group said they liked the woman significantly more than did subjects who were in a control condition and had not exercised. This result is consistent with Berscheid and Walster's theory. The effect is called the misattribution of arousal; that is, in a situation like this, the men misattribute their arousal—which is actually due to exercise—to their liking for the attractive woman.

Another study suggests that fear can increase a man's attraction to a woman (Dutton & Aron, 1974; see also Brehm et al., cited in Berscheid & Walster, 1974). An attractive female interviewer contacted male passersby either on a fear-arousing suspension bridge or on a non-fear-arousing bridge. The fear-arousing bridge was constructed of boards attached to cables and had a tendency to tilt, sway, and wobble; the handrails were low, and there was a 230-foot drop to rocks and shallow rapids below. The "control" bridge was made of solid cedar; it was firm, and there was only a 10-foot drop to a shallow rivulet below. The interviewer asked subjects to fill out questionnaires that included projective test items. These items were then scored for sexual imagery.

The men in the suspension-bridge group should have been in a state of physiological arousal, while those in the control-bridge group should not have been. In fact, there was more sexual imagery in the questionnaires filled out by the men in

> **Misattribution of arousal:**
> When one is in a state of physiological arousal (e.g., from exercising or being in a frightening situation), attributing these feelings to be love or attraction to the person present.

the suspension-bridge group, and these men made more attempts to contact the attractive interviewer after the experiment than the subjects on the control bridge. Intuitively, this might seem to be a peculiar result: that men who are in a state of fear are more attracted to a woman than men who are relaxed. But in terms of the Berscheid and Walster two-component theory, it makes perfect sense. The fearful men were physiologically aroused, while the men in the control group were not. And according to this theory, arousal is an important component of love or attraction.[2]

Now, of course, if the men (most of them heterosexuals) had been approached by an elderly man or a child, probably their responses would have been different. In fact, when the interviewer in the experiment was male, the effects discussed above did not occur. Society tells us what the appropriate objects of our love, attraction, or liking are. That is, we know for what kinds of people it is appropriate to have feelings of love or liking. For these men, feelings toward an attractive woman could reasonably be labeled "love" or "attraction," while such labels would probably not be attached to feelings for an elderly man. Thus in this experiment subjects were provided with a situation in which "love" or "liking" was a reasonable label for their feelings; however, only the suspension-bridge group also had the physiological arousal that is necessary to create the emotion. Our society generally encourages people to attach the label "love" to a wide variety of confused feelings (Berscheid & Walster, 1974).

The physical arousal that is important for love need not always be produced by unpleasant or frightening situations. Pleasant stimuli, such as sexual arousal or praise from the other person, may produce arousal and feelings of love. Indeed, Berscheid and Walster's theory does an excellent job of explaining why we seem to

---

[2] According to the terminology of Chapter 3, note that the Schachter and Singer study and the Dutton and Aron study are both examples of *experimental* research.

have such a strong tendency to associate love and sex. Sexual arousal is one method of producing a state of physiological arousal, and it is one that our culture has taught us to label as "love." Thus both components necessary to feel love are present: arousal and a label (see, for example, Stephan et al., 1971). On the other hand, this phenomenon may lead us to confuse love with lust, an all-too-common error.

INTIMACY

According to Sternberg's theory, intimacy is one of the three major components of romantic love. Today many people are seeking to increase the intimacy in their relationships. And so, in this section, we will explore intimacy in more detail to try to gain a better understanding of it.

Defining Intimacy

Psychologists have offered a number of definitions of intimacy, including the following (Perlman & Fehr, 1987, p. 17):

1. Intimacy's defining features include: "openness, honesty, mutual self-disclosure; caring, warmth, protecting, helping; being devoted to each other, mutually attentive, mutually committed; surrendering control, dropping defenses; becoming emotional, feeling distressed when separation occurs."

2. "Emotional intimacy is defined in behavioral terms as mutual self-disclosure and other kinds of verbal sharing, as declarations of liking and loving the other, and as demonstrations of affection."

3. Intimacy is defined as "a subjective appraisal that emerges out of a rational process between two individuals in which each comes to know the 'inner-most' aspects of the other, and is known in a like manner."

4. "The intimacy motive is a recurrent preference or readiness for *warm, close, and communicative exchange with others*—an interpersonal interaction perceived as an end in itself rather than a means to another end."

Notice in the definitions that some focus more on intimacy as a characteristic of a relationship and others focus on it as a characteristic of a person. One way to think about intimacy is as a quality of relationship between two people. But we can also think about certain persons as having more of a capacity for intimacy or engaging in more intimacy-promoting behaviors than others.

In one study, college students were asked to respond to an open-ended question asking what they thought made a relationship one of intimacy (Roscoe et al., 1987). The qualities that emerged, with great agreement, were sharing, sexual interaction, trust in the partner, and openness. Notice that these qualities are quite similar to the ones listed in the psychologists' definitions given earlier.

Intimacy and Self-Disclosure

One of the key characteristics of intimacy, appearing in psychologists' and college students' definitions, is self-disclosure, that is, telling personal information about oneself to the other person (Derlega, 1984). Consider the following scenario:

John is 41 years old and a professor at a state university. He has been dating Susan, a 35-year-old junior faculty member, for 3 months. He has felt depressed in the past year. His father died recently after a chronic illness. John has also felt unhappy about his teaching and research efforts. One evening he and Susan talked

for several hours about a wide range of topics. They talked most about John's uncertainties and pessimism about taking control over his life. Susan listened patiently as John talked in an open way about himself. She wished to understand him and to be supportive. Susan said she cared about John regardless of the personal problems he was having. John felt grateful and perceived that she understood him. He was much closer to her after their talk. (Derlega, 1984, p. 1)

This story illustrates how self-disclosure promotes intimacy in a relationship and makes us feel close to the other person. It also illustrates how important it is for the partner to be accepting in responses to self-disclosure. If the acceptance is missing, we can feel betrayed or threatened, and we certainly will not feel on more intimate terms with the partner.

Self-disclosure and intimacy, then, mutually build on each other. Self-disclosure promotes our feeling that the relationship is intimate, and when we feel that the relationship is intimate, we feel comfortable engaging in further self-disclosure.

Measuring Intimacy

Psychologists have developed some scales for measuring intimacy, and these scales can give us further insights. One such scale is the Personal Assessment of Intimacy in Relationships (PAIR) Inventory (Schaefer & Olson, 1981). It measures emotional intimacy in a relationship with items such as the following:

1. My partner listens to me when I need someone to talk to.
2. My partner really understands my hurts and joys.

Another scale measuring intimacy in a relationship includes items such as these (Miller & Lefcourt, 1982):

1. How often do you confide very personal information to him or her?
2. How often are you able to understand his or her feelings?
3. How often do you feel close to him or her?
4. How important is your relationship with him or her in your life?

If you are currently in a relationship, answer those questions for yourself and consider what the quality of the intimacy is in your relationship.

In summary, an intimate relationship is characterized by self-disclosure and feelings of closeness and trust. We can promote intimacy in our relationships by engaging in self-disclosure (providing, of course, that we trust the person, but it is quite difficult to develop intimacy when there is lack of trust) and being accepting of the other person's self-disclosures.

AN AFTERTHOUGHT

Senator William Proxmire, watchdogging the spending of federal funds for research, was very critical of research on sex and love. According to him, the last thing we need to do is understand love (Shaffer, 1977).

Personally, I think that it is one of the first things we should try to understand, and I hope that much more research will be done in this area. As Abraham Maslow put it, "We *must* understand love; we must be able to teach it, to create it, to predict it, or else the world is lost to hostility and to suspicion" (1970, p. 181).

Summary

Research indicates that we tend to be attracted to people who are similar to us (in terms of attitudes, intelligence, social status, and appearance). In first impressions, we are most attracted to people who are physically attractive; we also tend to be attracted to people whom we believe to be "within reach" of us, depending on our sense of our own attractiveness or desirability. Mere repeated exposure to another person also seems to facilitate attraction. Playing hard to get seems to work only if the person is able to convey the sense of being selectively hard to get. We tend to be attracted to those who give us many positive reinforcements.

According to Sternberg's theory, there are three components to love: intimacy, passion, and decision or commitment. He conceptualizes love as being a triangle, with each of these components as one of the points. Partners whose love triangles are substantially different are mismatched and are likely to be dissatisfied with their relationship.

According to the attachment theory of love, adults vary in their capacity for love as a result of their love or attachment experiences in infancy. This theory says that there are three types of lovers: secure lovers, avoidant lovers, and anxious-ambivalent lovers.

Zick Rubin has constructed a scale to measure romantic love and another scale to measure liking. They make it possible to do further scientific research on love. Research indicates that love shifts from passionate to compassionate as a relationship progresses. Research also indicates that men are more romantic and fall in love earlier in a relationship.

Berscheid and Walster have hypothesized that there are two basic components of romantic love: being in a state of physiological arousal and attaching the label "love" to the feeling.

1. Research indicates that we are more attracted to people whose attitudes are similar to ours than to people whose attitudes are different. True or false?

2. The mere-exposure effect refers to the tendency of women to be secretly attracted to exhibitionists. True or false?

3. According to Byrne's law of attraction, we tend to be attracted to people who give us many _____ and few punishments.

4. According to Sternberg's theory, love has three components: _____, _____, and decision or commitment.

5. According to the attachment theory of love, a person who, as an infant, experienced a secure, pleasant attachment to the parents, will be a _____ lover, finding it easy to form a close relationship with a partner.

6. As a relationship progresses, there is usually a shift from companionate love to passionate love, occurring when the relationship is between 6 and 30 months old. True or false?

7. Research indicates that men fall in love earlier in a relationship than women do, and that men cling longer to a dying love affair. True or false?

8. According to Berscheid and Walster's two-component theory, passionate love exists when two conditions exist simultaneously: _____ and attaching a cognitive label ("love") to the experience.

9. In one experiment, male subjects engaged in vigorous running in place and then met an attractive woman; they liked her significantly more than did a control group of subjects who didn't exercise. This effect is called the _____.

10. An _____ relationship is characterized by mutual self-disclosure and feelings of closeness.

(The answers to all review questions are at the end of the book, beginning on page 731.)

Questions for Thought, Discussion, and Debate

1. If you are currently in love with someone, how would you describe the kind of love you feel, using the various terms discussed in this chapter?

2. Do you agree with Senator Proxmire that the federal government should not be funding research on love? Why or why not?

Suggestions for Further Reading

Hendrick, Susan, & Hendrick, Clyde. (1992). *Liking, loving, and relating.* 2nd ed. Pacific Grove, CA: Brooks/Cole. This textbook explains psychologists' research on interpersonal attraction, love, and the formation and maintenance of relationships.

Lerner, Harriet G. (1989). *The dance of intimacy.* New York: Harper & Row. Lerner, a prominent psychotherapist and author, gives tips on how to promote intimacy in our relationships.

Rubin, Lillian B. (1983). *Intimate strangers: Men and women together.* New York: Harper & Row. A sociologist's insights on differences between men and women in their desire for intimacy and the barriers these differences create.

Trotter, Robert J. (1986, Sept.). The three faces of love. *Psychology Today,* 46–54. This article presents Sternberg's theory of love, written for a general audience.

14

Gender Roles, Female Sexuality, and Male Sexuality

C h a p t e r   H i g h l i g h t s

"The majority of women (happily for them) are not very much troubled with sexual feelings of any kind. What men are habitually, women are only exceptionally."*

Hoggity higgamous,
  men are polygamous,
Higgity hoggamous,
  women monogamous.†

A baby is born. What is the first statement made about it? "It's a boy" or "It's a girl," of course. Sociologists tell us that gender is one of the most basic of status characteristics. That is, in terms of both our individual interactions with people and the position we hold in society, gender is exceptionally important. The TV program *Saturday Night Live* carries a continuing sketch featuring Pat; no one can figure out whether Pat is a male or a female, and Pat's name is no help. The sketch illustrates the consternation we feel in those rare cases when we are uncertain of a person's gender. We do not know how to interact with the person, and we feel quite flustered, not to mention curious, until we can ferret out some clue as to whether the person is a male or a female. We seem to need to know a person's gender before we can figure out how to interact with the person.

GENDER ROLES AND STEREOTYPES

One of the basic ways societies codify this emphasis on gender is through gender roles.[1] A **gender role** is a set of norms, or culturally defined expectations, that define

Gender role: A set of norms, or culturally defined expectations, that define how people of one gender ought to behave.

* *Source:* Dr. William Acton, *The Functions and Disorders of the Reproductive Organs* (1857)

† *Source:* Dorothy Parker

[1] The distinction between sex and gender will be maintained in this chapter. Male-female roles—and thus gender roles—are being discussed here.

387

how people of one gender ought to behave. A closely related phenomenon is a stereotype, which is a generalization about a group of people (for example, men) that distinguishes those people from others (for example, women).

Psychologists are increasingly using the approaches of cognitive psychology (see Chapter 2) in investigating the complexities of gender stereotypes. Social psychologist Kay Deaux, for example, has found that there are four components of gender stereotypes (Deaux & Lewis, 1984):

1. *Personality traits*   For example, emotional expressiveness in women and self-confidence in men.
2. *Role behaviors*   For example, caring for children done by women, household repairs done by men.
3. *Occupations*   For example, registered nurse for women and construction worker for men.
4. *Physical appearance*   For example, small and graceful for women and tall and broad-shouldered for men.

Her research indicates that adults today view the male stereotype and the female stereotype as two overlapping categories rather than as two separate and distinct categories. For example, people no longer think that men are strong and women are weak. Rather, they believe that men are likelier to be stronger than women. To get at this idea, Deaux has her subjects estimate probabilities that a fictitious character will have a certain characteristic. For example, if subjects are given only the gender cue (the person is a man, or the person is a woman), they estimate the probability that a male is strong as .66 and that a woman is strong as .44 (Deaux & Lewis, 1983).

Deaux's research also indicates that as we learn about a person, gender per se has less influence on our impressions of that person (Deaux & Lewis, 1984). We are not totally ruled by gender stereotypes. They are most important in the very first impression we form of a person. But as we learn more about that person, that is, about his or her actual behavior and personality, these factors become far more important than stereotypes in our opinion of that person.

Gender Schema Theory

In Chapter 2 we discussed psychologist Sandra Bem's gender schema theory, her cognitive approach to understanding gender stereotypes. Recall that according to that theory, a gender schema is the set of ideas (about behaviors, personality, appearance, and so on) that we associate with males and females (Bem, 1981). The gender schema influences how we process information. It causes us to tend to dichotomize information on the basis of gender. It also leads us to distort or fail to remember information that is stereotype-inconsistent. Recall that children who were shown pictures of children engaging in stereotype-inconsistent activities such as boys baking cookies recalled, when tested a week later, that they had seen girls baking cookies.

Gender schema theory points out the extent to which gender stereotypes or gender schemas lead us to gender-dichotomized thinking. It also provides evidence that it is relatively difficult to change people's stereotyped notions because we tend to filter out information that contradicts stereotypes.

Socialization

Many adult women and men do behave as gender roles say they should. Why does this happen? Psychologists and sociologists believe that it is a result of gender-role socialization. **Socialization** refers to the ways in which society conveys to the individual its norms or expectations for his or her behavior. Socialization occurs especially in childhood, as children are taught to behave as they will be expected to in adulthood. Socialization may involve several processes. Children may be rewarded for behavior that is appropriate for their gender ("What a little man he is"), or they may be punished for behavior that is not appropriate to their gender ("Nice young ladies don't do that"). The adult models they imitate—whether these are parents of the same gender, teachers, or women and men on television—also contribute to their socialization. In some cases, simply telling children what is expected of males and females may be sufficient for role learning to take place. Socialization, of course, continues in adulthood, as society conveys its norms of appropriate behavior for adult women and men. These norms extend from appropriate jobs to who initiates sexual activity.

Who (or what) are society's agents in accomplishing this socialization? Certainly parents have an early, important influence, from buying dolls for girls and footballs or baseball bats for boys to giving boys more freedom to explore (Block, 1983). The parents' own conformity to their roles, which children may imitate, is also important. Parents are not the only socializing agents, though. The peer group can have a big impact in socializing for gender roles, particularly in adolescence. Other teenagers can be extremely effective in enforcing gender-role standards; for example, they may ridicule or shun the boy whose behavior is effeminate. Thus peers can exert great pressure for gender-role conformity.

The media can also be important as socializing agents. Many people assume that things have changed a lot in the last 20 years and that gender stereotypes are a thing of the past. On the contrary, an analysis of the Sunday comics in 1974 and again in 1984 indicates that not much changed (Brabant & Mooney, 1986). Males are still depicted more often—in 67 percent of the strips in 1974 and 74 percent in 1984, compared with women's 52 percent in 1974 and 59 percent in 1984. Women were shown in the home in 69 percent of the strips in 1974, compared with 32 percent for men; in 1984 the percentages were 72 percent for women and 33 percent for men.

Television—both the programs and the commercials—continues to show stereotyped roles (Bretl & Cantor, 1988; Kalisch & Kalisch, 1984; Mamay & Simpson, 1981). On prime-time series, women are seldom portrayed as being both employed and married (Weigel & Loomis, 1981). An analysis of television commercials from 1971 to 1985 indicated that in 1971, 89 percent of the commercials were narrated by men; in 1985, 91 percent were (Bretl & Cantor, 1988). On the other hand, this same analysis of commercials indicated that there have been some trends away from stereotyping. For example, men are increasingly being shown in the role of spouse or parent in commercials.

In sum, the evidence indicates that the media show less stereotyped gender roles than they did 20 years ago, but noticeable stereotyping still remains.

Does the stereotyping in the media have an effect on people? In one study, preschool children were individually read a picture book featuring a character of their own gender engaged in play with either a stereotypic or a nonstereotypic toy (doll or dump truck) (Ashton, 1983). Afterward, the children were given the opportunity to play in a playroom with six experimental toys: two female-stereotypic toys (doll and china set), two male-stereotypic toys (truck and gun), and two neutral toys (ball and pegboard). The girls who had been exposed to the stereotyped book played significantly more with the female-stereotypic toys than did the girls who had been exposed to the nonstereotyped book. And boys who had been exposed to the nonstereotyped books played significantly more with the female-stereotyped toys than did boys exposed to the stereotyped book. Gender stereotypes in the media, then, can affect behavior.

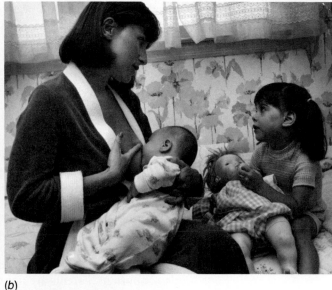

(a)

(b)

FIGURE 14.1
*Children are very interested
in achieving adult gender
roles.*

(c)

Finally, children may themselves be the agents of their own socialization. Once children have formed concepts of gender and know whether they are boys or girls, they typically acquire a very strong motivation to adopt their gender role (Kohlberg, 1966). That is, children actively seek out information about their gender role and then try to behave as they think boys or girls are supposed to behave. Thus not only are gender roles imposed on children by society, but children also strive to learn them.

Although gender roles themselves are universal (Rosaldo, 1974)—that is, all societies have gender roles—the exact content of these roles varies from one culture to the next, from one ethnic group to another, and from one social class to another. For example, Margaret Mead (1953) studied several cultures in which gender roles are considerably different from those in the United States. One such group is the Mundugumor of New Guinea. In that culture both females and males are extremely aggressive.

There is evidence that people's attitudes about gender roles have changed in the last 10 or 20 years in the United States. One study administered the Attitude Toward Women Scale to samples of college students in 1972, 1976, and 1980 (Helmreich et al., 1982). There was a large and significant shift toward more liberal, egalitarian attitudes from 1972 to 1976. However, from 1976 to 1980 there was no sigificant change in male attitudes, and females' attitudes actually changed slightly in the conservative direction. Thus it appears that there were substantial shifts toward approval of equality in gender roles, occurring in the early to mid-1970s, but this trend seems to have leveled off.

Gender-role expectations may change over the lifespan. Teenagers have fairly rigid concepts of gender roles (J. F. Adams, 1973), and young married couples, particularly those with small children, may follow very stereotyped roles (the woman takes care of the home and children, and the husband is the breadwinner). However, as people reach retirement age, there may be a considerable shifting of roles. After retiring, the husband may spend his time in the home, doing the marketing, cleaning, and cooking. As people get older, they are increasingly likely to be single, because of divorce or the death of a spouse, and thus they are more likely to assume both the male and the female roles (earn a living and take care of a home).

Having noted these gender-role variations, let us discuss the effect of gender roles on people as they grow up male or female. The role standards discussed will be mainly those of the white middle class in the United States. There are several reasons for this. First, most of the research has been done on this group. Second, white middle-class culture has an overwhelming impact on our culture as a whole through its domination of the media (television and children's readers, for example). We will also explore gender roles among African Americans, Hispanics, American Indians, and Asian Americans and how they differ from or are similar to gender roles for white Americans. As you read the following sections, you should keep in mind the effects that gender roles might have on sexuality.

GROWING UP FEMALE, GROWING UP MALE

Stereotypes About Females and Males

Psychologists have studied gender-role stereotypes in the United States (Deaux & Lewis, 1984; Ruble, 1983; Broverman et al., 1972; Rosenkrantz et al., 1968). The feminine traits that people consider desirable fall into a general category of "warmth" and "expressiveness." Feminine traits that are not valued include characteristics such as emotionality and lack of competitiveness. The traits that are valued in men fall into a general "competency" category, including traits such as independence, objectivity, competitiveness, logicalness, and skill in business. That is, a key expectation for men in our culture is that they be competent and possess the characteristics that go along with competence. A "macho" personality constellation also exists in our culture (Mosher & Tomkins, 1988). It includes the belief that men should have callous attitudes about sex, that violence is manly, and that danger is exciting.

Heterosexuality is another important part of gender roles. The "feminine" woman is expected to be sexually attractive to men and in turn to be attracted to them. Women who violate any part of this—for example, lesbian women—are viewed as violators of gender roles and are considered masculine (Storms et al., 1981). Heterosexuality is equally important in the male role. In one survey, 48 percent of the women felt that a "real man" should be a skilled lover (Tavris, 1977). Even in bed, men are required to be competent.

Two points of view have emerged in current debates over gender roles. Feminists note the stresses associated with women's low status, their restriction from high achievements, and the demand that they be wives and mothers. Men's liberationists argue that while women's low status does involve stresses, always having to be at the top is also stressful.

Current thinking among psychologists tends to support both of these points of view. More traditional psychological thought, extending from the 1930s to the 1960s, tended to be accepting and even encouraging of traditional gender roles. Conformity to gender roles and a strong sense of gender identity were thought to be essential to good adjustment (Pleck, 1981). In the 1970s and 1980s, however, psychologists shifted their thinking and their research toward the belief that gender roles are actually sources of stress or strain for people (Pleck, 1981); the view now is that the best-adjusted people may be those who manage to surmount gender roles and become androgynous, a topic to be discussed later in this chapter. That is, the view has shifted away from thinking that masculinity is best for men and femininity is best for women, toward thinking that androgyny is best for everyone.

Gender Roles and Ethnicity

Most of the research on gender roles discussed to this point in the chapter has been based on research with white or predominantly white samples. In the last decade, new research has emerged that helps us understand how gender roles may differ—or be the same—in other ethnic groups in the United States.

African Americans

Two factors are especially significant in the cultural heritage of African Americans: the heritage of African culture and the experience of slavery in America and subsequent racial oppression. Two characteristics of African women have been maintained to the present: an important economic function, and a strong bond between mother and child (Ladner, 1971; Dobert, 1975). African women have traditionally been economically independent, functioning in the marketplace and as traders. African American women in the United States continue to assume this crucial economic function in the family to the present day. Mother-child bonds also continue to be extremely important in the structure of African American society.

Both theories and research in the social sciences have traditionally viewed the African American man as being downtrodden and being psychologically castrated. There are several reasons that this view is neither very realistic nor very useful. First, the traditional view is based on historical tracing of the African American male role back to the days of slavery. This historical analysis has ignored the strong contributions of African American men to their families, even within the confines of slavery (Staples, 1978). For example, Alex Haley's *Roots* portrayed many male characters who were responsible and strong and who had a good sense of themselves.

The provider role is difficult for some African American men because of their high unemployment rate. For example, in 1989 the unemployment rate was 3.9 percent for adult white males; for adult black males, it was 10.0 percent (U.S. Department of Labor, 1990), more than double the rate for whites. The high unemployment rate creates a gender-role problem because the role of breadwinner or good provider is an important part of the male role in the United States. Not being able to fulfill this part of the male role may express itself in a number of ways. It may turn into antisocial behavior, violence, and crime, accounting for the high crime rate among male African American teenagers. It has been suggested that volunteering for the army becomes an alternative means of fulfilling the male role—one-third of army recruits are African American men (Staples, 1978).

The role of husband is closely tied to the breadwinner role. African American men are understandably reluctant to take on the responsibility of marriage when unemployment is such a justified fear, and the rules of the welfare system essentially force low-income men to be absent. Research shows that African American men have egalitarian attitudes toward marriage. Even African American male adolescents expect egalitarian roles for men and women in marriage, in areas such as authority, housekeeping, and child care (Rooks & King, 1973).

Hispanics

Hispanic Americans are currently the nation's second largest minority and are expected to be the largest by the year 2000 (Vasquez & Barron, 1988). When we speak of the cultural heritage of Hispanics, we must first understand the concept of *acculturation,* which is the process of incorporating the beliefs and customs of a new culture. The culture of Chicanos (those of Mexican heritage) is different from both the culture of Mexico and the dominant Anglo culture of the United States. Chicano culture is based on the Mexican heritage, modified through acculturation to incorporate Anglo components.

The family is the central focus of Hispanic life. Traditional Hispanics place a high value on family loyalty and on warm, mutually supportive relationships, so that family and community are highly valued. This emphasis on family places special stresses on employed Hispanic women, who are expected to be the preservers of family and culture and to do so by staying in the home.

As noted in Chapter 1, in traditional Latin American cultures, gender roles are rigidly defined (Comas-Diaz, 1987). Such roles are emphasized early in the socialization process for children. Boys are given greater freedom, are encouraged in sexual exploits, and are not expected to share in household work. Girls are expected to be passive, obedient, and weak, and to stay in the home. These rigid roles are epitomized in the concepts of machismo and marianismo, discussed in Chapter 1.

Asian Americans

Chinese—almost all of them men—were recruited first in the 1840s to come to America as laborers in the West and later in the 1860s to work on the transcontinental railroad (for an excellent summary of the cultural heritage of Asian Americans, see Tsai & Uemura, 1988). Racist sentiment against the Chinese grew, however, and there was a shift to recruiting first Japanese and Koreans and then Filipinos. Then, in the late 1960s and the 1970s, there was a mass exodus to the United States of refugees from war-torn Southeast Asia.

The cultural values of Asian Americans are in some ways consistent with white middle-class American values, but in other ways contradict them. Asian Americans share with the white middle class an emphasis on achievement and on the importance of education. For example, Asian American women actually have a higher level of education, on the average, than white American women (Hyde, 1991). On the other hand, Asian Americans place far more value on family and group interdependence, compared with the white American emphasis on individualism and self-sufficiency. For Asian Americans, the family is a great source of emotional nurturance. One has an obligation to the family, and the needs of the family must take precedence over the needs of the individual. For Asian American women, there can be a conflict in cultural values, between the traditional gender roles of Asian culture and those of modern Anglo culture, which increasingly prizes independence and assertiveness in women.

Just as the sexuality of African Americans has been stereotyped, so too has the sexuality of Asian Americans. The Asian American man has been stereotyped as asexual (lacking in sexuality), whereas the Asian American woman has been stereotyped as an exotic sex toy (Kim, 1990).

At least some Indian tribes, including the Cherokee, Navajo, Iroquois, Hopi, and Zuni, traditionally had relatively egalitarian gender roles (LaFromboise et al., 1990). That is, their roles were more egalitarian than that of white culture of the same period. The process of acculturation and adaptation to Anglo society seems to have resulted in increased male dominance among American Indians.

There is evidence that some tribes—such as the Canadian Blackfeet—institutionalized more than two gender roles, the male role and the female role. There was an additional role of the "manly hearted woman," a role that a woman who was exceptionally independent and aggressive could take on. There was a "warrior woman" role among the Apache, Crow, Cheyenne, Blackfoot, and Pawnee tribes (e.g., Buchanan, 1986). In both cases, women could express masculine traits or participate in male-stereotyped activities while continuing to live and dress as women.

In summary, new scholarship indicates that gender roles in the United States are not uniform. Different ethnic groups define gender roles differently.

MALE-FEMALE PSYCHOLOGICAL DIFFERENCES

Gender differences in personality and behavior have been studied extensively by psychologists (e.g., Hyde, 1991). Here we will focus on gender differences in two areas that are particularly relevant to gender and sexuality: aggressiveness and communication styles.

As has been noted, males and females differ in *aggressiveness*. Males are more aggressive than females. This is true for virtually all indicators of aggression (physical aggression such as fighting, verbal aggression, and fantasy aggression) (Hyde, 1984). It is also true at all ages; as soon as children are old enough to perform aggressive behaviors, boys are more aggressive, and adult males dominate the statistics on violent crimes. In some situations, it is possible for women to be as aggressive as men, but it is very rare for women to be more aggressive than men (Frodi et al., 1977). The gender difference in aggression tends to be largest among preschoolers, but it gets smaller with age, so that gender differences in adults' aggression are small (Hyde, 1984).

A number of scholars have noted that men and women differ in their style of communicating, both verbally and nonverbally (Mayo & Henley, 1981; Key, 1975; Lakoff, 1973).

In terms of total talking time, men consistently outdistance women. This is a good example of a stereotype—women as constant talkers—that turns out not to be true in reality. Men actually spend more time talking than women do. Men are also more likely to interrupt than women are (McMillan et al., 1977).

Social psychologists have also found gender differences in studies of self-disclosure. In these studies, people are brought into a laboratory and are asked to disclose personal information either to friends or to strangers. Women are much more willing to disclose information than men are, at least in situations like these (Cozby, 1973; Jourard & Lasakow, 1958).

Norms about self-disclosure are changing, though. Traditional gender roles favored emotional expressiveness for females, but emotional repressiveness and avoidance of self-disclosure for males. There is a new, emerging ethic, though, of good communication and openness which demands equal self-disclosure from males and females (Rubin et al., 1980). Research with college students who are dating

Self-disclosure: Telling personal information to another person.

couples confirms the emergence of this new norm; the majority of both males and females reported that they had disclosed their thoughts and feelings fully to their partners (Rubin et al., 1980). However, women revealed more in some specific areas, particularly their greatest fears. And couples with egalitarian attitudes disclosed more than couples with traditional gender-role attitudes. Thus the traditional expectation that men should not express their feelings seems to be shifting to a new expectation that they be open and communicative.

In studies of nonverbal communication, or "body language," gender differences have also been found. Men are more likely to touch others, while women are more likely to be touched (Henley, 1973a, 1973b). Men and women also differ in their reactions to being touched. In one ingenious study, the effects of being touched briefly, in an accidental way, were studied (Fisher et al., 1975). The investigators arranged to have library clerks (both male and female) either touch or not touch the hands of students who were checking out books. Soon after each student left the checkout desk, he or she was approached by an experimenter with a questionnaire concerning the library and its personnel. Women who had been briefly touched by the clerk reported feeling more positive than women who had not, and they reacted more favorably toward both the clerk and the library. However, being touched seemed to have no effect on the men's feelings. This study suggests, then, that being touched may be a more positive experience for women than it is for men.

There is a related finding from studies of interpersonal space. These studies indicate that American men prefer greater distances between themselves and another person than American women do (Deaux, 1976). For example, at public exhibits women stand closer to other women than men do to other men. Women also sit closer together when they are in an experimental laboratory.

Not only are there gender differences in nonverbal behaviors, there are also gender differences in people's ability to understand the nonverbal behaviors of others. The technical phrase for this is "decoding nonverbal cues"—that is, the ability to read others' body language correctly. It might be measured, for example, by accuracy of interpreting facial expressions. Research shows that women are better than men at decoding such nonverbal cues (Hall, 1978). Certainly this is consistent with the gender-related expectation of greater interpersonal sensitivity for women.

What are the implications of these gender differences in communication styles for sexuality? For example, if men are unwilling to disclose personal information about themselves, might this not hamper their ability to communicate their sexual needs to their partners (Jourard, 1971)? If women react more favorably to being touched than men do, might this suggest that women enjoy this aspect of sex and that men might be relatively hampered in their enjoyment of being touched sexually? Further research in this area should be intriguing.

MALE-FEMALE DIFFERENCES IN SEXUALITY

In the sections that follow, the discussion will focus on areas of sexuality in which there is some evidence of male-female differences. As I will point out, there are differences, but they are in a rather small number of areas—masturbation and attitudes about casual sex, especially, and to a lesser extent, anxiety and guilt about sex. There is a danger in focusing on these differences to the point of forgetting about gender similarities, which will be discussed later in the chapter. You should keep in mind that males and females are in many ways quite similar in their sexuality—for example, in the physiology of their sexual response (Chapter 9)—while considering the evidence on male-female differences that follows.

Masturbation

In a review of 177 studies of gender differences in sexuality conducted between the late 1960s and the 1980s, Mary Beth Oliver and I found that the largest gender difference was the incidence of masturbation (Oliver & Hyde, 1993).

Recall that in the Kinsey data, 92 percent of the males had masturbated to orgasm at least once in their lives, as compared with 58 percent of females. Not only did fewer women masturbate, but, in general, those who did masturbate had begun at a later age than the males. Virtually all males said they had masturbated before age 20 (most began between ages 13 and 15), but substantial numbers of women reported masturbating for the first time at age 25, 30, or 35. This gender difference shows no evidence of diminishing, according to more recent studies (e.g., Hunt, 1974). Every year I survey the students in my human sexuality course and, even in the 1990s, I still find this same pattern.

The data suggest, then, that there is a substantial gender difference in the incidence of masturbation; virtually all males masturbate to orgasm, whereas about one-third of women never do.

Attitudes About Casual Sex

The second largest gender difference we found was in attitudes toward casual sex—that is, premarital (or nonmarital) intercourse in a situation, such as a "one night stand," in which there is no emotionally committed relationship between the partners (Oliver & Hyde, 1993). Men are considerably more approving of such interactions, and women tend to be disapproving. Many women feel that premarital intercourse is ethical or acceptable only in the context of an emotionally committed relationship. For many men, that is a nice context for sex, but it isn't absolutely necessary.

In a related study, Janell Carroll, Kari Volk, and I surveyed 249 undergraduates about their motives for having sex (Carroll et al., 1985). The results illustrate the importance for women of relationship and emotional connectedness as prerequisites for sex. Men are less concerned about these prerequisites and focus more on the physical pleasure of sex. The actual sexual behavior of these students was relatively similar: 94 percent of the males and 80 percent of the females had engaged in sexual intercourse. However, their motives and attitudes were considerably different. When asked, "For you, is an emotional involvement a prerequisite for participating in sexual intercourse?" 45 percent of the females responded "Always," compared with only 8 percent of the males. Consistent with stereotypes, males and females gave considerably different responses to the question "What are your motives for having sexual intercourse?" Females emphasized love and emotional commitment, as in the following examples:

> Emotional feelings that were shared, wonderful way to express LOVE!!

> My motives for sexual intercourse would all be due to the love and commitment I feel for my partner.

Contrast those responses with the following typical responses from males:

> Need it.

> To gratify myself.

> When I'm tired of masturbation. (Carroll et al., 1985, p. 137)

Clearly males—at least in the college years—emphasize physical needs and pleasure as their motives for intercourse, whereas females emphasize love, relationships, and emotional commitment. No wonder there is some conflict in relationships between women and men!

Arousal to Erotica

Traditionally in our society most erotic material—sexually arousing pictures, movies, or stories—has been produced for a male audience. The corresponding assumption presumably has been that women are not interested in such things. Does the scientific evidence bear out this notion?

Kinsey found that the females in his sample were considerably less likely than the males to report responses to erotic materials. For example, about half of the males reported having been aroused at some time by erotic stories; although almost all the women had heard such stories, only 14 percent had been aroused by them. These data are often cited as evidence that women are not so easily aroused as men.[2]

Studies done in the last two decades, however, have provided little evidence that males and females differ in their arousal to erotic materials. For example, in one study the responses of 128 male and 128 female university students to erotic slides and movies were studied (Schmidt & Sigusch, 1970). The slides and movies showed petting and coitus. In several tests for gender differences, either there were no differences, or the differences were small, with about 40 percent of the females reporting a stronger arousal response than the average male. All the females and almost all the males reported genital responses to the slides and movies. And women—not men—showed an increase in petting and coitus in the 24 hours after seeing the erotic stimuli. Therefore, there seems to be little basis for saying that women are not erotically responsive to such materials.

An interesting study by psychologist Julia Heiman (1975, 1977; for a similar study with similar results, see Steinman et al., 1981) provides a good deal of insight into the responses of males and females to erotic materials. Her subjects were sexually experienced university students, and she studied their responses as they listened to tape recordings of erotic stories. Not only did Heiman obtain subjects' self-ratings of their arousal, as other investigators have done, but she also got objective measures of their physiological levels of arousal. To do this, she used two instruments: a penile strain gauge and a photoplethysmograph (Figure 14.2). The **penile strain gauge** (my students have dubbed this the "peter meter") is used to get a physiological measure of arousal in the male; it is a flexible loop that fits around the base of the penis. The **photoplethysmograph** measures physiological arousal in the female; it is an acrylic cylinder, about the size of a tampon, that is placed just inside the entrance to the vagina. Both instruments measure vasocongestion in the genitals, which is the major physiological response during sexual arousal (see Chapter 9). These physiological measures are a great advance, since they are not subject to the errors or distortions that may occur when subjects simply rate their own arousal.

Subjects heard one of four kinds of tapes. There is a stereotype that women are more turned on by romance, while men are more aroused by "raw sex." The

Penile strain gauge: A device used to measure physiological sexual arousal in the male; it is a flexible loop that fits around the base of the penis.

Photoplethysmograph (foh-toh-pleth-ISS-moh-graf): An acrylic cylinder that is placed inside the vagina in order to measure physiological sexual arousal in the female. Also called a photometer.

---

[2] Actually, though, the Kinsey data were not that simple. Kinsey noted wide variability in women's responses and speculated that perhaps one-third of all women are as erotically responsive as the average male. Further, there were no gender differences in certain behaviors; for example, about the same number of females as males reported having being aroused by erotic literary materials.

FIGURE 14.2
Two devices used to measure physiological sexual response in males and females. The penile strain gauge (left) consists of a flexible band that fits around the base of the penis. The photoplethysmograph (right) is an acrylic cylinder containing a photocell and light source, which is placed just inside the vagina.

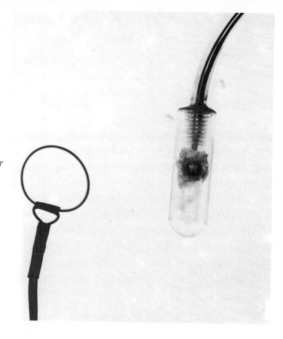

tapes varied according to which of these kinds of content they contained. The first group of tapes was *erotic;* they included excerpts from popular novels giving explicit descriptions of heterosexual sex. The second group of tapes was *romantic;* a couple were heard expressing affection and tenderness for each other, but they did not actually engage in sex. The third group of tapes was *erotic-romantic;* they included erotic elements of explicit sex and also romantic elements. Finally, the fourth group of tapes served as a *control;* a couple were heard engaging in conversation but nothing else. The plots of the tapes also varied according to whether the male or the female initiated the activity and whether the description centered on the female's physical and psychological responses or on the male's. Thus the tapes were male-initiated or female-initiated and female-centered or male-centered. Three important results emerged from the study:

1. Explicit heterosexual sex (the erotic and erotic-romantic tapes) was most arousing, both for women and for men. The great majority of both males and females responded most, both physiologically and in self-ratings, to the erotic and erotic-romantic tapes. Women, in fact, rated the erotic tapes as more arousing than men did. Neither men nor women responded—either physiologically or in self-reports—to the romantic tapes or to the control tapes (except for a couple of men who were aroused by a discussion of the relative merits of an anthropology major versus premed—ah, well).

2. Both males and females found the female-initiated, female-centered tape to be most arousing. Perhaps the female-initiated plot was most arousing because of its somewhat forbidden or taboo nature.

3. Women were sometimes not aware of their own physiological arousal. Generally there was a high correlation between self-ratings of arousal and objective physiological measures of arousal, both for men and for women. When men were physically aroused, they never made an error in reporting this in their self-ratings—it is pretty hard to miss an erection. But when the women were physically aroused, about half of them failed to report it in their self-ratings. (One might assume that women who were sophisticated enough to volunteer

for an experiment of this nature and who were willing to insert a photoplethysmograph into their vagina would not suddenly become bashful about reporting their arousal; that is, it seems likely that these women honestly did not know when they were physically aroused.)

In sum, then, Heiman's study indicates that males and females are quite similar in their responses to erotic materials but that women can sometimes be unaware of their own physical arousal.

In statistical terms, Heiman found a low correlation between women's self-reports of arousal and physiological measures of their arousal. In an interesting follow-up study, one experimental group of women was instructed to attend to their genital signs of sexual arousal ("While rating these slides, I would like you to attend to various changes that may occur in your genital area such as vaginal lubrication, pelvic warmth, and muscular tension"), and a second group was told to attend to nongenital signs of arousal ("While rating these slides, I would like you to attend to various changes that may occur in your body. These are heart rate increase, nipple erection, breast swelling, and muscular tension."), while a control group was given no instructions (Korff & Geer, 1983). Both experimental groups showed high correlations between self-reports and physiological measures of arousal, while the control group showed the same low correlation that Heiman found. This shows that women can be quite accurate in realizing their physical arousal if they are simply told to focus their attention on it. The broader culture, of course, does not give women such instructions, but rather tells them to focus on the environment outside themselves—the love, romance, partner—and so many women have not learned to focus on their body. But the experiment described here shows quite clearly that they can, and that there is no biological reason for women to be out of touch with their body's response.

WHY THE DIFFERENCES?

The previous section reviewed the evidence on differences between male and female sexuality. Two differences—the lower percentage of females, compared with males, who masturbate and women's more disapproving attitudes toward casual sex—seem to be fairly well documented and in need of explanation. Other stereotyped gender differences, such as differences in response to erotic materials, are not well documented by current data and thus are not in need of explanation. What factors, though, lead some women not to masturbate and to be disapproving of casual sex? Many different possible explanations have been suggested by a wide variety of scholars; these will be considered below.

Biological Factors

There has been some speculation that gender differences in sexuality are created by two biological factors: anatomy and hormones.

Anatomy

The male sexual anatomy is external and visible and has a very obvious response: erection. While the male is nude, he can easily see his sexual organs, either by looking down or by looking in a mirror. The female sexual organs, in contrast, are hidden. The nude female looks down and sees nothing except pubic hair (which really is not very informative); she looks in a full-length mirror and sees the same thing. Only by

Sexual Scripts: Female Sexuality in Marriage and Sex Manuals

Marriage and sex manuals are important to analyze for a number of reasons. They have enormous potential for influencing people's opinions, particularly because they are designed for mass consumption and do indeed enjoy enormous sales. For example, David Reuben's *Everything You Always Wanted to Know About Sex—But Were Afraid to Ask* (1966) sold more than 1 million copies in 1970, and *The Sensuous Woman* sold 600,000 copies in that same year. The old classic, *A Marriage Manual* (Stone & Stone, 1953), had 48 printings and sold more than 600,000 copies. These books essentially tell people what is sexually legitimate—that is, they provide sexual scripts. These manuals both reflect existing views of female sexuality in our culture and influence those views. Because of the important influence of these books, sociologists have analyzed their content to determine their assumptions and prescriptions about female sexuality.

The content of sex manuals published in the 1800s reflects the understanding that sex is a procreative necessity. Female sexual desire was thought to be virtually nonexistent:

> As a general rule, a modest women seldom desires any sexual gratification for herself. She submits to her husband, but only to please him; and, but for the desire of maternity, would far rather be relieved from his

attentions. The married woman has no wish to be treated on the footlings of a mistress. (Hayes, 1869, p. 227)

By the early years of the twentieth century, a change in thinking had occurred. Sex was now seen, in the context of marriage, not only as right and proper but also as an important part of married lfe. Female sexuality was now acknowledged. But women, supposedly, did not experience sexual desires until they were married, and then only when these were brought to the surface by the husband:

> No doubt women differ greatly, but in every woman who truly loves there lies dormant the capacity to become vibrantly alive in response to her lover, and to meet him as a willing and active participant in the sacrament of marriage. (Gray, 1922, p. 145)

Indeed, sex came to be seen as such an important part of marriage that by the 1930s a "cult of mutual orgasm" had developed.

Manuals of the 1950s and 1960s were based on the *different-equals-less* model. These manuals no longer assumed that sex was a distasteful duty. They encouraged women to enjoy sex. They portrayed women's sexuality as emotional and men's as physical and animalistic. Most importantly, they

doing the mirror exercise described in Chapter 4 can she get a good view of her own genitals. Further, the female's genitals do not have an obvious arousal response like the male's erection. As a result, she may be less aware of her own arousal, a notion that is supported by Heiman's research.

The anatomical explanation, then, is that because the woman's genitals are not in plain view and because their arousal response is less obvious than that of the man's genitals, she is less likely to masturbate and less likely to develop her full sexual potential. If this explanation is correct, or at least part of the answer, could steps be taken to help women develop their sexuality? Perhaps parents could show

portrayed the "sleeping beauty" view that women's sexuality is dormant until it is awakened by an experienced and skillful man.

The different-equals-less model disappeared from the scene by the 1970s for several reasons. Masters and Johnson's important books were published in 1966 and 1970 and provided a much different view of female sexual response. The introduction of the birth control pill, in 1960, allowed the separation of sex for procreation and sex for recreation. Radical social movements of the 1960s and 1970s led to more permissive sexual norms. And the feminist movement led many to question women's traditional roles, including their roles in sexual interactions.

The next wave of sex manuals, published in the 1970s and based on a *humanistic sexuality model,* reflected these radical changes. Perhaps the best known of these is Alex Comfort's *The Joy of Sex* (1972). These manuals no longer assumed that sex took place within marriage, and no longer referred to husband and wife, but to partners. They did assume a loving relationhip between the partners, and viewed sex as a part of human experience to be explored and experimented with. Women were viewed as equal participants and as active in the interaction. These manuals cited the research of Masters and Johnson on female orgasmic capacity and denounced female passivity. Many of today's sex manuals are also based on the humanistic sexuality model.

From 1975 to 1980, a new model, *sexual autonomy,* emerged in some manuals. This model arose from the feminist movement. The books were initially written by women authors for women, but these manuals gained widespread appeal. Their emphasis is on the woman as an independent sexual being, in contrast to other models that see the dyad or partnership as the focus. Thus independence and competence in sexuality are important for women to develop just as they develop independence and competence in careers and other aspects of their lives. These manuals view orgasm as every woman's right and provide exercises such as guided masturbation to help women learn or improve their orgasmic capacity. Furthermore, they urge women to take responsibility for their own sexual pleasure.

> To awaken your potential you must assume responsibility for *your own* sexual pleasure and the means of achieving *your own* orgasm. . . . He can give you his penis to enjoy, but the extent to which you enjoy it is *your responsibility.* (Newborn, 1973, p. 211, emphasis in original)

Most sex manuals today are based on the humanistic sexuality model or the sexual autonomy model.

The sexual scripts for women portrayed in these manuals have changed greatly in a century—from the passive woman with no sex drive, to the sleeping sexual beauty awakened by her husband, to an equal, growth-enhancing sexual partner, to an independently sexual woman.

Sources: Martin S. Weinberg, Rochelle Ganz Swensson, & Sue Kiefer Hammersmith (1983). Sexual autonomy and the status of women: Models of female sexuality in U.S. sex manuals from 1950 to 1980. *Social Problems,* 30, 312–324; Michael Gordon & Penelope J. Shankweiler. (1971). Different equals less: Female sexuality in recent marriage manuals. *Journal of Marriage and the Family,* 33, 459–466.

their daughters the mirror exercise at an early age and encourage them to become more aware of their own sexual organs. And parents may want to discuss the idea of masturbation with their daughters.

Hormones

The hormonal explanation rests on the finding that testosterone is related to sexual behavior. This evidence was reviewed in Chapter 9. Basically, the evidence comes from studies in which male animals are castrated (have their source of testosterone removed), with the result that their sexual behavior disappears, presumably reflecting a decrease in sex drive. If replacement injections of testosterone are given, the sexual behavior returns.

Females generally have lower levels of testosterone in their tissues than males do. Human females, for example, have about one-sixth the level of testosterone in their blood that human males do (Salhanick & Margulis, 1968).

The hormonal explanation, then, is that if testosterone is important in activating sexual behavior and if females have only one-sixth as much of it as males have, this might result in a lower level of sexual behavior such as masturbation in women, or a lower "sex drive."

There are several problems with this logic. First, it may be that cells in the hypothalamus or the genitals of women are more sensitive to testosterone than the comparable cells in men; thus a little testosterone may go a long way in women's bodies (Sherfey, 1966). Second, we must be cautious about making inferences to human males and females from studies done on animals. Although some recent studies demonstrate the effects of testosterone on sexual interest and behavior in human males, the effects are less consistent and more complex than in other species (Chapter 9).

Cultural Factors

Our culture has traditionally placed tighter restrictions on women's sexuality than it has on men's, and vestiges of these restrictions linger today. It seems likely that these restrictions have acted as a damper on female sexuality, and thus they may help to explain why some women do not masturbate and why they are wary about casual sex.

Double standard: The evaluation of male behavior and female behavior according to different standards; used specifically to refer to holding more conservative, restrictive attitudes toward female sexuality.

One of the clearest examples of the differences in restrictions on male and female sexuality is the **double standard.** The double standard says, essentially, that the same sexual behavior is evaluated differently, depending on whether a male or a female engages in it. An example is premarital sex. Traditionally in our culture, premarital sex has been more acceptable for males than for females. Indeed, premarital sexual activity might be a status symbol for a male but a sign of cheapness for a female.

These different standards have been reflected in behavior. For example, the Kinsey data, collected in the 1940s, indicated that over twice as many males (71 percent) as females (33 percent) had had premarital sex. Apparently, society's message got through to young women of that era. Most of them managed to keep themselves chaste before marriage, while their male contemporaries tended to get the experience that was expected of them.

Generally there seems to be less of a double standard today than there was in former times. For example, as the data in Chapter 11 indicate, people now approve of premarital sex for females about as much as they do for males. In Hunt's sample, 82 percent of the men felt that premarital sex was acceptable for males when the couple are in love, and 77 percent felt that it was acceptable for females under the same circumstances (Hunt, 1974). Interestingly, the females in the sample seemed to believe in a double standard more than the males did.

This change in attitudes is reflected in behavior. A much higher percentage of women report having engaged in premarital sex now than in Kinsey's time. In one sample, 80 percent of the males and 63 percent of the females had had premarital sex (Robinson et al., 1991). Thus there is much less of a difference between males and females now than there was a generation ago; the vast majority of both males and females are now engaging in premarital sex. Premarital sex still remains somewhat more common among males, though.

The decline of the double standard may help to explain why some of the gender differences found in older studies of sex behavior have disappeared in more recent studies. When cultural forces do not make such a distinction between male and female, males and females become more similar in their sexual behavior.

Gender roles are another cultural force that may contribute to differences in male and female sexuality, as was discussed earlier in this chapter. Gender roles dictate proper behavior for females and males in sexual interactions—that is, they specify the script. For example, there is a stereotype of the male as the initiator and the female as the passive object of his advances; surely this does not encourage the woman to take active steps to bring about her own orgasms. As a result of such stereotypes, the male has borne the whole weight of responsibility, both for his response and for the woman's response, and women have not been encouraged to take responsibility for producing their own pleasure.

Marital and family roles may play a part. When children are born, they can act as a damper on the parents' sexual relationship. The couple lose their privacy when they gain children. They may worry about their children bursting through an unlocked door and witnessing the "primal scene." Or they may be concerned that their children will hear the sounds of lovemaking. Generally, though, the woman is assigned the primary responsibility for child rearing, and so she may be more aware of the presence of the children in the house and more concerned about possible harmful effects on them of witnessing their parents engaging in sex. Once again, her worry and anxiety do not contribute to her having a satisfying sexual experience.

A related point is that a couple typically have sex in their own home or apartment; at least for the traditional homemaker, this is her place of work. Her homemaking responsibilities may then intrude into her sexual expression. For example, one hears of men complaining that their wives leap up in the middle of lovemaking to go and turn off the oven because they think the roast is overcooking. This understandably hurts a man's feelings, and it cannot be doing a thing to help the woman have an orgasm. The woman whose ear is cocked to hear whether a baby is crying or whose nose is sniffing to smell whether dinner is burning is not the woman who has an orgasm.

Other Factors

A number of other factors, not easily classified as biological or cultural, may also contribute to differences between male and female sexuality.[3]

Women get pregnant and men do not. Particularly in the days before highly effective contraceptives were available, pregnancy might be a highly undesirable consequence of sexuality for a woman. Thinking that an episode of lovemaking might result in a nine-month pregnancy and another mouth to feed could put a damper on anyone's sexuality. As the data in Figure 14.3 show, even today pregnancy fears can be a force (Rubenstein, 1983). For example, in one well-sampled study, 71 percent of sexually active 15- to 19-year-old girls used contraceptives not at all or inconsistently (Zelnik & Kantner, 1977). A woman who is worried about whether she will become pregnant—and, if she is not married, about whether others will find out that she has been engaging in sexual activity—is not in a state conducive to the enjoyment of sex, much less the experience of orgasm (although this scarcely explains why women do not masturbate).

Ineffective techniques of stimulating the woman may also be a factor. Kinsey found, for example, that women could masturbate to orgasm about as quickly as

---

[3] Other possible causes of orgasm problems in women are discussed in Chapter 19.

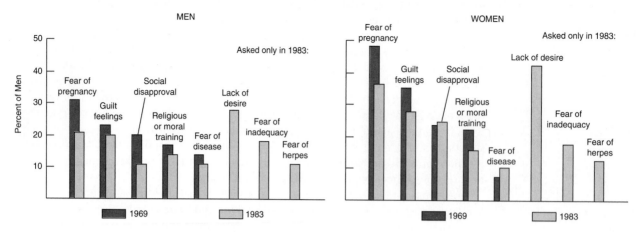

FIGURE 14.3

In 1969 and again in 1983 Psychology Today *surveyed its readers on the topic of love. These are the responses of men and women to the question, "What has prevented you from freely expressing your sexuality?" Notice that women are more likely to report being affected by fear of pregnancy, guilt feelings, and social disapproval.*

men could. This suggests that it is no harder for women to orgasm than it is for men, since they do it with about equal ease when they masturbate (and presumably they give themselves about ideal stimulation when they masturbate). The commonest techniques of intercourse, with the penis moving in and out of the vagina, may provide good stimulation for the male but not the female, since she is not getting sufficient clitoral stimulation. Perhaps the problem, then, is that women are expected to orgasm as a result of intercourse, when that is not a very effective technique for producing orgasms in women.

There may also be a relationship between the data on women not masturbating and gender differences in other aspects of sexuality. Childhood and adolescent experiences with masturbation are important early sources of learning about sexuality. Through these experiences we learn how our bodies respond to sexual stimulation and what the most effective techniques for stimulating our own bodies are. This learning is important to our experience of adult, two-person sex. For example, Kinsey's data suggested that women who masturbate to orgasm before marriage are more likely to orgasm in intercourse with their husbands;[4] 31 percent of the women who had never masturbated to orgasm before marriage had not had an orgasm by the end of their first year of marriage, while only 13 to 16 percent of the women who had masturbated had not had orgasms in their first year of marriage (Kinsey et al., 1953, p. 407). One woman spoke of how she discovered masturbation late and how this may be related to her orgasm capacity in heterosexual sex:

> I thought I was frigid, even after three years of marriage, until I read this book and learned how to turn myself on. After I gave myself my first orgasm, I cried for half an hour, I was so relieved. Afterwards, I did it a lot, for many months,

---

[4] Note that this is in direct contradiction to the old-fashioned advice given in manuals that suggested that "getting hooked" on masturbation might impair later marital sexuality; if anything, just the reverse is true.

and I talked to my doctor and to my husband, and finally I began to make it in intercourse. (Hunt, 1974, pp. 96–97)

Not only may women's relative inexperience with masturbation lead to a lack of sexual learning, but it also may create a kind of "erotic dependency" on men. Typically, boys' earliest sexual experiences are with masturbation, which they learn how to do from other boys. More important, they learn that they can produce their own sexual pleasure. Girls typically have their earliest sexual experiences in heterosexual petting. They therefore learn about sex from boys, and they learn that their sexual pleasure is produced by the male. As sex researcher John Gagnon commented:

> Young women may know of masturbation, but not know *how* to masturbate—how to produce pleasure, or even what the pleasures of orgasm might be. . . . Some young women report that they learned how to masturbate after they had orgasm from intercourse and petting, and decided they could do it for themselves. (1977, p. 152)

And Betty Dodson, in her book *Liberating Masturbation,* says:

> Masturbation is the way we discover our eroticism, the way we learn to respond sexually, the way we learn to love ourselves and build self-esteem. Sex is like any other skill—it has to be learned and practiced. When a woman masturbates, she learns to like her own genitals, to enjoy sex and orgasm, and furthermore, to become a proficient and independent about it. (1974, cited in Gagnon, 1977, p. 161)

Once again, these ideas might lead to a recommendation that girls be given information about masturbation.

Numerous factors that may contribute to shaping male and female sexuality have been discussed. My own feeling is that a combination of several of these factors produces the differences that do exist. I think that the early differences in experiences with masturbation are very important. Although these differences may result from differences in anatomy, they could be eliminated by giving girls information on masturbation. Women may enter into adult sexual relationships with a lack of experience in the bodily sensations of arousal and orgasm, and they may also be unaware of the best techniques for stimulating their own bodies. Put this lack of experience together with various cultural forces, such as the double standard and ineffective techniques of stimulation, and it is not too surprising that there are some gender differences in sexuality.

BEYOND THE YOUNG ADULTS

One of the problems with our understanding of gender differences in sexuality is that so much of the research has concentrated on college students or other groups of young adults (as is true of much behavioral research). For example, Schmidt and Sigusch used college students in their studies of male-female differences in arousal response to erotic materials, as did Heiman in her research. Using this population may provide a very narrow view of male-female differences; they are considered during only a very small part of the lifespan.

Female sexuality and male sexuality change in their nature and focus across the lifespan. For example, it is a common belief in our culture that men reach their sexual "peak" at around age 19, whereas women do not reach theirs until they are 35 or 40. There is some scientific evidence supporting this view. Kinsey found, for example, that women generally had orgasms more consistently at 40 than they did at 25.

Psychiatrist Helen Singer Kaplan, a specialist in therapy for sexual dysfunctions, has advanced an interesting view of differences between male sexuality and female sexuality across the lifespan (Kaplan & Sager, 1971). According to her analysis, the teenage male's sexuality is very intense and almost exclusively genital focused. As the man approaches age 30, he is still highly interested in sex, but not so urgently. He is also satisfied with fewer orgasms, as opposed to the adolescent male, who may have four to eight orgasms per day through masturbation. With age the man's refractory period becomes longer. By the age of 50, he is typically satisfied with two orgasms a week, and the focus of his sexuality is not so completely genital; sex becomes a more sensuously diffuse experience, and there is a greater emotional component.

In women, the process is often quite different. Their sexual awakening may occur much later; they may, for example, not begin masturbating until age 30 or 35. While they are in their teens and twenties, their orgasmic response is slow and inconsistent. However, by the time they reach their mid-thirties, their sexual response has become quicker and more intense, and they orgasm more consistently than they did during their teens and twenties. They initiate sex more frequently than they did in the past. Also, the greatest incidence of extramarital sex for women occurs among those in their late thirties. Vaginal lubrication takes place almost instantaneously in women in this age group.

Men, then, seem to begin with an intense, genitally focused sexuality and only later develop an appreciation for the sensuous and emotional aspects of sex. Women have an early awareness of the sensuous and emotional aspects of sex and develop the capacity for intense genital response later. To express this in another way, we might use the terminology suggested by Ira Reiss: **person-centered sex** and **body-centered sex**. Adolescent male sexuality is body-centered, and the person-centered aspect is not added until later. Adolescent female sexuality is person-centered, and body-centered sex comes later.

It is important to remember, though, that these patterns may be culturally, rather than biologically, produced. In some other cultures—for example, Mangaia in the South Pacific (see Chapter 1)—females have orgasms 100 percent of the time during coitus, even when they are adolescents.

Person-centered sex: Sexual expression in which the emphasis is on the relationship and emotions between the two people.

Body-centered sex: Sexual expression in which the emphasis is on the body and physical pleasure.

THE FUTURE

The data indicate that major changes in sexual behavior have occurred in the last several decades and that these changes have affected female and male sexuality. Will there by further changes in the future, and if so, what will they be?

Gender Similarities

A review of 22 surveys conducted between 1938 and 1975 indicates that there has been a trend toward gender similarities in the incidence of premarital intercourse (Hopkins, 1977). A survey of West German university students conducted in 1966 and again in 1981 confirms the trend toward gender similarities (Clement et al., 1984). Our review of 177 studies of sexual behavior between the 1960s and the 1980s indicated a trend toward gender similarities in rates of premarital intercourse, number of sexual partners, and attitudes toward premarital sex in a committed relationship (Oliver & Hyde, 1993). That is, male sexual behavior and female sexual behavior are becoming more similar than they were in former times. For example, premarital sex used to be much more common among males than among females, but now it is common among both.

The trend toward gender similarities, though, is not limited to females becoming more like males. Male sexuality is also changing and is showing some tendency to move in the direction of female patterns. For example, as noted earlier, some males now experience problems having orgasm in intercourse (Hunt, 1974). Men are now much less likely to have sex with prostitutes than they were a generation ago (Hunt, 1974).

Although the trend is toward gender similarities in *behavior,* the evidence suggests that substantial gender differences remain in some *attitudes,* and it may be that these differences will not disappear. Females are still considerably more disapproving of casual sex than males are (Oliver & Hyde, 1993). And patterns of sexual behavior are still most related to dominance in men, but to love and affection in women (Keller et al., 1982).

The "New Impotence"?

Some magazines have carried articles on the "new impotence." The idea is that with the rise of the women's movement, a sexually liberated, sexually demanding woman has emerged and that some men feel so threatened by this situation that they have become impotent. To give some data supporting this view, some psychotherapists and sex therapists feel that they are seeing a sharp rise in the number of men seeking help for problems of impotence (Ginsberg et al., 1972).

Does the sexual liberation of women create impotence in men? There really are not any good scientific data on either side of this arguent, and so I will simply offer my own opinion. I think that the apparent rise in cases of impotence is largely illusory. There have probably always been numerous cases of impotence; they appear to be more frequent now because of all the publicity given to sex therapy. Men probably now feel that it is more socially acceptable to admit they are having a problem and to seek therapy for it. Thus I doubt that more men are now impotent; there are simply more of them who are willing to ask for help with the problem. Masters and Johnson (1970) reported that they treated many cases of impotence during the 1960s and felt that sexual dysfunctions were quite common, and this was before the women's movement was really rolling. I agree with Masters and Johnson, who feel that men stand to gain much from the women's movement (1974).

Greater Sex Drive in Women?

Masters and Johnson, among others, have speculated that women actually have an innately stronger sex drive than men have, in direct opposition to the stereotype that women's sex drive is weaker (Masters & Johnson, 1966; see also Sherfey, 1966). As evidence, they cite the insatiable sex drive of female chimpanzees in estrus. A female chimpanzee, when in estrus, "presents" herself to one male after the next, perhaps copulating with a dozen in an hour. She appears to be nearly insatiable. Could it be that human females, who are capable of having sex at any phase in their cycle, are continuously insatiable? Another piece of evidence that is cited is the capacity of women to have multiple orgasms. Unlike men, who enter into a refractory period following orgasm, women may have one orgasm after another, which might suggest a greater, not a smaller, sexual capacity than men's. The argument then goes that in prehistoric, primitive human societies, the powerful sex drive of women created havoc—not to mention making the men feel insecure—and therefore societies instituted restrictions on female sexuality to bring it more in line with male sexuality; that explains the restrictions on female sexuality that persist to the present day. Since

Male Sexuality

Bernie Zilbergeld wrote *Male Sexuality,* published in 1978, on the basis of his experience as a sex therapist and psychotherapist. The book was much respected and had a large readership over more than a decade. In 1992 Zilbergeld wrote an updated version, *The New Male Sexuality,* to reflect trends in the 1990s.

He argues that the media have taught us a Fantasy Model of Sex, which is ultimately detrimental to men, and to women as well. He captures this idea in his chapter title, "It's Two Feet Long, Hard as Steel, Always Ready, and Will Knock Your Socks Off," describing the Fantasy Model of the erect penis and its power over women. The Fantasy Model of Sex creates unrealistic expectations and performance pressures on men.

Zilbergeld discusses a number of cultural myths based on the Fantasy Model. Here are some of them.

Myth 1. We're liberated folks who are very comfortable with sex. The media of the 1990s teach us that we have completely shed our Victorian heritage and everyone is totally comfortable with sex. The men and women in the movies and on TV never have any concerns or problems with sex. The women don't worry about their ability to have orgasms. The men don't worry about the size or hardness of their penis. But if all of that is true, why do we have such poor sex education in the United States? Why do parents have such difficulty talking about sex with their children? The truth is that, although public manifestations (like the movies) are very open about sex, in our private lives we have all kinds of discomforts and uncertainties about sex.

Myth 2. A real man isn't into sissy stuff like feelings and communicating. Boys are trained into the male role, which discourages the expression of emotions such as tenderness. Communicating about personal feelings becomes difficult if not impossible.

As one man said, "What it really comes down to is that I guess I'm not very comfortable with expressing my emotions—I don't think many men are—but I am pretty comfortable with sex, so I just sort of let sex speak for me" (Zilbergeld, 1992, p. 45). Men are crippled in forming emotional relationships, as a result, and sexual interactions are less than they might be if there were more communication.

Myth 3. All touching is sexual or should lead to sex. For men, touching is a means to an end: sex. For women, touch more often is a goal in itself, as when women hug each other. Men need to learn that sometimes they just need to be held or stroked, and that that can provide more emotional satisfaction than sexual intercourse.

Myth 6. Sex is centered on a hard penis and what's done with it. Adolescent boys have a fixation on their penis and its erections, and this fascination remains throughout life. This creates heavy performance pressure for an erection, and not just any old erection, but a really big one. As Zilbergeld puts it, "Penises in fantasyland come in only three sizes: large, extra large, and so big you can't get through the door." Men need to learn that the penis is not the only sexual part of their bodies, and that many very enjoyable forms of sexual behavior require no erection at all. That relieves a lot of performance pressure.

Zilbergeld's books are not based on a survey or laboratory research, but rather on his experiences as a sex therapist. That, of course, may bias his views insofar as he sees people having problems and seeking therapy. But his observations are tremendously insightful, and many people not seeking therapy have benefited from his books.

Sources: Bernie Zilbergeld. (1978). *Male sexuality.* New York: Bantam Books. Bernie Zilbergeld. (1992). *The new male sexuality.* New York: Bantam Books.

there are really no scientific data on this point, the whole idea is purely speculative, though intriguing. Perhaps, as restrictions on female sexuality lessen, future generations will regard women as having the greater sex drive.

ANDROGYNY

Androgyny: A combination of both masculine and feminine characteristics in an individual.

Androgyny[5] refers to a combination of both feminine and masculine traits in an individual. Thus if a person is androgynous, he or she possesses both masculine and feminine characteristics.

The traditional research on gender roles and masculinity-femininity was based on the assumption that all (or at least most) males are masculine and that all (or most) females are feminine; it was also assumed that females are not masculine and that males are not feminine. Further, it was assumed that the more masculine a person was, the less feminine that person would be, and vice versa. That is, if a woman learned how to repair cars, for example, that would make her more masculine and therefore less feminine. Similarly, if a man took up cooking, that made him more feminine and therefore decreased his masculinity.

But human beings are not that simple. Many men have a lot of masculine qualities but also "feminine" interests and talents as well, and many women possess both feminine traits and masculine traits. As the psychologist Walter Mischel has expressed it:

> When we observe a woman who seems hostile and fiercely independent some of the time but passive, dependent, and feminine on other occasions, our reducing valve usually makes us choose between the two syndromes. We decide that one pattern is in the service of the other, or that both are in the service of a third motive. She must be a really castrating lady with a facade of passivity—or perhaps she is a warm, passive-dependent woman with a surface defense of aggressiveness. But perhaps nature is bigger than our concepts and it is possible for the lady to be a hostile, fiercely independent, passive, dependent, feminine, aggressive, warm, castrating person all-in-one. Of course which of these she is at any particular moment would not be random and capricious—it would depend on who she is with, when, how, and much, much more. But each of these aspects of her self may be a quite genuine and real aspect of her total being. (1969, p. 1015)

Once this complexity is acknowledged, we can go beyond the simple idea that people can be filed into one of two categories: masculine or feminine. We can then recognize that there are at least four kinds of individuals: those who are very masculine (and they will not necessarily all be males), those who are very feminine (and they will not necessarily all be females), those who are really neither very masculine nor very feminine, and those who are both masculine and feminine, the last group being the androgynous people.

Psychologist Sandra Bem has done some important research that provides information on androgyny and androgynous people. The first step in her work was the construction of the Bem Sex Role Inventory, or BSRI (Bem, 1974), a paper-and-pencil test that measures a person's degree of androgyny. The BSRI contains 20 "masculine" items (for example, "aggressive," "ambitious," "willing to take risks") and 20 "feminine" items (for example, "affectionate," "loves children," "yielding"), as well as 20 "neutral" items (for example, "happy"). Items were included in the

---

[5] From the Greek roots *andro*, meaning "man" (as in "androgens"), and *gyn*, meaning "woman" (as in "gynecologist").

FIGURE 14.4
*Is androgyny the trend for
the future?*

masculine list on the basis of the criterion that in a preliminary study, subjects rated them as being significantly more desirable for males than for females in American society. A parallel criterion was used for the feminine items. To take the BSRI, subjects indicate, for each item on a seven-point scale, the extent to which the item characterizes them. Each person then gets both a masculinity score (average score on the masculine items) and a femininity score (average score on the feminine items). A person is considered androgynous if she or he has both a high masculinity score and a high femininity score. Bem finds that about one-third of the subjects in her college samples are androgynous.

Armed with the BSRI and its ability to detect androgynous people, Bem proceeded to see how androgynous people compare with strongly gender-typed people. She began with the assumption that gender roles constrict people and keep them from enjoying and doing well at certain kinds of activities, namely, activities supposedly reserved for the other gender. She believes that androgynous people are more liberated and do not allow gender roles to stifle their behavior. She tested these assumptions in several studies. For example, in one study subjects were under pressure to conform in their judgments on how funny some jokes were (Bem, 1975). Those who refused to conform would be showing the "masculine" trait of independence. As predicted, masculine subjects and androgynous subjects of both sexes showed significantly more independence than feminine subjects, who were more likely to conform. In another study, subjects listened to a student who poured out a list of troubles in adjusting to college life (Bem et al., 1976). The subjects were scored for their responsiveness to, and sympathy toward, the talker; this was a measure of their nurturance, nurturance being a "feminine" characteristic. As predicted, feminine subjects and androgynous subjects of both sexes were significantly more nurturant to the troubled student than the masculine subjects were.

These two studies, taken together, suggest that androgynous people have the flexibility to exhibit either masculine or feminine behaviors, depending on what the situation calls for; they can be independent when pressured to conform, and they can be nurturant to an unhappy person. On the other hand, the highly masculine person may do well in a situation that requires masculine behavior but may not do so well when feminine behavior is required; similarly, feminine people do well in situations that require feminine behavior but may not be able to function when masculine behavior is necessary. The results then serve to question the traditional assumption that very masculine men and very feminine women are well adjusted (Taylor & Hall, 1982). Instead, the results suggest that those who are androgynous, and thus transcend gender roles, are better able to function effectively in a wider range of situations.

What implications does androgyny have for sexual behavior? The ways in which gender roles might limit our abilities to respond sexually were discussed in a previous section. Androgyny may represent a new vision not only of personality but also of sexuality. Because androgynous people have both masculine and feminine behaviors in their bag of tricks, they should be more flexible and comfortable in their sexuality. For example, an androgynous person, whether male or female, should feel comfortable initiating sex but should also feel comfortable when the other person initiates sex. An androgynous person should be happy with a position in intercourse in which he or she is on top, as well as with a position in which she or he is on the bottom. An androgynous person would enjoy both the physical aspects of sex and the emotional aspects. Perhaps this androgyne, who integrates both masculinity and femininity, represents the vision of a truly liberated sexuality.

Is there any evidence that these speculations are true? Several studies have looked at the relation between gender-typing (whether one is androgynous or traditionally gender-typed) and sexual attitudes and behaviors. Three studies show positive results for androgynous people. In one, the results indicated that androgynous women have orgasms more frequently than feminine women (Radlove, 1983). In another study, androgynous women reported more sexual satisfaction than feminine women did (Kimlicka et al., 1983). And in the third study, androgynous subjects (both male and female) were less likely to stereotype the sexual behavior of others (Garcia, 1982). In yet another study, androgynous females were more comfortable with sex than feminine females, and androgynous males were more comfortable with sex than masculine males, just as Bem would predict (Walfish & Myerson, 1980). However, males were considerably more comfortable than females, so that masculine males were still more comfortable with sex than androgynous females were.

On the other hand, some studies on androgyny and sexuality do not produce the predicted results (Allgeier & Fogel, 1978). Some show the flexibility and benefits to sexuality Bem would predict, yet others show no difference between androgynous subjects and traditionally gender-typed subjects. Probably we should not set our expectations for androgyny too high. It will not be the cure to all of the sexual woes of our society. But it might help. And it may be that androgyny and changing gender roles will make their impact last in the area of sexuality, where we are most vulnerable, or where the rewards of relinquishing traditional behaviors are not obvious (Allgeier, 1981).

TRANSSEXUALISM

Many texts include transsexualism in the chapter on sexual variations or deviations. However, I have included it in the chapter on gender because it is fundamentally a problem of gender, and more specifically, a problem of gender identity.

A **transsexual** is a person who believes that he or she is trapped in the body of the other gender. This condition is also known as **gender dysphoria**, meaning unhappiness or dissatisfaction with one's gender. Transsexuals are the candidates for the sex-change operations that have received so much publicity, beginning with the case of Christine Jorgenson. The term "transsexual" is used to refer to the person both before and after the operation. There are, of course, two kinds of transsexuals: those with male bodies who think they are females (called **male-to-female transsexuals**) and those with female bodies who think they are males (called *female-to-male transsexuals*). Male-to-female transsexuals have been more likely to seek help at clinics and have more often been given sex-reassignment surgery (Abramowitz, 1986), in part because the surgery required in such cases is easier. Accordingly, most of the discussion that follows will focus on male-to-female transsexuals.[6]

Keeping in mind the distinction between sex and gender, it is important to note that transsexualism is a problem not of sexual behavior but of gender and gender identity. That is, the transsexual is preoccupied not with some special kind of sexual behavior but rather with wanting to be a female when her body is male. Sex, of course, is involved insofar as being sexually attracted to a member of the opposite gender (which is expected in our society) is concerned. But I also know of one transsexual who has never engaged in any sexual activity beyond kissing since she had surgery to make her a female. She is delighted with the results of the surgery and loves being a woman, but she is not particularly interested in sex.

References to transsexuals are found in much of recorded history, although of course they are not referred to by that modern, scientific term (Green, 1966). Philo, the Jewish philosopher of Alexandria, described them as follows: "Expending every possible care on their outward adornment, they are not ashamed even to employ every device to change artificially their nature as men into women. . . . Some of them . . . craving a complete transformation into women . . . have amputated their generative members." The American Indians had an institutionalized role for men who dressed as women and performed the functions assigned to women. Transsexualism is therefore by no means a phenomenon of modern, industrialized cultures.

Psychologically the transsexual is, to put it mildly, in an extreme conflict situation (Levine et al., 1976). The body says, "I'm a man," but the mind says, "I'm a woman." The person may understandably react with fright and confusion. Believing herself truly to be a female, she may try desperate means to change her body accordingly. Particularly in the days before the sex-change operation was performed, or among people who were unaware of it, self-castrations have been reported. The woman I mentioned above ate large quantities of women's face cream containing estrogens to try to bring about the desired changes in her body.

The Sex-Change Operation

Gender reassignment is rather complex and proceeds in several stages (Roberto, 1983). The first step in the process is very careful counseling and psychiatric evaluation. It is important to establish that the person is a true transsexual, that is, someone whose gender identity does not match her body type. Some people mistakenly seek gender reassignment; for example, a man who is simply poorly adjusted, unhappy, and not very successful might think that things would go better for him if he were a woman. Sometimes schizophrenics display such confused gender identity

[6] Because this kind of transsexual thinks of himself as a female, he prefers to be called "she," and to simplify matter in this discussion, "she" will be used to refer to the transsexual. Otherwise, figuring out which pronoun to use would be extremely difficult.

that they might be mistaken for transsexuals. It is important to establish that the person is a true transsexual before going ahead with a procedure that is fairly drastic.

The next step is hormone therapy. The male-to-female transsexual is given estrogen and must remain on it for the rest of her life. The estrogen gradually produces some feminization. The breasts enlarge. The pattern of fat deposits becomes feminine; in particular, the hips become rounded. Balding, if it has begun, stops. Secretions by the prostate diminish, and eventually there is no ejaculate. Erections become less and less frequent, a phenomenon with which the transsexual is pleased, since they were an unpleasant reminder of the unwanted penis. The female-to-male transsexual is given androgens, which bring about a gradual masculinization. A beard may then develop, to varying degrees. The voice deepens. The pattern of fat deposits becomes more masculine. The clitoris enlarges, although not nearly to the size of a penis, and becomes more erectile. The pelvic bone structure, of course, cannot be reshaped, and breasts do not disappear except with surgery.

Next comes the "real life test," which is the requirement that the person live as a member of the new gender for a period of one or two years. This is done to ensure that the person will be able to adjust to the role of the new gender; once again, the idea is to be as certain as possible that the person will not regret having had the operation. Some transsexuals, even before consulting a physician, spontaneously enter this "transvestite" stage in their efforts to become women. Problems may arise, though. Cross-dressing is illegal in many cities, and they may be arrested.

The final step is the surgery itself (transsexuals refer to it simply as "the operation"). For the male-to-female transsexual, the penis and testes are removed, but without severing the sensory nerves of the penis. The external genitalia are then reconstructed to look as much as possible like a woman's (see Figure 14.5). Next, an artificial vagina—a pouch 15 to 20 centimeters (6 to 8 inches) deep—is constructed. It is lined with the skin of the penis so that it will have sensory nerve endings that can respond to sexual stimulation. For about six months afterward, the vagina must be dilated with a plastic device so that it does not reclose. Other cosmetic surgery may also be done, such as reducing the size of the Adam's apple.

The female-to-male change is more complex and generally less successful. A penis and scrotum are constructed from tissues in the genital area (see Figure 14.6). The penis, unfortunately, does not have erectile capacity; in some cases a rigid silicone

FIGURE 14.5
The genitals following
male-to-female transsexual
surgery.

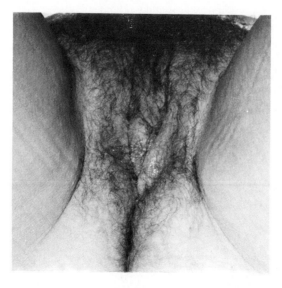

FIGURE 14.6
Female-to-male transsexual surgery. (a) A penile shaft is made from abdominal skin and fat and is skin-grafted. The labia majora are incised and closed over the clitoris to form a "scrotum." (b) Two months later the penile shaft is ready for detachment from the abdomen. A fan of abdominal skin has been partially released and resutured in preparation for final release and construction of the penile head. (c) The release is now complete and the penile head constructed from the smooth abdominal skin. Note the "urethral dimple" in the tip of the head: This is not functional, as the patient must still sit to urinate. Silicone testicles have been inserted into the "scrotum." Also a temporary silicone rod has been inserted down the hollow center of the penile shaft to allow this patient to "have an erection." This rod is removed most of the time and is used only for intercourse.

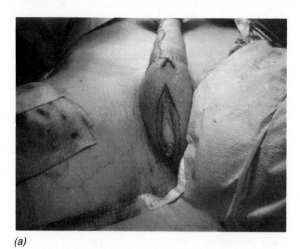

(a)

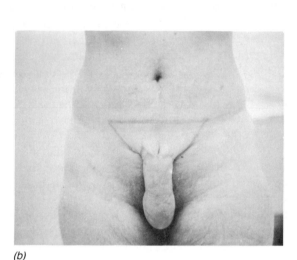

(b)

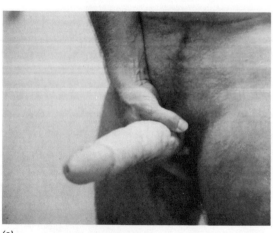

(c)

tube is implanted in the penis so that it can be inserted into a vagina, making coitus possible. Some female-to-male transsexuals choose not to have genital surgery and just go through breast removal and possibly hysterectomy.

What Causes Transsexualism?

Scientists have not found a definite cause of transsexualism. One speculation is that it might be due to some prenatal exposure to hormones of the wrong gender, causing improper brain differentiation. There is no direct evidence supporting this idea, though, and so it must remain speculative at present.

Two studies have investigated hormone levels in transsexuals before gender reassignment, one in male-to-female transsexuals and the other in female-to-male transsexuals (J. R. Jones, 1972; Migeon et al., 1968). In both studies the hormone levels were found to be within the normal range for the individuals' "original" gender (not the gender to which they wanted to be reassigned), suggesting that transsexualism does not result from a hormonal imbalance.

One idea for which there is some supporting evidence is that transsexualism results from early learning experiences. In one sample of 17 male-to-female transsexuals, all had had their gender treated inappropriately or ambiguously from infancy to puberty by their parent or parents (J. P. Driscoll, 1971; see also Green, 1975). Though they had the bodies of boys, they had been given girls' toys or had been dressed in girls' clothing. Feminine behavior, such as putting on the mother's high heels when guests were present, had been rewarded as "cute." When the interviewer asked whether they had been reared as boys or girls, one responded, "I was raised as a girl by my mother and aunts. My sex was discovered by a school nurse when I was six." It seems likely that such early learning experiences would be critical in giving the child a gender identity that is incongruent with her body. On the other hand, there are transsexuals who had no such learning experiences; thus learning theory does not seem adequate to explain every case.

By the time these transsexuals were of school age, they hated gym class and were labeled "freaks" by their peers. Not surprisingly, problems of adjustment arose. In adulthood, transsexuals often have trouble holding steady jobs, at least in part because they are so preoccupied with their gender problem.

Male-to-female transsexuals account for the great majority of cases, outnumbering female-to-male transsexuals by a ratio of 3:1 (Abramowitz, 1986; Green, 1975). Several explanations for this lopsided ratio have been offered. Perhaps male prenatal development is more complex and error-prone, or perhaps the problem is that preschool boys spend so much more time with their mothers than with their fathers.

Other Issues

Bucchal smear: A test of genetic sex, in which a small scraping of cells is taken from the inside of the mouth, stained, and examined under a microscope.

Barr body: A small, black dot appearing in the cells of genetic females; it represents an inactivated X chromosome.

The phenomenon of transsexualism raises a number of interesting psychological, legal, and ethical questions for our contemporary society.

One case that attracted attention is that of Dr. Renée Richards, formerly Richard Raskind, a physician who had her gender reassigned to that of a woman. When she was a man, she was a successful tennis player. In 1976 she attempted to enter a women's tennis tournament. The women players protested that she was not a woman, and she protested that she was. Officials subsequently decided to use the **bucchal smear** test for gender, which is also the one used in the Olympics. In this test a sample of cells is scraped from the inside of the mouth and is stained. If the sex chromosomes are XX, a **Barr body** should be present and will show up under the stain; if the chromosomes are XY, the Barr body should be absent. The test is

FIGURE 14.7
*Transsexual Renee
Richards before the sex-
change operation (left) as
tennis player Richard
Raskind and following
transsexual surgery (right)
as a female tennis player.*

therefore one of genetic gender. Dr. Richards protested that this was not the appropriate test to be used on her. Psychologically she is a female, she has female genitals, and she functions socially as a female, and she feels that these are the appropriate criteria. She does, though, have a male pelvic bone structure and other bone structures that are masculine, and these may have important consequences for athletic performance. The issue will require some time to settle. But the important question it raises is: What should the criteria be for determining a person's gender? Should it be chromosomal gender (XX or XY) as tested by the bucchal smear? Should it be the gender indicated by the external genitals? Should it be psychological gender identity?

Another question that might be raised concerns religious groups that do not permit women to become members of the clergy. Is a male-to-female transsexual, for example, qualified to be a priest before "the operation" but not after? Is the female-to-male transsexual qualified to be a priest by virtue of having had a sex-change operation?

Another problem arises in classifying the sexual behavior of the transsexual. For example, many male-to-female transsexuals prefer to engage in sex with men, even before gender reassignment. Is that sexual behavior homosexual (it is between two men), or is it heterosexual (because one of them thinks she is a woman)? Or is the behavior homosexual before surgery and heterosexual after surgery?

The transsexual also encounters a number of practical problems following gender reassignment. Official records, such as the social security card, must be changed to show not only the new name but also the new gender. Sometimes a new birth certificate is issued and the old one is sealed away. However, when the person reaches retirement age, it is not clear whether she should receive social security benefits beginning at age 62, the proper age for females, or age 65, the age for males. If the person was married before the sex change, often—though not always—the spouse must be divorced. Changing one's gender is, to say the least, a complicated process.

Transsexuals should be able to give us, through their own personal accounts, new insights into the nature of sex and gender. For example, most of us have wondered, at some time, how members of the other gender feel during sexual intercourse. The transsexual is in a unique position for giving us information on this question.

Criticisms of Sex-Change Surgery

A number of criticisms of sex-change surgery for transsexuals have been raised. One of these comes from a study by Johns Hopkins researcher Jon Meyer (1979). He did a follow-up study of the adjustment of 50 transsexuals, 29 of whom received surgery and 21 of whom did not. His conclusion, much publicized, was that there were no significant differences in the adjustment of the two groups. If that is the case, then transsexual surgery is unnecessary and should not be done.

Then criticisms of Meyer's study appeared (e.g., Fleming et al., 1980). Meyer's adjustment scale was somewhat peculiar and involved debatable values. After the Meyer study and also criticisms of it, some clinics ceased doing transsexual surgery, but most continue to do it. Almost surely we will see more attempts in the future to treat transsexualism with psychotherapy rather than surgery, but these methods remain to be worked out (see, e.g., Barlow et al., 1978). Unfortunately, attempts to use psychotherapy, such as psychoanalysis, as an alternative to surgery have generally been unsuccessful (Roberto, 1983). That is, trying to change the gender identity to match the anatomy—rather than the reverse as in the sex-change operation—does not seem to work very well. In contrast, adjustment of transsexuals has been shown to be significantly better following surgery (Fleming et al., 1981; Blanchard et al., 1983; Green & Fleming, 1990). Experts have concluded that approximately two-thirds of those who have sex reassignment surgery are improved by it in terms of adjustment indicators such as reduction in depression (Abramowitz, 1986). On the other hand, about 7 percent of the cases result in tragic outcomes such as suicide or a request for a reversal (Abramowitz, 1986).

In another vein, Janice Raymond offered a feminist ethical critique in her book *The Transsexual Empire: The Making of the She-Male* (1979). She argues that transsexualism itself is the product of a gender-role-stereotyped society. If we did not have two strictly defined roles, it would not be necessary for people to attempt drastic steps such as surgery to move from one to the other. They would simply behave as they pleased. It is ironic, as she notes, that at a time when gender-role stereotypes and their restrictiveness are being questioned by society, the transsexual movement goes in the opposite direction, defining gender in anatomical terms and assuming that roles should be sharply divided. Finally, Raymond questions the ethics involved in the enormous medical empire (some call it a $10 million per year growth industry) that has grown up around transsexual surgery. She raises the issues of unnecessary surgery and mutilation of the body.

One interesting empirical study bears on Raymond's critique. The Bem Sex Role Inventory, which measures androgyny, was administered to 72 self-defined transsexuals, all presurgery (Fleming et al., 1980). The results indicated that the female-to-male transsexuals had a gender-role pattern nearly identical to that of male college students—35 percent were masculine and 35 percent were androgynous. Male-to-female transsexuals showed a higher percentage of feminine people (60 percent) than college women do, but 22 percent still fell into the androgynous category. These results question Raymond's (and others') assumption that the transsexual is an overly gender-typed person—there are many who are androgynous. The results reaffirm the notion that transsexualism is an issue of gender identity, not of stereotyped role behaviors.

Nonetheless, Raymond's points about values and ethics involved in transsexualism and surgery for it are worth considering.

Summary

A gender role is a set of norms, or culturally defined expectations, that specify how people of one gender ought to behave. There are four components to gender stereotypes: personality traits, role behaviors, occupations, and physical appearance. Children are socialized into gender roles first by parents and later by other forces such as peers and the media. Stereotypes about females include warmth and expressiveness; for males, the stereotype focuses on competency. Heterosexuality is a key component of gender roles.

Gender roles are not uniform in the United States. They vary according to ethnic group and other factors. African American women, for example, have traditionally played an important economic role in their families. Among Hispanics, gender roles tend to be more rigidly defined than they are among Anglos. The sexuality of Asian Americans has been stereoptyped, with Asian American men seen as being sexless and Asian American women viewed as exotic sex toys. Some American Indian tribes traditionally had egalitarian gender roles compared with white culture.

Psychological gender differences have been documented in aggressiveness and communication styles.

The two largest male-female differences in sexuality are in the incidence of masturbation (males having the higher incidence) and attitudes toward casual sex (females being more disapproving). Heiman's study of arousal to erotic materials illustrates how males and females are in some ways similar and in some ways different in their responses.

Three sets of factors have been proposed to explain gender differences in sexuality: biological factors (anatomy, hormones); cultural factors (gender roles, the double standard); and other factors (fear of pregnancy, differences in masturbation patterns creating other gender differences).

Most research on gender and sexuality has been done with college-age samples. There is reason to believe that patterns of gender differences in sexuality change in middle age and beyond.

There is evidence of a trend toward gender similarities in some behaviors (e.g., incidence of premarital sex) and some attitudes (e.g., premarital sex in a committed relationship). However, a large gender gap remains in some others attitudes (e.g., attitudes about casual sex).

Research on androgyny (the combination of both masculine and feminine characteristics in one individual) suggests that it may provide a good alternative to being simply masculine or simply feminine. It also may permit a liberation in sexuality, although the evidence on this point is mixed.

Transsexuals—people who seek sex-reassignment surgery—represent an interesting variation in which gender identity does not match anatomy. Generally, their adjustment is good following the sex-change operation.

Review Questions

1. A _____ is a set of norms or culturally defined expectations that define how people of one gender ought to behave.

2. Traditionally, psychologists believed that gender roles were stressful to people, but in the 1970s and 1980s, psychologists shifted to viewing gender-role conformity as good for psychological adjustment. True or false?

3. _____ is the term for a combination of both feminine and masculine traits in an individual.

4. _____ is the term for a person who feels trapped in a body of the wrong gender.

5. Gender stereotypes vary according to ethnic group in the United States. For example, Asian American men have been stereotyped as asexual and Asian American women have been stereotyped as exotic sex objects. True or false?

6. The data indicate that the largest gender differences in sexuality are in _____ and _____.

7. According to Kinsey, _____ percent of males and _____ percent of females masturbate to orgasm at least once in their lives.

8. The _____ is a device that measures physiological sexual arousal in the male.

9. The alternative term for transsexualism is _____ .

10. Zilbergeld uses the phrase "It's two feet long, hard as steel, always ready, and will knock your socks off" to describe the ideal penis according to the Fantasy Model of Sex. True or false?

Questions for Thought, Discussion, and Debate

1. Do you think that transsexual surgery is the appropriate treatment for transsexuals? Why or why not?

2. Recalling from your childhood, do you think you were socialized in a stereotyped masculine or feminine way? What impact do you think those socialization experiences have had on your current sexual attitudes and behaviors?

3. Get a group of men and women together. Then separate them into subgroups, one composed entirely of men and the other of women. Instruct each group to write a list of questions they have always wanted to ask a member of the other gender. Then have the groups come together and ask and answer the questions for each other.

4. Do you think there is still a double standard for male and female sexuality today? Why?

Suggestions for Further Reading

Hyde, Janet S. (1991). *Half the human experience: The psychology of women.* (4th ed.). Lexington, MA: Heath. I am not in a very good position to give an objective appraisal of this book, but for what it's worth, I think it is an interesting, comprehensive summary of what is known about the psychology of women and gender roles.

Morris, Jan. (1974). *Conundrum.* New York: New American Library. A fascinating first-person account of the transsexual experience.

Kelley, Kathryn (Ed.). (1987). *Females, males, and sexuality: Theories and research.* Albany, NY: State University of New York Press. This collection of chapters presents current scholarship on many approaches to male and female sexuality, including hormonal influences, feminist perspectives, and sexual scripts.

Zilbergeld, Bernie. (1992). *The new male sexuality.* New York: Bantam Books. Zilbergeld's original *Male sexuality* was a great success, and this new version, updated for the 1990s, is every bit as insightful.

Sexual Orientation: Gay, Straight, or Bi?

Chapter Highlights

I. Stereotypes and Discrimination
   Attitudes Toward Homosexuality
   Stereotypes About Gays
   Gays as a Minority Group

II. Lesbian and Gay Lifestyles
   Coming Out
   Gay Relationships

III. How Many People Are Gay, Straight, or Bi?

IV. Sexual Orientation: Implications for Adjustment
   Sin and the Medical Model
   Research Results
   Can Sexual Orientation Be Changed by Psychotherapy?

V. Why Do People Become Homosexual or Heterosexual?
   Biological Theories
   Psychoanalytic Theory
   Learning Theory
   Interactionist Theory
   Sociological Theory
   Empirical Data

VI. Ethnicity and Sexual Orientation

VII. Bisexuality

The Western social norm proscribes homosexual activity and prescribes only heterosexual (fantasy and) intercourse, depending upon one's class, ethnic group, social situation, and historical period. However much individuals conform to this norm it is not universally valid. . . . In Melanesia, our Western norm does not apply; males who engage in ritual homosexual activities are not "homosexuals," nor have they ever heard the concept "gay." *

In June 1969, in response to police harassment, homosexuals rioted in a bar in Greenwich Village, in perhaps the first open group rebellion of homosexuals in history. Gay liberation was born. Since then, the public has been forced into an awareness of an issue—sexual orientation—that it had previously preferred to ignore. Gay liberationists proclaim that gay is good. Meanwhile, many Americans charitably maintain that homosexuals are sick (but can be cured).

Most of us want to know more about sexual orientation. The purpose of this chapter is to try to provide a better understanding of people's sexual orientations, whether homosexual, heterosexual, or bisexual, as well as an understanding of homophobia.

Sexual orientation is defined by whom we are sexually attracted to and also have the potential for loving. Thus a homosexual is a person whose sexual orientation is toward members of her or his own gender, a heterosexual is a person whose sexual orientation is toward members of the other gender, and a bisexual is a person whose sexual orientation is toward both genders. The word homosexual is derived from the Greek root *homo*, meaning "same" (not the Latin word *homo*, meaning "man"). The term "homosexual" may be applied in a general way to homosexuals of both genders or specifically to male homosexuals. The term lesbian, which is used to refer to female homosexuals, can be traced to the great Greek poet Sappho, who lived on the island of Lesbos (hence "lesbian") around 600 B.C. She is famous for

Sexual orientation: A person's erotic and emotional orientation toward members of his or her own gender or members of the other gender.

Homosexual: A person whose sexual orientation is toward members of the same gender.

Lesbian: A woman whose sexual orientation is toward other women.

* *Source:* Gilbert H. Herdt. (1984). *Ritualized Homosexuality in Melanesia*, pp. ix–x. Berkeley: University of California Press.

the love poetry that she wrote to other women. Sappho was actually married, apparently happily, and had one daughter, but her lesbian feelings were the focus of her life.

Several other terms are also used in conjunction with homosexuality. Gay activists prefer the term **gay** to "homosexual" because the latter emphasizes the sexual aspects of the lifestyle and can be used as a derogatory label, since there are so many negative connotations to homosexuality.[1] A heterosexual is then referred to as **straight.** Currently, the term "gay" is generally used for male homosexuals, and "lesbian" for female homosexuals. There are, of course, a number of derogatory slang terms for gays and lesbians, such as "queer," "fairy," "dyke," and "faggot" or "fag."

STEREOTYPES AND DISCRIMINATION

Your sexual orientation has implications for the attitudes people have toward you. First, there is the belief that all people are heterosexual, that heterosexuality is the norm. Further, just as there are stereotypes about other minority groups—for example, the stereotype that all blacks are stupid and lazy—so there are stereotypes about homosexuals. In this section we will examine some of these stereotyped ideas and attitudes and compare them with the scientific data.

Attitudes Toward Homosexuality

Most Americans disapprove of homosexuality. For example, as Table 15.1 shows, in a well-sampled 1991 survey of adult Americans, 71 percent expressed the opinion that sexual relations between two adults of the same sex are always wrong. In addition, 40 percent believe that a homosexual man should not be allowed to teach in a college or university. In a sample of university students, 30 percent said that homosexuality is always wrong (Leitenberg & Slavin, 1983).

Has the gay liberation movement succeeded in changing the negative attitudes of Americans? Apparently not. Table 15.1 shows that the percentage of people who believe that homosexual behavior is always wrong remained essentially unchanged from 1973 to 1991.

Some experts believe that many Americans' attitudes toward homosexuals can best be described as homophobic (Fyfe, 1983; Hudson & Ricketts, 1980). **Homophobia** may be defined as a strong, irrational fear of homosexuals and, more generally, as fixed negative attitudes and reactions to homosexuals (Fyfe, 1983). Some scholars dislike the term "homophobia" because, although certainly some people have antigay feelings so strong that they could be called a phobia, what is more common is negative attitudes and prejudiced behaviors. Therefore, some prefer the term **antigay prejudice.**

The most extreme expressions of antigay prejudice occur in *hate crimes* against lesbians and gays, as in the following case:

Gay: Homosexual; especially male homosexuals.

Straight: Heterosexual; that is, a person whose sexual orientation is toward members of the opposite gender.

Homophobia: A strong, irrational fear of homosexuals; negative attitudes and reactions to homosexuals.

Antigay prejudice: Negative attitudes and behaviors toward gays and lesbians.

---

[1] It is wise to have a good vocabulary on topics such as this. My husband had an aunt, a single lady, who frequently invited a pair of single young men who lived across the hall from her to her parties. The men were fairly open about their homosexuality. Aunt Mary, while an otherwise sophisticated person, was unaware of the usage of the term "gay." Greeting them at her parties, she typically complimented them on their appearance by saying, in a loud voice, "My, how gay you look."

Table 15.1
Attitudes of Adult Americans Toward Homosexuality, 1973 and 1991

Question and Responses	1973	1991
1. Are sexual relations between adults of the same sex:		
Always wrong	74	71
Almost always wrong	7	4
Wrong only sometimes	8	4
Not wrong at all	11	15
2. Should an admitted homosexual man be allowed to teach in a college or university?		
Yes	49	57
No	51	40

Percentage of Sample

Source: J. A. Davis and T. Smith. (1991). *General Social Surveys, 1972–1991: Cumulative data.* Storrs, CT: University of Connecticut, Roper Center for Public Opinion Research.

> Late one night in July, Heidi Dorow was embracing another woman on the corner of Bleecker and Carmine Streets in the West Village [of New York], when a teen-ager began to taunt them. As they shoved past him, Ms. Dorow said, "He swung around and punched me in the head."
>
> The youth and 10 other teen-agers then jumped on the women, felling them with their fists and kicking them as they lay on the pavement.
>
> Dazed and bleeding, Ms. Dorow and her friend staggered down the street in search of a cab, passing a man who shouted obscenities at them.
>
> At a nearby hospital, both women were treated for cuts and bruises, and Ms. Dorow's friend for a concussion, and released. Then the women, who are lesbians, went to the Sixth Precinct . . . to file a report. As they were leaving, someone on the street shouted more obscenities at them. (Hays, 1990)

In 1990, Congress passed the Hate Crimes Statistics Act in which gays and lesbians were included with ethnic minority persons as having a special status necessitating legal protection from hate-motivated crimes (Morin & Rothblum, 1991). Although this may seem like cold comfort to a person who has already been the victim of such a crime, it is a step in the direction of providing some legal protection.

In a thought-provoking illustration of the psychological impact of society's attitudes toward homosexuality on the gay person, the authors of a psychology text ask the reader to imagine that being anxious is as taboo as being gay:

> Imagine for a moment that you are an anxious person and that being anxious is against the law. You must try to hide your fears from others. Your own home may be a safe place to feel anxious, but a public display of apprehension can lead to arrest or at least to social ostracism. At work one day an associate looks at you suspiciously and says, "That's funny, for a crazy moment there I thought you were anxious." "Heck no," you exclaim a bit too loudly, "*not me.*" You begin to wonder if your fellow worker will report his suspicions to your boss. If he does, your boss may inform the police or will at least change your job to one that requires less contact with customers, especially with those who have children. (Davison and Neale, 1974, p. 293)

But we should also recognize the other side of the coin. As we can see from the statistics in Table 15.1, some Americans are tolerant of or supportive of homosexuals. For example, more than half of Americans approve of an overt homosexual teaching in a college or university. Thus Americans are a strange mixture of bigots and supporters on the issue of homosexuality. As one woman said,

> I really don't feel that I've ever been oppressed as a lesbian or suffered any abuse. I've been careful who I've told, but those people have been really accepting. (Jay and Young, 1979, p. 716)

Stereotypes About Gays

In addition to negative attitudes, many Americans have stereotyped ideas about gays and lesbians.

The Swish and the Dyke

One such stereotype is that all male homosexuals are effeminate; they are supposed to be limp-wristed, have a swishy walk, and talk with a lisp. The corresponding stereotype about the lesbian is that she is masculine; she has short hair and wears a man-tailored suit. Because people have these stereotyped ideas, they believe that it is easy to spot homosexuals and that it is always obvious who is a gay and who is a straight. In fact, these stereotypes are far from the truth, and people's abilities to spot gays and lesbians are not nearly so good as they think they are. In contrast to stereotypes, a study of male university athletes found that 40 percent of them had engaged in homosexual behavior to orgasm in the past two years (Garner & Smith, 1977). Most gay people look and behave just like everybody else. Except for a small percentage of cases, it is impossible to tell a gay person simply by appearance and mannerisms. Kinsey estimated that only about 15 percent of male homosexuals could be identified by their appearance. This is particularly true now because recent fashions in clothing have been stolen in part from gays: women now wear pants frequently. Mustaches are in style for male gays, as they are for male straights.

The belief that gay men are feminine and that lesbians are masculine represents a confusion of two important concepts: *gender identity* (sense of maleness or femaleness) and *sexual orientation* (heterosexual or homosexual). The gay person differs from the majority in who the erotic and emotional partner is, but the gay person does not typically differ from the majority in gender identity (Storms, 1980). That is, the gay man chooses a partner of the same gender, but his identity is quite definitely masculine. He thinks of himself as male and has no desire to be a female. The same holds true for the lesbian; although her erotic and emotional orientation is toward other women, she is quite definitely a woman and typically has no desire to be a man (Wolff, 1971). (Interestingly, this confusion of the concepts of sexual orientation and gender identity also occurs in some of the scientific theories to be discussed later in this chapter.)

The Role-Playing Stereotype

Another common stereotype is that in their relationships, lesbians and gays role-play heterosexual roles: that in a pair of gay men, one will assume the dominant role and the other the submissive role, and that in a lesbian couple, one will play the male role ("butch") and the other the female role ("femme"). In the sexual act itself, some people believe that the inserter is playing the active (or masculine) role, while the

(a)

(b)

FIGURE 15.1
*(a) Harvey Milk, a gay activist, was an elected member of San Francisco's Board of
Supervisors in 1978, representing a district including many gays. Milk fought for gay rights
throughout the state of California and was supported by San Francisco's mayor, George
Moscone. On November 17, 1978, Dan White, himself a former supervisor, entered City
Hall and fired shots that killed both Milk and Moscone. White confessed within hours. In
May 1979, a jury declined to convict White of first-degree murder, instead finding him
guilty of voluntary manslaughter, a lesser offense carrying a reduced jail sentence. The gay
community, as well as many sympathetic supporters, were shocked and furious. A protest
march and the White Night Riot ensued. The entire incident symbolizes the ambivalent
progress achieved by gay liberation: a gay liberationist can be elected to an important public
office, but he is then murdered. (b) Victims and killer—San Francisco Mayor George
Moscone (center), Milk (left), Dan White (right). White was a former city police officer,
firefighter, and city supervisor. In 1986 White was released from prison and later
committed suicide.*

insertee is playing the passive (or feminine) role. While such role playing does occur to some extent, in fact it is far from typical.

In regard to sexual practices, most gays engage in all forms of behavior and do not restrict themselves to one or another role. One study of a group of gay men (Hooker, 1965) found that 46 percent practiced all forms of sexual activity and varied their roles (inserter or insertee), depending on the preference of the partner, a wish for variety, and so on. Only 20 percent of the sample showed a distinct preference for given activities and for a particular role. Homosexual partners often switch roles during the sex act or engage in mutual oral-genital stimulation, further calling into question the notion that one plays the male role and one the female role.

In regard to role playing outside the sexual act itself, the practice seems to be far from typical (Peplau, 1981). In *The Gay Report* sample, 56 percent of the lesbian respondents had never played such roles, and an additional 23 percent had done so only infrequently (Jay & Young, 1979). The comparable statistics for the gay men were 47 percent and 23 percent. Thus only a minority of gays and lesbians engage in role playing with any substantial frequency.

The Child-Molester Stereotype

Another stereotyped belief is that gay men are child molesters. If an elementary school teacher or a high school teacher is discovered to be homosexual, there is an instant public outcry demanding that he be fired, based on the belief that he will try to seduce all the boys in the school. Strangely, the same people who worry about this never seem to worry that heterosexual male teachers will try to seduce young girls, although that seems to be just as logical a possibility. Actually, most child molesting is done by heterosexual men and involves little girls; 80 percent of child molesting is in that category, and only 20 percent is homosexual (McCaghy, 1971). According to *The Gay Report,* 93 percent of gay men have never had sex with someone 12 or under. The comparable statistic for lesbians is 98 percent (Jay & Young, 1979). Further, most adolescents are initiated into homosexual activity not by an adult but rather by another teenager (Sorensen, 1973). Therefore, there is no reason to assume that a given gay man is a child molester. (See Chapter 17 for a more complete discussion of child molestation.)

The "All-Gays-Have-AIDS" Stereotype

With media attention focused almost obsessively on AIDS, the spotlight has turned on gays, but not in a flattering manner. In the United States, gay men have been identified as the largest group of people having AIDS. Certainly it is true that gay men have borne a large share of the burden of the AIDS epidemic in America. On the other hand, growth in the spread of AIDS is currently fastest among heterosexuals. And AIDS is virtually unknown among lesbians. (Cases of female-to-female sexual transmission have only rarely been reported; Marmor et al., 1986; Monzon et al., 1987.)

Gays as a Minority Group

From the foregoing, it is clear that gay people are the subject of many stereotypes, just as other minorities are. They also have several other things in common with members of other minority groups. First, they suffer from job discrimination. Just as blacks and women have been denied access to certain jobs, so too have homosexuals. Homosexuality is grounds for a dishonorable discharge from the armed forces and there are many cases in which this rule has been applied, a fact that became an issue when President Bill Clinton took office in 1993. Homosexuality has also been grounds for firing a person from federal employment and for denial of a security clearance. The reason commonly given for the latter two rules is that homosexuals are susceptible to being blackmailed and therefore cannot be put in situations in which they have access to sensitive information. Actually, many heterosexuals might also be susceptible to blackmail because of their sexual activities—for example, the married man who is having an affair—although such factors are not grounds for denial of security clearance. In fact, in one sample 90 percent of lesbians and 86 percent of male homosexuals had never been the object of blackmail or threats of blackmail (Jay & Young, 1979). In addition, as homosexuals become more open, they will be less subject to blackmail.

In a spirit of reform in the 1980s, a number of states and cities passed laws prohibiting discrimination on the basis of sexual orientation. For example, in the state of Wisconsin it is illegal to discriminate against gays and lesbians in matters such as employment and housing. Massachusetts and Hawaii have similar laws.

There is an important way in which homosexuals differ from other minorities, though. In the case of most other minorities, appearance is a fairly good indicator of minority-group status. It is easy to recognize an African American or a woman, for example, but one cannot tell simply by looking at a person what his or her sexual orientation is. Thus homosexuals, unlike other minorities, can hide their status. There are certain advantages to this. It makes it fairly easy to get along in the heterosexual world—to "pass." However, it has the advantage of encouraging the person to live a lie and to deny her or his true identity; not only is this dishonest, but it may also be psychologically stressful.

Lest the picture seem bleak, it should also be noted that there are some advantages to being lesbian or gay. For example, lesbians claim that other women are better lovers; many men, they say, have a shaky knowledge of female anatomy and an even shakier knowledge of how to stimulate it. The female knows her own body and how to stimulate it best. Indeed, it has been reported that lesbians have greater orgasm consistency than heterosexual women (Kinsey et al., 1953). The same is true of gay men. Masters and Johnson (1979) held the opinion that lesbians and gays are better at lovemaking than straights.

LESBIAN AND GAY LIFESTYLES

Covert homosexual: A homosexual who is "in the closet," who keeps his or her sexual orientation a secret.

Overt homosexual: A homosexual who is "out of the closet," who is open about his or her sexual orientation.

In understanding lesbian and gay lifestyles, it is important to recognize that there is a wide variety of gay experiences. One of the most important aspects of this variability is whether the person is covert (in the closet) or overt (out of the closet) about his or her homosexuality. The covert homosexual may be heterosexually married, have children, and be a respected professional in the community, spending only a few hours a month engaging in secret same-gender sexual behavior. The overt homosexual, on the other hand, may live almost entirely within a homosexual community, particularly if he or she lives in a large city like New York or San Francisco where there is a large gay subculture, and may have relatively few contacts with heterosexuals. There are also various degrees of overtness (being "out") and covertness. Many lesbians and gays are out with trusted friends but not with casual acquaintances. The lifestyle of gay men differs considerably from that of lesbians, probably as a result of the different roles assigned to males and females in our society and the different ways that males and females are reared. In addition, there is more discrimination against gay men than there is against lesbians. For example, it is considered quite natural for two women to share an apartment, but if two men do so, eyebrows are raised.

Table 15.2
Some Slang Terms from the Gay Subculture

Term	Meaning
In the closet	Keeping one's homosexuality hidden, not being open or public
Coming out	Coming out of the closet, or becoming open about one's homosexuality
Queen	An effeminate gay man
Nellie	An effeminate gay man
Closet queen	A homosexual who is covert or in the closet
Drag queen	A gay man who dresses in women's clothing ("drag")
Butch	A masculine gay man or a masculine lesbian woman
Dyke	A masculine lesbian
Femme	A feminine lesbian
Trick	A casual sexual partner
Cruising	Looking for a sexual partner
Tearoom	A public rest room where gay men engage in casual sex

The lifestyles of gays are thus far from uniform. They vary according to whether one is male or female and overt or covert about the homosexuality and also according to social class, occupation, personality, and a variety of other factors.

Coming Out

As I noted earlier, there are significant variations in the gay experience depending on whether or not one is out of the closet. Being in the closet has some real disadvantages. One lesbian commented,

> I hate being in the closet. It's so boring having people ask if I have a boyfriend. I feel like putting the most horrified look possible on my face, and as if I'm deeply insulted exclaim, "I beg your pardon? I certainly hope not!" If I were sure of a job and safe living conditions, everyone would be fully informed that I am gay. I am seriously contemplating getting a T-shirt with "Support Gay Liberation" inscribed on it. (Jay & Young, 1979, p. 75)

Coming out: The process of acknowledging to oneself, and then to others, that one is gay or lesbian.

The process of coming out of the closet, or **coming out**, involves acknowledging to oneself, and then to others, that one is gay or lesbian (Coleman, 1982). The person is psychologically vulnerable during this stage. Whether the person experiences acceptance or rejection from friends and others to whom he or she comes out can be critical to self-esteem.

Following the period of coming out, there is a stage of exploration, in which the person experiments with the new sexual identity; the person makes contact with the lesbian and gay community and practices new interpersonal skills. Following the stage of exploration, there is typically a stage of forming first relationships. These relationships are often short-lived and characterized by jealousy and turbulence, much like many heterosexual dating relationships. Finally, there is the integration stage, in which the person becomes a fully functioning member of society and is capable of maintaining a long-term, committed relationship (Coleman, 1982).

Of course, before the coming out process can occur, the person must have arrived at a homosexual identity. This identity development seems to proceed in six stages (Cass, 1979):

1. *Identity confusion* The person most likely began assuming a heterosexual identity because heterosexuality is so normative in our society. As same-gender attractions or behaviors occur, there is confusion. Who am I?

2. *Identity comparison*   The person now thinks "I *may* be homosexual." There may be feelings of alienation because the comfortable heterosexual identity has been lost.

3. *Identity tolerance*   At this stage the person thinks "I probably am homosexual." The person now seeks out homosexuals and makes contact with the gay subculture, hoping for affirmation. The quality of these initial contacts is critical.

4. *Identity acceptance*   The person now can say "I am homosexual," and accepts rather than tolerates this identity.

5. *Identity pride*   The person dichotomizes the world into homosexuals (who are good and important people) and heterosexuals (who are not). There is a strong identification with the gay group, and an increased coming out of the closet.

6. *Identity synthesis*   The person no longer holds an "us versus them" view of homosexuals and heterosexuals, recognizing that there are some good and supportive heterosexuals. In this final stage, the person is able to synthesize public and private sexual identities.

Gay Relationships

Social scientists used to spend their time trying to figure out how many people are gay, or whether homosexuals are mentally ill or not. Today there is a recognition that gays and lesbians do form relationships—often long-term, committed ones—and current reearch focuses on understanding the nature of gay relationships.

When you hear the term "couple," what do you think of? Most likely a heterosexual married couple, or perhaps a heterosexual dating couple. Sociologists Philip Blumstein and Pepper Schwartz (1983) took an innovative approach in their major study, *American Couples*. They defined "couples" to include heterosexual married couples, heterosexual cohabiting couples, gay male couples, and lesbian couples. They found that many of the characteristics and problems of gay couples are similar to those of heterosexual couples. For example, the frequency of sex declines when the couple have been in the relationship for more than 10 years; this occurs for gay male couples, lesbian couples, and heterosexual married couples. For gay and lesbian couples, there are sometimes problems involved in who initiates sex, just as there are for straight couples. Among heterosexual couples, it is typically the man who initiates; among gay couples, the more emotionally expressive partner is the one who initiates sex.

In their relationships, lesbians attach great importance to emotional expressiveness, as do heterosexual women (Peplau & Amaro, 1982). For example, "being able to talk about my most intimate feelings" is rated as highly important by lesbians. Lesbians also tend to place a high value on equality in their relationships. In research on satisfaction in relationships, the most satisfying lesbian relationships are those in which the partners are equally committed, they are equally "in love," and there is equality of power between the two (Peplau, Padesky, & Hamilton, 1982).

In regard to satisfaction in relationships, comparisons of matched samples of lesbians, gay men, and heterosexuals indicate that lesbians and gay men rate their relationships as highly satisfying. There are no significant differences among lesbians, gay men, and heterosexuals in their satisfaction in the relationship, or in the love they feel for the partner (Peplau & Amaro, 1982). Thus, the research makes it clear—contrary to stereotypes that homosexuals specialize in promiscuous sex and one-night stands—that gay men and lesbians do form satisfying long-term relationships.

A major contribution to this new research on gay relationships is a study of male couples done by psychiatrist David McWhirter and psychologist Andrew Mat-

15.1

A Gay Couple: Tom and Brian

Tom and Brian have been living together as lovers for three years. Tom is 29, and Brian is 22; they live in a medium-sized midwestern city.

Tom grew up in a Roman Catholic family and attended parochial schools. His father was killed in an automobile accident when Tom was 4 days old. His mother remarried when he was 8 years old; although he gets along well with his stepfather, he feels that he has never had a real father. When asked why he thought he was gay, he said he felt it was because of the absence of a father in his early years.

After graduating from high school, Tom joined the army and served in Vietnam and Germany. His first sexual experience was with a Japanese prostitute. Though he enjoyed the physical aspects of sex with her, he felt that something was missing emotionally. When he was 23, after returning to the United States, he had his first homosexual experience with someone he met at a bar.

Tom had sex with about 20 different men before meeting Brian, including one with whom he had a long-term relationship. He is currently a student at a technical college and is working toward a career in electronics.

Brian also grew up in a Roman Catholic family and attended parochial schools. He has always gotten along well with both his parents and his four siblings, and he recalls his childhood as being uneventful. He realized he was gay when he was in his early teens, but he chose to ignore his feelings and instead tried to conform to what society expected of him. He had a girfriend when he was in high school. After he graduated from high school, he took a job; he had his first homosexual experience when he was 18 with a man he met at work. He currently works as a salesperson at Penney's. He had sex with eight different men before meeting Tom. He has never had intercourse with a woman.

Brian and Tom have not discussed their sexual orientation directly with their families. Both think their parents may have some vague ideas, but the parents apparently prefer not to have to confront the situation directly and instead prefer to think of their sons as just being "roommates." Both Brian and Tom wish they could be more honest about their gayness with their parents. However, they also do not want to hurt them, and so they have not pressed the matter.

Their relationship with each other is exclusive; that is, they have an agreement that they will be faithful to each other and that neither will have sex with anyone else. Both of them said they would feel hurt if they found out that the other had been seeing someone else on the sly. They both consider casual sex unfulfilling and want to have a real relationship with their sexual partner.

Household chores are allocated depending on who has the time and inclination to do them. Both like to cook, and so they share that duty about equally, as they do the laundry. Tom is good at carpentry, and therefore he tends to do things of that sort.

Tom and Brian feel that the greatest problem in their relationship is lack of communication, which sometimes creates misunderstandings and arguments. Brian feels that the greatest joy in their relationship is the security of knowing that they love each other and can count on each other. Tom agrees, and he also says that it is important to him to know that there is someone who really cares about him and loves him.

Source: Based on an interview conducted by the author.

FIGURE 15.2
*(a) A gay male couple. (b)
A lesbian couple in a long-
term relationship.*

(a)

(b)

tison (1984). They interviewed 312 gay men in 156 couples. On the average, the couples had been together 8.9 years; in fact, 8 of the couples had been together for 30 or more years, another striking contradiction to the stereotype that gay men are incapable of forming long-term relationships. Mattison and McWhirter came to the conclusion that gay couples pass through six identifiable stages as their relationship progresses through the years.

Stage 1, Blending, occurs in the first year they are together. This stage, according to Mattison and McWhirter, is characterized by merging, limerance, equalizing of the partnership, and a high level of sexual activity. In merging, the two separate men are joining together to form a couple. "Limerance" refers to the sense that one is falling in love, romantically and passionately. The men also work to equalize the relationship. Gender-role socialization in our culture ensures that men are brought up to be providers; when two men form a couple, they must work out new models, in which they share and equalize the work of providing.

Stage 2, Nesting, occurs in the second and third years of the relationship. It is characterized by homemaking, finding compatibility, a decline of limerance, and ambivalence. Stage 2 begins with a desire to make a home for the two of them together, to fix things up, to feather the nest. As one participant in the study said, "After a while I really wanted *our* home. You know, a place we were proud of, where we could have friends and family. We had a lot of fun fixing it up together" (1984, p. 41). This stage is also characterized by a decline of limerance, the passion and romance of the first stage. Because limerance declines, there are new efforts to find compatibility in the relationship; differences and flaws in the partner were ignored in the passion of Stage 1, but they can no longer be covered up in Stage 2, and so compatibility becomes an issue. As one man commented on this stage,

> It was real gradual, like I would feel aggravated which I had never felt before when he changed the TV channel, or I'd want to be alone in the bedroom and he'd follow me in, or suddenly I couldn't stand the noise he made chewing his food. I just wasn't floating on air as often as before. I got real scared thinking I was falling out of love. (1984, p. 52).

Because there is continued attraction to the partner, but also a recognition of flaws and problems, this stage is characterized by ambivalence, or mixed feelings.

Stage 3, Maintaining, occurs in the fourth and fifth years and is a time of the reappearance of the individual, taking risks, dealing with conflict, and establishing traditions. In contrast to the first two stages, where the emphasis was on oneness and togetherness, individuality and independence become important in the third stage, as the partners discover that too much togetherness can lead to stagnation. Because the relationship is longer and more stable than it was, the partners are willing to take risks, perhaps confessing dissatisfactions that they had covered up before. Couples in this stage evolve their own characteristic ways of dealing with conflicts in the relationship, such as compromise or establishing some fixed roles for each. The couple also begin establishing traditions—such as customs at holidays or birthdays—that enrich the relationship and increase the sense that it is permanent.

Stage 4, Building, occurs in the sixth through the tenth year of the relationship. It is characterized by collaborating, increasing productivity, establishing independence, and developing a sense of the dependability of the partners. In collaborating the couple work together, whether they finish each other's sentences because they know the other's thoughts so well, or open a business together. Because the relationship is now stable it is a source of strength for the individuals, and they are increasingly productive; the productivity may be in going back to school to get a new degree or in starting a new hobby like gardening. The sense of stability and dependability in the relationship also allows more independence for both.

Stage 5, Releasing, occurs from the eleventh through the twentieth year of the relationship. Its characteristics are trusting, merging of money and possessions, constricting, and taking each other for granted. Although there has always been trust in the relationship, it is greater and more salient now. Possessions and money are merged, and the couple no longer worry about who is paying for what or whether they are paying equally for the groceries; it is "our" money. There is often some constriction at this time, perhaps involving less of a social life for the couple, or one or both members going through a mid-life crisis. The partners also tend to take each other for granted.

Stage 6, Renewing, occurs after the couple have passed 20 years in the relationship, and it is characterized by achieving security, shifting perspectives, restoring the partnership, and remembering. Couples who move on to this stage and restore the partnership must take some active steps to move beyond the tendency to take each other for granted that occurred in Stage 5. As one respondent said,

> I almost lost him after his heart attack, and somehow we learned. We learned to take better care of ourselves, and we remembered to take better care of each other. I say "I love you" every night before we go to sleep now. And I mean it. We had stopped that ten years ago. It seemed like kid stuff, I suppose. But, I'll tell you, it's good medicine. (McWhirter & Mattison, 1984, p. 110)

Couples in this stage typically feel a sense of security, both in their relationships and in financial terms. Having pooled two male incomes and having had no dependents for 20 or more years, they are likely to have accumulated a good deal of money. Couples in this stage are also storytellers, remembering the many good times they have had together.

Because McWhirter and Mattison interviewed only gay male couples, they claim their stage theory only for that population. But it may well be that heterosexual couples and lesbian couples go through the same stages as their relationships progress. Only much more long-term research on relationships will be able to test those possibilities. Yet the thing that strikes me about all the research on gay relationships is how similar they are—in their satisfactions, loves, joys, and conflicts—to heterosexual relationships.

The Bars

Gay bar: A cocktail lounge catering to lesbians or gay men.

Gay bars are one aspect of the gay social life. These are cocktail lounges that cater exclusively to gays. Drinking, perhaps dancing, socializing, and the possibility of finding a sexual partner or a lover are the important elements. Some gay bars look just like any other bar from the outside, while others may have names—for example, The Open Closet—that indicate to the alert who the clientele is. Bars are typically gender-segregated—that is, they are for either gay men or lesbians—although a few are mixed. There are far more bars for gay men than for lesbian women. Typically, the atmosphere is different in the two, the male bars being more for finding sexual partners and the female bars more for talking and socializing. Lest the reader be unduly shocked at the none-too-subtle nature of pickup bars, it is well to remember that there are many bars—singles' bars—that serve precisely the same purpose for heterosexuals.

The Baths

Baths: Clubs for gay men that offer an opportunity for casual sex.

For some men, another feature of the gay lifestyle is the baths (or "steam baths" or "tubs"). The baths are clubs with many rooms in them, generally including a swimming pool or a whirlpool, as well as rooms for dancing, watching television, and socializing; most areas are dimly lit. On entering, the man rents a locker or a room, where he leaves his clothes; then he proceeds with a towel wrapped around his waist. When a sexual partner has been found, they go to one of a number of small rooms, furnished with beds, where they can engage in sexual activity. The baths feature impersonal sex, since a partner can be found and the act completed without the two even exchanging names, much less making any form of emotional commitment.

The majority of gay bathhouses closed during the 1980s because of AIDS. Public health officials believed that the baths encourage risky sex practices. Gay men

FIGURE 15.3
A "leather bar" on
Christopher Street in
New York.

simply are not interested in casual sex as much as they were before AIDS, and so a decline in business also helped to close many gay baths.

The Tearoom Trade

Tearoom trade: Impersonal sex in public places such as rest rooms.

A related aspect of the gay lifestyle is the "tearoom trade." This phenomenon was studied by sociologist Laud Humphreys and is reported in a book entitled *Tearoom Trade: Impersonal Sex in Public Places* (see Focus 15.2 on the ethics of sex research). As the title of the book implies, the "tearoom trade" refers to impersonal sexual acts in places like public rest rooms. Typically the man enters the rest room and conveys to another man who is already there an interest in having sex. He may do this by making certain signals while urinating or by making tapping sounds while in one of the stalls, for example. The sexual act is generally performed in a stall and may be accomplished without a single word being exchanged. The activity is typically fellatio, which can be done rapidly and with a minimum of encumberance, which is important in case the police or others intrude. The police have been very concerned with eliminating this behavior. There is some justification for their attempts, since the behavior is done in public rather than in private and may therefore be a nuisance to the bystander who happens on the scene. Police efforts to eliminate the phenomenon, though, have met with little success, but the clientele for the tearoom trade has reduced substantially in the AIDS era.

Humphreys's book provoked quite a controversy, not only because of the topic but also because of his findings that many of the men who engaged in this behavior were heterosexually married men, some of them respected leaders in the community. Apparently, the tearoom trade served a need for quick, impersonal sex, and the behavior of choice was homosexual. But the notion that "heterosexual," respectable men could engage in homosexual behavior was shocking to many. Indeed, many gays find the tearoom trade to be shocking. Because so much of the clientele is heterosexual men, one might even question whether the tearoom trade is part of gay culture.

The Ethics of Sex Research: The Tearoom Trade

Sociologist Laud Humphreys's study entitled *Tearoom Trade: Impersonal Sex in Public Places* (1970) is a classic in the field of sexuality. In light of concern on the part of both scientists and the general public about ethical standards in research, however, his methods of data collection appear somewhat questionable. Important issues are raised about the difficulty of doing good sex research within ethical bounds.

In the tearoom-trade situation, a third person generally serves as a "lookout" who watches for the police or other intruders while the other two engage in sex. To obtain his data, Humphreys became a lookout. Not only did he observe the behaviors involved in the tearoom trade, but he also wrote down the license-plate numbers of the participants. He then traced the numbers through government records and thus was able to get the addresses of the persons involved and to obtain census information about the neighborhood in which they lived. He also went to the homes of the people and administered a questionnaire (which included questions on sexual behavior) to them under the pretense of conducting a general survey.

The research provided some important data, particularly on the extent to which these sexual practices are engaged in by "respectable" citizens. Humphreys, of course, maintained the complete anonymity of the subjects in his report of the research. However, the ethical problems are still numerous. Was there invasion of privacy, particularly when Humphreys entered someone's home and obtained personal information under false pretenses? Was there a problem of deceiving subjects, and particularly of not "debriefing" them (explaining the true purpose of the research) afterward? Would the people have consented to being involved with the research had they known its true purpose? Could Humphreys have obtained good data within the bounds of ethics? On the other hand, these clearly negative aspects of the study have to be weighed against the benefits to society from knowing more about this form of sexual behavior.

Source: Laud Humphreys. (1970). *Tearoom trade: Impersonal sex in public places.* Chicago: Aldine.

Gay Liberation

Certainly in the last two decades the gay liberation movement has had a tremendous impact on the gay lifestyle. In particular, it has encouraged homosexuals to be more overt and to feel less guilty about their behavior. Gay liberation meetings and activities provide a social situation in which gay people can meet and discuss important issues rather than simply play games as a prelude to sex, which tends to be the pattern in the bars. Gay political meetings also provide an opportunity to discuss common experiences, thereby producing some consciousness raising. In addition, they provide a political organization that can attempt to bring about legal change, combat police harassment, and fight cases of job discrimination, as well as do public relations work. The National Gay and Lesbian Task Force[2] is the central clearing-house for all these groups; it can provide information on local organizations.

There are thus many places for gays to socialize besides bars, including the Metropolitan Community Church (a gay and lesbian church), gay athletic organizations, and gay political organizations.

Publications

Among other accomplishments, the gay liberation movement has succeeded in founding numerous gay newspapers and magazines. These have many of the same features as other newspapers: forums for political opinions, human-interest stories, and fashion news. In addition, the want-ads sections feature advertisements for sexual partners; similar ads for homosexual and heterosexual partners can be found in underground newspapers in most cities. Probably the best-known gay newspaper is *The Advocate,* published in Los Angeles and circulated throughout the United States. *New York Native* is an important newspaper, as is *The Ladder,* a publication of the Daughters of Bilitis, the largest organization of lesbians. There are also several publications that list all the gay bars and baths by city in the United States, which is handy for the traveler or for those newly arrived on the gay scene.

HOW MANY PEOPLE ARE GAY, STRAIGHT, OR BI?

Most people believe that homosexuality is rare. What percentage of people in the United States are gay or lesbian? As it turns out, the answer to this question is complex. Basically, it depends on how one defines "a homosexual" and "a heterosexual."

One source of information we have on this question is Kinsey's research (see Chapter 3 for an evaluation of the Kinsey data). Kinsey found that about 37 percent of all males had had at least one homosexual experience to orgasm in adulthood. This is a large percentage. Indeed, it was this statistic, combined with some of the findings on premarital sex, that led to the furor over the Kinsey report. The comparable figure for females was 13 percent. However, experts agree that, because of problems with sampling, Kinsey's statistics on homosexuality were probably inflated (e.g., Pomeroy, 1972).

In the last decade, especially in light of the AIDS epidemic, scientists have become increasingly concerned that we don't have more accurate statistics on this question. An important new study appeared in 1989 that attempted to provide better statistics (Fay et al., 1989). The researchers reanalyzed data from a 1970 probability sample of Americans. After applying statistical corrections, the researchers concluded that a minimum of 20 percent of the males had had sexual contact to orgasm with another male at some time in their life. Approximately 7 percent had had such contact in adulthood, and approximately 2 percent had had such contact in the past year. A comparable 1988 survey found essentially the same results (see also Rogers & Turner, 1991; Smith, 1991). The researchers stressed, however, that these should be regarded as minimum estimates because concealment is likely to be a special problem with self-reports of this particular behavior. This same study also found

[2] The National Gay and Lesbian Task Force, 1734 14th Street N.W., Washington, DC 20009; (202) 332-6483. See the Appendix at the end of this book for a list of other organizations dealing with various aspects of sexuality.

that never-married men were more likely than other men to have had same-gender sexual contact within the last year. Interestingly, though, among the men who had had same-gender sexual contact in the last year, approximately half were men who were or had been married. Unfortunately, this study did not report statistics for women.

The major new French survey found roughly the same statistic for men: 1.1 percent reported sexual relations with another man in the past year, compared with 0.3 percent for women (ACSF Investigators, 1992). The same statistic of 1.1 percent for men was found in the major British survey (Johnson et al., 1992). These and other surveys confirm the result that the incidence of homosexuality among men is considerably higher than the incidence among women. Probably twice as many men as women have a homosexual experience to orgasm in adulthood, and the same ratio is probably true for exclusive homosexuality.

After reading these statistics, though, you may still be left wondering how many people are homosexuals. As Kinsey soon realized in trying to answer this question, it depends on how you count. A prevalent notion is that like black and white, homosexual and heterosexual are two quite separate and distinct categories. This is what might be called a *typological conceptualization* (see Figure 15.4). Kinsey made an important scientific breakthrough when he decided to conceptualize homosexuality and heterosexuality not as two separate categories but rather as variations on a continuum (Figure 15.4, section 2). The black and white of heterosexuality and homosexuality have a lot of shades of gray in between: people who have had both some heterosexual and some homosexual experience, in various mixtures. To accommodate all this variety, Kinsey constructed a scale running from 0 (exclusively heterosexual) to 6 (exclusively homosexual), with the midpoint of 3 indicating equal amounts of heterosexual and homosexual experience.

Many sex researchers continue to use Kinsey's scale today, but the question remains, when is a person a homosexual? If you have had one homosexual experience, does that make you a homosexual, or do you have to have had substantial homosexual experience (say, a rating of 2 or 3 or higher)? Or do you have to be exclusively homosexual to be a homosexual? Kinsey dealt with this problem in part by devising the scale, but he also made another important point. He argued that we should not talk about "homosexuality" but rather about "homosexual behavior." "Homosexuality," as we have seen, is exceedingly difficult to define. "Homosexual behavior," on the other hand, can be scientifically defined as a sexual act between two people of the same gender. Therefore, we can talk more precisely about people who have engaged in varying amounts of homosexual behavior or who have had varying amounts of homosexual experience, thus avoiding the problem of deciding exactly when a person is a homosexual, which is difficult, if not impossible, to do.

Other theorists have suggested that Kinsey's one-dimensional scale is too simple (Storms, 1980). The alternative is to form a two-dimensional scheme, much like the two-dimensional scheme for recognizing androgyny as an alternative to masculinity-femininity (discussed in Chapter 14). The idea here is to have one scale for heteroeroticism (the extent of one's arousal to members of the opposite gender), ranging from low to high, and another for homoeroticism (extent of arousal to members of one's own gender), ranging from low to high (see Figure 15.4, section 3). Thus if one is high on both heteroeroticism and homoeroticism, one is a bisexual; the person high on heteroeroticism and low on homoeroticism is heterosexual; the person high on homoeroticism and low on heteroeroticism is homosexual; and finally, the person who is low on both scales is asexual. This scheme allows even more complexity in describing homosexuality and heterosexuality than Kinsey's scale did.

The answer to the original question—How many people are homosexual and how many are heterosexual?—is complex. Probably about 80 percent of men and

1 The typology

(*Heterosexual*)　　　　　　(*Homosexual*)

2 Kinsey's continuum

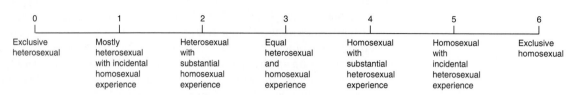

0	1	2	3	4	5	6
Exclusive heterosexual	Mostly heterosexual with incidental homosexual experience	Heterosexual with substantial homosexual experience	Equal heterosexual and homosexual experience	Homosexual with substantial heterosexual experience	Homosexual with incidental heterosexual experience	Exclusive homosexual

3 Two-dimensional scheme (Storms, 1980)

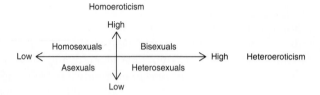

FIGURE 15.4
Three ways of conceptualizing homosexuality and heterosexuality.

90 percent of women are exclusively heterosexual. About 2 percent of men and 1 percent of women are exclusively homosexual. And the remaining group have had varying amounts of both heterosexual and homosexual experience.

One other statistic that is popularly cited for the incidence of homosexuality is 10 percent. In fact, there is a Ten Percent Society, a gay and lesbian organization. This statistic comes from no single study, but rather from an amalgamation of many. It represents those people whose orientation is predominantly homosexual, although they may have had some heterosexual experience. In view of the most recent surveys, the 10 percent figure may be a bit high, but it is probably not too far off.

SEXUAL ORIENTATION: IMPLICATIONS FOR ADJUSTMENT

As I noted earlier, many Americans believe that homosexuality is a kind of mental illness. Is this really true? Do psychologists and psychiatrists agree that homosexuals are poorly adjusted or deviant? Does research on homosexuality confirm the notion that the homosexual is sick? What are the implications of sexual orientation for a person's adjustment?

Sin and the Medical Model

Medical model: A theoretical model in psychology and psychiatry in which mental problems are thought of as sickness or mental illness; the problems in turn are often thought to be due to biological factors.

Actually, the belief that homosexuality is a form of mental illness is something of an improvement over previous beliefs about homosexuality. Before this century, the dominant belief in Europe and the United States was that homosexuality was a sin or a heresy. During the Inquisition, those accused of being heretics were also frequently accused of being homosexuals and were burned at the stake. Indeed, in those times, all mental illness was regarded as a sin. In the twentieth century, this view was replaced by the medical model, in which mental disturbance, and homosexuality in particular, is viewed as a sickness or illness. This view is widely held now by the general public.

Psychiatrist Thomas Szasz and others are critical of the medical model. In his well-known writing on "the myth of mental illness," Szasz argues that the medical model is now obsolete and that we need to develop a more humane and realistic way of dealing with mental disorders and variations from the norm. He has argued the case particularly for homosexuality (Szasz, 1965). Gay activists have joined in, saying that they do not like being called "sick" and that this is just another form of persecution of gays and lesbians.

Research Results

Theoretical and rhetorical approaches to the question are clearly diverse. What do the scientific data say? Once again, the answers provided by the data are complex and depend on the assumption of the particular investigator and the research design used. Basically, three kinds of research designs have been used, representing progressive sophistication and changing assumptions about the nature of homosexuality (see Rosen, 1974).

Clinical Studies

The first, and earliest, approach was clinical; homosexuals who were in psychotherapy were studied by the investigator (usually the therapist). He or she looked for disturbances in their current adjustment or in past experiences or home life. The data were then reported in the form of a case history of a single individual or a report of common factors that seemed to emerge in studying a group of homosexuals (for example, Freud, 1920; see also the review by Rosen, 1974). These clinical studies provided evidence that the homosexual was sick or abnormal; she or he typically was found to be poorly adjusted and neurotic. But the reasoning behind this research was clearly circular. The homosexual was assumed to be mentally ill, and then evidence was found supporting this view.

Studies with Control Groups

The second group of studies made significant improvements over the previous ones by introducing control groups. The question under investigation was rephrased. Rather than "Do homosexuals have psychological disturbances?" (after all, most of us have some problems) it became "Do homosexuals have more psychological disturbances than heterosexuals?" The research design then involved comparing a group of homosexuals in therapy with a group of randomly chosen heterosexuals not in therapy or perhaps with a group of heterosexuals matched with the homosexuals on some variables like age and education. These studies tended to agree with the earlier ones in finding more problems of adjustment among the homosexual group than among the heterosexual group (Rosen, 1974). The homosexuals tended to make more suicide attempts, to be more neurotic, and to have more disturbed family constellations. Once again, though, it became apparent that there were some problems with this research design. It compared a group of people in therapy with a group of people not in therapy and found, not surprisingly, that the people in therapy had more problems. It, too, was circular in assuming that homosexuals were abnormal (in therapy) and that heterosexuals were normal (not in therapy) and then finding exactly that. Of course, the investigator used the homosexuals in therapy as subjects at least in part because they were convenient, but this does not help to make the results any more accurate.

Nonpatient Research

A major breakthrough came with the third group of studies, which involved nonpatient research. In these studies, a group of homosexuals not in therapy (nonpatients) were compared with a group of heterosexuals not in therapy. The nonpatient homosexuals were generally recruited through homophile organizations, advertisements, or word of mouth. The results of these studies are mixed, but the general results seem to indicate that nonpatient homosexuals do not differ from nonpatient heterosexuals in their adjustment (Rosen, 1974). As a psychiatrist who has reviewed the literature on adjustment differences between homosexual and heterosexual women concluded, "The only difference between the lesbian and other women is the choice of love object" (Rosen, 1974; p. 65; see also Seigelman, 1979; and for similar results with male homosexuals, see Evans, 1970; Gagnon & Simon, 1973; Green, 1972).

Bell and Weinberg (1978) found similar results in their study. Lesbians and heterosexual women did not differ on most measures of psychological adjustment. Gay men were somewhat less self-accepting and more lonely, depressed, and tense than straight men. However, Bell and Weinberg's analysis of the variety of types of homosexual experience is helpful in understanding this difference. It is mostly those who are not in a stable, satisfying relationship who are less well off psychologically. Among men, those in long-term, committed relationships cannot be distinguished from heterosexuals on adjustment measures, and they actually scored higher on happiness. It seems clear that homosexuality per se does not cause adjustment difficulties—of more importance may be failure or success at establishing a long-term relationship with a partner.

Psychologist Evelyn Hooker did an important study that sheds considerable light on the question of differences in adjustment between heterosexuals and homosexuals. The assumption that the homosexual is poorly adjusted implies that there are considerable psychological differences between heterosexuals and homosexuals. If this is the case, such differences should be indicated on standard personality tests. Hooker (1957) obtained data on 30 overt nonpatient male homosexuals and on a group of 30 male heterosexuals matched for age, education, and IQ. The homosexuals were exclusively homosexual, except for three who had had minimal heterosexual experience. The heterosexuals, similarly, were exclusively heterosexual, except for three who had each had one homosexual experience. Hooker administered the Rorschach, a projective test, to all subjects. The Rorschach was used because it is considered a good measure of total personality and is sometimes used in the "diagnosis" of homosexuality. In the first phase of the experiment, the Rorschach responses were arranged in random order and were given to two highly skilled clinicians for interpretation. The clinicians assigned an adjustment rating from 1 (superior) to 5 (maladjusted) to each profile. According to these ratings, there were no differences in the adjustment of the homosexuals as compared with that of the heterosexuals; about two-thirds of each group were well adjusted. In the second phase, the clinicians received the profiles in the matched pairs and were asked to identify which of each pair was the heterosexual and which was the homosexual. One clinician identified 17 of the 30 pairs correctly, while the other was accurate for 18 of the 30. Since one would expect accuracy for 15 of the 30 merely by chance, the clinicians did not do better than chance in identifying the homosexuals and the heterosexuals. Apparently, even the skilled clinician cannot tell the gay from the straight without a scorecard. The notion that the homosexual has a disturbed personality receives no support in the results of this study.

On the basis of these studies, it must be concluded that the evidence does not support the notion that the homosexual is "sick" or poorly adjusted. This position

(a)

(b)

(c)

(d)

FIGURE 15.5
Gay and lesbian political issues: (a) The custody issue—lesbian mothers want the right to keep their children after a divorce; (b) the right to adoption—a gay couple with their two adopted children; (c) gays urge action on AIDS—to keep silent about the deadly disease means death; (d) the right to reproduce—a lesbian couple with a child born to the woman holding her, as a result of the use of artificial insemination.

441

has received official professional recognition by the American Psychiatric Association. Prior to 1973, the APA had listed homosexuality as a disorder under Section V, "Personality Disorders and Certain Other Nonpsychotic Mental Disorders," in its authoritative *Diagnostic and Statistical Manual of Mental Disorders.* In 1973, the APA voted to remove homosexuality from that listing; thus it is no longer considered a psychiatric disorder.

Can Sexual Orientation Be Changed by Psychotherapy?

Sexual dissatisfaction: Masters and Johnson's term for gays and lesbians who are unhappy with their sexual orientation and seek therapy to become heterosexual.

Masters and Johnson (1979) used the term **sexual dissatisfaction** to refer to lesbians and gays who seek therapy to become heterosexual. They treated 54 males and 13 females for this, using behavioral techniques similar to those described in Chapter 19. The report of the results of this therapy created much of the controversy over their book on homosexuality. Traditionally, psychologists have achieved a change rate of only 10 to 20 percent in "converting" gays to straights. Masters and Johnson, however, reported a failure rate of 21 percent immediately after therapy and 28 percent five years after therapy, translating to a 72 percent success rate. It was this high success rate that created the controversy over the book.

This research is subject to much the same criticism as that made in Chapter 19. For example, Masters and Johnson did not define clearly what they meant by a "success" or "failure." Low motivation has often been pinpointed as the cause of the traditional low success rate for therapy for sexual dissatisfaction; Masters and Johnson carefully screened applicants for therapy and probably kept only those with very high motivation. And many of their "homosexuals" might more accurately have been described as bisexuals at the beginning of therapy.

In sum, it is probably about as easy to change a gay man into a happy straight as it is to change a straight man into a happy gay—not very.

This whole concept of therapy for homosexuality, however, conflicts with the conclusion made earlier that homosexuality is not abnormal. If there is nothing wrong with homosexuality, trying to "cure" it makes no sense. Ethical issues are raised as well: Should a person be changed from a gay to a straight against his or her will? Perhaps the best resolution to this problem is that if a person freely requests therapy to help stop being a homosexual because the homosexual behavior is causing emotional distress, then the person should receive it, particularly in light of the fact that living as a gay or lesbian person in our society is difficult and that this alone might be sufficient reason for seeking therapy (but see Davison, 1976). Otherwise, there is no need for therapy.

WHY DO PEOPLE BECOME HOMOSEXUAL OR HETEROSEXUAL?

A fascinating psychological question is: Why do people become homosexual or heterosexual? Several theoretical answers to this quesiton, as well as the results of empirical research, are discussed below. You will notice that the older theorists and researchers considered it their task to explain homosexuality; more recent investigators, realizing that heterosexuality needs to be explained as well, are more likely to consider it their task to explain sexual orientation.

Biological Theories

There has been some speculation that homosexuality might be caused by biological factors. The likeliest candidates for these biological causes are genetic factors, prenatal factors, and endocrine imbalance.

Genetic Factors

Franz Kallman (1952a, 1952b) argued that there is a genetic predisposition to homosexuality, and he provided data to support his claim. He found perfect concordance for homosexuality (defined as a Kinsey rating between 3 and 6) among all the identical-twin pairs he studied (that is, if one was a homosexual, so was the other). Only 12 percent of the nonidentical twins were concordant. Numerous criticisms of this study could be made. The subjects were recruited from psychiatric institutions or prisons, so they were hardly a nonpatient sample. The identical twins were all reared together, and thus they shared not only common genes but also a common environment. Therefore, environmental factors might explain the similarities. Further, nonidentical twins are not genetically unrelated; they share, on the average, half of their genes. Hence if homosexuality were genetic, one would expect a moderate degree of concordance for them. Other investigators have found the concordance rate for identical twins to be far less than Kallman found (Heston & Shields, 1968).

The most recent and carefully done study on this question recruited gay and bisexual men who had a twin brother or an adopted brother (Bailey & Pillard, 1991). Among the 56 gay men who had an identical twin brother, 52 percent of the co-twins were themselves gay. Among the 54 gay men who had a nonidentical twin brother, 22 percent of the co-twins were themselves gay. Of the adoptive brothers of gay men, 11 percent were gay. The fact that the rate of concordance is substantially higher for identical twins than for nonidentical twins argues in favor of a genetic contribution to sexual orientation. On the other hand, if genetic factors absolutely *determined* sexual orientation, there would be 100 percent concordance for the identical twin pairs, and the rate of 52 percent is far from that. This indicates that factors other than genetics also play a role in influencing sexual orientation.

Prenatal Factors

Another speculation about a possible biological cause is that homosexuality develops as a result of factors during the prenatal period (Dörner, 1976). As was seen in Chapter 5, exposure to inappropriate hormones during fetal development can lead a genetic female to have male genitals, or a genetic male to have female genitals. It has been suggested that a similar process might account for homosexuality (and also for transsexualism—see Chapter 14).

According to the most recent theory, there is a critical time from the middle of the second month of fetal development to the middle of the fifth month of fetal development, during which the hypothalamus differentiates and sexual orientation is determined (Ellis & Ames, 1987). Any of several biological errors during this period will produce homosexuality. (Note that this theory views homosexuality as an error in development.)

One line of research that supports this theory has found evidence that severe stress to a mother during pregnancy tends to produce homosexual offspring. For example, exposing pregnant female rats to stress produces homosexual and bisexual male offspring (Ward, 1974). It is thought that the stress to the mother decreases the production of testosterone by the fetus. On the other hand, prenatal stress does not completely determine homosexuality because social rearing conditions after birth also have an effect (Ward & Reed, 1985). In research with humans, mothers of male homosexuals, bisexuals, and heterosexuals were interviewed and asked to recall stressful episodes that occurred during pregnancy, such as the death of a close relative, a divorce, or feelings of severe anxiety (Dorner et al., 1983). Approximately two-thirds of the mothers of homosexuals, compared with one-third of the mothers of bisexuals and less than one-tenth of the mothers of heterosexuals recalled such episodes. On the other hand, a similar study comparing lesbians and heterosexual women found no significant differences in mothers' stress during pregnancy (Ellis et al., 1988). And another study found no evidence of prenatal stress effects on sexual orientation for either males or females (Bailey et al., 1991).

This is an intriguing theory, but we need far stronger research with humans before the theory can be accepted. John Money (1987), for example, reviewing current research findings, argues that although there are prenatal hormone effects on sexual orientation, postnatal socialization influences are also important.

Brain Factors

Another line of theorizing has been that there are anatomical differences between the brains of gays and straights that produce the differences in sexual orientation. There have been a number of studies deriving from this point of view, all looking at somewhat different regions of the brain. A recent highly publicized study by neuroscientist Simon LeVay (1991) is a typical example. LeVay found significant differences between gay men and straight men in certain cells in the anterior portion of the hypothalamus. Anatomically, the hypothalamic cells of the gay men were more similar to those of women than those of straight men, according to LeVay. However, the study had a number of flaws: (1) The sample size was very small: only 19 gay men, 16 straight men, and 6 straight women were included. This small sample size was necessitated by the fact that the brains had to be dissected in order to examine the hypothalamus, so that the brains of living persons could not be studied. (2) All of the gay men in the sample, but only six of the straight men and one of the straight women, had died of AIDS. The groups are not comparable, then. Perhaps the brain differences were caused by the neurological effects of AIDS. (3) Lesbian women were omitted from the study, making them invisible in the research as they often have been in psychological and biological research. (4) The gay men were known to have been gay based on records at the time of death; the others, however, were just "presumed" to be heterosexual—if there was no record of sexual orientation, the assumption was that the person had been heterosexual, scarcely a sophisticated method of measurement. In short, the study is so flawed that we can't learn much from it.

Hormonal Imbalance

Investigating the possibility that endocrine imbalance is the cause, many researchers have tried to determine whether the testosterone ("male" hormone) levels of male homosexuals differ from those of male heterosexuals. These studies fail to find any hormonal differences between male homosexuals and male heterosexuals (Gooren et al., 1990; Meyer-Bahlburg, 1984). Of the 12 studies of testosterone levels in male homosexuals published since 1971, 8 found no significant differences between heterosexuals and homosexuals, 2 found heterosexuals to have higher levels of testosterone, and 2 found homosexuals to have higher levels (Gartrell, 1982).

Despite these results, some clinicians have attempted to cure male homosexuality by administering testosterone therapy (Glass & Johnson, 1944). This therapy fails; indeed, it seems to result in even more homosexual behavior than usual. This is not an unexpected result, since, as was seen in Chapter 9, androgen levels seem to be related to sexual responsiveness. As a clinician friend of mine replied to an undergraduate male who was seeking testosterone therapy for his homosexual behavior, "It won't make you heterosexual; it will only make you horny."

Other, more complex kinds of hormonal differences between heterosexuals and homosexuals are also being explored (e.g., Gladue et al., 1984); however, it is too early to be able to conclude much from these studies.

Virtually all these hormone studies have been done on male homosexuals. The two available studies on lesbians did find higher testosterone levels and lower estrogen levels among them than among a control group of heterosexual women (Loraine et al., 1971; Gartrell et al., 1977). The results have not been replicated yet, and so they should be viewed cautiously.

In conclusion, of the biological theories, the genetic theory, the prenatal theory, and the hormone theory have new evidence, but much more research is needed.

Psychoanalytic Theory

Freudian Theory

Since Freud believed sex to be the primary motivating force in human behavior, it is not surprising that he concerned himself with sexual orientation and its development (his classic work on the subject is *Three Essays on the Theory of Sexuality,* published in 1910).

Polymorphous perverse:
Freud's term for the infant's indiscriminate, undifferentiated sexuality.

According to Freud, the infant is **polymorphous perverse**; that is, the infant's sexuality is totally undifferentiated and is therefore directed at all sorts of objects, both appropriate and inappropriate. As the child grows up and matures into an adult, sexuality is increasingly directed toward "appropriate" objects (members of the other gender), while the desire for "inappropriate" objects (for example, members of the same gender) is increasingly repressed. Therefore, according to Freud, the homosexual is fixated at an immature stage of development.

Negative Oedipus complex:
Freud's term for the opposite of the Oedipus complex; in the negative Oedipus complex the child loves and sexually desires the parent of the same gender and identifies with the parent of the other gender.

According to Freud, homosexuality also stems from the **negative Oedipus complex**. In the (positive) Oedipus complex, discussed in Chapter 2, the child loves the parent of the opposite gender but eventually gives this up and comes to identify with the parent of the same gender, thereby acquiring a sense of gender identity. In the negative Oedipus complex, things are just the opposite: The child loves the parent of the same gender and identifies with the parent of the opposite gender. For example, in the negative Oedipus complex, a little boy would love his father and identify with his mother. In the process of maturation, once again, the child is supposed to repress this negative Oedipus complex. The homosexual person, however, fails to repress it and remains fixated on it. Thus according to Freud, for example, a woman becomes a homosexual because of a continuing love for her mother and identification with her father. In Freud's view, homosexuality is a continuation of love for the parent of the same gender.

Consistent with Freud's belief that the infant is polymorphous perverse was his belief that all humans are inherently bisexual; that is, he believed that all people have the capacity for both heterosexual and homosexual behavior. Thus he viewed homosexuality as very possible, if not desirable. This notion of inherent bisexuality also led to his concept of the *latent homosexual,* the person with a repressed homosexual component.

Bieber's Research

Because Freud had such a great influence on psychiatric thought, he inspired a great deal of theorizing and research, including research on homosexuality. Irving Bieber and his colleagues (1962) did one of the more important of these psychoanalytically inspired studies. They compared 106 male homosexuals with 100 male heterosexuals; all the subjects were in psychoanalysis, which makes the results somewhat questionable. The family pattern that Bieber and his colleages tended to find among the

Homoseductive mother:
Bieber's term for the mother who is seductive toward her son, traumatizing the boy and turning him into a homosexual.

homosexuals was that of a dominant mother and a weak or passive father. The mother was both overprotective and overly intimate. Bieber thus originated the concept of the **homoseductive mother** as an explanation of male homosexuality. This family pattern, according to Bieber, has a double effect: The man later fears heterosexual relations both because of his mother's jealous possessiveness and because her seductiveness produced anxiety. Bieber thus suggested that homosexuality results, in part, from fears of heterosexuality. While Bieber's findings on the homoseductive mother have received a great deal of attention, a more striking finding in his research was of a seriously disturbed relationship between the homosexual male and his father (Bieber, 1976). The fathers were described as detached and/or openly hostile; thus the homosexual son emerged into adulthood hating and fearing his father and yet deeply wanting the father's love and affection.

Wolff's Research

Charlotte Wolff, a British psychiatrist, has carried out a similar program of research and theorizing about the origins of lesbianism (1971). She studied over 100 nonpatient lesbians, comparing them with a control group of heterosexual women matched for family background, profession, and social class. The family characteristics that were more frequent among the homosexual women than among the heterosexual women were a rejecting or indifferent mother and a distant or absent father. Wolff theorized that lesbianism results from the girl's receiving inadequate love from the mother; as a result, she continues, throughout her life, to seek that missing love in other women. Secondarily, because her father was distant or absent, she may not have learned to relate to men.

Evaluation of Psychoanalytic Theories

Psychoanalytic theories of the genesis of homosexuality clearly operate under the assumption that homosexuality is deviant or abnormal. As Irving Bieber writes:

> We consider homosexuality to be a pathologic, bio-social, psycho-sexual adaption to pervasive fears surrounding the expression of heterosexual impulses. (Bieber et al., 1962, p. 22)

> All psychoanalytic theories assume that adult homosexuality is psycho-pathologic. (Bieber et al., 1962, p. 18)

Actually, in his later writings Freud came to consider homosexuality to be within the normal range of variation of sexual behavior; this view, however, appears not to have had much of an impact, compared with that of his earlier writings on the subject. Psychoanalytic theory could thus be criticized for the abnormality assumption, since, as has been seen, there is no strong evidence for the notion that the homosexual is poorly adjusted.

The psychoanalytic approach can also be criticized for its confusion of the concepts of "gender identity" and "sexual orientation." As was previously noted, the homosexual differs from the heterosexual in sexual orientation but not in gender identification: The male homosexual generally has a masculine identification, and the lesbian has a feminine identification. Psychoanalytic theory, however, assumes that the homosexual not only makes an inappropriate object choice but also has an abnormal gender identification—that the gay man has not identified with his father and has therefore not acquired a masculine identity and that the lesbian has not identified with her mother and has therefore not acquired a feminine identity. The basic assumption of abnormal gender identification is not supported by the data and is therefore another basis for criticizing psychoanalytic theories of homosexuality.

Learning Theory

Behaviorists emphasize the importance of learning in the development of sexual orientation. They note the prevalence of bisexual behavior both in other species and in young humans, and they argue that rewards and punishments must shape the individual's behavior into predominant homosexuality or predominant heterosexuality. The assumption, then, is that humans have a relatively amorphous, undifferentiated pool of sex drive which, depending on circumstances (rewards and punishments), may be channeled in any of several directions. In short, people are born sexual, not heterosexual or homosexual. Only through learning does one of these behaviors become more likely than the other. For example, a person who has early heterosexual experiences that are very unpleasant might develop toward homosexuality. Heterosexuality has essentially been punished and therefore becomes less likely. This might occur, for instance, in the case of a girl who is raped at an early age; her first experience with heterosexual sex was extremely unpleasant, and so she avoids it and turns to homosexuality. Parents who become upset about their teenagers' heterosexual activities might do well to remember this notion; punishing a young person for engaging in heterosexual behavior may not eliminate the behavior but rather rechannel it in a homosexual direction.

Another possibility, according to a learning-theory approach, is that if early sexual experiences are homosexual and pleasant, the person may become a homosexual. Homosexual behavior has essentially been rewarded and therefore becomes more likely.

The learning-theory approach treats homosexuality as a normal form of behavior and recognizes that heterosexuality is not necessarily inborn but must also, like homosexuality, be learned. There is a problem with the learning-theory approach, however (Whitam, 1977). The rewards in our society go overwhelmingly to heterosexuality. Society gives few rewards to homosexuality, and often punishes it. Why, then, does anyone become homosexual? While human sexual behavior is no doubt determined in part by reinforcement contingencies, it probably also has much more complex determinants which are not yet understood.

Interestingly, though, preliminary research indicates that children who grow up with a homosexual parent are not themselves likely to become gay (Green, 1978). In this sense, then, homosexuality is not "learned" from parents.

Interactionist Theory

Storms: Maturation Rates

Psychologist Michael Storms (1981; see also Bermant, 1972) has proposed a theory of the development of erotic orientation in which the rate of sexual maturation in adolescence is the critical factor. According to this theory, most people develop the sex drive in early adolescence, around the ages of 12 and 15. It is at that time that certain stimuli (e.g., a member of the same or the other gender) become conditioned to be arousing or erotic. As we discussed in Chapter 11, homosocial patterns (same-gender friendships and groups) predominate in preadolescence, reaching a peak at around age 12. Heterosexual interactions begin to emerge after that time, and most people have begun heterosexual dating by age 15. According to Storms, homosexuality results when individuals have an early maturing sex drive, at about age 12 when they are still in homosocial groupings, so that erotic conditioning is more likely to focus on members of their own gender with whom they spend time, since heterosexuality has not yet emerged as an alternative. Those whose sex drive emerges later are already immersed in a heterosexual culture of dating and friendships, so that they eroticize heterosexual experiences.

Supporting Storms's theory, data show that homosexual women are earlier sexual maturers than heterosexual women, as measured by age of beginning to masturbate, age of earliest feelings of sexual arousal, and age of first sexual fantasizing (Goode & Haber, 1977; Saghir & Robins, 1973).

This theory provides an explanation for why there are more men than women who have engaged in homosexual activity and who are exclusively homosexual: The sex drive in males emerges earlier, as evidenced by the earlier appearance of and more frequent masturbation of adolescent males (see Chapter 11). Thus males are more likely to experience the development of the sex drive while they are still in homosocial groupings. Females are more likely to experience the emergence of their sex drive later, after heterosexuality has become the norm in their lives.

In terms of the nature-nurture controversy, Storms's theory can be viewed as an interactionist theory. That is, it integrates biological factors (biological maturation of the sex drive) with environmental factors (learning and social interactions). One virtue of Storms's theory is that it is not based on an assumption that homosexuality is pathological. Rather, it seeks to explain both homosexuality and heterosexuality in terms of maturational patterns. The theory is very recent, and so it will take some time to accumulate enough data to determine its strengths and weaknesses.

Sociological Theory

Sociologists emphasize the effects of *labeling* in explaining homosexuality. The label "homosexual" has a big impact in our society. If you are a heterosexual, suppose that someone said to you, "I think that you are a homosexual." How would you react? Your immediate reaction would probably be negative: anger, anxiety, and embarrassment. The label "homosexual" has derogatory connotations and may even be used as an insult. This reflects our society's negative attitudes toward homosexuality.

A clever experiment demonstrated the effects of labeling someone a homosexual. Half of the subjects (all men) were led to believe that a particular member of their group was a homosexual. For the other half of the subjects (the control group), the man was not labeled. Subjects in the experimental group, in which the man was labeled, rated him as being significantly less clean, softer, more womanly, more tense, more yielding, more impulsive, less rugged, more passive, and quieter (Karr, 1978). Thus labeling a person a homosexual does influence people's perception of that person.

But the label "homosexual" may also act as a self-fulfilling prophecy. Suppose that a young boy—possibly because he is slightly effeminate, because he is poor in sports, or for no reason at all—is called a "homosexual." He reacts strongly and becomes more and more anxious and worried about his problem. He becomes painfully aware of the slightest homosexual tendency in himself. Finally he convinces himself that he is a homosexual. He begins engaging in homosexual behavior and associates with a gay group. In short, a homosexual has been created.

Sociologists also emphasize the importance of *roles* in explaining human behavior. Homosexuality might be a role people play, much like the male role or the female role (Goode, 1981; McIntosh, 1968; M. S. Weinberg & Williams, 1974). This view helps explain the apparent ease with which many homosexuals pass for heterosexuals in the straight world. They simply play the heterosexual role in certain situations and the homosexual role in others. Actually, there are two homosexual roles (Goode, 1981). One is the derogatory role ascribed to gays in American culture—limp wrists and so on. The other is the homosexual role defined by the gay subculture. In the developmental process of coming out, both these roles are important in shaping the gay person's identity.

Recall that in Chapter 2 we discussed Reiss's sociological theory of human sexuality. In his theorizing he has addressed the issue of sexual orientation, focusing particularly on gay men. Recognizing the need to explain cross-cultural differences in sexual patterns, he contends that it is male-dominant societies with great rigidity of gender roles that produce the highest incidence of homosexuality. In such societies, there is a rigid male role that must be learned and conformed to, but young boys have little opportunity to learn it from adult men precisely because the gender roles are rigid, so that women take care of children and men have little contact with them. It is therefore difficult to learn the heterosexual component of the male role. In addition, because the male role is rigid, there will be a certain number of males who dislike it and reject its heterosexual component. Cross-cultural studies support his observations (Reiss, 1986). Societies that have great maternal involvement with infants and low father involvement with infants and that have rigid gender roles are precisely those that have the highest incidence of same-gender sexual behavior in males.

This pattern describes the negative pathway to homosexuality. Reiss argues that there is also a positive pathway. It exists in less gender-rigid societies with more permissiveness about sexuality. In such societies, individuals will feel freer to experiment with same-gender behavior and may find it satisfying.

Empirical Data

Theoretical positions on the origins of sexual orientation are many and varied, as the previous sections indicate. Do any of these proposed explanations have a basis in fact? Unfortunately, most of the investigators who have collected data on the previous experiences of gays and lesbians have operated from a particular theoretical conviction; they then tended to obtain data supporting the theory in which they believed. Many of the early studies also have the problems of design mentioned in the discussion of whether homosexuality is abnormal. Many of the studies have been of either the first type (homosexuals in therapy, with no comparison group) or the second type (homosexuals in therapy compared with heterosexuals). Thus results of those studies should be interpreted cautiously.

Further, when studies do find differences between homosexuals and heterosexuals, the factors are generally not common enough among the homosexuals to make them the "explanation" of homosexuality. A good example is Charlotte Wolff's (1971) study of lesbians. Mothers of lesbians were more frequently indifferent or negligent, but indifference was characteristic of only 27 percent of the mothers of lesbians (as compared with 10 percent of the mothers of controls), and negligence was characteristic of only 10 percent of the mothers of lesbians (as compared with 0 percent of the mothers of controls). Hence, while maternal negligence and indifference were more common among lesbians, they certainly did not explain all cases of lesbianism.

The most comprehensive study of the causes of sexual orientation was done by Alan Bell, Martin Weinberg, and Sue Hammersmith, of the Kinsey Institute (1981). They interviewed 979 gay men and lesbian women and a comparison sample of 477 heterosexual men and women, all in San Francisco. The interviews, which took 3 to 5 hours, included approximately 200 questions about the person's childhood and adolescence; the questions were designed specifically to allow the researchers to test all the major theories that have been proposed as explanations for the development of sexual orientation. In general, their results indicated that all the environmental explanations are inadequate and are not supported by the data. Specifically, they concluded that:

1. The notion that disturbed parental relationships are influential—as proposed in psychoanalytic theory—is grossly exaggerated. Parental relationships seem

FIGURE 15.6
La Cage aux Folles II:
*Homosexuality has
received more open
coverage in mainstream
movies. The French film* La
Cage aux Folles *was so
commercially successful
that it inspired a sequel.*

to make little or no difference in whether one becomes heterosexual or homosexual.

2. The sociologists' notion that homosexuality results from labeling by others
received no support from the data.

3. The notion—proposed by learning theory—that homosexuality results from
early unpleasant heterosexual experience received no support. For example,
lesbians were no more likely to have been raped than heterosexual women
were.

4. The idea—proposed by learning theory—that homosexuality might result from
a boy or girl being seduced by an older member of his or her own gender (an
early positive homosexual experience) also was not supported.

Having shot down all the standard theories, Bell, Weinberg, and Hammersmith did
reach some positive conclusions. Two are especially important.

1. Sexual orientation seems to be determined before adolescence. This would be
important if, for example, it was discovered that the high school football coach
was gay. According to Bell and his colleagues, parents and the principal should
not worry that he will be a "bad influence" on the team members; their sexual
orientation is already determined.

2. It is likely that there is a biological basis for homosexuality. The researchers
reached this conclusion because none of the standard environmental explanations was supported by the data. They actually collected no biological data
(e.g., measurements of hormone levels). Thus this conclusion amounts to no
more than speculation, although it received a great deal of publicity.

In summary, when all the studies in this area are surveyed, no single factor
emerges consistently as a cause of male homosexuality or of lesbianism (the two

might have different causes). To be blunt, we do not know what causes sexual orientation. But there may be a good theoretical lesson to be learned from this somewhat frustrating statement. It has generally been assumed not only that gays form a distinct category (which, as has already been seen, is not very accurate) but also that they form a homogeneous category, that is, that all gays are fairly similar. Not so. Probably there are many different kinds or "types" of homosexuals. Indeed, one psychologist, expressing this notion, has suggested that we should refer not to "homosexuality" but rather to "the homosexualities" (A. P. Bell, 1974b; Bell and Weinberg, 1978). If this is the case, then one would not expect a single "cause" of homosexuality but rather many causes, each corresponding to its type. The next step in research, then, should be to identify the various types of homosexuals—not to mention the various types of heterosexuals—and the different kinds of development that lead to each.

ETHNICITY AND SEXUAL ORIENTATION

Just as different cultures around the world hold different views of same-gender sexual behavior (see Focus 15.3), so various American ethnic minority groups have different cultural definitions for same-gender behaviors.

Generally it is thought that there is less tolerance for homosexuality in the African American community. A survey of the attitudes of 2006 state employees confirmed this view (Ernst et al., 1991). In response to the statement "AIDS will help society by reducing the number of homosexuals (gay people)," African Americans were significantly more likely to agree, that is, to express a negative view of gays. Black women were especially negative about homosexuals, compared with white women. The researchers suggested that black women's more negative attitudes may be due to the perception, by some black women, that homosexuality is one of many sources draining the pool of eligible, marriageable black males (other factors including a higher rate of premature death among black males and a high rate of unemployment).

It is also true that black and Hispanic men are more likely than white men to engage extensively in homosexual behavior while still considering themselves to be heterosexual (Peterson & Marin, 1988). An interesting example of these different cultural definitions comes from a study of Mexican and Mexican American men and their same-gender sexual behavior (Magana & Carrier, 1991). In Mexico, there is a dichotomizing of same-gender sexual behaviors that parallels the rigidly defined gender roles. Anal intercourse, because it most resembles penis-in-vagina intercourse, is the preferred behavior, and fellatio is practiced relatively little. A man adopts the role either of receptive partner or inserting partner and does this exclusively. Those who take the receptive role are considered unmanly, feminine, and "homosexual." Those who take the inserting role are not labeled "homosexual," are considered masculine, and are not stigmatized. This approach differs substantially, of course, from that in Anglo culture, where men commonly switch roles. Among Mexican American men who have migrated to the United States, their views and sexual practices seem to be determined by whether their sexual socialization in adolescence occurred with Anglo peers or with Mexican American peers.

Latina lesbians also experience the complexities of ethnicity and sexual orientation (Espin, 1987). Although in Latin cultures emotional and physical closeness among women is considered acceptable and desirable, attitudes toward lesbianism are even more restrictive than in Anglo culture. The special emphasis on family—defined as mother, father, children, and grandparents—in Latin cultures makes the lesbian even more of an outsider. As a result, Latina lesbians often become part of

Ritualized Homosexuality in Melanesia

Melanesia is an area of the southwest Pacific that includes the islands of New Guinea and Fiji as well as many others.

Anthropologists' research on homosexual behavior in those cultures provides great insight into the ways in which sexual behaviors are the products of the scripts of a culture. This research is rooted in sociological and anthropological theory (see Chapter 2). As such, the analysis focuses on the norms of the society and the symbolic meaning that is attached to sexual behaviors.

Among Melanesians, homosexual behavior has a very different symbolic meaning from the one it has in Western culture. It is viewed as natural, normal, and indeed necessary. The culture actually prescribes the behavior, in contrast to Western cultures in which it is forbidden or proscribed.

Sociologists and anthropologists believe that most cultures are organized around the dimensions of social class, race, gender, and age. Among Melanesians, age organizes the homosexual behavior. It is not to occur among two men of the same age. Instead, it occurs between an adolescent and a preadolescent, or between an adult man and a pubertal boy. The older partner is always the inserter for the acts of anal intercourse and the younger partner is the insertee.

Ritualized homosexual behavior serves several social purposes in these cultures. It is viewed as a means by which a boy at puberty is incorporated into the adult society of men. It is also thought to encourage a boy's growth, so that it helps to "finish off" his growth in puberty. In these societies, semen is viewed as a scarce and valuable commodity. Therefore the homosexual behaviors are viewed as helpful and honorable, a means of passing on strength to younger men and boys. As one anthropologist observed,

> Semen is also necessary for young boys to attain full growth to manhood. . . . They need a boost, as it were. When a boy is eleven or twelve years old, he is engaged for several months in homosexual intercourse with a healthy older man chosen by his father. (This is always an in-law or unrelated person, since the same notions of incestuous relations apply to little boys as to marriageable women.) Men point to the rapid growth of adolescent youths, the appearance of peach fuzz beards, and so on, as the favorable results of this child-rearing practice. (Schieffelin, 1976, p. 124)

In all cases, these men are expected later to marry and father children. This points up the contrast between sexual identity and sexual behavior. The sexual behaviors are ones that we would surely term "homosexual," yet these cultures are so structured that the boys and men who engage in homosexual behaviors do not form a homosexual identity.

Ritualized homosexual behaviors are declining as these cultures are colonized by Westerners. It is fortunate that anthropologists were able to make their observations over the last several decades to document these interesting and meaningful practices before they disappear.

Source: Gilbert H. Herdt (Ed.). (1984). *Ritualized homosexuality in Melanesia.* Berkeley: University of California Press.

FIGURE 15.7
Ethnicity and sexual orientation. Among Latina women, warmth and physical closeness are very acceptable, but there are strong taboos against female-female sexual relationships.

an Anglo lesbian community while remaining in the closet with their family and among Latinos, creating difficult choices among identities. As one Cuban woman responded to a questionnaire, "I identify myself as a lesbian more intensely than as a Cuban/Latin. But it is a very painful question because I feel that I am both, and I don't want to have to choose" (Espin, 1987, p. 47).

BISEXUALITY

Here is a riddle: What is like a bridge that touches both shores but doesn't meet in the middle? The answer: Research and theories on sexual orientation (MacDonald, 1982; you'll have to admit that this is classier than the average riddle). The point of the riddle is that scientists, as well as lay people, focus on heterosexuals and homosexuals, ignoring all the bisexuals in between.

A **bisexual** is a person whose sexual orientation is toward both women and men, that is, toward members of the same gender and members of the other gender. Such a person is clearly not exclusively heterosexual or exclusively homosexual. He or she is called *bisexual* or, in slang, "ac–dc" (alternating current–direct current). Some scientists also call such a person **ambisexual.**

Bisexuality is really not at all rare; in fact, it is far more common than exclusive homosexuality (if a "bisexual" is defined as a person who has had at least one sexual experience with a male and one with a female). For example, earlier in this chapter it was noted that about 80 percent of all males are exclusively heterosexual and that about 2 percent are exclusively homosexual. That leaves a large number, perhaps 20 percent, who are bisexual according to the definition stated above.

The proponents of bisexuality argue that it has some strong advantages. It allows more variety in one's sexual and human relationships than either exclusive heterosexuality or exclusive homosexuality. The bisexual does not rule out any possibilities and is open to the widest variety of experiences, characteristics which are highly valued by today's young people.

On the other hand, the bisexual may be viewed with suspicion or downright hostility by the gay community (Blumstein & Schwartz, 1976). Radical lesbians refer to bisexual women as "fence sitters," saying that they betray the lesbian cause

Bisexual: A person whose sexual orientation is toward both men and women.

Ambisexual: Another term for bisexual.

453

Sexual identity: One's self-identity as homosexual, heterosexual, or bisexual.

because they can pretend to be straight when it is convenient and lesbian when it is convenient. Some gays even argue that there is no such thing as a true bisexual.

A consideration of the phenomenon of bisexuality will help illuminate several theoretical points and also provide some insights into homosexuality and heterosexuality. First, though, several concepts need to be clarified. A distinction has already been made between sex (sexual behavior) and gender (being male or female) and between gender identity (the male's association with the male role and the female's association with the female role) and sexual orientation (heterosexual, homosexual, or bisexual). To this, the concept of sexual identity should be added; this refers to one's self-label or self-identification as heterosexual, homosexual, or bisexual.[3] Sexual identity, then, is the person's concept of herself or himself as a heterosexual, homosexual, or bisexual.

Strangely, there may be contradictions between people's sexual identity (which is subjective) and their actual choice of sexual partners viewed objectively. Sociologists Philip Blumstein and Pepper Schwartz (1974) conducted a large program of research on bisexuals, and they have provided some good examples of these contradictions. For example, one of their subjects identified herself as a lesbian, and yet occasionally she sleeps with men. Objectively, her choice of sexual partners is bisexual, but her identity is lesbian. More common are persons who think of themselves as heterosexuals but who engage in both heterosexual and homosexual sex. A good example of this is the tearoom trade—the successful, heterosexually married men in gray flannel suits who occasionally stop off at a public rest room to have another male perform fellatio on them. Once again, the behavior is objectively bisexual, in contradiction to the heterosexual identity. Another example is the group of women who claim to have bisexual identities but who have experienced only heterosexual sex and never homosexual sex. These women, often as a result of feminist beliefs, claim bisexuality as an ideal which they are capable of attaining at some later time. Once again, identity contradicts behavior.

Just as we recognized a diversity of types of homosexuals, so there is a diversity of bisexuals (MacDonald, 1982). Some bisexuals, referred to as 50:50 bisexuals, have equal preferences for men and for women. Other bisexuals have a preference for one gender but are accepting of sex with the other gender. Some bisexuals are sequentially bisexual, whereas others are simultaneously bisexual; that is, some have only one lover at a time, sometimes a man and sometimes a woman, whereas other bisexuals have both a male and a female lover at the same time. And finally, some bisexuals are transitory bisexuals, passing through a bisexual phase on the way to becoming exclusively homosexual or heterosexual, whereas others are enduring bisexuals, maintaining their bisexual preferences throughout their lifespan.

Some bisexuals are heterosexually married. One study examined 26 married couples in which the husband was bisexual (Wolf, 1985; see also Matteson, 1985). The couples had, on the average, been married 13 years, and there had been open disclosure of the man's homosexuality for an average of 5.5 years. By and large, the marriages were happy. When asked to rate the quality of the marriage, 42 percent of the men and 32 percent of the women said it was outstanding, and an additional 34 percent of the men and 46 percent of the women said it was better than average. The majority of both husbands and wives said that they remained in the marriage because they valued the friendship of the spouse. Nonetheless, there were some conflicts, as there are in all marriages. Trust was one issue. One woman said, "I feel

---

[3] Clearly, the term "sexual identity" is not being used here the way it is generally used, which is to refer to one's sense of maleness or femaleness (for which the term "gender identity" is used in this book). However, it seems important to be able to talk about a person's sense that he or she is straight or gay, and "sexual identity" seems the most likely term to use for that purpose.

15.4

Joan, A Bisexual Woman

Joan, a professional woman in her middle thirties, considered herself exclusively heterosexual until about four years ago. Until that time she had never had homosexual fantasies or feelings, but she had been generally liberal about "sexual alternatives" and believed in equal rights for homosexuals. Four years ago, however, Joan became active in the women's liberation movement and developed closer friendships with some of the women with whom she worked. None of these relationships was sexualized, but her curiosity was aroused by sexual possibilities with women. Her approach to her own potential homosexual behavior was at this time still more intellectual than emotional and was not accompanied by graphic fantasies or feelings of attraction to other women whom she might meet or see in public.

During this period, Joan met another woman in her profession whom she found both intellectually and socially attractive. Vivian was also heterosexual, but she had had a few homosexual experiences. The relationship between the two women became closer, and during an exchange of confidences Joan learned that Vivian had had sexual experiences with women. At this point, Joan began to have sexual fantasies involving Vivian and began to be more overtly physical toward her, but she never crossed the bounds of female heterosexual friendship. The relationship intensified, and intimate dis-

cussions about sexuality turned to the possibility of sex between the two women. After about six months of such discussions, they slept together, first having overcome their initial worries concerning the effect that any guilt feelings about their "experimentation" might have on their friendship.

After the first successful sexual experience, Joan and Vivian repeated it approximately once every month for over a year. Vivian, however, continues to think of herself as a heterosexual, while Joan began to feel that she was in love with her friend and to want a more committed relationship. Joan stopped seeing Vivian when she realized that Vivian did not agree with her terms for the relationship. The two remained close friends, but Joan looked for someone else who might wish to share a committed relationship. She eventually fell in love with another woman, and an intense romantic and sexual relationship continued for two years. At the present, Joan is unsure of what sexual label to apply to herself, but she prefers "bisexual." At the time of her interview, she had both a male and a female lover.

Source: Philip W. Blumstein & Pepper Schwartz. (1976). Bisexual women. In J. P. Wiseman (Ed.), **The social psychology of sex.** New York: Harper & Row, pp. 154–162.

more suspicious and jealous at times since he lied in the past" (p. 142). On the other hand, others commented that their trust had deepened. One factor that seemed most related to positive adjustment in these marriages was communication. The couples expressing the most satisfaction with the marriage were the most likely to have very direct styles of communication and to have communicated about the homosexuality early in the marriage or from the beginning of the marriage. In the AIDS era, a different meaning may be attached to a husband's bisexuality; now it is not just an alternative sexual pattern, but also a potentially dangerous pattern that could introduce HIV infection into the marriage.

The available data on bisexual development (see Focus 15.4 about a bisexual woman) suggest several important points. First, they argue for the importance of late-occurring experiences in the shaping of one's sexual behavior and identity. As has been seen, most of the research on the development of homosexuality rests on the assumption that it is somehow determined by pathological conditions in childhood or even prenatally. Yet some females, as the story of the woman in Focus 15.4 illustrates, have their first homosexual encounter at age 30 or 40. It is difficult to believe that these behaviors were determined by some pathological conditions to which such women were exposed at age 5. Human behavior can be modified at any time throughout the lifespan. Deprivation homosexuality, or situational homosexuality, is also a good example of this. A heterosexual man who enters prison may engage in homosexual behavior and then return to heterosexuality after his release. Once again, it seems likelier that such a man's homosexual behavior was determined by his circumstances (being in prison) than by some problem with his Oedipus complex 20 years before. Unlike gender identity, which seems to be fixed in the preschool years, sexual identity continues to evolve throughout one's lifetime (Riddle, 1978). This contradicts Bell, Weinberg, and Hammersmith's assertion that sexual orientation is determined before adolescence. I think when sexual orientation is determined is still an open question.

Second, a question is raised as to whether heterosexuality is really the "natural" state. The pattern in some theories has been to try to discover those pathological conditions which cause homosexuality (for example, a father who is an inadequate role model or a homoseductive mother)—all on the basis of the assumption that heterosexuality is the natural state and that homosexuality must be explained as a deviation from it. As we have seen, this approach has failed; there appear to be multiple causes of homosexuality, just as there are multiple causes of heterosexuality. The important alternative to consider is that bisexuality is the natural state, a point acknowledged both by Freud and by the behaviorists. This chapter will close, then, with some questions. Psychologically, the real question should concern not the pathological conditions that lead to homosexuality but rather the causes of exclusive homosexuality and exclusive heterosexuality. Why do we eliminate some people as potential sex partners simply on the basis of their gender? Why is it that everyone is not bisexual?

Deprivation homosexuality: Homosexual activity that occurs in certain situations, such as prisons, when people are deprived of their regular heterosexual activity.

Summary

Homosexual behavior is sexual behavior with a member of the same gender; it is considerably more complex to define what a "homosexual" is. "Sexual orientation" is defined as whom we are sexually attracted to and have the potential to love.

Homosexuals suffer from discrimination and from a number of derogatory stereotypes. The majority of Americans believe that homosexual relations are always wrong. Although one stereotype is that male homosexuals are effeminate and lesbians are mannish, this is not true; in most cases one cannot tell a homosexual from a heterosexual on the basis of appearance. The belief that male homosexuals tend to be child molesters is also not true. Discrimination against homosexuals can take many forms; gay people may lose their jobs when their sexual practices become known, they may be the object of hate crimes, and some people believe that all gays have AIDS.

The gay lifestyle includes gay bars and political and social clubs. It is important to remember, however, that gays are not all identical and that they differ as much among themselves as heterosexuals do. In regard to satisfaction and love, long-term homosexual relationships are much like long-term heterosexual relationships. Research on long-term gay relationships—some of 20 or more years duration—indicates that there are predictable stages in the development of gay relationships.

In order to describe the homosexual behavior of the people in this sample, Kinsey devised a seven-point scale ranging from 0 (exclusively heterosexual) through 6 (exclusively homosexual), with the midpoint of 3 representing equal amounts of heterosexual and homosexual experience. Probably about 20 percent of men and 10 percent of women engage in at least some homosexual behavior in adulthood. Probably about 2 percent of men and 1 percent of women are exclusively homosexual.

Available data do not support the notion that homosexuals are poorly adjusted. Psychologially, they do not appear to differ substantially from heterosexuals except for their sexual orientation. The American Psychiatric Association no longer classifies homosexuality as a mental disorder.

Masters and Johnson have done therapy to change homosexuals to heterosexuals.

In regard to the causes of sexual orientation, biological explanations include hormone imbalance, prenatal factors, brain factors, and genetic factors. The genetic explanation has some support from the data, and there is some new, tentative evidence of prenatal factors and endocrine factors. According to the psychoanalytic view, homosexuality results from a fixation at an immature stage of development and a persisting negative Oedipus complex. Learning theorists stress that the sex drive is undifferentiated and is channeled, through experience, into heterosexuality or homosexuality. Storms's interactionist theory proposes that homosexuality results when the sex drive matures while the preadolescent is still in homosocial groupings; heterosexuality results when the sex drive matures later and heterosexual socializing is the norm. Sociologists emphasize the importance of roles and labeling in understanding homosexuality. They also note that gender-rigid, male-dominant societies are likely to produce a higher incidence of gay men. Available data do not point to any single factor as a cause of homosexuality but rather suggest that there may be many types of homosexuality ("homosexualities") with corresponding multiple causes.

Different ethnic groups in the United States hold different views of same-gender sexual behaviors.

Bisexuality is more common than exclusive homosexuality. A person's sexual identity may be discordant with his or her actual behavior. Bisexuality may be more "natural" than either exclusive heterosexuality or exclusive homosexuality.

Review Questions

1. Attitudes toward homosexuality have become more liberal in recent years, so that now a majority of Americans believe that sexual relations between two adults of the same gender are not wrong. True or false?

2. According to Reiss's sociological theory, the highest incidence of male homosexuality should occur in male-dominant cultures with rigid gender roles. True or false?

3. Homosexual couples tend to have stereotyped gender roles; for example, in a lesbian couple, one generally plays the butch role and the other plays the femme role. True or false?

4. Approximately _____ percent of child molesting is heterosexual (men molesting girls) and _____ percent is homosexual (men molesting boys).

5. _____ is the term for casual sex in a public place such as a rest room.

6. The process of "coming out" involves acknowledging to oneself and then to others that one is homosexual. True or false?

7. Lesbians and gay men rate their relationships as highly satisfying. True or false?

8. According to Kinsey's scale, someone who is a "3" is exclusively heterosexual. True or false?

9. In Melanesia, homosexual behavior is forbidden. True or false?

10. According to nonpatient research, there are no significant differences in adjustment between heterosexuals and homosexuals. True of false?

(The answers to all review questions are at the end of the book, beginning on page 731.)

Questions for Thought, Discussion, and Debate

1. Debate the following topic. Resolved: Homosexuals should not be discriminated against in employment, including such occupations as high school teaching.

2. Do you feel that you are homophobic, or do you feel that your attitude toward gays is positive? Why do you think your attitudes are the way they are? Are you satisfied with your attitudes or do you want to change them?

3. Does your college or university, in addition to prohibiting discrimination on the basis of race and sex, also prohibit discrimination on the basis of sexual orientation? Do you think it should?

Suggestions for Further Reading

Back, Gloria G. (1985). *Are you still my mother, are you still my family?* New York: Warner. This book aims at helping the parents of gays.

Clark, Don. (1987). *The new loving someone gay.* New York: Celestial Arts. A therapist offers some excellent thoughts for those who are coming out and for friends and spouses of lesbian women and gay men.

Herek, Gregory M., Kimmel, Douglas C., Amaro, Hortensia, & Melton, Gary B. (1991). Avoiding heterosexist bias in psychological research. *American Psychologist,* **46,** 957–963. This stimulating article on research methodology points out ways in which heterosexist bias can enter research and ways to avoid this bias.

Kohn, Barry, & Matusow, Alice. (1980). *Barry and Alice.* Englewood Cliffs, N.J.: Prentice-Hall. An autobiography of a bisexual married couple.

Variations in Sexual Behavior

16

Chapter Highlights

*Some men love women, some love other men, some love dogs and horses, and occasionally you find one who loves his raincoat.**

Most laypeople, as well as most scientists, have a tendency to classify behavior as normal or abnormal. There seems to be a particular tendency to do this with regard to sexual behavior. Many terms are used for abnormal sexual behavior, including "sexual deviance," "perversion," "sexual variance," and "paraphilias." The term "sexual variations" will be used in this chapter because it is currently favored in scientific circles and because defining exactly what is "deviant" or what is a "perversion" is rather difficult.

In Chapter 15 I argued that homosexuality per se is not an abnormal form of sexual behavior. This chapter will deal with some behaviors that more people might consider to be abnormal, and so it seems advisable at this point to consider exactly when a sexual behavior is abnormal. That is, what is a reasonable set of criteria for deciding what kinds of sexual behavior are abnormal?

Paraphilia (par-uh-FILL-ee-uh): Erotic attraction to unusual things or behaviors; sexual variations.

WHEN IS SEXUAL BEHAVIOR ABNORMAL?

As we saw in Chapter 1, sexual behavior varies a great deal from one culture to the next. There is a corresponding variation across cultures in what is considered to be "abnormal" sexual behavior. Given this great variability, how can one come up with a reasonable set of criteria for what is abnormal? Perhaps it is best to begin by considering the way others have defined "abnormal" sexual behavior.

One approach is to use a *statistical definition* (Pomeroy, 1966). According to this approach, an abnormal sexual behavior is one that is rare, that is, one that is not practiced by many people. Following this definition, then, standing on one's hands while having intercourse would be considered abnormal because it is rarely done, although it does not seem very "sick" in any absolute sense. This definition,

* *Source*: Max Schulman. *I was a teen-age dwarf.*

unfortunately, does not give us much insight into the psychological or social functioning of the person who engages in the behavior

In the *sociological approach,* the problem of culture dependence is explicitly acknowledged. A sociologist might define a deviant sexual behavior as a sexual behavior that violates the norms of society. Thus if a society says that a particular sexual behavior is deviant, it is—at least in that society. This approach recognizes the importance of the individual's interaction with society and of the problems that people must face if their behavior is labeled "deviant" in the culture in which they live.

A *psychological approach* was stated by Arnold Buss in his text entitled *Psychopathology* (1966). He says, "The three criteria of abnormality are discomfort, inefficiency, and bizarreness." The last of these criteria, bizarreness, has the problem of being culturally defined; what seems bizarre in one culture may seem normal in another. However, the first two criteria are good in that they focus on the discomfort and unhappiness felt by the person with a truly abnormal pattern of sexual behavior and also on inefficiency; for example, if a man has such a fetish for women's undies that he steals them, gets himself arrested, and cannot hold a job, that is inefficient functioning, and the behavior can reasonably be considered abnormal.

Buss's definition is the one that will be used in this chapter: A sexual behavior is abnormal when it is uncomfortable for the person, inefficient, and/or bizarre. A fourth criterion should also be added: that of doing harm, either physically or psychologically, to oneself or others. But it is clearly a complex matter to define "abnormal," and for this reason the less value-laden term "sexual variations" is used in this chapter.

FETISHISM

Fetishism: When a person becomes sexually fixated on some object other than another human being and attaches great erotic significance to that object.

One form of sexual variation is **fetishism.** In fetishism, a person becomes sexually fixated on some object other than another human being and attaches great erotic significance to that object. In extreme cases the person is incapable of becoming aroused and having an orgasm unless the fetish object is present. Typically, the fetish item is something closely associated with the body, such as clothing. Inanimate-object fetishes can be roughly divided into two subcategories: media fetishes and form fetishes.

Media Fetishes and Form Fetishes

Media fetish: When the fetish object is anything made of a particular substance, such as leather.

In the **media fetish,** it is the material out of which an object is made that is important in its erotic value. An example would be a leather fetish, in which any leather item is arousing to the person. Media fetishes can be subdivided into hard media fetishes and soft media fetishes. In the hard media fetish, the fetish is for a hard substance, such as leather or rubber. Hard media fetishes may often be associated with sadomasochism (see below). In the soft media fetish, the substance, is soft, such as fur or silk.

Form fetish: When the fetish item is an object with a particular shape, such as high-heeled shoes.

In the **form fetish,** it is the object and its shape that are important. An example would be a shoe fetish, in which shoes are highly arousing (see Focus 16.1). Often shoe fetishes require that the shoes be high-heeled; this fetish may be associated with sadomasochism, in which the fetishist derives sexual satisfaction from being walked on by a woman in high heels. Other examples of form fetishes are fetishes for boots (which also may be associated with sadomasochism), garters, and lingerie (almost all fetishists are men).

A Case History of a Shoe Fetishist

The following case history is taken directly from the 1886 book *Psychopathia Sexualis,* by von Krafft-Ebing, the great early investigator of sexual deviance. It should give you the flavor of his work.

Case 114. X., aged twenty-four, from a badly tainted family (mother's brother and grandfather insane, one sister epileptic, another sister subject to migraine, parents of excitable temperament). During dentition he had convulsions. At the age of seven he was taught to masturbate by a servant girl. X. first experienced pleasure in these manipulations when the girl happened to touch his member with her shoe-clad foot. Thus, in the predisposed boy, an association was established, as a result of which, from that time on, merely the sight of a woman's shoe, and finally, merely the idea of them, sufficed to induce sexual excitement and erection. He now masturbated while looking at women's shoes or while calling them up in imagination. The shoes of the school mistress excited him intensely, and in general he was affected by shoes that were partly concealed by female garments. One day he could not keep from grasping the teacher's shoes—an act that caused him great sexual excitement. In spite of punishment he could not keep from performing this act repeatedly. Finally, it was recognized that there must be an abnormal motive in play, and he was sent to a male teacher. He then revelled in the memory of the shoe scenes with his former school mistress and thus had erections, orgasms, and, after his fourteenth year, ejaculation. At the same time, he masturbated while thinking of a woman's shoe. One day the thought came to him to increase his pleasure by using such a shoe for masturbation. Thereafter he frequently took shoes secretly and used them for that purpose.

Nothing else in a woman could excite him; the thought of coitus filled him with horror. Men did not interest him in any way. At the age of eighteen he opened a shop and, among other things, dealt in ladies' shoes. He was excited sexually by fitting shoes for his female patrons or by manipulating shoes that came for mending. One day while doing this he had an epileptic attack, and, soon after, another while practicing onanism in his customary way. Then he recognized for the first time the injury to health caused by his sexual practices. He tried to overcome his onanism, sold no more shoes, and strove to free himself from the abnormal association between women's shoes and the sexual function. Then frequent pollutions, with erotic dreams about shoes occurred, and the epileptic attacks continued. Though devoid of the slightest feeling for the female sex, he determined on marriage, which seemed to him to be the only remedy.

He married a pretty young lady. In spite of lively erections when he thought of his wife's shoes, in attempts at cohabitation he was absolutely impotent because his distaste for coitus and for close intercourse in general was far more powerful than the influence of the shoe-idea, which induced sexual excitement. On account of his impotence the patient applied to Dr. Hammond, who treated his epilepsy with bromides and advised him to hang a shoe up over his bed and look at it fixedly during coitus, at the same time imagining his wife to be a shoe. The patient became free from epileptic attacks and potent so that he could have coitus about once a week. His sexual excitation by women's shoes also grew less and less.

Source: R. von Krafft-Ebing. (1886). *Psychopathia sexualis,* p. 288. (Reprinted by Putnam, New York, 1965.)

Perhaps reading that being aroused by lingerie is deviant has made you rather uncomfortable because you yourself find lingerie arousing. Fetishes are discussed first in this chapter because they provide an excellent example of the continuum from normal to abnormal sexual behavior. That is, normal sexual behavior and abnormal sexual behavior (like other normal and abnormal behaviors) are not two separate categories but rather gradations on a continuum. Many people have mild fetishes—they find things such as silk underwear arousing—and that is well within the range of normal behavior; only when the fetish becomes extreme is it abnormal. Indeed, in one sample of college men, 42 percent reported that they had engaged in voyeurism and 35 percent had engaged in frottage (sexual rubbing against a woman in a crowd (Templeman & Stinnett, 1991). Unfortunately, the researchers did not ask about fetishes. But the point is that many of these behaviors are common even in normal populations.

This continuum from normal to abnormal behavior might be conceptualized using the scheme shown in Figure 16.1. A mild preference, or even a strong preference, for the fetish object (say, silk panties) is within the normal range of sexual behavior. When the silk panties have become an absolute necessity—when the man cannot become aroused and have intercourse unless they are present—then we have probably crossed the boundary into abnormal behavior. In extreme forms, the silk panties may become a substitute for a human partner, and the man's sexual behavior consists of masturbating with the silk panties present. In these extreme forms, the man may commit burglary or even assault to get the desired fetish object, and this would certainly fit our definition of abnormal sexual behavior.

The continuum from normal to abnormal behavior holds for many of the sexual variations discussed in this chapter, such as voyeurism, exhibitionism, and sadism.

Why Do People Become Fetishists?

Psychologists are not completely sure what causes fetishes to develop. Here we will consider three theoretical explanations: learning theory, cognitive theory, and the sexual addiction model. These theories can be applied equally well to explaining many of the other sexual variations in this chapter.

According to learning theory (for example, McGuire, 1965), fetishes result from classical conditioning, in which a learned association is built between the fetish object and sexual arousal and orgasm. In some cases a single learning trial might serve to cement the association. For example, a 12-year-old boy might masturbate to orgasm for the first time while standing on a fuzzy bathroom rug and ever after require fuzzy objects to become aroused. Another example appears to be the shoe fetishist described in Focus 16.1. In this case, shoes were associated with sexual arousal as the result of an early learning experience. There is even an experiment

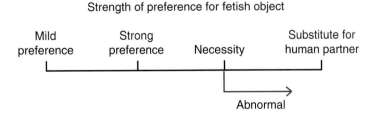

that demonstrated that males could, in the laboratory, be conditioned to become sexually aroused when viewing pictures of shoes (Rachman, 1966).

A second possible theoretical explanation comes from cognitive psychology, discussed in Chapter 2 (Walen & Roth, 1987). According to cognitive theorists, fetishists (or other paraphiliacs) have a serious cognitive distortion in that they perceive a nonconventional stimulus—such as black leather boots—as erotic. Further, their perception of arousal (Link 5 in the model, see Figure 9.4) is distorted. They feel "driven" to the sexual behavior when aroused, but the arousal may actually be caused by feelings of guilt and self-loathing. Thus there is a chain in which there are initial feelings of guilt at thoughts of the unconventional behavior, which produces arousal, which is misinterpreted as sexual arousal, which leads to a feeling that the fetish ritual must be carried out; it is, there is orgasm and temporary feelings of relief, but the evaluation of the event is negative, leading to further feelings of guilt and self-loathing, which perpetuates the chain.

A third theory that has been advanced to explain some paraphilias, especially those that seem compulsive, is the theory of sexual addictions, discussed in Focus 16.2.

Whatever the cause, fetishism typically develops early in life. In one sample of rubber fetishists, most of them first recognized their attraction to rubber when they were 4 to 10 years old (Gosselin & Wilson, 1980).

TRANSVESTISM

Transvestism: Deriving sexual gratification from dressing as a member of the other gender.

Drag queen: A male homosexual who dresses in women's clothing.

Female impersonator: A man who dresses up as a woman as part of a job in entertainment.

Transvestism ("trans" = "cross"; "vest" = "dressing") refers to dressing as a member of the other gender. Cross-dressing may be done by a variety of people for a variety of reasons. As has been noted, transsexuals may go through a stage of cross-dressing in the process of becoming women. Some male homosexuals—drag queens—dress up as women, and some lesbians dress in masculine clothes ("butch"); these practices, though, are basically caricatures of masculinity and femininity. Female impersonators are men who dress as women, often as part of their jobs as entertainers. For example, Jack Lemmon and Tony Curtis were female impersonators in the classic film with Marilyn Monroe *Some Like It Hot*. Finally, some—perhaps many—adolescent boys cross-dress, usually only once or a few times (Green, 1975). This behavior does not necessarily mean a life of transvestism; it may simply reflect the sexual drives, confusions, and frustrations of adolescence.

In contrast to people who engage in the kinds of cross-dressing discussed above, the true transvestite[1] is a person who derives sexual gratification from cross-dressing. Thus transvestism is probably basically a fetish (Pomeroy, 1975) and seems to be quite similar to a clothing fetish. The cross-dressing may often be done in private, perhaps even by a married man without his wife's knowledge.

As a result, no one has accurate data on the incidence of transvestism. One authority, though, estimates that more than a million males in the United States are involved in it, if all instances of men getting at least a temporary erotic reward from wearing female clothing are counted (Pomeroy, 1975). The vast majority of transvestites are heterosexuals; most are married and have children (Talamini, 1982).

Transvestism is almost exclusively a male sexual variation; it is essential unknown among women. There may be a number of reasons for this phenomenon,

[1] A common abbreviation for transvestism, used both by scientists and by members of the transvestite subculture, is TV. Therefore, if you see an ad in an underground newspaper placed by a person who is a TV, this is *not* someone who has delusions of broadcasting the six-o'clock news but rather a transvestite.

(a)

(b)

FIGURE 16.2
Two examples of cross-dressing; (a) A man in "drag." (b) Edward Hyde (1661–1723), governor of the colonies of New York and New Jersey from 1702 to 1708, who chose to be painted this way while he was governor.

including our culture's tolerance of women who wear masculine clothing and intolerance of men who wear feminine clothing. The phenomenon illustrates a more general point, namely, that many sexual variations are defined for, or practiced almost exclusively by, members of one gender; the parallel practice by members of the other gender is often not considered deviant. Most sexual variations are practiced mainly by males.[2]

Research indicates that there are four basic motivations for men engaging in transvestite activities (Talamini, 1982):

1. *Sexual arousal* As I noted earlier, transvestism appears to result from a conditioned association between sexual arousal and women's clothing. As one male transvestite commented,

   My older sister had beautiful clothes. When I was thirteen I wanted to see what I looked like when I dressed as a woman. We're about the same height. I put some of her lingerie on and I never had such powerful sexual feelings. It's twenty years later and I still dress up. (Talamini, 1982, p. 20)

2. *Relaxation* Transvestites report that they periodically need a break from the confining, pressured male role. Dressing up as women allows them to express emotionality and grace, traits that are taboo for men in our society.

[2] Two theories have been proposed as to why there are so many more male than female paraphiliacs (Flor-Henry, 1987; Wilson, 1987). According to one, the explanation lies in right-brain, left-brain differences between males and females. Sociobiologists, on the other hand, believe it lies in evolutionary selection of males to inseminate many partners and respond to novel sexual stimuli.

Sexual Addictions?

Patrick Carnes, in his book *The Sexual Addiction,* has advanced the theory that some cases of abnormal sexual behavior are actually a result of an addictive process much like alcoholism. One definition of alcoholism or other drug dependency is that the person has a pathological relationship with the mood-altering substance. In the case of the sexual addiction, the person has a pathological relationship to a sexual event or process, substituting it for a healthy relationship with others.

One common characteristic of alcoholics and sexual addicts is that they have a faulty belief system in which there is denial and distortion of reality. For example, the sexual addict may deny the possibility of sexual transmitted disease. Sexual addicts also engage in self-justification, such as "If I don't have it every few days, the pressure builds up." Like alcoholism, the addiction leads to many self-destructive behaviors. And, like alcoholism, the chief distinguishing feature of the sexual addiction is that the person has lost control of the behavior. Consider these examples:

- George had to take out a secret loan for $2700 to cover his frequent payments to prostitutes.

- Jeffrey, a respected lawyer, is arrested for the third time for flashing.

- In an example from film, Theresa (played by Diane Keaton in *Looking for Mr. Goodbar*) is murdered by one of her sexual partners as a consequence of her compulsive search for anonymous sex and bar pickups.

According to Carnes's analysis, each episode of the sexually compulsive behavior proceeds through a four-step cycle, and the cycle intensifies each time it is repeated.

1. *Preoccupation*   The person can think of nothing other than the sexual act to which he or she is addicted.

2. *Rituals*   The person enacts certain rituals that have become a prelude to the addictive act.

3. *Compulsive sexual behavior*   The sexual behavior is enacted and the person feels that he or she has no control over it.

4. *Despair*   Rather than feeling good after the sexual act is completed, the addict falls into a feeling of hopelessness and despair.

According to Carnes, it is important to understand that not all sexual variations are addictions, and therefore the addiction model will not explain all paraphilias. There are also addictions to some behaviors such as masturbation that in and of themselves are perfectly normal. Thus, for example, the man who masturbates while looking at pornographic magazines two times per week is probably not an addict, and the behavior is well within the normal range. However, the man who buys 20 porn magazines a week, masturbates four or five times a

3. *Role playing*   Just as many actors derive great satisfaction from playing roles in the theater, so transvestites get a great sense of achievement from being able to pass as women when in public.

4. *Adornment*   Men's clothes are relatively drab, whereas women's are more colorful and beautiful. Transvestites enjoy this sense of being beautiful.

day while looking at them, for a total of perhaps two or three hours, and can think of nothing else but where he can buy the next porn magazine and find the next private place to masturbate—that person is addicted. The key is the compulsiveness, the lack of control, the obsession (constant thoughts of the sexual scenario), and the obliviousness to danger or harmful consequences.

Interestingly, there is often a history of alcoholism in the families of sexual addicts. Sometimes, too, there is a history of the same sexual addiction, such as the father who sexually abuses his son, who in turn abuses his son, and the cycle perpetuates itself. Sexual addicts often report that as children they felt a sense of being abandoned and not loved.

Just as our culture celebrates alcohol and despises the alcoholic, so the culture celebrates sex and abhors the sexual addict. The media glorify alcohol. "You only go around once, so do it with Michelob." Advertising is filled with sexual messages (see Chapter 18). These sexual sells are difficult reminders for the sexual addict who is trying to recover.

According to Carnes, the most effective therapy for the sexual addict is the Alcoholics Anonymous program applied to sexual addictions. Several groups have adapted the AA program to sexual addiction, among them Sexaholics Anonymous (SA), Sex Addicts Anonymous (SAA), and Sex and Love Addicts Anonymous (SLAA). They can usually be found by calling the local phone number for Alcholics Anonymous. The first step in the process to recovery is admitting that one is sexually addicted, that the behavior is out of control, and that one's life has become unmanageable. These are hard admissions to make for someone who has spent years denying the existence of a problem. There are frequent meetings with a support group, and there is a strong emphasis on building feelings of self-worth.

There has generally been much praise for Carnes's analysis of sexual addictions. Criticism has come, however, from some gay activists, who feel the approach is homophobic in saying that gay men are addicted to sex. However, it is important to recognize that there are many possible addictions, many of them heterosexual (such as men addicted to anonmyous sex with prostitutes and women addicted to anonymous sex with bar pickups). Surely there are some gay men who are addicted to behaviors such as having impersonal tearoom sex, but the majority of gay men are not sexual addicts. The key feature, again, is that the behavior is out of control and compulsive.

Other criticisms have come from therapists and researchers in the field. The term "addiction," such as addiction to alcohol or heroin, has a very specific definition among professionals, and sexual addictions do not meet the definition in some ways. For example, if one is addicted to alcohol and suddenly stops using it, there is a withdrawl phenomenon that involves striking physical symptoms. If a person abstains from an addictive sexual behavior, there are no physiological withdrawal symptoms. A second criticism is that "addiction" may become an excuse for illegal, destructive behavior. For example, a rapist might say "I'm sexually addicted to raping and therefore can't stop myself."

In order to resolve this debate, some experts have suggested we use the term *compulsive sexual behavior* instead of "sexual addiction" (e.g., Coleman, 1991). The behavior is clearly compulsive and out of control, so it meets the definition of "compulsion" even though it may not meet the definition of "addiction."

These criticisms notwithstanding, Carnes's work has opened up a new way to think about out-of-control sexual behaviors and how to treat them.

Source: Patrick Carnes. (1983). *The sexual addiction*. Minneapolis: CompCare Publications.

How do the wives and children of the transvestite react to his unusual behavior? In one sample of 50 heterosexual transvestites, 60 percent of the wives were accepting of their husband's cross-dressing (Talamini, 1982). Most of these women commented that otherwise he was a good husband. Some of the wives felt fulfilled being supportive of the husband, and some even helped him in dressing and applying makeup. In the same sample, 13 of the couples had told their children about the cross-dressing.

They claimed that the relationship with the children was undamaged and that the children were tolerant and understanding.

Transvestism is one of the harmless, victimless sexual variations, particularly when it is done in private. Like other forms of fetishism, it is a problem only when it becomes so extreme that it is the person's only source of erotic gratification.

SADISM AND MASOCHISM

Sadist: A person who derives sexual satisfaction from inflicting pain on another person.

A sadist is a person who derives sexual satisfaction from inflicting pain on another person. The term "sadism" derives from the name of the historical character the Marquis de Sade, who lived around the time of the French Revolution. Not only did he practice sadism—several women apparently died from his attentions (Bullough, 1976)—but he also wrote novels about these practices (the best known is *Justine*), thus assuring his place in history.

Masochist: A person who derives sexual satisfaction from experiencing pain.

A masochist is a person who is sexually aroused by experiencing pain. This variation is named after Leopold von Sacher-Masoch (1836–1895), who was himself a masochist and who wrote novels expressing masochistic fantasies. Notice that the definitions of these variations make specific their *sexual* nature; the terms are often loosely used to refer to people who are cruel or to people who seem to bring misfortune on themselves, but these are not the meanings used here.

Bondage: A type of sadomasochism in which sexual pleasure is derived from feeling restricted, usually by being tied up with ropes.

Though many sadists and masochists trade on physical pain, another version of sadomasochism, bondage, depends on the person's feeling restricted; this is usually done by tying him or her up with ropes. In yet another psychological version, the sadist adopts a "master" role and the masochist a "slave" role. The master then exerts psychic dominance over the slave, who submits.

FIGURE 16.3
Sadomasochism in art: Aristotle and Phyllis.

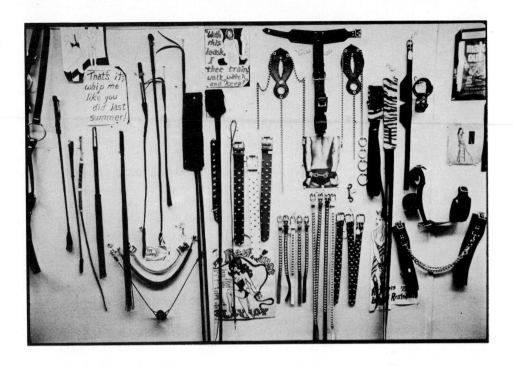

Sadomasochism is often accompanied by elaborate rituals and gadgetry, such as tight black leather clothing, pins and needles, ropes, whips, and hot wax (Figure 16.4). In the case of the psychological forms, the slave may actually wear a dog's collar and be led around on a leash by the master.

Interestingly, sadists and masochists do not consistently find experiencing pain and giving pain to be sexually satisfying. For example, the masochist who smashes a finger in a car door will yell and be unhappy just like anyone else. Pain is arousing for such people only when it is part of a carefully scripted ritual. As one woman put it,

> Of course, he doesn't *really* hurt me. I mean quite recently he tied me down ready to receive "punishment," then by mistake he kicked my heel with his toe as he walked by. I gave a yelp, and he said, "Sorry love—did I hurt you?" (Gosselin & Wilson, 1980, p. 55)

Sadomasochism (S-M) is a rare form of sexual behavior, although in its milder forms it is probably more common than many people think. Kinsey found that about 10 percent of males and 3 percent of females reported definite or frequent arousal responses to sadomasochistic stories. He also found that 26 percent of females and the same percentage of males had experienced definite or frequent erotic responses as a result of being bitten during sexual activity (Kinsey et al., 1953, pp. 677–678). Sadistic or masochistic fantasies appear to be considerably more common than real-life sadomasochistic behavior.

In one study, 178 S-M men filled out a questionnaire after responding to an ad in an S-M magazine or being contacted through an S-M support group (Moser & Levitt, 1987). The majority were heterosexual, well-educated, and interested in both dominant and submissive roles (switchable). The following are behaviors that the majority of them had both tried and enjoyed: humiliation, bondage, spanking, whipping, fetish behavior, tying up with ropes, and master and slave role playing.

Another study administered questionnaires to 130 males and 52 females who responded to ads placed in S-M magazines; the study focused particularly on the women respondents, who are often not recognized as part of the S-M subculture (Breslow et al., 1985). Thirty-three percent of the males and 28 percent of the females preferred the dominant role; 41 percent of the males and 40 percent of the females preferred the submissive role; and 26 percent of males and 32 percent of females were versatile. The majority of these S-M respondents were heterosexual.

The causes of sadism and masochism are not precisely known. The theories discussed in the section on fetishes can be applied here as well. For example, learning theory provides an explanation through conditioning. A little boy is being spanked over his mother's knee; in the process, his penis rubs against her knee, and he gets an erection. Or a little girl is caught masturbating and is spanked. In both cases, the child has learned to associate pain or spanking with sexual arousal, possibly setting up a lifelong career as a masochist. On the other hand, in one sample of sadomasochists, over 80 percent did *not* recall receiving erotic enjoyment from being punished as a child (Moser, 1979, cited in Weinberg, 1987). Thus forces besides conditioning must be at work.

Another psychological theory has been proposed to explain masochism specifically, although not sadism (Baumeister, 1988a, 1988b). According to the theory, the masochist is motivated by a desire to escape from self-awareness. That is, the masochistic behavior helps the individual escape from being conscious of the self in the same way that drunkenness or some forms of meditation do. In an era dominated by the "me generation," why would anyone want to escape from the self? Probably because high levels of self-awareness can lead to anxiety because of a focus on pressures on the self, responsibilities, the need to keep up a good image in front of others, and so on. Masochistic activity allows the person to escape from being an autonomous, separate individual. Masochism may be an unusually powerful form of escape because of its link to sexual pleasure. This theory can also explain why patterns of masochism seem to be so gender-linked (Baumeister, 1988b). According to the theory, the male role is especially burdensome because of the heavy pressures for autonomy, separateness, and individual achievement. Masochism accomplishes an escape from these aspects of the male role, explaining why masochism is more common among males than among females.

Sociologists emphasize that the key to the definition of S-M is not pain, but rather dominance and submission (D-S) (Weinberg, 1987). Thus it is not an individual phenomenon, but rather a social phenomenon embedded in a subculture and controlled by elaborate scripts.

Sociologists feel that to understand D-S, one must understand the social processes that create and sustain it (Weinberg, 1987). There is a distinct D-S subculture, involving magazines (such as *Corporal*), clubs, and bars. It creates culturally defined meanings for D-S acts. Thus a D-S act is not a wild outbreak of violence, but rather a carefully controlled performance with a script (recall the concept of scripts, Chapter 2). Within the play, people take on roles such as master, slave, or naughty child. Thus American men can play the submissive role in D-S culture, even though it contradicts the American male role, because it is really not them, but rather that naughty child, just as an actor can play the part of a murderer and know that he is not a murderer.

One interesting phenomenon, from a sociological point of view, is the social control of risk taking in D-S (Weinberg, 1987). That is, having allowed oneself to be tied up and whipped, one could be murdered, yet this is rare in the D-S subculture. Why? Research on the leather-sex subculture among gay men shows that there are complex social arrangements that reduce risk (Lee, 1979). First, initial contacts are usually made in protected territories such as leather bars, which are inhabited almost exclusively by other D-Sers who play by the same rules. Second, there are social networks among D-Sers, so that one can essentially get references on a potential partner to find out whether he is reliable. Finally, there is a negotiation of the D-S scenario as it begins, to ensure that both partners agree on how far they want to go.

VOYEURISM

Voyeur: A person who becomes sexually aroused from secretly viewing nudes.

Scoptophilia: A sexual variation in which the person becomes sexually aroused from others' sexual acts and genitals.

The term **voyeur** ("Peeping Tom")[3] generally refers to a person who derives sexual pleasure from watching others have sex. Actually, there are some variations within this category. In scoptophilia, sexual pleasure is derived from observing sexual acts and the genitals; in *voyeurism,* technically, the sexual pleasure comes from viewing nudes, often while the voyeur is masturbating.

Voyeurism appears to be much more common among males than among females, a fact that is reflected in the common name for it, "Peeping Tomism." According to FBI reports, nine men to one women are arrested on charges of "peeping."

Voyeurism provides another good illustration of the continuum from normal to abnormal behavior. For example, many men find it arousing to watch a nude woman—otherwise there would be no burlesque houses—and this is certainly well within the normal range of behavior. Some women are "crotch watchers," much as men are breast watchers (Friday, 1973, 1975). The voyeurism is abnormal when it replaces sexual intercourse or when the person commits a crime such as breaking and entering to observe others, thereby risking arrest.

Peepers typically want the woman they view to be a stranger and do not want her to know what they are doing (Yalom, 1960). The element of risk is also important; while one might think that a nudist camp would be heaven to a peeper, it is not, because the elements of risk and forbiddenness are missing (Sagarin, 1973).

Voyeurs may or may not be dangerous (Tuteur, 1984). Potentially dangerous voyeurs can be identified by the following characteristics: (1) They enter the confines of a building or other structure in order to view their subject, and (2) they draw the attention of their subject to the fact that they are watching (Yalom, 1960).

The voyeur is generally young and a "late bloomer" (R. S. Smith, 1976). He is typically a shy, sexually inadequate person who has difficulty establishing romantic relationships with others. It is rare to find a peeper who has a good sex life (Gebhard et al., 1965; Yalom, 1960).

In one study of arrested peepers, it was found that they were likely to be the youngest child in their family and to have good relationships with their parents but poor relationships with their peers (Gebhard et al., 1965). They had few sisters and few female friends. Few were married. This study, however, points up one of the major problems with the research on sexual variations: Much of it has been done only on people who have been arrested for their behavior. The "respectable paraphiliac" who has the behavior under somewhat better control or who is skilled enough or can pull enough strings not to get caught is not studied in such research. Thus the picture that research provides for us of these variations may be very biased.

EXHIBITIONISM

Exhibitionist: A person who derives sexual gratification from exposing his genitals to others in situations in which this is inappropriate.

The complement to voyeurism is **exhibitionism** ("flashing"), in which the person derives sexual pleasure from exposing his genitals to others in situations where this

---

[3] "Voyeur" comes from the French word *voir,* meaning "to see." "Peeping Tom" comes from the story of Lady Godiva; when she rode through town nude to protest the fact that her husband was raising his tenants' taxes, none of the townspeople looked except one, Tom of Coventry.

FIGURE 16.5
Exhibitionism.

is clearly inappropriate.[4] The pronoun "his" is used advisedly, since exhibitionism is defined exclusively for men. The woman who wears a dress that reveals most of her bosom is likely to be thought of as attractive rather than abnormal. When the male exposes himself, it is considered offensive. Once again, whether a sexual behavior is considered abnormal depends greatly on whether the person doing it is a male or a female. Homosexual exhibitionism is also quite rare, and so the prototype we have for exhibitionism is a man exposing himself to a woman. About 30 percent of all arrests for sexual offenses are for exhibitionism (Cox, 1988). According to one survey, 33 percent of college women have been the objects of indecent exposure (Cox, 1988).

The man generally begins exhibiting himself when he is in his early twenties,

[4]   Here is a classic limerick on exhibitionism:

There was a young lady of Exeter
So pretty, men craned their necks at her.
    One was even so brave
    As to take out and wave
The distinguishing mark of his sex at her.

472

although some may begin in adolescence (Blair & Lanyon, 1981). Exhibitionists generally recall their childhoods as being characterized by inconsistent discipline, lack of affection, and little training in appropriate forms of social behavior.

In adulthood, exhibitionists do not seem to be psychiatrically disturbed (Blair & Lanyon, 1981). However, they generally are timid and unassertive and lacking in social skills. They also seem to have trouble recognizing and handling their own feelings of hostility. Many are married, but they do not seem to be gratified with heterosexual sex.

One study indicated that exhibitionists have frequently been arrested previously for other sex offenses such as rape and voyeurism (Gebhard et al., 1965). However, this was a study of arrested exhibitionists, and this pattern might not hold for the more "normal" exhibitionist who doesn't get himself arrested.

The exact causes of exhibitionism are not known, but a social learning-theory explanation offers some possibilities (Blair & Lanyon, 1981). According to this view, the parents might have subtly (or perhaps obviously) modeled such behavior to the man when he was a child. In adulthood, there may be reinforcements for the exhibitionistic behavior because the man gets attention when he performs it. In addition, the man may lack the social skills to form an adult relationship, or the sex in his marriage may not be very good, so he receives little reinforcement for normal sex.

The learning-theory approach has been used to devise some programs of therapy that have been successful in treating exhibitionists. For example, in one therapy program exhibitionists were shown photos of scenes in which they typically engaged in exhibitionism; simultaneously, an unpleasant-smelling substance was placed at their nostrils (Maletzky, 1974, 1977, 1980). After 11 to 19 twice-weekly sessions of this conditioning and some self-administered home sessions, all but one of the men passed a temptation test in which they were placed in a naturalistic situation with a volunteer female and managed not to flash at her.

Many women, understandably, are alarmed by the exhibitionist. But since the exhibitionist's goal is to produce shock or some other strong emotional response, the woman who becomes extremely upset is gratifying him. Probably the best strategy for a woman to use in this situation is to remain calm and make some remark indicating her coolness, such as suggesting that he should seek professional help for his problem.

NYMPHOMANIA AND SATYRIASIS

Nymphomania (nim-foh-MANE-ee-uh): An excessive, insatiable sex drive in a woman.

Satyriasis (sat-ur-EYE-uh-sis): An excessive, insatiable sex drive in a man.

Nymphomania and satyriasis are both conditions in which there is an extraordinarily high level of sexual activity and sex drive, to the point where the person is apparently insatiable and where sexuality overshadows all other concerns and interests. When it occurs in women, it is called **nymphomania**; in men it is called **satyriasis** (or Don Juanism).[5] While this definition seems fairly simple, in practice it is difficult to say when a person has an abnormally high sex drive. As was seen in Chapters 11 and 12, there is a wide range in the frequencies with which people engage in coitus; therefore, the range we define as "normal" should also be broad. In real life, the "nymphomania" or "satyriasis" is often defined by the spouse. Some men, for example, might think that it was unreasonable for a wife to want intercourse once a day or even twice a week, and they would consider such a woman a nymphomaniac.[6]

[5] Satyriasis is named for the satyrs, who were part-human, part-animal beasts in Greek mythology. A part of the entourage of Dionysus, the god of wine and fertility, they were jovial and lusty and have become a symbol of the sexually active male.

[6] Someone once defined a nymphomaniac as a woman that a man can't keep up with.

Other men might think it would be wonderful to be married to a woman who wanted to make love every day. Labels like "nymphomaniac" can be used as weapons in marital squabbles. Because such terms are so loaded, some scholars think the term hypersexuality is preferable.

The term "nymphomaniac" is used particularly loosely by laypeople. A nymphomaniac is more than just a woman who likes sex. True nymphomania is very rare. What defines true hypersexuality, then? Probably it is the insatiability and the compulsiveness of the behavior. It is compulsive in the sense that the person feels driven to it even when there may be very negative consequences (Goldberg, 1987). The person is also never satisfied by the activity and may not be having orgasms, despite all the sexual activity. Such cases would meet the criteria for abnormal behavior discussed at the beginning of this chapter: The compulsiveness of the behavior leads it to become extremely inefficient, with the result that it impairs functioning in other areas of the person's life. Hypersexuality is probably best understood in terms of sexual addiction theory (Focus 16.2).

Once again, these variations illustrate the extent to which the person's gender is important in defining abnormality. Since the stereotype is that women have a very low sex drive, a woman with a high sex drive is classified as a "nympho," a term that is commonly used. Men, according to the stereotype, have a high sex drive; thus it is scarcely even recognized that a few men might have problems with an abnormally high sex drive, and the term "satyriasis" is rarely used.

OTHER SEXUAL VARIATIONS

The sexual variations discussed below are too rare to have had much research devoted to them; they are nonetheless interesting because of their bizarreness.

Troilism, or *triolism*, refers to three people having sex together.

Saliromania is a disorder found mainly in men; there is a desire to damage or soil a woman or her clothes or the image of a woman, such as a painting or statue. The man becomes sexually excited and may ejaculate during the act.

Asphyxiophilia is defined as a desire for oxygen deficiency in order to increase sexual arousal. It may involve placing a rope around the neck and tightening until the desired effect is obtained. This is a dangerous behavior; it is estimated that it causes between 250 and 1000 deaths per year in the United States (Innala & Ernuff, 1989).

Coprophilia and urophilia are both variations having to do with excretion. In coprophilia the feces are important to sexual satisfaction. In urophilia it is the urine that is important. The urophiliac may want to be urinated on as part of the sexual act.

Frotteurism is inappropriate sexual touching or rubbing. A man may approach a woman from the rear and covertly press his penis against her buttocks; sometimes she is not even aware of it, in a place like a crowded subway or elevator.

Necrophilia is sexual contact with a dead person. It is a very rare form of behavior and is considered by experts to be psychotic and extremely deviant. Necrophiliacs derive sexual gratification from viewing a corpse or actually having intercourse with it; the corpse may be mutilated afterward (Thorpe et al., 1961). The highly publicized murder and mutilation case involving Jeffrey Dahmer in Milwaukee may well fall into this category. Experts believe that he was motivated by necrophilia.

Zoophilia is sexual contact with an animal; this behavior is also called *bestiality* and *sodomy*, although the latter term is also used to refer to anal intercourse or even mouth-genital sex. About 8 percent of the males in Kinsey's sample reported sexual experiences with animals. Most of this activity was concentrated in adolescence and

---

Hypersexuality: An excessive, insatiable sex drive in either men or women.

Troilism (TROY-uhl-ism): Three people having sex together.

Saliromania: A desire to damage or soil a woman or her clothes.

Asphyxiophilia: A desire for a state of oxygen deprivation to enhance sexual arousal.

Coprophilia (cop-roh-FILL-ee-uh): Deriving sexual satisfaction from contact with feces.

Urophilia (YUR-oh-fill-ee-uh): Deriving sexual satisfaction from contact with urine.

Necrophilia: A sexual variation involving having sexual contact with a dead person.

Zoophilia: Sexual contact with an animal; also called bestiality or sodomy.

probably reflected the experimentation and diffuse sexual urges of that period. Not too surprisingly, the percentage was considerably higher among boys on farms; 17 percent of boys raised on farms had had animal contacts resulting in orgasm. Kinsey found that about 3 to 4 percent of all females have had some sexual contact with animals, and thus females appear to be less likely to engage in this behavior than males.

PREVENTION OF SEXUAL DISORDERS

The misery that many people—e.g., the sexually addicted S-Mer—suffer, not to mention the harm they may do to others (e.g., the child molester), is good reason to want to develop programs for preventing sexual disorders (Qualls, 1978). In preventive medicine, a distinction is made between primary prevention and secondary prevention. Applied to the sexual disorders, primary prevention would mean intervening in home life or in other factors in childhood to help prevent problems from developing or trying to teach people how to cope with crises or stress so that problems do not develop. In secondary prevention, the idea is to diagnose and treat the problem as early as possible, so that difficulties are minimized.

It would be highly advantageous to do primary prevention of sexual disorders—that is, head them off before they even develop. Unfortunately, this is proving to be difficult, for a number of reasons. One problem is in diagnostic categories. The categories for the diagnosis of sexual variations are not nearly so clear-cut as they may seem in this chapter, and multiple diagnoses for a person are not uncommon. That is, a given man might have engaged in incest, pedophilia, and exhibitionism. If it is unclear how to diagnose sexual variations, it is going to be rather difficult to figure out how to prevent them. If one is not sure if there is a difference between chicken pox and measles, it is rather difficult to start giving inoculations.

An alternative approach that seems promising—rather than figuring out ways to prevent each separate variation—is to analyze the *components of sexual development*. Disturbance in one or more of these components in development might lead to different variations. One proposal for these components is as follows (Bancroft, 1978):

1. *Gender identity*   The sense of maleness or femaleness developed in early childhood
2. *Sexual responsiveness*   Arousal to appropriate stimuli
3. *Formation of relationships with others*

It seems clear that different developmental components are disturbed in different variations. For example, in transsexualism, it is the first component, gender identity, that is disturbed. In the case of the fetishist, it is the second component, sexual responsiveness to appropriate stimuli, that is disturbed. And in the case of the exhibitionist, it may be that it is the last component, the ability to form relationships, that is disturbed.

The idea would then be to try to ensure that as children grow up, their development in each of these three components is healthy. Ideally, sexual variations should not occur then.

Space does not permit us to consider what prevention programs might look like for all the different variations (see Bancroft, 1978, for further discussion), so let us consider one example, transsexualism, in some detail (Green, 1978b; see Chapter 14 for a discussion of transsexualism).

Suppose that we have a typical case of a very feminine boy, Billy, whose parents bring him in for treatment. Billy prefers to dress in girls' clothes, wants to play with dolls and plays house, and dislikes playing with boys because they are too rough. He might be considered a high risk for becoming a transsexual, because virtually all transsexuals recall a sense of being trapped in the wrong body from earliest childhood.

What kind of therapy can be used? Some efforts are made at simple education—making sure Billy understands the anatomical differences between boys and girls, and that one cannot change gender magically. Positive aspects of maleness are emphasized. Male playmates are found who are not rough. Parents are encouraged not to engage in behavior that may reinforce his conflict—for example, commenting that he is cute when dressed up as a girl. The father-son relationship is encouraged, and a male therapist is used so that the boy can identify with him. Finally, intervention may simply be to help the child live with his own atypical behavior.

Such therapy raises a host of ethical issues. Is it right to make a traditional, stereotyped male out of a boy who might simply be androgynous? Is it right to intervene when one is not sure that he will become a transsexual? Indeed, in longitudinal follow-up studies of 26 feminine boys, 14 did become transsexuals, transvestites, or homosexuals, but 12 became heterosexuals. Therefore, one cannot be sure about a feminine 5-year-old. And even if superficial masculine behavior is successfully encouraged, what if a host of conflicts continues to simmer below the surface, creating a more seriously disturbed individual? Richard Green summarizes the complex problems this way:

> It may be argued that to induce intervention (which may be prevention) reinforces societal sexism. Regrettably, to a degree it does. But while we have a responsibility to reduce sexism, we have a responsibility to an individual child caught in the cross fire between sex role idealism and the real world in which he is embedded. (1978b, p. 88)

We have a long way to go in preventing sexual disorders, to say the least.

TREATMENT OF SEXUAL VARIATIONS

Some of the sexual variations discussed in this chapter—such as the mild fetishes—are well within the normal range of sexual expression. There is no need for treatment. Others, however, fall into the abnormal range, causing personal anguish to the individual and possibly harm to unwilling victims. Treatments are needed for this category of variations. Many different treatments have been tried, each based on a different theoretical understanding of the causes of sexual variations. We will look at four categories of treatments: biological-medical treatments, cognitive-behavioral therapies, skills training, and AA 12-step programs.

Biological-Medical Treatments

Based on the notion that sexual variations are caused by biological factors, various biological-medical treatments for sexual variations have been tried over the last century. Some of them look today like nothing other than cruel and unusual punishment. Nonetheless, people would love to have a "pill" that would cure some of these complex and painful or dangerous paraphilias, and so the search for such treatments continues.

Surgical castration was used fairly commonly in the United States in the 1800s as a treatment for various kinds of uncontrollable sexual urges (Bullough, 1976). The idea resurfaced recently in some court cases in which castration was proposed as a treatment for rapists, as discussed in Focus 9.3 in Chapter 9. Such treatments are based on the notion that removing a man's testosterone by removing the testes will lead to a drastic reduction in sex drive, which will in turn erase urges to commit sex offenses. However, as we saw in Chapter 9, reduction in testosterone levels in humans does not always lead to a reduction in sexual behavior. Surgical castration cannot be recommended as a treatment for sex offenders either on humanitarian grounds or on grounds of effectiveness.

An alternative strategy has been the use of various drugs that reduce testosterone levels or block the effects of testosterone. Cyproterone acetate (CPA) is one such drug. Studies indicate that it does inhibit sexual response to some extent. When used together with counseling, the drug seems to be effective with some sex offenders (Cooper, 1986). The best results are obtained with men who are highly motivated to change their behavior and have good relationships with some people who can provide social support for them.

Depo Provera, a drug used as a contraceptive for women, has also been used in treating male sex offenders (Walen & Roth, 1987). It, too, lowers testosterone levels and seems to cut the edge off the compulsiveness of the paraphilia so that the person can control the behavior.

Cognitive-Behavioral Therapies

Another approach is the use of various cognitive-behavioral therapies, which involve behavior therapy based on behaviorism and learning theory, together with cognitive therapies that focus on changing things such as perceptions, thoughts, and fantasies (Walen & Roth, 1987).

Although the media sometimes carry flashy stories about applications of behavior therapy that involve administering electric shocks to a sex offender if he becomes aroused at, say, a picture of a nude child, in fact much milder techniques have been used and are effective. *Covert sensitization* is one such therapy. It involves pairing aversive imagery (thoughts) with fantasies of the undesirable behavior. In the treatment of an exhibitionist, for example, he repeatedly practices a vivid fantasy in which, just as he imagines getting ready to expose himself, he experiences waves of nausea and vomiting. The details, of course, are individualized to the person and his particular problem. Case reports indicate that this approach has been effective in cases such as sadism, exhibitionism, and pedophilia (Walen & Roth, 1987; Barlow et al., 1969).

Another approach is *orgasmic reconditioning* (Walen & Roth, 1987; Marquis, 1970). The patient is told to masturbate to his usual paraphiliac fantasies. Then, just at the moment of orgasm, he switches to an acceptable fantasy. After practicing this for some time, he becomes able to have an orgasm regularly while having an acceptable fantasy. He then is told to move the fantasy progressively to an earlier time during masturbation. Gradually he becomes conditioned to experiencing sexual arousal in the context of acceptable behavior.

Skills Training

According to yet another theoretical understanding, paraphiliacs engage in their behavior because they have great difficulty forming healthy relationships in which they can find sexual satisfaction. For individuals who fall into this category, a treatment program might include social and dating skills training to enable them to master the early stages of forming a good relationship, together with training in such areas as communication skills, assertiveness training, and intimacy skills training.

AA 12-Step Programs

As we saw in Focus 16.2 earlier in this chapter, sexual addiction theory argues that many people who engage uncontrollable inappropriate sexual patterns are addicted to their particular sexual practice. The appropriate treatment, according to this approach, is one of the 12-Step programs modeled on Alcoholics Anonymous. There are Sexaholics Anonymous programs in most major cities today.

What Works?

What we need now is carefully controlled research on the effectiveness of these different treatment approaches so that we know which ones work at all, which work best, and which work best with different types of sexual problems.

It seems reasonable to define "abnormal sexual behavior" as behavior that is uncomfortable for the person, inefficient, bizarre, and/or physically or psychologically harmful to the person or others.

Four theoretical approaches have been used in understanding the paraphilias: learning theory, cognitive theory, the sexual addiction model, and sociological theory. Sociobiology has been used to explain why there are so many more male than female paraphiliacs.

A fetishist is a person who becomes erotically attached to some object other than another human being. Most likely, fetishism arises from conditioning, and it provides a good example of the continuum from normal to abnormal behavior.

The transvestite derives sexual satisfaction from dressing as a member of the opposite gender. Like many other sexual variations, transvestism is more common among men than among women.

The sadist derives sexual pleasure from inflicting pain, while the masochist is sexually excited by experiencing pain.

The voyeur is sexually aroused by looking at nudes or by watching others have sex; the exhibitionist displays his sexual organs to others. Both are generally harmless.

Nymphomania in women and satyriasis in men are conditions in which there is an extraordinarily high, insatiable sex drive. Both syndromes are very rare.

Other sexual variations include zoophilia, asphyxiophilia, and necrophilia.

The possibility of programs or therapies to prevent and treat sexual variations is being explored, although the topic is complex.

Review Questions

1. According to a psychological definition, sexual behavior can be considered abnormal if it causes discomfort to the person, if it is bizarre, or if it causes harm to the self or other. True or false?

2. ＿＿＿＿＿＿ is the term for becoming sexually fixated on some object other than another human being and attaching great erotic significance to that object.

3. Transvestism is considered to be a fetish, because the man becomes sexually aroused from dressing in women's clothes. True or false?

4. A ＿＿＿＿＿＿ is a person who becomes sexually aroused when experiencing pain.

5. A voyeur is a person who derives sexual gratification from exposing his or her genitals to others. True or false?

6. When a woman has an insatiable sex drive it is termed nymphomania, but the preferred scientific term is ＿＿＿＿＿＿.

7. According to Patrick Carnes, if a person's sexual ritual has become an obsession and can't be controlled, the person has a ＿＿＿＿＿＿.

8. It is rare to find a transvestite who is heterosexually married. True or false?

9. "Bondage" refers to a form of sadomasochism in which the pleasure is derived from one partner tying up the other one with ropes. True or false?

10. Covert sensitization is a treatment for sex offenders based on sexual addiction theory. True or false?

(The answers to all review questions are at the end of the book, beginning on page 731.)

1. What do you think of the idea about preventing sexual disorders presented at the end of this chapter? Do you think the schools or some other agency should institute a program to screen children, trying to detect those with characteristics that might indicate they would develop a sexual variation late in life, and then give therapy to those children?

2. Of the sexual variations in this chapter, which seems to you to be the most abnormal? Why? Does the one you have chosen fit the criteria for abnormality discussed at the beginning of the chapter?

Suggestion for Further Reading

Wilson, Glenn D. (Ed.). (1986). *Variant sexuality: Research and theory.* Baltimore: Johns Hopkins University Press. The chapters in this book review different theoretical explanations for sexual variations, from genetics and sociobiology to cross-cultural perspectives.

17

Sexual Coercion

Chapter Highlights

I. Rape
   Theoretical Views of Rape
   Attitudes Toward Rape
   Psychological Responses of the
      Rape Victim
   Female Socialization: Creating
      Rape Victims
   Rapists
   Date Rape
   Marital Rape
   Male Socialization: Creating Rapists
   Men Raped by Women
   Prison Rape
   Ethnicity and Rape
   Preventing Rape

II. Incest and Child Molestation
   Pedophilia
   Incidence of Incest
   Father-Daughter Incest
   Psychological Impact on the Victim
   Incest Taboos

III. Sexual Harassment
   Sexual Harassment at Work
   Sexual Harassment in Education: An A
      for a Lay
   Psychotherapist-Patient Sex

RAPE POEM

There is no difference between being raped
and being pushed down a flight of cement steps
except that the wounds also bleed inside.

There is no difference between being raped
and being run over by a truck
except that afterward men ask if you enjoyed it.

There is no difference between being raped
and being bit on the ankle by a rattlesnake
except that people ask if your skirt was short
*and why you were out alone anyhow.**

This chapter is about sexual activity that involves coercion and is not between consenting adults; specifically, we will consider rape, incest and child molestation, and sexual harassment at work and in education. All of these have been highly publicized topics in the last 10 or 15 years, and some good scientific research on them has quickly appeared.

RAPE

In 1990 there were 102,500 cases of reported rape in the United States; that means there were 80 reported rapes for every 100,000 women (FBI, 1991). However, according to the FBI, forcible rape is one of the most underreported crimes. One

* *Source:* Excerpted from Marge Piercy. (1976). Rape poem. In *Living in the open.* New York: Knopf. Reprinted by permission of Wallace & Sheil Agency, Inc. Copyright 1974, 1976 by Marge Piercy.

study found that about one in five (21 percent) stranger rapes had been reported, but only 2 percent of acquaintance rapes had been reported (Koss et al., 1988). Based on interviews with a random sample of San Francisco women, researchers concluded—after adjusting for age—that there is a 26 percent chance that a woman will be the victim of a completed rape at some time in her life (Russell & Howell, 1983). A well-sampled study of women college students found that 28 percent had experienced an act that met the legal definitions of rape (Koss et al., 1987).

We will examine what is known about the rape victim, about the rapist, and about what can be done to prevent rape. First, however, some terms need definition. Though the legal definition of rape varies from state to state, the following is typical of the definitions used in the United States (Snelling, 1975):

> . . . the perpetration of an act of sexual intercourse with a female, not one's wife, against her will and consent, whether her will is overcome by force or fear resulting from the threat of force, or by drugs or intoxicants; or when, because of mental deficiency, she is incapable of exercising rational judgment; or when she is below an arbitrary "age of consent." (Brownmiller, 1975, p. 368)

Rape: Sexual intercourse or other sex act (such as fellatio) that occurs without consent, whether by force or fear.

Statutory rape: Intercourse with a girl who is younger than the legal age of consent.

The last phrase refers to a specific kind of rape, statutory rape, which is intercourse with a girl who is below the legal age of consent. The idea is that in this particular offense, resistance or will is irrelevant, since the girl is simply too young to make a judgment; therefore, the man is automatically considered to have taken advantage of her. The legal age of consent varies from state to state; in most states, it ranges between 12 and 16 years.

Contemporary efforts at legal reform have led to the rewriting of rape laws. The victim may be referred to as a "person" to include male rape victims. The laws may also be worded so as to permit a wife to prosecute her husband for rape. Some states have changed to the terms "sexual assault" and "sexual battery" to emphasize that violence is the issue. However, many states have not rewritten their laws, and the definition given above would be typical for them.

Theoretical Views of Rape

To provide a perspective for the discussion that follows, we can distinguish among four major theoretical views of the nature of rape (Albin, 1977; Baron & Straus, 1989):

Victim-precipitated: The view that rape is a result of a woman "asking for it."

1. *Victim-precipitated* This view holds that a rape is always caused by a woman "asking for it." Rape, then, is basically the woman's fault. This view represents the tendency to "blame the victim."
2. *Psychopathology of rapists* This theoretical view holds that rape is an act committed by a psychologically disturbed man. His deviance is responsible for the crime occurring.
3. *Feminist* Feminist theorists view rapists as the product of gender-role socialization in our culture. They deemphasize the sexual aspects of rape and instead view rape as an expression of power and dominance by men over women. Gender inequality is both the cause and the result of rape.
4. *Social disorganization* Sociologists believe that crime rates, including rape rates, increase when the social organization of a community is disrupted and social disorganization results. Under such conditions the community cannot enforce its norms against crime.

You personally may subscribe to one of these views. It is also true that researchers in this area have generally based their work on one of these theoretical models, and this may influence their research. You should keep these models in mind as you continue to read the rest of this chapter.

Sociologists Larry Baron and Murray Straus (1989), experts in violence research, did an extensive study to test the last two theories listed above, feminist theory and social disorganization theory. Both theories deal with rape as a result of cultural context. Baron and Straus collected extensive data on each of the 50 states in the United States, seeing them as representing variations in cultural context (think for example, of the different cultures of Louisiana, New York, and North Dakota). To test feminist theory, they collected data on the extent of gender inequality in each state (for example, the gap beween men's and women's wages); they also examined the feminist hypothesis that use of pornography encourages rape, by collecting data on the circulation of pornographic magazines in each state. They also obtained measures of social disorganization, such as the number of people moving into or out of the state, the divorce rate, and even the number of tourists flowing into the state. Their data gave strong support to three conclusions: (1) Gender inequality is related to rape (the states with the greatest gender inequality had the highest rape rates); (2) pornography provides ideological support for rape (the states with the highest circulation of pornographic magazines tended to have the highest rape rates); and (3) social disorganization contributes to rape (those states with the greatest social disorganization tended to have the highest rape rates). This research shows that many complex factors may contribute to rape. It emphasizes how important cultural context is in creating a social climate that encourages or discourages rape.

Attitudes Toward Rape

Psychologist Hubert Feild (1978) investigated attitudes toward rape among police, rapists, rape-crisis counselors, and citizens from the general population. He began his research by constructing a paper-and-pencil questionnaire that would measure people's attitudes toward rape on a number of different dimensions. Items were ranked on a scale from 1 (strongly agree) to 6 (strongly disagree) and consisted of statements such as "A woman should be responsible for preventing her own rape." Once Feild had developed this attitude scale, he administered it to people from the groups listed above. He obtained a number of interesting results.

In general, there was strong agreement with the following statements: "A woman can be raped against her will" and "A woman should not feel guilty following a rape." There was strong disagreement with "A raped women is a less desirable woman"; "If a woman is going to be raped, she might as well relax and enjoy it"; "Most women secretly desire to be raped"; "It would do some women some good to get raped"; and "Rape serves as a way to put or keep women in their 'place.' " On the other hand, people on the average were fairly neutral (ratings around 3.5) on such items as "Women provoke rape by their appearance or behavior" and "The reason most rapists commit rape is for sex."

There were a number of gender differences in attitudes toward rape, as might be expected. Men indicated to a significantly greater extent that it was a woman's responsibility to prevent rape, that victims precipitate rape through their appearance or behavior, that rapists are mentally normal, that rapists are not motivated by a need for power over women, that a woman is less attractive as a result of being raped, and that women should not resist during rape. It was also true that attitudes toward rape were correlated with attitudes toward women; people with traditional, conservative attitudes toward women were more likely to blame the victim.

Comfortingly, there was a significant difference between rapists and rape-crisis counselors in their attitudes toward rape.

Distressingly, however, police officers' views of rape were more similar to the rapists' than they were to the counselors'. No significant differences were found between police and rapists on most dimensions. It was also true that citizens from the general population had attitudes more like those of rapists than those of counselors. The citizens generally seemed to hold a negative view of rape victims.

Psychological Responses of the Rape Victim

A number of researchers have investigated the psychological reactions of women following rape (e.g., Burgess & Holmstrom, 1974a, 1974b; Calhoun et al., 1982; Kilpatrick et al., 1981; Resick, 1983; review by Becker & Kaplan, 1991). This research shows that rape is a time of crisis for a woman and that the effects on her adjustment may persist for a year or more. The term rape trauma syndrome has been used to refer to the emotional and physical changes that a woman undergoes following a rape or an attempted rape (Burgess & Holmstrom, 1974a). Victims may experience posttraumatic stress disorder (PTSD) (Becker & Kaplan, 1991).

Emotional reactions immediately after the rape (the acute phase) generally are severe. At one month after the rape, victims are significantly more depressed than a control group of women (Resick, 1983). Victims are also very fearful and anxious.

Some women experience self-blame. The woman may spend hours agonizing over what she did to bring on the rape or what she might have done to prevent it: "If I hadn't worn that tight sweater, . . ." "If I hadn't worn that short skirt, . . ." "If I hadn't been stupid enough to talk on that dark street, . . ." "If I hadn't been dumb enough to trust that guy, . . ." This is an example of a tendency on the part of both the victim and others to blame the victim.

The woman also may have physical injuries from the rape, such as cuts and bruises. Women who have been forced to have oral sex may suffer irritation or damage to the throat, and rectal bleeding and pain are reported by women forced to have anal intercourse.[1]

After the immediate, acute phase, there is a *long-term reorganization phase* during which the woman makes efforts to cope and get her life back to normal, while still experiencing some serious psychological consequences. By four months after the rape, victims on the average are not significantly more depressed than a control group. However, fear and anxiety are still at heightened levels even one year after the rape (Resick, 1983). Problems with adjustment at work are still present eight months after the rape. And problems with sexual functioning can persist for a year or more. One woman reported, five months after being raped, "There are times I get hysterical with my boyfriend. I don't want him near me; I get panicked" (Burgess & Holmstrom, 1974a, p. 984).

On the other hand, not all victims of rape are severely traumatized. For example, in one study 26 percent of the victims reported no depressive symptoms two weeks after the rape (Resick, 1983). Researchers have tried to identify what factors determine who will experience the severe reactions (Resick, 1983). Contrary to what one might expect, the amount of trauma involved in the rape (e.g., the amount of physical injury) seems unrelated to psychological symptoms afterward. If the woman

Rape trauma syndrome: The psychological and physical damage that occurs to a woman who has been raped.

---

[1] Tests for sexually transmitted diseases should routinely be done as part of the hospital treatment of rape victims. Pregnancy tests can be done if the woman's period is late. Another alternative, if pregnancy seems likely, is to administer the morning-after pill immediately, although it has some serious side effects (see Chapter 8).

A Rape Victim Tells Her Story

High school was quite successful for me. I was a member of the group of about twenty who literally ran the school from the administration downward. I had several authoritative positions. The majority of my comrades were also female. This was very unusual, or so it seems, to have the student government of a school of two thousand primarily female. All of my friends went Ivy league or south to college. I was on my way to the University of Virgina as a National Merit Commended Scholar. I had the world by the tail, so I thought. . . .

I arrived there in August full of the usual freshman dreams of success and maybe even love. On October 12, my dreams were shattered. I was raped. My friend, Betsy, and I attended a toga party that night. I left the party to go outside to cool off from dancing. I thought I was alone. Apparently, I was followed from the party. My rapist caught me in a very dark place, threw me down, knocked me out and raped me.

It would have been to my advantage if I had remained unconscious. But, I regained consciousness just as he was climaxing. At that moment I hated everything that my femininity symbolized. He was deriving the utmost physical pleasure at the cost of my dignity and more importantly, at the cost of my future.

The cuts and bruises healed but the mental torture remained and will always be present. Because of him, I lost a year of my life. I was forced to withdraw from UVA and go home. I was mentally unable to return to school until a year later and am now a year behind my class. That is the least of it. The emotional aspects of it have been crippling.

Because of one single hateful act, I lost my security, my confidence, my trust, and my boyfriend. It was quite a price to pay for someone else's personality flaws. My loss of security arose from my loss of advantages—meaning my position in life. All that I worked to build was destroyed. My very base was blown out from under me. All this because I was the first woman to walk out a door alone. I had nothing to fall back on after I left UVA and transferred to another school.

As a result I lost every ounce of self-confidence I ever had. I had a low opinion of myself because I experienced something which many rape victims experience. I asked myself over and over again if I had "asked for it." For a while, I was convinced that I was a slut and had gotten what I had deserved. This is something which is extremely difficult to overcome. A year and a half later, I still have little self-confidence.

I was once a very trusting person. Now, however, I do not trust men, and I constantly have trouble trusting women. I question people's motives. In the back of my mind, I must feel that everyone has the hate for me that that one person exemplified. It is a very unhealthy and unfair attitude. I realize this, but I still judge harshly.

The person who took the brunt of all my inner unrest was my boyfriend of two and a half years. I mistrusted him and lashed out at him once too often because of my own insecurities. He and I gave up trying to regain what was once strong and beautiful because my ability to give and receive as before was lost along with the UVA and National Merit.

I was forced to realize my gender in a very brutal way. I would give anything to replace this experience with having been discriminated against for a job or something like that. But, my fate is mine and no one else but me can repair the damage done. I hope I live long enough to recapture myself. I miss me.

Source: From a student essay.

FIGURE 17.1
Rape crisis counseling.
Many women experience
severe emotional distress
after a rape, and it is
important that crisis
counseling be available to
them.

Silent rape reaction: The psychological responses of a woman when she doesn't tell anyone that she has been raped.

has a history of depression and anxiety, she is more likely to experience these symptoms after the rape. Also, social support from relatives and friends is important; women who receive poor support are more likely to have long-term problems with depression.

Researchers have also identified a **silent rape reaction,** in which the woman not only fails to report the rape to the police but also tells no one about it (Burgess & Holmstrom, 1974a). She, of course, experiences the same problems of adjustment that other rape victims do, but she has no way of expressing or venting her feelings. Counselors and psychotherapists need to be aware of this syndrome. For example, a woman may come for counseling complaining of quite different problems—perhaps inability to have orgasms, or anxiety and depression—when her real problem is that she has been raped but is unable to talk about it.

If a woman reports the rape and decides to press charges, the police investigation and the trial itself may be further crises for her. She must recall the traumatic experience in detail. The police and the courts have a history of callous or even abusive treatment of rape victims. The woman may be offered little sympathy, and the police may adopt a cynical attitude, as noted above, suggesting that she agreed to have sex but then changed her mind afterward. The attitudes of the police are not too surprising, for the police officers grew up in a culture that abounds with stereotypes about women, including the one that says that rape is only a situation in which a woman changed her mind. Of course, not all police officers have been guilty of such cynicism, but too many victims report treatment like this:

> They finally told me they thought I was lying. They said I'd probably been having sex with my boyfriend and probably was afraid I was pregnant. They also theorized that my boyfriend had set me up for it. They wanted to know if he'd ever asked me to have relations with his friends. (Brownmiller, 1975, p. 366)

The defense lawyer, in attempting to defend the rapist, may try to make it look as if the victim was actually the criminal—that she seduced him and later decided to call it rape, that she is a slut and therefore cannot be raped, and so on. She may be questioned about her prior sexual experiences, the idea being that if she has had premarital or extramarital sex, she is promiscuous and cannot be raped. As one women expressed it:

> They trotted out my whole past life, made me go through all these changes, while he just sat at the defendant's table, mute, surrounded by his lawyers. Of course that was his right by law, but it looked like I was the one who was on trial. (Brownmiller, 1975, p. 372)

In the last 15 years, some states have passed "reform" evidence laws, which do not permit the woman's previous sexual experience (except with the alleged rapist) to be a topic during a trial for rape.

In addition, perhaps partly as a result of several excellent television programs dramatizing the plight of the woman who has been raped, many police departments have tried to change their handling of rape victims. Some even have special "rape squads" composed of women police officers who record the woman's story and investigate the case; this spares the woman the embarrassment of describing the incident to a man.

Female Socialization: Creating Rape Victims

How do women become victims of rape? This section will discuss the notion that many of the qualities for which females are socialized make them vulnerable to rape (Russell, 1975; Weis & Borges, 1973).

For example, according to gender-role stereotypes, weakness is feminine, while strength is masculine. As a result, many women think of themselves as being physically weak, and those who do not exercise may actually be weak. This weakness is symbolized in many ways, as when men open doors for women or carry heavy bundles for them. To expect a person who needs such assistance to fight off a 220-pound attacker would be silly. Thus, the weakness and passivity for which females are socialized contribute to making them rape victims.

Females are also socialized for nurturance (taking care of others) and altruism (paying attention to the needs of others rather than one's own needs). The woman who has been socialized to be nurturant and who spends her days expressing her gentleness toward her children can scarcely be expected to attempt to gouge out a man's eyes with her fingernails, as some self-defense experts advise. Female altruism has an ironic effect in the rape situation. Some women report the rape but then choose not to press charges because they say they are afraid that the rapist might have to go to jail for a long time[2] or that his reputation will be ruined. Thus, the victim may adopt a nurturant, altruistic attitude toward her attacker, considering his needs and feelings first.

The feelings of altruism that lead to nonreporting are magnified by the fact that in most cases the victim knows her attacker at least casually. In one study, 89 percent of rapes were by acquaintances (Koss et al., 1988).

Females are also socialized for a group of qualities that might be called collectively "being ladylike." Ladies are neat and clean and pretty. Some women, immediately after a rape, go home to shower, wash their hair, and change their clothes; then they proceed to the police station. While their emotional need to get themselves clean is understandable, they have destroyed most of the evidence of the crime, and

---

[2] Those who worry about condemning a man to a long jail sentence may be interested to know that the average convicted rapist spends less than four years in jail for the offense (Brownmiller, 1975).

the skeptical reaction of the police is not surprising. If you look neat and clean and pretty, it is hard to believe that you have just been raped.

Children, and girls especially, are taught to fear sex crimes. They are told never to accept rides with strange men or to take candy from them. Yet the exact nature of the potential danger remains unknown and so the girl may build up an exceedingly great dread of a mysterious crime, perhaps thinking that it would be the worst thing that could happen to her. Thus, when she is attacked, she may be absolutely immobilized with fear. She freezes and is unable to wage an effective counterattack.

The reader can probably think of other examples of qualities that females are socialized for that contribute to making them rape victims. However, the imporant point is that conformity to traditional standards of femininity makes women more vulnerable to rape, at least when they are in a situation in which a man intends to rape them (Russell, 1975)

Further support for this gender-role socialization hypothesis comes from research that has found that people who hold traditional gender stereotypes are more accepting of rape myths and are more likely to blame the victim (Burt, 1980; Coller & Resick, 1987).

Rapists

What is the profile of the typical rapist? The basic answer to that question is that there is no typical rapist. Rapists vary tremendously from one to the next in occupation, education, marital status, previous criminal record, and motivation for committing the rape.

A few generalizations can be made about rapists or at least rapists who have been arrested and therefore can be studied. Most are young. According to the FBI *Uniform Crime Reports*, 61 percent are under 25. Many have a tendency to repeat their offense (M. L. Cohen et al., 1971). It is also true that most rapists are not murderers (Selkin, 1975). Probably no more than 1 rape in 500 is accompanied by a murder (Brownmiller, 1975).[3] This statistic is important for women who wonder how best to react in a rape situation. Statistically, although the rapist may threaten the woman with violence or murder, he is unlikely to carry through on this and is only using the threat to get her to submit. This may encourage women to resist the attacker rather than submit.

In an attempt to deal with the diversity in the personalities and approaches of rapists, some researchers have developed typologies, or schemes for categorizing rapists. According to one such typology, rapists vary according to whether their aim is primarily aggressive,[4] primarily sexual, or a mixture of the two (Cohen et al., 1971). The trouble with research of this kind is that it is based on reported rapes only and typically investigates rapists who have been arrested and sent to jail. It seems likely that these rapists are more deviant than those who escape being reported. Thus the research ignores the more common, "normal" rapist—the date rapist, the boss who rapes his secretary.

A massive program of research by Neil Malamuth, Mary Koss, and their colleagues identified four factors that predispose men to engage in sexual coercion with women (Malamuth et al., 1991):

[3] If anything, this is probably an *over*estimate of the number of rapes that end in murder, since rape murders are almost invariably discovered, whereas the rape in which the woman escapes with minor scratches is likely to go unreported.

[4] It is clear from the statistics that intercourse is not always the goal of the rapist. In one study, vaginal intercourse occurred in less than half the rape cases investigated (Selkin, 1975).

1. *Hostile home environment*   A boy who grows up in a hostile home environment has a higher likelihood of engaging in sexual aggression against women. Factors that create a hostile home environment include violence between the parents or abuse directed toward the child, whether battering or sexual abuse.

2. *Delinquency*   Being involved in delinquency is itself made more likely by coming from a hostile home. But the delinquency in turn increases the likelihood of engaging in sexual coercion—the boy associates with delinquent peers who, for example, encourage hostile attitudes and rationalizations for committing illegal acts and reward a tough, aggressive image.

3. *Sexual promiscuity*   The male, often in the context of the delinquent peer group, develops a heavy emphasis on sexual conquests to bring him self-esteem and status with the peer group. Coercion may seem to him a reasonable way of making conquests.

4. *A hostile masculine personality*   This personality constellation involves deep-seated hostility toward women together with negatively defined, exaggerated masculinity—masculinity defined as rejecting anything feminine such as nurturance, and emphasizing power, control, and "macho" characteristics.

Surprisingly, this research was not based on convicted rapists but rather on a national representative sample of male college students. The factors that contribute to sexual aggression against women can be present even in such apparently benevolent populations.

Date Rape

Incidents of forced sex on dates were investigated in one sample of 623 college students (Struckman-Johnson, 1988). Among the respondents, 22 percent of the women and 16 percent of the men said that they had experienced at least one incident of forced sexual intercourse on a date. In the same study, 10 percent of the men, but only 2 percent of the women, admitted that they had forced someone to have sex on a date. In a word, date rape is not a rare occurrence.

In some cases, date rape seems to result from male-female miscommunication. The traditional view in dating relationships has been that if she says "no," she really means "yes," Men need to learn that "no" means "no." Consider this example of miscommunication and different perceptions in a case of date rate:

Bob: Patty and I were in the same statistics class together. She usually sat near me and was always very friendly. I liked her and thought maybe she liked me, too. Last Thursday I decided to find out. After class I suggested that she come to my place to study for midterms together. She agreed immediately, which was a good sign. That night everything seemed to go perfectly. We studied for a while and then took a break. I could tell that she liked me, and I was attracted to her. I was getting excited. I started kissing her. I could tell that she really liked it. We started touching each other and it felt really good. All of a sudden she pulled away and said "Stop." I figured she didn't want me to think that she was "easy" or "loose." A lot of girls think they have to say "no" at first. I knew once I showed her what a good time she could have, and that I would respect her in the morning, it would be OK. I just ignored her protests and eventually she stopped struggling. I think she liked it but afterwards she acted bummed out and cold. Who knows what her problem was?

Patty: I knew Bob from my statistics class. He's cute and we are both good at statistics, so when a tough midterm was scheduled, I was glad that he suggested we study together. It never occurred to me that it was anything except a study date. That night everything went fine at first, we got a lot of studying done in a short amount of time, so when he suggested we take a break I thought we deserved it. Well, all of a sudden he started acting really romantic and started kissing me. I liked the kissing but then he started touching me below the waist. I pulled away and tried to stop him but he didn't listen. After a while I stopped struggling; he was hurting me and I was scared. He was so much bigger and stronger than me. I couldn't believe it was happening to me. I didn't know what to do. He actually forced me to have sex with him. I guess looking back on it I should have screamed or done something besides trying to reason with him but it was so unexpected. I couldn't believe it was happening. I still can't believe it did. (Hughes & Sandler, 1987, p. 1)

Kanin (1985) studied 71 unmarried college men who were self-disclosed date rapists, comparing them with a control group of unmarried college men. The date rapists tended to be sexually predatory. For example, when asked how frequently they attempt to seduce a new date, 62 percent of the rapists said "most of the time," compared with 19 percent of the controls. The rapists were also much more likely to report a variety of manipulative techniques with their dates, including getting them high on alcohol or marijuana, falsely professing love, and falsely promising "pinning," engagement, or marriage.

In summary, the consistent findings in studies of date rape are that such incidents are not rare but rather are fairly common even in "normal" populations.

Marital Rape

Marital rape: The rape of a woman by her husband.

The possibility that a man could rape his wife was brought to public attention when, in a 1978 Oregon case, Greta Rideout brought suit against her husband for marital rape. Defining marital rape is complicated by the fact that in many states, rape laws exclude the possibility of marital rape; the assumption seems to be that sex in marriage is always the husband's "right."

How common is marital rape? In a random sample of San Francisco women, 14 percent of those who had ever been married had been raped by a husband or ex-husband (Russell, 1983).

One phenomenon that emerges from the research is an association between marital violence and marital rape—that is, the man who batters his wife is also likely to rape her (Hanneke et al., 1986). For example, in a study of 137 women who had reported beatings from their husbands, 34 percent reported being raped by their husbands (Frieze, 1983). Reflecting the fact that some women are unwilling to define certain acts as marital rape, 43 percent of that sample said that sex was unpleasant because their husband forced them to have sex, a higher percentage than those admitting being raped. The response of the majority of the women was anger toward the husband. However, women who had been raped frequently began to experience self-blame. Marital rape also appeared to have consequences for the marriage: The raped women were more likely to say that their marriages had been getting worse over time.

What are the motivations for a man raping his wife? Three motives emerge in research: anger, power-domination, and sadism (Russell, 1983). In some cases the husband is extremely angry, perhaps in the middle of a family argument, and he expresses his anger toward his wife by raping her. In other cases, power and domination of the wife seem to be the motive—for example, the wife may be threatening to leave him, and he forces or dominates her into staying by rape. Finally, some rapes appear to occur because the husband is sadistic—enjoys inflicting pain—and is a psychiatrically disturbed individual.

The research shows that marital rape is a real and not uncommon phenomenon, that it is associated with wife battering, and that it has negative consequences, both for the woman and for the marriage.

Male Socialization: Creating Rapists

One view is that rapists are created as the result of gender-role socialization practices in our culture (Albin, 1977). To remedy the situation, radical changes in gender-role socialization practices would be necessary. The ideas in this section reflect this theoretical view.

A previous section reviewed the argument that many of the characteristics for which we socialize females contribute to making them rape victims. The parallel argument is also informative, namely, that males are socialized for characteristics that contribute to making them rapists (Russell, 1975; Weis & Borges, 1973).

Aggression, dominance, power, and strength are manly. In the study of gender-role stereotypes discussed in Chapter 14, it was found that Americans consider aggression to be a desirable characteristic of males. Having been socialized to be aggressive, it is not surprising that men commit the aggressive crime of rape. Further, rapists may themselves be victims of our culture's confusion of sex and aggression. For example, we often refer to the male as playing the "aggressive" role in sex, suggesting that sex is supposed to have an aggressive component. Sex and aggression are also combined in the violent pornography that is so common (see Chapter 18). The rapist's confusion of sex and aggression reflects a confusion existing in our society.

It may be, then, that rape is a means of proving masculinity or self-worth for the male who is insecure in his role (Geis, 1977). For this reason, the statistics on the youthfulness of rapists make sense; youthful rapists may simply be young men who are trying to adopt the adult male role, who feel insecure about doing this, and who commit a rape as proof of their manhood. Further, heterosexuality is an important part of manliness. Raping a woman is a flagrant way to prove that one is a heterosexual.

Kanin (1985) argues that date rapists are strongly influenced by a kind of hypersexual socialization process in their own peer group. They are part of a college peer group that pressures them and rewards them for being sexually active. Supporting Kanin's notion of the hypersexual peer group, 41 percent of the rapists (but only 7 percent of the controls) had been involved in a "gang bang," or sequential sharing of a female partner with one or more male friends. Over 67 percent of the rapists (compared with 13 percent of the controls) had had intercourse with a woman recommended by a friend as sexually willing.

Kanin (1985) also argues that the "relative deprivation hypothesis" helps to explain date rapists' behavior. Date rapists engage in plenty of sexual activity, so rape can hardly be viewed as their response to sexual frustration or deprivation. The issue probably is not deprivation, but relative deprivation. That is, it isn't how much sex they're getting, but rather how much they are getting relative to how much they think they need. If they set their level of aspiration unrealistically high, they may feel sexually deprived even though they are getting plenty of action. Kanin asked his sample of date rapists, "How many orgasms (ejaculations) per week, from any source, do you think you would require in order to give you sexual satisfaction?" Supporting Kanin's application of the relative deprivation hypothesis, the date rapists reported an average number of 4.5, compared with 2.8 for the controls. Thus the date rapists are dissatisfied because they are unable to achieve their overly ambitious goals, the goals themselves being a result of socialization for sexual hyperactivity.

Based on a series of samples of male college students at several universities, it was found, on the average, that about 35 percent indicated some likelihood that they would rape a woman if the opportunity was there and they were sure they would not be caught (Malamuth, 1981). This high percentage also supports the notion that rapists are the result of common male socialization practices in our culture. Consistent with this idea, too, is the finding that college men who hold traditional gender-role attitudes are more likely to have engaged in sexual aggression in a dating situation than men with liberated gender-role attitudes (Muehlenhard & Linton, 1987).

Cross-cultural research provides further evidence that rape is the product of social learning. As Margaret Mead observed, "Of rape the Arapesh know nothing beyond the fact that it is the unpleasant custom of the Nugum people to the southeast of them" (1935, p. 110). The Arapesh understanding of the nature of males—that they are nurturant, caring, gentle—is totally incompatible with the notion of rape, and so apparently it never occurs. Other cross-cultural research has found tribes that use rape precisely to punish women and enforce property rights (Chappell, 1976).

Rape, then, does seem to be a product, at least in part, of socialization patterns.

Men Raped by Women

Although it might seem to be a physical impossibility for a woman to rape a man, research shows that men may respond with an erection in emotional states such as anger and terror (Sarrel & Masters, 1982). In one study, 11 male victims of rape by women were interviewed (Sarrel & Masters, 1982). The cases fell into four categories: assault (the rape included physical constraint or threats of physical violence); "baby-sitter" abuse (a young boy is seduced by an older female who is not a relative); incestuous abuse (seduction of a boy by a female relative); and dominance rape (in which no physical violence is used but the male victim is intimidated or terrified). Some cases of female gang rape of males were even discovered. The research found that there was a rape trauma syndrome for men who had been raped which was much like the rape trauma syndrome discussed earlier for female victims. It is important for counselors and others in helping professions to recognize this possibility of male rape victims.

As noted earlier, in a study of date rape in a sample of college students, 13

Fraternity Gang Rape

Anthropologist Peggy Sanday (1990) has analyzed a widely publicized case of gang rape in a fraternity at a particular university, as well as many other similar cases documented at other universities.

Men join fraternities for many possible reasons. Some may anticipate establishing networks of friendships that will help them in their future careers. But often freshmen, insecure in a complex new environment, join the fraternity to find security. According to Sanday's analysis, the initiation rituals of many fraternities follow a sequence of creating high levels of anxiety in the new members, followed by a male bonding ritual that makes them "brothers." Essentially the young man's identity as an individual is undermined while loyalty to the group is prized, indeed enforced.

In the case investigated by Sanday, the XYZ fraternity (she used this name to guard the anonymity of the population being studied, as required by the ethical standards for anthropologists) had a practice called the "XYZ express," referring to an express train. It involved what would be classified as a gang rape in which a woman, typically drunk or surreptitiously drugged so that she was barely conscious, is raped successively by a series of brothers who stand in line to take their turn, just as cars in a train are in a line. Often this occurred toward the

end of a party, and the brothers themselves were drunk.

Sanday points out how this practice has two consequences: it establishes dominance over a woman, and it promotes strong bonds among the brothers. The practice, of course, fits the definition of rape and is illegal. Yet many of the brothers, when the case was brought to court, said that they had no idea that their activities were wrong or illegal. The culture of the fraternity had dulled their capacity for a rational judgment. The judge who heard the case was astounded that universities would tolerate, indeed support institutions that created the environment for such acts to occur.

Sanday notes anthropologists' findings that, cross-culturally, some societies are free of sexual assault while others are rape-prone. She concludes, "Social ideologies, not human nature, prepare men to abuse women" (Sanday, 1990, p. 192). The XYZ fraternity and others like it are essentially a subculture that socializes men to have sexist attitudes toward women and creates an environment in which gang rape is likely to occur.

Source: Peggy R. Sanday (1990). *Fraternity gang rape.* New York: New York University Press.

percent of the women and 9 percent of the men reported that they had experienced forced sex at some time while at the university (Struckman-Johnson, 1988). The type of coercion, however, was considerably different for men and women. The majority of men reported that they were coerced by psychological pressure, whereas the majority of women said they were coerced by physical force. One man reported,

> I was invited over for a party, unaware that it was a date. As the evening wore on, I got the message that the girl was my date. I didn't have to make a move on her because she was all over me. She wouldn't take no for an answer. Usually I like to get to know the person. I felt I was forced into sex. After, I felt terrible and used. (Struckman-Johnson, 1988, p. 238)

Another study investigated a broader category: unwanted sexual activity; that is, engaging in sexual activities when you really don't want to (Muehlenhard & Cook, 1988). The researchers actually found that more men (63 percent) than women (46 percent) had experienced unwanted intercourse. The most common reasons men gave for engaging in the unwanted activity were being enticed or seduced, altruism (wanting to satisfy the other person or not wanting the other person to feel rejected), inexperience (wanting to get experience or to have something to talk about with peers), and intoxication. Most of these incidents, of course, would not fit the legal definition of rape. However, they do indicate the ways in which men, too, can be coerced into sexual activity.

Having recognized the possibility of men being raped by women, it is important to note that the great majority of male rape victims are raped by men, not women, many of these incidents occurring in prisons (Calderwood, 1987).

Prison Rape

In most states, rape is legally defined as a crime that has a male offender and a female victim. However, this definition ignores a whole set of same-gender rapes of men by other men, many of which, in the United States, occur in prisons (Brownmiller, 1975). Indeed, for a male, one of the worst aspects of going to prison today is the danger of being the object of sexual violence.

A major study on this topic is Daniel Lockwood's *Prison Sexual Violence* (1980), based on interviews with aggressors and targets, as well as members of the prison staff. Readers wanting to pursue this topic should consult that book.

Prison rapes are the most tangible symbol of the dominance hierarchy among prisoners. Those at the bottom of the dominance hierarchy are the objects of this sexual violence, and, interestingly, they are called "girls." Prison rape is a particularly clear example of the way in which rape is an expression of power and aggression.

Ethnicity and Rape

We have seen how cultural context can promote or inhibit rape and affect the meaning people attach to rape. The different cultural heritages of the various ethnic groups in the United States provide different cultural contexts for people of those groups, and so it is important to consider patterns of rape in U.S. ethnic groups.

Rape has a highly charged meaning in the history of African Americans (Wyatt, 1992). In the time of slavery, an African American man convicted of rape or attempted rape of a white woman was typically castrated or sentenced to death. In sharp contrast, there was no penalty for a white man raping a black woman. Moreover, stereotypes originating at that time and continuing to the present portray both African American men and African American women as being highly sexual. Black women are so highly sexual, the reasoning goes, that they cannot be raped. The result is that African American women have a long history of nondisclosure of rape, a pattern of nondisclosure that exceeds even white women's. Many African American women think that no one will believe they can be raped and that they will have no credibility as a rape victim.

Research on a random sample of women in Los Angeles indicates that the rate of attempted or completed rape incidents was nearly the same for the two groups—25 percent for African American women and 20 percent for white women (Wyatt, 1992). However, only 23 percent of the black women reported the incident to the police or a rape crisis center, compared with 31 percent of the white women. Black women and white women were similar in the effects of the rape, such as its negative impact on their later sexual functioning.

FIGURE 17.3
Ethnicity and rape. Rape
has a highly charged
meaning in the history of
African Americans. In the
time of slavery, although
there was no penalty for a
white man raping a black
woman, a black man
convicted of raping a white
woman was typically
castrated or put to death.

Another survey of a random sample of Los Angeles women compared the rape experiences of Anglo and Hispanic women (Sorenson & Siegel, 1992). The results indicated that the Hispanics were considerably less likely to have been the victims of a sexual assault—8.1 percent of Hispanics compared with 19.9 percent of Anglos. The researchers interpreted this difference as being due to values in Hispanic culture, particularly among those born in Mexico, that place strong emphasis on the family and uphold partriarchal attitudes that insist that men should protect women.

Preventing Rape

Strategies for preventing rape fall into two categories: (1) avoiding situations in which there is a high risk of rape; and (2) if the first strategy has failed, knowing some self-defense techniques if a rape attempt is actually made.

The first and best strategy, of course, is to be alert to situations in which there is a high risk of rape and to avoid them. The Association of American Colleges, for example, recommends the following to avoid date rape situations (Hughes & Sandler, 1987, p. 3):

Set sexual limits. No one has a right to force you to do something with your body that you don't want to do. If you don't want to be touched, for example, you have a right to say "Don't touch me," and to leave if your wishes are not respected.

Decide early if you would like to have intercourse. The sooner you communicate your intentions firmly and clearly, the easier it will be for your partner to understand and accept your decision.

Do not give mixed messages; be clear. Say "yes" when you mean "yes" and "no" only when you mean "no."

Be forceful and firm. Do not worry about being polite if your wishes are being ignored.

Do not do anything you do not want to do just to avoid a scene or unpleasantness. Do not be raped because you were too polite to get out of a dangerous situation or because you are worried about hurting your date's feelings. If things get out of hand, be loud in protesting, leave, and go for help.

Be aware that alcohol and drugs are often related to date rape. They compromise your ability (and that of your date) to make responsible decisions.

How Can Friends Help a Rape Victim?

The victim needs to:

Obtain medical assistance.

Feel safe. Rape is a traumatic violation of the person. Especially in the beginning, it is often difficult for victims to be alone.

Be believed. With date rape especially, victims need to be believed that what occurred was, in fact, a rape.

Know it was not her fault. Most rape victims feel guilty and feel that the attack was somehow their fault.

Take control of her life. When a person is raped, she may feel completely out of control of what is happening to her. A significant step on the road to recovery is to regain a sense of control in little, as well as big, things.

Things You Can Do To Help

Listen, do not judge. Accept her version of the facts and be supportive.

Offer shelter. If possible, stay with her at her place or let her spend at least one night at your place. This is not the time for her to be alone.

Be available. She may need to talk at odd hours, or a great deal in the beginning. Also encourage her to call a hotline or go for counseling.

Give comfort. She needs to be nurtured.

Let her know she is not to blame.

Encourage action. For example, suggest she call a hotline, go to a hospital, and/or call the police. Respect her decision if she decides not to file charges. Do not make her decisions for her because she needs to regain a sense of control of her life.

Put aside your feelings and deal with them somewhere else. Although it is supportive for a rape survivor to know that others are equally upset with what happened, it does her no good if she also has to deal with, for example, your feelings of rage and anger. If you have strong feelings, talk to another friend or to a local hotline.

Source: Condensed from Jean O. Hughes & Bernice R. Sandler. (1987). *"Friends" raping friends: Could it happen to you?* Washington, DC: Association of American Colleges. Used with permssion.

Trust your gut-level feelings. If the situation feels risky to you, or if you feel you are being pressured, trust your feelings. Leave the situation or confront the person immediately.

Be careful when you invite someone to your home or you are invited to your date's home. These are the most likely places for date rapes to occur.

If this first set of strategies—avoiding rape situations—does not work, self-defense strategies are needed. Always remember that the goal is to get away from the attacker and run for help.

Many universities, YWCAs, and other organizations now offer self-defense classes for women, and I believe that every woman should take at least one such course. Many techniques are available. Judo (and aikido, which is similar) emphasizes throwing and wrestling. Tae kwon do (Korean karate) emphasizes kicking. Jujitsu uses combinations of these strategies. The exact method the woman chooses is probably not too important, as long as she does know some techniques. Related to this is the importance of getting exercise and keeping in shape; this gives a woman the strength to fight back and the speed to run fast.

Self-defense, though, is useful to the woman only in defending herself once an attack has been made. Feminists argue that it would be better if rape could be rooted out at a far earlier stage so that attacks never occurred. To do this, our society would need to make a radical change in the way it socializes males and females. If little boys were not so pressed to be aggressive and tough, perhaps rapists would never develop. If adolescent boys did not have to demonstrate that they are hypersexual, perhaps there would be no rapists. As we noted earlier, rape is unheard of in some societies where males are socialized to be nurturant rather than aggressive (Mead, 1935).

Changes would also need to be made in the way females are socialized, particularly if women are to become good at assertiveness and self-defense. Weakness is not considered a desirable human characteristic, and so it should not be considered a desirable feminine characteristic, especially because it makes women vulnerable to rape. Mothers particularly need to think of the kinds of role models they are providing for their daughters and should consider whether they are providing models of weakness. The stereotype of female weakness and passivity is so pervasive in our society that a complex set of strategies will be required to change it. Girls also need increased experience with athletics as they grow up. This change should have a number of beneficial effects: building strength, speed, and agility in women; building confidence in their ability to use their own bodies; and decreasing their fear of rough body contact. All of these should help them defend themselves against rape. While some people think that it is silly for the federal government to rule that girls must have athletic teams equal to boys' teams, it seems quite possible that the absence of athletic training for girls has contributed to making them rape victims.

Finally, for both males and females, we need a radical restructuring of our ideas concerning sexuality. As long as females are expected to pretend to be uninterested in sex and as long as males and females continue to play games on dates, rape will persist.

INCEST AND CHILD MOLESTATION

Here we discuss two situations in which children are sexually coerced: child molestation (pedophilia) and incest.

Pedophilia

Pedophiliac (peed-oh-FILL-ee-ak): An adult who engages in or desires sexual contact with a child; a child molester.

The pedophiliac[5] ("child molester") is an adult who engages in or desires sexual contact with a child. Pedophilia is typically regarded as one of the most despicable of sex offenses because of the naive trust of children and because the pedophiliac uses his power and authority as an adult over the child.

How common is child sexual abuse? The number of reported cases has increased dramatically in recent years, from 1975 in 1976 and 4327 in 1977 to 22,918 in 1982 (Finkelhor, 1984). However, these reported cases represent just the tip of the iceberg because the great majority of cases are not reported. In one survey of the general population, 3 percent of the males and 12 percent of the females reported

---

[5] Those of you who are interested in the roots of words might mistakenly guess that a pedophiliac is a foot fetishist. The root "ped-," however, refers to "child," as in "pediatrician."

having been sexually abused as children; in another general survey, the incidence was 6 percent for males and 15 percent for females (Finkelhor, 1984). Child sexual abuse is not uncommon, and females are more often its victims than males are.

Four factors seem to be necessary in explaining pedophilia (Finkelhor & Araji, 1986). First, the adult must find it emotionally satisfying to have a sexual experience with a child. Second, the person must find children sexually arousing. Social learning theory (see Chapter 2), and specifically imitation and modeling, may be important in explaining why some people would be aroused by children (Howells, 1981). Statistics show that an unusually large percentage of pedophiliacs were themselves sexually abused as children. Having witnessed the behavior as children, they may reenact it in adulthood, this time as the perpetrator, not the victim. However, this explanation does not make sense of the fact that the majority of victims are female, whereas the majority of perpetrators are male, a point to be discussed later. Third, the person must have some blockage in his or her ability to have emotional and sexual needs met by adult-adult relationships. The fourth factor is disinhibition. That is, there are many norms against child sexual abuse, and most people feel inhibited from engaging in such activities. The pedophiliac does not have such inhibitions.

Virtually all pedophiliacs are men; in one study, 94 percent of perpetrators were male (Finkelhor, 1984). A number of factors probably account for this great imbalance. Men in our culture are socialized more toward seeing sexuality as focused on sexual acts rather than seeing sexuality as a part of an emotional relationship. And, interestingly, men are socialized to believe that appropriate sexual partners are smaller and younger than themselves, whereas women are socialized to think that appropriate partners are larger and older than they are.

A number of factors in the family seem to increase the risk of a girl becoming a victim of child sexual abuse (Finkelhor, 1984): the presence of a stepfather, spending some period of time not living with the mother, not feeling emotionally close to the mother, the mother being uneducated, the mother being highly punitive about sex, and poverty. Mothers seem to be important in protecting daughters from sexual abuse. However, that doesn't mean that we should blame the mother when cases of abuse occur. She is important as protection only when a man is already predisposed to commit the act, and so the primary responsibility rests with him.

What effects does the abuse have on the child? Many therapists (for example, psychiatrists) have seen abundant evidence that child sexual abuse can have lasting effects, creating serious psychological problems in adulthood (Herman, 1981). On the other hand, people who seek help from therapists are probably a biased sample of sexual abuse victims, and results from them could be misleading. Research with samples from the general population shows that those who were sexually victimized as children have significantly lower levels of sexual self-esteem than those who were not victimized (Finkelhor, 1984). Someone with low sexual self-esteem would agree with such statements as "After sexual experiences, I often feel dissatisfied" or "I often find myself in awkward sexual situations." This negative view of the sexual self is a lasting consequence of child sexual abuse. On the other hand, on many other psychological measures, victims and nonvictims do not differ.

Some experts argue that the trauma of sexual victimization comes less from the experience itself than from the highly emotional reaction of the parents, or the police, or judicial procedures (McCaghy, 1971). It should not be assumed that every child who is abused is destined to difficulty, for the data show that some manage to cope and adjust. Indeed, as David Finkelhor, an expert on child sexual abuse, put it, "It may be that by providing a calm and supportive reaction to victimization, the risks of long-term effects on the child can be completely dissipated." (1984, p. 197)

It is important for parents to encourage open communication with their children so that the children will confide in them if molestation occurs. If a child does bring such a report to a parent, the parent should not overreact but rather should encourge the child to talk about the incident, while calmly reassuring the child.

Let us now turn to a particular kind of child sexual abuse—incest.

Incidence of Incest

Incest is typically defined as sexual relations between blood relatives, although the definition is often extended to include sex between nonblood relatives—for example, stepfather and stepdaughter (Maisch, 1972; Sagarin, 1977).

Traditionally it was thought that incest was a rare and bizarre occurrence. Early research confirmed this notion, indicating that the incidence of incest prosecuted by the police was only about one or two people per million per year in the United States (Weinberg, 1955). The catch, though, is that the overwhelming majority of cases go unreported to authorities and unprosecuted. To get a better idea of the true incidence of incest, it is necessary to do a survey of the general population. In one such survey, 7 percent of the sample had had sexual intercourse with a relative (Hunt, 1974). In a general survey of undergraduates, 15 percent of the females and 10 percent of the males said they had had a sexual experience with a sibling (Finkelhor, 1980). In most cases, the activity was limited to fondling and exhibiting the genitals. Intercourse occurred in only 5 percent of the incidents under age 8 and 18 percent of the incidents over age 13. The point is that incest, particularly if it is defined to include sexual contact other than intercourse, is not at all rare—perhaps 10 percent of people in the United States have been involved as children.

I have already mentioned the distinction between father-daughter incest and brother-sister incest. Which is more common? In a study of *reported* incest (reported to the police or other authorities), father-daughter cases were by far the most common: Father-daughter cases constituted 78 percent of the sample, 18 percent were brother-sister, 1 percent were mother-son, and the remaining 3 percent were multiple incestuous relationships (Weinberg, 1955). However, in surveys of the *general* population, brother-sister incest is far more common, outnumbering father-daughter incest cases by about 5 to 1 (Gebhard et al., 1965). Thus it appears that brother-sister is actually the most common form, but it is far less likely to be reported to the police than father-daughter incest. Because most research has been done on reported cases, most research is on father-daughter incest.

Father-Daughter Incest

What kind of man commits incest with his daughter? The stereotype is that such men are cases of extreme psychopathology. However, the research literature on incest shows that this stereotype is not true (Meiselman, 1978; Herman, 1981). Rather, the man who commits incest appears to be a classical patriarch within his family (Herman, 1981). He is a good provider, but he rules the family. The division of roles is traditional, and the mother is typically a full-time homemaker. She also seems to be somewhat isolated within the family, often because her health is poor. Within these family dynamics, the daughter-victim seems to take on the role of holding the family together and develops a "special" relationship with her father within which the incest occurs.

The sexual activity with his daughter appears to fulfill several needs for the father (Herman, 1981). He has feelings of dependency and a need for nurturance, which he receives in the relationship with his daughter (Justice & Justice, 1979). Doubtless he experiences a sense of power in the act, for he can control it exactly as he wishes and need not fear a rejection of his techniques as he might from a mature woman (Herman, 1981). The excitement coming from the secrecy may be pleasur-

FIGURE 17.4
Incest. Cheryl Pierson, 18, who paid a classmate to kill her father because, she said, he forced her to have sex with him. With her is her boyfriend, Robert Cuccio, 20. The former cheerleader served 3½ months of a 6-month sentence. There was general public sympathy for Cheryl as an incest survivor, and many people thought it was unfair when she was convicted and sentenced to 6 months imprisonment.

able. Finally, it has been suggested that the daughter's unhappiness with the sexual activity may contribute to pleasure in men who are basically expressing hostility.

One of the best accounts of the internal dynamics of father-daughter incest is Katherine Brady's autobiography, *Father's Days* (1978).

Psychological Impact on the Victim

Here we must keep in mind the distinction between father-daughter incest and brother-sister incest, because they may produce different effects on their victims.

Many therapists who are experienced with cases of incest feel that the effects of father-daughter incest on the victim are serious and long-lasting, despite the fact that the incidents were not reported and seem to have been repressed (Herman, 1981). Consider the following case:

> A 25-year-old office worker was seen in the emergency room with an acute anxiety attack. She was pacing, agitated, unable to eat or sleep, and had a feeling of impending doom. She related a vivid fantasy of being pursued by a man with a knife. The previous day she had been cornered in the office by her boss, who aggressively propositioned her. She needed the job badly and did not want to lose it, but she dreaded the thought of returning to work. It later emerged in psychotherapy that this episode of sexual harassment had reawakened previously repressed memories of sexual assaults by her father. From the age of 6 until midadolescence, her father had repeatedly exhibited himself to her and insisted that she masturbate him. The experience of being entrapped at work had recalled her childhood feelings of helplessness and fear. (Herman, 1981, p. 8)

Unfortunately, research in this area has not yet come to definitive conclusions about the effects on the victim, in part because the issue has been raised so recently and therefore little research has been done, and in part because there are some methodological difficulties in doing the research. Most of the research has been on reported or prosecuted cases, in which father-daughter incest is overrepresented, and in which police and court proceedings may have done as much damage to the victim as the act of incest itself, similar to what may happen with rape victims. Thus most research gives little information on sibling incest and its effects, or on the less traumatic cases that are never reported to the police or that never lead the victim to seek psychotherapy.

One study is worthy of note. In a general survey of 526 undergraduates, 17 percent of the students reported having had a sibling sexual encounter in childhood (Greenwald & Leitenberg, 1989; see also Finkelhor, 1980). There were no differences between this group and those who had had no such encounters, on a variety of measures of sexual behavior and adjustment, including incidence of premarital intercourse, age at first intercourse, number of sexual partners, sexual satisfaction, and sexual dysfunctions. The researchers concluded that childhood sexual experiences with a sibling close in age have no effect—positive or negative—on adult sexual adjustment.

What, then, are the psychological consequences of incest for the victim? Basically I think there is not enough good research to be able to tell right now. But I think the following conclusion is warranted: In some cases incest is highly damaging psychologically to the victim, but it is probably not damaging in every case (Renshaw, 1982). Many factors are probably involved in whether or not it is damaging: whether it is father-daughter or brother-sister incest (father-daughter being the more damaging), the age at which the victim experiences the incest, the age difference between the victim and the sibling if it is sibling incest, the extent to which coercion is used, how often the activity is repeated, and the extent to which the family is disrupted by the activity. In short, it depends.

Incest Taboos

Incest taboo: A social norm forbidding or banning incest.

Taboos against incest have been found in virtually all human societies, although some exceptions have been documented, including the Incan society and the societies of ancient Iran and ancient Egypt (Middleton, 1962; Murdock, 1949; Slotkin, 1947). It is possible that these taboos arose because people noted the harmful effects, either physical or social, of incest.

Genetically, incest may have bad consequences because it leads to inbreeding. In a study done in Japan in which marriages between cousins were compared with marriages of unrelated persons, it was found that the offspring of the cousin marriages did significantly worse in school performance and did worse on tests of physical performance, tests of intelligence, and some measures of health, although on some other measures there were no differences (Schull & Neel, 1965). Incest may also have bad social consequences; it can cause conflict and rivalry within the family, and it may also cause role strain ("Should I behave like a father or a boyfriend to her?" "How can I discipline her when I just had sex with her?").

SEXUAL HARASSMENT

Everyone in the country is aware of the issue of sexual harassment, following the dramatic and widely televised hearings involving Anita Hill and Clarence Thomas's confirmation to the Supreme Court in 1992. The issue is a powerful one—it can force a victim out of a job, but it also might force a perpetrator from a job.

The official definition of sexual harassment, given by the U.S. Equal Employment Opportunity Commission (EEOC), is as follows:

> Unwelcome sexual advances, requests for sexual favors, and other verbal or physical conduct of a sexual nature constitute sexual harassment when

A. Submission to such conduct is made either explicitly or implicitly a term or condition of an individual's employment or academic advancement,

B. Submission or rejection of such conduct by an individual is used as the basis for academic or employment decisions affecting that individual, or

C. Such conduct has the purpose or effect of unreasonably interfering with an individual's work or academic performance or creating an intimidating, hostile, or offensive working or educational environment.

The key ingredients for sexual harassment, then, are that the sexual advances are unwelcome and that they are coercive in the sense that the victim's job or grade is at stake. Point C of the definition also specifies that a "hostile environment" constitutes harassment—that is, if an employee is in a work environment that is so hostile (constant lewd innuendos, verbal intimidation, and so on) that he or she cannot work effectively, then that fits the definition of harassment, even if there has been no explicit sexual proposition directed to the employee.

The EEOC definition addresses sexual harassment at work and in education. Sexual harassment may occur in other contexts as well, such as in psychotherapy or on the street.

Sexual Harassment at Work

Sexual harassment at work may take a number of different forms. A prospective employer may make it clear that sexual activity is a prerequisite to being hired. Stories of such incidents are rampant among actresses. Once on the job, sexual activity may be made a condition for continued employment, for a promotion, or for other benefits such as a raise. Here is one case:

> A woman who works at a factory in Monroe, Wisconsin, has been subjected to an onslaught of outrageous conduct during the seven years she has been there.

FIGURE 17.5
In 1991, the televised hearings of Supreme Court nominee Clarence Thomas and Anita Hill captured the nation's attention and sparked much debate over sexual harassment.

(a)

(b)

FIGURE 17.6
Sexual harassment. A New York artist created a series of signs to educate men that sexual harassment is not acceptable. Although this is a serious issue, the artist uses humor effectively in getting men to change their behavior. The city of New York has now posted the signs at various locations.

For her birthday, her male coworkers constructed and presented her with an inflatable dildo. "I just laughed it off because, if I let them know it bothered me, they'd (harass me) more," she said.

She said the men call the women in the plant "office c---" in front of them and one woman is always being called "a life support system for a pr---."

One man came up to her and said that he was to be married in two weeks. "Last chance to f--- me," he said.

When she was pregnant, she was constantly asked who at the factory was the father.

Things got worse when she divorced six months ago; a coworker called her a whore when she declined his invitation to go out. Her managers ordered the man not to talk to her—but now everyone in the office ignores her. "I'm looked down on for turning him in," she said. "When you work with men and go up against them, you can't walk the halls without being talked about." Even the female coworkers think she lied about harassment, she said.

She said she feels like an "outsider" now. "It's very hard to show up at work every day." She can't quit, though, because she supports two children. (*Source:* Told to newspaper reporter, 1992)

It is clear in such incidents how damaging a hostile environment can be.

Surveys indicate that sexual harassment at work is far more common than many people realize. In one well-sampled study, 21 percent of women workers reported that they had been the object of incidents that an expert definitely classified as sexual harassment, compared with 9 percent of the men workers (Gutek, 1985). In a well-sampled survey of over 20,000 members of the federal work force, 42 percent of the women and 15 percent of the men reported having been sexually harassed at work within the preceding two years (Tangri et al., 1982; see also Levinson et al., 1988, for similar results). The preponderance of harassers (78 percent) were male.

Both women and men victims report that harassment has negative effects on their emotional and physical condition, their ability to work with others on the job, and their feelings about work (Tangri et al., 1982). However, men are more likely to feel that the overtures from women ended up being reciprocal and mutually enjoyable. Women, on the other hand, are more likely to report damaging consequences, including being fired or quitting their job (Gutek, 1985).

Although coworkers were reported as the most common harassers of both males and females, women were considerably more likely to have been harassed by a supervisor (37 percent of the cases with a female victim) than men were to have been harassed by a supervisor (14 percent of the cases with a male victim) (Tangri et al., 1982). Thus the power differential component of sexual harassment is more likely to be a factor for female victims.

Why does sexual harassment at work occur? One explanation derives from role theory in sociology. Applied to sexual harassment at work, this explanation is called the *gender-role spillover model* (Gutek, 1985). A work role can be defined as "a set of shared expectations about behavior in a job," and a gender role can be defined as "a set of shared expectations about the behavior of women and men" (Gutek, 1985, p. 17). Gender-role spillover occurs when gender roles are carried into the workplace, often in inappropriate ways—for example, when the woman in the work group is expected to make coffee for everyone or take notes at a meeting. Why don't work roles dominate in the workplace, and why does gender intrude? The answer in large part is because gender is a far more basic cognitive category than work (see Bem's gender schema theory, Chapter 2). Gender tends to dominate when we process information or when we act in a particular situation. Gender-role spillover explains sexual harassment at work in the following way. One part of the female role is being a sex object—a person who is sexually attractive and available to men. A part of the male role is being the sexual initiator. When these aspects of gender roles spill over into the workplace, harassment can easily occur, despite the fact that

FIGURE 17.7
Sexual harassment at work: This man has positioned himself so that the woman cannot avoid contact, and, if he is her supervisor, she may be hesitant to protest.

it clearly has negative effects for the individual and for the organization (Gutek, 1985).

Sexual harassment at work is more than just an annoyance. Particularly for women, because they are more likely to be harassed by supervisors, it can make a critical difference in career advancement. For the working-class woman who supports her family, being fired for sexual noncompliance is a catastrophe. The power of coercion is enormous.

Sexual Harassment in Education: An A for a Lay

Sexual harassment in education was brought to public attention when, in 1977, women students sued Yale University, complaining of sexual harassment, in the important case *Alexander v. Yale*. The case recognized that sexual harassment of women in education was a possible violation of Title IX of the Civil Rights Act.

A survey of a random sample of undergraduate women at Berkeley found that 30 percent had received unwanted sexual attention from at least one male instructor during their four years in college (Benson & Thomson, 1982; see also Adams et al., 1983). Table 17.1 shows the types of unwanted sexual attention reported by these women.

When the sexual harassment occurred with a professor with whom the woman student had had little previous contact, she generally reported coping with the situation by avoiding the man as much as possible; some of the respondents, for example, reported having their boyfriends pick them up after class (Benson & Thomson, 1982). When the harassment occurred after the woman had had a long-term academic relationship with the professor, it appeared to have more devastating effects on her. These women reported experiencing self-doubt and a loss of confidence in their academic ability, as well as disillusionment with male faculty in general.

As with sexual harassment at work, we must realize the serious consequences of such incidents. Women may lose opportunities, miss certain courses, or even be forced out of a graduate degree program because of sexual harassment.

In the wake of the Yale case and others, many universities have set up grievance procedures for sexual harassment cases. An important part of such procedures is that the victim's identity is kept anonymous so that she (or sometimes he) is reasonably protected from reprisals by the faculty member.

Table 17.1
Types of Unwanted Sexual Attention from Male Instructors Reported by Women Students at Berkeley

Behavior	Examples
Verbal advances	Explicit sexual propositions
Invitations	For dates, to one's apartment
Physical advances	Touching, kissing, fondling breasts
Body language	Leering, standing too close
Emotional come-ons	Writing long letters
Undue attention	Too helpful
Sexual bribery	Grade offered in exchange for affair

Source: D. J. Benson & G. E. Thomson. (1982). Sexual harassment on a university campus: The confluence of authority relations, sexual interest and gender stratification. *Social Problems,* **29,** 236–251.

Legal definitions of sexual harassment focus on these problems in the workplace or in education. However, there is another category of coercive and potentially damaging sexual encounters—those between a psychotherapist and patient, or between other professionals such as physicians and patients. Professional societies such as the American Psychological Association state clearly in their codes that such behaviors are unethical. Nonetheless, they occur, and can be damaging.

One survey of a sample of licensed Ph.D. psychologists found that 5.5 percent of the male and 0.6 of the female psychologists admitted having engaged in sexual intercourse with a client during the time the patient was in therapy, and an additional 2.6 percent of male and 0.3 percent of female therapists had intercourse with clients within three months of termination of therapy (Holroyd & Brodsky, 1977). These are probably best regarded as minimum figures because they are based on the self-reports of the therapists and some might not be willing to admit such activity even though the questionnaire was anonymous. Of those therapists who had intercourse with clients, 80 percent repeated the activity with other clients.

Experts regard this kind of situation as having the potential for serious emotional damage to the patient (Williams, 1992). Like the cases of sexual harassment discussed earlier, it is a situation of unequal power, in which the more powerful person, the therapist, imposes sexual activity on the less powerful person, the patient. The situation is regarded as particulary serious because patients in psychotherapy have opened themselves up emotionally to the therapist and therefore are extremely vulnerable emotionally.

Summary

This chapter explored three situations in which power or coercion is used to force sex on an unwilling victim: rape, incest, and sexual harassment.

There are four major theoretical views of rape: victim-precipitated, psychopathology of rapists, the feminist view, and social disorganization.

Rape victims often do not report the crime. Common psychological responses to being raped are fear, guilt, and depression. Research indicates that anxiety lasts for a year and, in some cases, longer. Social support from friends can help to reduce the psychological damage.

Although rapists vary tremendously, most are young, many repeat the offense, and most are not murderers. Date rape is common, and 14 percent of women who have been married report having been raped by a husband or an ex-husband. Men, too, can be victims of rape or unwanted intercourse. However, males are less often victims than females are, and the coercion is likelier to have been psychological for male victims, whereas physical force is more often used against female victims.

Patterns of gender-role socialization probably contribute to females becoming victims and males becoming rapists. Rape has different meanings among different U.S. ethnic groups.

Approximately 3 to 5 percent of males and 12 to 15 percent of females are victims of child sexual abuse. Over 90 percent of abusers are male.

Brother-sister incest is the most common form of incest and is less likely to be psychologically damaging than other forms. Father-daughter incest is the second most common form and is likely to be psychologically damaging to the daughter-victim.

Sexual harassment occurs both at work and in education. The most common pattern is that of a male harasser and a female victim, although the reverse pattern also occurs. Sexual harassment usually occurs in a context of unequal power between the harasser and the victim, as when the harasser is the victim's supervisor or professor. Sexual comments, propositions, and sexual touching, as well as coerced intercourse, are all classified as harassment. The consequences to the victim can be serious. There can also be serious consequences to therapist-patient sexual contact.

Review Questions

1. Based on a random sample of California women, one study concluded that there is a 26 percent chance that a woman will be the victim of a completed rape at some time in her life. True or false?

2. A person who believes that a raped woman is really a slut who got what she was asking for holds the _____ view of rape.

3. Research conducted with rape victims indicates that there is a rape trauma syndrome that typically lasts for about 10 years following the attack. True or false?

4. The typical rapist is in his forties and hypersexual. True or False?

5. Forced sexual intercourse on a date does not meet the legal definition of rape. True or false?

6. The typical motive for a man raping his wife is that they are not having intercourse as frequently as he would like. True or false?

7. In the 1800s, there were no penalties for a white man raping an African American woman. True or false?

8. "Pedophiliac" is the scientific term for a child molester. True or false?

9. Surveys of the general population indicate that the most common form of incest is father-daughter incest. True or false?

10. A job interviewer promising a woman she will get a job if she has intercourse with him is an example of sexual harassment. True or false?

(The answers to all review questions are at the end of the book, beginning on page 731.)

Questions for Thought, Discussion, and Debate

1. On your campus, what services are available for rape victims? Do these services seem adequate, given what you have read in this chapter about victim responses to rape? What could be done to improve the services?

2. Find out what procedures are available on your campus if a student is a victim of sexual harassment by a professor.

3. Apply the four theoretical views of rape to child sexual abuse.

Suggestions for Further Reading

Baron, Larry, & Straus, Murray A. (1989). *Four theories of rape*. These well-known violence researchers propose four theories of rape, focusing on feminist theory and social disorganization theory, and test them with an interesting data set.

Bart, Pauline B., & O'Brien, Patricia H. (1985). *Stopping rape: Successful survival strategies*. New York: Pergamon. This book is based on the authors' study of women who were the object of a rape attempt. The researchers compared the women who managed to avoid being raped and those who didn't. Their conclusion: Women should resist actively, and female socialization should be changed radically.

Brady, Katherine. (1979). *Father's days*. New York: Dell paperback. This autobiography of an incest victim is both moving and insightful.

Finkelhor, David. (1984). *Child sexual abuse: New theory and research*. New York: Free Press. This book, written for a general audience, provides an authoritative review of current research and theory on child sexual abuse.

White, Jacquelyn W., & Sorenson, Susan B. (1992). Adult sexual assault. *Journal of Social Issues,* **48**(1). The whole special issue of this journal is on sexual assault of adults and is packed with interesting articles.

Sex for Sale

C h a p t e r   H i g h l i g h t s

Pornography is an expression not of human erotic feeling and desire, and not a love of the life of the body, but of a fear of bodily knowledge, and a desire to silence eros. *

In this chapter we consider two ways in which sex can be bought and sold: prostitution and pornography. Both involve complex legal issues and public controversy, but also a steady stream of eager customers.

PROSTITUTION

Prostitute: A person who engages in sexual acts in return for money and does so in a promiscuous, fairly nondiscriminating fashion.

Prostitutes ("hookers," "whores") engage in sexual acts in return for money or some other payment such as drugs. As some social critics have pointed out, though, some marriages and dating arrangements would also fall into this category. Thus one should probably add the conditions that prostitutes are promiscuous and fairly nondiscriminating in their choice of partners. Female prostitutes will be discussed first.

Kinds of Prostitutes

There are many kinds of prostitutes; they vary in terms of social class, status, and the lifestyle they have.

Call girl: The most expensive and exclusive category of prostitutes.

The call girl is the elite of prostitutes. She is expensively dressed, lives in an attractive apartment in a good section of town, and probably charges a minimum of $100 for an hour's worth of her services (more if she is classier or is asked to engage in more exotic sexual acts, such as anal intercourse). She can thus earn over $75,000 a year, tax-free. But she does have high business expenses: an expensive wardrobe and apartment, high medical bills for prevention of sexually transmitted diseases, expenses for makeup and hairdressers, high tips for doormen and landlords, and the cost of an answering service or answering machine.

* *Source:* Susan Griffin. *Pornography and silence.* (1981). New York: Harper & Row.

She obtains her clients through personal referrals and may have many regular customers; thus she maintains close control over whom she services. She may also provide other than sexual services; for example, she may be an attractive companion for a party, or she may be part of a "reward" that businesses provide for executives. The contact is often made over the phone or perhaps in an expensive bar; the sexual activity may then take place in either her apartment or his.

The call girl is typically from a middle-class background, has more self-discipline than other prostitutes, and is better educated; some are college graduates. The movie *Klute,* starring Jane Fonda, provides a good look into the life of a call girl.

Other prostitutes work out of **brothels.** In the 1800s and early 1900s there were many successful brothels in the United States. They varied from clip joints, where the customer's money was stolen by an accomplice while he was sexually occupied, to sporting houses and mansions. There the women were beautifully dressed, and fine food and liquor were served. The customer could choose his partner in an attractive living room downstairs; the bedrooms were upstairs, and no time limits were imposed on the customer (Bess & Janus, 1976). Brothels have declined in number and success since World War II. In the last two decades, though, a replacement seems to have cropped up: the **massage parlor.**

Some women sell their sexual services in massage parlors (Perkins & Bennett, 1985). Massage parlors—and massages, of course—are perfectly legal, and so this setup has some advantages over more standard forms of prostitution, which are illegal. Once the customer is inside the private massage room, though, it is understood that he can get whatever services he pays for. Intercourse is not always possible, since massage parlors are not legally permitted to have beds, but fellatio and hand stimulation of the penis (a "local") are quite practical. Here, too, the customer may be fleeced. For example, he may pay for "oral sex" and find he is allowed to talk for several minutes and is then shown out.

Bar and hotel prostitutes are in the middle of the status hierarchy. Hotel prostitutes are expected to solicit subtly because, although the hotel management is generally aware of their presence, the hotel's facade of respectability must be maintained.

Another way in which a veneer of respectability is added to a sex business is through an "escort service," which may actually offer sexual services.

At the lower end of the status hierarchy is the **streetwalker,** which is the style of the majority of prostitutes. She sells her wares on the streets of cities. She is generally less attractive and less fashionably dressed than the call girl, and she charges correspondingly less for services, perhaps as little as $20 for a "quickie." She is more likely to impose strict time constraints on the customer. Because her mode of operation is obvious, she is likely to be arrested, and she is also more likely to be exposed to dangerous clients.

A **baby pro** is generally younger than 16 years old and works conventions, resorts, and hotels (Shoemaker, 1977). There has been an increasing demand in recent years for this kind of prostitute, especially because it is believed that they are less likely to be infected with STDs.

Pimps and Madams

The **pimp** ("The Man") is the companion-master of the prostitute. She supports him with her earnings, and in return he gives her companionship and sex, gets her out of jail, and provides her with food, clothing, shelter, and drugs, especially cocaine. He also provides protection against theft and other crimes, since the prostitute is scarcely in a position to go to the police if she is robbed by a customer. The *procurer,*

Brothel (BRAH-thul): A house of prostitution where prostitutes and customers meet for sexual activity.

Massage parlor: A place where massages, as well as sexual services, can generally be purchased.

Streetwalker: A lower-status prostitute who walks the streets selling her services.

Baby pro: A young prostitute, generally 16 years of age or younger.

Pimp: A prostitute's companion, protector, and master.

or panderer, helps the prostitute and client find each other. Pimps sometimes, though not always, function as panderers.

The prostitutes working for a pimp are called his "stable," and each is called a "wife." An "outlaw" is a prostitute who has no pimp. Typically, the pimp returns only 5 percent of the prostitute's earnings to her (Sheehy, 1973).

A madam is a woman who manages a brothel. Typically, she is quite intelligent and has excellent financial and social skills. The best-known madam of the 1970s was Xaviera Hollander, who managed a brothel in New York and wrote *The Happy Hooker*. The sensation of the 1980s was Manhattan's "Mayflower Madam," Sydney Biddle Barrows, who operated a phone-in escort service (Barrows, 1986).

Psychological Functioning of Prostitutes

Although most prostitutes are of average intelligence, the majority—with the exception of call girls—are not well educated (Bess & Janus, 1976). Given that they are of normal intelligence and sensitivity, they must surely perceive the low esteem in which society holds them. How do they cope with this degrading image of themselves?

According to one study, several rationalizing strategies may be adopted (Jackman et al., 1963). One group of prostitutes become a part of a criminal subculture and adopt its set of values. The prostitute then has a set of counterculture values and is critical of conventional values. She might say that middle-class, conventional mores are hypocritical and boring. A second group of women shift their lives between two worlds. They are middle-class, are often married and have children, and use prostitution as a means of supporting themselves and their families. These women have very conventional values and maintain a strict dissociation between their two worlds. One said:

> I think that I am a good mother who takes care of her children. I love my family very much. I have a normal family life other than being a prostitute. I hope that my husband can find a job and gets to working steadily again so I can be an ordinary housewife. (Jackman et al., 1963, p. 157)

Finally, Jackman and his colleagues described a third group as totally alienated. Their lives have no orientation and seem meaningless, and they have no well-defined set of values.

Prostitutes report that during sex with their customers, they typically turn off their emotions and try to dissociate themselves from the experience, concentrating on something else. As one said, "I do turn off. . . . My mind goes blank. . . . I never pretend to climax. I might think of the shopping tomorrow" (Perkins & Bennett, 1985, pp. 223–224).

The Career of a Prostitute

The first step in a prostitute's career is entry. There appear to be many reasons a woman enters prostitution (Bess & Janus, 1976). The most important is sheer economics. This factor is particularly likely during war, when prostitution may be the only means of survival. But even in times of peace, prostitution can be economically appealing, particularly for the woman who has no job skills. Why take a boring, restrictive job as a secretary for $300 a week when you can make that much in a day, or even a few hours, as a call girl? A related factor is a dislike of routine and regimen and an attraction for the glamour and excitement of the world of the

(a)

FIGURE 18.1
The oldest profession. (a)
Fifteenth-century
prostitutes "in the women's
house." (b) Modern
prostitutes "working the
street."

(b)

prostitute. For some women—for example, a poor but very attractive woman—prostitution is a means of attaining upward economic mobility. Some women become prostitutes in order to support a drug addiction. Another category of reasons involves gaining power. For example, a woman who serves as a call girl to famous politicians may think of herself as having access to real political power. As a woman who was involved in one of the Capitol Hill sex scandals uncovered in the 1970s said, "I was

Sexuality and the Media

The media are filled with images of sexuality. These images provide us with idealized characters and scripts, which both reflect and shape cultural values. Sexual messages were part of movies and advertising 50 years ago, just as they are today, but what is acceptable to show, and the standards of what is sexy, have changed considerably.

Entertainers are often sex symbols. Peggy Lee (above, left) and Pat Boone (above, right) epitomized attractiveness in the 1950s. Today they have been replaced by different stars with different styles: Madonna (below, left) and Prince (below, right). Peggy Lee's bare shoulders were the height of sensuousness in the fifties. Madonna shows us more, but is she more sensuous?

The standards for bedroom scenes in the movies have changed dramatically. Above: In *The Thin Man* (1934) William Powell and Myrna Loy are both thoroughly clad and in separate beds. Right: In *Basic Instinct* (1992) there is only one bed, and the couple are distinctly naked and about as close as they can get.

The teen beach scene has also changed over the past 30 years. Below: In *Where the Boys Are* (1960) direct expressions of sexuality are avoided by having the actors in group scenes, bodies covered by very generous swimsuits, and the body contact limited to a chaste arm linked to another arm. Right: When the cast of *90210* hits the beach (1993), the suits (at least the women's) are revealing, the body contact extensive and sexy, and arms link with body parts other than arms.

Gentleness means so much

Gentle moments come as a welcome pause in the hurry of modern living. And a gentle smoke brings needed solace, too. That's why this new Philip Morris, made gentle for modern taste, has such special appeal for our younger smokers. Enjoy the gentle pleasure—the *fresh unfiltered flavor*—of today's new Philip Morris. Ask for it in the smart new package.

New Philip Morris...*gentle for modern t...*

Gender roles portrayed in advertising have changed as well, reflecting and fostering the breakdown of traditional stereotypes. In the 1950s cigarette ad at left, the husband offers gentle strength as his wife sews a button on his shirt; she is passive and demure, with eyes downcast. Below: In the 1990s ad for "Yes" Clothing, there is an explicit reference to passion in selling the clothing, and the woman's approach is hardly demure.

YES CLOTHING CO.

to

*P*ASSION

Standards about the acceptability of conveying direct information about sex, contraception, and STDs have also changed dramatically. Below: Portraying a 1940s perspective, the movie *Summer of '42* shows adolescent boys sneaking away to pore over a medical book to learn the facts of life. Right: Today we can simply dial a telephone number found on our TV screen and get sex talk.

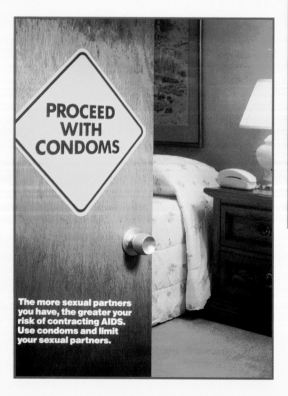

The more sexual partners you have, the greater your risk of contracting AIDS. Use condoms and limit your sexual partners.

Above: Again showing the 1940s perspective, a boy purchases his first condom and then secretively lets his friend see the forbidden treasure. Left: In contrast, explicit discussion of condoms is considered acceptable—indeed health-promoting—in today's advertising.

only a pillowcase away from the Presidency." Still other women gradually drift into prostitution, perhaps because they have a friend who is a prostitute who encourages them to do it.

On entering prostitution, some women—particularly if they want to be call girls—go through an apprenticeship in which they pay an experienced call girl to teach them the skills of the profession. The apprentice learns not only sexual techniques but also how to manage finances, how to control customers, how to avoid being robbed, and how to make contacts.

One problem with prostitution is that it is a short-lived career, in this respect bearing a resemblance to the career of a professional basketball or football player. Even a woman who starts as a high-priced call girl may find herself drifting down in status, either as she ages and begins to show wrinkles or if she gets hooked on alcohol or drugs. In prostitution, seniority is not rewarded.

"Squaring up" or "leaving the life" refers to giving up prostitution. Financially it is a difficult thing to do, particularly for the woman with no job skills; recognizing this, some rehabilitation programs provide job training, as well as a halfway house, to integrate the woman back into society (Winick & Kinsie, 1971).

The married prostitute may simply go back to being a housewife. The unmarried woman may escape through marriage, since she may get proposals from her regular customers.

Other reasons for leaving include arrest and the threat of a long-term jail sentence, government agencies' insistence that she give up her children, and the knowledge that a friend was the victim of violence while she worked as a prostitute (Bess & Janus, 1976). The major hazards associated with being a prostitute are violence (including rape, assault, and murder), drug addiction, sexually transmitted diseases, and arrest by the police (Perkins & Bennett, 1985).

Customers

At the time of the Kinsey research, about 69 percent of all white males had had some experience with prostitutes (Kinsey et al., 1948). The 1970s Hunt survey, however, found that the use of prostitutes had become less common in the under-35 age group, particularly among middle-class males; only 19 percent of the men under 35 with some college education had had premarital intercourse with a prostitute (Hunt, 1974). Thus the need of prostitutes seems to have declined.

Prostitutes refer to their customers as "johns." About 50 percent of the clients are occasional johns; they may be respectable businessmen who seek only occasional contacts with prostitutes, perhaps while on business trips. Another 50 percent are repeat clients who seek a regular relationship with a prostitute or a small group of prostitutes (Freund et al., 1991). Others are compulsive johns, who use prostitutes for their major sexual outlet. They are driven to them and cannot stay away. Some of these men are able to function sexually only with prostitutes (Bess & Janus, 1976). About 40 percent of the men are married (Freund et al., 1991).

Men use the services of prostitutes for a variety of reasons. Some are married but want sex more frequently than their wives do or want to engage in practices—such as fellatio—that they feel their wives would not be willing to do. Some use prostitutes to satisfy their exotic sexual needs, such as being whipped or having sex with a woman who pretends to be a corpse. The motivation for the unmarried man or the one who is away from home for a long period of time (for example, during a war) may simply be release of sexual tension. Others, particularly adolescents, may have sex with prostitutes to prove their manhood or to get sexual experience. Finally, some men enjoy sex with prostitutes because it is "forbidden."

An Australian Prostitute Tells Her Story

Zoe is a 25-year-old ex-prostitute who has worked in a parlor and as an escort girl. A member of the newly formed Australian Prostitutes Collective, she is anxious to help establish a movement in Australia similar to those in other countries. Zoe today is a social worker and active feminist, both areas of interest which she wants to incorporate with her concern for prostitute women. She says,

> My mother divorced my father when I was 6 years old, so there was my mother, myself, my twin sister, and my little sister in an all-female household. In the early stages we did miss our father and there used to be a lot of fights. We always got on well with our mother, who was very family-oriented. When I started going out with boys at age 14 she put me on the pill. She encouraged us to bring our boyfriends home and that way we didn't have to go screwing in the bicycle shed. At school I was always very much a tomboy, loved sport, and was always a leader of a group.
>
> My first sexual experience was at 15, with my mother's lover. He was living in our house since I was 11, and he used to give us cuddles. In looking back now it was sexual molestation I suppose, but my twin sister and I competed for his favors.

Mum was out a lot so she didn't know what was going on.

> In adolescence I had no stable relationships. I think I was fairly promiscuous and I know I was searching for something. Sex was a very important part of my adolescent identity. I experimented a lot with different boys, and I had my first sexual experience with a girl when I was 15 as well.
>
> In 1979 I came from England to Australia to meet my father. I hadn't seen him in 12 years. I came over by myself, did some painting and decorating for about 8 months, but became very bored with it as I wasn't meeting anybody so I did some bar work, receptionist work and waitressing, and then I was unemployed for 5 months. I was feeling really miserable at the time and wasn't getting on very well with my father. He had become an alcoholic.
>
> I was still unemployed, isolated, and lonely. I went for five interviews one day and the last one said "escort." I wondered if it were prostitution or not and when I went for the interview I knew it was a massage parlor. They told me the prices and what the job was, asked me if I wanted it. I said "Yes," and I walked out with $150 that night.

Gigolo (JIG-uh-loh): A male prostitute who sells his services to women; also refers to professional male escorts.

Hustler: A male prostitute who sells his services to men.

Male Prostitutes

Some male prostitutes serve a heterosexual clientele, selling their services to women; they are called gigolos. They often cater to wealthy, middle-aged women and provide them with escort as well as sexual services. Their approach is generally subtle and romantically flattering to their clients. The character played by Richard Gere in *American Gigolo* attempted to support himself in this way.

Hustlers are male prostitutes who cater to a homosexual clientele. Interestingly, some of them consider themselves to be heterosexual, not homosexual (Coombs,

A friend told my father. He offered me money to get out of it, but I refused because there were other reasons for remaining in prostitution than money, such as experimenting, being sexually anonymous, being independent, earning my own money rather than ask him for support.

We had clients coming in for mild, medium, and heavy bondage, but I couldn't do heavy. They were mostly businessmen, but we had army and navy guys as well asking for these. We had one navy guy, about 19, who used to come in for medium bondage. He wanted to be dressed up in a pink nightie and have a dildo shoved up his ass, while there were two of us who used to dress up in black leather raincoats with black underwear, high black shoes and whips. He would grovel around the room in the nightie and we would beat him on the bum while shouting abuse at him. That was $80 for half an hour.

When you're screwing the whole day it can be pretty heavy going, but with bondage it is good money where you don't have to have sex and it's without beating yourself around too much. Also it has the advantage of being able to abuse a guy rather than having the emotional pull of lying down and being fucked by a guy.

When the police closed the parlor, I applied for work at an escort agency. I would then phone up and tell them I would be on call that night. Then I got dressed ready to go out, and sat home waiting for the phone to ring. They might ring up and say there's a client at the _____

Hotel, a businessman with a bankcard, for two hours at $125 an hour. I would catch a cab to the hotel, meet the client in the bar, fill in the bankcard or take the money, phone through to the office to tell them I'd arrived, have a drink with the client, and go out or up to his room. Most of the work was fairly chatty, chat about his business or silly small talk, do the job in his room and phone through after it to let them know I'd finished.

The job risk is much higher than in parlors. You were very vulnerable in the client's room and have no control over the situation, which can be pretty frightening if things get nasty. You always let each client know that you have to phone the office before and after the job so that he is aware that you are being guarded. Nevertheless, it does not reduce the danger from clients who decide to mug you in the room.

I left the escort work when I fell in love with the guy I was going out with and I decided to set up a stable relationship with him. The relationship went on for 14 months, but I was totally frigid for six months after I gave up prostitution. I had lost myself in prostitution and had become so well established in my identity and role as a prostitute that once I had stopped I couldn't then relate to my lover as myself.

My immediate future plans are basically to finish my studies in humanities at university. I'd like to see all laws against prostitutes repealed, all of them.

Source: Roberta Perkins & Garry Bennett. (1985). *Being a prostitute.* London: Allen & Unwin, pp. 106–113.

1974). They may have strict rules for their customers to follow, such as only permitting the customer to perform fellatio on them. To indicate their masculinity, they may wear leather jackets and tight jeans. There is some market for "chickens" (young boys) as prostitutes.

Parallel to patterns of female prostitution, there are male homosexual escort services for a more upscale clientele (Salamon, 1989).

Male prostitutes seem to fall into four categories (Allen, 1980). First are the full-time street and bar hustlers, who operate much as female streetwalkers do. Second are full-time call boys or kept boys. They tend to have a more exclusive clientele and to be more attractive and more sexually versatile than the streetwalkers. Surprisingly, by far the largest group is the third: part-time hustlers, who are typically students or individuals employed in another occupation. They generally work at prostitution only when they need money. The part-time hustlers are notable because unlike those in the other groups, they are less likely to come from inadequate families. They also have the best long-term chance for getting an education and a stable job and achieving a good social adjustment. Finally, a fourth group is made up of delinquents; they use prostitution as an extension of other criminal activities, such as assault and robbery. They are taught by older gang members how to pick up homosexuals and then threaten, blackmail, or assault them.

In one study of adolescent male prostitutes in San Francisco, the main reason for engaging in prostitution, stated by 87 percent, was money (Weisberg, 1985). Most often they had left home because of conflict in the family, typically leaving when they were 15 or 16 years old, although some had done so when they were 11 or 12. The majority (72 percent) reported using drugs while engaging in acts of prostitution. The reason most often cited was the enjoyment of being high. Drugs were also used to reduce upset or fear from the scary nature of the work.

PORNOGRAPHY

A debate over pornography is currently raging. Fundamentalists and some feminists (strange bedfellows, indeed!) agree that some kinds of pornography should be made illegal, while civil liberties groups and some other feminists argue that freedom of expression, guaranteed in the Constitution, must be preserved and therefore pornography should not be restricted by law. Meanwhile, Joe Brown goes to his local newsstand, buys his monthly copy of *Playboy,* thinks a little longer about *Hustler,* buys it, too, and strolls back to his apartment for a pleasurable evening's entertainment. Here we will examine what the issues are, paying particular attention to social scientists' research on the effects of pornography on people who are exposed to it. First, we need to clarify some terminology.

Terms

Pornography: Sexually arousing art, literature, or films.

We can distinguish between pornography, obscenity, and erotica. **Pornography** comes from the Greek word "porneia," which means, quite simply, "prostitution"; in general usage today, it refers to literature, films, and so on, that are sexually arousing in nature.

Obscenity: Something that is offensive according to accepted standards of decency; the legal term for pornography.

In legal terminology the word used is "obscenity," not pornography. **Obscenity** refers to that which is foul, disgusting, or lewd, and it is used as a legal term for that which is offensive to the authorities or to society (Wilson, 1973). The U.S. Supreme Court has had a rather hard time defining exactly what is obscene and what can be regulated legally, a point to be discussed in more detail in Chapter 22.

In the current debate over pornography, some make the distinction between pornography (which is unacceptable to them) and erotica (which is acceptable). For example, sociologist Diana E. H. Russell defines *pornography* as "explicit representations of sexual behavior, verbal or pictorial, that have as a distinguishing characteristic the degrading or demeaning portrayal of human beings, especially women" (Russell, 1980, p. 218). In contrast, **erotica** is defined as differing from pornography "by virtue of not degrading or demeaning women, men, or children" (Russell, 1980, p. 218). According to this distinction, a movie of a woman being raped would be pornography, whereas a movie of two mutually consenting adults who are both enjoying having sexual intercourse together would be considered erotica.

Erotica: Sexually arousing material that is not degrading or demeaning to women, men, or children.

FIGURE 18.2
Sex for sale.

Beyond these definitions given by scholars in the area, it is interesting to see how typical Americans define pornography. Research shows that there is great diversity in what people consider pornography. *Time* magazine's well-sampled 1986 survey on this topic (July 21, 1986) showed that 56 percent of Americans consider books describing sex acts to be pornographic; that means that about half of Americans consider such books to be pornographic, but half do not. There are also substantial gender differences. Fifty-two percent of the women polled consider nude photos in magazines to be pornographic, whereas only 39 percent of men hold this view. There is not a clear consensus on what is pornographic, a difficult problem when one considers what laws we should or should not have on this issue. This same poll also showed that the majority of Americans have been exposed to various kinds of sexually explicit materials.

Types of Pornography

Pornography is a multimillion-dollar business in the United States. Included in that business are a number of products: magazines, films, kiddie porn, live sex shows, telephone porn, X-rated videocassettes, and the latest technological marvel, computer porn.

A large chunk of the pornography market consists of magazines, ranging from *Playboy* and *Penthouse* to *Hustler* and hundreds of others with less well-known names. The soft-core magazines mushroomed beginning in the early 1970s. In the

1990s the market is large and includes both general magazines and those catering to special tastes.

Most pornography is designed for the heterosexual male reader. Yet in the 1970s *Playgirl* appeared, featuring "beefcake" to please the heterosexual female customer. There is also a large gay pornography business.

Soft-core pornography is a lucrative business, to put it mildly. In 1981, the 10 best-selling soft-core magazines had a total monthly circulation of over 16 million, and in 1979 they brought in over $500 million in profit (Serrin, 1981).

Hard-core magazines have a no-holds-barred approach to what they present. Photographs may include everything from vaginal intercourse to anal intercourse, sadomasochism, bondage, and sex with animals. A study of the titles of magazines and books found in "adult" bookstores revealed that 17 percent were about a paraphilia or sexual variation (Lebeque, 1991). Of those, 50 percent featured sadomasochism. An additional 21 percent were about incest.

Here, again, the profit is great. The markups may be as high as 600 percent, and it is estimated that there are approximately 20,000 stores in the United States selling hard-core magazines. If run properly, such a business will have as much as $200,000 per year in gross sales (Serrin, 1981). Yet more profit comes from customers who have regular subscriptions for pornographic magazines by mail, and repeat, frequent customers account for a large part of the market.

Although sexually explicit movies were made as early as 1915, only in the last three decades have these films been slick and well produced. The *hard-core film* industry began to emerge in a big way around 1970. Two films were especially important in starting the revolution. *I Am Curious, Yellow,* appearing in 1970, showed sexual intercourse explicitly. In part because it was a foreign film with an intellectual tone, it became fashionable for people, including married couples, to see it. I remember long conversations in the faculty lounge among my psychology professor colleagues about their opinions after seeing it. The other important early film was *Deep Throat,* appearing in 1973. With its humor and creative plot, it was respectable and popular among the middle class. Linda Lovelace, the female star, gained national recognition and later appeared on the cover of *Esquire.*

After the success of *Deep Throat,* there was a rapid appearance of full-length technically well-done hard-core films. *Deep Throat* had made it clear that there were big profits to be made. It cost $24,000 to make, yet by 1982 it had yielded $25 million in profits ("Video turns big profit," 1982).

Loops are short (10-minute) hard-core films. They are set up in coin-operated projectors in private booths, usually in adult bookstores. The patron can enter and view the film in privacy and perhaps masturbate while doing so.

In the early 1980s, business declined at X-rated theaters. But this was more than offset by a booming new business: X-rated *videocassettes.* For example, *Deep Throat* became available on cassette in 1977, and, by 1982, 300,000 copies had been sold ("Video turns big profit," 1982; Cohn, 1983). Cable television has also entered the arena, with porn stations in some areas. The sexual content of MTV is unmistakable.

Live sex shows are yet another part of the sex industry. Strip shows, of course, have a long tradition in our culture. They have declined in popularity recently, but the new rage is male strippers, catering to a female audience. In the sex districts of many cities, there are also live sex shows featuring couples or groups engaging in sexual acts onstage.

Telephone sex is another recent development in this industry. The customer dials a number and hears sexual talk. Typically the customer can pay by credit card and is charged by the minute.

FIGURE 18.3
*One innovation in the sex
entertainment business is
male strippers.*

Kiddie porn: Pictures or
films of sexual acts with
children.

Finally, there is kiddie porn, which features pictures or films of sexual acts with children. It is viewed as the most reprehensible part of the porn industry because it produces such an obvious victim, the child model. Children, by virtue of their developmental level, cannot give true informed consent to participate in such activities, and the potential for doing psychological and physical damage to them is great. Many states have moved to outlaw kiddie porn, making it illegal to photograph or sell such material; as of 1984, 49 states prohibited the production of child pornography and 36 prohibited its distribution (Burgess, 1984, p. 202).

Again, the profit motives are strong. An advertisement in the magazine *Screw* offered $200 for young girl-child models, and dozens of parents responded. A reporter covering the scene said:

> Some parents appeared in the movie with their children; others merely allowed their children to have sex. One little girl, age 11, who ran crying from the bedroom after being told to have sex with a man of 40 protested, "Mommy I can't do it." "You have to do it," her mother answered. "We need the money." And of course the little girl did. (Anson, 1977)

Some major, well-known films could easily be classified as kiddie porn. *Taxi Driver* featured Jodie Foster as a 12-year-old prostitute. And *Pretty Baby* launched the career of Brooke Shields, playing the role of a 12-year-old brothel prostitute in New Orleans. Brooke herself was 12 years old when the film was made.

A major study of offenders (the people who produce child pornography) and victims profiled the offender as follows: All of the 69 offenders studied were male. They ranged in age from 20 to 70, with an average age of 43. And 38 percent had an already established relationship with the child before the illicit activity began—they were family friends or relatives, neighbors, teachers, or counselors (Burgess, 1984).

FIGURE 18.4
The making of a porn film.

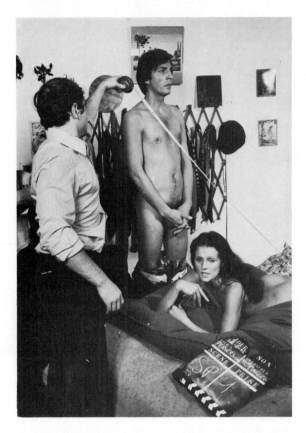

Sex ring: A group of children involved with an adult in sexual acts or producing kiddie porn.

One important part of the child pornography and prostitution business is the **sex ring** (Burgess, 1984). This refers to cases in which a group of children are involved with an adult, either engaging in sexual acts with the adult or posing as models in the filming of pornographic materials. In the *solo ring* one adult operates alone with a small group of children. In the *syndicated ring* there is a well-structured organization of adults formed for recruiting children, producing the pornography, delivering child prostitution services, and recruiting customers.

A study of 66 children who had been involved in sex rings documented the damaging psychological consequences for the children (Burgess, 1984). Because the child is forced so prematurely into adult sexual activity, there is difficulty integrating the physical, emotional, and psychological aspects of sexuality. Some children deal with the forced physical activity by separating their emotions from the physical aspects of sex. Some repress the events so that they cannot consciously remember their occurrence. Most learn that sex is to be shrouded in secrecy. And some become programmed to use sex to get attention and bolster their failing sense of self-esteem. In the din of public outrage over kiddie porn, we must not forget to care for the quiet child victims.

Yet we shouldn't leave our discussion of pornography with this most shocking aspect of it; let us instead close the discussion by considering a mating of sex and money that all of us encounter every day—*sex in advertising*. Both subtle and obvious sexual promises are used to sell a wide variety of products. A muscular young man wearing jeans—but no shirt—sells Calvin Kleins. Perfumes promise that they will make women instantly sexually attractive. There is a brand of coffee that seems to guarantee a warm, romantic, sensuous evening for the couple who drink it. An

Ernie: A Pedophile and Child Pornographer

In a study of child sexual abuse and child pornography, the investigators reported the following description of one offender:

In March 1979 contact was made with Ernie, a northern Indiana man, and arrangements were made to meet with him to share child pornography collections. Ernie arrived at a motel room carrying a small suitcase containing approximately 75 magazines and a metal file box containing twelve super-8-mm movies. The metal box was also filled with numerous photographs. Ernie then began to discuss his collection. He described himself as a pedophile and showed a series of instant photographs he had taken of his 7-year-old niece while she slept. The pictures revealed Ernie's middle finger inserted into the young girl's uncovered genitals, and he described how he had "worked" his finger up into her. Other photographs featured the girl being molested in various ways by Ernie while she remained asleep.

Despite the fact that he had engaged in numerous incidents of child molestation, Ernie had not been discovered because his victims remained asleep. He had molested and exploited both males and females, his own children, grandchildren, and neighborhood children. In order to photograph the uncovered genitals of his sleeping victims, Ernie had devised a string and hook mechanism. The hook was attached to the crotch of the panties, and he would uncover his sleeping victims' genitals as he photographed them with an instant-developing camera.

Ernie displayed his collection with the pride of a hobbyist. He exhibited photographs he had reproduced from magazines; he had reproduced these same photographs repeatedly and had engaged in a child pornography business from his residence.

While displaying his magazines and films, Ernie was arrested. A search warrant was obtained for his residence, and material seized from his one-bedroom apartment filled two pickup trucks. Numerous sexually explicit films, photographs, magazines, advertisements, and children's soiled underwear were confiscated. The panties had been encased in plastic, the child's school photograph featured with the panties. Also confiscated were nine cameras and a projector.

Several months passed before investigators found proof that Ernie had processed, through a central Indiana photographic lab, approximately 1500 photographs per week. It is believed that Ernie sold these pictures at $2 each, grossing an estimated $3000 per week.

Source: Ann W. Burgess. (1984). *Child pornography and sex rings.* Lexington, MA: Lexington Books of D. C. Heath, pp. 26–27.

important part of the presence of sexuality in the media is advertising. One study analyzed the sexual content of magazine advertising in 1964 and 1984 (Soley & Kurzbard, 1986). The percentage of ads with sexual content had not increased over that 20-year period, although the illustrations had become more explicit. In 1984, 23 percent of ads contained sexual content. And in those ads, female models were considerably more likely (41 percent) than male models (15 percent) to be shown partially clad or nude.

What is known about the customer of pornography? The stereotype is that he is a real sicko, living alone in a rundown apartment, obsessively reading and viewing pornography, and then slinking out to commit sex crimes against women and children. Yet scientific studies consistently indicate that the average customer of pornography is an educated, middle-class male between the ages of 22 and 34 (Mahoney, 1983). That is, the use of pornography is "typical" or "normal" (in the statistical sense) among males. Whether that fact is good or bad can be debated.

As an example, in one survey of university students 59 percent of the white males and 36 percent of the white females said they went to X-rated movies or read pornographic books (Houston, 1981). Over 5 percent of the females and 9 percent of the males said they did so frequently or very frequently. Repeat customers are a critical part of the success of the porn business.

Feminist Objections to Pornography

Beginning around 1978, some—though not all—feminists became very critical of pornography (e.g., Lederer, 1980; Griffin, 1981; Morgan, 1978). Why would feminists, who prize sexual liberation, be opposed to pornography?

There are three basic reasons some feminists object to pornography. First, they argue that pornography debases women. In the milder, soft-core versions it portrays women as sex objects whose breasts, legs, and buttocks can be purchased and then ogled. In the hard-core versions women may be shown being urinated upon or being chained. This scarcely represents a respectful attitude toward women. Second, pornography associates sex with violence toward women. As such, it contributes to rape and other forms of violence against women and girls. Robin Morgan put it bluntly: ". . . pornography is the theory and rape is the practice" (Morgan, 1980, p. 139). This is a point that can be tested with scientific data, and this evidence will be covered in the next section. Third, pornography shows, indeed glamorizes, unequal power relationships between women and men. A common theme in pornography is men forcing women to have sex, and so the power of men and subordination of women is emphasized. Consistent with this point, feminists do not object to sexual materials that portray women and men in equal, humanized relationships—what we have termed *erotica*.

Feminists also note the intimate relationship between pornography and traditional gender roles. Pornography is enmeshed as both cause and effect. That is, pornography in part results from traditional gender roles that make pornography socially acceptable for men to use and require hypersexuality and aggressiveness as part of the male role. Consistent with the idea that use of pornography is linked to traditional masculinity, one study of androgyny and the use of pornography among college students found that the likeliest users of pornography are traditionally gender-typed, masculine males and androgynous females (Kenrick et al., 1980). Yet the reverse process may also occur—that is, pornography may serve to perpetuate traditional gender roles. By seeing or reading about dominant males and submissive, dehumanized females, each new generation of adolescent boys is socialized to accept these roles.

The Effects of Pornography

Some of the assertions summarized above—for example, that violent pornography may predispose men to committing violent crimes against women—can be tested

(a)   (b)

FIGURE 18.5
*The controversy over
pornography has put some
members of the political
left wing on the same side
as some from the right
wing. (a) Feminists protest
pornography. (b) The
Meese Commission, which
included many
conservatives, urged
restrictions on
pornography and
encouraged citizens to
picket stores that sell
pornographic material.*

using the methods of social science. A number of social psychologists have been busy collecting data to test such assertions.

Two basic questions can be asked about the effects of pornography: Does it affect the sexual behavior of users; and does it affect the aggressive or criminal behavior of its users?

In 1967 Congress established the Commission on Obscenity and Pornography, which was charged with investigating these issues; the commission issued its report in 1970 (Commission on Obscenity and Pornography, 1970). The basic conclusion of the report was that pornography did not have bad effects on people. Soon after, there appeared a report of the "Denmark experiment"; Denmark completely legalized pornography, and the result seemed to be a reduction in sex crimes, notably child molestation (Kutchinsky, 1973). Thus most textbooks featured the conclusion that pornography is not harmful.

However, the 1970 Report of the Commission on Obscenity and Pornography has been criticized because aggressive-pornographic materials were relatively rare at the time, and thus the materials it investigated were relatively mild and soft-core and did not depict violence (Malamuth, 1984). Aggressive pornography might give much more cause for concern, and there is evidence that it increased in frequency in the 1970s, although it then decreased somewhat in the 1980s (Scott & Cuvelier, 1987). An analysis of the covers of pornographic magazines indicated that, in 1981, 17 percent of them featured bondage and domination imagery (Dietz & Evans, 1982). Certainly sexually explicit materials such as videocassettes are far more available now than they were in 1970. In short, the conclusions of the 1970 commission report may no longer be accurate, and so we turn to more recent studies.

In general, research indicates that pornography—whether violent or not—does not seem to have much of a long-term effect on people's *sexual behavior* (although there may be some short-term increases in arousal lasting from a few minutes to an hour). For example, in one study males were exposed to sexually explicit, but not violent, slides (Brown et al., 1976). In the week afterward there was no significant increase in sexual activity, although there was a large increase in masturbation on the day of exposure. Neither does exposure to aggressive pornography seem to produce increases in sexual arousal, even when the exposure is to five feature-length movies over a period of several weeks (Ceniti & Malamuth, 1984).

The effect of aggressive pornography on *aggressive behavior* is a different story. Here we do seem to find effects, with violent porn increasing aggressive behavior as well as affecting attitudes and perceptions of violence toward women. For example, in one study male subjects were assigned to one of three experimental conditions: reading aggressive pornography stories with pictures (from *Penthouse*, depicting a male pirate raping a woman); reading nonaggressive pornography with pictures (also from *Penthouse*, but showing a loving interaction); or reading a neutral selection (from *National Geographic*, but apparently not one of their selections featuring nude natives). Afterward all subjects were insulted by a woman who was actually a confederate of the experimenter's (Malamuth, 1978, cited in Malamuth, 1984). They were then placed in a situation in which they could aggress against her by delivering electric shocks to her—a standard way psychologists measure aggression—although in fact the shock did not reach her. Those who had been exposed to the aggressive pornography showed significantly higher levels of aggression than those exposed to the nonaggressive pornography. Other studies indicated that exposure to aggressive pornography increases the aggressive behavior of male subjects toward females but not toward males (Donnerstein, 1980, 1983; Donnerstein & Berkowitz, 1981).

Another, more naturalistic study investigated the impact of violent pornography on attitudes about violence against women (Malamuth & Check, 1981). Undergraduates volunteered to participate in a study that was supposedly about movie ratings. They viewed, on two different nights, either (1) the movies *Swept Away* and *The Getaway*, which show sexual aggression against women with "positive" consequences (the woman eventually becomes aroused by the aggressive sex); or (2) neutral feature-length films. The films were part of the university film series. Several days later the students completed a number of attitude scales, including some on sexual attitudes and acceptance of interpersonal violence. The results indicated that exposure to the films that showed sexual aggression with "positive" consequences significantly increased male subjects' acceptance of interpersonal violence against women and increased their acceptance of rape myths. Interestingly, these same increases did not occur for female subjects.

In sum, then, we can conclude that exposure to nonviolent pornography does not have much of an effect on people's sexual behavior or aggressive behavior. However, exposure to aggressive pornography does increase males' aggression toward women, as well as affecting males' attitudes, making them more accepting of violence against women. (For an excellent review, see Linz, 1989).

These are disturbing conclusions. What is the solution? Should pornography be censored or made illegal? Or would that only make it forbidden and therefore more attractive, and still available on a black market? Or should all forms of pornography be legal and readily available, and should we rely on other methods—such as education of parents and students through the school system—to abolish its use? Or should we adopt some in-between strategy, making some forms of pornography— kiddie porn and violent porn—illegal, while allowing free access to erotica? These are some of the questions that the Meese commission tried to answer.

The Meese Commission's Report

During the Reagan administration, Attorney General Edwin Meese appointed a commission to reevaluate the issue of pornography, updating the 1970 presidential commission's report. The Meese commission's report was published in 1986 and attracted widespread media attention (Attorney General's Commission on Pornography, 1986). The commission heard testimony from many sources, including judges, activists, victims, and social scientists such as Edward Donnerstein, and reviewed many research studies, including those discussed in the previous section. The commission recommended substantially greater regulation of pornography, including the following:

- Obscenity laws at federal, state, and local levels should be enforced more vigorously.
- There should be strict regulation of the production and distribution of child pornography.
- Congress should pass a law to ban obscene cable television programming and telephone pornography services.
- The Department of Justice should create a computer data base that would assist local officials in prosecutions. It would serve, for example, as a central storage unit for information on "known offenders."

The commission also urged private actions such as protests or picketing of stores that sell pornographic magazines.

The rationale for these recommendations was that the commission found evidence of substantial harm caused by pornography. However, social scientists who had given testimony to the commission quickly challenged the conclusions and the recommendations (Linz, Donnerstein, & Penrod, 1987). First, they pointed out that many of the studies on which the commission relied were laboratory experiments, usually with college students as subjects, and it is therefore not clear whether the results would generalize outside the laboratory or to other populations of subjects. But most importantly, the critics pointed out that research generally doesn't make it clear whether it is the sex or the violence in violent pornography that leads to its harmful effects (Linz et al., 1987). Indeed, in one study that tried to separate out the effects, men who saw a violence-only film (with no sexual content) were nearly as aggressive following it as men who viewed a sexually violent film; and those who viewed a sex-only film (with no violence) were no more aggressive than men who viewed a neutral film that had no sexual or aggressive content (Donnerstein et al., 1986, cited in Linz et al., 1987).

In conclusion, then, violent pornography may not be the problem, but rather violent media, whether sexually explicit or not. If that is the case, then the Meese commission's recommendations for restriction of pornography make no sense. They should have been concerned about violence in the media, not sex.

What Is the Solution?

We are nonetheless left with the unpleasant finding that pornography that depicts sexual aggression seems to have some harmful effects on men's attitudes toward women and aggressive behavior toward women, at least according to laboratory experiments. That is sufficent evidence to be concerned and to consider what can be done about the situation.

My own opinion is that legal restrictions—known less politely as censorship—are probably not the solution. I agree with the view of Donnerstein and his colleagues that education is the solution (Linz et al., 1987; Donnerstein et al., 1987). In their experiments, they have debriefed subjects at the conclusion of the procedures. They convey to subjects that media depictions are unreal and that the portrayal of women enjoying forced sex is fictitious. They dispel common rape myths, especially any that were shown in the film used in the experiment. Subjects who have been debriefed in this way show less acceptance of rape myths and more sensitivity to rape victims than subjects shown a neutral film (Donnerstein et al., 1987). It is also possible that *pre*briefings—telling subjects about the possible harmful effects even before they view the films—would be effective. We need more research on the effectiveness of these educational approaches. In the meantime, I am optimistic that education will be a considerably better solution than censorship.

Summary

There are several kinds of prostitutes, ranging from call girls to streetwalkers. The career of a prostitute begins with entry, usually for economic reasons. There may then be an apprenticeship, followed by a career that is generally short.

Male prostitutes are either gigolos (catering to women) or hustlers (catering to men).

There is a distinction between pornography (sexually arousing art, literature, or films), obscenity (the legal term), and erotica (sexual material that shows men and women in equal, humane relationships). Hard-core films and magazines form a multimillion-dollar business. Children—often runaways—are the star-victims in kiddie porn.

Some feminists object to pornography on the grounds that it debases women, that it encourages violence against women, and that it features unequal relationships between men and women.

Psychological research generally indicates that pornography has little long-term effect on people's sexual behavior, but that violent pornography can increase men's aggression toward women, as well as create more tolerant attitudes toward violence against women. The Meese commission advocated legal restrictions on pornography, but media education is probably a better solution.

Review Questions

1. The call girl is the most expensive and exclusive of prostitutes. True or false?
2. The _____ is a modern version of a brothel.
3. The _____ is the companion-master of the prostitute.
4. _____ are male prostitutes who sell their services to women.
5. The most important reason why women enter prostitution is economics. True or false?
6. Feminists distinguish between pornography and erotica, erotica being sexually explicit but not degrading to women, men, or children. True or false?
7. Kiddie porn is considered to be the worst part of the porn industry; it is illegal to produce kiddie porn in virtually all of the states. True or false?
8. The typical customer of pornography is a male in his forties or fifties who is psychiatrically disturbed, usually a psychopath. True or false?
9. Malamuth's research indicates that male subjects who are exposed to aggressive pornography are later more aggressive toward women than are a control group of males. True or false?
10. The Meese commission's report advocated legal restrictions or censorship of pornography, and social scientists agree with this recommendation. True or false?

(The answers to all review questions are at the end of the book, beginning on page 731.)

1. What is your position on the issue of censoring pornography? Do you think that all pornography should be illegal? Or should all pornography be legal? Or should some kinds—such as kiddie porn and violent porn—be illegal? What reasoning led you to your position?

Suggestions for Further Reading

Bullough, Vern, & Bullough, Bonnie. (1987). *Women and prostitution: A social history*. Buffalo, NY: Prometheus Books. A fascinating history of the oldest profession, from ancient Greece and Rome, through medieval times, India, and China, to the present.

Donnerstein, Edward, & Linz, Daniel. (1984, Jan.). Sexual violence in the media: A warning. *Psychology Today*, 14–15. This article discusses Donnerstein and others' research on the harmful effects of violent pornography.

Donnerstein, Edward, Linz, Daniel, & Penrod, Steven. (1987). *The question of pornography: Research findings and policy implications*. New York: Free Press. An excellent summary of social science research on pornography, with an analysis of legal issues and policy.

19

Sexual Dysfunction and Sex Therapy

Chapter Highlights

The only thing we have to fear is fear itself. *

Sexual dysfunctions such as premature ejaculation in men and inability to have orgasms in women have been the cause of a great deal of mental anguish, not to mention marital discord. A new era in understanding and treatment was ushered in with the publication, in 1970, of *Human Sexual Inadequacy,* by Masters and Johnson. This book reported not only their research on sexual dysfunctions and the causes of these dysfunctions but also their rapid-treatment program of therapy for such disorders. The work of Masters and Johnson, as well as many new developments in the field, will be discussed in this chapter.

Sexual dysfunction: A problem with sexual response that causes a person mental distress.

First, though, it is necessary to define the term "sexual dysfunction." A sexual dysfunction (the prefix "dys-" means "impaired") is any one of various disturbances or impairments of sexual functioning. A synonym might be "sexual malfunctioning." Examples are inability to get an erection (erectile dysfunction) in the male and inability to have an orgasm (orgasmic dysfunction, or anorgasmia) in the female. This definition seems fairly simple; as will be seen in the following sections, however, in practice it can be difficult to determine exactly when something is a sexual dysfunction.

No one knows exactly how many people have sexual dysfunctions. We know only about those who seek some kind of treatment for the problem, and they may be few in number compared with those who have a dysfunction but suffer quietly and never seek therapy, as a result of either ignorance or embarrassment. It seems safe to say that many Americans either have a sexual dysfunction or are affected by occasional instances of sexual dysfunction; most men, for example, occasionally experience problems in getting an erection.

In this section, the various kinds of sexual dysfunctions will be discussed: erectile dysfunction (impotence), premature ejaculation, and inhibited ejaculation in men; orgasmic dysfunction and vaginismus in women; and painful intercourse and problems of sexual desire, which may occur in men or women.

*Source: Franklin Delano Roosevelt, First Inaugural Address, March 4, 1933.

KINDS OF SEXUAL DYSFUNCTION

Erectile Dysfunction

Erectile dysfunction (also called *impotence* or *inhibited sexual excitement*) is the inability to have an erection or to maintain one. As a result, the man is not able to engage in sexual intercourse. Cases of erectile dysfunction can be further classified into primary erectile dysfunction and secondary erectile dysfunction. Primary erectile dysfunction refers to cases in which the man has never been able to have intercourse; secondary erectile dysfunction refers to cases in which the man has difficulty getting or maintaining an erection but has been able to have vaginal or anal intercourse at least once. Masters and Johnsons classified a man as secondarily dysfunctional if he has erection problems 25 percent or more of the time in sexual encounters.

Among men seeking sex therapy, erectile dysfunction is common, and secondary cases are more common than primary ones. It has been estimated that half of the general male population has experienced occasional episodes of erectile dysfunction, and this is certainly well within the range of normal sexual response (Kaplan, 1974). Erectile difficulties affect men of all ages, from teenagers to the elderly.

One problem of terminology is present. The word "impotence," which is often used, certainly carries negative connotations (the word means "lack of power"). A man who has erection problems has enough trouble without having people call him "impotent" besides. Further, the term is often confused with others, such as "sterility." There are many sterile men who do not have erectile dysfunction; they get fine, hard, lasting erections, but they just do not produce enough viable sperm to cause pregnancy. Conversely, many men with erectile dysfunction produce fine sperm and will be able to impregnate a woman as soon as they are able to have erections. The term "erectile dysfunction" is preferable to "impotence," since it gives a precise description of the problem but does not have the negative connotations.

Psychological reactions to erectile dysfunction may be severe. It is undoubtedly one of the most embarrassing things that can happen to a man. Depression may follow from repeated episodes. The situation can also be embarrassing to the man's partner.

The causes of erectile dysfunction and its treatment will be discussed later in the chapter.

Premature Ejaculation

Premature ejaculation (*ejaculatio praecox,* in medical terminology, or "PE," if you want to be on familiar terms with it) occurs when the man ejaculates too soon or is not able to postpone ejaculation long enough. In extreme cases, ejaculation may take place so soon after erection that it occurs before intercourse can even begin. In other cases, the man is able to delay the ejaculation to some extent, but not as long as he would like or not long enough for his partner to have an orgasm. Some experts prefer the term *early ejaculation* as having fewer negative connotations (McCarthy, 1989).

While the definition given above—ejaculating prematurely or too soon—seems simple enough, in practice it is much more difficult to define when a man is a premature ejaculator (McCarthy, 1989). What should the precise criterion for "too soon" be? Should the man be required to last for 30 seconds after erection? For 12 minutes? The definitions used by authorities in the field vary widely. One source defines "prematurity" as the occurrence of orgasm less than 30 seconds after the penis has been inserted into the vagina. Another group has extended this to $1\frac{1}{2}$

minutes; a third uses the criterion of ejaculation before there have been 10 pelvic thrusts. Masters and Johnson define premature ejaculation as inability to delay ejaculation long enough for the woman to have an orgasm at least 50 percent of the time. This last definition is interesting in that it stresses the importance of the interaction between the two partners; however, it carries with it the problem of how easily the woman is stimulated to orgasm. Psychiatrist Helen Singer Kaplan (1974) believes that the key to defining the premature ejaculator is the absence of voluntary control of ejaculation; that is, the premature ejaculator has little or no control over when he ejaculates, and this is what causes the problem. One of the best definitions, though, is self-definition; if a man finds that he has become greatly concerned about his ejaculatory control or that it is interfering with his ability to form intimate relationships, or if a couple agree that it is a problem in their relationship, then a dysfunction is present.

Premature ejaculation is a common dysfunction in the general male population. Approximately 50 percent of young adult men complain of early ejaculation, and about one-third of middle adult men say they ejaculate sooner than they would like (Frank et al., 1978).

Like erectile dysfunction, early ejaculation may create a host of related psychological problems. Because the ability to postpone ejaculation and the ability to "satisfy" a partner are so important in our concept of a man who is a competent lover, early ejaculation can cause a man to become anxious about his masculinity and sexual competence. Further, the condition may affect his partner and create friction in the relationship. The partner may be frustrated because she or he is not having a satisfying sexual experience either.

The negative psychological effects of early ejaculation are illustrated by a young man in one of my sexuality classes who handed in an anonymous question. He described himself as a premature ejaculator and said that after several humiliating experiences in intercourse with dates, he was now convinced that no woman would want him in that condition. He now did not have the courage to ask for dates, and so he had stopped dating. Basically, he wanted to know how the women in the class would react to a man with such a problem. The question was discussed in class, and most of the women agreed that their reaction to his problem would depend a great deal on the quality of the relationship they had with him. If they cared deeply for him, they would be sympathetic and patient and help him overcome the difficulty. The point is, though, that the early ejaculation had created problems so severe that the young man not only had stopped having sex but also had stopped dating.

Inhibited Male Orgasm

Inhibited male orgasm: A sexual dysfunction in which the male cannot have an orgasm, even though he is highly aroused and has had a great deal of sexual stimulation.

Inhibited male orgasm (retarded ejaculation) is the opposite of premature ejaculation. The man is uable to have an orgasm, even though he has a solid erection and has had more than adequate stimulation. The severity of the problem may range from only occasional problems ejaculating to a history of never having experienced an orgasm. In the most common version, the man is incapable of orgasm during intercourse but may be able to orgasm as a result of hand or mouth stimulation.

Inhibited ejaculation is far less common than premature ejaculation, accounting for only 1 to 2 percent of the cases among people seeking sex therapy and affecting about 4 to 10 percent of the general population (Apfelbaum, 1989; Spector & Carey, 1990).

Inhibited orgasm, to say the least, is a frustrating experience for the man. One would think that his partner, though, would be in an enviable position, being made love to by a man with a long-lasting erection that is not terminated by orgasm. In fact, though, some women react negatively to this condition in their partners, seeing the man's failure to have an orgasm as a personal rejection. Some men, anticipating these negative reactions, have adopted the practice of "faking" orgasm.

Let us now turn to some of the sexual dysfunctions in women.

Orgasmic Dysfunction

Orgasmic dysfunction: A sexual dysfunction in which the woman is unable to have an orgasm.

Anorgasmia: Another term for orgasmic dysfunction; the term "preorgasmic" is also used.

Primary orgasmic dysfunction: Cases of orgasmic dysfunction in which the woman has never in her life had an orgasm.

Situational orgasmic dysfunction: Cases of orgasmic dysfunction in which the woman is able to have an orgasm in some situations (e.g., while masturbating) but not in others (e.g., while having sexual intercourse).

Orgasmic dysfunction (or anorgasmia or *inhibited female orgasm*) in women is the condition of being unable to have an orgasm. The more commonly used term for this situation is "frigidity," but sex therapists reject this term because of its derogatory connotations, substituting the more neutral term "orgasmic dysfunction."[1] Like some other sexual dysfunctions, cases of orgasmic dysfunction may be classified as primary or secondary. Primary orgasmic dysfunction refers to cases in which the woman has never in her life experienced an orgasm (Andersen, 1983); *secondary orgasmic dysfunction* refers to cases in which the woman had orgasms at some time in her life but no longer does so. Situational orgasmic dysfunction refers to cases in which the woman has orgasms in some situations but not others. Some therapists prefer the term *preorgasmic,* suggesting that the woman has not yet learned to have orgasms but will be able to.

Once again, though, these definitions become more complicated in practice than they are in theory. Consider the case of the woman who has orgasms as a result of masturbation or of hand or mouth stimulation by a partner but who does not have orgasms in vaginal intercourse (what might be called "coital orgasmic inadequacy"). Is this really a sexual dysfunction? The notion that it is a dysfunction can be traced back to Freud's distinction between clitoral orgasms and vaginal orgasms and his belief that "mature" women should be able to have vaginal orgasms (see Chapter 2); both of these ideas have been debunked by Masters and Johnson. It can also probably be traced to beliefs that there is a "right" way to have sex—with the penis inside the vagina—and a corresponding "right" way to have orgasms. However, survey data indicate that this condition is quite common among women and may even characterize the majority of women (Hunt, 1974). Some authorities (for example, Wincze & Carey, 1991; Kaplan, 1974) consider such a condition to be well within the normal range of female sexual response. Perhaps the woman who orgasms as a result of hand or mouth stimulation, but not penile thrusting, is simply having orgasms when she is adequately stimulated and is not having them when she is inadequately stimulated. Thus there is some doubt as to whether "coital orgasmic inadequacy" is a dysfunction or an inadequacy at all and a corresponding doubt about whether it requires therapy.

On the other hand, there should be room for self-definition of dysfunctions. If a woman has coital orgasmic inadequacy, is truly distressed that she is not able to have orgasms during vaginal intercourse, and wants therapy, then it might be appropriate to classify her condition as a dysfunction and provide therapy for it, simply because she herself sees it as a problem (Zeiss et al., 1977). The therapist, however, should be careful to explain to her the issues and problems of definition raised above, in order to be sure that her request for therapy stems from her own dissatisfaction with her sexual responding rather than from a casual reading of Freud. Therapy in such cases probably is best viewed as an "enrichment experience" rather than "fixing a problem."

[1] The term "frigidity" is ambiguous, since it is used to refer to women who are unable to have orgasms and also to refer to women who show a total lack of sexual responsiveness and do not even become sexually aroused. The scientific term for this latter condition is "general sexual dysfunction."

A Case of Orgasmic Dysfunction in a Woman

Mr. and Mrs. F were referred for treatment six years after they were married. He was 29, and she was 24. They had one child, a girl, 3 years old.

Mrs. F came from a family of seven children; she remembers growing up in a warm, loving environment, with harried but happy parents.

Mr. F had a much different background. He was an only child who had been overindulged by his devoted parents. He began masturbating in his early teens, and he had a number of heterosexual experiences, including one relationship in which he had intercourse with his fiancée for six months before he broke the engagement.

The school years were uneventful for both Mr. and Mrs. F. When they first began dating, each was interested in someone else, but their mutual interest increased rapidly, and a courtship developed. They had intercourse regularly during the three-month period before their marriage.

During the courtship, Mr. F made every social decision, and he continued to exercise total control in the marriage. He insisted on making all decisions and was consistently concerned only with his own demands, paying little or no attention to his wife's needs. As a result, constant friction developed between the two.

Mrs. F did not have an orgasm before she was married. Afterward, she did have an orgasm on several occasions as a result of manual stimulation by her husband, but never during coitus. As the per-

sonal friction between the two increased, she found herself less and less responsive during coitus, although she occasionally had orgasms through manual stimulation. Pregnancy intervened at this time, distracting her for a year, but after that the problem became distressing to her and most embarrassing to her husband. He seemed to worry as much about his image as a sexually effective male as he did about his wife's frustration. Mrs. F's lack of sexual response was considered a personal affront by her uninformed husband.

Mr. F sent her to authorities to do something for "her" sexual inadequacy several times. The thought that the situation might have been in any way his responsibility was utterly foreign to him. When they were referred to Masters and Johnson for therapy, he at first refused to join her in treatment on the grounds that it was "her" problem. When he was told that the problem would not be accepted for treatment unless both partners cooperated, Mr. F grudgingly consented to participate.

According to Masters and Johnson's analysis, this was a case of secondary orgasmic dysfunction resulting from the woman's lack of identification with, or rejection of, her partner.

Source: William H. Masters & Virginia E. Johnson. (1970). *Human sexual inadequacy.* Boston: Little Brown, pp. 243–344.

Orgasmic dysfunctions in women are quite common (Wincze & Carey, 1991). They accounted for the vast majority—342 out of 371—of cases of female sexual dysfunction reported by Masters and Johnson. Surveys of the general population indicate that orgasmic dysfunction is quite common among women but that secondary orgasmic dysfunctions are probably more common than primary ones. These surveys indicate that probably about 5 to 10 percent of all women have orgasm problems and that inhibited female orgasm accounts for 25 to 35 percent of the cases seeking sex therapy (Spector & Carey, 1990).

In recent decades, particularly with the advent of the "Playboy ethic," female orgasm has come to be highly prized, and multiple orgasm may even be expected. In view of these pressures, it is not surprising that the woman who has difficulty having orgasms feels inadequate. Further, her partner may feel guilty if he cannot stimulate her to orgasm. Thus orgasmic dysfunctions in women are a cause for concern.

Vaginismus

Vaginismus[2] is a spastic contraction of the outer third of the vagina; in some cases it is so severe that the entrance to the vagina is closed, and the woman cannot have intercourse (Leiblum & Rosen, 1989) (see Figure 19.1). Vaginismus and dyspareunia (see below) may be associated. That is, if intercourse is painful, one result may be spasms that close off the entrance to the vagina.

Vaginismus is not a very common sexual dysfunction. Unfortunately, because the problem is rare and because it is often not discussed in the medical literature, physicians may fail to diagnose it or may misdiagnose it as something else, such as a small hymen.

Painful Intercourse

Painful intercourse, or **dyspareunia,** is often thought to be only a female problem, but it may affect males too. In women, the pain may be felt in the vagina, around the vaginal entrance and clitoris, or deep in the pelvis. In men, the pain is felt in the penis or testes. To put it mildly, dyspareunia decreases one's enjoyment of the sexual experience and may even lead one to abstain from sexual activity.

While complaints of occasional pain during intercourse are fairly common among women, persistent dyspareunia is not very common (Masters & Johnson, 1970). Painful intercourse may be related to a variety of physical causes, to be discussed below.

Problems of Sexual Desire

Sexual desire or *libido* refers to a set of feelings that lead the individual to seek out sexual activity or to be pleasurably receptive to it (Kaplan, 1979). When sexual desire is inhibited, so that the individual is not interested in sexual activity, the sexual dysfunction is termed *inhibited sexual desire* or **low sexual desire** (Leiblum & Rosen, 1988; LoPiccolo, 1980). People with inhibited sexual desire typically manage to avoid situations that will evoke sexual feelings. If, despite their best efforts, they find themselves in an arousing situation, they experience a rapid "turn-off" so that they feel nothing. The turn-off may be so intense that they report negative, unpleasant feelings; others simply report *sexual anesthesia*, that is, no feeling at all, even though they may respond to the point of orgasm.

The identification of low sexual desire as a sexual dysfunction by sex therapists began only about two decades ago. It arose from the study of patients who were failures with traditional sex therapy. Typically these patients had been misdiagnosed into one of the categories discussed earlier, and therapy was unsuccessful. Therapists

---

Vaginismus (Vaj-in-IS-mus): A sexual dysfunction in which there is a spastic contraction of the muscles surrounding the entrance to the vagina, in some cases so severe that intercourse is impossible.

Dyspareunia (dis-pah-ROO-nee-uh): Painful intercourse.

Low sexual desire: A sexual dysfunction in which there is a lack of interest in sexual activity; also termed "inhibited sexual desire."

---

[2] The suffix "-ismus" means "spasm."

FIGURE 19.1
Vaginismus. (a) A normal
vagina and other pelvic
organs, viewed from the
side, and (b) vaginismus, or
involuntary constriction of
the outer third of the
vagina.

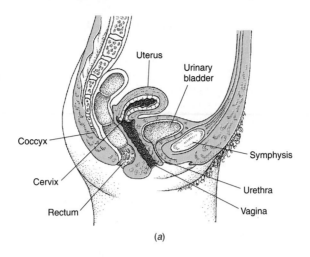

Uterus
Urinary bladder
Coccyx
Symphysis
Cervix
Urethra
Rectum
Vagina

(a)

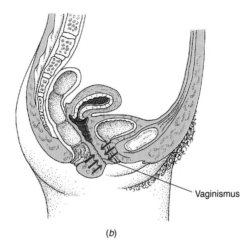

Vaginismus

(b)

came to realize that they were seeing a new, and increasingly frequent, disorder of desire rather than excitement or orgasm (e.g., Kaplan, 1979; LoPiccolo, 1980). Indeed, statistics indicate that low sexual desire is probably the most common dysfunction now. A survey of a "normal" (nonpatient) population indicated that 35 percent of the women and 16 percent of the men complained of disinterest in sex (Frank et al., 1978).

As with other dysfunctions, there are complex problems of definition. There are many circumstances when it is perfectly normal for a person's desire to be inhibited. For example, one cannot be expected to find every potential partner attractive. Kaplan (1979) recounts an example of a couple consisting of a shy, petite woman and an extremely obese (350 pounds, 5 feet 3 inches tall), unkempt man. He complained of her lack of desire, but one can hardly blame her, nor would one want to classify her as having a sexual dysfunction. One cannot expect to respond sexually at all times, in all places, and with all persons.

It is also true that the individual's absolute level of sexual desire is often not the problem—rather, the problem is a discrepancy between the partner's levels (Zilbergeld & Ellison, 1980). That is, if one partner wants sex less frequently than the other partner wants it, there is a conflict. This problem is termed a discrepancy of sexual desire.

Because recognition of this dysfunction is relatively recent, there is little agree-

Discrepancy of sexual desire: A sexual dysfunction in which the partners have considerably different levels of sexual desire.

ment in the field about definition or diagnosis. However, it seems likely that low sexual desire will turn out not to be a single category (LoPiccolo, 1980). Rather, it represents a single symptom that can be caused by many factors. The following have been implicated as determinants of desire problem: hormones, health problems, drugs, psychological factors (particularly anxiety and/or depression), cognitive factors (not having learned to perceive one's arousal accurately or having limited expectations for one's own ability to be aroused), and sexual trauma such as sexual abuse as a child (LoPiccolo, 1980; Rosen & Leiblum, 1987).

WHAT CAUSES SEXUAL DYSFUNCTION?

There are many causes of sexual dysfunction, varying from person to person and from one dysfunction to the next. Three general categories of factors may be related to sexual dysfunctions: organic causes, drugs, and psychological causes.

Organic Causes

Organic causes of sexual dysfunction: Physical factors, such as disease, that cause sexual dysfunctions.

Masters and Johnson held the opinion that only 10 to 20 percent of cases of sexual dysfunction result directly from organic (physical) factors. However, advances in physiological research make it clear that those estimates are too low. Because of this, a thorough physical examination may be suggested. It is useless to apply behavioral therapy if the dysfunction is a result of a physical condition, such as infection. Some specific organic factors that are known to cause sexual dysfunction are discussed below.

Erectile Dysfunction

Between 45 percent and 50 percent of cases of erectile dysfunction may be due to physical factors or have contributing physical factors (Richardson, 1991; Buvat et al., 1990).

Diseases associated with the heart and the circulatory system are particularly likely to be associated with the condition, since erection itself depends on the circulatory system. Any kind of vascular pathology (problems in the blood vessels supplying the penis) can produce erection problems (Tordjman et al., 1980). Erection depends on a great deal of blood flowing into the penis via the arteries, with a simultaneous constricting of the veins so that it cannot flow out as rapidly as it is coming in. Thus damage to either these arteries or veins may produce erectile dysfunction.

There is some association of erectile dysfunction with diabetes mellitus (Jensen, 1981). Either diabetes or a prediabetic condition may cause erectile dysfunction, although the exact mechanism by which this happens is not known. In fact, erectile dysfunction may in some cases be the earliest symptom of a developing case of diabetes. The incidence of erectile dysfunction among diabetic men is about two to five times higher than the incidence in the general population (Marmor, 1976b). Of course, this by no means suggests that all diabetic men have erectile dysfunction; indeed, the majority do not.

Any disease or accident that damages the lower part of the spinal cord may cause erectile dysfunction, since that is the location of the erection reflex center (see Chapter 9).

Alcoholism or problem drinking is often associated with erectile dysfunction; "brewer's droop" has been known since Shakespeare's time (Richardson, 1991).

Erectile dysfunction may also result from severe stress or fatigue. Some diseases of, or defects in, the genitals or reproductive tract may create erectile dysfunction. Finally, some—though not all—kinds of prostate surgery may cause the condition.

One of the methods sex therapists use to separate cases that are physically caused from cases that are psychologically caused is by using physiological recording instruments to measure *nocturnal penile tumescence* (NPT)—that is, whether the man has erections while he is asleep. The idea is that if he has erections while asleep, there must not be an organic cause. This method is generally useful, although it is not perfectly accurate (LoPiccolo & Stock, 1986).

It is also important to recognize that some cases of erectile dysfunction—as well as most other sexual dysfunctions—are caused by both organic and psychological factors (Buvat et al., 1990; LoPiccolo & Stock, 1986). For example, a man who has circulatory problems that initially cause him to have erection problems is likely to develop anxieties about erection as well. This notion of dual causes has importance implications for therapy. Sometimes people require both medical treatment and psychotherapy.

Premature Ejaculation

Early ejaculation is almost always caused by psychological, rather than physical, factors (Kaplan, 1974). Particularly in the man who has never been able to control his ejaculating, the causes are almost invariably psychological. In cases of secondary dysfunction, though, in which the man at one time had ejaculatory control but later lost it, physical factors may occasionally be involved. A local infection such as prostatitis may be the cause, as may a degeneration in the related parts of the nervous system, which may occur in degenerative neural disorders such as multiple sclerosis.

An intriguing explanation for early ejaculation comes from the sociobiologists (Hong, 1984). Their idea is that rapid ejaculation has been selected for in the process of evolution—what we might call "survival of the fastest." Focusing on monkeys and apes, the argument is that copulating and ejaculating rapidly would be advantageous in that the female would be less likely to get away and the male would be less likely to be attacked by other sexually aroused males while he was copulating. Thus males who ejaculated quickly were more likely to survive and to reproduce. Interestingly, among chimpanzees, our nearest evolutionary relatives, the average time from intromission (insertion of the penis into the vagina) to ejaculation is 7 seconds (Tutin & McGinnis, 1981). In modern U.S. society, of course, rapid ejaculation is not particularly advantageous and might even lead a man to have difficulty finding partners. Nonetheless, according to the sociobiologists, there are still plenty of genes for rapid ejaculation hanging around from natural selection occurring thousands of years ago.

Inhibited Male Orgasm

Inhibited male orgasm may be caused by various diseases attacking the nervous system (Munjack & Kanno, 1979), by Parkinson's disease, and by diabetes. It is most commonly caused, though, by psychological factors.

Orgasmic Dysfunction in Women

Orgasmic dysfunction in women may be caused by an extremely severe illness, by general ill health, or by extreme fatigue. Most cases of orgasmic dysfunction, though, are caused by psychological factors. They may also be a result of the loss of libido that occurs in severe depressions.

Hormonal factors are usually *not* the cause of orgasmic dysfunction in women, and treatment with estrogen is generally not effective (Marmor, 1976a).

Painful Intercourse

Dyspareunia in women is often caused by organic factors (Marmor, 1976a; Wabrek & Wabrek, 1975). These include:

1. *Disorders of the vaginal entrance* Intact hymen or irritated remnants of the hymen; painful scars, perhaps from an episiotomy; or infection of the Bartholin glands
2. *Irritation or damage to the clitoris*
3. *Disorders of the vagina* Vaginal infections; allergic reactions to douches, creams, jellies, or the latex in condoms and diaphragms; a thinning of the vaginal walls, which occurs naturally with age; or scarring of the roof of the vagina, which may occur after hysterectomy
4. *Pelvic disorders* Pelvic infection, endometriosis, tumors, cysts, or a tearing of the broad ligaments supporting the uterus

Painful intercourse in men can also be caused by a variety of organic factors. For an uncircumcised man, poor hygiene may be a cause; if the penis is not washed thoroughly, material may collect under the foreskin, causing infection. Proper hygiene practices require that the man frequently retract the foreskin completely and wash the penis thoroughly with soap and water. Phimosis, a condition in which the foreskin cannot be pulled back, can also cause painful intercourse. An allergic reaction to vaginal douches, creams, jellies, and foams may be also be involved. Vaginal infections may cause irritation, as may gonorrhea. Finally, various prostate problems may cause pain on ejaculation.

Vaginismus

Vaginismus generally results when a woman has learned to associate pain or fear with intercourse (Kaplan, 1974). In some cases vaginismus is a result of prior episodes of painful intercourse, which may itself be caused by organic factors; in such cases, vaginismus may be considered to be caused indirectly by the same physical factors that cause dyspareunia.

Drugs

Some drugs may have side effects causing sexual dysfunctions (Rosen, 1991; Segraves, 1988; Kaplan, 1979; Abel, 1985). For example, the drugs used in treating peptic ulcers may cause erectile dysfunction, and those used to treat allergies may in some cases decrease libido in women and erection capacity in men. A list of drugs that may decrease libido or impair sexual response is provided in Table 19.1.

The effects of illicit (illegal) drugs on sexual response vary widely. For example, some stimulants taken intravenously are powerful sexual stimulants (Rylander, 1969). One addict was quoted as saying that a shot of phenmetrazine "goes straight from the head to the scrotum." The opiates, on the other hand, can severely depress sexual behavior (Abel, 1985; Hollister, 1975; Isbell, 1965). In one report, nearly half of the 100 heroin addicts studied had erectile dysfunction (Chein et al., 1964, p. 166; see also Cushman, 1972; H. Jones & Jones, 1977). Because of their tendency to sharpen experiences, hallucinogens, such as LSD and marijuana, may increase the enjoyment of sexual activity.

Cocaine has been reported to create a variety of sexual dysfunctions, including loss of sexual desire and erection problems (Siegel, 1982; Cocores et al., 1986).

Marijuana

Most users report that smoking marijuana enhances sexual pleasure and increases sexual desire; sensations of touch and taste are particularly enhanced (Weller & Halikas, 1984). In a survey of 200 marijuana users, 44 percent said that their sexual desires were increased, and frequent users agreed that enjoyment was also enhanced (Goode, 1970; Halikas et al., 1971; see also Tart, 1970).

A study of the potential effects of marijuana on sexual responding, conducted at the Masters and Johnson Institute, received a great deal of publicity (Kolodny et al., 1974). The study compared the levels of testosterone in the blood of 20 men, aged 18 to 28, who smoked marijuana frequently (they smoked at least 4 days per week for a minimum of 6 months before the study) with the testosterone levels in the blood of 20 other men, matched for age, who had never smoked marijuana. All subjects used no other drugs at the time of the study, and none had ever used "hard" drugs. The investigators found that the smokers had significantly lower testosterone levels than nonsmokers. Further, testosterone levels were related to frequency of usage. Heavy smokers (10 or more joints per week) had significantly lower testosterone levels than light smokers (9 or fewer joints per week). Heavy smokers also had significantly lower sperm counts than light smokers. Two of the smokers (as compared with none of the nonsmokers) had erection problems. Finally, three of the smokers stopped smoking for 2 weeks; their testosterone levels rose considerably during that time (by 57 and 141 percent). This study raises serious questions about the effects of marijuana use on sexual and reproductive functioning, since testosterone is so important to both. On the other hand, the study suggests that the results are quickly reversible when use is discontinued. Another study found a 66 percent reduction in sperm count after 1 month of marijuana use (Hembree et al., 1976). And a study of female long-term users found that they had more anovulatory cycles (Kolodny et al., 1979). A report by the prestigious National Academy of Sciences (1982) concluded that long-term marijuana use can suppress testosterone production, decrease the size of the prostate and testes, and reduce sperm production, but the effects reverse rapidly after use is discontinued.

Alcohol

The effects of alcohol vary considerably. A small amount of alcohol may reduce anxiety and inhibitions, thereby improving responsiveness. A large amount of alcohol, however, acts as a depressant and reduces sexual arousal, thereby causing sexual dysfunction. Alcoholics, who are exposed to repeated high doses of alcohol, frequently have sexual dysfunctions, including erectile dysfunction and loss of desire (Leiblum & Rosen, 1984; Jones & Jones, 1977). As one alcoholic put it, "I started out Early Times, but quickly wound up as Old Granddad" (Lemere & Smith, 1973).

Carefully controlled experimental research has documented the effects of alcohol consumption on women's sexual response (Malatesta et al., 1982). Women

Table 19.1
Drugs That May Decrease Libido or Impair Sexual Response

Drug	How It Is Thought to Affect Sexual Functioning	Some Common Medical Indications*
Drugs That Act on the Brain†		
1. Sedatives		
Alcohol and barbiturates	Depress CNS activity in a single large dose; long-term heavy use leads to neural damage	Sedatives and hypnotics (sleep inducers)
Narcotics	General depression of the CNS plus depression of the sex centers. In high doses, produce impotence and inhibit orgasm	Analgesics (pain relievers); methadone used in treatment of narcotic addition; control of coughing, diarrhea
Heroin		
Morphine		
Codeine paregoric		
2. Antiandrogens	Oppose the stimulating action of androgen on the brain and sexual organs	
Estrogen	May decrease libido in women and decrease erections in men	Replacement therapy in postmenopausal women; birth control; men with prostatic cancer; after urinary-trace surgery, used to prevent erection
Cyproterone acetate	Decreases sexual arousal	Experimental—used in treatment of compulsive sexual disorders
Adrenal steroids	Decreases libido	Allergies and inflammatory disorders
Cortisone		
ACTH		
3. Antipsychotic drugs		Treatment of psychosis
Chlorpromazine		
Drugs That Act on the Genitals‡		
1. Anticholinergic drugs	Inhibit the parasympathetic nerves and so may cause erectile dysfunction	Peptic ulcers, dyskinesias, glaucoma and other eye problems
Banthine		
Probanthine		
Atropine		
Quaternary ammonium compounds		
2. Antiadrenergic drugs	Inhibit the sympathetic nerves and so may cause ejaculatory problems; may also diminish libido and erection	Hypertension (high blood pressure) and other vascular disorders
Phentolamine		
Ergo alkaloids		
Guanethidine (Ismelin)		
Methyl dopa (Aldomet)	Erectile dysfunction is a frequent complication; some women report loss of orgasm and decreased arousability	
Miscellaneous		
Disulfiram (Antabuse)	Occasional erectile dysfunction and delay of ejaculation reported	Alcohol abuse
Chlorphentermine (presate)	Occasional erectile dysfunction reported	Weight reduction

Drug	How It Is Thought to Affect Sexual Functioning	Some Common Medical Indications*
	Miscellaneous	
Antihistamines	Continuous use may interfere with sexual activity	Colds and allergies
Monoamine oxidase inhibitors (MAO) or tricyclics	Ejaculation problems; erection problems; anorgasmia in women	Depression

* "Medically indicated" means that a physician may prescribe it for the condition.
† These primarily decrease desire and the sexual responses.
‡ These block the nerves controlling the smooth muscles and blood vessels of the genital organs.
Sources: R. Taylor Segraves (1988). Drugs and desire. In S. R. Leiblum & R. C. Rosen (Eds.), *Sexual desire disorders.* New York: Guilford. Helen S. Kaplan. (1979). *Disorders of sexual desire.* New York: Simon & Schuster. Ernest L. Abel. (1985). *Psychoactive drugs and sex.* New York: Plenum. R. C. Kolodny, W. H. Masters, and V. E. Johnson. (1979). Drugs and sex. In R. C. Kolodny et al., *Textbook of sexual medicine.* Boston: Little Brown.

who have consumed small amounts of alcohol (compared with controls who have consumed none) report greater sexual arousal and more pleasurable orgasms, although their orgasms are slightly delayed. However, when a large amount of alcohol is consumed (blood alcohol concentration of 0.075 percent), orgasms take significantly longer to occur and subjects report that the orgasm is less intense.

Psychiatric Drugs

Some of the drugs used in treating psychiatric disorders may also affect sexual functioning. For example, "dry orgasm," an orgasm in which the man produces no ejaculate, may be a side effect of some of the drugs used in the treatment of schizophrenia (Mitchell & Popkin, 1983). Tranquilizers and antidepressants, while producing some cases of sexual dysfunction, often help improve sexual responding as a result of their improvement of the person's mental state. (For a more complete discussion, see Segraves, 1988; Abel, 1985; Kaplan, 1979; Leavitt, 1974.)

Psychological Causes

Prior learning: Things that people have learned earlier—for example, in childhood—that now affect their sexual response.

The psychological sources of sexual dysfunction have been categorized into immediate causes and prior learning (Kaplan, 1974). Prior learning refers to the things that people have learned earlier—for example, in childhood—which now inhibit their sexual response. Immediate causes are various things that happen in the act of lovemaking itself that inhibit the sexual response.

Immediate Causes

Immediate causes: Various factors that occur in the act of lovemaking that inhibit sexual response.

The following four factors have been identified as immediate causes of dysfunction: (1) anxieties such as fear of failure, (2) cognitive interference, (3) failure of the partners to communicate, and (4) failure to engage in effective, sexually stimulating behavior (Kaplan, 1974; Barlow, 1986).

543

A Case of Erectile Dysfunction

Mr. X was a handsome and successful 30-year-old businessman who had been divorced two years earlier. He and his fiancée, who was 26 years old, were planning to be married shortly.

The chief complaint was erectile dysfunction. The man was easily aroused and had an erection quickly upon commencing sex play. Almost invariably, though, his erection diminished when he was about to begin coitus. His fiancée had no sexual difficulty; she was easily aroused and orgastic on clitoral stimulation.

Neither had a history of psychiatric problems. In fact, they seemed to be very well adjusted individuals. Their relationship also seemed to be excellent.

In his prior marriage, which had lasted five years and produced two children, Mr. X had experienced no sexual difficulty. He and his wife had intercourse two or three times per week, and he invariably functioned well. His wife left him because she was in love with and wished to marry a close friend of the family.

The divorce was very traumatic for Mr. X. He became depressed and was left with deep feelings of insecurity. He kept wondering why his wife had left him and whether he was inferior to the other man.

Eight months after the separation he went to a party and met a woman who wanted to have sex with him right there. On her urging, they went to an upstairs room (which did not have a lock) and attempted to have intercourse on the floor. He became

Anxiety during intercourse can be a source of sexual dysfunction. Anxiety may be caused by fear of failure, that is, fear of being unable to perform. But anxiety itself can block sexual response. Often anxiety can create a vicious circle of self-fulfilling prophecy in which fear of failure produces a failure, which produces more fear, which produces another failure, and so on. For example, a man may have one episode of erectile dysfunction, perhaps after drinking too much at a party. The next time he has sex, he anxiously wonders whether he will "fail" again. His anxiety is so great that he cannot get an erection. At this point he is convinced that the condition is permanent, and all future sexual activity is marked by such intense fear of failure that erectile dysfunction results. The prophecy is fulfilled.

Similarly, anxiety in a woman may block arousal. If she is not aroused, she does not produce vaginal lubrication, and the result can be painful intercourse.

Fears of failure can also be created by a demand for performance by the partner. For example, some cases of erectile dysfunction apparently began when the woman demanded intercourse but the man did not feel aroused and therefore did not get an erection. Following that failure, anxiety built up in anticipation of future failures. Such a process is illustrated by the case history present in Focus 19.2. Demands for performance, of course, are generally harder on men than they are on women; to engage in intercourse, the man must be aroused and have an erection, and it is painfully obvious when this does not occur. Arousal is not an absolute necessity for a woman to have intercourse, though. The parallel demand for performance in

excited and erect, but for the first time in his life, he lost his erection. He tried to regain it, but his effort was of no avail.

Mr. X reacted to this experience with alarm. He felt depressed and extremely humiliated and embarrassed. He never saw this woman again. One month later he tried to make love to another woman, but again he lost his erection when the memory of his previous failure intruded into his mind.

From then on the problem escalated. He met his fiancée shortly thereafter, but initially he avoided making love to her. They attempted to have sex, but in most instances Mr. X was unable to function. Questioning revealed that he was preoccupied with thoughts about whether he would fail during lovemaking. He continued to feel humiliated and feared rejection, despite his fiancée's reassurance and sensitivity.

According to psychiatrist Helen Singer Kaplan's analysis, this was a case in which performance anxiety (an immediate cause) produced secondary erectile dysfunction.

In therapy Mr. X responded very readily to methods designed to dispel his performance anxiety.

Initially, intercourse was forbidden. During this time he and his fiancée engaged in mutual caressing. This proved most pleasurable to both. They then proceeded to gentle, teasing genital stimulation. Specifically, the woman stimulated the penis until it was erect. Then she stopped. When the erection abated, she resumed stimulation. This was repeated several times, still without orgasm for him.

Meanwhile, in the sessions with the therapist, Mr. X was told to stop watching the process of his erection and worrying about his "performance." He was confronted with the destructive effects of his spectatoring and his performance anxiety. In addition, the therapist was able to work through the dynamics of his reactions to his former wife's rejection of him, which seemed to be related to his current problems. The therapy thus combined elements of behavior therapy and psychotherapy, and is an example of Kaplan's psychosexual therapy.

Treatment of Mr. X proceeded to a successful conclusion.

Source: Helen S. Kaplan. (1974). *The new sex therapy.* New York: Brunner/Mazel, pp. 128–129.

women is the demand that they have orgasms. Once again, if the woman is unable to meet this demand, the result is anxiety and fear of failure, which further inhibit her response.

Cognitive interference is a second category of immediate cause of sexual dysfunction. "Cognitive interference" refers to thoughts that distract the person from focusing on the erotic experience. The problem is basically one of attention and of whether the person is focusing attention on erotic thoughts or on distracting thoughts (Will my technique be good enough to please her? Will my body be beautiful enough to arouse him?). Spectatoring, a term coined by Masters and Johnson, is one kind of cognitive interference. The person behaves like a spectator or judge of his or her own sexual "performance." People who do this are constantly (mentally) stepping outside the sexual act in which they are engaged, to evaluate how they are doing, mentally commenting, "Good job," or "Lousy," or "Could stand improvement." These ideas on the importance of cognition in sexual dysfunction derive from the cognitive theories of sexual responding discussed in Chapters 2 and 9.

Sex researcher David Barlow (1986) has done an elegant series of experiments to test the ways in which anxiety and cognitive interference affect sexual functioning. He has studied men who are functioning well sexually and men with sexual dysfunctions, particularly erectile dysfunction (to keep things simple, I will call these two groups the "functionals" and the "dysfunctionals"). He finds that functionals and dysfunctionals respond very different to stimuli in sexual situations. For exam-

Spectatoring: Masters and Johnson's term for acting as an observer or judge of one's own sexual performance; hypothesized to contribute to sexual dysfunction.

ple, anxiety (induced by the threat of being shocked) *increases* the arousal of functional men, but *decreases* the arousal of dysfunctional men while watching erotic films. Demands for performance (e.g., the experimenter says the subject must have an erection or he will be shocked) increase the arousal of functionals but are distracting (create cognitive interference) and decrease the arousal of dysfunctionals. When both self-reports of arousal and physiological measures of arousal (penile strain gauge) are used, dysfunctional men consistently underestimate their physical arousal, whereas functional men are accurate in their reporting.

From these laboratory findings, Barlow has constructed a model that describes how anxiety and cognitive interference act together to produce sexual dysfunctions such as erectile dysfunction (see Figure 19.2). When dysfunctionals are in a sexual situation, there is a performance demand. This causes them to feel negative emotions such as anxiety. They then experience cognitive interference and focus their attention on nonerotic thoughts, such as thinking about how awful it will be when they don't have an erection. This increases arousal of their autonomic nervous system. To them, that feels like anxiety, whereas a functional would experience it as sexual arousal. For the dysfunctionals, the anxiety creates further cognitive interference, and eventually the sexual performance is dysfunctional—they don't manage to get an erection. This leads them to avoid future sexual encounters or, when they are in one, to experience negative feelings, and the vicious cycle repeats itself.

This analysis is insightful and is backed by numerous well-controlled experiments. It fails to tell us, however, how the dysfunctionals got into this pattern in the first place. That explanation probably has to do with prior learning, to be discussed in a later section.

Failure to communicate is one of the most important causes of sexual dysfunction. Many people expect their partners to have ESP concerning their own sexual needs. You are the leading expert in the field of what feels good to you, and your partner will never know what turns you on unless you make this known, either verbally or nonverbally. But many people do not communicate their sexual desires. For example, a woman who needs a great deal of clitoral stimulation to have an orgasm may never tell her partner this; as a result, she does not get the stimulation she needs and consequently does not have an orgasm.

Another immediate cause of sexual dysfunction is a *failure to engage in effective sexually stimulating behavior*. Often this is a result of simple ignorance. For example, some couples seek sex therapy because of the wife's failure to have orgasms; the therapist soon discovers that neither the husband nor wife is aware of the location of the clitoris, much less of its fantastic erotic potential. Often such cases can be cleared up by simple educational techniques.

Prior Learning

The other major category of psychological sources of sexual dysfunction is prior learning and experience. This includes various things that were learned or experienced in childhood, adolescence, or even adulthood.

In some cases of sexual dysfunction, the person's first sexual act was a very traumatic experience. An example would be a young man who could not get an erection the first time he attempted intercourse and was laughed at by his partner. Such an experience sets the stage for future erectile dysfunction. Rape is another traumatic experience that may lead to sexual dysfunction.

Seductive parents may contribute to early traumatic sexual experiences. A parent may be seductive or may force the child to engage in intercourse; the child is in no position to refuse, but she or he feels terribly guilty. Once again, sex becomes

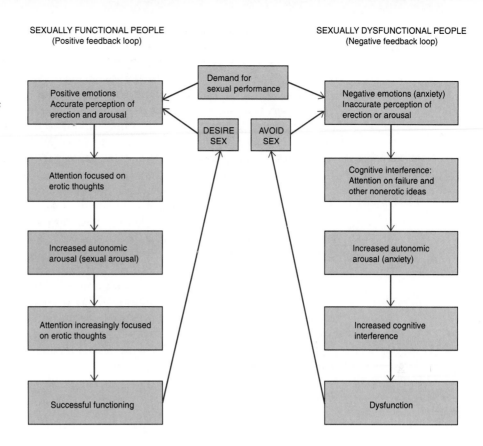

FIGURE 19.2
This model shows how anxiety and cognitive interference can produce erectile dysfunction and other sexual dysfunctions (Barlow, 1986).

SEXUALLY FUNCTIONAL PEOPLE
(Positive feedback loop)

SEXUALLY DYSFUNCTIONAL PEOPLE
(Negative feedback loop)

Demand for sexual performance

Positive emotions Accurate perception of erection and arousal

Negative emotions (anxiety) Inaccurate perception of erection or arousal

DESIRE SEX

AVOID SEX

Attention focused on erotic thoughts

Cognitive interference: Attention on failure and other nonerotic ideas

Increased autonomic arousal (sexual arousal)

Increased autonomic arousal (anxiety)

Attention increasingly focused on erotic thoughts

Increased cognitive interference

Successful functioning

Dysfunction

associated with psychic pain, laying the groundwork for a lack of sexual responsiveness later.

In other cases of sexual dysfunction, the person grew up in a very strict, religious family and was taught that sex was dirty and sinful. Such a person may grow up thinking that sex is not pleasurable, that it should be gotten over as quickly as possible, and that it is for purposes of procreation only. To say the least, such learning inhibits the enjoyment of a full sexual response. To use Byrne's terminology (Chapter 8) it may create an erotophobic personality.

Another source of dysfunction originating in the family occurs when parents punish children severely for sexual activity such as masturbation. An example is the little girl who is caught masturbing, is punished severely, and is told never to "touch herself" again; she obeys, and in adulthood she finds that she cannot have an orgasm through masturbation or as a result of manual stimulation by her partner.

Parents who teach their children the double standard may contribute to sexual dysfunction, particularly in their daughters. Women whose sexual response is inhibited in adulthood often have a history of being taught, when they were children, that no nice lady is interested in sex or enjoys it.

We should, though, note one major problem with the evidence of Masters and Johnson and others on these factors as causes of sexual dysfunction: The evidence comes from clinical data. This means that a group of people seeking therapy for their sexual problems were studied; certain factors emerged as common in their life histories, and it was therefore concluded that those factors must cause sexual dysfunction. The problem is that no data were collected on a comparison group of people who were functioning adequately in their sex lives to see whether those "causes" were also common in their histories. A classic example of this problem in logic is the following: A psychiatrist studies a group of schizophrenic patients and finds that every single one of them had a mother. The psychiatrist concludes that having a mother must cause schizophrenia. Had the psychiatrist also studied a comparison group of normal people, she or he would have discovered that they all had mothers too and that having a mother is therefore not a very likely cause of schizophrenia. We might apply this same critique to the statement that sexual dysfunction is caused by strong religious teachings. While strong religious teachings were common in the backgrounds of many of the patients with sexual dysfunctions, it might be that such a factor is also common among those who function quite well sexually; religious homes were, after all, quite common 30 or 40 years ago.

One study on female orgasm capacity provides some information that is relevant here. A large sample of adult women filled out a questionnaire about their own sexual behavior; they also provided other background information on such things as how religious they were (S. Fisher, 1973). The results indicated that the extent to which a woman was religiously devout had no relationship to her orgasm capacity. These findings seem to contradict Masters and Johnson.

The point is that the conclusions made by Masters and Johnson and other sex therapists concerning the causes of sexual dysfunction are not based on very good evidence. Our knowledge of exactly what factors in a person's past experience contribute to making that person sexually dysfunctional is highly speculative at the present time, and further research is needed.

Relationship Conflict

Although most sex therapists concentrate on treating the immediate and prior-learning causes of dysfunction, there are some other, more complex causes that are also worth considering. One of these is disturbances in the relationship between the two partners. If there is severe discord in a marriage, sexual dysfunction may develop. Anger and hating one's sexual partner do not create an optimal environment for sexual enjoyment. Sex can also be used as a weapon to hurt a partner; for example, a woman can hurt her husband by refusing to engage in a sexual behavior that he enjoys. Sexual dysfunction, then, may be one of many symptoms of marital discord.

Intrapsychic Conflict

Intrapsychic conflict: Psychological conflicts, often unconscious, that are believed by psychoanalysts to be the cause of sexual dysfunction.

In contrast to Masters and Johnson and other behavior therapists who view sexual dysfunction as a simple result of learning, Freudian analysts view sexual dysfunction as a result of unconscious intrapsychic conflict. The idea is that while humans have a strong craving for sexual expression, they also have unconscious anxieties about it and are afraid that they will be punished for engaging in sex. Put the two together, and you have conflict.

According to Freud, much of this conflict originates in childhood, specifically in the Oedipus complex. Resolving the Oedipus complex—identifying with the same-gender parent and repressing the incestuous sexual desires for the parent of the opposite gender—is essential for attaining mature, good adjustment. Sexual problems in adulthood result when an unresolved Oedipus complex, which has lain dormant for years, is reactivated. For example, an adult man is about to make love to a woman; suddenly, however, old castration anxieties are evoked, and he loses his erection. According to Freud, all sexual problems are caused by an unresolved Oedipus complex.

It follows from this theoretical model that sexual dysfunctions could be cured only by intensive, long-term psychoanalysis designed to uncover these unconscious, unresolved conflicts.

The success of the Masters and Johnson rapid-treatment program using behavior therapy provides evidence against the psychoanalytic model; according to Freud, their therapy techniques should not be successful. On the other hand, they do have a failure rate, and it is likely that those who fail in their treatment program are precisely the people whose dysfunction is caused by intrapsychic conflict. Accordingly, some therapists, such as Helen Singer Kaplan (1974, 1979), use a joint approach, combining the Masters and Johnson behavior therapy with psychotherapy for intrapsychic conflicts.

Fear of Intimacy

The fear of intimacy represents a peculiar blend of immediate causes, prior learning, and intrapsychic conflict, as documented by Helen Singer Kaplan (1979).

Some people actually seem to be fearful of intimacy—that is, of a deep emotional closeness to another person (Kaplan, 1979). Indeed, some people appear to fear intimacy more than they do sex. They would prefer to watch TV or talk about the weather or have sex rather than engage in a truly intimate, emotionally vulnerable, and trusting conversation with another person. If such persons are single, they typically progress in a relationship to a certain degree of closeness and then lose interest. This pattern is repeated with many partners. The fear of intimacy may be a result of negative or disappointing intimate relationships—particularly with the parents—in early childhood. The fear of intimacy causes a person to draw back from a sexual relationship before it becomes truly fulfilling.

TWO MODELS OF THERAPY

In the treatment of psychological problems, including sexual problems, there are two basic theoretical models that may be used, each leading to a different type of therapy. These are the psychoanalytic approach and the behavioral approach (see, for example, Meissner, 1980; Fensterheim & Kantor, 1980).

Psychoanalytic Approach

Psychoanalytic therapy: A system of therapy originated by Freud, based on uncovering and resolving unconscious conflicts.

The assumption of psychoanalysts is that sex problems are caused by unconscious intrapsychic conflict, often the result of childhood experiences. Following this assumption, sex problems can be cured only by long-term (perhaps several years), intensive psychoanalytic therapy designed to uncover the unconscious conflicts, gain insight into them, and resolve them. Often the problems are seen to be the result of a lack of resolution of the Oedipus complex. The idea is that if the unconscious conflicts are resolved, the problem sexual behavior should disappear.

This psychodynamic approach was essentially the only form of therapy available for sexual dysfunctions until the mid-1960s, with the advent of the Masters and Johnson work.

Behavioral Approach

Behavior therapy: A system of therapy based on learning theory, in which the focus is on the problem behavior and how it can be modified or changed.

In contrast to the psychoanalytic approach is the behavioral approach, or behavior therapy, with its roots in behaviorism and learning theory. The basic assumption is that sex problems are the result of learning in the past and that they are maintained by ongoing reinforcements and punishments (the immediate causes). It follows that these problem behaviors can be unlearned by new conditioning. Note that the focus is on the problem *behavior* and how to recondition it. There is no concern whatsoever with the unconscious or with intrapsychic conflicts.

THE MASTERS AND JOHNSON SEX THERAPY PROGRAM

The Format and Basic Principles

In 1970, Masters and Johnson reported on their development of a new set of techniques for sex therapy. Today, more than 20 years later, their methods are still used widely. Masters and Johnson operate out of a behavior therapy model because they see sexual dysfunction as a learned behavior rather than a psychiatric illness. If sexual dysfunction is learned, it can be unlearned. Thus Masters and Johnson use a two-week, rapid-treatment program of intensive therapy. The therapy consists mainly of discussions and specific behavioral exercises, or "homework assignments."

One of the most basic goals of Masters and Johnson's therapy is to eliminate goal-oriented sexual performance. Many patients believe that in sex they must perform and achieve certain things. If sex is an achievement situation, it also can become the scene of failure, and it is perceived failures that lead people to believe they have a sexual problem. Spectatoring contributes to the problem. The idea is to reduce anxiety.

In part, Masters and Johnson eliminate the couple's goal-oriented attitude toward sex by forbidding, from the beginning of therapy, any sexual activity not explicitly ordered by the therapists. Then they assign exercises, such as the sensate focus exercise, that reduce the demands on the patients. As the patients successfully complete these exercises, they are given assignments in which the sexual components are gradually increased. The couple continue to chalk up successes until eventually they are having intercourse and the dysfunction has disappeared.

One distinctive feature of the Masters and Johnson therapy format is that both members of the couple must participate in therapy. For example, a man cannot simply come to the therapists with a problem of erectile dysfunction and be treated. His wife must participate also. There are two reasons behind this requirement. First, many of the therapy techniques, such as the "homework" exercises, require the cooperation of the other partner as well as some training of the partner. For example, the "squeeze technique" is used in treating premature ejaculation, but it must be performed by the man's partner, and thus she must be trained to do it. The second reason for the requirement that both persons participate in therapy is that each is almost invariably affected by the other's dysfunction and thus needs therapy as well. For example, the wife of a man with erection problems is probably having some difficulties with orgasm herself and thus will benefit from therapy. The husband of a woman who has orgasmic dysfunction may be feeling that he is inadequate as a lover, and thus the therapy will help him also. As Masters and Johnson put it, "There is no such thing as an uninvolved partner in any marriage in which there is some form of sexual inadequacy" (1970, p. 2).

The requirement that both persons participate in the therapy raises one problematic issue, however. Should therapy be denied to the married person who has a sexual dysfunction but whose spouse absolutely refuses to participate? Or should a single person who has no steady relationship but who nonetheless has a sexual dysfunction also be denied therapy? One strategy that Masters and Johnson developed for dealing with such people was the use of a **surrogate**, or a third member of

Sensate focus exercise: A part of sex therapy developed by Masters and Johnson in which one partner caresses the other, the other communicates what is pleasurable, and there are no performance demands.

Surrogate (SIR-oh-get): An extra member of a sex theapy team who serves as a sexual partner for the client, allowing the client to do the prescribed exercises if no other partner is available.

the therapy team who served as a sexual partner for the patient during the two-week therapy program. The surrogates were a group of volunteers carefully chosen by Masters and Johnson. They were not prostitutes; rather, they were people who were sincerely concerned with helping those with sexual dysfunctions. In fact, one of the female surrogates was a physician. The use of surrogates proved to be effective, judged by the success rate for people in this type of therapy, which was the same as the success rate for married couples in therapy. The use of surrogates did attract considerable publicity, though, and it remains a controversial practice to the present day, as well as opening up a confused mass of legal difficulties, such as the possibility of being charged with prostitution. Nonetheless, the use of surrogates does seem to be a reasonable solution to the problem of treating certain people who otherwise would be denied sex therapy.

Other therapists are exploring other techniques—such as masturbation therapy, biofeedback, and hypnosis—for persons without partners.

Basic Therapy Techniques

Masters and Johnson (1970) use several basic techniques in therapy.

One is simple education. The couple is given thorough instruction in the anatomy and physiology of the male and female sexual organs. Some couples, for example, have no idea of what or where the clitoris is. There is also an opportunity to clear up some of the misunderstandings that either the man or the woman may have had since childhood. For example, a man with problems of erectile dysfunction may have learned as a child that men can have only a fixed number of orgasms in their lifetime. As he approaches middle age, he starts to worry about whether he may have used up almost all his orgasms, and this inhibits his sexual response. It is important for such men to learn that nature has imposed no such quota on them.

The *sensate focus* exercises are perhaps the most important of the Masters and Johnson therapy techniques. They are based on the notion that touching and being touched are important forms of sexual expression and that touching is also an important form of communication; for example, a touch can express affection, desire, understanding, or lack of caring. In the exercises, one member of the couple plays the "giving" role (touches the other), while the other person plays the "getting" role (is touched by the other). The giving partner is instructed to massage or fondle the other, while the getting partner is instructed to communicate to the giver what is most pleasurable. Thus the exercise fosters communication between the two. The couple then switch roles after a certain period of time. At the beginning, the giver is not to stroke the genitals or breasts but may touch any other area. As the couple progress through the exercises, they are instructed to begin touching the genitals and breasts. These exercises also encourage the persons to focus their attention or concentrate on the sensuous pleasures they are receiving. Many people's sexual response is dulled because they are distracted; for example, they are thinking about what to cook for dinner, or they are spectatoring on their own performance. To use Barlow's terminology, they are victims of cognitive interference. The sensate focus exercises train people to focus on their sexual experience, thereby increasing their pleasure.

Masters and Johnson combine these basic therapy techniques with specific treatments for specific dysfunctions. These specific treatments will be discussed later in the chapter.

The Success Rate

Masters and Johnson have collected data on the success and failure rates of their therapy. In *Human Sexual Inadequacy* they reported on the treatment of 790 individuals. Of these, 142 were still dysfunctional at the end of the 2-week therapy program. This yields a failure rate of 18 percent, or *a success rate of 82 percent.* While the failure rate ran around 18 percent for most dysfunctions, there were two exceptions: therapy for premature ejaculation had a very low failure rate (2.2. percent), and therapy for primary erectile dysfunction had a very high failure rate (40.6 percent). That is, premature ejaculation seems to be quite easy to cure, whereas primary erectile dysfunction is very difficult. In addition, research shows that there are significant increases in couples' communication skills by the end of the 2-week therapy program (Tullman et al., 1981). Masters and Johnson's success rate is impressive and is considerably higher than the success rate in many forms of traditional psychotherapy, although some have questioned their results, as we shall see later in this chapter.

Masters and Johnson also followed up 226 people 5 years after therapy. The former patients were interviewed about their current sexual functioning. After the 5 years, the failure rate had risen to only about 25.5 percent; that is, the therapy seems to have lasting effects, and few people seem to develop their old problems again afterward.

OTHER THERAPIES

Variations of the Masters and Johnson Method

One of the problems with the Masters and Johnson treatment program is that it is expensive. The 2-week treatment program costs $5000, although reduced fees or free care are available to people with low incomes. A number of therapists have developed variations on their program with the goal of making treatment available more cheaply to more people. Having two therapists essentially doubles the price of the therapy, and so some people use a single therapist, apparently with good results. Others have explored group therapy, in which 5 or 10 people, all with the same dysfunction, are treated together in a group (see, for example, Schneidman & McGuire, 1976; Zilbergeld, 1975). Therapy for a group with a mixture of dysfunctions has also been explored (Leiblum et al., 1976). The Masters and Johnson program is also expensive because it requires taking off 2 weeks from work, traveling to St. Louis, and staying in a motel for 2 weeks. Most therapists have therefore changed from the 2-week, rapid-treatment program to a format of one or two sessions per week for 10 to 15 weeks. Many major-medical health insurance programs now cover psychiatric treatment and therefore sex therapy, which makes cost somewhat less of a problem for many people.

Specific Treatments for Specific Problems

Squeeze Technique

Squeeze technique: A form of sex therapy for premature ejaculation in which the partner squeezes the man's penis, stopping his orgasm just when he felt he was about to orgasm.

A method that is used to treat premature ejaculators is the **squeeze technique.** The woman sits on the bed with her back against the backboard, propped by pillows. The man lies on his back, facing her, with his feet outside her thighs (Figure 19.3). The woman caresses his genitals until he gets an erection. When he has a full erection, she holds his penis between the thumb and first two fingers of her hand. The thumb is placed on the lower surface of the penis, just below the corona, and the two fingers are placed on the opposite side of the penis, one above the coronal ridge and the other below it. When he feels that ejaculation is about to happen, he tells her, and she then squeezes the penis fairly hard for 3 to 4 seconds. This causes the man to lose his urge to ejaculate. He may also lose some of his erection. After waiting 15 to 30 seconds, the woman again stimulates him to a full erection, squeezes, and so on. The couple may thus engage in 15 to 20 minutes of continuous sex play, and the man gradually gains some control over his orgasm. Lest this technique sound like cruel and unusual punishment, it should be noted that the squeeze, when done properly, does not hurt.

After the man has gained some control with this method, the couple assume the woman-on-top position (see Figure 19.4), and he inserts his penis into her vagina; however, no pelvic thrusting is permitted. If the man feels that he is about to ejaculate, the woman simply raises her body and uses the squeeze technique. After there is control in this situation, the man is instructed to begin some pelvic thrusting. As he gradually gains more control, they may proceed to the side-to-side position for intercourse and finally to the man-on-top position.

The squeeze technique is actually a variant on the *stop-start technique,* which was originally devised by James Semans (1956) and is used by Helen Singer Kaplan and others. The woman uses her hand to stimulate the man to erection. Then she stops the stimulation. Gradually he loses his erection. She then starts stimulation again, he gets another erection, she stops, and so on. Kaplan finds that this procedure is less uncomfortable than the squeeze technique and that couples respond better to it in the treatment of premature ejaculation.

Masturbation

The most effective form of therapy for women with orgasmic dysfunction is a program of directed masturbation (Andersen, 1983; LoPiccolo & Stock, 1986). The

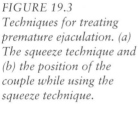

FIGURE 19.3
Techniques for treating
premature ejaculation. (a)
The squeeze technique and
(b) the position of the
couple while using the
squeeze technique.

FIGURE 19.4
*The woman-on-top
position is used in treating
sexual dysfunctions in both
women and men.*

data indicate that masturbation is the technique most likely to produce orgasm in women. Kinsey found that the average woman reaches orgasm 95 percent of the time when masturbating, as opposed to 73 percent of the time in intercourse. Masters and Johnson found that masturbation produces the most intense orgasm in women. Masturbation therefore seems to be a likely treatment for women with primary orgasmic dysfunction. Masturbation is sometimes recommended as therapy for men as well (Zilbergeld, 1978).

Kegel Exercises

Kegal (KAY-gul) exercises:
A part of sex therapy for women with orgasmic dysfunction, in which the woman exercises the muscles surrounding the vagina; also called pubococcygeal or PC muscle exercises.

One technique that is used with women is the Kegel exercises, named for the physician who devised them (Kegel, 1952). They are designed to exercise and strengthen the *pubococcygeal muscle,* or PC muscle, which runs along the sides of the entrance of the vagina (see Figure 4.9 in Chapter 4). The exercises are particularly helpful for women who have had this muscle stretched in childbirth and for those who simply have poor tone in the muscle. The woman is instructed first to find her PC muscle by sitting on a toilet with her legs spread apart, urinating, and stopping the flow of urine voluntarily. The muscle that stops the flow is the PC muscle. After that, the woman is told to contract the muscle 10 times during each of six sessions per day. Gradually she can work up to more.[3] The most important effect of these exercises

[3]   Students should recognize the exciting possibilities for doing these exercises. For example, they are a good way to amuse yourself in the middle of a boring lecture, and no one will ever know you are doing them.

FIGURE 19.5
A position used in treating
female sexual dysfunction.

is that they seem to increase women's sexual pleasure by increasing the sensitivity of the vaginal area (Messé & Geer, 1985). They also permit the woman to stimulate her partner more, and they are a cure women who have problems with involuntarily urinating as they orgasm. Kegel exercises are sometimes also used with men.

Marital Therapy

While the above approaches are essentially all forms of behavior therapy, based on a learning-theory model, another approach is marital therapy. Marital therapy rests on the assumption that sexual dysfunction is caused by a problem in the marital relationship, that is, that the dysfunction is a symptom of interpersonal conflict between the husband and wife. In marital therapy, the relationship between them is treated, with the goal of reducing the antagonisms and tensions in the marriage. The idea is that as the marital relationship improves, the sexual dysfunction should disappear.

Individual Psychotherapy

If one believes that sexual dysfunction is caused by intrapsychic conflict, the appropriate form of therapy is psychotherapy or psychoanalysis. The idea is that the sexual dysfunction is a symptom of poor adjustment or a disordered personality. The therapy would then treat the person's individual adjustment, with the goal of trying to resolve conflicts. Sexual functioning should improve as adjustment improves.

David Reuben, in his popular *Everything You Always Wanted to Know About Sex,* voiced this viewpoint when he said, "The only effective treatment for total orgasmic impairment is psychotherapy, because the condition is a psychiatric one. The sexual difficulty is simply a manifestation of a deeper emotional dysfunction" (1969, p. 129).

Kaplan: Psychosexual Therapy

Prominent sex therapist Helen Singer Kaplan (1974, 1979) advocates the combining of psychotherapy with the Masters and Johnson type of behavioral sex therapy into what she calls psychosexual therapy for the treatment of sexual dysfunctions (see also Hartman & Fithian, 1974). That is, she assigns specific sexual exercises, but she also believes that the symptoms may have deeper roots, and thus in psychotherapy she confronts the patient's resistances, unconscious conflicts, and so on.

Her analyses of the outcomes of sex therapy indicate that some dysfunctions, such as orgasmic dysfunction in women, are relatively easy to cure using the Masters and Johnson approach. Problems of sexual desire, however, fall at the opposite end of the spectrum and have a very low success rate with behavior therapy. Psychosexual therapy, combining behavioral exercises with a heavy focus on psychotherapy aimed at developing insights into unconscious conflicts, is necessary for such persons.

Psychosexual therapy: A form of sex therapy advocated by Helen Singer Kaplan, in which both behavior therapy exercises (like Masters and Johnson's) and psychotherapy are combined.

Cognitive Therapy

As we discussed in Chapter 2, cognitive theories are increasingly important in psychology. Paralleling this increased importance in theory, cognitive approaches in psychotherapy are also becoming important. Sometimes cognitive and behavioral treatments are combined (e.g., McCarthy, 1989).

Cognitive restructuring is an important technique in a cognitive approach to sex therapy (Wincze & Carey, 1991). In cognitive restructuring, the therapist essentially helps the client restructure his or her thought patterns, helping them to become more positive (for an example see Focus 19.3). In one form of cognitive restructuring, the therapist challenges the client's negative attitudes. These attitudes may be as general as a woman who has negative, distrusting attitudes toward all men, or as specific as a man's negative attitudes about masturbation. The client can then reshape these attitudes to be more positive.

Earlier in this chapter we noted that cognitive interference is one of the immediate causes of sexual dysfunction. That is exactly the kind of issue that a cognitive therapist likes to address. The general idea is to reduce the presence of interfering thoughts during sex. First the therapist must help the client identify the presence of such thoughts. The therapist then suggests techniques for reducing these thoughts, generally by replacing them with erotic thoughts—perhaps focusing attention on a

particular part of one's body and how it is responding with arousal, or perhaps having an erotic fantasy. Out go the bad thoughts, in come the good thoughts.

Surgical Therapy: The Inflatable Penis

Penile prosthesis (prahs-THEE-sis): A surgical treatment for erectile dysfunction, in which inflatable tubes are inserted into the penis.

For severe cases of erectile dysfunction, surgical therapy is possible. The surgery involves implanting a **prosthesis** into the penis (see Figure 19.7). A sac or bladder of water is implanted in the lower abdomen, connected to two inflatable tubes running the length of the corpus spongiosum, with a pump in the scrotum. Thus the man can literally pump up or inflate his penis so that he has a full erection.

The surgery takes approximately one and a half hours and requires only one incision, where the penis and scrotum meet. The total cost is about $10,000.

It should be emphasized that this is a radical treatment and that it should be reserved only for those cases that have not been cured by sex therapy. Typically it should be a case of primary erectile dysfunction that is due to organic factors such as diabetes. The patient must understand that the surgery itself destroys some portions of the penis, so that a natural erection will never again be possible. Research shows that about one-fourth of men who have had this treatment are dissatisfied afterward. Reasons for dissatisfaction include the penis being smaller when erect than it was presurgery, different sensations during arousal, and different sensations during ejaculation (Steege et al., 1986). There is concern that unnecessary implants are being performed when less drastic therapy could be used (Shaw, 1989). Although the treatment is radical and should be used conservatively, it is a godsend for some men who have been incapable of erection because of organic difficulties. Indeed,

A Case of Low Sexual Desire

Mr. and Mrs. Brown were in their early thirties, had middle-class backgrounds, and were college-educated; they had been married for four years when they entered therapy. The presenting complaint was this: Mr. Brown never initiated sexual contact and rarely appeared interested in sex. Sexual intercourse had occurred only once during the past seven months. He never experienced erectile dysfunction. He professed love for his wife and denied interest in any other women.

Mrs. Brown expressed a similarly positive picture of her marriage during her separate interview. She loved her husband very much, was interested in and enjoyed sex, had no interests in other men, and could not identify any problems in their relationship other than her husband's lack of sexual interest. She felt his lack of sexual interest was the likely result of his strict religious background. Whenever she tried

to act sexy, such as wearing erotic undergarments, Mr. Brown would laugh and discourage her. Currently, she said that she had just shut down and didn't bother thinking of sex any more. She was worried about this because she wanted to become pregnant.

The medical assessment by a urologist revealed no medical factors that could explain Mr. Brown's low desire. The interview with Mr. Brown revealed some factors that might be contributors to his lack of sexual initiative and low arousal. Although Mr. Brown's religious upbringing did not affect his overall interest in sex, it did seem to dichotomize in his mind sex with "good girls" versus "bad girls." He had had some very arousing sexual experiences with a number of women before marriage. In his words, if the women were very "slutty" and sexually demanding, he became highly aroused. On the other

more than a dozen children have been born as a result of this surgery, to women whose partners had previously been incapable of intercourse.

Which Therapy Is Best?

At the present time we have no definitive evidence on which of the three basic therapy approaches—behavior therapy (the Masters and Johnson program being an example), marital therapy, or individual psychotherapy—is the "right" one for treating sexual dysfunction. (For a critical review, see Sotile & Kilmann, 1977.) The success of the Masters and Johnson program argues for the assumptions and methods of behavior therapy. But probably there is no "right" method. Marital therapy or psychotherapy may be just what is needed by people who are not helped in the Masters and Johnson program. Indeed, many therapists who use behavior therapy refuse to treat people with severe adjustment problems or those whose marital relationships are severely disturbed; such people may be referred for marital therapy or psychotherapy. It may also be desirable to combine behavior therapy with marital

hand, if a woman was "proper" and deserving of respect, he found it very difficult to become aroused. His wife was very attractive but very wholesome; this wholesome image seemed to contribute to a restrained approach to sex on his part.

Other possible factors emerged. Mrs. Brown used to initiate sex, but during the past two years she had left the responsibility up to Mr. Brown. Furthermore, Mr. Brown never used sexual fantasies to enhance his arousal and did not expose himself to erotic materials. Finally, Mr. Brown said that he would approach his wife for sex only if he felt fully aroused. It did not occur to him that arousal would evolve as a by-product of sexual activity.

All of these possible etiological factors were discussed with Mr. and Mrs. Brown. The Browns were encouraged to try sensate focus, with Mr. Brown taking the initiative. He was reminded that he did *not* have to be sexually aroused to start. He had a great deal of trouble initiating any kind of physical activity; in fact, after failing to initiate during home practice, he disclosed in therapy that he had *never* initiated contact with any female. By not initiating, he never took the chance of being rejected. He also had difficulty in expressing his emotions and found it unmanly to do so. These issues were discussed at length, with a focus on his cognitions, and he was encouraged to continue with his initiation of the sensate focus sessions.

Mrs. Brown was encouraged to be expressive of her sexual feelings in dress and in action, whereas Mr. Brown was encouraged to work on accepting her sexuality. Cognitive restructuring with Mr. Brown focused on his longstanding beliefs regarding women and sexual expression, especially as these related to Mrs. Brown's sexual behavior.

Mr. Brown was also encouraged to practice bringing erotic thoughts into his life. He was given assignments to read erotic passages and to enjoy sexual material he viewed on TV rather than turning away from it.

Fifteen therapy sessions were held over 10 months, and the couple experienced a very positive change in their sexual relationship. Mr. Brown became much more emotionally expressive and felt comfortable initiating sexual contacts. At the end of therapy, the couple was participating in sexual intercourse approximately once a week, and both partners were satisfied with this rate. Both took equal responsibility for initiating sex.

Source: John P. Wincze, & Michael P. Carey (1991). *Sexual dysfunction: A guide for assessment and treatment.* New York: Guilford, pp. 174–175.

therapy or psychotherapy—what Kaplan calls psychosexual therapy—when this seems appropriate, a practice illustrated in Focus 19.2.

SEX THERAPY FOR LESBIANS AND GAY MEN

Masters and Johnson were among the first to write about the notion that gays might have problems with erection or orgasm. Thus they initiated a program of therapy for gays, using the same methods as were described earlier for heterosexuals. They reported the results in their 1979 book on homosexuality (see also McWhirter & Mattison, 1980).

They treated 57 homosexual men for erectile dysfunction. At the 5-year follow-up, four of them were categorized as failures, leading to a 7 percent failure rate or a 93 percent success rate. This is phenomenally high. Notice that it is higher than the success rate for heterosexuals. Masters and Johnson speculated that they obtained a higher success rate with homosexuals for two reasons: (1) They were treating two

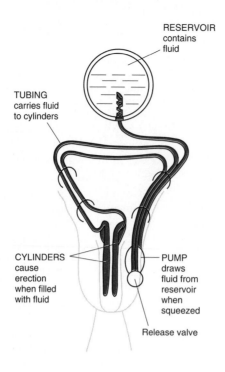

FIGURE 19.7
A surgically implanted prosthesis can be used in treating erectile dysfunction, although it should be regarded as a treatment of last resort.

RESERVOIR
contains
fluid

TUBING
carries fluid
to cylinders

CYLINDERS
cause
erection
when filled
with fluid

PUMP
draws
fluid from
reservoir
when
squeezed

Release valve

people who have the same body—this leads to intrinsic advantages in communication and knowing what techniques will be most effective; and (2) there is less performance pressure for erection in male homosexuals, since intercourse is not required. Nonetheless, they noted that the pattern of casual sex that was common with gay men does impose some serious performance pressures, and they cited instances in which the man's unwillingness to give up casual sex created a failure in therapy.

They also treated 27 lesbians for anorgasmia. At the 5-year follow-up, only 2 cases were classified as failures, once again for a 93 percent success rate. This, too, is higher than the success rate in treating heterosexual women. However, Masters and Johnson note that lesbians have no demand for orgasm from intercourse—which is generally hardest for heterosexual women—so that essentially lesbians have an easier criterion to meet.

Sex therapy with gays and lesbians is now a standard part of the repertoire of many sex therapists, and some therapists specialize particularly in treating gay or lesbian couples (Nichols, 1989; Coleman & Reece, 1988).

CRITIQUES OF SEX THERAPY

In 1980, two important critiques of sex therapy, and of Masters and Johnson's work in particular, were published. It is interesting to note that these did not appear until a full 10 years after the publication of *Human Sexual Inadequacy* in 1970. Why did a critical assessment take so long? Probably partly because everyone was so enthusiastic about the successes of Masters and Johnson, and partly because their previous work on the physiology of sexual response had established them as respected scientists.

Psychologists Bernie Zilbergeld and Michael Evans (1980) did an extensive critique of the research methods used by Masters and Johnson in evaluating the success of their sex therapy. Zilbergeld and Evans concluded that there are a number of substantial problems. In brief, the criticisms suggest that we really do not know what the success rate of Masters and Johnson's therapy is, and it is almost surely lower than 80 percent. A discussion of the specific criticisms follows.

First, Masters and Johnson never actually reported a *success* rate for the therapy. Instead, they reported a *failure* rate of about 20 percent. Thus, most people have concluded, as I did earlier in the chapter (and you probably thought it was logical as you read it), that this implies a success rate of about 80 percent. But Masters and Johnson say that this is not the case. That is, the 80 percent apparently includes a mixture of clear successes and cases that are ambiguous as to whether they are successes or failures—in short, they have 80 percent nonfailures, but that does not mean 80 percent successes.

Further, Masters and Johnson never defined what they meant by a "success" in therapy. This is an important point. How improved does a person have to be to be counted as a success? Suppose a woman seeks help for anorgasmia; she has never had an orgasm. By the end of therapy, she is able to have orgasms from a vibrator, but not from hand stimulation or mouth stimulation by her partner, nor by intercourse. Is that a success? How would Masters and Johnson have classified her? We cannot tell from their book.

Masters and Johnson did define what they meant by failure: "Initial failure is defined as indication that the two-week rapid treatment phase has failed to initiate reversal of the basic symptomatology of sexual dysfunction." (This will give you a flavor of Masters and Johnson's writing style and will help explain why people have often accepted their results without reading the original book.) The problem is that this, too, is vague—for example, how would we classify the anorgasmic woman described above?

Zilbergeld and Evans initiated their critical appraisal after finding that they and other sex therapists were unable to get success rates as dramatic as the ones Masters and Johnson reported. The obvious possibility is that other sex therapists have been using definitions of therapy success that are much stricter and more precise than the definition used by Masters and Johnson.

Masters and Johnson did not report clearly how the initial population of patients for therapy was chosen. They said that they rejected some people from therapy, but they not specify who made the decision, how the decision was made, and how many people were thus rejected. It seems quite possible that Masters and Johnson weeded out the most difficult cases, leaving themselves with the easier ones and a high success rate.

With their 5-year follow-up of patients, Masters and Johnson reported an amazingly low relapse rate of 7 percent, but other sex therapists find much higher relapse rates. Once again, Masters and Johnson did not specify their criterion for relapse clearly, and so it is hard to evaluate or replicate the 7 percent figure.

Masters and Johnson were also somewhat misleading about the duration of their therapy. They described it as two weeks of rapid treatment. Other therapists typically find that patients need more sessions than that. What Masters and Johnson failed to highlight is the fact that patients were instructed to call Masters and Johnson if they ran into problems; in addition, there were regularly scheduled telephone calls between the couple and the cotherapists. Essentially, a couple could get a great deal more than two weeks of therapy.

Finally, Masters and Johnson never discussed the possible harmful effects of their therapy. They made fleeting references to a couple of cases in which the therapy apparently ended in divorce, but they made no systematic attempt to assess problems of this sort. Their five-year follow-up was of "successes" only, not failures. It seems likely that the failures were precisely those who might have been harmed, yet there is no information on them.

In contrast to the scientific criticisms by Zilbergeld and Evans is the criticism by psychiatrist Thomas Szasz. In his book *Sex by Prescription* (1980) he criticizes the philosophical basis of sex therapy. Szasz has long been an outspoken critic of psychotherapy. He is particularly critical of the medical model in dealing with psychological problems (see, for example, his classic *The Myth of Mental Illness*). His essential argument is that psychologists and psychiatrists take people who have problems in living, or perhaps freely chosen lifestyles, and classify them as "sick" or "mentally ill" (the medical model) and in need of therapy. Although the professionals may think they are being helpful, they may do more harm than good. For example, once persons are classified as "sick," the implication is that they need a psychologist to fix them up; it might be better for them simply to make active efforts to solve their own problems.

Applying this thinking to the sex therapy field, Szasz argues that the sex therapists have essentially created a lot of illnesses by creating the (somewhat arbitrary) diagnostic categories of the sexual dysfunctions. For example, the man who cannot have intercourse because he cannot manage an erection is said to have "erectile dysfunction," yet the man who cannot bring himself to perform cunnilingus is not regarded as having any dysfunction. Why should the first problem be an "illness" and the second one not? A man who ejaculates rapidly is termed a "premature ejaculator" and considered in need of therapy, but what exactly is wrong with ejaculating rapidly? Szasz believes that instead of regarding the so-called sexual dysfunctions as diseases, it would be better to see them as individuals' solutions to various life situations.

Szasz criticizes Masters and Johnson for presenting their work as medical and scientific; he believes that it is moral and political and laden with values. For example, Masters and Johnson claim that homosexuality is not a disease but that nonetheless they can cure it in two weeks. Further, there is a confusion of science and ethics. For example, Masters and Johnson claim that their finding of the same physiology of sexual response in homosexuals as in heterosexuals should improve public opinion about homosexuals. But the physiology of homosexuals is in fact irrelevant to the question of whether homosexuality is ethical or sinful.

Szasz summarizes his arguments as follows:

> I do not deny that sexual problems exist or are real. . . . I maintain only that such problems—including sexual problems—are integral parts of people's lives. . . .
>
> As some of the examples cited in the book illustrate, one medical epoch's or person's sexual problem may be another epoch's or person's sexual remedy. Today, it is dogmatically asserted—by the medical profession and the official opinion-makers of our society—that it is healthy or normal for people to enjoy sex, that the lack of such enjoyment is the symptom of a sexual disorder, that such disorders can be relieved by appropriate medical (sex-therapeutic) interventions, and that they ought, whenever possible, to be so treated. This view, though it pretends to be scientific, is, in fact, moral or religious: it is an expression of the medical ideology we have substituted for traditional religious creeds. (1980, pp. 164–165)

Where do these criticisms leave us? In my opinion they do not completely invalidate the work of Masters and Johnson or other sex therapists. Rather, they urge us to be cautious. We probably cannot expect cure rates as high as Masters and Johnson reported; the 63 percent found by Kaplan (1979) may be more realistic. The relapse rate is probably higher than Masters and Johnson claimed. Their rapid, behavioral treatment probably works well with the "easy" dysfunctions; the harder dysfunctions will require longer and deeper therapy. Finally, we must be sensitive to the values expressed in labeling something or someone "dysfunctional."

SEX THERAPY IN THE AIDS ERA

The threat of AIDS—not to mention herpes and genital warts (HPV)—puts modern sex therapy into a new cultural context (Leiblum & Rosen, 1989). Here are a few examples of some of these new factors that are changing sex therapy.

People are now more interested in maintaining a long-term, monogamous relationship and less interested in giving up on a partner and finding a new one just because the sex has lost some excitement. Sex therapists are seeing more couples who want help in rejuvenating their sex lives.

Communication skills training (see Chapter 10), which is a standard part of sex therapy, has become increasingly important. Being able to communicate directly, openly, and effectively with a partner about condom use can literally be a matter of life or death. There will surely be increased demand for communication skills training.

If you go to a sex therapist, you have no partner, and the therapist feels you need work with a surrogate, you should definitely demand to see a recent HIV test result from the surrogate—and the surrogate should ask you for one, too.

Sex therapists will need to do more work with people on how to have pleasurable sex using condoms. Therapists have documented case histories of men who have such negative feelings about using a condom that they literally lose their erection if they try to put one on (Leiblum & Rosen, 1989). As condoms become an increasing necessity, this might even become a sexual dysfunction—condom-induced erectile dysfunction! Sex therapists can work with such people to diminish uncomfortable feelings and substitute comfortable—perhaps even erotic—feelings about condoms.

SOME PRACTICAL ADVICE

Avoiding Sexual Dysfunction

Since I was raised by a father who worked for the National Safety Council, I learned well their motto: "Prevention is better than cure." It seems to me that this principle could be applied not only to accidents but also to sexual dysfunction. That is, people could use some of the principles that emerge from sex therapists' work to avoid having sexual dysfunctions in the first place. The following are some principles of good sexual mental health.

1. *Communicate with your partner.* Don't expect him or her to be a mind reader concerning what is pleasurable to you. One way to do this is to make it a habit to talk to your partner while you are having sex; verbal communication then does not come as a shock. Some people, though, feel uncomfortable talking at such times; nonverbal communication, such as placing your hand on top of your partner's and moving it where you want it, works well too (see Chapter 10 for more detail).

2. *Don't be a spectator.* Don't feel as if you are putting on a sexual performance that you constantly need to evaluate. Concentrate as much as possible on the giving and receiving of sensual pleasures, not on how well you are doing.

3. *Don't set up goals of sexual performance.* If you have a goal, you can fail, and failure can produce dysfunctions. Don't set your heart on having simultaneous orgasms or, if you are a woman, on having five orgasms before your partner has one. Just relax and enjoy yourself.

4. *Be choosy about the situations in which you have sex.* Don't have sex when you are in a terrific hurry or are afraid you will be disturbed. This produces anxiety, and anxiety can produce dysfunction, as in the case of a man whose first sexual experiences were "quickies" in the back seats of cars and who became a premature ejaculator as a result. Also be choosy about who your partner is. Trusting your partner is essential to good sexual functioning; similarly, a partner who really cares for you will be understanding if things don't go well and will not laugh or be sarcastic.

5. *"Failures" will occur.* They do in any sexual relationship. What is important is how you deal with them. Don't let them ruin the relationship. Instead, try to think, "How can we make this turn out well anyhow?"

Choosing a Sex Therapist

Unfortunately, most states do not have licensing requirements for sex therapists (most states do have requirements for marriage counselors and psychologists). Particularly with the popularizing of Masters and Johnson's work, quite a few quacks have hung out shingles saying "Sex Therapist," and many states make no attempt to regulate this. Some of these "therapists" have no more qualifications than having had a few orgasms themselves.

How do you go about finding a good, qualified sex therapist? Your local medical association or psychological association can provide a list of psychiatrists or psychologists and may be able to tell you which have special training in sex therapy. There are also professional organizations of sex therapists. The American Association of Sex Educators, Counselors, and Therapists certifies sex therapists (see Appendix A for complete information on this organization and many other useful ones).

Summary

In men, the major kinds of sexual dysfunction are erectile dysfunction, early ejaculation, and inhibited orgasm; in women, the major dysfunctions are orgasmic dysfunction and vaginismus. Dyspareunia and sexual desire problems may occur in men or women.

Sexual dysfunction may be caused by a variety of organic (physical) factors such as some illnesses, infections, and damage to the spinal cord. Certain drugs may also create problems of sexual functioning. Other cases are caused by various psychological factors. Some of these are immediate causes—anxieties about failure, cognitive interference, and failure to communicate. Others may result from prior experiences such as an early traumatic sexual experience. Some theorists believe that relationship discord or intrapsychic conflict may cause dysfunctions.

Masters and Johnson's program is a kind of behavior therapy based on the assumption that sexual dysfunction is learned and can therefore be unlearned. One of their major goals in therapy was the elimination of goal-directed sexual performance. Some of the therapy techniques they used were education, sensate focus exercises, Kegel exercises, and the squeeze technique. Their overall success rate in therapy was about 80 percent.

Others have developed variations of the basic Masters and Johnson techniques, often in an effort to reduce the cost of therapy. Directed masturbation is particularly effective for preorgasmic women. Marital therapy and psychotherapy, which are based on different theoretical models, are two other approaches to treating sexual dysfunction. Cognitive therapy can be used, sometimes in conjunction with behavior therapy. Sex therapy for gays is being explored.

Criticisms of Masters and Johnson's work question their high reported success rate, focusing on their lack of definition of what actually constitutes a "success" or "failure" in therapy, their lack of specification of whom they accepted and whom they rejected for therapy, and their lack of consideration of the possible harmful effects of therapy. Szasz rejects the medical model of sexual dysfunction.

Review Questions

1. _____ is the proper term for the inability to have an erection or maintain one.

2. Orgasmic dysfunction or anorgasmia in women is the condition of being unable to have an orgasm. True or false?

3. According to sex therapists, the most common sexual dysfunction now is low sexual desire. True or false?

4. A large quantity of alcohol acts as a depressant and can thus cause sexual dysfunction. True or false?

5. _____ is the term for acting as an observer or judge of one's own sexual performance, thus contributing to sexual dysfunction.

6. The Masters and Johnson approach to sex therapy can be classified as psychoanalytic. True or false?

7. Sensate focus exercises are prescribed to reduce performance demands and encourage communication. True or false?

8. Masturbation is recommended for women with orgasmic dysfunction. True or false?

9. Cognitive restructuring is used in _____ therapy.

10. Masters and Johnson's research on the effectiveness of their program of sex therapy has been criticized on several grounds, including the fact that they never define what they mean by a "success" in therapy. True or false?

(The answers to all review questions are at the end of the book, beginning on page 731.)

Questions for Thought, Discussion, and Debate

1. When (if) you engage in sexual activity with a partner, do you feel that you are under pressure to perform and do you feel you engage in spectatoring? If so, what can you do to change the pattern?

2. Considering the prior learning causes of sexual dysfunction, what are the implications for parents who want to raise sexually healthy children? Could parents do certain things that would avoid or prevent sexual dysfunctions in their children?

Barbach, Lonnie G. (1975). *For yourself: The fulfillment of female sexuality.* Garden City, NY: Doubleday. Provides good information for women with orgasmic dysfunction, based on the author's program of group therapy for sexually dysfunctional women. Still the classic in the field.

Francoeur, Robert. (1983, July). Drugs that screw up sex. *Forum.* Reprinted in O. Pocs (Ed.). (1985). *Human sexuality 85/86.* Guilford, CT: Dushkin. pp. 52–54. A thought-provoking article on common prescription drugs that can create sexual dysfunctions.

Kilmann, Peter R., & Mills, Katherine H. (1983). *All about sex therapy.* New York: Plenum. These two recognized therapists have written this book to educate the general public about sex therapy. Helpful for those considering sex therapy.

20
Sexually Transmitted Diseases

Chapter Highlights

*Maria and Luis get home after an evening on the town and enter the house hungry for passion. The two embrace, clinging to each other, longing for each other. Luis slowly undresses Maria, hungry for the silky flesh he feels beneath him. As their passion grows, she begins reaching for him, ripping his clothes off as she explores his body with her tongue. As Luis gets more and more excited, Maria rips a condom package open with her teeth and slowly slides the condom over Luis's erect penis. After an hour of incredible lovemaking, Luis, exhausted with pleasure, turns to Maria and says, "You were right, the BEST sex is SAFE sex with LATEX!"** *

The sexual scene is not the same as it was 20 years ago. Herpes and AIDS pose real threats. We need to do many things to combat these dangers. One is that we must rewrite our sexual scripts, as the quotation above illustrates. We also need to inform ourselves, and the goal of this chapter is to provide you with the important information you need to make decisions about your sexual activity.

Your health is very important, and a good way to ruin it or cause yourself a lot of suffering is to have an untreated case of a sexually transmitted disease (STD). Consequently, it is very important to know the symptoms of the various kinds of STDs so that you can seek treatment if you develop any of them. Also, there are some ways to prevent STDs or at least reduce your chances of getting them, and these are certainly worth knowing about. Finally, after you have read some of the statistics on how many people contract STDs every year and on your chances of getting one, you may want to modify your sexual behavior somewhat. If you love, love wisely.

GONORRHEA

Gonorrhea (gon-uh-REE-uh): A sexually transmitted disease that usually causes symptoms of a puslike discharge and painful, burning urination in the male but is frequently asymptomatic in the female.

Historical records indicate that **gonorrhea** ("the clap," "the drip") is the oldest of the sexual diseases. Its symptoms are described in the Old Testament, Leviticus 15

---

* *Source:* From a student essay.

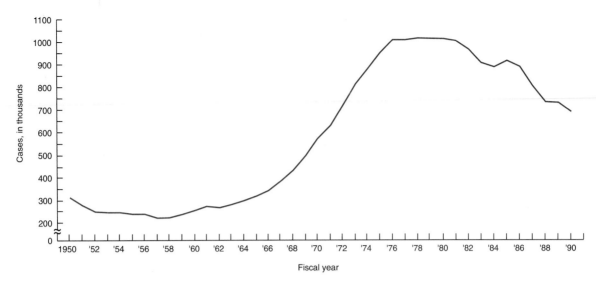

FIGURE 20.1
Reported cases of gonorrhea in the United States, 1950 to 1990. Note how sharply the number rose during the 1960s and 1970s, although rates fell in the 1980s.

(about 1500 B.C.E.[1]). The Greek physician Hippocrates (400 B.C.E.) believed that gonorrhea resulted from "excessive indulgence in the pleasures of Venus," the goddess of love (hence the name "venereal" disease). Albert Neisser identified the bacterium that causes it, the gonococcus *(Neisseria gonorrhoeae),* in 1879.

Gonorrhea has always been a particular problem in wartime, when it spreads rapidly among the soldiers and the prostitutes they patronize. In this century, a gonorrhea epidemic occurred during World War I, and gonorrhea was also a real problem during World War II. Then, with the discovery of penicillin and its use in treating gonorrhea, the disease became much less prevalent in the 1950s; indeed, public health officials thought that it would be virtually eliminated.

Then there was a resurgence of gonorrhea. By 1971 there were 620,000 *reported* cases of gonorrhea in the United States; however, since public health officials believe that only about 25 percent of the cases are reported, it is estimated that there were about 2.5 million cases (Millar, 1972).[2] The incidence peaked at slightly over a million cases in 1978 and then fell back to about 700,000 cases by 1990, still a very large number (Centers for Disease Control, 1991).

The resurgence of gonorrhea seems to be due to a number of factors. One factor was the shift in contraceptive practices from 1950 to 1970. The condom, which provides some protection against gonorrhea, was largely replaced by the pill and the IUD. Also, increased sexual permissiveness probably contributed. If everyone were completely monogamous, there would be no gonorrhea; it is spread only when

---

[1] Some argue that the traditional abbreviations B.C. (before Christ) and A.D. (anno Domini, or "in the year of our Lord") create too much of a Christian-centered bias in dates. They have suggested the substitution of B.C.E. (before the Common era) for B.C. and C.E. (Common era) for A.D., and I will follow that suggestion.

[2] These statistics are even more remarkable when one realizes that gonorrhea is not 100 percent contagious. For example, the chances of a man catching it from one act of intercourse with an infected woman is 25 percent, and the chances are 50 percent of a woman getting it from a single act of intercourse with an infected man (Hooper et al., 1978; Platt et al., 1983); that is, you do not always get it. Thus an even greater number of people were exposed to it, but some were lucky and did not contract it. (I debated for a long time over whether to mention these statistics. I fear it will create an "it can't happen to me" attitude. But don't count on it. And remember that the more times you have intercourse with an infected partner, the greater your chances of getting the disease.)

a person has intercourse (or other intimate sexual contact such as mouth-genital sex or anal intercourse) with an infected person and then does so with someone else.

Symptoms

Most cases of gonorrhea result from penis-in-vagina intercourse. In the male, the gonococcus invades the urethra, producing gonococcal urethritis (inflammation of the urethra). White blood cells rush to the area and attempt to destroy the bacteria, but the bacteria soon win the battle. In most cases, symptoms appear three to five days after infection, although they may appear as early as the first day or as late as two weeks after infection. Initially a thin, clear mucous discharge seeps out of the meatus (the opening at the tip of the penis). Within a day or so it becomes thick and creamy and may be white, yellowish, or yellow-green. This is often referred to as a "purulent" (puslike) discharge. The area around the meatus may become swollen. There is a painful burning sensation when urinating, and the urine may contain pus or blood. In some cases, the lymph glands of the groin become enlarged and tender.

Because the early symptoms of gonorrhea in the male are painful and obvious, most men seek treatment immediately and are cured. If the disease is not treated, however, the urethritis spreads up the urethra, causing inflammations in the prostate (prostatitis), seminal vesicles (seminal vesiculitis), urinary bladder (cystitis), and epididymis (epididymitis). Pain on urination becomes worse and is felt in the whole penis. Then these early symptoms may disappear as the disease spreads to the other organs. If the epididymitis is left untreated, it may spread to the testicles, and the resulting scar tissue may cause sterility.

Asymptomatic gonorrhea (gonorrhea with no symptoms) does occur in males, but its incidence is low (Handsfield et al., 1974). In some studies, though, as many as 50 percent of men with gonorrhea have been asymptomatic or have had only slight symptoms (Handsfield et al., 1974). This high rate is due to the fact that these men do not seek treatment and therefore continue to have gonorrhea and continue to appear in the statistics, unlike men who are treated and cured and drop out of the statistics. These asymptomatic carrier males are an important source of transmission of the disease to women.

About 60 to 80 percent of women infected with gonorrhea are asymptomatic during the early stages of the disease. Many women are unaware of their infection unless they are told by a male partner. Therefore, it is extremely important for any male who is infected to inform all his contacts.

The gonorrheal infection in the woman invades the cervix. Pus is discharged, but the amount may be so slight that it is not noticed. When present, it is yellow-green and irritating to the vulva, but it is generally not heavy (it is not to be confused with normal cervical mucus, which is clear or white and nonirritating, or with discharges resulting from the various kinds of vaginitis—discussed later in this chapter—which are irritating but white). Although the cervix is the primary site of infection, the inflammation may also spread to the urethra, causing burning pain on urination (not to be confused with cystitis).

If the infection is not treated, the Bartholin glands may become infected and, in rare cases, swell and produce pus. The infection may also be spread to the anus and rectum, either by a heavy cervical discharge or by the menstrual discharge.

Because so many women are asymptomatic in the early stages of gonorrhea, many receive no treatment, and thus there is a high risk of serious complications. In about 20 percent of women who go untreated, the gonococcus moves up into the uterus, often during the menstrual period. From there it infects the fallopian tubes, causing *salpingitis*[3] (Hook & Hansfield, 1990). The tissues become swollen and

Asymptomatic (ay-simp-toh-MAT-ik): Having no symptoms.

---

[3] "Salpinx" is another name for the fallopian tubes.

Pelvic inflammatory disease (PID): An infection and inflammation of pelvic organs, such as the fallopian tubes and the uterus, in the female.

inflamed, and thus the condition is also called pelvic inflammatory disease (PID—although PID can be caused by diseases other than gonorrhea). The major symptom is pelvic pain and, in some cases, irregular or painful menstruation. If the salpingitis is not treated, scar tissue may form, blocking the tubes and leaving the woman sterile. Indeed, untreated gonorrhea is one of the commonest causes of sterility in women. If the tubes are partially blocked, so that sperm can get up them but eggs cannot move down, ectopic pregnancy can result, since the fertilized egg is trapped in the tube.

In rare cases, in both males and females, the gonococcus may enter the bloodstream and travel to the joints, causing *gonococcal arthritis,* or it may travel to the heart valves.

There are three other major sites for nongenital gonorrhea infection: the mouth and throat, the anus and rectum, and the eyes. If fellatio is performed on an infected person, the gonococcus may invade the throat. (Cunnilingus is less likely to spread gonorrhea, and mouth-to-mouth kissing rarely does.) Such an infection is often asymptomatic; the typical symptom, if there is one, is a sore throat. Rectal gonorrhea is contracted through anal intercourse and thus affects both women in heterosexual relations and, more commonly, men in homosexual relations. Symptoms include some discharge from the rectum and itching, but many cases are asymptomatic. Gonorrhea may also invade the eyes. This occurs only rarely in adults, when they touch the genitals and then transfer the bacteria-containing pus to their eyes by touching them. This eye infection is much more common in newborn infants *(gonococcal ophthalmia neonatorum).* The infection is transferred from the mother's cervix to the infant's eyes during birth. For this reason, most states require that silver nitrate, or erythromycin or some other antibiotic, be put in every newborn's eyes to prevent any such infection. If left untreated, the eyes become swollen and painful within a few days, and there is a discharge of pus. Blindness was a common result in the preantibiotic era.

Diagnosis

In males, the physician can generally make a "clinical diagnosis" by inspecting the genitals and the discharge; absolute confirmation, however, must be based on a laboratory analysis of the discharge. A sample is obtained by inserting a swab about $\frac{1}{2}$ inch up the urethra (this causes some pain, but it is not severe).

The simplest laboratory test of the discharge is performed by wiping the coated swab across a microscope slide. The slide is then treated with Gram stain, and the gonococcus should show up, stained by the dye. Unfortunately, this test is somewhat inaccurate for men and highly inaccurate for women. The alternative is a somewhat more complex, time-consuming test, in which the bacteria are grown ("cultured") by wiping the swab onto a medium on a culture plate.

If gonorrhea in the throat is suspected, a swab should be taken and cultured using the same technique. People who suspect that they may have rectal gonorrhea should request that a swab be taken from the rectum, since most physicians will not automatically think to do this.

In females, the vulva is first inspected for inflammations. Then a speculum is inserted into the vagina, and a sample of the cervical discharge is obtained by inserting a cotton-tipped swab into the cervix, a procedure that may be uncomfortable but is usually painless. This discharge is then cultured as described above. A pelvic examination should also be performed. Pain during this exam may indicate salpingitis. Women who suspect throat or rectal infection should request that samples be taken from those sites as well.

At the present time there is no good blood test for gonorrhea available, as there is for syphilis. This is unfortunate, since a blood test would permit routine diagnosis, especially in asymptomatic cases and in pregnant women.

Treatment

The traditional treatment for gonorrhea has been a large dose of penicillin, or tetracycline for those who are allergic to penicillin. However, strains resistant to penicillin and to tetracycline have become so common that a new antibiotic, ceftriaxone, is now in use (Hook & Handsfield, 1990). It is highly effective, even against resistant strains.

CHLAMYDIA

Chlamydia (klah-MIH-dee-uh): An organism causing a sexually transmitted disease; the symptoms in males are a thin, clear discharge and mild pain on urination; females are frequently asymptomatic.

Nongonococcal urethritis (non-gon-oh-COK-ul yur-ith-RITE-is): An infection of the male's urethra usually caused by chlamydia; also called NGU.

Chlamydia trachomatis is an organism that is spread by sexual contact and infects the genital organs of both males and females. The female is said to have a chlamydia infection. Men with a chlamydia infection in the urethra are said to have chlamydia or nongonococcal urethritis, NGU (also known as *nonspecific urethritis* or *NSU*). NGU is any inflammation of the male's urethra that is not caused by a gonorrhea infection. (For reviews, see Stamm & Holmes, 1990; Felman & Nikitas, 1981.) *Chlamydia* is one organism known to cause it, but it may be caused by several other organisms.

Recent statistics indicate that chlamydia has become one of the major sexually transmitted diseases. The Centers for Disease Control estimated that there were approximately 2.6 million cases of chlamydia in women in 1986 and 1.8 million in men, compared with 1 million cases of gonorrhea in men (Cates & Wasserheit, 1991; Washington et al., 1987). Chlamydia is more prevalent in higher socioeconomic groups and among university students. When a man consults a physician because of a urethral discharge, his chances of having chlamydia are about as good as his chances of having gonorrhea. It is important that the correct diagnosis be made since chlamydia does not respond to some of the drugs used to cure gonorrhea.

Symptoms

The main symptoms are a thin, usually clear discharge and mild discomfort on urination. The symptoms are somewhat similar to the symptoms of gonorrhea in the male. However, gonorrhea tends to produce more painful urination and a more profuse, puslike discharge. Diagnosis is made from a scraping of cells from the genitals; a chemical test is then done which is both fast and accurate (Boffey, 1984).

Treatment

Chlamydia is treated with tetracycline or erythromycin since it does not respond to penicillin. Poorly treated or undiagnosed cases may lead to a number of complications: urethral damage, epididymitis (infection of the epididymis), Reiter's syndrome,[4] and proctitis in men who have had anal intercourse. Female partners of men with NGU are likely to harbor *Chlamydia* and may experience the following serious complications if not treated: damage to the cervix, salpingitis (infection of the fallopian tubes), pelvic inflammatory disease, and possibly infertility. Chlamydia infec-

---

[4] Reiter's syndrome involves the following symptoms: urethritis, eye inflammations, and arthritis.

FIGURE 20.2
The lesions remaining after herpes blisters burst.

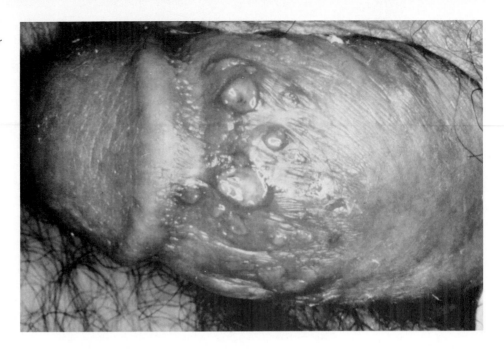

tion is associated with an increased risk of ectopic pregnancy and with increased rates of prematurity and low-birth-weight babies (Cohen et al., 1990; Chow et al., 1990; Sherman et al., 1990). A baby born to an infected mother may develop pneumonia or an eye infection. It is essential to treat female partners, both so that they do not suffer complications and so that they do not reinfect the man.

GENITAL HERPES

Genital herpes (HER-pees): A sexually transmitted disease, the symptoms of which are small, painful bumps or blisters on the genitals.

Genital herpes is a disease of the genital organs caused by the herpes simplex virus Type II in 85 percent of the cases, and otherwise by the Type I virus (Gunby, 1983). Herpes simplex Type I usually causes symptoms on nongenital parts of the body: cold sores and fever blisters, for instance. Genital herpes is transmitted by sexual intercourse, although there are people who have it whose only sexual partner does not. Herpes simplex Type I may be transmitted to the genitals during oral-genital sex (Gunby, 1983).

Symptoms

The symptoms are small, painful bumps or blisters on the genitals. In women, they are usually found on the vaginal lips; in men, they usually occur on the penis. They may be found around the anus if the person has had anal intercourse. The blisters burst and can be quite painful. Fever, painful urination, and headaches may occur. The blisters heal on their own in about three weeks in the first episode of infection. The virus continues to live in the body, however. It may remain dormant for the rest of the person's life. But the symptoms may recur unpredictably so that the person repeatedly undergoes 7- to 14-day periods of sores. On the average, herpes patients have four recurrences per year (Corey & Spear, 1986). The disease may also be transmitted from a pregnant woman to the fetus. Some infants recover, but others develop a brain infection that rapidly leads to death. (For an excellent review, see Corey & Spear, 1986.)

FIGURE 20.3
Herpes infection of the vulva.

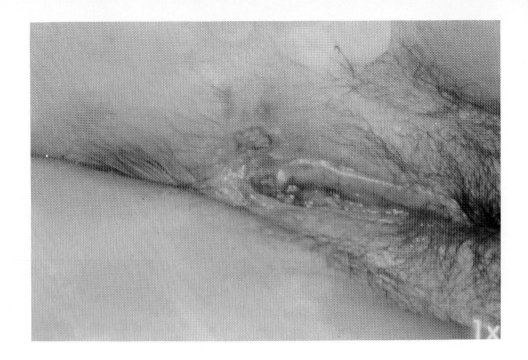

With an estimated 600,000 new cases of herpes per year (Gunby, 1983), it approaches gonorrhea and chlamydia in frequency. This does not count recurrent cases, which may number 5 million to 10 million. One study found that 16 percent of Americans between the ages of 15 and 74 are infected with herpes (13 percent of whites and 41 percent of blacks) (Johnson et al., 1989).

People with herpes are most infectious when they are having an active outbreak. However, there is new evidence that people may be somewhat infectious even when there is no outbreak. It is not entirely clear if there is a "safe" period.

Treatment

Unfortunately, there is not yet any known drug that kills the virus. In short, once you have genital herpes, you have it for the rest of your life. Researchers are pursuing two solutions: drugs that would cure symptoms in someone who is already infected, and vaccinations that would prevent herpes. The drug acyclovir prevents or reduces the recurring symptoms, although it does not actually "cure" the disease (Corey, 1990). When applied in ointment form early in a person's first episode of the disease, it speeds up the healing process and the disappearance of the symptoms. Acyclovir in capsule form seems to reduce pain and swelling in recurrent episodes (Gunby, 1983). Other drugs—and even the use of lasers—are also being investigated, as are vaccines.

Long-Term Consequences

The major long-term risk associated with the disease is cervical cancer. Women who have been exposed to herpes genitalis have an increased risk of getting cervical cancer and should have a Pap smear every six months. In addition, a pregnant woman with an active outbreak of herpes can transmit the infection to her infant during birth. For this reason, C-sections are typically performed on women in this situation.

Although the medical consequences of herpes are serious, the psychological consequences are no less serious (Luby & Klinge, 1985). The disease is, presently, incurable. The patient has to face recurrences that will occur unpredictably and uncontrollably and are especially likely to occur at times of excessive stress. Infected persons must face the idea that they can infect another person and, although people are most infectious when there is an active outbreak of blisters, it is not entirely clear when a person is infectious and when the "safe" periods are. Not surprisingly, a sample of herpes patients reported that the disease had the strongest effect on their lives in the area of sexual relations (Luby & Klinge, 1985); they reported that it interfered with their sexual freedom, frequency, and spontaneity. The respondents expressed worries about their ability to establish future intimate relationships, fearing a rejection when the potential partner discovered that they were infected. On the other hand, many people adjust very well to having herpes. Approximately one-third of the people in this sample reported that they had made a successful adjustment to herpes. The human capacity to cope with adversity never ceases to impress me!

Psychologists are exploring therapies for herpes patients. One highly effective treatment program consists of a combination of information on herpes, relaxation training, instruction in stress management, and instruction in an imagery technique in which the patient imagines that the genitals are free of lesions and that he or she is highly resistant to the virus (Longo et al., 1988). Patients given six sessions in this program (compared with an untreated control group and a group that participated in a social support group only) showed significantly less depression and anxiety and even had a significant reduction in the number of herpes outbreaks per year.

HIV INFECTION AND AIDS

In 1981, a physician in Los Angeles reported a mysterious and frightening new disease identified in several gay men. Within two years, the number of cases escalated sharply, the gay community had become both frightened and outraged, and Washington had funded a major public health effort aimed at understanding and eradicating the disease.

The disease was named AIDS, an abbreviation for acquired immune deficiency syndrome. As the name implies, the disease destroys the body's natural system of immunity to diseases. Once AIDS has damaged an individual's immune system, opportunistic disease may take over, and the person usually dies within a few months to a few years. The two most common of these diseases found in AIDS patients are one form of pneumonia (Pneumocystis carinii pneumonia or PCP) and a rare form of cancer that produces purplish lesions on the skin (Kaposi's sarcoma or KS). Both are killers.

A major breakthrough came in 1984 when Robert Gallo, of the National Institutes of Health (NIH), announced that he had identified the virus causing AIDS. A French team, headed by Luc Montagnier of the Pasteur Institute, simultaneously announced the same discovery. The virus was initially named HTLV-3 but is now called HIV for human immune deficiency virus. A new strain of the virus has now emerged, HIV-2, although it is found almost exclusively in Africa. HIV-1 accounts for almost all infections in North America.

An Epidemic?

As of March 1993, more than 289,000 persons in the United States had been diagnosed as having AIDS, and more than half of them had died from it. However, public health officials believe that these statistics represent only the tip of the iceberg, for they do not count persons who are just infected with the HIV virus, nor do they count persons who have mild symptoms of the disease but whose symptoms are not

Acquired immune deficiency syndrome (AIDS): A sexually transmitted disease that destroys the body's natural immunity to infection so that the person is susceptible to and may die from a disease such as pneumonia or cancer.

Pneumocystis carinii (noo-moh-SIST-is kay-RIN-ee-eye) pneumonia: A form of pneumonia that may cause death and to which AIDS victims are particularly susceptible.

Kaposi's sarcoma (KAP-oh-seez sar-COH-muh): A rare form of skin cancer to which AIDS victims are particularly susceptible.

HIV: Human immune deficiency virus, the virus that causes AIDS.

severe enough to be classified as AIDS. Experts estimate that 5 to 10 million persons worldwide are affected with the HIV virus, although the majority of them show no symptoms yet and are unaware that they are infected (Liskin & Blackburn, 1986). Thus the term "global epidemic" has been used with reason. The term "pandemic" (a widespread epidemic) has also been used to describe the situation.

On the other hand, there is a current of hysteria over AIDS in the United States that does not seem completely justified, given the nature of the disease. It is a disease that is spread only in certain ways, and we know what those ways are. I will detail them below. Most important, the disease is not spread by casual contact. You can't get it from someone sneezing on you, from shaking hands with someone, or from sitting next to an infected person on the bus. It simply isn't going to spread like the common cold. What we need to do is remain calm and focus our efforts on education and research.

Transmission

When people speak of AIDS being transmitted by exchange of body fluids, the body fluids they are referring to are semen and blood and possibly secretions of the cervix and vagina. AIDS is spread in four ways: (1) by sexual intercourse (either penis-in-vagina intercourse or anal intercourse[5]); (2) by contaminated blood (a risk for people who receive a blood transfusion if the blood has not been screened); (3) by contam-

---

[5]   There is also a chance that mouth-genital sex can spread AIDS, particularly if semen is swallowed.

inated hypodermic needles (a risk for those who abuse intravenous drugs); and (4) from an infected woman to her baby during pregnancy or childbirth.

Supporting these assertions, statistics for cases of AIDS in the United States as of March 1992 indicated that those affected were in the following groups: 58 percent were homosexual or bisexual men; 23 percent were heterosexuals who use intravenous (IV) drugs; 6 percent were homosexual or bisexual IV drug users; 6 percent were heterosexual partners of people with AIDS; and 3 percent were hemophiliacs and others receiving blood transfusions. Although approximately 90 percent of U.S. cases are men, in Africa 35 to 57 percent of cases are women, indicating that the disease can definitely be transmitted by heterosexual intercourse (Liskin & Blackburn, 1986).

How great is your risk of contracting AIDS? In essence, it depends on who you are and what your sexual practices are (leaving aside issues of drug abuse, which are beyond the scope of this book). Suppose you are a gay man. The San Francisco Men's Health Study provides relevant data (Winkelstein et al., 1987). The study sampled 1034 single men from neighborhoods in San Francisco where the AIDS epidemic is most serious. Among the homosexual or bisexual participants, 48.5 percent had positive blood tests, meaning they were infected with the virus. Among the heterosexual participants, none had positive blood tests. On the other hand, even among the gay men there was considerable variability. Among those gay men who had had no sexual partners in the previous 2 years, only 18 percent had positive blood tests; in contrast, for those gay men who had had more than 50 partners in the previous 2 years, 71 percent had positive blood tests. One simple lesson is, *the greater your number of sexual partners, the greater the risk of getting AIDS.*

The San Francisco Men's Health Study also makes it clear that *the sexual behavior most likely to spread AIDS is anal intercourse, and being the receiving partner puts one most at risk* (Winkelstein et al., 1987). For example, among those men who had been receiving partners, approximately 50 percent tested positive for HIV, compared with 27 percent for those who had been inserters only and 21 percent for those who had not engaged in anal intercourse.

Let's suppose, instead, that you are heterosexual. Table 20.1 shows some risk statistics for different situations in which you might have intercourse; these statistics were based on carefully collected data and were computed by expert scientists in the field. I believe that they are the best statistics we have to go on at the present time. Notice that *sexual behavior is riskier if it is with a person who is infected with the HIV virus (seropositive), if the person is in a high-risk group (gay, IV drug user, or hemophiliac), or if condoms are not used.* Thus the range of risk is wide. If you have heterosexual intercourse with a person chosen at random and you use a condom, your chance is only 1 in 50 million of becoming infected. At the other end of the spectrum, if you have heterosexual intercourse 500 times with an infected person and you don't use condoms, the chances are 2 in 3 that you will become infected.

The Disease

In 1986 the Centers for Disease Control established the following categorization for four broad classes of infection with the HIV virus:

1. Initial infection with the virus and development of antibodies to it. Usually people who have been infected show no immediate symptoms, but they do develop antibodies in the blood within two to eight weeks after infection.

2. Asymptomatic carrier state (the person is infected with the virus but shows no symptoms). The mean asymptomatic period in adults is seven to nine years (Hirsch, 1990). These asymptomatic carriers can nonetheless infect other persons, which is a dangerous situation.

3. Lymphadenopathy. This is a more severe condition in which infected persons develop symptoms, although they are not immediately life-threatening. Symptoms are swollen lymph nodes, night sweats, fever, diarrhea, weight loss, and fatigue.

4. AIDS. According to the 1986 standards of the U.S. Centers for Disease Control, the diagnosis of AIDS was applied when the person is affected by life-threatening opportunistic infections (infections that occur only in people with severely reduced immunity), such as pneumocystis carinii pneumonia or Kaposi's sarcoma. The diagnosis is also used when other opportunistic infections or cancers of the lymph tissue are present and the person shows a positive test for HIV antibodies. Neurological problems can occur in AIDS patients because the virus can infect the cells of the brain; symptoms may include seizures and mental problems. Other infections in this stage include herpes, candida in the mouth and throat, and human papillomavirus (HPV).

The Centers for Disease Control have developed a new definition of AIDS that is designed to be an improvement on the original definition, which required the patient to have an opportunistic infection such as Kaposi's sarcoma (KS) or pneumocystis carinii pneumonia (PCP). Some activists have argued that the original definition is particularly inadequate for infected women, who are unlikely to get Kaposi's sarcoma but are likely to develop cervical cancer, precancerous cervical disease, or pelvic inflammatory disease (PID) (Stephens, 1991).

The CDC's new definition depends on the person's T4 helper cell count (Stein-

Table 20.1
*The Risk of Becoming Infected with the AIDS Virus as a Result of
Heterosexual Intercourse*

Risk Category of Partner	Estimated Risk of Infection	
	1 Act of Intercourse	500 Acts of Intercourse
HIV Serostatus Unknown*		
Not in any high-risk group†		
Using condoms	1 in 50,000,000	1 in 110,000
Not using condoms	1 in 5,000,000	1 in 16,000
High-risk group†		
Using condoms	1 in 10,000	1 in 21
Not using condoms	1 in 1,000	1 in 3
HIV Seronegative		
No history of high-risk behavior†		
Using condoms	1 in 5,000,000,000	1 in 11,000,000
Not using condoms	1 in 500,000,000	1 in 1,600,000
Continuing high-risk behavior		
Using condoms	1 in 500,000	1 in 1,100
Not using condoms	1 in 50,000	1 in 160
HIV Seropositive		
Using condoms	1 in 5,000	1 in 11
Not using condoms	1 in 500	2 in 2

* Serostatus refers to the outcome of the blood test for AIDs. "Seropositive" means that the person
is infected. "Seronegative" means that the person is not infected.
† High-risk groups are gay men, IV drug users, and hemophiliacs. High-risk behaviors consist of
sexual intercourse or needle sharing with someone in a high-risk group.
Source: N. Hearst & S. B. Hulley (1988). Preventing the heterosexual spread of AIDS: Are we giving
our patients the best advice? *Journal of the American Medical Association,* **259,** 2428–2432.

berg, 1993). The normal count is approximately 1000 cells per cubic millimeter of
blood. The early stage of the disease would be defined as the time from infection so
long as the person keeps feeling well and the T4 cell count stays around 1000. In
the middle stage, the T4 cell count drops by half, to around 500, but the person still
may have no outward symptoms. The immune system is silently failing, however.
Treatment with AZT, DDI, and other drugs may begin at this time because the
treatments may be more effective if begun early. In the late stage, the T4 cell count
drops to 200 or less and, although the person may initially have no symptoms, he
or she becomes increasingly vulnerable to bacterial, viral, and fungal infections. Early
in this stage people may show weight loss, develop diarrhea, and experience fatigue
and fevers. Later the person may develop serious opportunistic infections including
KS, PCP, and toxoplasmosis, a parasitic infection that attacks the brain. According
to the new definition, a T4 cell count below 200 is by itself an indication of AIDS.
Other new indicators have been added for people who are HIV positive, including
cervical cancer.

The Virus

The HIV virus is one of a group of retroviruses. Retroviruses reproduce only in living cells of the host species, in this case humans. They invade a host cell, and each time the host cell divides, copies of the virus are produced along with more host cells, each containing the genetic code of the virus. Current research is aimed at finding drugs that will prevent the virus from infecting new cells.

HIV invades particularly a group of white blood cells (lymphocytes) called T-helper cells or T4 cells. These cells are critical to the body's immune response in fighting off infections. When HIV reproduces, it destroys the infected T-helper cell. Eventually the infected person's number of T4 cells is so reduced that infections cannot be fought off.

AIDS: Women, Children, and Racial Minorities

More than 90 percent of the cases of AIDS in the United States have been men, and so most attention has been focused on them. However, AIDS infects men and women in Africa nearly equally, and the number of infected women in the United States is rising rapidly, so there is an increasing need to address the needs of women with AIDS.

In a study of women with AIDS, more than half had been infected by intravenous drug use (Guinan & Hardy, 1987). However, the second largest group, and the fastest growing group, had contracted the disease through sexual intercourse with infected men. As noted earlier, women may show different symptoms of HIV infection and the disease may progress differently for them than it does for men.

AIDS also exists in children (Rogers, 1985). It is contracted in one of two ways. Babies born to infected mothers are often, although not always, infected. And children who receive transfusions with unscreened blood may become infected. In babies

FIGURE 20.5
The AIDS tragedy has highlighted the strength of caring in gay male couples, as a healthy partner nurtures a sick partner.

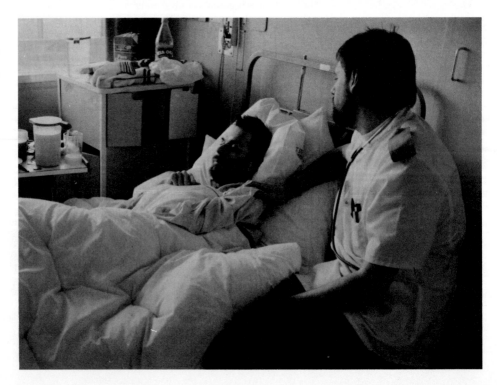

born to infected mothers, symptoms usually appear around four months after birth. Opportunistic infections develop, as they do in adults, and typically the baby dies.

There is also cause for concern about the spread of AIDS among people of color in the United States. As one writer put it, "HIV has become a scourge within Black and Latin communities" (Fullilove, 1988, p. 3). For example, in mass testing of Army recruits from 1985 to 1987, 0.07 percent of white recruits tested positive for the AIDS antibody, compared with 0.51 percent of black recruits and 0.22 percent of Latin recruits. Although blacks make up only 12 percent of the American population, they account for 27 percent of reported cases of AIDS (CDC, 1992). The pattern of spread of the disease among black Americans is somewhat different than it is for white Americans. Among blacks, fewer cases are accounted for by gay and bisexual men, and more are accounted for by intravenous drug use and heterosexual intercourse. Hispanics account for 16 percent of reported cases and are therefore also overrepresented; the incidence is low among Asian Americans (0.6 percent of the cases) and Native Americans (0.2 percent).

In short, AIDS is not just a disease of gay white men.

There is an urgent need to develop education and prevention programs for the black and Latin communities in the same way that these programs have been launched for the gay community. The programs need to focus on the elimination of needle sharing and unsafe sex practices.

AIDS: Psychological Considerations

Psychological issues for the AIDS patients are profound. Focus 20.1 is provided as a personal view of the psychological struggles of such a person. There are some analogies to people who receive a diagnosis of an incurable cancer, for AIDS is—at least at present—incurable. Many patients experience the typical reactions for such situations, including a denial of the reality, and then anger and/or depression. However, the analogy to cancer patients is not perfect, for AIDS is a socially stigmatized disease in a way that cancer is not. Thus the revelation that one has AIDS often involves an announcement that one is homosexual or drug-addicted. Also, as the patient becomes sicker, he or she probably cannot continue to hold a job, and financial burdens become an additional strain.

There is a great need to be sensitive to the psychological needs of AIDS patients. In most cities, support groups for AIDS patients and their families have formed. Social and psychological support from others is essential as people weather this crisis.

Interestingly, AIDS patients who adopt a fighting spirit survive, on the average, longer than those who do not (Mays & Cochran, 1987).

Progress in Diagnosis and Treatment

An important advance was the development, in March 1985, of a blood test that detects the presence of antibodies to HIV. The test is called ELISA (for enzyme-linked immunosorbent assay). It is easy and cheap to perform. It can be used in two important ways: (1) to screen donated blood; all donated blood in the United States is now screened with ELISA, so that infections because of transfusions should rarely occur, although some did occur before ELISA was developed and a tiny risk remains with ELISA[6] (Ward et al., 1988); and (2) to help people determine whether they are

[6] The risk that ELISA will miss occasional cases of infected blood results from the fact that it detects antibodies to HIV, not HIV itself. It takes six to eight weeks for antibodies to form. Thus if a person donates blood within a few weeks of becoming infected and before antibodies form, ELISA will not detect the infection.

An HIV-Positive Person Tells His Story

Scott Christensen is 25 and a graduate of the University of Wisconsin. He moved to Madison in 1990 from a small town in Minnesota. In Madison he found his first opportunity to be openly gay and began relationships with two lovers.

In the spring of 1990 he tested positive for HIV. The very next day he began to attend a support group organized by the Madison AIDS Support Network. He had had some early warning about the possible infection because he had been very ill for five weeks, including swollen lymph nodes and night sweats (an unusual occurrence at such an early stage of infection). During those five weeks he came to grips with the idea that he had the disease and that he was going to go on living rather than just giving up and dying.

One of his lovers from that time still tests negative for HIV. Scott believes that the other person is positive and knew at the time and did not tell him.

Scott quite openly acknowledges that he hates that man.

A physican monitors Scott's health status and prescribes drugs for him. Often Scott hears of a new drug just being tested even before the physician does because of the communication network among HIV-infected people. By January 1991 his T-cell count had dropped to 211, so he began treatment with AZT and continued it for nine months. He suffered no side effects from it. Then he was given Bactrim for pneumonia prevention. The two drugs interacted and lowered his red blood cell count so far that he had to be hospitalized for transfusions. He stopped all medications at that time. In January 1992, he started treatment with another antipneumonia drug, dapsone, which continues to work well for him. He has been invited to be part of a clinical trial of the newest antiretroviral drug, D4T. The study will test it against DDI, so he will receive one drug or the

asymptomatic carriers. The latter use is important because if people suspect that they are infected and find through the blood test that they are, they should either abstain from sexual activity or, at the very least, use a condom consistently, in order not to spread the disease to others. Only by responsible behavior of this kind can we get the epidemic under control.

ELISA is a very sensitive test; that is, it is highly accurate in detecting the antibody (it has a very low rate of false negatives, in statistical language). However, it does produce a substantial number of false positives—the test saying the HIV antibody is present when it really is not. Thus positive results on ELISA should always be confirmed by a second, more specific test.

The other major test, the Western blot or immunoblot, is used for this purpose. It is more expensive and difficult to perform, and so it is not practical for mass screening of blood, as ELISA is. However, it is highly accurate (false positives are rare), and thus it is very useful in confirming or disconfirming a positive test from ELISA.

It should be emphasized that both tests detect only the presence of HIV antibodies. They do not predict whether the person will develop symptoms or will progress to the AIDS classification.

other. He is deciding whether he wants to be part of that clinical trial. Currently he feels healthy.

One month after his diagnosis, he began a relationship that lasted two and a half years and ended only recently. The relationship was an enormous psychological boost to him, as he came to grips with being infected. His partner is HIV-negative. Scott let him know that he was infected even before their first date. They practiced safe sex, and there seem to have been no problems. He has just started a new relationship, again with an HIV-negative man. Again, the man knew about Scott's infection before they began the relationship. Scott says that he doesn't want a relationship with an HIV-positive person because he is very nurturant and would exhaust himself caring for an infected partner. He has never had a potential partner reject him because he is HIV-positive. Scott believes that everyone, gay and straight, male and female, should practice safe sex because the disease is so widespread.

Scott has worked for the Madison AIDS Support Network. He spends much of his time speaking to groups about being HIV-positive. He feels that it is important for him to talk openly with as many people as possible about HIV. He has also been working with a research program that has provided 70 HIV-positive people with access to networked computers in their homes so that they can easily communicate with each other. This allows them to share information rapidly and efficiently. A physician has been placed on the network to answer questions. One strength of this experimental program is that it allows these individuals to be in contact with others while remaining anonymous if they so wish.

When asked how he deals emotionally with his situation and with the future, Scott replied that he recognizes his own mortality, but that he still has many plans for the future. He does best when he concentrates on the present moment—How can I best utilize my time now? Sometimes he feels like he is waiting for the other shoe to drop. He thinks that he has come to grips with his anger and expresses it openly. He feels he needs to come to grips with his sadness, which he doesn't handle as well. So far this year he has attended the funerals of six of his friends. He has benefited a great deal from being in an art therapy program (his college major was art) run for HIV-positive people. He plans to go to graduate school to become an art therapist so he can give back to the HIV community some of what he has received.

Source: Based on an interview conducted by the author.

There is not yet any cure for AIDS. However, some progress is being made in developing treatments to control the disease. One antiviral drug, *AZT* (azidothymidine), has been used widely (Chaisson, 1986). It has the effect of stopping the virus from multiplying. However, even if the virus is stopped, there is still a need to repair the person's badly damaged immune system. Unfortunately, AZT is somewhat toxic and cannot be used by some patients, or can be used for only limited periods of time. Therefore there has been a concerted effort to find new drugs that will slow or stop the progression of the disease.

DDI (dideoxyinosine) is the promising new drug on the block (Hooper & Barnes, 1989). It was released for clinical trials in late 1989 after less testing than usual, owing to the urgency of finding additional drugs to treat HIV-infected persons. It was made available particularly to those patients who could no longer take AZT. One of the early DDI side effects to be reported is inflammation of the pancreas. Like AZT, DDI slows the progression of the disease by preventing replication of the HIV virus. DDC (dideoxycytidine) is another drug being developed in tandem with DDI; it, too, stops the AIDS virus from replicating. It will be very helpful for use with patients who develop problems taking AZT and DDI (Flaskerud & Ungvarski, 1992).

AZT: A drug used to treat HIV-infected persons.

DDI: A drug used to treat HIV-infected persons.

DDC: A drug used to treat HIV-infected persons.

Progress is also being made with drugs that will prevent the opportunistic infections that strike people with AIDS. The drug pentamidine, in aerosol form, is a standard treatment designed to prevent pneumocystis carinii pneumonia.

It would be wonderful to have a vaccine against AIDS. Researchers are energetically pursuing this goal, but experts agree that a vaccine will not be available until at least the late 1990s. The reason for the long development period is that there are actually many forms of the HIV virus and, further, the virus mutates rapidly (Marx, 1988). Therefore, as soon as a vaccine against one form of the virus is developed, a new mutant may appear against which the vaccine is ineffective. Monkeys are being used in the development of potential vaccines. Late in 1989 Murphey-Corb and her colleagues reported on results with a vaccine that protected eight of nine rhesus monkeys from infection with simian immunodeficiency virus (SIV), the monkey analog of HIV (Murphey-Corb et al., 1989; Agnew & Stein, 1990). Previously, so many efforts at a vaccine had tried and failed that researchers had become pessimistic, so this study was a real breakthrough. Over the next two years, several research groups demonstrated that several vaccine candidates worked against SIV in monkeys (Nowak, 1991). The next step is a big one, though: moving from laboratory tests with monkeys to large-scale clinical trials with humans in the real world. People are exposed to multiple strains of the virus, strains that may not have been in the vaccine, and 80 percent of human HIV infections result from sexual transmission (Nowak, 1991). That means that the person may be exposed repeatedly, over a long or short time, and that the virus enters not through injection into the bloodstream as in the laboratory tests but through the mucosal membranes of the genitals. Little is known scientifically about what occurs when the virus enters through mucosal tissue of the genitals. Another promising line of research that is being pursued involves boosting the immunity of the mucosal tissues of the genitals so that the virus is fought off before it gets too far into the body (e.g., Forrest, 1991).

SYPHILIS

Syphilis (SIFF-ih-lis): A sexually transmitted disease that causes a chancre to appear in the primary stage.

There has been considerable debate over the exact origins of syphilis. The disease, called "The Great Pox," was present in Europe during the 1400s and became a pandemic by 1500.

The organism causing syphilis was identified by the German scientists Shauddin and Hoffman in 1905. The bacterium they identified is called *Treponema pallidum* (*T. pallidum,* if you want to be on cozy terms with it). It is spiral-shaped and is thus often called a *spirochete* (see Figure 20.7). In 1906, Wassermann, Neisser, and Bruck described a test for diagnosing syphilis; this was known as the *Wassermann test* or *Wassermann reaction*. This test has been replaced by more modern blood tests, but the "Wassermann" label hangs on.

The incidence of syphilis is much less than that of gonorrhea and chlamydia. There were 50,000 reported cases in 1990 compared with 690,000 reported cases of gonorrhea (Centers for Disease Control, 1990). It is also true that syphilis rates rose sharply in the late 1980s and early 1990s. Although the disease is not nearly so common as gonorrhea, the effects of syphilis are much more serious than those of gonorrhea. In most cases, gonorrhea causes only discomfort and, sometimes, sterility; syphilis can kill.

Symptoms

Chancre (SHANK-er): A painless, ulcerlike lesion with a hard, raised edge that is a symptom of syphilis.

The major early symptom of syphilis is the chancre. It is a round, ulcerlike lesion with a hard, raised edge, resembling a crater (see Figure 20.8 on page 588). One of the distinctive things about it is that although it looks terrible, it is painless. The

Safer Sex in the AIDS Era

The AIDS virus is now widespread enough to mean that everyone needs to think about positive health practices to prevent, or at least reduce the chances of, infection. Technically, these practices are called "safer sex," there being no true safe sex except no sex. But at least health experts agree that the following practices will make sex safer:

FIGURE 20.6
Quality control of condoms.

1. If you choose to be sexually active (and abstinence is one alternative to consider), have sex only in a stable, faithful, monogamous relationship with an uninfected partner.

2. If you are sexually active with more than one partner, always use latex condoms. They have a good track record in preventing many sexually transmitted diseases. Laboratory tests indicate that condoms are effective protection against the AIDS virus (Conant et al., 1986). Condoms have a failure rate in preventing disease just as they do in preventing pregnancy, but they are still much better than nothing.

3. If there is any risk that you are infected or that your partner is, abstain from sex, always use condoms, or consider alternative forms of sexual expression such as hand-genital stimulation.

4. Spermicides (specifically, nonoxynol 9) kill the HIV virus (Peterman & Curran, 1986) and can be used with condoms to make sex even safer.

5. Do not have sexual intercourse with someone who has had many previous partners.

6. Do not engage in anal intercourse if there is even the slightest risk that your partner is infected.

7. Remember that both vaginal intercourse and anal intercourse transmit AIDS. Mouth-genital sex may, also, particularly if semen enters the mouth.

8. If you think that you may be infected, have a blood test to determine whether you are. If you find that you are infected, at the very least use a condom every time you engage in anal or vaginal intercourse or, preferably, abstain from these behaviors.

9. If you are a woman and you think that you might be infected, think carefully before getting pregnant, because of the risk of transmitting the disease to the baby during pregnancy and childbirth.

chancre appears about three to four weeks (as early as ten days or as late as three months) after intercourse with the infected person. The chancre appears at the point where the bacteria entered the body. Typically, the bacteria enter through the mucous membranes of the genitals as a result of intercourse with an infected person. Thus in men the chancre often appears on the glans or corona of the penis, or it may

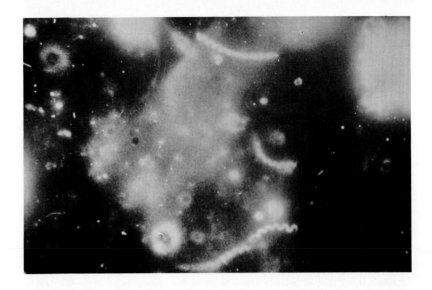

appear anywhere on the penis or scrotum. In women, the chancre often appears on the cervix, and thus the woman does not notice it and is unaware that she is infected (Nature's sexism again; this may be a good reason for a woman to do the pelvic self-exam with a speculum as described in Chapter 4). The chancre may also appear on the vaginal walls or, externally, on the vulva.

If oral sex or anal intercourse with an infected person occurs, the bacteria can also invade the mucous membranes of the mouth or rectum. Thus the chancre may appear on the lips, tongue, or tonsils or around the anus. Finally, the bacteria may enter through a cut in the skin anywhere on the body. Thus it is possible (though this happens rarely) to get syphilis by touching the chancre of an infected person. The chancre would then appear on the hand at the point where the bacteria entered through the break in the skin.

The progress of the disease once the person has been infected is generally divided into four stages: primary-stage syphilis, secondary-stage syphilis, latent syphilis, and late (tertiary) syphilis. The phase described above, in which the chancre forms, is primary-stage syphilis. If left untreated, the chancre goes away by itself within one to five weeks after it appears. This marks the end of the primary stage. The important thing to remember is that the disease has not gone away just because the chancre has healed. The disease has only gone underground.

By the time the chancre has appeared, the bacteria are well into the bloodstream and have circulated throughout the body. Beginning one to six months after the original appearance of the chancre, a generalized body rash develops, marking the beginning of secondary-stage syphilis. The rash is very variable in its appearance, the most distinctive feature being that it does not itch or hurt. It generally appears as raised bumps on various parts of the body. When the rash appears on the palms of the hands or the soles of the feet, it is a particularly distinctive symptom of syphilis. On white skin the bumps are first cherry- or ham-colored and then become coppery or brown. On black skin the bumps are grayish blue. In the moist areas the bumps may form large growths called *condylomata lata*. When these break, a thick fluid oozes out; this fluid is highly infectious because it contains many of the bacteria.

Hair loss may also occur during the secondary stage. Other symptoms of secondary syphilis are a sore throat; headaches; loss of appetite; nausea; constipation; pain in the bones, muscles, or joints; and a low, persistent fever. For this reason, syphilis is sometimes called "the great imitator," since its symptoms in the secondary and later stages look like those of so many other diseases.

Usually the symptoms are troublesome enough to cause the person to seek

Primary-stage syphilis: The first few weeks of a syphilis infection during which the chancre is present.

Secondary-stage syphilis: The second stage of syphilis, occurring several months after infection, during which the chancre has disappeared and a generalized body rash appears.

Cool Lines About Safer Sex

The journal *Medical Aspects of Human Sexuality* (March 1987) thoughtfully published some responses you can give to a partner who is resistant to safer sex practices. Here are some of their ideas.

If the partner says
I'm on the pill; you don't need a condom.

You can say
I'd like to use it anyway. We'll both be protected from infections we may not realize we have.

I'll lose my erection by the time I stop and put it on.

I'll help you put it on—that'll help you keep it up.

Condoms are unnatural, fake, a total turnoff.

What kinds of alternatives?

None of my other boyfriends uses a condom. A *real* man isn't afraid.

Just this once.

Please let's try to work this out—an infection isn't great either. So let's give the condom a try. Or maybe we can look for alternatives.

Maybe we'll just pet, or postpone sex for a while.

Please don't compare me to them. A real man cares about the woman he dates, himself, and their relationship.

Once is all it takes.

medical help. With appropriate treatment at this stage, the disease can still be cured, and there will be no permanent effects.

Even without treatment, the secondary-stage symptoms go away in two to six weeks, leading people to believe mistakenly that the disease has gone away. Instead, it has entered a more dangerous stage.

After the symptoms of the secondary stage have disappeared, the disease is in the latent stage; latent-stage syphilis may last for years. While there are no symptoms in this stage, *T. pallidum* is busily burrowing into the tissues of the body, especially the blood vessels, central nervous system (brain and spinal cord), and bones. After the first year or so of the latent stage, the disease is no longer infectious, except that a pregnant woman can still pass it on to the fetus.

About half of the people who enter the latent stage remain in it permanently, living out the rest of their lives without further complications. The remaining half, however, move into the dangerous *late (tertiary-stage) syphilis*. There are three major kinds of late syphilis. In *benign late syphilis,* the skin, muscles, digestive organs, liver, lungs, eyes, or endocrine glands may be affected. The characteristic effect is the formation of a *gumma*—a large, destructive ulcer—on the affected organ. With prompt treatment, the gumma can heal and the patient recovers completely. In *cardiovascular late syphilis* the heart and major blood vessels are attacked; this occurs 10 to 40 years after the initial infection. Cardiovascular syphilis can lead to death. In *neurosyphilis* the brain and spinal cord are attacked, leading to insanity and paralysis, which appear 10 to 20 years after infection. Neurosyphilis may be fatal.

Latent (LAY-tent)-stage syphilis: The third stage of syphilis, which may last for years, during which symptoms disappear although the person is still infected.

Late syphilis: The fourth and final stage of syphilis, during which the disease does damage to major organs of the body such as the lungs, heart, or brain; also called tertiary-stage syphilis.

If a pregnant woman has syphilis, the fetus may be infected when the bacteria cross the placental barrier, and the child gets **congenital** (from birth) **syphilis.** The infection may cause early death of the fetus (spontaneous abortion) or severe illness at or shortly after birth. It may also lead to late complications which show up only at 10 or 20 years of age. Women are most infectious to their baby when they have primary- or secondary-stage syphilis, but they may transmit the infection to the fetus in utero as long as 8 years after the mother's initial infection. If the disease is diagnosed and treated before the fourth month of pregnancy, the fetus will not develop the disease. For this reason, a syphilis test is done as a routine part of the blood analysis in a pregnancy test.

Diagnosis

Syphilis is somewhat difficult to diagnose from symptoms because, as noted above, its symptoms are like those of many other diseases.

The physical exam should include inspection not only of the genitals but also of the entire body surface. Women should have a pelvic exam so that the vagina and the cervix can be checked for chancres. If the patient has had anal intercourse, a rectal exam should also be performed.

If a chancre is present, some of its fluid is taken and placed on a slide for inspection under a dark-field microscope. If the person has syphilis, *T. pallidum* should be present with its characteristic shape (Figure 20.7).

The most common tests for syphilis are the blood tests, which can be used either for individual diagnosis or for mass screening (as with everyone who obtains a marriage license). The VDRL (named for the Venereal Disease Research Laboratory of the U.S. Public Health Service, where the test was developed) is one of these blood tests, all of which are based on antibody reactions. The VDRL is fairly accurate, cheap, and easy to perform. However, it has some limitations. It does not give accurate results until at least 4 to 6 weeks after the person has been infected. Even then, it correctly diagnoses only about 75 percent of the cases of primary syphilis; in the other 25 percent it gives a "false negative." It is completely accurate in detecting secondary syphilis. The VDRL may give a "false positive" in the case of people who have recently had diseases like measles or chicken pox and in the case of drug addicts.

FIGURE 20.8
The chancre characteristic of primary-stage syphilis (a) on the labia majora, and (b) on the penis.

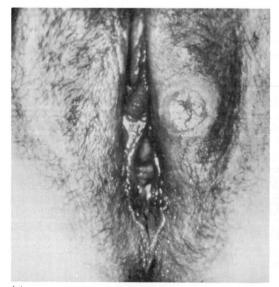

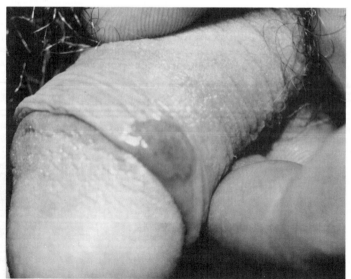

(a)

(b)

FIGURE 20.9
The skin rash characteristic
of secondary-stage syphilis.

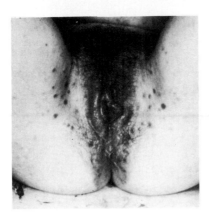

Treatment

The treatment of choice for syphilis is penicillin. *Treponema pallidum* is actually rather fragile, and so large doses are not necessary in treatment; however, the bacteria may survive for several days, and therefore a long-acting penicillin is used. The recommended dose is two shots of benzathine penicillin, of 1.2 million units each, one in each of the buttocks. Latent, late, and congenital syphilis require larger doses.

For those allergic to penicillin, doxycycline is the recommended treatment, but it should not be given to pregnant women. They can be given erythromycin.

Follow-up exams should be performed to make sure that the patient is completely cured.

PUBIC LICE

Pubic lice: Tiny lice that attach themselves to the base of pubic hairs and cause itching; also called crabs or pediculosis pubis.

Pubic lice ("crabs" or pediculosis pubis) are tiny lice that attach themselves to the base of pubic hairs and there feed on blood from their human host. They are about the size of a pinhead and, under magnification, resemble a crab (see Figure 20.10). They live for about 30 days, but they die within 24 hours if they are taken off a human host. They lay eggs frequently, the eggs hatching in 7 to 9 days. Crabs are transmitted by sexual contact, but they may also be picked up from sheets, towels, sleeping bags, or toilet seats. (Yes, Virginia, there are some things you can get from toilet seats.)

FIGURE 20.10
A public louse, enlarged.

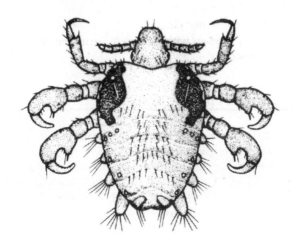

589

The major symptom of pubic lice is an itching in the region of the pubic hair, although some people do not experience the itching. Diagnosis is made by finding the lice or the eggs attached to the hairs.

Pubic lice are treated with the drug gamma benzene hexachloride, which is available by prescription only as a cream, lotion, or shampoo under the brand name Kwell (Kwellada in Canada). A-200 Pyrinate is also effective and is available without prescription. Both kill the lice. After treatment, the person should put on clean clothing. Since the lice die within 24 hours, it is not necessary to disinfect clothing that has not been used for over 24 hours. However, the eggs can live up to 6 days, and in difficult cases it may be necessary to boil or dry-clean one's clothing (Hatcher et al., 1980).

GENITAL WARTS

Genital warts: A sexually transmitted disease causing warts on the genitals.

HPV: Human papilloma virus, the organism that causes genital warts.

Genital warts are cauliflower-like warts appearing on the genitals, usually around the urethral opening of the penis, the shaft of the penis, or the scrotum in the male, and on the vulva, the walls of the vagina, or the cervix in the female (Figure 20.11); warts may also occur on the anus (Oriel, 1990). Typically they appear two to three months after intercourse with an infected person, although they may appear as late as nine months later. They are caused by the human papilloma virus (HPV), similar to the one that causes common skin warts.

Experts say that, if AIDS were not around, the big news story of the decade would be genital warts. New data show that there is widespread infection with HPV. Moreover, HPV, like herpes, increases the risk of cervical cancer in women, so the disease has potentially serious consequences. The disease is also highly infectious. About two-thirds of the sex partners of persons with genital warts develop the disease, with an average incubation period of two to three months (Oriel, 1990).

In one study, researchers randomly selected 454 women attending an STD clinic and 545 college women undergoing a routine annual examination (Kiviat et al., 1989). HPV infection was found in 11 percent of the STD clinic patients and 2 percent of the college women. There were cervical abnormalities in 40 to 50 percent of the women infected with HPV.

Another study capitalized on Finland's program of mass screening for cervical cancer (Syrjanen et al., 1990). For this research, 1289 22-year-old women were screened in 1985 and then again 1 year later. At the time of the first testing, 3 percent

FIGURE 20.11
Genital warts (a) on the penis, and (b) on the vulva.

(a)

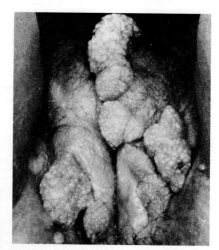

(b)

showed HPV infection. One year later the incidence had risen to 7 percent, a dramatic increase. The researchers estimated that half of the sexually active women in Finland would experience at least one HPV infection within the next 10 years.

These studies provide strong evidence of how widespread the disease is, and of its strong association with cervical cancer. Because of the increased risk of cervical cancer, any woman with recurrent genital warts should have a Pap smear every six months. Additional evidence indicates that HPV infection is associated not only with cancer of the cervix but also with cancer of the vagina, vulva, penis, and anus (Kiviat et al., 1989).

Diagnosis

Diagnosis can generally be made simply by inspecting the warts, because their appearance is distinctive (Figure 20.11). However, new strains of warts are sometimes flat and less obvious. Also, the warts may grow inside the vagina and may not be detected there. A new test involves analysis of the DNA from a sample of cells taken from the cervix and vagina and tests directly for the presence of the HPV virus.

Treatment

Several treatments for genital warts are available. Podophyllin resin or trichloroacetic acid (TCA) can be applied directly to the warts. Typically these treatments have to be repeated several times, and the warts then fall off. With cryotherapy (e.g., using liquid nitrogen), the warts are frozen off; again it is typically necessary to apply more than one treatment. Laser therapy can also be used to destroy the warts. Interferons are antiviral agents that are injected; they are advantageous in treating cases where the infection is very widespread. One expert recommends TCA for localized warts (Gall, 1991). Laser therapy is recommended for more extensive infections of the vulva or anus. Interferon alone or combined with laser therapy may be the best new approach (Gall, 1991).

VIRAL HEPATITIS

Viral hepatitis is a disease of the liver. One symptom is an enlarged liver that is somewhat tender. It can vary greatly in severity from asymptomatic cases to cases in which there is a high fever, fatigue, jaundice (yellowish skin), vomiting, and abdominal pain, much as one might experience with a serious case of the flu. There are three types of viral hepatitis: hepatitis A, hepatitis B, and non-A non-B hepatitis. The one that is of most interest in a discussion of sexually transmitted diseases is hepatitis B.

Hepatitis B (which used to be called serum hepatitis) can be transmitted through blood, saliva, semen, vaginal secretions, and other body fluids. The behaviors that spread it include needle sharing by intravenous drug users, anal intercourse, and oral-anal sex. The disease is found among male homosexuals and among heterosexuals. It has many similarities to AIDS, although hepatitis B is more contagious.

Hepatitis B is more common than most people think because it receives relatively little publicity compared with AIDS and herpes. There are approximately 200,000 new cases in the United States every year. People who have had the disease continue to have a positive blood test for it for the rest of their lives. Thus in samples of the general population, 40 to 60 percent of homosexual men test positive, compared with 4 to 18 percent of heterosexual men (Alter et al., 1986; Dietzman et al., 1977; Schreeder et al., 1982). Among heterosexual university students, those who had had more than three sexual partners in the past four months were likelier to test positive (14 percent) than were students with fewer partners (1.5 percent) (Alter et al., 1986). This raises the important point—which is relevant not only to hepatitis B, but also to all sexually transmitted diseases—that having many sexual partners increases your risk of contracting a disease, not only because you have a higher probability of being exposed but also because you are being exposed to a riskier group of partners—namely, people who engage in casual sex with many partners.

Treatment for hepatitis B is complex; there is no cure except rest, and treatments are aimed mainly at relieving the individual symptoms. The good news is that a vaccine against hepatitis B, which is safe and effective, is now available (Francis et al., 1982; Hadler et al., 1986). I urge people in high-risk groups (gay men, IV drug users, heterosexual men or women who have many different partners) to be vaccinated.

PREVENTING STDs

While most of the literature one reads concentrates on the rapid diagnosis and treatment of STDs, prevention would be much better than cure, and there are some ways in which one can avoid getting STDs, or at least reduce one's chances of getting them. The most obvious, of course, is limiting yourself to a monogamous relationship or abstaining from sexual activity. This would not be a strategy acceptable to some of you, but there are other techniques you might be willing to follow.

The condom, in addition to being a decent contraceptive, gives some protection against AIDS, gonorrhea, herpes, syphilis, and other STDs. With some concerns over birth control pills and the rise of the STD epidemic, the condom is again becoming popular. Contraceptive foams, creams, and jellies that contain nonoxynol-9 help to kill STD bacteria and viruses.

Some simple health precautions are also helpful. Successful prostitutes, who need to be careful about STDs, take such precautions. Washing the genitals before intercourse helps remove bacteria. This may not sound like a romantic prelude to lovemaking, but prostitutes make a sensuous game out of soaping the man's genitals. You can do this as part of taking a shower or bath with your partner. The other important technique is inspecting your partner's genitals. If you see a chancre, a wart, a herpes blister, or a discharge, put on your clothes and leave (do not fall for the "it's only a pimple" routine). This technique may sound a little crude or embarrassing, but it seems to me that if you are intimate enough with someone to make love with that person, you ought to be intimate enough to look at her or his genitals. Once again, if you are cool about it, you can make this an erotic part of foreplay.

Urinating both before and after intercourse helps to keep bacteria out of the urethra.

Finally, each person needs to recognize that it is his or her social responsibility to get early diagnosis and treatment. Probably the most important responsibility is that of informing prospective partners if one has an STD and of informing past partners if one discovers that one has it. For example, because so many women are asymptomatic for gonorrhea and chlamydia, it is particularly important for men to take the responsibility for informing their female partners if they find that they have the disease.

OTHER INFLAMMATIONS

Vaginitis (vaj-in-ITE-is): An irritation or inflammation of the vagina, usually causing a discharge.

Vaginitis (vaginal inflammation or irritation) is very common among women and is endemic in college populations. Three kinds of vaginitis, as well as cystitis (inflammation of the urinary bladder) and prostatitis, will be considered here. Strictly speaking, vaginitis is not always an STD because it is generally not transmitted by sexual contact; it is, however, a common inflammation of the sex organs.

Monilia

Monilia (Moh-NILL-ee-uh): A form of vaginitis causing a thick, white discharge; also called candida or yeast infection.

Monilia (also called *candida, yeast infection, fungus,* and *moniliasis*) is a form of vaginitis caused by the yeast fungus *Candida albicans. Candida* is normally present in the vagina, but if the delicate environmental balance there is disturbed (for example, if the pH is changed), the growth of *Candida* can get out of hand. Conditions that encourage the growth of *C. albicans* include long-term use of birth control pills, menstruation, diabetes or a prediabetic condition, pregnancy, and long-term doses of antibiotics such as tetracycline. It is not a sexually transmitted disease, although intercourse may aggravate it.

The major symptom is a thick, white, curdlike vaginal discharge, found on the vaginal lips and the walls of the vagina. The discharge can cause extreme itching, to the point where the woman is not interested in having intercourse. Because monilia can be very uncomfortable, physicians need to take their patients' complaints about it seriously.

Treatment is by the drug nystatin (Mycostatin or other drugs) in vaginal suppositories. The problem sometimes resists treatment, though. Women, especially those who have frequent bouts of monilia, may want to take some steps to prevent it (see Focus 20.4). A drug to treat yeast infections is now available in drugstores without prescription.

If a woman has monilia while she is pregnant, she can transmit it to her baby during birth. The baby gets the yeast in its digestive system, a condition known as *thrush.* Thrush can also result from oral-genital sex.

Trichomoniasis

Trichomoniasis (trick-oh-moh-NY-us-is): A form of vaginitis causing a frothy white or yellow discharge with an unpleasant odor.

Trichomoniasis ("trich") is caused by a single-celled organism, *Trichomonas vaginalis;* it has four strands protruding from it that whip back and forth, propelling it.

Trichomoniasis can be passed back and forth from the man to the woman, and so it is technically an STD (for this reason, it is important for the man as well as the woman to be treated), but it can also be transmitted by such objects as toilet seats and washcloths. As with gonorrhea, some women are asymptomatic.

The symptom is an abundant, frothy, white or yellow vaginal discharge which irritates the vulva and also has an unpleasant smell. There are usually no symptoms in the male.

It is extremely important that accurate diagnoses of the different forms of vaginitis be made, since the drugs used to treat them are different and since the long-term effects of untreated trichomoniasis can be bad (see below). A drop of the vaginal discharge should be put on a slide and examined under a microscope. If the infection is trichomoniasis, then *Trichomonas vaginalis* should clearly be present. Cultures can also be grown.

The treatment of choice is metronidazole (Flagyl) taken orally.

If left untreated for long periods of time, trichomoniasis may cause damage to the cells of the cervix, making them more susceptible to cancer.

Nonspecific Vaginitis

Nonspecific vaginitis: A form of vaginitis caused by an anaerobic bacterium.

Nonspecific vaginitis occurs when there is a vaginal infection, with accompanying discharge, but it is not a case of monilia or trichomoniasis. This diagnosis can be made only when microscopic examination of the discharge, as well as other labo-

Preventing Vaginitis

The following steps help to prevent vaginitis:

1. Wash the vulva carefully and dry it thoroughly.

2. Do *not* use feminine hygiene deodorant sprays. They are not necessary, and they can irritate the vagina.

3. Wear cotton underpants. Nylon and other synthetics retain moisture, and vaginitis-producing organisms thrive on moisture. Consider cutting out the center panel in the crotch of panty hose, even in those with cotton crotches, which still do not allow much air to curculate.

4. Avoid wearing pants that are too tight in the crotch; they increase moisture and may irritate the vulva. Loose-fitting clothes are best, since they permit air to circulate.

5. Keep down the amount of sugar and carbohydrates in your diet.

6. Wipe the anus from front to back so that bacteria from the anus do not get into the vagina. For the same reason, never go immediately from anal intercourse to vaginal intercourse. After anal intercourse, the penis must be washed before it is put into the vagina.

7. Douching with a mildly acidic solution (1 or 2 tablespoons of vinegar in a quart of water) can help to prevent vaginitis.

ratory tests, has eliminated all the other common causes of vaginitis (trichomoniasis, monilia, gonorrhea) as possibilities. A distinctive symptom is often the foul odor of the discharge. Treatment is by Flagyl taken orally (Hatcher et al., 1980).

Cystitis

Cystitis (sis-TY-tis): An infection of the urinary bladder in women, causing painful, burning urination.

Cystitis is an infection of the urinary bladder that occurs almost exclusively in women. In most cases it is caused by the bacterium *Escherichia coli*. The bacteria are normally present in the body (in the intestine), and in some cases, for unknown reasons, they get into the urethra and the bladder. Sometimes frequent, vigorous sexual intercourse will irritate the urethral opening, permitting the bacteria to get in. For this reason, it used to be called "honeymoon cystitis" since many women got it on their honeymoons. But with the demise of the virgin bride and the "wedding night," the name no longer seems appropriate.

The symptoms are a desire to urinate every few minutes, with a burning pain on urination. The urine may be hazy or even tinged with red; this is caused by pus and blood from the infected bladder. There may also be backache. Diagnosis can usually be made simply on the basis of these symptoms. A urine sample should be taken and analyzed, though, to confirm that *E. coli* is the culprit.

Treatment is usually with a sulfa drug (such as Gantrisin or ampicillin) taken orally. The drug may include a dye that helps relieve the burning sensation on urination; the dye turns the urine bright orange-red. If the cause is a bacterium other than *E. coli*, ampicillan is typically prescribed.

If cystitis is left untreated (which it seldom is, since the symptoms are so unpleasant), the bacteria may get up to the kidneys, causing a kidney infection, which is dangerous.

To prevent cystitis or prevent recurring bouts of it, drink lots of water and urinate frequently, especially just before and after intercourse. This will help flush any bacteria out of the bladder and urethra.

Prostatitis

Prostatitis (pros-tuh-TY-tis): An infection or inflammation of the prostate gland.

Prostatitis is an inflammation of the prostate gland. As with cystitis in women, the infection is usually caused by the bacterium *E. coli.* The symptoms are fever, chills, pain around the anus and rectum, and a need for frequent urination. It may produce sexual dysfunction, typically painful ejaculation. In some cases, prostatitis may be chronic (long-lasting) and may have no symptoms, or only lower-back pain. Antibiotics are used in treatment.

Summary

STDs are at epidemic levels in the United States.

Chlamydia and gonorrhea are the most common of the sexually transmitted diseases. The primary symptoms of gonorrhea in the male, appearing three to five days after infection, are a white or yellow discharge from the penis and a burning pain on urination. The majority of all women with gonorrhea are asymptomatic. Gonorrhea is caused by a bacterium, the gonococcus; it is treated quite successfully with an injection of an antibiotic. If left untreated, it may lead to sterility.

Chlamydia may be symptomatic or asymptomatic in women and men. In men, it produces nongonococcal urethritis. NGU has symptoms similar to those of gonorrhea, except that the pain on urination is mild. In women, chlamydia may cause cervicitis, PID, or urethritis.

Genital herpes is a virus infection that produces bouts of painful blisters on the genitals that may recur for the rest of the person's life. Currently there is no known cure, although the drug acyclovir minimizes the symptoms.

AIDS is an incurable disease that destroys the body's natural immune system and leaves the person vulnerable to certain kinds of infections and cancer that lead to death. It is found mostly among gay men, intravenous drug abusers, and heterosexual partners of infected persons. The drugs AZT and DDI are used to treat it. Education and safe sex practices are important in combating the disease.

Syphilis is caused by the bacterium *Treponema pallidum.* The first symptom is a chancre, which appears three to four weeks after infection, generally on the sexual organs. Treatment with penicillin is very successful. If left untreated, the disease progresses past the primary stage to the secondary stage, and then to the latent stage; however, it may reappear as late-stage syphilis, in which various body organs—including the heart, blood vessels, and nervous system—are attacked, leading to death.

Pubic lice are tiny lice that infect the pubic hair; they are spread through sexual contact.

Genital warts, caused by the HPV virus, are becoming nearly as common as chlamydia and gonorrhea. Like herpes, they increase the risk of cervical cancer. Hepatitis B is another STD; a vaccine against it is available.

Techniques for preventing STDs include thorough washing of both partners' genitals before intercourse, urination both before and after intercourse, inspecting the partner's genitals for symptoms like a chancre, a wart, or urethral discharge, and the use of a condom or contraceptive foam or cream.

Three types of vaginitis (vaginal inflammation), all of which lead to irritating vaginal discharges, are monilia, trichomoniasis, and nonspecific vaginitis. Cystitis is an infection of the urinary bladder in women, leading to frequent, burning urination.

Review Questions

1. HPV causes _____.
2. A puslike discharge from the penis and burning, painful urination are symptoms of _____.
3. Gonorrhea is frequently asymptomatic in women, but it is never asymptomatic in men. True or false?
4. If left untreated, chlamydia in women can cause sterility. True or false?
5. Small, painful bumps or blisters on the genitals are symptoms of _____.
6. Currently there is no known cure for genital herpes. True or false?
7. Small, cauliflowerlike growths on the genitals are symptoms of _____.
8. Pubic lice are tiny lice that attach themselves to the base of pubic hairs and may cause cancer if left untreated. True or false?
9. AIDS is found exclusively among male homosexuals. True or false?
10. Oral-anal sex can spread hepatitis B. True or false?

(The answers to all review questions are at the end of the book, beginning on page 731.)

Questions for Thought, Discussion, and Debate

1. Contact the student health service on your campus and see whether they are willing to share with you the number of cases of chlamydia, gonorrhea, genital warts, and herpes they diagnose per year; then share the information with your class.
2. Design a program to reduce the number of cases of sexually transmitted disease on your campus.

Suggestions for Further Reading

Breitman, Patti, Knutson, Kim, & Reed, Paul. (1987). *How to persuade your lover to use a condom . . . And why you should.* Rocklin, CA: Prima Publishing. This book provides a rationale for the use of condoms, both for the prevention of STDs and for birth control. It also provides a thorough discussion of how to communicate with a partner about this issue.

Fettner, Ann G., & Check, William A. (1985). *The truth about AIDS.* New York: Holt, Rinehart, & Winston. There are already many books out on AIDS, and new ones appear almost weekly, so it is risky to choose a "best" one. This one is at least excellent, providing a history of the disease and an explanation of the immune system for the layperson. It also provides a useful list of agencies for AIDS patients and their loved ones.

Jones, James H. (1981). *Bad blood: The Tuskegee syphilis experiment.* New York: Free Press. The shocking story of the study in which black people in Alabama were left untreated for syphilis to determine how the disease would run its course.

Langston, Deborah. (1983). *Living with herpes.* New York: Doubleday. This is one of the best of the many books on herpes, covering everything from medical to emotional issues.

21

Ethics, Religion, and Sexuality

C h a p t e r   H i g h l i g h t s

I. Sexuality In Great Ethical Traditions
Classical Greek Philosophy
Judaism
Christianity
Humanism
Sexuality in Other Religions

II. Contemporary Issues In Sexual Ethics
Sex Outside Marriage
Contraception
Abortion
Homosexuality
AIDS

III. Technology and Sexual Ethics

IV. Toward An Ethics Of Human Sexuality

Sex is intended to be a langage of love.*

A high school student is in love with her boyfriend and wonders whether they ought to begin sleeping together. A corporation executive hears rumors that one of his employees is a homosexual, and he tries to decide what to do about it. A minister is asked to counsel a husband and wife, one of whom is involved in an affair. A presidential candidate is confronted by a right-to-life group demanding support for a constitutional amendment to ban abortion. All these people are facing the need to make decisions that involve sexuality, and they find that issues of values make the decisions difficult. The two principal conceptual frameworks for dealing with questions of value are religion and ethics, which are therefore the topics of this chapter.

Ethics: A system of moral principals, a way of determining right and wrong.

There are two concerns that give force to our consideration of the religious and ethical aspects of human sexuality. First, there is the scientific concern to explain sexual phenomena. Since religion and ethics are important influences on people's behaviors, especially in matters of sex, one cannot fully appreciate why people do what they do without looking at these influences. Second, there is also a personal side to this coin. We are all ethical decision makers; we all have a personal system of values. Each of us must make decisions with respect to our own sexuality. Therefore, we would do well to consider how such decisions are made.

An ethical system is a priority of values, a way of deciding what is most important to us, particularly when there is a conflict between things we value or desire highly. Sexual gratification may be an important value for one person and something to be avoided for another. However, regardless of the importance we attach to sex, we need a way of integrating our sexuality into our patterns of decision making. To do this we use such categories as "right or wrong," "good or bad," "appropriate or inappropriate," and "moral or immoral." These are the kinds of

* *Source:* James B. Nelson. (1978). *Embodiment: An approach to sexuality and Christian theology.* Minneapolis: Augsburg.
Major contributions to this chapter were made by Clark Hyde, M. Div., S.T.M., an Episcopal priest.

Hedonism: A moral system based on maximizing pleasure and avoiding pain.

Asceticism: An approach to life emphasizing discipline and impulse control.

Legalism: Ethics based on the assumption that there are rules for human conduct and that morality consists of knowing the rules and learning to apply them.

Situationism: Ethics based on the assumption that there are no absolute rules, or at least very few, and that each situation must be judged individually.

distinctions made in the field of ethics; since we use them every day, we are all practical ethicists.

Religion enters the picture as a source of values, attitudes, and ethics. For believers, religion sets forth an ethical code and provides sanctions (rewards and punishments) that motivate them to obey the rules. When a particular religion is practiced by many people in a society, it helps create culture, which then influences even those who do not accept the religion. Therefore, it is important to study the relationship of religion to sexuality for two reasons. First, it is a powerful influence on the sexual attitudes of many individuals. And second, as a creator of culture, it often forms a whole society's orientation toward human sexuality.

Let us begin by defining some terms that will be useful in discussing ethics, religion, and sexuality. Hedonism and asceticism have to do with one's approach to the physical and material aspects of life in general and to sexuality in particular. The word "hedonism" comes from the Greek word meaning "pleasure" and may be used to refer to the belief that the ultimate goal of human life is the pursuit of pleasure, the avoidance of pain, and the fulfillment of physical needs and desires: "Eat, drink, and be merry, for tomorrow we die." Asceticism, in contrast, holds that there is more to life than its material aspects, which must be transcended to achieve true humanity. Ascetics are likely to view sexuality as neutral at best and evil at worst; they prize self-discipline, the avoidance of physical gratification, and the cultivation of spiritual values. Orders of monks and nuns, found in Eastern religions as well as in Christianity, are good examples of institutionalized asceticism, with their affirmation of celibacy, virginity, poverty, and so on.

Two other terms, legalism and situationism, refer to methods of ethical decision making. As an approach to ethics, legalism is concerned with following a moral law, or set of principles, which comes from a source outside the individual, such as nature or religion. Legalistic ethics are focused on the rightness or wrongness of specific acts and set forth a series of rules—"Do this" and "Don't do that"—that persons are to follow. The term "situationism" has been used since it was coined by Joseph Fletcher in his 1966 book *Situation Ethics.* Also called contextual ethics, this approach suggests that although there may be broad general guidelines for ethical behavior, each ethical decision should be made according to the individuals and situations involved. Situationism is based in human experience and, in matters of sexual morality, tends to focus on relationships rather than rules. Whereas legalism deals in universal laws, situationism decides matters on a case-by-case basis, informed by certain guiding principles, such as love. Traditional religious ethical systems (which we might call the Old Morality) have tended to be quite legalistic, and many continue to be today (e.g., Orthodox Judaism, Roman Catholicism, and Evangelical Protestantism). However, with the advent of the modern empirical scientific world view, the situationist approach (the New Morality) has attracted many adherents (Nelson, 1987).

Of course, few ethical systems are purely hedonistic or ascetic or entirely legalistic or situationist; most lie between these extremes. However, the terms are useful in pointing to tendencies and will be used for that purpose in this chapter. The concluding section will try to put them into perspective and offer a critique of their strengths and weaknesses as approaches to sexual ethics.

SEXUALITY IN GREAT ETHICAL TRADITIONS

With these ways of looking at ethics, especially sexual ethics, as background, let us examine certain great ethical traditions to see how they deal with norms for sexual behavior. Although some attention will be given to non-Western sexual ethics, the thrust of this section will be on ethical traditions of Western culture, primarily because this is a text for American undergraduates, who are part of that culture. We are understandably interested in *our* story, in the world of ideals and practice in which *we* live. That culture can, at the risk of oversimplification, be seen as originating in the confrontation of Greek culture, preserved and developed by the Romans, and Jewish tradition, extended by Christianity. From that point on until rather recently, Western culture was Christian, at least officially. Even self-conscious revolts against Christian culture in the West are part of that tradition because of their roots.

Classical Greek Philosophy

During the Golden Age of Greek culture, covering roughly the fifth and fourth centuries B.C.E., philosophers such as Socrates, Plato, and Aristotle pondered most of the great ethical questions that have continued to interest Western intellectuals. These Athenians regarded the beautiful and good as the chief goal of life, and they admired the figure of the warrior-intellectual, who embodied the virtues of wisdom, courage, temperance, justice, and piety.

While nothing in Greek culture rejected sex as evil—the gods and goddesses of Greek mythology are often pictured enjoying it—the great philosophers did develop a kind of asceticism that assumed an important place in Western thought. They thought that virtue resulted from wisdom, and they believed that people would do right if they could, failing to live morally only through ignorance. To achieve wisdom and cultivate virtue, violent passions must be avoided, and these might well include sex. Plato believed that love (*eros*) led toward immortality and was therefore a good thing. However, since this kind of love was rather intellectual and more like friendship than vigorous sexuality, the term "platonic love" has come to mean sexless affection. There was also, among the warrior class, a certain approval of pederasty, that is, a sexual relationship between an older man and a younger one. However, the practice was far from universal and was frequently ridiculed (Brinton, 1959).

Pederasty: Sex between an older man and a younger man, or a boy; sometimes called "boy love."

FIGURE 21.1
The ancient Greeks not only approved of, but idealized, pederasty.

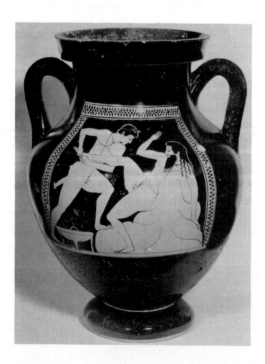

Later, Greek philosophy became even more ascetic than in the Golden Age. Epicurus (341–270 B.C.E.) taught that the goal of life was *ataraxia,* a tranquil state between pleasure and pain in which the mind is unaffected by emotion. The Stoics of the same period valued detachment from worldly anxieties and pleasures and, indeed, a total indifference to either life or death. Sex was seen not necessarily as evil but as less important than wisdom and virtue, something to be transcended to achieve the beautiful and good.

Judaism

The basic source of the Judeo-Christian tradition, which is the religious foundation of Western culture, is the Hebrew scriptures or the Old Testament of the Bible, which is the basis for Judaism and a major source for Christianity as well. Written between approximately 800 and 200 B.C.E. the Old Testament has a great deal to say about the place of sexuality in human life and society. However, sexuality and all aspects of life are always seen in religious terms.

To begin, the Old Testament view of sexuality is fundamentally positive. In the Genesis myth of creation we read, "So God created man in his own image, in the image of God he created him; male and female he created them" (Genesis 1:27). Human sexual differentiation is not an afterthought or an aberration; it is part and parcel of creation, which God calls "good." Judaism sees sexuality as a gift to be used responsibly and in obedience to God's will, never as something evil in itself. Looking at the Old Testament as a whole, we can find three themes in this view of sexuality.

First, sex is seen not as just another biological function but as a deep and intimate part of a *relationship* between two people. The very ancient story of Adam and Eve states that "a man leaves his father and cleaves to his wife and the two become one flesh" (Genesis 2:24). Frequently, biblical Hebrew uses the verb "to know" to mean sexual intercourse (as in "Adam knew Eve and she conceived a child"). It also uses the word "knowledge," with this suggestion of deep intimacy, to describe the relationship between God and his people.[1] The use of sexual imagery in describing both marital and divine-human relationship testifies to the positive view of the Old Testament toward sex.

Second, in the Old Testament, sexuality could never be separated from its *social consequences.* Historically, Israel began as a small group of nomadic tribes fighting to stay alive in the near-desert of the Arabian peninsula. Sheer survival demanded that there be enough children, especially males, so that there would be enough herdsmen and warriors.[2] Thus, nonprocreative sex could not be allowed. Further, since the tribes were small and close-knit, sex had to be regulated to prevent jealousy over sexual partners, which could have divided and destroyed the group. It is not surprising, then, that so much of the Old Testament is concerned with laws regarding people living together in society and that these laws often include the regulation of sexual practices.

Finally, the Old Testament sees sexual behavior as an aspect of *national and religious loyalty.* When the Israelites settled in what is now the state of Israel, about 1200 to 1000 B.C.E., they came into contact with the original inhabitants, whom they called Canaanites. Like many agricultural peoples of the time, the Canaanites sought

---

[1] See, for example, Hosea, The Song of Solomon, and, in the New Testament, Revelation.

[2] Note that the heart of God's promise to the patriarch Abraham was descendants as numberless as the grains of sand or the stars in the sky (Genesis 13:14–17, among many other places).

to encourage the growth of their crops through their religion. In this fertility cult Baal, the Sky Father, was encouraged to mate with Asherah (Astarte or Ishtar), the Earth Mother, so that crops would grow. This mating was encouraged by ritual sex, and temple prostitutes (male and female) were very much a part of Canaanite religion. Hebrew religious leaders saw in the fertility cult a threat to their religion, and many sexual practices are forbidden in the Old Testament because they were found among the Canaanites and might lead to infidelity to Israel's God.

The many sexual regulations of the Old Testament need to be seen both in the context of the times and against this historical background. From Israel's struggle for survival during the nomadic period came institutions such as polygamy (many wives) and concubinage (slaves kept for childbearing purposes) designed to produce many children, and also laws against illegitimacy and nonprocreative sex. From the confrontation with the fertility cult, Israel derived prohibitions against sexual laxity, nakedness, cultic prostitution, and other such typically Canaanite practices. Both themes are present in this passage from Leviticus 20:10–19:

> If a man commits adultery with his neighbor's wife, both adulterer and adulteress shall be put to death. The man who has intercourse with his father's wife has brought shame on his father. They shall both be put to death; their blood shall be on their own heads. . . . A man who has intercourse with any beast shall be put to death, and you shall kill the beast. . . . If a man takes his sister, his father's daughter or his mother's daughter, and they see one another naked, it is a scandalous disgrace. They shall be cut off in the presence of their people. . . . If a man lies with a woman during her monthly period and brings shame upon her, he has exposed her discharge and she has uncovered the source of her discharge; they shall both be cut off from their people.

Adultery and incest are threats to the harmony of the group. Not only is bestiality "unnatural," but it is also nonprocreative and may have been a feature of Canaanite religion. The menstrual taboo is typical of many societies (see Chapter 6).

It should be noted that all societies have had laws regulating sex (Chapter 1) and that these laws, however exotic they may seem to us, made sense in their historical context and were, for the most part, remarkably humane for the time. The Old Testament is also marked by a great regard for married love, affection, and sexuality; this is in marked contrast to, for example, the Greek view of marriage as an institution for breeding and housekeeping. Old Testament Judaism is highly legalistic but not particularly ascetic in its high regard for responsible sexuality as a good and integral part of human life.

Christianity

As the discussion turns to Christianity, which grew in three centuries from an obscure Jewish sect to the dominant religion in the West, the complex conditions of the Mediterranean world between 100 B.C.E. and 100 C.E. must be noted. The world in which Christianity developed was one of tremendous ferment in the spheres of philosophy, religion, and morals. Although Stoicism remained popular among intellectuals, ordinary folks preferred various blends of mythology, superstition, and religion. Few people were much concerned with the pursuit of wisdom and virtue. There were many strange cults, often characterized by some sort of dualism. This was the notion that body and spirit were unalterably separate and opposed to each other and that the goal of life was to become purely spiritual by transcending the physical and material side of life. Public morals were notably decadent, and even ethical pagans were shocked by a society in which people, at least those who could afford it, prized pleasure above all things (Brinton, 1959).

FIGURE 21.2
*The Virgin Mary. During
the Middle Ages, a great
devotion to the mother of
Jesus developed,
emphasizing her perpetual
virginity, purity, and
freedom from all sin.*

Revulsion at the excesses of Roman life affected Judaism, which became markedly more dualistic and antisex by the time of Jesus' birth and the growth of the Christian Church. That Church's ethical tradition is rooted in Old Testament Judaism and was given its direction by the teachings of Jesus, the writings of St. Paul, and the theology of the Fathers of early Christianity. From these beginnings, Christian ethics has evolved and developed over 2000 years in many and various ways. This makes oversimplification a real danger, and yet it is possible to speak in general terms of a Christian tradition of sexual ethics and morality.

The New Testament

At the heart of the Christian scriptures are the Gospels, which describe the life and teachings of Jesus. Since Jesus said almost nothing on the subject of sex, it is difficult to elaborate a sexual ethic from the Gospels alone. Jesus' ethical teaching is based on the tradition of the Old Testament prophets, and his view of sexuality does not seem to differ from that of mainstream Judaism. He urged his followers to strive for ethical perfection, and he spoke strongly against pride, hypocrisy, injustice, and the misuse of wealth. Toward penitent sinners, including those whose sins were sexual, the Gospels show Jesus as compassionate and forgiving (see, for example, his dealings with "fallen women" in John 4:1–30, John 8:53–9:11, and Luke 7:36–50). He did not put any particular emphasis on sexual conduct, apparently regarding it as a part of a whole moral life based on the love of God and neighbor.

The task of first applying the principles of Jesus in concrete situations fell to St. Paul, whose letters form the earliest part of the New Testament. Paul's view of sexuality and women was rather ambivalent, deriving both from the immorality of much Greco-Roman culture and from the expectation he shared with most early Christians that Jesus would return soon, bringing the world to an end. Paul advocated celibacy, not necessarily because he was opposed to sex but because marriage might prove a distraction from prayer, worship, and the proclamation of the Gospel. As a Jew, Paul opposed all sexual expression outside marriage and judged sexual immorality harshly. However, he did not single out sexual sin. He condemned the "sins of the flesh," but by this he meant all aspects of fallen humanity, such as "immorality, impurity, sorcery, enmity, strife, jealousy, anger, selfishness, party spirit, envy, drunkenness, carousing and the like" (Galatians 5:19–21). Later Christian theologians tended to understand the "sins of the flesh" primarily in sexual terms and thus gave Christianity a bias against sexuality beyond what Paul probably intended.

Other New Testament writings show a concern that Christians behave in a manner which is above reproach and morally distinctive. Again, sexual morality is part of this concern for ethical perfection but not necessarily the most important. Given the times, it is not surprising that the New Testament is ambivalent about sexuality, probably more so than the Old Testament.

The Early Christian Church

The "Fathers of the Church," who wrote roughly between 150 and 600 C.E., completed the basic theological shape of the Christian faith. During this time, Christian ethics became increasingly ascetic for several reasons: its natural tendencies, the assimilation of often dualistic Greek philosophy (especially Stoicism), the decadence of Roman society, and the conversion of the Roman Emperor Constantine in 325. As the Church became the official religion of the Roman Empire, much of its original fervor was lost and the Church began to grow corrupt and worldly.

Serious Christians revolted against this situation by moving to the desert to become monks and hermits, to fast, to pray, and to practice all sorts of self-denial, including, of course, **celibacy**. From this point on, monks and monasticism became a permanent reform movement within the Church, a vanguard of ascetics calling Christians to greater rigor. Their success can be seen in the twelfth-century requirement that all clergy in the West be celibate, a departure from early Church practice.[3] The Fathers of the Church, almost all of whom were celibates, allowed that marriage was good and honorable but thought virginity to be a much superior state.

Celibate (SEL-ih-bit): A person who remains unmarried, usually for religious reasons. (Celibacy: the practice of remaining celibate.) Sometimes used to refer to abstaining from sexual intercourse, the correct term for which is "chastity."

The Middle Ages

During the Middle Ages, these basic principles continued to be elaborated and extended. The most important figure of the period, and even today the basic source of Catholic moral theology, was St. Thomas Aquinas (1225–1274). His great achievement was the *Summa Theologica*, a synthesis of Christian theology with Aristotelian philosophy which answered virtually any question a Christian might have on any topic. Thomas combined reason with divine revelation to discern the moral law of the universe, which was to be obeyed as God's intention for creation. This "natural law" approach to ethics was normative in Western Christianity for many centuries and remains so for Roman Catholicism.

Thomas believed that sex was obviously intended for procreation and that, therefore, all nonprocreative sex violates the natural law and is sinful, being opposed to both human nature and the will of God. In the *Summa*, Thomas devoted a chapter

---

[3]   The First Epistle of Timothy, Chapter 3, shows the clear expectation that clergy will be married and father children.

to various sorts of lust and condemned as grave sin such things as fornication (premarital intercourse), nocturnal emissions, seduction, rape, adultery, incest, and "unnatural vice," which includes masturbation, bestiality, and homosexuality.

The theology of Aquinas and other moralists was communicated to the ordinary Christian through the Church's canon law, which determined when intercourse was or was not sinful. All sex outside marriage was, by definition, a sin. Even within marriage the Church forbade intercourse during certain times in a woman's physiological cycle (during menstruation, pregnancy, and up to 40 days postpartum) as well as on certain holy days, fast days (such as Fridays), and even during whole liturgical seasons (such as Advent and Lent). These rules were "enforced" through the *Penitentials,* guidebooks for priests hearing confessions, which instructed them on how to judge certain sins and what penances to assign for them (Brundage, 1984). All of this communicated to the ordinary person that the Church regarded sex as basically evil, for procreation only, and probably not something one should enjoy!

The Protestants

The Protestant Reformation in the sixteenth century destroyed the Christian unity of Europe and shook the theological foundations of the Catholic Church. However, in matters of sexual ethics there were only rather modest changes. The Protestant churches abandoned clerical celibacy, regarding it as unnatural and the source of many abuses, and placed a higher value on marriage and family life. However, Reformers feared illegitimacy and saw sexuality only in the confines of matrimony. Even then, they were often ambivalent. For example, Martin Luther, who was the founder of the Reformation and was happily married to a former nun, called marriage "a hospital for the sick" and saw its purpose as being to "aid human infirmity and prevent unchastity" (quoted in Thielicke, 1964, p. 136)—scarcely an enthusiastic approach.

A significant contribution of Reformation Protestantism to Christianity was a renewed emphasis on the individual conscience in matters such as the interpretation of the Bible and ethical decision making. Such an emphasis on freedom and individual responsibility has led to the serious questioning of legalistic ethics and, in part, to today's ethical debates.

The Reformation also gave rise to Puritanism. The Puritans followed Augustine in emphasizing the doctrine of "original sin" and the "total depravity" of fallen humanity. This led them to use civil law to regulate human behavior in an attempt to suppress frivolity and immorality. As will be seen in the next chapter, this urge to make people good by law has many sexual applications, although the Puritans were probably no more sexually repressive than other Christians of the time. What we often think of as "Puritan" sexual rigidity is probably more properly referred to as "Victorian." During the reign of Queen Victoria (1819–1901), English society held sexual expression in exaggerated disgust and probably exaggerated its importance. While strict public standards of decency and purity were enforced, many Victorians indulged in private vices of pornography, prostitution, and the rest. It is against this typically Victorian combination of repressiveness and hypocrisy that many people of the twentieth century have revolted, wrongly thinking the Victorian period to be representative of the whole Christian ethical tradition.

Current Trends

Across Western history there has been a fairly stable consensus on the fundamentals of sexual ethics, which I have called the Old Morality. Sex has been understood as a good part of divine creation but also as a source of temptation that needs to be

FIGURE 21.3
The most notable of the Western Fathers was St. Augustine (354–430 B.C.E.), who had had a promiscuous youth and overreacted after his conversion to Christianity. For Augustine, sexuality was a consequence of the Fall, and every sexual act was tainted by concupiscence (from the Latin word concupiscentia, *meaning "lust" or "evil desire of the flesh"). Even sex in marriage was sinful, and in* The City of God, *he wrote that "children could not have been begotten in any other way than they know them to be begotten now, i.e., by lust, at which even honorable marriage blushes" (1950 ed., Article 21). The stature of Augustine meant that his negative view of sexuality was perpetuated in subsequent Christian theology.*

controlled. Although at various times chastity has been exalted, marriage and the family have always been held in esteem, and sex outside marriage condemned, in theory if not always in practice. The only approved purpose for sex has been procreation, and nonprocreative sex has been regarded as unnatural and sinful. However, this consensus has largely broken down in this century, and sexual ethics is now a topic of considerable debate. Several factors, both within the religious community and outside it, have contributed to this ferment.

The rise of historical-critical methods in biblical scholarship has led to a questioning of the absoluteness of scriptural norms. Many scholars see them as conditioned by the time and culture in which they were written and not necessarily binding today. Further, traditional understandings of biblical treatments of sexuality have been questioned as more is known about the original historical context. The Reformation emphasis on the Bible and individual conscience has called the natural-law approach into question. The religious community has also been influenced by the behavioral sciences, which suggest that sexuality is much more complex than had been thought, and question older assumptions about what is "natural" or "normal." Technology has made it possible, for the first time in human history, to prevent conception reliably and to terminate pregnancy safely, which, for example, blunts the force of arguments against premarital intercourse on the basis of the fear of illegitimacy. Indeed, technology itself has raised a host of ethical issues as humans gain more and more control over what had been a matter of "doing what comes naturally."

All this has led religious groups, and others concerned with ethics, into serious debate and even conflict. Within Judaism, the Orthodox who still live by the rabbinic interpretation of the Old Testament law may be in serious conflict with the Conservative and Reformed groups. Protestants are deeply divided among conservatives who hold to the Old Morality, liberals inclined to the New Morality, and others who come out somewhere in between. Perhaps no single religious community has experienced as much tension over sexual morality as the Roman Catholic Church in America (see Focus 21.1). Controversy in matters of sexuality tends to be heated, as we shall see when we examine specific topics.

Humanism

It would be misleading to suggest that within Western culture, at least since the Renaissance, all ethical thinking has been religious in origin. Many ethicists have quite consciously tried to find a framework for moral behavior that does not rely on divine revelation or any direction from a source outside or beyond human intellect and personality. Nonreligious ethics covers the whole spectrum; however, we can look at a fairly broad mainstream called humanism.

Humanism: A religious or philosophical system which denies a divine origin for morality and holds that ethical judgments must be made on the basis of human experience and human reason.

Humanistic ethics accepts no supernatural source for direction and insists that values can be found only in human experience in this world, as observed by the philosopher or social scientist. Most humanists would hold that the basic goals of human life are happiness, self-awareness, the avoidance of pain and suffering, and the fulfillment of human needs. Of course, the individual pursuit of these ends must be tempered by the fact that no one lives in the world alone and that some limitation of individual happiness may be required for the common good. Another important humanistic principle is that the individual must make his or her own decisions and accept responsibility for them and their consequences, without appeal to some higher authority, such as God.

In the area of human sexuality, humanism demands a realistic approach to human behavior that does not create arbitrary or unreasonable standards and expectations; it is very distrustful of the legalistic approach. It seeks real intimacy between persons and condemns impersonal and exploitative relationships, though probably not with the vigor that marks religious ethics. It tends to be tolerant, compassionate, and skeptical of claims of absolute value.

Sexuality in Other Religions

The discussion so far has been mostly concerned with Western culture and the Judeo-Christian tradition. It will broaden our outlook if we consider human sexuality in religious traditions outside dominant American culture. Obviously, this could be the topic for a very large book itself, and the reader will have to be content with a rather brief look at the three non-Western religions with the largest number of adherents: Islam, Hinduism, and Buddhism.

Islam

Geographically, and in terms of its roots, Islam is the closest faith to the Judeo-Christian heritage. It was founded by the Prophet Muhammad, who lived from 570 to 632 in what is now Saudi Arabia. Its followers are called *Moslems* (or *Muslims*),

Dissent in the Roman Catholic Church

In the 1980s and 1990s the Roman Catholic Church in the United States has experienced a number of serious controversies over the Church's teaching, many of them in the area of sexual ethics. The Church's traditional teaching on sexuality has been vigorously reasserted by Pope John Paul II in the face of calls for a less legalistic and rigorous approach. He has repeatedly condemned all sexual activity outside marriage and all nonprocreative sex. In 1983, for example, the Vatican issued *Educational Guidance in Human Love*, a pamphlet for parents and teachers. In this document procreation is seen as the essential purpose of conjugal love; masturbation, extramarital sex, and homosexuality are all described as "grave moral disorders." However, such teaching has not always been welcomed, either by ethicists or by ordinary Catholics. Thus the debate within American Catholicism mirrors the controversy that has been going on in the society at large. At issue are such topics as contraception, abortion, homosexuality, and reproductive technologies.

Contraception

Although the Vatican and the American hierarchy have not moved from the condemnation of "artificial" birth control as set forth in Pope Paul VI's encyclical *Humanae Vitae* (1968), there is evidence that many American Catholics ignore the condemnation and use contraceptives, often with the tacit approval of their priests. Since *Humanae Vitae* was not an infallible teaching, some Catholic ethicists still treat contraception as an open question.

Abortion

On the whole, American Catholics support their Church's strong, organized opposition to abortion, but there is a vocal minority within the Church calling for reconsideration. In October 1984, Catholics for a Free Choice paid for an ad in the *New York Times* headlined, "A Diversity of Opinion Regarding Abortion Exists Among Committed Catholics." The 97 signers of the ad, which sought to open a freer discussion of the issue, included clergy, members of religious orders, and lay theologians. The Vatican responded by ordering the priests, brothers, and nuns to retract their views or face discipline, including possible expulsion from their orders. Twenty-four nuns refused, and although none was actually dismissed, the controversy ended in a stalemate. Several academic signers of the ad had speaking engagements at Catholic colleges canceled and were subjected to other forms of official disapproval.

Homosexuality

In 1976 Jesuit priest and psychotherapist John J. McNeill published *The Church and the Homosex-*

and its sacred scripture is the Koran. Islam shares some of its basic precepts with a neighboring faith, Judaism, but it has a flavor all its own. Classical Islam values sexuality very positively, and Muhammad saw intercourse, especially in marriage, as the highest good of human life. Islam sanctions both polygamy and concubinage, and the Prophet had several wives. In legend, great sexual prowess is attributed to him, although it may be exaggerated. He opposed celibacy, and Islam has very little ascetic tradition. A male-dominated faith, Islam has a strong double standard but

FIGURE 21.4
The Reverend Charles Curran, professor of theology at Catholic University, holds a news conference in response to the Vatican action stripping him of his right to teach Catholic theology.

ual, in which he questioned the Church's traditional teaching on homosexuality and its scriptural and theological bases. At the time, Fr. McNeill was forbidden by his Jesuit superiors from speaking or writing further on the subject. He obeyed the order for

10 years, until his superiors ordered him to cease all ministry to the gay community, at which point he left the Jesuits and the priesthood.

Reproductive Technologies

In 1987, the Congregation for the Doctrine of the Faith issued an "Instruction on Respect for Human Life in Its Origin and on the Dignity of Procreation," which roundly condemned in vitro fertilization, surrogate motherhood, artificial insemination, and other aspects of new procreative technologies. The document was severely criticized by many American Catholic ethicists, who found it too rigid and ill-informed.

The Curran Controversy

In 1986 Father Charles Curran, one of the nation's leading Catholic ethicists, was removed from his professorship at Catholic University (Washington, DC). Father Curran had raised some rather mild questions about the Church's teaching on the subjects of contraception, abortion, and homosexuality but claimed that he was not challenging any infallible doctrine of the Church. The Vatican responded that Curran, by publicly rejecting the *magisterium* (Church's teaching authority) in these areas, had forfeited his claim to be a teacher of Catholic moral theology. The *Christian Century,* a leading ecumenical weekly, made the Vatican efforts to curb dissent in the American Church its leading religious news story of 1986 (**103**, pp. 1163–1165).

Sources: The Christian Century, Grammick (1986), Reuther (1985), McNeill (1987), Curran (1988).

recognizes a number of rights and prerogatives for women as well. Although sex outside either marriage or concubinage is viewed as a sin, Islam can be ethically quite moderate and rather tolerant of sexual sin, including homosexuality. All these aspects combine to create a "sex-positive" religion (Bullough, 1976, p. 205).

Islam is not a monolithic faith, and there is great variety in the ways in which the laws of the Koran are carried out in societies throughout the Moslem world. Some Arab states (e.g., Saudi Arabia) are theocracies in which the religious law is

enacted in civil law. In these nations sexual offenses are likely to be more stringently punished, and women have very little freedom. The best-known example of such a state is Iran (see Figure 21.5). Other Islamic countries (such as Egypt and Syria) are secular states in which Western values have been adopted to some extent. In these, women have more rights and sexual mores are more pluralistic. Moreover, there is considerable variation in the interpretation of the Koran, especially between Sunnis and Shi'ites, the two principal Islamic "denominations."

Hinduism

"Hinduism" is a rather inclusive term which refers to a highly varied complex of mythology and religious practice founded on the Indian subcontinent. Here can be found virtually every approach to sexuality the human species has yet invented. However, certain themes are worth mentioning. In Hinduism, four possible approaches to life are acceptable: Kama, the pursuit of pleasure; Artha, the pursuit of power and material wealth; Dharma, the pursuit of the moral life; and Moksha, the pursuit of liberation through the negation of the self in Nirvana. Kama is notable because it has produced an extensive literature on the achievement of sexual pleasure, notably the *Kama Sutra* of Vatsyayana, a masterpiece of erotic hedonism. This testifies to the highly positive view of sexuality to be found in Hinduism.

However, in contrast, the ways of Dharma and Moksha can be as rigorously ascetic as anything in Christianity. By avoiding all passions, including sex, the follower of these ways of renunciation seeks to pass out of the cycle of continual rebirth to absorption into the godhead. Part of this is *brahmacarya*, or celibacy, which is to be cultivated at the beginning of life (for the purposes of education and discipline) and at the end of life (for the purpose of finding peace). It is interesting to note that in between it is permissible to marry and raise a family, and thus this form of

Hinduism makes active sexuality and asceticism possible in the same lifetime (Noss, 1963).

Buddhism

Buddhism was a development of Hinduism; it originated in the life and thought of Guatama (560–480 B.C.E.) and has been elaborated in many forms since then. There is little discussion of sex in the teachings of the Buddha; his way is generally ascetic and concentrates on the achievement of enlightenment and on escape from the suffering of the world. Two main traditions, Therevada and Mahayana, are found in contemporary Buddhism, and they differ greatly. The ethics of Therevada includes the strict nonindulgence of the desires that bring joy; understanding, morals, and discipline are emphasized. The ethics of Mahayana is more active and directed toward love of others. Both encourage men to live celibate lives as monks. Originally, Buddha sought a "middle way" between extreme asceticism and extreme hedonism, but today the situation is rather like that of medieval Christianity: The masses live ordinary and usually married lives, and the monks cultivate ascetic wisdom.

Tantric Buddhism, found particularly in Tibet, is a form of Buddhism which is of particular interest. There is a devotion to natural energy *(shakti),* and followers are taught that passion can be exhausted by passion. For example, sexual desire can be overcome while engaging in intercourse according to occult knowledge. Sexuality

FIGURE 21.6
A yoga master's view of sex: "Sexual life is not unnatural nor condemned by God. Those who are interested in it should get into matrimonial life and experience it in moderation. Overindulgence in anything will be detrimental to both physical and mental health. Others whose interest is in serving God and his creation full-time should stay away from matrimony to avoid personal obligations and to conserve and redirect their sexual, physical and mental energies toward their service." In this statement Sri Swami Satchidananda summarizes much Hindu teaching on sexuality.

can therefore be used as a means of transcending the limitations of human life. This sexual mysticism is by no means common, but it is one of the various forms which Eastern religion may take (Parrinder, 1980).

CONTEMPORARY ISSUES IN SEXUAL ETHICS

It cannot be said too frequently that human sexuality is a heavily value-laden subject and, therefore, is likely to be the subject of strongly and emotionally held convictions. It is also likely to be the focal point of conflicts in society, if there is no broad consensus on the norms of sexual behavior. This is clearly the case in contemporary American society. Rapid change in all aspects of life has been the rule for the last several decades, and this change includes the "sexual revolution." This change is perceived by many people as a threat to all they hold dear and, not surprisingly, they respond with fear and anger. The backlash against the more liberal view of sexuality and the greater freedom of sexual behavior which has come about in the last 25 years, accelerated by the spread of AIDS and herpes, has resulted in explosive public debate, organized attempts at legislating the Old Morality back into force, and a reassertion of a highly legalistic view of the Judeo-Christian ethic. The debate promises to continue for some time and to generate much heat (Nelson, 1987).

This debate over the limits, if any, of individual sexual freedom can be seen as the clash between the New Morality and the Old Morality, but let us propose a more helpful model. The Old Morality is, to a great extent, supported by people who believe that there are clearly and objectively defined standards of right and wrong and that a society has a right to insist that all its members conform, at least outwardly, to them. We might call this view **moralism;** and it has many proponents in the religious community who see the objective standard of morality as deriving from divine law. Opposed to this view are the proponents of **pluralism;** they see the question of public morality as being much more complex. Pluralists deny that there are objective standards which everyone can know, and they are likely to contend that truth is to be discovered in the clash of differing opinions and convictions. A society is, therefore, according to this view, wise to allow many points of view to be advocated and expressed. The conscience and rights of the individual are to be stressed over the needs of society for order and uniformity. Pluralists are much less likely than moralists to appeal to either law or religion for the enforcement of their views, and they are more likely to allow freedom to individuals even if society might be endangered by their actions. The debate between moralist and pluralist has been going on for a very long time, both in the religious community itself and throughout American history. It will not be settled any time soon.

An illustration of the above can be found in the emergence of a "profamily" position which is rooted in religious conservatism and is increasingly attempting to influence the legislative process. Profamily activists are against the Equal Rights Amendment and other bars to sex discrimination, in favor of an absolute constitutional ban on abortion, against any kind of legal tolerance of the cohabitation of unmarried persons, and in favor of legal discrimination against homosexuals in such areas as housing, child custody, and employment.

This position is essentially that of the New Religious Right, a coalition of conservative religious and political groups. Members of this movement, largely but not exclusively fundamentalist Protestants, argue that the New Morality has sapped the moral vigor of American society, leaving the country open to inner decay, Communist infiltration, and divine judgment. Their efforts to enforce their religious convictions by legislation have created one of the most intense church-state contro-

Moralism: A religious or philosophical attitude which emphasizes moral behavior, usually according to strict standards, as the highest goal of human life. Moralists tend to favor strict regulation of human conduct to help make people good.

Pluralism: A philosophical or political attitude which affirms the value of many competing opinions and believes that the truth is discovered in the clash of diverse perspectives. Pluralists, therefore, believe in the maximum human freedom possible.

FIGURE 21.7
Pat Robertson, profamily presidential candidate in 1988.

versies of the twentieth century (see Chapter 22). Their position is clearly odious to pluralists and to those who have benefited by the liberalization of laws and attitudes concerning sexuality. These persons and groups will fight to keep what they consider to be gains, while profamily and New Right activists will seek to turn the clock back to what they perceive to have been a healthier and more moral time.

This conflict can be found within most religious communities today. Even liberal "mainline" Protestant groups, which have tended to accommodate at least some of the New Morality, have been under attack from portions of their own membership on such issues as abortion, premarital sex, and homosexuality. Reports in the Church press of national gatherings of American religious groups reveal a remarkable number of debates related to human sexuality, debates which parallel those in society at large. We will illustrate this ferment by a discussion of the ethical issues posed by sex outside marriage, contraception, abortion, homosexuality, and AIDS. Looking toward a future rapidly becoming the present, we will also consider the ethical dilemmas posed by technology.

Sex Outside Marriage

The biblical tradition underlying Western ethics has almost always limited sexual intercourse to marriage. This is rooted in a religious understanding of marriage as God's will for most men and women, the way in which sin is avoided and children are cared for. In theological terms, then, there has been a requirement that the relationship and procreative aspects of sex be joined, at least potentially, in every sexual act. Thus, the tradition has condemned both sex before marriage (which the Bible calls fornication) and sex by persons married to others (adultery). Today, this position continues to be held by theological conservatives among Jews, Protestants, and Roman Catholics. A 1976 Roman Catholic statement on the subject is typical of this position:

Fornication: The biblical term for sex by unmarried persons and, more generally, all immoral sexual behavior.

Adultery: Voluntary sexual intercourse by a husband or wife with someone not one's spouse; thus, betrayal of one's marriage vows.

> Today there are many who vindicate the right to sexual union before marriage, at least in those cases where a firm intention to marry and an affection which is already in some way conjugal in the psychology of the subjects require this completion which they judge to be connatural. . . . This option is contrary to Christian doctrine, which states that every genital act must be within the frame-work of marriage. (Congregation for the Doctrine of the Faith, 1976, p. 11)

However, trends in society have caused many ethicists to reopen the question and to take less dogmatic positions. Among these are the development of safe and reliable contraception, later marriage, the fact that many people experience the singleness of divorce and widowhood, and empirical evidence to suggest significant sexual experimentation and activity among the young. These ethicists are concerned that people be given more helpful guidance than "thou shalt not." For them, the quality of the relationship is more important ethically than its legal status.

Criteria for judging the morality of nonmarital sexual acts could include the following. First, is there a genuine respect for the personhood of all involved? Virtually all ethicists would agree that sexual exploitation of one person by another (whether married or not)—the use of human beings merely for one's pleasure—is wrong. Further, most would require genuine affection and serious commitment from both parties. This commitment would be manifested in responsible behavior such as the use of contraceptives if the couple were not willing or able to have children and taking precautions against disease (such as herpes or AIDS). Finally, many ethicists would insist that moral sexual behavior must include genuine openness and honesty toward one another. Public and private institutions, in this view, should be involved in helping people to make good ethical choices about sexual behavior in a culture that tends to glorify and exploit sex (Lebacqz, 1987; Moore, 1987).[4]

Extramarital sex (adultery) has always been regarded as a grave matter in the Judeo-Christian tradition. In the Hebrew Scriptures, the penalty for it was to be stoned to death; in the New Testament, it is the only grounds for divorce allowed by Jesus (Matthew 6:21–22). Adultery has been understood as a serious breach of trust by a spouse, as well as an act of unfaithfulness to God (a violation of religiously significant promises). Few contemporary ethicists would modify this position, but many would argue for a less judgmental, more humane approach to those involved. In this view, people in extramarital relationships should be helped to find the root causes and to move toward a reconciliation with their spouses based on forgiveness and love. This approach would suggest that counseling is more helpful than condemnation. Above all, some would argue, religious organizations need to assist people in establishing and maintaining good marriages based on mutual respect, communication, and commitment.

Contraception

The situation today with respect to birth control is clearer than the situation with respect to some of the other topics dealt with here. Roman Catholics and Orthodox Jews oppose any "artificial" means of contraception; other Jews and most Protestants favor responsible family planning by married couples. Moreover, most ethicists would suggest that unmarried persons who are sexually active ought to be using some means to prevent pregnancy.

Those who oppose birth control for religious reasons see it as being contrary to the will of God, against the natural law, or both. Orthodox Judaism cites the biblical injunction to "be fruitful and multiply" (Genesis 1:26) as God's command to his people, not to be disobeyed in any way. Further, some members of other Jewish communities warn that limiting family size threatens the future existence of the Jewish people, and they call for a return to the traditionally large Jewish family.

The Roman Catholic position is best articulated in Pope Paul VI's 1968 encyclical, *Humanae Vitae*:

---

[4] A fine discussion of these issues from different perspectives (liberal Protestant and Roman Catholic, respectively) can be found in Nelson (1978) and Genovesi (1987).

Marriage and conjugal love are by their nature ordained toward the begetting and educating of children. . . . In the task of transmitting life, therefore, they are not free to proceed completely at will, as if they could determine in a wholly autonomous way the honest path to follow, but they must conform their activity to the creative intention of God, expressed in the very nature of marriage and by its acts, and manifested by the constant teaching of the Church. (Pope Paul VI, 1968, p. 20).

The encyclical continued the Church's approval of "natural family planning," that is, abstinence during fertile periods, popularly known as the "rhythm method" or "Vatican roulette." *Humanae Vitae* was not enthusiastically accepted by all Catholics and, as noted in Chapter 8, there is evidence to suggest that many Catholic couples, often with the encouragement or tacit approval of their priest, ignore these teachings and use contraceptives anyway. Nonetheless, the teachings of *Humanae Vitae* have been repeatedly and resoundingly reiterated by the current Pope, John Paul II, all over the world.

Those in the religious community who favor the use of contraceptives do so for a variety of reasons. Many express a concern that all children who are born should be "wanted," and they see family planning as a means to this end. Others, emphasizing the dangers that the population explosion poses to the quality and future of human life, the need for a more equitable distribution of natural resources, and the needs of the emerging nations, call for family planning as a matter of justice. Another point of view regards the use of contraceptives as part of the responsible use of freedom. In this view, any couple who are unwilling or unready to assume the responsibility of children have a duty to use contraceptives. For these groups, the decision to use contraceptives is a highly individual one, and the government must allow each individual the free exercise of his or her conscience (Curran, 1988).

Abortion

One of the most convulsive debates of our time is being waged over the issue of abortion. Prolife and prochoice activists are well organized and deeply convinced of the rightness of their positions. The conflict is a clash of religious belief, political conviction, and world view in the realm of public policy, one that allows for no easy solutions.[5]

Two distinctions should be made at the outset. First, there is no consensus on the relation between abortion and contraception. For the Roman Catholic Church, and others within the prolife movement, the two are the same in intention; indeed many prolife activists wish to ban all contraception except natural family planning. In the other camp, there are some prochoice advocates who also regard abortion as a variety of contraception—less desirable, perhaps, but better than unwanted pregnancy. However, most centrist ethicists do distinguish between abortion and contraception, typically favoring the latter while raising ethical questions about the former. Second, a distinction is frequently made between therapeutic abortion and abortion on demand. Therapeutic abortion is a termination of pregnancy when the life or mental health of the woman is threatened or when there is trauma, such as in cases of rape or incest. Many ethical theorists are willing to endorse therapeutic abortion as the lesser of two evils but do not sanction abortion on demand, i.e., abortion whenever requested by a woman for any reason (see, for example, Thielicke, 1964, pp. 226–244).

[5] For a thorough and careful study of what prolife and prochoice activists believe they have at stake, see Luker (1984).

The leadership of the antiabortion movement clearly comes from the Roman Catholic Church, for which the end of abortion is a major policy goal. For many Catholics, opposition to abortion is seen as part of an overall commitment to respect for life, what Joseph Cardinal Bernardin has called the "seamless garment" that includes opposition to capital punishment, euthanasia (mercy killing), and social injustice, and a very positive stance toward peace (Cahill, 1985). The underlying principle of this position is that all life is a gift from God that human beings are not permitted to take. It is the position of the prolife movement that human life begins at the moment of conception and that the fetus is, from that beginning, entitled to full rights and protections. The Roman Catholic position is shared by Orthodox Jews, Eastern Orthodox Christians, and many conservative, or fundamentalist, Protestants (Enquist, 1983). An end to legalized abortion is at the top of the political agenda of many theologically conservative groups and has been a major issue in the past several presidential and congressional elections and Supreme Court appointments.

Nonetheless, there has been some significant dissent from this position even within the Catholic Church. Prochoice Catholics point out that for most of its history, the Church accepted Aristotle's teaching, reaffirmed by St. Thomas Aquinas, that "ensoulment," that is, the entry into the fetus of its distinctively human soul, takes place 40 days after conception for a male and 80 or 90 days after conception for a female. Theoretically, this permits abortions at least until the fortieth day. In 1869, Pope Pius IX eliminated the concept of ensoulment, holding that life begins at conception and that all abortion is therefore murder (Luker, 1984). Though regularly denounced by the Vatican and the American hierarchy, some Catholic ethicists insist that the Church's position is not unchangeable and argue that the concerns and needs of women should be more carefully considered in the matter (Maguire, 1983; Kolbenschlag, 1985; Reuther, 1985).

The prochoice position takes at least two forms: absolute and modified. The absolute position argues that pregnancy is solely the concern of a woman and that she should have the absolute right to control her own body and determine whether to carry a fetus to term or not. Ethically, this position is based on the conviction that the individual must be free and autonomous in all personal decisions. It is also inspired by feminism, which regards such autonomy as necessary if women are to be truly equal. Feminists also observe that, historically, the rules about abortion were made by men, who do not become pregnant, and thus are deeply suspect. Indeed, for many feminists abortion on demand is an absolute value for women's liberation. Concerns for autonomy and individualism have formed a significant part of Western ethics and American social theory for over two centuries.

For those who hold the modified prochoice position—and this includes most liberal Protestants and Jews—the issue is more complex and means balancing several goods against one another. They affirm that human life is good and ought to be preserved but also argue that the quality of life is important. They argue that an unborn child may have a right to life, but ask if it does not also have the right to be wanted and cared for. In high-risk situations, might not the danger to the well-being of a woman already alive take precedence over the well-being of an unborn fetus? Few in this camp would regard abortion as a good thing but suggest that there may be many situations in which it is the least bad choice. Moreover, these ethicists tend to observe that since there is no real consensus in society over the morality of abortion, the government ought to keep out and let the individual woman make up her own mind.

The "prolife" position is, as is typical with moralism, much more absolute and apparently simple, while the pluralist "prochoice" position is subtle and differentiated. Both positions agree on the value and dignity of human life, but are sharply

FIGURE 21.8
The abortion controversy.
Prolife and prochoice
advocates are both
adamant about their
positions.

divided on when life begins, how various conflicting interests are to be balanced, and how human life is best preserved and enhanced. Several factors ensure that the debate will continue for some time. Advances in neonatal medicine are pushing back the threshold of "viability" (the survival of premature infatns), and this may affect the ethical acceptability of second-trimester abortions for some people (Callahan, 1986). The politicalization of the issue will keep it in the public consciousness, and legal challenges will undoubtedly continue (see Chapter 22). The apparent shift of public opinion in a more conservative direction may also influence the course of the debate and its outcome. Certainly, the intensity is not likely to diminish, as it is a clash about life, law, freedom, and values, and few people are neutral on these great issues (Callahan & Callahan, 1984) (see Focus 21.2).

Homosexuality

Mirroring society as a whole, the religious community has been engaged in a vigorous debate on the subject of homosexuality. Until recently, it was assumed that all homosexual acts and persons were condemned by the Judeo-Christian tradition. However, many contemporary ethicists, and some religious bodies, are reexamining their attitudes toward homosexuality. This change has occurred in part because some recent biblical and historical scholarship suggests the traditional interpretation is not accurate, and in part because the impact of social science has led many ethicists to question whether homosexuality is truly abnormal and unnatural and therefore against the will of God. There are three positions, broadly speaking, on the issue: rejection, modified rejection or qualified acceptance, and full acceptance.[6]

It has generally been presumed that the weight of the Judeo-Christian tradition absolutely opposes any sexual acts between persons of the same gender and regards those committing such acts as dreadful sinners, utterly condemned by God. Although there are few references in the Bible, all are negative, the most famous being the passage about the destruction of Sodom (see Figure 21.9). (See also Leviticus 20:13.)

In the Hebrew Scriptures, homosexual practices are included on lists of offenses

⁶ Here I have slightly modified the very helpful scheme of James Nelson (1978, chap. 8).

Prolife Versus Prochoice

The following statements suggest some of the arguments and rhetoric of the abortion debate. In reading them it is useful to keep in mind the Gallup poll (Table 21.1) which has recorded some increases over time in support for legal abortion but also a remarkable lack of consensus.

Prolife Statements

Our opposition to abortion derives from the conviction that whatever is opposed to life is a violation of man's [sic] inherent rights, a position that has a strong basis in the history of American law. The U.S. Bill of Rights guarantees the right to life to every American and the U.N. Declaration of the Rights of the Child, which our nation endorses, affirms that every child, because of his dependent status, should be accorded a special protection under the law before as well as after birth. (National Conference of Catholic Bishops, 1979)

All human beings ought to value every person for his or her uniqueness as a creature of God, called to be a brother or sister of Christ by reason of the incarnation and universal redemption. For us, the sacredness of human life is based on these premises. And it is on the same premises that there is based our celebration of human life—all human life. This explains our efforts to defend human life against every influence or action that threatens or weakens it, as well as our endeavors to make every life more human in all its aspects. (Pope John Paul II, 1979)

Human life in all is forms is sacred, and every means must be used for its preservation, protection and defense. (Orthodox Church in America, 1983)

Abortion is not a moral option, except as a tragically unavailable by-product of medical procedures necessary to prevent the death of another human being, viz., the mother. (Lutheran Church—Missouri Synod, 1979)

Be it finally resolved that we favor legislation and/or a constitutional amendment prohibiting abortion except to save the life of the mother. (Southern Baptist Convention, 1980)

Prochoice Statements

The question of when life begins is basic to the abortion debate. It is primarily a

against God. Jesus made no comment on the subject, but St. Paul was unambiguously against homosexual acts, seeing them as perverse behavior by fundamentally heterosexual persons. Thus he included them in lists of sexual sins, along with adultery and fornication, that are in opposition to the will of God and symptomatic of human depravity. However, Paul does not seem to have found homosexuality any more dreadful than other sexual sins (Thielicke, 1964).

Homosexuality was not uncommon in the Hellenistic world of the early Church, and the Fathers condemned it as part of the immoral world in which they found themselves. They saw it as a crime against nature that might bring down the wrath of God upon the whole community (Kosnik, 1977). In the Middle Ages,

Table 21.1
The Gallup Poll Has Repeatedly Surveyed Americans on Their Attitudes Toward Abortion

	Percentage		
	1975	1980	1992
Abortion should be:			
Legal under any circumstances	21	25	31
Legal under only certain circumstances	54	53	53
Illegal under all circumstances	22	18	14
No opinion	3	4	2

theological question, on which denominations or religious groups must be permitted to establish and follow their own teachings. Every woman must have the personal freedom of choice to follow her personal religious and moral convictions concerning the completion or termination of her pregnancy. (United Chuch of Christ, General Synod, 1981)

Our belief in the sanctity of unborn human life makes us reluctant to approve abortion. But we are equally bound to respect the sacredness of life and well-being of the mother for whom devastating damage may result from an unacceptable pregnancy. (United Methodist Church, General Conference, 1976, 1984)

We affirm the moral right of women to be-come pregnant by choice and to become mothers by choice. We affirm the moral right of women to freely choose a termination of unwanted pregnancies. We oppose actions by individuals, organizations and governmental bodies that attempt to restrict and limit the woman's moral right and obligation of responsible parenthood. (American Humanist Association, Annual Conference, 1977)

The American Jewish Congress has long recognized that reproductive freedom is a fundamental right, grounded in the most basic notions of personal privacy, individual integrity and religious liberty. Jewish religious traditions hold that a woman must be left free to her own conscience and God to decide for herself what is morally correct. The fundamental right to privacy applies to contraception to avoid unintended pregnancy as well as to freedom of choice on abortion to prevent unwanted birth. (American Jewish Congress, Biennial Convention, 1982)

While we acknowledge that in this country it is the legal right of every woman to have a medically safe abortion, as Christians we believe strongly that if this right is exercised, it should be used only in extreme situations. We emphatically oppose abortion as a means of birth control, family planning, sex selection or any reason of mere convenience. (Episcopal Church, General Convention, 1988)

Sources: The Right to Life Society and the Religious Coalition for Abortion Rights.

Thomas Aquinas stated that "unnatural vice . . . flouts nature by transgressing its basic principle of sexuality and is in this matter the gravest of sin" (1968 ed., II-II, q. 154, a. 12). Thielicke notes a similar attitude among Reformation theologians and quotes a seventeenth-century Lutheran, Benedict Carpzov, as listing the following results of homosexuality: "earthquakes, famine, pestilence, Saracens, floods, and very fat voracious field mice" (1964, p. 276). The rejectionist position continues to be held by many members of the religious community who condemn homosexual acts and reject homosexual persons unless they repent and become heterosexual. An example of this stance is a 1987 resolution of the Southern Baptist Convention that states: "Homosexuality is a perversion of divine standards and a violation of nature

FIGURE 21.9

In Genesis 19:4–11, God sends two angels to the city of Sodom to investigate its alleged immorality. The angels are granted hospitality by Lot, but his house is surrounded by a crowd of men demanding that he send the angels out, "that we may know them." Lot offers his virgin daughters instead, but the men of Sodom insist, the angels strike them blind, and God destroys the city. This story has been understood to condemn all homosexual acts. However, some modern scholars question this interpretation, noting that at most it condemns homosexual rape. Moreover, scholars point out that in other portions of the Bible and in Jewish history, the sin of Sodom is never seen as homosexuality, but rather as general immorality and lack of hospitality (a serious offense in the ancient Near East).

and of natural affections. . . . [While] God loves the homosexual and offers salvation, homosexuality is not a normal lifestyle and is an abomination in the eyes of God" (Associated Press, June 1987).

However, many religious groups would modify this position somewhat, through a distinction between homosexual orientation and behavior. In essence this stance of modified rejection or qualified acceptance regards homosexual orientation, when it cannot be changed, as morally neutral, but rejects homosexual acts. Thus, an ethical homosexual person may be fully obedient to the will of God, as long as she or he remains abstinent. This is the official position of the Roman Catholic Church, recently reiterated in a Vatican directive entitled "The Pastoral Care of Homosexual Persons" which states in part:

Although the particular inclination of the homosexual person is not a sin, it is a more or less strong tendency ordered toward an intrinsic moral evil and thus the inclination itself must be seen as an objective disorder. Therefore special concern and pastoral attention should be directed toward those who have this condition, lest they be led to believe that the living out of this orientation in homosexual activity is a morally acceptable opinion. It is not. (Congregation for the Doctrine of the Faith, 1986, p. 379)

As a result of this instruction, many chapters of Dignity, an organization of lesbian and gay Catholics, were denied the use of church facilities by American bishops. Various Protestant groups have taken the same stance—that is, being gay per se may not be sinful, but homosexual acts are—and a statement by the 1976 General Conference of the United Methodist Church is typical: "We do not condone the practice of homosexuality and consider this practice incompatible with Christian teaching" (*The Christian Century*, 1976, 93, 557). Farther down the road to some sort of acceptance is the 1985 statement of the Episcopal Church's General Convention, in which that body committed itself

to find an effective way to foster a better understanding of homosexual persons, to dispel myths and prejudices about homosexuality, to provide pastoral support, and to give life to the claim of homosexual persons upon the love, acceptance, and pastoral care and concern of the Church. (*Journal of the General Convention*, 1985, p. 505)

The Episcopal Church stands, with many other religious groups, for full civil rights and liberties for homosexual persons, although it is officially opposed to the ordination of practicing homosexuals (see below). Thus, rejection can be modified and acceptance qualified in a variety of ways.

At the other end of the spectrum, there are those in the religious community who favor full acceptance of lesbian and gay persons, usually basing this on a revisionist view of the Bible and Church tradition. Some scholars question whether the apparent condemnation in the Scriptures is really relevant to homosexuality as it is generally understood today. New Testament scholar Robin Scroggs, for example, says that the only form of same-gender behavior known to the world of the New Testament involved older men and youths (often prostitutes or slaves), and he concludes that "what the New Testament was against was the image of homosexuality as pederasty and primarily here its more sordid and dehumanizing dimensions" (1983, p. 126). Yale historian John Boswell's detailed research into early and medieval Christianity has led him to conclude that up until about the thirteenth century the Christian church was relatively neutral toward homosexuality and, when it did see homosexual behavior as sinful, did not regard it as any worse than heterosexual transgressions. Boswell found a gay subculture that flourished throughout this period and argues that it was known to the Church, that clergy and church officials were often part of it, and that it was not infrequently tolerated by religious and civil authorities alike (Boswell, 1980). This sort of reinterpretation has led theologians, such as the Roman Catholic John McNeil and the Anglican Norman Pittenger, to question whether the tradition has been understood properly and to conclude that sexual relationships which are characterized by mutual respect, concern, and commitment—by love in its fullest sense—are to be valued and affirmed, whatever the gender of the partners (Pittenger, 1970; McNeill, 1988). The revisionist view has not captured the religious community, but it has been articulated well enough to keep the debate going.

Institutional expression of the position of full acceptance has been varied. In

FIGURE 21.10
The Reverend Troy Perry founded the Universal Fellowship of Metropolitan Community Churches in 1968 as part of his coming out—the story of which is told in his book, The Lord Is My Shepherd and He Knows I'm Gay. *Providing a home for over 30,000 members, in 1983 the UFMCC applied for membership in the National Council of Churches, the major American organization of Christian bodies. After much debate, its application was placed on permanent hold.*

1963 a group of English Friends challenged traditional thinking about sexuality, including homosexuality, in *Toward a Quaker View of Sex*. Since that time, Quakers and Unitarians have been notable for their acceptance not only of the homosexual person but also of her or his sexual behavior, as long as it is conscientious. Within virtually all the mainline churches, gay caucuses and organizations have been formed in an effort to move fellow believers toward greater understanding and tolerance. A considerable number of lesbians and gays have simply left the established religious organizations and founded their own churches, synagogues, temples, covens, etc.— of which the largest is the Metropolitan Community Church (see Figure 21.10). On the other hand, many homosexual persons reject all forms of religion as oppressive and invalid, making religion as controversial within the gay community as homosexuality is within religious bodies.

Three issues in particular seem to provoke the most debate: ordination, the "marriage" of homosexual people, and AIDS. During the 1970s and early 1980s, most major American Protestant denominations debated the appropriateness of ordaining lesbians and gays to the ministry. The debates were emotional and explosive, and nearly all resulted in legislation forbidding homosexual ordination. The 1984 debate at the General Conference of the United Methodist Church was typical. That body required all clergy and candidates for ordination to observe "fidelity in marriage and celibacy in singleness" and added a specific prohibition against the ordination of "self-avowed practicing homosexuals" to its *Book of Discipline* (*The Christian Century*, 1984, **101**, 565). At present only the Unitarian-Universalist Association and the United Church of Christ seem willing to ordain gay people openly, and the lines are pretty clearly drawn in other religious groups.

Many who favor full acceptance of homosexual persons have argued for formal recognition of committed relationships along the lines of matrimony. The Metropolitan Community Church frequently performs such "holy unions," but so far no mainline church has officially approved of such a rite, although they do occur without permission of ecclesiastical authorities.

Finally, the religious community has shared fully in the public debate over how to respond to AIDS, and that controversy is unlikely to abate for some time (see below). Since the issue of homosexuality raises fundamental questions about the nature of creation, the purpose of sexuality, human relationships, and the will of God—all matters of deep concern to believers—the religious community will be wrestling with the issue for some time to come (Harper & Harper, 1988).

AIDS

Acquired immune deficiency syndrome raises, and will continue to raise, a host of complex and difficult ethical issues for individuals, religious communities, and the society as a whole. These issues are being debated in an atmosphere of fear, anger, and ignorance, which is focused on the fatality of the disease and the fact that the vast majority of sufferers in the United States are either homosexual males or intravenous drug users, two populations about which the society has profound ambivalence. Religious groups, like the rest of society, have struggled to develop effective ways of ministering to persons with HIV infection or AIDS, in view of the great need (Meyer, 1986; Shelp & Sunderland, 1987; Cherry & Mitulski, 1988). Responses have ranged from declaring AIDS to be God's punishment on sinners to actively organizing to minister to persons with AIDS and seeking to educate members of churches and synagogues about the disease and how they may respond compassionately (Godges, 1986; Countryman, 1987).

Broadly speaking, the major ethical conflicts center around the dignity and autonomy of the person, on the one hand, and the welfare of society on the other. This issue has both personal and public aspects. For the person who has AIDS or who is HIV-positive, a primary issue is confidentiality. Given that disclosure can lead to the loss of job, housing, friends, and family, such persons may well wonder if anyone has a right to know about their condition. On the other hand, many people argue that the public, or at least groups within society, have a right to know who is infected in order to be protected from them.

It has been proposed that children with HIV infection should not be allowed to attend public schools and that infected persons should be registered for the protection of emergency medical personnel, health care workers, coroners, and morticians. Several large populations, including military personnel, would-be immigrants, and some prisoners have been required to undergo mandatory testing for the AIDS virus. Many public health officials and AIDS researchers oppose such measures because they fear that persons at risk would be driven underground. They argue that the public health is best protected by voluntary testing and fairly stringent protection of confidentiality (Levine & Bermel, 1985; Levine & Bermel, 1986).

Ethically, a solid middle position would encourage persons in high-risk categories to be responsible for themselves by undergoing voluntary testing and practicing safe sex. This position would argue that infected persons have a right to confidentiality but should voluntarily disclose their status to anyone put at risk by it—notably health care personnel and sexual partners. For health care workers, there is the personal ethical problem of whether to treat persons who are HIV-positive. It is probable that there is an ethical obligation to treat, but that there is also an obligation to take appropriate precautions (Zuger, 1987).

FIGURE 21.11
*Pope John Paul II
embraces 5-year-old
Brendan O'Rourke, a San
Francisco AIDS patient
who contracted the disease
from a blood transfusion.*

Many of the ethical issues of public policy revolve around the very high cost of the disease—both treating its victims and seeking a medical solution. Who should pay this cost? Insurance companies have sought ways in which to deny life and health coverage to persons in high-risk groups. People with AIDS often cannot work and so lose job-related insurance benefits. Who should pay for their care—hospitals, cities, states, the federal government? Specialized services and facilities—such as home care and hospices—are needed. Who is responsible for providing them? Given limited funds available for research, what should the focus of that research be? Should resources be concentrated on prevention through a vaccine or on treatment of those who already have the disease? Who should develop treatments, public agencies or private drug companies? And again, who will pay?

Public education for prevention, generally regarded as the only really effective response at present, raises some ethical problems, particularly given public hostility toward the high-risk groups (Kayal, 1985). What kind of education is appropriate? At what age should it begin? How graphic should it be? Does government advocacy of "safe sex" mean endorsement of sexual practices abhorrent to many Americans? Because of its stand on birth control, the Roman Catholic Church absolutely opposes the use of condoms. Should Catholics have to support government programs to make them generally available? Some public health officials, alarmed by the rapid spread of AIDS among intravenous drug users, suggest the reversal of a long-time policy of fighting drug abuse by restricting the availability of syringes. They argue that if addicts could readily obtain clean needles, they would not have to share and risk infection. However, this strategy outrages the sensibilities of many who believe that drug addiction is a grave moral and social evil.

Most of the choices that must be made in dealing with AIDS are unappealing, expensive, or both. For the rest of the century, American society will be challenged very deeply to maintain its own values and to deal compassionately and effectively with what many have described as the greatest health crisis since the bubonic plague.

TECHNOLOGY AND SEXUAL ETHICS

A major challenge to ethicists in the late twentieth century is the rapid development of technologies that raise new moral issues before the old ones have been resolved, in matters of human sexuality as in anything else. We have already discussed several issues in which technology has played a major role. Although sex outside of marriage is hardly a problem unique to our time, the availability of reliable birth control techniques has probably increased the incidence of premarital and extramarital sex. The fact that millions of people can enjoy vigorous sex lives without ever conceiving children, unless they choose to, has markedly changed the basic moral climate.

The issue of abortion is also intensified by technological advances of the past few decades and will only get more complicated in the future. The developing medical science of neonatology means that fetuses are viable outside the uterus earlier and earlier. Some late-pregnancy abortions produce a fetus that can be kept alive, and hospital staffs are faced with agonizing questions about what should be done in such cases. Traditional ethics suggest that such unwanted children be kept alive, yet this can be incredibly costly and the children are often severely handicapped. Hospitals may find it prudent to limit, or even forbid, second-trimester abortions to deal with the issue (Callahan, 1986).

Another complex of ethical issues arises out of the host of new reproductive technologies which enable people to conceive children outside of the "normal" process of sexual intercourse in what is often called "collaborative parenting." These include artificial insemination, either by husband or donor (AIH or AID), in vitro fertilization (IVF), embryo transfer, and surrogate motherhood.

For many ethicists, these technologies can be tentatively approved because they enable otherwise infertile people to have children with at least one partner's genes (Robertson, 1983). Certainly, having children of one's own has had a very high value for most people throughout history and barrenness has been seen as a curse in most cultures. On the other hand, these technologies bring with them a number of ethical problems.

Chief among the objections to these techniques is that they involve "playing God." That is, they exercise human control over things best left up to nature and raise serious problems of who will decide how they are to be used. It is also argued that separating conception from marital intercourse may denigrate human dignity, confuse the parenthood of children, and have a negative effect on the family. Another concern is the possibility of the exploitation of others, particularly in the case of surrogacy. Some ethicists, especially those taking a feminist perspective, fear that rich couples will "rent wombs" or "buy babies" from low-income women. Many question the morality of conceiving and/or carrying a child one never intends to raise. Others wonder if AID and IVF might not be used to select the sex of a child or predetermine other characteristics, ushering in a "Brave New World" that is less than human (Krimmel, 1983; McDowell, 1983; Schneider, 1985; Boyd, Callaghan, & Shotter, 1986).

Two religious communities have condemned most or all of these technologies, though on somewhat different grounds. Orthodox Judaism might permit the use of techniques which would allow an otherwise infertile couple to have a child if both egg and sperm come from the couple, e.g., in AIH or IVF with implantation in the wife's uterus. On the other hand, any technique involving a third party is condemned as being de facto adultery and confusing the parentage of the child (Rosner, 1983; Green, 1984). The Roman Catholic position was given very clear statement in a 1987 Vatican "Instruction on Respect for Human Life in Its Origin and on the Dignity of Procreation." The statement admitted as an open moral question fertility techniques which remained within the woman's body using her husband's sperm not collected by masturbation. Otherwise all techniques such as AID, IVF, and surrogacy were unequivocally condemned as an assault on the dignity of the embryo (in Catholic theology a human person) and on the sanctity of marriage as the only licit means of procreation (Congregation for the Doctrine of the Faith, 1987).

There is no way to stop the development of technology, or its speed, and it would not be desirable. Nonetheless, it is important to recognize that decisions about human life and reproduction ought not to be made on purely scientific grounds. By definition, they have the deepest moral implications, and these implications must be adequately addressed if the essential values of human life are to be preserved.

TOWARD AN ETHICS OF *HUMAN* SEXUALITY

The combined forces of the sexual revolution and the New Morality have attacked the traditional Judeo-Christian sexual ethic as narrow and repressive. This may be true, but it has not yet been proved to everyone's satisfaction that the alternatives proposed are a real improvement upon the Old Morality. Whether the debate will be resolved, and how, remains to be seen. Some of the arguments and possibilities are considered below.

The Old Morality tends to be ascetic and legalistic and, at its worst, reduces ethical behavior to following a series of rules. Its asceticism may downgrade the goodness of human sexuality and negate the very real joys of physical pleasure. A healthy personality needs to integrate the physical side of life and affirm it, and this kind of self-acceptance may be made more difficult by the Old Morality. Further, if morality is simply a matter of applying universal rules, there is no real choice, and human freedom is seriously undermined. In short, opponents of the Old Morality might argue, this approach diminishes the full nature of humanity and impoverishes human life. On the other hand, the traditional approach deserves a few kind words as well. For one thing, with the traditional morality people almost always know where they stand. Right and wrong and good and bad are clearly, if somewhat inflexibly, spelled out. Moreover, asceticism does witness to the fact that the human is more than merely the body.

The New Morality, with its situational approach and tendencies toward hedonism, has its own share of pluses and minuses. It affirms quite positively the physical and sexual side of human nature as an integral part of the individual. This is helpful, but if it is pushed too far, it can also leave people under no control and thus less than fully human. Situation ethics quite properly calls for an evaluation of every ethical decision on the basis of the concrete aspects of the personalities involved and the context of the decision. Its broad principles of love, respect, and interpersonal responsibility are sound, but it can be argued that situationism does not take sufficiently into account the problem of human selfishness. Dishonesty about our real motives may blind us to the actual effects of our actions, however sincere we profess to be. Further, situationism is a much less certain guide than the older approach, since so many situations are ambiguous.

There is a middle way between these two extremes, one that may prove to be the synthesis that sexual ethics seems to be searching for. This approach would use the traditional principles (laws) as guidelines for actions while insisting that they must be applied in concrete situations and occasionally reworked to conform to changes in the human situation. This approach differs from the Old Morality by stating that ethical principles must be flexible, and it differs from the New Morality by holding that departures from tradition must be based on very strong evidence that the old rules do not apply. For those adopting this position, healthy decision-making functions in the tensions between the rigid "thou shalt not" of the legalist and the "do your own thing" of the situationist.

In the specific case of sexual ethics, such a middle-of-the-road approach would affirm the goodness of human sexuality but insist that sexual behavior needs to be responsible, and based on reason, experience, and conscience. It would accept sexuality as a vital part of human personality but not the sum total of who we are. Such an approach to sexual ethics would indeed be consistent with what was shown earlier in this chapter to be the heart of the Judeo-Christian tradition, shorn of some of its rigidity and distrust of sexuality. If, as is sometimes claimed, the sexual revolution is over, and there is a movement toward relationship and commitment, this might prove to be just the sexual morality that people in our time are looking for.

Summary

It is important to study religion and ethics in conjunction with human sexuality because they frequently provide the framework within which people judge the rightness or wrongness of sexual activity. They give rise to attitudes that influence the way members of a society regard sexuality, and they are therefore powerful influences on behavior. Religion and ethics may be hedonistic (pleasure oriented) or ascetic (emphasizing self-discipline). They may be legalistic (operating by rules) or situational (making decision in concrete situations, with few rules).

In the great ethical traditions, the Greeks tended toward a philosophical asceticism, while ancient Judaism had a positive, though legalistic, view of sexuality. Christian sources are ambivalent about sexuality, with Jesus saying little on the subject and with St. Paul, influenced by the immorality of Roman culture and his expectation of the end of the world, being somewhat negative. Later, Christianity became much more ascetic; this is reflected in the writings of Augustine and Thomas Aquinas, who also placed Catholic moral theology in the natural-law mold. The Protestant Reformation abolished clerical celibacy and opened to door to greater individual freedom in ethics. Today, technological development and new forms of biblical scholarship have led to a wide variety of positions on issues of sexual ethics.

Humanistic ethics rejects external authority, replacing it with a person-centered approach to ethics. A variety of approaches to sexuality can be found in Islam, Hinduism, and Buddhism.

Six ethical issues involving human sexuality have provoked lively debate recently. Although the Western ethical tradition opposes sex outside marriage, some liberals are open to sex among the unmarried under certain conditions. Contraception is opposed by Roman Catholicism and Orthodox Judaism on scriptural and natural-law grounds, but it is positively valued by other groups. Abortion provokes a very emotional argument, with positions ranging from condemnation on the grounds that it is murder to a view that asserts the moral right of women to control their own bodies. Although the traditional view condemns homosexuality absolutely, there is some movement toward either a qualified approval of at least civil rights for gay people or a more complete acceptance of their lifestyle. The spread of AIDS poses serious ethical problems, which involve a balancing of individual needs with the welfare of society. Developments in the technology of human reproduction are creating complex ethical issues with few clear norms.

A possible resolution of the conflict between the Old Morality and the New Morality involves an ethics of *human* sexuality, neither hedonistic nor rigidly ascetic, which takes seriously the historical tradition of ethical thinking while insisting that decisions be made on the basis of the specific situation.

Review Questions

1. The ethics of the Old Morality tend to be _____, and those of the New Morality are often called _____.

2. Jewish teaching, as found in the Old Testament, is uniformly negative about sex. True or false?

3. Much Christian teaching, from the Apostle Paul through the Middle Ages, favored _____ over marriage for ordinary Christians, and required it for the clergy.

4. Engagement in sexual intercourse and family life at one time in life and extreme asceticism at others is characteristic of the _____ religion.

5. A political and religious position found in contemporary society that opposes abortion, women's liberation, and gay rights is often called _____.

6. Roman Catholicism opposes all sexual intercourse outside of marriage on the basis of _____ law.

7. Abortion is uniformly condemned by all religious groups in the United States. True or false?

8. Areas of debate on homosexuality in many religious groups center on the issues of _____, _____, and _____.

9. Ethical debate over AIDS includes discussion about whether an individual who is HIV-positive should be able to keep that information _____.

10. Which of the following reproductive technologies has been approved for use by Roman Catholics: AID, IVF, surrogacy?

(The answers to all review questions are at the end of the book, beginning on page 731.)

Questions for Thought, Discussion, and Debate

1. If you are a member of a religious group, investigate your group's beliefs on the issues discussed in this chapter (sex outside marriage, contraception, abortion, homosexuality, AIDS, and technology). Do you agree with those positions? If you are not a member of a religious group, see if you can state a view of sexual ethics that is consistent with your philosophy of life.

2. Seek out a person, group, or written material which takes the opposite of your position on abortion and carefully consider those arguments. What effect does this have on your views?

Suggestions for Further Reading

Boswell, John. (1980). *Christianity, social tolerance, and homosexuality*. Chicago: University of Chicago Press. A very sophisticated reassessment of Christian attitudes toward gays and their place in Western society through the Middle Ages.

Callahan, Sidney, & Callahan, Daniel. (1984). *Abortion: Understanding differences*. New York: Plenum Press. A thought-provoking collection of essays from all viewpoints on this significant controversy.

Countryman, L. William (1988). *Dirt, greed, and sex: Sexual ethics in the New Testament and their implications for today*. This seminary professor carefully examines biblical statements about sexuality to gain a better understanding of their meaning and their relevance today.

Genovesi, Vincent J. (1987). *In pursuit of love: Catholic morality and human sex-

uality. Wilmington, DE: Michael Glazier. Well-written, scholarly work treating the whole field from the mainline Roman Catholic point of view.

Nelson, James B. (1978). *Embodiment: An approach to sexuality and Christian theology*. Minneapolis: Augsburg. Well-written, scholarly work treating the whole field from the mainline Protestant point of view.

Parrinder, Geoffrey. (1980). *Sex in the world's religions*. New York: Oxford University Press. A superb and concise treatment of the variety of religious approaches to human sexuality. The best short book in the field.

22

Sex and the Law

Chapter Highlights

The AIDS epidemic challenges the law to face up to our irrational as well as our rational selves; to structure procedures and fashion rules that, simultaneously, give vent to our fears and life to our aspirations.

One day in the late 1960s, I stood chatting on a Berkeley street corner with David and Ken, who are gay. David leered at his companion and announced in mock conspiratorial tones, "We're going to commit an illegal act." And they were. And so, that day, were a great many other people—gay and straight, male and female, single and married. All would be violating one or another of various state laws telling them, in effect, what they might do, how, where, and with whom. The average citizen might be very surprised by what the law has, over the years and even today, seen fit to regulate in this most private act. In 1965, legal scholar Ralph Slovenko concluded in a massive study that "Americans commonly and regularly engage in sexual practices which are technically forbidden by law" (1965, p. 5). The past generation has seen fast-moving and remarkable change in sex laws, and today fewer Americans probably commit crime in the bedroom. Nonetheless, the number of laws regulating sexual behavior is still substantial. This chapter will consider why there are such laws, what sorts of behaviors are affected, how these laws are enforced, how they are changing, and what the future prospects for sex-law reform might be.

WHY ARE THERE SEX LAWS?

To begin, we might well ask why there are laws regulating sexual conduct in the first place. This actually is a very modern question, for throughout most of Western history such laws were taken for granted. Sexual legislation is quite ancient, dating

* *Source:* Harlon L. Dalton, Scott Burris, & the Yale AIDS Project (1987). *AIDS and the law.* New Haven: Yale University Press.

Major contributions to this chapter were made by Clark Hyde, M. Div., S.T.M.

back certainly to the time of the Old Testament (see Chapter 21). Since then, in countries where the Judeo-Christian tradition is influential, attempts to regulate morals have been the rule. Today we are likely to regard sex as a private matter, of concern only to those involved. However, historically it has been seen as a matter that very much affects society and therefore as a fit subject for law. Most societies regulate sexual behavior, both by custom and by law.

Even today, certain kinds of sex laws are probably legitimate and necessary. Stanford University law professor Herbert Packer argues that the following might be rationally included in law: protection "against force and equivalent means of coercion to secure sexual gratification," "protection of the immature against sexual exploitation," and, although this is somewhat problematic, "the prevention of conduct that gives offense or is likely to give offense to innocent bystanders" (1968, p. 306). It sems obvious that people ought to be free from sexual assault and coercion and that children should not be sexually exploited; individual rights and the interests of society are here in agreement.

However, sex laws have been designed for other purposes which may be more open to question. Historically, the rationale was to preserve the family as the principal unit of the social order by protecting its integrity from, for example, adultery or desertion of a spouse. Sex laws also seek to ensure children of a supportive family by prohibiting conduct such as **fornication,** which is likely to result in out-of-wedlock births. Changing social conditions may call for revision of these statutes, but the principles behind them are understandable.

There is yet another realm of motivation behind sex laws which is highly problematic, and that is the protection of society's morals. However, this tends to become a matter of religion, and the constitutional separation of church and state in the United States is designed to prevent one religious group from enforcing its tenets on others. The concern for public morality results in laws against nonprocreative sex, for reasons outlined in Chapter 21. Thus there have been laws against homosexual acts, bestiality, and contraception. Religious beliefs as to what is "unnatural," "immoral," or "sinful" have found expression in law, as it was often held that the state had a duty to uphold religion as a pillar of civilized society, using the law to make people good. The example of England is instructive, since American law derives so extensively from English law. Church and state in England have historically been seen as identical, and the state had an obligation to protect the interests of the Church. A secular government not tied to the church, such as the United States, was unthinkable, and an individual's morals were a matter of public concern. Sin and crime have often been confused in the public mind, and this confusion has found its way into law (Parker, 1983; Katz, 1982).

It can be argued that another principal source of sex laws is *sexism*, which is deeply rooted in Western culture. One scholar has suggested that the history of the regulation of sexual activity could as well be called the history of the double standard. He goes on to note that:

> The law of marriage and the law controlling sexual expression are really the same question looked at from different angles. Women have always been looked upon as the property of men—whether fathers or husbands. Marriage has frequently in history been a commercial transaction or a way in which the fabric of society could be maintained. The male insistence on chastity was simply an attempt to regulate social relations, to cement dynasties, to ensure the orderly succession of property (particularly real property) and to perpetuate male domination. (Parker, 1983, p. 190)

It is probably not coincidental that the movement for sex-law reform has gone hand in hand with the movement for the liberation of women.

Fornication: Sex between two unmarried persons.

The American tradition of moralism in politics, the prudery of the Victorian period (during which much of the American legal system came into being), and the zealousness of such individuals as Anthony Comstock (see Focus 22.1) combined to provide the United States with an enormous amount of sexual legislation. This legislation refects a great deal of ambiguity in our attitudes toward sex, which is perhaps unsurprising in such a varied population. It also contrasts with other societies in which the trend since 1800 has been away from such laws. According to one authority, "The United States apparently has more laws on the subject than all of the European countries combined" (Slovenko, 1965, p. 9).[1] The U.S. legal tradition assumes both the right of the state to enforce morals and a consensus in society as to which morals are to be enforced. However, contemporary citizens have come to question the legitimacy of government interference in what they regard as their private affairs. This tension has led to a widespread demand for a radical overhaul of laws that regulate sexual conduct. It all makes for a fascinating, if frustrating, field of study, for law has a way of reflecting the ambiguities and conflicts of society.

WHAT KINDS OF SEX LAWS ARE THERE?

Cataloging the laws pertaining to sexual conduct would be a difficult project. It is possible that no one really knows how many such laws there are, given the large number of jurisdictions in the American legal system. When one considers federal law, the Uniform Code of Military Justice, state laws, municipal codes, county ordinances, and so on, the magnitude of the problem becomes clear. In addition to *criminal* law, portions of civil law that may penalize certain sexual behaviors—such as licensing for professions, personnel rules for government employees, and immigration regulations—must also be considered. Further, these laws are changing all the time, and any list would be obsolete before it went to press. Therefore, what is offered here is not so much a statistical summary of specific sex laws as a look at the *kinds* of laws that are, or have been, on the statute books.[2] The subheadings, all of which contain the word "crime," have been chosen with care, as a reminder that we are discussing legal offenses which can carry with them the penalty of going to jail, loss of reputation, monetary fines, or all of these. However quaint and amusing some of these laws may seem, they are a serious matter.

Crimes of Exploitation and Force

Recalling our earlier discussion about the kinds of laws that seem to make sense in a pluralistic society, let us begin with those seeking to prevent the use of force or exploitation in sexual relations—chiefly laws against rape and sexual relations with the young. In the past two decades, there has been a movement toward seeing such crimes not so much as sex crimes but as crimes of violence and victimization, with laws being revised to accommodte this different understanding and to protect the victims (see Chapter 17).

---

[1] For a good comparison with another English-based North American legal system, see the history of Canadian sex laws (Parker, 1983).

[2] A general discussion of the kinds of laws may be found in MacNamara & Sagarin (1977). State-by-state listings appear in Bernard et al. (1985), Boggan et al. (1983), Mueller (1980), and Rivera (1979).

Anthony Comstock:
Crusader Against Vice

In any discussion of laws regulating sexual behavior, the name of Anthony Comstock looms large. His zeal for moral reform is reflected in the use of the term "Comstock laws" for the kinds of restrictive statutes considered here.

Comstock was born in Connecticut in 1844 and was reared as a strict Puritan Congregationalist; he had a well-developed sense of his own sinfulness—and of others' as well. He served in the Union Army during the Civil War and worked as a dry-goods salesperson. While still a young man, he became very active in the Young Men's Christian Association, seeking the arrest and conviction of dealers in pornography. He helped found the Committee for the Suppression of Vice within the YMCA. This later became an independent society, as his efforts gained him national attention.

Comstock's most noteworthy success was probably a comprehensive antiobscenity bill which passed the U.S. Congress in 1873. The law prohibited the mailing of obscene matter within the United States, as well as advertisements for obscenity, which included matter "for the prevention of conception." Comstock initiated the passage of a similar law in New York, making it illegal to give contraceptive information verbally, and many other states followed suit. At the same time, Comstock received an appointment as a special agent of the U.S. Post Office, and this gave him the authority personally to enforce the Comstock Law. He did, with a vengeance, claiming at the end of his career to have been personally responsible for the jailing of over 3600 offenders against public decency.

Comstock's energies were directed not only against pornography but also against abortionists, fraudulent advertisers and sellers of quack medicines, lotteries, saloonkeepers, artists who painted nude subjects, and advocates of free love. Among the objects of his wrath were many of the most famous advocates of unpopular opinions of his day. He carried on a crusade against women's movement pioneers Victoria Woodhull and her sister Tennessee Claflin; he helped jail William Sanger, husband of Margaret Sanger, the birth control crusader; he attacked Robert Ingersoll, the atheist; and he tried to prevent the New York production of George Bernard Shaw's play about a prostitute, *Mrs. Warren's Profession*. For the last of these efforts, Shaw rewarded him by coining the word "Comstockery."

Anthony Comstock was a controversial figure during his own lifetime and has often been blamed for all legislation reflecting his views. However, it is important to understand that he had a great deal of support from the public, without which he could not have jailed his 3600 miscreants. He will probably go down in history as a symbol of the effort to make people moral by legislation. He died in 1915 shortly after representing the United States at an International Purity Congress.

Anthony Comstock may be long dead, but comstockery has always been a feature of American society and seems to have made a comeback in the 1980s and 1990s. He might very well be a patron saint for the Moral Majority.

Source: Heywood Broun & Margaret Leech (1927). *Anthony Comstock: Roundsman of the Lord*. New York: Boni.

For generations, the classical definition of (forcible) rape was:

Rape: In the broadest sense, sexual intercourse when one of the parties is unwilling.

> The act of sexual intercourse with a female person not the wife of, or judicially separated from bed and board from, the offender, committed without her lawful consent. Emission is not necessary; and any sexual penetration, however slight, is sufficient to accomplish the crime. (Slovenko, 1965, p. 48)

In trials under this definition, the principal issue was the consent of the victim, and many states allowed the victim's prior sexual activities to be considered as evidence of her consent, in effect putting the victim on trial. The Model Penal Code of the American Law Institute, attempting to deal with some of the problems of the older definition, proposed this law:

> Rape. A male who has sexual intercourse with a female not his wife is guilty of rape if: (a) he compels her to submit by force or by threat of imminent death, serious bodily injury, extreme pain or kidnapping, to be inflicted on anyone; or (b) he has substantially impaired her power to appraise or control her conduct by administering or employing without her knowledge drugs, intoxicants or other means for the purpose of generating compliance; or (c) the female is unconscious; or (d) the female is less than ten years old. Rape is a felony of the second degree unless (i) in the course thereof the actor inflicts serious bodily injury upon anyone, or (ii) the victim was not a voluntary social companion of the actor upon the occasion of the crime and had not previously permitted him sexual liberties, in which cases the offense is a felony of the first degree. Sexual intercourse includes intercourse per os or per anum [in the mouth or rectum], with some penetration however slight; emission is not required. (MacNamara & Sagarin, 1977, p. 31).

Even by this statute, only a woman can be the victim of a rape and a husband cannot be tried for raping his wife, however unwilling she may be. Some states, however, have revised their laws so that a husband can be tried for raping his wife (Mueller, 1980). The 1979 Rideout case in Oregon was the first prosecution under such a law, although the husband was acquitted. Some states have also revised the language of their statutes to eliminate the word rape, choosing instead "criminal sexual assault," which permits prosecution of men for raping men and even of women for raping men (Searles & Berger, 1987; Jaffe & Becker, 1984).

Laws that seek to prevent the sexual exploitation of children and young people are complicated by the issues of consent, coercion, and immaturity, all of which are rather difficult to define. Most states have laws against *statutory rape,* or carnal knowledge of a juvenile. These laws presume that all intercourse by an adult male (normally one over 17 or 18) with any female under a certain age is, by definition, illicit because she cannot give genuine consent. That age, the "age of consent," varies from state to state, ranging between 12 and 18. Many states have laws that also include a reference to the difference in ages between the male and the female, on the assumption that there is a difference in criminality between a 16-year-old girl having intercourse with her 18-year-old boyfriend and with a man in his thirties or forties (MacNamara & Sagarin, 1977; Mueller, 1980).

There are a great variety of laws against the *sexual abuse of children,* called variously child molestation, carnal abuse of a child, or impairing the morals of a child. These general terms usually cover all sexual contact between adult and child, heterosexual and homosexual, and can include the use of sexual language, exhibitionism, showing pornography to a child, having a child witness intercourse, or taking a child to a brothel or gay bar (MacNamara & Sagarin, 1977). Such statutes attempt to protect children, a reasonable goal, but are often so vague as either to be ineffective or to criminalize innocuous behavior. With the great increase recently in public awareness of the extent of child sexual abuse, it is likely that more precise and effective laws will be developed.

Incest: Sexual relations between persons closely related to each other.

Finally, every state includes laws against **incest** in its penal code. Although incestuous sexual relations can take place between adults, the law seems far more concerned where children are involved. The nearly universal taboo against incest seems to have as its purpose the guarantee to children that the home will be a place where they can be free from sexual pressure. In many states, the closer the relationship, the more severe the penalties against incest (Mueller, 1980). Incest laws also seek to prevent the alleged genetic problems of inbreeding. Again, greater public awareness of the extent of incest (see Chapter 17) is likely to lead to a reexamination of laws on the subject.

Criminal Consensual Acts

Cohabitation: Unmarried persons living together (with sexual relations assumed).

Adultery: Intercourse between persons, at least one of whom is married to someone else.

Miscegenation: Sex between members of different races.

Sodomy: From the alleged homosexuality of the men of Sodom in the Bible, homosexual acts, often expanded to include all "unnatural" sexual acts, especially oral or anal sex.

Bestiality: Sex with animals.

Necrophilia: Sexual acts with a dead person.

Although it is not hard to see the logic of laws against force and exploitation of the young, many people are amazed to discover the number of sexual acts forbidden to consenting adults. These laws have been justified on the grounds of the prevention of illegitimacy, the preservation of the family, the promotion of public health, and the enforcement of morality (Bernard et al., 1985). With respect to heterosexuals, there are a number of laws against fornication, **cohabitation,** and **adultery.** As of 1985, fornication was illegal in 13 states and the District of Columbia; cohabitation was outlawed in 13. Adultery, in addition to being grounds for divorce in all jurisdictions, was a crime in 23 states and the District of Columbia. It is also disconcerting to realize that until 1967, when the Supreme Court invalidated them in the case of *Loving v. Virginia,* there were laws against **miscegenation,** whether the parties were married or not, in 25 states, not all of them in the Deep South.

Besides specifying with whom one might have sex, laws have also attempted to regulate what acts are permissible, even in the case of a legally married couple. Until quite recently, virtually all states had laws prohibiting **sodomy,** or "crimes against nature."[3] These laws attempt to prohibit "unnatural" sex acts, even between consenting adults. Sodomy laws are many and varied, and they differ widely in terms of specificity, acts prohibited, and the severity of the penalties. They prohibit such things as oral-genital and anal-genital acts, as well as **bestiality** and, in some jurisdictions, **necrophilia.**

One cogent example is the Georgia statute, which defines sodomy as "any act involving the mouth or anus of one person, and the sex organs of another." It is a felony and is punishable by not less than 1 year, or more than 20 years, in jail (Boggan et al., 1983, p. 140). This statute was upheld by the U.S. Supreme Court in the 1986 case of *Bowers v. Hardwick,* in which the Court affirmed the right of states to enact such statutes. Sodomy laws are on the books in 25 states and the District of Columbia.

Although in theory most sodomy laws are supposed to prohibit "unnatural acts" between any two persons, when they are enforced, which is not very often, the prosecution is almost invariably against gay people. Sodomy laws are only the tip of the iceberg in a legal structure of discrimination against homosexual persons (Rivera, 1981–1982; Rivera, 1979; Boggan et al., 1983). In most places gay persons may be denied private employment. However, the federal civil service regulations

---

[3] Beginning with Illinois in 1961, roughly half the states have decriminalized consensual sodomy, either by direct repeal or through a revision of the criminal code, most in the last two decades (Boggan et al., 1983; Rivera, 1979). For a complete list of the remaining laws and their penalties, see Boggan et al. (1983).

Table 22.1
Results of a Well-Sampled Poll on Americans' Attitudes Toward Gay Rights

	Percentage		
	Yes	No	Not Sure
1. Do you think homosexual couples should be legally allowed to inherit each other's property?	65	27	8
2. Do you think homosexual couples shoud be permitted to receive medical- and life-insurance benefits from a partner's policies?	54	37	9
3. Do you think marriages between homosexual couples should be recognized by the law?	23	69	8
4. Do you think homosexual couples should be legally permitted to adopt children?	17	75	8

Source: A telephone poll of 1000 adult Americans, October 1989, reported in *Time*, November 20, 1989.

forbid such discrimination in public employment, and some state governors have forbidden sexual orientation discrimination by executive order. Gays are still denied security clearances and the right to serve in the military. Many professional and occupational licensing requirements have "good character" or morality clauses which seem to invite discrimination. For example, a number of public school teachers have been dismissed when their homosexuality became known. No right to gay marriage is supported by statute, and gay relationships have very little legal support. This means that homosexual couples cannot inherit each other's property, although a well-sampled poll indicates that the majority of Americans support this right to inheritance (see Table 22.1). The homosexuality of a parent is a serious disadvantage in child custody proceedings. Homosexual persons may be denied entry to the United States or deported despite long residence. Surveying this landscape, legal scholar Rhonda Rivera documented

> systematic and pervasive discrimination against homosexual individuals in our courts. . . . Homosexuals are penalized in all aspects of their lives because of their sexual preference. They lose their jobs, their children, and numerous other precious rights as a result of many current judicial policies. (Rivera, 1979, p. 947)

With this in mind, gay activists have pursued a variety of strategies aimed at overcoming discrimination. They had hoped that the Supreme Court would eventually expand the "right of privacy" (discussed below) to include consensual sodomy and even homosexuality as a lifestyle. The decision in *Bowers v. Hardwick* seems to close that door for the present (Leading Cases, 1986). Another judicial approach would be to seek to define sexual orientation as a "suspect classification" protected from discrimination under the "equal protection of the laws" clause of the Fourteenth Amendment. However, the courts have shown very little inclination to move in that direction. Some states and municipalities have passed laws and ordinances forbidding

FIGURE 22.1
*Gays and the law. (a) This
lesbian/gay rights march in
San Francisco is one of
many to protest laws
criminalizing homosexual
acts. (b) President Clinton
meets with General Colin
Powell in 1993 over the
ban on gays in the military.*

(a)

(b)

discrimination on the basis of sexual orientation, notably in housing and employment. These laws have withstood court tests but are often unpopular and subject to repeal by referendum. And in 1990 the Supreme Court upheld the military's right to ban lesbians and gays from the armed forces. Particularly with public sentiment inflamed by the AIDS crisis, significant increases in legal protection for gays seem unlikely at this time (Conkle, 1986; Notes, 1987), although the more tolerant attitudes expressed in President Clinton's administration may have an impact.

Crimes Against Good Taste

Exhibitionism: Showing one's genitals to passersby; indecent exposure.

Voyeurism: Viewing people engaged in sexual activity.

Another broad category of sex offenses can be viewed as crimes against community standards of good taste and delicacy. In this company we find laws against exhibitionism, voyeurism, solicitation, disorderly conduct, being a public nuisance, and "general lewdness." These statutes are by and large quite vague and punish acts which are offensive, or *likely* to be offensive, to someone. Over half the states have such laws, and they carry penalties of from 30 days to 5 years in jail, with fines of $5 to $5000 (Boggan et al., 1983). As will be seen below, unequal enforcement of these laws, their vagueness, and the difference between what is offensive and what is actually criminal make these statutes suspect.

Crimes Against Reproduction

As was noted in Focus 22.1, the Comstock laws included a ban on the giving of information concerning the prevention of conception. Comstock apparently regarded contraception and abortion as identical. These issues will be discussed more fully in the section on the right to privacy, below; here it will be mentioned only that until 1973 abortion was prohibited or severely limited in all jurisdictions, and contraception was prohibited in many. These laws are clear examples of the values of another day enshrined in statute books. They arise from an understanding of reproduction as the only legitimate purpose of sex and a belief in the necessity of vigorous propagation of the species. Such laws were overturned by Supreme Court action, but continuing agitation, at least in the case of abortion, ensures that public debate will continue for some time.

Criminal Commercial Sex

The law has also deemed it illegal to make money from sex, at least in certain circumstances. It is not illegal to sell products with subtle promises of sexual fulfillment, but it is illegal actually to provide such fulfillment, either in direct form (that is, prostitution) or on paper, as in pornography. Both will be treated in greater detail below; first, however, the kinds of laws on these subjects should be noted.

Prostitution is the exchange of sex for money or other payment such as drugs. Except in Nevada, where counties may allow it, prostitution is illegal in every jurisdiction in the United States, though not in many other countries. The law also forbids activities related to it, such as solicitation, pandering (pimping, procuring), renting premises for prostitution, and enticing minors into prostitution (Perry, 1980). Laws against vagrancy and loitering are also used against prostitutes. However, the prostitute's client is almost never charged or chargeable with a crime. These laws have proved very difficult to enforce, and so the "oldest profession" goes on unabated.

Obscenity: That which is offensive to decency or modesty, or calculated to arouse sexual excitement or lust.

Obscenity will be discussed in more detail in a later section. Suffice it to say here that in most jurisdictions it is a crime to sell material or to present a play, film, or other live performance which is "obscene." That much is fairly simple, although many civil libertarians attack censorship as an infringement on freedom of the press. The real problem comes in deciding *what* exactly is obscene and how that will be determined without doing violence to the First Amendment. So far, no satisfactory answer has been found. Obscenity laws seem to have a twofold basis. First, they attempt to prevent the corruption of morals by materials that incite sexual thoughts and desires. Second, they attempt to ensure that no one will profit by the production and distribution of such materials. Whether either can be done, or is worth doing, is a question that will be taken up in a later section.

SEX-LAW ENFORCEMENT

From the foregoing, it is clear that the law has intruded into areas that the reader may well have thought were his or her own business. We can now ask: How are sex

FIGURE 22.2
The oldest profession. A prostitute sets up an appointment.

laws enforced? The answer is simple: With *great* inconsistency. One authority estimated that "the enforcement rate of private consensual sex offenders must show incredibly heavy odds against arrest—perhaps one in ten million" (Packer, 1968, p. 304). The contrast between the number and severity of the laws themselves and the infrequency and capriciousness of their enforcement reflects the ambiguity of society's attitude toward the whole subject.

This contrast leads to serious abuses and to demands for radical reform of sex laws. A summary of the arguments for reform will be presented later in this chapter. First, however, it should be noted that as long as the laws are on the books, the *threat* of prosecution, or even of arrest, can exact a great penalty from the "offender." Loss of job, reputation, friendship, family, and so on, can result from the sporadic enforcement of sex laws. For persons engaging in the prohibited acts, especially gay and lesbian persons, the threat of blackmail is ever present. Of course, for those actually convicted on "morals charges," the situation is even worse. That individuals should be subjected to such punishments for private acts is questionable.

Second, the uneven enforcement of sex laws may have a very bad effect on law enforcement generally. It invites arbitrary and unfair behavior and abuse of authority by police and prosecutors, and it may even lead them to corruption and extortion. One serious abuse is entrapment, in which an undercover police agent, posing, for example, as a homosexual or a prostitute's potential client, actually solicits the commission of a crime. Since a sexual act between consenting parties means that there is no one to report the act to the authorities, undercover agents must create the crime in order to achieve an arrest for it. Such entrapment hardly leads to respect for the law. Moreover, the knowledge that sex laws are violated with impunity creates a general disrespect for the law, particularly among those who know that they are, strictly speaking, "criminals" under it. If nothing else, the failure of Prohibition ought to demonstrate that outlawing activities of which a substantial proportion of the population approves is bad public policy. It may well be said that more violations of the public good result from the enforcement of sex laws than from the acts they seek to prevent.[4] Keeping this in mind, let us turn to the prospects for the future.

TRENDS IN SEX-LAW REFORM

It has been difficult to specify the number and details of certain types of sex laws because change is very rapid in this area. My distaste for these attempts to regulate human behavior leads me to call this "reform," although many in our society would contend that the change is for the worse. Since sex is a topic heavily laden with values, such reform is not likely to be accomplished without a good deal of conflict. This makes it difficult to predict either the precise directions of change or its speed. However, some important legal principles are used to bring about changes in sex laws; these trends in reform are discussed below.

Early Efforts at Sex-Law Reform

In recent years, there have been two landmark efforts to get oppressive sexual legislation off the statute books—one English and one American. In 1954, largely at the instigation of the Moral Welfare Council of the Church of England, a blue-ribbon Committee on Homosexual Offenses and Prostitution was appointed to advise Parliament on possible reform of the laws in these two areas. After much careful research and deliberation, in 1957 the committee issued its report, commonly known by the name of its chair, J. F. Wolfenden. The recommendations were rather startling, most notably that "homosexual behavior between consenting adults in private be no longer a criminal offense" and that prostitution be decriminalized, leaving laws only against public nuisance (Great Britain Committee on Homosexual Offenses and Prostitution, 1963, p. 187). Essentially, the Wolfenden report concluded that private sex ought to be a private matter, and the British Parliament gradually came to agree with it.

On this side of the Atlantic, the American Law Institute's Model Penal Code recommended **decriminalization** of many kinds of sexual behavior previously outlawed. Under the section dealing with sexual offenses, it includes only rape, deviate sexual intercourse by force or imposition, corruption and seduction of minors, sexual assault, and indecent exposure (American Law Institute, 1962, Article 213). With the notable exception of prostitution, which it still makes illegal, the American Law Institute follows the principle that private sexual behavior between consenting adults is not really the law's business. The recommendation of the Model Penal Code has been followed by nearly half the states.

While there are exceptions, a state is more likely to reform its sex laws as part of a complete overhaul of its criminal code than it is to make specific repeal of such laws. The reason for this is political and is grounded in the distinction between legalization and decriminalization.[5] If legislators "legalize" unconventional sexual practices, people are likely to become upset and accuse the state of "condoning" them. It is therefore important to note that what is advocated is decriminalization; that is, ceasing to define certain acts as criminal or removing the penalties attached to them. Decriminalization is morally neutral; it neither approves nor disapproves, and it simply revises the definitions.

> **Decriminalization:**
> Removing some act from those prohibited by law, ceasing to define it as a crime.

---

[4] For a good discussion of these and other arguments, see Packer (1968, pp. 301–306).

[5] One exception is in California, where laws prohibiting adulterous cohabitation, sodomy, and oral copulation were specifically rescinded by the narrowest possible margin in the state senate (*Sexual Law Reporter*, 1975, p. 18).

A legal principle which has been very important in sex-law reform is the constitutional right to privacy. This has come into play chiefly in attacks on sex laws through the courts. Interestingly enough, although the right to privacy is invoked in connection with an amazing variety of matters—criminal records, credit bureaus and banks, school records, medical information, government files, wiretapping, and the 1974 amendment to the Freedom of Information Act (known as the Privacy Act), to name a few—the definitive articulation of the constitutional principle came in a sex-related case (Brent, 1976).

In 1965 the Supreme Court decided the case of *Griswold v. Connecticut* and invalidated a state law under which a physician was prosecuted for providing information and medical advice concerning contraception for a married couple. Justice Douglas stated flatly that "we deal with a right of privacy older than the Bill of Rights, older than our political parties, older than our school system" (*Griswold v. Connecticut,* 1965, p. 486). The problem that Douglas, and the six justices who voted with him, faced was finding the specific provisions of the Constitution which guaranteed this right. Douglas found it not in any actual article of the Bill of Rights but in "penumbras, formed by emanations from those guarantees that help give them life and substance" (*Griswold v. Connecticut,* 1965, p. 484). Critics have found this a splendid example of constitutional double-talk, and the debate over the application of the right to privacy continues. Nonetheless, in invalidating the Connecticut law, the Court defined a constitutional right to privacy which was, in this instance, abridged when a married couple was denied access to information on contraception.

While the decision in the Griswold case declared the marriage bed an area of privacy, in the 1972 case of *Eisenstadt v. Baird,* the Court invalidated a Massachusetts law forbidding the dissemination of contraception information to the unmarried. In doing so, the Court stated that "if the right of privacy means anythng, it is the right of the individual, married or single, to be free from unwarranted governmental intrusion into matters as fundamentally affecting a person as the decision whether to bear or beget a child" (*Eisenstadt v. Baird,* 1972, p. 453). Other decisions have established one's home as a protected sphere of privacy which the law cannot invade (Brent, 1976).

The right to privacy was also invoked by the Court in 1973 in one of its most controversial cases, *Roe v. Wade,* which invalidated laws prohibiting abortion. Suing under the assumed name of Jane Roe, a Texas resident argued that her state's law against abortion denied her a constitutional right. The Court agreed that "the right of personal privacy includes the abortion decision" (*Roe v. Wade,* 1973, p. 113). However, it held that such a right is not absolute and that the state has certain legitimate interests that it may preserve through law, such as the protection of the viable fetus. Nonetheless, the Court declared that a fetus is not a person and therefore not entitled to constitutional protection. The effect of the Roe case, and of related litigation, was to invalidate most state laws against abortion. The Court limited second- and third-trimester abortions to reasons of maternal health but made a woman's right to a first-trimester abortion nearly absolute. However, the 1989 decision in *Webster v. Reproductive Health Services* and the 1992 decision in *Planned Parenthood v. Casey* changed the shape of abortion laws as discussed later in this chapter.

The *Roe* decision was based on the right to privacy, but the Supreme Court has not chosen to extend the right of sexual privacy much further. The reasoning in *Bowers v. Hardwick* is interesting in this regard. Michael Hardwick was arrested for sodomy in his own bedroom. Though he was not prosecuted, he sued the state of Georgia, arguing that the existence of the sodomy law violated his right to privacy.

FIGURE 22.3
On April 5, 1992,
prochoice advocates rallied
in Washington, D.C., to
demonstrate against
restrictions on abortion
rights resulting from
decisions by the Supreme
Court.

The Court, in a 5 to 4 decision, appealed to long-standing societal and legal antipathy toward homosexual acts. In doing so, it affirmed the right of a state to appeal to the common values of society and to write them into law. The *Hardwick* case suggests that the right to privacy is limited to the traditional categories of marriage, family, and procreation (Leading Cases, 1986; Conkle, 1986).

Victimless Crimes

In the past two decades, a great deal of legislative change has taken place involving the principle of "victimless crimes"—a concept that has broad applicability beyond sexual behavior. It is asserted that when an act does no legal harm to anyone or does not provide a demonstrable victim, it cannot reasonably be defined as a crime. The thrust of the argument is well articulated by University of Chicago Law School Dean Norval Morris:

> Most of our legislation concerning drunkenness, narcotics, gambling and sexual behavior is wholly misguided. It is based on an exaggerated conception of the capacity of the criminal law to influence men and, ironically, on a simultaneous belief in the limited capacity of men to govern themselves. We incur enormous collateral costs for that exaggeration and we overload our criminal justice system to a degree that renders it grossly defective where we really need protection— from violence and depredations on our property. But in attempting to remedy this situation, we should not substitute a mindless "legalization" of what we now proscribe as crime. Instead, regulatory programs, backed up by criminal sanctions, must take the place of our present unenforceable, crime-breeding and corrupting prohibitions. (1973, p. 11)

The victimless-crime argument should appeal not only to the public's sense of privacy but also to its pocketbooks. Crimes in which there is no readily identifiable victim account for over half the cases handled by U.S. courts (Boruchowitz, 1973). If the court dockets could be cleared and law enforcement officers reassigned, protection against violent crimes would be rendered more efficient and less expensive.

The application of the principle to some of the issues discussed above should

643

FIGURE 22.4
A cartoonist's view of
victimless crime.

"Be right with you, ma'am, soon as I've brought these lawbreakers to justice."

be obvious. A sexual act performed by consenting adults, whatever it might be, produces neither a victim nor legal harm. The only conceivable end served by criminalizing such an act is the protection of "public morals," which, in a society with many values, seems an end not worth the cost, if it is even possible. If sodomy laws, for example, are removed by a state legislature, the victimless-crime argument is likely to be used, by itself or in combination with an appeal to the right to privacy.

The most common reference to the decriminalization of victimless acts is with respect to prostitution. Police efforts at curbing the "oldest profession" seem to be ineffective, open to corruption and questionable practices, and tremendously expensive. Since prosecution is normally of the prostitute and not her customer, there seems to be a clear pattern of discrimination against women which violates the constitutional principle of equal protection. Finally, as all manner of adult consensual behavior is decriminalized, the legitimacy of distinguishing between commercial and noncommercial consensual sex has been questioned (Parnas, 1981). It has been suggested that much of the demonstrable harm associated with prostitution, such as the committing of robbery and other crimes by prostitutes and pimps and the connections with organized crime, has resulted *because* the practice is illegal (Caughey, 1974). Thus, it has been argued that all would benefit if prostitution were no longer defined as a crime—the prostitute, her patron, the police, and society at large (Parnas, 1981; Rosenbleet & Pariente, 1973).

The argument against the criminalization of prostitution assumes that if prostitution were legal it could be regulated and the problems of crime, public offense, and the spread of sexually transmitted diseases associated with it might be avoided. In this case, then, there would be no victims and no societal need to ban the practice. However, this argument can be countered by suggestions that there may be victims.

644

First, as AIDS spreads to the heterosexual population, prostitutes may be carriers. Second, a feminist analysis of prostitution suggests that the prostitute herself may be a victim of the profession. Some assert that prostitution is inherently degrading and that many prostitutes would welcome alternative means of livelihood. At the moment, the "victimless crime" appeal seems less persuasive than it did a decade ago.

The Problem of Obscenity and Pornography

Among the most controversial topics in the area of sexual regulation, is obscenity and pornography. A substantial portion of the American populace apparently finds pornography offensive and wishes it suppressed. Many others do not share this view and find any form of censorship outrageous and unconstitutional. Antivice crusaders consider "smut" dangerous to the average citizen. Legislators are swamped with demands that something be done, while the courts have labored unsuccessfully for years to balance the First Amendment right of freedom of speech with the desire of some to outlaw, or at least regulate, pornography.

The discussion will begin with a problem of definition. Here it is helpful to distinguish between "pornography" as a popular term and "obscenity" as a legal concept. "Pornography" comes from the Greek word *porneia,* which means, quite simply, "prostitution." In general usage today, it refers to literature, art, films, speech, and so on, that are sexually arousing, or presumed to be arousing, in nature. Pornography may be "soft-core," that is, suggestive, or "hard-core," which usually means that there is explicit depiction of some sort of sexual activity. Pornography, as such, has never been illegal, but obscenity is. The word "obscene" suggests that which is foul, disgusting, or lewd, and it is used as a legal term for that which is offensive to the authorities or to society (Wilson, 1973).

Obscenity has been a legal issue ever since the Supreme Court decided the Roth case in 1957. The Court explicitly stated that obscenity was not protected by the First Amendment—which guarantees freedom of speech and the press and which, by long-recognized extensions, includes films, pictures, literature, and other forms of artistic expression. However, it also ruled that not all sexual expression is obscene, defining obscenity as material "which deals with sex in a manner appealing to prurient interest" (*U.S. v. Roth,* 1957, p. 487). The Roth decision evoked much controversy, both from those who thought the Court had opened the floodgates of pornography and from civil libertarians who found the definition too limiting of freedom. The Court continued to try to refine the test for obscenity. In the 1966 Memoirs case, obscenity was additionally defined as that which is "utterly without redeeming social value." In the Ginzburg decision the same year, the Court upheld the obscenity conviction of a publisher for "pandering" in his advertising; that is, flagrantly exploiting the sexually arousing nature of his publication. However, none of these tests was persuasive to more than five members of the Court, much less to the public at large.[6]

The current standard definition of obscenity by the Supreme Court came in the 1973 case of *Miller v. California.* Rejecting the "utterly without redeeming social value" test, Chief Justice Burger and the four justices concurring with him proposed the following definition:

---

[6] Perhaps the frustration of defining obscenity is best expressed by Justice Potter Stewart in *Jacobelis v. Ohio* (1964): "I shall not further attempt to define [hard-core pornography], and perhaps I could not ever succeed in intelligibly doing so. But I know it when I see it" (378 U.S. 197).

FIGURE 22.5

The production and sale of pornography have become a major commercial enterprise. Most large cities have areas in which such businesses are concentrated, as in this photo taken near New York's Times Square.

(a) whether "the average person, applying contemporary community standards," would find that the work, taken as a whole, appeals to the prurient interest, (b) whether the work depicts or describes, in a patently offensive way, sexual conduct specifically defined by the applicable state law, and (c) whether the work, taken as a whole, lacks serious literary, artistic, political or scientific value. (*Miller v. California*, 1973, p. 24)

The goals of this decision seem to be to define as obscenity "hard-core pornography" in the popular sense, to require from state statutes precise descriptions of that which is to be outlawed, and to give governments more power to regulate it (Gruntz, 1974). The notable problem in the Miller standards, at least for civil libertarians, is the "contemporary community standards" provision. This allows the local community to determine what is obscene, rather than using national norms, making it impossible to predict what a given jury in a particular town might find obscene.

One important factor which has affected the law on pornography is the extent to which legislators, law enforcement officers, and courts believe that it causes harm to the general population. For evidence, they have often turned to social science and found a mixture of data and conclusions. Some social science research in the late 1960s indicated that pornography did little harm and led the Commission on Obscenity to issue a 1970 report which favored the availability of pornography to consenting adults, while keeping it from children and unconsenting adults (Kemp, 1974). On the other hand, the Commission on Pornography appointed by Attorney General Edwin Meese, in its 1986 *Final Report,* using personal testimony and different studies, concluded that pornography is harmful and linked it to the abuse of children and women (see Chapter 18). The Commission's controversial recommendations affirmed the existing antiobscenity statutes and urged their vigorous enforcement. It also seemed to approve other strategies for combating pornography (U.S. Department of Justice, 1986).

The least controversial of these strategies is concerned with the problem of child pornography, which is widespread and damaging to the young people involved in it (Burgess, 1984). In the 1982 case of *New York v. Ferber,* the U.S. Supreme

Court ruled unanimously that child pornography, whether or not it is obscene under the prevailing legal standards, is not protected by the Constitution. This decision gives states broader latitude in legislation, based on the government's obligation to protect children from abuse (Shewaga, 1983). The Court required states to be precise about whether they were prohibiting the production, processing, or distribution of child pornography, and to develop clear definitions of what was to be outlawed. This has proved difficult, but efforts will no doubt continue. Another approach to the problem is to make tougher and more precise laws against child sexual abuse, without which "kiddy porn" could not be made. This approach would criminalize the very production of such material and sidestep the more complicated constitutional issue of distribution and sale (Shouvlin, 1981).

Far more problematic is a strategy advocated by some feminists which seeks to define pornography as inherently discriminatory against women, and thus a matter of civil rights. This approach takes the results of studies, such as those cited in Chapter 18, and feminist analysis as a basis for arguing that pornography, especially the more violent kind, is indeed harmful to women. Writer Andrea Dworkin and legal scholar Catherine MacKinnon drafted a model city ordinance which defines pornography as "the graphic sexually explicit subordination of women through pictures and/or words," and goes on to describe this subordination (Dworkin, 1985, p. 25). A version of this ordinance was adopted in 1982 in Minneapolis amid much controversy but was vetoed by the mayor. Subsequently, it was adopted by Indianapolis and tested in the courts in the case of *American Booksellers v. Hudnut*. Feminists filed friend-of-the-court briefs on both sides of the issue. Both the Federal District Court and the U.S. Court of Appeals rejected the ordinance on First Amendment grounds. While recognizing the possible harm to women in pornography, the courts would not accept limitation on free, constitutionally permitted, expression as an allowable remedy. In 1968, the Supreme Court affirmed the lower-court opinions without comment, and further efforts to fight pornography in this manner have not been successful (Brest & Vandenberg, 1987; Benson, 1986).

A more fruitful approach for those who oppose pornography has been the attempt to regulate, or eliminate, its sale through zoning. The city of Renton, Washington, in an effort to keep adult movie theaters out of the community, passed an ordinance forbidding adult film theaters within 1000 feet of any residential zone, single- or multiple-family dwelling, church, park, or school. Citing precedents and a municipality's right to prevent crime and protect property values, the Supreme Court upheld the Renton ordinance in 1986. Such zoning laws are content-neutral and thus can avoid First Amendment issues. It is likely that more such laws will be passed in the future (Clarke, 1986).

The Supreme Court has not abandoned the Miller test, but it seems likely that various attempts will continue to be made to reduce or eliminate the availability of what some see as harmful pornography. The complexity of the legal issues and the continuing debate over what is appropriate for Americans to read and view will undoubtedly keep the matter of pornography, obscenity, and erotica controversial for some time to come.[7]

The Controversy over Reproductive Freedom

An even more convulsive controversy is to be found in the matter of abortion. Although the Supreme Court's decision in the Roe case was quite clear, it was under continuous attack. Opposition comes from a broad coalition of antiabortion groups

---

[7] For a clear survey of the issues and recent court decisions, see Sunstein (1986).

that prefer to call themselves "prolife" and include the Roman Catholic Church, Evangelical Protestants, various "New Right" organizations, and the Republican Party. The controversy has been carried on in recent elections, in the courts, in state legislatures, and in the Congress. The prolife movement is well organized and well financed and has proved to be an effective lobbying force, instrumental in the defeat of a number of legislators who have not supported the antiabortion cause. Those seeking to preserve the right of women to legal abortions, who choose to call themselves "prochoice," have also organized and been effective as well. In the 1980s and 1990s the prolife movement has used five basic strategies to eliminate or reduce abortions: funding restrictions, parental consent and notification, procedural requirements, the Human Life Amendment, and disruptive action against those performing abortions.

The most notable example of funding restrictions is the "Hyde amendment," annually proposed by Congressman Henry Hyde (no relation to the author of this text). This is a rider to the appropriations bill for the Department of Health and Human Services forbidding the expenditure of any federal money for abortions under Medicaid. This approach was ruled constitutional in the 1980 case of *Harris v. McRae,* and subsequently poor women have been denied this means of obtaining abortions (Milbauer, 1983). Various states have also introduced similar restrictions on state money that has been used to cover the gap left in federal funds. Another strategy involves regulations in Title X of the Public Health Act denying funds to organizations such as family planning agencies which make referrals for abortions and granting funds to organizations that oppose abortions (Paul & Klassel, 1987). In 1991 the Bush administration issued regulations called the *Gag Rule,* which were attached to Title X funding for family planning agencies. The regulations prohibited physicians or other clinic personnel from even discussing abortion as an option with patients; more precisely, the regulations withdrew federal funding from any clinic at which such discussions occurred. The regulations survived a court test of their constitutionality; the challenge was based on the right to free speech of clinic employees and the right of patients to choose whether to end a pregnancy. In 1991 the Supreme Court ruled that the regulations were permissible (Greenhouse, 1991). Planned Parenthood decided it would not compromise its right to provide abortion counseling for patients and continued this practice despite the threat of loss of funding. The battle went back and forth, as the administration started to implement its regulations and Congress responded with legislation overturning the Gag Rule, requiring family planning providers to inform women with unwanted pregnancies about all their options, including abortion. Then in January 1993, newly elected President Bill Clinton reversed Bush's Executive Order and eliminated the Gag Rule.

The second strategy has been to restrict abortion by requiring *parental consent* for a minor to have an abortion, or *notification* of a husband by a woman seeking an abortion. This is part of a strategy to make abortion more difficult to obtain. In the 1992 case of *Planned Parenthood v. Casey,* discussed below, the Supreme Court ruled that states could require parental consent for unmarried girls under 18 seeking abortions. However, it struck down the requirement that married women must notify their husbands.

A third strategy to restrict abortion by making it more difficult or unpleasant is to require that women seeking an abortion be given certain information, for example, that they be informed about fetal development or the medical or psychological consequences of abortion. Some laws along these lines have specified information that is reasonably accurate scientifically, whereas others specify information that is propaganda with little scientific basis. In 1983 the Supreme Court struck down the "Akron Ordinance," which required information of the propaganda variety (Fox, 1983; Mereson, 1983). However, in the 1992 *Planned Parenthood v. Casey* decision, the Supreme Court upheld Pennsylvania's requirement that women seeking abortion be informed about fetal development during the three trimesters of pregnancy and the possible viability of fetuses during the third trimester.

The waning of the Supreme Court majority recognizing a woman's right to an abortion became clear in the important 1989 decision *Webster v. Reproductive Health Services.* The case concerned a Missouri law that (a) prohibited state employees from assisting in abortions and prohibited abortions from being performed in state-owned hospitals, and (b) banned abortions of "viable" fetuses. The Court upheld the Missouri law. Thus it essentially said that states may pass certain kinds of laws regulating abortions. For example, states might require doctors to perform a "viability-test" on any fetus if a woman is believed to be 20 weeks or more pregnant and make it illegal to perform an abortion if the test shows that the fetus could live (such tests are not 100 percent accurate). Ironically, abortions of genetically defective fetuses might be prevented by this ruling because amniocentesis does not provide results until the eighteenth or nineteenth week of pregnancy. The broader effect of the Court's decision, however, is to throw the hot potato back to state legislatures.

By 1992 the membership of the Supreme Court had shifted to a majority of conservatives as a result of appointments made during the Reagan and Bush administrations. Another important abortion case was decided, *Planned Parenthood v. Casey.* The case concerned a Pennsylvania law that placed many obstacles in the way of a woman seeking abortion. She had to be given information about fetal development and then wait 24 hours before the abortion could be performed. Unmarried girls under 18 had to get the consent of at least one parent, or a state judge had to rule that she was mature enough to make the decision herself (called a judicial bypass). Married women had to notify their husbands before obtaining an abortion. The Court's decision was complex. It did not overturn *Roe v. Wade,* as many had expected. Instead, it reaffirmed a woman's constitutional right to an abortion before the fetus is viable. On the other hand, it upheld all the restrictions in the Pennsylvania law except the one requiring a married woman to notify her husband. The Court was again ruling that states could pass laws placing restrictions on abortion, although abortion itself could not be outlawed, and the laws could not place "undue burden" on a woman seeking an abortion.

In summary, then, *Roe v. Wade* (1973) decriminalized abortion and said that states could not restrict access to first-trimester abortion. The two recent decisions have chipped away at *Roe v. Wade* without overturning it completely. In *Webster v. Reproductive Health Services* (1989) the Court said that states could restrict abortion in some ways, namely, by forbidding it in state-owned hospitals and by banning abortion of viable fetuses. In *Planned Parenthood v. Casey* (1992) the Court again upheld a state law placing restrictions on abortion, involving parental consent, information, and a waiting period. However, requiring a woman to notify her husband was going too far, according to the decision, and laws could not place an undue burden on women seeking an abortion.

A fourth strategy used by opponents of abortion has been to champion the Human Life Amendment to the Constitution. This amendment, which would prohibit all abortions, was defeated in the Senate in 1983, falling 18 votes short of the necessary two-thirds majority. However, it is likely to remain on the prolife agenda.

A fifth strategy adopted by some prolife activists such as Operation Rescue is that of disruption such as picketing and civil disobedience outside abortion clinics, Planned Parenthood offices, or the homes of physicians who perform abortions. At the most extreme, abortion clinics have been bombed, although most leaders of the prolife movement disapprove of such tactics.

FIGURE 22.6
It is important that women
of color have equal access
to abortion.

Ethnicity and Sex Laws

Although the Constitution promises equal protection to people of all races, in practice people of color and low-income people are often at a disadvantage, and this is no less true in the area of sexuality than elsewhere. Here we will consider abortion as an example (Nsiah-Jefferson, 1989).

There is little information on abortion or the reproductive needs of women of color. For example, published abortion statistics come in only two categories: white and black. Therefore, we have no data on Native American, Asian American, or Hispanic women. Given the different cultural heritages of these groups, discussed in previous chapters, abortion must have a different meaning for women from these groups, yet we lack data on the specifics.

Although it has been common for many decades for white women to control their reproduction, for many women of color this is a new step. They may be wary because of the history of negative experiences of women of color in this area, such as the experimental work on the introduction of the birth control pill, which was done with poor women in Puerto Rico. Therefore, women of color need far more access to information and education, and it is critical that this information be sensitive to their cultural heritage.

A significantly higher percentage of women of color obtain abortions after the first trimester than do white women (Nsiah-Jefferson, 1989). Statistics indicate that 8.6 percent of all abortions obtained by white women are done after the first trimester (that is, 91.4 percent were done in the first trimester). By comparison, 12.0 percent of all abortions obtained by nonwhite women are done after the first trimester. It seems clear that the Hyde Amendment, which prohibits the use of federal Medicaid funds to pay for abortions for low-income women, is a key factor in this difference. Women of color, who are disproportionately represented in the low-income group, must often spend a good deal of time raising the funds for an abortion because Medicaid is denied them, and this process of raising funds delays the abortion into the second trimester.

In some cases, women of color may have significantly less access to abortion (Nsiah-Jefferson, 1989). For example, Native American women living on reservations are denied federal funding for abortion and, to make matters worse, no Indian Health Service clinics or hospitals may perform abortions even when paid for with private funds. Native American women can therefore be literally hundreds of miles away from access to an abortion.

Abortion is only one example of ways in which people of color are disadvantaged under the present system of sex laws. This example, however, illustrates that efforts at sex-law reform need to include a consideration of the impact on people of color.

SEX AND THE LAW IN THE FUTURE

Nothing seems riskier than to predict with any degree of confidence how society's views of sex, and the laws that express those views, will develop and change. Thus, any look ahead is at best a guess of what might happen, based on what has happened. Unforeseen events have a way of upsetting our calculations and introducing new variables into the mix. For example, in the first edition of this text (1978), I predicted that sex-law reform would go on as it had in the 1970s, with the extension of the right to privacy and wide use of the "victimless-crime argument" for decriminalization of various sexual practices. The election of 1980 in which Ronald Reagan became President, the rise of the New Right, and the increasing appeal of its "social agenda" rendered that prophecy unsound. Likewise, the third edition (1986) was written without any attention to the complex legal issues posed by AIDS and the new reproductive technologies. As we focus our attention on these issues, you might well speculate on what will need to be included in the next edition.

Sex-Law Reform and Backlash

At this writing, it appears that the movement toward more permissive sex laws, which probably had its roots in the civil rights movement, the sexual revolution, and feminism, has achieved virtually all the gains it is likely to for the time being. The Supreme Court has limited the right to privacy in sexual matters, and even a woman's right to an abortion is threatened. The decriminalization of sex offenses had essentially ceased by 1980. New strategies for combating pornography have been tried, and some have succeeded. The New Right and its allies in the conservative evangelical sector of the religious community have, it would seem, taken the initiative away from those who had favored less restrictive sex laws. The latter now find themselves seeking to defend and preserve gains already made, rather than extending them.

While the "profamily" coalition has by no means attained all its goals, it has certainly stopped sex-law reform and may be on the way to reversing it. The mood of the nation in the 1990s is far less hospitable to such reform and to the extension of legal protection to sexual minorities. Above all, fear of AIDS (see Focus 22.2) may be the motivating force behind increasingly restrictive laws regulating sexual behavior. This would be very much in the tradition of the American legal system, which has always tended to reflect both the values and the conflicts of the society.

The Legal Challenge of New Reproductive Technologies

Very complex legal questions are being raised by the proliferation of techniques enabling previously infertile people, and others, to have children. These include

AIDS and the Law

The growing incidence of AIDS (see Chapter 20) poses a serious threat not only to American society but to its law as well. None of the choices facing legislators and judges is easy. Any reflection on AIDS and the law must take into account two factors, both of them rendering the issue more complex and emotional. AIDS is identified, both statistically and in the popular mind, with persons who are already disliked, feared, and discriminated against: homosexuals, intravenous drug users, and prostitutes. Second, at this writing, there is no vaccine for AIDS and no lasting treatment, and it is judged to be 100 percent fatal. This combination of factors has led some commentators to write of the "two epidemics": the medical epidemic of the disease and the social epidemic of fear (Lazzo & McElgunn, 1986).

The fact of the twin epidemics makes the legal balancing act even more difficult. Government has two very strong responsibilities with respect to HIV infection and those who suffer from it. On the one hand, the state is obligated to protect individual rights and defend its citizens from discrimination and injustice. On the other, it is equally obliged to protect the general welfare of the public. AIDS is one of those tragic cases in which these two obligations may be in severe conflict. It is difficult to predict how government will resolve this tension, although past history suggests that it is more likely to err on the side of the general welfare than on individual rights, especially given the current climate.

There is significant case law, much of it from the early twentieth century when cities were swept with epidemics of tuberculosis and other infectious diseases, affirming the right and responsibility of the state to protect the populace. As one scholar notes, "Courts have traditionally deferred to public health authorities in their struggle to control epidemics, even when these efforts infringed on the constitutional rights of individual citizens" (Nanula, 1986, p. 330). Measures approved include the reporting of cases to local public health officials, mass vaccination programs, quarantine, and other restrictions on suspected carriers. Nonetheless, public health officials must demonstrate that any measure is directly aimed at the disease in question and is not arbitrary, capricious, or oppressive (Lazzo & McElgunn, 1986).

There has been much debate on the mandatory testing of certain populations. So far, it has been required of all military personnel, prison inmates in some states, would-be immigrants, and, in Illinois, those applying for marriage licenses, although Illinois later changed this regulation; so far none of these practices has been invalidated by the courts. Public health authorities in several cities have closed gay bathhouses. However, many other traditional measures are rendered suspect both by the huge number of people thought to be potential carriers and by the relatively restricted ways in which the disease is transmitted. It is argued that widespread mandatory testing will only serve to keep those who should be tested away or drive them underground (Closer et al., 1986; Nanula, 1986). Thus, the best case for state activity can be made for research, education, and prevention.

Protection of individual rights poses a thorny problem. To have AIDS, or even to be thought to have the disease, has led to individuals being fired

FIGURE 22.7
A police officer guards a closed gay bathhouse. In several cities the public health authorities have closed the baths to prevent the spread of AIDS.

from their jobs, divorced parents losing custody or visitation rights, persons losing health insurance or even being deprived of medical care, and children being barred from attending school, not to mention all sorts of informal harassment and discrimination. Federal regulations and ordinances in several municipalities and counties have forbidden discrimination against those with AIDS or thought to have AIDS.

A major issue is the confidentiality of test results and medical records. Three states—California, Wisconsin, and Florida—have passed laws to protect the confidentiality of antibody test records. Persons with positive tests have a reasonable fear of losing their jobs, and the insurance industry has made efforts to find ways of denying coverage to those thought to carry the virus, and even to high-risk groups (Schatz, 1987). Some legal scholars argue that the constitutional right to privacy should afford protection to individuals infected with the AIDS virus, but the extent of that protection is by no means clear, especially given the decision in *Bowers v. Hardwick.*

Another approach is to seek protection for in-fected persons under the Rehabilitation Act of 1973, which prohibits discrimination against the handicapped. In the 1987 case of *School Board of Nassau County v. Arline,* the Supreme Court ruled that the Rehabilitation Act applied to a schoolteacher who suffered from chronic tuberculosis. Legal scholars regard this as an indication that AIDS might well be seen as a handicapping condition under the meaning of the act (Fagot-Diaz, 1988; Gentemann, 1988).

In the future, legislatures and courts will struggle to resolve a host of questions such as these. Who has a right to know if a person may be carrying the HIV virus? Who is going to pay the enormous costs of this disease? Should people be held legally liable if they knowingly (or even unknowingly) infect others with the disease? Should there be registries of infected persons, and who should have access to these registries? How, indeed, are the rights of the public and individuals to be balanced and protected?

Sources: Dalton & Burris (1987), Schatz (1987), Closer et al. (1986), Nanula (1986), Lazzo & McElgunn (1986).

artificial insemination, in vitro fertilization (IVF), surrogate motherhood, and various kinds of embryo fertilization and transfer. There are few state laws on the subject, with the exception of statutes regulating artificial insemination in 27 states and laws in all jurisdictions aginst trafficking in children ("baby buying"), which may impinge on surrogacy. There are likewise few federal standards other than regulations on IVF experimentation (Taub, 1987; Shapiro, 1986). However, the issues must be addressed, and very soon.

A fundamental difficulty is that these technologies bring a very public quality to what has always been one of the most private of all human activities, the conception of children. Some of them involve a third party, as a donor of sperm, egg, embryo, or uterus, to what had been solely between a man and a woman. Even the nomenclature is complicated. In this section we adopt the convention of designating as "parent(s)" the person(s) who will rear the child and accept legal responsibility for her or him. Those who provide some necessary aspect of the process we will call "donors," or in the special case at women in whose wombs embryos are implanted, "surrogates." In the absence of clear legislation or case law, we are mostly able to point to the questions raised.

Perhaps the foremost question is whether or not there is a fundamental right to conception. If there is, it is hard to argue against the use of any appropriate technique to achieve that end, including third-party participation, or what some call "collaborative conception." On the other hand, if there is no such fundamental right, it may be reasonable to limit or even prohibit the use of such technology. Unfortunately, this question cannot be answered definitively at present. There is a well-established right not to conceive under the right to privacy, but the converse has not been established. Since our ancestors did not face this problem, their legacy is not much help.

Closely related is the question of the legal status of an embryo, since in several of these techniques fertilization and conception take place outside the uterus. Those who assert that life begins at conception would accord full personhood and legal rights to the embryo from the first cell division. Many states have recently enacted laws aimed at protecting embryos. For example, a new Louisiana law specifies that an embryo, even if outside anyone's body, is a person and shall not intentionally be destroyed (Andrews, 1989). At the other extreme are those who regard an embryo merely as tissue, to be disposed of at will. This view would put no limits on reproductive technologies. A moderate view would see the embryo as less than a person

FIGURE 22.8
The law has not yet dealt adequately with the consequences of new reproductive technologies, as this cartoon indicates.

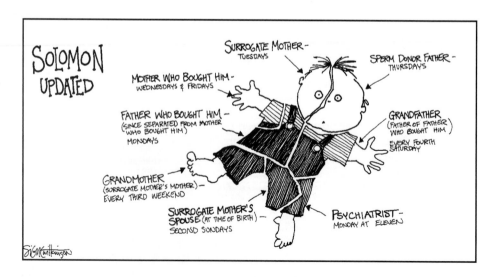

but more than mere tissue and would argue that it should be treated with the respect due potential human life. This view would seem to lead to some regulation of reproductive technology short of prohibition (Robertson, 1986). The question of what can be done with embryos not implanted also arises and is related. An embryo's status—even in the maternal womb, much less outside it—is a question the Supreme Court has explicitly avoided in its abortion decisions.

Another complex of questions is to be found in the matter of kinship, parental rights, and responsibilities. When a child is born as a result of these techniques, who exactly are the parents? One commentator notes that there can be five: an egg donor, a sperm donor, the donor of a uterus for all or part of the gestation, and the couple who rear the child (Shapiro, 1986, p. 54). This is a particularly thorny question in the case of a surrogate mother who has donated her egg and her uterus for nine months and then is required to give up the child. Do donors have any legal claim to further contact with "their" children after birth? (See Figure 22.9.)

Surrogacy and surrogacy contracts raise particularly complex issues, especially if the woman has contributed not only her uterus but an egg as well. A man who donates his sperm to a sperm bank renounces any right to further contact with children who may be conceived; however, no equivalent principles have been established for those who donate eggs or a uterus. Some argue that state laws against trafficking in children ("buying babies") make surrogacy contracts, especially surrogacy for pay, illegal. Others have raised the concern that commercializing reproduction is inherently corrupting and should be prohibited because it turns children into commodities. There is a concern that surrogacy leads to the exploitation of low-income women, who will rent their wombs because they need the money, despite the possible psychological stresses and health risks (Andrews, 1989; Taub, 1987; O'Brien, 1986). Responding to some of these concerns, in 1988 Michigan became the first state to outlaw surrogacy contracts for pay.

Taking a broad perspective, there are a number of alternatives for legal approaches to the issue of surrogacy (Andrews, 1989). The most restrictive one is to outlaw all surrogacy contracts for pay, as Michigan did. A second alternative would be to have courts scrutinize all surrogacy contracts to ensure, for example, that the woman has not been coerced. Some proposed laws require that a mental health professional interview all participants—surrogate, egg donor, sperm donor, potential rearing parents—to be sure that all are truly giving informed consent. Another alternative, to address the concern that the surrogate may be exploited, is to require that surrogates must have their own legal counsel when they enter into a contract. Some suggest that all surrogacy arrangements and contracts should be handled by nonprofit agencies, as adoptions are, to discourage profit making. Another possibility is to declare surrogacy to be a special case of adoption. That is, the surrogate is treated the same as any other birth mother who arranges to give her child up for adoption. This ensures that she has a period of 6 weeks or so after the birth to decide whether she wants to keep the baby, and it clearly establishes whose baby it is.

A final possibility, at the other end of the spectrum, is that government stay out of this matter entirely, based on the argument that this is a private matter between the people involved. I don't see this as a viable option, because contested surrogacy cases, such as that of Mary Beth Whitehead and Baby M (see Figure 22.9) are already reaching the courts. The government is already involved. It would be far better to have some well-thought-out legislation on this matter to provide guidance and reduce the number of painful contested cases.

Finally, there are a host of procedural issues that will inevitably arise if any of these reproductive techniques are legally permitted and regulated. What will the standards of confidentiality be, especially with regard to the identity of nonparent donors? If something goes wrong during one of these procedures—and they are

(a)   (b)

FIGURE 22.9

Real-life Solomon updated. (a) William Stern and Baby M; (b) Mary Beth Whitehead and Baby M. In 1985 Mary Beth Whitehead signed a contract with William Stern to be artificially inseminated with his sperm, to surrender the resulting child to him, and to renounce all parental rights to that child, in return for expenses and compensation of $10,000. Other parties to the contract were the parties' spouses and the Infertility Center of New York, which acted as broker. The child, named "Baby M" by the courts, was born in 1986, but Whitehead refused to surrender her. The Sterns brought suit to uphold the contract and obtain full custody of the child. The trial judge found for the Sterns and immediately granted the adoption of the child by Elizabeth Stern. However, the New Jersey Supreme Court unanimously ruled that surrogacy contracts cannot be enforced. In doing so, the court invalidated the adoption of Baby M by Elizabeth Stern and sent the case back to a lower court to determine Whitehead's visitation rights (Recht, 1988; Taub, 1987).

risky—who is liable? Who will take responsibility for a defective child born through one of these techniques? Who will bear the expense? They are expensive. Must insurance companies pay for artificial insemination, IVF, embryo transfer, or even surrogacy? Should such procedures be covered under Medicaid for the poor? Many more such questions will develop in the future.

Underlying all these issues are the root questions: What is the government's interest, if any, in human reproduction, and how shall it be expressed? What procedures shall be used to put into law society's concerns, if this is not deemed to be strictly a private matter? And, above all, who is to decide these issues? Legislatures and courts have shown a marked disinclination to enter this field, but that strategy cannot be viable much longer.[8]

[8] For a fuller development of these issues, see Cohen & Taub (1989), Taub (1987), Robertson (1986), Shapiro (1986), O'Brien (1986), Mallory & Rich (1986).

Summary

It is reasonable to suggest that laws to protect adults from coercion, children from sexual exploitation, and the public from offensive behavior are justifiable. However, many laws against sexual conduct originated in a desire to promote public morality and perpetuate sexism, and it is hard to justify them.

The laws governing sexual conduct include laws against crimes of exploitation and force (such as rape, carnal knowledge of a juvenile, and child molestation), against various consensual acts (such as fornication, adultery, sodomy, and other "unnatural acts"), against gays, against offending public taste (exhibitionism, voyeurism, solicitation, disorderly conduct, lewdness, and the like), against crimes affecting reproduction (contraception and abortion), and against criminal commercial sex (notably prostitution and obscenity). These laws are often capriciously enforced, and this unequal enforcement has high social costs that may require reform.

Certain trends can be discerned in the reform of such sex laws. The British Wolfenden report and the American Model Penal Code are early examples of proposals to decriminalize consensual sexual behavior. The legal principle which has accounted for much court action to reform laws against contraception and abortion is the "right to privacy," but it has not been broadened to include consensual acts by adults. A factor that has influenced legislators is the movement for the decriminalization of "victimless crimes." The issue of pornography and obscenity, which includes such problems as definition, conflicting societal values, and actual demonstration of effects, is a confusing one. Abortion remains a volatile and highly controversial matter. Sex-law reform will move more slowly in the 1990s than it did in the previous decade, and there are signs of a conservative backlash. In the future, the law will need to balance individual rights and the public interest in issues such as AIDS and new reproductive technologies.

Review Questions

1. The regulation of sexual conduct by law is a fairly new development in American history. True or false?

2. Until recently a husband could not be prosecuted for raping his wife. True or false?

3. By and large, the law allows consenting adults to do in private whatever they want to do. True or false?

4. Laws which, in theory, may apply to many forms of sexual conduct, such as oral and anal sex, but which are usually enforced only against homosexuals, are _____ laws.

5. _____ was the 1965 Supreme Court decision that struck down state laws that had made it illegal for a physician to discuss or prescribe contraceptives for married persons.

6. In legal terms, what is often called pornography is not protected by the Constitution if it can be shown to be _____.

7. _____ was the 1992 Supreme Court case that upheld a woman's right to abortion while also upholding a Pennsylvania law's restrictions, including parental notification for minors.

8. The reform of sex laws and the extension of the right of privacy are likely to continue in the future with little controversy. True or false?

9. The law recognizes the validity of surrogacy contracts. True or false?

10. A woman has an absolute right to an abortion, at any age and with public funds. True or false?

(The answers to all review questions are at the end of the book, beginning on page 731.)

Questions for Thought, Discussion, and Debate

1. Find out what sort of laws relate to sexual activity in the state in which you live or go to school. Are there any moves to change those laws?

2. What aspects of human sexuality do you think it is reasonable for the law to regulate?

3. How do you think young children can best be protected from sexual abuse and exploitation?

4. If you were a state legislator, what kinds of laws would you favor regarding AIDS and surrogate parenthood?

Suggestions for Further Reading

Bernard, M., Levine, E., Presser, S., & Steich, M. (1985). *The rights of single people*. New York: Bantam Books. Boggan, E. C., Haft, M. G., Lister, D., Rupp, J. H., & Stoddard, T. B. (1983). *The rights of gay people* (revised ed.). New York: Bantam Books. Prepared by the American Civil Liberties Union, these guides cover most laws regarding sexuality.

Dalton, Harlon L., & Burris, Scott (Eds.). (1987). *AIDS and the law*. New Haven: Yale University Press. Produced by the Yale AIDS Law Project, this excellent book discusses all the various legal issues regarding AIDS.

Messer, Ellen, & May, Kathryn E. (1988). *Backrooms: Voices from the illegal abortion era*. New York: St. Martin's Press. This book is based on interviews with 24 women, all of whom had unwanted pregnancies before *Roe v. Wade*. The women tell the stories of their illegal abortions and their consequences. It is important reading, especially for those who have grown up in the era of legal abortions.

Tribe, Laurence H. (1990). *Abortion: The clash of absolutes*. New York: Norton. Constitutional scholar Tribe analyzes the arguments on the two sides of the abortion debate and explains why we make no progress in finding a compromise on this issue.

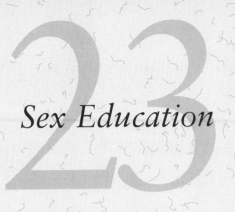

Sex Education

Chapter Highlights

That gets me very nervous; that people like this [conservatives] want to take sex education out of the schools. Reagan wanted to take it out. He said he believed sex education caused promiscuity: if you had the knowledge, you'd use it. Hey—I took algebra; I never do math. *

Children are curious about sex. That is perfectly normal and good, and it motivates them to learn. The only problem is that adults often do not know what to do about it. This chapter is about concepts and methods that are useful in sex education, both in a formal school curriculum and in informal sex education in the home or some other situation.

IN THE HOME, IN THE SCHOOL, OR SOMEWHERE ELSE?

When concerned parents get together and urge a school system to begin a sex education curriculum, invariably some upright citizens of the community raise a protest. They might say that sex education promotes promiscuity, communism, or some other disaster, and they are sure that it should take place only in the home (or possibly the church), but certainly not in the schools.

What these upright citizens overlook is the realistic alternative to sex education in the schools. For most teenagers, the primary source of sex information is friends (see Table 23.1), and that is the classic case of the blind leading the blind. Parents come in a poor second as actual sources of sex information. Interestingly, young people would prefer to hear about sex from their parents (J. H. Gagnon, 1965b).

The fact is that many children are given no sex education in the home. Rather, they learn about sex in the street, and the result is a massive amount of misinformation. Thus, people who say that sex education should be carried out in the home, not in the school, are not making a sensible argument.

* *Source:* Elayne Boosler, *Best of Comic Relief 3*

Table 23.1
People's Main Source of Sex Information as a Teenager

	Percentage
Friends	40
Parents	23
Sex education courses in school	9
From experience	8
Books	4
Older brother/sister	3
Other sources, not sure	13

Source: From a well-sampled survey of U.S. adults by *Time* and Clancy Shulman Yankelovich, November 10, 1986.

Of course, the times are changing, and many of today's parents are precisely the people who participated in the sexual revolution of the 1960s and 1970s. Perhaps they will be better sex educators. But some experts feel these parents are still too unclear about their changing attitudes and lifestyles to be helpful to their children (Roberts et al., 1978).

Surveys have shown repeatedly that the majority of parents are in favor of sex education in the schools. One well-sampled survey found that 86 percent of U.S. adults favor sex education in the schools (*Time*/Yankelovich, November, 1986). The results of *Time* magazine's well-sampled 1986 survey of adult Americans (July 21, 1986) showed that the great majority favor sex education for 12-year-olds and favor teaching them about a number of very explicit topics, including AIDS and other sexually transmitted diseases, birth control, premarital sex, abortion, and homosexuality. The great majority believe that school health clinics should make birth control information available, although only a minority believe that the clinics should provide contraceptives. The point is that there is strong support for detailed sex education in the schools, beginning at least when children are 12 years old (sixth or seventh grade).

FIGURE 23.1
Although some parents claim that sex education belongs in the home, it rarely happens there effectively.

Sex education in the schools was given a major boost when, in 1986, then Surgeon General C. Everett Koop, responding to the AIDS epidemic, went on record as advocating sex education—including AIDS education—in the schools for children beginning at age 8, a recommendation that most sex educators would support. In 1988 Koop then took the unprecedented step, one not expected in the conservative Reagan administration, of mailing an informational brochure on AIDS to every household in the country. Ironically, the horror of AIDS may yield at least some benefits if it fosters a commitment in the United States to sound sex education in the schools.

EFFECTS OF SEX EDUCATION

One argument made by people opposed to sex education in the schools is that it leads to terrible consequences, particularly increases in premarital sex and promiscuity. Is there any scientific evidence backing this assertion? (For comprehensive reviews of the effects of sex education courses, see Voss, 1980; Kilmann et al., 1981).

A national probability sample of 1177 college students were interviewed about their current sexual behavior and their previous sources of sex information (Spanier, 1976, 1977). The results indicated that having sex education in the schools had had little effect on the students' premarital sexual activity; current factors—such as dating patterns—seemed to be much more important influences (Spanier, 1976). Thus, the evidence does not support the contention that sex education encourages premarital sexual experimentation (for similar results, see Eisen & Zellman, 1987).

In contrast, there is evidence that responsible sex education may have a number of desirable effects. A large-scale study of numerous junior high and high school sex education programs indicated that students' knowledge of factual information about sex increased from the beginning to the end of the courses, and that the increased knowledge was maintained five months after the courses (Kirby, 1984). In another well-conducted survey of teenagers in metropolitan areas, those who had had sex education were no more or no less likely to have had sexual intercourse than those who had not had sex education; this refutes the argument that sex education promotes promiscuity. Furthermore, sexually active young women who had had sex education were less likely to have become pregnant than sexually active young women who had not had sex education (Zelnik & Kim, 1982).

PURPOSES OF SEX EDUCATION

The Sex Information and Education Council of the United States (SIECUS) has been one of the most active groups promoting quality sex education. According to SIECUS, the goals of sex education should be:

1. *Information* To provide accurate information about human sexuality, including: growth and development, human reproduction, anatomy, physiology, masturbation, family life, pregnancy, childbirth, parenthood, sexual response, sexual orientation, contraception, abortion, sexual abuse, HIV/AIDS and other sexually transmitted diseases.
2. *Attitudes, values, and insights* To provide an opportunity for young people to question, explore, and assess their sexual attitudes in order to develop their own values, increase self-esteem, develop insights concerning relationships with members of both genders, and understand their obligations and responsibilities to others.
3. *Relationships and interpersonal skills* To help young people develop interpersonal skills, including communication, decision-making, assertiveness, and peer refusal skills, as well as the ability to create satisfying relationships. Sexuality education programs should prepare students to understand their sexuality effectively and creatively in adult roles. This would include helping young people develop the capacity for caring, supportive, non-coercive, and mutually pleasurable intimate and sexual relationships.
4. *Responsibility* To help young people exercise responsibility regarding sexual relationships, including addressing abstinence, how to resist pressures to become prematurely involved in sexual intercourse, and encouraging the use of contraception and other sexual health measures. Sexuality education should be a central component of programs designed to reduce the prevalence of sexually-related medical problems, including teenage pregnancies, sexually transmitted diseases including HIV infection, and sexual abuse. (SIECUS, 1991)

THE TEACHER

Suppose you have decided to start a program of sex education. Whether it is to be carried out in the school, in the home, or someplace else, the first thing you need is a teacher. What qualifications should this person have?[1]

First, the person should be fairly well educated in sexual matters. Reading a text such as this one or taking a university course in sexuality would be a good way to acquire the knowledge that is needed. But do not assume that a teacher has to have a Ph.D. in sex; the important qualifications are a good basic knowledge, a willingness to admit when he or she does not know the answer, and the patience to look things up (and a knowledge of where to look).

---

[1] The American Association of Sex Educators, Counselors, and Therapists is a professional organization that can provide further information. See the Appendix at the back of this book for addresses and telephone numbers.

Conservative Sex Education: Sex Respect

A new sex education curriculum has come on the market recently, and it has a considerably different approach from the one in this book. It is called *Sex Respect* (there are actually several similar curricula now, but this is the most well known), and it is a political conservative's approach to sex education. Federally funded, it is targeted at middle-school audiences and, as of 1991, there were 1600 school districts nationwide using it.

The major goal of this curriculum is to teach that abstinence is the only thing that is moral and the only thing that is safe. The curriculum uses a variety of attention-grabbing techniques, including cartoons. (A cartoon would have been reprinted here, but the publisher would not grant us permission to use it.) There are catchy slogans that children must chant in class, such as

> Don't be a louse, wait for your spouse!
> Do the right thing, wait for the ring!
> Pet your dog, not your date!

There is a "chastity pledge" that all students take, and a chart of physical intimacy in which a prolonged kiss is characterized as the "beginning of danger." The curriculum teaches that condoms can be the road to ruin because many fail.

Sex Respect throws in a lot of gender-role stereotypes as well, characterizing boys as "sexual aggressors" and girls as "virginity protectors." It presents the two-parent, heterosexual couple as "the sole model of a healthy, 'real' family."

Wisconsin's American Civil Liberties Union (ACLU), on behalf of parents who object to the curriculum, is demanding that it be removed from all public schools using it. The ACLU is arguing that the curriculum amounts to discrimination based on gender, marital status, sexual orientation, and religion—all of which are illegal under Wisconsin laws.

In fairness to *Sex Respect*, it may have some good points in that it teaches students skills in resisting peer pressure. On the other hand, it includes a lot of "facts" that are really misinformation (for example, condoms frequently fail, when they actually have a very low failure rate), and it seems out of touch with today's teenagers.

The widespread adoption of this curriculum points out how important it is for parents to examine the sex education materials being presented to their children.

Sources: Newsweek, June 17, 1991; *Wall Street Journal,* February 20, 1992.

Equally important is the teacher's comfort with sexual topics. Even when parents or other adults willingly give accurate factual information to a child about sex, they may still convey negative attitudes because they become anxious or blush while answering the child's questions or because they use euphemisms rather than direct sexual terms. Thus, it is important for the teacher to feel relaxed and comfortable in discussing sex. Some people are that way; others must work to learn this attitude. There are a number of ways to do this. For example, the teacher can role play, with another adult, having sexual discussions with children. Comfort is gained with practice.

A good teacher is also a good listener who can assess what the child knows from the questions asked and who can understand what a child really wants to know when she or he asks a question. According to a joke, little Billy ran into the kitchen

FIGURE 23.3
*Sex education around the
world: (a) The use of the
condom is explained in a
sex education class in
Kingston, Jamaica. The
teenage pregnancy rate in
Jamaica dropped by 80
percent two years after this
sex education program was
initiated. (b) Family
planning clinic in
Colombia.*

(a)

(b)

in his home one day after kindergarten and asked his mother where he had come from; she gritted her teeth, realized the time had come, and proceeded with a 15-minute discussion of intercourse, conception, and birth, blushing the whole time. Billy listened, but at the end he appeared somewhat confused and walked away shaking his head and saying, "That's funny. Jimmy says he came from Illinois."

WHAT TO TEACH
AT DIFFERENT AGES

Sex education is not something that can be carried out all at once in one week during fifth grade. Like teaching math, it is a process that must begin when children are small. They should learn simple concepts first, progressing to more difficult ones as they grow older. What one teaches at any particular age depends on the child's sexual behavior (see Chapter 11), sexual knowledge, and sexual interests at that age. This section will concentrate on theories and research that provide information on these last two points.

Children's Sex Knowledge

A few researchers have investigated what children know about sex and reproduction at various stages.

In one study, Israeli children aged 4 to 5½ were questioned about sex and reproduction (Kreitler & Kreitler, 1966). About 60 percent of the children could describe the sex organs of the other gender. More than 90 percent knew that a baby came from the mother's enlarged belly. But when asked what the mother does in order to get a baby, many of them responded that she must eat a lot or that she swallows a baby. Only about 2 percent of the boys and one of the girls mentioned intercourse. When the children were asked how the baby gets out, most said that the mother's belly had to be cut open. One wonders what the effects are when children hold such an alarming view of birth.

The children were also asked how the father helps in this process. Their answers typically involved things like feeding the mother, earning money, and helping the mother, once again demonstrating that they had no knowledge of intercourse.

Probably the most comprehensive study of children's sex knowledge is described in Focus 23.2.

Stages of Understanding

Psychologist Anne Bernstein (1976; Bernstein & Cowan, 1975) investigated children's understanding of reproduction, basing her research on Piaget's idea that children go through various stages in their understanding. She found that children do proceed through the following levels (stages) of understanding about reproduction.

LEVEL 1: GEOGRAPHY   Most 3- to 4-year-olds believe that a baby has always existed and may believe that it was located somewhere else (geographically) before it got inside the mother. The following is an example of the responses of a Level 1 child:

> (How did the baby happen to be in your Mommy's tummy?) It just grows inside. (How did it get there?) It's there all the time. Mommy doesn't have to do anything. She waits until she feels it. (You said that the baby wasn't in there when you were there.) Yeah, then he was in the other place . . . in America. (In America?) Yeah, in somebody else's tummy. (Bernstein & Cowan, 1975, p. 86)

LEVEL 2: MANUFACTURING   At around age 4, children begin to understand that something causes babies to come into existence. However, they think a manufacturing process is involved, as in the production of a refrigerator or a TV. A Level 2 child described how people get babies as follows:

> Maybe they just paint the right bones. . . . Maybe they just paint the bones and paint the blood, and paint the blue blood. . . . (Bernstein & Cowan, 1975, p. 86)

LEVEL 3: TRANSITIONAL   By age 7 or 8, children explain reproduction as a mixture of technology and physiology, but they stick to feasible occurrences. They no longer think that the mother opens up her tummy to let the baby out. Level 3 children may know that three things are involved in making a baby: a social relationship between two people, such as love or marriage; sexual intercourse; and the union of sperm and egg.

The combination of manufacturing ideas and biology ideas is illustrated by a Level 3 child's explanation of why the male's contribution is necessary:

> Well, the father puts the shell. I forget what it's called, but he puts something in for the egg. If he didn't then a baby couldn't come. Because it needs the stuff that the father gives. It helps it grow. I think that the stuff has the food part, maybe, and maybe it helps protect it. I think he gives the shell part, and the shell part, I think, is the skin. (Bernstein, 1976, p. 34)

In Piaget's terms, these children are in a transitional phase between the preoperational and the concrete operational stages of thought.

LEVEL 4: CONCRETE PHYSIOLOGY   Level 4 and the successive levels are qualitatively different from the previous ones because children now have an understanding of the physical facts of life and of the importance of sperm and egg. At Levels 4 through 6 they come increasingly closer to scientific understandings, although they still don't have it quite right.

Although Level 4 children know about egg and sperm, they may not know why they have to unite. An 8-year-old said:

> The man and the woman get together, and then they put a speck, then the man has his seed and the woman has an egg. They have to come together or else the baby won't really get hatched very well. The seed makes the egg grow. It's just like plants. If you plant a seed, a flower will grow. (Bernstein, 1976, p. 34)

LEVEL 5: PREFORMATION   At level 5, children (usually 11- or 12-year-olds) believe that the baby already exists (is preformed) in either the sperm or the egg. They think that the other germ cell or intercourse simply makes conditions suitable for the baby to grow. For example:

> Well, if they're the man that made love to your mother, then your father because you really originally came out of him, and then went into your mother. Well, you were a sperm inside of him, there. So that you're the, you're really his daughter or son. 'Cause he was the one that really had you first. (Why must the egg be there for the sperm to develop into a baby?) 'Cause otherwise the sperm will have, uh, nothing to nourish it, or sort of keep it warm or, you know, able to move or something. Just has, it's not, just has to have the egg to be able to do something, develop. It just dies if it doesn't have the egg. (Bernstein & Cowan, 1975, p. 89)

LEVEL 6: PHYSICAL CAUSALITY   Level 6 children, who are generally 12 or older, give a good physiological explanation of reproduction that includes the idea that the embryo begins its biological existence at the moment of conception and that it is the product of genetic material from both parents. A Level 6 child said:

> The sperm encounters one ovum, and one sperm breaks into the ovum which produces, the sperm makes like a cell, and the cell separates and divides. And so it's dividing, and the ovum goes through a tube and embeds itself in the wall of the, I think it's the fetus of the woman. (Bernstein & Cowan, 1975, p. 89)

Are American Children Sexual Illiterates?

Ronald and Juliette Goldman (1982) did a massive cross-cultural study of children's understanding of sexual matters. From their results, they concluded that American children are sexual illiterates.

The Goldmans did face-to-face interviews with children aged 5, 7, 9, 11, 13, and 15 in four different cultures: Australia, England, North America, and Sweden. A total of 838 children were interviewed. The Swedish sample is particularly interesting because there is compulsory sex education for all children in Swedish schools, beginning at age 8. It is also worth noting that the North American sample was originally planned to be a United States sample, but school officials in the United States were so uncooperative that the Goldmans had to go across the border from upstate New York to Canada (where they obtained more cooperation) in order to complete the sample. Therefore, the North American sample is a mixture of children from Canada and the United States.

The Goldmans were careful to avoid contro-versial topics such as homosexuality in the interview, and they questioned children only about their understanding of sexual concepts, not about their own sexual behavior. They called the study "Children's Concepts of Development." These precautions were taken in order to produce a high rate of cooperation from parents. Parents in general were cooperative; only 20 percent of parents overall refused to allow their children to participate.

A comparison of the results from the North American children with those from children in the other three cultures led the Goldmans to conclude that American children are strikingly lacking in sexual information. Some of the results are shown in Table 23.2. Notice, for example, that only 23 percent of North American 9-year-olds, but 60 percent of Australian 9-year-olds, know the genital differences beween newborn baby boys and girls. The Swedish children are consistently more knowledgeable than the American children, indicating the positive effects of sex education.

Bernstein's findings have important implications for sex education (Bernstein, 1976). Educators should be aware of the level of the child's understanding and should not inundate him or her with information appropriate for a child three or four levels higher. Instead, there should be an attempt to clarify misunderstandings inherent in the child's beliefs. For example, a Level 1 child believes that a baby has always existed. To such a child, you might say, "To make a baby person, you need two grown-up persons, one a man and one a woman." To the Level 2 child, who believes that babies are manufactured, you might say, "That's an interesting way of looking at things. That's the way you'd make a doll. You would buy a head and some hair and put it all together. But making a real, live baby is different from making a doll or a cake or an airplane" (Bernstein, 1976, p. 35).

Children's Questions About Sex

Children's knowledge of and interest in sex are reflected in the questions they ask. In a study of children's questions about sex, it was found that many questions are

Table 23.2
Responses of 9-Year-Olds in Four Cultures in the Goldman Study

Concept	Percentage of Correct Answers Among			
	Australians	British	North Americans	Swedish
Knowing physical sex differences of newborn babies	60	35	23	40
Knowing correct terms for the genitals	50	33	20	*
Knowing length of gestation is 8 to 10 months	35	32	30	67
Knowing that one purpose of coitus is enjoyment	6	10	4	60
Knowing the meaning of the term "uterus"	0	0	0	23

* Owing to the difficulties of translating from the Swedish language, this percentage is not available.
Source: Ronald Goldman & Juliette Goldman (1982). *Children's sexual thinking.* London: Routledge & Kegan Paul, pp. 197, 213, 240, 263, 354.

Some of the children's responses can only be classified as amusing. In response to the question "How can anyone know a newborn baby is a boy or a girl?" an 11-year-old English boy said, "If it's got a penis or not. If it has it's a boy. Girls have a virginia." And in all cultures there seems to be a lot of confusion about contraception. Here are some responses:

The pill goes down the stomach and dissolves the baby and it goes out in the bowels. You should take three pills a day. (American boy, 7 years old)

If you don't want to start one, you don't get married. There's no other way. (English girl, 7 years old)

The tubes are tied, the vocal cords. (Australian girl, 15 years old)

If the Goldmans' conclusion is right, that American children are sexual illiterates, the remedy seems to be a massive program of sex education in the United States.

Source: Ronald Goldman and Juliette Goldman. (1982). *Children's sexual thinking.* London: Routledge & Kegan Paul.

asked at around age 5, a time when children are generally asking questions. Boys also tended to ask a lot of questions at around age 9, and girls at ages 9 and 13 (Byler, 1969). The areas of sexual curiosity were (beginning with the most common) the origin of babies, the coming of another baby, intrauterine growth, the process of birth, the organs and functions of the body, physical gender differences, the relation of the father to reproduction, and marriage.

It is important that the sex education curriculum for a particular age group address the questions of that age group, rather than questions they haven't thought of yet or questions they thought about and answered long ago.

Children's Dirty Jokes

We can also tell something about children's sexual knowledge and interest by the dirty jokes they tell.

Anthropologist Rosemary Zumwalt collected dirty jokes from girls between

A Sample Sex Education Curriculum

This set of curriculum guidelines for sex education, developed by SIECUS, is based on teaching about six key concepts, and teaching about each concept at each age level, with age-appropriate material. The age levels are as follows:

- Level 1: ages 5 to 8; early elementary school
- Level 2: ages 9 to 12; upper elementary school
- Level 3: ages 12 to 15; middle school or junior high
- Level 4: ages 15 to 18; high school.

The guidelines recommend that the following material be taught:

Key Concept 1: Human Development

Topic 1: Reproductive Anatomy and Physiology

Level 1: Each body part has a correct name and a specific function. Boys and men have a penis, scrotum, and testicles. Girls and women have a vulva, clitoris, vagina, uterus, and ovaries. Both girls and boys have body parts that feel good when touched.

Level 2: The maturation of external and internal reproductive organs occurs during puberty. At puberty, boys begin to ejaculate and girls begin to menstruate.

Level 3: The sexual response system differs from the reproductive system. Some of the reproductive organs provide pleasure as well as reproductive capability.

Level 4: Chromosomes determine whether a developing fetus will be male or female. For both sexes, hormones influence growth and development as well as sexual and reproductive function. A woman's ability to reproduce ceases after menopause; a man can usually reproduce throughout his life. Both men and women can experience sexual pleasure throughout their life. Most people enjoy giving and receiving pleasure.

Topic 2: Reproduction

Level 1: Reproduction requires both a man and a woman. Men and women have reproductive organs that enable them to have a child. Not all men and women decide to have children. When a woman is pregnant, the fetus grows inside her body in her uterus. Babies usually come out of a woman's body through an opening called a vagina. Women have breasts that can provide milk for a baby. Sexual intercourse occurs when a man and a woman place the penis inside the vagina.

Level 2: Sexual intercourse provides pleasure. Whenever genital intercourse occurs, it is possible for the woman to become pregnant. There are ways to have genital intercourse without causing pregnancy.

Level 3: People should use contraception during sexual intercourse unless they want to have a child. Conception is most likely to occur midway between a woman's menstrual periods. Ovulation can occur any time during the month; therefore a woman may become pregnant at any time. When a girl begins to menstruate, she can become pregnant. When a boy produces sperm and can ejaculate, he can cause a pregnancy. An important first sign of pregnancy is a missed menstrual period.

Level 4: Menopause is when a woman's reproductive capacity ceases. Some people are unable to reproduce due to physiological reasons. Medical procedures can help some people with fertility problems. People who cannot reproduce can choose to adopt children. New reproductive technologies, such as artificial insemination, in vitro fertilization, and surrogate motherhood allow people with fertility problems to have children.

Topic 3: Puberty

Level 1: Bodies change as children grow older. People are able to have babies only after they have reached puberty.

Level 2: Puberty begins and ends at different ages for different people. Most changes in puberty are similar for boys and girls. Girls often begin pubertal changes before boys. Early adolescents often feel uncomfortable, clumsy, and/or self-conscious because of the rapid changes in their bodies. The sexual and reproductive systems mature during puberty. During puberty, girls begin to ovulate and menstruate, and boys begin to produce sperm and ejaculate. During puberty, many people begin to develop sexual and romantic feelings.

Level 3: Some people will not reach full puberty until their middle or late teens.

Topic 4: Body Image

Level 1: Individual bodies are different sizes, shapes, and colors. Male and female bodies are equally special. All bodies are special, including those that are disabled. Good health habits, such as diet and exercise, can improve the way a person looks and feels. Each person can be proud of the special qualities of his or her own body.

Level 2: A person's appearance is determined by heredity, environment, and health habits. The media portrays beautiful people, but most people do not fit these images. The value of a person is not determined by his or her appearance.

Level 3: The size and shape of the penis or breasts does not affect reproductive ability or the ability to be a good sexual partner. The size and shape of a person's body may affect how others feel about and behave toward that person. People with physical disabilities have the same feelings, needs, and desires as people without disabilities.

Level 4: Physical appearance is only one factor that attracts one person to another. A person who accepts and feels good about his or her body will seem more likeable and attractive to others. Physical attractiveness should not be a major factor in choosing friends or dating partners.

Topic 5: Sexual Identity and Orientation

Level 1: Everyone is born a boy or a girl. Boys and girls grow up to be men and women. Most men and women are heterosexual, which means they will be attracted to and fall in love with someone of the other gender. Some men and women are homosexual, which means they will be attracted to and fall in love with someone of the same gender. Homosexuals are also known as gay men and lesbian women.

Level 2: Sexual orientation refers to whether a person is heterosexual, homosexual, or bisexual. A bisexual person is attracted to men and women. It is not known why a person has a particular sexual orientation. Homosexual, heterosexual, and bisexual people are alike except for their sexual attraction. Homosexual and bisexual people are often mistreated, called hurtful names, or denied their rights because of their sexual orientation. Some people are afraid to admit they are homosexual because they fear they will be mistreated. Homosexual love relationships can be as fulfilling as heterosexual relationships. Gay men and lesbians can form families by adopting children or having their own chidren.

Level 3: Many young people have brief sexual experiences (including fantasies and dreams) with the same gender, but they mainly feel attracted to the other gender. When a homosexual person accepts his or her sexual orientation, gains strength and pride as a gay or lesbian person, and tells others, it is known as "coming out." People do not choose their sexual orientation. Sexual orientation cannot be changed by therapy or medicine.

Level 4: One's understanding and identification of one's sexual orientation may change during life. Teenagers who have questions about their sexual orientation should consult a trusted and knowledgeable adult.

The curriculum guidelines continue with equally detailed content for the remaining four key concepts:

Key Concept 2: Relationships

Key Concept 3: Personal Skills

Key Concept 4: Sexual Behavior

Key Concept 5: Sexual Health

Space does not permit me to list all the details under each of these concepts, so interested readers may want to consult the source listed below.

Source: Condensed from SIECUS (1991). *Guidelines for Comprehensive Sexuality Education.* New York: Sex Information and Education Council of the United States.

FIGURE 23.4
Children often have
inaccurate ideas about sex.

DENNIS the MENACE

"THAT'S FUNNY... MY DAD CAN TELL IF IT'S A BOY OR A GIRL JUST BY LOOKIN' AT THE BOTTOM OF ITS FEET."

the ages of 7 and 10 as part of her study of children's folklore (1976). The following is typical of the jokes they told her:

> There's this little boy, and he wanted to take a bath with his dad. And his dad said, "If you promise not to look under the curtain." And then he took a shower, and he looked under the curtain. And he said, "Dad, what's that long hairy thing?" And the father says, "That's my banana."
>
> Then he asks his Mom, "Can I take a shower with you, Mom?" She says, "If you promise not to look under the curtain." And they get into the shower, and he looks under the curtain. And he says, "Mom, what's that thing?" And she says, "That's my fruit bowl." And he says, "Mom, can I sleep with you and Dad?" And she says, "Yes, if you promise not to look under the covers." And he looks under the covers and says, "Mom, Dad's banana is in your fruit bowl!" (Zumwalt, 1976, p. 261)

Children's dirty jokes reflect several themes in their attitudes toward sexuality and in their interactions with their parents on the issue. First, children seem to view their parents as always trying to keep sex a secret from them. The parents consistently tell children not to look under the cover, for example. Second, the jokes reflect children's fascination with sex, particularly with the penis, the vagina, the breasts, and intercourse. The jokes generally revolve around these topics and children's attempts to find out about them. Third, the jokes seem to satirize adults' use of euphemisms for sexual terms. The joke above hinges on a parent's using a term such as "banana" instead of "penis." Most frequently, the fanciful names used for the sexual organs involve food (banana, hot dog), power (light bulbs, light sockets), or animals (gorilla). Commenting on the bathtub-shower form of dirty joke, an authority said, "In all forms of the . . . joke, the wonderful humor to the child is the mocking of the parents' evasions, which are somehow so foolishly phrased . . ." (Legman, 1968, p. 53).

Teenagers have outgrown this sort of joke, but they tell a parallel one:

> This little boy walks into the bathroom, and he catches his mother naked. She was a little embarrassed. He said, "Mommy, what's that?" And she says, "Oh,

that's where God hit me with an axe." And the little kid says, "Got you right in the cunt, eh?" (Zumwalt, 1976, p. 267)

Once again, this joke has the theme of a parent's embarrassment and use of evasions and euphemisms when dealing with sex. But now the child (teenager) reflects a sophistication about sex, perhaps even a greater sophistication than the parent has.

Sex educators should remember that children are aware of adults' attempts to "cover up" and of their embarrassment and their use of euphemisms, as these jokes indicate.

CURRICULUM

Space does not permit outlining a complex sex education curriculum here. Instead, a brief outline of major concepts to be covered in one major curriculum is given in Focus 23.3. Further references to curriculum materials are provided at the end of this chapter in "Suggestions for Further Reading."

Note that the sample curriculum in Focus 23.3 exemplifies several principles. First, sex education must be carried out at all grade levels. It cannot be provided all at once in a week (or a day) during the fifth or sixth grade. Curriculum materials are therefore geared to the age of the child and build on each other from year to year. For example, by the time conception and intercourse are discussed in grade 6 or 7, the child is already familiar with parts of the anatomy and understands terms such as "penis," "vagina," and "uterus." Second, correct terminology should be taught from the beginning. Even children in kindergarten and first grade should learn terms such as "penis" and "vagina."[2] Third, the curriculum should reflect the need to teach children about the emotional and social aspects of sex—such as dealing with sexual feelings and going on dates—as well as the biological and health aspects. These are important principles for any sex education curriculum.

Summary

Most children receive their sex education from their peers, not from their parents; as a result, those who argue for sex education in the home rather than in the school are not being realistic. Most Americans actually do favor sex education in the school, including education about AIDS. Further, the presumed negative effects of sex education are not substantiated by the available data.

The purposes of sex education include providing children with an adequate knowledge of the physical and emotional aspects of sex and eliminating unwarranted fears and anxieties.

Sex Respect is a new, politically conservative sex education curriculum that teaches abstinence.

A good instructor in sex education must have some accurate knowledge about

[2] The use of euphemisms and analogies by adults can cause children to have somewhat confused understandings of sex. One 4-year-old girl, when asked how a lady would get a baby to grow in her tummy, responded, "Get a duck." As it turns out, one widely distributed sex education book for children begins with a pencil dot (representing an ovum) and then proceeds through the sex lives of flowers, bees, rabbits, giraffes, chickens, and dogs before getting to humans. No wonder the little girl thought that in order to have a baby, you have to begin with a duck (Bernstein, 1976).

sex, must be comfortable discussing it, and must be good at listening to children's questions.

What one teaches in sex education at each age depends on what children are thinking about at that age. Children pass through various stages in their understanding of sex. First, they believe that a baby has always existed. Later they realize that the parents caused the baby's creation, though they have little idea of exactly how. Older children acquire a more and more scientific understanding of reproduction.

Children generally do not know the correct names of the sexual organs. American children have a relatively poor understanding of sexual concepts.

Children's dirty jokes reflect their parents' attempts to hide sex from them, their parents' use of euphemisms rather than accurate terms, and their great fascination with sexual organs and intercourse.

Review Questions

1. For most children, the major source of sex information is the mother. True or false?

2. Approximately 35 percent of American parents favor sex education in the schools. True or false?

3. Research on the effects of sex education indicates that those teenagers who had sex education in high school are more likely to engage in premarital intercourse and have a higher incidence of premarital pregnancies. True or false?

4. Sex Respect is a model sex education curriculum sponsored by SIECUS and favored by most sex education experts. True or false?

5. On the basis of their research, the Goldmans argue that North American children are sexual illiterates who possess less sexual knowledge than their counterparts in other cultures such as Australia and Sweden. True or false?

6. According to Bernstein's research on children's stages of understanding about sexual intercourse and conception, most children do not have a good physiological understanding until they reach Stage 6, when they are 12 years of age or older. True or false?

7. Analyses of children's dirty jokes indicate that children realize their parents try to keep sex a secret from them. True or false?

(The answers to all review questions are at the end of the book, beginning on page 731.)

Questions for Thought, Discussion, and Debate

1. Design a sample sex education curriculum for the schools, indicating what you think would be important to teach at various age levels and what your reasoning is behind your choices.

2. Debate the following topic. Resolved: A sex education unit, at least a week long, should be included in all grades in all schools.

Suggestions for Further Reading

Calderone, Mary S., & Ramey, James W. (1983). *Talking with your child about sex: Questions and answers for children from birth to puberty*. New York: Random

House. An excellent guide for parents. Mary Calderone is one of America's leading sex educators.

Fischer, H. L., Krajicek, M. J., & Borthick, W. A. (1973). *Sex education for the developmentally disabled.* Baltimore: University Park Press. Children with developmental disabilities need sex education just as much as other children do, and this book provides a guide.

Gordon, Sol. (1986, Oct.) What kids needs to know. *Psychology Today.* Reprinted in O. Pocs (Ed.), *Human Sexuality 88/89.* Guilford, CT: Dushkin. Sol Gordon, a leading sex educator, provides a humorous view of what sex education ought to be accomplishing.

Mayle, P., Robins, A., & Walter, P. (1973). *Where did I come from?* Secaucus, N.J.: Lyle Stuart. A delightful sex education book for young children. Its companion volume—*What's happening to me?*—is for children approaching puberty.

Epilogue

In the AIDS era, the challenge for us is to create joyous, intimate, fulfilling sex. I am convinced that there are two courses of action that are absolute folly. One is to be so overwhelmed by the threat of AIDS that sex becomes locked in the icy grip of anxiety. The other absolute folly is to hide our heads in the sand, ignore the threat of AIDS (and herpes and genital warts), and continue with sex as usual. The AIDS epidemic will then only intensify. We need to steer a middle course in which we take AIDS and other STDs seriously, while keeping sex joyful and satisfying.

One day in 1988 when my son was approaching his seventh birthday, he asked me, quite out of the blue, "Mommy, how can you make love without getting AIDS?" Rather irrelevantly, I was pleased about several features of his question—the fact that I'd done a good enough job with his sex education so far that he knew about making love, that he knew he could talk with me about it, and that making love was something he looked forward to in the future. But the question itself was terribly sad, for it indicated that an elementary school child growing up in the late 1980s not only knew about AIDS but actually assumed that it was the necessary consequence of making love. I certainly had not conveyed that belief to him. He had leaped to the conclusion based on educational TV ad campaigns about AIDS. Although I applaud the ad campaigns, I am saddened about the sexual environment in which he is growing up. Certainly I will not tell either him or my daughter the same things about sex that I had planned to at the time of their births.

I confess that I have no easy answers to the challenge I posed at the beginning of this epilogue. I am certain that sex education is one part of the solution, as is drug education. Continued funding for both medical and psychological research is essential. We might even need to consider wild and crazy lifestyles like monogamy. Meanwhile, we need to remember that sex can and should be joyous.

Directory of Resources
in Human Sexuality

I. Health Issues: Pregnancy, Contraception, Abortion, Diseases

American Cancer Society
1599 Clifton Road, N. E.
Atlanta, GA 30329-4251
(404) 320-3333
1-800-227-2345
Offers information and funds research on cancer.

American Foundation for the Prevention of
Venereal Disease, Inc.
799 Broadway, Suite 638
New York, NY 10003
(212) 759-2069
Provides a complete guide, *STD Prevention,*
emphasizing sex education and personal hygiene.

Association for Voluntary Surgical Contraception
79 Madison Avenue
New York, NY 10016
(212) 561-8000
Offers information on sterilization.

CDC National AIDS Clearinghouse
P.O. Box 6003
Rockville, MD 20849-6003
1-800-458-5231
Operated by the U.S. Public Health Service, this
clearinghouse provides information and referrals on
AIDS/HIV.

La Leche League International
9616 Minneapolis Avenue
P.O. Box 1209
Franklin Park, IL 60131-8209
(708) 455-7730
An organization devoted to encouraging
breast-feeding.

National Abortion Rights Action League (NARAL)
1101 14th Street, N.W.
Washington, DC 20005
(202) 408-4600
A political action organization working at both state
and national levels, dedicated to preserving a
woman's right to safe and legal abortion and also to
teaching its members effective use of the political
process to ensure abortion rights.

Divison of STD/HIV Prevention
National Center for Prevention Services
Centers for Disease Control
Atlanta, Georgia 30333
(404) 639-2564
Offers the most up-to-date information on
prevention-related issues for sexually transmitted
diseases and the human immunodeficiency virus;
administers federal programs for the prevention of
STD and HIV infection.

National Resource Center on Women and AIDS
2000 P Street N.W., Suite 508
Washington, DC 20036
(202) 872-1770
A project, located at the Center for Women Policy
Studies, devoted to the special problems of women
and AIDS.

National Right to Life Committee, Inc.
Suite 500
419 7th Street, N.W.
Washington, DC 20004
(202) 626-8800
An organization based on the belief that human life
begins at conception and that abortion should
therefore be opposed.

National Women's Health Resource Center
2440 M Street, N.W.
Washington, DC 20037
(202) 293-6045
An organization dedicated to the betterment of
women's health. Publishes a newsletter, *National
Women's Health Report.*

Planned Parenthood Federation of America (PPFA)
810 Seventh Avenue
New York, NY 10019
(212) 541-7800
PPFA is the nation's oldest and largest voluntary
family planning agency. Through local clinics (check
your telephone book), it offers birth control
information and services, pregnancy testing,
voluntary sterilization, prenatal care, early abortion,
pelvic and breast exams, and other reproductive
health services, including sexuality education.

PMS Access
P.O. Box 9326
Madison, WI 53715
1-800-222-4PMS
Provides a toll-free line to talk to a pharmacist
about PMS, as well as physician referrals and
programs.

Population Information Program
Johns Hopkins Center for Communication Programs
527 St. Paul Place
Baltimore, MD 21202
FAX (410) 659-6366
Publishes *Population Reports,* frequent, up-to-date
reports on contraception and family planning with
emphasis on developing countries.

II. Sex Education, Sex Research, and Sex Therapy

Alan Guttmacher Institute
111 Fifth Avenue
New York, NY 10003-1089
(212) 254-5656
An organization devoted to promoting family
planning and sex education. It produces many
excellent, informative publications.

American Association of Sex Educators, Counselors,
and Therapists (AASECT)
435 North Michigan Avenue, Suite 1717
Chicago, IL 60611
(312) 644-0828
This organization certifies sex educators,
sex counselors, and sex therapists and provides
other services associated with sex education and
sex therapy.

Masters and Johnson Institute
24 South Kingshighway
St. Louis, MO 63108
(314) 361-2377
FAX (314) 361-8390
Human Sexuality Information Hotline
1-900-463-4636
A public foundation committed to sex research,
sex therapy, and education.

Sex Information and Education Council of the
United States (SIECUS)
130 West 42nd Street, Suite 2500
New York, NY 10036
(212) 819-9770
Provides a library and information service on
sex education, including curricula. Publishes
bibliographies and maintains a database of titles of
books and journals on human sexuality, currently
consisting of over 8000 entries.

Society for the Scientific Study of Sex
P.O. Box 208
Mount Vernon, IA 52314
(319) 895-8407
An organization devoted to promoting quality sex
research; publishes the *Journal of Sex Research*.

III. Lifestyle Issues

Coalition on Sexuality and Disability, Inc.
380 2nd Avenue, 4th Floor
New York, NY 10010
(212) 242-3900
Educational and advocacy organization related to
sexuality and socialization and people with
disabilities.

Harry Benjamin International Gender Dysphoria
Association
1515 El Camino Real
Palo Alto, CA 94306
Society for professionals interested in the study and
care of transsexualism and gender dysphoria.

J2CP Information Services
P.O. Box 184
San Juan Capistrano, CA 92693-0184
Information on transsexualism and professional
referrals

Lambda Legal Defense and Education Fund
666 Broadway
New York, NY 10012-2317
(212) 995-8585
and
606 S. Olive St. #580
Los Angeles, CA 90014
(213) 629-2728
Advances the legal rights of lesbians, gay men, and
people with AIDS through test case litigation and
public education. Publishes many resource manuals,
newsletters, bibliographies, and articles on current
topics for lesbian, gay, and HIV/AIDS communities.

National Council on Sexual Addiction and
Compulsivity
P.O. Box 20249
Wickenburg, AZ 85358
An organization dedicated to promoting public
understanding of sexual addiction and
compulsivities.

National Gay and Lesbian Task Force (NGLTF)
1734 14th Street, N.W.
Washington, DC 20009-3409
(202) 332-6483
The oldest national gay and lesbian civil rights
advocacy organization. Lobbying, grassroots
organizing, publications (call or write for listing),
and referrals.

Society for the Second Self
Box 194
Tulare, CA 93275
(209) 688-6386
An organization for heterosexual men who cross-
dress and their wives.

IV. Media

Multi-Focus, Inc.
1525 Franklin Street
San Francisco, CA 94109-4592
1-800-821-0514
Has one of the largest selections of sex education and sex therapy films and videos avaiable.

Focus International
14 Oregon Drive
Huntington Station, NY 11746
(516) 549-2066
Another organization with a large selection of sex education and sex therapy films and videos.

V. Sexual Victimization

Antisocial and Violent Behavior Branch
National Institute of Mental Health
5600 Fishers Lane, Room 18-105
Rockville, MD 20857
(301) 443-3728
This branch is the focal point at the National Institute of Mental Health for research on violent behavior, including sexual abuse and sexual assault.

VI. Feminism and Gender Issues

National Organization for Changing Men
794 Penn Avenue
Pittsburgh, Pennsylvania 15221
(412) 432-3010
Provides a network of support and services for men and women committed to positive changes in men's roles and relationships. Publishes *Men's Studies Newsletter* and *Brother Magazine.*

National Organization for Women (NOW)
1000 Sixteenth St., N.W., Suite 700
Washington, DC 20036
(202) 331-0066
NOW seeks to take action to bring women into full participation in the mainstream of U.S. society, exercising all the privileges and responsibilities thereof in truly equal partnership with men.

VII. Journals

Annual Review of Sex Research
Society for the Scientific Study of Sex
P.O. Box 208
Mount Vernon, IA 52314

Archives of Sexual Behavior
Plenum Publishing Corporation
233 Spring Street
New York, NY 10013

Gender & Society
Sage Publications
2455 Teller Road
Newbury Park, CA 91320

Journal of Gay and Lesbian Psychotherapy
Haworth Press
12 West 32nd Street
New York, NY 10001

Journal of Homosexuality
Haworth Press
12 West 32nd Street
New York, NY 10001

Journal of Men's Studies
Men's Studies Press
P.O. Box 32
Harriman, TN 37748-0032

Journal of Sex and Marital Therapy
Brunner/Mazel, Inc.
19 Union Square West
New York, NY 10003
(212) 924-3344

Journal of Sex Education and Therapy
American Association of Sex Educators, Counselors, and Therapists
435 North Michigan Avenue, Suite 1717
Chicago, IL 60611

Journal of Sex Research
Society for the Scientific Study of Sex
P.O. Box 208
Mount Verson, IA 52314

Journal of the History of Sexuality
University of Chicago Press
P.O. Box 37005
Chicago, IL 60637

Psychology of Women Quarterly
Cambridge University Press
40 West 20th Street
New York, NY 10011

Sex Roles: A Journal of Research
Plenum Press
233 Spring Street
New York, NY 10013

Sexuality and Disability
Human Sciences Press
233 Spring Street
New York, NY 10013-1578
(212) 620-8000

Bibliography

Abel, Ernest L. (1980). Fetal alcohol syndrome. *Psychological Bulletin, 87,* 29–50.

Abel, Ernest L. (1984). *Fetal alcohol syndrome and fetal alcohol effects.* New York: Plenum.

Abplanalp, Judith M. (1983). Premenstrual syndrome: A selective review. In S. Golub (Ed.), *Lifting the curse menstruation* (pp. 107–123). New York: Haworth.

Abramowitz, Stephen I. (1986). Psychosocial outcomes of sex reassignment surgery. *Journal of Consulting and Clinical Psychology 54,* 183–189.

Abramson, Paul R. (1977). Ethical requirements for research on human sexual behavior: From the perspectives of participating subjects. *Journal of Social Issues, 33,* 184–192.

Abramson, Paul R., & Mechanic, Mindy B. (1983). Sex and the media: Three decades of best-selling books and major motion pictures. *Archives of Sexual Behavior, 12,* 185–206.

ACSF Investigators (1992). AIDS and sexual behaviour in France. *Nature, 360,* 407–409.

Adams, Catherine G., & Turner, Barbara F. (1985). Reported change in sexuality from young adulthood to old age. *Journal of Sex Research, 21,* 126–141.

Adams, James F. (1973). *Understanding adolescence.* Boston: Allyn and Bacon.

Adams, J. W., et al. (1983). Sexual harassment of university students. *Journal of College Student Personnel, 24,* 484–490.

Addiego, F., Belzer, E. G., Comolli, J., Moger, W., Perry, J. D., & Whipple, B. (1981). Female ejaculation: A case study. *Journal of Sex Research, 17,* 13–21.

Adler, N. E., David, H. P., Major, B. P., Roth, S. H., Russo, N. F., & Wyatt, G. E. (1992). Psychological factors in abortion: A review. *American Psychologist, 47,* 1194–1204.

Adler, N. E., & Dolcini, P. (1986). Psychological issues in abortion for adolescents. In G. B. Melton (Ed.), *Adolescent abortion: Psychological and legal issues* (pp. 74–95). Lincoln: University of Nebraska Press.

Adler, N. E., et al. (1990). Psychological responses after abortion. *Science, 248,* 41–44.

Agnew, Bruce, & Stein, Rob. (1990, Jan.). Getting closer to an AIDS vaccine. *Journal of NIH Research, 2,* 33.

Aiken, D. L. (1973, Sept. 26). Ex-sailor charges jail rape, stirs up storm. *Advocate,* 5.

Albee, George W. (1977). The Protestant ethic, sex, and psychotherapy. *American Psychologist, 32,* 150–161.

Albin, Rochelle S. (1977). Psychological studies of rape. *Signs, 3,* 423–435.

Alexander, Pamela C., & Lupfer, Shirley L. (1987). Family characteristics and long-term consequences associated with sexual abuse. *Archives of Sexual Behavior, 16,* 235–246.

Allen, David F., & Allen, Victoria S. (1979). *Ethical issues in mental retardation.* Nashville, TN: Abingdon Press.

Allen, Donald M. (1980). Young male prostitutes: A psychological study. *Archives of Sexual Behavior, 9,* 399–426.

Allgeier, Elizabeth Rice, & Fogel, Arthur. (1978). Coital position and sex roles: Responses to cross-sex behavior in bed. *Journal of Consulting and Clinical Psychology, 46,* 588–589.

Allgeier, Elizabeth R. (1976, May). Heterosexuality and sex-typing. Paper presented at meetings of the Midwestern Psychological Association, Chicago.

Allgeier, Elizabeth R. (1981). The influence of androgynous identification on heterosexual relations. *Sex Roles, 7,* 321–330.

Allgeier, Elizabeth R., & McCormick, Naomi B. (Eds.) (1982). *Changing boundaries: Gender roles and sexual behavior.* Palo Alto, CA: Mayfield.

Alter, Miriam J., et al. (1986). Hepatitis B virus transmission between heterosexuals. *Journal of the American Medical Association, 256,* 1307–1310.

Altman, I., & Taylor, D. A. (1973). *Social penetration: The development of interpersonal relationships.* New York: Holt, Rinehart & Winston.

Alzate, Heli, & Londono, M. L. (1984). Vaginal erotic sensitivity. *Journal of Sex and Marital Therapy, 10,* 499–506.

Amberson, J. Ingrid, & Hoon, Peter W. (1985). Hemodynamics of sequential orgasm. *Archives of Sexual Behavior, 14,* 351–360.

American Cancer Society. (1980). *Cancer facts & figures.* New York: American Cancer Society.

American Cancer Society. (1987). *Cancer facts & figures—1987.* New York: American Cancer Society.

American Cancer Society. (1988). *Facts on testicular cancer.* New York: American Cancer Society.

American Cancer Society. (1991). *Facts on breast cancer.* New York: American Cancer Society.

American Law Institute. (1962). *Model penal code: Proposed official draft.* Philadelphia: ALI.

American Psychological Association, Ad hoc Committee on Ethical Standards in Psychological Research. (1973). *Ethical principles in the conduct of research with human participants.* Washington, DC: APA.

Amick, Angelynne, E., & Calhoun, Karen S. (1987). Resistance to sexual aggression: Personality, attitudinal, and situational factors. *Archives of Sexual Behavior, 16,* 153–164.

Amir, Menachem. (1971). *Patterns in forcible rape.* Chicago: University of Chicago Press.

Andersen, Barbara L. (1981). A comparison of systematic desensitization and directed masturbation in the treatment of primary orgasmic dysfunction in females. *Journal of Consulting and Clinical Psychology, 49,* 568–570.

Andersen, Barbara L. (1983). Primary orgasmic dysfunction: Diagnostic considerations and review of treatment. *Psychological Bulletin, 93,* 105–136.

Andrews, Eva, & Cappon, Daniel. (1957). Autism and schizophrenia in a child guidance clinic. *Canadian Psychiatric Association Journal, 2,* 1–25.

Andrews, Lori B. (1989). Alternative modes of reproduction. In S. Cohen & N. Taub (Eds.), *Reproductive laws for the 1990s* (pp. 361–404). Clifton, NJ: Humana Press.

Angrist, Shirley S. (1969). The study of sex roles. *Journal of Social Issues, 25,* 215–232.

Anonymous. (1975). When a woman is attacked. In L. G. Schultz (Ed.), *Rape victimology.* Springfield, IL: Charles C. Thomas.

Anson, Robert S. (1977, Oct. 25). *San Francisco Chronicle.*

Antle, Katharyn. (1978). Active involvement of expectant fathers in pregnancy: Some further considerations. *Journal of Obstetric, Gynecologic and Neonatal Nursing, 7*(2), 7–12.

Apfelbaum, Bernard. (1989). Retarded ejaculation: A much-misunderstood syndrome. In S. Leiblum & R. Rosen (Eds.), *Principles and practice of sex therapy* (2nd ed.) (pp. 168–206). New York: Guilford.

Aquinas, St. Thomas. (1968). *Summa theologica* (Vol. 43). (Thomas Gilly, Trans.). New York: McGraw-Hill.

Arafat, Ibtihaj S., & Cotton, Wayne L. (1974). Masturbation practices of males and females. *Journal of Sex Research, 10,* 293–307.

Araoz, Daniel L. (1982). *Hypnosis and sex therapy.* New York: Brunner/Mazel.

A regular check for testicular tumors. (1980, Oct. 15). *Emergency Medicine 12,* 167–168.

Arehart-Treichal, J. (1974, May 11). Sperm don't like it hot. *Science News, 105,* 309–310.

Aristotle. (1925). *Nicomachean ethics.* (W. D. Ross, Trans.) Oxford: Clarendon Press.

Ashton, Eleanor. (1983). Measures of play behavior: The influence of sex-role stereotyped children's books. *Sex Roles, 9,* 43–47.

Associated Press. (1971, Aug. 28). German drug may reduce sex offenses. *Houston Chronicle.*

Associated Press. (1984, Mar. 25). Baby girl is born from transferred embryo. *New York Times.*

Athanasiou, Robert, et al. (1970). Sex. *Psychology Today, 4*(2), 39–52.

Atkeson, Beverly M., et al. (1982). Victims of rape: Repeated assessment of depressive symptoms. *Journal of Consulting and Clinical Psychology, 50,* 96–102.

Attorney General's Commission on Pornography. (1986). *Final report.* Washington, DC: U.S. Department of Justice.

Bach, G., & Wyden, P. (1969). *The intimate enemy: How to fight fair in love and marriage.* New York: Morrow.

Bader, Louis. (1981). Constitutional Law—Police Power—Equal Protection—Voluntary Sexual Deviate Intercourse Statute. *Duquesne Law Review, 19,* 793–800.

Badgley, R. F., Caron, D. F., & Powell, M. G. (1977). *Report of the Committee on the Operation of the Abortion Law.* Ottawa: Minister of Supply and Services Canada.

Bailey, J. Michael, & Pillard, Richard C. (1991). A genetic study of male sexual orientation. *Archives of General Psychiatry, 48,* 1089–1096.

Bailey, J. M., Pillard, R. C., Neale, M. C., & Agyei, Y. (1993). Heritable factors influence sexual orientation in women. *Archives of General Psychiatry, 50,* 217–223.

Bailey, J. M., Willerman, L., & Parks, C. (1991). A test of the maternal stress theory of human male homosexuality. *Archives of Sexual Behavior, 20,* 277–294.

Baldwin, John D., & Baldwin, Janice I. (1989). The socialization of homosexuality and heterosexuality in a non-Western society. *Archives of Sexual Behavior, 18,* 13–30.

Bancroft, John. (1974). *Deviant sexual behavior: Modification and assessment.* New York: Oxford University Press.

Bancroft, John. (1978). The prevention of sexual offenses. In C. B. Qualls et al. (Eds.), *The prevention of sexual disorders.* (pp. 95–116). New York: Plenum.

Bancroft, John. (1987). A physiological approach. In J. H. Geer & W. T. O'Donohue (Eds.), *Theories of human sexuality.* (pp. 411–421). New York: Plenum.

Bandura, Albert. (1969). *Principles of behavior modification.* New York: Holt.

Bandura, Albert J. (1977). *Social learning theory.* Englewood Cliffs, NJ: Prentice-Hall.

Bandura, Albert, & Walters, Richard H. (1963). *Social learning and personality development.* New York: Holt.

Barash, David P. (1977a). *Sociobiology and behavior.* New York: Elsevier.

Barash, David P. (1977b). Sociobiology of rape in mallards: Response of the mated male. *Science, 197,* 788–789.

Barash, David P. (1982). *Sociobiology and behavior* (2d ed.). New York: Elsevier.

Barbach, Lonnie G. (1975). *For yourself: The fulfillment of female sexuality.* Garden City, NY: Anchor/Doubleday.

Barclay, Andrew M. (1973). Sexual fantasies in men and women. *Medical Aspects of Human Sexuality. 7,* 209–212.

Bardwick, Judith M. (1971). *Psychology of women: A study of biocultural conflicts.* New York: Harper & Row.

Barker, William J., & Perlman, Daniel. (1975). Volunteer bias and personality traits in sexual standards research. *Archives of Sexual Behavior, 4,* 161–171.

Barlow, David H. (1973). Increasing heterosexual responsiveness in the treatment of sexual deviation: A review of the clinical and experimental evidence. *Behavior Therapy, 4,* 655–671.

Barlow, David H. (1986). Causes of sexual dysfunction: The role of cognitive interference. *Journal of Consulting and Clinical Psychology, 54,* 140–148.

Barlow, D. H., Abel, G. G., & Blanchard, E. B. (1978). Gender identity change in transsexuals: Follow-up and replication. *Archives of General Psychiatry.*

Barlow, David H., & Agras, W. S. (1973). Fading to increase heterosexual responsiveness in homosexuals. *Journal of Applied Behavior Analysis, 6,* 355–366.

Barlow, D. H., Leitenberg, H., & Agras, W. S. (1969). Experimental control of sexual deviation through manipulation of noxious scenes in covert sensitization. *Journal of Abnormal Psychology, 74,* 596–601.

Barlow, D. H., Sakheim, D. K., & Beck, J. G. (1983). Anxiety increases sexual arousal. *Journal of Abnormal Psychology, 92,* 49–54.

Barnett, W. (1973). *Sexual freedom and the Constitution.* Albuquerque: University of New Mexico Press.

Baron, Larry, & Straus, Murray A. (1989). *Four theories of rape in American society.* New Haven: Yale University Press.

Barrows, Sydney B. (1986). *Mayflower madam.* New York: Arbor House.

Bart, Pauline B. (1971). Depression in middle-aged women. In V. G. Gornick & B. K. Moran (Eds.), *Women in sexist society.* New York: Basic Books.

Bart, Pauline B., & O'Brien, P. H. (1985). *Stopping rape: Successful survival strategies.* New York: Pergamon.

Bartell, Gilbert D. (1970). Group sex among the mid-Americans. *Journal of Sex Research, 6,* 113–130.

Batra, Ashok K., & Lue, Tom F. (1990). Physiology and pathology of penile erection. *Annual Review of Sex Research, 1,* 251–264.

Baulieu, Etienne-Emile. (1989). Contragestion and other clinical applications of RU486, an antiprogesterone at the receptor. *Science, 245,* 1351–1357.

Baumeister, Roy F. (1988a). Masochism as escape from the self. *Journal of Sex Research, 25,* 28–59.

Baumeister, Roy F. (1988b). Gender differences in masochistic scripts. *Journal of Sex Research, 25,* 478–499.

Beach, Frank A. (1947). Evolutionary changes in the physiological control of mating behavior in mammals. *Psychological Review, 54,* 297–315.

Beach, Frank A. (Ed.). (1976). *Human sexuality in four perspectives.* Baltimore, MD: Johns Hopkins University Press.

Beach, Frank, & Merari, A. (1970). Coital behavior in dogs. V. Effects of estrogen and progesterone on mating and other forms of social behavior in the bitch. *Journal of Comparative and Physiological Psychology Monograph, 70*(1), Part 2, 1–22.

Becker, Judith V., et al. (1986). Level of postassault sexual functioning in rape and incest victims. *Archives of Sexual Behavior, 15,* 37–50.

Becker, Judith V., & Kaplan, Meg S. (1991). Rape victims: Issues, theories, and treatment. *Annual Review of Sex Research, 2,* 267–292.

Behrman, Richard E., & Rosen, Tove S. (1976). HEW Publication No. 05 76-128, 12-1–12-116.

Beir, E. G., & Sternberg, D. P. (1977). Marital communication. *Journal of Communication, 27,* 92–103.

Belcastro, Philip A. (1985). Sexual behavior differences between black and white students. *Journal of Sex Research, 21,* 56–67.

Bell, Alan P. (1974a, Summer). Childhood and adolescent sexuality. Address delivered at the Institute for Sex Research, Indiana University.

Bell, Alan P. (1974b). Homosexualities: Their range and character. In *Nebraska symposium on motivation 1973.* Lincoln: University of Nebraska Press.

Bell, Alan P., & Weinberg, Martin S. (1978). *Homosexualities.* New York: Simon & Schuster.

Bell, A. P., Weinberg, M. S., & Hammersmith, S. K. (1981). *Sexual preference.* Bloomington: Indiana University Press.

Bell, N. J., & Carver, W. (1980). A reevaluation of gender label effects: Expectant mothers' responses to infants. *Child Development, 51,* 925–927.

Bell, Robert R. (1966). *Premarital sex in a changing society.* Englewood Cliffs, NJ: Prentice–Hall.

Bell, R. R., Turner, S., & Rosen, L. (1975). A multivariate analysis of female extramarital coitus. *Journal of Marriage and the Family, 37,* 375–384.

Belliveau, Fred, & Richter, Lin. (1970). *Understanding human sexual inadequacy.* New York: Bantam.

Belzer, E. G. (1981). Orgasmic expulsions of women: A review and heuristic inquiry. *Journal of Sex Research, 17,* 1–12.

Bem, Sandra L. (1974). The measurement of psychological androgyny. *Journal of Consulting and Clinical Psychology, 42,* 155–162.

Bem, Sandra L. (1975). Sex-role adaptability: One consequence of psychological androgyny. *Journal of Personality and Social Psychology, 31,* 634–643.

Bem, Sandra L. (1981). Gender schema theory: A cognitive account of sex typing. *Psychological Review, 88,* 354–364.

Bem, Sandra L., & Bem, D. J. (1970). Case study of nonconscious ideology: Training the woman to know her place. In D. J. Bem (Ed.), *Beliefs, attitudes, and human affairs.* Belmont, CA: Brooks/Cole.

Bem, S. L., Martyna, W., & Watson, C. (1976). Sex-typing and androgyny: Further explorations of the expressive domain. *Journal of Personality and Social Psychology, 34,* 1016–1023.

Bendet, Peggy. (1986, Aug.–Sept.). Hostile eyes: What is behind the anger and fear triggered by homosexuality? *Campus Voice,* 30–36.

Benjamin, Harry, & Masters, R. E. L. (1964). *Prostitution and morality.* New York: Julian Press.

Benkert, O., Witt, W., & Leitz, A. (1979). Effects of testosterone undecanoate on sexual potency and the hypothalamic-pituitary-gonadal axis of impotent males. *Archives of Sexual Behavior, 8,* 471–480.

Benney, M., Riesman, D., and Star, S. (1956). Age and sex in the interview. *American Journal of Sociology, 62,* 143–152.

Benson, Donna J., & Thomson, Gregg E. (1982). Sexual harassment on a university campus: The confluence of authority relations, sexual interest and gender stratification. *Social Problems, 29,* 236–251.

Benson, Rebecca. (1986). Pornography and the first amendment. *Harvard Women's Law Journal, 9,* 153–172.

Bentler, Peter M., & Abramson, Paul R. (1981). The science of sex research: Some methodological considerations. *Archives of Sexual Behavior, 10,* 225–252.

Berardo, Felix. (1968). Widowhood status in the United States: Perspective on a neglected aspect of the family life-cycle. *Family Coordinator, 17,* 191–203.

Berg, J. H., & Derlega, V. J. (1987). Themes in the study of self-disclosure. In V. J. Derlega & J. H. Berg (Eds.), *Self-*

disclosure: Theory, research and therapy (pp. 1–8). New York: Plenum.

Berg, Phyllis, A., & Hyde, Janet S. (1976, Aug.). Race and sex differences in causal attributions of success and failure. Paper presented at meeting of the American Psychological Association, Washington, DC.

Berger, Charles J. (1980). Medical risks associated with "natural" family planning. *Advances in Planned Parenthood, 15*(1), 1–2.

Berger, Raymond M. (1982). *Gay and gray: The older homosexual man.* Champaign, IL: University of Illinois Press.

Bergquist, Christer, et al. (1979). Inhibition of ovulation in women by intranasal treatment with a luteinizing hormone agonist. *Contraception, 19,* 497–506.

Bergstrom-Walan, Maj-Briht, & Nielsen, Helle. (1990). Sexual expression among 60–80 year-old men and women: A sample from Stockholm, Sweden. *Journal of Sex Research, 27,* 289–295.

Berk, Bernard. (1977). Face-saving at the singles dance. *Social Problems,* 530–544.

Bermant, Gordon. (1972). Behavior therapy approaches to modification of sexual preferences: Biological perspective and critique. In J. Bardwick (Ed.), *Readings on the psychology of women.* New York: Harper & Row.

Bermant, Gordon, & Davidson, Julian M. (1974). *Biological bases of sexual behavior.* New York: Harper & Row.

Bernard, Jesse. (1981). The good provider role: Its rise and fall. *American Psychologist, 36,* 1–12.

Bernard, M., Levine, E., Presser, S., & Stecich, M. (1985). *The rights of single people.* New York: Bantam Books.

Berne, Eric. (1970). *Sex in human loving.* New York: Simon & Schuster.

Bernstein, Anne C. (1976). How children learn about sex and birth. *Psychology Today, 9*(8), 31.

Bernstein, Anne C., & Cowan, Philip, A. (1975). Children's concepts of how people get babies. *Child Development, 46,* 77–92.

Berscheid, Ellen, & Walster, Elaine. (1974a). A little bit about love. In T. L. Huston (Ed.), *Foundations of interpersonal attraction.* New York: Academic.

Berscheid, Ellen, & Walster, Elaine. (1974b). Physical attractiveness. *Advances in Experimental Social Psychology, 7,* 157–215.

Berscheid, Ellen, et al. (1971). Physical attractiveness and dating choice: A test of the matching hypothesis. *Journal of Experimental Social Psychology, 7,* 173–189.

Bess, Barbara E., & Janus, Samuel S. (1976). Prostitution. In B. J. Sadock, et al. (Eds.), *The sexual experience.* Baltimore: Williams & Wilkins.

Bibring, Grete, et al. (1961). A study of the psychological processes in pregnancy and of the earliest mother-child relationship. *The psychoanalytic study of the child* (Vol. XVI, pp. 9–72). New York: International Universities Press.

Bieber, Irving. (1976). A discussion of "Homosexuality: The ethical challenge." *Journal of Consulting and Clinical Psychology, 44,* 163–166.

Biller, Henry, & Meredith, D. (1975). *Father power.* New York: Anchor Books.

Billings, Andrew. (1979). Conflict resolution in distressed and non-distressed married couples. *Journal of Consulting and Clinical Psychology, 47,* 368–376.

Billings, E. L., Billings, J. J., & Catarinch, M. (1974). *Atlas of the ovulation method.* Collegeville, MN: Liturgical Press.

Billy, J. O. G., Tanfer, K., Grady, W. R., & Klepinger, D. H. (1993). The sexual behavior of men in the United States. *Family Planning Perspectives, 25*(2), 52–60.

Bingham, H. C. (1928). Sex development in apes. *Comparative Psychology Monographs, 5,* 1–165.

Bingol, N., Fuchs, M., Diaz, V., Stone, R., & Gromish, D. (1987). Teratogenicity of cocaine in humans. *Journal of Pediatrics, 110,* 93–96.

Birchler, Gary R., Weiss, R. L., & Vincent, J. P. (1975). Multimethod analysis of social reinforcement exchange between maritally distressed and nondistressed spouse and stranger dyads. *Journal of Personality and Social Psychology, 31,* 349–360.

Birnbaum, Judith A. (1976). Life patterns and self-esteem in gifted family-oriented and career-committed women. In M. Mednick, L. W. Hoffman, & S. Tangri (Eds.), *Women: Social psychological perspectives on achievement.* New York: Psychological Dimensions.

Biskind, Morton S. (1947). The relation of nutritional deficiency to impaired libido and potency in the male. *Journal of Gerontology, 2,* 303–314.

Blair, C. David, & Lanyon, Richard I. (1981). Exhibitionism: Etiology and treatment. *Psychological Bulletin, 89,* 439–463.

Blanchard, R., Clemmensen, L. H., & Steiner, B. W. (1983). Gender reorientation and psychosocial adjustment in male-to-female transsexuals. *Archives of Sexual Behavior, 12,* 503–510.

Blanchard, R., Racansky, I. G., & Steiner, B. W. (1986). Phallometric detection of fetishistic arousal in heterosexual male cross-dressers. *Journal of Sex Research, 22,* 452–462.

Blanchard, Ray, & Steiner, Betty W. (1983). Gender reorientation, psychological adjustment, and involvement with female partners in female-to-male transsexuals. *Archives of Sexual Behavior, 12,* 149–158.

Blanchard, W. H. (1959). The group process in gang rape. *Journal of Social Psychology, 49,* 259–266.

Blechman, E. A., Clay, C. J., Kipke, M. D., & Bickel, W. K. (1988). The premenstrual experience. In E. Blechman & K. Brownell (Eds.), *Handbook of behavioral medicine for women.* (pp. 80–91). New York: Pergamon.

Block, Jeanne H. (1976). Issues, problems, and pitfalls in assessing sex differences. *Merrill-Palmer Quarterly, 22,* 283–308.

Block, Jeanne H. (1983). Differential premises arising from differential socialization of the sexes: Some conjectures. *Child Development, 54,* 1335–1354.

Blood, R., & Wolfe, D. N. (1960). *Husbands and wives.* Glencoe, IL: Free Press.

Blumstein, Philip W., & Schwartz, Pepper. (1974). Lesbianism and bisexuality. In E. Goode (Ed.), *Sexual deviance and sexual deviants.* New York: Morrow.

Blumstein, Philip W., & Schwartz, Pepper. (1976). Bisexual women. In J. P. Wiseman (Ed.), *The social psychology of sex.* New York: Harper & Row.

Blumstein, Philip, & Schwartz, Pepper. (1983). *American couples.* New York: Morrow.

Boffey, Philip M. (1984, Oct. 9). Fast and accurate chlamydia test reported. *New York Times,* C2.

Boggan, E. C., Haft, M. G., Lister, C., & Rupp, J. P. (1975). *The rights of gay people.* New York: Discus Books, Avon.

Bohmer, Carol. (1974). Judicial attitudes toward rape victims. *Judicature, 57,* 303–307.

Bonaparte, Marie. (1965). *Female sexuality.* New York: Grove. (First published by International Universities Press, 1953.)

Booth, Cathryn L., & Meltzoff, Andrew N. (1984). Expected and actual experience in labour and delivery and their relationship to maternal attachment. *Journal of Reproductive and Infant Psychology, 2,* 79–91.

Bornstein, Robert F. (1989). Exposure and affect: Overview and meta-analysis of research, 1968–1987. *Psychological Bulletin, 106,* 265–289.

Boruchowitz, Robert C. (1973). Victimless crimes: A proposal to free the courts. *Judicature, 57,* 69–78.

Boston Lesbian Psychologies Collective. (Eds.) (1987). *Lesbian psychologies: Explorations and challenges.* Champaign, IL: University of Illinois Press.

Boston Women's Health Book Collective. (1976). *Our bodies, ourselves.* New York: Simon & Schuster.

Boston Women's Health Book Collective. (1984). *The new our bodies, ourselves.* New York: Simon & Schuster.

Boswell, John. (1980). *Christianity, social tolerance, and homosexuality.* Chicago: University of Chicago Press, 1980.

Boyd, K., Callaghan, B., & Shotter, E. (1986). *Life before birth.* London: SPCK.

Brabant, Sarah, & Mooney, Linda. (1986). Sex role stereotyping in the Sunday comics: Ten years later. *Sex Roles, 14,* 141–148.

Brady, Katherine. (1978). *Father's days.* New York: Dell.

Breast cancer: Second thoughts about routine mammography. (1976). *Science, 193,* 555.

Breasted, Mary. (1970). *Oh, sex education.* New York: Praeger.

Brecher, Edward M. (1975, Mar.–Apr.). Marijuana. *Consumer Reports, 40,* 3–4.

Brecher, Edward M. (1984). *Love, sex, and aging.* Mount Vernon, NY: Consumers Union.

Brecher, Ruth, & Brecher, Edward. (Eds.). (1966). *An analysis of human sexual response.* New York: Signet Books, New American Library.

Breitman, P., Knutson, K., & Reed, P. (1987). *How to persuade your lover to use a condom . . . and why you should.* Rocklin, CA: Prima Publishing.

Brent, Jonathan. (1976). A general introduction to privacy. *Massachusetts Law Quarterly, 61,* 10–18.

Brenton, Myron. (1972). *Sex talk.* New York: Stein and Day.

Breslow, N., Evans, L., & Langley, J. (1985). On the prevalence and roles of females in the sadomasochistic subculture: Report of an empirical study. *Archives of Sexual Behavior, 14,* 303–318.

Brest, Paul, & Vandenberg, Ann. (1987). Politics, feminism, and the Constitution. *Stanford Law Review, 39,* 607–671.

Bretl, Daniel J., & Cantor, Joanne. (1988). The portrayal of men and women in U.S. television commercials: A recent content analysis and trends over 15 years. *Sex Roles, 18,* 595–610.

Bretschneider, Judy G., & McCoy, Norma L. (1988). Sexual interest and behavior in healthy 80- to 102-year-olds. *Archives of Sexual Behavior, 17,* 109–130.

Brim, O. G. (1976). Theories of the male mid-life crisis. *Counseling Psychologist, 6*(1), 2–9.

Brinton, Crane. (1959). *A history of Western morals.* New York: Harcourt Brace Jovanovich.

Broderick, Carlfred B. (1966a). Sexual behavior among preadolescents. *Journal of Social Issues, 22*(2), 6–21.

Broderick, Carlfred B. (1966b). Socio-sexual development in a suburban community. *Journal of Sex Research, 2,* 1–24.

Broderick, Carlfred B., & Bernard, Jessie. (1969). *The individual, sex, and society.* Baltimore: Johns Hopkins University Press.

Brodsky, Carroll M. (1976). Rape at work. In M. J. Walker & S. L. Brodsky (Eds.), *Sexual assault: The victim and the rapist.* Lexington, MA: Lexington Books.

Bronson, F. (1968). Pheromonal influences on mammalian reproduction. In M. Diamond (Ed.), *Perspectives in reproduction and sexual behavior.* Bloomington: Indiana University Press.

Brotman, Harris. (1984, Jan. 8). Human embryo transplants. *New York Times Magazine,* 42ff.

Broun, Heywood, & Leech, Margaret. (1927). *Anthony Comstock: Roundsman of the Lord.* New York: Boni.

Broverman, Inge K., et al. (1972). Sex-role stereotypes: A current appraisal. *Journal of Social Issues, 28*(2), 59–78.

Brown, C., et al. (1978). Community standards, conservatism, and judgements of pornography. *Journal of Sex Research, 14,* 81–95.

Brown, Daniel G. (1966). Female orgasm and sexual inadequacy. In R. Brecher & E. Brecher (Eds.), *An analysis of human sexual response.* New York: Signet Books, New American Library.

Brown, M., Amoroso, D. M., & Ware, E. E. (1976). Behavioral effects of viewing pornography. *Journal of Social Psychology, 98,* 235–245.

Browne, Angela, & Finkelhor, D. (1986). Impact of child sexual abuse: A review of the research. *Psychological Bulletin, 99,* 66–77.

Brownmiller, Susan. (1975). *Against our will: Men, women, and rape.* New York: Simon & Schuster.

Bruce, H. M. (1969). Pheromones and behavior in mice. *Act Neurological Belgica, 69,* 529–538.

Brueschke, Erich E., et al. (1979). Development of a reversible vas deferens occlusive device. VI. Long-term evaluation of flexible prosthetic devices. *Fertility and Sterility, 31,* 575–586.

Bruser, M. (1969). Sporting activities during pregnancy. Cited in Sports and pregnancy. *Briefs: Footnotes on Maternity Care, 33*(4), 51–53.

Brussel, J. A. (1971). Comment following Menachem Amir, Forcible rape. *Sexual Behavior, 1,* 8.

Bryan, James H. (1965). Apprenticeships in prostitution. *Social Problems, 12,* 278–297.

Buchanan, K. M. (1986). *Apache women warriors.* El Paso: Texas Western Press.

Budoff, Penny W. (1980). *No more menstrual cramps and other good news.* New York: Putnam.

Bullough, Vern L. (1976). *Sexual variance in society and history.* New York: Wiley.

Bullough, Vern, & Bullough, B. (1978). *Prostitution: An illustrated social history.* New York: Crown.

Bureau of the Census. (1990). Marital status and living arrangements: March 1990. *Current Population Reports,* Series P-20, No. 450.

Burgess, Ann W. (1984). *Child pornography and sex rings.* Lexington, MA: Lexington Books (D. C. Heath).

Burgess, Ann W., & Holmstrom, Lynda L. (1974a). Rape trauma syndrome. *American Journal of Psychiatry, 131,* 981–986.

Burgess, Ann W., & Holmstrom, Lynda L. (1974b). *Rape: Victims of crisis.* Bowie, MD: Robert J. Brady.

Burgess, Ann W., & Holmstrom, Lynda, L. (1979). *Rape: Crisis and recovery.* Bowie, MD: Robert J. Brady.

Burkett, G., Yasin, S., & Palow, D. (1990). Perinatal implications of cocaine exposure. *Journal of Reproductive Medicine, 35,* 35–42.

Burnell, G. M., & Norfleet, M. A. (1987). Women's self-reported responses to abortion. *Journal of Psychology, 121,* 71–76.

Burt, Martha R. (1980). Cultural myths and supports for rape. *Journal of Personality and Social Psychology, 38,* 217–230.

Burton, Frances D. (1970). Sexual climax in *Macaca mulatta. Proceedings of the Third International Congress on Primatology, 3,* 180–191.

Bush, Trudy L., et al. (1983). Estrogen use and all-cause mortality. *Journal of the American Medical Association, 249,* 903–906.

Buss, Arnold. (1966). *Psychopathology.* New York: Wiley.

Buss, David M. (1988). The evolution of human intrasexual competition: Tactics of mate attraction. *Journal of Personality and Social Psychology, 54,* 616–628.

Buunk, Bram, & Hupka, Ralph B. (1987). Cross-cultural differences in the elicitation of sexual jealousy. *Journal of Sex Research, 23,* 12–22.

Buvat, Jacques, et al. (1990). Recent developments in the clinical assessment and diagnosis of erectile dysfunction. *Annual Review of Sex Research, 1,* 265–308.

Byler, Ruth V. (1969). *Teach us what we want to know.* New York: Mental Health Materials Center (for the Connecticut State Board of Education).

Byne, William, & Parsons, Bruce (1993). Human sexual orientation: The biologic theories reappraised. *Archives of General Psychiatry, 50,* 228–239.

Byrne, Donn. (1971). *The attraction paradigm.* New York: Academic.

Byrne, Donn. (1977, July). A pregnant pause in the sexual revolution. *Psychology Today, 11*(2), 67–68.

Byrne, Donn. (1977). Social psychology and the study of sexual behavior. *Personality and Social Psychology Bulletin, 3,* 3–30.

Byrne, Donn. (1983). Sex without contraception. In D. Byrne & W. A. Fisher (Eds.), *Adolescents, sex, and contraception.* Hillsdale, NJ: Lawrence Erlbaum.

Byrne, Donn, Ervin, C. E., & Lamberth, J. (1970). Continuity between the experimental study of attraction and real-life computer dating. *Journal of Personality and Social Psychology, 16,* 157–165.

Cado, Suzanne, & Leitenberg, Harold. (1990). Guilt reactions to sexual fantasies during intercourse. *Archives of Sexual Behavior, 19,* 49–64.

Cahill, Lisa Sowle. (1985). The "seamless garment": Life in its beginnings. *Theological Studies, 46,* 64–80.

Calderwood, Deryck. (1987, May). The male rape victim. *Medical Aspects of Human Sexuality,* 53–55.

Calhoun, K. S., Atkeson, B. M., & Resick, P. A. (1982). A longitudinal examination of fear reactions in victims of rape. *Journal of Counseling Psychology, 29,* 655–661.

Callahan, Daniel. (1986, Feb.). How technology is reframing the abortion debate. *Hastings Center Report,* 33–42.

Callahan, Sidney, & Callahan, Daniel. (1984). *Abortion: Understanding differences.* New York: Plenum.

Campbell, A., Converse, P. E., & Rodgers, W. L. (1975). *The quality of American life.* Ann Arbor, MI: ISR Social Science Archive.

Carani, Cesare, et al. (1990). Effects of androgen treatment in impotent men with normal and low levels of free testosterone. *Archives of Sexual Behavior, 19,* 223–234.

Carpenter, C. R. (1942). Sexual behavior of free ranging rhesus monkeys (*Macaca mulatta*). *Journal of Comparative and Physiological Psychology, 33,* 113–162.

Carpenter, Mary. (1979, Sept. 24). Physicians ponder popularity of pregnancy self-test kits. *Medical News, 3*(14), 18.

Carroll, Janell, Volk, K., & Hyde, J. S. (1984). Differences between males and females in motives for engaging in sexual intercourse. *Archives of Sexual Behavior, 14,* 131–139.

Cass, Vivienne C. (1979). Homosexual identity formation: A theoretical model. *Journal of Homosexuality, 4,* 219–235.

Catalona, William J., et al. (1991). Measurement of prostate-specific antigen in serum as a screening test for prostate cancer. *New England Journal of Medicine, 324,* 1156–1161.

Catania, Joseph A. et al. (1992). Prevalence of AIDS-related risk factors and condom use in the United States. *Science, 258,* 1101–1106.

Catania, Joseph A., Gibson, D., Marin, B., Coates, T., & Greenblatt, R. (1990a). Response bias in assessing sexual behaviors relevant to HIV transmission. *Evaluation and Program Planning, 13,* 19–29.

Catania, Joseph A., Gibson, D. R., Chitwood, D. D., & Coates, T. J. (1990b). Methodological problems in AIDS behavioral research: Influences on measurement error and participation bias in studies of sexual behavior. *Psychological Bulletin, 108,* 339–362.

Catania, Joseph A., & White, Charles B. (1982). Sexuality in an aged sample: Cognitive determinants of masturbation. *Archives of Sexual Behavior, 11,* 237–246.

Cates, R. M., et al. (1982). Premarital abuse: A social psychological perspective. *Journal of Family Issues, 3*(1), 79–90.

Cates, Willard, & Wasserheit, Judith N. (1991). Genital chlamydial infections: Epidemiology and reproductive sequelae. *American Journal of Obsetrics and Gynecology, 164,* 1771–1781.

Catterall, R. D. (1974). *A short textbook of venereology.* Philadelphia: Lippincott.

Caughey, Madeline S. (1974). The principle of harm and its application to laws criminalizing prostitution. *Denver Law Journal, 51,* 235–262.

Ceniti, J., & Malamuth, N. (1984). Effects of repeated exposure to sexually violent or nonviolent stimuli on sexual arousal to rape or nonrape depictions. *Behavior Research and Therapy, 22,* 535–548.

Centers for Disease Control. (1987). *Sexually transmitted disease statistics.* Atlanta, GA: CDC.

Centers for Disease Control. (1983, Jan. 6). Acquired Immune Deficiency Syndrome (AIDS)—United States. *Morbidity and Mortality Weekly Report, 32,* 688–691.

Centers for Disease Control. (1991). *Sexually transmitted disease surveillance 1990*. Atlanta, GA: CDC.

Centers for Disease Control (1992). Selected behaviors that increase risk for HIV infection, other sexually transmitted diseases, and unintended pregnancy among high school students—United States, 1991. *Morbidity and Mortality Weekly Reports, 41*(50), 945–950.

Chafetz, Janet S. (1974). *Masculine/feminine or human? An overview of the sociology of sex roles*. Itasca, IL: F. E. Peacock.

Chaikin, A. L., & Derlega, V. J. (1976). Norms affecting self-disclosure in men and women. *Journal of Consulting and Clinical Psychology, 44*, 376–380.

Chaisson, Richard E., et al. (1986). Significant changes in HIV level in the serum of patients treated with azidothymidine. *New England Journal of Medicine, 315*, 1610–1611.

Chambless, Dianne L., et al. (1982). The pubococcygeus and female orgasm: A correlational study with normal subjects. *Archives of Sexual Behavior, 11*, 479–490.

Chappell, Duncan. (1976). Cross-cultural research on forcible rape. *International Journal of Criminology and Penology, 4*, 295–304.

Chappell, D., Geis, G., & Fogarty, F. (1974). Forcible rape: Bibliography. *Journal of Criminal Law and Criminology, 65*, 248–263.

Check, James V. P., & Malamuth, N. M. (1985). An empirical assessment of some feminist hypotheses about rape. *International Journal of Women's Studies, 8*, 414–423.

Check, James V. P., & Malamuth, Neil M. (1984). Can there be positive effects of participation in pornography experiments? *Journal of Sex Research, 20*, 14–31.

Chein, Isidor, Gerard, D., Lee, R., & Rosenfeld, E. (1964). *Narcotics, delinquency, and social policy*. London: Tavistock.

Cherry, Kittredge, & Mitulski, James. (1988). We are the church alive, the Church with AIDS. *Christian Century, 105*, 85–88.

Chesler, Phyllis. (1972). *Women and madness*. Garden City, NY: Doubleday.

Chiazze, L., Jr., et al. (1968). The length and variability of the human menstrual cycle. *Journal of the American Medical Association, 203*, 6.

Chow, J. M., et al. (1990). The association between *Chlamydia trachomatis* and ectopic pregnancy: A matched-pair, case-control study. *Journal of the American Medical Association, 263*, 3164.

Christensen, Cornelia V. (1971). *Kinsey: A biography*. Bloomington: Indiana University Press.

Church, Cathleen, & Geller, Judith S. (1990). Voluntary female sterilization: Number one and growing. *Population Reports*, Series C, No. 10, 1–23.

Cimbalo, R. S., Faling, B., & Mousaw, P. (1976). The course of love: A cross-sectional design. *Psychological Reports, 38*, 1292–1294.

Clanton, Gordon. (1973). The contemporary experience of adultery: Bob and Carol and Updike and Rimmer. In R. W. Libby & R. N. Whitehurst (Eds.), *Renovating marriage*. Danville, CA: Consensus Publishers.

Clanton, Gordon, & Smith, Lynn G. (Eds.). (1986). *Jealousy*. Lanham, MD: University Press of America.

Clark, Alexander L., & Wallin, Paul. (1964). The accuracy of husbands' and wives' reports of the frequency of marital coitus. *Population Studies, 18*, 165–173.

Clarke, C. H. (1986). Freedom of speech and the problem of the lawful harmful public reaction. *Adron Law Review, 20*, 187–208.

Clarren, S. K., & Smith, D. W. (1978). The fetal alcohol syndrome. *New England Journal of Medicine, 298*, 1063–1067.

Clatworthy, Nancy M. (1980). Morals and the ever-changing college student. Paper presented at North Central Sociological meetings, Dayton, OH.

Clement, Ulrich. (1990). Surveys of heterosexual behavior. *Annual Review of Sex Research, 1*, 45–74.

Clement, U., Schmidt, G., & Kruse, M. (1984). Changes in sex differences in behavior: A replication of a study on West German students (1966–1981). *Archives of Sexual Behavior, 13*, 99–120.

Cochran, S. D., Mays, V. M., & Leung, L. (1991). Sexual practices of heterosexual Asian American young adults: Implications for risk of HIV infection. *Archives of Sexual Behavior, 20*, 381–392.

Cochran, W. G., Mosteller, F., & Tukey, J. W. (1953). Statistical problems of the Kinsey report. *Journal of the American Statistical Association, 48*, 673–716.

Cocores, J. A., Dackis, C. A., & Gold, M. S. (1986). Sexual dysfunction secondary to cocaine abuse in two patients. *Journal of Clinical Psychiatry, 47*, 384–385.

Cohen, I., et al. (1990). Improved pregnancy outcome following successful treatment of chlamydial infection. *Journal of the American Medical Association, 263*, 3160.

Cohen, Michael W., & Friedman, Stanford B. (1975). Nonsexual motivation of adolescent sexual behavior. *Medical Aspects of Human Sexuality, 9*(9), 9–31.

Cohen, M. L., Garofalo, R., Boucher, R., & Seghorn, T. (1971). The psychology of rapists. *Seminars in Psychiatry, 3*, 307–327.

Cohn, Frederick. (1974). *Understanding human sexuality*. Englewood Cliffs, NJ: Prentice-Hall.

Cohn, Lawrence. (1983, Nov. 16). Pix less able but porn is stable. *Variety, 313*(3), 1–2.

Cole, Theodore M. (1975). Sexuality and the spinal cord injured. In R. Green (Ed.), *Human sexuality: A health practitioner's text*. Baltimore: Williams & Wilkins.

Cole, Theodore M., & Cole, S. (1978). The handicapped and sexual health. In A. Comfort (Ed.), *Sexual consequences of disability*. Philadelphia: G. F. Stickley.

Coleman, Eli. (1982a). Changing approaches to the treatment of homosexuality: A review. In W. Paul et al. (Eds.), *Homosexuality: Social, psychological, and biological issues*. Beverly Hills, CA: Sage.

Coleman, Eli. (1982b). Developmental stages of the coming-out process. In W. Paul et al. (Eds.), *Homosexuality: Social, psychological, and biological issues*, Beverly Hills, CA: Sage.

Coleman, Eli. (1991). Compulsive sexual behavior: New concepts and treatments. *Journal of Psychology and Human Sexuality, 4*(2), 37–51.

Coleman, Eli, & Reece, Rex. (1988). Treating low sexual desire among gay men. In S. R. Leiblum & R. C. Rosen (Eds.), *Sexual desire disorders*. New York: Guilford.

Coleman, S., Piotrow, P. T., & Rinehart, W. (1979, Mar.). Tobacco: Hazards to health and human reproduction. *Population Reports,* Series L(1).

Coles, Robert, & Stokes, Geoffrey. (1985). *Sex and the American teenager.* New York: Harper.

Coller, Sarah A., & Resick, Patricia A. (1987). Women's attributions of responsibility for date rape: The influence of empathy and sex-role stereotyping. *Violence and Victims, 2,* 115–125.

Comas-Diaz, Lillian. (1987). Feminist therapy with mainland Puerto Rican women. *Psychology of Women Quarterly, 11,* 461–474.

Comfort, Alex. (1971). Likelihood of human pheromones. *Nature, 230,* 432–433.

Comfort, Alex. (1972). *The joy of sex.* New York: Crown.

Comfort, Alex. (1978). *Sexual consequences of disability.* Philadelphia: G. F. Stickley.

Comfort, Alex. (1991). *The new joy of sex: A gourmet guide to lovemaking for the nineties.* New York: Crown.

Commission on Obscenity and Pornography (1970). *The report of the Commission on Obscenity and Pornography.* New York: Bantam Books.

Conant, M., et al. (1986). Condoms prevent transmission of AIDS-associated retrovirus. *Journal of the American Medical Association, 25,* 1706.

Condy, Sylvia R., et al. (1987). Parameters of sexual contact of boys with women. *Archives of Sexual Behavior, 16,* 379–394.

Congregation for the Doctrine of the Faith. (1986). The pastoral care of homosexual persons. *Origins, 26,* 378–382.

Congregation for the Doctrine of the Faith. (1987). Instruction on respect for human life in its origin and on the dignity of procreation. *Origins, 16,* 198–711.

Conkle, D. O. (1987). The second death of substantive due process. *Indiana Law Journal, 62,* 215–242.

Constantine, Larry L., & Constantine, Joan M. (1973). *Group marriage: A study of contemporary multilateral marriage.* New York: Macmillan.

Coombs, N. R. (1974). Male prostitution: A psychosocial view of behavior. *American Journal of Orthopsychiatry, 44,* 782.

Cooper, A. J. (1986). Progestogens in the treatment of male sex offenders: A review. *Canadian Journal of Psychiatry, 31,* 73–79.

Corey, Lawrence. (1990). Genital herpes. In K. Holmes et al. (Eds.), *Sexually transmitted diseases.* (pp. 391–414). New York: McGraw-Hill.

Corey, Lawrence, & Spear, Patricia G. (1986). Infections with herpes simplex virus—Part two. *New England Journal of Medicine, 314,* 749–757.

Corrales, R. (1974). The influence of family life's cycle categories, marital power, spousal agreement, and communication styles upon marital satisfaction in the first six years of marriage. Unpublished doctoral dissertation, University of Minnesota.

Countryman, L. William. (1987). The AIDS crisis: Theological and ethical reflections. *Anglican Theological Review, 69,* 125–134.

Couzinet, Beatrice, et al. (1986). Termination of early pregnancy by the progesterone antagonist RU486 (mifepristone). *New England Journal of Medicine, 315,* 1565–1569.

Cox, D. J. (1983). Menstrual symptoms in college students: A controlled study. *Journal of Behavioral Medicine, 6,* 335–338.

Cox, Daniel J. (1988). Incidence and nature of male genital exposure behavior as reported by college women. *Journal of Sex Research, 24,* 227–234.

Cox, Harvey (Ed.) (1968). *The situation ethics debate.* Philadelphia: Westminster Press.

Cozby, P. C. (1973). Self-disclosure: A literature review. *Psychological Bulletin, 79,* 73–91.

Cranston-Cuebas, Margaret A., & Barlow, David H. (1990). Cognitive and affective contributions to sexual functioning. *Annual Review of Sex Research, 1,* 119–162.

Craven, J., & Polak, A. (1954). Cantharidin poisoning. *British Medical Journal, 2,* 1386–1388.

Creighton, James. (1992). *Don't go away mad.* New York: Doubleday.

Croughan, Jack L., et al. (1981). A comparison of treated and untreated male cross-dressers. *Archives of Sexual Behavior, 10,* 515–528.

Cunningham, F. Gary, MacDonald, Paul C., & Gant, Norman F. (1989). *Williams obstetrics* (18th ed.) Norwalk, CT: Appleton & Lange.

Curran, Charles E. (1988). Roman Catholic sexual ethics: A dissenting view. *Christian Century, 105,* 1139–1142.

Cushman, P. (1961). Sexual behavior in heroin addiction and methadone maintenance. *New York State Medical Journal, 1972,* 27.

Cutler, Winnifred B., et al. (1986). Human axillary secretions influence women's menstrual cycles: The role of donor extract from men. *Hormones and Behavior, 20,* 463–473.

Dalton, Harlon L., & Burris, Scott (Eds.). (1987). *AIDS and the law: A guide for the public.* New Haven: Yale University Press.

Dalton, Katharina. (1979). *Once a month.* Ramona, CA: Hunter House.

Darling, C. A., Davidson, J. K., & Conway-Welch, C. (1990). Female ejaculation: Perceived origins, the Gräfenberg spot/area, and sexual responsiveness. *Archives of Sexual Behavior, 19,* 29–48.

Darling, C. A., Davidson, J. K., & Jennings, D. A. (1991). The female sexual response revisited: Understanding the multiorgasmic experience of women. *Archives of Sexual Behavior, 20,* 527–540.

Darney, Philip D., et al. (1990). Acceptance and perceptions of Norplant among users in San Francisco, USA. *Studies in Family Planning, 21,* 152–160.

Darrow, William. (1984). Meeting the AIDS dilemma. Address to the AASECT/SSSS Convention, Boston.

Davenport, William H. (1987). An anthropological approach. In J. H. Geer & W. T. O'Donohue (Eds.), *Theories of human sexuality.* (pp. 197–236.) New York: Plenum.

David, Henry P. (1986). Population, development, and reproductive behavior: Perspectives for population and health psychology. *American Psychologist, 41,* 309–312.

David, Henry P. (1992). Born unwanted: Long-term developmental effects of denied abortion. *Journal of Social Issues, 48(3),* 163–181.

David, H. P., Dytrych, Z., Matejcek, Z., & Schuller, V. (Eds.). (1988). *Born unwanted: Developmental effects of denied abortion.* New York: Springer.

David, Henry P., & Matejcek, Z. (1981). Children born to women denied abortion: An update. *Family Planning Perspectives, 13,* 32–34.

Davidson, J. Kenneth, & Hoffman, Linda E. (1986). Sexual fantasies and sexual satisfaction: An empirical analysis of erotic thought. *Journal of Sex Research, 22,* 184–205.

Davidson, Julian M., et al. (1983). Maintenance of sexual function in a castrated man treated with ovarian steroids. *Archives of Sexual Behavior, 12,* 263–274.

Davis, J. A., & Smith, T. (1991). *General social surveys, 1972–1991.* Storrs, CT: University of Connecticut, Roper Center for Public Opinion Research.

Davis, John D. (1978). When boy meets girl: Sex roles and the negotiation of intimacy in an acquaintance exercise. *Journal of Personality and Social Psychology, 36,* 684–692.

Davis, Keith E., & Braucht, G. Nicholas. (1973). Exposure to pornography, character and sexual deviance: A retrospective study. *Journal of Social Issues, 29,* 183–196.

Davison, G. C. (1976). Homosexuality: The ethical challenge. *Journal of Consulting and Clinical Psychology, 44,* 157–162.

Davison, G. C., & Neale, J. M. (1974). *Abnormal psychology: An experimental clinical approach.* New York: Wiley.

Davison, Gerald C. (1982). Politics, ethics, and therapy for homosexuality. In W. Paul et al. (Eds.), *Homosexuality: Social, psychological, and biological issues.* Beverly Hills, CA: Sage.

Deaux, Kay. (1976). *The behavior of women and men.* Belmont, CA: Brooks/Cole.

Deaux, Kay, & Lewis, Laurie, L. (1983). Components of gender stereotypes. *Psychological Documents, 13,* 25. (Ms. No. 2583).

Deaux, Kay, & Lewis, Laurie L. (1984). Structure of gender stereotypes: Interrelationships among components and gender label. *Journal of Personality and Social Psychology, 46,* 991–1004.

DeBuono, B. A., Zinner, S. H., Daamen, M., & McCormack, W. M. (1990). Sexual behavior of college women in 1975, 1986, and 1989. *New England Journal of Medicine, 322,* 821–825.

DeLamater, John. (1981). The social control of sexuality. *Annual Review of Sociology, 7,* 263–290.

DeLamater, John. (1982). Response effects of question content. In W. Dijkstra & J. Van derZouwen (Eds.), *Response behavior in the survey-interview.* London: Academic.

DeLamater, John. (1987). A sociological perspective. In J. H. Geer & W. T. O'Donohue (Eds.), *Theories of human sexuality.* (pp. 237–256). New York: Plenum.

DeLamater, John, & MacCorquodale, Patricia. (1979). *Premarital sexuality: Attitudes, relationships, behavior.* Madison: University of Wisconsin Press.

Delaney, J., Lupton, M. J., & Toth, E. (1976). *The curse: A cultural history of menstruation.* New York: Dutton.

DeLora, Joann S., & Warren, Carol, A. B. (1977). *Understanding sexual interaction.* Boston: Houghton Mifflin.

D'Emilio, John, & Freedman, Estelle B. (1988). *Intimate matters: A history of sexuality in America.* New York: Harper & Row.

Derlega, Valerian J. (Ed.). (1984). *Communication, intimacy, and close relationships.* New York: Academic.

Derogatis, Leonard R., & Kind, Katherine M. (1981). The coital coronary: A reassessment of the concept. *Archives of Sexual Behavior, 10,* 325–336.

Deschin, C. S. (1963). Teen-agers and venereal disease: A sociological study of 600 teen-agers in NYC social hygiene clinics. *American Journal of Nursing, 63,* 63–67.

Dewsbury, Donald A. (1981). Effects of novelty on copulatory behavior: The Coolidge effect and related phenomena. *Psychological Bulletin, 89,* 464–483.

de Zalduondo, Barbara O. (1991). Prostitution viewed cross-culturally: Toward recontextualizing sex work in AIDS intervention research. *Journal of Sex Research, 28,* 223–248.

Diamond, Milton. (1965). A critical evaluation of the ontogeny of human sexual behavior. *Quarterly Review of Biology, 40,* 147–175.

Diamond, Milton. (1979). Sexual identity and sex roles. In V. Bullough (Ed.), *The frontiers of sex research.* Buffalo, NY: Prometheus Books.

Diamond, Milton. (1982). Sexual identity, monozygotic twins reared in discordant sex roles, and a BBC followup. *Archives of Sexual Behavior, 11,* 181–186.

Diewtz, P. E., & Evans, B. (1982). Pornographic imagery and prevalence of paraphilia. *American Journal of Psychiatry, 139,* 1493–1495.

Dietzman, D. E., et al. (1977). Hepatitis B surface (HBsAg) and antibody of HBsAg: Prevalence in homosexual and heterosexual men. *Journal of the American Medical Association, 238,* 2625–2626.

Dion, K. (1977). The incentive value of physical attractiveness for young children. *Personality and Social Psychology Bulletin, 3,* 67–70.

Dion, K. K. (1973). Young children's stereotyping of facial attractiveness. *Developmental Psychology, 9,* 183–188.

Dishotsky, N., Loughman, W., Mogar, R., and Lipscomb, W. (1971). LSD and genetic damage. *Science, 172,* 431–440.

Ditkoff, Mitchell. (1978). Child pornography. *American Humane Society Magazine, 16*(4), 30.

Ditman, Keith. (1964). Inhibition of ejaculation of chlorprothixens. *American Journal of Psychiatry, 120,* 1004–1005.

Dixon, Joan K. (1984). The commencement of bisexual activity in swinging married women over age thirty. *Journal of Sex Research, 20,* 71–90.

Djerassi, Carl. (1989). The bitter pill. *Science, 245,* 356–361.

Dobert, Margarete. (1973). Tradition, modernity, and woman power in Africa. In M. S. Mednick, L. W. Hoffman, & S. S. Tangri (Eds.), *Women: Psychological perspectives on achievement.* Washington, DC: Hemisphere.

Dodson, Betty. (1987). *Sex for one: The joy of self-loving.* NY: Harmony Books (Crown).

Doering, Charles, et al. (1975). A cycle of plasma testosterone in the human male. *Journal of Clinical Endocrinology and Metabolism, 40,* 492.

Doering, Charles, et al. (1978). Plasma testosterone levels and psychologic measures in men over a 2-month period. In R. Friedman et al. (Eds.), *Sex differences in behavior.* Huntington, NY: Krieger.

Donnerstein, Ed. (1980). Aggressive-erotica and violence against women. *Journal of Personality and Social Psychology, 39,* 269–277.

Donnerstein, Ed, & Berkowitz, Leonard. (1981). Victim reactions in aggressive-erotic films as a factor in violence against women. *Journal of Personality and Social Psychology, 41,* 710–724.

Donnerstein, Ed. (1983). Erotica and human aggression. In R. Geen and E. Donnerstein (Eds.), *Aggression: Theoretical and empirical reviews* (Vol. 2). New York: Academic.

Donnerstein, E., Linz, D., & Penrod, S. (1987). *The question of pornography: Research findings and policy implications.* New York: Free Press.

Doran, Terence A. (1990). Chorionic villus sampling as the primary diagnostic tool in prenatal diagnosis. *Journal of Reproductive Medicine, 35,* 935–940.

Dorner, G. (1969, Feb. 2). Prophylaxie and therapie angeborener sexual deviationen. *Deutsche Medizinische Wochenschrift Sonderdruck.*

Dorner, G. (1976). *Hormones and brain differentiation.* Amsterdam: Elsevier.

Dorner, Gunter, et al. (1983). Stressful events in prenatal life of bi- and homosexual men. *Experimental and Clinical Endocrinology, 81,* 83–87.

Doshi, Mary L. (1986). Accuracy of consumer-performed in-home tests for early pregnancy detection. *American Journal of Public Health, 76,* 512–514.

Dotti, A., & Reda, M. (1975). Major tranquilizers and sexual function. In M. Sandler and G. L. Gessa (Eds.), *Sexual behavior: Pharmacology and biochemistry.* New York: Raven.

Doty, Richard L., et al. (1975). Changes in the intensity and pleasantness of human vaginal odors during the menstrual cycle. *Science, 190,* 1316–1318.

Douglas, Mary. (1970). *Purity and danger: An analysis of concepts of pollution and taboo.* Baltimore: Penguin.

Downs, James F. (1990). Nudity in Japanese visual media: A cross-cultural observation. *Archives of Sexual Behavior, 19,* 583–594.

Doyle, J. A. (1983). *The male experience.* Dubuque, IA: W. C. Brown.

Dreger, Ralph M., et al. (1964). Behavioral classification project. *Journal of Consulting Psychology, 28,* 1–13.

Driscoll, James P. (1971, Mar.–Apr.). Transsexuals. *Transaction,* 28–31.

Driscoll, R., Davis, K. E., & Lipetz, M. E. (1972). Parental interference and romantic love: The Romeo and Juliet effect. *Journal of Personality and Social Psychology, 24,* 1–10.

Dunn, H. G., et al. (1977). Maternal cigarette smoking during pregnancy and the child's subsequent development. II. Neurologic and intellectual maturation to the age of $6\frac{1}{2}$ years. *Canadian Journal of Public Health, 68,* 43–50.

Dunn, Marian E., & Trost, Jan E. (1989). Male multiple orgasms: A descriptive study. *Archives of Sexual Behavior, 18,* 377–388.

Dutton, Donald G., & Aron, Arthur P. (1974). Some evidence for heightened sexual attraction under conditions of high anxiety. *Journal of Personality and Social Psychology, 30,* 470–517.

Dworkin, Andrea. (1985). Against the flood. *Harvard Women's Law Journal, 8,* 1–29.

Eagly, A. H., Ashmore, R. D., Makhijani, M. G., & Longo, L. (1991). What is beautiful is good, but . . .: A meta-analytic review of research on the physical attractiveness stereotype. *Psychological Bulletin, 110,* 109–128.

Earls, Christopher M., & David, Helene. (1989). A psychosocial study of male prostitution. *Archives of Sexual Behavior, 18,* 401–420.

Eastman, N. J. (1968, Nov.). The geographical distribution of pregnancy in the United States. National Research Council, Working Group on Relation of Nutrition to the Toxemias of Pregnancy. Cited in L. M. Hellman and J. A. Pritchard, *Williams obstetrics* (14th ed.). New York: Appleton-Century-Crofts.

Ebomayi, Ehigie (1987). Prevalence of female circumcision in two Nigerian communities. *Sex Roles, 17,* 13–152.

Edelman, D. A., et al. (1983). Comparative trial of the contraceptive sponge and diaphragm: A preliminary report. *Journal of Reproductive Medicine, 28,* 781–784.

Edelman, D. A., McIntyre, S. L., & Harper, J. (1984). A comparative trial of the Today contraceptive sponge and diaphragm. *American Journal of Obstetrics and Gynecology, 150,* 869–876.

Edwards, John N., & Booth, Alan. (1976). Sexual behavior in and out of marriage: An assessment of correlates. *Journal of Marriage and the Family,* 73–81.

Ehrhardt, Anke, et al. (1985). Sexual orientation after prenatal exposure to exogenous estrogen. *Archives of Sexual Behavior, 14,* 57–78.

Ehrhardt, A. A., Yingling, S., & Warne, P. A. (1991). Sexual behavior in the era of AIDS: What has changed in the United States? *Annual Review of Sex Research, 2,* 25–48.

Ehrlich, June, & Riesman, David. (1961). Age and authority in the interview. *Public Opinion Quarterly, 23,* 39–56.

Ehrlich, Paul A., & Ehrlich, Anne H. (1972). *Population, resources, environment* (2d ed.). San Francisco: Freeman.

Eisen, Marvin, & Zellman, Gail L. (1987). Changes in incidence of sexual intercourse of unmarried teenagers following a community-based sex education program. *Journal of Sex Research, 23,* 527–533.

Elder, Glen. (1969). Appearance and education in marriage mobility. *American Sociological Review, 34,* 519–533.

Elias, James, & Gebhard, Paul. (1969). Sexuality and sexual learning in childhood. *Phi Delta Kappan, 50,* 401–405.

Ellis, Albert, & Brancale, Ralph. (1956). *Psychology of sex offenders.* Springfield, IL: Charles C. Thomas.

Ellis, Albert. (1962). *The American sexual tragedy.* New York: Grove.

Ellis, Bruce J., & Symons, Donald. (1990). Sex differences in sexual fantasy: An evolutionary psychological approach. *Journal of Sex Research, 27,* 527–555.

Ellis, Henry Havelock. (1939). *My life.* Boston: Houghton Mifflin.

Ellis, Lee, & Ames, M. Ashley. (1987). Neurohormonal functioning and sexual orientation: A theory of homosexuality-heterosexuality. *Psychological Bulletin, 101,* 233–258.

Ellis, L., Ames, M. A., Peckham, W., & Burke, D. (1988). Sexual orientation of human offspring may be altered by severe maternal stress during pregnancy. *Journal of Sex Research, 25,* 152–157.

Enquist, Roy J. (1983). The churches' response to abortion. *Word and World, 5,* 414–425.

Entwisle, Doris R., & Doering, Susan G. (1981). *The first birth: A family turning point.* Baltimore: Johns Hopkins University Press.

Erikson, Erik H. (1950). *Childhood and society.* New York: Norton.

Erikson, Erik H. (1968). *Identify: Youth and crisis.* New York: Norton.

Erikson, W. D., Walbek, N. H., & Seely, R. K. (1988). The behavior patterns of child molesters. *Archives of Sexual Behavior, 17,* 77–86.

Ernst, Frederick A., et al. (1991). Condemnation of homosexuality in the black community: A gender-specific phenomenon? *Archives of Sexual Behavior, 20,* 579–585.

Erwin, J., & Maple, Terry. (1976). Ambisexual behavior with male-male anal penetration in male rhesus monkeys. *Archives of Sexual Behavior, 5,* 9–14.

Evans, R. B. (1970). Sixteen personality factor questionnaire scores of homosexual men. *Journal of Consulting and Clinical Psychology, 34,* 212–215.

Everett, Guy M. (1975). Amyl nitrate ("poppers") as an aphrodisiac. In M. Sandler and G. L. Gessa (Eds.), *Sexual behavior: Pharmacology and biochemistry.* New York: Raven.

Everitt, Barry J., & Bancroft, John. (1991). Of rats and men: The comparative approach to male sexuality. *Annual Review of Sex Research, 2,* 77–118.

Eysenck, H. J., & Nias, D. K. B. (1978). *Sex, violence, and the media.* New York: Harper & Row.

Fagot-Diaz, Jose G. (1988). Employment discrimination against AIDS victims: Rights and remedies available under the Federal Rehabilitation Act of 1973. *Labor Law Journal, 39,* 148–166.

Falk, Patricia J. (1989). Lesbian mothers: Psychosocial assumptions in family law. *American Psychologist, 44,* 941–947.

Farkas, G. M., Sine, L. G., & Evans, I. M. (1978). Personality, sexuality, and demographic differences between volunteers and nonvolunteers for a laboratory study of male sexual behavior. *Archives of Sexual Behavior, 7,* 513–520.

Fasteau, Marc F. (1974). *The male machine.* New York: McGraw-Hill.

Fay, R. E., Turner, C. F., Klassen, A. D., & Gagon, J. H. (1989). Prevalence and patterns of same-gender sexual contact among men. *Science, 243,* 338–348.

Feder, H. H. (1984). Hormones and sexual behavior. *Annual Review of Psychology, 35,* 165–200.

Federal Bureau of Investigation. (1973, 1975, 1979). *Uniform crime reports.* Washington, DC: FBI.

Federal Bureau of Investigation. (1988). *Uniform crime reports 1987.* Washington, DC: U.S. Department of Justice.

Federal Bureau of Investigation. (1991). *Uniform crime reports.* Washington, DC: U.S. Department of Justice.

Feild, Hubert S. (1978). Attitudes toward rape: A comparative analysis of police, rapists, crisis counselors, and citizens. *Journal of Personality and Social Psychology, 36,* 156–179.

Feingold, Alan. (1988). Matching for attractiveness in romantic partners and same-sex friends: A meta-analysis and theoretical critique. *Psychological Bulletin, 104,* 226–235.

Feingold, Allen. (1990). Gender differences in effects of physical attractiveness on romantic attraction. *Journal of Personality and Social Psychology, 59,* 981–993.

Felman, Yehudi M., & Nikitas, James A. (1981). Nongonococcal urethritis. *Journal of the American Medical Association, 245,* 381–386.

Felton, Gary, & Segelman, Florrie. (1978). Lamaze childbirth training and changes in belief about personal control. *Birth and the Family Journal, 5,* 141–150.

Fensterheim, Herbert, & Kantor, Jerry S. (1980). The behavioral approach to sexual disorders. In B. J. Wolman and J. Money (Eds.), *Handbook of human sexuality.* Englewood Cliffs, NJ: Prentice-Hall.

Feorino, P. M., et al. (1985). Transfusion-associated acquired immunodeficiency syndrome: Evidence for persistent infection in blood donors. *New England Journal of Medicine, 312,* 1293–1296.

Feshbach, Seymour, & Malamuth, Neal. (1978, Nov.). Sex and aggression: Proving the link. *Psychology Today, 12*(6), 110.

Fettner, Ann G., & Check, William A. (1985). *The truth about AIDS.* New York: Holt, Rinehart & Winston.

Finkelhor, David. (1980). Sex among siblings: A survey on prevalence, variety and effects. *Archives of Sexual Behavior, 9,* 171–194.

Finkelhor, David. (1984). *Child sexual abuse: New theory and research.* New York: Free Press.

Finkelhor, David, & Araji, Sharon. (1986). Explanations of pedophilia: A four factor model. *Journal of Sex Research, 22,* 145–161.

Fischer, Gloria J. (1986). College student attitudes toward forcible date rape. I. Cognitive predictors. *Archives of Sexual Behavior, 15,* 457–466.

Fisher, C., et al. (1983). Patterns of female sexual arousal during sleep and waking: Vaginal thermo-conductance studies. *Archives of Sexual Behavior, 12,* 97–122.

Fisher, J. D., et al. (1975, Sept.). Hands touching hands: Affective and evaluative effects of an interpersonal touch. Paper presented at meetings of the American Psychological Association, Chicago.

Fisher, Seymour. (1973). *Understanding the female orgasm.* New York: Basic Books.

Fisher, William A. (1986). A psychological approach to human sexuality: The sexual behavior sequence. In D. Byrne & K. Kelley (Eds.), *Alternate approaches to the study of sexual behavior* (pp. 131–171). Hillsdale, NJ: Lawrence Erlbaum.

Fisher, W. A., Branscombe, N. R., & Lemery, C. R. (1983). The bigger the better? Arousal and attributional responses to erotic stimuli that depict different size penises. *Journal of Sex Research, 19,* 377–396.

Fisher, W. A., Byrne, D., & White, L. A. (1983). Emotional barriers to contraception. In D. Byrne and W. A. Fisher (Eds.), *Adolescents, sex, and contraception.* Hillsdale, NJ: Lawrence Erlbaum.

Fisher, W. A., Byrne, D., White, L. A., & Kelley, K. (1988). Erotophobia-erotophilia as a dimension of personality. *Journal of Sex Research, 25,* 123–151.

Fishman, J. (1978). *Sex in prison.* New York: Hartwick Publications.

Fishman, Jack. (1980). Fatness, puberty, and ovulation. *New England Journal of Medicine, 303,* 42–43.

Flaskerud, Jacquelyn H., & Ungvarski, Peter J. (1992). *HIV/AIDS: A guide to nursing care.* Philadelphia: Saunders.

Fleming, Michael Z., Jenkins, S. R., & Bugarin, C. (1980). Questioning current definitions of gender identity: Implications of the Bem sex-role inventory for transsexuals. *Archives of Sexual Behavior, 9,* 13–26.

Fleming, M., Steinman, C., & Boeknok, G. (1980). Methodological problems in assessing sex reassignment surgery: A reply to Meyer and Reter. *Archives of Sexual Behavior, 9,* 451–456.

Fleming, Michael, et al. (1981). A study of pre- and postsurgical transsexuals: MMPI characteristics. *Archives of Sexual Behavior, 10,* 161–170.

Fletcher, Joseph. (1966). *Situation ethics.* Philadelphia: Westminster Press.

Fletcher, Joseph. (1967). *Moral responsibility: Situation ethics at work.* Philadelphia: Westminster Press.

Flor-Henry, Pierre. (1987). Cerebral aspects of sexual deviation. In G. D. Wilson (Ed.), *Variant sexuality: Research and theory.* Baltimore: Johns Hopkins University Press.

Ford, Clellan S., & Beach, Frank A. (1951). *Patterns of sexual behavior.* New York: Harper & Row.

Ford, Kathleeen, & Norris, Anne. (1991). Methodological considerations for survey research on sexual behavior: Urban African American and Hispanic youth. *Journal of Sex Research, 28,* 539–555.

Forer, Bertram R. (1972). Use of physical contact. In L. N. Soloman & B. Berzon (Eds.), *New perspectives on encounter groups.* San Francisco: Jossey-Bass.

Forgac, Gregory E., & Michaels, Edward J. (1982). Personality characteristics of two types of male exhibitionists. *Journal of Abnormal Psychology, 91,* 287–293.

Forrest, Bruce. (1991). Women, HIV, and mucosal immunity. *Lancet, 337,* 835.

Forrest, Jacqueline D., & Henshaw, Stanley K. (1983, Aug.). What U.S. women think and do about contraception. *Family Planning Perspectives, 15*(5), 157–166.

Forrest, Jacqueline D., & Singh, Susheela. (1990). The sexual and reproductive behavior of American women, 1982–1988. *Family Planning Perspectives, 22*(5), 206–214.

Forssman, H., & Thuwe, I. (1966). One hundred and twenty children born after application for therapeutic abortion refused. *Acta Psychiatrica Scandinavica, 42,* 71–85.

Fox, C. A., et al. (1972). Studies on the relationship between plasma testosterone levels and human sexual activity. *Journal of Endocrinology, 52,* 51–58.

Fox, Laura. (1983). The 1983 abortion decisions. *University of Richmond Law Review, 18,* 137–159.

Fox, Maurice, & Lipton, Helene L. (1983). AIDS—Two years later. *New England Journal of Medicine, 309,* 609–610.

Francis, D. P., et al. (1982). The prevention of hepatitis B with vaccine: Report of the Centers for Disease Control multicenter efficacy trial among homosexual men. *Annals of Internal Medicine, 97,* 362–366.

Francoeur, Anna K., & Francoeur, Robert T. (1974). Hot and cool sex: Closed and open marriage. In R. T. Francoeur and A. K. Francoeur (Eds.), *The future of sexual relations.* Englewood Cliffs, NJ: Prentice-Hall.

Francoeur, Robert. (1983, July). Drugs that screw up sex. *Forum.*

Francoeur, Robert T. (1974). The technologies of man-made sex. In R. T. Francoeur and A. K. Francoeur (Eds.), *The future of sexual relations.* Englewood Cliffs, NJ: Prentice-Hall.

Frank E., Anderson, C., & Rubinstein, D. (1978). Frequency of sexual dysfunction in "normal" couples. *New England Journal of Medicine, 299*(3), 111–115.

Frank, Lawrence K. (1961). *The conduct of sex.* New York: Morrow.

Frank, R. T. (1931). The hormonal causes of premenstrual tension. *Archives of Neurological Psychiatry, 26,* 1053.

Frayser, Suzanne G. (1985). *Varieties of sexual experience: An anthropological perspective on human sexuality.* New Haven, CT: Human Relations Area Files Press.

Freedman, A. M. (1976). Drugs and sexual behavior. In B. J. Sadock et al. (Eds.)., *The sexual experience.* Baltimore: Williams & Wilkins.

Freedman, Mark. (1975). Homosexuals may be healthier than straights. *Psychology Today, 8*(10), 28–32.

Freud, Sigmund. (1924). *A general introduction to psychoanalysis.* New York: Permabooks, 1953. (Boni & Liveright edition, 1924).

Freud, S. (1948). The psychogenesis of a case of homosexuality in a woman (1920). In *The collected papers* (Vol. II, pp. 202–231). London: Hogarth.

Freund, Kurt, & Watson, Robin. (1990). Mapping the boundaries of courtship disorder. *Journal of Sex Research, 27,* 589–606.

Freund, M, Lee, N., & Leonard, T. (1991). Sexual behavior of clients with street prostitutes in Camden, NJ. *Journal of Sex Research, 28,* 579–591.

Friday, Nancy. (1973). *My secret garden: Women's sexual fantasies.* New York: Simon & Schuster.

Friday, Nancy. (1975). *Forbidden flowers: More women's sexual fantasies.* New York: Simon & Schuster.

Fried, Peter A. (1986). Marijuana use in pregnancy. In I. J. Chasnott (Ed.), *Drug use in pregnancy: Mother and child.* Boston: MTP Press.

Frieze, Irene H. (1983). Causes and consequences of marital rape. *Signs, 8,* 532–553.

Frisch, R. E., & McArthur, J. W. (1974). Menstrual cycles: Fatness as a determinant of minimum weight for height necessary for their maintenance or onset. *Science, 185,* 949–951.

Fritz, G. S., Stoll, K., & Wagner, N. M. (1981). A comparison of males and females who were sexually molested as children. *Journal of Sex and Marital Therapy, 7,* 54–59.

Frodi, A., Macaulay, J., & Thome, P. R. (1977). Are women always less aggressive than men? A review of the experimental literature. *Psychological Bulletin, 84,* 634–660.

Fromm, Erich. (1956). *The art of loving.* New York: Harper & Row.

Fullilove, M. T., Fullilove, R. E., Haynes, K., & Gross, S. (1990). Black women and AIDS prevention: A view towards understanding the gender rules. *Journal of Sex Research, 27,* 47–64.

Fullilove, Robert E. (1988). Minorities and AIDS: A review of recent publications. *Multicultural Inquiry and Research on AIDS Newsletter, 2,* 3–5.

Fulton, Gere B. (1974). *Sexual awareness.* Boston: Holbrook Press.

Furby, L., Weinrott, M. R., & Blackshaw, L. (1989). Sex offender recidivism: A review. *Psychological Bulletin, 105,* 3–30.

Furstenberg, F. F., Brooks-Gunn, J., & Morgan, S. P. (1987). *Adolescent mothers in later life.* New York: Cambridge University Press.

Fyfe, B. (1983). "Homophobia" or homosexual bias reconsidered. *Archives of Sexual Behavior, 12,* 549–554.

Gagnon, F. (1950). Contribution to study of etiology and prevention of cancer of cervix of uterus. *American Journal of Obstetrics and Gynecology, 60,* 516.

Gagnon, John H. (1965a). Female child victims of sex offenses. *Social Problems, 13,* 176–192.

Gagnon, John H. (1965b). Sexuality and sexual learning in the child. *Psychiatry, 28,* 212–228.

Bibliography

Gagnon, John H. (1977). *Human sexualities.* Glenview, IL: Scott, Foresman.

Gagnon, John H. (1985). Attitudes and responses of parents to pre-adolescent masturbation. *Archives of Sexual Behavior, 14,* 451–466.

Gagnon, John H. (1990). The explicit and implicit use of the scripting perspective in sex research. *Annual Review of Sex Research, 1,* 1–44.

Gagnon, John H., & Simon, William. (1973). *Sexual conduct: The social origins of human sexuality.* Chicago: Aldine.

Gall, Stanley A. (1991, Oct.). Update on HPV infection and how to manage it. *Contemporary OB/GYN,* 37–48.

Gallo, Maria Teresa de, & Alzate, Heli. (1976). Brothel prostitution in Colombia. *Archives of Sexual Behavior, 5,* 1–7.

Galston, A. W. (1975). Here come the clones. *Natural History, 84,* 72–75.

Garcia, Luis T. (1982). Sex-role orientation and stereotypes about male-female sexuality. *Sex Roles, 8,* 863–876.

Garfinkel, Harold. (1967). *Studies in ethnomethodology.* Englewood Cliffs, NJ: Prentice-Hall.

Garner, Brian, & Smith, Richard W. (1977). Are there really any gay male athletes? An empirical survey. *Journal of Sex Research, 13,* 22–34.

Gartrell, Nanette K. (1982). Hormones and homosexuality. In W. Paul et al. (Eds.), *Homosexuality: Social, psychological, and biological issues.* Beverly Hills, CA: Sage.

Gartrell, N. K., Loriaux, D. L., & Chase, T. N. (1977). Plasma testosterone in homosexual and heterosexual women. *American Journal of Psychiatry, 134,* 1117–1119.

Gay, Peter. (1984). *The bourgeois experience: Victoria to Freud.* New York: Oxford University Press.

Gebhard, Paul H. (1968). Postmarital coitus among widows and divorcees. In P. Bohannan (Ed.), *Divorce and after.* Garden City, NY: Doubleday.

Gebhard, Paul H. (1969, Mar.). Misconceptions about female prostitutes. *Medical Aspects of Human Sexuality, 3,* 24–30.

Gebhard, Paul H. (1971). Human sexual behavior: A summary statement. In D. S. Marshall & R. C. Suggs (Eds.), *Human sexual behavior.* New York: Basic Books.

Gebhard, Paul H. (1976). The Institute. In M. S. Weinberg (Ed.), *Sex research: Studies from the Kinsey Institute.* New York: Oxford University Press.

Gebhard, P. H., Gagnon, J. H., Pomeroy, W. B., & Christenson, C. V. (1965). *Sex offenders: An analysis of types.* New York: Harper & Row.

Geis, Gilbert. (1977). Forcible rape: An introduction. In D. Chappell and R. Geis (Eds.), *Forcible rape.* New York: Columbia University Press.

Genovesi, Vincent J. (1987). *In pursuit of love: Catholic morality and human sexuality.* Wilmington: DE: Michael Glazier.

Gentemann, Evelynn M. (1988). After *School Board of Nassau County v. Arline:* Employees with AIDS and the concerns of the "worried well." *American University Law Review, 37,* 838–913.

George, Linda K., & Weiler, Stephen J. (1981). Sexuality in middle and late life. *Archives of General Psychiatry, 38,* 919–923.

Gerrard, Meg. (1987). Sex, sex guilt, and contraceptive use revisited: The 1980s. *Journal of Personality and Social Psychology, 52,* 975–980.

Gil, Vincent E. (1991). An ethnography of HIV/AIDS and sexuality in the People's Republic of China. *Journal of Sex Research, 28,* 521–537.

Gilligan, Carol (1982). *In a different voice: Psychological theory and women's development.* Cambridge, MA: Harvard University Press.

Gilmartin, Brian G. (1975). The swinging couple down the block. *Psychology Today, 8*(9), 54.

Ginsberg, Barry G., & Vogelsong, Edward. (1977). Premarital relationship improvement by maximizing empathy and self-disclosure. The PRIMES program. In B. G. Guerney (Ed.), *Relationship enhancement.* San Francisco: Jossey-Bass.

Ginsberg, G. L., Frosch, W. A., & Shapiro, T. (1972). The new impotence. *Archives of General Psychiatry, 26*(3), 218–220.

Gittelson, Natalie. (1980, Jan.). Marriage: What women expect and what they get. *McCall's,* 87–89.

Gladue, B. A., Green, R., & Helman, R. E. (1984). Neuroendocrine response to estrogen and sexual orientation. *Science, 225,* 1496–1498.

Glass, S. J., Deuel, H. J., & Wright, C. A. (1940). Sex hormone studies in male homosexuality. *Endocrinology, 26,* 590–594.

Glass, S. J., & Johnson, R. W. (1944). Limitations and complications of organotherapy in male homosexuality. *Journal of Clinical Endocrinology, 4,* 540–544.

Glassberg, B. Y. (1970). The quandary of a virginal male. *Family Coordinator, 19,* 82–85.

Godges, John. (1986). Religious groups meet the San Francisco AIDS challenge. *Christian Century, 103,* 771–775.

Goergen, Donald. (1974). *The sexual celibate.* New York: Seabury Press.

Goffman, Erving. (1961). *Encounters: Two studies in the sociology of interaction.* Indianapolis, IN: Bobbs-Merrill.

Gold, Alice R., & Adams, David B. (1981). Motivational factors affecting fluctuations of female sexual activity at menstruation. *Psychology of Women Quarterly, 5,* 670–680.

Gold, Dolores, & Reis, Myrna. (1982). Male teacher effects on young children: A theoretical and empirical consideration. *Sex Roles, 8,* 493–514.

Goldberg, Daniel C., et al. (1983). The Gräfenberg spot and female ejaculation: A review of initial hypotheses. *Journal of Sex and Marital Therapy, 9,* 27–37.

Goldberg, M. (1987). Understanding hypersexuality in men and women. In G. R. Weeks & L. Hof (Eds.), *Integrating sex and marital therapy.* New York: Brunner-Mazel.

Goldberg, Susan. (1983). Parent-infant bonding: Another look. *Child Development, 54,* 1355–1382.

Golde, Peggy, & Kogan, Nathan. (1959). A sentence completion procedure for assessing attitudes toward old people. *Journal of Gerontology, 14,* 355–363.

Goldfoot, D. A., Westerberg-van Loon, W., Groeneveld, W., & Koos Slob, A. (1980). Behavioral and physiological evidence of sexual climax in the female stump-tailed macaque (*Macaca arctoides*). *Science, 208,* 1477–1478.

Goldman, Ronald J., & Goldman, Juliette D. G. (1982a). How children perceive the origin of babies and the roles of mothers and fathers in procreation: A cross-national study. *Child Development, 53,* 491–504.

Goldman, Ronald J., & Goldman, Juliette D. G. (1982b). *Children's sexual thinking.* London: Routledge & Kegan Paul.

Goldstein, Bernard. (1976). *Human sexuality.* New York: McGraw-Hill.

Bibliography

Goldstein, Marc. (1986, Fall). The future of male birth control. *Planned Parenthood Review*, 11–12.

Goldstein, Marc, & Feldberg, Michael (1982). *The vasectomy book: A complete guide to decision making.* Los Angeles: J. P. Tarcher (distributed by Houghton Mifflin).

Goldstein, Michael J. (1973). Exposure to erotic stimuli and sexual deviance. *Journal of Social Issues, 29*, 197–219.

Goldstein, Michael J., & Kant, Harold. (1973). *Pornography and sexual deviance.* Berkeley: University of California Press.

Golub, Sharon. (1976). The effect of premenstrual anxiety and depression on cognitive function. *Journal of Personality and Social Psychology, 34*, 99–104.

Golub, Sharon. (1992). *Periods: From menarche to menopause.* Newbury Park, CA: Sage.

Goode, Erich. (1970). *The marijuana smokers.* New York: Basic Books.

Goode, Erich. (1981). Comments on the homosexual role. *Journal of Sex Research, 17*, 54–65.

Goode, E., & Haber, L. (1977). Sexual correlates of homosexual experience: An exploratory study of college women. *Journal of Sex Research, 13*, 12–21.

Gooren, L., Fliers, E., & Courtney, K. (1990). Biological determinants of sexual behavior. *Annual Review of Sex Research, 1*, 175–196.

Gordon, E. M. (1967). Acceptance of pregnancy before and since oral contraception. *Obstetrics and Gynecology, 29*, 144–146.

Gordon, Linda. (1976). *Woman's body, woman's right: A social history of birth control in America.* New York: Penguin Books.

Gordon, M., & Shankweiler, P. J. (1971). Different equals less: Female sexuality in recent marriage manuals. *Journal of Marriage and the Family, 33*, 459–466.

Gordon, R. E., & Gordon, K. K. (1967). Factors in postpartum emotional adjustment. *American Journal of Orthopsychiatry, 37*, 359–360.

Gordon, R. E., Kapostons, E. F., & Gordon, K. K. (1965). Factors in postpartum emotional adjustment. *Obstetrics and Gynecology, 25*, 158–166.

Gordon, Sol. (1986, Oct.). What kids need to know. *Psychology Today.* Reprinted in O. Pocs (Ed.), *Human Sexuality 88/89.* Guilford, CT: Dushkin.

Gosselin, Chris, & Wilson, Glenn. (1980). *Sexual variations: Fetishism, sadomasochism, transvestism.* New York: Simon & Schuster.

Gottman, J., Markman, H., & Notarius, C. (1977). The topography of marital conflict: A sequential analysis of verbal and nonverbal behavior. *Journal of Marriage and the Family, 39*, 461–478.

Gottman, J., Notarius, C., Gonso, J., & Markman, H. (1976). *A couple's guide to communication.* Champaign, IL: Research Press.

Gottman, John M. (1979). *Marital interaction: Experimental investigations.* New York: Academic.

Gottman, John M. (1980). Consistency of nonverbal affect and affect reciprocity in marital interaction. *Journal of Consulting and Clinical Psychology, 48*, 711–717.

Gottman, John M., & Porterfield, A. L. (1981). Communicative competence in the nonverbal behavior of married couples. *Journal of Marriage and the Family, 43*, 817–824.

Gould, R. (1974, Apr.). Vasectomy complications (a 1110 patient study). Paper presented at the twelfth annual meeting of the American Association of Planned Parenthood Physicians, Memphis, TN.

Gould, Stephen J. (1987). *An urchin in the storm.* New York: Norton.

Gove, W. R., & Tudor, Jeannette F. (1973). Adult sex roles and mental illness. *American Journal of Sociology, 78*, 812–835.

Grammick, Jeannine. (1986). The Vatican's battered wives. *Christian Century, 103*, 17–20.

Grady, W. R., Klepinger, D. H., Billy, J. O. G., & Tanfer, K. (1993). Condom characteristics: The perceptions of men in the United States. *Family Planning Perspectives, 25*(2), 67–73.

Gray, A. H. (1922). *Men, women, and God.* New York: Associated Press.

Great Britain Committee on Homosexual Offenses and Prostitution. (1963). *The Wolfenden report* (American ed.). New York: Stein and Day.

Green, B. L., Lee, R. R., & Lustig, N. (1974, Sept.). Conscious and unconscious factors in marital infidelity. *Medical Aspects of Human Sexuality*, 87–91, 97–98, 104–105.

Green, Richard M. (1966). Mythological, historical, and cross-cultural aspects of transsexualism. In H. Benjamin (Ed.), *The transsexual phenomenon.* New York: Julian Press.

Green, Richard. (1972). Homosexuality as mental illness. *International Journal of Psychiatry, 10*, 77–98.

Green, Richard. (1975). Adults who want to change sex; adolescents who cross-dress; and children called "sissy" and "tomboy." In R. Green (Ed.), *Human sexuality: A health practitioner's text.* Baltimore: Williams & Wilkins.

Green, Richard. (1978). Sexual identity of 37 children raised by homosexual or transsexual parents. *American Journal of Psychiatry, 135*, 692–687.

Green, Richard. (1978). Intervention and prevention: The child with cross-sex identity. In C. B. Qualls et al. (Eds.), *The prevention of sexual disorders.* (pp. 75–94). New York: Plenum.

Green, Richard, et al. (1986). Lesbian mothers and their children: A comparison with solo parent heterosexual mothers and their children. *Archives of Sexual Behavior, 15*, 167–184.

Green, Richard, & Fleming, Davis T. (1990). Transsexual surgery follow-up: Status in the 1990s. *Annual Review of Sex Research, 1*, 163–174.

Green, Ronald M. (1984). Genetic medicine in Jewish legal perspective. *Annual of the Society of Christian Ethics, 1984*, 249–272.

Greene, F., Kirk, R. M., & Thompson, I. M. (1970). Retrograde ejaculation. *Medical Aspects of Human Sexuality, 4*(12), 59–65.

Greenhouse, Linda. (1991, May 24). Five justices uphold U.S. rule curbing abortion advice. *New York Times*, 1.

Greenspan, Stanley, & Greenspan, Nancy T. (1985). *First feelings.* New York: Penguin.

Greenwald, Evan, & Leitenberg, Harold. (1989). Long-term effects of sexual experiences with siblings and nonsiblings during childhood. *Archives of Sexual Behavior, 18*, 389–400.

Gregersen, Edgar. (1983). *Sexual practices: The story of human sexuality.* New York: Franklin Watts.

Gregor, Thomas. (1985). *Anxious pleasures: The sexual lives of an Amazonian people.* Chicago: University of Chicago Press.

Grieco, Alan. (1987). Scope and nature of sexual harassment in nursing. *Journal of Sex Research, 23,* 261–265.

Griffin, Bernard Cardinal. (1956). Report of the Roman Catholic Advisory Commission on Prostitution and Homosexual Offenses and the Present Law. *Dublin Review, 471,* 60–65.

Griffin, Susan. (1981). *Pornography and silence.* New York: Harper & Row.

Griffit, W. (1970). Environmental effects on interpersonal affective behavior: Ambient effective temperature and attraction. *Journal of Personality and Social Psychology, 15,* 240–244.

Gross, Alan E. (1978). The male role and heterosexual behavior. *Journal of Social Issues, 34*(1), 87–107.

Gross, Alan E., & Bellew-Smith, Martha. (1983). A social psychological approach to reducing pregnancy risk in adolescence. In D. Byrne & W. A. Fisher (Eds.), *Adolescents, sex, and contraception.* Hillsdale, NJ: Lawrence Erlbaum.

Gruber, K. J., Jones, R. J., & Freeman, M. H. (1982). Youth reactions to sexual assault. *Adolescence, 17,* 541–551.

Gruntz, Louis G., Jr. (1974). Obscenity 1973: Remodeling the house that Roth built. *Loyola Law Review, 20,* 159–174.

Guerney, Bernard G. (1977). *Relationship enhancement.* San Francisco: Jossey-Bass.

Guinan, Mary E., & Hardy, Ann. (1987). Epidemiology of AIDS in women in the United States, 1981 through 1986. *Journal of the American Medical Association, 257,* 1039–2042.

Gunby, Phil. (1983). Genital herpes research. *Journal of the American Medical Association, 250,* 2417–2427.

Gunderson, B. H., et al. (1981). Sexual behavior of preschool children. In L. L. Constantine & F. M. Martinson (Eds.), *Children and sex* (pp. 45–62). Boston: Little, Brown.

Gutek, Barbara A. (1985). *Sex and the workplace.* San Francisco: Jossey-Bass.

Haavio-Mannila, Elina. (1967). Sex differentiation in role expectations and performance. *Journal of Marriage and the Family, 29,* 568–578.

Hackett, C. J. (1963). On the origin of the human treponematoses. *Bulletin of the World Health Organization, 29,* 7–41.

Hadler, Stephen C., et al. (1986). Long-term immunogenicity and efficacy of hepatitis B vaccine in homosexual men. *New England Journal of Medicine, 315,* 209–214.

Hafez, E. S. E. (Ed.). (1980). *Human reproduction: Conception and contraception.* Hagerstown, MD: Harper & Row.

Hahn, S. R., & Paige, K. E. (1980). American birth practices: A critical review. In J. E. Parsons (Ed.), *The psychobiology of sex differences and sex roles.* New York: McGraw-Hill, Hemisphere.

Haider, I. (1966). Thioridazine and sexual dysfunctions. *International Journal of Neuropsychiatry,* 255–257.

Hair, Paul. (1972). *Before the bawdy court.* London: Elek.

Halikas, J. A., Goodwin, P. H., & Guze, S. B. (1971). Marijuana effects: A survey of regular users. *Journal of the American Medical Association, 217,* 692.

Hall, Judith A. (1978). Gender effects in decoding nonverbal cues. *Psychological Bulletin, 85,* 845–857.

Halleck, S. (1967). Sex and mental health on the campus. *Journal of the American Medical Association, 200,* 684.

Halverson, H. M. (1940). Genital and sphincter behavior of the male infant. *Journal of Genetic Psychology, 43,* 95–136.

Hamilton, G. V. (1914). A study of sexual tendencies in monkeys and baboons. *Journal of Animal Behavior, 4,* 295–318.

Hamilton, R. (1980). *The herpes book.* Los Angeles: J. P. Tarcher.

Hammond, Charles B., & Maxson, Wayne S. (1982). Current status of estrogen therapy for the menopause. *Fertility and Sterility, 37,* 5–25.

Hand, J. R. (1970). Surgery of the penis and urethra. In M. F. Campbell & J. H. Harrison (Eds.), *Urology* (Vol. 3). Philadelphia: Saunders.

Handsfield, H. H. (1984, Jan. 20). Cause of acquired immune deficiency syndrome. *Journal of the American Medical Association, 251,* 341.

Handsfield, H. H., Lipman, T. O., Harnisch, J. P., Tronca, E., & Holmes, K. K. (1975). Asymptomatic gonorrhea in men: Diagnosis, natural course, prevalence, and significance. *New England Journal of Medicine, 290*(3), 117–123.

Hanneke, C. R., Shields, N. M., & McCall, G. J. (1986). Assessing the prevalence of marital rape. *Journal of Interpersonal Violence, 1,* 350–362.

Harbison, R. D., & Mantilla-Plata, B. (1972). Prenatal toxicity, maternal distribution and placental transfer of tetrahydrocannabinol. *Journal of Pharmacology and Experimental Therapeutics, 180,* 446–453.

Hariton, E. Barbara. (1973). The sexual fantasies of women. *Psychology Today, 6*(10), 39–44.

Harlow, Harry F. (1959, June). Love in infant monkeys. *Scientific American, 200,* 68–70.

Harlow, Harry F., Harlow, M. K., & Hause, F. W. (1963). The maternal affectional system of rhesus monkeys. In H. L. Rheingold (Ed.), *Maternal behavior in mammals.* New York: Wiley.

Harper, Ruth, & Harper, George Lea, Jr. (1988). Homosexuality: UMC's turn to vote. *Christian Century, 105,* 356–358.

Harris, Carol, et al. (1983, May 19). Immunodeficiency in female sexual partners of men with the acquired immuno-deficiency syndrome. *New England Journal of Medicine, 308.*

Harris, G. W., & Levine, S. (1965). Sexual differentiation of the brain and its experimental control. *Journal of Physiology, 181,* 379–400.

Harry Benjamin International Gender Dysphoria Association (1985). Standards of care: The hormonal and surgical sex reassignment of gender dysphoric persons. *Archives of Sexual Behavior, 14,* 79–90.

Hart, Linda L. (1990). Accuracy of home pregnancy tests. *Annals of Pharmacotherapy, 24,* 712–713.

Hartley, Ruth E. (1959). Sex-role pressures in the socialization of the male child. *Psychological Reports, 5,* 457–468.

Hartman, William E., & Fithian, Marilyn A. (1974). *Treatment of sexual dysfunction.* New York: Jason Aronson.

Hartman, William, & Fithian, Marilyn (1984). *Any man can: The multiple orgasmic technique for every loving man.* New York: St. Martin's Press.

Hass, Aaron. (1979). *Teenage sexuality.* New York: Macmillan.

Hatcher, Robert A., et al. (1976). *Contraceptive technology, 1976–1977* (8th ed.). New York: Irvington.

Hatcher, Robert A., et al. (1984). *Contraceptive technology 1984–1985* (12th ed.). New York: Irvington.

Hatcher, Robert A., et al. (1986). *Contraceptive technology 1986–1987* (13th ed.). New York: Irvington.

Hatcher, Robert A., et al. (1988). *Contraceptive technology 1988–1989* (14th ed.). New York: Irvington.

Hatcher, Robert A., et al. (1990). *Contraceptive technology 1990–1992* (15th ed.). New York: Irvington.

Hatfield, Elaine, & Sprecher, Susan (1986). *Mirror, mirror . . .: The importance of looks in everyday life.* Albany, NY: State University of New York Press.

Hatfield, Elaine, & Walster, G. William. (1978). *A new look at love.* Reading, MA: Addison-Wesley.

Hatfield, Elaine, Walster, G. W., & Berscheid, E. (1978). *Equity theory and research.* Boston: Allyn and Bacon.

Hattendorf, K. W. (1932). A study of the questions of young children. *Journal of Social Psychology, 3,* 37–65.

Hayes, A. (1869). *Sexual physiology of woman.* Boston: Peabody Medical Institute.

Hays, Constance L. (1990, Sept. 30). Reports of assaults on homosexuals increase. *New York Times.*

Hazan, C., & Shaver, P. (1987). Love conceptualized as an attachment process. *Journal of Personality and Social Psychology, 52,* 511–524.

Hearst, Norman, & Hulley, Stephen B. (1988). Preventing the heterosexual spread of AIDS: Are we giving our patients the best advice? *Journal of the American Medical Association, 259,* 2428–2432.

Heath, Robert C. (1972). Pleasure and brain activity in man. *Journal of Nervous and Mental Disease, 154,* 3–18.

Heilbrun, Carolyn G. (1973). *Toward a recognition of androgyny.* New York: Knopf.

Heim, Nikolaus. (1981). Sexual behavior of castrated sex offenders. *Archives of Sexual Behavior, 10,* 11–20.

Heiman, Julia R. (1975). The physiology of erotica: Women's sexual arousal. *Psychology Today, 8*(11), 90–94.

Heiman, J., LoPiccolo, L., & LoPiccolo, J. (1976). *Becoming orgasmic: A sexual growth program for women.* Englewood Cliffs, NJ: Prentice-Hall.

Heiman, Julia R., et al. (1991). Psychophysiological and endocrine responses to sexual arousal in women. *Archives of Sexual Behavior, 20,* 171–186.

Hellerstein, Herman K., & Friedman, Ernest H. (1969, Mar.). Sexual activity and the post coronary patient. *Medical Aspects of Human Sexuality, 3,* 70–74.

Hellman, L. M., & Pritchard, J. A. (1971). *Williams obstetrics* (14th ed.). New York: Appleton-Century-Crofts.

Helmreich, R. L., Spence, J. T., & Gibson, R. H. (1982). Sex-role attitudes: 1972–1980. *Personality and Social Psychology Bulletin, 8,* 656–663.

Hembree, W. C., et al. (1976). Marihuana effects upon gonadal function. In G. G. Nahas et al. (Eds.), *Marihuana: Chemistry, biochemistry, and cellular effects.* New York: Springer-Verlag.

Henahan, John. (1984). Honing the treatment of early breast cancer. *Journal of the American Medical Association, 251,* 309–310.

Henderson, B. E., et al. (1978). Risk factors for cancer of the testis in young men. *International Journal of Cancer, 23,* 598–602.

Hendrick, Susan S. (1981). Self-disclosure and marital satisfaction. *Journal of Personality and Social Psychology, 40,* 1150–1159.

Hendrick, Susan, & Hendrick, Clyde. (1992). *Liking, loving, and relating* (2d ed). Pacific Grove, CA: Brooks/Cole.

Hendrick, S. S., Hendrick, Clyde, & Adler, N. L. (1988). Romantic

relationships: Love, satisfaction, and staying together. *Journal of Personality and Social Psychology, 54,* 980–988.

Henley, Nancy M. (1973a). The politics of touch. In P. Brown (Ed.), *Radical psychology.* New York: Harper & Row.

Henley, Nancy M. (1973b). Status and sex: Some touching observations. *Bulletin of the Psychonomic Society, 2,* 91–93.

Henshaw, S. K. (1987). Characteristics of U.S. women having abortions, 1982–1983. *Family Planning Perspectives, 19,* 5–9.

Henshaw, Stanley K. (1990, Apr.). Induced abortion: A world review, 1990. *Family Planning Perspectives, 22,* 76–89.

Herbert, J. (1966). The effect of estrogen applied directly to the genitalia upon the sexual attractiveness of the female rhesus monkey. *Excerpta Medica International Congress Series, 3,* 212.

Herbst, A. (1972). Clear cell adenocarcinoma of the genital tract in young females. *New England Journal of Medicine, 287*(25), 1259–1264.

Herbst, Arthur L. (1979). Coitus and the fetus. *New England Journal of Medicine, 301,* 1235–1236.

Herdt, Gilbert H. (1984). *Ritualized homosexuality in Melanesia.* Berkeley: University of California Press.

Herek, Gregory M. (1990). Gay people and government security clearances: A social science perspective. *American Psychologist, 45,* 1035–1042.

Herman, Judith L. (1981). *Father-daughter incest.* Cambridge: Harvard University Press.

Herold, E. S., & Way, L. (1983). Oral-genital sexual behavior in a sample of university females. *Journal of Sex Research, 19,* 327–338.

Heron, Alastair (Ed.) (1964). *Toward a Quaker view of sex* (rev. ed.). London: Friends Service Committee.

Hersey, R. B. (1931). Emotional cycles in man. *Journal of Mental Science, 77,* 151–169.

Heston, Leonard, & Shields, J. (1968). Homosexuality in twins: A family study and a registry study. *Archives of General Psychiatry, 18,* 149–160.

Higgins, Glenn E. (1978). Aspects of sexual response in adults with spinal-cord injury: A review of the literature. In J. LoPiccolo & L. LoPiccolo (Eds.), *Handbook of sex therapy* (pp. 387–410). New York: Plenum.

Higham, Eileen. (1980). Sexuality in the infant and neonate: Birth to two years. In B. B. Wolman & J. Money (Eds.), *Handbook of human sexuality.* Englewood Cliffs, NJ: Prentice-Hall.

Hill, C. T., Rubin, Z., & Peplau, L. A. (1976). Breakups before marriage: The end of 103 affairs. *Journal of Social Issues, 32*(1).

Hirsch, Martin S. (1990). Clinical manifestations of HIV infection in adults in industrialized countries. In K. Holmes et al. (Eds.), *Sexually transmitted diseases* (pp. 331–342). New York: McGraw-Hill.

Hite, Shere. (1976). *The Hite report.* New York: Macmillan.

Hite, Shere. (1981). *The Hite report on male sexuality.* New York: Knopf.

Hite, Shere. (1987). *Women and love.* New York: Knopf.

Hobart, C. Q. (1958). The incidence of romanticism during courtship. *Social Forces, 36,* 364.

Hoff, Gerard A., & Schneiderman, Lawrence J. (1985, Dec.). Having babies at home: Is it safe? Is it ethical? *Hastings Center Report,* 19–27.

Hofferth, Sandra L. (1990). Trends in adolescent sexual activity, contraception, and pregnancy in the United States. In J.

Bancroft & J. Reinisch (Eds.), *Adolescence and puberty* (pp. 217–233).

Hoffman, Lois W. (1974). Effects of maternal employment on the child: A review of the research. *Developmental Psychology, 10,* 204–228.

Hollister, Leo E. (1975). The mystique of social drugs and sex. In M. Sandler & G. L. Gessa (Eds.), *Sexual behavior: Pharmacology and biochemistry.* New York: Raven.

Holmberg, A. R. (1946). The Siriono. Unpublished doctoral dissertation, Yale University. Cited in Clellan S. Ford & Frank A. Beach, *Patterns of sexual behavior.* New York: Harper & Row.

Holmes, King K., et al. (Eds.). (1990). *Sexually transmitted diseases* (2d ed.). New York: McGraw-Hill.

Holmstrom, Lynda Lytle, & Burgess, Ann Wolbert (1980). Sexual behavior of assailants during reported rapes. *Archives of Sexual Behavior, 9,* 427–440.

Holroyd, Jean C., & Brodsky, Annette M. (1977). Psychologists' attitudes and practices regarding erotic and nonerotic physical contact with patients. *American Psychologist, 34,* 843–849.

Hong, Lawrence K. (1984). Survival of the fastest: On the origin of premature ejaculation. *Journal of Sex Research, 20,* 109–122.

Hook, Edward W., & Handsfield, H. Hunter. (1990). Gonococcal infections in adults. In K. Holmes et al. (Eds.), *Sexually transmitted diseases.* (pp. 149–160). New York: McGraw-Hill.

Hooker, Evelyn. (1957). The adjustment of the male overt homosexual. *Journal of Projective Techniques, 21,* 18–31.

Hooker, Evelyn. (1965). An empirical study of some relations between sexual patterns and gender identity in male homosexuals. In J. Money (Ed.), *Sex research: New developments.* New York: Holt.

Hoon, P. W., Bruce, K., & Kinchloe, B. (1982). Does the menstrual cycle play a role in sexual arousal? *Psychophysiology, 19,* 21–26.

Hooper, Celia, & Barnes, Deborah. (Nov.-Dec. 1989). DDI approved for clinical trials and almost-parallel track. *Journal of NIH Research, 1,* 50–52.

Hooper, R. R., et al. (1978). Cohort study of venereal disease. I. The risk of gonorrhea transmission from infected women to men. *American Journal of Epidemiology, 108,* 136–144.

Hopkins, J., Marcues, M., & Campbell, S. B. (1984). Postpartum depression: A critical review. *Psychological Bulletin, 95,* 498–515.

Hopkins, J. Ray. (1977). Sexual behavior in adolescence. *Journal of Social Issues, 33*(2), 67–85.

Hopkins, June H. (1969). The lesbian personality. *British Journal of Psychiatry, 115,* 1433–1436.

Hopkins, June R. (1977). Sexual behavior in adolescence. *Journal of Social Issues, 33*(2), 67–85.

Hopwood, Nancy J., et al. (1990). The onset of human puberty: Biological and environmental factors. In J. Bancroft & J. M. Reinisch (Eds.), *Adolescence and puberty.* New York: Oxford University Press.

Horner, Matina S. (1972). Toward an understanding of achievement-related conflicts in women. *Journal of Social Issues, 28*(2), 157–175.

Horney, Karen. (1973). The flight from womanhood (1926). In K. Horney, *Feminine psychology.* New York: Norton.

Horstman, W. (1972). Homosexuality and psychopathology. Unpublished doctoral dissertation. University of Oregon.

Hosken, Fran P. (1988, Feb.). Female genital mutilation and AIDS. *Sojourner, 7.*

Householder, Joanne, et al. (1982). Infants born to narcotic-addicted mothers. *Psychological Bulletin, 92,* 453–468.

Houston, L. N. (1981). Romanticism and eroticism among black and white college students. *Adolescence, 16,* 263–272.

Howard, D. R., Lott, B., & Reilly, M. E. (1982). Sexual assault and harassment: A campus community study. *Signs,* 321.

Hudson, Walter W., & Ricketts, Wendell A. (1980). A strategy for the measurement of homophobia. *Journal of Homosexuality, 5,* 357–372.

Hughes, J. (1964). Failure to ejaculate with chlordiazepoxide. *American Journal of Psychiatry, 121,* 610–611.

Hughes, Jean O., & Sandler, Bernice R. (1987). "Friends" raping friends: Could it happen to you? Washington, DC: Association of American Colleges.

Humphreys, Laud. (1970). *Tearoom trade: Impersonal sex in public places.* Chicago: Aldine.

Hunt, Morton. (1966). *The world of the formerly married.* New York: McGraw-Hill.

Hunt, Morton. (1974). *Sexual behavior in the 1970s.* Chicago: Playboy Press.

Hunt, Morton, & Hunt, Bernice. (1977). *The divorce experience.* New York: McGraw-Hill.

Hurst, John. (1977, May 26). Children—A big profit item for the smut producers. *Los Angeles Times.*

Huston, T. L., & Levinger, G. (1978). Interpersonal attraction and relationships. In M. R. Rosenzweig & L. W. Porter (Eds.), *Annual Review of Psychology* (Vol. 29). Palo Alto: Annual Reviews.

Huttel, F., et al. (1972). A quantitative evaluation of psychoprophylaxis in childbirth. *Journal of Psychosomatic Research, 16,* 81–92.

Hyde, Janet S. (1981). How large are cognitive gender differences? A meta-analysis using omega squared and d. *American Psychologist, 36,* 892–901.

Hyde, Janet S. (1984). How large are gender differences in aggression? A developmental meta-analysis. *Developmental Psychology, 20,* 722–736.

Hyde, Janet S. (1985). *Half the human experience: The psychology of women* (3rd ed.). Lexington, MA: D. C. Heath.

Hyde, Janet S., & Linn, Marcia C. (1988). Gender differences in verbal ability: A meta-analysis. *Psychological Bulletin, 104,* 53–69.

Hyde, Janet S., & Rosenberg, B. G. (1976). *Half the human experience: The psychology of women.* Lexington, MA: Heath.

Idanpaan-Heikkila, J., et al. (1969). Placental transfer of tritiated-1 tetrahydrocannabinol. *New England Journal of Medicine, 281,* 330.

Iffy, L., & Wingate, M. D. (1970). Risks of rhythm method of birth control. *Journal of Reproductive Medicine, 3*(1), 11.

Imperato-McGinley, J., et al. (1974). Steroid 5 reductase deficiency in man: An inherited form of male pseudohermaphroditism. *Science, 186,* 1213–1215.

Innala, Sune M., & Ernulf, Kurt E. (1989). Asphyxiophilia in Scandinavia. *Archives of Sexual Behavior, 18,* 181–190.

Intelligence report. (1971, July 25). *Parade.*

Isbell, H. (1965). Prospectus in research on opiate addiction. In D. M. Wilner & G. G. Kasserbaum (Eds.), *Narcotics.* New York: McGraw-Hill.

Israel, R. G., Sutton, M., & O'Brien, K. F. (1985). Effects of aerobic training on primary dysmennorhea symptomatology in college females. *Journal of American College Health, 33,* 241–244.

Israel, Spencer L. (1967). *Diagnosis and treatment of menstrual disorders and sterility* (15th ed.). New York: Harper & Row.

Ivey, M. E., & Bardwick, Judith M. (1968). Patterns of affective fluctuation in the menstrual cycle. *Psychosomatic Medicine, 30,* 336–345.

"J." (1969). *The sensuous woman.* New York: Lyle Stuart.

Jackman, N. R., O'Toole, R., & Geis, G. (1963). The self-image of the prostitute. *Sociological Quarterly, 4,* 150–161.

Jacob, Kathyrn A. (1981). The Mosher report. *American Heritage,* 57–64.

Jacobson, N. S. (1978). Specific and non-specific factors in the effectiveness of a behavioral approach to marital discord. *Journal of Consulting and Clinical Psychology, 46,* 442–452.

Jaffe, A., & Becker, R. E. (1984). Four new basic sex offenses: A fundamental shift in emphasis. *Illinois Bar Journal, 72,* 400–403.

Jaffe, H. W., et al. (1985). Persistent infection with human T-lymphotropic virus III/lymphadenopathy-associated virus in apparently healthy homosexual men. *Annals of Internal Medicine, 102,* 627–628.

Jaffee, David, & Straus, Murray A. (1987). Sexual climate and reported rape: A state-level analysis. *Archives of Sexual Behavior, 16,* 107–125.

Jamison, K. R., Wellisch, D. K., & Pasnau, R. O. (1978). Psychosocial aspects of mastectomy. I. The woman's perspective. *American Journal of Psychiatry, 135,* 432–436.

Jay, Karla, & Young, Allen (1979). *The gay report.* New York: Summit Books.

Jemail, Jay Ann, & Geer, James (1977). Sexual scripts. In R. Gemme & C. C. Wheeler (Eds.), *Progress in sexology.* New York: Plenum.

Jenkins, J. S., & Nussey, S. S. (1991). The role of oxytocin: Present concepts. *Clinical Endocrinology, 34,* 515–525.

Jenks, Richard J. (1985). Swinging: A replication and test of a theory. *Journal of Sex Research, 21,* 199–210.

Jenks, Richard J. (1985). Swinging: A test of two theories and a proposed new model. *Archives of Sexual Behavior, 14,* 517–528.

Jensen, Gordon D. (1976a). Adolescent sexuality. In B. J. Sadock et al. (Eds.), *The sexual experience.* Baltimore: Williams & Wilkins.

Jensen, Gordon D. (1976b). Cross-cultural studies and animal studies of sex. In B. J. Sadock et al. (Eds.), *The sexual experience.* Baltimore: Williams & Wilkins.

Jensen, Soren B. (1981). Diabetic sexual dysfunction. *Archives of Sexual Behavior, 10,* 493–504.

Jick, Hershel, et al. (1981). Vaginal spermicides and congenital disorders. *Journal of the American Medical Association, 245,* 1329–1332.

John, E. M., Savitz, D. A., & Sandler, D. P. (1991). Prenatal exposure to parents' smoking and childhood cancer. *American Journal of Epidemiology, 133,* 123–132.

Johnson, Anne M., Wadsworth, J., Wellings, K., Bradshaw, S., & Field, J. (1992). Sexual lifestyles and HIV risk. *Nature, 360,* 410–412.

Johnson, Robert E., et al. (1989). A seroepidemiologic survey of the prevalence of herpes simplex virus type 2 infection in the United States. *New England Journal of Medicine, 321,* 7–12.

Jones, Hardin, & Jones, Helen. (1977). *Sensual drugs.* New York: Cambridge University Press.

Jones, Jennifer C., & Barlow, David H. (1990). Self-reported frequency of sexual urges, fantasies, and masturbatory fantasies in heterosexual males and females. *Archives of Sexual Behavior, 19,* 269–280.

Jones, J. R. (1972). Plasma testosterone concentrations in female transsexuals. *Archives of Sexual Behavior, 2.*

Jones, W. C. (1976). *Doe v. Commonwealth Attorney:* Closing the door to a fundamental right to sexual privacy. *Denver Law Journal, 53,* 553–576.

Jorgensen, S. R. (1980). Contraceptive attitude-behavior consistency in adolescence. *Population and Environment, 3,* 174–194.

Jost, A. (1970). Hormonal factors in the sex differentiation of the mammalian foetus. *Philosophical Transactions of the Society of London, Series B, 259,* 119–131.

Jourard, Sidney M. (1971). Some lethal aspects of the male role. In S. M. Jourard, *The transparent self.* Princeton, NJ: Van Nostrand.

Jourard, Sidney M., & Lasakow, P. (1958). Some factors in self-disclosure. *Journal of Abnormal and Social Psychology, 56,* 91–98.

Justice, Blair, & Justice, Rita. (1979). *The broken taboo: Sex in the family.* New York: Human Sciences Press.

Kaats, Gilbert, & Davis, Keith. (1971). Effects of volunteer biases in studies of sexual behavior and attitudes. *Journal of Sex Research, 7,* 26–34.

Kaeser, Lisa. (1989, Dec.). Reconsidering the age limits on pill use. *Family Planning Perspectives, 21,* 273–274.

Kalisch, Philip A., & Kalisch, Beatrice J. (1984). Sex-role stereotyping of nurses and physicians on prime-time television. *Sex Roles, 10,* 533–554.

Kallman, Franz J. (1952a). Comparative twin study on the genetic aspects of male homosexuality. *Journal of Nervous and Mental Disease, 115,* 283–298.

Kallman, Franz J. (1952b). Twin and sibship study of overt male homosexuality. *American Journal of Human Genetics, 4,* 136–146.

Kando, Thomas. (1973). *Sex change: The achievement of gender identity among feminized transsexuals.* Springfield, IL: Charles C. Thomas.

Kanin, Eugene J. (1969). Selected dyadic aspects of male sex aggression. *Journal of Sex Research, 5.*

Kanin, Eugene J. (1985). Date rapists: Differential sexual socialization and relative deprivation. *Archives of Sexual Behavior, 14,* 219–232.

Kanin, E. J., Davidson, K. D., & Scheck, S. R. (1970). A research note on male-female differentials in the experience of heterosexual love. *Journal of Sex Research, 6,* 64–72.

Kantner, John F., & Zelnik, Melvin. (1972). Sexual experience of young unmarried women in the United States. *Family Planning Perspectives, 4*(4), 9–18.

Kantner, John F., & Zelnik, Melvin. (1973). Contraception and pregnancy: Experience of young unmarried women in the United States. *Family Planning Perspectives, 5*(1), 21–35.

Kaplan, Helen S. (1974). *The new sex therapy.* New York: Brunner/Mazel.

Kaplan, Helen Singer. (1979). *Disorders of sexual desire.* New York: Simon & Schuster.

Kaplan, Helen S., & Sager, C. J. (1971, June). Sexual patterns at different ages. *Medical Aspects of Human Sexuality,* 10–23.

Karpman, Benjamin. (1954). *The sexual offender and his offenses.* New York: Julian Press.

Karr, Rodney K. (1978). Homosexual labeling and the male role. *Journal of Social Issues, 34*(3), 73–83.

Katz, Kathryn D. (1982). Sexual morality and the Constitution: *People v. Onofre. Albany Law Review, 46,* 311–362.

Kayal, Philip M. (1985). "Morals," medicine, and the AIDS epidemic. *Journal of Religion and Health, 24,* 218–238.

Kegel, A. H. (1952). Sexual functions of the pubococcygeus muscle. *Western Journal of Surgery, 60,* 521–524.

Keller, J. F., Elliott, S. S., & Gunberg, E. (1982). Premarital sexual intercourse among single college students. A discriminant analysis. *Sex Roles, 8,* 21–32.

Kemp, Karl H. (1974). Comment: Recent obscenity cases. *Arkansas Law Review, 28,* 335–356.

Kempf, E. J. (1971). The social and sexual behavior of infrahuman primates with some comparable facts in human behavior. *Psychoanalytic Review, 4,* 127–154.

Kenrick, D., et al. (1980). Sex differences, androgyny and approach responses to erotica: A new variation on an old volunteer problem. *Journal of Personality and Social Psychology, 38,* 517–524.

Kestelman, Philip, & Trussell, James. (1991, Oct.). Efficacy of the simultaneous use of condoms and spermicides. *Family Planning Perspectives, 23,* 226–232.

Key, Mary R. (1975). *Male/female language.* Metuchen, NJ: Scarecrow Press.

Kilmann, Peter R., et al. (1981). Sex education: A review of its effects. *Archives of Sexual Behavior, 10,* 177–206.

Kilmann, Peter R., & Mills, Katherine H. (1983). *All about sex therapy.* New York: Plenum.

Kilpatrick, Allie C. (1986). Some correlates of women's childhood sexual experiences: A retrospective study. *Journal of Sex Research, 22,* 221–242.

Kilpatrick, Allie C. (1987). Childhood sexual experiences: Problems and issues in studying long-range effects. *Journal of Sex Research, 23,* 173–196.

Kilpatrick, D. G., Resick, P. A., & Veronen, L. J. (1981). Effects of a rape experience: A longitudinal study. *Journal of Social Issues, 37*(4), 105–122.

Kim, Elaine H. (1990, Winter). "Such opposite creatures": Men and women in Asian American literature. *Michigan Quarterly Review, 29,* 68–93.

Kimlicka, Thomas, Cross, H., & Tarnai, J. (1983). A comparison of androgynous, feminine, masculine, and undifferen-

tiated women on self-esteem, body satisfaction, and sexual satisfaction. *Psychology of Women Quarterly, 1,* 291–294.

Kinsey, A. C., Pomeroy, W. B., & Martin, C. E. (1948). *Sexual behavior in the human male.* Philadelphia: Saunders.

Kinsey, A. C., Pomeroy, W. B., Martin, C. E., & Gebhard, P. H. (1953). *Sexual behavior in the human female.* Philadelphia: Saunders.

Kirby, Douglas. (1977). The methods and methodological problems of sex research. In J. S. DeLora & C. A. B. Warren, *Understanding sexual interaction.* Boston: Houghton Mifflin.

Kirby, Douglas. (1984). *Sexuality education: An evaluation of programs and their effects.* Santa Cruz, CA: Network Publications.

Kirkendall, Lester A. (1965). *Sex education.* SIECUS Study Guide No. 1. New York: Sex Information and Education Council of the United States.

Kiviat, Nancy B., et al. (1989). Prevalence of genital papillomavirus infection among women attending a college student health clinic or a sexually transmitted disease clinic. *Journal of Infectious Diseases, 159,* 293–302.

Klaus, Marshall A., et al. (1972). Maternal attachment: Importance of the first postpartum days. *New England Journal of Medicine, 286,* 460–463.

Klaus, Marshall, & Kennell, John. (1976). Human maternal and paternal behavior. In M. Klaus & J. Kennell (Eds.), *Maternal infant bonding.* St. Louis: Mosby.

Klaus, Marshall, & Kennell, John (1976). *Maternal-infant bonding.* St. Louis: Mosby.

Klepinger, D. H., Billy, J. O. G., Tanfer, K., & Grady, W. R. (1993). Perceptions of AIDS risk and severity and their association with risk-related behavior among U.S. men. *Family Planning Perspectives, 25*(2), 74–82.

Klitsch, Michael. (1988, Jan.–Feb.). The return of the IUD. *Family Planning Perspective, 20,* 19–24.

Knopp, Fay H. (1984). *Retraining adult sex offenders: Methods and models.* New York: Safer Society Press.

Kohlberg, Lawrence. (1966). A cognitive-developmental analysis of children's sex-role concepts and attitudes. In E. E. Maccoby (Ed.), *The development of sex differences.* Stanford, CA: Stanford University Press.

Kolata, Gina. (1986). Maleness pinpointed on Y chromosome. *Science, 234,* 1076–1077.

Kolbenschlag, Madonna. (1985). Abortion and moral consensus: Beyond Solomon's choice. *Christian Century, 102,* 179–183.

Kolker, Aliza. (1989). Advances in prenatal diagnosis. *International Journal of Technology Assessment in Health Care, 5,* 601–617.

Kolodny, R. C., Masters, W. H., & Johnson, V. E. (1979). Drugs and sex. In R. C. Kolodny et al., *Textbook of sexual medicine.* Boston: Little, Brown.

Kolodny, R. C., Masters, W. H., Kolodny, R. M., & Toro, G. (1974). Depression of plasma testosterone levels after chronic intensive marihuana use. *New England Journal of Medicine, 290,* 872–874.

Kolodny, Robert C., et al. (1979). Chronic marihuana use by women. Cited in Rosen, R. C. (1991). Alcohol and drug effects on sexual response. *Annual Review of Sex Research, 2,* 119–180.

Kon, Igor S. (1987). A sociocultural approach. In J. H. Geer & W.

T. O'Donohue (Eds.), *Theories of human sexuality* (pp. 257–286). New York: Plenum.

Koonin, L. M., Atrash, H. K., Lawson, H. W., & Smith, J. C. (1991a, July). Maternal mortality surveillance, United States, 1979–1986. *Morbidity and Mortality Weekly Report, 40,* No. SS-1, 1–13.

Koonin, L. M., Kochanek, K. D., Smith, J. C., & Ramick, M. (1991b, July). Abortion surveillance, United States, 1988. *Morbidity and Mortality Weekly Report, 40,* No. SS-1, 15–42.

Korff, Janice, & Geer, James H. (1983). The relationship between sexual arousal experience and genital response. *Psychophysiology, 20,* 121–127.

Kosnick, Anthony, et al. (1977). *Human sexuality: New directions in American Catholic thought.* New York: Paulist Press.

Koss, M. P., Dinero, T. E., Siebel, C. A., & Cox, S. L. (1988). Stranger and acquaintance rape: Are there differences in the victim's experience? *Psychology of Women Quarterly, 12,* 1–24.

Koss, M. P., Gidycz, C. A., & Wisniewski, N. (1987). The scope of rape: Incidence and prevalence in a national sample of higher education students. *Journal of Consulting and Clinical Psychology, 55,* 162–170.

Koss, Mary P., & Oros, Cheryl J. (1982). Sexual experiences survey: A research instrument investigating sexual aggression and victimization. *Journal of Consulting and Clinical Psychology, 50,* 455–457.

Kost, K., Forrest, J. D., & Harlap, S. (1991, April). Comparing the health risks and benefits of contraceptive choices. *Family Planning Perspectives, 23,* 54–61.

Kraemer, D., Moore, G., & Kramen, M. (1976). Baboon infant produced by embryo tansfer. *Science, 192,* 1246–1247.

Krauss, D. (1983). The physiologic basis of male sexual dysfunction. *Hospital Practice, 2,* 193–222.

Kreitler, Hans, & Kreitler, Shulamith. (1966). Children's concepts of sex and birth. *Child Development, 37,* 363–378.

Krimmel, Herbert T. (1983, Oct.). The case against surrogate parenting. *Hastings Center Report,* 35–39.

Kronhausen, Phyllis, & Kronhausen, Eberhard. (1964). *The sexually responsive woman.* New York: Grove.

Kumar, R., Brant, H. A., & Robson, K. M. (1981). Childbearing and maternal sexuality: A prospective survey of 119 primiparae. *Journal of Psychosomatic Research, 25,* 373–383.

Kutchinsky, Berl. (1973). The effect of easy availability of pornography on the incidence of sex crimes: The Danish experience. *Journal of Social Issues, 29,* 163–181.

Kweskin, Sally L., & Cook, Alicia S. (1982). Heterosexual and homosexual mothers' self-described sex-role behavior and ideal sex-role behavior in children. *Sex Roles, 8,* 967–976.

Ladas, A. K., Whipple, B., & Perry, J. D. (1982). *The G spot and other recent discoveries about human sexuality.* New York: Holt, Rinehart, Winston.

Ladner, Joyce A. (1971). *Tomorrow's tomorrow: The black woman.* Garden City, NY: Doubleday.

LaFromboise, T. D., Heyle, A. M., & Ozer, E. J. (1990). Changing and diverse roles of women in American Indian cultures. *Sex Roles,* 455–476.

Lakoff, Robin. (1973). Language and woman's place. *Language in Society, 2,* 45–79.

Lamb, Michael. (1982, Apr.). Second thoughts on first touch. *Psychology Today,* 9–1.

Lamb, Michael E., & Hwang, C. (1982). Maternal attachment and mother-neonate bonding: A critical review. In M. E. Lamb & A. L. Brown (Eds.), *Advances in developmental psychology* (Vol. 2). Hillsdale, NJ: Lawrence Erlbaum.

Landesman, S. H., & Vierra, J. (1983). Acquired immune deficiency syndrome (AIDS): A review. *Archives of Internal Medicine, 143,* 2307–2309.

Laner, M. R., & Thompson, J. (1982). Abuse and aggression in courting couples. *Deviant Behavior: An Interdiscipline Journal, 3,* 229–244.

Lange, James D., et al. (1981). Effects of demand for performance, self-monitoring of arousal and increased sympathetic nervous system activity on male erectile response. *Archives of Sexual Behavior, 10,* 443–464.

Langer, Ellen J., & Dweck, Carol S. (1973). *Personal politics: The psychology of making it.* Englewood Cliffs, NJ: Prentice-Hall.

Langevin, R., et al. (1979). Experimental studies of the etiology of genital exhibitionism. *Archives of Sexual Behavior, 8,* 307–332.

Langfeldt, Thore. (1981). Childhood masturbation. In L. L. Constantine & F. M. Martinson (Eds.), *Children and sex* (pp. 63–74). Boston: Little Brown.

Lanson, Lucienne. (1975). *From woman to woman.* New York: Knopf.

Lantz, H. R., Keyes, J., & Schultz, H. (1975). The American family in the preindustrial period: From baselines in history to change. *American Sociological Review, 40,* 21–36.

Laumann, Edward O. (1969). Friends of urban men: An assessment of accuracy in reporting their socioeconomic attributes, mutual choice, and attitude agreement. *Sociometry, 32,* 54–69.

Leading cases: Right to privacy. (1986). *Harvard Law Review, 100,* 200–220.

Leavitt, Fred. (1974). *Drugs and behavior.* Philadelphia: Saunders.

Lebacqz, Karen. (1987). Appropriate vulnerability: A sexual ethic for singles. *Christian Century, 104,* 435–438.

Lebegue, Breck. (1991). Paraphilias in U.S. pornography titles: "Pornography made me do it" (Ted Bundy). *Bulletin of the American Academy of Psychiatry and Law, 19,* 43–48.

Lecos, Chris. (1980, Oct.). Caution light on caffeine. *FDA Consumer,* 6–9.

Lederer, Laura. (Ed.). (1980). *Take back the night: Women on pornography.* New York: Morrow.

Lee, J. A. (1979). The social organization of sexual risk. *Alternative Lifestyles, 2,* 69–100.

Lee, John Alan. (1974). Styles of loving. *Psychology Today, 8*(5), 43–51.

Lee, John Alan. (1977). A typology of styles of loving. *Personality and Social Psychology Bulletin, 3,* 173–182.

Legman, Gershon. (1968). *Rationale of the dirty joke.* New York: Grove.

Leiblum, Sandra R., & Pervin, L. A. (Eds.) (1980). *Principles and practice of sex therapy.* New York: Guilford.

Leiblum, Sandra R., & Rosen, Raymond C. (1984). Alcohol and human sexual response. *Alcoholism Treatment Quarterly, 3,* 1–16.

Leiblum, Sandra R., & Rosen, Raymond C. (Eds.) (1988). *Sexual desire disorders.* New York: Guilford.

Leiblum, Sandra R., & Rosen, Raymond C. (1989). *Principles and practice of sex therapy* (2d ed.). New York: Guilford.

Leiblum, S. R., Rosen, R. C., & Pierce, D. (1976). Group treatment format: Mixed sexual dysfunctions. *Archives of Sexual Behavior, 5,* 313–322.

Leifer, Myra. (1980). *Psychological effects of motherhood: A study of first pregnancy.* New York: Praeger.

Leigh, Barbara C. (1989). Reasons for having and avoiding sex: Gender, sexual orientation, and relationship to sexual behavior. *Journal of Sex Research, 26,* 199–209.

Leitenberg, H., Greenwald, E., & Tarran. M. J. (1989). The relation between sexual activity among children during preadolescence and/or early adolescence and sexual behavior and sexual adjustment in young adulthood. *Archives of Sexual Behavior, 18,* 299–314.

Leitenberg, Harold, & Slavin, Lesley. (1983). Comparison of attitudes toward transsexuality and homosexuality. *Archives of Sexual Behavior, 12,* 337–346.

LeMagnen, J. (1952). Les pheromones olfactosexuals chez le rat blanc. *Archives des Sciences Physiologiques, 6,* 295–332.

Lemere, Frederick, & Smith, James W. (1973). Alcohol-induced sexual impotence. *American Journal of Sex Research, 8,* 268–285.

Lerman, Hannah. (1986). From Freud to feminist personality theory. *Psychology of Women Quarterly, 10,* 1–18.

Lerner, Harriet G. (1989). *The dance of intimacy.* New York: Harper & Row.

LeVay, Simon. (1991). A difference in hypothalamic structure between heterosexual and homosexual men. *Science, 253,* 1034–1037.

Levin, Robert J., & Levin, Amy. (1975, Sept.). Sexual pleasure: The surprising preferences of 100,000 women. *Redbook, 51.*

Levin, Robert J., & Levin, Amy. (1975, Oct.). The *Redbook* report on premarital and extramarital sex. *Redbook, 38.*

Levin, Saul M., & Stava, Lawrence. (1987). Personality characteristics of sex offenders: A review. *Archives of Sexual Behavior, 16,* 57–80.

Levine, Carol, & Bermal, Joyce. (Eds.). (1985, Aug.). AIDS: The emerging ethical dilemmas. *Hastings Center Report Special Supplement,* 1–31.

Levine, Carol, & Bermel, Joyce. (Eds.). (1986, Dec.). AIDS: Public health and civil liberties. *Hastings Center Report Special Supplement,* 1–36.

Levine, E. M., Gruenewald, D., & Shaiova, C. H. (1976). Behavioral differences and emotional conflict among male-to-female transsexuals. *Archives of Sexual Behavior, 5,* 81–86.

Levine, M. I. (1970). Sex education in the public elementary and high school curriculum. In D. L. Taylor (Ed.), *Human sexual development.* Philadelphia: Davis.

Levinson, Daniel J. (1978). *The seasons of a man's life.* New York: Ballantine.

Levinson, D. R., Johnson, M. L., & Devaney, D. M. (1988). *Sexual harassment in the federal government: An update.* Washington, DC: U.S. Merit Systems Protection Board.

Levinson, Ruth A. (1986). Contraceptive self-efficacy: A perspective on teenage girls' contraceptive behavior. *Journal of Sex Research, 22,* 347–369.

Levitt, E. E., & Klassen, A. D. (1974). Public attitudes toward homosexuality. *Journal of Homosexuality, 1,* 29–43.

Levitt, Eugene E. (1983). Estimating the duration of sexual behavior. A laboratory analog study. *Archives of Sexual Behavior, 12,* 329–336.

Lewis, C. S. (1960). *The four loves.* New York: Harcourt Brace Jovanovich.

LeWitter, Maximillian, & Abarbanel, Albert. (1973). Aging and sex. In A. Ellis and A. Abarbanel (Eds.), *The encyclopedia of sexual behavior.* New York: Jason Aronson.

Libby, Roger W. (1980). Make love not war? Sex, sexual meanings, and violence in a sample of university students. *Archives of Sexual Behavior, 9,* 133–148.

Libby, Roger W., & Nass, Gilbert D. (1971). Parental views on teenage sexual behavior. *Journal of Sex Research, 7,* 226–236.

Licklider, S. (1961). Jewish penile carcinoma. *Journal of Urology, 86,* 98.

Liebmann-Smith, Joan. (1987). *In pursuit of pregnancy: How couples discover, cope with, and resolve their fertility problems.* New York: Newmarket Press.

Lightfoot-Klein, Hanny. (1989). *Prisoners of ritual: An odyssey into female genital circumcision in Africa.* New York: Haworth.

Lindsey, Robert. (1988, Feb. 1). Circumcision under criticism as unnecessary to newborn. *New York Times.* A1.

Linz, Daniel. (1989). Exposure to sexually explicit materials and attitudes toward rape: A comparison of study results. *Journal of Sex Research, 26,* 50–84.

Linz, D., Donnerstein, E., & Penrod, S. (1987). The findings and recommendations of the Attorney General's Commission on Pornography: Do the psychological "facts" fit the political fury? *American Psychologist, 42,* 946–953.

Liskin, Laurie. (1984). After contraception: Dispelling rumors about later childbearing. *Population Reports,* Series J, No. 28, J697–J731.

Liskin, Laurie. (1985, Nov.–Dec.). Youth in the 1980s: Social and health concerns. *Population Reports,* XIII, No. 5, M350–M388.

Liskin, L., Beroit, E., & Blackburn, R. (1992). Vasectomy: New opportunities. *Population Reports,* Series D, No. 5. Baltimore: Johns Hopkins University Population Information Program.

Liskin, Laurie, & Blackburn, Richard. (1986, July–Aug.). AIDS: A public health crisis. *Population Reports,* Series L, No. 6, L193–L228.

Liskin, L., Wharton, C., & Blackburn, R. (1990). Condoms—Now more than ever. *Population Reports,* Series H, No. 8, 1–35.

Little, B. B., et al. (1989). Cocaine abuse during pregnancy: Maternal and fetal implications. *Obstetrics & Gynecology,*

Lobitz, W. Charles, & LoPiccolo, Joseph. (1972). New methods in the behavioral treatment of sexual dysfunction. *Journal of Therapy and Experimental Psychiatry, 3,* 265–271.

Lobsenz, Norman. (1974, Jan. 20). Sex and the senior citizen. *New York Times Magazine,* 87–91.

Lockwood, Daniel. (1980). *Prison sexual violence.* New York: Elsevier.

Lodl, K., McGettigan, & Bucy, J. (1984). Women's responses to abortion: Implications for postabortion support groups. *Journal of Social Work and Human Sexuality,* 119–132.

Longo, D. J., Clum, G. A., & Yaeger, N. J. (1988). Psychosocial treatment for recurrent genital herpes. *Journal of Consulting and Clinical Psychology, 56,* 61–66.

LoPiccolo, Joseph, & Lobitz, Charles. (1972). The role of masturbation in the treatment of sexual dysfunction. *Archives of Sexual Behavior, 2,* 163–171.

LoPiccolo, Joseph, & Stock, Wendy E. (1986). Treatment of sexual dysfunction. *Journal of Consulting and Clinical Psychology, 54,* 158–167.

LoPiccolo, Leslie. (1980). Low sexual desire. In S. R. Leiblum & L. A. Pervin (Eds.), *Principles and practice of sex therapy.* New York: Guilford.

LoPresto, C. T., Sherman, M. F., & Sherman, N. C. (1985). The effects of a masturbation seminar on high school males' attitudes, false beliefs, guilt, and behavior. *Journal of Sex Research, 21,* 142–156.

Loraine, J. A., Adampopoulos, D. A., Kirkhan, K. E., Ismail, A. A., & Dove, G. A. (1971). Patterns of hormone excretion in male and female homosexuals. *Nature, 234,* 552–554.

Lorenz, Konrad. (1966). *On aggression.* New York: Harcourt Brace Jovanovich.

Louria, Donald B. (1970, Jan.). Sexual use of amyl nitrate. *Medical Aspects of Human Sexuality, 89.*

Louv, W. C., et al. (1989). Oral contraceptive use and risk of chlamydial and gonococcal infections. *American Journal of Obstetrics and Gynecology, 160,* 396.

Lowenthal, M. F., et al. (1975). *Four stages of life: A comparative study of women and men facing transitions.* San Francisco: Jossey-Bass.

Lu, Y. (1952). Marital roles and marital adjustment. *Sociology and Social Research, 36,* 364–368.

Luby, Elliot C., & Klinge, Valerie. (1985). Genital herpes: A pervasive psychosocial disorder. *Archives of Dermatology, 121,* 494–497.

Luker, Kristin. (1975). *Taking chances: Abortion and the decision not to contracept.* Berkeley: University of California Press.

Luker, Kristin. (1984). *Abortion and the politics of motherhood.* Berkeley: University of California Press.

Lumby, M. E. (1978). Men who advertise for sex. *Journal of Homosexuality, 4,* 63–72.

Lyons, Richard D. (1983, Oct. 4). Promiscuous sex believed declining in recent years. *New York Times,* C1.

Maccoby, Eleanor E., & Jacklin, Carol N. (1974). *The psychology of sex differences.* Stanford, CA: Stanford University Press.

MacDonald, A. P. (1982). Research on sexual orientation: A bridge that touches both shores but doesn't meet in the middle. *Journal of Sex Education and Therapy, 8*(1), 9–13.

MacDougald, D. (1961). Aphrodisiacs and anaphrodisiacs. In A. Ellis & A. Abarbanel (Eds.), *The encyclopedia of sexual behavior* (Vol. I). New York: Hawthorn.

MacFarlane, J. A., et al. (1978). The relationship between mother and neonate. In S. Kitzinger & J. A. Davis (Eds.), *The place of birth.* Oxford: Oxford University Press.

MacKinnon, Catharine A. (1979). *Sexual harassment of working women.* New Haven: Yale University Press.

MacLean, Paul. (1962). New findings relevant to the evolution of psychosexual functions of the brain. *Journal of Nervous and Mental Disease, 135,* 289–301.

MacLusky, Neil J., & Naftolin, Frederick. (1981). Sexual differentiation of the central nervous system. *Science, 211,* 1294–1303.

MacNamara, Donald E. J., & Sagarin, Edward. (1977). *Sex, crime and the law.* New York: Free Press.

Magana, J. R., & Carrier, J. M. (1991). Mexican and Mexican American male sexual behavior and spread of AIDS in California. *Journal of Sex Research, 28,* 425–441.

Maguire, Daniel C. (1983). Abortion: A question of Catholic honesty. *Christian Century, 100,* 803–807.

Mahoney, E. R. (1983). *Human sexuality.* New York: McGraw-Hill.

Maisch, Herbert. (1972). *Incest.* New York: Stein and Day.

Mallory, Tammie E., & Rich, Katherine E. (1986). Human reproductive technologies: An appeal for brave new legislation in a brave new world. *Washburn Law Journal, 25,* 458–504.

Malamuth, Neil M. (1981a). Rape proclivity in males. *Journal of Social Issues, 37*(4), 138–157.

Malamuth, Neil M. (1981b). Rape fantasies as a function of exposure to violent sexual stimuli. *Archives of Sexual Behavior, 10,* 33–48.

Malamuth, Neil M. (1984). Aggression against women: Cultural and individual causes. In N. Malamuth & E. Donnerstein (Eds.), *Pornography and sexual aggression.* New York: Academic.

Malamuth, Neil M., & Check, J. V. P. (1981). The effects of mass media exposure on acceptance of violence against women: A field experiment. *Journal of Research in Personality, 15,* 436–446.

Malamuth, N., Feshbach, S., & Jaffe, Y. (1977). Sexual arousal and aggression: Recent experiments and theoretical issues. *Journal of Social Issues, 33,* 110–133.

Malamuth, N. M., Heim, M., & Feshbach, S. (1980). Sexual responsiveness of college students to rape depictions: Inhibitory and disinhibitory effects. *Journal of Personality and Social Psychology, 38,* 399–408.

Malamuth, N. M., Sockloskie, R. J., Koss, M. P., & Tanaka, J. S. (1991). Characteristics of aggressors against women: Testing a model using a national sample of college students. *Journal of Consulting and Clinical Psychology, 59,* 670–781.

Malamuth, Neil M., & Spinner, B. (1980). A longitudinal content analysis of sexual violence in the best-selling erotic magazines. *Journal of Sex Research, 16,* 226–237.

Malatesta, V. J., Pollack, R. H., Crotty, T. D., & Pecock, L. J. (1982). Acute alcohol intoxication and female orgasmic response. *Journal of Sex Research, 18,* 1–17.

Maletzky, B. M. (1974). "Assisted" covert sensitization in the treatment of exhibitionism. *Journal of Consulting and Clinical Psychology, 42,* 34–40.

Maletzky, B. M. (1977). "Booster" sessions in aversion therapy: The permanency of treatment. *Behavior Therapy, 8,* 460–463.

Maletzky, B. M. (1980). Assisted covert sensitization. In D. J. Cox & R. J. Daitzman (Eds.), *Exhibitionism: Description, assessment, and treatment.* New York: Garland.

Malinowski, Bronislaw. (1929). *The sexual life of savages.* New York: Harcourt Brace Jovanovich.

Mamay, Patricia D., & Simpson, Richard L. (1981). Three female roles in television commercials. *Sex Roles, 1,* 1223–1232.

Manabe, Y. (1969). Artificial abortion at mid-trimester by mechanical stimulation of the uterus. *American Journal of Obstetrics and Gynecology, 105,* 132–146.

Margolis, Stephen. (1984). Genial warts and molluscum contagiosum. *Urologic Clinics of North America, 11,* 163–170.

Marin, Peter. (1983, July). A revolution's broken promises. *Psychology Today, 17*(7), 50–57.

Markman, Howard J. (1979). Application of a behavioral model of marriage in predicting relationship satisfaction of couples planning marriage. *Journal of Consulting and Clinical Psychology, 47,* 743–749.

Markman, Howard J., & Floyd, Frank. (1980). Possibilities for the prevention of marital discord: A behavioral perspective. *American Journal of Family Therapy, 8,* 29–48.

Markman, Howard J. (1981). Prediction of marital distress: A 5-year follow-up. *Journal of Consulting and Clinical Psychology, 49,* 760–762.

Marks, Isaac, & Gelder, Michael. (1967). Transvestism and fetishism: Clinical and psychological changes during faradic aversion. *British Journal of Psychiatry, 113,* 711–729.

Marmor, Judd. (1969). Sex for nonsexual reasons. *Medical Aspects of Human Sexuality, 3*(6), 8–21.

Marmor, Judd. (1976). Frigidity, dyspareunia, and vaginismus. In B. J. Sadock et al. (Eds.), *The sexual experience.* Baltimore: Williams & Wilkins.

Marmor, J. J., et al. (1986). Possible female to female transmission of human immunodeficiency virus. *Annals of Internal Medicine, 105,* 969.

Marquis, J. N. (1970). Orgasmic reconditioning: Changing sexual object choice through controlling masturbation fantasies. *Journal of Behavior Therapy and Experimental Psychiatry, 1,* 263–272.

Marshall, P., Surridge, D., & Delva, N. (1981). The role of nocturnal penile tumescence in differentiating between organic and psychogenic impotence: The first stage of validation. *Archives of Sexual Behavior, 10,* 1–10.

Marsiglio, William, & Menaghan, Elizabeth G. (1987). Couples and the male birth control pill: A future alternative in contraceptive selection. *Journal of Sex Research, 23,* 34–49.

Martin, Carol L., & Halverson, C. F. (1983). The effects of sex-typing schemas on young children's memory. *Child Development, 54,* 563–574.

Martin, Clyde E. (1981). Factors affecting sexual functioning in 60–79-year-old married males. *Archives of Sexual Behavior, 10,* 399–420.

Martin, Del, & Lyon, Phyllis. (1972). *Lesbian/woman.* San Francisco: Glide Publications.

Martinez, G. A., & Nalezienski, J. P. (1981). 1980 update: The recent trend in breastfeeding. *Pediatrics, 67*(2), 260–263.

Martinson, Floyd M. (1973). *Infant and child sexuality: A sociological perspective.* St. Peter, MN: Book Mark.

Martinson, Floyd M. (1981). Eroticism in infancy and childhood. In L. L. Constantine & F. M. Martinson (Eds.), *Children and sex.* Boston: Little, Brown.

Marx, Jean L. (1988). The AIDS virus can take on many guises. *Science, 241,* 1039–1040.

Maslow, Abraham H. (1968). *Toward a psychology of being* (2d ed.). Princeton, NJ: Van Nostrand.

Maslow, Abraham H. (1970). *Motivation and personality* (2d ed.). New York: Harper & Row.

Maslow, Abraham, & Sakoda, J. (1952). Volunteer-error in the Kinsey study. *Journal of Abnormal and Social Psychology, 47,* 259–267.

Massey, Frank J., et al. (1984). Vasectomy and health: Results from a large cohort study. *Journal of the American Medical Association, 252,* 1023–1029.

Masters, William H., & Johnson, Virginia. (1966). *Human sexual response.* Boston: Little, Brown.

Masters, William H., & Johnson, Virginia. (1970). *Human sexual inadequacy.* Boston: Little, Brown.

Masters, William H., & Johnson, Virginia. (1974). What men stand to gain from women's liberation. In W. H. Masters & V. Johnson, *The pleasure bond.* Boston: Little, Brown.

Masters, William H., & Johnson, Virginia. (1979). *Homosexuality in perspective.* Boston: Little, Brown.

Masters, W. H., Johnson, V. E., & Kolodny, R. C. (1982). *Human sexuality.* Boston: Little, Brown.

Masters, W., Johnson, V., & Kolodny, R. (1988). *Crisis: Heterosexual behavior in the age of AIDS.* New York: Grove.

Matteson, David R. (1985). Bisexual men in marriage: Is a positive homosexual identity and stable marriage possible? In F. Klein & T. J. Wolf (Eds.), *Bisexualities: Theory and Research.* New York: Haworth.

Maugh, Thomas H. (1981). Male "pill" blocks sperm enzyme. *Science, 314.*

May, Rollo. (1974). *Love and will.* New York: Dell Books.

Mayes, L. C., Granger, R. H., Bornstein, M. H., & Zuckerman, B. (1992). The problem of prenatal cocaine exposure: A rush to judgment. *Journal of the American Medical Association, 267,* 406–408.

Mays, Vickie M., & Cochran, Susan D. (1987). Acquired immunodeficiency syndrome and black Americans: Special psychosocial issues. *Public Health Reports, 102,* 224–231.

Maykovich, M. K. (1976). Attitudes versus behavior in extramarital sexual relations. *Journal of Marriage and the Family, 38,* 693–699.

Mayo, Clara, & Henley, Nancy M. (Eds.). (1981). *Gender and nonverbal behavior.* New York: Springer-Verlag.

Mazur, Allan. (1986). U.S. trends in feminine beauty and overadaptation. *Journal of Sex Research, 22,* 281–303.

Mazur, Ronald. (1973). *The new intimacy.* Boston: Beacon Press.

McArthur, Leslie Z., & Resko, Beth G. (1975). The portrayal of men and women in American television commercials. *Journal of Social Psychology, 97,* 209–220.

McBride, Arthur F., & Hebb, D. O. (1948). Behavior of the captive bottlenose dolphin, *Tursiops truncatus. Journal of Comparative and Physiological Psychology, 41,* 111–123.

McCaghy, Charles H. (1971). Child molesting. *Sexual Behavior, 1,* 16–24.

McCarthy, Barry W. (1989). Cognitive-behavioral strategies and techniques in the treatment of early ejaculation. In S. R. Leiblum & R. C. Rosen (Eds.), *Principles and practice of sex therapy* (2d ed). New York: Guilford.

McCary, James L. (1972, Nov.). Nymphomania: A case history. *Medical Aspects of Human Sexuality, 6,* 192–202.

McCary, James L. (1973). *Human sexuality.* Princeton, NJ: Van Nostrand.

McClintock, Martha K. (1971). Menstrual synchrony and suppression. *Nature, 229,* 244–245.

McConaghy, Nathaniel. (1987). A learning approach. In J. H. Geer & W. T. O'Donohue (Eds.), *Theories of human sexuality* (pp. 287–334). New York: Plenum.

McCormick, Naomi B. (1979). Come-ons and put-offs: Unmarried students' strategies for having and avoiding sexual intercourse. *Psychology of Women Quarterly, 4,* 194–211.

McCormick, Naomi B. (1987). Sexual scripts: Social and therapeutic implications. *Sexual and Marital Therapy, 2,* 3–27.

McCrary, J., & Gutierrez, L. (1979/80). The homosexual person in the military and in national security employment. *Journal of Homosexuality, 5*(1/2), 115–146.

McDowell, Janet Dickey. (1983). Ethical implications of in vitro fertilization. *Christian Century, 100,* 936–938.

McGlothlin, W., Sparkes, R., & Arnold, D. (1970). Effect of LSD on human pregnancy. *Journal of the American Medical Association, 212,* 1483–1487.

McGuire, R. J., Carlisle, J. M., & Young, B. G. (1965). Sexual deviations as conditioned behavior: A hypothesis. *Behavioral Research and Therapy, 2,* 185–190.

McIntosh, Mary. (1968). The homosexual role. *Social Problems, 16*(2), 185–190.

McKinlay, Sonja M., & Jeffreys, Margot. (1974). The menopausal syndrome. *British Journal of Preventive and Social Medicine, 28*(2), 108.

McKusick, Leon, et al. (1985). Reported changes in the sexual behavior of men at risk for AIDS, San Francisco, 1982–84: The AIDS behavioral research project. *Public Health Reports, 100,* 622–628.

McMillan, Julie R., et al. (1977). Women's language: Uncertainty or interpersonal sensitivity and emotionality? *Sex Roles, 3,* 545–560.

McNeill, John J. (1976). *The church and the homosexual.* Kansas City: Sheed, Andrews, & McMeel.

McNeill, John J. (1987). Homosexuality: Challenging the Church to grow. *Christian Century, 104,* 242–246.

McWhirter, David P., & Mattison, Andrew M. (1980). Treatment of sexual dysfunction in homosexual male couples. In S. R. Leiblum & L. A. Pervin (Eds.), *Principles and practice of sex therapy.* New York: Guilford.

McWhirter, David P., & Mattison, Andrew M. (1984). *The male couple: How relationships develop.* Englewood Cliffs, NJ: Prentice-Hall.

Mead, Margaret. (1935). *Sex and temperament in three primitive societies.* New York: Morrow.

Mead, Margaret, & Newton, Niles. (1967). Fatherhood. In S. A. Richardson & A. F. Guttmacher (Eds.), *Childbearing: Its social and psychological aspects.* Baltimore: Williams & Wilkins.

Meiselman, Karin. (1978). *Incest.* San Francisco: Jossey-Bass.

Meissner, William W. (1980). Psychoanalysis and sexual disorders. In B. J. Wolman & J. Money (Eds.), *Handbook of human sexuality.* Englewood Cliffs, NJ: Prentice-Hall.

Melbye, M. (1986). The natural history of human T lymphotropic virus-III infection: The cause of AIDS. *British Medical Journal, 292,* 5–12.

Melton, Gary B. (Ed.). (1986). *Adolescent abortion.* Lincoln: University of Nebraska Press.

Mendelsohn, Jack H, et al. (1974). Plasma testosterone levels before, during and after chronic marihuana smoking. *New England Journal of Medicine, 291,* 1051–1055.

Meredith, Nikki. (1984, Jan.). The gay dilemma. *Psychology Today,* 56–62.

Mereson, Amy. (1983). Court throws out Akron ordinance, reaffirms abortion rights. *Civil Liberties,* No. 347, 8.

Messe, Madelyn R., & Geer, James H. (1985). Voluntary vaginal musculature contractions as an enhancer of sexual arousal. *Archives of Sexual Behavior, 14,* 13–28.

Meyer, J. K. (1979). Sex reassignment. *Archives of General Psychiatry, 36,* 1010–1015.

Meyer-Bahlburg, Heino F. L. (1980). Homosexual orientation in women and men: A hormonal basis? In J. E. Parsons (Ed.), *The psychobiology of sex differences and sex roles.* New York: McGraw-Hill.

Meyer-Bahlburg, Heino F. L. (1984). Psychoendocrine research on sexual orientation: Current status and future options. *Progress in Brain Research, 61,* 367–390.

Meyerowitz, Beth E. (1980). Psychosocial correlates of breast cancer and its treatments. *Psychological Bulletin, 87,* 108–131.

Michael, R. P., Bonsall, R. W., & Warner, P. (1974). Human vaginal secretions: Volatile fatty acid content. *Science, 186,* 1217–1219.

Michael, Richard P., & Keverne, E. B. (1968). Pheromones in the communication of sexual status in primates. *Nature, 218,* 746–749.

Middleton, R. (1962). Brother-sister and father-daughter marriage in ancient Egypt. *American Sociological Review, 27,* 603–611.

Migeon, C. J., Rivarola, M. A., & Forest, M. G. (1968). Studies of androgens in transsexual subjects: Effects of estrogen therapy. *Johns Hopkins Medical Journal, 123,* 128–133.

Milan, Richard J., & Kilmann, Peter R. (1987). Interpersonal factors in premarital contraception. *Journal of Sex Research, 23,* 289–321.

Milbauer, Barbara. (1983). *The law giveth: Legal aspects of the abortion controversy.* New York: Atheneum.

Millar, J. D. (1972). The national venereal disease problem. *Epidemic venereal disease: Proceedings of the Second International Symposium on Venereal Disease.* St. Louis: American Social Health Association and Pfizer Laboratories.

Millenson, Michael L. (1992, Jan. 13). Women's condom in clinical trials. *Wisconsin State Journal,* 3A.

Miller, Eleanor M. (1986). *Street woman.* Philadelphia: Temple University Press.

Miller, Rickey S., & Lefcourt, Herbert M. (1982). The assessment of social intimacy. *Journal of Personality Assessment, 46,* 514–518.

Miller, S., Corrales, R., & Wachman, D. B. (1975). Recent progress in understanding and facilitating marital communication. *Family Coordinator, 24,* 143–152.

Miller, S., Nunnally, E., & Wachman, D. (1975). *Alive and aware.* Minneapolis: Interpersonal Communications Programs.

Millett, Kate. (1969). *Sexual politics.* New York: Doubleday.

Mirotznick, Jerrold, et al. (1987). Genital herpes: An investigation of its attitudinal and behavioral correlates. *Journal of Sex Research, 23,* 266–272.

Mischel, Walter. (1969). Continuity and change in personality. *American Psychologist, 24,* 1012–1018.

Mitchell, James, & Popkin, Michael. (1983). The pathophysiology of sexual dysfunction associated with antipsychotic drug therapy in males: A review. *Archives of Sexual Behavior, 12,* 173–183.

Money, John, & Ehrhardt, Anke. (1972). *Man and woman, boy and girl.* Baltimore: Johns Hopkins University Press.

Money, John. (1986). *Venuses penuses: Sexology, sexosophy, and exigency theory.* Buffalo, NY: Prometheus Books.

Money, John. (1987). Sin, sickness, or status: Homosexual gender identity and psychoneuroendocrinology. *American Psychologist, 42,* 384–399.

Money, John, & Yankowitz, R. (1967). The sympathetic-inhibiting effects of the drug Ismelin on human male eroticism with a note on Mellaril. *Journal of Sex Research, 3,* 69–82.

Montagu, Ashley. (1971). *Touching.* New York: Columbia University Press.

Monzon, O. T., & Capellan, J. M. B. (1987, July). Female-to-female transmission of HIV. *Lancet.*

Moffatt, Michael. (1989). *Coming of age in New Jersey.* New Brunswick, NJ: Rutgers University Press.

Moodbidri, S. B., et al. (1980). Measurement of inhibin. *Archives of Andrology, 5,* 295–303.

Moore, Allen J. (1987). Teenage sexuality and public morality. *Christian Century, 104,* 747–750.

Moore, Dianne S., & Erickson, Pamela I. (1985, Nov.). Age, gender, and ethnic differences in sexual and contraceptive knowledge, attitudes, and behavior. *Family & Community Health, 8*(3), 38–51.

Moore, James E., & Kendall, Diane G. (1971). Children's concepts of reproduction. *Journal of Sex Research, 7,* 42–61.

Moore, K. A., Simms, M. C., & Betsey, C. L. (1986). *Choice and circumstance: Racial differences in adolescent fertility.* New Brunswick, NJ: Transaction Books.

Morgan, Robin. (1978, Nov.). How to run the pornographers out of town (and preserve the first amendment). *Ms. 55,* 78–80.

Morgan, Robin. (1980). Theory and practice: Pornography and rape. In L. Lederer (Ed.), *Take back the night: Women on pornography.* New York: Morrow.

Morgentalev, Henry. (1982). *Abortion and contraception.* Toronto: General Publishing.

Morin, Jack. (1981). *Anal pleasure and health.* Burlingame, CA: Down There Press.

Morin, Stephen F., & Garfinkle, Ellen M. (1978). Male homophobia. *Journal of Social Issues, 34*(1), 29–47.

Morin, Stephen F., & Rothblum, Esther D. (1991). Removing the stigma: Fifteen years of progress. *American Psychologist, 46,* 947–949.

Morrell, M. J., Dixen, J. M., Carter, S., & Davidson, J. (1984). The influence of age and cycling status on sexual arousability in women. *American Journal of Obstetrics and Gynecology, 148,* 66–71.

Morris, Norval J. (1973, Apr. 18). The law is a busy-body. *New York Times Magazine,* 58–64.

Morrison, Diane M. (1985). Adolescent contraceptive behavior: A review. *Psychological Bulletin, 98,* 538–568.

Morokoff, Patricia J. (1986). Volunteer bias in the psychophysiological study of female sexuality. *Journal of Sex Research, 22,* 35–51.

Morrison, Eleanor S., et al. (1980). *Growing up sexual.* New York: Van Nostrand.

Moser, Charles, & Levitt, Eugene E. (1987). An exploratory-descriptive study of a sadomasochistically oriented sample. *Journal of Sex Research, 23,* 322–337.

Moses, Stephen, et al. (1990). Geographical patterns of male circumcision practices in Africa: Association with HIV seroprevalence. *International Journal of Epidemiology, 19,* 693–697.

Mosher, Donald L. (1973). Sex differences, sex experience, sex guilt and explicitly sexual films. *Journal of Social Issues, 29,* 95–112.

Mosher, Donald L. (1991). Macho men, machismo, and sexuality. *Annual Review of Sexuality, 2,* 199–248.

Mosher, Donald L., & Tomkins, Silavan S. (1988). Scripting the macho man: Hypermasculine socialization and enculturation. *Journal of Sex Research, 25,* 60–84.

Mosher, William D. (1990, Oct.). Contraceptive practice in the United States, 1982–1988. *Family Planning Perspectives, 22,* 198–205.

Muehlenhard, Charlene L., & Cook, Stephen W. (1988). Men's self-reports of unwanted sexual activity. *Journal of Sex Research 24,* 58–72.

Muehlenhard, Charlene L., & Linton, Melaney A. (1987). Date rape and sexual aggression in dating situations: Incidence and risk factors. *Journal of Counseling Psychology, 34,* 186–196.

Mueller, G. O. W. (1980). *Sexual conduct and the law* (2d ed.). Dobbs Ferry, NY: Oceana Publications.

Mulvihill, D. J., et al. (1969). Crimes of violence: A staff report to the National Commission on the Causes and Prevention of Violence. Washington, DC: GPO.

Munjack, Dennis, J., & Kanno, Pamela H. (1979). Retarded ejaculation: A review. *Archives of Sexual Behavior, 8,* 139–150.

Murdock, George P. (1949). *Social structure.* New York: Macmillan.

Murnen, S. K., Perot, A., & Byrne, D. (1989). Coping with unwanted sexual activity: Normative responses, situational determinants, and individual differences. *Journal of Sex Research,* 85–106.

Murphey-Corb, Michael, et al. (1989). A Formalin-inactivated whole SIV vaccine confers protection in macaques. *Science, 246,* 1293–1297.

Murstein, Burnard I. (1976). *Who will marry whom?* New York: Springer.

Myers, Barbara J. (1984). Mother-infant bonding: The status of this critical-period hypothesis. *Developmental Review, 4,* 240–274.

Naeye, Richard L. (1979). Coitus and associated amniotic-fluid infections. *New England Journal of Medicine, 301,* 1198–1200.

Narod, Steven A., et al. (1988). Human mutagens: Evidence from paternal exposure? *Environmental and Molecular Mutagenesis, 11,* 401–415.

National Academy of Sciences. (1982). *Marihuana and health.* Washington, DC: National Academy Press.

National Coordinating Group on Male Antifertility Agents. (1978). Gossypol—A new antifertility agent for males. *Chinese Medical Journal, 4,* 417–428.

Neiger, S. (1968). Sex potions. *Sexology,* 730–733.

Nelson, James B. (1978). *Embodiment: An approach to sexuality and Christian theology.* Minneapolis: Augsburg.

Nelson, Joan A. (1986). Incest: Self-report findings from a nonclinical sample. *Journal of Sex Research, 22,* 463–477.

Neugarten, Bernice L. (1974). The roles we play. In American Medical Association (Ed.), *Quality of life: The Middle years.* Acton, MA: Publishing Sciences Group.

Neugarten, Bernice L., & Kraines, Ruth J. (1965). "Menopausal symptoms" in women of various ages. *Psychosomatic Medicine, 27,* 266.

New studies find no link between spermicide use and heightened risk of congenital malformations. *Family Planning Perspectives*, 20, 1988 (Jan.–Feb.), 42–43.

Newcomer, Susan F., & Udry, J. Richard. (1985). Oral sex in an adolescent population. *Archives of Sexual Behavior, 14*, 41–46.

Newhorn, Paula. (1973). *Primal sensuality: New horizons and explorations for lovers*. New York: Putnam.

Newton, Niles A. (1972). Childbearing in broad perspective. In Boston Children's Medical Center, *Pregnancy, birth and the newborn baby*. New York: Delacorte Press.

Nichols, Margaret. (1989). Sex therapy with lesbians, gay men, and bisexuals. In S. R. Leiblum & R. C. Rosen (Eds.), *Principles and practice of sex therapy* (2d ed). New York: Guilford.

Nickolls, L., & Teare, D. (1954). Poisoning by cantharidin. *British Medical Journal*, Part 2, 1384–1386.

Noller, P. (1984). *Nonverbal communication and marital interaction*. New York: Pergamon.

Norton, Arthur J. (1987, July–Aug.). Families and children in the year 2000. *Children Today*, 6–9.

Norton, Arthur J., & Moorman, Jeanne E. (1987). Current trends in marriage and divorce among American women. *Journal of Marriage and the Family, 49*, 3–14.

Norton, G. R., & Jehu, D. (1984). The role of anxiety in sexual dysfunctions: A review. *Archives of Sexual Behavior, 13*, 165–183.

Noss, John B. (1963). *Man's religions* (3d ed.). New York: Macmillan.

Note: The constitutional status of sexual orientation. (1985). *Harvard Law Review, 98*, 1285–1309.

Notzon, Francis C. (1990). International differences in the use of obstetric interventions. *Journal of the American Medical Association, 263*, 3286–3291.

Notzon, Francis C., Placek, P. J., & Taffel, S. M. (1987). Comparison of national cesarean section rates. *New England Journal of Medicine, 316*, 386–389.

Novak, E. R., Jones, G. S., & Jones, H. W. (1975). *Novak's textbook of gynecology* (9th ed.). Baltimore: Williams & Wilkins.

Novell, H. A. (1965). Psychological factors in premenstrual tension and dysmenorrhea. *Clinical Obstetrics and Gynecology, 8*, 222–232.

Nowak, Rachel. (Sept. 1991). AIDS vaccines: Key questions still unanswered. *Journal of NIH Research, 3*, 37–39.

Nsiah-Jefferson, Laurie. (1989). Reproductive laws, women of color, and low-income women. In S. Cohen & N. Taub (Eds.), *Reproductive laws for the 1990s* (pp. 23–68). Clifton, NJ: Humana Press.

Nyberg, K. L., & Alston, J. S. (1976/77). Analysis of public attitudes toward homosexual behavior. *Journal of Homosexuality, 2*, 99–107.

O'Brien, Shari. (1986). Commercial conceptions: A breeding ground for surrogacy. *North Carolina Law Review, 65*, 127–153.

Obzrut, L. (1976). Expectant fathers' perceptions of fathering. *American Journal of Nursing, 76*, 1440–1442.

O'Hara, Michael W. (1986). Social support, life events, and depression during pregnancy and the puerperium. *Archives of General Psychiatry, 43*, 569–573.

Olds, James. (1956). Pleasure centers in the brain. *Scientific American, 193*, 105–116.

Olds, James, & Milner, Peter. (1954). Positive reinforcement produced by electrical stimulation of the septal area and other regions of the rat brain. *Journal of Comparative and Physiological Psychology, 47*, 419–427.

Olds, Sally, & Eiger, M. S. (1973). *The complete book of breastfeeding*. New York: Bantam.

Oliver, Mary Beth, & Hyde, Janet S. (1993). Gender differences in sexuality: A meta-analysis. *Psychological Bulletin, 114*, 29–51

O'Neill, George, & O'Neill, Nena. (1972). *Open marriage: A new life style for couples*. New York: M. Evans.

O'Neill, Nena, & O'Neill, George. (1976). Marriage: A contemporary model. In B. J. Sadock et al. (Eds.), *The sexual experience*. Baltimore: Williams & Wilkins.

Oriel, David. (1990). Genital human papillomavirus infection. In K. Holmes et al. (Eds.), *Sexually transmitted diseases* (pp. 433–442). New York: McGraw-Hill.

Ory, H. W. (1982). The noncontraceptive health benefits from oral contraceptive use. *Family Planning Perspectives, 14*, 182–184.

Osofsky, Joy D., & Osofsky, Howard J. (1972). The psychological reactions of patients to legalized abortions. *American Journal of Orthopsychiatry, 42*, 48–60.

Otto, H. A. (1963). Criteria for assessing family strengths. *Family Process, 2*, 329–337.

Packer, H. L. (1968). *The limits of the criminal sanction*. Stanford, CA: Stanford University Press.

Page, David C., et al. (1987). The sex-determining region of the human Y chromosome encodes a finger protein. *Cell, 51*, 1091–1104.

Paige, Karen E. (1971). Effects of oral contraceptives on affective fluctuations associated with the menstrual cycle. *Psychosomatic Medicine, 33*, 515–537.

Paige, Karen E. (1973). Women learn to sing the menstrual blues. *Psychology Today, 7*(4), 41.

Palmer, Craig T. (1991). Human rape: Adaptation or by-product? *Journal of Sex Research, 28*, 365–386.

Parke, Ross D. (1979). Perspectives on father-infant interaction. In J. D. Osofsky (Ed.), *Handbook of infant development*. New York: Wiley.

Parker, Graham. (1983). The legal regulation of sexual activity and the protection of females. *Osgoode Hall Law Journal, 21*, 187–244.

Parlee, Mary Brown. (1973). The premenstrual syndrome. *Psychological Bulletin, 80*, 454–465.

Parlee, Mary B. (1978, April). The rhythms in men's lives. *Psychology Today*, 82–91.

Parnas, Raymond I. (1981). Legislative reform of prostitution laws: Keeping commercial sex out of sight and out of mind. *Santa Clara Law Review, 21*, 669–696.

Parrinder, Geoffrey. (1980). *Sex in the world's religions*. New York: Oxford University Press.

Patterson, Charlotte. (1992). Children of lesbian and gay parents. *Child Development, 63*, 1025–1042.

Paul, Eva W., & Klassel, Dara. (1987). Minors' rights to confidential contraceptive services. *Women's Rights Law Reporter, 10*, 45–64.

Paul, William, et al. (Eds.). (1982). *Homosexuality: Social, psychological, and biological issues.* Beverly Hills, CA: Sage.

Peplau, Letitia Anne. (1981, Mar.). What homosexuals want in relationships. *Psychology Today, 15*(3), 28–38.

Peplau, L. Anne, et al. (1978). Loving women: Attachment and autonomy in lesbian relationships. *Journal of Social Issues, 34*(3), 7–27.

Peplau, Letitia Anne, & Amaro, Hortensia. (1982). Understanding lesbian relationships. In W. Paul et al. (Eds.), *Homosexuality: Social, psychological and biological issues.* Beverly Hills, CA: Sage.

Peplau, L. A., Padesky, C., & Hamilton, M. (1982). Satisfaction in lesbian relationships. *Journal of Homosexuality, 8,* 23–35.

Perkins, Roberta, & Bennett, Garry (1985). *Being a prostitute: Prostitute women and prostitute men.* London: Allen & Unwin.

Perlman, Daniel, & Fehr, B. (1987). The development of intimate relationships. In D. Perlman & S. Dack (Eds.), *Intimate relationships: Development, dynamics, and deterioration.* Newbury Park, CA: Sage.

Perper, T. (1985). *Sex signals: The biology of love.* Philadelphia: ISI Press.

Perry, Catherine D. (1980). Right of privacy challenges to prostitution statutes. *Washington University Law Quarterly, 58,* 439–480.

Perry, John D., & Whipple, Beverly. (1981). Pelvic muscle strength of female ejaculators: Evidence in support of a new theory of orgasm. *Journal of Sex Research, 17,* 22–39.

Persson, Goran. (1980). Sexuality in a 70-year-old urban population. *Journal of Psychosomatic Research, 24,* 335–342.

Peterman, Thomas A., & Curran, James W. (1986). Sexual transmission of human immunodeficiency virus. *Journal of the American Medical Association, 256,* 2222–2226.

Peterson, Gail, et al. (1979). The role of some birth related variables in father attachment. *American Journal of Orthopsychiatry, 40,* 330–338.

Peterson, J., & Marin, G. (1988). Issues in the prevention of AIDS among Black and Hispanic men. *American Psychologist, 43,* 871–877.

Peterson, W., Morese, K., & Kaltreider, D. (1965). Smoking and prematurity: A preliminary report based on a study of 7740 Caucasians. *Obstetrics and Gynecology, 26,* 775–779.

Peyster, A. (1979). Gossypol-proposed contraceptive for men passes the Ames test. *New England Journal of Medicine, 301,* 275–276.

Pfeiffer, Eric (1975). Sex and aging. In L. Gross (Ed.), *Sexual issues in marriage.* New York: Spectrum.

Pfeiffer, E., Verwoerdt, A., & Wang, H. S. (1968). Sexual behavior in aged men and women. *Archives of General Psychiatry, 19,* 753–758.

Phillips, Leslie. (1977, Sept. 9). For women sexual harassment is an occupational hazard. *Boston Globe.*

Phoenix, C. H., Goy, R. W., Gerall, A. A., & Young, W. C. (1959). Organizing action of prenatally administered testosterone proprionate on the tissues mediating mating behavior in the female guinea pig. *Endocrinology, 65,* 369–382.

Pietropinto, A., & Simenauer, J. (1977). *Beyond the male myth.* New York: Times Books.

Pittenger, W. Norman. (1970). *Making sexuality human.* Philadelphia: Pilgrim Press.

Pittenger, W. Norman. (1974). *Love and control in sexuality.* Philadelphia: United Church Press.

Pittenger, W. Norman. (1976). A theological approach to understanding homosexuality. In R. T. Barnhouse & U. T. Holmes, III (Eds.), *Male and female.* New York: Seabury Press.

Plato. (1956). Symposium. In Irwin Edman (Ed.), *The works of Plato.* New York: Modern Library.

Platt, R., Rice, P. A., & McCormack, W. M. (1983). Risk of acquiring gonorrhea and prevalance of abnormal adnexal findings among women recently exposed to gonorrhea. *Journal of the American Medical Association, 250,* 3205–3209.

Pleck, Joseph H. (1981). *The myth of masculinity.* Cambridge, MA: MIT Press.

Pleck, Joseph H., & Sawyer, Jack. (1974). *Men and masculinity.* Englewood Cliffs, NJ: Prentice-Hall.

Pomeroy, Wardell B. (1966). Normal vs. abnormal sex. *Sexology, 32,* 436–439.

Pomeroy, Wardell B. (1972). *Dr. Kinsey and the Institute for Sex Research.* New York: Harper & Row.

Pomeroy, Wardell B. (1975). The diagnosis and treatment of transvestites and transsexuals. *Journal of Sex and Marital Therapy, 1,* 215–224.

Pope Paul VI. (1968, July 30). *Humanae vitae.* (English text in the *New York Times,* 20.)

Population Information Program. (1982). IUDs: An appropriate contraceptive for many women. *Population Reports,* Series B, No. 4, B101–B135.

Population Information Program. (1983). Vasectomy—Safe and simple. *Population Reports,* Series D, No. 4, D61–D100.

Powdermaker, Hortense. (1933). *Life in Lesu.* New York: Norton.

Pratt, W. F., Mosher, W. D., Bachrach, C. A., & Horn, M. C. (1984, Dec.). Understanding U.S. fertility: Findings from the National Survey of Family Growth. *Population Bulletin, 39,* 1–42.

Presser, H. B., & Bumpass, L. L. (1972). The acceptability of contraceptive sterilization among U.S. couples: 1970. *Family Planning Perspectives, 4*(4), 18.

Preti, George, Cutler, Winnifred B., et al. (1986). Human axillary secretions influence women's menstrual cycles: The role of donor extract of females. *Hormones and Behavior, 20,* 474–482.

Price, James H. (1981). Toxic shock syndrome—An update. *Journal of School Health.*

Prince, Virginia, & Butler, P. M. (1972). Survey of 504 cases of transvestism. *Psychological Reports, 31,* 903–917.

Pritchard, J. A., & MacDonald, P. C. (1980). *Williams Obstetrics* (16th ed.). New York: Appleton-Century-Crofts.

Pritchard, J. A., MacDonald, P. C., & Grant, N. F. (1985). *Williams Obstetrics* (17th ed.). Norwalk, CT: Appleton-Century-Crofts.

Quadagno, D., et al. (1991). The menstrual cycle: Does it affect athletic performance? *Physician and Sports Medicine, 19,* 121–124.

Qualls, C. B., Wincze, J. P., & Barlow, D. H. (1978). *The prevention of sexual disorders.* New York: Plenum.

Rachman, S. (1966). Sexual fetishism: An experimental analogue. *Psychological Record, 16,* 293–296.

Radlove, Shirley. (1983). Sexual response and gender roles. In E. R. Allgeier & N. B. McCormick (Eds.), *Changing boundaries: Gender roles and sexual behavior*. Palo Alto, CA: Mayfield.

Rainwater, Lee. (1965). *Family design*. Chicago: Aldine.

Rainwater, Lee. (1971). Marital sexuality in four "cultures of poverty." In D. S. Marshall & R. C. Suggs (Eds.), *Human sexual behavior*. New York: Basic Books.

Ramcharan, S., Pellegrin, F. S., Ray, R., & Hsu, J.-P. (1980). *The Walnut Creek contraceptive drug study: A prospective study of the side effects of oral ccontraceptives* (Vol. III). Washington, DC: Government Printing Office.

Ramey, Estelle. (1972, Spring). Men's cycles. *Ms.*, 8–14.

Ramsey, Glen V. (1943a). The sex information of younger boys. *American Journal of Orthopsychiatry, 13*, 347–352.

Ramsey, Glen V. (1943b). The sexual development of boys. *American Journal of Psychology, 56*, 217–233.

Raphael, Bette-Jane. (1973, Oct. 25). The myth of the male orgasm. *Village Voice*. [Reprinted in *Psychology Today, 7*(8), 1974.]

Ravenholt, R., & Levinski, M. (1965). Smoking during pregnancy. *Lancet, 1*, 961.

Raymond, Janice G. (1979). *The transsexual empire: The making of the she-male*. Boston: Beacon Press.

Recht, Steven N. (1988). "M" is for money: Baby M and the surrogate motherhood controversy. *American University Law Review, 39*, 986–1013.

Reevy, William R. (1967). Child sexuality. In A. Ellis & A. Abarbanel (Eds.), *The encyclopedia of sexual behavior*. New York: Hawthorn.

Reilly, T., Carpenter, S., Dull, V., & Bartlett, K. (1982). The factorial survey technique: An approach to defining sexual harassment on campus. *Journal of Social Issues, 38*(4), 99–110.

Reis, H. T., Senchak, M., & Solomon, B. (1985). Sex differences in the intimacy of social interaction: Further examination of potential explanations. *Journal of Personality and Social Psychology, 48*, 1204–1217.

Reisenzein, Rainer. (1983). The Schachter theory of emotion: Two decades later. *Psychological Bulletin, 94*, 239–264.

Reiss, Ira L. (1960). *Premarital sexual standards in America*. New York: Free Press.

Reiss, Ira L. (1961, Nov.). Sexual codes in teenage culture. *Annals*, 53–62.

Reiss, Ira L. (1967). *The social context of premarital sexual permissiveness*. New York: Holt.

Reiss, Ira L. (1986). *Journey into sexuality: An exploratory voyage*. Englewood Cliffs, NJ: Prentice-Hall.

Reiss, Ira L., & Leik, Robert K. (1989). Evaluating strategies to avoid AIDS: Number of partners vs. use of condoms. *Journal of Sex Research, 26*, 411–433.

Renshaw, Domeena C. (1982). *Incest: Understanding and treatment*. Boston: Little, Brown.

Resick, Patricia, et al. (1981). Social adjustment of victims of sexual assault. *Journal of Consulting and Clinical Psychology, 49*, 705–712.

Resick, Patricia A. (1983). The rape reaction: Research findings and implications for intervention. *Behavior Therapist, 6*, 129–132.

Reuben, David. (1969). *Everything you always wanted to know about sex but were afraid to ask*. New York: Bantam Books.

Reuther, Rosemary Radford. (1985). Catholics and abortion: Authority vs. dissent. *Christian Century, 102*, 859–862.

Reynolds, Barry S. (1980). Biofeedback and facilitation of erection in men with erectile dysfunction. *Archives of Sexual Behavior, 9*, 101–114.

Rhodes, Richard. (1972, Aug.). Sex and sin in Sheboygan. *Playboy*, 186–190.

Ribble, Margaret A. (1955). *The personality of the young child*. New York: Columbia University Press.

Rice, Berkeley. (1974). Rx: Sex for senior citizens. *Psychology Today, 8*(1), 18–20.

Richards, David A. J. (1979). Sexual autonomy and the constitutional right to privacy: A case study in human rights and the unwritten constitution. *Hastings Law Journal, 30*, 957–1018.

Richards, D. A. J. (1979/80). Homosexual acts and the constitutional right to privacy. *Journal of Homosexuality, 5*(1/2), 43–66.

Richardson, J. Derek. (1991). I. Medical causes of male sexual dysfunction. *Medical Journal of Australia, 155*, 29–33.

Richardson, Stephan A. (1972). People with cerebral palsy talk for themselves. *Developmental Medicine and Child Neurology, 14*, 524–535.

Richwald, Gary A., et al. (1988). Sexual activities in bathhouses in Los Angeles County: Implication for AIDS prevention education. *Journal of Sex Research, 25*, 169–180.

Riddle, Dorothy I. (1978). Relating to children: Gays as role models. *Journal of Social Issues, 34*(3), 38–58.

Riportella-Mueller, Roberta. (1989). Sexuality in the elderly: A review. In K. McKinney & S. Sprecher (Eds.), *Human sexuality: The societal and interpersonal context* (pp. 210–236). New York: Ablex.

Ritzer, George. (1983). *Sociological theory*. New York: Knopf.

Rivera, Rhonda. (1979). Our straight-laced judges. The legal position of homosexual persons in the U.S. *Hastings Law Journal, 30*, 799–955.

Rivera, Rhonda. (1980–81). Recent developments in sexual preference law. *Drake Law Review, 30*, 311–346.

River, Rhonda. (1982). Homosexuality and the law. In W. Paul et al. (Eds.), *Homosexuality: Social, psycholological, and biological issues*. Beverly Hills, CA: Sage.

Roberto, Laura G. (1983). Issues in diagnosis and treatment of transsexualism. *Archives of Sexual Behavior, 12*, 445–473.

Roberts, Elizabeth J. (Ed.). (1980). *Childhood sexual learning: The unwritten curriculum*. Cambridge, MA: Ballinger.

Roberts, Elizabeth, Kline, D., & Gagnon, J. (1978). *Family life and sexual learning: A summary report* (Vol. I). Cambridge, MA: Population Education.

Robertson, John A. (1983, Oct.). Surrogate mothers: Not so novel after all. *Hastings Center Report*, 28–34.

Robertson, John A. (1986). Embryos, families and procreative liberty: The legal structure of the new reproduction. *Southern California Law Review, 59*, 942–1041.

Robins, M. B., & Jensen, G. G. (1978). Multiple orgasm in males. *Journal of Sex Research, 13*, 21–26.

Robinson, D., & Rock, J. (1967). Intrascrotal hyperthermia induced by scrotal insulation: Effect on spermatogenesis. *Obstetrics and Gynecology, 29*, 217.

Robinson, I., Ziss, K., Ganza, B., & Katz, S. (1991). Twenty years of the sexual revolution, 1965–1985: An update. *Journal of Marriage and the Family, 53*, 216–220.

Rogers, Carl R. (1951). *Client-centered therapy: Its current practice, implications, and theory.* Boston: Houghton Mifflin.

Rogers, Martha F. (1985). AIDS in children: A review of the clinical, epidemiological and public health aspects. *Centers for Disease Control: Current Issues in Pediatrics, 4,* 230–236.

Rogers, Rex S. (1974). *Sex education: Rationale and reaction.* New York: Cambridge University Press.

Rogers, Susan M., & Turner, Charles F. (1991). Male-male sexual contact in the U.S.A.: Findings from five sample surveys, 1970–1990. *Journal of Sex Research, 28,* 491–519.

Rooks, E., & King, R. (1973). A study of the marriage role expectations of black adolescents. *Adolescence, 8,* 317–324.

Rosaldo, Michelle A. (1974). Woman, culture, and society: A theoretical overview. In M. S. Rosaldo & L. Lamphere (Eds.), *Woman, culture, and society.* Stanford, CA: Stanford University Press.

Roscoe, B., Kennedy, D., & Pope, T. (1987). Adolescents' views of intimacy: Distinguishing intimate from nonintimate relationships. *Adolescence, 22,* 511–516.

Rose, R. M. (1975). Testosterone, aggression, and homosexuality: A review of the literature and implications for future research. In E. J. Sachar (Ed.), *Topics in psychoendocrinology.* New York: Grune & Stratton.

Rosebury, Theodor. (1971). *Microbes and morals: The strange story of venereal disease.* New York: Viking.

Rosen, David H. (1974). *Lesbianism: A study of female homosexuality.* Springfield, IL: Charles C. Thomas.

Rosen, Raymond C. (1991). Alcohol and drug effects on sexual response: Human experimental and clinical studies. *Annual Review of Sex Research, 2,* 119–180.

Rosen, Raymond C., & Beck, J. Gayle (1988). *Patterns of sexual arousal.* New York: Guilford.

Rosen, Raymond C., & Leiblum, Sandra R. (1987). Current approaches to the evaluation of sexual desire disorders. *Journal of Sex Research, 23,* 141–162.

Rosen, Raymond C., & Leiblum, Sandra R. (1992). *Erectile disorders.* New York: Guilford.

Rosenbleet, C., & Pariente, B. J. (1973). The prostitution of the criminal law. *American Criminal Law Review, 11,* 373–427.

Rosenkrantz, P. S., et al. (1968). Sex role stereotypes and self-concepts in college students. *Journal of Consulting and Clinical Psychology, 32,* 287–295.

Rosner, Fred. (1983). In vitro fertilization and surrogate motherhood: The Jewish view. *Journal of Religion and Health, 22,* 139–160.

Rotkin, I. D. (1962). Relation of adolescent coitus to cervical cancer risk. *Journal of the American Medical Association, 179,* 110.

Rotkin, I. K. (1973). A comparison review of key epidemiological studies in cervical cancer related to current searches for transmissible agents. *Cancer Research, 33,* 1353.

Rousseau, S., et al. (1983). The expectancy of pregnancy for "normal" infertile couples. *Fertility and Sterility, 40,* 768–772.

Ruan, Fang-fu. (1991). *Sex in China.* New York: Plenum.

Ruan, F., Bullough, V. L., & Tsai, Y. (1989). Male transsexualism in mainland China. *Archives of Sexual Behavior, 18,* 517–522.

Rubenstein, Carin. (1983, July). The modern art of courtly love. *Psychology Today,* 40–49.

Rubin, Arline M., & Adams, James R. (1986). Outcomes of sexually open marriages. *Journal of Sex Research, 22,* 311–319.

Rubin, Isadore. (1965). *Sexual life after sixty.* New York: Basic Books.

Rubin, Isadore. (1966). Sex after forty—and after seventy. In Ruth Brecher & Edward Brecher (Eds.), *An analysis of human sexual response.* New York: Signet Books, New American Library.

Rubin, Lillian B. (1979). *Women of a certain age: The midlife search for self.* New York: Harper & Row.

Rubin, Robert T., Reinisch, J. M., & Haskett, R. F. (1981). Postnatal gonadal steroid effects on human behavior. *Science, 211,* 1318–1324.

Rubin, Zick. (1970). Measurement of romantic love. *Journal of Personality and Social Psychology, 16,* 265–273.

Rubin, Zick. (1973). *Liking and loving: An invitation to social psychology.* New York: Holt.

Rubin, Zick, et al. (1980). Self-disclosure in dating couples: Sex roles and the ethic of openness. *Journal of Marriage and the Family, 42,* 305–317.

Rubin, Z. Peplau, L. A., & Hill, C. T. (1981). Loving and leaving: Sex differences in romantic attachments. *Sex Roles, 1,* 821–836.

Ruble, Diane N. (1977). Premenstrual symptoms: A reinterpretation. *Science, 197,* 291–292.

Ruble, Diane N., & Stangor, Charles (1986). Stalking the elusive schema: Insights from developmental and social-psychological analyses of gender schemas. *Social Cognition, 4,* 227–261.

Ruble, D. N., Brooks-Gunn, J., & Clarke, A. (1980). Research on menstrual-related psychological changes: Alternative perspectives. In J. E. Parsons (Ed.), *The psychobiology of sex differences and sex roles.* New York: McGraw-Hill.

Ruble, Thomas L. (1983). Sex stereotypes: Issues of change in the 1970s. *Sex Roles, 9,* 397–402.

Rush, Florence. (1980). Child pornography. In L. Lederer (Ed.), *Take back the night: Women on pornography.* New York: William Morrow.

Russell, Diana. (1975). *The politics of rape: The victim's perspective.* New York: Stein & Day.

Russell, Diana E. H. (1980). Pornography and violence: What does the new research say? In L. Lederer (Ed.), *Take back the night: Women on pornography.* New York: Morrow.

Russell, Diana E. H. (1983). *Rape in marriage.* New York: Macmillan.

Russell, Diana E. H., & Howell, Nancy. (1983). The prevalence of rape in the United States revisited. *Signs, 8,* 688–695.

Ryan, Alan A., et al. (1991). Recent declines in breast-feeding in the United States, 1984 through 1989. *Pediatrics, 88,* 719–727.

Rylander, Gosta. (1969). Clinical and medico-criminological aspects of addiction to central stimulating drugs. In Folke Sjoqvist & Malcolm Tottie (Eds.). *Abuse of central stimulants.* New York: Raven.

Sabatelli, R. M., Buck, R., & Dreyer, A. (1982). Nonverbal communication accuracy in married couples: Relationships with marital complaints. *Journal of Personality and Social Psychology, 43,* 1088–1097.

Sacred Congregation for the Doctrine of the Faith. (1976, Jan. 16).

Declaration on certain questions concerning sexual ethics. (English text in The *New York Times, 2.*)

Sadock, Benjamin J., & Sadock, Virginia A. (1976). Techniques of coitus. In B. J. Sadock et al. (Eds.), *The sexual experience.* Baltimore: Williams & Wilkins.

Saegert, S., Swap, W., & Zajonc, R. B. (1973). Exposure, context, and interpersonal attraction. *Journal of Personality and Social Psychology, 25,* 234–242.

Safran, C. (1976, Nov.). What men do to women on the job: A shocking look at sexual harassment. *Redbook,* 148.

Sagarin, Edward. (1973). Power to the peephole. *Sexual Behavior, 3,* 2–7.

Sagarin, Edward. (1977). Incest: Problems of definition and frequency. *Journal of Sex Research, 13,* 126–135.

Saghir, M., & Robins, E. (1973). *Male and female homosexuality.* Baltimore: Williams & Wilkins.

Salamon, Edna. (1989). The homosexual escort agency: Deviance disavowal. *British Journal of Sociology, 40,* 1–21.

Salhanick, H. A., & Margulis, R. H. (1968). Hormonal physiology of the ovary. In J. J. Gold (Ed.), *Textbook of gynecologic endocrinology.* New York: Harper & Row.

Sanday, Peggy R. (1981). The socio-cultural context of rape: A cross-cultural study. *Journal of Social Issues, 37*(4), 5–27.

Sanday, Peggy R. (1990). *Fraternity gang rape.* New York: New York University Press.

Saral, Rein, et al. (1981). Acyclovir prophylaxis of herpes-simplex-virus infection. *New England Journal of Medicine, 305,* 63–67.

Sarrel, Lorna, & Sarrel, Philip (1984). *Sexual turning points: The seven stages of adult sexuality.* New York: Macmillan.

Sarrel, Philip, & Masters, William. (1982). Sexual molestation of men by women. *Archives of Sexual Behavior, 11,* 117–132.

Saunders, D. M., Fisher, W. A., Hewitt, E. C., & Clayton, J. P. (1985). A method for empirically assessing volunteer selection effects: Recruitment procedures and responses to erotica. *Journal of Personality and Social Psychology, 49,* 1703–1712.

Sayers, Dorothy. (1946). *Unpopular opinions.* London: Gollancz.

Scanzoni, John. (1982). *Sexual bargaining* (2d ed). Chicago: University of Chicago Press.

Schachter, Stanley. (1964). The interaction of cognitive and physiological determinants of emotional state. In L. Berkowitz (Ed.), *Advances in experimental social psychology* (Vol. I). New York: Academic.

Schachter, Stanley, & Singer, J. F. (1962). Cognitive, social, and physiological determinants of emotional state. *Psychological Review, 69,* 379–399.

Schaefer, Mark T., & Olson, David H. (1981). Assessing intimacy: The PAIR Inventory. *Journal of Marital and Family Therapy,* 47–60.

Schafer, Sigrid. (1977). Sociosexual behavior in male and female homosexuals: A study in sex differences. *Archives of Sexual Behavior, 6,* 355–364.

Schaffer, H. R., & Emerson, Peggy E. (1964). Patterns of response to physical contact in early human development. *Journal of Child Psychology and Psychiatry, 5,* 1–13.

Schegloff, Emanuel A. (1979). Identification and recognition in telephone conversation openings. In G. Psathas (Ed.), *Everyday language: Studies in ethnomethodology.* New York: Irvington.

Schenker, J. G., & Evron, S. (1983). New concepts in the surgical management of tubal pregnancy and the consequent postoperative results. *Fertility and Sterility, 40,* 709–723.

Schiavi, Raul C. (1990). Sexuality in aging men. *Annual Review of Sex Research, 1,* 227–250.

Schieffelin, E. L. (1976). *The sorrow of the lonely and the burning of the dancers.* New York: St. Martin's Press.

Schmidt, Gunter. (1977). Personal communication.

Schmidt, Gunter, & Schorsch, Eberhard. (1981). Psychosurgery of sexual deviant patients: Review and analysis of new empirical findings. *Archives of Sexual Behavior, 10,* 301–323.

Schmidt, Gunter, & Sigusch, Volkmar. (1970). Sex differences in response to psychosexual stimulation by films and slides. *Journal of Sex Research, 6,* 268–283.

Schmidt, Gunter, Sigusch, V., & Schafer, S. (1973). Responses to reading erotic stories: Male-female differences. *Archives of Sexual Behavior, 2,* 181–199.

Schmidt, Madeline H. (1970). Superiority of breast-feeding: Fact or fancy? *American Journal of Nursing, 70,* 1488–1493.

Schneider, Edward D. (Ed.). (1985). *Questions about the beginning of life.* Minneapolis: Augsburg.

Schneidman, Barbara, & McGuire, Linda. (1976). Group therapy for nonorgasmic women: Two age levels. *Archives of Sexual Behavior, 5,* 239–248.

Schofield, Alfred T., & Vaughan-Jackson, Percy. (1913). *What a boy should know.* New York: Cassell.

Schoof-Tams, K., Schlaegel, J., & Walczak, L. (1976). Differentiation of sexual morality between 11 and 16 years. *Archives of Sexual Behavior, 5,* 353–370.

Schreeder, M. T., et al. (1982). Hepatitis B in homosexual men: Prevalence of infection and factors related to transmission. *Journal of Infectious Diseases, 146,* 7–15.

Schull, William J., & Neel, James F. (1965). *The effects of inbreeding on Japanese children.* New York: Harper & Row.

Schultz, W. C. M., et al. (1989). Vaginal sensitivity to electric stimuli: Theoretical and practical implications. *Archives of Sexual Behavior, 18,* 87–96.

Schwartz, M. F., Kolodny, R. C., & Masters, W. H. (1980). Plasma testosterone levels of sexually functional and dysfunctional men. *Archives of Sexual Behavior, 9,* 355–366.

Sciarra, John J. (1991). Infertility: A global perspective on the role of infection. *Annals of the New York Academy of Sciences, 626,* 478–483.

Sciarra, J. J., Markland, C., & Speidel, J. J. (1975). *Control of male fertility.* New York: Harper & Row.

Scott, John Paul. (1964). The effects of early experience on social behavior and organization. In W. Etkin (Ed.), *Social behavior and organization among vertebrates.* Chicago: University of Chicago Press.

Scott, Joseph E., & Cuvelier, Steven J. (1987). Sexual violence in *Playboy* magazine. *Journal of Sex Research, 23,* 534–539.

Scroggs, Robin. (1983). *The New Testament and homosexuality.* Philadelphia: Fortress.

Searles, Patricia, & Berger, Ronald J. (1987). The current status of rape reform legislation. *Women's Rights Law Reporter, 10,* 25–44.

Seavey, C. A., Katz, P. A., & Zalk, S. R. (1975). Baby X: The effect of gender labels on adult responses to infants. *Sex Roles, 1,* 103–109.

Seeley, T. T., & Abramson, P. R., Perry, L. B., Rothblatt, A. B., &

Seeley, D. M. (1980). Thermographic measurement of sexual arousal: A methodological note. *Archives of Sexual Behavior, 9,* 77–86.

Segraves, R. Taylor. (1988). Drugs and desire. In S. R. Leiblum & R. C. Rosen (Eds.), *Sexual desire disorders* (pp. 313–347). New York: Guilford.

Selkin, J. (1975). Rape. *Psychology Today, 8*(8), 70.

Semans, J. (1956). Premature ejaculation: A new approach. *Southern Medical Journal, 49,* 353–358.

Serbin, Lisa A., & Sprafkin, Carol H. (1987). A developmental approach: Sexuality from infancy through adolescence. In J. H. Geer & W. T. O'Donahue (Eds.), *Theories of human sexuality* (pp. 163–196). New York: Plenum.

Serrin, W. (1981, Feb. 9). Sex is a growing multimillion dollar business. *New York Times,* B1–B6.

Shaffer, Leigh S. (1977). The golden fleece: Anti-intellectualism and social science. *American Psychologist, 32,* 814–823.

Shapiro, E. Donald. (1986). New innovations in conception and their effects upon our law and morality. *New York Law Review, 21,* 37–59.

Shaw, Jeanne. (1989). The unnecessary penile implant. *Archives of Sexual Behavior, 18,* 455–460.

Sheehy, Gail. (1973). *Hustling: Prostitution in our wide open society.* New York: Delacorte Press.

Shelp, Earl E., & Sunderland, Ronald H. (1987). The challenge of AIDS to the church. *St. Luke's Journal of Theology, 30,* 273–280.

Sherfey, Mary Jane. (1966). The evolution and nature of female sexuality in relation to psychoanalytic theory. *Journal of the American Psychoanalytic Association, 14,* 28–128.

Sherman, Julia. (1971). *On the psychology of women: A survey of empirical studies.* Springfield, IL: Charles C. Thomas.

Sherman, Karen J., et al. (1990). Sexually transmitted diseases and tubal pregnancy. *Sexually Transmitted Diseases, 17,* 115–121.

Sherwin, Barbara B. (1991). The psychoendocrinology of aging and female sexuality. *Annual Review of Sex Research, 2,* 181–198.

Sherwin, Robert, & Corbett, Sherry (1985). Campus sexual norms and dating relationships: A trend analysis. *Journal of Sex Research, 21,* 258–274.

Shewaga, Duane. (1983). Note on *New York Ferber. Santa Clara Law Review, 23,* 675–694.

Shields, W. M., & Shields, L. M. (1983). Forcible rape: An evolutionary perspective. *Ethology and Sociobiology, 4,* 115–136.

Shoemaker, Donald J. (1977). The teeniest trollops: "Baby pros," "chickens," and child prostitutes. In C. D. Bryant (Ed.), *Sexual deviancy in social context* (pp. 241–254). New York: Franklin Watts.

Shope, David F. (1975). *Interpersonal sexuality.* Philadelphia: Saunders.

Shore, M. F. (1970, Dec.). Drugs can be dangerous during pregnancy and lactation. *Canadian Pharmaceutical Journal.*

Shostak, Arthur B. (1984). *Men and abortion: Lessons, losses, and love.* New York: Praeger.

Shouvlin, David P. (1981). Preventing the sexual exploitation of children: A model act. *Wake Forest Law Review, 17,* 535–560.

Shusterman, L. R. (1979). Predicting the psychological consequences of abortion. *Social Science and Medicine, 13,* 683–689.

SIECUS. (1991). *Guidelines for comprehensive sexuality education.* New York: Sex Information and Education Council of the United States.

Siegel, Karolynn, & Glassman, Marc. (1989). Individual and aggregate level change in sexual behavior among gay men at risk for AIDS. *Archives of Sexual Behavior, 18,* 335–348.

Siegel, Ronald K. (1982). Cocaine and sexual dysfunction: The curse of Mama Coca. *Journal of Psychoactive Drugs, 14,* 71–74.

Siegelman, Marvin. (1979). Adjustment of homosexual and heterosexual women: A cross-national replication. *Archives of Sexual Behavior, 8,* 121–126.

Silber, Sherman. (1981). *The human male: From birth to old age.* New York: Scribner's.

Silvestre, Louise, et al. (1990). Voluntary interruption of pregnancy with mifepristone (RU 486) and a prostaglandin analogue: A large-scale French experience. *New England Journal of Medicine, 322,* 645.

Simon, William, & Gagnon, John H. (1986). Sexual scripts: Permanence and change. *Archives of Sexual Behavior, 15,* 97–120.

Simpson, J. A. (1990). Influence of attachment styles on romantic relationships. *Journal of Personality and Social Psychology, 59,* 971–980.

Simpson, J. A., Campbill, B., & Berscheid, E. (1986). The association between romantic love and marriage. *Personality and Social Psychology Bulletin, 12,* 363–372.

Singer, Peter, & Wells, Deane. (1985). *Making babies: The new science and ethics of conception.* New York: Scribner's.

Sivin, Irving. (1989). IUDs are contraceptives, not abortifacients: A comment on research and belief. *Studies in Family Planning, 20,* 355–359.

Slater, Philip E. (1973, Dec.). Sexual adequacy in America. *Intellectual Digest,* 132–135.

Sloane, Ethel. (1985). *Biology of women.* New York: Wiley.

Slob, A. K., et al. (1991). Menstrual cycle phase and sexual arousability in women. *Archives of Sexual Behavior, 20,* 567–578.

Slotkin, J. S. (1947). On a possible lack of incest regulations in Old Iran. *American Anthropologist, 49,* 612–617.

Slovenko, Ralph. (1965). *Sexual behavior and the law.* Springfield, IL: Charles C. Thomas.

Smith, D., Wesson, D., & Apter-Marsh, M. (1984). Cocaine and alcohol-induced sexual dysfunctions in patients with addictive disease. *Journal of Psychoactive Drugs, 14,* 91–99.

Smith, D. G. (1976). The social content of pornography. *Journal of Communication, 26,* 16–33.

Smith, R. Spencer. (1976). Voyeurism: A review of literature. *Archives of Sexual Behavior, 5,* 585–608.

Smith, Stuart L. (1975). Mood and the menstrual cycle. In E. J. Sachar (Ed.), *Topics in psychoendocrinology.* New York: Grune & Stratton.

Smith, Tom W. (1991). Adult sexual behavior in 1989: Number of partners, frequency of intercourse and risk of AIDS. *Family Planning Perspectives, 23*(3), 102–107.

Snelling, H. A. (1975). What is rape? In L. G. Schultz (ed.). *Rape victimology.* Springfield, IL: Charles C. Thomas.

Soley, Lawrence C., & Kurzbard, Gary. (1986). Sex in advertising: A comparison of 1964 and 1984 magazine advertisements. *Journal of Advertising, 15*(3), 46–54.

Somers, A. (1982). Sexual harassment in academe: Legal issues and definitions. *Journal of Social Issues, 38*(4), 23–32.

Sommer, Barbara. (1973). The effect of menstruation on cognitive and perceptual-motor behavior: A review. *Psychomatic Medicine, 35,* 515–534.

Sonenstein, F., Pleck, J. H., & Ku, L. C. (1989). Sexual activity, condom use and AIDS awareness among adolescent males. *Family Planning Perspectives, 21*(4), 152–158.

Sorensen, Robert C. (1973). *Adolescent sexuality in contemporary America.* New York: World.

Sorenson, Susan B., & Siegel, Judith M. (1992). Gender, ethnicity, and sexual assault: Findings from a Los Angeles study. *Journal of Social Issues, 48*(1), 93–104.

Sotile, Wayne M., & Kilmann, Peter R. (1977). Treatments of psychogenic female sexual dysfunctions. *Psychological Bulletin, 84,* 619–633.

Spahn, William C. (1988). The moral dimension of AIDS. *Theological Studies, 49,* 88–110.

Spanier, Graham B. (1976). Formal and informal sex education as determinants of premarital sexual behavior. *Archives of Sexual Behavior, 5,* 39–67.

Spanier, Graham B. (1977). Sources of sex information and premarital sexual behavior. *Journal of Sex Research, 13,* 73–88.

Spanier, Graham B. (1979). Mate swapping: Marital enrichment or sexual experimentation? In G. B. Spanier (Ed.), *Human sexuality in a changing society.* Minneapolis, MN: Burgess.

Spanier, Graham. (1983). Married and unmarried cohabitation in the United States: 1980. *Journal of Marriage and the Family, 45,* 277–288.

Spector, Ilana P., & Carey, Michael P. (1990). Incidence and prevalence of the sexual dysfunctions: A critical review of the empirical literature. *Archives of Sexual Behavior, 19,* 389–408.

Speidel, J. J. (1983). Steroidal contraception in the 80's: The role of current and new products. *Journal of Reproductive Medicine, 28,* 759–769.

Spencer, S. Lee, & Zeiss, Antonette M. (1987). Sex roles and sexual dysfunction in college students. *Journal of Sex Research, 23,* 338–347.

Speroff, L., Glass, R. H., & Kase, N. G. (1973). *Clinical gynecologic endocrinology and infertility.* Baltimore: Williams & Wilkins.

Spira, A., et al. (1992). AIDS and sexual behavior in France. *Nature, 360,* 407.

Spitz, Rene A. (1949). Autoeroticism: Some empirical findings and hypotheses on three of its manifestations in the first year of life. *The Psychoanalytic Study of the Child* (Vols. III–IV, pp. 85–120). New York: International Universities Press.

Spivack, G., & Spotts, J. (1965). The Devereux Child Behavior Scale: Symptom behaviors in latency age children. *American Journal of Mental Retardation, 69,* 839–853.

Sprecher, Susan. (1987). The effects of self-disclosure given and received on affection for an intimate partner and stability of the relationship. *Journal of Social and Personal Relationships, 4,* 115–127.

Spring-Mills, E., & Hafey, E. S. (1980). Male accessory sexual organs. In E. S. Hafey (Ed.), *Human reproduction* (pp. 60–90). New York: Harper & Row.

Srivastava, A., Borries, C., & Sommer, V. (1991). Homosexual mounting in free-ranging female Hanuman langurs. *Archives of Sexual Behavior, 20,* 487–512.

Stack, Steven, & Gundlach, James H. (1992). Divorce and sex. *Archives of Sexual Behavior, 21,* 359–368.

Stamm, Walter E., & Holmes, King K. (1990). *Chlamydia trachomatis* infections of the adult. In K. K. Holmes (Ed.), *Sexually transmitted diseases* (pp. 181–194). New York: McGraw-Hill.

Staples, Robert. (1972). Research on black sexuality: Its implication for family life education and public policy. *Family Coordinator, 21,* 183–188.

Staples, Robert. (1978). Masculinity and race: The dual dilemma of black men. *Journal of Social Issues, 34*(1), 169–183.

St. Augustine. (1950). *The city of God.* (Marcus Dods, Trans.). New York: Modern Library.

Steege, J. F., Stout, A. L., & Carson, C. C. (1986). Patient satisfaction in Scott and Small-Carrion penile implant recipients. *Archives of Sexual Behavior, 15,* 393–400.

Stein, Richard A. (1980). Sexual counseling and coronary heart disease. In S. R. Leiblum & L. A. Pervin (Eds.), *Principles and practice of sex therapy* (pp. 301–320). New York: Guilford.

Steinberg, Jennifer. (Feb. 1993). CDC broadens AIDS definition. *Journal of NIH Research, 5,* 32.

Steinberg, Karen K., et al. (1991). A meta-analysis of the effect of estrogen replacement therapy on the risk of breast cancer. *Journal of the American Medical Association, 265,* 1985–1990.

Steinman, Debra L., et al. (1981). A comparison of male and female patterns of sexual arousal. *Archives of Sexual Behavior, 10,* 529–548.

Stephan, W., Berscheid, E., & Walster, E. (1971). Sexual arousal and heterosexual perception. *Journal of Personality and Social Psychology, 20,* 83–101.

Stephens, Tim. (1991, Feb.). AIDS in women reveals health-care deficiencies. *Journal of NIH Research, 3,* 27–30.

Stephens, Tim. (1992, Feb.). RU 486: New studies, same old politics. *Journal of NIH Research, 4,* 44–46.

Stephens, W. N. (1961). A cross-cultural study of menstrual taboos. *Genetic Psychology Monographs, 64,* 385–416.

Sternberg, Robert J. (1986). A triangular theory of love. *Psychological Review, 93,* 119–135.

Sternberg, Robert J. (1987). Liking versus loving: A comparative evaluation of theories. *Psychological Bulletin, 102,* 331–345.

Stevens-Simon, Catherine, & White, Marguerite M. (1991). Adolescent pregnancy. *Pediatric Annals, 20*(6), 322–331.

Stewart, W. F. R. (1979). *The sexual side of handicap: A guide for the caring professions.* Cambridge, England: Woodhead-Faulkner.

Stone, Abraham. (1931). *The practice of contraception.* Baltimore: Williams & Wilkins.

Storms, Michael D. (1980). Theories of sexual orientation. *Journal of Personality and Social Psychology, 38,* 783–792.

Storms, Michael D. (1981). A theory of erotic orientation development. *Psychological Review, 88,* 340–353.

Storms, Michael D., et al. (1981). Sexual scripts for women. *Sex Roles, 1,* 699–708.

Stout, J. (1973, Aug. 25). Quaker tells of rape in D.C. jail. *Washington Star-News.*

Streissguth, A. P., Sampson, P., & Barr, H. M. (1989). Neurobehavioral dose-response effects of prenatal alcohol exposure in humans from infancy to adulthood. *Annals of the New York Academy of Sciences, 562,* 145–158.

Struckman-Johnson, Cindy. (1988). Forced sex on dates: It happens to men, too. *Journal of Sex Research, 24,* 234–241.

Sullivan, W. (1971, Jan. 24). Boys and girls are now maturing earlier. *New York Times.*

Sunstein, Cass R. (1986). Pornography and the first amendment. *Duke Law Journal, 1986,* 589–629.

Symons, Donald. (1979). *The evolution of human sexuality.* New York: Oxford University Press.

Symons, Donald. (1987). An evolutionary approach: Can Darwin's view of life shed light on human sexuality? In J. H. Geer & W. T. O'Donohue (Eds.), *Theories of human sexuality* (pp. 91–126). New York: Plenum.

Syrjanen, Kari, et al. (1990). Prevalence, incidence, and estimated life-time risk of cervical human papillomavirus infections in a nonselected Finnish female population. *Sexually Transmitted Diseases, 17,* 15–19.

Szasz, Thomas S. (1965). Legal and moral aspects of homosexuality. In J. Marmor (Ed.), *Sexual inversion: The multiple roots of homosexuality.* New York: Basic Books.

Szasz, Thomas S. (1980). *Sex by prescription.* Garden City, NY: Anchor/Doubleday.

Taberner, Peter V. (1985). *Aphrodisiacs: The science and the myth.* Philadelphia: University of Pennsylvania Press.

Taffel, Selma M., et al. (1991, June). 1989 U.S. cesarean section rate steadies—VBAC rate rises to nearly one in five. *Birth, 18,* 73–77.

Talamini, John T. (1982). *Boys will be girls: The hidden world of the heterosexual male transvestite.* Washington, DC: University Press of America.

Tamir, Lois M. (1982). *Men in their forties: The transition to middle age.* New York: Springer.

Tanfer, K., Grady, W. R., Klepinger, D. H., & Billy, J. O. G. (1993). Condom use among U.S. men, 1991. *Family Planning Perspectives, 25(2),* 61–66.

Tanfer, Koray, & Horn, Marjorie C. (1985, Jan.–Feb.). Contraceptive use, pregnancy and fertility patterns among single American women in the 20s. *Family Planning Perspectives, 17,* 1–19.

Tanfer, Koray, & Schoorl, Jeannette J. (1992). Premarital sexual careers and partner change. *Archives of Sexual Behavior, 21,* 45–68.

Tangri, S., Burt, M. R., & Johnson, L. B. (1982). Sexual harassment at work: Three explanatory models. *Journal of Social Issues, 38(4),* 33–54.

Tannen, Deborah. (1986). *That's not what I meant! How conversational style makes or breaks relationships.* New York: Ballantine Books.

Tanner, James M. (1967). Puberty. In A. McLaren (Ed.), *Advances in reproductive physiology* (Vol. II). New York: Academic.

Tart, Charles. (1970). Marijuana intoxication: Common experiences. *Nature, 226,* 701–704.

Tart, Charles. (1971). *On being stoned.* Palo Alto, CA: Science and Behavior Books.

Taub, Nadine. (1987). Amicus brief: In the matter of Baby M. *Women's Rights Law Reporter, 10,* 7–24.

Tavris, Carol. (1977). Masculinity. *Psychology Today, 10(8),* 34.

Tavris, C., & Sadd, S. (1975). *The Redbook report on female sexuality.* New York: Dell.

Taylor, Marylee C., & Hall, Judith A. (1982). Psychological androgyny: Theories, methods, and conclusions. *Psychological Bulletin, 92,* 347–366.

Taylor, Robert. (1990, Jan.). Zona pellucida peptide blocks fertilization. *Journal of NIH Research, 2,* 30.

Teen-age sex: Letting the pendulum swing. (1972, Aug. 21). *Time,* 34–38.

Templeman, Terrel L., & Stinnett, Ray D. (1991). Patterns of sexual arousal and history in a "normal" sample of young men. *Archives of Sexual Behavior, 20,* 137–150.

Terman, Lewis M. (1948). Kinsey's *Sexual behavior in the human male:* Some comments and criticisms. *Psychological Bulletin, 45,* 443–459.

Terman, Lewis M. (1951). Correlates of orgasm adequacy in a group of 556 wives. *Journal of Psychology, 32,* 115–172.

Terman, Lewis, et al. (1938). *Psychological factors in marital happiness.* New York: McGraw-Hill.

Thielicke, Helmut. (1964). *The ethics of sex.* New York: Harper & Row.

Thin, R. N. T., Williams, I. A., & Nicol, C. S. (1970). Direct and delayed methods of immunofluorescent diagnosis of gonorrhea in women. *British Journal of Venereal Disease, 47,* 27–30.

Thomas, David J. (982). San Francisco's 1979 White Night riot. In W. Paul et al. (Eds.), *Homosexuality: Social, psychological, and biological issues.* Beverly Hills, CA: Sage.

Thomas, Patricia. (1988, Mar. 14). Contraceptives: Break due after decade of drought. *Medical World News,* 49–68.

Thompson, Anthony P. (1983). Extramarital sex: A review of the research literature. *Journal of Sex Research, 19,* 1–22.

Thorpe, L. P., Katz, B., & Lewis, R. T. (1961). *The psychology of abnormal behavior.* New York: Ronald Press.

Tiefer, Leonore. (1991). Historical, scientific, clinical, and feminist criticisms of "The Human Sexual Response Cycle" model. *Annual Review of Sex Research, 2,* 1–24.

Tiefer, Leonore. (1991). New perspectives in sexology: From rigor (mortis) to richness. *Journal of Sexual Research, 28,* 593–602.

Tietze, Christopher. (1984). The public health effects of legal abortion in the United States. *Family Planning Perspectives, 16,* 26–28.

Todd, J., et al. (1978). Toxic-shock syndrome associated with phase-group-I staphylococci. *Lancet, 2,* 1116–1118.

Tordjman, Gilbert, et al. (1980). Advances in the vascular pathology of male erectile dysfunction. *Archives of Sexual Behavior, 9,* 391–398.

Touchette, Nancy. (1991, July). HIV-1 link prompts circumspection on circumcision. *Journal of NIH Research, 3,* 44–46.

Towne, J. E. (1955). Carcinoma of cervix in nulliparous and celibate women. *American Journal of Obstetrics and Gynecology, 69,* 606.

Tsai, M., Feldman-Summers, S., & Edgar, M. (1979). Childhood molestation: Variables related to differential impacts on psychosexual functioning in adult women. *Journal of Abnormal Psychology, 88,* 407–417.

Tsai, Mavis, & Uemura, Anne. (1988). Asian Americans: The struggles, the conflicts, and the successes. In P. Bronstein & K. Quina (Eds.), *Teaching a psychology of people*. Washington, DC: American Psychological Association.

Tullman, Gerald M., et al. (1981). The pre- and post-therapy measurement of communication skills of couples undergoing sex therapy at the Masters & Johnson Institute. *Archives of Sexual Behavior, 10*, 95–109.

Turner, Barbara F., & Adams, Catherine G. (1988). Reported change in preferred sexual activity over the adult years. *Journal of Sex Research, 25*, 289–303.

Turner, R. (1990). Vaginal ring is comparable in safety and efficacy to other low-dose, progestogen-only methods. *Family Planning Perspectives, 22*(5), 236–237.

Tutin, C. E. G., & McGinnis, P. R. (1981). Chimpanzee reproduction in the wild. In C. E. Graham (Ed.), *Reproductive biology of the great apes* (pp. 239–264). New York: Academic.

Tutuer, W. (1984). Dangerousness of peeping toms. *Medical Aspects of Human Sexuality, 18*, 97.

Udry, J. Richard. (1988). Biological predispositions and social control in adolescent sexual behavior. *American Sociological Review, 53*, 709–722.

Udry, J. Richard, et al. (1985). Serum androgenic hormones motivate sexual behavior in adolescent boys. *Fertility and Sterility, 43*, 90–94.

Udry, J. Richard, & Eckland, Bruce K. (1984). Benefits of being attractive. Differential payoffs for men and women. *Psychological Reports, 54*, 47–56.

Udry, J. Richard, & Morris, N. M. (1968). Distribution of coitus in the menstrual cycle. *Nature, 220*, 593–596.

Ulmann, A., Teutsch, G., & Philibert, D. (1990, June). RU 486. *Scientific American, 262*, 42–48.

U.P.I. (1981, Nov. 5). Toxicologist warns against butyl nitrite. *Delaware Gazette*, 3.

Upton. (1983). The phasic approach to oral contraception: The triphasic concept and its clinical application. *International Journal of Fertility, 28*(3), 121–140.

U.S Department of Commerce. (1973). *Some demographic aspects of aging in the U.S.: Growth of the population 65 years and over*. Washington, DC: GPO.

U.S. Department of Justice. (1986). *The Attorney General's Commission on Pornography: Final report*. Washington, DC: U.S. Department of Justice.

U.S. Department of Labor. (1982). *20 facts on women workers*. Washington, DC: U.S. Department of Labor.

U.S. Department of Labor. (1988). *20 facts on women workers*. Washington, DC: U.S. Department of Labor.

U.S. Department of Labor. (1990). *20 facts on women workers*. Washington, DC: U.S. Department of Labor.

U.S. Public Health Service, Centers for Disease Control. (1976, Nov. 26). Comparative risks of three methods of midtrimester abortion. *Morbidity and Mortality Weekly Report*, 370.

U.S. Public Health Service, Centers for Disease Control. (1977). *Abortion surveillance 1975*. Atlanta: CDC.

Vacek, Edward W. (1988). Vatican instruction on reproductive technology. *Theological Studies, 49*, 111–130.

Vance, Ellen B., & Wagner, Nathaniel N. (1976). Written descriptions of orgasm: A study of sex differences. *Archives of Sexual Behavior, 5*, 87–98.

Vandenberg, Steven G. (1972). Assortative mating, or who marries whom? *Behavior Genetics, 2*, 127–158.

Vasquez, Melba, & Baron, Augustine. (1988). The psychology of the Chicano experience: A sample course structure. In P. Bronstein & K. Quina (Eds.), *Teaching a psychology of people*. Washington, DC: American Psychological Association.

Verhey, Allen. (1985). The morality of genetic engineering. *Christian Scholars Review, 14*, 124–139.

Velarde, Albert H., & Warick, Mark. (1973). Massage parlors. The sensuality business. *Society, 11*(1), 63–74.

Veronesi, Umberto, et al. (1981). Comparing radical mastectomy with quadrantectomy, axillary dissection, and radiotherapy in patients with small cancers of the breast. *New England Journal of Medicine, 305*, 6–11.

"Video turns big profit for porn products." (1982, Mar. 10). *Variety, 306*, 35.

Vincent, J. P., Friedman, L. C., Nugent, J., & Messerly, L. (1979). Demand characteristics in observations of marital interaction. *Journal of Consulting and Clinical Psychology, 47*, 557–566.

Voeller, Bruce. (1991). AIDS and heterosexual anal intercourse. *Archives of Sexual Behavior, 20*, 233–276.

Von Krafft-Ebing, Richard. (1886). *Psychopathia sexualis*. (Reprinted by Putnam, New York, 1965).

Vorherr, H., Messer, R. H., & Reid, D. (1983). Complications of tubal sterilization: Menstrual abnormalities and fibrocystic breast disease. *American Journal of Obstetrics and Gynecology, 145*, 644–645.

Voss, Jacqueline R. (1980). Sex education: Evaluation and recommendations for future study. *Archives of Sexual Behavior, 9*, 37–59.

Wabrek, Alan J., & Wabrek, Carolyn J. (1975). Dyspareunia. *Journal of Sex and Marital Therapy, 1*, 234–241.

Wabrek, Alan J., & Burchell, R. Clay. (1980). Male sexual dysfunction associated with coronary heart disease. *Archives of Sexual Behavior, 9*, 69–75.

Wagner, Nathanial, & Solberg, Don. (1974). Pregnancy and sexuality. *Medical Aspects of Human Sexuality, 8*(3), 44–79.

Walfish, Steven, & Myerson, Marilyn. (1980). Sex role identity and attitudes toward sexuality. *Archives of Sexual Behavior, 9*, 199–204.

Walen, Susan R., & Roth, David. (1987). A cognitive approach. In J. H. Geer & W. T. O'Donohue (Eds.), *Theories of human sexuality* (pp. 335–362). New York: Plenum.

Walker, Alexander M., et al. (1981). Hospitalization rates in vasectomized men. *Journal of the American Medical Association, 245*, 2315–2317.

Wallerstein, Edward. (1980). *Circumcision: An American health fallacy*. New York: Springer.

Wallin, Paul. (1949). An appraisal of some methodological aspects of the Kinsey report. *American Sociological Review, 14*, 197–210.

Walling, M., Andersen, B. L., & Johnson, S. R. (1990). Hormonal replacement therapy for postmenopausal women: A review of sexual outcomes and related gynecologic effects. *Archives of Sexual Behavior, 19*, 119–138.

Walster, Elaine. (1978). Equity and extramarital sexuality. *Archives of Sexual Behavior, 7*, 127–141.

Bibliography

Walster, Elaine, et al. (1973). "Playing hard-to-get": Understanding an elusive phenomenon. *Journal of Personality and Social Psychology, 26,* 113–121.

Walster, E., Walster, G. W., & Traupmann, J. (1978). Equity and premarital sex. *Journal of Personality and Social Psychology, 36,* 82–92.

Walters, C., Shurley, J. T., & Parsons, O. A. (1962). Differences in male and female responses to underwater sensory deprivation: An exploratory study. *Journal of Nervous and Mental Disease, 135,* 302–310.

Wampler, Karen S. (1982). The effectiveness of the Minnesota Couple Communication Program: A review of research. *Journal of Marital and Family Therapy,* 345–355.

Ward, Ingeborg L. (1974). Sexual behavior differentiation: Prenatal hormonal and environmental control. In R. C. Friedman et al. (Eds.), *Sex differences in behavior* (pp. 3–17). New York: Wiley.

Ward, Ingeborg L., & Reed, J. (1985). Prenatal stress and prepubertal social rearing conditions interact to determine sexual behavior in male rats. *Behavioral Neuroscience, 99,* 301–309.

Ward, et al. (1988). Transmission of human immunodeficiency virus (HIV) by blood transfusions screened as negative for HIV antibody. *New England Journal of Medicine, 318,* 473–478.

Warden, C. J. (1931). *Animal motivation: Experimental studies on the albino rat.* New York: Columbia University Press.

Warga, Claire. (1987, Aug.). Pain's gatekeeper. *Psychology Today, 21*(8), 50–56.

Washington, E. E., Johnson, E. R. E., & Sanders, L. L. (1987). *Chlamydia trachomatis* infections in the United States: What are they costing us? *Journal of the American Medical Association, 257,* 2070–2072.

Wass, Debbie M., et al. (1991). Completed follow-up of 1,000 consecutive transcervical chorionic villus samplings performed by a single operator. *Australia New Zealand Journal of Obstetrics and Gynecology, 31,* 240–245.

Weideger, Paula. (1976). *Menstruation and menopause.* New York: Knopf.

Weigel, R. H., & Loomis, J. W. (1981). Televised models of female achievement revisited: Some progress. *Journal of Applied Social Psychology, 11,* 58–63.

Weinberg, Martin S., Swensson, Rochelle G., & Hammersmith, Sue K. (1983). Sexual autonomy and the status of women: Models of female sexuality in U.S. sex manuals from 1950 to 1980. *Social Problems, 30,* 312–324.

Weinberg, Martin S., & Williams, Colin. (1974). *Male homosexuals: Their problems and adaptations.* New York: Oxford University Press.

Weinberg, Martin S., & Williams, Colin J. (1988). Black sexuality: A test of two theories. *Journal of Sex Research, 25,* 197–218.

Weinberg, Samuel K. (1955). *Incest behavior.* New York: Citadel Press.

Weinberg, Thomas S. (1987). Sadomasochism in the United States: A review of recent sociological literature. *Journal of Sex Research, 23,* 50–69.

Weiner, L., et al. (1951). Carcinoma of the cervix in Jewish women. *American Journal of Obstetrics and Gynecology, 61,* 418.

Weis, David L. (1983). Affective reactions of women to their initial experience of coitus. *Journal of Sex Research, 19,* 209–237.

Weis, Kurt, & Borges, Sandra S. (1973). Victimology and rape: The case of the legitimate victim. *Issues in Criminology, 8*(2), 71–115.

Weisbert, D. Kelly. (1984). *Children of the night: A study of adolescent prostitution.* Lexington, MA: Lexington Books.

Weiss, Howard D. (1973). Mechanism of erection. *Medical Aspects of Human Sexuality, 7*(2), 21–40.

Weiss, Noel S., et al. (1976). Increasing incidence of endometrial cancer in the United States. *New England Journal of Medicine, 294,* 1259–1261.

Weissman, Myrna, & Klerman, G. (1977). Sex differences and the epidemiology of depression. *Archives of General Psychiatry, 34,* 98–111.

Weitzman, L. J., Eifles, D., Hokada, E., & Ross, C. (1972). Sex role socialization in picture books for preschool children. *American Journal of Sociology, 72,* 1125–1150.

Weizman, R., & Hart, J. (1987). Sexual behavior in healthy married elderly men. *Archives of Sexual Behavior, 16,* 39–44.

Weller, Ronald A., & Halikas, James A. (1984). Marijuana use and sexual behavior. *Journal of Sex Research, 20,* 186–193.

Wennberg, Robert N. (1985). *Life in the balance: Exploring the abortion controversy.* Grand Rapids, MI: Eerdmans.

Werry, J. S., & Quay, H. S. (1971). The prevalence of behavior symptoms in younger elementary school children. *American Journal of Orthopsychiatry, 41,* 136–143.

Wertz, R. W., & Wertz, D. C. (1977). *Lying-in: A history of childbirth in America.* New York: Free Press.

Wesson, D. R. (1982). Cocaine use by masseuses. *Journal of Psychoactive Drugs, 14,* 75–76.

Westoff, Charles. (1974). Coital frequency and contraception. *Family Planning Perspectives, 6*(3), 136–141.

Westoff, Charles, & Bumpass, Larry. (1973). The revolution in birth control practices of U. S. Roman Catholics. *Science, 179,* 41–44.

Westoff, Charles F., & Jones, Elise F. (1977). Contraception and sterilization in the United States, 1965–1975. *Family Planning Perspectives, 9,* 153–157.

Wharton, Chris, & Blackburn, Richard. (1988). Lower-dose pills. *Population Reports,* Series A, No. 7, 1–31.

Wheeler, Garry D., et al. (1984). Reduced serum testosterone and prolactin levels in male distance runners. *Journal of the American Medical Association, 252,* 514–516.

Wheeler, John, & Kilmann, Peter R. (1983). Comarital sexual behavior: Individual and relationship variables. *Archives of Sexual Behavior, 12,* 295–306.

Whitam, Frederick L. (1977). The homosexual role: A reconsideration. *Journal of Sex Research, 13,* 1–11.

Whitam, Frederick L. (1983). Culturally invariable properties of male homosexuality: Tentative conclusions from cross-cultural research. *Archives of Sexual Behavior, 12,* 207–226.

White, Charles B. (1982). Sexual interest, attitudes, knowledge, and sexual history in relation to sexual behavior in the institutionalized aged. *Archives of Sexual Behavior, 11,* 11–22.

White, David. (1981, Sept.). Pursuit of the ultimate aphrodisiac. *Psychology Today, 15*(9), 9–12.

White, Gregory L., Fishbein, S., & Rutstein, J. (1981). Passionate love and the misattribution of arousal. *Journal of Personality and Social Psychology, 41,* 56–62.

White, Gregory L., & Knight, T. D. (1984). Misattribution of arousal and attraction: Effects of salience of explanations for arousal. *Journal of Experimental Social Psychology, 20,* 55–64.

White, Gregory L., & Mullen, Paul E. (1989). *Jealousy: Theory, research, and clinical strategies.* New York: Guilford.

White, Susan E., & Reamy, Kenneth. (1982). Sexuality and pregnancy: A review. *Archives of Sexual Behavior, 11,* 429–444.

Whitehurst, R. N. (1972). Extramarital sex: Alienation or extension of normal behavior. In J. N. Edwards (Ed.), *Sex and society.* Chicago: Rand McNally.

Whiteside, D. C., et al. (1983). Factors associated with successful vaginal delivery after cesarean section. *Journal of Reproductive Medicine, 28,* 785–788.

Wickler, Wolfgang. (1973). *The sexual code.* New York: Anchor Books. (Original in German, 1969).

Wielandt, Hanne, et al. (1989). Age of partners at first intercourse among Danish males and females. *Archives of Sexual Behavior, 18,* 449–454.

Williams, Colin H., & Weinberg, Martin S. (1971). *Homosexuals and the military: A study of less than honorable discharge.* New York: Harper & Row.

Williams, Martin H. (1992). Exploitation and inference: Mapping the damage from therapist-patient sexual involvement. *American Psychologist, 47,* 412–421.

Willmuth, Mary E. (1987). Sexuality after spinal cord injury: A critical review. *Clinical Psychology Review, 7,* 389–412.

Wilson, E. O. (1975). *Sociobiology: The new synthesis.* Cambridge: Harvard University Press.

Wilson, Glenn D. (1987). An ethological approach to sexual deviation. In G. D. Wilson (Ed.), *Variant sexuality: Research and theory.* Baltimore: Johns Hopkins University Press.

Wilson, Glenn D. (Ed.). (1987). *Variant sexuality: Research and theory.* Baltimore: Johns Hopkins University Press.

Wilson, G. T., & Lawson, D. M. (1978). Expectancies, alcohol, and sexual arousal in women. *Journal of Abnormal Psychology, 87,* 358–367.

Wilson, R. D., et al. (1991). Chorionic villus sampling: Analysis of fetal losses to delivery, placental pathology, and cervical microbiology. *Prenatal Diagnosis, 11,* 539–550.

Wilson, W. Cody. (1973). Pornography: The emergence of a social issue and the beginning of psychological study. *Journal of Social Issues, 29,* 7–17.

Wincze, John P., & Carey, Michael P. (1992). *Sexual dysfunction: A guide for assessment and treatment.* New York: Guilford.

Winick, Charles, & Kinsie, Paul M. (1971). *The lively commerce.* New York: Quadrangle.

Winick, Charles, & Kinsie, Paul M. (1972). Prostitutes. *Psychology Today, 5*(9), 57.

Winkelstein, Warren, et al. (1987a). The San Francisco Men's Health Study. III. Reduction in human immunodeficiency virus transmission among homosexual/bisexual men, 1982–86. *American Journal of Public Health, 76,* 685–688.

Winkelstein, Warren, et al. (1987b). Sexual practices and risk of infection by the human immunodeficiency virus: The San Francisco Men's Health Study. *Journal of the American Medical Association, 257,* 321–325.

Winkelstein, Warren, et al. (1987c). Selected sexual practices of San Francisco heterosexual men and risk of infection by the human immunodeficiency virus. *Journal of the American Medical Association, 257,* 1470.

Winn, Rhonda L., & Newton, Niles. (1982). Sexuality in aging: A study of 106 cultures. *Archives of Sexual Behavior, 11,* 283–298.

Wiswell, T. E., Enzenauer, R. W., Cornish, J. D., & Hawkins, C. T. (1987). Declining frequency of circumcision: Implications for changes in the absolute incidence of and male to female sex ratio of urinary tract infections in early infancy. *Pediatrics, 79,* 338–342.

Wolchik, S. A., Braver, S. L., & Jensen, K. (1985). Volunteer bias in erotica research: Effects of intrusiveness of measure of sexual background. *Archives of Sexual Behavior, 14,* 93–107.

Wolchik, S. A., Spencer, S. L., & Lisi, I. S. (1983). Volunteer bias in research employing vaginal measures of sexual arousal. *Archives of Sexual Behavior, 12,* 399–408.

Wolf, Timothy J. (1985). Marriages of bisexual men. In F. Klein & T. J. Wolf (Eds.), *Bisexualities: Theory and Research.* New York: Haworth.

Wolfe, L. (1980, Sept.). The sexual profile of that *Cosmopolitan* girl. *Cosmopolitan,* 254–265.

Wolff, Charlotte. (1971). *Love between women.* New York: Harper & Row.

Women on Words and Images. (1972). *Dick and Jane as victims: Sex stereotyping in children's readers.* Princeton, NJ: WWI.

Woods, James S. (1975). Drug effects on human sexual behavior. In N. F. Woods (Ed.), *Human sexuality in health and illness.* St. Louis: Mosby.

Wright, A. L., Holberg, C., & Taussig, L. M. (1988). Infant-feeding practices among middle-class Anglos and Hispanics. *Pediatrics, 82,* 496–503.

Wright, L., Schaefer, A. B., & Solomons, G. (1979). *Encyclopedia of pediatric psychology.* Baltimore: University Park Press.

Wyatt, Gail E. (1991). Child sexual abuse and its effects on sexual functioning. *Annual Review of Sex Research, 2,* 249–266.

Wyatt, Gail E. (1992). The sociocultural context of African American and White American women's rape. *Journal of Social Issues, 48*(1), 77–92.

Wyatt, Gail E., & Dunn, Kristi M. (1991). Examining predictors of sex guilt in multiethnic samples of women. *Archives of Sexual Behavior, 20,* 471–486.

Wyatt, G. E., Peters, S. D., & Guthrie, D. (1988). Kinsey revisited. Part I: Comparisons of the sexual socialization and sexual behavior of white women over 33 years. *Archives of Sexual Behavior, 17,* 201–240.

Wysor, Bettie. (1974). *The lesbian myth.* New York: Random House.

Yalom, Irvin D. (1960). Aggression and forbiddenness in voyeurism. *Archives of General Psychiatry, 3,* 317.

Yarbro, E. Scott, & Howards, Stuart S. (1987). Vasovasostomy. *Urologic Clinics of North America, 14,* 515–526.

Yerushalmy, J. (1964). Mother's cigarette smoking and survival of infant. *American Journal of Obstetrics and Gynecology, 88,* 505–518.

Young, B. K., Katz, M., & Klein, S. (1983). Pregnancy after spinal cord injury: Altered maternal and fetal responses to labor. *Obstetrics & Gynecology, 62,* 59–63.

Young, Wayland. (1970). Prostitution. In J. D. Douglas (Ed.), *Observations of deviance.* New York: Random House.

Zabin, L. S., Hirsch, M. B., Smith, E. A., & Harcy, J. B. (1984). Adolescent sexual attitudes and behaviors: Are they consistent? *Family Planning Perspectives, 4,* 181–185.

Zaslow, Martha J., et al. (1985). Depressed mood in new fathers: Association with parent-infant interaction. *Genetic, Social, and General Psychology Monographs, 111*(2), 133–150.

Zax, M., Sameroff, A., & Farnum, J. (1975). Childbirth education, maternal attitude and delivery. *American Journal of Obstetrics and Gynecology, 123,* 185–190.

Zeiss, A. M., Rosen, G. M., & Zeiss, R. A. (1977). Orgasm during intercourse: A treatment strategy for women. *Journal of Consulting and Clinical Psychology, 45,* 891–895.

Zelnik, Melvin, & Kantner, John F. (1977). Sexual and contraceptive experience of young unmarried women in the United States, 1976 and 1971. *Family Planning Perspectives, 9*(2), 55–71.

Zelnik, Melvin, & Kantner, John F. (1980). Sexual activity, contraceptive use and pregnancy among metropolitan-area teenagers: 1971–1979. *Family Planning Perspectives, 12*(5), 230–237.

Zelnik, Melvin, & Kim, Young J. (1982). Sex education and its association with teenage sexual activity, pregnancy and contraceptive use. *Family Planning Perspectives, 14*(3).

Zelnik, Melvin, & Shah, Farida K. (1983, Mar.–April). First intercourse among young Americans. *Family Planning Perspectives, 15*(2), 64–70.

Zilbergeld, Bernie. (1975). Group treatment of sexual dysfunction in men without partners. *Journal of Sex and Marital Therapy, 1,* 204–214.

Zilbergeld, Bernie. (1978). *Male sexuality.* Boston: Little, Brown.

Zilbergeld, Bernie. (1992). *The new male sexuality.* New York: Bantam Books.

Zilbergeld, Bernie, & Ellison, Carol Rinklieb. (1980). Desire discrepancies and arousal problems in sex therapy. In S. R. Leiblum & L. A. Pervin (Eds.), *Principles and practice of sex therapy* (pp. 65–104). New York: Guilford.

Zilbergeld, Bernie, & Evans, Michael. (1980, Aug.). The inadequacy of Masters and Johnson. *Psychology Today, 14*(3), 28–43.

Zimmer, D. (1983). Interaction patterns and communication skills in sexually distressed, and normal couples: Two experimental studies. *Journal of Sex and Marital Therapy, 9,* 251–265.

Zuger, Abigail. (1987, June). AIDS on the wards: A residency in medical ethics. *Hastings Center Report,* June 16–20.

Zumpe, Doris, & Michael, R. P. (1968). The clutching reaction and orgasm in the female rhesus monkey (*Macaca mulatta*). *Journal of Endocrinology, 40,* 117–123.

Zumwalt, Rosemary. (1976). Plain and fancy: A content analysis of children's jokes dealing with adult sexuality. *Western Folklore, 35,* 258–267.

Zussman, L., Zussman, S., Sunley, R., & Bjornson, E. (1981). Sexual response after hysterectomy-oophorectomy. *American Journal of Obstetrics and Gynecology, 140,* 725–729.

Glossary

Abortion The ending of a pregnancy and the expulsion of the contents of the uterus; may be spontaneous or induced by human intervention.

Abstinence (sexual) Not engaging in sexual activity.

Acculturation The process of incorporating the beliefs and customs of a new culture.

Acquired immune deficiency syndrome (AIDS) A sexually transmitted disease that destroys the body's natural immunity to infection.

Adrenogenital syndrome See *congenital adrenal hyperplasia*

Adultery Sexual intercourse between a married person and someone other than her or his spouse.

Afterbirth The placenta and amnoitic sac, which come out after the baby during childbirth.

Agape A Greek word meaning selfless love of others.

AIDS See *acquired immune deficiency syndrome.*

Ambisexual See *bisexual.*

Amenorrhea The absence of menstruation.

Amniocentesis A test done to determine whether a fetus has birth defects; done by removing amniotic fluid from the pregnant woman's uterus.

Amniotic fluid The watery fluid surrounding a developing fetus in the uterus.

Amyl nitrate A drug, usually inhaled, that some people use to prolong or intensify orgasm.

Anal intercourse Sexual behavior in which one person's penis is inserted into another's anus.

Analogous organs Organs in the male and female that have similar functions.

Anaphrodisiac A substance that decreases sexual desire.

Androgens "Male" sex hormones, produced in the testes; an example is testosterone. In females, the adrenal glands produce androgens.

Androgyny Having both feminine and masculine characteristics.

Anilingus Mouth-anus stimulation.

Anorgasmia The inability of a woman to orgasm; a sexual dysfunction.

Antigay prejudice Negative attitudes and behaviors toward gays and lesbians.

Anus The opening of the rectum, located between the buttocks.

Aphrodisiac A substance that increases sexual desire.

Areola The dark circular area of skin surrounding the nipple of the breast.

Artificial insemination Artificially putting semen into a woman's vagina or uterus for the purpose of inducing pregnancy.

Asexual Without sexual desires.

Asphyxophilia A desire for a state of oxygen deprivation to enhance sexual arousal.

Asymptomatic Having no symptoms.

Attachment A psychological bond that forms between an infant and the mother, father, or other care giver.

Autoeroticism Sexual self-stimulation; masturbation is one example.

Axillary hair Underarm hair.

Barr body A small, black dot appearing in the cells of genetic females; it represents an inactivated X chromosome.

Bartholin's glands Two tiny glands located on either side of the vaginal entrance.

Basal body temperature method One method of rhythm birth control.

Behavior therapy A system of therapy based on learning theory and focusing on the problem behavior, not the unconscious.

Bestiality Sexual contact with an animal; also called *zoophilia*.

Bisexual A person who has some sexual contacts with males and some with females.

Blastocyst A small mass of cells that results after several days of cell division by the fertilized egg.

Braxton-Hicks contractions Contractions of the uterus during pregnancy that are not part of actual labor.

Breech presentation Birth of a baby with buttocks or feet first.

Brothel A house of prostitution.

Buccal smear A test of genetic gender.

Bulbourethral glands See *Cowper's glands*.

Butch A very masculine lesbian; may also refer to a very masculine male homosexual.

Candida albicans A yeast or fungus in the vagina; if its growth gets out of control, it causes vaginitis, or irritation of the vagina, with an accompanying discharge.

Carpopedal spasm A spastic contraction of the hands or feet which may occur during orgasm.

Castration The removal (usually by means of surgery) of the gonads (the testes in men or the ovaries in women).

Celibate Unmarried; also used to refer to someone who abstains from sexual activity.

Cervical cap A birth control device similar to the diaphragm.

Cervix The lower part of the uterus; the part next to the vagina.

Cesarean section Surgical delivery of a baby through an incision in the abdominal wall.

Chancre A painless open sore with a hard ridge around it; it is an early symptom of syphilis.

Chancroid A sexually transmitted disease.

Chastity Sexual abstinence.

Chlamydia An organism causing a sexually transmitted disease.

Chorionic villus sampling (CVS) A new technique for early detection of birth defects.

Cilia Tiny hairlike structures lining the vas deferens and the fallopian tubes.

Circumcision Surgical removal of the foreskin of the penis.

Classical conditioning A learning process whereby a previously neutral stimulus (CS) is repeatedly paired with an unconditioned stimulus (US) that reflexively elicits an unconditioned response (UR). Eventually the CS will evoke the response.

Climacteric See *menopause*.

Climax An orgasm.

Clitoridectomy Removal of the clitoris.

Clitoris A small, highly sensitive sexual organ in the female, located in front of the vaginal entrance.

Cloning Producing genetically identical individuals from a single parent.

Cognitive Relating to mental activity, such as thought, perception, understanding.

Cohabitation Living together.

Coitus Sexual intercourse, insertion of the penis into the vagina.

Coitus interruptus See *withdrawal*.

Coitus reservatus Sexual intercourse in which the man intentionally refrains from ejaculating.

Colostrum A watery substance that is secreted from the breast at the end of pregnancy and during the first few days after delivery.

Coming out The process of acknowledging to oneself, and then to others, that one is gay or lesbian.

Conceptus The product of conception; sometimes used to refer to the embryo or fetus.

Condom A male contraceptive sheath that is placed over the penis; also used in the prevention of sexually transmitted diseases.

Congenital adrenal hyperplasia A condition in which a genetic female has an abnormally functioning adrenal gland that produces an excess of androgens so that she is born with genitals that look like a male's.

Contraceptive sponge A polyurethane sponge containing a spermicide, which is placed in the vagina for contraceptive purposes.

Contraceptive technique A method of preventing conception.

Coprophilia A sexual variation in which arousal is associated with defecation or feces.

Copulation Sexual intercourse.

Corona The rim of tissue between the glans and the shaft of the penis.

Corpora cavernosa Two cylindrical masses of erectile tissue running the length of the penis; also present in the clitoris.

Corpus luteum The mass of cells remaining after a follicle has released an egg; it secretes progesterone.

Corpus spongiosum A cylinder of erectile tissue running the length of the penis.

Correlation A number that measures the relationship between two variables.

Couvade The experiencing of the symptoms of pregnancy and labor by a male.

Cowper's glands A pair of glands that secrete substances into the male's urethra.

Crabs See *Pediculosis pubis.*

Cramps Painful menstruation, or dysmenorrhea.

Cremaster muscle A muscle in the scrotum.

Cryptorchidism Undescended testes.

Cul-de-sac The end of the vagina, past the cervix.

Culdoscopy A female sterilization procedure.

Culpotomy A female sterilization procedure.

Cunnilingus Mouth stimulation of the female genitals.

Cystitis Inflammation of the urinary bladder; the major symptom is a burning sensation while urinating.

Dartos muscle A muscle in the scrotum.

Decriminalization Removing criminal penalties for an activity that was previously defined as illegal.

Defloration The rupture of a virgin's hymen, through intercourse or other means.

Depo-Provera A drug containing synthetic hormones; used as a form of birth control in women, as well as a treatment for male sex offenders.

Detumescence The return of an erect penis to the flaccid (unaroused) state.

Diaphragm A cap-shaped rubber contraceptive device that fits inside a woman's vagina over the cervix.

Diethylstilbestrol (DES) A potent estrogen drug used in the "morning-after" pill.

Dilate To enlarge; used to refer to the enlargement of the cervical opening during childbirth.

Dildo An artificial penis.

Don Juanism Hypersexuality in a male.

Douche To flush out the inside of the vagina with a liquid.

Drag queen A male homosexual who dresses in women's clothing.

Ductus deferens See *vas deferens.*

Dysmenorrhea Painful menstruation.

Dyspareunia Painful intercourse.

Ectopic pregnancy A pregnancy in which the fertilized egg implants somewhere other than the uterus.

Edema An excessive accumulation of fluid in a part of the body.

Effacement Thinning out of the cervix during childbirth.

Ejaculation The expulsion of semen from the penis, usually during orgasm.

Electra complex In Freudian theory, a little girl's sexual desires for her father; the female analogue of the Oedipus complex.

Embryo In humans, the term used to refer to the unborn young from the first to the eighth week after conception.

Embryo transfer A technique in which a fertilized, developing egg (embryo) is transferred from the uterus of one woman to the uterus of another woman.

Endocrine gland A gland that secretes substances (hormones) directly into the bloodstream.

Endometriosis A condition in which the endometrium grows in some place other than the uterus, such as the fallopian tubes.

Endometrium The inner lining of the uterus.

Epididymis Highly coiled tubules located on the edge of the testes; the site of sperm maturation.

Episiotomy An incision that is sometimes made at the vaginal entrance during delivery.

Erectile dysfunction The inability to get or maintain an erection.

Erection An enlargement and hardening of the penis which occurs during sexual arousal.

Erogenous zones Areas of the body that are particularly sensitive to sexual stimulation.

Eros The Greeks' term for passionate or erotic love.

Erotica Sexually arousing material that is not degrading to women, men, or children.

Erotophilia Feeling comfortable with sex, the opposite of erotophobia.

Erotophobia Feeling guilty and fearful about sex.

Estrogens A small group of "female" sex hormones; also produced in smaller quantities in males.

Estrus The period of ovulation and sexual activity in nonhuman female mammals.

Eunuch A castrated male.

Exhibitionist A person who derives sexual gratification from exposing his or her genitals to others.

Extramarital sex Sexual activity by a married person with someone other than her or his spouse.

Fallopian tube The tube extending from the uterus to the ovary.

Fellatio Mouth stimulation of the penis.

Female circumcision Amputation of the clitoris.

Femme A feminine lesbian.

Fertilization The union of sperm and egg, resulting in conception.

Fetal alcohol syndrome Disease of a newborn born to an alcoholic mother.

Fetishism A sexual variation in which an inanimate object causes sexual arousal.

Fetus In humans, the term used to refer to the unborn young from the third mouth after conception until birth.

Fimbriae Fingerlike projections at the end of the fallopian tube near the ovary.

Fitness In evolutionary theory, an individual's reproductive success.

Flaccid Not erect.

Follicle The capsule of cells surrounding an egg in the ovary.

Follicle-stimulating hormone (FSH) A hormone secreted by the pituitary; it stimulates follicle development in females and sperm production in males.

Follicular phase The first phase of the menstrual cycle, beginning just after menstruation.

Foreskin The sheath of skin covering the tip of the penis or clitoris

Fornication Sexual intercourse between two unmarried people.

Fourchette The place where the inner lips come together behind the vaginal opening.

Frenulum A highly sensitive area of skin on the underside of the penis next to the glans.

Frigidity Lack of sexual response in a woman.

Gamete intra-fallopian transfer (GIFT) A procedure in which sperm and eggs are collected and then inserted together into the fallopian tube.

Gametes Sperm or eggs.

Gay Homosexual; particularly a male homosexual.

Gender The state of being male or female.

Gender dysphoria See *transsexual*.

Gender identity The psychological sense of one's own maleness or femaleness.

Gender role A cluster of socially defined expectations that people of one gender are expected to fulfill.

Genitals The sexual or reproductive organs.

Genital warts A sexually transmitted disease causing warts on the genitals.

Gerontophilia Sexual attraction to the elderly.

Gestation The period of pregnancy; the time from conception until birth.

GIFT See *Gamete intra-fallopian transfer*.

Gigolo A male who sells his sexual services to women.

Glans The tip of the penis or clitoris.

Gonadotropin-releasing hormone (Gn-RH) A hormone secreted by the hypothalamus that regulates the pituitary's secretion of hormones.

Gonadotropins Pituitary hormones (FSH, LH) that stimulate the activity of the gonads.

Gonads The ovaries or testes.

Gonorrhea A common sexually transmitted disease.

Gossypol A substance used as a male contraceptive in China.

Gräfenberg spot A hypothesized small gland on the front wall of the vagina, emptying into the urethra, which may be responsible for female ejaculation.

Granuloma inguinale A rare sexually transmitted disease.

Gynecomastia Temporary enlargement of a male's breasts during puberty.

Hegar's sign A sign of pregnency based on a test done by a physician, in which a softening of the uterus is detected.

Hepatitis B A disease that can be transmitted by anal intercourse or oral-anal sex.

Hermaphrodite A person with both male and female sex glands, that is, both ovaries and testicular tissue (see also *pseudohermaphrodite*).

Herpes genitalis A disease characterized by painful bumps on the genitals.

Heterosexual A person who is sexually attracted to, or engages in sexual activity primarily with, members of the other gender.

HIV Human immune deficiency virus, the virus that causes AIDS.

Homologous organs Organs in the male and female that develop from the same embryonic tissue.

Homophobia Irrational fear of homosexuality.

Homosexual A person who is sexually attracted to, or engages in sexual activity primarily with, members of her or his own gender.

Homosocial A pattern of social grouping in which males associate with other males and females associate with other females.

Hormones Chemical substances secreted by the endocrine glands.

Human chorionic gonadotropin (HCG) A hormone produced by the placenta; HCG is what is detected in most pregnancy tests.

Human papilloma virus (HPV) The organism that causes genital warts.

Hustlers Male prostitutes who sell their services to other males.

Hyaluronidase An enzyme secreted by the sperm that allows it to penetrate the egg.

Hymen A member that partially covers the vaginal opening.

Hypersexuality An excessive, insatiable sex drive.

Hypothalamus A part of the brain which is important in regulating certain body functions including sex hormone production.

Hysterectomy Surgical removal of the uterus.

Hysterotomy A method of abortion sometimes used during the second trimester.

Id In Freudian theory, the part of the personality containing the libido or sex drive.

Imperforate hymen A condition where the hymen is unusually thick and covers the vaginal entrance completely.

Implantation The burrowing of the fertilized egg into the lining of the uterus.

Impotence See *erectile dysfunction.*

Impregnate To make pregnant.

Incest Sexual activity between close relatives, such as a brother and sister.

Incest taboo A regulation prohibiting sexual activity between blood relatives.

Incidence The percentage of people giving a particular response.

Infibulation A ritual practice of cutting off the inner lips and sewing together the outer lips, making intercourse impossible.

Inguinal canal In the male, the passageway from the abdomen to the scrotum through which the testes usually descend shortly before birth.

Inhibin Substance produced by the testes, which regulates FSH levels.

Inner lips Thin folds of skin on either side of the vaginal entrance.

Intercourse (sexual) Sexual activity in which the penis is inserted into the vagina; coitus (see also *anal intercourse.*)

Interfemoral intercourse Sexual activity in which the penis moves between the thighs.

Interstitial cells Cells in the testes which manufacture male sex hormones; also called *Leydig cells.*

Intimacy A quality of relationship characterized by self-disclosure and feelings of closeness and trust.

Intrauterine device (IUD) A plastic or metal device that is inserted into the uterus for contraceptive purposes.

Introitus Entrnce to the vagina.

Intromission Insertion of the penis into the vagina.

In vitro fertilization (IVF) A technique in which sperm and egg are mixed outside the body in a laboratory dish, so that conception can occur.

John Slang term for a prostitute's customer.

Kaposi's sarcoma A rare form of skin cancer to which AIDS patients are susceptible.

Kegel exercises Exercises to strengthen the muscle surrounding the genitals.

Kiddie porn Pictures or films of sexual acts with children.

Labia majora See *outer lips.*

Labia minora See *inner lips.*

Labor The series of processes involved in giving birth.

Lactation Secretion of milk from the female's breasts.

Lamaze method A method of "prepared" childbirth.

Laparoscopy A method of female sterilization.

Lesbian A female homosexual.

Leydig cells See *interstitial cells.*

Libido The sex drive.

Limbic system A set of structures in the interior of the brain, including the amygdala, hippocampus, and fornix; believed to be important for sexual behavior in both animals and humans.

Limerance Romantic love marked by preoccupation with the loved one.

Lochia A discharge from the uterus and vagina that occurs during the first few weeks after childbirth.

Low sexual desire A sexual dysfunction in which there is a lack of interest in sexual activity.

Lumpectomy A surgical treatment for breast cancer in which only the lump and a small bit of surrounding tissue are removed.

Luteinizing hormone (LH) A hormone secreted by the pituitary. In females, it causes ovulation.

Lymphogranuloma venereum (LGV) A virus-caused disease affecting the lymph glands in the genital region.

Mammary gland The milk-producing part of the breast.

Mammography X-rays for diagnosing breast cancer.

Masochism A sexual variation in which the person derives sexual pleasure from experiencing physical or mental pain.

Mastectomy Surgical removal of the breast.

Masturbation Self-stimulation of the genitals to produce sexual arousal.

Menage à trois A sexual relationship involving three people.

Menarche The first menstruation.

Menopause The gradual cessation of menstruation in a woman, generally at around age 50.

Menses The menstrual flow.

Menstruation A bloody discharge of the lining of the uterus, generally occurring about once a month in women.

Midwife A person (often a nurse) trained as a birth attendant.

Mini-pill A birth control pill containing a low dose of progesterone and no estrogen.

Miscarriage A pregnancy that terminates on its own; spontaneous abortion.

Miscegenation Sex between two people of different races.

Mittelschmerz Abdominal cramps at the time of ovulation.

Monilia A yeast infection of the vagina.

Monogamy The pairing of one person with just one other person in a long-term relationship in which neither engages in sexual activity with anyone else.

Mons pubis The fatty pad of tissue under the pubic hair; also called the *mons* or *mons veneris*.

Morning-after pill A pill containing a high dose of DES, which can be used in emergency situations for preventing pregnancy after intercourse has occurred.

Mucosa Mucous membrane.

Müllerian ducts In the embryo, a pair of ducts that eventually become part of the female reproductive system.

Multiparous A term used to refer to a woman who has had more than one baby.

Myotonia Muscle tension.

Necrophilia A sexual variation in which there is attraction to a corpse.

Nipples The pigmented tip of the breast, through which milk goes when a woman is breast-feeding.

Nocturnal emission Involuntary orgasm and ejaculation while asleep.

Nongonococcal urethritis An inflammation of the male's urethra not caused by gonorrhea.

Norplant An implanted progestin-only contraceptive for women.

Nulliparous A term used to refer to a woman who has never given birth to a baby.

Nymphomania An extraordinarily high, insatiable sex drive in a woman.

Obscenity Something that is offensive according to accepted standards of decency; the legal term for pornography.

Oedipus complex In Freudian theory, the sexual attraction of a little boy to his mother.

Onanism Withdrawal of the penis from the vagina before ejaculation; sometimes also used to refer to masturbation.

Operant conditioning The process of changing the frequency of a behavior (the operant) by following it with reinforcement or punishment.

Operational definition Defining a concept or term by how it is measured.

Oral-genital sex Sexual activity in which the mouth is used to stimulate the genitals.

Orchidectomy Surgical removal of the testes.

Orgasm An intense sensation that occurs at the peak of sexual arousal and is followed by release of sexual tensions.

Orgasmic platform The thickening of the walls of the outer third of the vagina that occurs during sexual arousal.

Outer lips The fatty pads of tissue lying on either side of the vaginal opening and inner lips.

Ovaries The paired sex glands in the female which produce ova (eggs) and sex hormones.

Oviduct Fallopian tube.

Ovulation Release of an egg by the ovaries.

Ovum Egg.

Oxytocin A hormone secreted by the pituitary which stimulates the contractions of the uterus during childbirth; also involved in breast-feeding.

Pander To produce a prostitute for a client; sometimes used to mean any catering to another's sexual desires.

Pap test The test for cervical cancer.

Paraphilia A sexual variation; erotic attraction to unusual things or behaviors.

Parturition Childbirth.

Pederasty Sexual relations between a man and a boy; sometimes also used to mean anal intercourse.

Pediculosis pubis Lice attaching themselves to the roots of the pubic hair; crabs.

Pedophilia A sexual variation in which an adult is sexually attracted to children; child molesting.

Pelvic inflammatory disease Infection of the pelvic organs such as the fallopian tubes.

Penis A male sexual organ.

Perineum The area between the vaginal opening and the anus.

Period The menstrual period.

Perversion A sexual deviation.

Phallus Penis.

Pheromones Chemical substances secreted outside the body that are important in communication between animals.

Phimosis A condition in which the foreskin is so tight that it cannot be pulled back.

Photoplethysmograph A device used to measure physiological sexual arousal in the female.

Pimp A prostitute's protector; one who procures a prostitute's services for another.

Pituitary gland A gland located on the lower surface of the brain; it secretes several hormones important to sexual and reproductive functioning.

Placenta An organ formed on the wall of the uterus through which the fetus receives oxygen and nutrients and gets rid of waste products.

Plateau phase Masters and Johnson's term for the second phase of sexual response, occurring just before orgasm.

Polygamy Marriage in which a man has more than one wife or a woman has more than one husband.

Population A group of people a researcher wants to study and make conclusions about.

Pornography Sexually arousing art, literature, or films.

Postpartum The period of time following childbirth.

Postpartum depression Mild to moderate depression in women following the birth of a baby.

Premarital intercourse Intercourse before marriage.

Premature ejaculation A sexual dysfunction in which the male ejaculates too soon.

Premenstrual syndrome (PMS) A combination of severe physical and psychological symptoms (such as depression and irritability) occurring in some women just before menstruation.

Prenatal Before birth.

Prepuce Foreskin.

Preterm birth An infant born weighing only 2500 grams ($5\frac{1}{2}$ pounds) or less.

Priapism A rare condition in which erections are long-lasting and painful.

Primipara A woman having her first baby.

Progesterone A female sex hormone produced by the corpus luteum in the ovary.

Prolactin A hormone secreted by the pituitary; it is involved in lactation.

Promiscuous A term used to refer to someone who engages in sexual activity with many different people.

Prophylactic A drug or device used to prevent disease, often specifically sexually transmitted disease; often used to mean "condom."

Prostaglandins Chemicals that stimulate the muscles of the uterus.

Prostate The gland in the male, located below the bladder, that secretes some of the fluid in semen.

Prostatitis An infection or inflammation of the prostate gland.

Prostitution Indiscriminate sexual activity for payment.

Pseudocyesis False pregnancy.

Pseudohermaphrodite An individual who has a mixture of male and female reproductive structures, so that it is not clear whether the individual is a male or a female.

Psychoanalytic theory A psychological theory originated by Freud; its basic assumption is that part of the human psyche is unconscious.

Puberty The period of time during which the body matures from that of a child to that of an adult capable of reproducing.

Pubic hair Hair on the lower abdomen and genital area, appearing at puberty.

Pubic lice See *Pediculosis pubis*.

Pubococcygeal muscle A muscle around the vaginal entrance.

Pudendum The external genitals of the female.

Radical mastectomy A surgical treatment for breast cancer in which the entire breast, as well as underlying muscle and lymph nodes, are removed.

Rape Forcible sexual relations with an individual without that person's consent.

Refractory period The period following orgasm during which the person cannot be sexually aroused.

Resolution phase Masters and Johnson's term for the last phase of sexual response, in which the body returns to the unaroused state.

Retarded ejaculation A sexual dysfunction in which the male cannot have an orgasm even though he is highly aroused.

Retrograde ejaculation A condition in which orgasm in the male is not accompanied by an external ejaculation; instead, the ejaculate goes into the urinary bladder.

Rhythm method A method of birth control that involves abstaining from sexual intercourse during the fertile days of the woman's menstrual cycle.

RU-486 A new pill that produces a very early abortion.

Sadism A sexual variation in which the person derives sexual pleasure from inflicting pain on someone else.

Salpingectomy See *tubal ligation*.

Salpingitis Infection of the fallopian tubes.

Satyriasis An extraordinarily high level of sex drive in a male.

Schema A general knowledge framework a person has about a given topic, e.g., a gender schema.

Scripts What we have learned to be appropriate sequences of behavior.

Scrotum The pouch of skin that contains the testes.

Secondary sex characteristics The physical characteristics, other than the sex organs, that distinguish the male from the female; examples are the woman's breasts and the man's beard.

Semen The fluid that is ejaculated from the penis during orgasm; it contains sperm.

Seminal vesicles The two organs lying on either side of the prostate, which secrete much of the fluid in semen.

Seminiferous tubules Highly coiled tubules in the testes that manufacture sperm.

Sensate focus exercises Exercises prescribed by sex therapists to increase sexual response.

Sex-change operation The surgery done on transsexuals to change their anatomy to the other gender.

Sex flush A rashlike condition on the skin that occurs during sexual arousal.

Sexual dissatisfaction Masters and Johnson's term for homosexuals who are unhappy with their sexual orientation and seek therapy to become heterosexual.

Sexual dysfunction A problem with sexual responding that causes a person mental distress; examples are erectile dysfunction in men and anorgasmia in women.

Sexual harrassment Unwanted imposition of sexual requirements in the context of a relationship of unequal power, such as an employer and an employee.

Sexual identity A person's sense of his or her own sexual orientation, whether heterosexual, homosexual, or bisexual.

Sexual orientation A person's erotic and emotional orientation toward members of his or her own gender or members of the other gender.

Sexual selection An evolutionary theory proposed to explain gender differences.

Skene's glands Glands opening into the urethra.

Smegma A cheesy substance formed under the foreskin of the penis.

Sociobiology A theory that applies evolutionary biology to understanding the social behavior of animals, including humans.

Sodomy An ambiguous legal term which may refer to anal intercourse, sexual relations with animals, or mouth-genital sex.

Spectatoring Acting as an observer or judge of one's own sexual performance.

Sperm The mature male reproductive cell, capable of fertilizing an egg.

Spermatogenesis The production of sperm.

Sperm bank A place that stores frozen sperm for later use.

Spermicide A substance that kills sperm.

Spirochete A spiral-shaped bacterium; one kind causes syphilis.

Sponge See *contraceptive sponge*.

Squeeze technique A form of therapy for premature ejaculation.

Statutory rape Sexual relations with a person who is below the legal "age of consent."

Stereotype A generalization about a group of people (e.g., men) that distinguishes them from others (e.g., women).

Sterile Incapable of reproducing.

Sterilization technique A procedure by which an individual is made incapable of reproducing.

Steroids A group of chemical substances including the sex hormones estrogen, progesterone, and testosterone.

Straight Heterosexual.

Structural-functionalism A sociological theory that views society as an interrelated set of structures that function together to maintain that society.

Superego According to Fued, the part of the personality containing the conscience.

Surrogate An extra member of a sex tharapy team who serves as a sexual partner for the client while in therapy.

Surrogate mother A woman who, through artificial insemination or in vitro fertilization, gestates a fetus for someone else.

Swinging An exchange of sex partners between married couples.

Syphilis A sexually transmitted disease.

Tearoom trade Impersonal sex in public places such as restrooms.

Teratogenic Producing defects in the fetus.

Test-retest reliability A method for determining whether self-reports are reliable or accurate; subjects are tested and then tested a second time some time later to determine whether their answers are the same both times.

Testes The sex glands of the male, located in the scrotum; they manufacture sperm and sex hormones.

Testicle A testis.

Testis-determining factor (TDF) A gene on the Y chromosome that causes testes to differentiate prenatally.

Testosterone A hormone secreted by the testes in the male; it maintains secondary sex characteristics.

Toxemia A dangerous disease of pregnancy.

Toxic shock syndrome A sometimes fatal disease associated with tampon use.

Transsexual A person who feels that he or she is trapped in the body of the wrong gender; a person who undergoes a sex-change operation.

Transvestism Dressing in the clothing of the other gender.

Tribadism A sexual technique in which one woman lies on top of another, moving rhythmically to produce sexual pleasure.

Trichomoniasis A vaginal infection.

Trimester Three months.

Troilism A sexual variation in which three people engage in sexual activity together.

Tubal ligation A surgical method of female sterilization; also called salpingectomy.

Tumescence Swelling due to congestion with body fluids; erection.

Tyson's glands Glands under the foreskin of the penis that secrete a cheesy substance called smegma.

Umbilical cord The tube that connects the fetus to the placenta.

Urethra The tube through which urine leaves the bladder and passes out of the body; in males, also the tube through which semen is discharged.

Urophilia (or urolagnia) A sexual variation in which the person derives sexual pleasure from urine or urination.

Uterus The organ in the female in which the fetus develops.

Vacuum curettage A method of abortion that is performed during the first trimester.

Vagina The barrel-shaped organ in the female into which the penis is inserted during intercourse and through which a baby passes during birth.

Vaginal ring An experimental device for contraception.

Vaginismus A strong, spastic contraction of the muscles around the vagina, closing off the vaginal entrance and making intercourse impossible.

Vaginitis An inflammation or irritation of the vagina, usually due to infection.

Varicocele Essentially, varicose veins in the testes; may be related to infertility in men.

Vas deferens The ducts through which sperm pass on their way from the testes to the urethra.

Vasectomy A surgical procedure for male sterilization involving severing of the vas deferens.

Vasocongestion An accumulation of blood in the blood vessels of a region of the body, especially the genitals; a swelling or erection results.

Venereal disease A disease transmitted primarily by sexual contact.

Viral hepatitis See *hepatitis B.*

Virgin A person who has never had sexual intercourse.

Volunteer bias A problem in sex research caused by some people refusing to participate, thus making it impossible to have a random sample.

Voyeurism A sexual variation in which the person derives sexual pleasure from watching nudes or watching others having sexual intercourse; also called *scoptophilia* and *Peeping Tomism.*

Vulva The collective term for the external genitals of the female; includes the mons, clitoris, inner and outer lips, and vaginal and urethral openings.

Warts See *genital warts.*

Wassermann test A blood test for syphilis.

Wet dream See *nocturnal emission.*

Withdrawal A method of birth control in which the male withdraws his penis from the vagina before he ejaculates.

Wolffian ducts Embryonic ducts which form part of the male's reproductive system.

Womb See *uterus.*

Zoophilia See *bestiality.*

Zygote The fertilized egg.

Zygote intra-fallopian transfer (ZIFT) A procedure in which an egg fertilized by sperm in a laboratory dish (zygote) is placed into the fallopian tube.

Answers to Review Questions

Chapter 1. Sexuality in Perspective
1. True
2. False
3. False
4. True
5. True
6. False
7. True
8. Gender
9. True
10. True

Chapter 2. Theoretical Perspectives on Sexuality
1. Sociobiology
2. Libido
3. False
4. True
5. False
6. True
7. True
8. Macro level, subcultural level, interpersonal level, individual level
9. True
10. Self-disclosure

Chapter 3. Sex Research
1. True
2. Volunteer bias
3. True
4. Direct observation
5. False
6. True
7. False
8. Participant-observer study
9. False
10. False

Chapter 4. Sexual Anatomy
1. Clitoris
2. Hymen
3. False
4. Endometrium
5. Estrogen, progesterone
6. True
7. Circumcision
8. Interstitial cells
9. True
10. 80

Chapter 5. Sex Hormones and Sexual Differentiation
1. Hypothalamus
2. Pituitary gland
3. True
4. False
5. Hypothalamus
6. Ovaries
7. True
8. False
9. False
10. True

Chapter 6. Menstruation and Menopause
1. Luteal phase
2. True
3. True
4. Prostaglandins
5. True
6. False
7. True
8. Estrogen-replacement therapy
9. True
10. True

Chapter 7. Conception, Pregnancy, and Childbirth
1. False
2. False
3. Placenta
4. Human chorionic gonadotropin (HCG)
5. True
6. True
7. Lamaze method
8. False
9. In vitro fertilization
10. Gamete intra-fallopian transfer (GIFT)

Chapter 8. Contraception and Abortion
1. Estrogen and progestin (progesterone)
2. True
3. False
4. Tubal ligation (minilaparotomy)
5. False
6. True
7. False
8. Rhythm
9. Condoms and vasectomy (male sterilization)
10. False

Chapter 9. The Physiology of Sexual Response
1. Excitement, plateau, orgasm, resolution
2. Vasocongestion
3. True
4. Cognitive
5. False
6. True
7. G spot (Gräfenberg spot)
8. Organizing
9. Pheromones
10. False

Chapter 10. Techniques of Arousal and Communication
1. False
2. True
3. False
4. Cunnilingus
5. False
6. True
7. True
8. Leveling
9. False
10. Validating

Answers to Review Questions

Chapter 11. Sexuality and the Life Cycle: Childhood and Adolescence
1. Birth or even prenatally
2. False
3. True
4. True
5. True
6. True
7. False
8. Testosterone
9. False
10. True

Chapter 12. Sexuality and the Life Cycle: Adulthood
1. True
2. True
3. True
4. False
5. False
6. Swinging
7. Equity theory
8. True
9. True
10. Regular sexual expression

Chapter 13. Attraction, Love, and Intimacy
1. True
2. False
3. Positive reinforcements (rewards)
4. Intimacy, passion
5. Secure
6. False
7. True
8. Physiological arousal
9. Misattribution of arousal
10. Intimate

Chapter 14. Gender Roles, Female Sexuality, and Male Sexuality
1. Gender role
2. False
3. Androgyny
4. Transsexual (gender dysphoria)
5. True
6. Masturbation, attitudes about casual sex
7. 92, 58
8. Penile strain gauge
9. Gender dysphoria
10. True

Chapter 15. Sexual Orientation: Gay, Straight, or Bi?
1. False
2. True
3. False
4. 80, 20
5. Tearoom trade
6. True
7. True
8. False
9. False
10. True

Chapter 16. Variations in Sexual Behavior
1. True
2. Fetishism
3. True
4. Masochist
5. False
6. Hypersexuality
7. Sexual addiction
8. False
9. True
10. False

Chapter 17. Sexual Coercion
1. True
2. Victim-precipitated
3. False
4. False
5. False
6. False
7. True
8. True
9. False
10. True

Chapter 18. Sex for Sale
1. True
2. Massage parlor
3. Pimp
4. Gigolos
5. True
6. True
7. True
8. False
9. True
10. False

Chapter 19. Sexual Dysfunction and Sex Therapy
1. Erectile dysfunction
2. True
3. True
4. True
5. Spectatoring
6. False
7. True
8. True
9. Cognitive sex
10. True

Chapter 20. Sexually Transmitted Diseases
1. Genital warts
2. Gonorrhea
3. False
4. True
5. Herpes
6. True
7. Genital warts
8. False
9. False
10. True

Chapter 21. Ethics, Religion, and Sexuality
1. Legalistic, situationist
2. False
3. Celibacy
4. Hindu
5. Profamily
6. Natural
7. False
8. Ordination, marriage of homosexuals, and AIDS
9. Confidential
10. None

Chapter 22. Sex and the Law
1. False
2. True
3. False
4. Sodomy
5. *Griswold v. Connecticut*
6. Obscenity
7. *Planned Parenthood v. Casey*
8. False
9. False
10. False

Chapter 23. Sex Education
1. False
2. False
3. False
4. False
5. True
6. True
7. True

Acknowledgments

PHOTO AND ART

CHAPTER 1:

1.1   (a) AP/Wide World; (b) Culver
1.2   The Kinsey Institute for Research in Sex, Gender, and Reproduction, Inc.
1.4   (a) Hector R. Acebes/Photo Researchers; (b) Robert A. Isaacs/Photo Researchers
1.5   © 1987 Thomas H. Gregor/The University of Chicago Press
1.6   Ronald D. Nadler/Yerkes Regional Primate Research Center
1.7   From Philip Rawson, *Primitive Erotic Art*

CHAPTER 2:

2.1   O. S. Penttingill, Jr./Photo Researchers
2.2   Richard Frieman/Photo Researchers
2.3   Adapted from Martin & Halverson (1983). The effects of sex-typing schemas on young children's memory. *Child Development, 54,* pp. 563–574.
2.4   Adapted from J. DeLamater (1987). A sociological approach. In J. H. Greer and W. T. O'Donohue (Eds.), *Theories of Human Sexuality*. Reprinted by permission of Plenum Publishing.
2.5   Alice Kandell/Photo Researchers
2.6   Pamela Price/Picture Group

CHAPTER 3:

3.1   Copyright © Punch/Rothco Cartoons, Inc.
3.2   Reproduced by permission of the Kinsey Institute for Research in Sex, Gender and Reproduction, Inc. Photo by Dellenback.
3.3   United Artists Corp.
3.4   Carolina Population Center, University of North Carolina, Chapel Hill, North Carolina
3.6   Reprinted by permission of The Kinsey Institute for Research in Sex, Gender, and Reproduction, Inc.
3.7   Mitro, Rothco original. Rothco Cartoons, Inc. © Mitro/Rothco.

CHAPTER 4:

4.1   D. Luciano, A. J. Vander, J. H. Sherman, *Human Anatomy and Physiology: Structure and Function* (2d ed.). New York: McGraw-Hill, 1983. Reproduced with permission of McGraw-Hill, Inc.
4.3   Betty Dodson, *Liberating Masturbation: A Meditation on Self-Love.* Copyright © 1974 by Betty Dodson.
4.4   Kathy Bendo
4.6, 4.7, 4.12   D. Luciano, A. J. Vander, and J. H. Sherman, *Human Anatomy and Physiology: Structure and Function* (2d ed.). New York: McGraw-Hill, 1983. Reproduced with permission of McGraw-Hill, Inc.
4.14   Ann Pomaska
4.16   Randolph H. Buthrie, Jr., M.D., P.C.
4.17   Hazel Hankins/Stock, Boston

CHAPTER 5

5.2, 5.3   Adapted from A. J. Vander, J. H. Sherman, and D. Luciano, *Human Physiology: The Mechanisms of Body Function* (2d ed.). New York: McGraw-Hill, 1975. Reproduced with permission of McGraw-Hill, Inc.
5.5   AP/Wide World
5.6   From J. Money and A. Ehrardt, *Man and Woman, Boy and Girl.* Baltimore: Johns Hopkins, 1972.
5.7   W. A. Marshall. Sex differences at puberty. *Journal of Biosocial Science,* Supplement, 1970, 2, pp. 31–41. Reprinted by permission of *Journal of Biosocial Science.*
5.8   Alice Kandell/Photo Researchers

CHAPTER 6:

6.1   Adapted from A. J. Vander, J. H. Sherman, and D. Luciano, *Human Physiology: The Mechanism of Body Function* (2d ed.). New York: McGraw-Hill, 1975. Reproduced with permission of McGraw-Hill, Inc.
6.2   R. J. Demarest and J. J. Sciarra, *Conception, Birth, and Contraception: A Visual Presentation* (2d ed.). New York: McGraw-Hill, 1976. Reproduced with permission of McGraw-Hill, Inc.

6.4   (*a*) © 1992 Hallmark Cards, Inc. Used by permission.
6.5   Flying Fish, Inglewood
6.6   Will McIntyre/Photo Researchers

CHAPTER 7:

7.4   Spencer Grant/Monkmeyer
7.5   James W. Hanson, M.D., Professor of Pediatrics, Division of Medical Genetics, University of Iowa
7.7   (*a*) Hella Hammid/Photo Researchers; (*b*) Eugene Richards/Magnum.
7.9   George Malave/Stock, Boston
7.10   Fred Ward/Black Star
7.11   Mary M. Thatcher/Photo Researchers
7.13   By permission of Rothco Cartoons.
7.14   Dana Summers. © 1983, Washington Post Writers Group. Reprinted with permission.
7.15   AP/Wide World
7.16   (*a*) Hank Morgan/Science Source/Photo Researchers, (*b*) Phillip Hayson/Science Source/Photo Researchers

CHAPTER 8:

8.2   Culver
8.3   (*a*) Planned Parenthood of NYC; (*b*) Johns Hopkins University, Population Communication Services; (*c-d*) Randy Matusow.
8.4   Joel Gordon
8.5   Gyno Pharma, Inc.
8.8   Courtesy Pharmacists Planning Service, Inc., Sausalito, CA.
8.9   Jonathan Shrorey, 1984.
8.13   Wisconsin Pharmacal Company
8.14   (*a*) J. L. Atlan/SYGMA; (*b*) Reuters/Bettman

CHAPTER 9:

9.3   UPI/Bettman
9.4   Adapted from S. Walen and D. Roth (1987). A cognitive approach. In J. H. Geer and W. T. O'Donohue (Eds.), *Theories of Human Sexuality* (New York: Plenum, 1987). Reprinted by permission of David Roth and Susan Walen.
9.5   Leonard Freed/Magnum
9.8   Time, Inc.
9.10   (*a*) Abraham Menashe/Photo Researchers; (*b*) Joel Gordon; (*c*) AP/Wide World.
9.11   Time Magazine
9.12   (*a*) Guy Gilette/Photo Researchers; (*b*) Randy Matusow.

CHAPTER 10:

10.1   Reprinted by permission of the Putnam Publishing Group from Philip Rawson, *Erotic Art of the East,* copyright 1968 by Philip Rawson.
10.2   (*a-b*) Randy Matusow
10.4   Art Resource
10.10 Randy Matusow
10.11 Reprinted with special permission of North American Syndicate.
10.12 Mort Walker and Dick Browne. Reprinted with special permission of North American Syndicate.
10.13 (*a*) Ellen Sheffield/Woodfin Camp & Associates; (*b*) Lynne Weinstein/Woodfin Camp & Associates.

CHAPTER 11:

11.1   Tana Hoban
11.2   Monkmeyer
11.3   Frederick D. Bodin/Stock, Boston
11.4   Bob Daemmrich/Tony Stone Worldwide
11.5   Alfred C. Kinsey, Wardell B. Pomeroy, & Clyde F. Martin (1984). *Sexual Behavior in the Human Male* and *Sexual Behavior in the Human Female.* Reprinted by permission of The Kinsey Institute for Research in Sex, Gender, and Reproduction, Inc.
11.6   Katrina Thomas/Photo Researchers
11.7   *Journal of Marriage and the Family,* "Twenty Years of the Sexual Revolution, 1965–1985: An Update," Ira Robinson, Ken Ziss, Bill Ganza, Stuart Katz, and Edward Robinson; 53:1, pp. 216–220. Copyrighted © 1991 by the National Council on Family Relations, 3989 Central Avenue NE, Suite 550, Minneapolis, MN 55421. Reprinted by permission.

CHAPTER 12:

12.1   (*a*) Joel Gordon; (*b*) Chester Higgins, Jr./Photo Researchers
12.2   Philip Blumstein & Pepper Schwartz (1983). *American Couples.* Copyright © 1983 by Philip Blumstein and Pepper Schwartz. By permission of William Morrow & Co., Inc.
12.3   Randy Matusow
12.4   Spencer Grant/Photo Researchers
12.5   Bruce Davidson/Magnum

CHAPTER 13:

13.1   Cartoon: Peanuts featuring "Good Ol' Charlie Brown" by Schulz. PEANUTS reprinted by permission of United Feature Syndicate, Inc.
13.2   Adapted from R. Sternberg (1986). *Psychological Review,* **93,** Fig. 6, p. 128. Copyright © 1986 by the American Psychological Association. Reprinted by permission.
13.3   Adapted from R. Sternberg (1986). *Psychological Review,* **93,** Fig. 8, p. 129. Copyright © 1986 by the American Psychological Association. Reprinted by permission.
13.4   Guy LeQuerrec/Magnum
13.5   Copyright © 1983, reprinted from *Psychology Today* magazine, American Psychological Association.
13.6   Randy Matusow
13.7   Toni Michaels/Image Works

CHAPTER 14:

14.1   (*a*) Victor Friedman/Photo Researchers; (*b*) Erika Stone/Photo Researchers; (*c*) Ulrike Welsch/Photo Researchers
14.2   Photo courtesy of J. R. Heinman
14.3   Reprinted with permission of the American Psychological Association, 1969, 1983.
14.4   AP/Wide World

14.5 Courtesy Dr. D. Laub, Gender Dysphoria Program, Department of Plastic and Reconstructive Surgery, Stanford University.

14.6 Courtesy David W. Foerster, M.D., and Charles L. Reynolds, M.D.

14.7 New Times Magazine and Wide World Photos

CHAPTER 15:

15.1 (*a–b*, left) Joyce R. Wilson/Photo Researchers; (*b*, middle and right) AP/Wide World

15.2 Joel Gordon

15.3 Joel Gordon

15.5 (*a*) Bettye Lane/Photo Researchers; (*b*) S. Gazin/Image Works; (*c*) Pamela Price/Picture Group; (*d*) Hella Hammid/Photo Researchers.

15.6 Photofest

15.7 Randy Matusow

CHAPTER 16:

16.2 (*a*) Reuters/Bettmann; (*b*) Courtesy The New York Historical Society

16.3 Bettmann

16.4 Joel Gordon

16.5 Randy Matusow

16.6 (*a*) Randy Matusow; (*b*) Jeff MacNelly, *Shoe* Cartoon, Jefferson Communications, Inc., 1982. Reprinted by permission of Tribune Media Services.

CHAPTER 17:

17.1 Bettye Lane/Photo Researchers

17.2 Monique Manceau/Photo Researchers

17.4 UPI/Bettmann

17.5 Reuters/Bettmann

17.6 Ilona Granet, 1988. All rights reserved. Photos by Fred Krughoff.

17.7 Randy Matusow

CHAPTER 18:

18.1 (*a*) Courtesy The New York Public Library; (*b*) John Maher/Stock, Boston

18.3 Richard Sobol/Stock, Boston

18.4 Guy LeQuerrec/Magnum

18.5 (*a*) UPI/Bettmann; (*b*) Gamma Liason

CHAPTER 19:

19.2 David H. Barlow (1986). *Journal of Consulting and Clinical Psychology, 54,* pp. 140–148. Copyright 1986 by the American Psychological Association. Reprinted by permission.

19.6 Tony Guccione

19.7 V. Puglisi, Time, Inc. 1979.

CHAPTER 20:

20.2 Centers for Disease Control, Atlanta

20.3 Centers for Disease Control, Atlanta

20.4 New York City Department of Health

20.5 Stuart Franklin/Magnum

20.6 Stuart Franklin/Magnum

20.7 Centers for Disease Control, Atlanta

20.8 (*a*) Centers for Disease Control, Atlanta; (*b*) CNRI/Phototake

20.9 Centers for Disease Control, Atlanta

20.11 Centers for Disease Control, Atlanta

CHAPTER 21:

21.1 The Metropolitan Museum of Art, Rogers Fund, 1919.

21.2 Alinari/Art Resource

21.3 Bettmann

21.4 UPI/Bettmann

21.5 Marc Riboud/Magnum

21.6 Office of Sri Guradav, International Headquarters Integral Yoga Institute

21.7 UPI/Bettmann

21.8 Left, Sylvia Johnson.Woodfin Camp & Associates; right, Jerry Berndt/Stock, Boston

21.9 Culver

21.10 Universal Fellowship of Metropolitan Community Churches

21.11 UPI/Bettmann

CHAPTER 22:

22.1 Top, Peter Fredin/Gamma Liaison; bottom, Reuters/Bettmann

22.2 Gianfranco Gorgoni/Woodfin Camp & Associates

22.3 Reuters/Bettmann

22.4 Bill Mauldin, cartoon, 1976. Reprinted with special permission of North America Syndicate.

22.5 Ira Berger/Woodfin Camp & Associates

22.6 Joel Gordon

22.7 UPI/Bettmann

22.8 Sigy Hutkinson, cartoon: Solomon updated.

22.9 UPI/Bettmann

CHAPTER 23:

23.1 Margulies cartoon by Rothco. Reprinted by permission of Rothco Cartoons.

23.3 *Dennis the Menace* cartoon by T. M. 1983. *Dennis the Menace*® used by permission of Hank Ketcham and © by North American Syndicate.

23.4 (*b*) U.S. Agency for International Development

INSERT I:

7.3 (*a*) Dr. Landrum B. Shettles; (*b*) Dr. Landrum B. Shettles; (*c*) Petit Format/Nestle/Science Source/Photo Researchers; (*d*) Petit Format/Nestle/Science Source/Photo Researchers; (*e*) Petit Format/Nestle/Science Source/Photo Researchers; (*f*) Lennart Nilsson, from A CHILD IS BORN, Dell Publishing Company; (*g*) Lennart Nilsson, from A CHILD IS BORN, Dell Publishing Company; (*h*) Lennart Nilsson, from BEHOLD MAN, Little, Brown & Company; (*i*) Lennart, Nilsson, from BEHOLD MAN, Little, Brown & Company.

INSERT II:

II-1   Top left, Photofest
II-1   Top right, FPG International
II-1   Bottom left, M. Hicks/Gamma Liaison
II-1   Bottom right, Frank Micelotta/Retna
II-2   Top left, Bettmann
II-2   Top right, Everett Collection
II-2   Bottom left, Photofest
II-2   Bottom right, Everett Collection
II-3   Top, Phillip Morris Companies
II-3   Bottom, Courtesy Outdoor Advertising Association of America, Inc.
II-4   Top left, Photofest
II-4   Top right, Mark Antman/Image Works
II-4   Bottom right, Rhoda Sidney/Stock, Boston
II-4   Bottom left, Photofest

TABLES

CHAPTER 1:

Table 1.1: Koray Tanfer and Marjorie C. Horn, *Family Planning Perspectives, 17,* No. 1, pp. 10–19, January/February 1985. Reproduced with the permission of the Alan Guttmacher Institute.

CHAPTER 5:

Table 5.2: Bernard Goldstein. 1976. *Introduction to Human Sexuality,* pp. 80–81. Reprinted by permission of Bernard Goldstein.

CHAPTER 7:

Table 7.1: Reprinted from *Journal of Psychosomatic Research, 25,* pp. 373–383, R. Kumar, H. A. Brant, and K. M. Robson, 1981. With permission from Pergamon Press, Ltd., Headington Hill Hall, Oxford OX3 OBW, UK.

CHAPTER 8:

Table 8.1: London, K., Cushing, J., Cleland, J., Anderson, J. E., Morris, L., Moore, S. H., and Rutstein, S. O. (1985). Fertility and family planning surveys: An update. *Population Reports,* Series M, No. 8, M-291–M-348. Baltimore: Johns Hopkins University, Population Information Program, September/October 1985.

Table 8.4: Stanley K. Henshaw, *Family Planning Perspectives, 22* (2), March/April 1990, pp. 76–78. Reproduced with the permission of the Alan Guttmacher Institute.

Table 8.5: Table from Robert A. Hatcher et al. (1990). *Contraceptive technology, 1990–1992.* Reprinted by permission of Irvington Publishers, Inc.

CHAPTER 10:

Table 10.1: Morton Hunt, pp. 91–93. Reproduced with permission from Playboy Enterprises, Inc., from *Sexual Behavior in the 1970s* by Morton Hunt. Copyright © 1974 by Morton Hunt.

CHAPTER 11:

Table 11.2: D. A. Moore and P. I. Erickson, *Family and Community Health,* **8** (3), pp. 38–51, November 1985. Reprinted with permission of Aspen Publishers, Inc., © 1985.

Table 11.3: John DeLamater and Patricia MacCorquodale (1973). *Premarital sexuality: Attitudes, relationships, behavior.* Reprinted by permission of University of Wisconsin Press, Madison.

Table 11-4: Liskin, L., Kak, N., Rutledge, A. H., Smit, L.C., and Stewart, L. Youth in the 1980's: Social and health concerns. *Population Reports,* Series M, No. 9. Baltimore, Johns Hopkins University, Population Information Program, November/December 1985.

Table 11.5: Morton Hunt (1974). *Sexual Behavior in the 1970s,* p. 144. Copyright © 1974 by Morton Hunt. Reproduced with permission from Playboy Enterprises, Inc.

Table 11.7: J. D. Forrest and S. Singh (1990). *Family Planning Perspectives,* **22** (5), pp. 206–214. Reproduced with the permission of the Alan Guttmacher Institute.

CHAPTER 12:

Table 12.3: "Love, Sex and Aging," by Edward M. Brecher and the Editors of Consumer Report Books. Copyright 1984 by Consumers Union of U.S., Inc., Yonkers, NY 10703-1057. Reprinted by permission from Consumer Report Books.

CHAPTER 13:

Table 13.1: Stanley Schachter and J. F. Singer (1962). Cognitive, social, and physiological determinants of emotional state. *Psychological Review,* **69,** pp. 379–399.

CHAPTER 15:

Table 15.1: J. A. Davis and T. Smith (1991). *General Social Surveys, 1972–1991: Cumulative Data.* Storrs, CT: University of Connecticut, Roper Center for Public Opinion Research.

CHAPTER 17:

Table 17.1: D. J. Benson and G. E. Thomson (1982). © 1982 by the Society for the Study of Social Problems. Reprinted from *Social Problems,* vol. 29, pp. 236–251 by permission.

CHAPTER 20:

Table 20.1: N. Hearst and S. B. Hulley, "Preventing the heterosexual spread of AIDS: Are we giving our patients the best advice?" Modified from the *Journal of the American Medical Association,* **259,** 2428–2432. Copyright 1988, American Medical Association.

CHAPTER 21:

Table 21.1: From Gallup poll on Americans on their attitudes toward abortion (1975, 1977, 1980, 1992). By permission of The Gallup Organizations, Inc.

CHAPTER 22:

Table 22.1: A telephone poll of 1000 adult Americans, October 1989, reported in *Time,* November 20, 1989. Copyright 1989, Time Inc. Reprinted by permission.

CHAPTER 23:

Table 23.1: Yankelovich, 1986. From a well sampled survey of U.S. adults by *Time* and Clancy Shulman Yankelovich, 11/10/86.

Table 23.2: Ronald Goldman and Juliette Goldman. 1982, pp. 197, 213, 240, 263, 354, *Children's sexual thinking*. London: Routledge and Kegan Paul, by permission.

QUOTATIONS FROM TEXT:

Page 10: J. C. Messenger, Sex and repression in an Irish folk community. In D. S. Marshall and R. C. Suggs (Eds.). *Human Sexual Behavior,* 1971. Copyright © 1971 by the Institute of Sexual Research, Inc. Excerpted by permission of Basic Books, Inc., a division of HarperCollins Publishers.

Page 11: Thomas Gregor, *Anxious pleasures: The sexual lives of an Amazonian people,* 1985. Reprinted by permission of The University of Chicago Press.

Page 16: Bronislaw Malinowski, *The sexual life of savages,* 1929. Copyright © 1929 by Bronislaw Malinowski. Reprinted by permission of John Hawkins & Associates, Inc.

Page 50: "Too Darn Hot" (Cole Porter) © 1949 Chappell and Co. (Renewed). All Rights Reserved. Excerpted and used by permission.

Pages 60–61: Cochran et al. (1953). Evaluating the Kinsey reports. *Journal of the American Statistical Association.* Copyright 1953 by the American Statistical Association. All rights reserved.

Page 100: American Cancer Society. "The Breast Self-Exam." Reprinted by permission of the American Cancer Society.

Pages 104–105: American Cancer Society. "The Testicular Self-Exam." Reprinted by permission of the American Cancer Society.

Page 109: Excerpt from "An Odd Gastropod," by Milton Hildebrand from *Laugh and Love,* 1979, p. 134. Exposition Press.

Pages 120–121: John Money and Anke Ehrhardt, *Man and women, boy and girl,* 1972, pp. 154–156. © John Money.

Page 153: Boston Women's Health Book Collective. *The new our bodies, ourselves,* pp. 344–351, 1992. Copyright © 1984, 1992 by the Boston Women's Health Book Collective. Excerpted by permission of Simon & Schuster, Inc.

Page 276: E. Barbara Hariton (1973). The sexual fantasies of women. *Psychology Today,* 6(10), pp. 39–44.

Page 291: P. E. Slater, Sexual adequacy in America. *Intellectual Digest,* pp. 132–135, December 1973.

Page 314: Floyd M. Martinson, *Infant and child sexuality: A sociological perspective,* pp. 31 and 39, Book Mark, 1973. Excerpted with permission of the author.

Page 315: Boston Women's Health Book Collective. *The new our bodies, ourselves,* p. 40, 1992. Copyright © 1984, 1992 by The Boston Women's Health Book Collective. Excerpted by permission of Simon & Schuster, Inc.

Page 315: Floyd M. Martinson. *Infant and child sexuality: A sociological perspective,* p. 40, Book Mark, 1973. Excerpted with permission of the author.

Pages 316, 319: Morton Hunt (1974). *Sexual behavior in the 1970s,* pp. 79 and 95, 1974. Copyright © 1974 by Morton Hunt. Reproduced with permission from Playboy Enterprises, Inc.

Pages 321–322: Boston Women's Health Collective. *The new our bodies, ourselves,* p. 64, 1976. Copyright © 1984, 1992 by the Boston Women's Health Collective. Excerpted by permission of Simon & Schuster, Inc.

Pages 327, 343, 344, 345, 348: Morton Hunt (1974). *Sexual behavior in the 1970s,* pp. 98, 163, 200, 220, 183, 225–226, 286. Copyright © 1974 by Morton Hunt. Reproduced with permission from Playboy Enterprises, Inc.

Page 349: Gilbert D. Bartell, Group sex among the mid-Americans. *Journal of Sex Research,* 6, pp. 115, 122. Excerpted from *The Journal of Sex Research,* a publication of The Society for the Scientific Study of Sex, P.O. Box 208, Mount Vernon, Iowa 52314.

Pages 358, 359: Edward M. Brecher, Love, sex and aging, p. 21, 33, 1984. "Love, Sex and Aging." Copyright 1984 by Consumers Union of U.S., Inc., Yonkers, NY 10703-1057. Reprinted by permission from Consumer Report Books.

Page 382: Daniel Perlman and B. Fehr, 1987. The development of intimate relationships. In D. Perlman and S. Dack (eds.), *Intimate relationships: Development, dynamics, and deterioration,* p. 17. Reprinted by permission of Sage Publications Inc.

Pages 382–383: Valerian J. Derlega (ed.), 1984. *Communication, intimacy, and close relationship,* p. 1. Excerpted by permission of Valerian J. Derlega and Academic Press.

Page 396: Carroll et al., 1985, p. 137.

Page 399: Korff & Geer (1983). The relationship between arousal, experience and genital response. *Psychophysiology, 20,* 121–127. Copyright 1983, The Society for Psychophysiological Research. Reprinted with permission of the publisher and author.

Pages 404–405: Morton Hunt (1974). *Sexual behavior in the 1970s,* pp. 96–97, 1974. Copyright © 1974 by Morton Hunt. Reproduced with permission from Playboy Enterprises, Inc.

Page 409: Walter Mischel (1969). Continuity and change in personality. *American Psychologist,* **24,** 11: p. 1015. © 1969 American Psychological Association.

Page 423: Gerald C. Davison and John M. Neale (1974). *Abnormal psychology: An experimental clinical approach* (New York: John Wiley & Sons), p. 293.

Page 460: Max Schulman, excerpt from *I was a teenage dwarf.*

Page 482: Excerpt from "Rape Poem" by Marge Piercy from *Circles on the water: Selected poems of Marge Piercy.* Copyright © 1975, 1976, 1982 by Marge Piercy and Middlemarsh Inc. Reprinted by permission of Alfred A. Knopf, Inc., and the Wallace Literary Agency, Inc.

Pages 490–491: Jean O. Hughes and Bernice R. Sandler (1987). *"Friends" raping friends: Could it happen to you?,* p. 1. Excerpted by permission of the Center for Women Policy Studies.

Page 494: Struckman-Johnson, Forced sex on dates: It happens to men, too. *Journal of Sex Research, 24,* p. 238. Reprinted from *The Journal of Sex Research,* a publication of The Society for the Scientific Study of Sex, P. O. Box 208, Mount Vernon, Iowa 52314.

Page 513: Jackman, et al. The self-image of the prostitute. *The Sociological Quarterly,* 4, pp. 150–161. Reprinted with permission of *The Sociological Quarterly.*

Pages 516-517: Roberta Perkins and Garry Bennett, *Being a pros-*

titute, pp. 106–113. Excerpted by permission of Allen & Unwin Australia Pty, Ltd.

Page 521: Robert S. Anson, **excerpt from article in the** *San Francisco Chronicle,* 10/25/77.

Page 611: Reprinted by permission of Sri Swami Satchidananda.

Pages 613, 615: Reprinted by permission of the Vatican Embassy, Washington, D.C.

Page 619: Reprinted by permission of the United Church of Christ, Cleveland, OH.

Page 619: Reprinted by permission of the American Humanist Association, New York.

Page 619: Reprinted with permission of the Episcopal Church Center, New York.

Page 619: Reprinted with permission of the American Jewish Congress, New York.

Page 619: From *The book of discipline* of the United Methodist Church, 1992. Copyright © 1992 by The United Methodist Publishing House. Used by permission.

Pages 620–621: Vatican directive, "The Pastoral Care of Homosexual Persons," Congregation for the Doctrine of the Faith, 1986, *Origins,* 16, pp. 378–382. Excerpted with permission of *Origins,* CNS Documentary Service, Washington, D.C.

Page 632: Graham Parker, "The legal regulation of sexual activity and the protection of females," 1983, *Osgoode Hall Law Journal, 21,* 187–244. Reprinted with permission of the *Osgoode Hall Law Journal.*

Page 643: Norval Morris, The law is a busy-body. *New York Times Magazine,* pp. 58–64, April 18, 1973. Copyright © 1973 by The New York Times Company. Reprinted by permission.

Page 663: "Sex education." Sex Information and Education Council of the United States.

Pages 667–668: Anne C. Bernstein, How children learn about sex and birth. *Psychology Today, 9*(8), p. 31, January 1976. Reprinted with permission from *Psychology Today* magazine. Copyright © 1976 (Sussex Publishers, Inc.).

Pages 667, 669, 670: Anne C. Bernstein and Philip A. Cowan, 1975. Children's concepts of how people get babies. *Child Development,* 46, pp. 77–92. © The Society for Research in Child Development, Inc.

Page 671: Rosemary Zumwait, Plain and fancy: A content analysis of children's jokes dealing with adult sexuality, 1976. *Western Folklore, 35,* pp. 261, 267. Reprinted by permission of Western Folklore. Copyright © 1976.

FOCUS BOXES

Focus 1.2: D. S. Marshall and R. S. Suggs (Eds.). *Human sexual behavior.* Copyright © 1971 by the Institute for Sexual Research, Inc. Reprinted by permission of Basic Books, Inc., a division of HarperCollins Publishers.

Focus 8.1: P. Van Preagh (1982). The Hamilton birth control clinic: In response to need. *News/Nouvelles, Journal of Planned Parenthood Federation of Canada,* 3 (2). Excerpted by permission of Planned Parenthood Federation of Canada.

Focus 8.3: Robert A. Hatcher et al. (1976). *Contraceptive Technology,* 1976–1977, 8/e. Reprinted with permission of Irvington Publishers, Inc.

Focus 9.1: Ruth Brecher and Edward Brecher (Eds.) (1966). *An analysis of human sexual response.* Reprinted with permission of Jeremy Brecher.

Focus 15.4: P. W. Blumstein and P. Schwartz. (1976). Bisexual women. In J. P. Wiseman (Ed.), *The Social Psychology of Sex,* New York: Harper & Row, pp. 154–162.

Focus 18.2: A. W. Burgess (1984). *Child pornography and sex rings.* Lexington, MA: Lexington Books of D. C. Heath, pp. 26–27.

Focus 20.3: From *Medical Aspects of Human Sexuality,* Cahners Publishing Co. ©.

Index